KT-452-463

MARY BERRY'S COMPLETE COOK BOOK

MARY BERRY'S COMPLETE COOK BOOK

DORLING KINDERSLEY
London • New York • Stuttgart • Moscow

A DORLING KINDERSLEY BOOK

Created and produced by
CARROLL & BROWN LIMITED
5 Lonsdale Road
London NW6 6RA

Editorial Consultant Jeni Wright

Project Editor Vicky Hanson

Editors Jo-Anne Cox, Stella Vayne, Anne Crane,
Sophie Lankenau, Trish Shine

Cookery Consultants Valerie Cipollone
and Anne Hildyard

Art Editors Louisa Cameron and Gary Edgar-Hyde
Designers Alan Watt, Karen Sawyer, Lucy De Rosa

Photography David Murray and Jules Selmes

Production Wendy Rogers and Amanda Mackie

Published in Great Britain by
Dorling Kindersley Limited,
9 Henrietta Street, London WC2E 8PS

First UK edition, 1995
8 10 9

Visit us on the World Wide Web at
http://www.dk.com

A CIP catalogue record for this book is available from the British Library.

ISBN 0-7513-0205-8

Reproduced by Colourscan, Singapore
Printed in China by Toppan Printing Co., (Shenzhen) Ltd

FOREWORD

MARY BERRY'S COMPLETE COOK BOOK is a comprehensive collection of recipes suitable for every occasion. The opportunity to bring together in a single volume tried and tested favourites, as well as innovative new recipes, has been very satisfying. These recipes, both old and new, have been assembled in order to meet today's requirements for healthy, quick dishes made with fresh ingredients. The emphasis is on choice and flexibility: my intention has been to make the book the perfect companion for the person who needs to prepare meals for a family each day, as well as for those who find entertaining a pleasure. I hope you will enjoy using this book as much as I have enjoyed creating it.

Each chapter provides a varied selection of recipes, incorporating the traditional and the new and has been designed to accommodate elegant entertaining as well as family meals. There is such a wonderful variety of new ingredients to be found in today's supermarkets – a large selection of fresh herbs, exotic ingredients such as papayas, unusual types of fish, and a wide range of meat and poultry – that I have been able to gain inspiration from the recipes and cooking techniques used all over the world.

Finally, I would like to say a special thank you to Fiona Oyston for her expertise in writing and testing recipes, and for all her hard work helping me produce this exciting new cookery book.

Mary Berry

Contents

Introduction

HOME COOKING with fresh ingredients is the best way to ensure your meals are well-prepared and delicious. Despite the popularity of so-called convenience foods, time spent shopping for and cooking fresh, good-quality ingredients is time well spent.

Home-cooked meals need not be labour intensive – when modern gadgets can save you time, their use has been incorporated in the recipes in this book. Tricky techniques that may be *de rigueur* for professionals, but impractical for everyday cooking, have been avoided. If there's a short cut that gives good results, its use has been explained. By the same token, a well-stocked store cupboard and a few good tools are important parts of the process as well – saving you precious time.

The aim of this book is to make cooking the pleasurable experience it should be, and meals as enjoyable to prepare as they are to eat.

The store cupboard

With a supply of useful ingredients always to hand, you'll never be short of ideas for an impromptu meal. Canned chopped tomatoes, fish such as tuna and anchovies, and ready-cooked beans, such as kidney beans, can be added to a whole host of dishes. Dried pasta and noodles, different types of rice, and a variety of pulses can form the basis of many meals. Olives and capers will pep up numerous dishes, a variety of oils can be used for cooking and flavouring, while flavoured vinegars add distinction to salad dressings and marinades. And of course you should have a good supply of spices and dried herbs. Keep jars of chutneys, pickles, and mustards, and bottles of soy sauce, chilli sauce, and Worcestershire sauce for adding spice to savoury meals; and jams, marmalades, and honeys for adding a sweet, fruity note to all kinds of dishes.

With a constant supply of sugars, flours, nuts, and dried fruits, you'll be able to bake cakes at a moment's notice. Dry ingredients, such as flour, dried pasta, and spices should be kept in a dark cupboard.

You'll find advice on storing different foods in the Know-How pages of the chapters. Be sure to keep a check on use-by dates, and remember that foods at the back of the cupboard won't last indefinitely – try to rotate goods so that the first to be stored in the cupboard are the first to be used.

BASIC EQUIPMENT

Good equipment makes cooking easy. With high-quality knives, pots and pans, and other utensils, you will be able to cook efficiently and with pleasure. If you are equipping your first kitchen, an investment in a few basic items is all that's required – you don't need many fancy utensils to turn out delicious meals. Then, as your skills and experience grow, you can add to your collection of kitchen equipment, buying more unusual items to prepare the food you like to cook. It's important to buy the best tools and equipment you can afford. High-quality, well-made equipment is a worthwhile investment because it will last for many years, giving good service. The cheaper alternatives will need to be replaced more often, as they will dent, break, or wear out. And, using a thin pan in which food always sticks and burns, or trying to chop vegetables with a flimsy knife, can turn cooking into a chore.

YOUR KITCHEN

Although there is no lack of appliances on the market, kitchens vary from being under-equipped to over-equipped. The basics, of course, are most important, and well-built appliances should last a good while.

A refrigerator-freezer, and conventional oven are all that is really needed, although many homes are now equipped with microwave ovens and free-standing freezers as well. There's advice on microwaving and freezing in the Know-How pages at the beginning of each chapter, and you'll find additional information on pages 492–495.

Traditional ovens are still the norm, whether gas or electric, conventional or fan-assisted. Ovens are all slightly different and may be hotter or cooler than you expect. Use an oven thermometer for the most accurate reading.

Fan-assisted ovens can cook foods quicker than conventional ovens. To compensate, you can reduce the temperature given in a recipe, but it's best to consult the manufacturer's handbook. Fan-assisted ovens have an even temperature throughout; in conventional ovens, the heat rises, so that the top of the oven is hotter than the bottom.

MEASURING EQUIPMENT

Even experienced cooks need accurate measuring tools to ensure ingredients are in correct proportion to one another. The following are essential in the kitchen and can be found in any good kitchenware shop. Look for equipment that will stand up to use:

- **Kitchen scales:** either electronic and run on batteries, spring-operated, or balance-based. Electronic scales will register very small quantities, and will normally display both metric and imperial weights; balance scales are very accurate but are not able to measure small quantities.
- **Measuring jug:** a clear glass 600 ml (1 pint) jug, with metric and imperial calibrations is best.
- **Set of metric measuring spoons:** 1.25 ml (1/4 tsp), 2.5 ml (1/2 tsp), 5 ml (1 tsp), and 15 ml (1 tbsp).
- **Meat thermometer:** to measure the internal temperature of meat and poultry during cooking.
- **Deep-frying thermometer:** to check the temperature of oil. Electric deep-fat fryers usually contain their own built-in thermometers.
- **Oven thermometer:** to check oven temperature; some ovens can exceed or fall short of the desired temperature.

POTS & PANS

Pans used on top of the stove need to be heavy enough to sit securely on the burner without tipping, yet not so heavy that you have trouble lifting them. A heavy base is particularly important for gentle, even heat distribution. Pots and pans also need to have lids that fit tightly and sturdy handles that stay cool. Ovenproof handles make it easy to transfer pots and pans from the stove top to the oven, when necessary.

- **Three straight-sided saucepans:** 1 litre (1$^3/_4$ pint), 2 litre (3$^1/_2$ pint), and 3 litre (5 pint) capacity with tightly fitting lids.
- **Two non-stick frying pans:** one 20 cm (8 ins) in diameter and the other 30 or 35 cm (12 or 14 ins) in diameter, preferably with lids so that foods can be covered and allowed to simmer.
- **Large, heavy, flameproof casserole:** preferably cast iron coated in enamel, which disperses a gentle heat, with a tight-fitting lid. Use for stewing and braising.

- **Wok:** for stir-fries and steaming. A wok with a single, long handle is easier to use than a wok with 2 small handles. The more authentic Chinese woks are made from steel, although non-stick models are also available. A wok with a lid is the most versatile.
- **Steamer:** for cooking vegetables and fish. Available as a pan with a perforated base which forms a tier between 2 saucepans, as a folding steaming basket that fits in a saucepan, or a bamboo steamer to use in a wok.
- **Omelette pan:** 18 or 20 cm (7 or 8 ins) in diameter is the most convenient with curved sides.
- **Crêpe pan:** with a flat bottom and shallow, sloping side for making crêpes and pancakes.
- **Small, non-stick milk pan:** with a spout for easy pouring.
- **Large, lightweight stock pot:** for making stock and cooking pasta. The best ones are tall and narrow, in order to contain a large amount of water but to limit the evaporation of water and keep the flavours in.
- **Stove-top grill pan:** used for cooking steaks and chops on top of the stove. The base of this heavy, flat, cast iron pan is ridged to keep the meat out of the fat – there is also a spout for pouring off the fat. It gives results similar to cooking on a barbecue or grill.

Uncoated cast iron pans, omelette pans, and crêpe pans should all be seasoned before using for the first time: cover with a thin layer of oil and heat until very hot, then wipe the oil away with paper towels. The pan need never be washed – simply wipe with paper towels after every use. If you do have to wash it, soak in hot water only and wipe clean, don't use detergent or scouring pads, and season as before.

CUTTING & CHOPPING

A set of sturdy, well-made knives that are kept sharp is essential for efficient food preparation.

- **Chef's or cook's knife:** with a rigid, heavy, wide blade 20 or 25 cm (8 or 10 ins) long.
- **Sharp knife:** with a blade 12 or 15 cm (5 or 6 ins) long, for cutting fruit and vegetables.
- **Small knife:** with a 7 or 10 cm (3 or 4 ins) blade. Use to trim and peel fruit and vegetables.

Knives made of high-carbon stainless steel combine the best of both their components: the carbon enables the knife to take a sharp edge and the stainless steel prevents rusting. Ideally, the metal of the blade should run all the way through the handle and the handle should be well riveted. Keep knives in a knife block or on a magnetic strip: knives lying in a kitchen drawer are dangerous, and can become damaged. Use a sharpening steel regularly, and have your knives sharpened professionally once or twice a year. Blunt knives cause accidents.

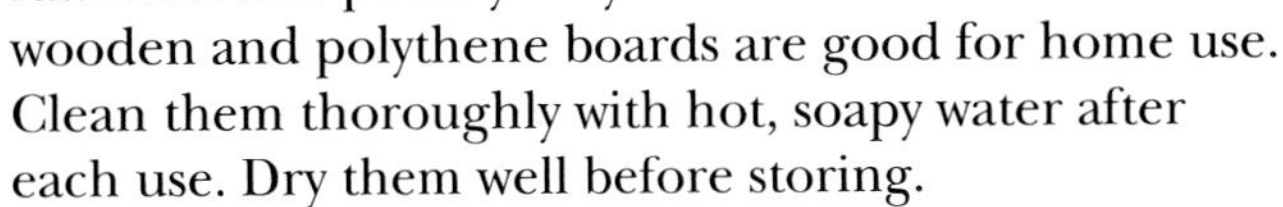

- **Sharpening steel:** to hone or refresh your sharpened knives.
- **Two-pronged carving fork:** some have a guard to protect your hand in case the knife slips.
- **Cutting boards:** these are indispensable, and you should have at least two, keeping one for raw meat and poultry only. Both wooden and polythene boards are good for home use. Clean them thoroughly with hot, soapy water after each use. Dry them well before storing.

OVENWARE

Cooking in the oven requires sturdy tins and dishes that conduct and retain heat efficiently. Baking tins and trays are now available with non-stick coatings, although these are liable to become scratched if you use metal implements. For added convenience, choose oven dishes – casseroles, baking dishes and gratin dishes – that are attractive enough to be used for serving at the table too.

- **Roasting tin:** made of heavy stainless steel or aluminium. If possible, have tins in 2 sizes. Roasting in a tin that is too large will cause juices to evaporate and burn; if the tin is too small, it will be difficult to baste the meat or poultry properly.
- **Two flat baking trays:** for biscuits and meringues.
- **Two loaf tins:** one 500 g (1 lb) and the other 1 kg (2 lb), for breads and cakes, moulding mousses and terrines.
- **12-hole bun tin or muffin tin:** for baking American muffins, fruit buns, and Yorkshire puddings.
- **Deep, loose-bottomed cake tin:** 20 or 23 cm (8 or 9 in) in diameter, for large cakes such as fruit cakes.
- **Springform cake tin:** for making cheesecakes, gateaux, and mousses. The sides open out and the bottom is loose, to allow easy removal.
- **Individual soufflé dishes or ramekins:** used for small soufflés, baked puddings such as crème caramel, baked eggs, savoury pâtés and terrines, and mousses.
- **Two 20 cm (8 in) sandwich tins:** for making layered cakes such as Victoria sandwich cakes.
- **Swiss roll tin:** with shallow sides and a non-stick coating. Swiss roll tins usually measure 23 x 33 cm (9 x 13 in), and are used for both sweet and savoury sponge mixtures and roulades.
- **Shallow, fluted flan tin:** 20 or 23 cm (8 or 9 ins) in diameter, for making quiches and sweet and savoury flans. Metal flan tins conduct heat more efficiently than ceramic dishes, and ensure crisp pastry. The bottoms of the tins are usually loose so that the flans are easy to remove.
- **Individual tartlet tins:** for sweet and savoury tartlets. Available in a variety of shapes, including round-, diamond-, and boat-shaped.
- **Straight-sided soufflé dish:** 1.25 litre (2 pint) capacity. The dish can double as a baking dish for crumbles and other puddings.
- **Large gratin dish:** for making vegetable and other gratins. Also useful for puddings, and for baking fish.
- **Oval pie dish:** with a wide lip for deep-dish sweet and savoury pies.

MATERIALS FOR COOKWARE

As it is important to have pots and pans in a variety of shapes and sizes, it is important that they are made from a variety of materials. A well-stocked kitchen has some cookware made of each of these materials. Buy the best you can afford.

Copper is an excellent heat conductor. Copper pans lined with nickel, tin, or stainless steel are truly the best, preferred by many professional chefs. Copper pans are very expensive and heavy, however, and have to be kept polished.

Aluminium is another efficient heat conductor, but it has certain disadvantages. It scratches easily and can react with acidic foods, giving them a metallic taste. As recent research suggests that aluminium may also contaminate foods, it is usually covered with another material, such as stainless steel.

Porcelain pans both hold and conduct heat well.

Stainless steel is lightweight and durable, but not a very good heat conductor. To compensate, the bases of stainless steel pans are usually reinforced with aluminium or copper.

Cast iron can be heated to a high temperature and retains heat well. Plain cast-iron pans need to be seasoned before use. Enamelled cast-iron pans retain heat well and do not need to be seasoned – perfect for long, slow cooking. Both materials are very heavy.

Non-stick pans are easy to clean and can be used with little or no fat. The coating is quite easily scratched however, and will wear off with time.

ELECTRICAL EQUIPMENT

The wide variety of machines now available takes much of the hard work out of food preparation. Though not absolutely necessary, these machines quite often speed the cook's progress.

- **Hand-held electric mixers:** compact in size and easy to use. An electric mixer allows you to whisk egg whites or cream in seconds.
- **Tabletop mixers:** bulkier than hand-held mixers but will quickly mix cake batters and bread doughs.
- **Blenders:** purée soups, sauces, and other liquids. They cannot be used for solids alone.
- **Food processors:** by changing the blade, you can chop, grate, slice, or purée all kinds of ingredients, and even mix pastry and bread doughs.
- **Electric grinders:** these will quickly produce freshly ground coffee, spices, and peppercorns. They are also useful for grinding nuts and citrus zest.

UTENSILS

You can get by in the kitchen with relatively few utensils and small pieces of equipment. Here is a list of those I use most often. All these tools are readily available.

- **Several wooden spoons and spatulas:** in varying sizes.
- **Two rubber spatulas:** for scraping bowls clean.
- **Long, heavy rolling pin:** 5–7 cm (2–3 ins) in diameter. Wooden ones are fine, although marble ones stay cooler for rolling pastry and chocolate.
- **Pastry brush:** for glazing pastry, greasing cake tins, and brushing meats with marinades.
- **Set of at least 4 mixing bowls:** in varying sizes. These can double as pudding basins.
- **Wire rack:** for cooling cakes, biscuits, and breads.
- **Pastry cutters:** plain and fluted, for biscuits, scones, and tartlets.
- **Piping bag and nozzles:** for piping whipped cream and icing on to cakes and desserts, and shaping meringues and choux pastry.
- **Slotted spoon:** for draining foods and skimming stocks.
- **Fish slice:** for turning and lifting large items of food.
- **Tongs:** for turning meat during cooking without piercing it.
- **Wire balloon whisk:** about 30 cm (12 ins) long, for whisking eggs, cream, and sauces.
- **Long-handled ladle:** for transferring liquids such as stocks and soups.
- **Flexible palette knife:** with a 25 cm (10 in) blade, for turning and lifting foods.
- **Box grater:** with 3 or 4 different cutting surfaces, from coarse to fine, for grating cheese, citrus zest, and nutmeg.
- **Vegetable peeler with a fixed blade:** for peeling potatoes and other round fruits and vegetables. A swivel-bladed peeler is also useful for straight-sided vegetables such as carrots. (When using peeler with a fixed blade, draw it towards you; use a swivel-bladed peeler in the opposite way, working it in downward strokes away from your body.)
- **Sieves:** rigid metal mesh for sifting dry ingredients, flexible nylon for straining sauces and purées.
- **Kitchen scissors:** made from stainless steel for easy cleaning.
- **Juice squeezer:** preferably with a guard to catch pips.
- **Colander:** with legs or a base, so it is free-standing.
- **Pestle and mortar:** ideal for grinding herbs.

AND DON'T FORGET

Here's a reminder of those items that no cook can do without.

- **paper towels**
- **foil**
- **cling film**
- **greaseproof paper**
- **baking parchment**
- **fine white string** for trussing and tying
- **wooden cocktail sticks**
- **can opener**
- **corkscrew and bottle opener**
- **pepper mill** is a must for grinding black pepper
- **kitchen timer** is useful when baking cakes
- **metal skewers** for testing cakes, and meat and poultry
- **ice-cube trays**

HOW TO USE THIS BOOK

EACH CHAPTER BEGINS with a COLOUR INDEX that provides a colour photograph and a clear description of each recipe. The recipes are divided into 3 colour-coded categories according to the preparation and cooking time of each dish. Details such as the number of servings, the number of calories, and the page on which the recipe can be found are also included. The KNOW-HOW pages contain practical information relating to the recipes in the chapter and step-by-step pictures explaining some of the more specialized cooking techniques. The RECIPE PAGES which follow make up the bulk of each chapter. Every recipe has a comprehensive list of ingredients and easy to follow step-by-step instructions. In addition, every recipe page is packed with special features designed to make your cooking simple, enjoyable, and very successful.

COLOUR INDEX

Colour-coded time band

Photograph of each dish

Number of servings

Calories

Total preparation and cooking time

Special band for extra information

Recipe description

Page number

KNOW-HOW

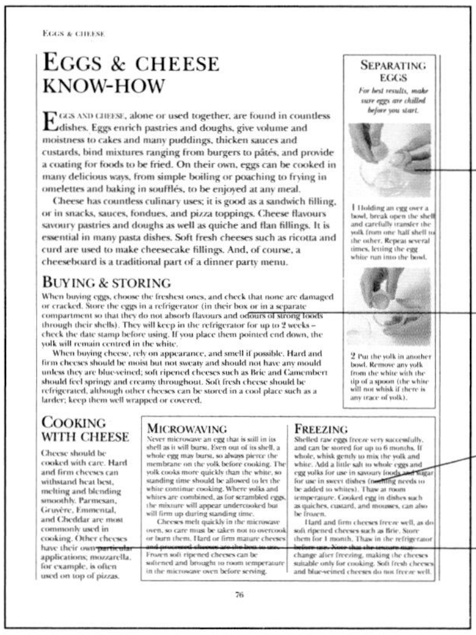

Step-by-step guide to basic cooking techniques

Buying and storing advice

Microwaving and freezing information

Practical hints and tips

RECIPE PAGES

Complete list of ingredients with metric and imperial measurements

Each stage of the recipe given in concise steps

"Cook's know-how" provides professional tips

Simple variations of the main recipe offer even more choice

Full-colour photograph of the finished dish

Additional information about certain dishes

Any special equipment needed listed with ingredients

Illustrated explanation of specific techniques

1

HOT & CHILLED SOUPS

UNDER 30 MINUTES

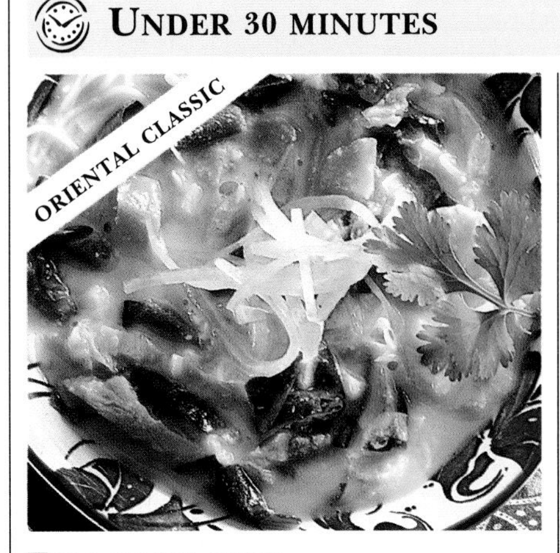

THAI SPICED SOUP

Fresh and chunky: shredded chicken, bean sprouts, and leafy vegetables simmered in coconut milk and stock. Served over noodles.

SERVES 4 238 calories per serving
Takes 25 minutes **PAGE 37**

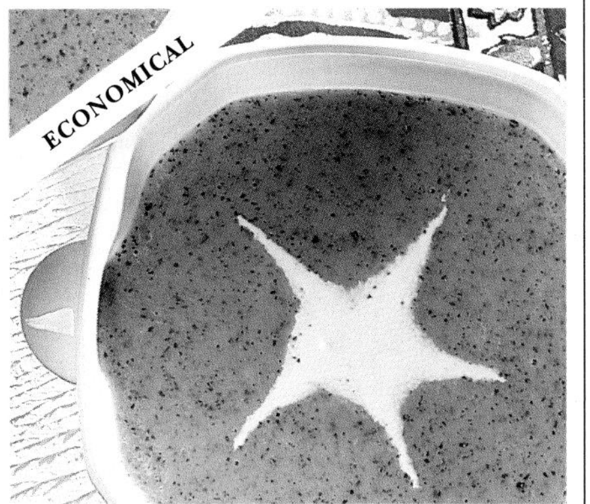

WATERCRESS SOUP

Smooth and creamy: blended onion, potatoes, watercress, stock, and milk, lightly flavoured with a bay leaf. Can be served hot or cold.

SERVES 6 140 calories per serving
Takes 25 minutes **PAGE 25**

SOMERSET MUSHROOM SOUP

Mushrooms, garlic, and onion cooked with stock and white wine, and generously flavoured with thyme and marjoram.

SERVES 4–6 109–73 calories per serving
Takes 25 minutes **PAGE 23**

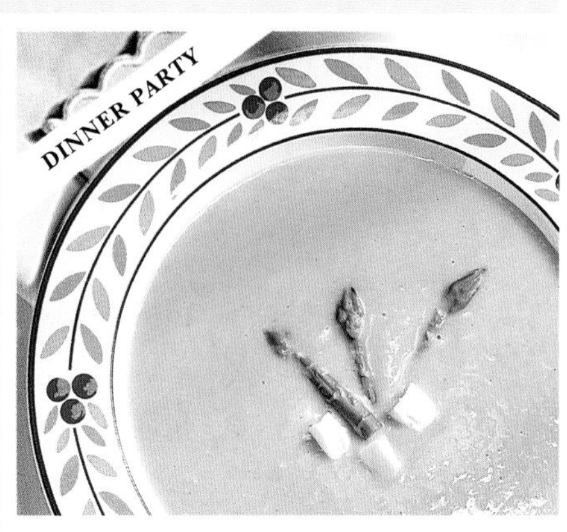

ASPARAGUS SOUP

Fresh asparagus blended with stock and potatoes, and richly flavoured with garlic. Garnished here with nuggets of butter.

SERVES 6 96 calories per serving
Takes 25 minutes **PAGE 24**

TOMATO SOUP

Tomatoes, onions, and garlic blended with stock. Enriched with ready-made pesto and flavoured with a bay leaf.

SERVES 6–8 134-101 calories per serving
Takes 25 minutes **PAGE 27**

CHINESE CRAB & SWEETCORN SOUP

Blended sweetcorn kernels cooked with crabmeat and stock, and flavoured with soy sauce, spring onions, garlic, and ginger.

SERVES 4 216 calories per serving
Takes 20 minutes **PAGE 37**

30–60 MINUTES

LOW FAT

FRENCH PEA SOUP

Smooth and summery: onion and lettuce blended with fresh peas and stock, and flavoured with mint sprigs.

SERVES 4–6 253–169 calories per serving
Takes 35 minutes **PAGE 22**

CUBAN SWEETCORN & SEAFOOD SOUP

Hot and spicy: firm white fish added to sweetcorn, pumpkin, potato, stock, and passata, and simmered with chilli and garlic.

SERVES 4 379 calories per serving
Takes 40 minutes **PAGE 32**

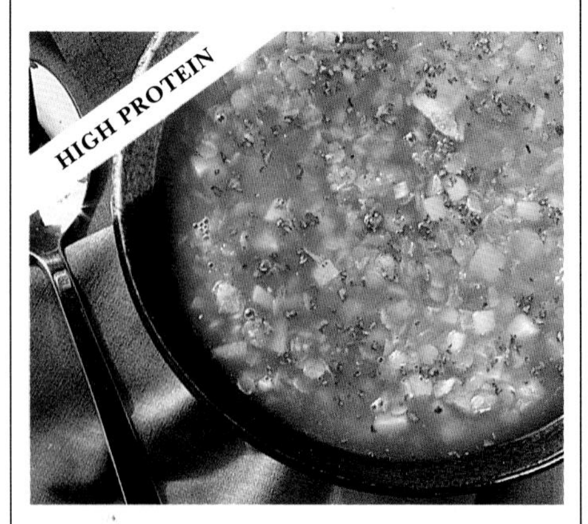

LENTIL & BACON SOUP

Nourishing and hearty: diced vegetables, bacon, and lentils simmered in stock, and richly flavoured with garlic and herbs.

SERVES 4–6 301–201 calories per serving
Takes 50 minutes **PAGE 35**

30–60 MINUTES

CLAM CHOWDER

Fresh clams cooked in fish stock, then simmered with milk, onion, and potatoes, and flavoured with bacon and bay leaf.

SERVES 4 497 calories per serving

Takes 50 minutes **PAGE 30**

MULLIGATAWNY SOUP

Vegetables and spices, simmered with chick peas and stock and combined with yogurt, make a rich and piquant soup.

SERVES 4–6 274–182 calories per serving

Takes 50 minutes **PAGE 28**

PUMPKIN SOUP

Nourishing and smooth: blended pumpkin, leeks, and stock, enriched with cream, and combined with petits pois and spinach.

SERVES 6 329 calories per serving

Takes 50 minutes **PAGE 34**

GAME SOUP

Rich and aromatic: bacon and mushrooms simmered in game stock, flavoured with a citrus and herb bouquet and redcurrant jelly.

SERVES 4 223 calories per serving

Takes 50 minutes **PAGE 35**

CURRIED PARSNIP SOUP

Smooth and spicy: parsnips blended with mild curry powder, onion, garlic, and stock, and enriched with single cream.

SERVES 6–8 197–147 calories per serving

Takes 35 minutes **PAGE 26**

SPICED AUTUMN SOUP

Potatoes, carrots, dessert apples, orange zest and juice, tomatoes, and stock blended with onion, garlic, curry powder, and dried basil.

SERVES 8 171 calories per serving

Takes 50 minutes **PAGE 29**

BLUE STILTON & ONION SOUP

Creamy and rich: finely sliced onions combined with stock, blue Stilton cheese, bay leaves, and nutmeg make a tasty soup.

SERVES 6–8 340–255 calories per serving

Takes 50 minutes **PAGE 29**

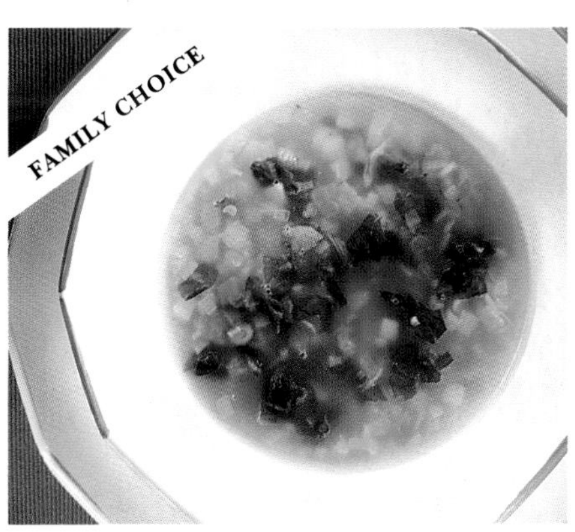

WINTER VEGETABLE SOUP

Assortment of seasonal vegetables simmered with stock, seasoned with dill and turmeric, and coloured with spinach.

SERVES 6 153 calories per serving

Takes 55 minutes **PAGE 26**

HOT & SOUR SOUP

Rich and tangy: dried mushrooms, sliced cabbage, tofu, bamboo shoots, and chicken simmered with stock, and enriched with eggs.

SERVES 4–6 249–166 calories per serving

Takes 50 minutes **PAGE 36**

OVER 60 MINUTES

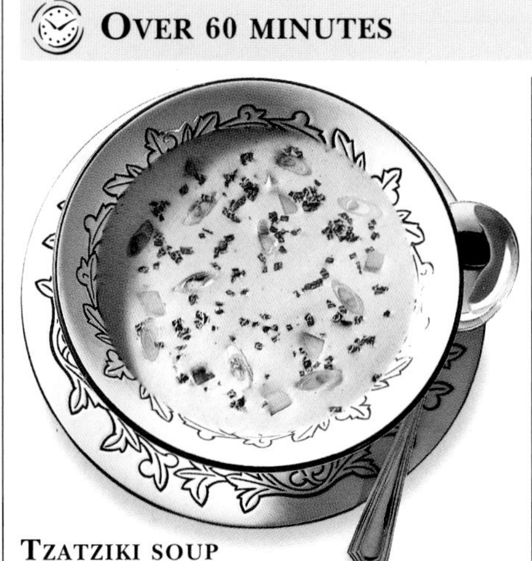

TZATZIKI SOUP

Cool and refreshing: yogurt, cucumber, and garlic blended with olive oil, white wine vinegar, and mint, and served chilled.

SERVES 4–6 138–92 calories per serving

Takes 15 minutes, plus chilling **PAGE 38**

BORSCHT

Beetroot, cabbage, potatoes, and tomatoes simmered with stock, vinegar, sugar, and dill for a rich sweet-sour flavour.

SERVES 4 244 calories per serving

Takes 1 1/4 hours **PAGE 27**

BOUILLABAISSE

Mediterranean favourite: assorted white fish and shellfish simmered in stock with vegetables, orange zest, and Provençal herbs.

SERVES 8 337 calories per serving

Takes 1 1/4 hours **PAGE 33**

GAZPACHO

Tomatoes, pimientos, and garlic blended with stock, olive oil, and red wine vinegar make a rich iced soup. Served with garlic croûtons.

SERVES 4–6 249–166 calories per serving

Takes 15 minutes, plus chilling **PAGE 39**

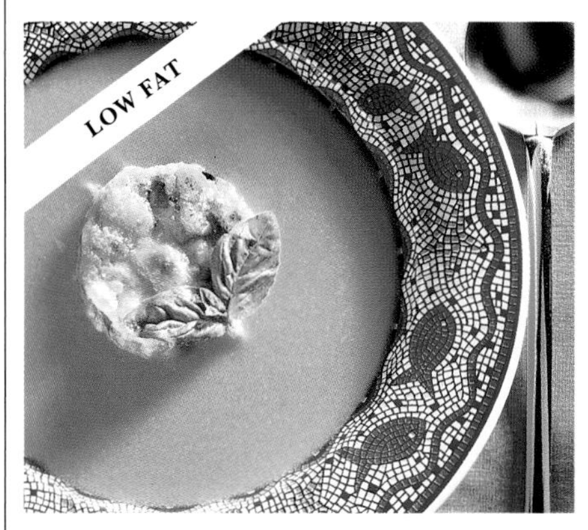

RICH FISH SOUP

White fish fillets blended with stock, dry white wine, and mixed vegetables, and richly flavoured with garlic and herbs.

SERVES 4 419 calories per serving

Takes 1 1/4 hours **PAGE 30**

PRAWN GUMBO

Red pepper and tomatoes cooked with chorizo, stock, and okra make a piquant base for prawns. Served with a rice timbale.

SERVES 4 512 calories per serving

Takes 1 1/4 hours **PAGE 32**

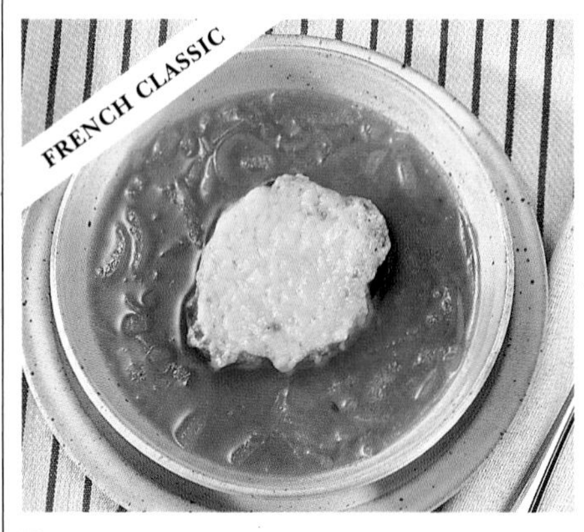

FRENCH ONION SOUP

Thinly sliced caramelized onions simmered in beef stock and topped with a traditional Gruyère croûte.

SERVES 8 353 calories per serving

Takes 1 1/4 hours **PAGE 24**

CREAMY CARROT & ORANGE SOUP

Smooth and tangy: carrots and stock mixed with crème fraîche, orange zest and juice, and flavoured with fresh chives.

SERVES 6–8 308–231 calories per serving

Takes 1 1/4 hours **PAGE 22**

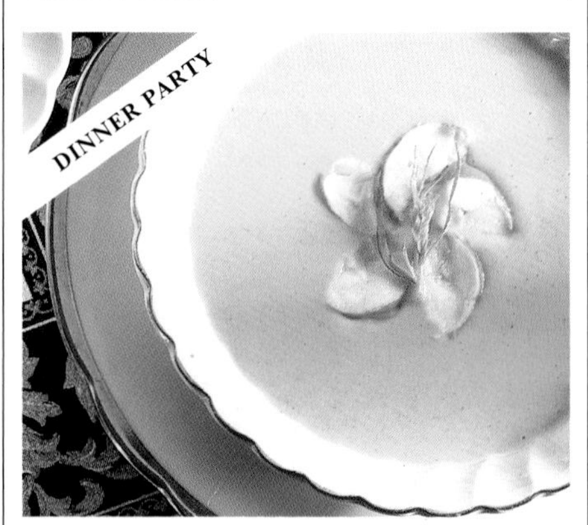

LOBSTER BISQUE

Rich and luxurious: lobster tails, shallots, brandy, wine, stock, and tarragon combined with cream and lemon juice.

SERVES 4 449 calories per serving

Takes 1 1/2 hours **PAGE 31**

OVER 60 MINUTES

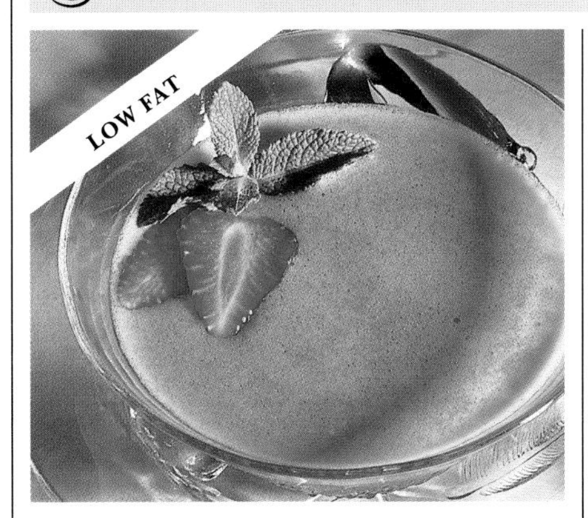

CHILLED STRAWBERRY SOUP

White wine sweetened with caster sugar and blended with strawberries and orange juice, then chilled for a refreshing, sweet soup.

SERVES 4 169 calories per serving
Takes 15 minutes, plus chilling **PAGE 40**

GOULASH SOUP

Rich and wholesome: beef, roasted red peppers, onions, potatoes, and tomatoes cooked in stock, and flavoured with paprika.

SERVES 4–6 544–363 calories per serving
Takes 2¼ hours **PAGE 34**

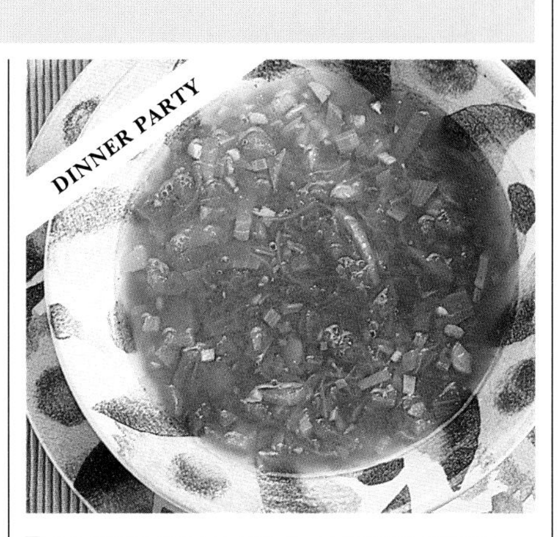

ROASTED TOMATO & GARLIC SOUP

Light and well flavoured: roasted ripe tomatoes cooked with onion and stock, and richly flavoured with garlic.

SERVES 4 127 calories per serving
Takes 40 minutes, plus standing **PAGE 23**

BLUEBERRY & RED WINE SOUP

Chilled and fruity: cranberry juice, red wine, cinnamon, and sugar simmered with blueberries, and enriched with cream.

SERVES 4 364 calories per serving
Takes 30 minutes, plus chilling **PAGE 39**

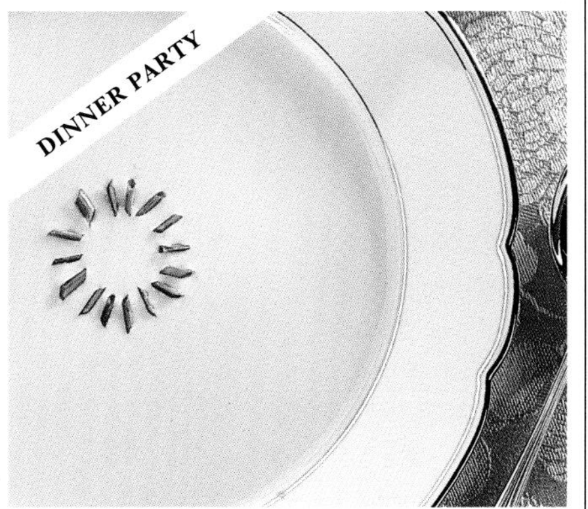

VICHYSSOISE

Leeks, onion, and potatoes blended with chicken stock, chilled, then combined with cream, result in this renowned velvety soup.

SERVES 4–6 251–167 calories per serving
Takes 45 minutes, plus chilling **PAGE 38**

VEGETABLE MINESTRONE

Hearty soup: dried beans cooked and added to a tomato sauce with stock, leeks, cabbage, and arborio rice.

SERVES 4–6 250–167 calories per serving
Takes 1¾ hours, plus soaking **PAGE 25**

CHILLED CURRIED APPLE & MINT SOUP

Apples blended with onion, curry powder, stock, mango chutney, and lemon juice, and combined with yogurt and mint.

SERVES 6 110 calories per serving
Takes 40 minutes, plus chilling **PAGE 40**

CHICKEN NOODLE SOUP

Rich and warming: simmered chicken, carrots, and stock, flavoured with garlic, parsley, and dill, and served over noodles.

SERVES 4 391 calories per serving
Takes 2½ hours **PAGE 36**

SPLIT PEA & GAMMON SOUP

Green split peas and flavoursome gammon, simmered with onion, celery, potatoes, and leeks, make a substantial meal.

SERVES 6–8 451–338 calories per serving
Takes 3¾ hours, plus soaking **PAGE 28**

SOUPS KNOW-HOW

HOME-MADE SOUPS are highly nutritious and wonderfully versatile. They may be simple and quick to prepare, or cooked gently and slowly to extract maximum flavour from the ingredients. They may be hot and warming or cold and refreshing; light and delicate or rich and hearty. There are even sweet and fruity soups.

First-course soups should stimulate the appetite and not be too filling. Puréed vegetable soups are ideal as first courses, as are clear soups, particularly those with attractive garnishes. Main-course soups are designed to be sustaining, and they normally contain ingredients such as meat, poultry, fish, pulses, and pasta. Some good bread is usually the only accompaniment they need to make a well-balanced meal. Fruit soups, which are often served chilled, can double up as delicious desserts.

STOCKS

A well flavoured stock forms the base of many soups, and nothing tastes as good as home-made stock. Stock is economical to make because it is based on meat or fish bones, trimmings, and vegetables. Although it takes time to make stock – several hours of gentle simmering – it is easy to prepare, and can be made well in advance and in large quantities. It can then be frozen until needed. Recipes for stocks can be found on pages 104, 148, 209, and 276. If you don't have any home-made stock, there are fresh stocks available in the chilled cabinets in supermarkets, or you can use stock made from a cube. Remember that stock cubes are often strong and salty, and some contain artificial colourings and flavourings. Another quick alternative is to use canned consommé.

MICROWAVING

For many soups, a microwave oven cannot give the same results as long, slow cooking, but it can produce light vegetable soups in minutes and is useful for thawing frozen stocks and soups, and for reheating soups. The most efficient way is to transfer the soup to individual bowls because soup in larger containers takes longer to heat up than in a pan on top of the stove.

For cooking, use a container that is large enough to allow the soup to rise up slightly during heating. Stir the soup once or twice during cooking, especially just before serving, as the soup at the edge will be hot and bubbling long before that in the centre. Add single cream, soured cream, or yogurt and any garnish just before serving.

FREEZING

Soups taste best if freshly made, but most can be frozen without impairing flavour or texture. Avoid freezing soups containing ingredients such as pasta, potatoes, and rice as they become mushy. It is always best to underseason, as further seasoning can be added when reheating. Add any cream, eggs, and milk at the reheating stage, as freezing could cause separation or curdling.

To thaw a soup to be served hot, heat from frozen in a heavy saucepan over a low heat, stirring occasionally. If the soup appears to be separating, whisk briskly until smooth or work in a blender or food processor for a few seconds. Thaw soup to be served cold in its freezer container, in the refrigerator.

PUREEING SOUPS

Soups are often puréed to give a velvety texture. Starchy vegetables or flour help to thicken them.

Blender or food processor
Either of these can be used to process the cooked ingredients in batches. Scrape the sides to ensure there are no solid pieces left unprocessed.

Hand blender
Use this to purée directly in the saucepan, but only for small quantities of soup. It is ideal for blending in a final addition of cream.

Sieve
Work soup through a fine sieve with a wooden spoon. If soup has been puréed in a blender, it can be sieved afterwards to make it smoother, or to remove any fibres, seeds, or skins.

THICKENING SOUPS

Many smooth soups reach a slightly thickened consistency simply by being puréed. Puréed soups containing starchy ingredients such as rice and potatoes will be even thicker. In some recipes, a little flour is added to the softened vegetables, to bind the fat and juices together before puréeing.

Soups that are not puréed may also be thickened with the addition of a little flour before the stock is stirred in. A classic thickening method is to start with a butter and flour mixture called a roux, just as you do when making a béchamel sauce.

GARNISHES

Fresh herbs, either chopped or as whole leaves, are widely used to garnish soups – mint, chives, thyme, parsley, basil, tarragon, and coriander are all popular. Choose a herb that complements or mirrors any herbs in the soup, and add at the last minute so that it retains its freshness.

Other garnishes include grated or crumbled cheese, chopped hard-boiled egg, crisp pieces of bacon, shredded or diced meat or poultry, toasted nuts, croûtons, chopped spring onions, and sliced or diced cucumber.

A spoonful of a sauce such as pesto adds contrast in colour and flavour. Or create a pattern on the surface of a smooth soup, using double cream for hot or cold soups (see box, below). Greek-style yogurt can be used instead of cream for cold soups.

SKIMMING SOUPS

As a soup is brought to the boil, foam or scum may form on the surface. This is most likely with soups that contain meat or poultry, particularly on the bone, or root vegetables and pulses. This foam, which contains impurities, should be removed as it forms.

Use a large metal spoon or skimmer (slotted if there are herbs and whole spices in the soup) to skim off foam.

If there is a lot of fat on the surface of a soup, skim it off with a large metal spoon, or blot it with paper towels, before serving.

Adding cream & yogurt

Double cream and crème fraîche can be added to a hot soup and cooked further, with no danger of curdling.

◆

Single cream, soured cream, and yogurt will curdle if overheated, so add them just before serving and warm through over a low heat. For chilled soups, add cream or yogurt once the soup has been chilled, before serving.

GARNISHING WITH CREAM

Many attractive garnishes can be added to a soup just before serving. Cream adds a decorative and enriching touch. Whipped cream or soured cream can be simply spooned in the centre of a soup or you can try your hand at one of these simple patterns.

Star
Put a spoonful of cream in the centre. Draw the tip of a knife from the centre towards the edge of the soup, to make 5 points.

Ring of hearts
Drip cream from the tip of a teaspoon to form a circle of drops. Draw the tip of a small knife through the centre of each drop.

Flower
Drizzle cream from the tip of a teaspoon to make a circle. Draw the tip of a knife through it outwards, then inwards.

FRENCH PEA SOUP

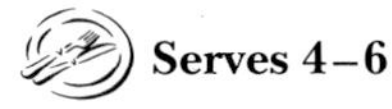

Serves 4–6

30 g (1 oz) butter
1 large onion, coarsely chopped
375 g (12 oz) lettuce leaves, coarsely chopped
1 tbsp plain flour
1.5 kg (3 lb) fresh peas, shelled
1.25 litres (2 pints) chicken or vegetable stock
1/2 tsp caster sugar
2 large mint sprigs
salt and black pepper
shredded fresh mint to garnish

1 Melt the butter in a large saucepan, add the onion, and cook gently, stirring occasionally, for a few minutes until soft but not coloured.

2 Add the lettuce to the pan, and cook, stirring constantly, for 2 minutes. Add the flour and stir for a further 1–2 minutes, then add the peas, stock, sugar, and sprigs of mint. Bring to a boil, cover, and simmer, stirring occasionally, for 20 minutes or until the peas are soft.

3 Remove the mint sprigs and discard. Purée the soup in a food processor or blender until smooth.

4 Return the soup to the rinsed-out pan, reheat, and add salt and pepper to taste. Serve hot, garnished with shredded fresh mint.

Cook's know-how

When fresh peas are out of season, substitute frozen peas. As the pods make up about half the weight of unshelled peas, you will need about 750 g (1 1/2 lb) frozen peas.

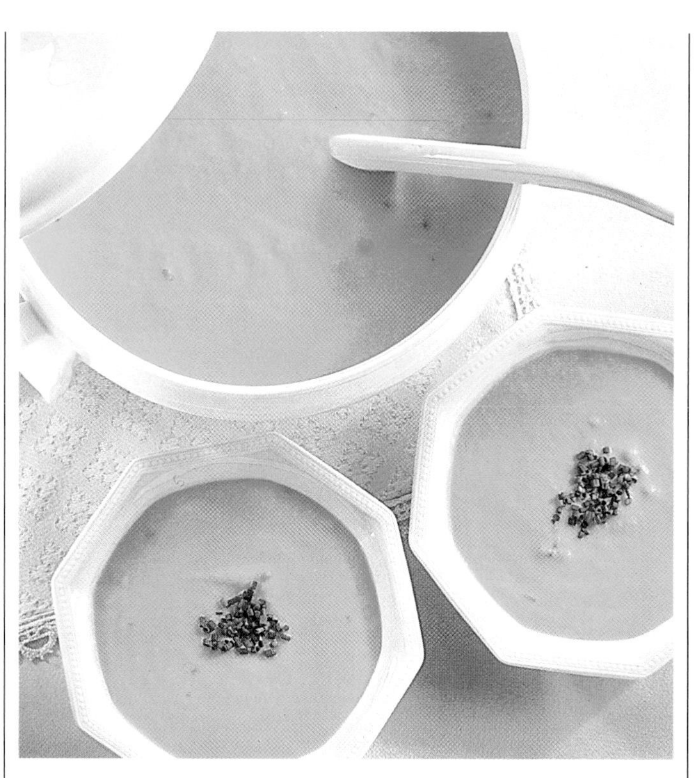

CREAMY CARROT & ORANGE SOUP

Serves 6–8

30 g (1 oz) butter
1 onion, coarsely chopped
1 kg (2 lb) carrots, thickly sliced
1.5 litres (2 1/2 pints) vegetable stock
grated zest of 1/2 orange (see box, right)
300 ml (1/2 pint) orange juice
salt and black pepper
300 ml (1/2 pint) crème fraîche
3 tbsp snipped fresh chives

1 Melt the butter in a large saucepan, add the onion, and cook gently, stirring occasionally, for a few minutes until soft but not coloured. Add the carrots, cover, and cook gently, stirring from time to time, for 10 minutes.

2 Add the stock and bring to a boil. Cover and simmer, stirring from time to time, for 30–40 minutes until the carrots are soft.

3 Purée the soup in a food processor or blender until smooth. Return the soup to the rinsed-out pan, add the orange zest and juice, and salt and pepper to taste. Stir in the crème fraîche and then gently reheat the soup.

4 Stir in half of the snipped chives; garnish individual servings with the remaining chives.

Grating orange zest

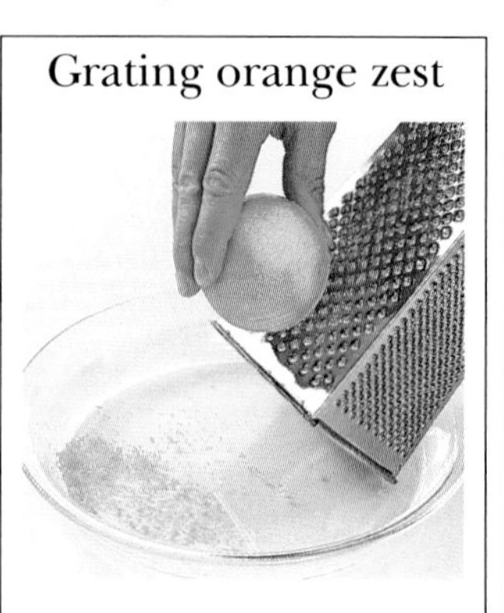

Using the medium grid of a grater, grate the zest, leaving the pith behind.

ROASTED TOMATO & GARLIC SOUP

This soup is light in consistency but full of flavour, making it perfect for late summer when tomatoes are at their best. Charring the tomato skins under a hot grill gives the soup its delicious smoky flavour.

Serves 4

1 kg (2 lb) ripe tomatoes
2 tbsp olive oil
1 onion, chopped
5 garlic cloves, coarsely chopped
1.5 litres (2 1/2 pints) chicken or vegetable stock
salt and black pepper
ready-made pesto to serve

1 Cut the tomatoes in half and arrange them, cut-side down, in a single layer in a flameproof baking dish. Place the tomato halves under a hot grill, close to the heat, for 3 minutes or until the skins are charred.

2 Roast the tomatoes in a preheated oven at 180°C (350°F, Gas 4) for 15–20 minutes until soft. Remove the tomatoes from the oven and leave to stand for at least 4 hours.

3 Peel the tomatoes, and squeeze the skins tightly into the baking dish to extract all the juice. Discard the tomato skins, then coarsely chop the flesh, adding it to the juices in the baking dish.

4 Heat the oil in a large saucepan, add the onion and half of the garlic, and cook gently, stirring from time to time, for a few minutes until soft but not coloured.

5 Add the stock, the tomato flesh and juices, and the remaining garlic, and bring to a boil. Lower the heat and simmer for 5 minutes, then add salt and pepper to taste.

6 Serve at once, with a bowl of pesto so that everyone can stir in a spoonful just before they eat.

MEXICAN ROASTED TOMATO SOUP

Add 1/4 tsp ground cumin and 1/4 tsp crushed mild red chillies to the seasoning and proceed as directed. Instead of pesto, serve with a relish made with 3–4 tbsp chopped fresh coriander leaves, 1 tbsp chopped raw onion, and 1–2 tbsp lime or lemon juice.

SUN-DRIED TOMATO SOUP

Add 2–3 chopped sun-dried tomatoes with the onion and garlic in step 4 and cook as directed. Garnish with finely shredded fresh basil.

SOMERSET MUSHROOM SOUP

Serves 4–6

30 g (1 oz) butter
1 small onion, finely chopped
1 garlic clove, crushed
500 g (1 lb) mushrooms, sliced
1.25 litres (2 pints) chicken or beef stock
150 ml (1/4 pint) dry white wine
2 tbsp chopped fresh thyme
2 tsp chopped fresh marjoram
salt and black pepper

1 Melt the butter in a large saucepan, add the onion and garlic, and cook gently, stirring occasionally, for a few minutes until soft but not coloured. Add the mushrooms and cook, stirring from time to time, for 10 minutes.

2 Add the stock, wine, 1 tbsp of the thyme, the marjoram, and salt and pepper to taste. Bring to a boil, cover, and simmer gently for 10 minutes. Taste for seasoning.

3 Serve hot, sprinkled with the remaining fresh thyme.

Asparagus soup

Serves 6

250 g (8 oz) potatoes, chopped
1.5 litres (2 1/2 pints) chicken or vegetable stock
500 g (1 lb) asparagus
2 garlic cloves, crushed
2 tbsp chopped fresh basil (optional)
salt and black pepper
30 g (1 oz) butter (optional)

1 Put the potatoes into a large saucepan, add the stock, and bring to a boil. Cover and simmer for 15 minutes or until the potatoes are tender.

2 Meanwhile, trim the asparagus and discard any tough stalks. Chop into chunky pieces.

3 Add the chopped asparagus and garlic to the pan and cook, stirring from time to time, for 5 minutes or until the asparagus is tender. Remove 9 tips; reserve for garnish.

4 Purée the soup in a food processor or blender until smooth.

5 Return the soup to the rinsed-out pan and reheat. Add the basil, if using, and salt and pepper to taste. Slice the reserved asparagus tips lengthwise in half. Serve the soup at once, garnished with the asparagus tips and small nuggets of butter, if wished.

Courgette soup

Substitute sliced courgettes for the asparagus, reserving a few slices for garnish. For a lighter soup, omit the potatoes.

Artichoke soup

Substitute 1 x 400 g (13 oz) can artichoke hearts or bottoms, drained and diced, for the asparagus, reserving a few dice for garnish.

French onion soup

Serves 8

45 g (1 1/2 oz) butter
4 tbsp sunflower oil
1 kg (2 lb) large onions, thinly sliced
1 tbsp caster sugar
30 g (1 oz) plain flour
1.8 litres (3 pints) beef stock
salt and black pepper
8 Gruyère croûtes (page 31)

1 Melt the butter with the oil in a large saucepan, and caramelize the onions with the sugar (see box, right). Sprinkle the flour into the pan and cook, stirring constantly, for 1–2 minutes.

2 Gradually stir in the stock and bring to a boil. Add salt and pepper to taste, cover, and simmer, stirring from time to time, for 35 minutes.

3 Taste the soup for seasoning, then ladle into warmed bowls. Float a Gruyère croûte in each bowl and serve at once.

Cook's know-how

Cooking with sugar is the key to developing a rich, golden brown colour and sweet caramel flavour in onions. It is this process that produces the characteristic taste and appearance of the soup.

Caramelizing onions

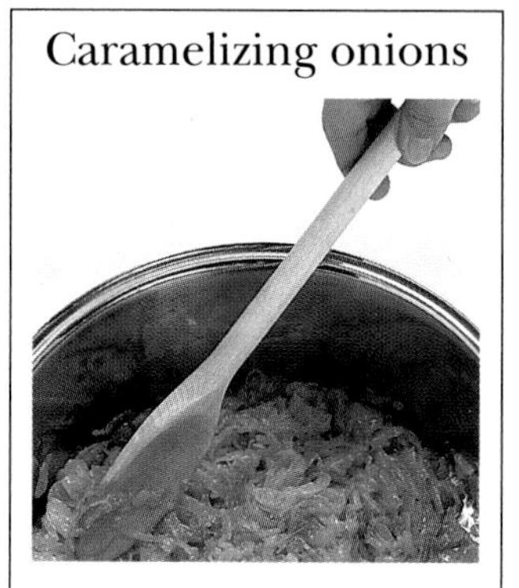

Cook the onions in the butter and oil for a few minutes until soft. Add the sugar and continue cooking over a low heat, stirring occasionally, for 20 minutes or until the onions are golden brown.

VEGETABLE MINESTRONE

Serves 4–6

125 g (4 oz) dried cannellini or borlotti beans
2 tbsp olive oil
1 onion, chopped
2 celery stalks, chopped
2 carrots, diced
1 x 400 g (13 oz) can plum tomatoes, drained and chopped
1 tbsp tomato purée
1 garlic clove, crushed
salt and black pepper
1.5 litres (2½ pints) chicken or vegetable stock
250 g (8 oz) leeks, trimmed and finely sliced
125 g (4 oz) Savoy cabbage, finely shredded
2 tbsp arborio rice
grated Parmesan cheese to serve

1 Put the dried beans into a large bowl and cover with cold water. Leave to soak overnight.

2 Drain the beans, put them into a saucepan, and cover with fresh cold water. Boil rapidly for 10 minutes, then simmer for 35 minutes or until soft.

3 Meanwhile, heat the oil in a large saucepan, add the onion, celery, and carrots, and cook over a high heat, stirring, for 3 minutes.

4 Add the tomatoes, tomato purée, garlic, and salt and pepper to taste. Cover and cook very gently, stirring from time to time, for 20 minutes. Drain the cooked beans and set aside.

5 Pour the stock into the tomato mixture, and continue to simmer, covered, for 15 minutes. Add the leeks, cabbage, rice, and cooked beans, and simmer for 20 minutes. Taste for seasoning.

6 Serve at once, sprinkled with grated Parmesan cheese.

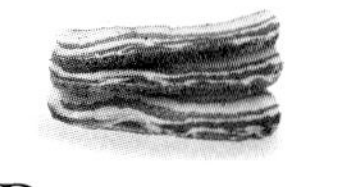

PANCETTA MINESTRONE

Pancetta, Italian cured pork, is sometimes used in minestrone. Dice 60 g (2 oz) pancetta and fry it in the oil over a high heat for 5 minutes before adding the onion, celery, and carrots.

WATERCRESS SOUP

Serves 6

30 g (1 oz) butter
1 onion, finely chopped
2 potatoes, coarsely chopped
125 g (4 oz) watercress, tough stalks removed
900 ml (1½ pints) chicken or vegetable stock
300 ml (½ pint) milk
1 bay leaf
salt and black pepper
single cream to garnish

1 Melt the butter in a large saucepan, add the onion, and cook gently, stirring from time to time, for a few minutes until soft but not coloured.

2 Add the potatoes and the watercress to the saucepan and cook for about 5 minutes until the watercress is wilted.

3 Pour in the chicken or vegetable stock and milk, add the bay leaf, and salt and pepper to taste.

4 Bring the mixture to a boil, cover, and then simmer very gently for 15 minutes or until the potatoes are tender.

5 Remove the bay leaf and discard. Purée the soup in a food processor or blender until smooth. Return the soup to the rinsed-out pan, reheat, then taste for seasoning.

6 Serve immediately, garnished with a little single cream.

Cook's know-how

Watercress is a member of the mustard family and has a distinctive peppery flavour. Watercress soup is delicious served chilled in summer. After puréeing, pour the soup into a large bowl, then cover, cool, and chill for at least 3 hours. Taste for seasoning before serving.

CURRIED PARSNIP SOUP

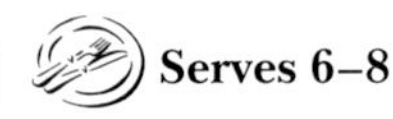 **Serves 6–8**

30 g (1 oz) butter

750 g (1½ lb) parsnips, coarsely chopped

1 large onion, chopped

1 large garlic clove, crushed

2 tsp mild curry powder

1.8 litres (3 pints) chicken or vegetable stock

salt and black pepper

200 ml (7 fl oz) single cream

fresh chives to garnish

1 Melt the butter in a large saucepan, add the chopped parsnips, onion, and crushed garlic, and cook gently, stirring occasionally, for 5 minutes or until the onion is softened but not coloured.

2 Stir in the curry powder, and cook for 1 minute, then blend in the stock, and add salt and pepper to taste. Bring to a boil, stirring, then cover, and simmer gently for 20 minutes or until the parsnips are tender.

3 Purée the soup in a food processor or blender until smooth. Return the soup to the rinsed-out pan, heat gently to warm through, stirring constantly, then taste for seasoning.

4 Stir in the single cream and reheat gently. Serve at once, garnished with fresh chives.

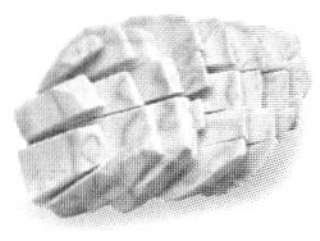

CURRIED CELERIAC SOUP

Substitute 750 g (1½ lb) celeriac, coarsely chopped, for the parsnips, and cook as directed.

WINTER VEGETABLE SOUP

Serves 6

45 g (1½ oz) butter

1 leek, trimmed and diced

1 onion, chopped

1 celery stalk, diced

1 small potato, diced

1 turnip, diced

1 small carrot, diced

3 garlic cloves, crushed

1.5 litres (2½ pints) chicken or vegetable stock

250 g (8 oz) spinach, coarsely shredded (see box, right)

3 spring onions, thinly sliced

¼ tsp dill

¼ tsp turmeric

salt and black pepper

2 hard-boiled eggs, peeled and chopped, to serve

1 Melt the butter in a large saucepan, add the leek, and cook gently, stirring occasionally, for 5 minutes or until softened. Add the onion, celery, potato, turnip, carrot, and garlic, and cook for 8 minutes.

2 Add the stock, and bring to a boil. Cover and simmer, stirring occasionally, for 25 minutes or until the vegetables are tender.

3 Add the spinach, spring onions, dill, and turmeric, and cook for 3 minutes or until the spinach is cooked through but still bright green. Add salt and pepper to taste.

4 Serve the soup at once, with a bowl of chopped hard-boiled eggs handed separately.

Shredding spinach

Remove the stalks and stack several spinach leaves. Roll up tightly, and cut crosswise into shreds.

TOMATO SOUP

Serves 6–8

30 g (1 oz) butter
2 onions, coarsely chopped
1 garlic clove, crushed
1 tbsp plain flour
1.25 litres (2 pints) chicken or vegetable stock
2 x 400 g (13 oz) cans tomatoes
1 bay leaf
salt and black pepper
4 tbsp ready-made pesto
single cream and fresh basil leaves to garnish

Garnishing with cream

With a teaspoon, quickly swirl the single cream in a spiral on each serving.

1 Melt the butter in a large saucepan, add the onions and garlic, and cook gently, stirring from time to time, for a few minutes until soft but not coloured.

2 Add the flour to the pan and cook, stirring constantly, for 1 minute.

3 Pour in the stock and add the tomatoes and their juice, the bay leaf, and salt and pepper to taste. Bring to a boil, cover the pan, and simmer gently for 20 minutes.

4 Remove the bay leaf and discard. Purée the soup in a food processor or blender until smooth.

5 Return the soup to the rinsed-out pan, add the pesto, and heat through. Taste for seasoning.

6 Serve at once, garnished with cream (see box, above) and fresh basil leaves.

QUICK TOMATO SOUP

Passata, Italian sieved tomatoes, makes a beautiful deep red soup. Substitute 750 ml (1¼ pints) of bottled or canned passata for the canned tomatoes and then cook as directed.

BORSCHT

Serves 4

5 raw beetroot, peeled
½ cabbage, coarsely chopped
2 waxy potatoes, diced
175 g (6 oz) tomatoes, peeled (page 39), seeded, and diced
½ carrot, chopped
¼ small onion, chopped
1.5 litres (2½ pints) chicken or vegetable stock, more if needed
3–4 dill sprigs
30 g (1 oz) sugar
2 tbsp red wine vinegar
salt and black pepper
soured cream and dill sprigs to garnish

Grating beetroot

Using the coarse grid of a grater, grate the beetroot on to a plate with firm downward strokes.

1 Dice 4 of the beetroot, and coarsely grate the remaining beetroot (see box, right).

2 Put the diced beetroot, cabbage, potatoes, tomatoes, carrot, and onion into a large pan with the stock. Bring to a boil, then simmer for 30–40 minutes until the vegetables are very tender. Add extra stock if necessary.

3 Add the dill, sugar, and vinegar, and simmer for 10 minutes to let the sweet-sour flavours develop. Add the grated beetroot, salt and pepper to taste, and more sugar and vinegar if necessary.

4 Serve at once, garnished with spoonfuls of soured cream and sprigs of dill.

SPLIT PEA & GAMMON SOUP

Serves 6–8

500 g (1 lb) green split peas
500 g (1 lb) gammon knuckle
2.5 litres (4 pints) water
1 large onion, finely chopped
4 celery stalks, finely chopped
3 potatoes, diced
3 leeks, trimmed and sliced
3 tbsp chopped parsley (optional)
salt and black pepper

1 Put the green split peas and the gammon knuckle into 2 separate large bowls and cover with cold water. Leave to soak overnight.

2 Drain the split peas and gammon knuckle, then put them into a large saucepan with the measured water. Bring to a boil, then simmer, uncovered, for about 1 hour.

3 Add the onion, celery, potatoes, and leeks to the pan, cover, and simmer gently for 2½ hours until the gammon is tender and the peas are cooked. Add more water, if needed, during cooking.

4 Skim the surface if necessary. Remove the gammon knuckle from the saucepan and let it cool slightly. Pull the meat away from the knuckle bone, discarding any skin and fat.

5 Coarsely chop the meat and return it to the saucepan. Add the parsley, if using, and salt and pepper to taste. Heat the soup gently to warm through, and serve immediately.

SPLIT PEA, GAMMON, & CHORIZO SOUP

Add 60 g (2 oz) sliced chorizo sausage when returning the cooked meat to the pan.

MULLIGATAWNY SOUP

Serves 4–6

45 g (1½ oz) butter
½ onion, chopped
1 celery stalk, diced
1 small apple, peeled and diced
1 small carrot, diced
1 small green pepper, cored, seeded, and diced
3–5 garlic cloves, crushed
3 tbsp plain flour
2–3 tsp curry powder
¼ tsp each ground ginger, cinnamon, and turmeric
1.25 litres (2 pints) chicken or vegetable stock
1 x 400 g (13 oz) can chick peas, drained and lightly mashed
1 x 400 g (13 oz) can chopped tomatoes
1 bay leaf
1 tbsp chopped parsley
1 tbsp lemon juice
175 g (6 oz) plain yogurt
chopped parsley and flat-leaf parsley leaves to garnish

1 Melt the butter in a pan, add the onion, and cook gently, stirring from time to time, for a few minutes until soft but not coloured.

2 Add the celery, apple, carrot, green pepper, and garlic. Cook, stirring from time to time, for 8 minutes.

3 Add the flour, curry powder, ginger, cinnamon, and turmeric, and cook for 2 minutes. Stir in the stock, chick peas, tomatoes, and bay leaf, and bring to a boil. Cover and simmer for 20 minutes, until the vegetables are tender.

4 Remove the bay leaf and discard. Add the chopped parsley and lemon juice to the saucepan. Combine a little of the soup with the yogurt, then stir it back into the hot soup. Serve the soup immediately, garnished with the chopped parsley and parsley leaves.

Mulligatawny

This spiced soup dates from the days of the British Raj and was introduced to Britain by nabobs returning from India in the 18th and 19th centuries. The name comes from a Tamil word, milagutannir, *which means "pepper water".*

SPICED AUTUMN SOUP

Serves 8

60 g (2 oz) butter
2 large onions, coarsely chopped
2 potatoes, coarsely chopped
2 carrots, coarsely chopped
3 garlic cloves, crushed
pared zest and juice of 1 orange
2 tsp mild curry powder
1.8 litres (3 pints) chicken or vegetable stock
2 x 400 g (13 oz) cans chopped tomatoes
2 dessert apples, peeled and chopped
1 tbsp dried basil
salt and black pepper
herb croûtes (page 31) to serve

1 Melt the butter in a large saucepan, add the onions, potatoes, carrots, garlic, and orange zest, and cook gently, stirring from time to time, for about 5 minutes.

2 Add the curry powder, and cook, stirring constantly, for 1–2 minutes.

3 Add the stock, orange juice, tomatoes, apples, basil, and salt and pepper to taste. Bring to a boil, cover, and simmer gently for 30 minutes or until the vegetables are tender. Discard the orange zest.

4 Purée the soup in a food processor or blender until smooth. Return to the rinsed-out pan, reheat, and taste for seasoning. Serve at once, with herb croûtes.

Paring orange zest

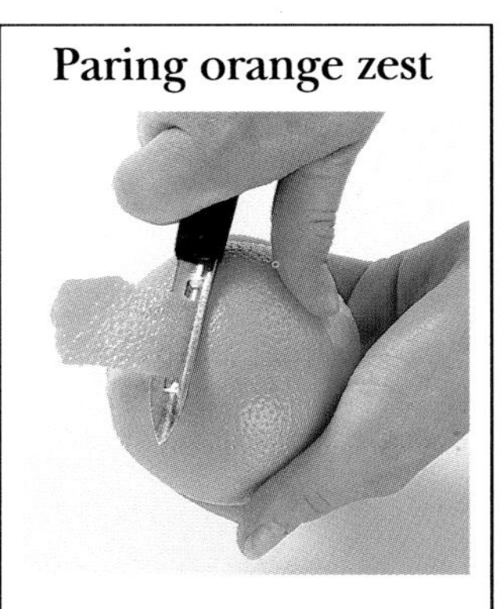

With a vegetable peeler, remove strips of zest, excluding the pith.

BLUE STILTON & ONION SOUP

Serves 6–8

600 ml (1 pint) milk
2 bay leaves
1/4 tsp grated nutmeg
90 g (3 oz) butter
2 large onions, finely sliced
75 g (2 1/2 oz) plain flour
1.5 litres (2 1/2 pints) chicken or vegetable stock
salt and black pepper
150 g (5 oz) blue Stilton cheese, crumbled
single cream to serve (optional)

1 Pour the milk into a saucepan, add the bay leaves and nutmeg, and bring almost to a boil. Remove from the heat, cover, and leave to infuse for 20 minutes.

2 Meanwhile, melt the butter in a large pan, add the onions, and cook very gently, stirring occasionally, for 10 minutes or until they are soft but not coloured.

3 Add the flour, and cook, stirring, for 2 minutes. Strain the infused milk and gradually blend it into the onion and flour mixture. Add the stock, and salt and pepper to taste. Bring to a boil, then simmer, partially covered, for 10 minutes.

4 Add the cheese to the pan and stir over a very low heat until it is melted; do not let the soup boil or the cheese will become stringy. Taste for seasoning. If you wish, stir in a little single cream. Serve at once.

Blue Stilton

This cheese originated in the 18th century in Leicestershire, but was first sold at The Bell, a famous coaching inn in Stilton in Huntingdonshire, 30 miles away. Travellers referred to it as Stilton cheese and the name stuck.

CLAM CHOWDER

Serves 4

500 g (1 lb) clams in shells, cleaned (page 106)
250 ml (8 fl oz) fish stock
45 g (1½ oz) butter
1 onion, chopped
3 unsmoked bacon rashers, rinds removed, diced
2 tbsp plain flour
2 potatoes, diced
750 ml (1¼ pints) milk
1 bay leaf
salt and black pepper

1 Put the clams into a large saucepan, add the fish stock, and bring to a boil. Lower the heat, cover, and cook over a medium heat for 5–8 minutes until the clam shells open.

2 Discard any clams that have not opened. Set aside 12 clams in their shells for garnish and keep warm. Remove the remaining clams from their shells. Discard the shells and strain the cooking juices.

3 Melt the butter in a large pan, add the onion, and cook gently, stirring, for a few minutes until soft but not coloured. Add the bacon, and cook for 1 minute, then add the flour, and cook, stirring, for 1–2 minutes.

4 Add the potatoes, milk, strained clam juices, and bay leaf to the pan. Bring to a boil, then lower the heat and simmer for 15 minutes. Add the shelled clams, and reheat gently for about 5 minutes. Remove the bay leaf and discard.

5 Add salt and pepper to taste. Serve at once, garnished with the reserved clams in their shells.

Which chowder?

Some people hold very firm views about the best way to make this classic American recipe. This version is for New England clam chowder; Manhattan clam chowder omits the milk but adds tomatoes and green peppers.

RICH FISH SOUP

Serves 4

4 tbsp olive oil
2 leeks, trimmed and chopped
1 celery stalk, chopped
1 potato, chopped
1 carrot, chopped
½ red pepper, chopped
3 garlic cloves, chopped
375 g (12 oz) tomatoes, peeled (page 39), seeded, and chopped
500 g (1 lb) mixed white fish fillets, chopped (see right)
1 litre (1¾ pints) fish stock
500 ml (16 fl oz) dry white wine
5 basil sprigs
1 tsp chopped parsley
¼ tsp dried mixed herbs
¼ tsp cayenne pepper
salt and black pepper
Gruyère croûtes (page 31) and basil sprigs to garnish

1 Heat the oil in a large saucepan, add the leeks, celery, potato, carrot, red pepper, and garlic, and cook gently, stirring occasionally, for 5 minutes or until the vegetables are just soft.

2 Add the tomatoes and fish, and cook for 3 minutes. Add the stock, wine, basil, parsley, and mixed herbs, and bring to a boil. Simmer for 35 minutes.

Cook's know-how

This delicious soup is based on the French soupe de poisson. *For an interesting flavour in the finished soup, use several types of white fish, such as cod, haddock, monkfish, and red and grey mullet. The soup is puréed, so small pieces and scraps of fish will do very well.*

3 Purée the soup in a food processor or blender until smooth. For a very smooth consistency, work the soup through a sieve after puréeing.

4 Return the soup to the rinsed-out pan and reheat gently. Add the cayenne pepper and salt and pepper to taste.

5 Serve at once, garnished with Gruyère croûtes and basil sprigs.

LOBSTER BISQUE

A bisque is a purée flavoured with brandy, white wine, and cream, prepared by a complex process which brings out the maximum flavour. When made with lobster, it is perfect for a special occasion.

 **Serves 4**

- *45 g (1 1/2 oz) butter*
- *6 shallots, coarsely chopped*
- *1/2 carrot, coarsely chopped*
- *1 live lobster, halved (see Cook's know-how, right)*
- *1 bay leaf*
- *4 tbsp brandy*
- *1.5 litres (2 1/2 pints) fish stock*
- *250 ml (8 fl oz) dry white wine*
- *125 g (4 oz) long grain rice*
- *1–2 tsp chopped fresh tarragon*
- *175 ml (6 fl oz) single cream*
- *1 tbsp lemon juice*
- *pinch of cayenne pepper*
- *salt and black pepper*
- *tarragon sprigs to garnish*

1 Melt half of the butter in a large saucepan, add the shallots and carrot, and cook gently for 5 minutes until softened. Add the lobster and bay leaf and cook for 5 minutes, or until the lobster turns bright red.

2 Add the brandy and boil until it has reduced to about 2 tbsp, then add the stock and wine. Cook the lobster for another 5 minutes, then remove from the pan and leave until cool enough to handle.

3 Using a mallet, crack the lobster shells, remove the meat (page 107), and set aside. Add the lobster shells, rice, and chopped tarragon to the soup, and cook for 15–20 minutes until the rice is tender.

4 Remove the lobster shells and bay leaf from the soup and discard. Cut the cooked lobster into several slices and add half to the soup, reserving the other half for garnish.

5 Purée the soup in a food processor or blender until smooth. Pour the purée through a sieve to make sure that no tiny pieces of lobster shell remain.

6 Return the purée to the pan. Add the cream, lemon juice, cayenne pepper, and salt and pepper to taste, then reheat. Stir in the remaining butter.

7 Serve at once, garnished with the reserved lobster meat and tarragon sprigs.

Cook's know-how

To kill and cut up the lobster, start by piercing through the cross on the centre of the head. Split the lobster in half lengthwise, and remove and discard the intestinal vein and the sack of grit which is found in the head. Scoop out the tomalley (greenish liver) and either discard or reserve for a sauce. Crack the claws, but do not shell them.

CROUTES & CROUTONS

These need not be reserved for special occasions. They can add colour, texture, and interest to the most basic everyday soups.

HERB CROUTES

Trim the crusts from slices of bread. Cut each slice into a square or decorative shape. Heat a 5 mm (1/4 in) layer of oil in a frying pan, add the bread, and brown all over. Finely chop some parsley or separate into small sprigs. Drain the croûtes on paper towels. Roll the edges of the croûtes in the parsley or put a leaf on top of each one.

GARLIC CROUTONS

Trim the crusts from slices of bread and cut into 1 cm (1/2 in) cubes. Heat a 5 mm (1/4 in) layer of oil in a frying pan. Peel and crush 1 garlic clove and cook for 1 minute. Add the bread cubes and cook, stirring occasionally, until brown all over. Remove, and drain on paper towels.

GRUYERE CROUTES

Cut slices from a baguette and toast on one side under a hot grill. Remove from the heat and turn the slices over. Grate some Gruyère cheese and sprinkle it evenly on top of the bread slices. Return to the grill and cook until the cheese has melted and is softly bubbling.

CUBAN SWEETCORN & SEAFOOD SOUP

Serves 4

30 g (1 oz) butter
1 small onion, chopped
2 garlic cloves, crushed
500 g (1 lb) frozen sweetcorn kernels
125 g (4 oz) piece of pumpkin, peeled and cut into chunks
1 waxy potato, cut into chunks
1 mild, fresh red chilli, cored, seeded, and chopped
1.25 litres (2 pints) fish, chicken, or vegetable stock
250 ml (8 fl oz) passata
1 bay leaf
1/4 tsp dried thyme
salt and black pepper
250 g (8 oz) firm white fish, cut into large chunks
lime wedges to serve

1 Melt the butter in a large pan, add the onion and garlic, and cook gently for a few minutes until soft but not coloured. Add the sweetcorn, pumpkin, potato, and chilli, and cook, stirring occasionally, for 5 minutes.

2 Add the stock, passata, bay leaf, thyme, and salt and pepper to taste, and bring to a boil. Simmer, uncovered, stirring occasionally, for 15 minutes or until the pumpkin and potato pieces are just tender.

3 Add the fish to the soup, and heat through gently, cooking just until the chunks become opaque.

4 Remove the bay leaf and discard. Taste for seasoning. Serve the soup immediately, accompanied by wedges of lime.

Cook's know-how

Any firm white fish or shellfish may be used in this soup. Be careful not to overcook the pieces of fish or they will disintegrate.

PRAWN GUMBO

Serves 4

3 tbsp sunflower oil
1 small onion, diced
1 red pepper, cored, seeded, and diced
1 celery stalk, diced
3 garlic cloves, crushed
2 tbsp chopped parsley
30 g (1 oz) plain flour
1/2 tsp paprika
1/4 tsp each ground cumin and dried oregano
750 g (1 1/2 lb) tomatoes, peeled (page 39), seeded, and diced
175 g (6 oz) chorizo, sliced
1.25 litres (2 pints) fish stock
250 g (8 oz) okra, sliced
250–375 g (8–12 oz) cooked peeled prawns
pinch of cayenne pepper
salt and black pepper
rice timbales (see box, right) to serve
large cooked prawns and spring onions to garnish

1 Heat the oil, add the onion, red pepper, celery, garlic, and parsley, and cook for 8 minutes or until softened. Add the flour, and cook, stirring all the time, for 1 minute.

2 Sprinkle in the paprika, cumin, and oregano, and cook, stirring, for 1 minute, then add the tomatoes, chorizo, and stock. Bring to a boil, then simmer, stirring occasionally, for 30 minutes or until the soup has thickened slightly.

3 Add the okra, and cook for 5–7 minutes until tender, then add the prawns and heat through. Add the cayenne pepper, and salt and pepper to taste.

4 Serve the gumbo hot, with rice timbales. Garnish with large cooked prawns and spring onions.

Making a rice timbale

Oil a small bowl, fill with cooked rice, and press down lightly. Turn upside down on to a warmed soup plate and lift off the bowl.

BOUILLABAISSE

Bouillabaisse, the classic fish dish with the authentic flavours of Provence, is one of the most satisfying and delectable dishes you can bring to your table. This rich stew-soup is served with thick slices of toasted bread spread with rouille, a chilli-flavoured mayonnaise.

Serves 8

- *2 tbsp olive oil*
- *2 leeks, trimmed and diced*
- *1 small onion, chopped*
- *1 small fennel bulb, sliced*
- *4 garlic cloves, crushed*
- *1 tbsp chopped parsley*
- *1 bay leaf*
- *1 litre (1 3/4 pints) water*
- *600 ml (1 pint) fish stock*
- *500 g (1 lb) tomatoes, peeled (page 39), seeded, and diced*
- *1/4 tsp herbes de Provence*
- *5 cm (2 in) piece of orange zest*
- *1/4 tsp fennel seeds*
- *2–3 potatoes, cut into chunks*
- *1 kg (2 lb) assorted fish, cut into bite-sized pieces*
- *1 kg (2 lb) assorted shellfish, shelled*
- *1/2 tsp saffron threads*
- *salt and black pepper*
- *8 slices of baguette, toasted, to serve*

ROUILLE

- *3 garlic cloves*
- *125 ml (4 fl oz) mayonnaise*
- *2 tsp paprika*
- *1 tsp mild chilli powder*
- *1/4 tsp ground cumin*
- *3 tbsp olive oil*
- *1 small fresh red chilli, cored, seeded, and finely chopped*
- *1 tbsp lemon juice*
- *salt*

1 Heat the olive oil in a large, heavy saucepan. Add the diced leeks, chopped onion, fennel, garlic, parsley, and bay leaf, and cook, stirring occasionally, for 5 minutes.

2 Pour in the measured water and stock. Add the tomatoes, herbes de Provence, orange zest, and fennel seeds. Bring to a boil, and simmer for 30 minutes.

3 Meanwhile, make the rouille (see box, right). Chill until needed.

4 Add the potatoes to the soup, and simmer for 10 minutes. Do not stir or the potatoes will break up.

5 Add the fish, shellfish, saffron, and salt and pepper to taste, and cook for a few minutes until the fish becomes opaque.

6 Remove the bay leaf and orange zest and discard. Serve the bouillabaisse with slices of toasted baguette spread with the rouille.

Making rouille

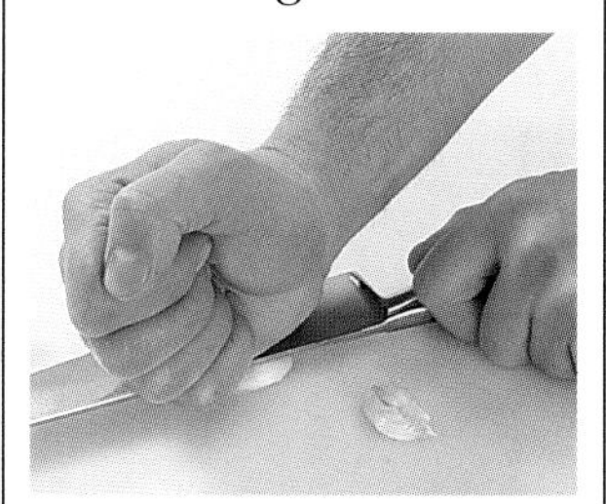

Use a knife blade to crush the garlic. Put into a bowl with the mayonnaise, paprika, chilli powder, and ground cumin.

Pour in the olive oil, drop by drop, whisking constantly as the oil is absorbed into the spicy mayonnaise.

Add the red chilli and lemon juice to the sauce; add salt to taste, and stir well to combine.

Cook's know-how

Bouillabaisse is made with an assortment of firm-fleshed fish, which can include monkfish and John Dory, and shellfish, such as mussels, prawns, and small crab.

PUMPKIN SOUP

Serves 6

- *1.5 kg (3 lb) pumpkin*
- *150 g (5 oz) butter*
- *2 leeks, trimmed and sliced*
- *1 litre (1¾ pints) chicken or vegetable stock*
- *¼ tsp grated nutmeg*
- *salt and black pepper*
- *30 g (1 oz) petits pois*
- *250 g (8 oz) spinach leaves, finely chopped*
- *300 ml (½ pint) single cream*

1 Cut out the flesh from the pumpkin, discarding the seeds and fibres. Cut the pumpkin flesh into 2 cm (¾ in) chunks.

2 Melt 100 g (3½ oz) of the butter in a large saucepan. Add the leeks, and cook very gently, covered, for 10 minutes or until soft.

3 Add the stock, pumpkin chunks, nutmeg, and salt and pepper to taste. Bring to a boil, cover, and simmer for 30 minutes or until the vegetables are very soft.

4 Meanwhile, cook the petits pois in boiling salted water for 5 minutes. Drain thoroughly.

5 Melt the remaining butter in a saucepan, add the spinach and cook very gently, covered, for 3 minutes or until soft.

6 Purée the soup in a food processor or blender until smooth, in batches if necessary. Return to the pan and stir in the cream. Stir the petits pois and spinach into the soup, heat through, and serve immediately.

Cook's know-how

For individual servings as illustrated above, use small hollowed-out pumpkins, or a single large pumpkin in place of a soup tureen. When removing the pumpkin flesh, leave a scalloped border to make the container look attractive.

GOULASH SOUP

Serves 4–6

- *2 red peppers*
- *2 tbsp sunflower oil*
- *500 g (1 lb) stewing beef, trimmed and cut into 3.5 cm (1½ in) pieces*
- *2 large onions, thickly sliced*
- *1 tbsp plain flour*
- *2 tsp paprika*
- *1.5 litres (2½ pints) beef stock*
- *1 x 400 g (13 oz) can chopped tomatoes*
- *2 tbsp tomato purée*
- *1 tbsp red wine vinegar*
- *1 garlic clove, crushed*
- *1 bay leaf*
- *salt and black pepper*
- *750 g (1½ lb) potatoes, coarsely chopped*
- *dash of Tabasco sauce*
- *soured cream and snipped fresh chives to garnish*

1 Roast and peel the red peppers (page 354). Cut the flesh into chunks.

2 Heat the oil in a large pan. Add the beef and brown all over. Add the onions, peppers, flour, and paprika, and stir over a high heat for 1–2 minutes.

3 Add the stock, tomatoes, tomato purée, vinegar, garlic, bay leaf, and salt and pepper to taste. Bring to a boil, cover tightly, and simmer for 1½ hours.

4 Add the potatoes and cook for 30 minutes or until the beef and potatoes are tender. Remove the bay leaf and discard.

5 Add a little Tabasco sauce and taste for seasoning. Serve at once, garnished with soured cream and snipped chives.

Goulash

From a 9th century nomadic tribal meal of slowly stewed meat, Hungarian goulash has developed into an internationally acclaimed dish, distinctively flavoured with paprika, onions, and red peppers, and enriched with potatoes, tomatoes, and soured cream.

LENTIL & BACON SOUP

 **Serves 4–6**

30 g (1 oz) butter
1 onion, chopped
1 carrot, diced
1 celery stalk, diced
3 garlic cloves, crushed
2–3 lean back bacon rashers, rinds removed, diced
175 g (6 oz) red lentils
60 g (2 oz) swede or turnip, peeled and diced
1 small potato, diced
2 bay leaves
1/4 tsp chopped fresh sage
1/4 tsp cumin seeds (optional)
2 litres (3 1/2 pints) chicken or vegetable stock
salt and black pepper
chopped parsley to garnish

1 Melt the butter in a large saucepan, add the onion, carrot, celery, and garlic, and cook, stirring, for 5–6 minutes until soft and lightly coloured. Add the bacon, lentils, swede or turnip, potato, bay leaves, sage, and cumin, if using, and cook for 15 minutes.

2 Pour in the stock, bring to a boil, then simmer gently, uncovered, for 20 minutes or until the lentils and vegetables are tender. Add salt and pepper to taste.

3 Remove the bay leaves and discard. Serve at once, sprinkled with chopped parsley.

LENTIL & FRANKFURTER SOUP

For a hearty main meal soup, add 250 g (8 oz) frankfurters. Chop them into 1 cm (1/2 in) pieces and add to the soup about 5 minutes before the end of cooking time, so that they are warmed through but not overcooked. Smoked sausages may also be used in this way.

GAME SOUP

Serves 4

30 g (1 oz) butter
125 g (4 oz) smoked streaky bacon rashers, rinds removed, diced
1 onion, sliced
125 g (4 oz) chestnut mushrooms, sliced
1 tbsp plain flour
1.25 litres (2 pints) game stock (page 148)
salt and black pepper
1 tbsp redcurrant jelly

ORANGE & HERB BOUQUET
6 parsley stalks
pared zest of 1 orange
1 bay leaf
1 large thyme or marjoram sprig

1 Melt the butter in a large saucepan, add the bacon, and cook over a high heat, stirring occasionally, for 5–7 minutes until crisp.

2 Lower the heat, add the onion to the pan, and cook gently, stirring from time to time, for a few minutes until softened but not coloured.

3 Make the orange and herb bouquet (see box, above) and set aside.

4 Add the mushrooms to the pan, and cook for 5 minutes, then add the flour and cook, stirring constantly, for 1 minute. Add the stock, the herb bouquet, and salt and pepper to taste, then bring to a boil. Cover and simmer for 30 minutes.

5 Remove and discard the orange and herb bouquet, then stir in the redcurrant jelly. Taste for seasoning, and serve at once.

Making a bouquet

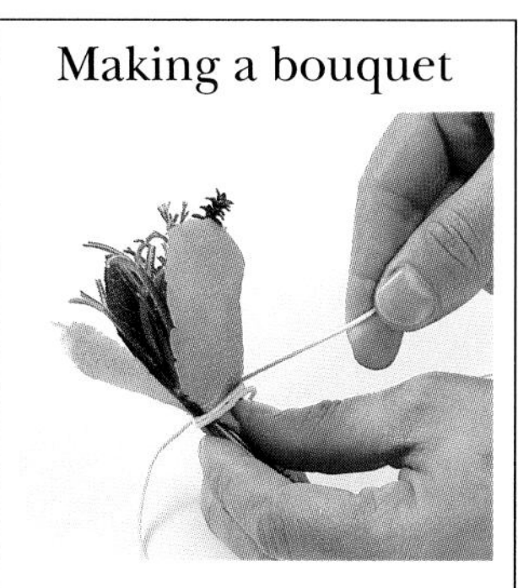

Tie the parsley, orange zest, bay leaf, and thyme or marjoram with a piece of white string. Leave a length of string to tie to the saucepan handle, so that the orange and herb bouquet can be easily lifted from the pan at the end of cooking.

CHICKEN NOODLE SOUP

 **Serves 4**

1 kg (2 lb) chicken pieces
500 g (1 lb) carrots, sliced
1/2 head celery, chopped
1 small onion, peeled but left whole
5 garlic cloves, coarsely chopped
a few parsley sprigs
3 litres (5 pints) water
2–3 chicken stock cubes
salt and black pepper
125 g (4 oz) thin noodles
chopped fresh dill to garnish

1 Put the chicken pieces into a large saucepan with the carrots, celery, onion, garlic, and parsley. Pour in the measured water and bring to a boil. Using a slotted spoon, skim off the foam that rises to the top of the pan.

2 Lower the heat, add the stock cubes, and salt and pepper to taste. Simmer gently, covered, for 2 hours, adding extra water if the liquid reduces too much.

3 Meanwhile, break the noodles into 5 cm (2 in) lengths. Simmer in boiling salted water for about 2 minutes or until just tender. Drain and set aside.

4 Skim any fat from the surface of the soup. With a slotted spoon, remove the parsley, onion, and chicken, and discard the parsley, chicken bones and skin. Chop the onion and chicken and return to the soup. Taste for seasoning.

5 Divide the noodles among warmed soup plates. Ladle the soup over the noodles, garnish with dill, and serve at once.

Cook's know-how

This soup is best made with chicken thighs and drumsticks; these are more moist and have considerably more flavour than breast meat when cooked for a long time.

HOT & SOUR SOUP

Serves 4–6

2 dried Chinese mushrooms
1/4 head Chinese cabbage, sliced
1.5 litres (2 1/2 pints) chicken or vegetable stock
60 g (2 oz) Chinese noodles, such as rice sticks
salt
125 g (4 oz) firm tofu, diced
90 g (3 oz) bamboo shoots, sliced
90 g (3 oz) cooked chicken, diced
30 g (1 oz) bean sprouts
3 tbsp cornflour mixed with 3 tbsp water
2 eggs, lightly beaten
2 tbsp white wine vinegar
1 tbsp dark soy sauce
1/4 tsp each white pepper and cayenne pepper

TO SERVE

2 tsp sesame oil
2 spring onions, thinly sliced
coriander sprigs

1 Put the mushrooms into a bowl, cover with hot water, and leave to soak for about 30 minutes.

2 Meanwhile, put the sliced cabbage into a large saucepan, add the stock, and bring to a boil. Simmer for 15 minutes. Set aside.

3 Break the noodles into pieces. Simmer in boiling salted water for 3–4 minutes until just tender. Drain and set aside.

4 Drain the mushrooms, reserving the soaking liquid. Pour the liquid through a sieve lined with a paper towel to remove any grit. Squeeze the mushrooms dry, then cut them into thin strips. Reserve the mushrooms and their liquid.

5 Add the tofu, bamboo shoots, chicken, bean sprouts, noodles, and the mushrooms and their liquid to the cabbage and stock. Heat until almost boiling, then stir in the cornflour mixture. Simmer until the soup thickens slightly, then drizzle in the beaten eggs to form strands.

6 Combine the vinegar, soy sauce, white and cayenne peppers, and pour into the soup. Taste for seasoning. Drizzle a little sesame oil over each serving, and garnish with spring onion slices and coriander sprigs. Serve at once.

CHINESE CRAB & SWEETCORN SOUP

Serves 4

375 g (12 oz) frozen sweetcorn kernels, thawed
1 litre (1³/4 pints) chicken stock
3 spring onions, thinly sliced
1 cm (¹/2 in) piece of fresh root ginger, peeled and chopped
1 garlic clove, crushed
1 tbsp light soy sauce
250 g (8 oz) cooked crabmeat
1 tbsp cornflour mixed with 2 tbsp water
salt and black pepper
sesame oil and coriander sprigs to serve

1 Purée the sweetcorn with one-quarter of the stock in a food processor or blender until smooth.

2 Pour the remaining stock into a pan, and add the spring onions, ginger, garlic, and soy sauce. Heat until bubbles form at the edge.

3 Add the crabmeat and the sweetcorn purée, and continue to heat until bubbles form again. Blend the cornflour mixture into the soup, and cook, stirring occasionally, for 10 minutes or until it thickens slightly. Add salt and pepper to taste.

4 Drizzle a little sesame oil over each serving, garnish with coriander sprigs, and serve at once.

THAI SPICED SOUP

Serves 4

90 g (3 oz) thin noodles
salt and black pepper
500 ml (16 fl oz) chicken stock
1 x 400 ml (13 fl oz) can coconut milk
¹/2 carrot, coarsely chopped
30 g (1 oz) French beans, cut into 1 cm (¹/2 in) pieces
3 spring onions, thinly sliced
250 g (8 oz) cooked chicken, shredded
125 g (4 oz) mixed green leaves, such as spinach and Chinese leaves, thinly sliced
30 g (1 oz) bean sprouts
2 tbsp fish sauce
¹/4 tsp turmeric
¹/4 cucumber, cut into matchstick-thin strips, and coriander sprigs to garnish

1 Cook the noodles in boiling salted water for 2–3 minutes, or according to package instructions, until just tender. Drain and rinse in cold water. Set aside while preparing the soup.

2 Put the stock, coconut milk, carrot, French beans, and spring onions into a large saucepan, and bring to a boil.

3 Lower the heat, add the chicken, green leaves, bean sprouts, fish sauce, and turmeric, and cook for 2 minutes or until the green leaves are tender. Add salt and pepper to taste.

4 To serve, divide the cooked noodles among warmed bowls. Ladle the hot soup over the noodles, and garnish with cucumber strips and coriander sprigs.

Cook's know-how

For a vegetarian version, omit the cooked chicken and use a vegetable stock instead of the chicken stock. You could also vary the vegetables, but be sure to make allowance for their different cooking times. Try shredded white cabbage instead of Chinese leaves and mangetout instead of French beans. Sliced courgettes, Swiss chard, a small quantity of sweetcorn kernels, or even a little diced aubergine would also be good in this soup.

VICHYSSOISE

Serves 4–6

60 g (2 oz) butter

3 large leeks, trimmed and sliced

1 small onion, chopped

2 potatoes, coarsely chopped

1.25 litres (2 pints) chicken stock

salt and black pepper

TO SERVE

150 ml (1/4 pint) single cream

milk (optional)

2 tbsp fresh snipped chives

1 Melt the butter in a large saucepan, add the leeks and onion, and cook very gently, stirring occasionally, for 10–15 minutes until soft but not coloured.

2 Add the potatoes, stock, and salt and pepper to taste, and bring to a boil. Cover and simmer gently for 15–20 minutes until the potatoes are tender.

3 Purée the soup in a food processor or blender until smooth. Pour into a large bowl or pass through a sieve for a smoother finish. Cover and chill for at least 3 hours.

4 To serve, stir in the cream. If the soup is too thick, add a little milk. Taste for seasoning. Garnish with snipped chives before serving.

Vichyssoise

This soup is the sophisticated chilled version of a peasant recipe for leek and potato soup. It was created in 1917 by the French chef Louis Diat when he was working at the Ritz-Carlton Hotel in New York. Inspired by memories of his mother's cooking, he named it after Vichy, the spa town near his childhood home.

TZATZIKI SOUP

Serves 4–6

600 g (1 lb 3 oz) plain yogurt

250 ml (8 fl oz) water

1 cucumber, seeded (see box, right) and diced

4 garlic cloves, coarsely chopped

1 tbsp olive oil

1 tsp white wine vinegar

1 tsp dried mint

salt and black pepper

2–3 tbsp chopped fresh mint and 3 spring onions, thinly sliced, to garnish

1 Purée the yogurt, measured water, one-quarter of the diced cucumber, the garlic, oil, vinegar, and mint in a food processor or blender until smooth. Season well with salt and add pepper to taste.

2 Transfer the soup to a large bowl and stir in the remaining cucumber. Cover and chill for at least 1 hour.

3 Taste for seasoning. Sprinkle the soup with chopped mint and spring onions before serving.

Seeding a cucumber

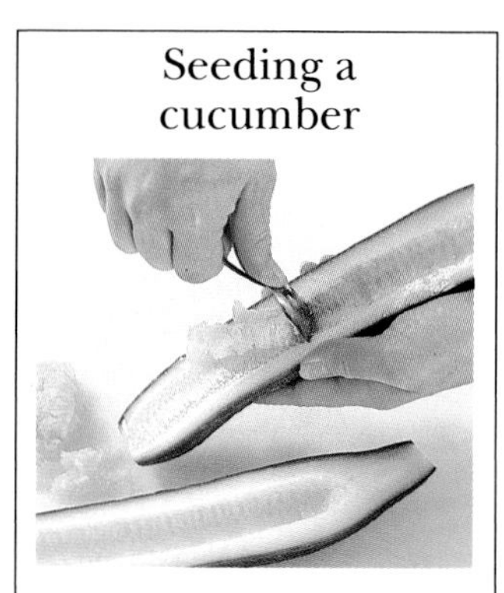

Trim the cucumber with a small knife, then cut it in half lengthwise. With a teaspoon, scoop out and discard the seeds from each cucumber half.

Tzatziki

Tzatziki is best known as a cooling Greek salad, but it is even more refreshing when served as a chilled soup. Dried mint is used in the soup because of its intense flavour, although fresh mint is used for the garnish.

GAZPACHO

Serves 4–6

1 kg (2 lb) tomatoes, peeled (see box, right) and seeded
1 large Spanish onion
200 g (7 oz) can sweet red pimientos, drained
2 large garlic cloves
600 ml (1 pint) cold chicken stock
75 ml (2½ fl oz) olive oil
4 tbsp red wine vinegar
juice of ½ lemon
salt and black pepper
TO GARNISH
½ cucumber, diced
1 small green pepper, cored, seeded, and diced
garlic croûtons (page 31)

1 Coarsely chop the tomatoes, onion, pimientos, and garlic. Purée in a food processor or blender with the stock, oil, and vinegar until smooth.

2 Turn the mixture into a bowl and add the lemon juice, and salt and pepper to taste. Cover and chill for at least 1 hour.

3 Garnished with spoonfuls of diced cucumber, green pepper, and garlic croûtons before serving.

Peeling tomatoes

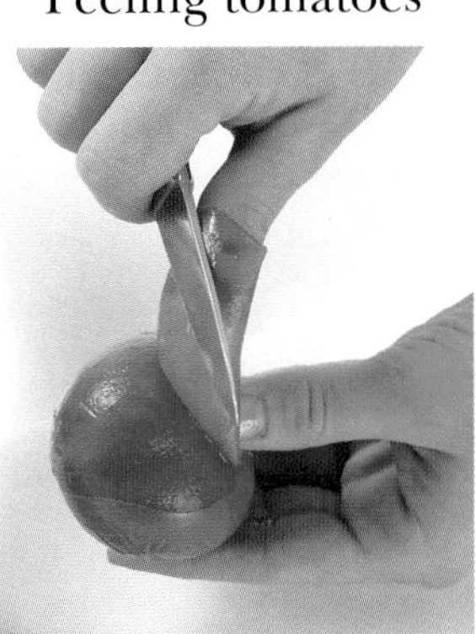

Cut the cores from the tomatoes and score an "x" on the base. Immerse the tomatoes in boiling water for 8–15 seconds until their skins start to split. Transfer at once to cold water. When the tomatoes are cool enough to handle, peel off the skin with a small knife.

BLUEBERRY & RED WINE SOUP

Serves 4

350 ml (12 fl oz) cranberry juice
250 ml (8 fl oz) red wine
1 cinnamon stick
about 125 g (4 oz) caster sugar
250 g (8 oz) blueberries
1 tbsp cornflour mixed with 2 tbsp water
125 ml (4 fl oz) soured cream
125 ml (4 fl oz) single cream

1 Put the cranberry juice, wine, and cinnamon stick into a large saucepan. Add the sugar (the amount depends on the sweetness of the fruit), bring to a boil, and simmer for 15 minutes.

2 Stir the blueberries into the pan, reserving a few for garnish, and cook for 5 minutes. Add more sugar to taste, if necessary.

3 Gradually blend the cornflour mixture into the soup, and return to a boil. Cook for 3 minutes or until the soup thickens slightly. Remove the pan from the heat and discard the cinnamon stick. Pour the soup into a bowl and leave to cool for about 30 minutes.

4 Combine the soured cream and single cream and stir into the soup. Cover and chill for at least 3 hours. Garnish with the reserved blueberries before serving.

Cook's know-how

Red wine adds a richness and depth of flavour to this creamy American soup and prevents it from tasting too sweet. Choose a robust red wine, such as a Californian Zinfandel or a Bulgarian Cabernet Sauvignon. If blueberries are not available, use dark sweet cherries instead.

CHILLED CURRIED APPLE & MINT SOUP

Serves 6

30 g (1 oz) butter
1 onion, coarsely chopped
1 tbsp mild curry powder
900 ml (1 1/2 pints) vegetable stock
750 g (1 1/2 lb) cooking apples, peeled, cored, and coarsely chopped
2 tbsp mango chutney
juice of 1/2 lemon
7–8 sprigs of fresh mint
salt and black pepper
100 g (3 1/2 oz) plain yogurt
a little milk, if needed

1 Melt the butter in a large saucepan, add the onion, and cook gently, stirring occasionally, for a few minutes until soft but not coloured. Add the curry powder and cook, stirring constantly, for 1–2 minutes.

2 Add the stock and chopped apples and bring to a boil, stirring. Cover and simmer for 15 minutes or until the apples are tender.

3 Purée the apple mixture, mango chutney, and lemon juice in a food processor or blender until very smooth.

4 Strip the mint leaves from the stalks, reserving 6 small sprigs for garnish. Finely chop the mint leaves.

5 Pour the soup into a large bowl, stir in the chopped mint, and add salt and pepper to taste. Cover and chill in the refrigerator for at least 3 hours.

6 Whisk in the yogurt, then taste for seasoning. If the soup is too thick, add a little milk. Garnish with the reserved mint before serving.

Cook's know-how

This soup is equally delicious served hot. After puréeing, reheat the soup. Stir in the chopped mint, whisk in the yogurt, and heat through gently. Serve at once.

CHILLED STRAWBERRY SOUP

Serves 4

250 ml (8 fl oz) dry white wine
90 g (3 oz) caster sugar
very small piece of lime zest (optional)
250 g (8 oz) strawberries
250 ml (8 fl oz) orange juice
mint sprigs to garnish

1 Put the wine and sugar into a saucepan; bring to a boil, and boil for 5 minutes. Remove the pan from the heat, add the lime zest, if using, and let cool.

2 Remove the lime zest from the pan. Hull and chop the strawberries, reserving 4 for garnish.

3 Purée the wine syrup and strawberries in a food processor or blender until very smooth.

4 Turn the purée into a large bowl and stir in the orange juice. Cover and chill for at least 3 hours.

5 Garnish with the reserved strawberries and mint sprigs just before serving.

STRAWBERRY & CHAMPAGNE SOUP

Omit the white wine and lime zest. Purée the strawberries, reserving a few for garnish, with the sugar and orange juice. Divide the mixture between chilled glass serving bowls, and top with chilled Champagne or dry sparkling wine. Garnish and serve.

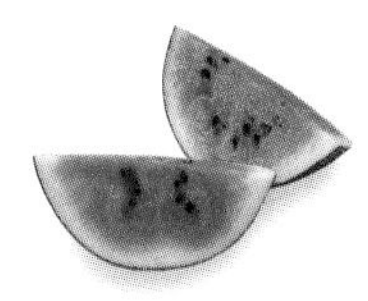

STRAWBERRY & WATERMELON SOUP

Substitute a 1 kg (2 lb) piece of watermelon for the orange juice. Remove and discard the seeds, scoop out and purée the melon flesh until smooth, then combine with the wine syrup, strawberries, and a little lime juice.

FIRST COURSES

UNDER 30 MINUTES

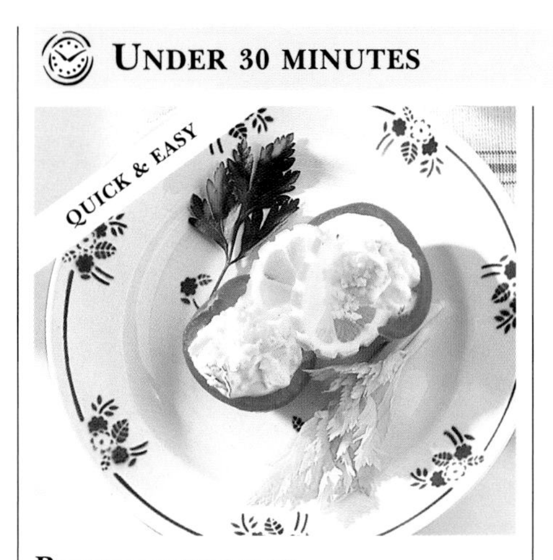

RUSSIAN FISH SALAD

Rich creamy salad of white fish fillets, soured cream, hard-boiled egg, mayonnaise, and parsley. Served on tomato quarters.
SERVES 4 213 calories per serving
Takes 10 minutes **PAGE 64**

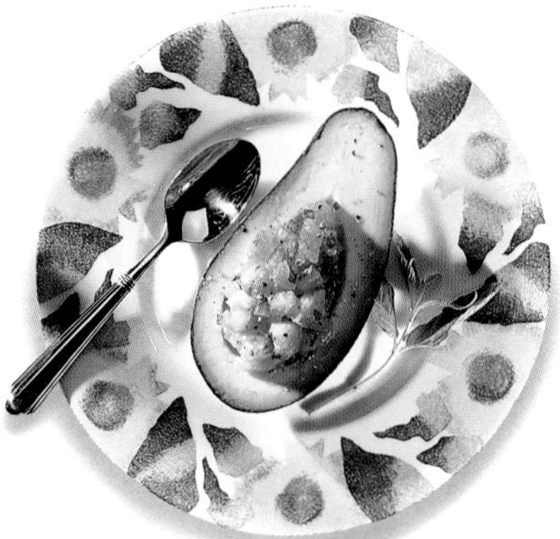

AVOCADO WITH TOMATOES & MINT

Light and refreshing: chopped tomatoes combined with mint and vinaigrette dressing, and piled into avocado halves.
SERVES 4 232 calories per serving
Takes 15 minutes **PAGE 68**

SCALLOPS WITH CHEESE SAUCE

Rich and luxurious: scallops poached with white wine and bay leaf, then stirred into a Mornay sauce flavoured with Gruyère cheese.
SERVES 4 297 calories per serving
Takes 25 minutes **PAGE 60**

WHITE BEAN PATE

Smooth and summery: cannellini beans blended with rosemary, olive oil, and lemon juice, and richly flavoured with garlic.
SERVES 6 150 calories per serving
Takes 10 minutes **PAGE 57**

CHEVRE CROUTES

Goat's cheese and pesto, on toasted baguette slices and sprinkled with olive oil, give a tangy flavour to this inviting appetizer.
SERVES 4 450 calories per serving

Takes 20 minutes **PAGE 48**

SARDINES WITH CORIANDER

Lightly grilled sardines, flavoured with a butter combining coriander and shallot with lime juice, make a refreshing starter.
SERVES 4 511 calories per serving
Takes 25 minutes **PAGE 62**

PIQUANT PRAWNS

Prawns in a dressing of mayonnaise, creamed horseradish, and tomato purée, spiked with lemon juice and Tabasco sauce.
SERVES 4 338 calories per serving
Takes 10 minutes **PAGE 63**

JUMBO PRAWNS WITH AIOLI

Stir-fried jumbo prawns served with a Provençal mayonnaise combining garlic, egg yolks, mustard, olive oil, and lemon juice.
SERVES 4 482 calories per serving
Takes 20 minutes **PAGE 62**

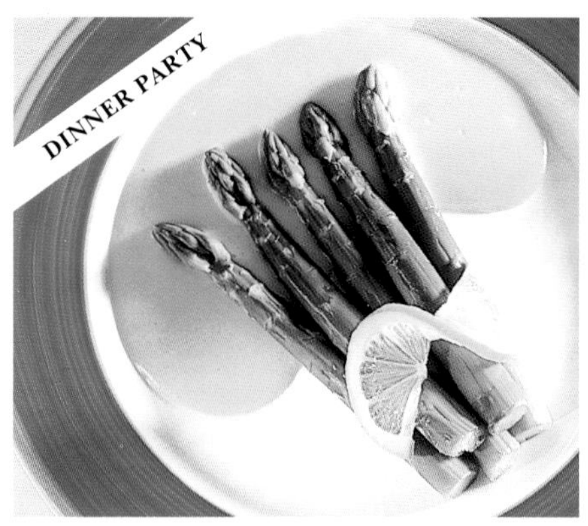

ASPARAGUS WITH QUICK HOLLANDAISE

Tender spears of fresh asparagus served with a simple version of hollandaise sauce, and garnished with lemon twists.
SERVES 4 384 calories per serving
Takes 20 minutes **PAGE 66**

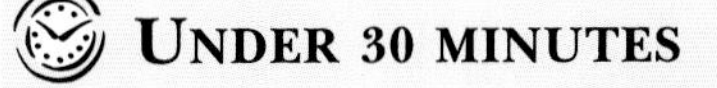

UNDER 30 MINUTES

BRIOCHES WITH WILD MUSHROOMS & WATERCRESS

Light-textured, rich bread filled with a mixture of mushrooms, watercress, and cream.

SERVES 6 295 calories per serving
Takes 20 minutes **PAGE 66**

WARM SALAD WITH BACON & SCALLOPS

Light and crunchy: bacon and scallops with salad leaves tossed in walnut oil. Dressed with shallots and hot wine vinegar.

SERVES 4 276 calories per serving
Takes 20 minutes **PAGE 65**

SPICY MEATBALLS

Tiny warm meatballs seasoned with garlic, onion, paprika, fresh coriander, and tomato purée. Served with a sesame dip.

SERVES 6 481 calories per serving
Takes 25 minutes **PAGE 47**

SMOKED CHICKEN SALAD WITH WALNUTS

Sliced smoked chicken, tossed in an orange dressing, and served on a bed of salad leaves, orange segments, and walnuts.

SERVES 6 472 calories per serving
Takes 15 minutes **PAGE 65**

MOULES MARINIERE

Traditional French dish: mussels cooked with dry white wine, onion, garlic, parsley, thyme, and a bay leaf. Served in a light sauce.

SERVES 6 302 calories per serving
Takes 25 minutes **PAGE 60**

CHEESE AIGRETTES

Warm nuggets of choux pastry, flavoured with mature Cheddar cheese, then deep-fried and served warm.

SERVES 10–12 238–198 calories per serving
Takes 25 minutes **PAGE 49**

30–60 MINUTES

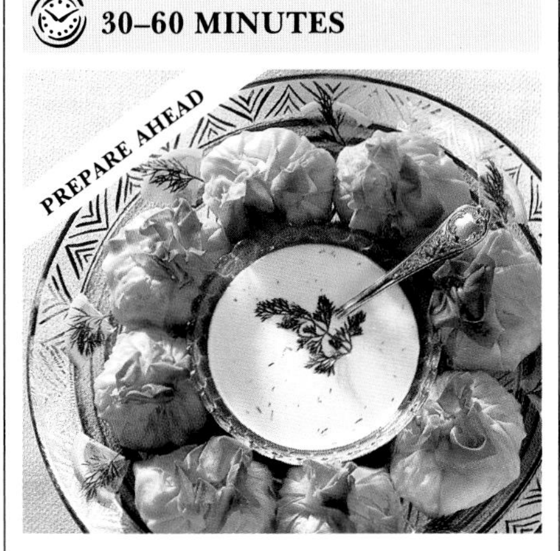

SALMON & PRAWN FILO PURSES

Bite-sized pieces of salmon combined with prawns in light-textured filo pastry purses. Served with a wine, cream, and dill sauce.

SERVES 8 448 calories per serving
Takes 55 minutes **PAGE 53**

CANAPES

Lightly toasted bread served with a selection of toppings: anchovy and prawn, cheese and spring onion, salami, and asparagus.

SERVES 4 251 calories per serving
Takes 40 minutes **PAGE 47**

CHEESE & OLIVE BITES

Pimiento-stuffed olives wrapped in cheese pastry flavoured with paprika and mustard. Baked, then served warm or cold.

SERVES 4 317 calories per serving
Takes 40 minutes **PAGE 48**

30–60 MINUTES

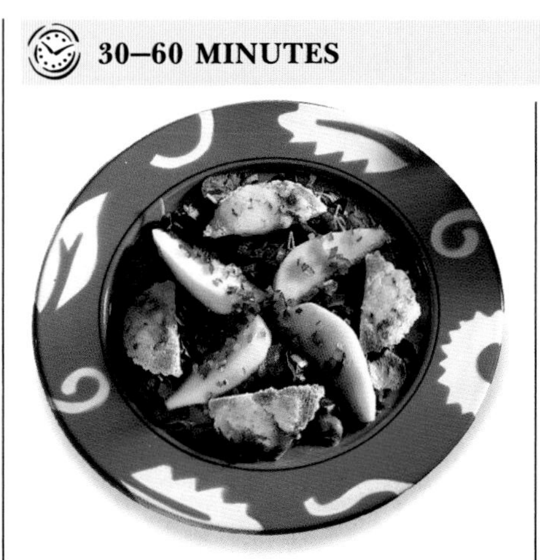

WARM SALAD WITH PEARS & STILTON

Toast topped with Stilton cheese on a bed of watercress and pears. Served with a warm red onion and balsamic vinegar dressing.

SERVES 4 563 calories per serving

Takes 35 minutes **PAGE 70**

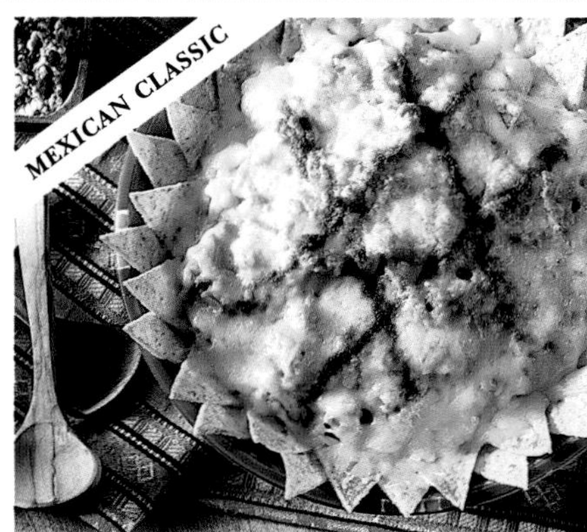

NACHOS GRANDE

Spicy and nourishing: refried beans, tomatoes, chilli, onion, garlic, and green pepper, enclosed by tortilla chips. Topped with cheese.

SERVES 4–6 594–396 calories per serving

Takes 45 minutes **PAGE 52**

SARDINE PATE

Individual pâtés of sardines blended with butter, low-fat soft cheese, and lemon juice, seasoned with black pepper, then chilled.

SERVES 8 197 calories per serving

Takes 10 minutes, plus chilling **PAGE 54**

LEEK PARCELS WITH PROVENÇAL VEGETABLES

Layers of aubergine, pesto, red pepper, courgette, and tomato, wrapped in leek strips.

SERVES 4 283 calories per serving

Takes 40 minutes **PAGE 59**

ANTIPASTI

Two popular Italian starters: crostini, made from thin slices of baguette brushed with garlic and olive oil and baked until crispy, then topped with sun-dried tomato purée; mozzarella, tomato, and basil salad, dressed with olive oil and balsamic vinegar.

SERVES 8 311 calories per crostini serving

180 calories per salad serving

Takes 45 minutes **PAGE 69**

OVER 60 MINUTES

PAN-FRIED PATES

Blended chicken livers with bacon, spinach, shallots, parsley, garlic, and sage. Moulded into ovals and wrapped in bacon.

SERVES 4 392 calories per serving

Takes 60 minutes **PAGE 57**

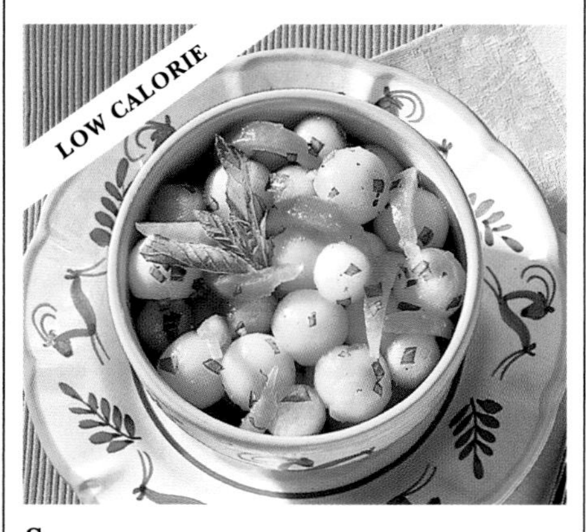

SUMMER MELONS

Contrastingly coloured melon balls, mixed with tomato strips, and dressed in vinaigrette. Chilled and served with mint.

SERVES 4 282 calories per serving

Takes 15 minutes, plus chilling **PAGE 68**

EGG PATE

Hard-boiled eggs mixed with crème fraîche, consommé, and whipped double cream, and garnished with large prawns.

SERVES 8 243 calories per serving

Takes 45 minutes, plus chilling **PAGE 59**

OVER 60 MINUTES

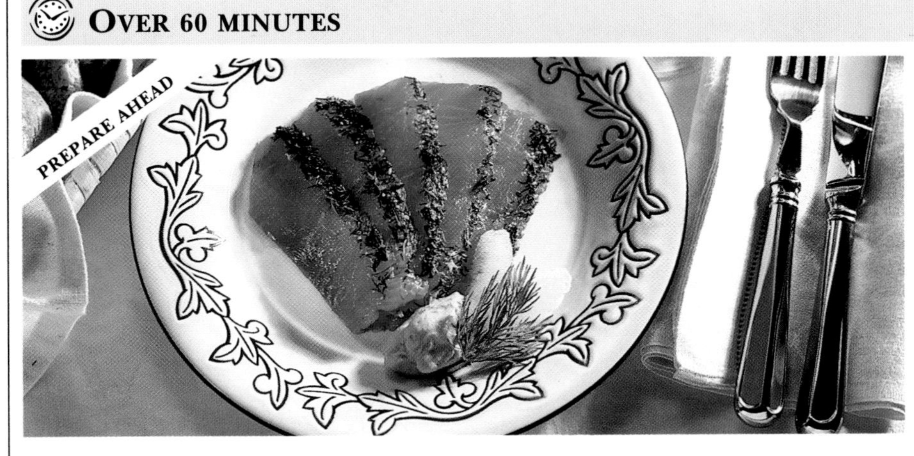

GRAVADLAX

Scandinavian speciality: fresh salmon fillets pickled in sugar, sea salt, dill, and black pepper, sandwiched together, and chilled. Served in slices, with a rich sauce combining mustard, sugar, white wine vinegar, egg yolk, sunflower oil, and dill.

SERVES 16 395 calories per serving
Takes 30 minutes, plus chilling **PAGE 63**

CAPONATA

Aubergine cooked with celery, onions, tomato purée, sugar, and vinegar, then mixed with olives, garlic, and parsley.

SERVES 4–6 297–198 calories per serving
Takes 35 minutes, plus standing **PAGE 70**

SALMON QUENELLES

Little dumplings of salmon, egg whites, and cream, shaped and poached, and served with a luxurious asparagus sauce.

SERVES 4–6 766–511 calories per serving
Takes 30 minutes, plus chilling **PAGE 61**

LIGHT CHICKEN PATE

Diced chicken breast combined with wine, olives, garlic, breadcrumbs, and egg. Baked in a dish lined with bacon rashers.

SERVES 6 277 calories per serving
Takes 1¼ hours, plus chilling **PAGE 56**

CARROT MOUSSE

Fresh and creamy: carrots blended with tomatoes, cumin seeds, and fromage frais. Served with a tomato salsa.

SERVES 6 124 calories per serving
Takes 45 minutes, plus chilling **PAGE 58**

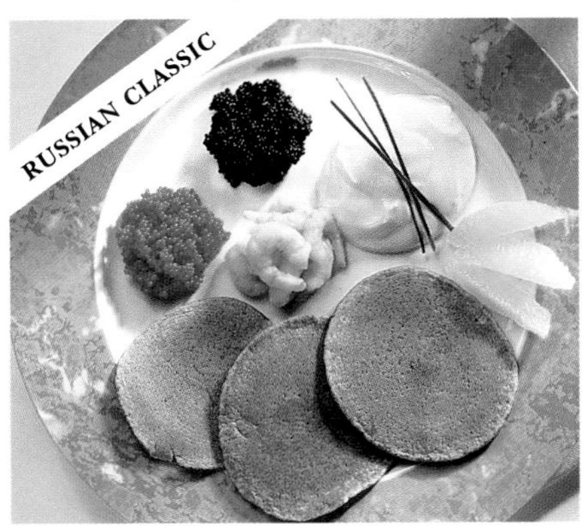

PRAWN BLINI

Russian pancakes made with yeast and buckwheat flour. Served with red and black lumpfish roe, prawns, and crème fraîche.

SERVES 6–8 369–277 calories per serving
Takes 35 minutes, plus standing **PAGE 64**

THREE FISH TERRINE

Layers of smoked fish pâtés – trout with cream cheese and lemon juice; salmon with lemon juice, tomato purée, cream cheese, and dill; mackerel with cream cheese and lemon juice – wrapped in smoked salmon slices. Served here on a bed of watercress.

SERVES 10 424 calories per serving
Takes 40 minutes, plus chilling **PAGE 55**

OVER 60 MINUTES

SMOKED SALMON PINWHEELS

Savoury spinach roulade layered with smoked salmon, a mixture of cream cheese, yogurt, spring onions, and tomatoes.

SERVES 4–6 407–271 calories per serving

Takes 45 minutes, plus chilling **PAGE 67**

INDIVIDUAL FISH PATES

Rich and delicate: haddock blended with smoked salmon, white sauce, mayonnaise, and cream, and flavoured with white wine.

SERVES 8 176 calories per serving

Takes 50 minutes, plus chilling **PAGE 54**

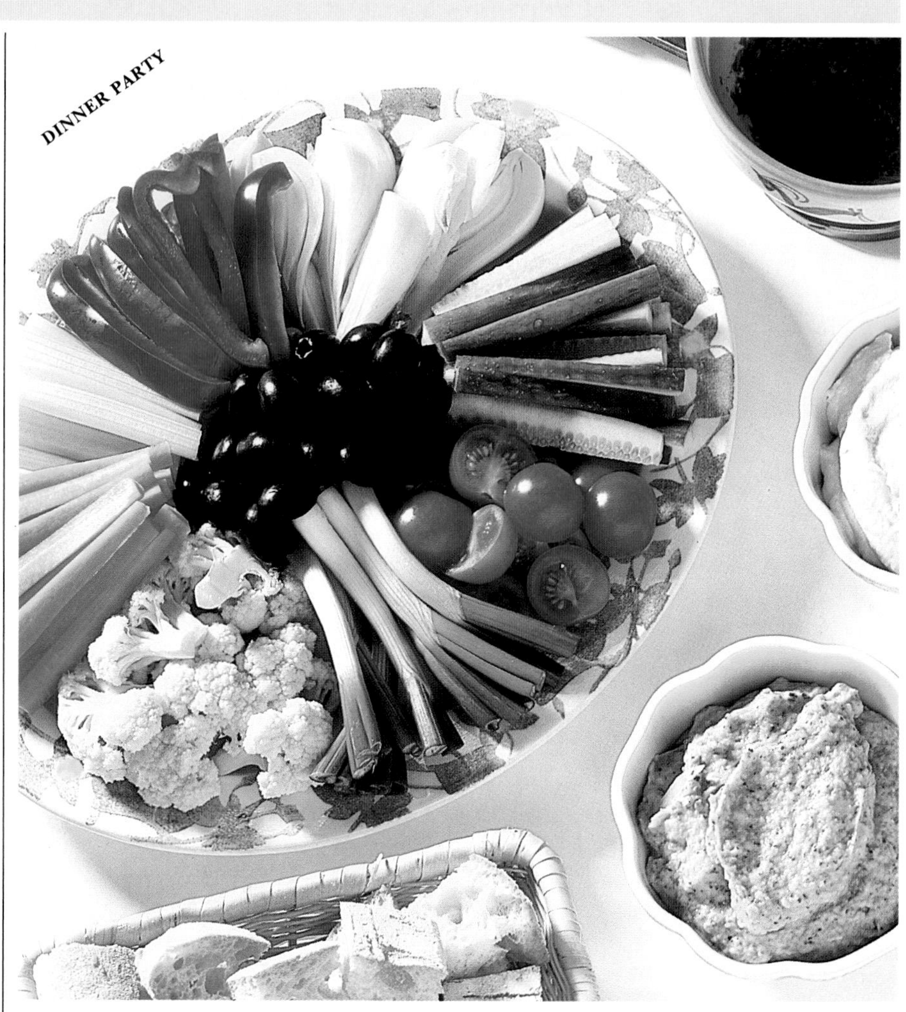

SAVOURY DIPS WITH CRUDITES

Three popular dips: bagna cauda, a warm anchovy and garlic dip; taramasalata, a chilled mixture of smoked cod's roe, lemon juice, garlic, and oil; and an aubergine dip, in which aubergines, shallots, and garlic are mixed with parsley and tahini paste.

SERVES 12 120 calories per serving

Takes 1½ hours, plus chilling **PAGE 49**

SPICY CHICKEN WINGS

Authentic American recipe: chicken wings marinated in oil, lemon juice, and spices, then baked. Served with blue cheese dressing.

SERVES 4–6 206–137 calories per serving

Takes 60 minutes, plus marinating **PAGE 52**

BROCCOLI TERRINE

Broccoli florets blended with milk and egg yolk, flavoured with grated nutmeg, and set with gelatine and double cream.

SERVES 4–6 236–157 calories per serving

Takes 50 minutes, plus chilling **PAGE 58**

BRANDIED CHICKEN LIVER PATE

Chicken livers blended with bread, bacon, thyme, egg, and nutmeg, and flavoured with brandy. Baked, then chilled.

SERVES 8 268 calories per serving

Takes 1¼ hours, plus chilling **PAGE 56**

CANAPES

Home-made canapés are an excellent accompaniment for drinks, or they can be served as an appetizer before dinner. These use toasted bread as a base, but if you prefer, fry the bread in a mixture of oil and butter instead.

Serves 4

4 slices of white bread, crusts removed

ANCHOVY TOPPING

1 tbsp mayonnaise

1 or 2 spring onion tops

8 anchovy fillets, drained

4 cooked peeled prawns

CHEESE & SPRING ONION TOPPING

30 g (1 oz) cream cheese

2 spring onion tops, very finely sliced

4 capers

SALAMI TOPPING

15 g (1/2 oz) butter

2 slices of Danish salami

4 slices of gherkin

ASPARAGUS TOPPING

1 tbsp mayonnaise

6 asparagus tips, cooked and drained

2 slices of radish

a few parsley leaves to garnish

1 Make the canapé bases: toast the white bread lightly on both sides. Remove from the heat and leave to cool.

2 Make the anchovy topping: spread 1 piece of toast with mayonnaise and cut into 4 squares. Cut the spring onion tops into 4 pieces, then make vertical cuts to separate each piece into strands. Cut the anchovies in half and arrange in a lattice pattern on each square. Place a prawn on top, and insert a spring onion tassel through each prawn.

3 Make the cheese and spring onion topping: spread 1 piece of toast with cream cheese and cut into 4 squares. Arrange the spring onion slices diagonally across the cream cheese. Place a caper on each square.

4 Make the salami topping: butter 1 piece of toast and cut into 4 rounds with a pastry cutter.

5 Make the salami cornets (see box, below). Put 1 cornet and 1 piece of gherkin on each canapé.

6 Make the asparagus topping: spread 1 piece of toast with mayonnaise and cut into 4 squares. Halve the asparagus tips lengthwise. Halve the radish slices and cut away the centres to form 4 crescents. Put 3 halved asparagus tips on each square, arrange the radish on top, and garnish.

Making a salami cornet

Cut each slice of salami in half, using a chef's knife. Roll each half to form a point at the straight end. Press to seal.

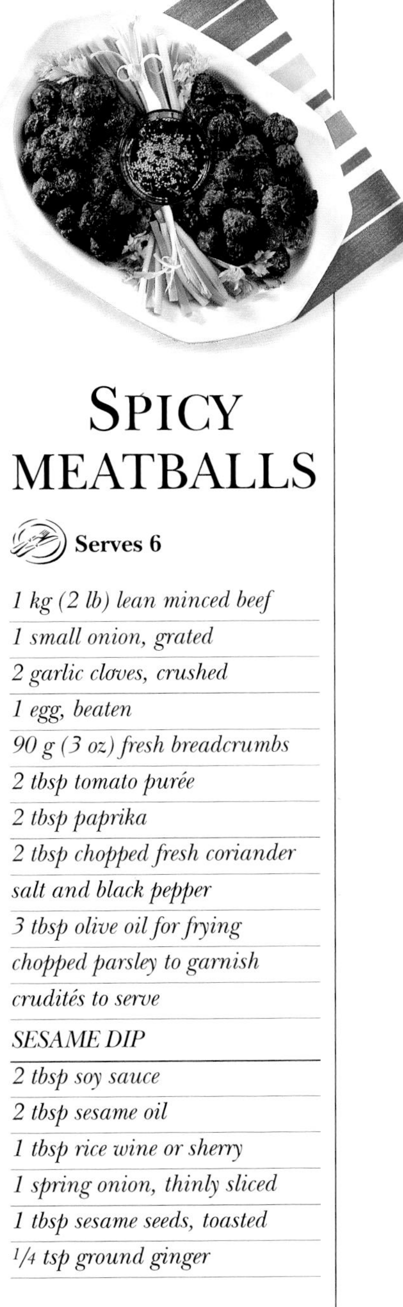

SPICY MEATBALLS

Serves 6

1 kg (2 lb) lean minced beef

1 small onion, grated

2 garlic cloves, crushed

1 egg, beaten

90 g (3 oz) fresh breadcrumbs

2 tbsp tomato purée

2 tbsp paprika

2 tbsp chopped fresh coriander

salt and black pepper

3 tbsp olive oil for frying

chopped parsley to garnish

crudités to serve

SESAME DIP

2 tbsp soy sauce

2 tbsp sesame oil

1 tbsp rice wine or sherry

1 spring onion, thinly sliced

1 tbsp sesame seeds, toasted

1/4 tsp ground ginger

1 Make the sesame dip: whisk all the ingredients together and set aside.

2 Combine the meatball ingredients in a bowl. Using your hands, roll the mixture into little balls.

3 Heat the oil in a frying pan, and cook the meatballs, in batches, over a medium heat for 5 minutes or until browned, firm, and cooked through. Garnish, and serve warm with the sesame dip and crudités.

CHEVRE CROUTES

Serves 4

1/2 baguette
about 2 tbsp ready-made pesto
1 log-shaped goat's cheese
olive oil for sprinkling
black pepper
radicchio and frisée leaves to serve
chervil sprigs to garnish

1 Cut the baguette into 8 slices, 1 cm (1/2 in) thick, and toast under a hot grill on one side only. Lightly spread the untoasted sides of the baguette slices with the ready-made pesto.

2 Cut the goat's cheese into 8 slices, 1 cm (1/2 in) thick, and arrange on top of the pesto. Toast the topped croûtes under the hot grill, about 7 cm (3 ins) from the heat, for 3 minutes or until the cheese just begins to soften. Remove the grill pan from the heat.

3 Lightly sprinkle a little olive oil and grind a little pepper over each cheese croûte. Return the croûtes to the hot grill, close to the heat, for 3 minutes or until the cheese begins to bubble and is just tinged golden brown.

4 Line a serving platter with radicchio and frisée leaves, arrange the croûtes on top, and garnish with chervil sprigs. Serve at once.

CHEVRE CROUTES ITALIAN STYLE

Substitute 8 slices of Italian ciabatta for the baguette. After toasting the topped croûtes, sprinkle chopped black olives over each croûte before lightly sprinkling with olive oil, and proceed as directed.

CHEESE & OLIVE BITES

Serves 4

175 g (6 oz) mature Cheddar cheese, grated
90 g (3 oz) plain flour
15 g (1/2 oz) butter, plus extra for greasing
1 tsp paprika
1/2 tsp mustard powder
20 pimiento-stuffed green olives
cayenne pepper and parsley sprigs to garnish

1 Work the cheese, flour, butter, paprika, and mustard powder in a food processor until the mixture resembles fine breadcrumbs.

2 Flatten the dough mixture, and wrap around the olives (see box, right).

3 Butter a baking tray. Add the wrapped olives and bake in a preheated oven at 200°C (400°F, Gas 6) for 15 minutes until the pastry is golden.

4 Remove the cheese and olive bites from the baking tray and leave to cool slightly.

5 Serve warm or cold, sprinkled with cayenne pepper and garnished with parsley sprigs.

Wrapping the olives in the dough

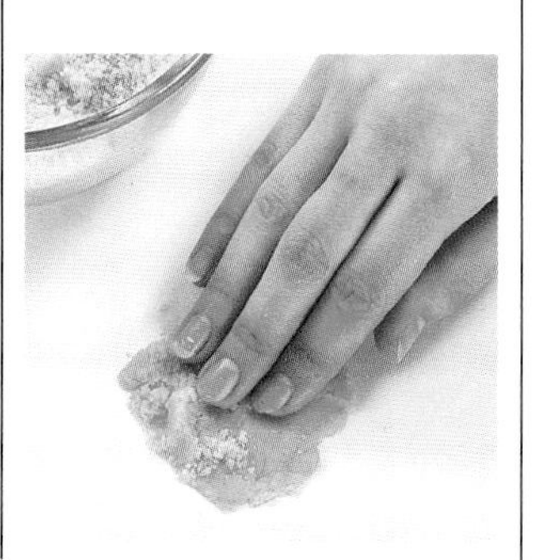

Take a thumb-sized piece of the dough mixture and flatten on a work surface.

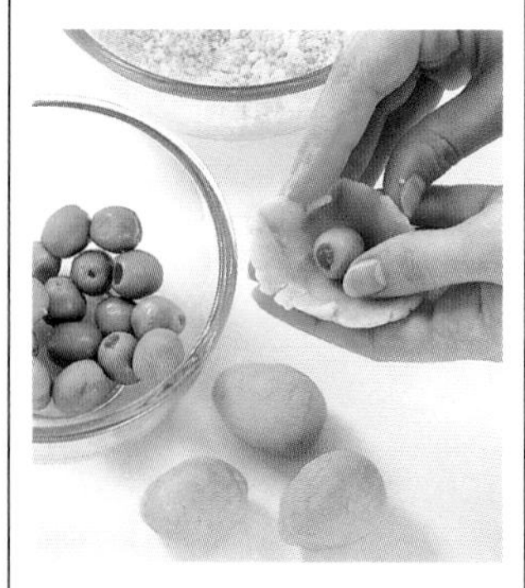

Place an olive in the middle of the dough. Wrap the dough around the olive, pressing to make it stick. If the pastry is too crumbly and will not stick, add a little water. Repeat with the remaining dough and olives.

Savoury dips with crudites

For an informal start to a meal, a selection of dips served with fresh, crisp vegetables is hard to beat. Bagna cauda, meaning "hot bath", is a rustic Italian dip which should be put over a gentle heat to keep it warm.

Aubergine dip

Serves 4

750 g (1 1/2 lb) aubergines
salt and black pepper
2 shallots, halved
1–2 garlic cloves
4 tbsp lemon juice
4 tbsp olive oil
4 tbsp chopped parsley
2 tbsp tahini paste

1 Cut the aubergines in half lengthwise. Score the flesh in a lattice pattern, sprinkle with salt, and leave to stand for 30 minutes.

2 Rinse the aubergine halves with cold water, and pat dry with paper towels. Place on a baking tray and bake in a preheated oven at 200°C (400°F, Gas 6) for 20 minutes.

3 Add the shallots and garlic to the baking tray, and bake for 15 minutes.

4 Purée the aubergines, shallots, and garlic with the lemon juice, oil, parsley, tahini paste, and salt and pepper to taste in a food processor until smooth.

5 Turn the dip into a bowl. Cover and chill for at least 1 hour before serving.

Taramasalata

Serves 4

500 g (1 lb) smoked cod's roe, skinned and coarsely chopped
4 small slices of white bread, crusts removed
4 tbsp lemon juice
1 large garlic clove, coarsely chopped
250 ml (8 fl oz) olive oil
salt and black pepper

1 Purée the cod's roe in a food processor or blender until smooth.

2 Break the bread into a bowl, add the lemon juice, and let the bread soak for 1 minute. Add to the cod's roe with the garlic, and purée until smooth.

3 Pour the oil into the mixture, a little at a time, and purée until all the oil has been absorbed. Add salt and pepper to taste.

4 Turn the taramasalata into a bowl. Cover and chill for at least 1 hour before serving.

Bagna cauda

Serves 4

150 ml (1/4 pint) olive oil
45 g (1 1/2 oz) butter
2 garlic cloves, crushed
1 x 60 g (2 oz) can anchovy fillets, drained and chopped
black pepper

1 Heat the oil and butter in a frying pan, add the garlic, and cook gently, stirring occasionally, for a few minutes until soft but not coloured. Add the anchovies and cook over a very low heat until they dissolve in the oil. Season with black pepper.

2 To serve, transfer the bagna cauda to an earthenware pot placed on a candle-heated tray, or to a fondue pot.

Cheese aigrettes

Serves 10–12

300 ml (1/2 pint) water
60 g (2 oz) butter
125 g (4 oz) self-raising flour
2 egg yolks
2 eggs
125 g (4 oz) mature Cheddar cheese, grated
salt and black pepper
oil for deep-frying

1 Put the water and butter into a saucepan and bring to a boil. Remove from the heat, and add the flour. Beat well until the mixture is smooth and glossy and leaves the side of the pan clean. Leave to cool slightly.

2 In a bowl, lightly mix the yolks and eggs, then beat into the flour mixture a little at a time. Stir in the cheese. Add salt and pepper to taste.

3 Heat the oil to 190°C (375°F). Lower mixture a teaspoonful at a time into the oil, and cook very gently until golden brown. Lift out and drain on paper towels. Serve warm.

Aigrettes

Cheese is the the most common flavouring ingredient for these little deep-fried choux pastry savouries, but chopped anchovies may also be used.

Tapas

Tapas are Spanish hors d'oeuvre: little plates of savoury foods traditionally served in bars, and accompanied by glasses of wine and good conversation. All sorts of hot or cold dishes make excellent tapas: just make sure they can be eaten with the fingers or a fork.

Vegetables with Garlic Dips

Serves 4

- *750 g (1 1/2 lb) small new potatoes*
- *1 aubergine, thinly sliced lengthwise*
- *olive oil for brushing*
- *1 red pepper, roasted and peeled (page 354)*
- *small bunch of watercress to serve*
- *rouille and aïoli (pages 33 and 62) to serve*

1 Boil the potatoes for 10–15 minutes until just tender. Drain and leave to cool, or keep warm, as desired.

2 Arrange the aubergine slices on a baking tray and brush with olive oil. Cook under a hot grill, 10 cm (4 ins) from the heat, for 10 minutes or until lightly browned on each side. Cut the pepper into strips.

3 Arrange the vegetables on a serving plate, garnish with the watercress, and serve with rouille and aïoli.

Chick Pea & Red Pepper Salad

Serves 4

- *1 x 400 g (13 oz) can chick peas, drained*
- *1/2 red onion or 3 spring onions, chopped*
- *3 garlic cloves, crushed*
- *3 tbsp olive oil*
- *2 tbsp white wine vinegar*
- *salt and black pepper*
- *a few sprigs of flat-leaf parsley*
- *1 red pepper, roasted and peeled (page 354)*
- *25 pimiento-stuffed olives*

1 Combine the chick peas with the onion, garlic, oil, vinegar, and salt and pepper to taste. Remove the parsley leaves from the stems and stir in.

2 Cut the red pepper into strips. Stir into the chick pea mixture with the olives until evenly mixed.

Tuna Tostados

Serves 4

- *1/2 baguette, cut diagonally into thin slices*
- *1 garlic clove, crushed*
- *3 tbsp olive oil*
- *2 ripe tomatoes, thinly sliced*
- *30 g (1 oz) tuna, drained*
- *90 g (3 oz) Gouda or Cheddar cheese, thinly sliced*
- *1 tbsp chopped flat-leaf parsley*

1 Under a hot grill, lightly toast the bread on both sides. Meanwhile, combine the garlic with the olive oil.

2 Brush each slice of toasted bread with a little of the garlic oil, then top with a thin slice of tomato. Place a little tuna on each, then top with a slice of cheese and a sprinkling of parsley.

3 Return to the grill and cook, 10 cm (4 ins) from the heat, for 2–3 minutes, until the cheese has melted.

Traditional tapas

An appetizing selection of tapas need not involve a whole day in the kitchen. The following authentic dishes require little or no preparation:

- pan-fried and salted almonds
- black or green olives
- manchego cheese
- Spanish omelette (page 81)
- slices of chorizo (spicy sausage)
- chunks of crusty bread
- jumbo prawns

Andalucian Mushrooms

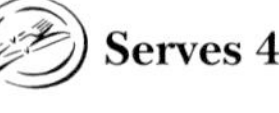

Serves 4

- *250 g (8 oz) button mushrooms*
- *2 tbsp olive oil*
- *30 g (1 oz) butter*
- *6 shallots, chopped*
- *3 garlic cloves, crushed*
- *30 g (1 oz) serrano ham or prosciutto, cut into strips*
- *1/4 tsp mild chilli powder*
- *1/4 tsp paprika*
- *4 tbsp water*
- *1 tsp lemon juice*
- *90 ml (3 fl oz) dry red wine*
- *4 tbsp chopped fresh coriander or parsley to garnish*

1 Pull the mushroom stems from the caps. Heat the olive oil and butter in a frying pan. When the butter is foaming, add the shallots and half of the garlic, and cook, stirring, for about 5 minutes until soft but not coloured. Add the mushroom caps and stems, and cook, stirring, for 3 minutes until lightly browned.

2 Add the serrano ham, chilli powder, and paprika, and cook, stirring constantly, for 1 minute.

3 Add the water and lemon juice, and cook over a high heat for a few minutes until the liquid has almost evaporated and the mushrooms are just tender.

4 Add the red wine and continue to cook over a high heat until the liquid is reduced and flavourful. Stir in the remaining garlic, sprinkle with the chopped coriander or parsley, and serve at once.

Clockwise from top: *Vegetables with Garlic Dips, Aïoli, Andalucian Mushrooms, Tuna Tostados, Rouille, Chick Pea & Red Pepper Salad.*

SPICY CHICKEN WINGS

Serves 4–6

500 g (1 lb) chicken wings
2 tbsp sunflower oil
1 tsp lemon juice
1 tsp onion salt
1 tsp garlic granules
1 tsp ground cumin
1/2 tsp dried oregano
1/2 tsp mild chilli powder
1/2 tsp paprika
1/4 tsp cayenne pepper
black pepper
parsley sprigs and cress to garnish

TO SERVE

1/2 red pepper, cut into strips
1/2 head celery, cut into sticks, plus leaves
blue cheese dressing (page 338)

1 Cut the chicken wings in half (see box, right). Arrange in a shallow dish.

2 In a large bowl, combine the oil, lemon juice, onion salt, garlic granules, cumin, oregano, chilli powder, paprika, cayenne pepper, and black pepper to taste. Brush the mixture over the chicken, cover, and leave to marinate at room temperature for at least 1 hour.

Cutting a chicken wing in half

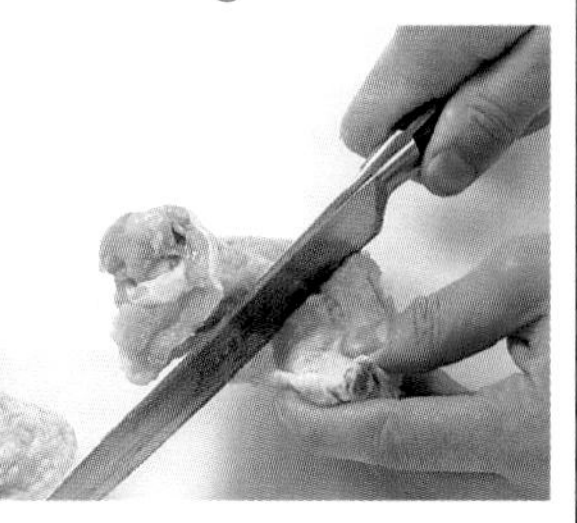

Tilt the chicken wing, raising the double end slightly off the chopping board. Using a chef's knife, cut the chicken wing into 2 pieces at the main joint, making a drumstick-like piece and a mini-wing.

3 Line a large baking tray with foil and place a rack on top. Arrange the chicken wings in a single layer on the rack, and cook in a preheated oven at 200°C (400°F, Gas 6) for 40 minutes, or until browned, sizzling hot, and crispy.

4 Remove the chicken from the rack and drain on paper towels. Serve with red pepper strips, celery sticks, and blue cheese dressing, and garnish with parsley and cress.

NACHOS GRANDE

Serves 4–6

2 tbsp sunflower oil
1 onion, finely chopped
1/2 green pepper, chopped
3 garlic cloves, crushed
125 g (4 oz) canned chopped tomatoes
1/2 –1 fresh green chilli, cored, seeded, and finely chopped
1/2 tsp chilli powder
1/2 tsp paprika
1 x 400 g (13 oz) can refried beans
75 ml (2 1/2 fl oz) water
75 g (2 1/2 oz) packet tortilla chips
1/4 tsp ground cumin
175 g (6 oz) Cheddar cheese, grated
paprika to garnish

1 Heat the oil in a frying pan, add the onion, green pepper, and garlic, and cook gently, stirring occasionally, for 5 minutes or until softened.

2 Add the tomatoes and chilli and cook over a medium heat for a further 5 minutes, or until most of the liquid has evaporated.

3 Stir in the chilli powder and paprika and cook for 3 minutes, then add the refried beans, breaking them up with a fork. Add the measured water and cook, stirring from time to time, for 8–10 minutes, until the mixture thickens.

4 Spoon the beans into the middle of a baking dish, arrange the tortilla chips around the edge, and sprinkle with cumin. Sprinkle the cheese over the beans and tortilla chips.

5 Bake in a preheated oven at 200°C (400°F, Gas 6) for 15–20 minutes until the cheese has melted. Sprinkle paprika in a lattice pattern on top.

Tortilla chips

These are traditionally made from round, flat, soft tortillas that are cut into segments and deep-fried. When covered with melted cheese and perhaps refried beans, salsa, or other toppings, the dish is known as nachos.

SALMON & PRAWN FILO PURSES

These crisp, golden purses and their creamy sauce are ideal for a party as they can be prepared up to 24 hours ahead, kept covered with a damp tea towel in the refrigerator, and cooked at the last minute. For a really special occasion, use scallops instead of prawns.

Makes 8 purses

500 g (1 lb) tail end of salmon, boned, skinned, and cut into bite-sized pieces

250 g (8 oz) cooked peeled prawns

lemon juice for sprinkling

250 g (8 oz) packet filo pastry

60 g (2 oz) butter, melted

butter for greasing

salt and black pepper

lemon slices and dill sprigs to garnish

WHITE WINE SAUCE

100 ml (3½ fl oz) dry white wine

300 ml (½ pint) double cream

1 tsp chopped fresh dill

1 Combine the salmon pieces and prawns. Sprinkle with lemon juice and add salt and pepper to taste. Set aside.

2 Cut the filo pastry into sixteen 18 cm (7 in) squares. Brush 2 squares with the melted butter, covering the remaining squares with a damp tea towel. Make a filo purse (see box, right). Repeat to make 8 purses.

3 Butter a baking tray. Add the filo purses, lightly brush with the remaining melted butter, and bake in a preheated oven at 190°C (375°F, Gas 5) for 15–20 minutes, until crisp and golden.

4 Meanwhile, make the sauce: pour the wine into a saucepan and boil rapidly until it has reduced to about 3 tbsp. Add the cream and simmer until it reaches a light coating consistency. Remove from the heat and add the dill and salt and pepper to taste.

5 Pour the sauce into a small bowl and garnish with a dill sprig. Garnish the purses with the lemon slices and dill sprigs and serve with the warm sauce.

VEGETABLE & GARLIC FILO PURSES

Heat 1 tbsp sunflower oil in a frying pan, add 175 g (6 oz) each carrot and celery, and 125 g (4 oz) spring onions, all cut into matchstick-thin strips. Stir-fry over a high heat for 2–3 minutes. Add salt and pepper to taste and leave to cool slightly. Prepare the purses as directed, filling them with the vegetable mixture and 125 g (4 oz) soft garlic cheese. Proceed as directed.

Making a filo purse

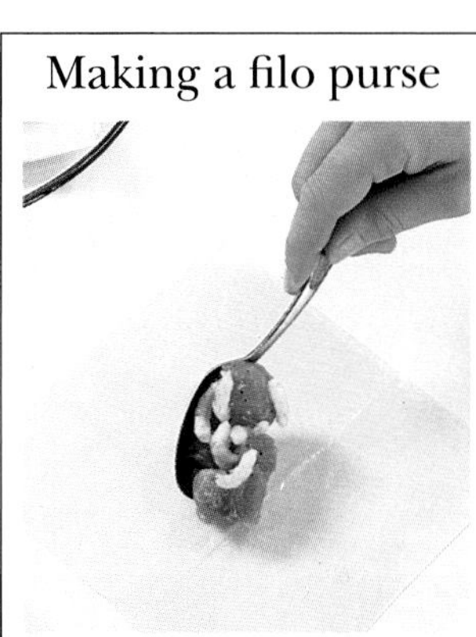

Place one-eighth of the salmon and prawn mixture in the middle of one buttered filo square.

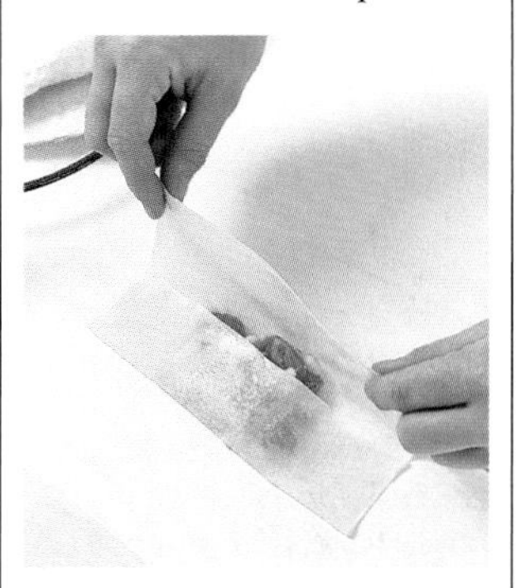

Fold 2 sides of filo pastry over the mixture to form a rectangle. Take the 2 open ends and fold one over the filling and the other underneath.

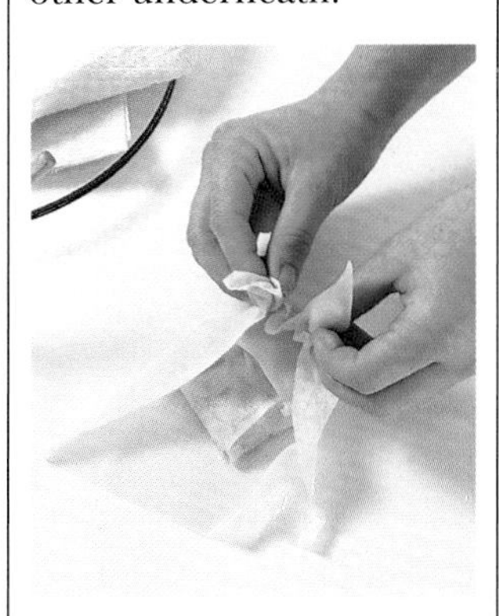

Place this parcel on the second buttered pastry square and draw up the edges. Squeeze the pastry together at the neck to seal the purse.

INDIVIDUAL FISH PATES

Rich in flavour, these little pâté parcels make an ideal starter for a special occasion. With the gelatine, they are firm enough to be sliced. For softer pâtés, omit the gelatine and wine and serve in ramekin dishes.

Serves 8

250 g (8 oz) haddock fillets
150 ml (1/4 pint) milk
20 g (3/4 oz) butter
20 g (3/4 oz) plain flour
1 tsp gelatine
4 tbsp dry white wine
250 g (8 oz) smoked salmon pieces
2 tbsp mayonnaise
4 tbsp double cream
dash of lemon juice
black pepper
oil for greasing
smoked salmon petals (see box, right), lemon slices, and dill sprigs to garnish

1 Put the haddock into a saucepan, and add the milk. Bring almost to a boil, then simmer gently for 10 minutes or until the fish is opaque and flakes easily.

2 Lift the haddock out of the pan, remove the skin and bones and discard. Flake the fish and leave to cool. Reserve the cooking liquid.

3 Melt the butter in a small pan, add the flour, and cook, stirring, for 1 minute. Gradually blend in the reserved cooking liquid, and bring to a boil, stirring constantly, until the mixture thickens. Place a piece of damp greaseproof paper over the surface of the sauce to prevent a skin forming, and leave to stand until cold.

4 Sprinkle the gelatine evenly over the wine in a small bowl. Leave to stand for 3 minutes or until the gelatine becomes spongy.

5 Put the bowl into a saucepan of gently simmering water for 3 minutes or until the gelatine has dissolved. Leave to cool slightly.

6 Purée the haddock, cold white sauce, smoked salmon pieces, and mayonnaise in a food processor or blender until almost smooth. Gradually add the gelatine mixture, processing between each addition. Add the cream, lemon juice, and pepper to taste, then purée briefly.

7 Grease 8 small moulds. Spoon the pâté into the moulds, cover, and chill for at least 2 hours.

8 To serve, unmould each pâté and garnish with smoked salmon petals, lemon slices, and dill sprigs.

Making smoked salmon petals

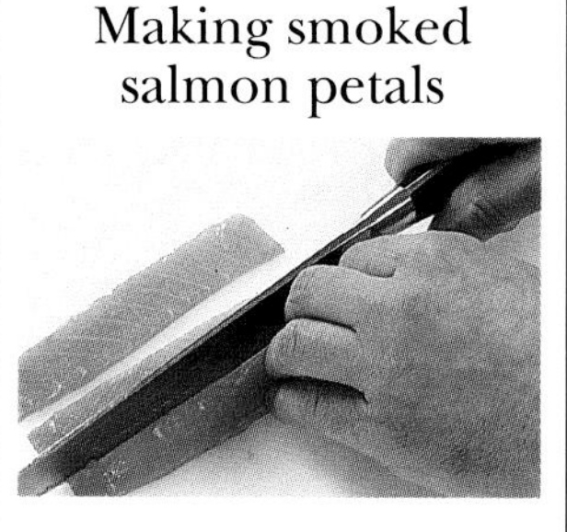

Cut the salmon into strips 2 cm (3/4 in) wide, using a chef's knife.

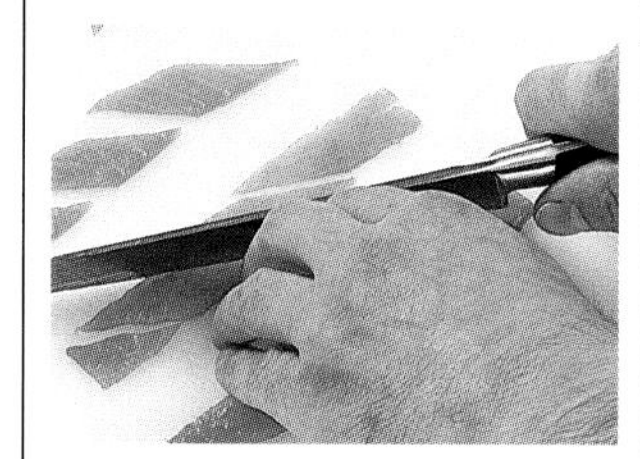

Cut diagonally across the strips to make 40 diamond-shaped pieces to represent petals.

SARDINE PATE

Serves 8

2 x 125 g (4 oz) cans sardines in oil, drained, bones removed
125 g (4 oz) butter, softened
125 g (4 oz) low-fat soft cheese
3 tbsp lemon juice
black pepper
lemon twists and parsley sprigs to garnish

1 Purée the sardines, butter, soft cheese, and lemon juice in a food processor until almost smooth. Add pepper to taste, and a little more lemon juice if needed.

2 Divide the sardine mixture between 8 small ramekins (or put into 1 large bowl) and level the surface. Cover and chill in the refrigerator for at least 30 minutes.

3 Serve chilled, garnished with lemon twists and parsley sprigs.

PRAWN PATE

Substitute 250 g (8 oz) cooked peeled prawns for the sardines, and proceed as directed.

THREE FISH TERRINE

Three smoked fish pâtés, made from trout, salmon, and mackerel blended with soft cheese, are arranged in layers and then wrapped in slices of smoked salmon, providing a subtle variety of flavours and colours. The finished terrine can be frozen for up to 1 month.

Serves 10

sunflower oil for greasing

175–250 g (6–8 oz) smoked salmon slices

salt and black pepper

watercress to serve

TROUT PATE

175 g (6 oz) smoked trout

90 g (3 oz) butter

90 g (3 oz) cream cheese

1½ tbsp lemon juice

SALMON PATE

125 g (4 oz) smoked salmon pieces

60 g (2 oz) butter

60 g (2 oz) cream cheese

1½ tbsp lemon juice

1 tbsp tomato purée

1 tbsp chopped fresh dill

MACKEREL PATE

175 g (6 oz) smoked mackerel

90 g (3 oz) butter

90 g (3 oz) cream cheese

1½ tbsp lemon juice

☆ *1.25 litre (2 pint) loaf tin or terrine*

1 Make the trout pâté: remove the skin and bones from the trout and purée with the butter, cream cheese, lemon juice, and salt and pepper to taste in a food processor until smooth and well blended. Turn into a bowl, cover, and chill.

2 Make the salmon pâté: purée the smoked salmon pieces, butter, cream cheese, lemon juice, tomato purée, dill, and salt and pepper to taste in a food processor until smooth and well blended. Turn into a bowl, cover, and chill.

3 Make the mackerel pâté: remove the skin and bones from the mackerel and purée with the butter, cream cheese, lemon juice, and salt and pepper to taste in a food processor until smooth and well blended. Turn into a bowl, cover, and chill.

4 Assemble the terrine (see box, right). Cover and chill overnight.

5 To serve, carefully turn out the terrine, cut into thick slices, and arrange on beds of watercress on individual serving plates.

Terrine

Named after the long, narrow container in which it was traditionally made, a terrine may be made from fish and seafood, a variety of meats, or even vegetables. Once firm, the mixture is either removed from the container in slices, or turned out of the mould and then sliced.

Assembling the terrine

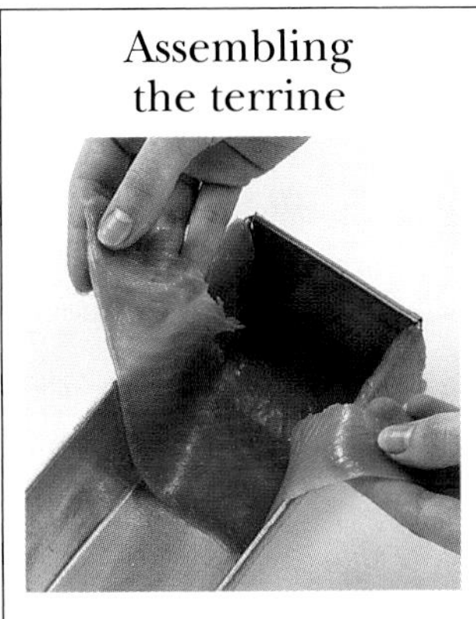

Oil the loaf tin and line with overlapping slices of smoked salmon, arranging them crosswise and allowing 3.5–5 cm (1½–2 ins) to overhang the sides of the tin.

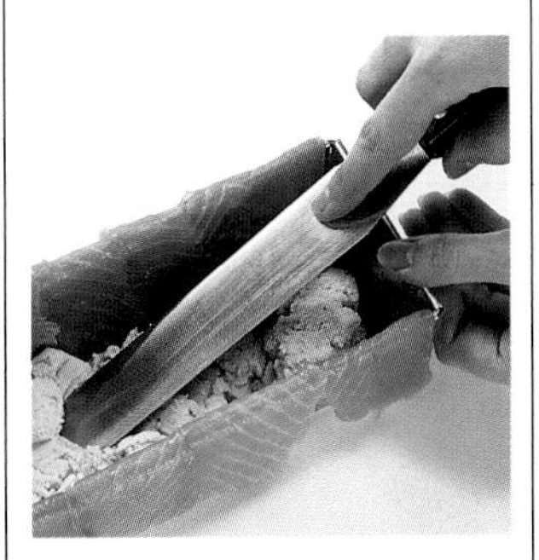

Turn the trout pâté into the loaf tin, spreading it evenly with a palette knife and levelling the surface. If necessary, wet the knife to prevent sticking. Add the salmon pâté in the same way, and then add the mackerel pâté.

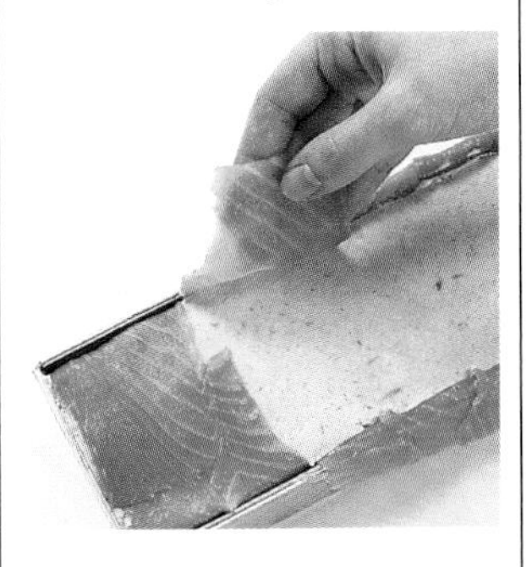

Fold the smoked salmon over the mackerel pâté, tucking in the ends.

LIGHT CHICKEN PATE

Serves 6

375 g (12 oz) boneless chicken breasts, skinned and diced

275 ml (9 fl oz) dry white wine

60 g (2 oz) pitted black olives

4 garlic cloves, crushed

salt and black pepper

3 tbsp fresh breadcrumbs

1 egg, lightly beaten

175 g (6 oz) unsmoked streaky bacon rashers, rinds removed

⋆ 23 cm (9 in) round ovenproof dish, 6 cm (2 1/2 ins) deep

1 In a bowl, combine the diced chicken with the wine, pitted black olives, garlic, and salt and pepper to taste. Stir in the fresh breadcrumbs and egg.

2 Line the base and side of the dish with the bacon rashers. Add the chicken mixture, then cover tightly with foil.

3 Place the dish in a roasting tin, pour in boiling water to come about halfway up the side of the dish, and bake in a preheated oven at 180°C (350°F, Gas 4) for about 1 hour until the pâté is firm. Leave to cool.

4 Remove the foil from the pâté, and pour off the cooking juices and fat. Replace the foil and put a plate on top that fits inside the rim of the dish. Weigh down with kitchen weights or heavy cans, and chill overnight. To serve, cut the pâté into slices.

Cook's know-how

Fat is used as much for preserving as for flavouring, so a low-fat pâté such as this one does not have the keeping qualities of one encased in fat. Keep this pâté chilled, and use within 3 days.

BRANDIED CHICKEN LIVER PATE

Serves 8

125 g (4 oz) white bread, crusts removed

1 garlic clove, coarsely chopped

125 g (4 oz) streaky bacon rashers, rinds removed, coarsely chopped

2 tsp chopped fresh thyme

500 g (1 lb) chicken livers, trimmed

1 egg

4 tbsp brandy

1/2 tsp grated nutmeg

salt and black pepper

60 g (2 oz) butter, melted

⋆ 1.25 litre (2 pint) loaf tin or terrine

1 Line the loaf tin with foil, leaving 5 cm (2 ins) foil overhanging on each side.

2 Cut the bread into thick chunks, and work them with the garlic in a food processor to form fine breadcrumbs. Add the bacon and thyme, and work until finely chopped.

3 Add the chicken livers, egg, brandy, nutmeg, and salt and pepper to taste, and purée until smooth. Add the butter and purée again.

4 Put the pâté mixture into the prepared loaf tin, level the surface, and fold the foil over the top. Place in a roasting tin, pour in boiling water to come about halfway up the side of the loaf tin, and bake in a preheated oven at 160°C (325°F, Gas 3) for 1 hour.

5 Test the pâté for doneness (see box, below). Leave the pâté to cool completely, then cover, and leave to chill in the refrigerator overnight.

6 To serve, cut the pâté into slices.

Testing the pâté

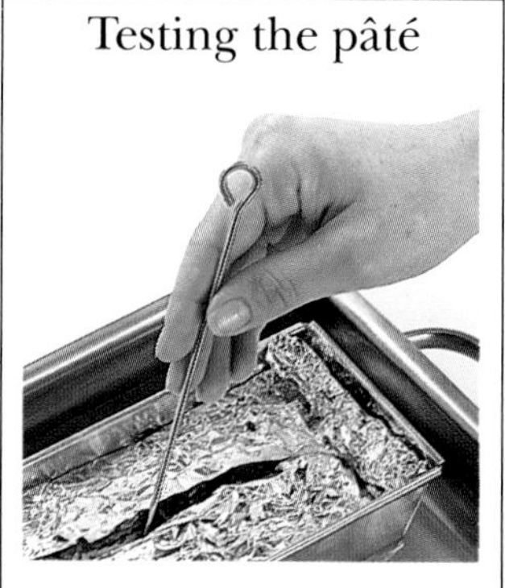

Insert a skewer into the pâté at the end of cooking time. If it comes out clean, the pâté is cooked.

PAN-FRIED PATES

These little bacon-wrapped chicken liver and spinach pâtés are a speciality of Burgundy. They are easy to make and at their most delicious when served with a tangy salad of sliced tomatoes and chopped onions in a herb vinaigrette dressing.

Serves 4

30 g (1 oz) butter
125 g (4 oz) chicken livers, trimmed
5 shallots, coarsely chopped
125 g (4 oz) lean bacon rashers, rinds removed, coarsely chopped
60 g (2 oz) spinach leaves, shredded
2 tbsp chopped parsley
1 garlic clove, chopped
1 tsp dried sage
1/2 tsp chopped fresh thyme
1/4 tsp ground cloves
salt and black pepper
8 streaky bacon rashers, rinds removed

1 Melt half of the butter in a frying pan, add the chicken livers, and cook gently, stirring occasionally, for 3 minutes or until they are browned on the outside but still pink inside.

2 Purée the chicken livers in a food processor until smooth. Turn into a large bowl and set aside.

3 Melt the remaining butter in the frying pan, add the shallots, and cook gently, stirring occasionally, for a few minutes until soft but not coloured.

4 Add the shallots to the chicken livers with the chopped bacon, spinach, parsley, garlic, sage, thyme, cloves, and salt and pepper to taste. Purée half of this mixture until smooth, then stir it into the remaining mixture in the bowl.

5 Shape and wrap the chicken liver pâtés (see box, right).

6 Heat a frying pan, add the pâtés, and cook them gently until browned all over. Lower the heat, cover, and cook over a very gentle heat for 35–40 minutes.

7 Serve the pan-fried pâtés either warm or at room temperature.

Cook's know-how

To trim the chicken livers, use a small sharp knife to cut away any membranes.

Shaping and wrapping the pâtés

Mould the pâté into 8 ovals, using your hands or 2 tablespoons.

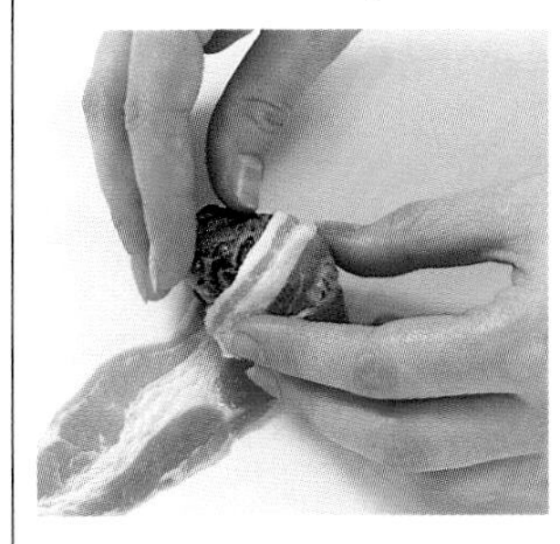

Place a bacon rasher on a work surface and roll it around one oval.

Twist the rasher round the ends to cover the pâté. Tuck it in to secure. Roll a bacon rasher around each of the remaining ovals.

WHITE BEAN PATE

Serves 6

2 x 400 g (13 oz) cans cannellini beans, drained
2–3 garlic cloves, coarsely chopped
1 tbsp chopped fresh rosemary
3 tbsp olive oil
juice of 1 lemon
salt and black pepper

TO GARNISH

6 rosemary sprigs
1 red pepper, cored, seeded, and cut into strips
12 small black olives

1 Purée the cannellini beans, garlic, rosemary, oil, and lemon juice in a food processor or blender until smooth.

2 Add salt and pepper to taste, then spoon the mixture into 6 small dishes, and level the surfaces.

3 Garnish each pâté with a rosemary sprig, strips of red pepper, and 2 olives.

Cook's know-how

Before chopping fresh rosemary, strip the leaves from the woody stems and discard the stems.

CARROT MOUSSE

 **Serves 6**

250 g (8 oz) carrots, sliced
salt and black pepper
1/2 vegetable stock cube
1 1/2 tsp gelatine
2 tbsp olive oil, plus extra for greasing
1 onion, chopped
3 garlic cloves, chopped
2 ripe tomatoes, peeled (page 39), seeded, and diced
1 tsp cumin seeds
75 ml (2 1/2 fl oz) fromage frais
coriander leaves and watercress to garnish

TOMATO SALSA
2 ripe tomatoes, peeled (page 39), seeded, and diced
1/2 onion, finely chopped
1 tbsp olive oil
1 tsp balsamic vinegar or wine vinegar
1 tbsp chopped fresh coriander
☆ 6 small ramekins

1 Make the tomato salsa: combine the tomatoes, onion, oil, vinegar, and coriander. Cover and chill.

2 Cook the carrots in boiling salted water until tender. Drain, reserving 125 ml (4 fl oz) of the cooking liquid in a bowl.

3 Crumble the 1/2 stock cube into the reserved cooking liquid and stir to dissolve. Sprinkle the gelatine over the top. Leave to stand for 3 minutes or until the gelatine becomes spongy.

4 Put the bowl into a pan of simmering water and heat for 3 minutes or until the gelatine has dissolved.

5 Heat the oil in a frying pan, add the onion and garlic, and cook gently, stirring occasionally, for a few minutes until soft but not coloured. Add the tomatoes and cumin seeds, and cook for 5–7 minutes until the mixture is thick.

6 Purée the carrots and the tomato mixture in a food processor until smooth, then add the fromage frais and salt and pepper to taste, and purée again. Add the gelatine mixture and purée once more.

7 Oil the ramekins and spoon in the carrot mixture. Cover and chill for at least 3 hours.

8 Garnish with the coriander leaves and watercress, and serve with the tomato salsa.

BROCCOLI TERRINE

Serves 4–6

500 g (1 lb) broccoli florets
salt and black pepper
1 tbsp gelatine
125 ml (4 fl oz) milk
1 egg yolk
pinch of grated nutmeg
125 ml (4 fl oz) double cream
oil for greasing
carrot julienne salad (page 357) to serve
☆ 1.25 litre (2 pint) loaf tin

1 Cook the broccoli in boiling salted water for 6 minutes or until just tender. Drain, reserving 75 ml (2 1/2 fl oz) of the cooking liquid, and rinse in cold water.

2 Pour the reserved cooking liquid into a small bowl, leave to cool slightly, then sprinkle the gelatine over the top. Leave to stand for 3 minutes or until the gelatine becomes spongy. Put the bowl into a pan of gently simmering water for 3 minutes or until the gelatine has dissolved.

3 Put the milk and egg yolk into a small saucepan and beat together. Heat gently, stirring, until the mixture thickens enough to coat the back of the spoon. Leave to cool slightly.

4 Reserve a few broccoli florets for garnish. Roughly chop half of the broccoli, and purée the remainder with the milk and egg mixture in a food processor until smooth. Pour the puréed broccoli mixture into a large bowl, add the chopped broccoli, gelatine mixture, nutmeg, and salt and pepper to taste, and mix together.

5 Whip the cream until it forms firm peaks, then fold it into the broccoli mixture. Oil the loaf tin and pour in the broccoli mixture. Cover and chill for at least 3 hours.

6 Turn out the terrine and cut into slices. Garnish with the reserved broccoli florets, and serve the terrine with the carrot julienne salad.

LEEK PARCELS WITH PROVENÇAL VEGETABLES

In this appealing starter, the addition of pesto to the dressing, with its delicious flavours of basil, pine nuts, garlic, and Parmesan cheese, complements the pesto inside the parcels, where it enhances the aubergine slices.

Serves 4

1 large leek, green part only, trimmed and cut in half lengthwise

1 aubergine, cut into 8 slices

1 courgette, sliced

olive oil for brushing

1/2 tsp herbes de Provence

salt and black pepper

1 red pepper, cored, seeded, roasted, and peeled (page 354)

200 g (7 oz) canned tomatoes, drained

3 tbsp ready-made pesto

2 garlic cloves, chopped

carrot julienne to garnish

PESTO DRESSING

3 tbsp olive oil

3 tbsp white wine vinegar

1 tsp ready-made pesto

1 Blanch the leek for 1 minute. Drain and rinse. Separate the green layers to give 13 strips.

2 Brush the aubergine and courgette slices with the oil, and sprinkle with herbes de Provence, and salt and pepper to taste. Cook under a hot grill, 10 cm (4 ins) from the heat, for 5 minutes.

3 Cut the pepper and tomatoes into chunks. Brush aubergine with pesto.

4 Cut one of the strips of leek into 4 long strands and set aside. Take 3 strips of leek and place on top of one another in a star formation. Assemble the leek parcels (see box, right).

5 Put the parcels on to a baking tray and bake in a preheated oven at 180°C (350°F, Gas 4) for 10 minutes.

6 Make the pesto dressing: whisk the oil, vinegar, and pesto. Spoon the dressing on to 4 serving plates, place a parcel on top, garnish, and serve at once.

Assembling the leek parcels

Place a slice of aubergine where the strips of leek cross. Place a piece of red pepper on top, then 1–2 slices of courgette, a little of the chopped garlic, a piece of tomato, and finish with another slice of aubergine.

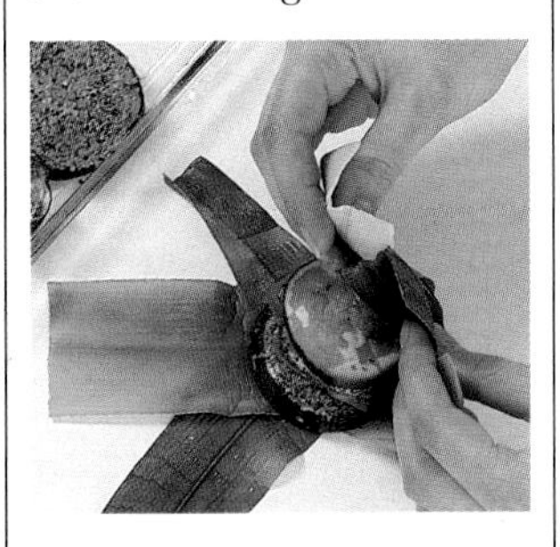

Fold the ends of the leek strips up over the filling, so that they meet in the middle and enclose the vegetable filling.

Tie the parcel with one of the long strands of leek or with a length of string. Repeat the assembling steps with the remaining leek strips and vegetables to make 4 parcels.

EGG PATE

Serves 8

1 tbsp gelatine

2 tbsp water

1 x 400 g (13 oz) can consommé

150 ml (1/4 pint) double cream

6 hard-boiled eggs, peeled and chopped

150 ml (1/4 pint) crème fraîche

salt and black pepper

8 large cooked prawns in their shells, lemon slices, and dill sprigs to garnish

1 Sprinkle the gelatine over the water in a bowl. Leave to stand for 3 minutes or until the gelatine becomes spongy. Put the bowl into a saucepan of simmering water for 3 minutes or until the gelatine has dissolved.

2 Pour the consommé into a jug and stir in the gelatine liquid.

3 Whip the cream in a large bowl until it forms soft peaks. Fold in the eggs, crème fraîche, and three-quarters of the consommé. Add salt and pepper to taste.

4 Divide the mixture between 8 ramekins and level the surfaces. Leave to stand for about 30 minutes until set. If it has already set, reheat the remaining consommé gently. Spoon it over the pâté. Chill for at least 3 hours.

5 To serve, turn out the pâté, and garnish with the prawns, lemon slices, and dill sprigs.

SCALLOPS WITH CHEESE SAUCE

Serves 4

8 scallops, cleaned, 4 shells reserved
150 ml (1/4 pint) water
4 tbsp medium dry white wine
1 bay leaf
salt and black pepper
lemon wedges and bay leaves to garnish

MORNAY SAUCE
45 g (1 1/2 oz) butter
3 tbsp plain flour
4 tbsp single cream
60 g (2 oz) Gruyère cheese, grated

1 Cut each scallop into 2–3 pieces. Put the measured water, wine, and bay leaf into a small pan, and add salt and pepper to taste. Bring to a boil, then lower the heat and add the scallops.

2 Poach for 1 minute or until the scallops are just tender when tested with the tip of a knife. Lift out the scallops with a slotted spoon, strain the cooking liquid, and reserve.

3 Make the Mornay sauce: melt the butter in a saucepan, add the flour, and cook, stirring, for 1 minute. Gradually stir in the reserved cooking liquid, and bring to a boil, stirring constantly, until the mixture thickens. Simmer gently for about 5 minutes. Lower the heat, and stir in the cream and half of the grated cheese. Taste for seasoning.

4 Stir the scallops into the sauce, divide among the shells, and sprinkle with the remaining cheese.

5 Place the filled shells under a hot grill, 7 cm (3 ins) from the heat, for about 5 minutes until the cheese has melted and the sauce is golden and bubbling. Garnish with lemon wedges and bay leaves.

MOULES MARINIERE

Serves 6

90 g (3 oz) butter
1 small onion, finely chopped
1 garlic clove, crushed
3 kg (6 lb) mussels, cleaned (page 106)
450 ml (3/4 pint) dry white wine
6 parsley sprigs
3 thyme sprigs
1 bay leaf
salt and black pepper
1 tbsp plain flour
3 tbsp chopped parsley to garnish

1 Melt two-thirds of the butter in a large saucepan, add the onion and garlic, and cook gently, stirring occasionally, for a few minutes until soft but not coloured.

2 Add the mussels, wine, parsley, thyme, bay leaf, and salt and pepper to taste. Cover the saucepan tightly and bring to a boil.

3 Cook, shaking the saucepan frequently, for 5–6 minutes or until the mussels open.

4 Throw away any mussels which have not opened: do not try to force them open. Transfer the remaining mussels to a warmed tureen.

5 Strain the cooking juices into a small saucepan. Boil until reduced by about one-third.

6 Work the remaining butter and the flour together on a plate, until a paste is formed.

7 Whisk the kneaded butter into the cooking liquid, and bring to a boil, stirring constantly. Taste the sauce for seasoning, and pour over the mussels. Garnish with the parsley, and serve at once.

Marinière

Derived from the French word marin, *which means sailor, the term* marinière *may refer to any type of seafood cooked with white wine and herbs.*

SALMON QUENELLES

Quenelles are delicate little dumplings, traditionally oval but sometimes round, which can be made with fish, meat, or chicken. The name comes from Knödel, *the German word for dumpling. They look difficult to make, but in fact they are quite simple, and make a most elegant starter.*

Serves 4–6

500 g (1 lb) salmon fillet, skinned, boned, and cut into chunks

2 egg whites

salt and white pepper

150 ml (1/4 pint) double cream

lemon slices and flat-leaf parsley sprigs to garnish

ASPARAGUS SAUCE

90 ml (3 fl oz) dry white wine

250 g (8 oz) young asparagus, trimmed, woody parts removed

300 ml (1/2 pint) double cream

1 Make the quenelles: purée the salmon, egg whites, and salt and pepper to taste in a food processor until completely smooth.

2 With the machine still running, pour in the cream in a steady stream until it is thoroughly blended. Turn the mixture into a large bowl, cover, and chill for about 2 hours.

3 Bring a saucepan of salted water to a simmer. Shape and cook the quenelles (see box, right). Keep the quenelles warm while you make the sauce.

4 Make the asparagus sauce: pour the wine into a saucepan and boil rapidly for about 2 minutes until it is reduced to a thin syrup.

5 Cook the asparagus in a pan of boiling salted water for 3–5 minutes until tender. Drain, then cut off the asparagus tips, and reserve them for garnish.

6 Purée the reduced wine and the asparagus stalks until very smooth.

7 Boil the cream in a saucepan for 4 minutes or until it is thick enough to coat the back of a metal spoon. Stir in the purée, and taste for seasoning.

8 Pour the sauce on to warmed plates, arrange the quenelles on top, and garnish with the reserved asparagus tips, lemon slices, and parsley sprigs.

Cook's know-how

When blending the quenelle mixture, take care not to overprocess the purée or the cream may curdle.

Shaping and cooking the quenelles

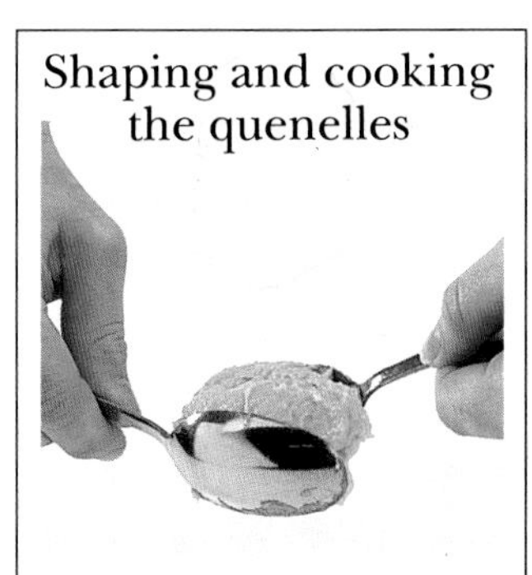

Dip a dessertspoon into the simmering water, then take a spoonful of the chilled quenelle mixture. Using a second warm wetted dessertspoon or your fingers, mould into an oval. Repeat with the remaining mixture.

Lower some quenelles into the simmering water and cook for 6–10 minutes until they are firm when pressed with a finger. Do not put too many into the pan at one time.

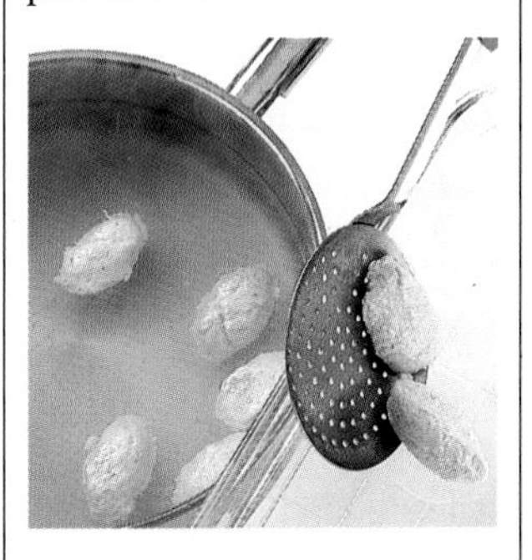

Remove the quenelles with a slotted spoon, drain well, and keep them warm while you cook the remainder.

SARDINES WITH CORIANDER

Serves 4

12–16 large sardines

olive oil for brushing

salt and black pepper

lime wedges and flat-leaf parsley sprigs to garnish

CORIANDER LIME BUTTER

1 tsp ground coriander

60 g (2 oz) unsalted butter, at room temperature

1½ tsp lime juice

1 shallot, finely chopped

¼ tsp finely grated lime zest

1 Scale the sardines with the back of a kitchen knife. With a sharp knife, cut the stomachs open, and scrape out the contents, particularly any dark blood.

2 Rinse the sardines inside and out, and pat dry. Brush all over with oil, and sprinkle with salt and pepper.

3 Prepare the coriander lime butter: heat a heavy pan, add the coriander and toast lightly. Transfer the coriander to a bowl and leave to cool slightly.

4 Add the butter and lime juice to the coriander and whisk until thick. Stir in the shallot and lime zest, and salt and pepper to taste.

5 Place the sardines under a hot grill, 10 cm (4 ins) from the heat, and grill for 1½–2 minutes on each side until they begin to feel firm.

6 Transfer the sardines to a platter, and spread a little coriander lime butter on each one. Garnish with lime wedges and flat-leaf parsley sprigs, and serve at once.

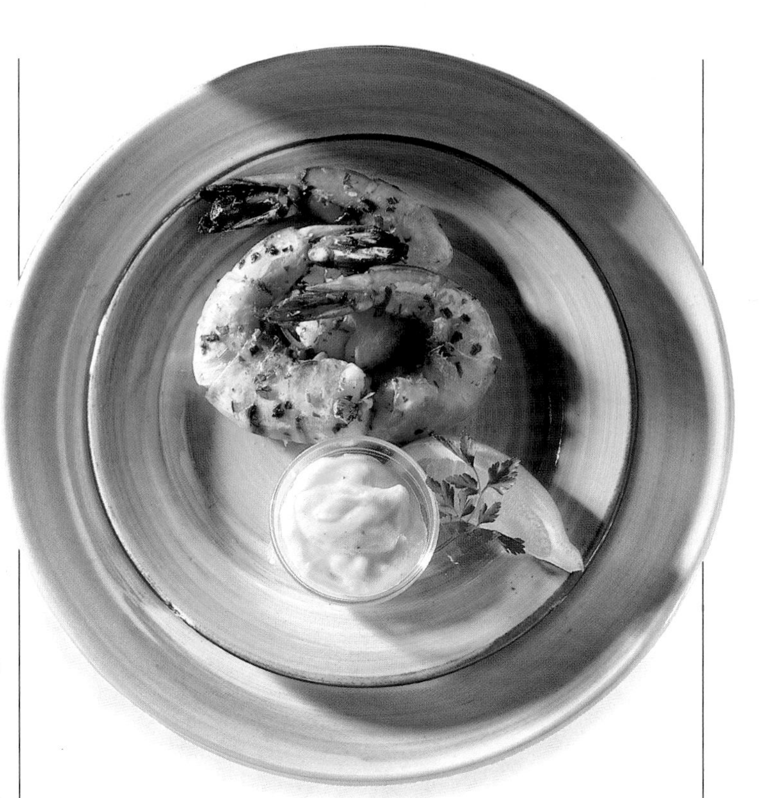

JUMBO PRAWNS WITH AIOLI

Serves 4

2 tbsp olive oil

12 uncooked jumbo prawns in their shells

1 tbsp chopped parsley

lemon wedges and flat-leaf parsley sprigs to garnish

AIOLI

2 garlic cloves, coarsely chopped

salt and black pepper

1 egg yolk

1 tsp mustard powder

150 ml (¼ pint) olive oil

1 tbsp lemon juice

1 Make the aïoli: in a small bowl, crush the garlic with a pinch of salt until it forms a smooth paste. Add the egg yolk and mustard powder, and beat well. Beat in the oil, drop by drop, whisking constantly until the mixture is thick and smooth, and all the oil has been absorbed. Beat in the lemon juice, and add pepper to taste.

2 Heat the oil in a large frying pan, add the prawns, and toss over a high heat for 4–5 minutes until the shells turn bright pink. Remove the prawns from the frying pan and drain on paper towels.

3 To serve, arrange the prawns on warmed plates, sprinkle with chopped parsley, and garnish with lemon wedges and parsley sprigs. Serve with individual bowls of aïoli.

Aïoli

This is a garlic-flavoured mayonnaise from Provence, where it is served with cold fish, hard-boiled eggs, cold meats, and fish soups.

GRAVADLAX

This is a Scandinavian method of pickling fresh salmon, and a lovely recipe for a party. Serve it with thin slices of dark rye bread. You will find it easier to slice if it has been frozen for about 4 hours beforehand.

Serves 16

2.25 kg (4½ lb) whole fresh salmon, boned and cut into 2 fillets

dill sprigs and lemon segments to garnish

PICKLING MIXTURE

75 g (2½ oz) granulated sugar

4 tbsp coarse sea salt

4 tbsp chopped fresh dill

MUSTARD DILL SAUCE

3 tbsp Dijon mustard

2 tbsp caster sugar

1 tbsp white wine vinegar

1 egg yolk

150 ml (¼ pint) sunflower oil

salt and black pepper

2 tbsp chopped fresh dill

1 Make the pickling mixture: put the granulated sugar, sea salt, and chopped dill into a small bowl, season generously with black pepper, and stir to mix.

2 Sandwich together the salmon fillets (see box, right).

3 Wrap the fillets in a double thickness of foil and place in a large dish. Weigh down with kitchen weights or heavy cans, and chill in the refrigerator for 1–3 days, turning the salmon over every day.

4 Make the mustard dill sauce: in a medium bowl, whisk together the mustard, sugar, vinegar, and egg yolk, then whisk in the oil a little at a time. The sauce should have the consistency of mayonnaise. Add salt and pepper to taste, and stir in the chopped dill.

5 Unwrap the gravadlax. A lot of sticky, salty liquid will drain from the fish when it has been pickled: this is quite normal. Remove the fish from the pickling liquid, and dry well. Separate the 2 salmon fillets.

6 To serve, slice each fillet on the slant, cutting the flesh away from the skin. The slices should be a little thicker than for smoked salmon and each one should have a fringe of dill. Garnish with dill sprigs and lemon segments, and serve with the mustard dill sauce.

Sandwiching the salmon

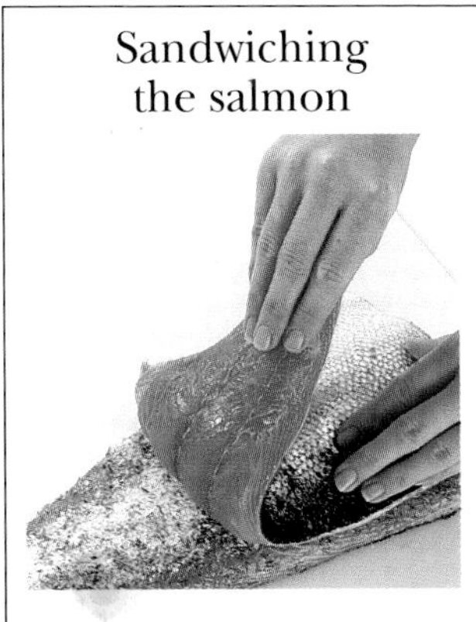

Put 1 salmon fillet skin-side down on a board, cover the surface with the pickling mixture, and place the second fillet on top, skin-side up.

PIQUANT PRAWNS

Serves 4

150 ml (¼ pint) mayonnaise

2 tbsp creamed horseradish

1 tbsp lemon juice

1 tsp Worcestershire sauce

1 tsp tomato purée

¼ tsp caster sugar

few drops of Tabasco sauce

black pepper

250 g (8 oz) cooked peeled prawns

salad leaves to serve

thin lemon wedges, parsley sprigs, and 4 large cooked prawns in their shells to garnish

1 Make the dressing: in a medium bowl, combine the mayonnaise, creamed horseradish, lemon juice, Worcestershire sauce, tomato purée, caster sugar, and Tabasco sauce, and season well with a little black pepper.

2 Add the peeled cooked prawns and stir to coat with the dressing.

3 Line 4 individual glass serving bowls with the salad leaves and top with the prawn mixture. Garnish each serving with a thin lemon wedge, a parsley sprig, and a large prawn.

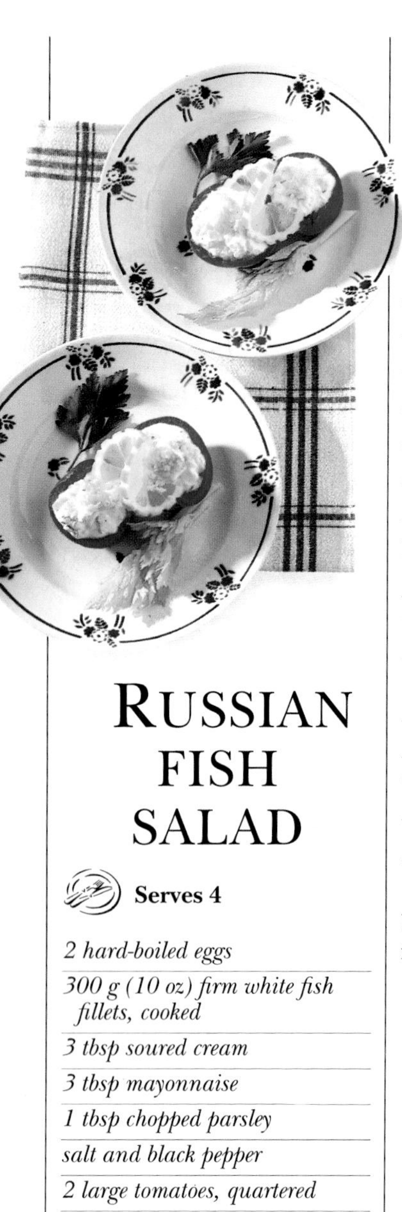

RUSSIAN FISH SALAD

Serves 4

2 hard-boiled eggs

300 g (10 oz) firm white fish fillets, cooked

3 tbsp soured cream

3 tbsp mayonnaise

1 tbsp chopped parsley

salt and black pepper

2 large tomatoes, quartered

lemon twists, flat-leaf parsley sprigs, and celery leaves to garnish

1 Remove the yolk from one egg and reserve. Chop the white and the remaining egg.

2 Put the fish into a bowl and flake with a fork. Stir in the chopped egg, soured cream, mayonnaise, parsley, and salt and pepper to taste.

3 Arrange the tomatoes on 4 plates and top with the fish mixture. Push the egg yolk through a sieve and sprinkle over the mixture. Garnish with lemon twists, parsley, and celery leaves.

PRAWN BLINI

Blini are small traditional Russian pancakes made with yeast and buckwheat flour. Buckwheat flour is available from health food shops but if you cannot find any, use wholemeal flour instead. This mixture makes about 24 blini.

Serves 6–8

BLINI

125 g (4 oz) plain flour

125 g (4 oz) buckwheat flour

1/2 tsp salt

1/2 tsp fast-action dried yeast

450 ml (3/4 pint) milk, warmed

1 egg, separated

sunflower oil for frying

TO SERVE

2 x 75 g (2 1/2 oz) jars lumpfish roe (1 red, 1 black)

125 g (4 oz) cooked peeled prawns

125 ml (4 fl oz) crème fraîche

lemon segments and fresh chives to garnish

1 In a large bowl, mix together the plain and buckwheat flours, salt, and fast-action dried yeast.

2 Gradually beat in the warm milk to make a smooth batter. Cover and leave in a warm place for about 40 minutes until the mixture is frothy and has doubled in volume.

3 Beat the egg yolk into the flour and yeast mixture. In a second bowl, whisk the egg white until stiff but not dry, then fold into the mixture.

4 Heat a large non-stick frying pan or griddle, brush with oil, and heat until the oil is hot. Spoon about 2 tbsp batter into the pan for each blini; you should be able to cook 3 or 4 at a time. Cook the blini over a moderate heat for 2–3 minutes, or until bubbles rise to the surface and burst.

5 Turn the blini over with a palette knife and cook for a further 2–3 minutes until golden on the other side. Wrap the cooked blini in a tea towel and keep them warm.

6 Cook the remaining batter in batches until all the batter is used up, lightly oiling the pan between each batch.

7 To serve, arrange the blini on warmed plates, with spoonfuls of red and black lumpfish roe, prawns, and crème fraîche. Garnish with lemon segments and fresh chives.

SMOKED CHICKEN SALAD WITH WALNUTS

Serves 6

1 smoked chicken, weighing about 1.25 kg (2½ lb)
100 ml (3½ fl oz) sunflower oil
2 tbsp walnut oil
75 ml (2½ fl oz) orange juice
¼ tsp ground coriander
¼ tsp caster sugar
salt and black pepper
375 g (12 oz) mixed salad leaves
4 oranges, peeled and segmented
60 g (2 oz) walnut pieces

1 Remove the meat from the chicken carcass, and discard the skin and any gristle. Cut the meat into thin, neat slices. Put the chicken slices into a shallow non-metallic dish.

2 In a small bowl, combine the sunflower and walnut oils, orange juice, ground coriander, sugar, and salt and pepper to taste. Pour the mixture over the chicken slices and toss them gently until evenly coated.

3 Arrange the salad leaves, orange segments, and chicken slices on individual serving plates, scatter the walnut pieces over the top, and serve immediately.

Smoked chicken

In the past, foods were smoked to preserve them, but flavour is now one of the prime reasons for smoking foods. The chicken is first cold-smoked, then briefly hot-smoked, before being rested to let the flavour mature. It is darker than fresh chicken.

WARM DUCK SALAD

Substitute 375 g (12 oz) smoked duck or turkey breast for the chicken. Gently heat the poultry slices in the dressing, and add warm croûtons (page 31) to the salad.

WARM SALAD WITH BACON & SCALLOPS

Serves 4

375 g (12 oz) mixed salad leaves, such as radicchio, lamb's lettuce, frisée, and rocket
8 shallots, finely chopped
1 tbsp sunflower oil
250 g (8 oz) lean unsmoked bacon rashers, rinds removed, diced
12 scallops, halved
3 tbsp white wine vinegar
2 tbsp walnut oil
salt and black pepper

Tossing a salad

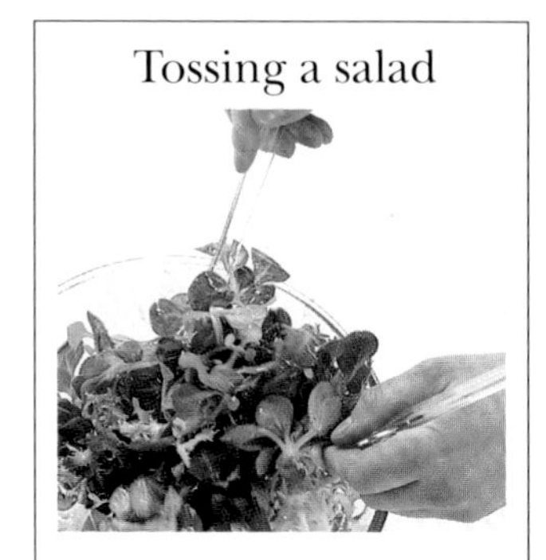

Pour the oil over the salad leaves. Lift a portion of the leaves and turn them over as you drop them back into the bowl. Repeat until all the leaves are evenly coated.

1 Put the salad leaves into a large bowl and sprinkle with half of the shallots.

2 Heat the oil in a frying pan, add the bacon, and cook quickly, stirring occasionally, for 5 minutes or until crisp. Add the scallops and cook quickly for 1–2 minutes until just opaque. Remove from the pan and keep warm.

3 Add the remaining shallots and cook for 1 minute. Add the vinegar and boil rapidly, stirring to incorporate the pan juices.

4 Toss the salad with the walnut oil (see box, above). Add the bacon and scallops, hot vinegar and shallots, and season to taste.

Cook's know-how

Stirring vinegar into the frying pan loosens and dissolves the flavoursome juices on the bottom of the pan so they are not wasted. This is called deglazing.

Asparagus with Quick Hollandaise

Serves 4

625 g (1¼ lb) asparagus

salt and black pepper

lemon twists to garnish

QUICK HOLLANDAISE

600 ml (1 pint) hot water

1 tbsp lemon juice

1 tbsp white wine vinegar

4 egg yolks, at room temperature

150 g (5 oz) unsalted butter, melted

1 Trim the asparagus, cut off the woody ends, and tie into 4 bundles with string.

2 Stand the asparagus upright in a deep pan with enough boiling salted water to come halfway up the stems, allowing the tips to steam rather than boil. Cover and cook for 8–10 minutes until the asparagus is tender but still firm.

3 Meanwhile, make the quick hollandaise: put the measured hot water into a food processor or blender and work briefly, to warm the bowl. Discard the water and dry the bowl.

4 Put the lemon juice and vinegar into the food processor, add the egg yolks and process briefly. With the machine running, gradually pour in the melted butter, and work until thick and creamy. Season to taste.

5 To serve, drain and untie the asparagus. Ladle the hollandaise sauce on to warmed plates, arrange the asparagus on top, and garnish with lemon twists.

Asparagus

One of the most prized of all vegetables, asparagus is known as "grass" in the British greengrocery trade, after its old name, sparrowgrass. Select spears with a good colour, that are crisp, straight, and firm with tightly closed tips. Ideally, asparagus should be cooked and eaten on the day it is picked, but if you need to keep it longer than 12 hours, wrap the bottoms of the stalks in wet paper towels, seal tightly in a polythene bag, and store in the refrigerator. Use within 4 days.

Brioches with Wild Mushrooms & Watercress

Serves 6

30 g (1 oz) butter

250 g (8 oz) wild mushrooms, trimmed and sliced

60 g (2 oz) watercress, finely chopped

4 tbsp double cream

squeeze of lemon juice

salt and black pepper

6 brioches (page 380)

watercress sprigs to garnish

1 Melt the butter in a large frying pan, add the mushrooms, and cook gently, stirring from time to time, for 3 minutes or until tender. Add the watercress, cream, lemon juice, and salt and pepper to taste, and cook until the watercress is just wilted.

2 Remove the tops and insides from the brioches (see box, right). Spoon in some of the mixture.

Preparing brioches

Remove brioche top and set aside. Using your fingers, pull out the soft inside, leaving a 5 mm (¼ in) crust. Repeat with the remaining brioches.

3 Transfer the brioches to warmed serving plates, replace the brioche tops, and spoon the remaining mushroom and watercress mixture on to the plates beside the brioches. Garnish with watercress sprigs, and serve at once.

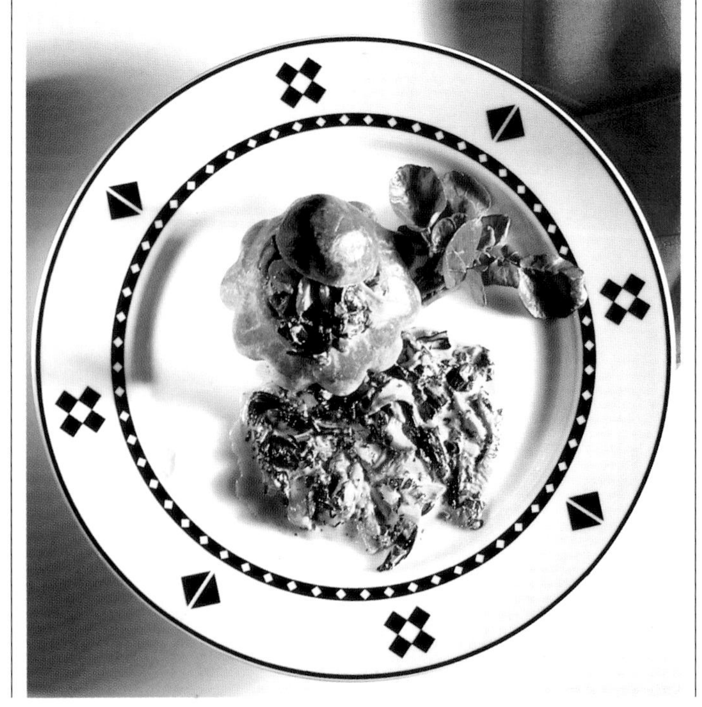

SMOKED SALMON PINWHEELS

The pinwheel pattern of the roulade is almost as delightful as its flavour. Since both the cream cheese and smoked salmon layers are quite rich, the inclusion in the roulade of a very thin layer of tomatoes provides a fresh contrast.

Serves 4–6

15 g (1/2 oz) butter
1 garlic clove, crushed
150 g (5 oz) spinach, cooked, squeezed dry, and chopped
4 eggs, separated
1 tsp chopped fresh rosemary
pinch of grated nutmeg
salt and black pepper
salad leaves and lemon slices to garnish

FILLING

200 g (7 oz) cream cheese
3 tbsp Greek yogurt
4 spring onions, thinly sliced
125 g (4 oz) smoked salmon
2 ripe tomatoes, thinly sliced
⋆ 33 x 23 cm (13 x 9 in) Swiss roll tin

1 Line the Swiss roll tin with a sheet of baking parchment, cutting the corners of the paper so that it fits snugly into the tin.

2 Put the butter into a saucepan, add the garlic, and cook gently until the butter melts. Remove from the heat. Stir in the spinach.

3 Add the egg yolks, rosemary, and nutmeg, season to taste, and beat into the spinach mixture.

4 In another bowl, whisk the egg whites until firm but not dry. Fold 2–3 spoonfuls into the spinach mixture, then fold in the remainder.

5 Spread the mixture in the Swiss roll tin, and bake in a preheated oven at 190°C (375°F, Gas 5) for 10–12 minutes until the mixture feels firm. Remove from the oven, cover with a damp tea towel, and leave to cool.

6 Meanwhile, make the filling: beat together the cream cheese and yogurt until smooth, then stir in the spring onions.

7 Turn out the cooled roulade and peel off the paper. Fill and roll the roulade (see box, right).

8 Wrap the roulade in foil, then overwrap with a damp tea towel, and chill overnight.

9 To serve, trim off the hard edges of the roulade, cut into thick slices, and arrange on a serving platter. Garnish with salad leaves and lemon slices.

PARMA HAM PINWHEELS

Substitute 150 g (5 oz) broccoli, cooked and puréed, for the spinach, and 125 g (4 oz) thinly sliced Parma ham for the smoked salmon. Proceed as directed.

Filling and rolling the roulade

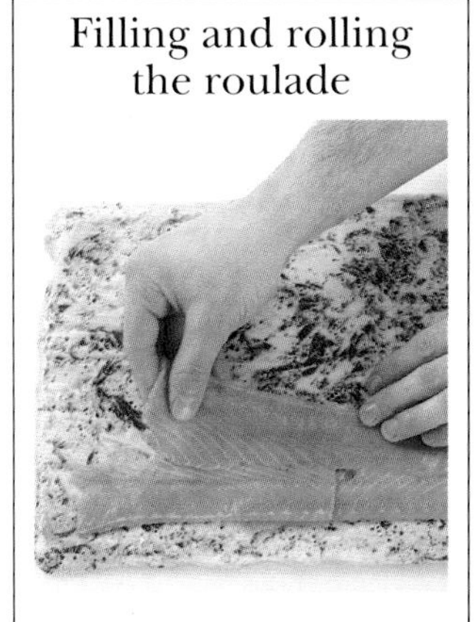

Arrange the slices of smoked salmon on top of the roulade, leaving a 2.5 cm (1 in) border on each side.

Spread the cream cheese filling over the smoked salmon, using a palette knife. Arrange the tomato slices over half of the cream cheese filling.

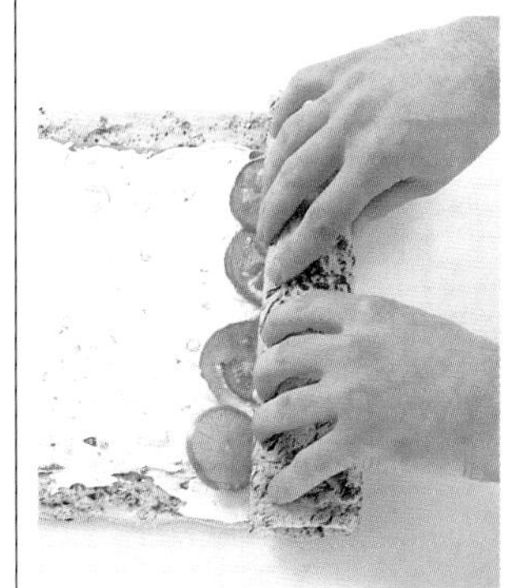

Roll up the roulade, starting from the end where the tomato slices have been placed.

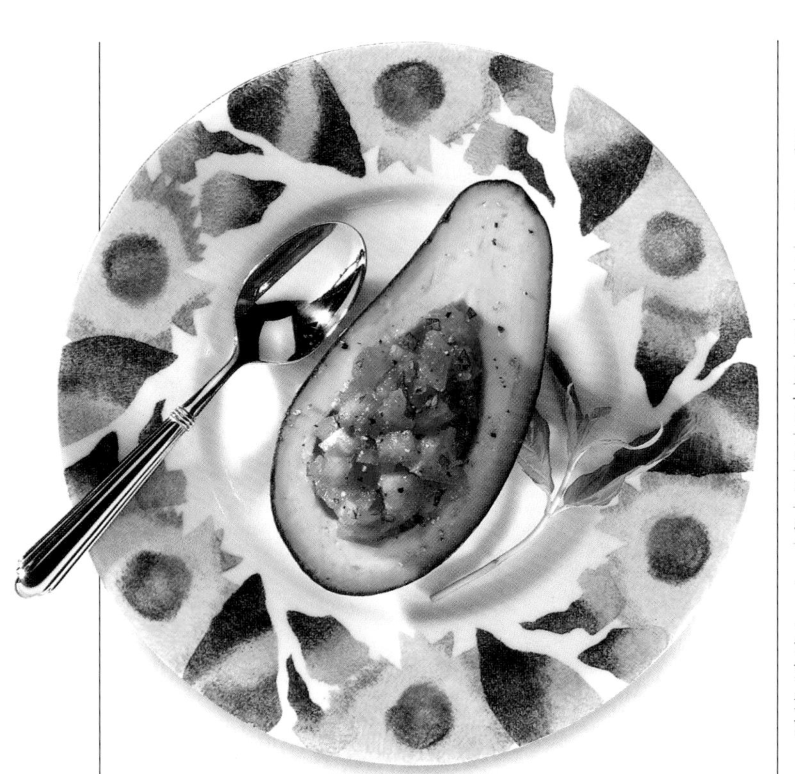

AVOCADO WITH TOMATOES & MINT

Serves 4

4 small firm tomatoes
2 ripe avocados
1 tbsp chopped fresh mint
mint sprigs to garnish

DRESSING

2 tsp white wine vinegar
1 tsp Dijon mustard
2 tbsp olive oil
¼ tsp caster sugar
salt and black pepper

1 Peel the tomatoes: cut out the cores and score an "x" on the base of each one, then immerse in a bowl of boiling water until the skins start to split. Transfer at once to a bowl of cold water. Peel, seed, and then coarsely chop the tomato flesh.

2 Make the dressing: in a small bowl, whisk together the vinegar and mustard. Gradually whisk in the oil, then add the caster sugar, and salt and pepper to taste.

Stoning an avocado

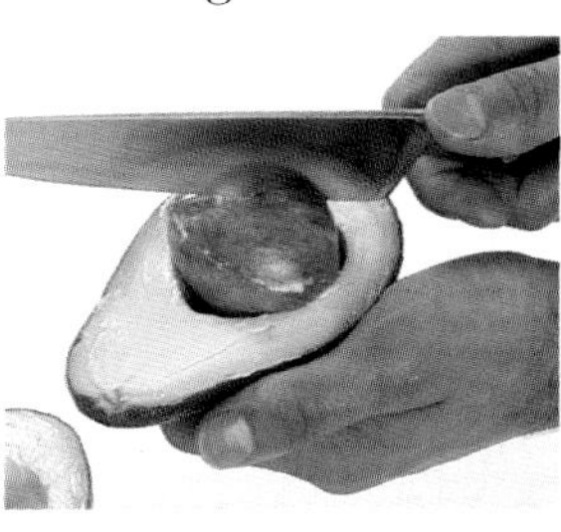

Cut the avocado in half lengthwise, through to the stone. Twist the halves and then pull them apart. Embed the blade of a chef's knife in the stone and lift it out.

3 Halve and stone the avocados (see box, above). Brush at once with a little dressing to prevent discoloration.

4 Combine the tomatoes, chopped mint, and dressing. Pile the tomato mixture into the avocado halves, garnish with mint sprigs, and serve at once.

SUMMER MELONS

Serves 4

2 x 750 g (1½ lb) ripe melons with differently coloured flesh
500 g (1 lb) tomatoes
1 tbsp chopped fresh mint
mint sprigs to garnish

DRESSING

90 ml (3 fl oz) sunflower oil
2 tbsp white wine vinegar
¼ tsp caster sugar
salt and black pepper

1 Cut the melons in half, and remove and discard the seeds. Using a melon baller, cut balls from the flesh of each half into a bowl, or cut into neat cubes.

2 Peel the tomatoes: cut out the cores and score an "x" on the base of each one, then immerse in a bowl of boiling water until the skins start to split. Transfer at once to a bowl of cold water. Peel and seed the tomatoes, then cut the flesh into long strips. Add the strips to the melon.

3 Make the dressing: in a small bowl, whisk together the sunflower oil and vinegar, then add the caster sugar, and salt and pepper to taste. Pour the dressing over the melon and tomato mixture. Cover and chill for at least 1 hour.

4 To serve, stir the chopped mint into the melon and tomato mixture, spoon the salad into chilled bowls, and garnish each serving with a mint sprig.

Cook's know-how

Choose two or three varieties of melon to make an attractive colour combination. Honeydew has pale greenish yellow flesh, cantaloupe has either pale green or orange flesh, ogen has pale yellow or green flesh, while Charentais has deep orange flesh.

ANTIPASTI

This is the Italian equivalent of hors d'oeuvre – a selection of hot and cold appetizers. In Italy, you are most likely to find lavish displays of antipasti in restaurants; at home, only one or two simple appetizers are served.

MOZZARELLA, TOMATO, & BASIL SALAD

Serves 8

4 slicing or beefsteak tomatoes
250 g (8 oz) mozzarella cheese
4 tbsp shredded fresh basil
4 tbsp olive oil
1 tbsp balsamic vinegar or wine vinegar
salt and black pepper
basil sprig to garnish

1 Peel the tomatoes: cut out the cores and score an "x" on the base of each one, then immerse in boiling water until the skins start to split. Transfer at once to cold water; when cool, peel off the skin. Thinly slice the tomatoes.

2 Slice the mozzarella cheese. Arrange the tomato and cheese slices alternately on a plate, overlapping one another. Sprinkle with the basil, olive oil and vinegar, and salt and pepper to taste. Garnish with a basil sprig and serve.

Mozzarella

This is an unripened white cheese. Traditionally made with buffalo milk, less expensive varieties made with cow's milk are now widely available, and often used in the place of mozzarella di bufala.

SUN-DRIED TOMATO CROSTINI

Serves 8

1 baguette
2 garlic cloves, crushed
about 3 tbsp olive oil
4 sun-dried tomatoes in oil
30 g (1 oz) butter
salt and black pepper
12 pitted black olives, chopped
1/4 tsp dried rosemary

1 Cut the baguette into 24 thin slices and arrange them on 2 baking trays. Add the garlic to the olive oil, then brush about half of the mixture on to the slices of bread. Bake in a preheated oven at 180°C (350°F, Gas 4) for 10 minutes.

2 Remove the baking trays from the oven, turn the slices of bread over, brush with a little more garlic oil, and bake for a further 10 minutes or until crisp and golden. Leave to cool.

3 Dry the sun-dried tomatoes with a paper towel and cut them into pieces. Put the tomato and butter in a food processor and work until finely chopped. Season with salt and pepper to taste.

4 Spread the sun-dried tomato purée over the crostini, arrange the chopped olives on top, and sprinkle with rosemary.

Cook's know-how

Italian delicatessens are a wonderful hunting ground for ready-prepared antipasti. Make up a large platter of preserved meats, such as prosciutto di Parma *(Parma ham),* mortadella *(a stewed pork sausage from Bologna),* bresaola *(dried, salted beef), or some slices of salami. Among the many varieties are* salame milano, *traditionally made of pork, sometimes a combination of pork and beef;* salame genoa, *pork studded with white peppercorns; and* salame finocchiona, *made from pork flavoured with fennel. Serve a selection of bowls containing green olives stuffed with anchovies or pimientos; green and black olives marinated in olive oil, herbs, and spices; roasted red peppers marinated in olive oil, garlic, and parsley; and ready-prepared mixtures of prawns, mussels, squid, and other seafood in a herb dressing.*

CAPONATA

Serves 4–6

1 large aubergine
salt and black pepper
about 4 tbsp olive oil
1/2 head celery, diced
2 onions, thinly sliced
125 g (4 oz) tomato purée
60 g (2 oz) sugar
125–175 ml (4–6 fl oz) red wine vinegar
125 g (4 oz) pitted green olives
30 g (1 oz) capers (optional)
1–2 garlic cloves, crushed
30 g (1 oz) parsley, chopped

1 Cut the aubergine into 1 cm (1/2 in) chunks, and sprinkle generously with salt. Leave to stand for 30 minutes to draw out the bitter juices, then rinse well with cold water, and dry thoroughly with paper towels.

2 Heat three-quarters of the oil in a large saucepan, add the aubergine, and cook gently, stirring, for 8 minutes or until tender. Remove the aubergine from the pan with a slotted spoon.

3 Heat the remaining oil in the pan, add the celery, and cook gently, stirring occasionally, for 7 minutes or until browned.

4 Return the aubergine to the pan with the onions, tomato purée, sugar, and vinegar. Cook over a medium heat for 10 minutes to reduce the harshness of the vinegar. Add a little water if the mixture becomes too thick and starts sticking to the pan.

5 Remove from the heat, and add the green olives, capers, if using, garlic, and half of the parsley. Add pepper to taste. Cover and leave to cool. To serve, transfer to serving plates and sprinkle with the remaining parsley.

Capers

These are the flower buds of a Mediterranean shrub, preserved by pickling in vinegar and salt. They have a tangy, sour taste.

WARM SALAD WITH PEARS & STILTON

Serves 4

8 thin slices of white bread
2 garlic cloves, halved
250 g (8 oz) blue Stilton cheese, sliced
2 bunches of watercress, trimmed and chopped
2 pears, peeled and cut into thin wedges
4 tbsp sunflower oil
1 small red onion, finely chopped
2 tbsp balsamic vinegar
☆ 7 cm (3 in) pastry cutter

1 With the pastry cutter, cut out decorative shapes from the slices of bread.

2 Toast the bread shapes on both sides under a hot grill. Rub both sides of the bread with the garlic cloves and arrange the slices of Stilton cheese on top of each piece. Set aside.

3 Arrange the chopped watercress and pear wedges on 4 individual serving plates, then set aside.

4 Heat the sunflower oil in a frying pan, add the onion, and cook gently for 5 minutes or until soft but not coloured.

5 Meanwhile, put the Stilton-topped toasts under the hot grill, close to the heat, for 1–2 minutes until the cheese is melted and warmed through. Cut the toasts in half.

6 Add the vinegar to the onion in the frying pan, and let it heat through, stirring occasionally. Pour the onion mixture over the watercress and pears. Arrange the toasts on the plates and serve at once.

WARM SALAD WITH PEARS & BRIE

For a milder flavour, substitute 250 g (8 oz) Brie, thickly sliced, for the Stilton.

3

EGGS & CHEESE

UNDER 30 MINUTES

SPINACH & MUSHROOM FRITTATA

Firm and chunky Italian omelette enclosing bacon, mushrooms, and spinach, sprinkled with Parmesan, and browned under the grill.

SERVES 2 673 calories per serving

Takes 25 minutes **PAGE 80**

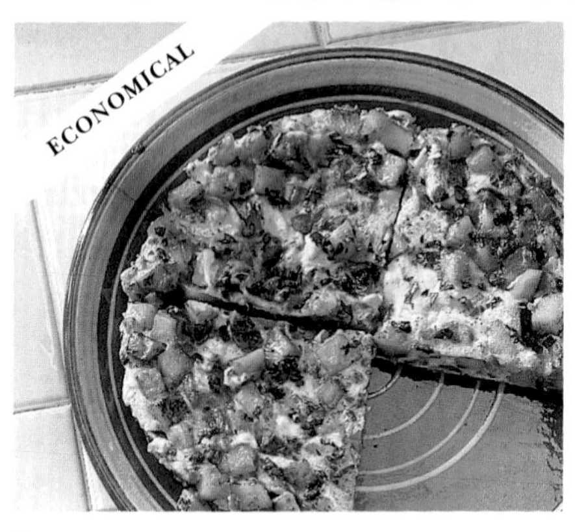

SPANISH OMELETTE

Traditional Spanish dish: diced potatoes, onions, and eggs cooked slowly make a nourishing and simple meal.

SERVES 4 389 calories per serving

Takes 25 minutes **PAGE 81**

RACLETTE

Boiled new potatoes topped with Swiss raclette cheese, and heated in the oven until sizzling. Served with gherkins and onions.

SERVES 4 446 calories per serving

Takes 25 minutes **PAGE 93**

OEUFS EN COCOTTE

Warm creamy snack: whole eggs in ramekins, topped with double cream and parsley, and steamed or baked.

SERVES 4 176 calories per serving

Takes 25 minutes **PAGE 96**

COURGETTE FRITTATA

Light and easy to make: thinly sliced courgettes and diced prosciutto cooked with eggs make a colourful Italian omelette. Browned under the grill, cut into wedges, and garnished with shredded fresh basil. Served hot or cold.

SERVES 4 270 calories per serving

Takes 25 minutes **PAGE 81**

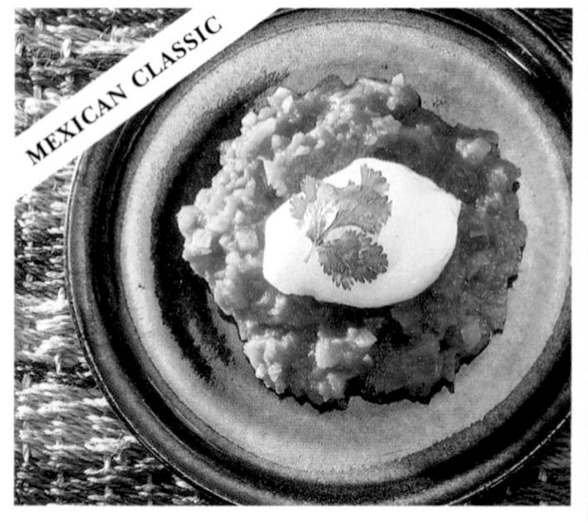

HUEVOS RANCHEROS

Classic Mexican dish of tomatoes simmered with onion, garlic, green pepper, fresh chilli, and cumin. Topped with a poached egg.

SERVES 4 196 calories per serving

Takes 25 minutes **PAGE 96**

MUSHROOM OMELETTE WITH CIABATTA

Italian ciabatta bread, filled with an omelette brimming with sliced shiitake mushrooms.

SERVES 2 673 calories per serving

Takes 25 minutes **PAGE 80**

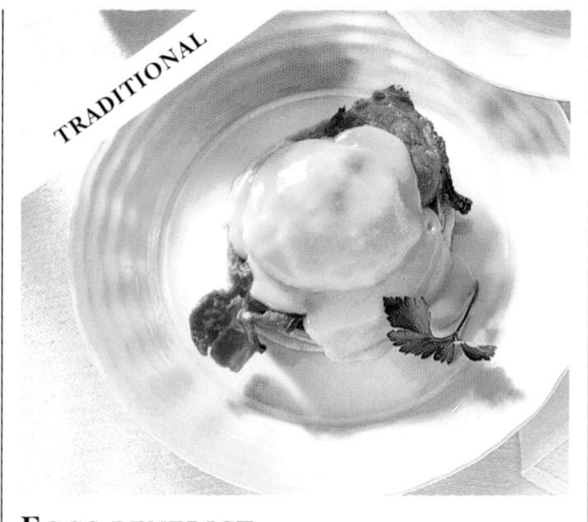

EGGS BENEDICT

Hearty snack: poached eggs and bacon rashers on toasted muffins, topped with lemon-flavoured hollandaise sauce.

SERVES 4 602 calories per serving

Takes 25 minutes **PAGE 95**

30–60 MINUTES

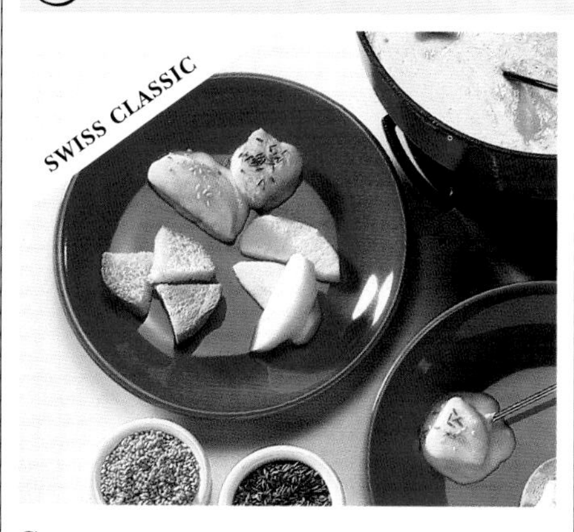

CHEESE FONDUE

Gruyère and Emmental cheeses melted in a fondue pot with wine, garlic, and kirsch. Served with bread and apple for dipping.

SERVES 4–6 1219–813 calories per serving

Takes 30 minutes **PAGE 93**

SAVOURY SOUFFLE OMELETTE

Light and summery: courgette, red pepper, and tomatoes combined with soufflé mixture. Flavoured with garlic, onion, and thyme.

MAKES 2 479 calories per serving

Takes 35 minutes **PAGE 79**

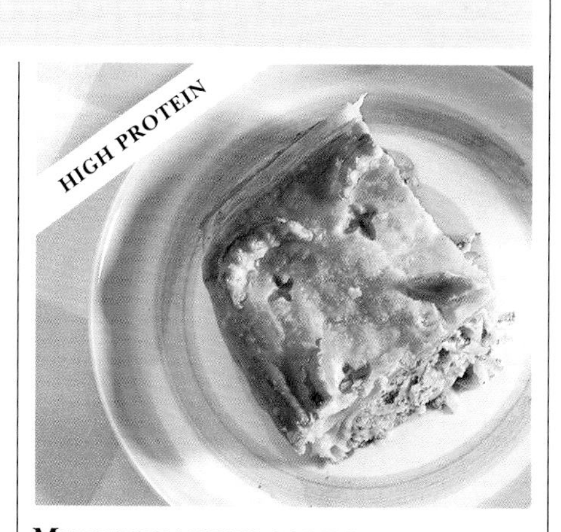

MEDITERRANEAN COURGETTE PIE

Wholesome and rich: courgettes mixed with Parmesan and mozzarella cheeses, eggs, pesto, garlic, and mint. Topped with puff pastry.

SERVES 4 545 calories per serving

Takes 50 minutes **PAGE 84**

CROQUE SENOR

Sandwich of Cheddar cheese and ham given a Mexican flavour with salsa of tomatoes, chilli, and red pepper. Cooked until golden.

SERVES 4 413 calories per serving

Takes 30 minutes **PAGE 94**

MEXICAN OMELETTE

Classic omelette with a substantial filling of onion and garlic cooked with green pepper, tomatoes, mushrooms, and Tabasco.

MAKES 2 547 calories per serving

Takes 50 minutes **PAGE 79**

BROCCOLI SOUFFLES

Broccoli, shallots, and blue cheese combined with soufflé mixture and flavoured with nutmeg and cayenne pepper.

SERVES 4 499 calories per serving

Takes 45 minutes **PAGE 91**

EGGS FLORENTINE

Nutritious and creamy: spinach mixed with spring onions and double cream, topped with a poached egg and Parmesan cheese sauce.

SERVES 4 475 calories per serving

Takes 30 minutes **PAGE 95**

ITALIAN CHEESE & RED PESTO TARTLETS

Rich and tangy: tomatoes, black olives, and Fontina cheese, complemented by the Mediterranean flavours of garlic and oregano, set in shortcrust pastry tartlet shells spread with pesto. Sprinkled with Parmesan cheese to give a tasty, crispy finish.

MAKES 12 198 calories each

Takes 55 minutes **PAGE 85**

30–60 MINUTES

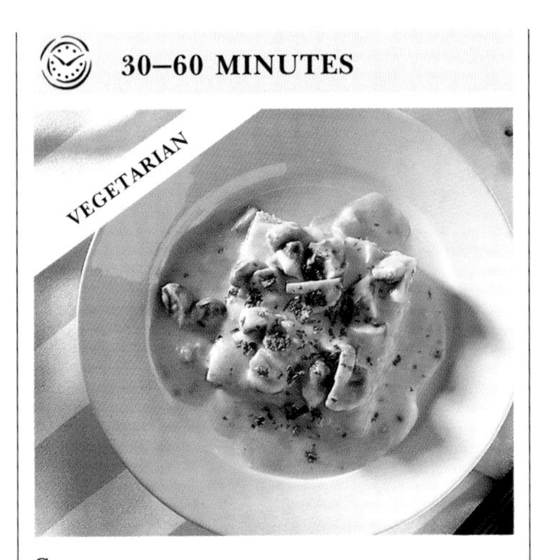

SWISS TOMATO RAREBIT

Variation of Welsh rarebit: tomatoes and wine cooked with Gruyère cheese and mushrooms. Served on buttered toast.

SERVES 4 640 calories per serving

Takes 30 minutes **PAGE 94**

STRATA WITH CHEESE AND PESTO

Savoury custard of eggs, crème fraîche, and milk, poured over slices of bread and pesto. Sprinkled with Italian cheeses.

SERVES 4 896 calories per serving

Takes 50 minutes **PAGE 86**

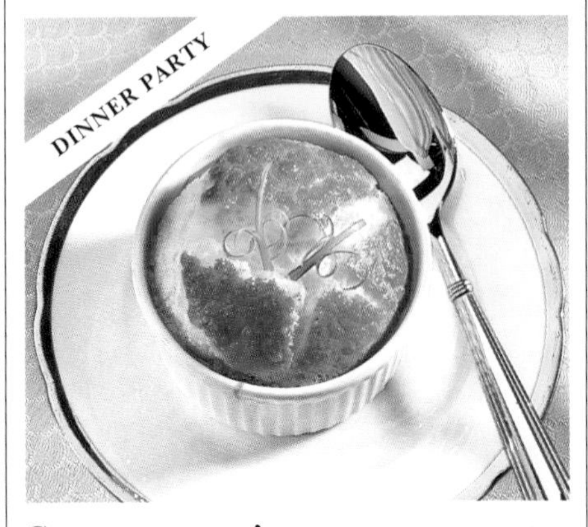

GARLIC & GOAT'S CHEESE SOUFFLES

Tangy soufflés combining garlic-flavoured milk with butter, flour, goat's cheese, egg yolks, and whisked egg whites.

SERVES 6 267 calories per serving

Takes 55 minutes **PAGE 92**

OVER 60 MINUTES

SOUFFLE PANCAKES WITH BROCCOLI & CHEESE

Pancakes with a soufflé filling combining tiny broccoli florets, Cheddar cheese, and mustard.

MAKES 8 300 calories per serving

Takes 45 minutes, plus standing **PAGE 90**

BROCCOLI & RICOTTA TART

Ricotta, Cheddar, and Parmesan cheeses mixed with broccoli, eggs, garlic, and thyme, baked in a buttered breadcrumb crust.

SERVES 4–6 689–460 calories per serving

Takes 1 hour 5 minutes **PAGE 86**

QUICHE LORRAINE

Classic savoury tart: shortcrust pastry shell spread with lightly cooked onion and crispy pieces of streaky bacon. Sprinkled with grated Gruyère cheese, then filled with an egg and cream mixture, and baked until golden brown. Served warm or cold.

SERVES 4–6 756–504 calories per serving

Takes 60 minutes, plus chilling **PAGE 82**

OVER 60 MINUTES

CREAMY SEAFOOD PANCAKES

Pieces of cod fillet cooked with onion, garlic, tomatoes, dill seeds, cream, and prawns, and flavoured with fresh basil. The creamy filling is spread over pancakes, which are then folded into triangles, and garnished with prawns, sprigs of basil, and lemon coronets.

SERVES 6 308 calories per serving
Takes 50 minutes, plus standing **PAGE 87**

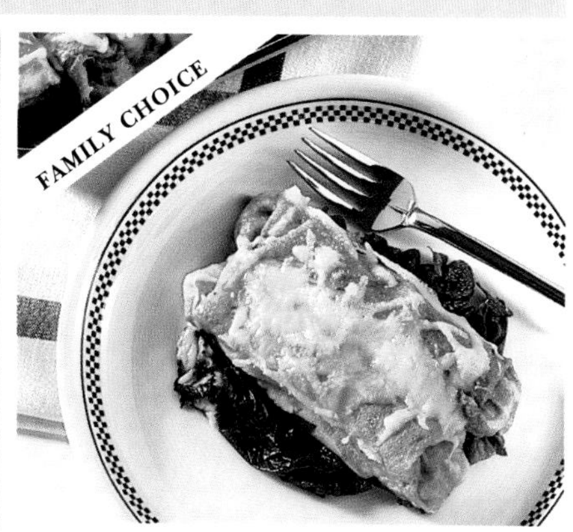

CHICKEN PANCAKES FLORENTINE

Pancakes filled with chicken, mushrooms, and thyme, served on a bed of spinach. Sprinkled with Gruyère cheese and baked.

SERVES 4 721 calories per serving
Takes 50 minutes, plus standing **PAGE 90**

SPINACH, LEEK, & GRUYERE TART

Nourishing and creamy: leek and spinach in a shortcrust pastry shell with a mixture of eggs, milk, cream, and Gruyère cheese.

SERVES 4–6 721–480 calories per serving
Takes 60 minutes, plus chilling **PAGE 84**

SMOKED SALMON & ASPARAGUS QUICHE

Salmon and asparagus set in a shortcrust pastry shell with a savoury custard of Greek yogurt, eggs, and dill.

SERVES 6–8 321–241 calories per serving
Takes 1 1/4 hours, plus chilling **PAGE 83**

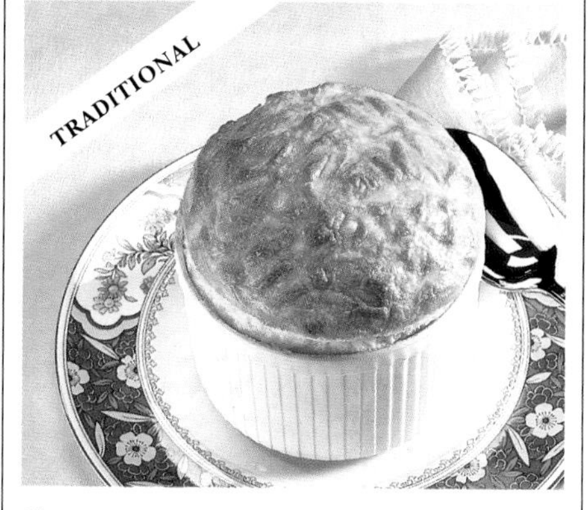

CLASSIC CHEESE SOUFFLE

Delicate and light: milk flavoured with bay leaf and a clove-studded onion, combined with butter, flour, eggs, and Cheddar cheese.

SERVES 4 640 calories per serving
Takes 1 1/4 hours **PAGE 91**

SWISS DOUBLE CHEESE SOUFFLES

Rich and very creamy: individual soufflés flavoured with Gruyère cheese and chives. Baked until golden and firm, then unmoulded and topped with double cream and Parmesan cheese. Baked again until golden, and garnished with snipped fresh chives.

SERVES 6 465 calories per serving
Takes 1 hour 5 minutes **PAGE 92**

ROQUEFORT QUICHE

Roquefort and low-fat soft cheese combined with eggs, crème fraîche, and chives, set in a shortcrust pastry shell, and baked.

SERVES 4–6 504–336 calories per serving
Takes 1 hour 5 minutes **PAGE 83**

EGGS & CHEESE KNOW-HOW

EGGS AND CHEESE, alone or used together, are found in countless dishes. Eggs enrich pastries and doughs, give volume and moistness to cakes and many puddings, thicken sauces and custards, bind mixtures ranging from burgers to pâtés, and provide a coating for foods to be fried. On their own, eggs can be cooked in many delicious ways, from simple boiling or poaching to frying in omelettes and baking in soufflés, to be enjoyed at any meal.

Cheese has countless culinary uses; it is good as a sandwich filling, or in snacks, sauces, fondues, and pizza toppings. Cheese flavours savoury pastries and doughs as well as quiche and flan fillings. It is essential in many pasta dishes. Soft fresh cheeses such as ricotta and curd are used to make cheesecake fillings. And, of course, a cheeseboard is a traditional part of a dinner party menu.

BUYING & STORING

When buying eggs, choose the freshest ones, and check that none are damaged or cracked. Store the eggs in a refrigerator (in their box or in a separate compartment so that they do not absorb flavours and odours of strong foods through their shells). They will keep in the refrigerator for up to 2 weeks – check the date stamp before using. If you place them pointed end down, the yolk will remain centred in the white.

When buying cheese, rely on appearance, and smell if possible. Hard and firm cheeses should be moist but not sweaty and should not have any mould unless they are blue-veined; soft ripened cheeses such as Brie and Camembert should feel springy and creamy throughout. Soft fresh cheese should be refrigerated, although other cheeses can be stored in a cool place such as a larder; keep them well wrapped or covered.

SEPARATING EGGS

For best results, make sure eggs are chilled before you start.

1 Holding an egg over a bowl, break open the shell and carefully transfer the yolk from one half shell to the other. Repeat several times, letting the egg white run into the bowl.

2 Put the yolk in another bowl. Remove any yolk from the white with the tip of a spoon (the white will not whisk if there is any trace of yolk).

COOKING WITH CHEESE

Cheese should be cooked with care. Hard and firm cheeses can withstand heat best, melting and blending smoothly. Parmesan, Gruyère, Emmental, and Cheddar are most commonly used in cooking. Other cheeses have their own particular applications; mozzarella, for example, is often used on top of pizzas.

MICROWAVING

Never microwave an egg that is still in its shell as it will burst. Even out of its shell, a whole egg may burst, so always pierce the membrane on the yolk before cooking. The yolk cooks more quickly than the white, so standing time should be allowed to let the white continue cooking. Where yolks and whites are combined, as for scrambled eggs, the mixture will appear undercooked but will firm up during standing time.

Cheeses melt quickly in the microwave oven, so care must be taken not to overcook or burn them. Hard or firm mature cheeses and processed cheeses are the best to use. Frozen soft ripened cheeses can be softened and brought to room temperature in the microwave oven before serving.

FREEZING

Shelled raw eggs freeze very successfully, and can be stored for up to 6 months. If whole, whisk gently to mix the yolk and white. Add a little salt to whole eggs and egg yolks for use in savoury foods and sugar for use in sweet dishes (nothing needs to be added to whites). Thaw at room temperature. Cooked egg in dishes such as quiches, custard, and mousses, can also be frozen.

Hard and firm cheeses freeze well, as do soft ripened cheeses such as Brie. Store them for 1 month. Thaw in the refrigerator before use. Note that the texture may change after freezing, making the cheeses suitable only for cooking. Soft fresh cheeses and blue-veined cheeses do not freeze well.

BAKING WITH EGGS

Eggs are used in a variety of dishes to set, thicken, aerate, or emulsify. For most preparations, eggs should be warmed to room temperature before using. This helps to maximize the volume if the eggs are whisked, and it will discourage the eggs from curdling, which can occur as a result of any abrupt temperature changes.

BOILING

Put the eggs into a pan of boiling salted water (if you use eggs at room temperature, the shells are less likely to crack). Bring back to a boil, then simmer gently. Cooking times are calculated from the time the water comes back to a boil, and can vary according to individual taste and on the freshness of the eggs. For soft-boiled eggs, simmer gently for $3^1/_2$–5 minutes. For hard-boiled eggs, allow 10–12 minutes, crack to allow steam to escape, then plunge the eggs into iced water and leave to cool. Peel and keep in a bowl of cold water or store, unpeeled, in the refrigerator.

Salmonella & listeria

There is a slight risk of salmonella poisoning from eggs. Listeria bacteria has been found in soft cheeses such as Brie and Camembert, in some blue-veined cheeses and in goat's and sheep's cheese. The Department of Health recommends that pregnant women and the immuno-compromised should avoid these cheeses and undercooked eggs, and that no one should eat raw eggs.

SCRAMBLING

Scrambled eggs can be served plain, or made with herbs, cheese, ham, or smoked salmon. Allow 2 eggs per person.

1 Lightly beat the eggs with salt and pepper to taste and a little milk, if you like. Melt a knob of butter in a pan. Add the eggs.

2 Cook over a medium heat, stirring constantly with a wooden spatula or spoon until almost set – they will continue to cook after they have been removed from the heat. Serve at once.

FRYING

Fresh eggs are essential for successful frying because they keep their shape during cooking. Fry fresh eggs in oil, dripping, or bacon fat, with a little butter added if you like.

1 Heat a thin layer of oil in a heavy frying pan. When the oil is very hot and starting to sizzle, slip in an egg and cook over a medium heat.

2 Spoon the oil over once or twice to give a white top. Remove and serve, or turn over and cook for a few seconds, to set the yolk a little more.

POACHING

The classic method for poaching eggs is in a pan of simmering water. Adding a small quantity of vinegar to the water prevents the egg white from breaking up.

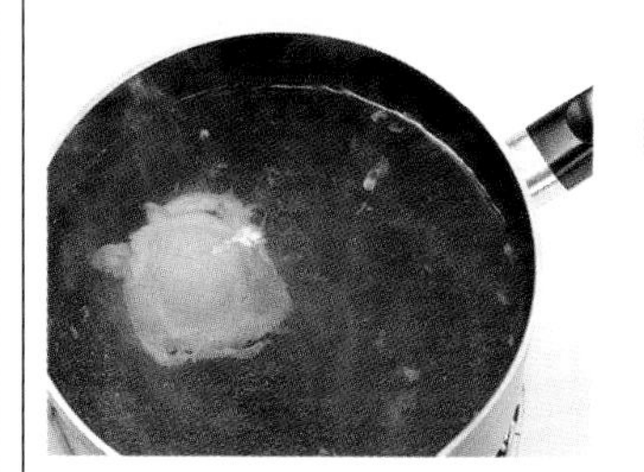

1 Add 2 tbsp vinegar to a pan of boiling water. Lower the heat so that the water is simmering, and slide in an egg. Swirl the water round the egg to make a neat shape. Simmer for about 4 minutes until yolk is set.

2 Lift out the egg with a slotted spoon and drain briefly on paper towels. To keep poached eggs warm, or to reheat them if they have been prepared ahead of time, immerse them in a bowl of warm water.

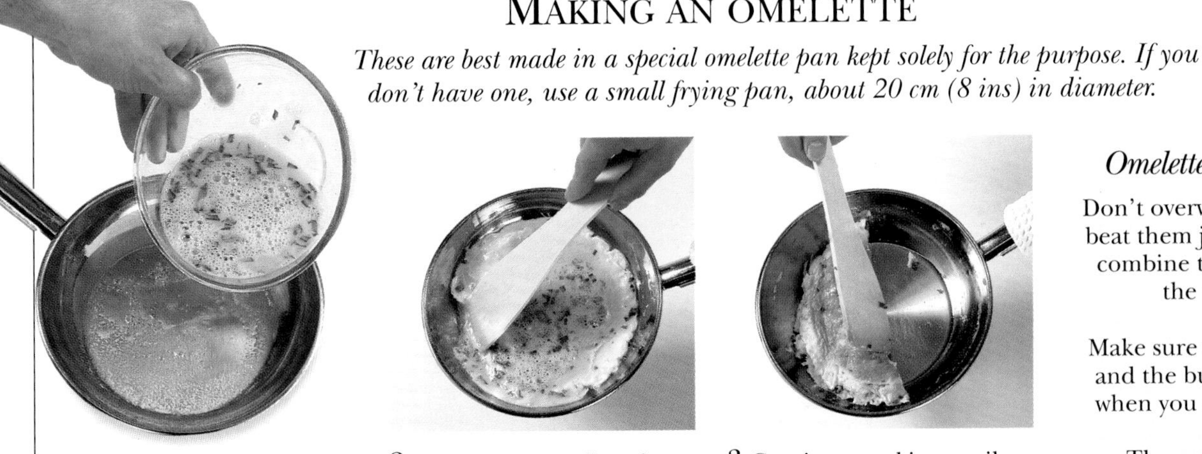

MAKING AN OMELETTE

These are best made in a special omelette pan kept solely for the purpose. If you don't have one, use a small frying pan, about 20 cm (8 ins) in diameter.

1 Beat *2–3 eggs* with *1 tbsp water, salt and pepper to taste* and *chopped herbs, if you like.* Heat the pan, then add *a knob of butter.* When butter is foaming, pour in the eggs.

2 Cook over a medium heat. As the eggs begin to set, lift and pull back the edge of the omelette, tilting the pan so the liquid egg can run to the side of the pan.

3 Continue cooking until the omelette is just set and the underside is golden brown. Loosen the edge and flip over one half, to fold it. Slide on to a plate and serve.

Omelette know-how

Don't overwhisk the eggs; beat them just enough to combine the yolks with the whites.

◆

Make sure the pan is hot and the butter foaming when you add the eggs.

◆

The omelette will continue to cook when you remove it from the heat, so the centre should still be a little moist.

MAKING PANCAKES

These are easy and fun to make. The quantities given here will make enough batter for about 12 pancakes, using an 18–20 cm (7–8 in) pan. If you don't need 12 pancakes, use up all the batter and just freeze the pancakes that are not used. Don't worry if the first pancake is a failure: it acts as a test for the consistency of the batter and the heat of the pan.

1 Sift *125 g (4 oz) plain flour* into a bowl and make a well in the centre. Whisk together *1 egg, 1 egg yolk,* and *a little milk* taken from *300 ml (1/2 pint),* pour into the well, and whisk.

2 Whisk in half of the remaining milk, drawing in the flour, a little at a time, to make a smooth batter. Stir in the remaining milk. Cover and leave to stand for 30 minutes.

3 Heat the frying pan and brush with *a little oil.* Ladle about 3 tbsp batter into the pan, tilting the pan so that the batter spreads out evenly over the base.

4 Cook the pancake over a medium-high heat for 45–60 seconds, until small holes appear in the surface, the underside is lightly browned, and the edge has started to curl. Loosen the pancake and turn it over to cook the other side by tossing or flipping it with a palette knife.

5 Cook the other side for about 30 seconds until golden. Slide the pancake out of the pan. Heat and lightly grease the pan again before making the next pancake. Serve the pancakes as they are made, or stack them on a plate, and reheat before serving.

MEXICAN OMELETTE

An omelette is one of the most useful of all egg dishes, quick and easy to make, and delicious either plain or with a filling. This recipe combines a classic French omelette with a piquant filling, but you can add whatever filling you like.

Makes 2

6 eggs
2 tbsp water
30 g (1 oz) butter
chopped parsley to garnish

FILLING
2 tbsp olive oil
1 onion, finely chopped
1 garlic clove, crushed
1 green pepper, cored, seeded, and finely chopped
2 ripe tomatoes, peeled (page 39), seeded, and finely chopped
125 g (4 oz) button mushrooms, thinly sliced
1/4 tsp Worcestershire sauce
few drops of Tabasco sauce
salt and black pepper

1 Make the filling: heat the oil in a frying pan, add the onion and garlic, and cook for 5 minutes or until softened. Add the pepper, and cook, stirring, for 5 minutes.

2 Add the tomatoes and mushrooms, and cook, stirring, for 10 minutes. Add the Worcestershire and Tabasco sauces, and salt and pepper to taste, and simmer for 5 minutes. Keep warm.

3 Beat 3 of the eggs with 1 tbsp of the measured water. Heat an omelette pan or small frying pan and add half of the butter.

4 When the butter is foaming, add the eggs, and cook over a medium heat, pulling back the edge as the eggs set, and tilting the pan to allow the uncooked egg to run to the side of the pan. Continue until lightly set and golden.

5 Spoon half of the filling on to the half of the omelette farthest from the pan handle. With a palette knife, lift the uncovered half of the omelette and flip it over the filling.

6 Slide the omelette on to a warmed plate, and garnish with chopped parsley. Make the second omelette in the same way, reheating the pan before adding the butter.

MUSHROOM OMELETTE

Substitute 175 g (6 oz) sliced button mushrooms for the filling. Cook in a little melted butter, and season with salt and pepper to taste. Proceed as directed.

SMOKED CHICKEN OMELETTE

Substitute 125 g (4 oz) diced smoked chicken and 1 tbsp snipped fresh chives for the filling. Proceed as directed in the recipe.

TOMATO OMELETTE

Substitute 5 peeled (page 39), seeded, and chopped tomatoes for the filling. Cook the tomatoes in a little butter for 2–3 minutes. Season well, and stir in a few snipped fresh chives. Proceed as directed.

SAVOURY SOUFFLE OMELETTE

Makes 2

4 eggs, separated
30 g (1 oz) butter

FILLING
2 tbsp olive oil
1/2 onion, thinly sliced
1 garlic clove, crushed
1 courgette, sliced
1 red pepper, cored, seeded, and sliced
1 x 200 g (7 oz) can chopped tomatoes
1 tbsp chopped fresh thyme
salt and black pepper

1 Make the filling: heat the oil in a frying pan, add the onion and garlic, and cook gently for 5 minutes or until softened. Add the courgette and red pepper, and cook for 2 minutes. Add the tomatoes, thyme, and salt and pepper to taste, and simmer for 20 minutes.

2 Whisk together the egg yolks and salt and pepper to taste. Whisk the egg whites until stiff, then fold into the yolks.

3 Melt half of the butter in an omelette pan. When it foams, add half of the egg mixture, and cook over a gentle heat for 3 minutes. Add half of the filling, fold the omelette in half, and serve. Repeat with the remaining eggs and filling.

MUSHROOM OMELETTE WITH CIABATTA

 **Serves 2**

4 eggs

salt and black pepper

2 tbsp water

30 g (1 oz) butter

60 g (2 oz) shiitake mushrooms, sliced

1 tsp chopped fresh thyme

1 loaf of ciabatta bread, warmed and split lengthwise

1 Break the eggs into a small bowl, add salt and black pepper to taste, and beat in the measured water with a fork.

2 Melt half of the butter in a small frying pan, add the mushrooms, and cook quickly, stirring, for 3–5 minutes until tender. Add the thyme, and salt and pepper to taste. Keep the mushrooms warm while you make the omelette.

3 Heat an omelette pan or small frying pan until very hot. Add the remaining butter and swirl the pan to evenly coat the base and side. When the butter is foaming, pour in the seasoned egg mixture.

4 Cook the omelette over a medium heat, pulling back the edge as the eggs set, and tilting the pan to allow the uncooked egg to run to the side of the pan. Continue until the omelette is lightly set and the underside is golden brown. Remove from the heat.

5 Put the mushrooms on the half of the omelette furthest from the pan handle, and flip the uncovered half over the filling. Fill the warmed split ciabatta with the omelette, cut the ciabatta in half crosswise, and serve at once.

SPINACH & MUSHROOM FRITTATA

Serves 2

3 tbsp olive oil

60 g (2 oz) thick-cut smoked bacon rashers, rinds removed, diced

250 g (8 oz) chestnut mushrooms, quartered

125 g (4 oz) spinach leaves, coarsely chopped

6 eggs

salt and black pepper

2 tbsp grated Parmesan cheese

1 Heat the oil in a large frying pan. Add the bacon and mushrooms and cook over a high heat, stirring, for 7 minutes or until the bacon is crisp. Add the spinach and turn in the oil for 1–2 minutes. Do not allow the spinach to wilt. Lower the heat.

2 Break the eggs into a bowl, add salt and pepper to taste, and beat with a fork.

3 Pour the eggs over the mushroom and spinach mixture and cook over a medium heat for about 10 minutes. As the eggs set, lift the frittata with a spatula and tilt the pan to allow the uncooked egg to run underneath.

4 When the eggs are set, sprinkle with grated Parmesan, and place the pan under a hot grill, 10 cm (4 ins) from the heat, for 1–2 minutes until the top is golden brown and firm when pressed. Serve at once, cut in half.

Frittata

This is an Italian omelette. Unlike the classic French omelette, it is first cooked in a pan until set, then it is put under a hot grill until firm. A frittata is always served flat rather than folded over.

Courgette frittata

 **Serves 4**

2 tbsp olive oil

625 g (1¼ lb) courgettes, thinly sliced

6 eggs

salt and black pepper

60 g (2 oz) prosciutto, diced

shredded fresh basil to garnish

1 Heat the olive oil in a large frying pan. Add the courgettes and cook gently for 5 minutes or until just tender.

2 Break the eggs into a bowl, add salt and pepper to taste, and beat with a fork.

3 Add the prosciutto to the courgettes in the frying pan, then pour over the eggs. Cook over a medium heat for about 10 minutes. As the eggs set, lift the frittata with a spatula and tilt the pan to allow the uncooked egg to run underneath. Continue until almost set and the underside is golden brown.

4 Place the frying pan under a hot grill, 10 cm (4 ins) from the heat, for 1–2 minutes until the top is a light golden brown colour and the egg is cooked through and quite firm when pressed.

5 Cut the courgette frittata into wedges, and lightly garnish with shredded fresh basil. Delicious served both hot or cold.

Sweetcorn & pepper frittata

Substitute 1 red pepper, cut into strips, 1 x 200 g (7 oz) can sweetcorn kernels, and 3 chopped spring onions for the courgettes and prosciutto. Cook the pepper strips for 3 minutes, add the sweetcorn and spring onions, and cook for 1 minute. Remove with a slotted spoon, and proceed as directed.

Spanish omelette

 **Serves 4**

3 tbsp olive oil

2 large potatoes, diced

2 large onions, chopped

6 eggs

salt and black pepper

1 tbsp chopped parsley

1 Heat the oil in a frying pan, add the potatoes and onions, and stir until coated with the oil. Cook gently for about 10 minutes until golden brown. Pour the excess oil from the pan.

2 Break the eggs into a bowl, season with salt and pepper to taste, and beat with a fork.

3 Pour the eggs into the pan, and mix with the vegetables. Cook for about 10 minutes until the eggs are almost set, then brown the top of the omelette under a hot grill for 1–2 minutes.

4 Slide the omelette on to a warmed plate, and cut into quarters. Sprinkle with chopped parsley and serve warm or cold.

Tortilla

Omelettes are a traditional part of the Spanish tapas – a selection of small, tasty dishes often served with sherry or other cocktails. This substantial omelette, known in Spain as "tortilla", can be served warm or cold, but not chilled.

Mixed bean omelette

Lightly cook 60 g (2 oz) French beans and 125 g (4 oz) shelled broad beans. Add to the pan after cooking the potatoes and onions, and stir to coat in the oil. Add the eggs, and proceed as directed.

QUICHE LORRAINE

A quiche is a flat, open tart filled with a savoury egg custard. This most famous of all quiches is named after the area it comes from – Alsace Lorraine in north-eastern France – where it was traditionally served on May Day, following a dish of roast suckling pig.

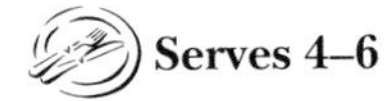 **Serves 4–6**

30 g (1 oz) butter
1 onion, chopped
175 g (6 oz) unsmoked streaky bacon rashers, rinds removed, diced
125 g (4 oz) Gruyère cheese, grated
250 ml (8 fl oz) single cream
2 eggs, beaten
salt and black pepper

SHORTCRUST PASTRY
125 g (4 oz) plain flour
60 g (2 oz) butter
about 1 tbsp cold water
⋆ *20 cm (8 in) flan dish or tin*
⋆ *baking beans*

1 Make the pastry with the flour, butter, and water (see box, right). Wrap in cling film and chill for 30 minutes.

2 Roll out the pastry on a lightly floured work surface, and use to line the flan dish or tin. Prick the bottom of the pastry shell with a fork.

3 Line the pastry shell with foil or greaseproof paper, and fill with baking beans. Place the flan dish on a heated baking tray and bake the shell in a preheated oven at 220°C (425°F, Gas 7) for 15–20 minutes, removing the foil and baking beans for the final 10 minutes.

4 Meanwhile, make the filling: melt the butter in a frying pan, add the onion and bacon, and cook gently, stirring occasionally, for 10 minutes or until the onion is golden brown and the bacon is crisp.

5 Spoon the onion and bacon mixture into the pastry shell, and sprinkle the cheese on top. Mix the cream and eggs in a jug, add salt and pepper to taste, and pour into the pastry shell.

6 Reduce the oven temperature to 180°C (350°F, Gas 4), and bake the quiche for 25–30 minutes until the filling is golden and set. Serve warm or cold.

Making shortcrust pastry

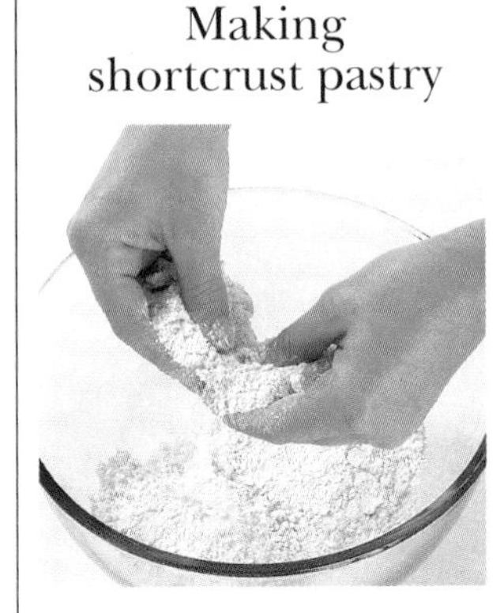

Sift the flour into a bowl. Add the butter and rub in lightly with your fingertips until the mixture looks like fine breadcrumbs.

Add the water and mix with a round-bladed knife to form a soft but not sticky dough.

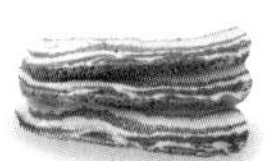

PANCETTA & SUN-DRIED TOMATO QUICHE

Make the shortcrust pastry shell and the filling as directed, using 125 g (4 oz) chopped pancetta instead of the bacon. Add 60 g (2 oz) drained and coarsely chopped sun-dried tomatoes in oil after cooking the pancetta and onion, and cook for 1 minute. Proceed as directed.

SMOKED SALMON & ASPARAGUS QUICHE

Serves 6–8

125 g (4 oz) fine asparagus, cooked, drained, and cut into 3.5 cm (1½ in) lengths

90 g (3 oz) smoked salmon, cut into strips

300 g (10 oz) Greek yogurt

2 eggs

1 tbsp chopped fresh dill

black pepper

SHORTCRUST PASTRY

175 g (6 oz) plain flour

90 g (3 oz) butter

about 2 tbsp cold water

⭑ 23 cm (9 in) flan dish or tin

⭑ baking beans

1 Make the pastry: put the flour in a bowl, add the butter, and rub in with the fingertips. Add enough water to bind to a soft dough. Wrap in cling film and chill for 30 minutes.

2 Roll out the pastry, and use to line the dish. Prick the pastry with a fork.

3 Line the pastry shell with foil or greaseproof paper, and fill with baking beans. Place the flan dish on a heated baking tray and bake in a preheated oven at 220°C (425°F, Gas 7) for 15–20 minutes, removing the foil and baking beans for the final 10 minutes.

4 Arrange the asparagus and half of the salmon in the pastry shell. Mix the yogurt, eggs, dill, and plenty of pepper, and pour into the shell. Arrange the remaining salmon on top.

5 Reduce the oven temperature to 180°C (350°F, Gas 4), and bake for 35 minutes or until golden and set. Serve warm or cold.

ROQUEFORT QUICHE

Serves 4–6

90 g (3 oz) Roquefort or other blue cheese, crumbled

175 g (6 oz) low-fat soft cheese

2 eggs, beaten

150 ml (¼ pint) crème fraîche

1 tbsp snipped fresh chives

salt and black pepper

SHORTCRUST PASTRY

125 g (4 oz) plain flour

60 g (2 oz) butter

about 1 tbsp cold water

⭑ 20 cm (8 in) flan dish or tin

⭑ baking beans

1 Make the pastry: put the flour in a bowl, add the butter, and rub in with the fingertips. Add enough water to bind to a soft dough. Wrap in cling film and chill for 30 minutes.

2 Roll out the shortcrust pastry, and use to line the flan dish. Prick the bottom of the pastry shell with a fork.

3 Line the pastry shell with foil or greaseproof paper, and fill with baking beans. Place the flan dish on a heated baking tray, and bake in a preheated oven at 220°C (425°F, Gas 7) for 15–20 minutes, removing the foil and baking beans for the final 10 minutes.

4 Meanwhile, make the filling: mix the Roquefort and low-fat cheese in a bowl, then beat in the eggs, crème fraîche, chives, and salt and pepper to taste. Take care not to add too much salt as blue cheese is already quite salty.

5 Pour the mixture into the pastry shell, reduce the oven temperature to 180°C (350°F, Gas 4), and bake the quiche for about 30 minutes until golden and set. Serve warm or cold.

SPINACH, LEEK, & GRUYERE TART

Serves 4–6

30 g (1 oz) butter
175 g (6 oz) leeks, trimmed and finely sliced
250 g (8 oz) spinach leaves, coarsely chopped
2 eggs, beaten
150 ml (1/4 pint) milk
150 ml (1/4 pint) double cream
90 g (3 oz) Gruyère cheese, grated
salt and black pepper

SHORTCRUST PASTRY

175 g (6 oz) plain flour
90 g (3 oz) butter
about 2 tbsp cold water
⋆ 23 cm (9 in) flan dish or tin
⋆ baking beans

1 Make the pastry: put the flour in a bowl, add the butter, and rub in with the fingertips. Add enough water to bind to a soft dough. Wrap in cling film and chill for 30 minutes.

2 Roll out the pastry on a lightly floured work surface, and use to line the flan dish. Prick the bottom of the pastry shell with a fork.

3 Line the pastry shell with foil or greaseproof paper, and fill with baking beans. Put the flan dish on a heated baking tray, and bake the shell in a preheated oven at 220°C (425°F, Gas 7) for 15–20 minutes, removing the foil and baking beans for the final 10 minutes.

4 Make the filling: melt the butter in a frying pan, add the leeks, and cook over a high heat for 5 minutes or until just beginning to turn golden brown. Add the spinach and cook for about 2 minutes until it just begins to wilt. Arrange the filling in the pastry shell.

5 Mix together the eggs, milk, cream, and Gruyère cheese in a jug, add salt and pepper to taste, and pour into the pastry shell.

6 Reduce the oven temperature to 180°C (350°F, Gas 4), and bake for 25 minutes or until the filling is golden and set. Serve warm or cold.

MEDITERRANEAN COURGETTE PIE

Serves 4

500 g (1 lb) courgettes
90 g (3 oz) Parmesan cheese, grated
90 g (3 oz) mozzarella or Fontina cheese, grated
2 eggs, lightly beaten
2–3 tbsp ready-made pesto
2–3 garlic cloves, crushed
1 tsp dried mint
salt and black pepper
250 g (8 oz) puff pastry
beaten egg for glazing
⋆ 23 cm (9 in) square baking dish or tin

1 Grate the courgettes (see box, right). Put them into a colander to drain for about 10 minutes. (If they seem bitter or very wet, toss them with a little salt, and leave for a further 10 minutes, then rinse with cold water.) Squeeze dry, then blot with paper towels.

2 In a large bowl, combine the courgettes with the Parmesan and mozzarella cheeses, eggs, pesto, garlic, mint, and salt and pepper to taste. Spoon the mixture into the baking dish.

Grating courgettes

Grate courgettes on to a plate, using the coarse grid of a grater, and making firm, downward strokes.

3 Roll out the pastry into a rough square, about 2.5 cm (1 in) larger than the dish and 3–5 mm (1/8–1/4 in) thick. Cover the dish with the pastry, trimming the edges. Cut slits in the top with a knife.

4 Using a pastry cutter, cut out shapes from the trimmings. Brush the top of the pie with beaten egg, arrange the pastry shapes on top, and glaze them with the beaten egg.

5 Bake the pie in a preheated oven at 200°C (400°F, Gas 6) for 15–20 minutes until lightly browned on top and puffy. Serve at once.

ITALIAN CHEESE & RED PESTO TARTLETS

These tartlets, with their tangy Italian flavours, will serve 4 people as a light lunch or supper dish, accompanied by a crisp, green salad. They also make a tasty appetizer to serve with pre-dinner drinks. They taste just as good cold as hot, so they can be prepared well in advance.

Makes 12

90 g (3 oz) ready-made red pesto or sun-dried tomato purée

250 g (8 oz) tomatoes, peeled (page 39), seeded, and chopped

9 black olives, pitted and quartered

125 g (4 oz) Fontina or mozzarella cheese, grated

2–3 garlic cloves, crushed

2–3 tbsp grated Parmesan cheese

1 tsp dried oregano

SHORTCRUST PASTRY

175 g (6 oz) plain flour

90 g (3 oz) butter

about 2 tbsp cold water

1 Make the pastry: put the flour in a bowl, add the butter, and rub in with the fingertips. Add enough water to bind to a soft dough. Wrap in cling film and chill for 30 minutes.

2 Make the tartlet shells (see box, right).

3 Spread the red pesto in the tartlet shells, then fill the shells with the tomatoes, garlic, black olives, and Fontina cheese.

4 Sprinkle the grated Parmesan cheese over the tartlets, covering the pastry edges as well as the filling. Sprinkle the dried oregano on top.

5 Bake the tartlets in a preheated oven at 200°C (400°F, Gas 6) for 20–30 minutes until the edges are a golden brown colour and the cheese topping has melted and become crispy.

6 Serve the tartlets warm or cold.

GOAT'S CHEESE TARTLETS

Substitute 90 g (3 oz) ready-made green pesto for the red pesto, and 12 slices from a log of goat's cheese for the grated Fontina. Proceed as directed.

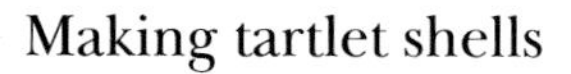

Making tartlet shells

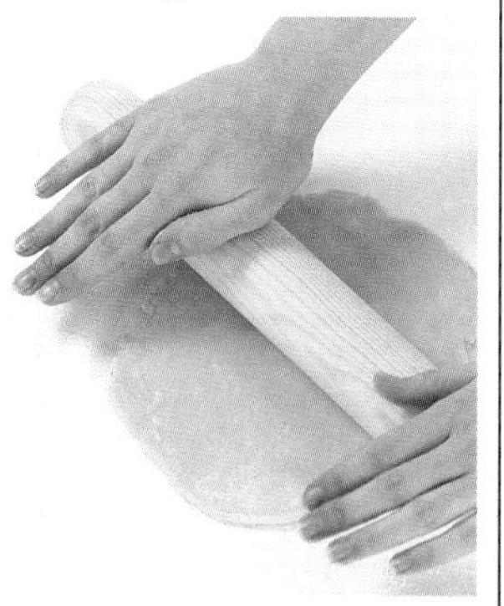

Sprinkle a work surface with flour, then roll out the shortcrust pastry to a 3–5 mm (1/8–1/4 in) thickness.

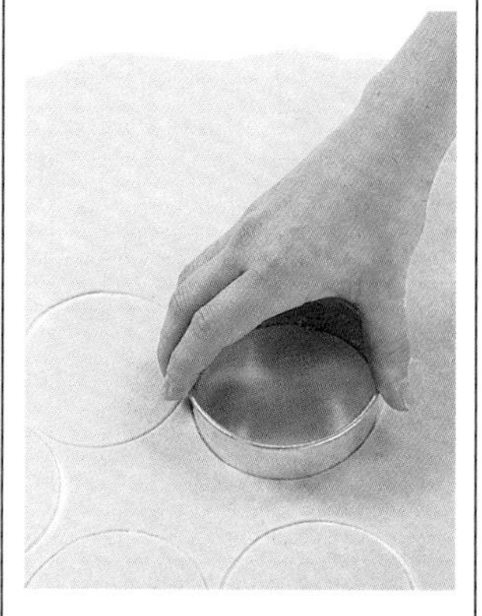

Cut out 12 rounds from the pastry, using a 10 cm (4 in) pastry cutter.

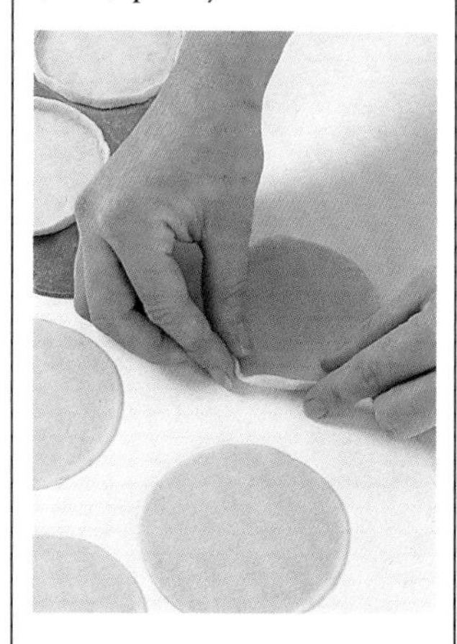

Fold up the edges of the rounds to form rims; put on a baking tray.

STRATA WITH CHEESE & PESTO

 **Serves 4**

4–6 thick slices of stale bread

60–90 g (2–3 oz) ready-made green pesto

4 eggs, lightly beaten

125 ml (4 fl oz) crème fraîche

125 ml (4 fl oz) milk

375 g (12 oz) Fontina, mozzarella, or mature Cheddar cheese, grated

3 tbsp grated Parmesan cheese

1 Cut off and discard the crusts from the bread. Spread the slices with pesto, then arrange them in a single layer in a baking dish or roasting tin.

2 In a bowl, combine the eggs with the crème fraîche and milk, then pour over the bread. Sprinkle with the cheeses.

3 Bake the strata in a preheated oven at 200°C (400°F, Gas 6) for 35–40 minutes until golden brown. It will puff up slightly as it bakes but, unlike a soufflé, it can be safely left to stand for about 5 minutes before serving.

Cook's know-how

This is an excellent way of using up stale bread. In fact for this recipe, the staler the bread the better, although if it is very hard you will have to make the savoury custard more liquid. If you do not have any leftover bread, dry slices of fresh bread in a low oven for 15 minutes or so.

BROCCOLI & RICOTTA TART

 **Serves 4–6**

250 g (8 oz) broccoli

salt and black pepper

375 g (12 oz) ricotta or cottage cheese, lightly mashed

125 g (4 oz) mature Cheddar cheese, grated

60 g (2 oz) Parmesan cheese, grated

2 eggs, lightly beaten

2–3 garlic cloves, crushed

1 tsp chopped fresh thyme

75 g (2½ oz) butter

175 g (6 oz) fresh breadcrumbs

** 23 cm (9 in) flan dish*

1 Trim the broccoli and cut the stalks from the heads. Peel and dice the stalks, and break the heads into small florets. Plunge the florets and stalks into a pan of boiling salted water for 1 minute. Drain, rinse under cold water, and drain again.

2 Put the ricotta cheese into a large bowl with the Cheddar and Parmesan, the eggs, garlic, thyme, and salt and pepper to taste. Mix until smooth, then add the broccoli stalks.

3 Melt the butter in a saucepan, remove it from the heat, and stir in the breadcrumbs.

4 Line the baking dish with about three-quarters of the buttered breadcrumbs, pushing them up the side of the dish to form a loose crust. Spoon in the cheese mixture, and then sprinkle with the remaining breadcrumbs. Arrange the broccoli florets on top.

5 Bake in a preheated oven at 180°C (350°F, Gas 4) for about 40 minutes until the tart is quite firm. Serve warm or cold.

SPINACH & RICOTTA TART

Substitute 250 g (8 oz) chopped cooked spinach for the broccoli, or use a mixture of chopped cooked spinach and sautéed diced red pepper.

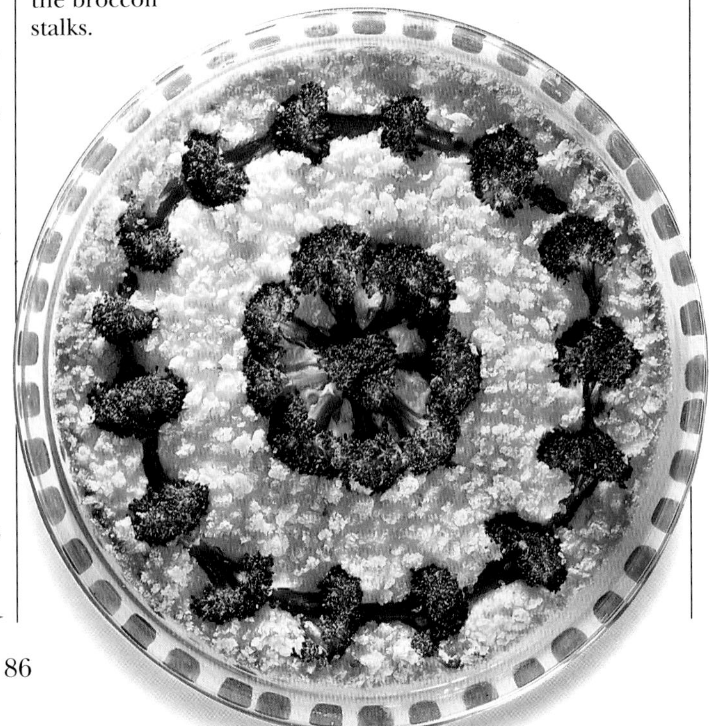

CREAMY SEAFOOD PANCAKES

A succulent filling of prawns and white fish in a herby cream sauce makes these pancakes an excellent light lunch dish or dinner party first course. The unfilled pancakes can be made in advance and stored in the freezer for up to 1 month: leave them to cool after frying, layer them with greaseproof paper, and wrap in foil.

Serves 6

FILLING

- *250 g (8 oz) cod fillet, skinned*
- *375 g (12 oz) cooked prawns in their shells*
- *2 tbsp olive oil*
- *1 small onion, finely chopped*
- *1 garlic clove, crushed*
- *4 tomatoes, peeled (page 39), seeded, and finely chopped*
- *1 tbsp dill seeds, crushed*
- *salt and black pepper*
- *3 tbsp single cream*
- *2 tbsp chopped fresh basil*
- *basil sprigs and lemon coronets to garnish*

PANCAKES

- *125 g (4 oz) plain flour*
- *1 egg, plus 1 egg yolk*
- *300 ml (1/2 pint) milk*
- *sunflower oil for frying*

1 Make the pancake batter: sift the flour into a large bowl, and make a well in the middle. Add the egg, extra egg yolk, and a little of the milk.

2 Gradually blend in the flour, beating until smooth. Add the remaining milk to give the batter the consistency of thin cream. Leave to stand for about 30 minutes.

3 Meanwhile, make the filling: cut the cod into 1 cm (1/2 in) pieces. Reserve 12 of the prawns for garnish, and peel the remainder.

4 Heat the oil in a medium saucepan, add the onion and garlic, and cook gently, stirring occasionally, for a few minutes until soft but not coloured.

5 Add the cod, tomatoes, dill seeds, and salt and pepper to taste. Cook over a medium heat, stirring, for 10 minutes or until the mixture is thick and rich.

6 Stir in the cream and prawns and heat gently. Remove from the heat and stir in the basil. Keep warm.

7 Heat a small frying pan, and brush with a little oil. Ladle about 3 tbsp batter into the pan and cook for 1 minute until the underside is golden. Turn and cook the second side. Keep warm. Repeat to make 12 pancakes.

8 Fill the pancakes with the seafood mixture, and fold (see box, right). Garnish with the reserved prawns, basil sprigs, and lemon coronets.

Filling and folding the pancakes

Put a pancake on a board or clean serving plate. Put 2–3 spoonfuls of the seafood filling on to one half of the pancake and spread it to within 5 mm (1/4 in) of the edge.

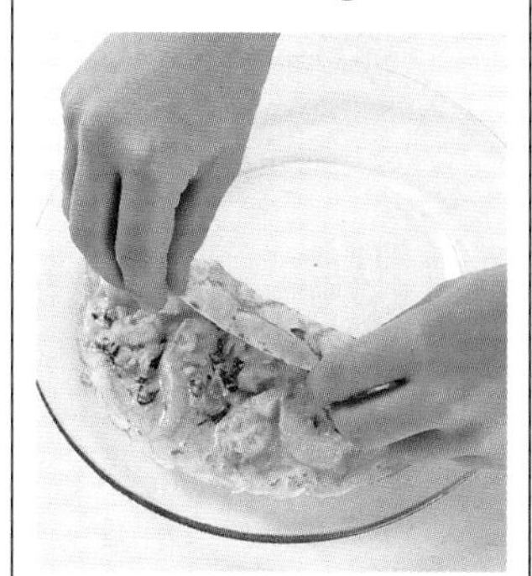

Fold the unfilled half of the pancake over the seafood filling to enclose it.

Fold the pancake in half again, to form a triangle. Transfer to a serving plate and keep warm. Repeat with the remaining pancakes and filling.

BUFFET PANCAKES

With no more than a basic pancake recipe, some simple fillings, and a little dexterity, you can create a stunning buffet display, whether you decide to make only one of these recipes or choose two or three. Each recipe makes enough for 6–8 guests when served as an appetizer with other small dishes.

BASIC PANCAKES

Makes 16

250 g (8 oz) plain flour
3 eggs, lightly beaten
250 ml (8 fl oz) milk
250 ml (8 fl oz) water
75 ml (2 1/2 fl oz) sunflower oil, plus extra for frying
** 20–23 cm (8–9 in) crêpe pan or small frying pan*

1 Sift the flour into a bowl and make a well in the middle. Add the eggs and a little of the milk and gradually blend in the flour. Whisk together the remaining milk, the measured water, and oil and stir in to the flour mixture. Leave to stand for 30 minutes.

2 Heat the crêpe pan. Brush with a little oil and add 2–3 tbsp batter, tilting the pan to coat with batter. Cook for 1 minute, turn, and cook the second side until golden.

CHICKEN & DILL PARCELS

175 g (6 oz) cooked chicken, finely diced
3 tbsp frozen petits pois, thawed
2 tbsp mayonnaise
1 tbsp chopped fresh dill
1 tsp Dijon mustard
3 spring onions, thinly sliced
salt and black pepper
4 pancakes (see above), cooled

1 Combine the chicken, petits pois, mayonnaise, chopped fresh dill, mustard, spring onions, and salt and pepper to taste.

2 Cut each pancake into quarters. Place a little of the chicken mixture in the middle of each quarter. Fold 1 long edge of each quarter towards the middle and overlap with the other long edge to enclose the filling.

BLUE CHEESE CORNUCOPIA

4 pancakes (see left), cooled
125 g (4 oz) blue cheese
60 g (2 oz) butter
fresh basil and walnut halves to garnish

1 Cut each pancake into eight. Blend together the blue cheese and butter. Place a little blue cheese mixture in the middle of each piece of pancake.

2 Fold the point up over the filling, then fold over the 2 sides. Tuck in a basil leaf and top with a walnut half.

MULTI-COLOURED PINWHEELS

125 g (4 oz) frozen sweetcorn kernels, thawed
125 g (4 oz) garlic and herb cream cheese
90 g (3 oz) mature Cheddar cheese, grated
1 spring onion, chopped
1 garlic clove, crushed
1/4 tsp ground cumin
dash of Tabasco sauce
pinch of salt
4 pancakes (see left), cooled
3–4 tbsp fresh coriander leaves
1 tomato, finely diced

1 Mix the sweetcorn with 1–2 tbsp of the cream cheese, to bind together. Mix in the Cheddar cheese, spring onion, garlic, cumin, Tabasco, and salt, and stir to combine.

2 Spread a little cream cheese over each pancake. Arrange a quarter of the sweetcorn mixture in a strip across the middle of the pancake. To one side of this, arrange a strip of coriander, then a strip of diced tomato, leaving a little space between each strip.

3 Beginning at the side with the tomato, tightly roll each pancake. Chill, then slice crosswise into rounds.

MUSHROOM TRIANGLES

6–8 mushrooms, finely chopped
125 g (4 oz) mature Cheddar cheese, grated
2 tsp chopped fresh tarragon
salt and black pepper
4 pancakes (see left), cooled

1 Mix together the mushrooms, cheese, tarragon, and salt and pepper to taste. Cut each pancake into quarters. Place a little of the filling in the middle of each quarter. Fold 1 long edge over the other and enclose the filling to form a triangle.

2 Heat a non-stick frying pan, add the triangles, and cook on both sides.

BASIL PANCAKES WITH GOAT'S CHEESE

175 g (6 oz) plain flour
3 eggs lightly beaten
125 ml (4 fl oz) milk
125 ml (4 fl oz) water
3 tbsp olive oil, plus extra for frying
30 g (1 oz) fresh basil, finely chopped
150 g (5 oz) goat's cheese, cut into 20 wedges
1 tbsp chopped parsley
1 tsp paprika

1 Make a pancake batter (see left) with the flour, eggs, milk, measured water, oil, and basil.

2 Heat a frying pan and brush with oil. Add 1 tbsp batter, to form a pancake about 7 cm (3 ins) in diameter. Cook over a gentle heat for 2 minutes on each side. Repeat with the remaining batter to make 20 pancakes.

3 Top each pancake with a wedge of goat's cheese, and sprinkle with parsley and paprika.

Clockwise from top; *Blue Cheese Cornucopia, Chicken & Dill Parcels, Mushroom Triangles, Multi-coloured Pinwheels, Basil Pancakes with Goat's Cheese.*

SOUFFLE PANCAKES WITH BROCCOLI & CHEESE

 **Makes 8**

8 pancakes (page 78)
butter for greasing
2 tbsp grated Parmesan cheese

FILLING

125 g (4 oz) tiny broccoli florets
salt and black pepper
45 g (1½ oz) butter
45 g (1½ oz) plain flour
300 ml (½ pint) milk
½ tsp Dijon mustard
125 g (4 oz) mature Cheddar cheese, grated
4 eggs, separated

1 Make the filling: blanch the broccoli florets in boiling salted water for about 1 minute. Drain, rinse under cold running water, and drain again.

2 Melt the butter in a small saucepan, add the flour, and cook, stirring occasionally, for about 1 minute.

3 Remove the pan from the heat, and gradually blend in the milk. Bring to a boil, stirring until thickened. Remove from the heat, and add the mustard, cheese, and salt and pepper to taste. Leave to cool slightly.

4 Beat the egg yolks into the sauce. In a large bowl, whisk the egg whites until soft peaks form, then fold into the cheese sauce with the broccoli florets.

5 Put the pancakes on 2 lightly buttered baking trays. Divide the soufflé mixture among the pancakes, arranging it down the middle of each one. Fold the sides of each pancake loosely over the top of the filling, and sprinkle with grated Parmesan cheese.

6 Bake in a preheated oven at 200°C (400°F, Gas 6) for 15–20 minutes, until the soufflé mixture has risen and the pancakes are crisp.

CHICKEN PANCAKES FLORENTINE

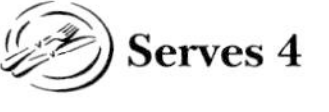 **Serves 4**

500 g (1 lb) spinach leaves, coarsely chopped
30 g (1 oz) butter
pinch of grated nutmeg
8 pancakes (page 78)
125 g (4 oz) Gruyère cheese, grated

FILLING

60 g (2 oz) butter
375 g (12 oz) chestnut mushrooms, quartered
45 g (1½ oz) plain flour
300 ml (½ pint) chicken stock
375 g (12 oz) cooked chicken, cut into bite-sized pieces
1 tbsp chopped fresh thyme
salt and black pepper

1 Make the filling: melt the butter in a heavy pan, add the mushrooms, and cook, stirring occasionally, for 2–3 minutes.

2 Add the flour, and cook, stirring, for 1 minute. Remove the pan from the heat, and gradually blend in the stock. Bring to a boil, stirring, and simmer for 2–3 minutes. Add the chicken, thyme, and salt and pepper to taste.

3 Rinse the spinach and put into a saucepan with only the water that clings to the leaves. Cook for about 2 minutes until tender. Drain well, squeezing to extract any excess water, then stir in the butter and nutmeg. Spoon into a shallow ovenproof dish.

4 Divide the chicken and mushroom mixture between the 8 pancakes. Roll up the pancakes, and place them in a single layer on top of the spinach.

5 Sprinkle with the cheese, and bake in a preheated oven at 190°C (375°F, Gas 5) for about 25 minutes until golden. Serve hot.

Cook's know-how

Ready-made pancakes or crêpes, available in packets at supermarkets and delicatessens, are a convenient alternative to home-made pancakes. They work particularly well in recipes such as this one, in which they are rolled around a filling and baked in the oven.

CLASSIC CHEESE SOUFFLE

Serves 4

250 ml (8 fl oz) milk
1 bay leaf
1/2 onion, studded with several cloves
salt and black pepper
30 g (1 oz) butter, plus extra for greasing
2 tbsp plain flour
6 eggs, separated
2 tbsp Dijon mustard
375 g (12 oz) mature Cheddar cheese, grated
⋆ *1.4 litre (2 1/4 pint) soufflé dish*

1 Pour the milk into a small saucepan, add the bay leaf and clove-studded onion half, and bring to a boil. Remove from the heat, cover, and leave to infuse for 20 minutes. Strain the milk, and season to taste.

2 Melt the butter in a large pan, add the flour, and cook, stirring, for 1 minute. Remove the pan from the heat, gradually blend in the infused milk, then bring to a boil, stirring until thickened. Simmer for 2–3 minutes. Leave to cool for 10 minutes.

3 Beat the egg yolks in a bowl. Stir them into the cooled white sauce, then stir in the mustard and all but 30 g (1 oz) of the Cheddar.

4 Whisk the egg whites until they form firm but not dry peaks. Fold 1–2 tbsp of the egg whites into the cheese mixture until evenly combined, then fold in the remaining egg whites.

5 Lightly butter the soufflé dish and then pour in the egg and cheese mixture. Sprinkle with the remaining cheese and bake in the top half of a preheated oven at 180°C (350°F, Gas 4) for 30 minutes. Serve the soufflé at once.

CORN & CUMIN SOUFFLE

Substitute 375 g (12 oz) coarsely puréed cooked sweetcorn kernels or drained and puréed canned sweetcorn kernels, for the Cheddar cheese, and add 2 tsp cumin seeds.

BROCCOLI SOUFFLES

Serves 4

45 g (1 1/2 oz) butter, plus extra for greasing
3 tbsp plain flour
250 ml (8 fl oz) milk
pinch of grated nutmeg
salt and cayenne pepper
375 g (12 oz) broccoli florets
3–4 shallots, finely chopped
2 tbsp grated Parmesan cheese
4 egg yolks
175 g (6 oz) blue cheese, crumbled
6 egg whites
⋆ *4 x 250 ml (8 fl oz) soufflé dishes*

1 Melt 30 g (1 oz) butter in a large pan, add the flour, and cook, stirring, for 1 minute. Remove from the heat, gradually blend in the milk, then bring to a boil, stirring, until thickened. Add the nutmeg, and salt and cayenne pepper to taste. Leave to cool for 10 minutes.

2 Steam the broccoli for 2–3 minutes until just tender. Rinse in cold water, then chop coarsely.

3 Heat the remaining butter in a pan, add the shallots, and cook gently for 3 minutes or until soft.

4 Prepare the soufflé dishes (see box, below).

5 Beat the egg yolks and add to the cooled sauce with the broccoli, shallots, and blue cheese.

6 Whisk the egg whites until they form firm but not dry peaks. Fold 1–2 tbsp of the egg whites into the broccoli mixture, then fold in the remaining egg whites.

7 Pour the mixture into the soufflé dishes. Bake the soufflés in the top half of a preheated oven at 180°C (350°F, Gas 4) for 30 minutes. Serve at once.

Preparing the soufflé dishes

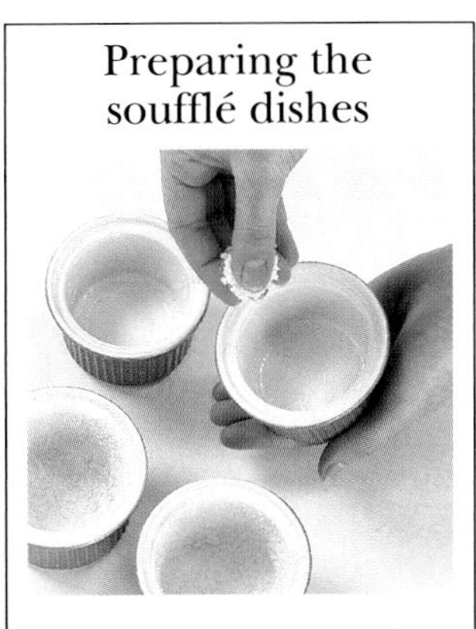

Butter the bottoms and sides of the soufflé dishes. Sprinkle with a thin layer of grated Parmesan cheese.

GARLIC & GOAT'S CHEESE SOUFFLES

Serves 6

1 head of garlic

250 ml (8 fl oz) milk

125 ml (4 fl oz) water

30 g (1 oz) butter, plus extra for greasing

2 tbsp plain flour

150 g (5 oz) goat's cheese, diced

6 eggs, separated

salt and black pepper to taste

fresh chives to garnish

⋆ *6 x 150 ml (1/4 pint) soufflé dishes*

1 Separate and peel the garlic cloves. Put the milk, measured water, and all but one of the garlic cloves into a saucepan. Bring to a boil, then simmer for 15–20 minutes until the garlic is tender and the liquid has reduced to 250 ml (8 fl oz). Leave to cool. Lightly mash the garlic in the milk.

2 Melt the butter in a saucepan, add the flour, and cook, stirring, for 1 minute. Remove from the heat, and gradually blend in the garlic milk.

3 Return to the heat and bring to a boil, stirring constantly, until the mixture thickens. Simmer for 2–3 minutes. Transfer to a large bowl and leave to cool for 10 minutes. Chop the remaining garlic clove.

4 Add the chopped garlic, diced goat's cheese, egg yolks, and salt and pepper to taste to the cooled sauce.

5 In a large bowl, whisk the egg whites until stiff but not dry. Stir 1 tbsp of the egg whites into the garlic and cheese mixture, then fold in the remaining egg whites.

6 Lightly butter the soufflé dishes, pour in the soufflé mixture, and bake in a preheated oven at 180°C (350°F, Gas 4) for 15–20 minutes. Serve at once, garnished with chives.

SWISS DOUBLE CHEESE SOUFFLES

Serves 6

45 g (1 1/2 oz) butter, plus extra for greasing

30 g (1 oz) plain flour

300 ml (1/2 pint) milk

60 g (2 oz) Gruyère cheese, grated

2 tbsp snipped fresh chives

salt and black pepper

3 eggs, separated

60 g (2 oz) Parmesan cheese, grated

300 ml (1/2 pint) double cream

snipped fresh chives to garnish

1 Melt the butter in a large saucepan, add the flour, and cook, stirring, for 1 minute. Remove from the heat and gradually blend in the milk. Return to the heat and bring to a boil, stirring until the mixture thickens.

2 Remove the pan from the heat and beat in the Gruyère cheese and chives. Add salt and pepper to taste, and stir in the egg yolks.

3 Whisk the egg whites until stiff but not dry. Stir 1 tbsp into the mixture, then fold in the rest.

4 Generously butter 6 small ramekins, and divide the mixture equally among them. Place the ramekins in a small roasting tin, and pour boiling water into the tin to come halfway up the sides of the ramekins.

5 Bake the soufflés in a preheated oven at 220°C (425°F, Gas 7) for 15–20 minutes until golden and springy to the touch. Leave the soufflés to stand for 5–10 minutes; they will shrink by about one-third.

6 Butter a large shallow gratin dish. Sprinkle half of the Parmesan cheese over the bottom. Run a palette knife around the edge of each soufflé, unmould carefully, and arrange on top of the Parmesan in the gratin dish.

7 Season the cream with salt and pepper, and pour over the soufflés. Sprinkle the remaining Parmesan over the top, and return to the oven for 15–20 minutes until golden. Garnish with snipped chives.

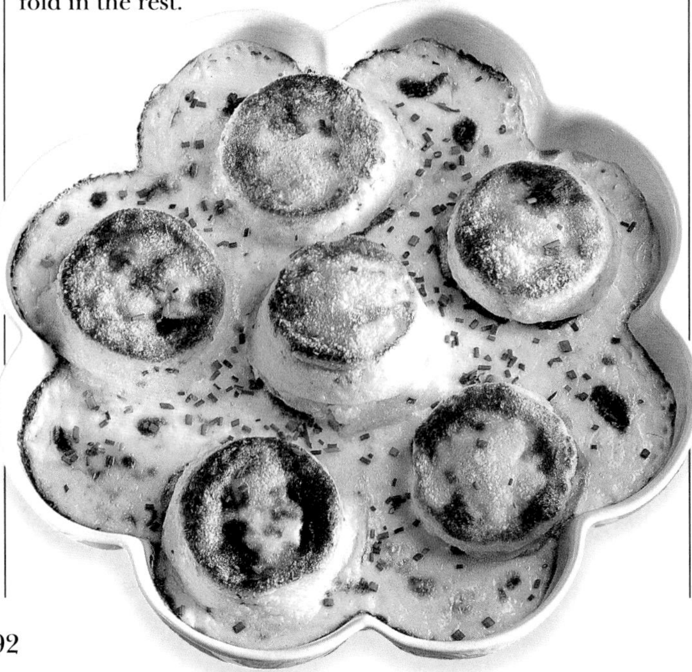

RACLETTE

Serves 4

1 kg (2 lb) new potatoes, halved

salt

250 g (8 oz) Swiss raclette cheese, cut into 16 thin slices

1 red onion, thinly sliced

12 small gherkins

12 cocktail pickled onions

1 Cook the potatoes in boiling salted water for 12–15 minutes until just tender. Drain, and keep the potatoes warm.

2 Put 4 heavy, ovenproof serving plates into a preheated oven at 240°C (475°F, Gas 9) to warm for 3–5 minutes.

3 Divide the potatoes among the plates, and arrange 4 slices of raclette cheese on top of each serving. Return the plates to the oven for 1–2 minutes until the cheese is melted and sizzling.

4 Divide the red onion slices, gherkins, and pickled onions among the plates, and serve at once.

Raclette

This is a Swiss speciality where raclette cheese is melted over potatoes and served with gherkins and onions. The name means "scraper", as raclette was traditionally eaten by holding half a cheese in front of an open fire and scraping off the cheese as it melted. Gruyère or Emmental can be used instead of raclette.

CHEESE FONDUE

Serves 4–6

1 large loaf of crusty bread, crusts left on, cut into 2.5 cm (1 in) triangles

250 g (8 oz) Gruyère cheese, coarsely grated

250 g (8 oz) Emmental cheese, coarsely grated

30 g (1 oz) plain flour

500 ml (16 fl oz) dry white wine

1 garlic clove, lightly crushed

2 tbsp kirsch

pinch of grated nutmeg

salt and black pepper

2 tart apples, quartered and sliced

60 g (2 oz) sesame seeds, lightly toasted

30 g (1 oz) cumin seeds, lightly toasted

⋆ *1 fondue set*

1 Place the pieces of bread on a large baking tray and put into a preheated oven at 160°C (325°F, Gas 3) for 3–5 minutes until dried out slightly.

2 Put the Gruyère and Emmental cheeses into a medium bowl, and toss with the flour.

3 Put the wine and garlic into a fondue pot and boil for 2 minutes, then lower the heat so that the mixture is barely simmering. Add the cheese mixture, a spoonful at a time, stirring constantly with a fork and letting each spoonful melt before adding the next.

4 When the fondue is creamy and smooth, stir in the kirsch, nutmeg, and salt and pepper to taste.

5 To serve, put the fondue pot on to a small burner, and set the heat on low so that the mixture barely simmers. Arrange the bread, apple slices, and sesame and cumin seeds in dishes for your guests to dip into as desired.

CROQUE SENOR

Serves 4

8 slices of white bread

4 slices of mature Cheddar cheese

4 slices of ham

30 g (1 oz) butter, softened

lemon wedges and coriander sprigs to serve

SPICY TOMATO SALSA

3 tomatoes, peeled (page 39), seeded, and finely chopped

1 red pepper, cored, seeded, roasted, and peeled (page 354), finely chopped

1 garlic clove, crushed

2 spring onions, thinly sliced

1 fresh green chilli, cored, seeded, and chopped

1 tbsp red wine vinegar

salt

1 Make the salsa: combine the tomatoes, red pepper, garlic, spring onions, chilli, and vinegar in a bowl. Add salt to taste and set aside.

2 Put 4 slices of bread on to a board, and arrange the cheese slices, then the ham slices, on top. Spoon the salsa over the ham.

3 Lightly spread the butter over one side of the remaining slices of bread and put them, butter-side up, on top of the salsa.

4 Heat a heavy frying pan, and cook each sandwich, butter-side down, over a medium-high heat until the cheese begins to melt and the bread becomes golden. Lightly spread the second side of each sandwich with butter. Turn over and cook the other side until golden.

5 Garnish with lemon wedges, coriander sprigs, and any remaining spicy tomato salsa. Serve at once.

Croque señor

This is an unusual variation of croque monsieur, *the classic French toasted cheese and ham sandwich. The spicy tomato salsa adds a tangy Mexican flavour to the filling.*

SWISS CHEESE & TOMATO RAREBIT

Serves 4

3 garlic cloves

15 g (1/2 oz) butter, plus extra for spreading

2 tbsp plain flour

250 g (8 oz) ripe tomatoes, peeled (page 39), seeded, and chopped

125 ml (4 fl oz) dry white wine

375 g (12 oz) Gruyère cheese, grated

125 g (4 oz) mushrooms, chopped

1 tbsp chopped fresh tarragon

salt and black pepper

4 slices of bread, crusts removed

chopped parsley to garnish

1 Crush 2 of the garlic cloves. Melt the butter in a saucepan, add the crushed garlic, and cook gently, stirring, for 1–2 minutes. Add the flour, and cook, stirring, for 1 minute. Add the chopped tomatoes and cook for 2 minutes.

2 Pour in the wine, and cook, stirring, for 5 minutes or until the mixture thickens. Add the Gruyère cheese, a little at a time, and stir until it has melted. Add the chopped mushrooms, tarragon, and salt and pepper to taste, and cook for 3 minutes or until the mushrooms are tender.

3 Cut the remaining garlic clove in half. Toast the bread on both sides under a hot grill. Rub one side of the toast with the cut garlic.

4 Spread the garlic side of the toast with butter, place on warmed plates, and top with the cheese mixture. Serve at once, sprinkled with chopped parsley.

EGGS BENEDICT

Serves 4

8 lean back bacon rashers, rinds removed

2 muffins, halved

4 eggs

2 tbsp vinegar

butter for spreading

flat-leaf parsley to garnish

HOLLANDAISE SAUCE

2 tsp lemon juice

2 tsp white wine vinegar

3 egg yolks, at room temperature

125 g (4 oz) unsalted butter, melted

salt and black pepper

1 Cook the bacon under a hot grill, 7 cm (3 ins) from the heat, for 5–7 minutes until crisp. Keep the bacon warm.

2 Toast the cut sides of the muffin halves under the grill. Keep warm.

3 Make the hollandaise sauce: put the lemon juice and wine vinegar into a small bowl, add the egg yolks, and whisk with a balloon whisk until light and frothy.

4 Place the bowl over a pan of simmering water and whisk until the mixture thickens. Gradually add the melted butter, whisking constantly until thick. Season. Keep warm.

5 Poach the eggs: add the vinegar to a large pan of boiling water. Lower the heat so that the water is simmering, and slide in the eggs. Swirl the water round the eggs to make neat shapes. Simmer for about 4 minutes. Lift out with a slotted spoon.

6 Butter the muffin halves and put on to warmed plates. Put 2 bacon rashers and an egg on each one, and top with the sauce. Serve at once, garnished with parsley.

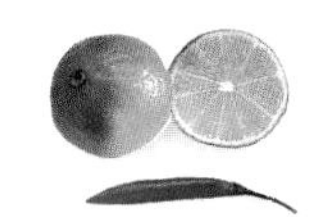

SPICY LIME HOLLANDAISE

Substitute 2 tsp lime juice for the lemon juice in the hollandaise sauce, and add 1/2 tsp each of paprika and mild chilli powder.

EGGS FLORENTINE

Serves 4

250 g (8 oz) spinach leaves

3 spring onions, thinly sliced

2 tbsp double cream

4 eggs

2 tbsp vinegar

3 tbsp grated Parmesan cheese

CHEESE SAUCE

30 g (1 oz) butter

1 tbsp plain flour

250 ml (8 fl oz) milk

175 g (6 oz) mature Cheddar cheese, grated

pinch each of cayenne pepper and grated nutmeg

salt and black pepper

1 Rinse the spinach, and put into a saucepan with only the water that clings to the leaves. Cook for about 2 minutes until tender. Drain, and set aside.

2 Make the cheese sauce: melt the butter in a saucepan, add the flour, and cook, stirring, for 1 minute. Remove from the heat and gradually blend in the milk. Bring to a boil, stirring constantly until the mixture thickens. Simmer for 2–3 minutes.

3 Stir in the Cheddar cheese, cayenne pepper, nutmeg, and salt and pepper to taste. Keep warm.

4 In a bowl, combine the spinach with the spring onions, cream, and salt and pepper to taste. Set aside.

5 Poach the eggs: add the vinegar to a large pan of boiling water. Lower the heat so that the water is simmering, and slide in the eggs, one at a time. Swirl the water round the eggs to make neat shapes. Lift out with a slotted spoon.

6 Divide the spinach and spring onion mixture among 4 warmed flameproof dishes. Arrange the poached eggs on the spinach, and spoon the cheese sauce over the eggs.

7 Sprinkle the grated Parmesan cheese over the sauce, then place the dishes under a hot grill, 7 cm (3 ins) from the heat, until the cheese has melted and is lightly browned, and the whole dish is heated through. Serve hot.

OEUFS EN COCOTTE

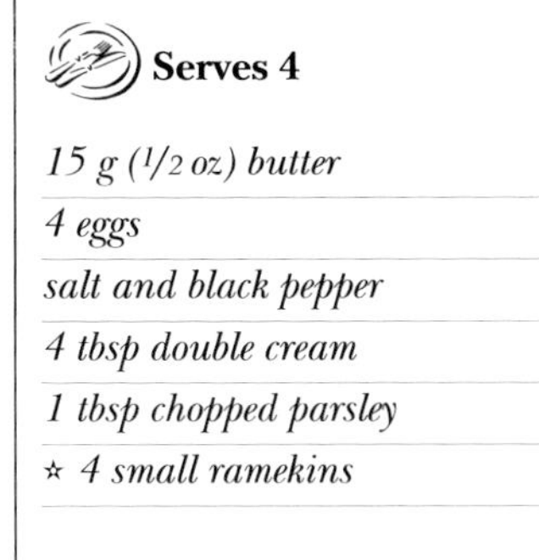

Serves 4

15 g (1/2 oz) butter

4 eggs

salt and black pepper

4 tbsp double cream

1 tbsp chopped parsley

☆ *4 small ramekins*

1 Melt the butter, and pour a little into each ramekin.

2 Break each egg into a saucer, then slide into a prepared ramekin. Add salt and pepper to taste, and top each egg with 1 tbsp cream.

3 Place the ramekins in a roasting tin and pour in boiling water to come halfway up the sides of the ramekins. Cover with foil.

4 Bake in a preheated oven at 200°C (400°F, Gas 6) for 10 minutes or until the whites are opaque and firm but the yolks still soft. Or, put the ramekins into a large frying pan, add boiling water to come halfway up the sides, cover, and cook over a medium heat for 10 minutes, letting the water boil and gently steam the eggs.

5 Sprinkle a little parsley over each baked egg 1–2 minutes before the end of cooking time.

FETA CHEESE COCOTTES

After pouring the butter into the ramekins, divide 125 g (4 oz) diced feta cheese, marinated in chopped fresh herbs and diced fresh red chilli, among the ramekins. Proceed as directed, substituting 2–3 thinly sliced spring onions for the parsley.

HUEVOS RANCHEROS

Serves 4

2 tbsp sunflower oil

1 onion, finely chopped

3 garlic cloves, crushed

1 green pepper, cored, seeded, and chopped

1–2 fresh green chillies, cored, seeded, and chopped

500 g (1 lb) tomatoes, peeled (page 39), seeded, and diced

1 tsp ground cumin

1/4 tsp sugar

salt

2 tbsp vinegar

4 eggs

coriander sprigs to garnish

1 Heat the oil in a frying pan, add the onion, garlic, green pepper, and chillies, and cook gently, stirring occasionally, for about 5 minutes until the onion is soft.

2 Add the tomatoes, cumin, sugar, and salt to taste, and simmer, stirring occasionally, for 10 minutes or until the mixture is thick.

3 Meanwhile, poach the eggs: add the vinegar to a large pan of boiling water. Lower the heat so that the water is simmering, and slide in the eggs, one at a time. Swirl the water round the eggs to make neat shapes. Simmer for 4 minutes. Lift out with a slotted spoon.

4 Taste the tomato sauce for seasoning, and ladle on to serving plates. Top each of the servings with a poached egg, and garnish with a coriander sprig.

HUEVOS RANCHEROS WITH CHEESE

Fry the eggs instead of poaching them. Transfer the eggs to serving plates, top with the sauce, and sprinkle with 60 g (2 oz) grated mature Cheddar cheese. Serve at once.

4

FISH & SHELLFISH

UNDER 30 MINUTES

THAI PRAWN STIR-FRY

Spicy oriental dish: prawns, red pepper, ginger, chilli, and lemon grass, stir-fried with rice noodles, soy sauce, and lime juice.

SERVES 4 522 calories per serving
Takes 15 minutes **PAGE 109**

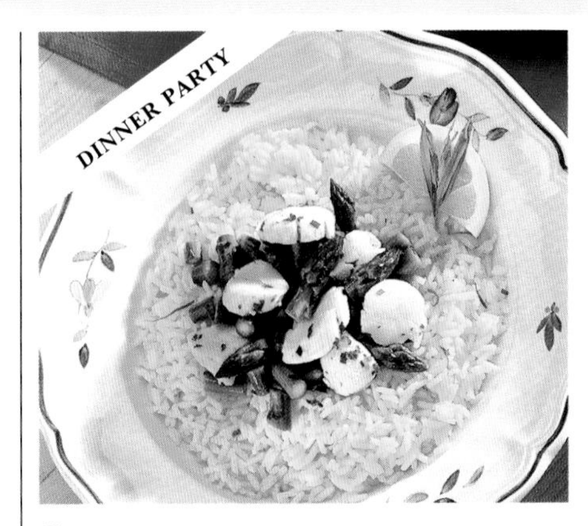

SCALLOPS WITH ASPARAGUS & LEMON

Fresh and aromatic: scallops cooked with asparagus and garlic, with a parsley, lemon, and tarragon sauce.

SERVES 4 342 calories per serving
Takes 20 minutes **PAGE 112**

DEVILLED CRAB

Crabmeat in a sauce flavoured with nutmeg, sherry, spring onion, and Tabasco sauce. Topped with breadcrumbs and baked.

SERVES 4 502 calories per serving
Takes 25 minutes **PAGE 110**

TIGER PRAWNS WITH TARRAGON SAUCE

Prawns simmered with wine, garlic, and parsley. Served with a tarragon sauce.

SERVES 4 252 calories per serving
Takes 20 minutes **PAGE 108**

HERRINGS WITH OATMEAL

Crispy and wholesome: herrings coated in oatmeal and mustard, then grilled. Served with deep-fried parsley.

SERVES 4 461 calories per serving
Takes 15 minutes **PAGE 117**

OYSTER STEW WITH PERNOD & SAFFRON

An unusual Mediterranean-style dish: fresh oysters simmered with Pernod, single cream, white wine, fish stock, leek, carrot, watercress, saffron, and lemon juice. Lightly seasoned with cayenne pepper, and garnished with fresh chervil.

SERVES 4 251 calories per serving
Takes 25 minutes **PAGE 115**

UNDER 30 MINUTES

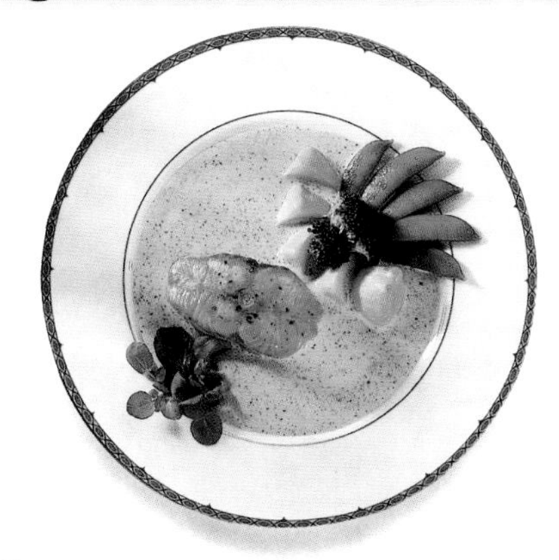

SEVERN SALMON
Baked salmon flavoured with pepper, in a pool of sauce made from cream, watercress, lemon juice, butter, and egg yolk.
SERVES 6 414 calories per serving
Takes 25 minutes  **PAGE 122**

GRILLED TROUT WITH CUCUMBER & DILL
Trout with a stuffing of lightly cooked cucumber, dill, and lemon juice.
SERVES 4 435 calories per serving
Takes 25 minutes **PAGE 118**

SCALLOPS WITH SPICY CASHEW SAUCE
Scallops stir-fried with mustard seeds and garlic, served in a cashew and chilli sauce.
SERVES 4 414 calories per serving
Takes 25 minutes **PAGE 112**

CHINESE-STYLE OYSTERS
Oysters wrapped in bacon and stir-fried with green pepper, garlic, and water chestnuts, then sprinkled with spring onion slices.
SERVES 4 248 calories per serving
Takes 25 minutes **PAGE 115**

SALMON WITH SPINACH
Grilled salmon served with a salsa of lightly cooked spring onions mixed with spinach, lemon juice, and mustard.
SERVES 4 454 calories per serving
Takes 25 minutes **PAGE 122**

BEST-EVER FRIED FISH
Crispy and nourishing: plaice fillets coated in flour, beaten egg, and fresh breadcrumbs. Cooked until golden and served with lemon.
SERVES 4 298 calories per serving
Takes 25 minutes **PAGE 128**

HERRINGS WITH MUSTARD SAUCE
Baked herrings served with a classic sauce made from mustard powder, sugar, and white wine vinegar.
SERVES 4 479 calories per serving
Takes 25 minutes **PAGE 117**

FILLETS OF SOLE MEUNIERE
Fresh and summery: lemon sole fillets lightly floured and cooked in butter, then served with parsley and lemon-flavoured butter.
SERVES 4 274 calories per serving
Takes 20 minutes **PAGE 126**

PRAWN TACOS
Crispy and hot: taco shells with a spicy filling of prawns, coriander, tomatoes, onion, garlic, green pepper, and paprika.
SERVES 4 414 calories per serving
Takes 25 minutes **PAGE 108**

30–60 MINUTES

CAJUN-SPICED RED SNAPPER

Red snapper fillets marinated in a piquant mixture of garlic, paprika, cumin, and chilli powder. Topped with coriander butter.

SERVES 4 258 calories per serving

Takes 15 minutes, plus marinating **PAGE 132**

HOT & SOUR MACKEREL

Red pepper, fresh chilli, carrots, and spring onions stir-fried, then grilled with mackerel fillets. Served with a hot and sour sauce.

SERVES 4 539 calories per serving

Takes 35 minutes **PAGE 116**

MUSSEL GRATIN

Mussels simmered with wine, shallot, and garlic, topped with cream and parsley sauce, and breadcrumbs, then grilled.

SERVES 4 448 calories per serving

Takes 35 minutes **PAGE 113**

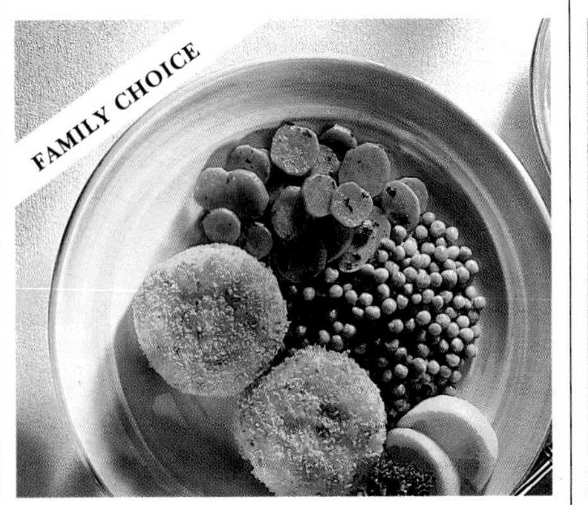

GOLDEN FISH CAKES

Cod or haddock simmered in milk flavoured with bay leaf and peppercorns. Mixed with potato and coated in fresh breadcrumbs.

SERVES 4 613 calories per serving

Takes 50 minutes **PAGE 136**

LOBSTER WITH BLACK BEAN SALSA

Lobster tails spread with garlic and oregano-flavoured butter and grilled. Served with black bean salsa.

SERVES 4 531 calories per serving

Takes 35 minutes **PAGE 111**

CHEESE-TOPPED BAKED BREAM

Bream fillets baked with finely grated lemon zest and juice. Covered in a white sauce and sprinkled with Cheddar cheese, then grilled.

SERVES 4 401 calories per serving

Takes 40 minutes **PAGE 133**

MACKEREL WITH GOOSEBERRY SAUCE

Grilled mackerel served with a tangy sauce made from gooseberries, simmered with water and sugar, and mixed with butter and ginger.

SERVES 4 489 calories per serving

Takes 35 minutes **PAGE 116**

SALMON WITH AVOCADO

Succulent salmon steaks baked with tarragon, and served with a rich sauce of avocado, yogurt, and lime zest and juice.

SERVES 4 543 calories per serving

Takes 35 minutes **PAGE 123**

MUSHROOM-STUFFED SOLE FILLETS

Sole fillets rolled and stuffed with onion and mushrooms. Baked with tarragon and wine, which form the base for a cream sauce.

SERVES 4 568 calories per serving

Takes 35 minutes **PAGE 126**

30–60 MINUTES

CLAMS IN SALSA VERDE

Clams cooked in a delicious sauce made of fish stock, olive oil, sherry, garlic, onion, and chopped parsley.

SERVES 4 291 calories per serving

Takes 40 minutes **PAGE 114**

SPICED FISH WITH COCONUT

Sweet and spicy: monkfish pieces lightly coated in flour, cooked with coconut milk, onion, coriander, cumin, and turmeric.

SERVES 4 389 calories per serving

Takes 45 minutes **PAGE 131**

SPICY CLAMS WITH CORIANDER PESTO

Clams cooked with tomatoes and stock, richly flavoured with garlic, paprika, chilli powder, and cumin. Served with coriander pesto.

SERVES 4–6 349–233 calories per serving

Takes 45 minutes **PAGE 114**

CITRUS MONKFISH

Light and tangy: monkfish fillets cooked with satsumas, ginger, spring onions, and stock; served with a sauce spiked with lime.

SERVES 4 221 calories per serving

Takes 40 minutes **PAGE 130**

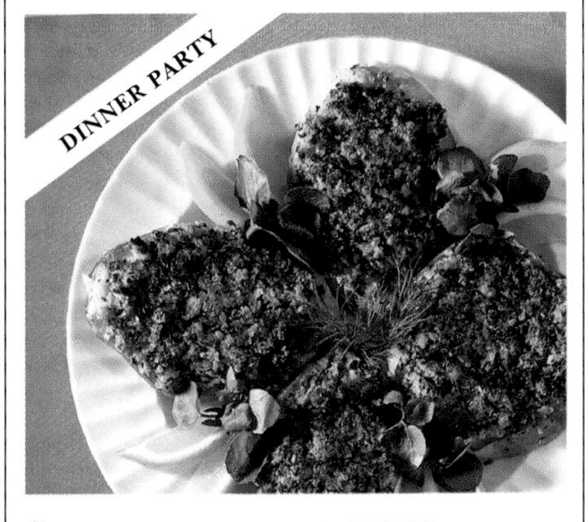

COD STEAKS WITH ANCHOVY & FENNEL

Cod steaks baked with a topping of anchovies, fennel, parsley, and breadcrumbs.

SERVES 4 429 calories per serving

Takes 40 minutes **PAGE 132**

SEA BASS WITH LEMON BUTTER SAUCE

Fresh and aromatic: sea bass baked in foil with tarragon, lemon, and wine. Served with a warm and creamy lemon sauce.

SERVES 4 363 calories per serving

Takes 40 minutes **PAGE 135**

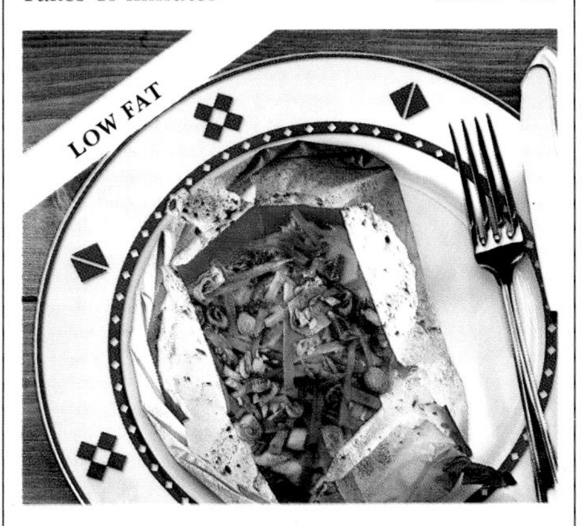

FISH EN PAPILLOTE

An aromatic oriental dish: white fish fillets sprinkled with ginger, spring onion, soy sauce, and rice wine, baked in a parcel.

SERVES 4 312 calories per serving

Takes 35 minutes **PAGE 135**

BLACK BREAM NIÇOISE

Baked black bream on a bed of fennel, onion, and garlic, sprinkled with lemon juice, olives, and chopped parsley.

SERVES 4 356 calories per serving

Takes 50 minutes **PAGE 133**

CRISPY-TOPPED SEAFOOD PIE

Cod poached in milk, then baked with prawns, leeks, and broccoli. Topped with white sauce, Gruyère, and crispy pastry.

SERVES 4 575 calories per serving

Takes 55 minutes **PAGE 136**

30–60 MINUTES

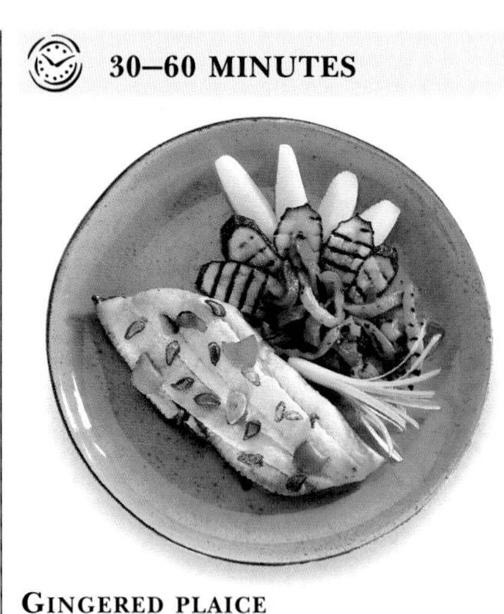

GINGERED PLAICE

Light and tangy: plaice fillets marinated in sunflower and sesame oils, fresh root ginger, garlic, sherry, and vinegar, then grilled.

SERVES 4 247 calories per serving

Takes 15 minutes, plus marinating **PAGE 127**

STUFFED SQUID

Baked squid pouches filled with breadcrumbs, onion, garlic, tomato juice, chopped squid, olives, parsley, rosemary, egg, and vinegar.

SERVES 4 410 calories per serving

Takes 40 minutes **PAGE 109**

MUSSELS WITH POTATOES & CHORIZO

Mussels cooked with potatoes, spicy Spanish chorizo sausage, garlic, stock, sherry, and cumin seeds.

SERVES 4 784 calories per serving

Takes 40 minutes **PAGE 113**

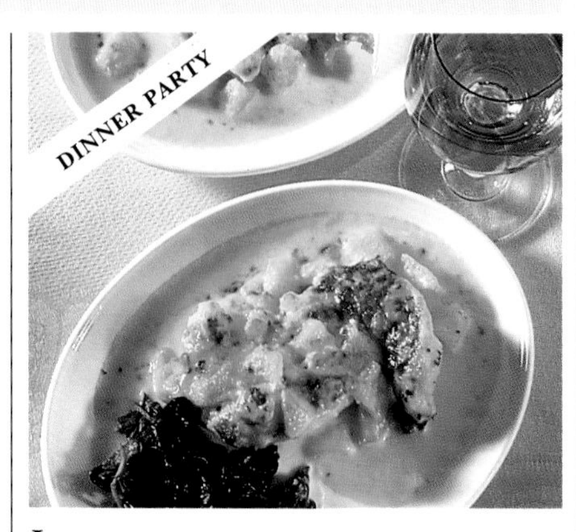

LOBSTER TAILS WITH MANGO & LIME

Lobster tail meat coated in a sauce of wine, cream, mango, and grated lime zest and juice. Sprinkled with Parmesan cheese and baked.

SERVES 4 442 calories per serving

Takes 40 minutes **PAGE 110**

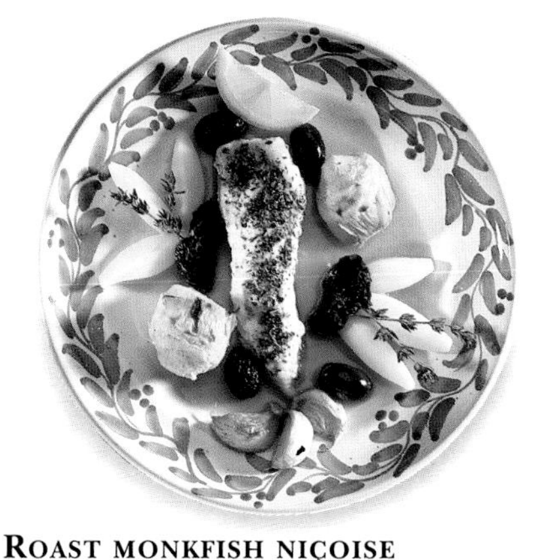

ROAST MONKFISH NIÇOISE

Richly flavoured monkfish cooked with roasted garlic, lemon, wine, artichoke hearts, herbs, olives, and sun-dried tomatoes.

SERVES 4 448 calories per serving

Takes 50 minutes **PAGE 130**

HADDOCK WITH MUSHROOMS & CREAM

Baked haddock topped with mushrooms, a creamy sauce, breadcrumbs, and Parmesan.

SERVES 4–6 429–286 calories per serving

Takes 55 minutes **PAGE 129**

OVER 60 MINUTES

SEAFOOD & AVOCADO SALAD

Poached monkfish with crabmeat and prawns on a bed of salad leaves, avocado, and tomatoes, dressed with crème fraîche.

SERVES 4 396 calories per serving

Takes 35 minutes, plus cooling **PAGE 111**

LEMON SOLE FLORENTINE

Lemon sole fillets baked on a bed of white sauce and spinach and topped with Parmesan. Served with hot lemon bread.

SERVES 4 422 calories per serving

Takes 1 hour 5 minutes **PAGE 127**

HALIBUT IN FILO PARCELS

Delicate and moist: leek and carrot strips cooked with wine, stock, and saffron, form a bed for halibut wrapped in filo pastry.

SERVES 4 564 calories per serving

Takes 1 hour 5 minutes **PAGE 134**

OVER 60 MINUTES

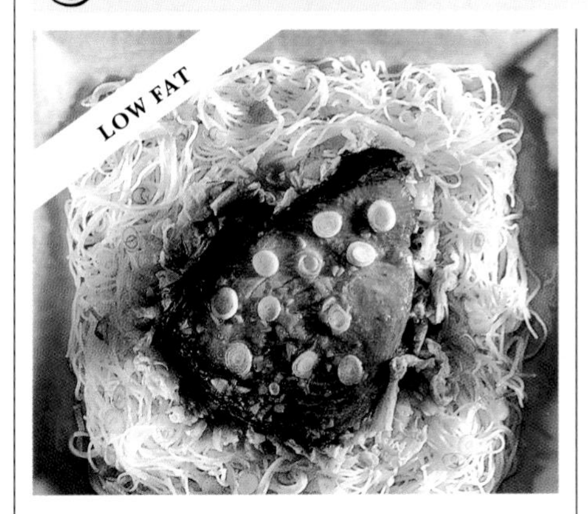

TUNA TERIYAKI

Light and simple: tuna steaks marinated in garlic, ginger, soy sauce, and sesame oil. Grilled, and sprinkled with spring onion.

SERVES 4 339 calories per serving

Takes 15 minutes, plus marinating **PAGE 119**

TUNA WITH FENNEL & TOMATO RELISH

Tuna marinated in oil, lemon juice, garlic, and herbs, grilled, and topped with relish.

SERVES 4 467 calories per serving

Takes 25 minutes, plus marinating **PAGE 119**

MONKFISH KEBABS

Pieces of monkfish marinated in oil, lemon zest and juice, and dill, threaded with lightly cooked cucumber, lemon, and bay leaves.

SERVES 4 286 calories per serving

Takes 30 minutes, plus marinating **PAGE 131**

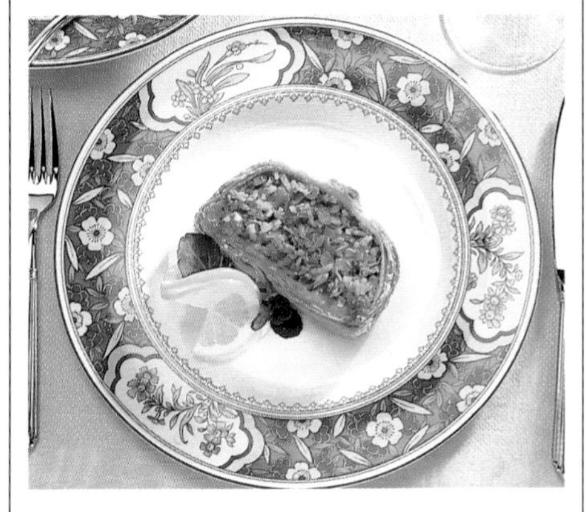

KOULIBIAC

Flaked salmon mixed with rice, onion, tomatoes, parsley, and lemon. Wrapped in puff pastry and decorated with a pastry plait.

SERVES 8–10 518–414 calories per serving

Takes 1 1/4 hours **PAGE 121**

INDIAN SPICED HADDOCK

Pieces of haddock marinated in a mixture of coriander, cayenne, and turmeric. Simmered with ginger, chilli, and potato.

SERVES 4 365 calories per serving

Takes 40 minutes, plus marinating **PAGE 129**

SALMON EN CROUTE

Salmon fillets marinated in dill and lemon zest and juice, baked in puff pastry with spinach, spring onions, and soft cheese.

SERVES 6 993 calories per serving

Takes 1 1/2 hours, plus marinating **PAGE 123**

SWORDFISH WITH ORANGE RELISH

Swordfish steaks marinated in orange and lemon juices, olive oil, and garlic. Grilled, then served with an orange relish.

SERVES 4 429 calories per serving

Takes 20 minutes, plus marinating **PAGE 120**

SHARK WITH TROPICAL SALSA

Shark steaks marinated in cumin, garlic, lemon juice, and coriander. Served with a salsa of pineapple, papaya, and chilli.

SERVES 4 534 calories per serving

Takes 25 minutes, plus marinating **PAGE 120**

BAKED TROUT WITH ORANGE

Fresh and hearty dish: trout stuffed with mushrooms, shallots, orange zest and juice, white wine vinegar, thyme, and parsley.

SERVES 4 378 calories per serving

Takes 45 minutes, plus chilling **PAGE 118**

FISH & SHELLFISH KNOW-HOW

SEAFOOD IS ONE OF THE MOST delicious, versatile, and nutritious foods we can eat. Compared with other protein foods it is excellent value for money – usually there is very little wastage – and it is easy to prepare and quick to cook. Fish and shellfish are good sources of essential nutrients, but oily fish are particularly rich in vitamins A and D and should be a regular part of a healthy diet.

Seafood is divided into two broad categories: fish and shellfish. Fish can be sub-divided into "round white fish", such as cod or whiting; "flat white fish", like plaice and turbot; and "oily fish", which includes herring and mackerel. All of these are vertebrates with fins and gills. Among shellfish, crab, prawns, and mussels have shells on the outside, while squid have reduced internal shells.

BUYING & STORING

When choosing fish and shellfish, smell and appearance are your guides. Fresh fish should smell like the sea. If it smells at all unpleasant or ammonia-like, it is not fresh. Whole fresh fish should have clean, red gills, the scales should be shiny, and it should feel firm and elastic. The flesh of fillets and steaks should look moist and lustrous. If buying pre-packaged fish, check the colour of any liquid that has accumulated in the pack: it should not be cloudy or off-white.

Shellfish is sold both in the shell and shelled, raw and cooked. The shells of crabs, lobsters, and prawns become pink or red when cooked. Live shellfish, such as mussels, clams, and oysters should have tightly closed shells. Open shells should close if lightly tapped; if they do not, the shellfish is dead and should be discarded. Shelled oysters, scallops, and clams should be plump; scallops should smell slightly sweet. Prawns should also smell faintly sweet, and feel firm.

Keep the fish or shellfish cool until you get home, then unwrap it, cover with a wet cloth or wet paper towels and store in the coldest part of the refrigerator. Use the same day, or within 1 day at the most.

MICROWAVING

Fish and shellfish cook well in a microwave, retaining their texture, flavour, and juices. But care must be taken not to overcook the delicate flesh. Whether cooking or thawing, arrange pieces of fish so that the thicker areas are at the outside of the dish; overlap thin areas or fold them under. With whole fish, shield delicate areas, such as the tail and head, with smooth strips of foil. If thawing seafood, again protect thin, delicate areas by shielding them with smooth strips of foil.

FREEZING

It's best to buy fish ready-frozen, as it is frozen very soon after catching – often while still at sea – and won't have begun to deteriorate. Some fresh seafood, particularly prawns, may have been frozen already then thawed, so should not be frozen again.

Clean fish before freezing, wrap tightly, and, for the best flavour, store for no longer than 2 months. Fish can be cooked very successfully from frozen but if you need to thaw it, do so slowly in the refrigerator or quickly in the microwave.

FISH STOCK

Ask your fishmonger for heads, bones, and trimmings from lean white fish only (oily fish make a bitter-tasting stock).

1 Rinse *750 g (1½ lb) trimmings* and put them into a large pan. Add *1 litre (1¾ pints) water* and *250 ml (8 fl oz) dry white wine*. Bring to a boil, skimming the surface.

2 Add *1 sliced onion, 1 sliced carrot, 1 chopped celery stalk, 1 bay leaf, a few parsley sprigs,* and *a few black peppercorns*. Simmer for 20–25 minutes. Strain. Use immediately or cool, cover, and refrigerate. Use within 2 days or freeze for up to 3 months.

SCALING

Unless the fish is to be skinned, remove the scales before cooking. Dip your fingers in salt to ensure a firm grip and grasp the fish tail. Using the blunt side of a knife, with firm strokes scrape off the scales, from the tail to the head. Rinse the fish well under cold running water.

CLEANING & FILLETING ROUND FISH

Fishmongers will clean and fillet fish for you, but if you have to do it yourself, here's how. Round fish such as trout, mackerel, herring, or even salmon, are often cooked whole, and boning makes them easier to serve and eat.

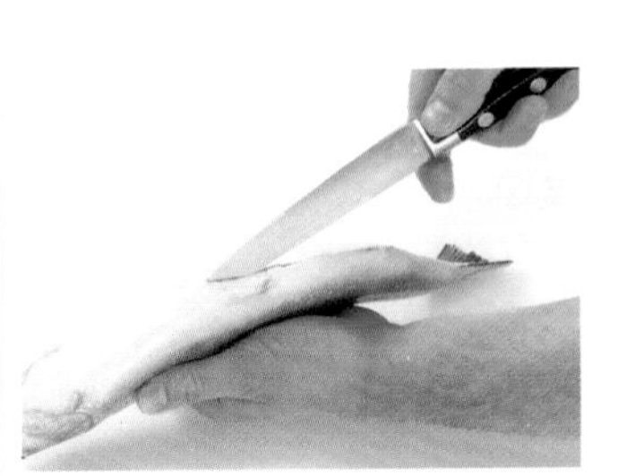

1 Snip off the fins. Cut along the belly, from the vent end to just below the head. Remove the innards, scraping away any dark blood. Lift the gill covering and remove the concertina-shaped gills. Rinse well.

2 Extend the belly opening so that it goes all the way to the tail. Hold the belly open and carefully run the knife between the flesh and the bones along one side, from tail to head, to cut the flesh from the ribcage.

3 Turn the fish around and cut the flesh from the ribcage on the other side. Snip through the backbone at each end and gently pull it away from the flesh, removing it with the ribcage in one piece.

4 If the head and tail have been cut off, open out the fish and lay it skin-side up. Press along the backbone to loosen the bones. Turn over and lift out the ribcage and backbone, freeing it with a knife if necessary.

SKINNING A FLAT FISH

A flat fish may be skinned before filleting.

1 With the dark-side up, make a shallow cut between the tail and the body. Gently cut a little of the skin from the flesh.

2 Holding the tail with one hand, grip the skin with salted fingers and pull it away. Repeat on the other side.

FILLETING FLAT FISH

Either 2 or 4 fillets may be cut from a small flat fish, depending on whether you would like 2 wide or 4 narrow fillets. Larger flat fish yield 4 fillets.

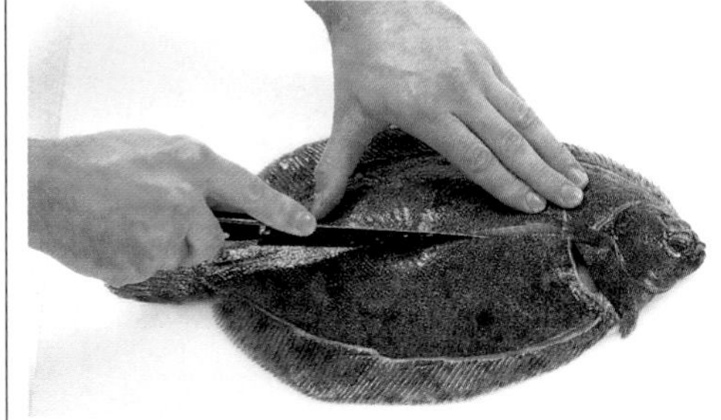

1 Make a shallow cut around the edge of the fish, where the fin bones meet the body. Cut across the tail and make a curved cut around the head. Cut along the centre of the fish, cutting through to the bone.

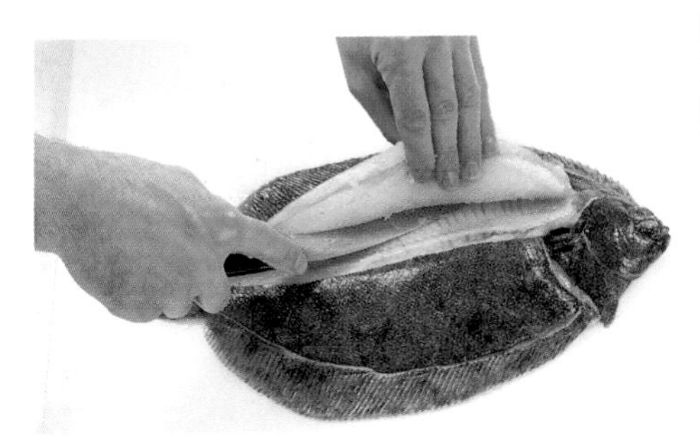

2 Insert the knife between the flesh and the bones at the head end, keeping it almost parallel to the fish. Cut, close to the bones, to remove the flesh.

3 Continue cutting, to detach the flesh in one piece. Repeat to remove the second fillet. Turn the fish over and remove the fillets on the other side in the same way. Check the flesh for any stray bones.

4 To skin, lay each fillet skin-side down, hold the tail with salted fingers to ensure a firm grip, and pull away. Cut through the flesh at the tail end, then hold the knife at an angle and cut the flesh from the skin.

PREPARING PRAWNS

Both cooked and uncooked prawns can be used successfully in a variety of tasty dishes. Prawns lose at least half of their weight when the heads and shells are removed.

1 Gently pull off the head and then the legs. Peel the shell from the body, starting at the head end. When you reach the tail, pull it out of the shell.

2 Make a shallow cut along the centre of the back of the prawn. Lift out the black intestinal vein and rinse the prawn under cold running water.

PREPARING MUSSELS & CLAMS

Most mussels and clams are sold live and are cooked by steaming in their shells. They must be scrubbed before cooking. The anchoring threads found on mussels, known as beards, must also be removed.

1 To clean the shells of mussels and clams, hold under cold running water and scrub with a small stiff brush. Use a small knife to scrape off any barnacles.

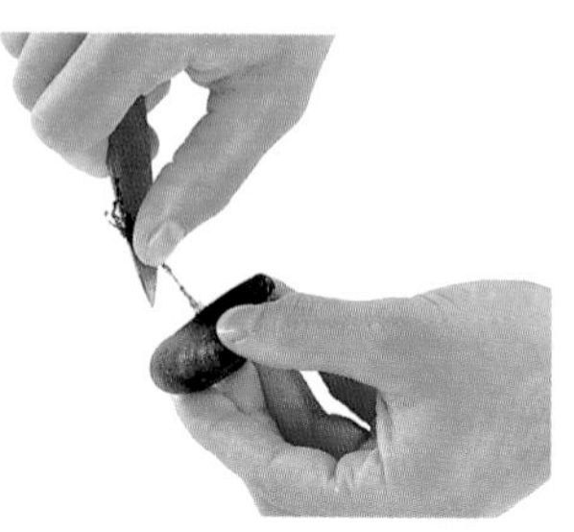

2 To remove the beard from a mussel, hold the beard firmly between your thumb and the blade of a small knife and pull the beard away from the shell.

PREPARING A COOKED CRAB

The meat inside a crab is of two types – a soft, rich, brown meat and a chewier white meat. When a crab is "dressed", the meat is removed from the shell, and the two types kept separate.

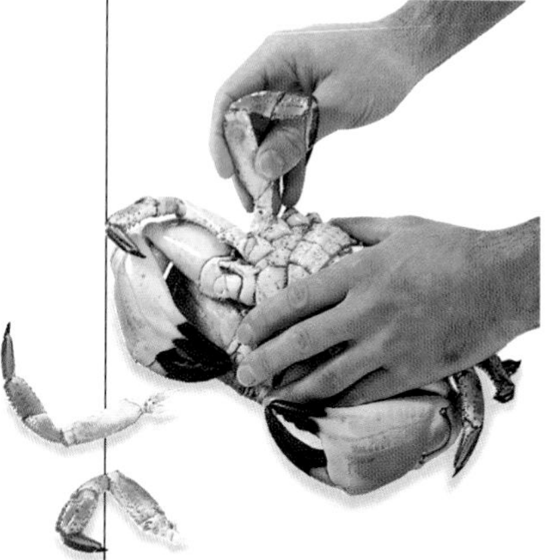

1 Put the crab on its back and twist off the legs and claws, close to the body.

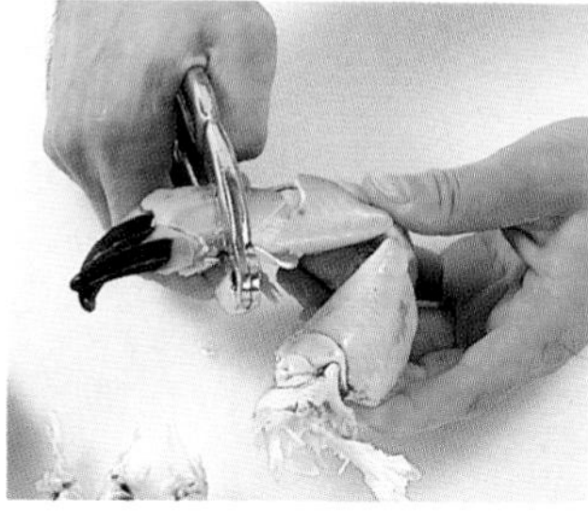

2 Using nutcrackers, a small hammer, or a rolling pin, crack the shells of the claws without crushing them. Break open the shells and carefully remove the meat, using a small fork or skewer.

3 Press your thumbs along the "perforation" to crack the central section of the shell and prise it apart. Remove and discard the "apron" flap from the underside of the body.

4 Pull the central body section up and away from the shell. Scoop the creamy-textured brown meat out of the shell and put it into a bowl (keeping it entirely separate from the white claw and leg meat). Scoop out any roe. Discard the stomach sac which is located between the eyes.

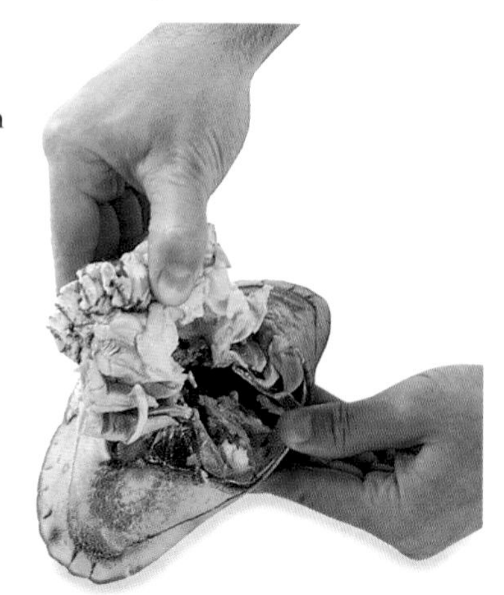

5 Pull the spongy gills (known as "dead man's fingers") from the body and discard them.

6 Cut the body in half with a large knife and pick out all the meat from the crevices. Add to the meat in the bowl.

PREPARING A COOKED LOBSTER

Ready-cooked lobster can be added to cooked dishes, or served cold with mayonnaise, in which case the shell is simply cut into 2 halves and the flesh loosened and returned to the shell.

Removing the meat

1 Twist off the large claws. Using a sturdy nutcracker, small hammer, or rolling pin, crack the shells of the claws without crushing them. Pick out the meat, in 1 or 2 large pieces. If the shell is not to be used for serving, pull apart the body and tail. Twist off the small legs and remove the meat with a skewer or lobster pick.

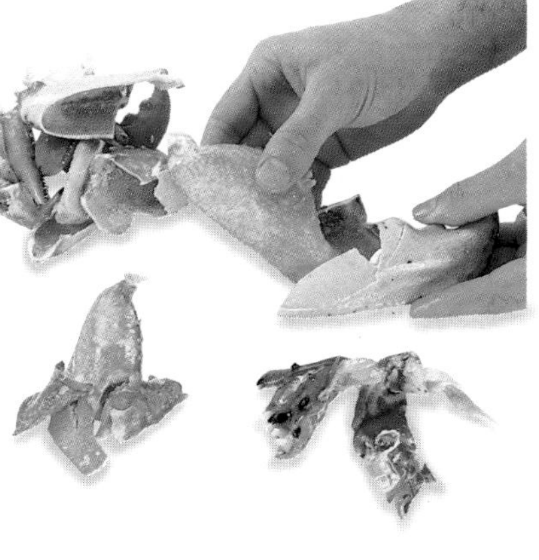

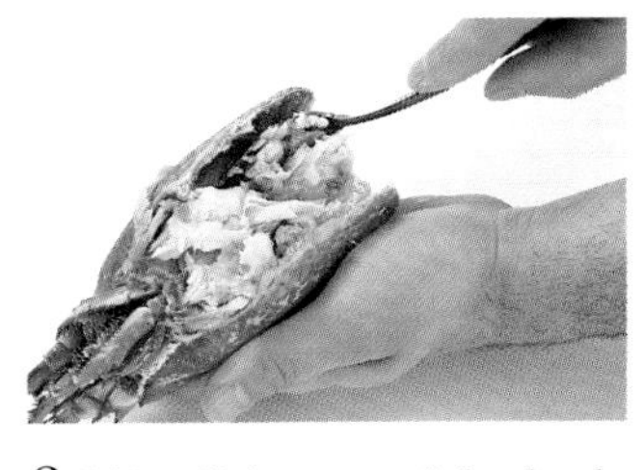

2 Lift off the top of the body shell, scoop out the grey-green liver (tomalley) and any coral-coloured roe, both of which are edible, and reserve. Discard the stomach and spongy gills ("dead man's fingers").

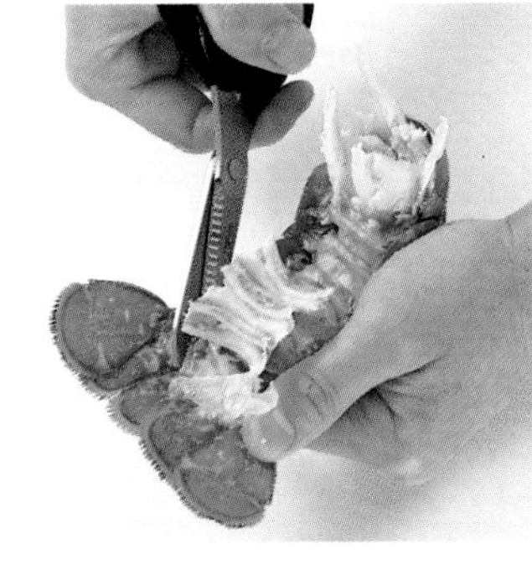

3 With scissors or a sharp knife, cut along the soft underside of the tail.

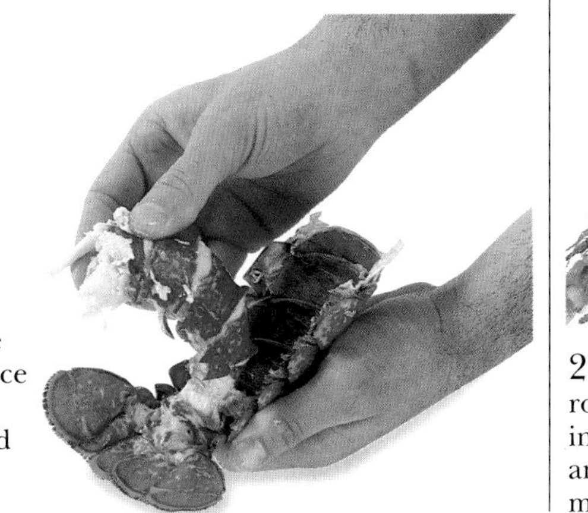

4 Bend back the flaps and carefully remove the tail meat, keeping it in 1 piece. Remove and discard the intestine that runs through the centre of the tail meat. Slice the tail meat, or prepare as required and serve with the claw and leg meat.

To serve in the shell

1 Use a knife to cut the lobster in half lengthwise, cutting from the head to the tail. Keep the shell for serving.

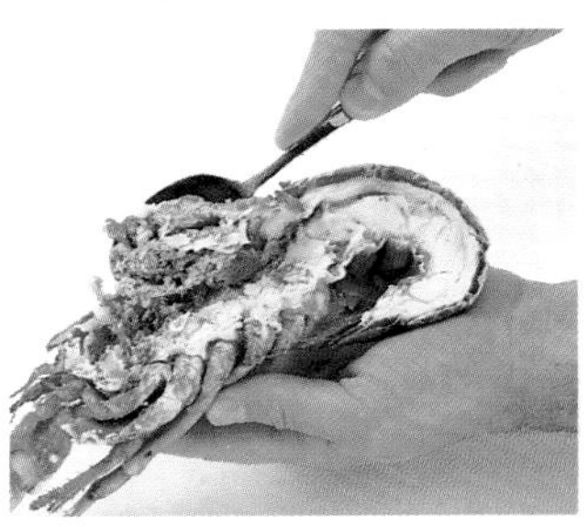

2 Scoop out the liver and roe and discard the intestine. Twist off the legs and claws and remove the meat. Loosen the tail meat.

PREPARING OYSTERS

To shuck oysters, use an oyster knife or small, sturdy knife.

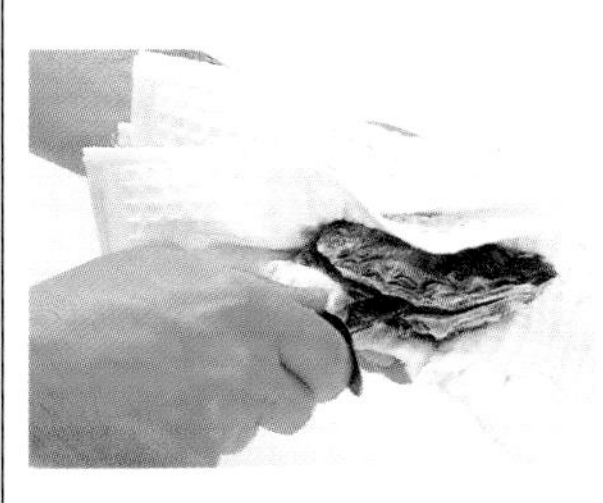

Hold oyster round-side down, and insert the knife near the hinge. Lever the shells apart. Slide in the knife to sever the top muscle. Lift off the shell. Run the knife under the oyster to loosen.

PREPARING A SQUID

Once cleaned, fresh squid yields an empty, tube-like body and separate tentacles. The body may be stuffed before cooking, or sliced and cooked with the tentacles.

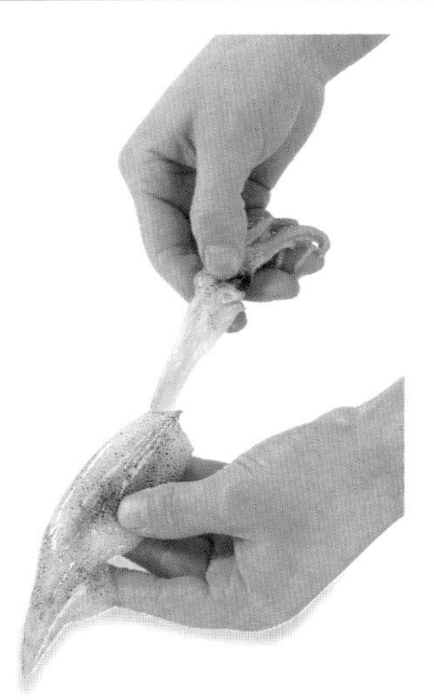

1 Pull the body of the squid away from the head and tentacles. The innards will come away with the head. Cut off the tentacles, just in front of the eyes.

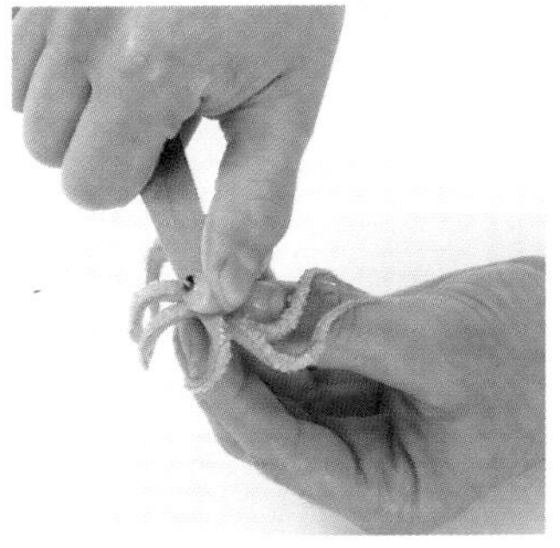

2 Squeeze the tentacles near the cut end to remove the hard beak and then discard it. Rinse the tentacles well and set aside. Discard the head and innards.

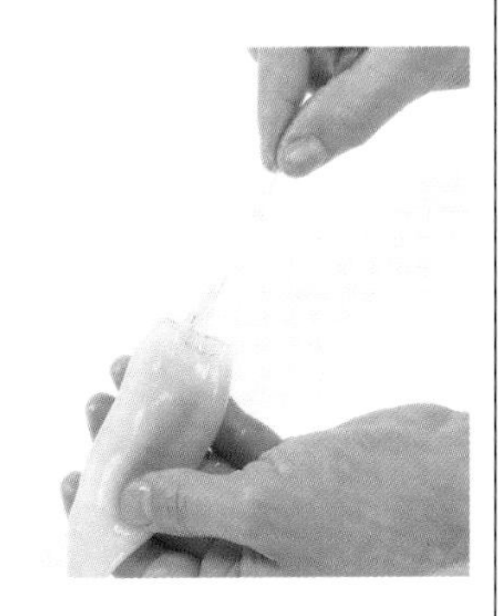

3 Peel the skin from the body. Pull the quill out of the body and discard. Rinse the body thoroughly, dislodging any remaining innards with your fingers.

PRAWN TACOS

Serves 4

2 tbsp sunflower oil
2 onions, chopped
3 garlic cloves, crushed
1 green pepper, cored, seeded, and diced
1 tbsp paprika
2 tsp mild chilli powder
1/2 tsp ground cumin
4 tomatoes, peeled (page 39), seeded, and chopped
500 g (1 lb) cooked peeled prawns
2 tbsp chopped fresh coriander
salt and black pepper
12 taco shells
1 round lettuce, shredded
sliced pickled chillies, large cooked peeled prawns, and coriander leaves to garnish

1 Heat the oil in a large frying pan, add the onions, and cook gently, stirring occasionally, for 3–5 minutes until softened but not coloured. Add the garlic and diced green pepper, and cook, stirring occasionally, for 3 minutes or until the pepper is soft.

2 Stir in the paprika, chilli powder, and cumin, and cook, stirring, for 1 minute. Add the tomatoes and cook for 3–5 minutes until soft.

3 Lower the heat and stir in the prawns, chopped coriander, and salt and pepper to taste.

4 Meanwhile, heat the taco shells in a preheated oven at 180°C (350°F, Gas 4) for 3 minutes or according to packet instructions.

5 Spoon the prawn mixture into the taco shells, top with the shredded lettuce, and garnish with chillies, prawns, and coriander. Serve at once.

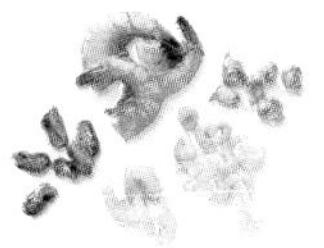

SEAFOOD TACOS

Substitute 1 diced snapper fillet and shellfish, such as mussels, cockles, or thinly sliced rings of squid, for 300 g (10 oz) of the prawns.

TIGER PRAWNS WITH TARRAGON SAUCE

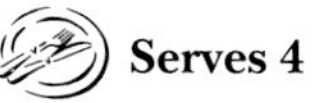
Serves 4

12 uncooked tiger prawns in their shells
olive oil for brushing
300 ml (1/2 pint) dry white wine
1 garlic clove, crushed
4 tbsp chopped parsley
lemon and tarragon to garnish

TARRAGON SAUCE
150 ml (1/4 pint) soured cream
4 tbsp chopped fresh tarragon
1 tsp Dijon mustard
squeeze of lemon juice
salt and black pepper

1 Make the tarragon sauce: combine the soured cream, tarragon, mustard, lemon juice, and salt and pepper to taste.

2 Heat a heavy frying pan. Brush the prawns with oil, add to the pan, and cook the prawns over a high heat for 2 minutes or until pink.

3 Keeping the heat high, add 150 ml (1/4 pint) of the wine and the garlic. Boil rapidly for 2–3 minutes, then stir in 2 tbsp of the parsley.

4 When the wine has reduced slightly, lower the heat, and add the remaining wine, with salt and pepper to taste. Simmer for 5 minutes or until the prawns have released their juices into the wine.

5 Spoon the cooking juices over the prawns, sprinkle with the remaining parsley, and garnish with lemon and tarragon. Serve hot, with the tarragon sauce.

Tiger prawns

Originally from the Far East, tiger prawns are the largest prawns available. They may also be sold as jumbo prawns.

STUFFED SQUID

Serves 4

3 tbsp olive oil
1 onion, chopped
3–4 garlic cloves, crushed
8 small squid, cleaned (page 107)
60 g (2 oz) fresh breadcrumbs
90 ml (3 fl oz) tomato juice
2 tsp chopped fresh rosemary
10 pitted black olives, sliced
2 tbsp chopped parsley
1 egg, lightly beaten
2 tsp balsamic or red wine vinegar
salt and black pepper
cayenne pepper
lemon slices and chopped parsley to garnish

1 Make the stuffing: heat 2 tbsp of the oil in a saucepan, add the onion and garlic, and cook gently, stirring occasionally, for 3–5 minutes until the onion is soft but not coloured.

2 Chop the squid tentacles very finely. Add them to the pan and cook, stirring, for 2 minutes, then add the breadcrumbs, tomato juice, and chopped rosemary and stir well.

3 Remove the pan from the heat, and stir in the olives, parsley, beaten egg, and vinegar. Add salt, pepper, and cayenne pepper to taste. Mix well to combine. Fill the squid with the stuffing, and secure the tops (see box, below).

4 Arrange the squid in an ovenproof dish, sprinkle with the remaining oil, and season with salt and pepper. Bake in a preheated oven at 220°C (425°F, Gas 7) for about 20 minutes until the squid and filling are quite firm to the touch. Garnish the squid with the lemon slices and parsley, and serve at once.

Securing the squid

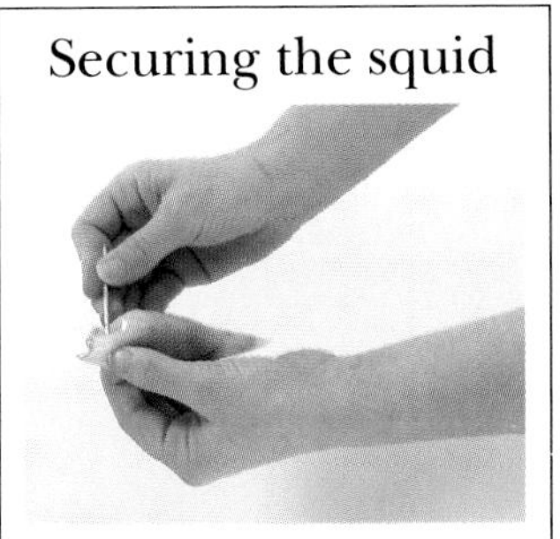

Thread a cocktail stick through the top of each stuffed squid to secure the opening.

THAI PRAWN STIR-FRY

Serves 4

250 g (8 oz) rice noodles
salt
3 tbsp sunflower oil
1 red pepper, cored, seeded, and cut into thin strips
1 carrot, cut into thin strips
1 fresh green chilli, cored, seeded, and cut into thin strips
2.5 cm (1 in) piece of fresh root ginger, peeled and cut into thin strips
1 garlic clove, crushed
8 spring onions, sliced
2 lemon grass stalks, trimmed, peeled, and sliced
500 g (1 lb) cooked peeled tiger prawns
2 tbsp white wine vinegar
2 tbsp soy sauce
juice of 1/2 lime
1 tbsp sesame oil
3 tbsp chopped fresh coriander to garnish

1 Put the rice noodles into a large saucepan of boiling salted water, stir to separate the noodles, then turn off the heat, cover, and leave to stand for 4 minutes. Drain well and set aside.

2 Heat 1 tbsp of the sunflower oil in a wok or large frying pan. Add the red pepper, carrot, chilli, ginger, garlic, spring onions, and lemon grass, and then stir-fry over a high heat for 2 minutes.

3 Add the prawns, and stir-fry for 1 minute, then stir in the noodles. Add the remaining sunflower oil, the vinegar, soy sauce, lime juice, and sesame oil, and stir-fry for 1 minute.

4 Sprinkle with the chopped fresh coriander, and serve at once.

SCALLOP STIR-FRY

Substitute 750 g (1 1/2 lb) scallops for the tiger prawns. Stir-fry for about 5 minutes, then add the red pepper, carrot, chilli, fresh root ginger, garlic, spring onions, and lemon grass, and stir-fry for a further 2 minutes. Add the drained noodles and proceed as directed in the recipe.

DEVILLED CRAB

 **Serves 4**

- *75 g (2 1/2 oz) butter*
- *1 1/2 tbsp plain flour*
- *175 ml (6 fl oz) milk*
- *1/4 tsp mustard powder*
- *1/4 tsp grated nutmeg*
- *1 egg yolk*
- *1 1/2 tbsp dry sherry*
- *1 tsp Worcestershire sauce*
- *2–3 dashes of Tabasco sauce*
- *4 small cooked crabs, meat removed (page 106) and shells and claws reserved*
- *1 spring onion, thinly sliced*
- *salt and black pepper*
- *125 g (4 oz) fresh breadcrumbs*
- *paprika and lemon wedges to garnish*

1 Melt 45 g (1 1/2 oz) of the butter in a saucepan, add the flour, and cook, stirring, for 1 minute. Remove from the heat, and gradually blend in the milk. Bring to a boil, stirring constantly until the mixture thickens. Simmer for 2–3 minutes. Remove from the heat, and stir in the mustard and nutmeg.

2 Put the egg yolk into a small bowl, and whisk in a little of the sauce. Stir this mixture back into the sauce.

3 Add the dry sherry, Worcestershire sauce, Tabasco sauce, crabmeat, spring onion, and salt and pepper to taste, and stir to mix. Spoon the mixture into the reserved crab shells.

4 Melt the remaining butter in a saucepan, add the breadcrumbs, and cook, stirring, for 5 minutes or until golden brown.

5 Spoon the breadcrumbs over the crabmeat mixture, replace the claws, and bake in a preheated oven at 200°C (400°F, Gas 6) for 10 minutes or until the top is brown and bubbling. Sprinkle with paprika, garnish with lemon wedges, and serve at once.

Cook's know-how

If you cannot find fresh crabs, 750 g (1 1/2 lb) frozen or canned crabmeat can be used instead, or even diced crab sticks. Serve the devilled crab in individual ovenproof ramekins instead of the crab shells, if you prefer.

LOBSTER TAILS WITH MANGO & LIME

 **Serves 4**

- *4 cooked lobster tails*
- *90 ml (3 fl oz) dry white wine*
- *250 ml (8 fl oz) double cream*
- *1 small mango, peeled, stoned, and cut into cubes (page 430)*
- *grated zest and juice of 1 lime*
- *30 g (1 oz) Parmesan cheese, grated*

1 Remove the flesh from the lobster tails (see box, below). With a large, sharp knife, cut the lobster flesh in half lengthwise. Arrange the lobster tail halves cut-side up in a large shallow ovenproof dish.

2 Pour the wine into a small saucepan and boil rapidly until it has reduced to about 2 tbsp.

3 Add the double cream to the saucepan and boil until the mixture has reduced to a coating consistency. Stir in the mango cubes and grated lime zest and juice.

4 Spoon the mixture over the lobster tail halves. Lightly sprinkle with the Parmesan cheese and bake in a preheated oven at 220°C (425°F, Gas 7) for about 20 minutes. Serve at once.

Removing the flesh from a lobster tail

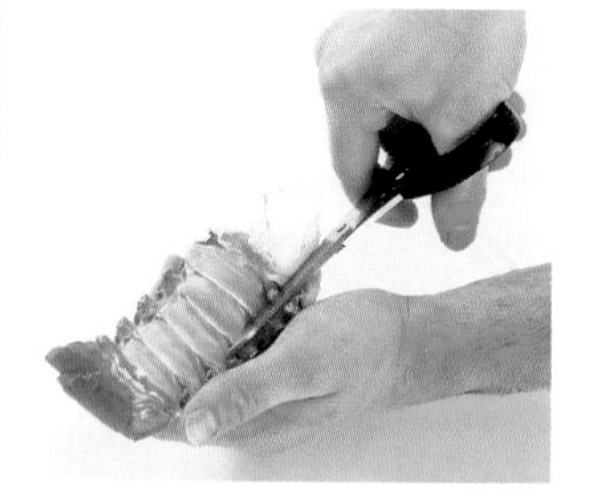

Hold the tail in 1 hand. With a pair of scissors, cut along both sides of the underside of the shell, towards the end, without damaging the flesh.

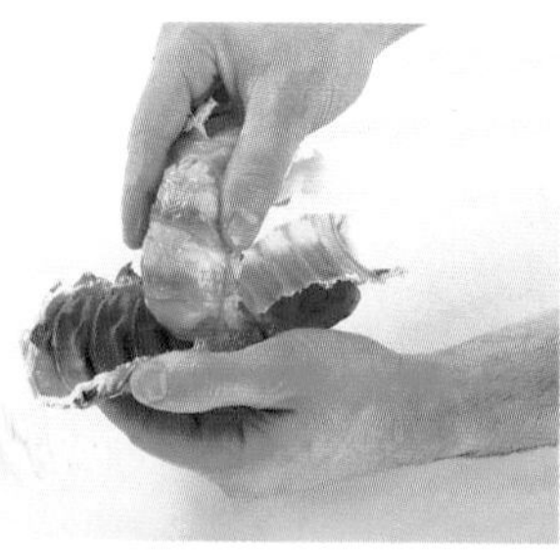

Pull back the underside of the shell, and lift out the lobster flesh, making sure it is all in 1 piece.

Lobster with Black Bean Salsa

Serves 4

4 cooked lobster tails

lime twists and coriander sprigs to garnish

BLACK BEAN SALSA

4 tomatoes, peeled (page 39), seeded, and diced

1/2 onion, chopped

1 garlic clove, crushed

2 tbsp chopped fresh coriander

1 mild fresh green chilli, cored, seeded, and chopped

1/4 tsp ground cumin

1 x 375 g (12 oz) can black beans, drained

salt and black pepper

GARLIC BUTTER

150 g (5 oz) butter

5 garlic cloves, crushed

2 tsp finely chopped fresh oregano

1 Make the black bean salsa: in a bowl, combine the tomatoes, onion, garlic, coriander, chilli, and cumin. Add the beans, and salt and pepper to taste.

2 With a sharp knife, cut each lobster tail in half lengthwise and loosen the flesh, keeping it in the shell.

3 Make the garlic butter: cream the butter in a bowl, add the garlic, oregano, and salt and pepper to taste, and mix well. Spread half of the butter mixture over the lobster flesh.

4 Place the lobster under a hot grill, 10 cm (4 ins) from the heat, and grill for 5 minutes or until slightly browned in patches and heated through.

5 Spread the lobster with the remaining garlic butter, and then garnish with lime twists and coriander sprigs. Serve the lobster at once with the black bean salsa.

Lobster with Refried Beans

Substitute refried beans for the salsa. Heat 1 x 375 g (12 oz) can refried beans with a little water, and 1/4 tsp each ground cumin and chilli powder, then lightly sprinkle with grated Cheddar cheese. Proceed as directed.

Seafood & Avocado Salad

Serves 4

500 g (1 lb) monkfish, trimmed and skinned

150 ml (1/4 pint) fish stock

1 slice of onion

6 black peppercorns

squeeze of lemon juice

1 bay leaf

mixed salad leaves, such as frisée, radicchio, and rocket

2 avocados

lemon juice for brushing

2 large tomatoes, peeled (page 39), seeded, and cut into strips

125 g (4 oz) cooked peeled prawns

90 g (3 oz) white crabmeat

flat-leaf parsley to garnish

CREME FRAICHE DRESSING

125 ml (4 fl oz) crème fraîche

3 tbsp lemon juice

salt and black pepper

1 Put the monkfish into a saucepan with the stock, onion, peppercorns, lemon juice, and bay leaf. Bring to a boil, cover, and poach very gently, turning once, for 10–15 minutes until opaque throughout and firm.

2 Lift the monkfish out of the liquid, leave to cool slightly, then cut the flesh into bite-sized pieces. Leave to cool completely.

3 Make the crème fraîche dressing: put the crème fraîche and lemon juice into a bowl, add salt and pepper to taste, and stir to mix.

4 To serve, arrange the salad leaves on individual plates. Halve, stone (page 68), and peel the avocados, and brush with lemon juice. Slice lengthwise and arrange in a fan shape on the leaves. Add the strips of tomato, the monkfish, prawns, and crabmeat. Spoon the crème fraîche dressing over the salad, garnish with the parsley, and serve at once.

Cook's know-how

The liquid in which the monkfish is poached can be re-used as a good fish stock. When cool, strain the liquid, and freeze it in a small container.

SCALLOPS WITH ASPARAGUS & LEMON

Serves 4

500 g (1 lb) baby asparagus
45 g ($1^1/_2$ oz) butter
3–4 garlic cloves, crushed
750 g ($1^1/_2$ lb) scallops, sliced
juice of 1 lemon
$1^1/_2$ tbsp finely chopped parsley
$1^1/_2$ tbsp chopped fresh tarragon
salt and black pepper

1 Steam the asparagus for 3 minutes or until just tender. Chop and set aside.

2 Melt half of the butter in a pan, add the garlic, and cook for 1 minute. Add the scallops, and cook, stirring, for 1 minute or until opaque and firm to the touch. Add the asparagus and cook for a further 3 minutes. Remove from the pan with a slotted spoon, and keep warm.

3 Add the remaining butter to the pan with the lemon juice, parsley, tarragon, and salt and pepper to taste. Cook, stirring, until the butter melts. Pour the sauce over the scallops and asparagus, and serve at once.

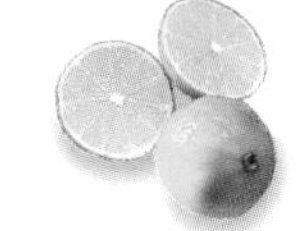

SCALLOPS WITH LIME

Substitute lime juice for the lemon juice, and equal quantities of chopped fresh coriander and mint for the parsley and tarragon. To serve as a starter, simply omit the asparagus, and proceed as directed in the recipe.

SOFT-SHELLED CRABS WITH LEMON

Omit the asparagus, and substitute 4 soft-shelled crabs for the scallops. Dip into seasoned flour. Melt 60 g (2 oz) butter in a large frying pan, then cook the crabs for 4 minutes on each side. Remove from the pan with a slotted spoon, and make the sauce as in step 3 (left).

SCALLOPS WITH SPICY CASHEW SAUCE

Serves 4

100 g ($3^1/_2$ oz) toasted, salted cashew nuts
3 tbsp sunflower oil
1 tsp black mustard seeds
3 garlic cloves, crushed
500 g (1 lb) scallops
1 onion, chopped
1 green pepper, cored, seeded, and cut into thin strips
1 fresh red chilli, cored, seeded, and finely chopped
$^1/_2$ tsp turmeric
250 ml (8 fl oz) fish stock
salt and black pepper

1 Work the cashew nuts in a food processor until smooth.

2 Heat the oil in a large frying pan, add the mustard seeds, and cook until they just begin to pop. Add the garlic and scallops, and stir-fry for 2 minutes or just until the scallops turn opaque. Remove with a slotted spoon, and reserve.

3 Add the onion, green pepper, and chilli to the frying pan, and cook gently, stirring occasionally, for 3–5 minutes until the onion is soft but not coloured. Add the turmeric and cook, stirring, for 1 minute.

4 Add the ground cashew nuts and stock to the mixture in the frying pan, bring to a boil, and simmer for 5–10 minutes until the sauce thickens.

5 Stir the scallops into the sauce, add salt and pepper to taste, and heat gently to warm through. Serve at once.

Cook's know-how

Black mustard seeds, known for their distinctive pungent flavour, are often used in Indian dishes. Brown mustard seeds are more common, however, and may be substituted if black ones are not available.

Mussels with Potatoes & Chorizo

Serves 4

2 tbsp olive oil

2 large potatoes, diced

375 g (12 oz) chorizo sausage, diced

3 garlic cloves, crushed

125 ml (4 fl oz) fish stock

4 tbsp dry sherry

about 2 dozen large mussels, cleaned (page 106)

1/2 tsp cumin seeds

salt and black pepper

chopped fresh coriander to garnish

1 Heat the olive oil in a large saucepan, add the potatoes, and cook gently, stirring from time to time, for 12–15 minutes until golden and softened. Add the chorizo sausage and garlic, and cook, stirring constantly, for about 2 minutes.

2 Add the fish stock, sherry, mussels, cumin seeds, and salt and pepper to taste, cover the saucepan tightly, and bring to a boil. Cook, shaking the saucepan frequently, for 8–10 minutes until the mussels have opened.

3 Discard any mussels that have not opened; do not try to force them open.

4 Transfer the mussel, potato, and chorizo mixture to a large serving dish, and pour the cooking juices over the top. Garnish with coriander and serve hot.

Mussels with Broad Beans

Substitute 375 g (12 oz) young broad beans for the potatoes, and proceed as directed.

Cook's know-how

Chorizo, the Spanish sausage flavoured with paprika and garlic, adds a russet colour to this simple peasant dish of sautéed mussels and potatoes. If chorizo is not available, use another spiced sausage, such as the North African merguez or Polish kabanos.

SPICY CLAMS WITH CORIANDER PESTO

Serves 4–6

4 tbsp olive oil

6 tomatoes, peeled (page 39), seeded, and diced

4 garlic cloves, crushed

2 tbsp paprika

1 tbsp mild red chilli powder

1 tsp ground cumin

about 4 dozen baby clams, cleaned (page 106)

600 ml (1 pint) fish stock

juice of 1/2 lime

CORIANDER PESTO

12 coriander sprigs

2 tbsp olive oil

1 large garlic clove, coarsely chopped

1 mild fresh green chilli, cored, seeded, and chopped

salt and black pepper

1 Make the coriander pesto: strip the coriander leaves from the stalks. Purée the coriander leaves, olive oil, garlic, and green chilli in a food processor or blender until smooth. Add salt and pepper to taste; set aside.

2 Heat the oil in a large saucepan, add the tomatoes and garlic, and cook gently, stirring occasionally, for 8 minutes or until slightly thickened. Stir in the paprika, chilli powder, and ground cumin.

3 Add the clams and stir them in the hot spices for 1 minute, then pour in the stock. Cover the pan tightly, and cook the clams over a medium heat, shaking the pan frequently, for about 12 minutes until the clams open. Discard any that have not opened; do not try to force them open.

4 Using a slotted spoon, transfer the clams to a warmed bowl.

5 Pour the cooking juices into a small pan, and boil until reduced by about half. Add the lime juice, and season to taste, then pour the sauce over the clams.

6 Serve the clams at once, topped with the coriander pesto.

CLAMS IN SALSA VERDE

 **Serves 4**

about 3 dozen clams, cleaned (page 106)

salt and black pepper

chopped parsley to garnish

SALSA VERDE

350 ml (12 fl oz) fish stock

4 tbsp olive oil

3 tbsp dry sherry

5 garlic cloves, chopped

1/2 onion, chopped

60 g (2 oz) plain flour

4 tbsp chopped parsley

1 Make the salsa verde: purée the stock, oil, sherry, garlic, onion, flour, and parsley in a food processor until smooth.

2 Transfer to a pan, bring to a boil, then simmer for 8 minutes or until thickened.

3 Add the clams, cover the pan, and bring to a boil. Cook, shaking the pan, for about 12 minutes until the clams open. Discard any that have not opened; do not try to force them open.

4 Using a slotted spoon, transfer the clams to a warmed tureen. Stir the salsa thoroughly, adding more liquid if it is too thick, or boiling to reduce it if it is not thick enough.

5 Taste the salsa for seasoning. Pour the salsa over the clams, garnish with the chopped parsley, and serve at once.

Cook's know-how

Salsa verde, *meaning "green sauce" in Spanish, also goes very well with grilled fish such as swordfish or tuna. To give it a slightly different flavour, add 3 tbsp pastis or another aniseed-flavoured apéritif instead of the dry sherry.*

CHINESE-STYLE OYSTERS

Serves 4

8 streaky bacon rashers, rinds removed, cut in half

100 g (3 1/2 oz) can smoked oysters, drained

1 small green pepper, cored, seeded, and cut into bite-sized pieces

1 garlic clove, crushed

250 g (8 oz) canned water chestnuts, drained

1 spring onion, thinly sliced

lemon wedges, spring onion tassels (see box, right), and Tabasco sauce to serve

1 Wrap half a bacon rasher around each oyster, and fasten securely with wooden cocktail sticks.

2 Heat a frying pan, add the bacon-wrapped oysters, and cook gently for 6–8 minutes until browned and crisp. Add the green pepper, garlic, and water chestnuts, and stir-fry over a high heat for 2 minutes.

3 Sprinkle with the spring onion slices, and serve with lemon wedges, spring onion tassels, and Tabasco.

Making spring onion tassels

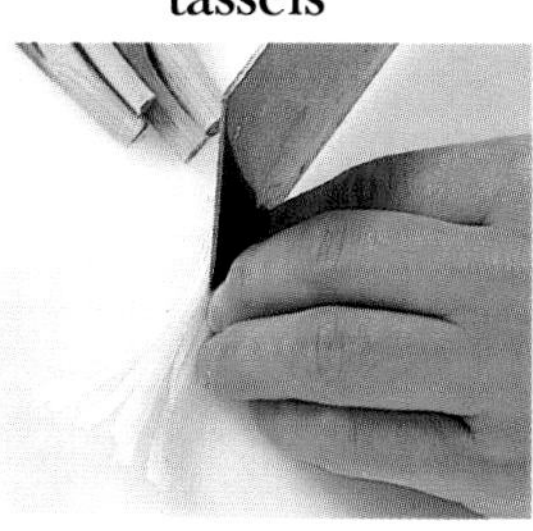

Trim the root end of each spring onion and cut into 5 cm (2 in) lengths. Make several lengthwise cuts at both ends of each piece of onion.

Put into iced water, and chill for 30 minutes or until the ends curl. If you prefer, swirl the tassels in the water to make them open out and curl more.

OYSTER STEW WITH PERNOD & SAFFRON

Serves 4

12 oysters in their shells

350 ml (12 fl oz) single cream

250 ml (8 fl oz) dry white wine

250 ml (8 fl oz) fish stock

1 leek, trimmed and chopped

1/2 carrot, diced

30 g (1 oz) watercress, tough stalks removed, coarsely chopped

pinch of saffron threads

1 tbsp Pernod

1 tbsp lemon juice

salt

pinch of cayenne pepper (optional)

chervil sprigs to garnish

1 Remove the oysters from their shells (page 107), and strain their liquid into a jug. Set aside.

2 Put the cream, wine, stock, leek, and carrot into a saucepan, and bring to a boil. Simmer for 7–10 minutes until the vegetables are just tender.

3 Add the reserved oyster liquid, watercress, saffron, Pernod, lemon juice, salt, and cayenne pepper, if using, to the pan. Bring to a boil, add the oysters, and simmer until the oysters heat through and curl slightly at the edges.

4 Serve at once, garnished with chervil sprigs.

Saffron

Made from the dried stigmas of the saffron crocus, this is the most expensive spice in the world. Over 250,000 flowers must be picked, by hand, to produce 500 g (1 lb) of saffron. Saffron is cultivated in many Mediterranean countries, although Spain is the main producer.

HOT & SOUR MACKEREL

Serves 4

2 carrots

1 red pepper, cored and seeded

1 fresh green chilli, cored and seeded

6 garlic cloves

8 spring onions

1 lemon grass stalk, trimmed and peeled

2 tbsp sunflower oil

4 x 175 g (6 oz) mackerel fillets

coriander sprigs to garnish

HOT AND SOUR SAUCE

4 tbsp Thai fish sauce or light soy sauce

4 tbsp cider vinegar

2 tbsp lime juice

2 tbsp sugar

1 Make the hot and sour sauce: in a small bowl, combine the fish sauce, vinegar, lime juice, and sugar. Cover and set aside.

2 Cut the carrots, red pepper, green chilli, and garlic into matchstick-thin strips. Slice the spring onions, and finely slice the lemon grass.

3 Line a grill pan with foil. Arrange the mackerel on the foil, and cook under a hot grill, 10 cm (4 ins) from the heat, for 3 minutes on each side. Continue to grill until the fish is opaque and the flesh flakes easily. Meanwhile, stir-fry the vegetables.

4 Heat the sunflower oil in a wok or large frying pan. Add the carrots, red pepper, chilli, garlic, spring onions, and lemon grass, and stir-fry over a high heat for 3 minutes or until the vegetables are just tender.

5 Arrange the vegetable mixture on top of the fish, pour the sauce over, garnish with the coriander sprigs, and serve at once.

MACKEREL WITH GOOSEBERRY SAUCE

Serves 4

4 x 250 g (8 oz) mackerel, cleaned, with heads removed (page 105)

salt and black pepper

GOOSEBERRY SAUCE

375 g (12 oz) gooseberries

2 tbsp water

30 g (1 oz) caster sugar, more if needed

30 g (1 oz) butter

1/2 tsp ground ginger

1 Cut the fins off the mackerel, and make 3–4 diagonal cuts on both sides of each fish. Season the mackerel inside and out with salt and pepper.

2 Make the gooseberry sauce: top and tail the gooseberries, and put them into a pan with the water and sugar. Cover tightly and simmer very gently, shaking the pan occasionally, for 5 minutes or until tender.

3 Reserve 12 of the cooked gooseberries for garnish, then work the remainder through a nylon sieve. Beat in the butter and ginger and add more sugar if necessary. Return the sauce to the pan and keep warm.

4 Cook the mackerel under a hot grill, 10 cm (4 ins) from the heat, for 7–8 minutes on each side until the fish is opaque and the flesh flakes easily.

5 Serve the mackerel hot, garnished with the reserved gooseberries. Hand the sauce separately.

MACKEREL WITH CRANBERRY SAUCE

Substitute 375 g (12 oz) fresh or frozen cranberries for the gooseberries, and proceed as directed.

HERRINGS WITH OATMEAL

Serves 4

125 g (4 oz) medium oatmeal
2 tsp mustard powder
salt and black pepper
4 x 175–250 g (6–8 oz) herrings, cleaned (page 105), heads removed, and filleted
8 parsley sprigs
sunflower oil for deep-frying
chopped parsley and lemon wedges to garnish

1 In a shallow dish, combine the oatmeal, mustard powder, and salt and pepper to taste. Open out the herrings and press them into the oatmeal mixture to coat well on both sides.

2 Grill the herrings under a hot grill, 10 cm (4 ins) from the heat, for about 4 minutes on each side or until the fish is opaque and the flesh flakes easily.

3 First making sure they are dry, deep-fry the parsley sprigs (see box, below). Arrange the grilled herrings and deep-fried parsley sprigs on a warmed serving platter, and garnish with the chopped parsley and lemon wedges. Serve the herrings at once.

Deep-frying parsley

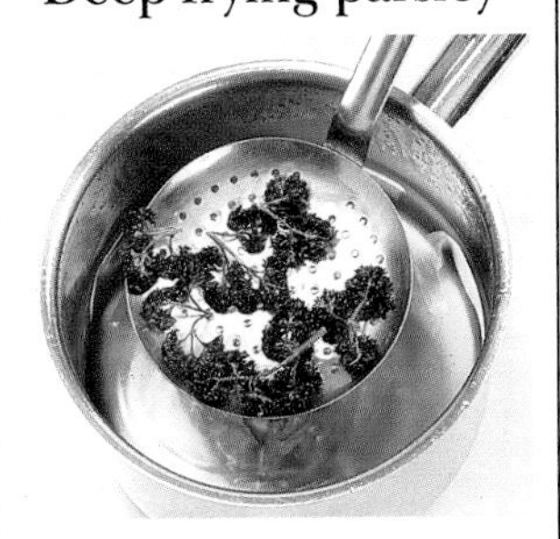

Heat 5 cm (2 ins) oil in a large saucepan. Add the parsley sprigs, and deep-fry for 30 seconds or until crisp. Lift out with a slotted spoon and drain on paper towels.

HERRINGS WITH MUSTARD SAUCE

Serves 4

4 x 175–250 g (6–8 oz) herrings, cleaned (page 105), heads removed, and filleted
salt and black pepper
butter for greasing
lemon wedges and parsley sprigs to garnish

MUSTARD SAUCE
30 g (1 oz) butter
30 g (1 oz) plain flour
300 ml (1/2 pint) milk
2 tsp mustard powder
1 tsp caster sugar
2 tsp white wine vinegar

1 Season the herrings inside and out with salt and black pepper, fold the fish over, and place in a single layer in a buttered ovenproof dish.

2 Cover and bake in a preheated oven at 200°C (400°F, Gas 6) for 12 minutes or until the fish is opaque and the flesh flakes easily.

3 Meanwhile, make the mustard sauce: melt the butter in a saucepan, add the flour, and cook, stirring, for 1 minute. Remove from the heat and gradually blend in the milk. Bring to a boil, stirring constantly until the mixture thickens. Simmer for 2–3 minutes. Add the mustard powder, sugar, vinegar, and salt and pepper to taste, and cook for a further minute.

4 To serve, garnish the herrings with lemon wedges and parsley sprigs, and hand the mustard sauce separately.

Cook's know-how

For a milder tasting sauce, substitute 2 tsp Dijon mustard for the mustard powder.

BAKED TROUT WITH ORANGE

Serves 4

- *4 x 375–425 g (12–14 oz) trout, cleaned (page 105)*
- *4 large thyme sprigs*
- *4 large parsley sprigs*
- *125 g (4 oz) button mushrooms, sliced*
- *2 shallots, chopped*
- *4 tbsp white wine vinegar*
- *grated zest and juice of 1 orange*
- *salt and black pepper*
- *orange slices and thyme sprigs to garnish*

1 With a knife, make 2 diagonal cuts in the flesh on both sides of each trout.

2 Strip the thyme and parsley leaves from their stalks. In a bowl, combine the mushrooms, shallots, white wine vinegar, orange zest and juice, thyme and parsley leaves, and salt and pepper to taste.

3 Reserve one-quarter of the mushroom and herb mixture to spoon over the stuffed trout.

4 Stuff the trout with the remaining mushroom and herb mixture (see box, below).

5 Arrange the trout in a non-metallic ovenproof dish and spoon over the reserved mushroom mixture. Cover and chill for 4 hours.

6 Bake in a preheated oven at 180°C (350°F, Gas 4) for 20–25 minutes until the fish is opaque and the flesh flakes easily. Garnish with orange slices and thyme sprigs, and serve at once.

Stuffing the trout

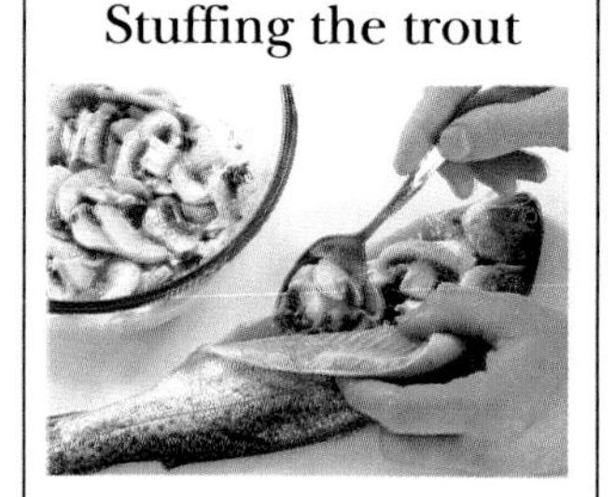

Hold open the stomach of each trout with 1 hand, and spoon in one-quarter of the mushroom and herb mixture.

GRILLED TROUT WITH CUCUMBER & DILL

Serves 4

- *1 cucumber, peeled*
- *30 g (1 oz) butter*
- *small bunch of fresh dill, chopped*
- *salt and black pepper*
- *juice of 1 lemon*
- *4 x 375–425 g (12–14 oz) trout, cleaned (page 105)*
- *dill sprigs and fresh chives to garnish*
- *dill cream sauce (page 128) to serve*

1 Cut the cucumber in half lengthwise, scoop out the seeds, and cut the flesh into 5 mm (1/4 in) slices. Melt the butter in a saucepan, add the cucumber, and cook gently for 2 minutes.

2 In a bowl, combine two-thirds of the cooked cucumber with the chopped dill, add salt and pepper to taste, and sprinkle with the lemon juice. Stuff the trout with the mixture.

3 Line a grill pan with foil. Arrange the trout on the foil, and put the remaining cucumber around them.

4 Grill the trout under a hot grill, 10 cm (4 ins) from the heat, for 4–7 minutes on each side until the flesh flakes easily.

5 Garnish the trout with dill sprigs and fresh chives, and serve at once, with dill cream sauce handed separately.

TROUT WITH ALMONDS

Dip the trout in seasoned flour. Melt 60 g (2 oz) butter in a large frying pan, and cook the trout, in batches if necessary, for 6–8 minutes on each side until the fish is opaque and the flesh flakes easily. Drain on paper towels, and keep warm. Wipe the pan, melt 15 g (1/2 oz) butter, and fry 60 g (2 oz) flaked almonds until lightly browned. Add a squeeze of lemon juice, then pour the lemon and almond mixture over the trout. Serve at once.

TUNA WITH FENNEL & TOMATO RELISH

 **Serves 4**

4 tbsp olive oil
juice of 1/2 lemon
3 garlic cloves, crushed
1/2 tsp herbes de Provence
4 x 175 g (6 oz) tuna steaks, about 2.5 cm (1 in) thick
salt and black pepper
lime wedges and dill sprigs to garnish

FENNEL AND TOMATO RELISH
1 small fennel bulb, chopped
2 tomatoes, peeled (page 39), seeded, and diced
2 tbsp olive oil
1 tbsp lemon juice
1 tbsp black olive paste
1 garlic clove, chopped

1 Combine the olive oil, lemon juice, garlic, and herbes de Provence in a large non-metallic dish. Add the tuna steaks and turn to coat. Cover and leave to marinate in the refrigerator, turning occasionally, for about 1 hour.

2 Meanwhile, make the relish: put the fennel, tomatoes, olive oil, lemon juice, black olive paste, and garlic into a bowl, and stir well to combine.

3 Remove the tuna steaks from the marinade, reserving the marinade. Cook the steaks under a hot grill, 7 cm (3 ins) from the heat, basting once or twice with the reserved marinade, for 3–4 minutes on each side.

4 Season the steaks with salt and pepper to taste, and top with the fennel and tomato relish. Garnish with lime wedges and dill sprigs, and serve at once.

Black olive paste

This originally comes from Provence, where it is commonly known as tapenade. *It is a deliciously tangy blend of olives, anchovies, and capers, puréed with olive oil.*

TUNA TERIYAKI

Serves 4

4 x 175 g (6 oz) tuna steaks, about 2.5 cm (1 in) thick
2 spring onions, thinly sliced, to garnish

MARINADE
3 tbsp dark soy sauce
2 tbsp sesame oil
1 tbsp Japanese rice wine or sweet sherry
3 garlic cloves, chopped
1 tbsp caster sugar
1 cm (1/2 in) piece of fresh root ginger, peeled and chopped

1 Make the marinade: put the soy sauce, sesame oil, rice wine, garlic, sugar, and ginger into a non-metallic dish. Add the tuna steaks to the marinade and turn to coat. Cover and marinate in the refrigerator for 8 hours.

2 Reserve the marinade. Cook the steaks under a hot grill, 7 cm (3 ins) from the heat, brushing with the marinade, for 3–4 minutes on each side. Serve at once, garnished with spring onions.

BARBECUED SALMON TERIYAKI

Make the marinade as directed. Cut 750 g (1 1/2 lb) salmon fillet into 2.5 cm (1 in) cubes. Cover and leave to marinate in the refrigerator for 8 hours. Thread on to metal skewers. Cook over a hot barbecue, turning and brushing frequently with the marinade, for 6–8 minutes.

Teriyaki

This is a traditional Japanese marinade, used to flavour meat, poultry, or fish that is to be grilled, barbecued, or fried. When heated, the sugar in the marinade makes a thick and glossy glaze.

SWORDFISH WITH ORANGE RELISH

 **Serves 4**

4 x 175 g (6 oz) swordfish steaks

MARINADE

3 tbsp olive oil

juice of 1 orange

juice of 1 lemon

3 garlic cloves, crushed

salt and black pepper

ORANGE RELISH

2 oranges, peeled, separated into segments, and diced

3 tbsp olive oil

2 tbsp chopped fresh basil

1 Make the marinade: in a shallow non-metallic dish, combine the olive oil, orange and lemon juices, garlic, and salt and pepper to taste. Turn the swordfish steaks in the marinade, cover, and leave to marinate in the refrigerator for at least 1 hour.

2 Make the orange relish: in a bowl, combine the oranges, olive oil, basil, and season with salt and pepper to taste.

3 Remove the swordfish from the marinade, reserving the marinade. Place the steaks under a hot grill, 7 cm (3 ins) from the heat, and grill, basting once or twice with the marinade, for 5 minutes on each side or until the fish is opaque and the flesh flakes easily. Serve at once, with the relish.

TUNA WITH ORANGE RELISH

Substitute tuna steaks for the swordfish steaks, and fresh coriander for the basil, and proceed as directed.

Cook's know-how

Swordfish has a meaty texture and a mild flavour. Its firmness makes it ideal for grilling, baking, or poaching.

SHARK WITH TROPICAL SALSA

Serves 4

4 x 175 g (6 oz) shark steaks

MARINADE

125 ml (4 fl oz) olive oil

juice of 1/2 lemon

3 garlic cloves, crushed

1 tbsp shredded fresh coriander

1 tsp ground cumin

pinch of cayenne pepper

salt and black pepper

TROPICAL SALSA

1 x 275 g (9 oz) can pineapple pieces in natural juices, drained

1 small ripe papaya, peeled, seeded, and diced

1 small red pepper, cored, seeded, and diced

1 mild fresh red or green chilli, cored, seeded, and diced

2 tbsp chopped fresh coriander

1 tbsp white wine vinegar

sugar (optional)

1 Make the marinade: in a shallow non-metallic dish, combine the oil, lemon juice, garlic, coriander, cumin, cayenne pepper, and salt and black pepper to taste.

2 Turn the shark steaks in the marinade, cover, and marinate in the refrigerator for at least 1 hour.

3 Make the tropical salsa: in a large bowl, combine the pineapple, papaya, red pepper, chilli, coriander, vinegar, and salt and pepper to taste. If the fruit is tart, add a little sugar.

4 Remove the steaks from the marinade, reserving the marinade. Place the steaks under a hot grill, 7 cm (3 ins) from the heat, basting once or twice with the marinade, for 3–4 minutes on each side until the fish is opaque and the flesh flakes easily. Serve with the salsa.

SHARK WITH FRUITY SALSA

Peel, segment, and finely chop 1 orange. Mix with 250 g (8 oz) chopped cranberries and 125 g (4 oz) sugar. Chill for a few hours. Cook the shark as directed above, and serve with the fruity salsa.

KOULIBIAC

This is a type of salmon kedgeree enclosed in crisp puff pastry, which makes an impressive dish for a dinner party or other special occasion. In Russia, its country of origin, there is a saying, "Houses make a fine street, pies make a fine table".

Serves 8–10

75 g (2 1/2 oz) long grain rice

salt and black pepper

60 g (2 oz) butter, plus extra for greasing

1 large onion, chopped

1 x 400 g (13 oz) can chopped tomatoes, drained

500 g (1 lb) salmon, cooked and flaked

2 tbsp chopped parsley

grated zest and juice of 1 lemon

500 g (1 lb) puff pastry

1 egg, beaten

60 g (2 oz) butter, melted, and juice of 1/2 lemon to serve

lemon twists and watercress sprigs to garnish

1 Cook the rice in boiling salted water, covered tightly, for 12 minutes or until just tender.

2 Meanwhile, melt the butter in a saucepan, add the onion, and cook gently for a few minutes until soft but not coloured. Add the tomatoes and cook for 15 minutes. Leave to cool.

3 Drain the rice thoroughly, and combine with the onion and tomato mixture, the flaked salmon, parsley, lemon zest and juice, and salt and pepper to taste.

4 Roll out 425 g (14 oz) of the puff pastry into a 28 x 40 cm (11 x 16 in) rectangle.

5 Arrange the salmon mixture down the middle of the rectangle, leaving a 7 cm (3 in) border on each side. Brush the border with a little of the beaten egg, and wrap and decorate the koulibiac (see box, right).

6 Bake the koulibiac in a preheated oven at 220°C (425°F, Gas 7) for 30–45 minutes until golden.

7 Transfer to a warmed serving dish, and pour the melted butter and lemon juice into the cuts. Serve in thick slices, garnished with lemon twists and watercress.

Koulibiac

This became popular in western Europe in the mid 19th century. Described as "a salmon pie in the Russian manner", authentic versions contain layers of fish, buckwheat, hard-boiled eggs, and vesiga, *the dried spinal cord of the sturgeon. In Russia, other fish, such as sturgeon and pike-perch, were sometimes used instead of salmon.*

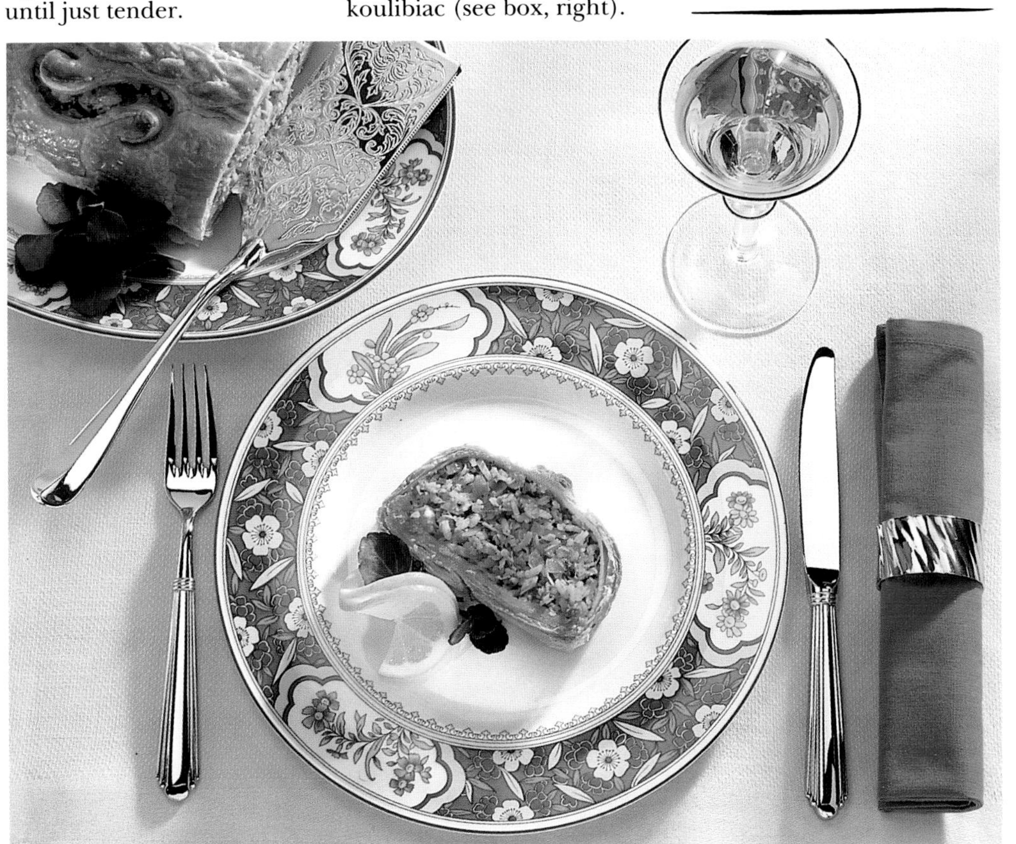

Wrapping and decorating the koulibiac

Fold the shortest ends of pastry over the salmon filling and brush the top of the folded pastry with beaten egg.

Fold the longest sides over the filling to make a long parcel. Turn the parcel over and place on a lightly buttered baking tray. Brush all over with beaten egg.

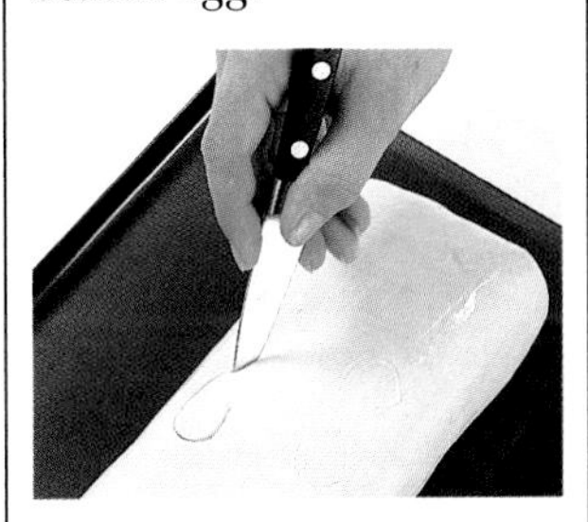

Make 2 decorative cuts in the top of the pastry. Roll the remaining pastry into a 5 x 30 cm (2 x 12 in) piece, trim, then cut into 3 equal strips. Press the ends together and plait the strips. Lay the plait down the middle of the parcel, and glaze with beaten egg.

SALMON WITH SPINACH

Serves 4

4 x 175 g (6 oz) salmon steaks

salt and black pepper

15 g (1/2 oz) butter

lemon twists to garnish

SPINACH SALSA

2 tbsp olive oil

8 spring onions, finely sliced

1 garlic clove, crushed

4 tbsp lemon juice

1 tsp wholegrain mustard

500 g (1 lb) spinach, finely chopped

1 Season the salmon steaks with black pepper and dot with the butter.

2 Cook the salmon steaks under a hot grill, 7 cm (3 ins) from the heat, for 5–6 minutes on each side until the fish is opaque and the flesh flakes easily.

3 Meanwhile, make the spinach salsa: heat the oil in a frying pan, add the spring onions and garlic, and cook, stirring, for about 1 minute. Stir in the lemon juice, mustard, and spinach, and cook, stirring, for about 2 minutes. Transfer to a bowl, and season with salt and pepper to taste.

4 Garnish the salmon with lemon twists and serve at once, with the salsa.

SEVERN SALMON

Tail end of salmon served with a creamy watercress sauce makes an excellent dish for a summer dinner, simple to prepare, elegant to look at, and delicious to eat. The salmon is baked in the oven with a foil covering to keep it moist.

Serves 6

750 g (1 1/2 lb) tail end of salmon, skinned

butter for greasing

salt and black pepper

watercress sprigs to garnish

WATERCRESS CREAM SAUCE

300 ml (1/2 pint) single cream

60 g (2 oz) watercress, tough stalks removed

90 g (3 oz) butter, melted

1 tsp plain flour

juice of 1 lemon

1 egg yolk

1 Divide the salmon into 6 pieces (see box, right).

2 Butter a roasting tin. Arrange the salmon pieces in a single layer, and sprinkle with black pepper.

3 Cover tightly with foil, and bake in a preheated oven at 180°C (350°F, Gas 4) for 15–20 minutes until the fish is opaque and the flesh flakes easily.

4 Meanwhile, make the watercress cream sauce: purée the cream, watercress, butter, flour, lemon juice, egg yolk, and salt and pepper to taste in a food processor until smooth.

5 Transfer the cream and watercress mixture to a small saucepan, and cook over a gentle heat, stirring, until the sauce thickens. Taste for seasoning.

6 Serve the salmon at once, on a bed of watercress cream sauce, garnished with watercress sprigs.

Dividing a salmon tail into 6 pieces

Put the salmon on to a chopping board, and slice it crosswise in half.

Cut the tail end crosswise in half. Cut the thicker section crosswise in half, then lengthwise in half, making 4 pieces.

SALMON EN CROUTE

Serves 6

- *1.7–2 kg (3½–4 lb) salmon, cleaned and filleted (page 105), skinned*
- *1 tbsp chopped fresh dill*
- *grated zest and juice of 1 lemon*
- *salt and black pepper*
- *30 g (1 oz) butter*
- *8 spring onions, sliced*
- *250 g (8 oz) spinach, coarsely shredded*
- *250 g (8 oz) low-fat soft cheese*
- *plain flour for dusting*
- *750 g (1½ lb) puff pastry*
- *1 egg, beaten*
- *lemon slices, cherry tomatoes, and parsley sprigs to garnish*

1 Put the salmon fillets into a shallow non-metallic dish and sprinkle with the dill, lemon zest and juice, and salt and pepper to taste. Cover and leave to marinate in the refrigerator for at least 1 hour.

2 Melt the butter in a small saucepan, add the spring onions, and cook gently for 2–3 minutes until soft but not coloured.

3 Add the spinach, toss in the butter, and remove from the heat. Leave to cool, then stir in the cheese. Add salt and pepper to taste.

4 Lightly dust a work surface with flour, and roll out half of the pastry to a 20 x 38 cm (8 x 15 in) rectangle. Put the pastry on a baking tray, and place 1 salmon fillet on top. Spread with the spinach and cheese mixture, then put the second salmon fillet on top. Brush the pastry border with a little of the beaten egg.

5 Roll out the remaining pastry to a slightly larger rectangle, cover the salmon completely, then seal the edges.

6 Decorate and trim the pastry (see box, right). Brush the pastry with the beaten egg and bake in a preheated oven at 200°C (400°F, Gas 6) for 40–45 minutes until the pastry is well risen and golden brown.

7 Garnish with lemon slices, cherry tomatoes, and parsley sprigs.

Decorating and trimming the pastry

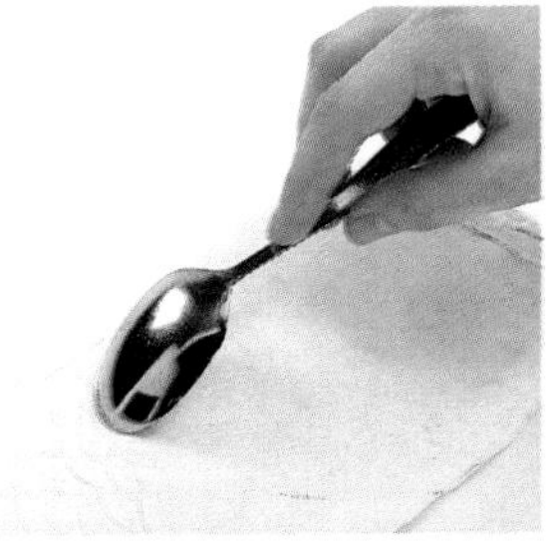

Mark "scales" all over the fish, using the rounded edge of a dessertspoon. Make 2 small holes in the top of the pastry to allow the steam to escape.

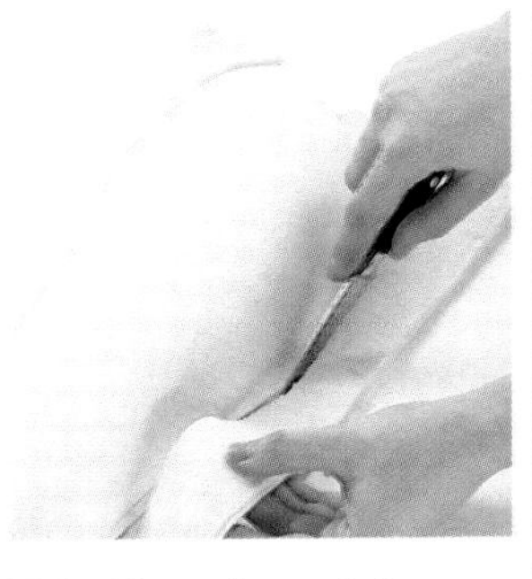

Trim the edges of the pastry to form a fish shape. If you prefer, make fins from the trimmings and attach with beaten egg.

SALMON WITH AVOCADO

Serves 4

- *30 g (1 oz) butter, melted*
- *4 x 175 g (6 oz) salmon steaks*
- *salt and black pepper*
- *4 tarragon sprigs*
- *4 slices of lime*

AVOCADO SAUCE

- *2 avocados, halved, stoned (page 68), and peeled*
- *150 ml (¼ pint) plain yogurt*
- *grated zest and juice of 1 lime*

1 Brush 4 large squares of foil with melted butter. Put a salmon steak on each square, season, and top with a tarragon sprig and a slice of lime. Wrap the foil around the salmon. Put on a baking tray, and bake in a preheated oven at 150°C (300°F, Gas 2) for 25 minutes or until the fish is opaque and the flesh flakes easily.

2 Meanwhile, make the avocado sauce: put the flesh of 1 avocado into a food processor with the yogurt, lime zest and juice, and salt and pepper to taste, and purée until smooth. Transfer to a serving bowl. Dice the remaining avocado, and stir into the sauce.

3 Unwrap the salmon, transfer to warmed serving plates, and serve with the avocado sauce.

Poached Salmon with Dill Mayonnaise

This is the perfect dish for a buffet party. The salmon is gently poached, with the skin and head for added flavour, and left to cool in the cooking liquid to keep it moist. Fish kettles can be hired from good fishmongers or from the fish counters of some large supermarkets.

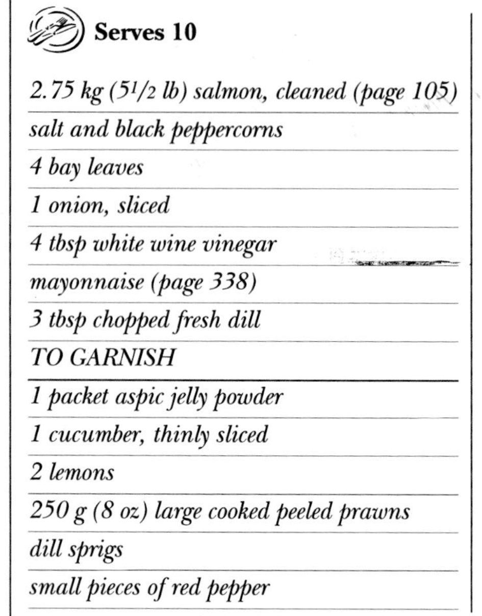

Serves 10

- *2.75 kg (5½ lb) salmon, cleaned (page 105)*
- *salt and black peppercorns*
- *4 bay leaves*
- *1 onion, sliced*
- *4 tbsp white wine vinegar*
- *mayonnaise (page 338)*
- *3 tbsp chopped fresh dill*

TO GARNISH

- *1 packet aspic jelly powder*
- *1 cucumber, thinly sliced*
- *2 lemons*
- *250 g (8 oz) large cooked peeled prawns*
- *dill sprigs*
- *small pieces of red pepper*

1 Lift out the rack from a fish kettle and set aside. Half fill the kettle with cold water and add 2 tbsp salt, 12 black peppercorns, the bay leaves, onion, and vinegar.

2 Put the salmon on to the rack, and lower into the kettle. Bring to a boil, then simmer for 1 minute only. Remove from the heat, cover, and leave to stand for about 2 hours, until the fish is just warm.

3 Lift the rack and salmon out of the fish kettle. Strain the cooking liquid and reserve. Cover the salmon with a large piece of cling film and flip the fish over on to the cling film. Bone and skin the salmon (see box, below). Cover and chill in the refrigerator for at least 1 hour.

4 Reserve 2 tbsp of the mayonnaise. Add the dill to the remaining mayonnaise, put into a serving bowl, and chill until ready to serve.

5 Make up the aspic according to packet instructions, using 600 ml (1 pint) of the cooking liquid. Arrange the cucumber slices over the fish to represent scales. When the aspic has just started to thicken, brush a thin glaze over the fish and cucumber. Leave to set, then brush another layer of aspic over the fish and cucumber.

6 Cut lengthwise grooves in the lemons with a canelle knife, cut in half lengthwise and slice. Garnish the salmon with the lemon slices, prawns, reserved mayonnaise, dill sprigs, and red pepper. Serve with the mayonnaise.

Boning and skinning a salmon

1 Using a chef's knife, neatly remove the head from the salmon.

2 Run the knife along the backbone of the fish to loosen the top fillet.

3 Flip the top fillet over and remove the bones from the fish.

4 Use the cling film to flip the bottom fillet back on to the top and remove the skin and any dark flesh.

5 Use the cling film to flip the fish on to a large serving plate, and remove the remaining skin.

6 With a small knife, gently scrape away the brownish flesh, leaving behind only the pink flesh.

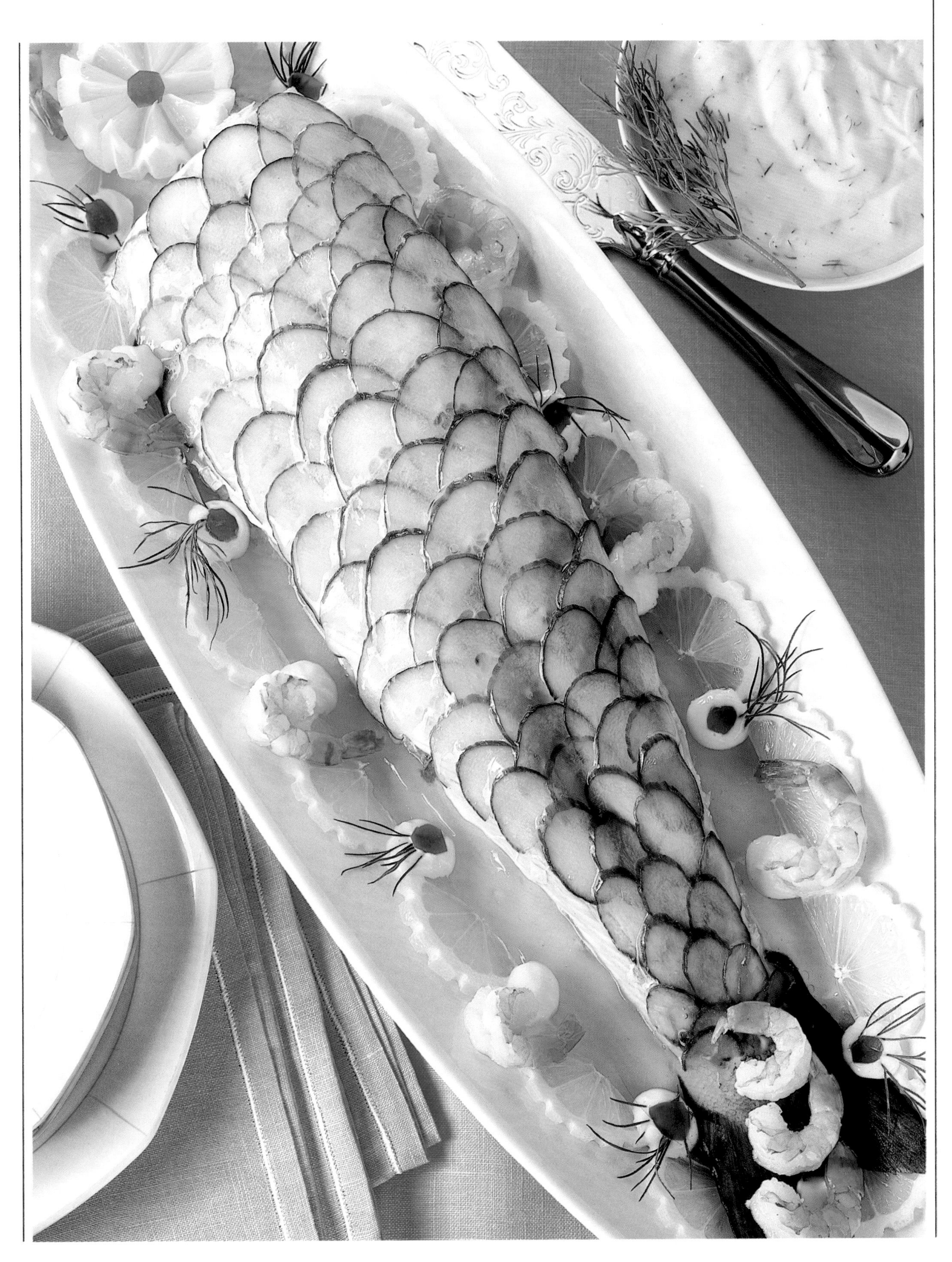

Fillets of Sole Meuniere

Serves 4

- *60 g (2 oz) plain flour*
- *salt and black pepper*
- *4 small lemon sole, skinned, each cut into 4 fillets (page 105)*
- *60 g (2 oz) butter*
- *1 tbsp chopped parsley*
- *juice of 1/2 lemon*
- *lemon twists and parsley sprigs to garnish*

1 Sprinkle the flour on to a plate and season with salt and pepper. Dip the fillets into the seasoned flour and shake off any excess.

2 Melt half of the butter in a large frying pan. When it is foaming, add the fillets, and cook for 2 minutes on each side or until the fish is opaque and the flesh flakes easily. Transfer to warmed serving plates and keep warm.

3 Wipe the pan with paper towels. Melt the remaining butter and heat quickly until golden. Stir in the parsley and lemon juice, then pour over the fillets. Serve at once, garnished with lemon twists (see box, below) and parsley sprigs.

Making a lemon twist

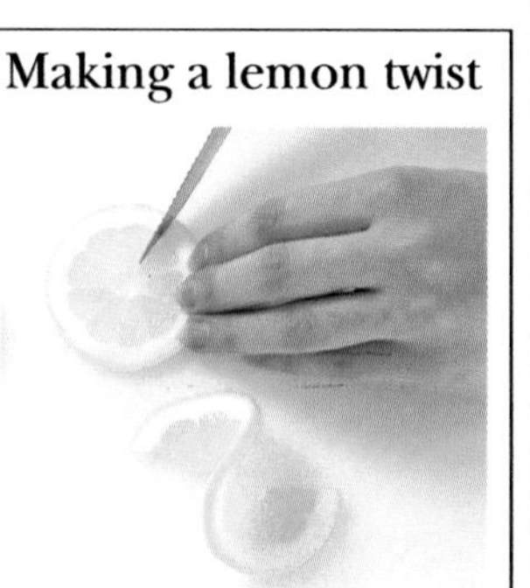

Slice a lemon thinly, then cut from the centre to the edge of each slice. Gently twist the lemon to form a curved shape.

Mushroom-Stuffed Sole Fillets

Serves 4

- *60 g (2 oz) butter*
- *1 onion, finely chopped*
- *375 g (12 oz) mushrooms, finely chopped*
- *2 large sole, skinned, each cut into 4 fillets (page 105)*
- *250 ml (8 fl oz) dry white wine*
- *2 tsp chopped fresh tarragon*
- *salt and black pepper*
- *250 ml (8 fl oz) double cream*
- *squeeze of lemon juice*

1 Melt half of the butter in a saucepan, add the onion and mushrooms, and cook gently for 5 minutes.

2 Roll the fillets (see box, right). Stand the rolls in a shallow ovenproof dish and fill them with the mushroom mixture.

3 Add the wine, tarragon, and salt and pepper to taste. Cover with foil and bake in a preheated oven at 180°C (350°F, Gas 4) for 15 minutes or until opaque and the flesh flakes easily.

4 Remove the fish from the dish and keep warm. Pour the juices into a saucepan and boil for 3 minutes or until reduced by half. Stir in the cream and lemon juice, taste for seasoning, and serve at once.

Rolling the fillets

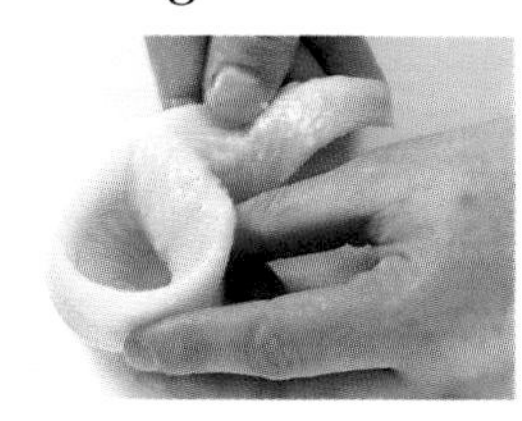

Bring round the 2 ends of each fillet to form a circle, with the smaller tail end on the outside.

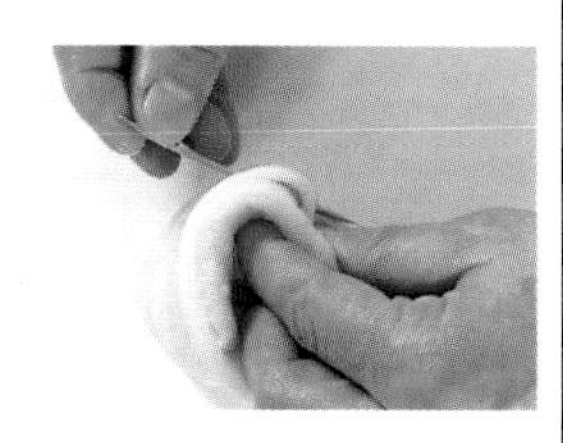

Thread a wooden cocktail stick through both ends of each fillet, to secure.

LEMON SOLE FLORENTINE

Fillets of lemon sole are topped with a cheese sauce and baked on a bed of spinach, so they stay moist while cooking. Slices of hot lemon bread – an interesting variation of garlic bread – make an unusual accompaniment.

Serves 4

4 large lemon sole fillets, skinned (page 105)

juice of 1/2 lemon

salt and black pepper

45 g (11/2 oz) butter

45 g (11/2 oz) plain flour

450 ml (3/4 pint) milk

750 g (11/2 lb) spinach

30 g (1 oz) Parmesan cheese, grated

hot lemon bread to serve (see box, below)

1 Sprinkle the lemon sole fillets with the lemon juice and salt and pepper. Fold the fillets in half crosswise, and set aside.

2 Melt the butter in a saucepan, add the flour, and cook, stirring, for 1 minute. Remove from the heat and gradually blend in the milk. Bring to a boil, stirring constantly until the white sauce mixture thickens. Simmer for 2–3 minutes, then add salt and pepper to taste.

3 Wash the spinach and put into a pan with only the water remaining on the leaves. Cook for 2 minutes or until wilted. Drain well.

4 Stir half of the sauce into the cooked spinach and spoon into a shallow ovenproof dish. Arrange the sole on top. Pour the remaining sauce over the top and sprinkle with the cheese. Bake in a preheated oven at 200°C (400°F, Gas 6) for 30–40 minutes. Serve hot, with hot lemon bread.

Hot lemon bread

Beat the *grated zest of 1/2 lemon* into *125 g (4 oz) softened butter,* using a fork. Slowly add the *juice of 1/2 lemon,* beating between each addition. Add *salt and pepper to taste.*

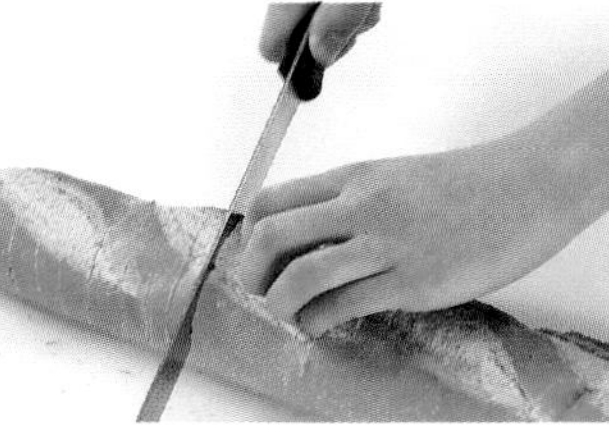

Cut *1 baguette* into 1 cm (1/2 in) slices, leaving the slices attached at the bottom.

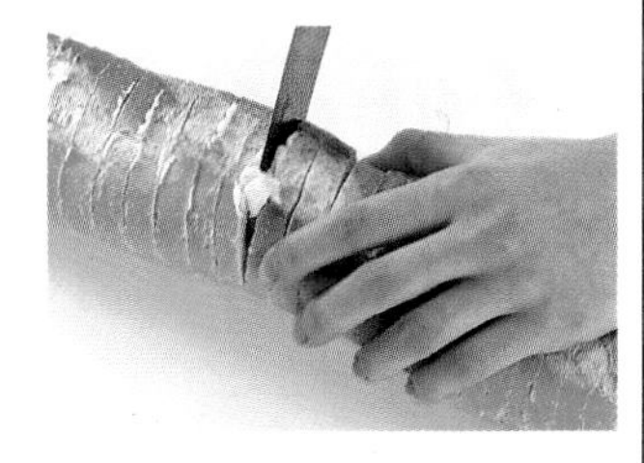

Spread the butter over the slices, and a little over the top. Wrap in foil and bake in a preheated oven at 200°C (400°F, Gas 6) for 20 minutes, opening the foil for the last 5 minutes to crisp the top.

GINGERED PLAICE

Serves 4

4 large plaice fillets

sliced spring onions and spring onion tassels (page 115) to garnish

GINGER MARINADE

2.5 cm (1 in) piece of fresh root ginger, peeled and finely sliced

1 large garlic clove, sliced

2 tbsp sunflower oil

1 tbsp sesame oil

1 tbsp dry sherry

1 tbsp sherry vinegar

2 tsp light soy sauce

1 Put the plaice fillets into a shallow non-metallic dish.

2 Make the marinade: combine the ginger, garlic, sunflower and sesame oils, sherry, sherry vinegar, and soy sauce, and pour over the fish.

3 Cover the fish and leave to marinate in the refrigerator, turning once, for 30 minutes.

4 Grill the fillets, skin-side down, under a hot grill, 7 cm (3 ins) from the heat, for 4–5 minutes, until the fish is opaque and the flesh flakes easily.

5 Serve hot, garnished with sliced spring onions and spring onion tassels.

BEST-EVER FRIED FISH

These plaice fillets are shallow-fried in a crisp coating of fresh breadcrumbs. This is far superior to a batter coating in both flavour and texture, and it protects the fish from the heat of the fat, and keeps it moist, in the same way as batter.

 **Serves 4**

- *3 tbsp plain flour*
- *salt and black pepper*
- *1 large egg, beaten*
- *30 g (1 oz) fresh white breadcrumbs*
- *4 large plaice fillets, skinned*
- *2 tbsp sunflower oil*
- *lemon wedges to garnish*

1 Sprinkle the flour into a shallow dish and season with salt and pepper. Pour the beaten egg into another dish, and sprinkle the breadcrumbs into a third.

2 Lightly coat the fish fillets with breadcrumbs (see box, below).

3 Heat the oil in a large frying pan, add the coated fillets, in 2 batches if necessary, and fry over a high heat for 2–3 minutes on each side until they are crisp, golden, and juicy inside.

4 Lift the fillets out of the frying pan with a fish slice and then leave to drain briefly on paper towels. Serve the fish at once, garnished with the lemon wedges.

Fish and chips

Fried fish was first served with chips in the 19th century. In 1968 the National Federation of Fish Fryers presented a plaque to Malin's, in the East End of London, to mark 100 years of fish and chips, describing the shop as the world's oldest purveyor of fish and chips.

Coating a fish fillet

Dip the fillet into the seasoned flour, to coat. Shake off any excess.

Dip the floured fillet into the beaten egg, letting any excess drain off.

Dip the fillet into the breadcrumbs, making sure it is evenly coated.

SAUCES FOR FISH

DILL CREAM SAUCE

Purée *300 ml (1/2 pint) single cream, 90 g (3 oz) butter, 1 egg yolk, the juice of 1 lemon,* and *1 tsp plain flour* in a food processor until smooth. Transfer the mixture to a small saucepan and heat very gently, stirring constantly, until the sauce has thickened and will coat the back of a spoon. Add *salt and pepper to taste,* then stir in *2 tbsp chopped fresh dill* and *1 tbsp snipped fresh chives.*

TARTARE SAUCE

Purée *1 egg, 1 1/2 tsp sugar, 1/2 tsp mustard powder,* and *salt and pepper to taste* in a food processor or blender until smooth. Add *300 ml (1/2 pint) sunflower oil,* pouring in a steady stream, and purée until the mixture is very thick and all of the oil has been incorporated. Add *the juice of 1 lemon,* and purée. Transfer to a bowl, and stir in *1 tbsp each chopped gherkins, capers, and parsley,* and *2 tbsp chopped fresh tarragon.* Cover and leave to stand for at least 1 hour to allow the flavours to blend.

INDIAN SPICED HADDOCK

Serves 4

750 g (1½ lb) thick pieces of haddock fillet, skinned
1 tsp cumin seeds
1 tsp coriander seeds
pinch of cayenne pepper
¼ tsp turmeric
1 tsp salt
2 tbsp sunflower oil
1 small onion, sliced
2.5 cm (1 in) piece of fresh root ginger, peeled and finely chopped
1 fresh green chilli, cored, seeded, and finely chopped
1 small cauliflower, cut into small florets
2 potatoes, diced
1 large green pepper, cored, seeded, and cut into strips
150 ml (¼ pint) water
black pepper
Greek yogurt to serve

1 Cut the haddock into 5 cm (2 in) squares and put them into a bowl.

2 Crush the spices and salt (see box, right). Sprinkle the mixture over the haddock, stir to coat evenly, cover, and leave to marinate in the refrigerator for 1 hour.

Crushing the spices

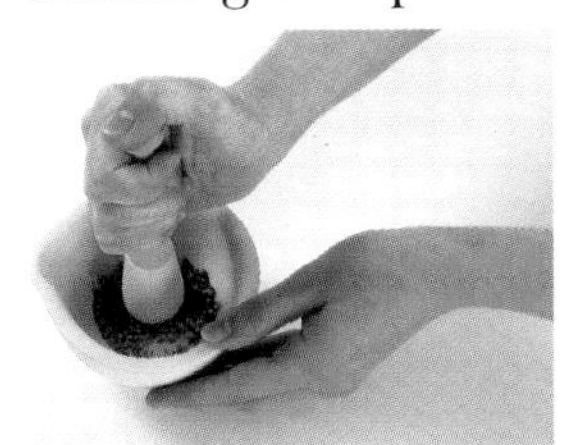

Crush the cumin and coriander seeds, cayenne pepper, turmeric, and salt until finely ground, using a pestle and mortar.

3 Heat half of the oil in a frying pan, add the onion, and cook over a high heat for 5 minutes. Stir in the ginger and chilli and cook for 2 minutes. Add the cauliflower, potatoes, and green pepper and cook for 5–7 minutes. Remove the vegetables with a slotted spoon and set aside.

4 Heat the remaining oil, add the haddock and brown lightly all over. Add the cooked vegetables and measured water, and simmer for 10 minutes or until the fish is cooked and the vegetables are tender. Taste for seasoning. Serve at once, with the Greek yogurt.

HADDOCK WITH MUSHROOMS & CREAM

Serves 4–6

300 ml (½ pint) milk
1 slice of onion
6 black peppercorns
1 bay leaf
60 g (2 oz) butter, plus extra for greasing
750 g (1½ lb) haddock fillet, skinned
salt and black pepper
squeeze of lemon juice
250 g (8 oz) button mushrooms, sliced
30 g (1 oz) plain flour
3 tbsp single cream
30 g (1 oz) fresh white breadcrumbs
30 g (1 oz) Parmesan cheese, grated
chopped parsley to garnish

1 Put the milk into a small saucepan with the onion, peppercorns, and bay leaf, and bring just to a boil. Remove from the heat, cover, and leave to infuse for 10 minutes. Lightly butter a shallow ovenproof dish.

2 Cut the haddock into 7 cm (3 in) pieces, and place in a single layer in the dish. Sprinkle with salt and pepper to taste.

3 Melt half of the butter in a saucepan, add the lemon juice, mushrooms, and salt and pepper to taste, and cook gently, stirring occasionally, for 3 minutes or until just tender. Remove the mushrooms with a slotted spoon and put them on top of the fish.

4 Strain the infused milk and set aside. Melt the remaining butter in a saucepan, add the flour, and cook, stirring, for 1 minute. Remove from the heat and gradually blend in the infused milk. Bring to a boil, stirring constantly until the mixture thickens. Simmer for 2–3 minutes. Stir in the cream, and add salt and pepper to taste.

5 Pour the sauce over the fish and mushrooms, then sprinkle with the breadcrumbs and Parmesan. Bake in a preheated oven at 190°C (375°F, Gas 5) for 25–30 minutes until the fish is cooked and the top is golden and bubbling. Garnish with parsley, and serve at once.

ROAST MONKFISH NIÇOISE

 **Serves 4**

3 tbsp olive oil

1 head of garlic, separated

1 lemon, thickly sliced

4 x 175 g (6 oz) monkfish fillets, skinned

1 tsp herbes de Provence

250 ml (8 fl oz) dry white wine

125 ml (4 fl oz) fish stock

1 x 400 g (13 oz) can artichoke hearts, drained and rinsed

15 pitted black olives

10 sun-dried tomatoes in oil, drained

squeeze of lemon juice

salt and black pepper

lemon wedges and thyme sprigs to garnish

1 Put 1 tbsp of the oil into an ovenproof dish, add the garlic cloves, and roast in a preheated oven at 190°C (375°F, Gas 5) for about 10 minutes until softened.

2 Arrange the lemon slices in the dish, and put the garlic and monkfish on top. Sprinkle with the remaining oil and the herbs, and pour in the wine and stock. Return to the oven for 15 minutes.

3 Add the artichoke hearts, olives, and sun-dried tomatoes, and cook for 5 minutes to heat through.

4 Transfer the fish and vegetables to a serving dish, discarding the lemon slices. Keep warm.

5 Pour the cooking juices into a small saucepan, and boil for about 8 minutes until reduced to about 125 ml (4 fl oz). Add the lemon juice, and salt and pepper to taste, and pour over the fish. Garnish with lemon and thyme, and serve at once.

ROAST MONKFISH BASQUAISE

Substitute 1 yellow and 1 red pepper for the artichoke hearts. Core, seed, and cut into strips, and roast with the garlic cloves. Proceed as directed.

CITRUS MONKFISH

 **Serves 4**

2 unpeeled satsumas or tangerines, washed and thinly sliced

1 onion, chopped

1 cm (1/2 in) piece of fresh root ginger, peeled and finely chopped

500 g (1 lb) monkfish fillets, skinned

3 spring onions, thinly sliced

250 ml (8 fl oz) fish stock

grated zest of 1/2 lime

75 ml (2 1/2 fl oz) lime juice

salt and cayenne pepper

60 g (2 oz) unsalted butter, chilled and cubed

satsuma slices to garnish

1 Put the satsumas, onion, and ginger into a pan. Add the monkfish, spring onions, and stock. Bring to a boil, and simmer, without stirring, for 10 minutes or until the fish is firm. With a slotted spoon, transfer to a serving dish. Keep warm.

2 Put a sieve over a bowl and work through the remaining contents of the pan, pressing hard with the back of a spoon to extract all the juices.

3 Pour the juices into a small saucepan and boil rapidly, uncovered, for about 12 minutes until the liquid has reduced to about 2 tbsp.

4 Add the lime zest and juice, salt and cayenne pepper to taste, and heat gently, stirring, to warm through. Remove the pan from the heat and finish the sauce (see box, below).

5 Pour the citrus sauce over the monkfish and serve at once, garnished with satsuma slices.

Finishing the sauce

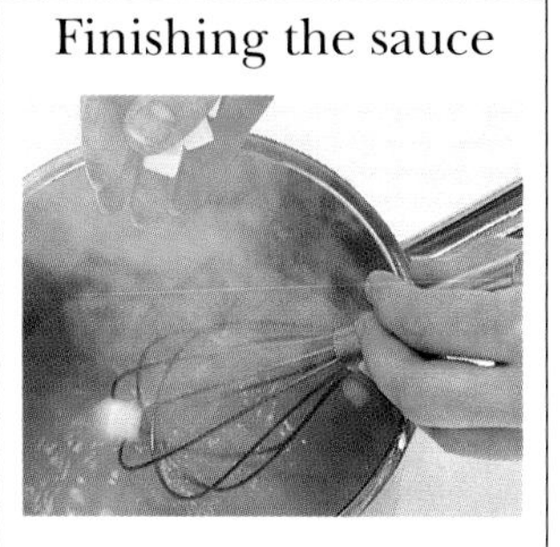

Add the cubes of butter, one at a time, to the citrus sauce, whisking constantly between each addition, until the butter melts and the sauce thickens slightly and becomes glossy.

MONKFISH KEBABS

Serves 4

500 g (1 lb) monkfish fillets, skinned

4 tbsp olive oil

grated zest and juice of 1 large lemon

1 tbsp chopped fresh dill

salt and black pepper

1/2 cucumber

30 g (1 oz) butter

12 fresh bay leaves

2 lemons, thinly sliced

dill sprigs to garnish

1 Cut the monkfish fillets into 2.5 cm (1 in) pieces and put them into a bowl. Whisk together the olive oil, lemon zest and juice, dill, and salt and pepper to taste, and pour over the fish. Cover and leave to marinate in the refrigerator for about 4 hours.

2 Peel the cucumber, and cut it in half lengthwise. Scoop out the seeds from each half, and cut the flesh across into 2 cm (3/4 in) slices. Melt the butter in a small saucepan, add the cucumber slices, and cook gently for 2 minutes or until they begin to soften.

3 Lift the monkfish out of the marinade with a slotted spoon, reserving the marinade. Thread the kebabs (see box, below).

4 Brush the kebabs with marinade, and put under a hot grill, 7 cm (3 ins) from the heat. Cook the kebabs, brushing them occasionally with the marinade, for 5–6 minutes on each side until the fish is cooked through. Serve at once, garnished with dill sprigs.

Threading the kebabs

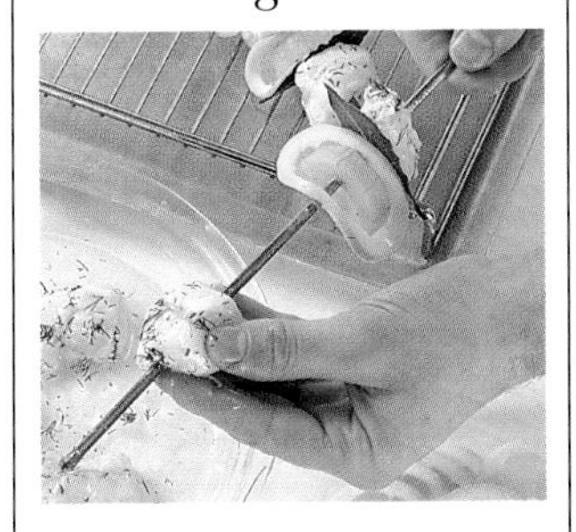

Push a piece of fish and a bay leaf on to a skewer. Fold a lemon slice around a cucumber slice and push on to the skewer. Keep threading the fish, bay leaves, and lemon and cucumber until 4 skewers are filled.

SPICED FISH WITH COCONUT

Serves 4

750 g (1 1/2 lb) monkfish fillets, skinned

1 tbsp plain flour

salt and black pepper

90 g (3 oz) creamed coconut, coarsely chopped

150 ml (1/4 pint) boiling water

2 tbsp sunflower oil

1 onion, finely sliced

1 garlic clove, crushed

1/2 tsp ground coriander

1/2 tsp ground cumin

1/4 tsp turmeric

500 g (1 lb) tomatoes, peeled, seeded, and cut into strips

3 tbsp chopped fresh coriander

coriander sprigs to garnish

1 Cut the monkfish into 5 cm (2 in) squares. Season the flour with salt and pepper. Lightly coat the monkfish with the flour.

2 Put the creamed coconut into a jug, add the boiling water, and stir until the coconut has dissolved.

3 Heat the oil in a large frying pan, add the onion, garlic, coriander, cumin, and turmeric, and cook gently, stirring from time to time, for 3 minutes or until the onions begin to soften. Stir in the dissolved creamed coconut mixture and cook for 1 minute.

4 Add the monkfish and tomatoes, cover, and cook gently, stirring occasionally, for 15 minutes or until the fish is opaque and the flesh flakes easily. Add the chopped coriander, and taste for seasoning. Serve hot, garnished with coriander sprigs.

Cook's know-how

Coconut milk, as prepared in this recipe, can be made from creamed, fresh, or desiccated coconut. The liquid inside a coconut is a thin watery fluid and should not be confused with coconut milk.

CAJUN-SPICED RED SNAPPER

Serves 4

4 x 150–175 g (5–6 oz) red snapper fillets

30 g (1 oz) butter

coriander butter (page 221) and watercress sprigs to serve

CAJUN SPICE MIXTURE

2–3 tbsp plain flour

1 tsp garlic granules

1 tsp paprika

1 tsp onion salt

1 tsp ground cumin

1 tsp mild chilli powder

1/2 tsp dried oregano

1/4 tsp each black and cayenne pepper

1 Make the Cajun spice mixture: combine the flour, garlic granules, paprika, onion salt, cumin, chilli powder, oregano, and black and cayenne peppers. Rub over the red snapper fillets, cover, and leave to marinate in the refrigerator for at least 30 minutes.

2 Melt the butter in a large frying pan, add the fillets, and cook gently for 2–3 minutes on each side until the fish is opaque and the flesh flakes easily.

3 Top the fillets with pats of coriander butter, garnish with watercress sprigs, and serve at once.

Red snapper

This is a pinkish-red fish found in tropical waters. It has a large head, plump body, and firm, juicy flesh. While fresh garlic is usually preferable to dried granules, in Cajun spice mixtures granules are used for their texture as well as their particularly pungent flavour.

COD STEAKS WITH ANCHOVY & FENNEL

Serves 4

1 x 60 g (2 oz) can anchovy fillets

30 g (1 oz) butter, plus extra for greasing

1 small onion, finely chopped

1 small fennel bulb, finely chopped

30 g (1 oz) parsley, chopped

125 g (4 oz) fresh white breadcrumbs

salt and black pepper

4 x 250 g (8 oz) cod steaks

dill sprigs, lemon wedges, and watercress sprigs to garnish

1 Drain the anchovy fillets, reserving the oil. Cut the anchovies into small pieces and set aside.

2 Melt the butter in a pan, add the onion and fennel, and cook over a medium heat, stirring, for 5 minutes or until soft but not browned. Remove from the heat, stir in the anchovies, parsley, and breadcrumbs, and salt and pepper to taste.

3 Put the cod steaks into a buttered ovenproof dish and top each one with the anchovy and fennel mixture, pressing it down firmly with your hand.

4 Drizzle a little of the reserved anchovy oil over each steak. Bake the steaks in a preheated oven at 200°C (400°F, Gas 6) for 15–20 minutes until the cod is opaque and the flesh flakes easily from the bone.

5 Transfer to a warmed serving plate. Garnish the cod steaks with dill sprigs, lemon wedges, and watercress sprigs, and serve at once.

COD STEAKS WITH SUN-DRIED TOMATOES

Omit the anchovies, fennel, parsley, and breadcrumbs. Peel (page 39), seed, and chop 4 tomatoes. Drain 30 g (1 oz) sun-dried tomatoes in oil, and snip them into small pieces. Add the tomatoes to the softened onion in step 2, with 12 pitted and chopped black olives, and salt and pepper to taste. Drizzle the cod steaks with 1 tbsp olive oil, then top with the tomato mixture, and bake as directed.

CHEESE-TOPPED BAKED BREAM

Serves 4

2 x 560 g (1 lb 2 oz) black bream, filleted and skinned

grated zest and juice of 1/2 lemon

salt and black pepper

150 ml (1/4 pint) water

butter for greasing

30 g (1 oz) mature Cheddar cheese, grated

lemon zest and parsley sprigs to garnish

WHITE SAUCE

30 g (1 oz) butter

1 tbsp plain flour

150 ml (1/4 pint) milk

1 Cut the black bream fillets in half lengthwise, and arrange them in a single layer in a large ovenproof dish.

2 Sprinkle the fish fillets evenly with the grated lemon zest and salt and pepper to taste. Pour the lemon juice and measured water over the fish fillets. Cover the dish with buttered greaseproof paper.

3 Bake in a preheated oven at 160°C (325°F, Gas 3) for about 20 minutes until the flesh flakes easily.

4 Transfer the bream to a warmed flameproof platter, cover, and keep warm. Strain the cooking liquid and reserve.

5 Make the white sauce: melt the butter in a small saucepan, add the flour, and cook, stirring, for 1 minute. Remove from the heat, and gradually blend in the milk and the reserved cooking liquid. Bring to a boil, stirring constantly until the mixture thickens. Simmer for 2–3 minutes. Taste for seasoning.

6 Pour the white sauce over the fish, sprinkle with the cheese, and place under a hot grill, 10 cm (4 ins) from the heat, for 3–5 minutes until heated through and golden.

7 Serve the bream at once, garnished with lemon zest and parsley sprigs.

BLACK BREAM NIÇOISE

Serves 4

2 x 560 g (1 lb 2 oz) black bream, cleaned (page 105), with heads removed

salt and black pepper

3 tbsp olive oil

1 large onion, sliced

1 small fennel bulb, sliced

1 garlic clove, crushed

12 pitted black olives

2 tbsp chopped parsley

juice of 1 lemon

lemon segments and parsley sprigs to garnish

1 Prepare the bream (see box, below).

2 Heat 2 tbsp of the oil in a frying pan, add the onion, fennel, and garlic, and cook gently, stirring occasionally, for 5–8 minutes until the vegetables are soft but not coloured.

3 Spoon the vegetables into an ovenproof dish, and place the bream on top. Scatter the olives and parsley over the fish, sprinkle with the lemon juice, and drizzle with the remaining olive oil.

4 Cover the fish loosely with foil, and bake in a preheated oven at 200°C (400°F, Gas 6) for about 20 minutes.

5 Remove the foil and bake for 10 minutes or until the fish is cooked. Garnish with lemon segments and parsley sprigs before serving.

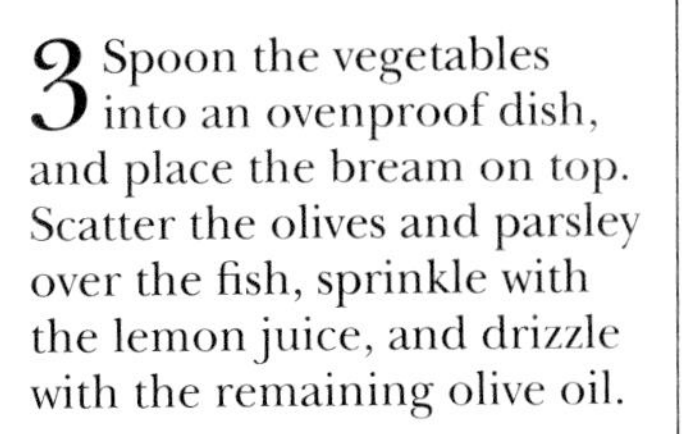

Black bream

A relatively inexpensive salt-water fish with dark grey skin and a flattish body. The firm flesh has a sweet flavour.

Preparing the bream

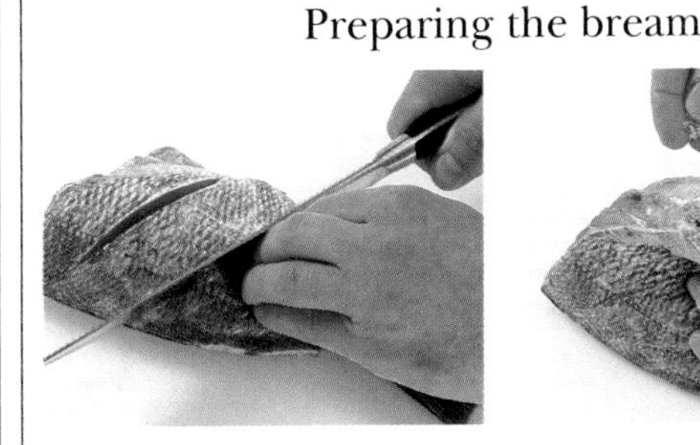

Make 2 deep diagonal cuts in the flesh on both sides of each bream, using a sharp knife.

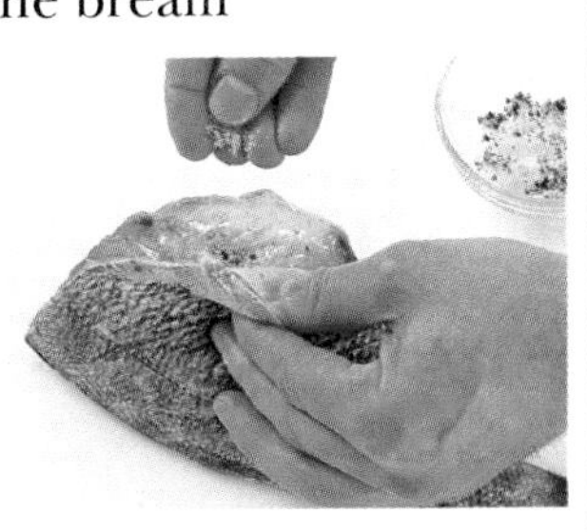

Put salt and pepper into a bowl and combine. Sprinkle on the inside and outside of the bream.

HALIBUT IN FILO PARCELS

Halibut is a very fine fish with a delicate flavour and firm texture. Enclosing the halibut steaks in filo parcels with matchstick-thin vegetables keeps the fish moist and seals in all the flavours, while the pastry trimmings on top provide an attractive, crunchy finish.

Serves 4

- *2 x 375 g (12 oz) halibut steaks, skinned and boned*
- *1 carrot*
- *1 leek, trimmed*
- *150 ml (1/4 pint) fish stock*
- *2 tbsp dry white wine*
- *2 tsp lemon juice*
- *3 strands of saffron or 1/4 tsp turmeric*
- *salt and black pepper*
- *8 large sheets of filo pastry*
- *60 g (2 oz) butter, melted*
- *lemon slices and dill sprigs to garnish*

1 Halve the halibut steaks crosswise, and set aside. Cut the carrot and leek into matchstick-thin strips.

2 Put the vegetables into a pan with the stock, wine, lemon juice, and saffron.

3 Bring to a boil, and cook, uncovered, for 5 minutes or until the vegetables are just tender. Drain, and add salt and pepper to taste.

4 Cut the filo pastry into eight 25 cm (10 in) squares, and reserve the trimmings. Brush 1 square with a little melted butter, put a second square on top, and brush with more melted butter. Make a filo parcel (see box, right). Repeat to make 4 filo parcels.

5 Place the filo parcels on a baking tray, and bake in a preheated oven at 200°C (400°F, Gas 6) for 20 minutes or until golden and crispy. Garnish with lemon slices and dill sprigs, and serve at once.

Cook's know-how

Sheets of filo pastry are usually sold in a roll, fresh or frozen. The size of the sheets may vary with different brands, so don't worry if they are slightly smaller than 25 cm (10 ins) wide – just be sure there is sufficient pastry to cover the filling.

HADDOCK IN FILO PARCELS

Substitute skinned haddock fillets for the halibut, and 1 courgette and 4 spring onions, cut into matchstick-thin strips, for the carrot and leek. Proceed as directed.

Making a filo parcel

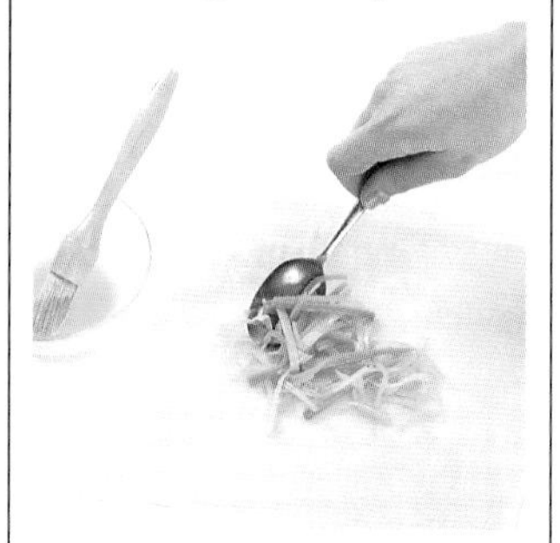

Spoon one-quarter of the vegetable mixture into the middle of the pastry square. Put 1 piece of halibut on top of the vegetable mixture.

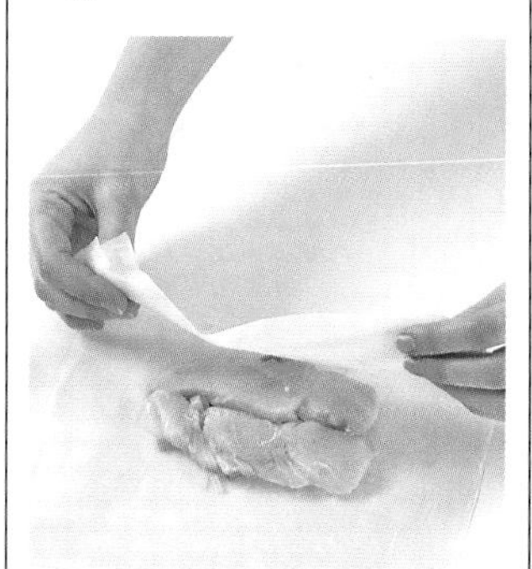

Fold 2 sides of the filo pastry over the halibut and vegetables, and tuck the remaining 2 ends underneath to form a neat parcel. Brush the top of the parcel with a little melted butter.

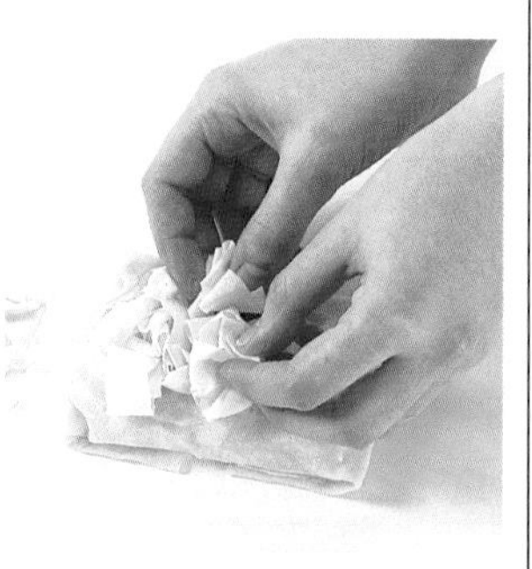

Crumple some of the reserved filo trimmings, and arrange them on top of the filo parcel. Brush with melted butter.

SEA BASS WITH LEMON BUTTER SAUCE

Serves 4

sunflower oil for greasing

1.1 kg (2¼ lb) sea bass, cleaned and filleted (page 105)

4 tarragon sprigs

1 lemon, sliced

salt and black pepper

2 tbsp dry white wine

LEMON BUTTER SAUCE

150 ml (¼ pint) single cream

juice of ½ lemon

45 g (1½ oz) butter, melted

1 egg yolk

1 tsp plain flour

white pepper

1 tsp chopped fresh tarragon

1 Put a large piece of foil on to a baking tray and brush lightly with oil. Put the sea bass on to the foil, tuck 3 of the tarragon sprigs and all but 1–2 of the lemon slices inside the stomach cavity, and sprinkle with salt and black pepper to taste.

2 Season the outside of the fish, and lift up the sides of the foil. Pour the wine over the fish, then seal the foil into a loose parcel. Bake in a preheated oven at 200°C (400°F, Gas 6) for 30 minutes or until the flesh is opaque and flakes easily.

3 Meanwhile, make the sauce: whisk the cream in a pan with the lemon juice, butter, egg yolk, and flour until mixed. Heat very gently, stirring constantly, until the mixture is thick enough to coat the back of a spoon. Add salt and white pepper to taste, and stir in the tarragon. Keep warm.

4 Remove the sea bass from the foil and arrange on a warmed serving dish. Pour over the cooking juices. Garnish with the remaining lemon slices and tarragon sprig, and serve at once. Serve the warm lemon butter sauce separately.

FISH EN PAPILLOTE

Serves 4

45 g (1½ oz) butter

4 x 250 g (8 oz) white fish fillets, such as sole or grouper, skinned

2 cm (¾ in) piece of fresh root ginger, peeled and thinly sliced

3 spring onions, thinly sliced

2–3 garlic cloves, crushed

2 tbsp light soy sauce

1 tbsp rice wine or dry sherry

½ tsp sugar

⋆ *4 sheets of baking parchment*

1 Cut the sheets of baking parchment into four 30 x 37 cm (12 x 15 in) rectangles, and cut out 4 hearts (see box, right).

2 Melt 30 g (1 oz) of the butter in a small saucepan. Brush the paper hearts and 2 large baking trays with the butter.

3 Place a fish fillet on one half of each heart. Top each one with ginger, spring onions, and garlic, and dot with the remaining butter. Whisk together the soy sauce, rice wine, and sugar, and drizzle over the fish. Fold the paper over the fish, pleat the edges, and twist the pointed ends to seal.

4 Put the paper cases on to the prepared baking trays and bake the fish in a preheated oven at 230°C (450°F, Gas 8) for 8–10 minutes until the paper has turned brown and the cases have puffed up.

5 Transfer the paper cases to warmed individual plates, and serve at once.

Cutting a paper heart

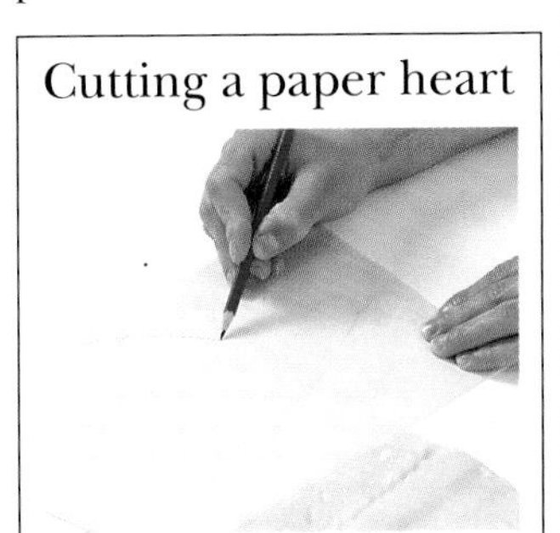

Fold a baking parchment rectangle in half, and draw a curve to make a heart when unfolded.

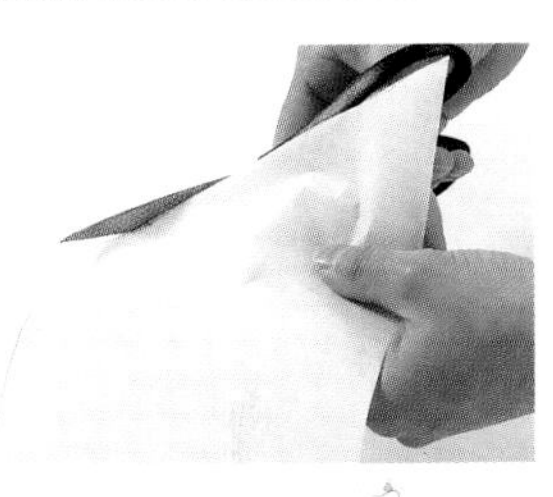

Cut out the heart shape just inside the pencilled line, and unfold.

GOLDEN FISH CAKES

Serves 4

500 g (1 lb) potatoes, roughly chopped

salt and black pepper

500 g (1 lb) cod or haddock fillets

300 ml (1/2 pint) milk

1 bay leaf

9 black peppercorns

60 g (2 oz) butter

4 tbsp chopped parsley

175 g (6 oz) fresh breadcrumbs

1 egg, beaten

sunflower oil for frying

tartare sauce (page 128) to serve

1 Cook the potatoes in boiling salted water for 15–20 minutes until tender.

2 Meanwhile, put the fish into a pan with the milk, bay leaf, and peppercorns. Bring slowly to a boil, and simmer for 10 minutes or until the fish is just opaque.

3 Drain the fish, reserving the liquid. Leave the fish to cool, then remove and discard the skin and bones, and flake the fish.

4 Drain the potatoes. Turn into a large bowl, add the butter and 3 tbsp of the reserved fish cooking liquid, and mash until smooth and creamy. Add the flaked fish, parsley, and salt and pepper to taste, and mix well.

5 Spread the breadcrumbs on a plate. With your hands, shape the fish and potato mixture into 8 flat cakes, 7 cm (3 ins) in diameter. Dip each fish cake into the beaten egg, then coat with breadcrumbs.

6 Heat a little oil in a frying pan and fry the fish cakes, a few at a time, for about 5 minutes on each side until golden brown. Serve at once, with the tartare sauce.

CRISPY-TOPPED SEAFOOD PIE

Serves 4

500 g (1 lb) cod fillet

300 ml (1/2 pint) milk

1 bay leaf

2 leeks, trimmed and sliced

175 g (6 oz) broccoli, cut into florets

175 g (6 oz) cooked peeled prawns

15 g (1/2 oz) butter

15 g (1/2 oz) plain flour

salt and black pepper

250 g (8 oz) ready-made shortcrust pastry, chilled

30 g (1 oz) Gruyère cheese, grated

1 Put the cod into a saucepan with the milk and bay leaf, bring slowly to a boil, and poach gently for about 10 minutes until the fish flakes easily.

2 Meanwhile, blanch the leeks and broccoli for 3 minutes in a saucepan of boiling salted water. Drain.

3 Lift out the fish, remove and discard the skin and bones, and flake the fish. Strain and reserve the milk.

4 Put the leeks and broccoli into a pie dish, and add the cod and prawns.

5 Melt the butter in a small saucepan, add the flour, and cook, stirring, for 1 minute. Remove from the heat and gradually blend in the reserved milk. Bring to a boil, stirring constantly until thickened. Simmer for 2–3 minutes. Season to taste and pour over the pie filling.

6 Grate the pastry (see box, below), and sprinkle over the sauce. Sprinkle with the grated cheese. Bake in a preheated oven at 200°C (400°F, Gas 6) for 25–30 minutes. Serve at once.

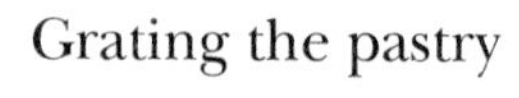

Grating the pastry

Grate the pastry on to a plate, using the coarse grid of a grater. Ensure the pastry is well chilled.

5

POULTRY & GAME

UNDER 30 MINUTES

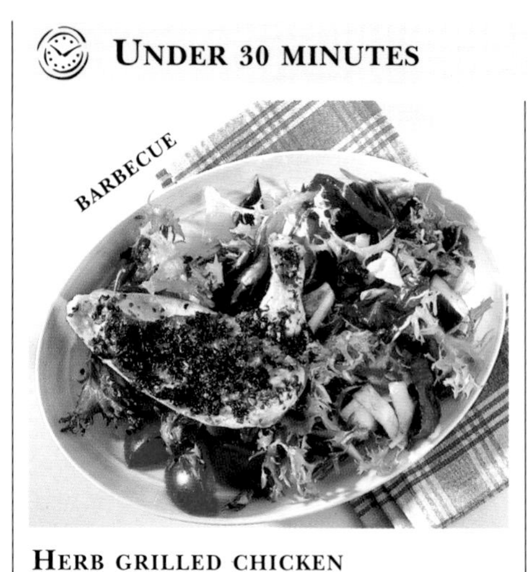

HERB GRILLED CHICKEN

Fresh and summery: chicken quarters brushed with parsley, chives, and garlic in melted butter, then barbecued or grilled.

SERVES 8 297 calories per serving
Takes 25 minutes **PAGE 160**

CHICKEN KEBABS

Pieces of chicken marinated in soy sauce, vinegar, oil, and thyme. Grilled with green pepper, mushrooms, and cherry tomatoes.

SERVES 4 662 calories per serving
Takes 25 minutes **PAGE 166**

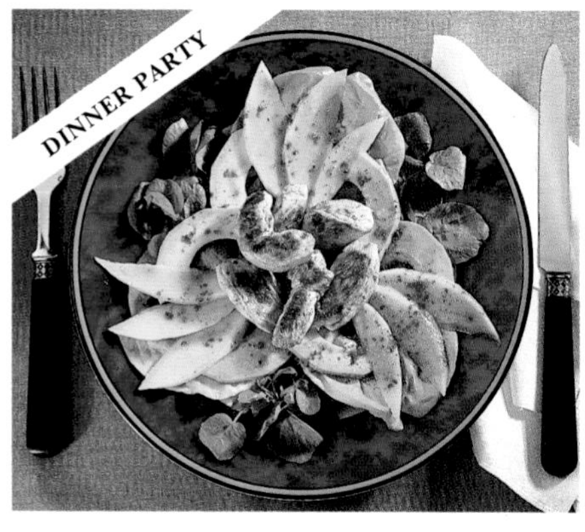

WARM CHICKEN SALAD WITH MANGO & AVOCADO

Marinated chicken with mango and avocado, and rum-flavoured cooking juices.

SERVES 4 411 calories per serving
Takes 25 minutes **PAGE 176**

MUSTARD CHICKEN

Hot and creamy: strips of chicken coated with garlic, in a cream sauce piquantly flavoured with mustard.

SERVES 4 380 calories per serving
Takes 25 minutes **PAGE 165**

TURKEY WITH SOURED CREAM & CHIVES

Strips of turkey breast in a bacon, mushroom, and soured cream sauce.

SERVES 4 542 calories per serving
Takes 25 minutes **PAGE 180**

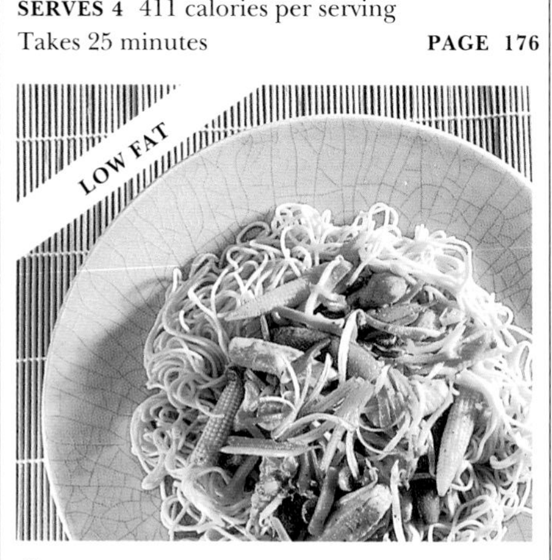

STIR-FRIED CHICKEN WITH VEGETABLES

Strips of chicken dry marinated in ginger, mustard, sugar, turmeric, and curry powder. Stir-fried with mixed vegetables.

SERVES 4 405 calories per serving
Takes 25 minutes **PAGE 164**

GREEK SPICED CHICKEN

Creamy and intensely flavoured with herbs: pieces of cooked chicken coated in yogurt, crème fraîche, spring onions, and herbs.

SERVES 6 264 calories per serving
Takes 15 minutes **PAGE 176**

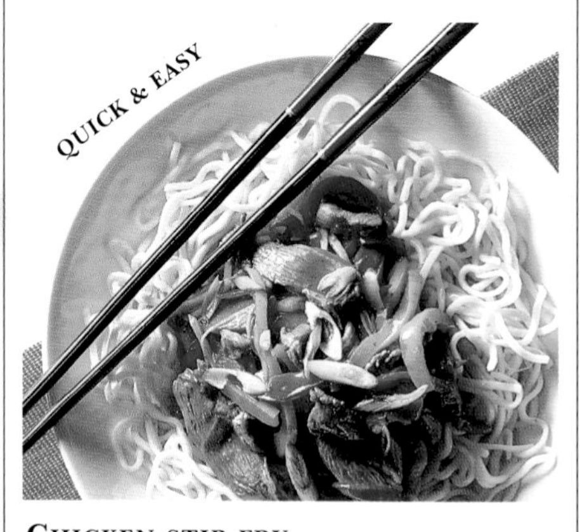

CHICKEN STIR-FRY

Light oriental dish: strips of chicken stir-fried with spring onions, ginger, carrots, and peppers. Flavoured with soy sauce and sherry.

SERVES 4 381 calories per serving
Takes 15 minutes **PAGE 167**

HOT & SPICY STIR-FRIED DUCK

Strips of duck marinated in soy sauce, vinegar, ginger, chilli, and orange. Stir-fried with vegetables and water chestnuts.

SERVES 4 453 calories per serving
Takes 25 minutes **PAGE 189**

30–60 MINUTES

CORONATION CHICKEN

Bite-sized pieces of chicken in a sauce made from spring onions, curry paste, wine, lemon, apricot jam, mayonnaise, and yogurt.

SERVES 6 580 calories per serving
Takes 15 minutes, plus cooling PAGE 175

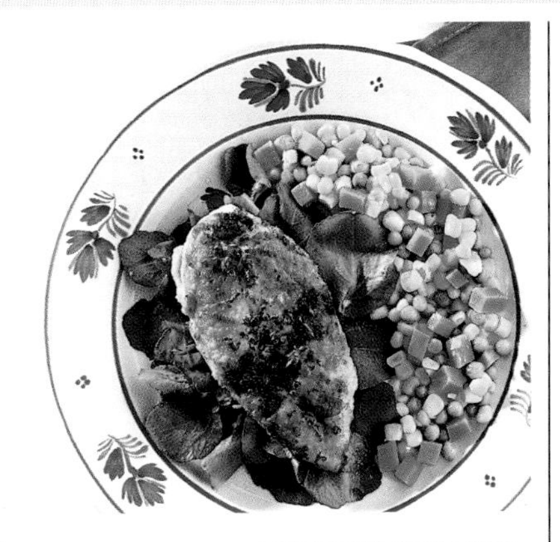

HERB-MARINATED CHICKEN BREASTS

Chicken breasts marinated in lemon juice, herbs, and garlic. Cooked until crispy, and served with a hot stock sauce.

SERVES 4 641 calories per serving
Takes 30 minutes, plus marinating PAGE 170

THAI CHICKEN WITH WATER CHESTNUTS

Aromatic stir-fry: chicken with water chestnuts, lemon grass, garlic, ginger, coriander, chilli, and tofu.

SERVES 4 272 calories per serving
Takes 30 minutes PAGE 164

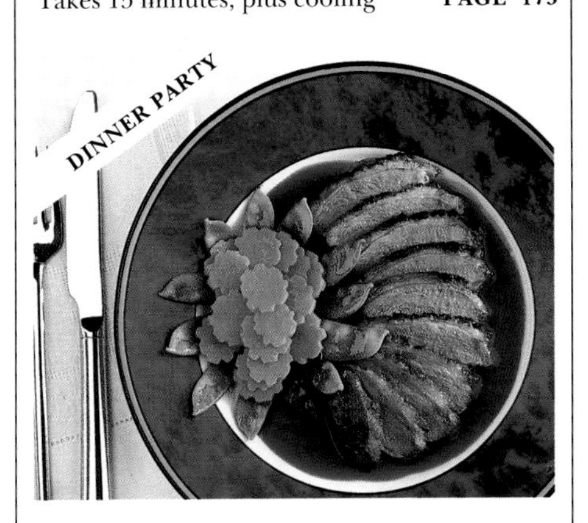

DUCK BREASTS WITH RASPBERRY SAUCE

Rich and fruity: slices of grilled duck breast served with a sauce of raspberries mixed with port, sugar, and orange juice.

SERVES 4 975 calories per serving
Takes 45 minutes PAGE 188

STIR-FRIED TURKEY MEATBALLS

Mixture of minced turkey, garlic, soy sauce, and ginger, stir-fried with onion, pepper, courgette, mushrooms, and bean sprouts.

SERVES 4 232 calories per serving
Takes 30 minutes PAGE 183

TARRAGON CHICKEN WITH LIME

Chicken breasts coated with lime butter and sprinkled with lime juice and tarragon. Baked, and served with a crème fraîche sauce.

SERVES 4 428 calories per serving
Takes 45 minutes PAGE 168

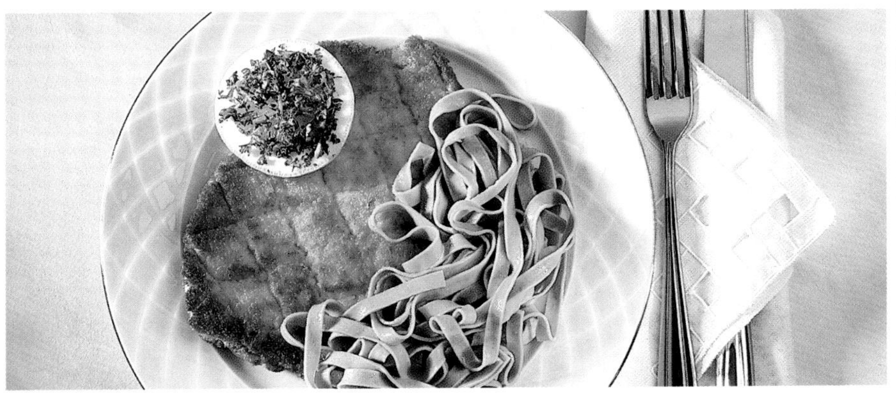

TURKEY SCHNITZEL

Golden and tender: turkey breast escalopes coated in seasoned flour, beaten egg, and fresh breadcrumbs, and decorated with a criss-cross pattern. Chilled in the refrigerator, then cooked until golden. Garnished with lemon slices and chopped parsley.

SERVES 4 394 calories per serving
Takes 25 minutes, plus chilling PAGE 181

CHEESE & GARLIC STUFFED CHICKEN

Chicken breasts stuffed with soft cheese, onion, garlic, fresh tarragon, egg yolk, and nutmeg, then baked. Served cut into slices.

SERVES 6 628 calories per serving
Takes 45 minutes PAGE 168

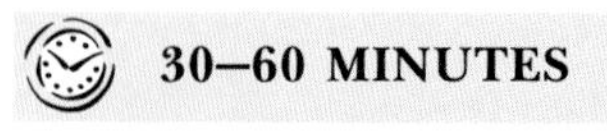

30–60 MINUTES

DEVILLED CHICKEN DRUMSTICKS

Crispy and piquant: chicken drumsticks covered with a mixture of wine vinegar, ketchup, mustard, and sugar, then baked.

MAKES 12 138 calories each

Takes 45 minutes **PAGE 174**

TURKEY WITH CHEESE & PINEAPPLE

Bite-sized pieces of turkey with a cheese and pineapple sauce, sprinkled with fresh brown breadcrumbs, then baked.

SERVES 6 450 calories per serving

Takes 40 minutes **PAGE 184**

CHICKEN SATAY

Pieces of chicken marinated in soy sauce, lemon juice, garlic, and spring onions. Served with a peanut and coconut sauce.

SERVES 4 815 calories per serving

Takes 25 minutes, plus marinating **PAGE 166**

CHICKEN THIGHS NORMANDE

Chicken thighs baked with leeks, bacon, cider, and thyme, richly flavoured with garlic. Served with a crème fraîche sauce.

SERVES 4 599 calories per serving

Takes 55 minutes **PAGE 171**

BACON-WRAPPED CHICKEN BREASTS

Tender and tangy: boneless chicken breasts spread with coarse-grain mustard, and wrapped in bacon rashers.

SERVES 6 528 calories per serving

Takes 50 minutes **PAGE 169**

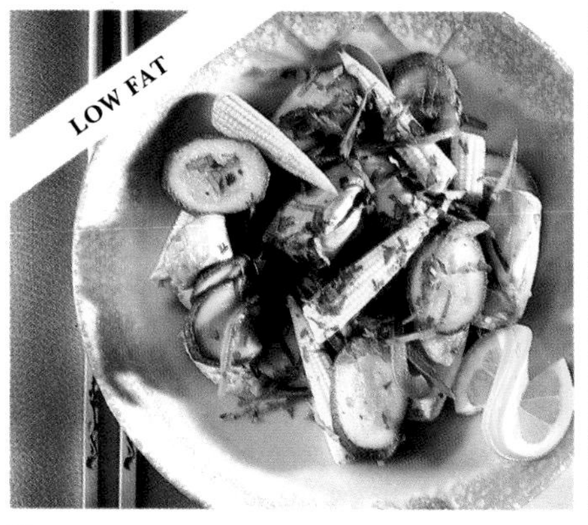

TURKEY & LEMON STIR-FRY

Turkey breast strips marinated in white wine and lemon zest and juice, stir-fried with courgettes, green pepper, and baby sweetcorn.

SERVES 4 342 calories per serving

Takes 20 minutes, plus marinating **PAGE 181**

CHICKEN PINWHEELS

Pounded chicken breasts spread with a cheese and basil mixture, rolled up, simmered, then sliced. Served with a tomato and herb sauce.

SERVES 4 423 calories per serving

Takes 50 minutes **PAGE 167**

FRAGRANT CHICKEN CURRY WITH ALMONDS

Chicken breasts cooked in an authentic blend of Indian spices, including cinnamon, cardamom seeds, cloves, cumin seeds, ginger, and garam masala, with a creamy yogurt sauce. Served with a sprinkling of sultanas and toasted almonds.

SERVES 4 527 calories per serving

Takes 45 minutes **PAGE 162**

30–60 MINUTES

ORIENTAL POUSSINS

Tangy and succulent: poussins brushed with soy and hoisin sauces, sherry, garlic, and ginger, and baked.

SERVES 4 395 calories per serving

Takes 50 minutes **PAGE 157**

CHICKEN THIGHS WITH CHESTNUT STUFFING

Delicious and filling: boneless chicken thighs stuffed with diced bacon, chestnuts, onion, fresh brown breadcrumbs, chopped parsley, and egg yolk, and then roasted until a golden brown colour. Served with a fruity cranberry jelly sauce.

SERVES 4 598 calories per serving

Takes 55 minutes **PAGE 171**

TURKEY BURGERS HOLSTEIN

Golden and tasty: minced turkey combined with chopped ham, parsley, and onion, then shaped into burgers. Served with a fried egg.

SERVES 4 429 calories per serving

Takes 30 minutes, plus chilling **PAGE 183**

JERK CHICKEN

Crispy and spicy: chicken pieces spread with blended lime juice, rum, spring onions, chilli, garlic, and spices, then barbecued.

SERVES 4 304 calories per serving

Takes 30 minutes, plus marinating **PAGE 161**

LEMON & HERB DRUMSTICKS

Fresh and easy to make: chicken drumsticks marinated in olive oil, lemon juice and zest, onion, garlic, and parsley, then grilled.

MAKES 12 200 calories each

Takes 25 minutes, plus marinating **PAGE 174**

TEX-MEX CHICKEN

Chicken breasts marinated in oil, orange juice, and cumin, then grilled. Served with sliced avocado, and a tomato and lime salsa.

SERVES 4 659 calories per serving

Takes 30 minutes, plus marinating **PAGE 161**

ORIENTAL DUCK WITH GINGER

Duck marinated in orange, soy sauce, sesame oil, rice wine, honey, and ginger. Served with baby sweetcorn and toasted sesame seeds.

SERVES 4 445 calories per serving

Takes 30 minutes, plus marinating **PAGE 189**

TURKEY MOLE

Hot and spicy: turkey pieces cooked with a blended sauce of tomatoes, almonds, chocolate, chilli, cinnamon, and cloves.

SERVES 4 501 calories per serving

Takes 55 minutes **PAGE 182**

30–60 MINUTES

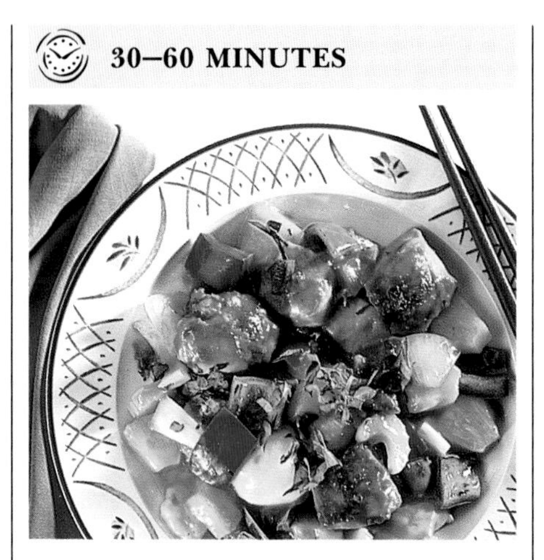

SWEET & SOUR CHINESE CHICKEN

Pieces of chicken marinated in soy sauce and rice wine. Stir-fried with peppers, celery, onion, ketchup, pineapple, and lychees.

SERVES 4–6 458–305 calories per serving

Takes 30 minutes, plus marinating **PAGE 165**

SAFFRON CHICKEN

Chicken breasts marinated in saffron, ginger, lemon, cardamom, coriander, and cinnamon, then roasted. Served with crème fraîche sauce.

SERVES 6 527 calories per serving

Takes 40 minutes, plus marinating **PAGE 163**

CHICKEN WITH SAGE & ORANGE

Fresh and tangy: chicken breasts marinated in orange juice, soy sauce, sage, and ginger. Served with a sage and orange sauce.

SERVES 6 435 calories per serving

Takes 40 minutes, plus marinating **PAGE 169**

OVER 60 MINUTES

DUCK BREASTS WITH RED WINE SAUCE

Duck marinated in garlic, balsamic vinegar, and rosemary, then cooked, sliced, and served with a wine sauce.

SERVES 4 906 calories per serving

Takes 40 minutes, plus chilling **PAGE 188**

POUSSINS WITH ROMESCO SAUCE

Spatchcocked poussins and spring onions marinated in oil, vinegar, and cinnamon. Served with sauce of tomatoes and almonds.

SERVES 2 845 calories per serving

Takes 60 minutes, plus marinating **PAGE 157**

MOROCCAN POUSSINS

Spatchcocked poussins marinated in lime, garlic, coriander, paprika, curry powder, cumin, and saffron, then grilled.

SERVES 2 467 calories per serving

Takes 45 minutes, plus marinating **PAGE 156**

PERFECT AMERICAN FRIED CHICKEN

Pieces of buttermilk-soaked chicken coated in flour seasoned with paprika. Cooked until golden, and served with bacon.

SERVES 4 683 calories per serving

Takes 40 minutes, plus standing **PAGE 160**

CHICKEN TIKKA

Chicken marinated in yogurt, tomato purée, garlic, tamarind paste, paprika, and ginger. Served with cucumber raita.

SERVES 4 266 calories per serving

Takes 20 minutes, plus marinating **PAGE 163**

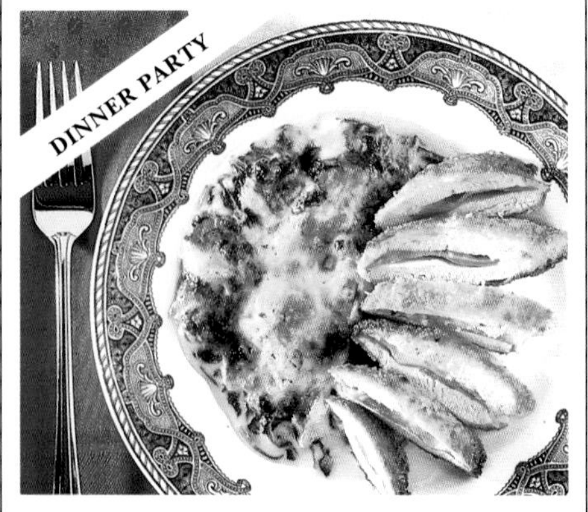

CHICKEN CORDON BLEU

Golden and tender: pounded chicken breasts filled with ham and Gruyère cheese, and folded. Coated with egg and breadcrumbs.

SERVES 4 602 calories per serving

Takes 45 minutes, plus chilling **PAGE 170**

OVER 60 MINUTES

LEMON POUSSINS WITH MARINATED ARTICHOKE HEARTS

Roasted poussins served with artichokes marinated in lemon, garlic, and parsley.

SERVES 4 555 calories per serving

Takes 1 1/4 hours **PAGE 156**

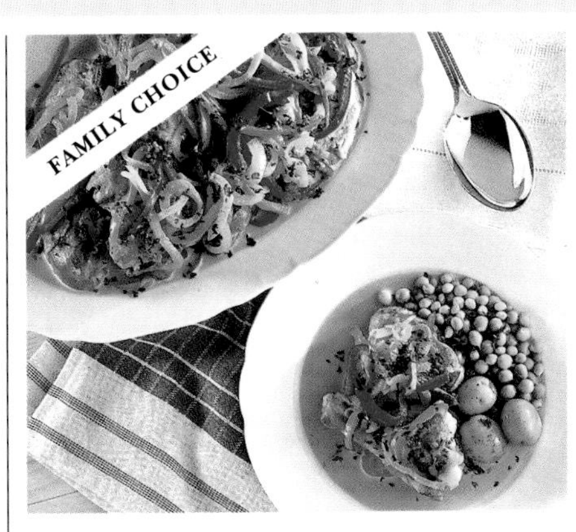

TURKEY CASSEROLE WITH PEPPERS & CIDER

Turkey pieces cooked with cider, red and yellow peppers, onion, and garlic.

SERVES 4 351 calories per serving

Takes 1 1/2 hours **PAGE 182**

PROVENÇAL POT ROAST CHICKEN

Chicken stuffed with garlic and parsley, cooked with red pepper, carrot, and stock which form the basis of a sauce.

SERVES 4 298 calories per serving

Takes 1 1/2 hours **PAGE 154**

COQ AU VIN

Rich and nourishing: chicken pieces cooked with bacon, shallots, mushrooms, red wine, stock, and a medley of fresh herbs.

SERVES 4 531 calories per serving

Takes 1 1/2 hours **PAGE 159**

TRADITIONAL ROAST PHEASANT

Two pheasants, buttered and covered with bacon rashers, then roasted and served with redcurrant-flavoured gravy, and the traditional accompaniments of game chips, fried breadcrumbs, and bread sauce. Garnished with watercress sprigs.

SERVES 4 660 calories per serving

Takes 1 1/2 hours

PAGE 191

MUSHROOM-STUFFED QUAIL

Whole boned quail stuffed with shallots, mushrooms, and breadcrumbs, and served with a lime and crème fraîche sauce.

SERVES 6 651 calories per serving

Takes 1 1/4 hours **PAGE 190**

TURKEY SALAD WITH MANGO & GRAPES

Turkey breast poached with parsley and peppercorns, coated in lemon mayonnaise. Served with mango, grapes, and walnuts.

SERVES 4 734 calories per serving

Takes 1 1/2 hours, plus cooling **PAGE 184**

CHICKEN MARENGO

Chicken pieces cooked with shallots, wine, stock, tomatoes, mushrooms, garlic, parsley, thyme, bay leaf, and prawns.

SERVES 4 479 calories per serving

Takes 1 3/4 hours **PAGE 159**

OVER 60 MINUTES

NORMANDY PHEASANT

Rich and tangy: pheasant cooked with apples, celery, onion, stock, and wine. Served with a creamy sauce and apple rings.
SERVES 6–8 751–563 calories per serving
Takes 1$\frac{3}{4}$ hours **PAGE 192**

BRAISED RABBIT WITH MUSHROOMS & CIDER

Rabbit cooked with shallots, mushrooms, cider, herbs, and enriched with cream.
SERVES 4 506 calories per serving
Takes 2 hours **PAGE 194**

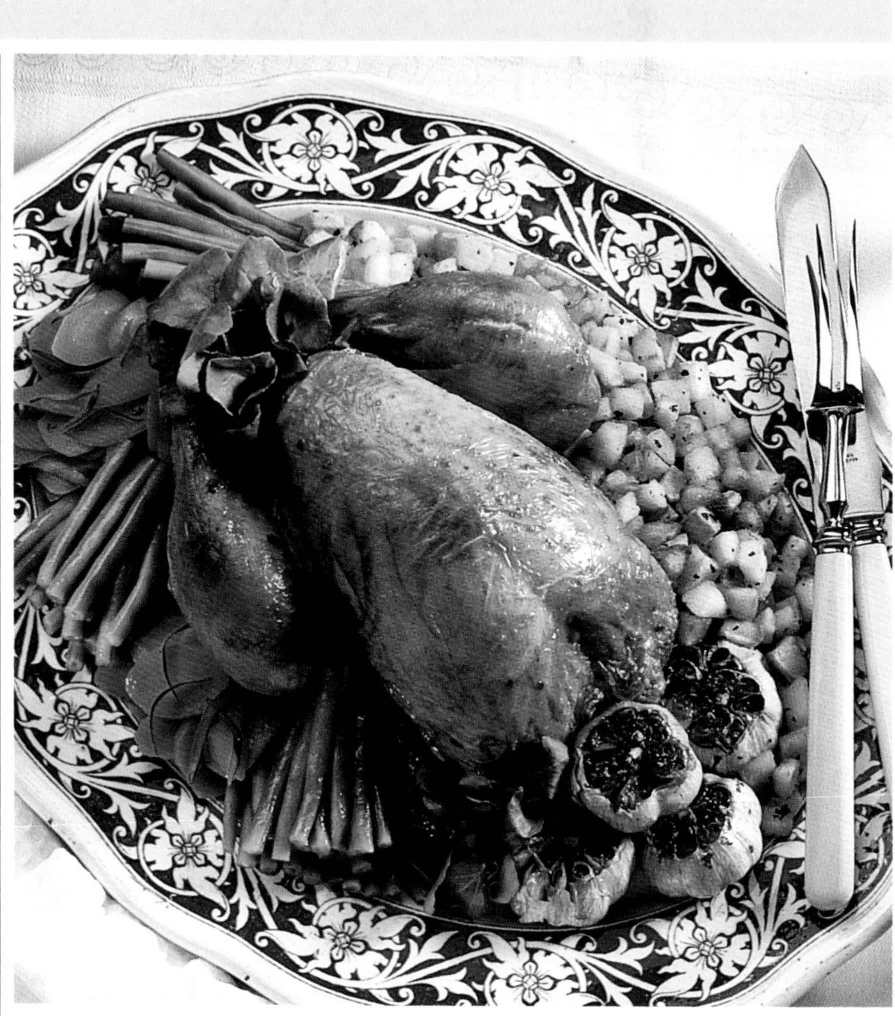

FRENCH ROAST CHICKEN

Tender and succulent: a whole chicken spread with softened butter, seasoned with black pepper, and roasted with chicken stock and a sprig of tarragon. Served with gravy made from the cooking juices, and garlic flowers, drizzled with olive oil, then roasted.
SERVES 4 433 calories per serving
Takes 2 hours **PAGE 153**

FAMILY CHICKEN CASSEROLE

Popular wholesome meal: chicken quarters cooked with bacon, carrots, celery, onion, stock, bay leaf, thyme, and parsley.
SERVES 4 659 calories per serving
Takes 1$\frac{3}{4}$ hours **PAGE 158**

ROAST CHICKEN WITH ORANGE & PEPPERS

Chicken with red pepper and garlic, flambéed with brandy, and served with orange sauce.
SERVES 4 411 calories per serving
Takes 1$\frac{3}{4}$ hours **PAGE 154**

SUNDAY ROAST CHICKEN

Traditional English Sunday lunch: chicken flavoured with parsley and thyme, and cooked with an apple, lemon, and herb stuffing.
SERVES 4 534 calories per serving
Takes 2 hours, plus cooling **PAGE 152**

OVER 60 MINUTES

ROAST TURKEY WITH GARLIC & TARRAGON

Turkey joint marinated in lemon, tarragon, thyme, and garlic, roasted with the marinade.

SERVES 4 296 calories per serving

Takes 1 3/4 hours, plus marinating **PAGE 180**

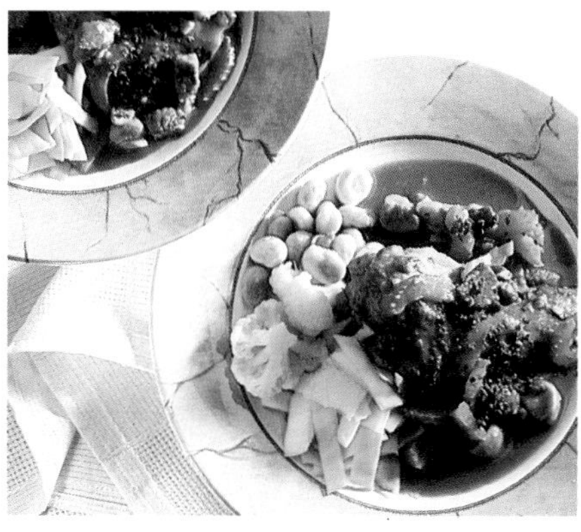

PHEASANT STEW

Pieces of pheasant simmered with red wine, game stock, bacon, celery, mushrooms, shallots, and garlic.

SERVES 6–8 633–475 calories per serving

Takes 2 hours **PAGE 192**

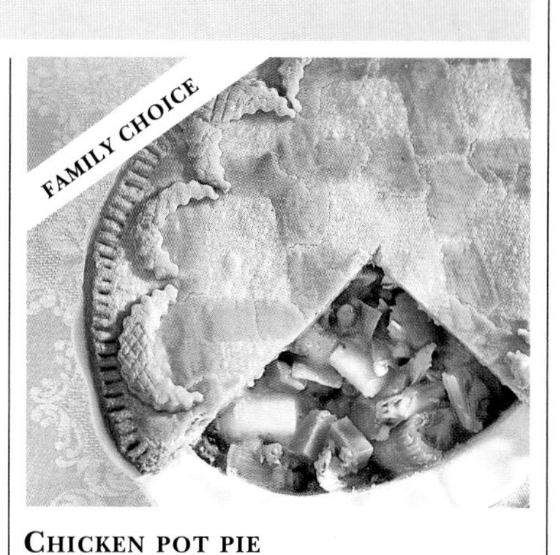

CHICKEN POT PIE

Hearty meal: chicken simmered with stock, garlic, carrots, and potatoes. Flavoured with nutmeg and parsley, and baked with pastry.

SERVES 6 508 calories per serving

Takes 2 hours, plus cooling **PAGE 155**

MARINATED CHICKEN WITH PEPPERS

Chicken roasted with strips of red and yellow peppers, cooled, then tossed with a honey and herb marinade. Served with black olives.

SERVES 4–6 563–376 calories per serving

Takes 1 3/4 hours, plus cooling **PAGE 175**

PIGEON PIE WITH FENNEL & CARROTS

Strips of pigeon breast cooked with fennel, carrots, onion, stock, and wine, and baked with a puff pastry lid.

SERVES 6 672 calories per serving

Takes 2 hours **PAGE 193**

GUINEA FOWL MADEIRA

Pieces of guinea fowl cooked with shallots, stock, wine, and Madeira, enriched with double cream and green grapes.

SERVES 6 613 calories per serving

Takes 1 3/4 hours **PAGE 190**

RABBIT WITH MUSTARD & MARJORAM

Pieces of rabbit marinated in mustard and marjoram, and cooked with garlic, bacon, and stock. Served with a mustard sauce.

SERVES 4 548 calories per serving

Takes 2 hours, plus marinating **PAGE 194**

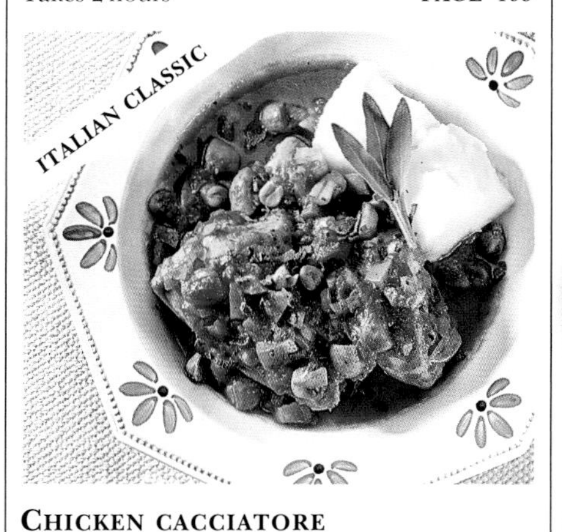

CHICKEN CACCIATORE

Pieces of chicken sprinkled with thyme, and cooked with bacon, onion, green pepper, garlic, mushrooms, wine, tomatoes, and sage.

SERVES 4 540 calories per serving

Takes 1 3/4 hours **PAGE 158**

CASSEROLE OF HARE

Rich and full of flavour: hare marinated in port, and cooked with shallots, bacon, chestnut mushrooms, and herbs.

SERVES 6 712 calories per serving

Takes 2 1/2 hours, plus marinating **PAGE 193**

OVER 60 MINUTES

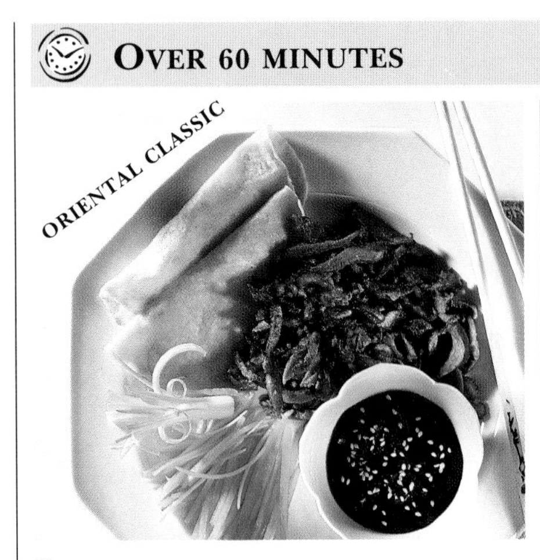

PEKING DUCK

Oriental speciality: whole duck brushed before cooking with sherry, honey, and soy sauce. Served with Chinese pancakes.

SERVES 6 848 calories per serving
Takes 2½ hours, plus drying **PAGE 186**

POT ROAST VENISON

Rolled shoulder of venison marinated in red wine, orange and lemon zests, and juniper berries, and slowly braised in the marinade with chopped carrots, celery, and onions. Redcurrant jelly is added to the sauce just before serving.

SERVES 4–6 681–454 calories per serving
Takes 3½ hours, plus marinating **PAGE 195**

ROAST DUCK WITH CRANBERRIES

Duck with a stuffing of onion, fresh brown breadcrumbs, and cranberries, roasted until crisp-skinned. Served with cranberry sauce.

SERVES 4 580 calories per serving
Takes 2½ hours, plus cooling **PAGE 187**

HEARTY VENISON CASSEROLE

Rich stew: cubes of venison marinated in wine, parsley, and allspice, and cooked with celery, mushrooms, and carrots.

SERVES 4 699 calories per serving
Takes 2¼ hours, plus marinating **PAGE 195**

TRADITIONAL GAME PIE

A selection of game, chicken, and pork marinated in port. Baked in a pastry case filled with jellied stock, then chilled.

SERVES 18 563 calories per serving
Takes 6 hours, plus marinating **PAGE 196**

BALLOTINE OF CHICKEN

Boned chicken pounded and stuffed with pork, liver, bacon, brandy, ham, and pistachio nuts. Rolled, cooked, chilled, and sliced.

SERVES 8–10 617–494 calories per serving
Takes 2¾ hours, plus chilling **PAGE 177**

CHRISTMAS ROAST GOOSE

Succulent and fruity: goose stuffed with pork sausagemeat, sage, and apple, and roasted. Served with wine-flavoured gravy, enriched with goose stock, and baked apples with a stuffing of Calvados, ground cinnamon, ground allspice, and prunes.

SERVES 8 921 calories per serving
Takes 5¼ hours, plus cooling **PAGE 185**

POULTRY & GAME KNOW-HOW

POULTRY IS THE TERM applied to all domesticated farmyard birds and includes chicken, turkey, geese, and duck. Chicken is sold whole, in joints, or cut into boneless strips, and lends itself to an infinite variety of recipes. Turkey is equally versatile and you can now enjoy whole birds, breast joints, and breast fillets or escalopes at any time of year. Though eaten less frequently, the richer, fattier meat of duck and goose has a truly wonderful flavour, as does the leaner meat of game and game birds.

BUYING & STORING

Poultry and game birds should have a plump breast and moist skin. Poultry should smell fresh and sweet. Game birds, which are left to hang to tenderize their flesh and to enhance their "gamey" flavour, should nevertheless have an appealing odour. They should be hung in a cool, draughty place for 2 days during warm and muggy weather and for up to 2 weeks during cold weather.

There is a great variety of poultry available. With chicken, for instance, the cook can choose free-range birds which have been allowed to roam in the open air and have been fed on a diet of grain. They are more expensive but are thought to have a superior flavour. Corn-fed chickens are another option. They are raised on a diet of maize, which gives their flesh a yellow colour and a delicious flavour. Chickens range in size from poussins, which serve 1–2, to oven-ready birds weighing from 1.5 kg (3 lb) up to 3 kg (6 lb). Turkeys can weigh as much as 15 kg (30 lb).

Poultry and game are very perishable so they must be kept cool. Remove any tight plastic wrapping and giblets and refrigerate the bird, loosely wrapped, immediately. It's a very good idea to set the bird on a plate to collect any drips. Cook smaller birds within 2 days of purchase and store goose and turkey for up to 4 days.

MICROWAVING

Casseroles and stews made from poultry and game can be cooked quite easily in the microwave oven. They are quick to prepare and when cooked properly, the meat stays tender and juicy. You may choose to brown the poultry or game and any vegetables on top of the stove first, then transfer the dish to finish cooking in the microwave oven. If you use two different pans, be sure to transfer the flavoursome pan drippings to the casserole in the microwave as well.

Roasted game and poultry are best cooked in a conventional oven; however, the microwave oven can speed up the process by quickly thawing meat that has been frozen.

FREEZING

To freeze poultry and plucked, oven-ready game at home, wrap it well and freeze without delay. When buying frozen poultry and game, check that it is completely frozen and transport it home as quickly as possible. Chicken, turkey, game birds, and small game animals can be stored for 6 months; duck, goose, and guinea fowl can be kept for 4 months; and large game animals for 8 months.

Poultry and game must be thoroughly thawed before cooking. Pierce the wrapping and set the bird on a plate, in the refrigerator (or use the microwave). Remove the giblets as soon as possible. Never re-freeze raw poultry or game.

Poultry safety

Raw poultry can carry bacteria such as salmonella. To reduce the risk of food poisoning, it is vital to store and handle poultry properly, and to cook it thoroughly. Wash your hands and all utensils in hot soapy water. Keep a chopping board just for raw poultry (preferably one that can be scalded, or washed in a dishwasher). Never let raw poultry (or its preparation utensils) come into contact with cooked poultry or meat. Don't stuff a bird until just before cooking, make sure the stuffing is cold, and stuff the neck end only: stuffing in the body cavity can inhibit heat penetration and prevent thorough cooking.

THOROUGH COOKING

Cook poultry thoroughly to kill any bacteria.

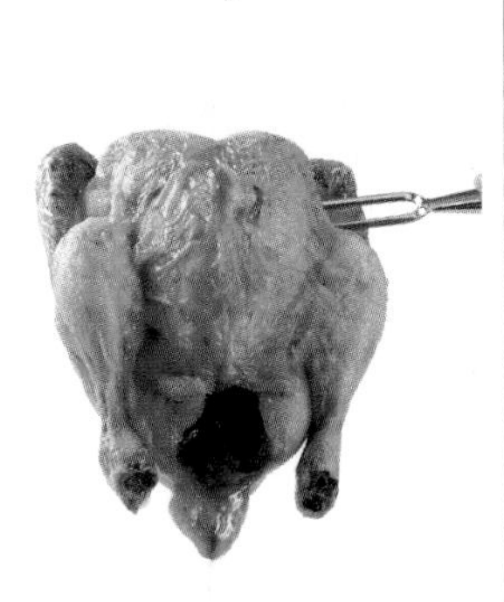

If you are roasting a whole bird, lift it on a long fork – the juices that run out should be clear. Insert a skewer into the thickest part of the meat and check the colour of the juices. Large birds are best tested with a meat thermometer – the internal temperature should be 90°C (190°F) when properly cooked.

POULTRY OR GAME STOCK

To make 2.5 litres (4 pints) stock, use 1.5 kg (3 lb) poultry or game pieces, the carcasses and trimmings from 3–4 chickens, or a turkey, or a whole chicken.

1 Put the cooked or uncooked bones into a stockpot or large pan with *2 or 3 halved, unpeeled onions.* Cook until browned. If using a whole chicken, brown just the onions, not the bird.

2 Add *4 litres (7 pints) water.* Bring to a boil, skimming off any scum from the surface. Add *3 chopped carrots, 3 chopped celery stalks, 1 large bouquet garni,* and *a few black peppercorns.*

3 Half cover the pan and simmer for 2½–3 hours. Strain the stock into a bowl. Leave to cool, then remove the solidified fat from the surface of the stock and discard. Cover and keep in the refrigerator for up to 3 days, or freeze for up to 3 months.

GIBLET STOCK

Use the giblets from 1 or 2 birds (poultry or game), excluding the liver.

1 In a stockpot or large saucepan, cook the giblets until lightly browned. Stir in *1 litre (1¾ pints) water* (or previously made stock). Bring to a boil, skimming off any scum that forms on the surface.

2 Add *1–2 quartered, unpeeled onions, 1 chopped carrot, 1 chopped celery stalk, 1 bouquet garni,* and *a few black peppercorns.* Simmer for about 1 hour. Cool, cover, and keep in the refrigerator for 3 days or freeze for 3 months. Strain before use.

JELLIED STOCK

This stock is used in cold dishes such as raised pies, where it forms a jelly around the meat. Make it in the same way as other stocks, but use bones only, rather than a whole chicken or other meats, as they contain a high level of gelatine. Crack the bones before adding them to the pot. The stock will set when cool.

Stock know-how

Do not add salt when making stock because it may be reduced in recipes to concentrate the flavour.

◆

Peppercorns, instead of ground black pepper, are used in stock. Prolonged cooking can turn ground black pepper bitter.

◆

Skim fat with a large spoon, soak it up with paper towels, or allow to cool and lift it off.

JOINTING A CHICKEN

Chicken portions are widely available, but cutting a bird into 4 or 8 serving pieces is not at all difficult to do yourself, and it can be done before or after cooking. A pair of special poultry shears makes the job particularly easy, otherwise use good, strong scissors or a sharp chef's knife.

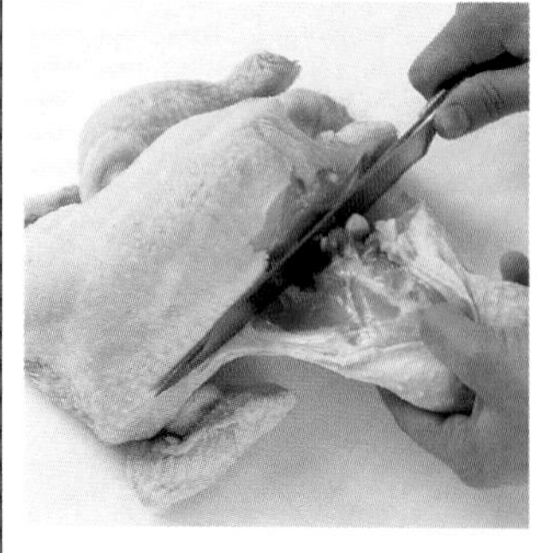

1 Cut through to the joint between one of the legs and the body. Twist the leg out and away from the body to pop the ball and socket joint, then cut through the joint to remove the leg. Remove the second leg.

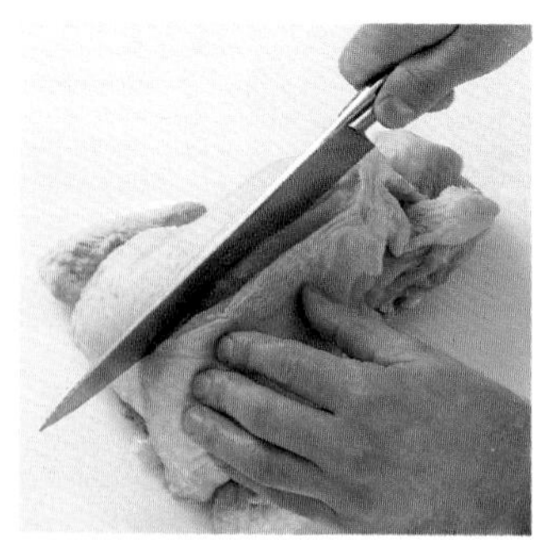

2 To remove the breasts, cut through the skin and flesh along both sides of the breastbone. Cut through the bones of the ribcage where it joins the sides of the breastbone, then remove the breastbone.

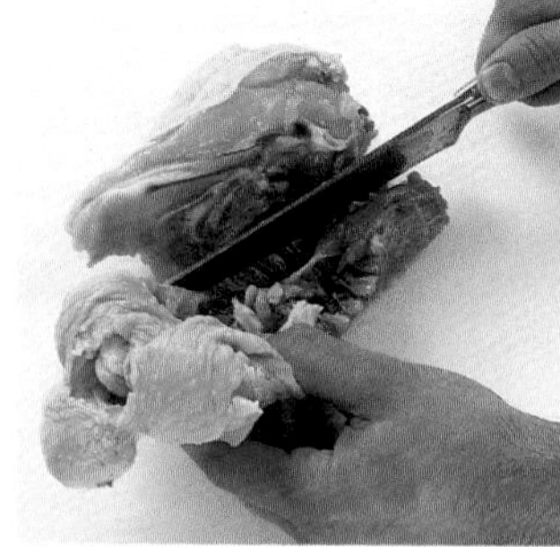

3 Open up the bird and cut along the backbone, to give 2 breasts with wings attached. For 8 pieces, cut each breast diagonally in two: the wing half should be slightly smaller. Cut each leg through the joint.

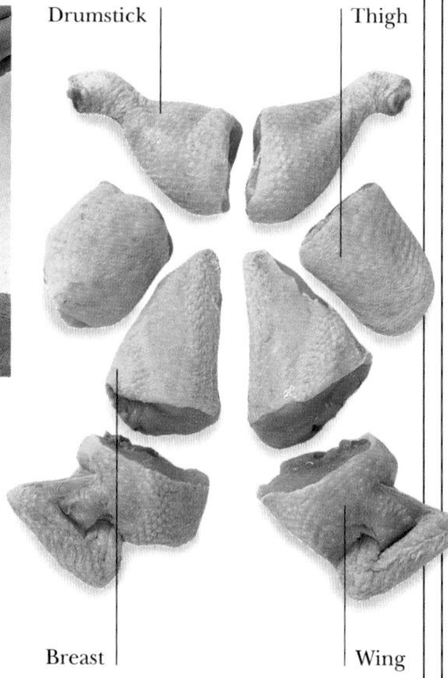

BONING A WHOLE CHICKEN

Although boning a chicken requires a little time and effort, the result is impressive. Stuffed and rolled into a ballotine, it is ideal for entertaining because it is so easy to carve. Other birds can be boned in the same way.

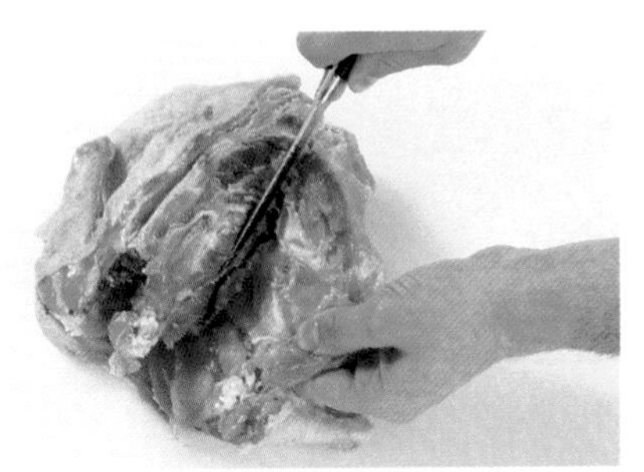

1 Set the bird breast-side down and slit the skin along the backbone. Remove the wishbone (page 150). Slide the knife into the cut and gently pull and scrape the flesh away from the ribcage. Continue cutting away the flesh until you reach the leg and wing joints.

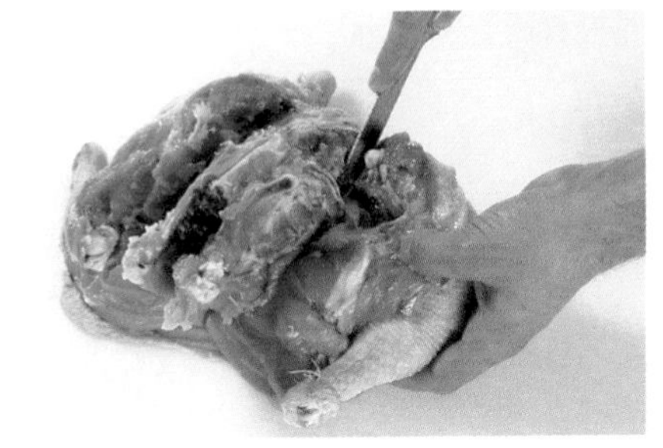

2 Scrape away the flesh from the other side of the ribcage. Take care not to make any holes in the skin as you bone the bird. Cut through the ball and socket joints connecting the thighs to the bird.

3 Keep cutting until you reach the breastbone in the middle. Cut the breastbone free without cutting through the skin. Press each leg out and away from the body to pop the ball and socket joint.

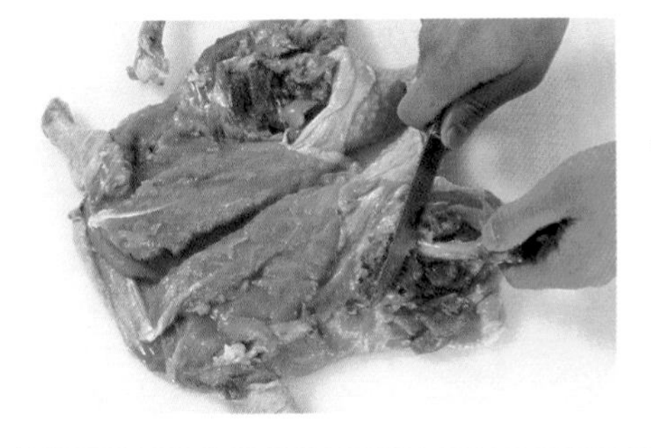

4 Cut through the tendons that join the legs to the body. Cut and scrape back the flesh until the bones of each leg have been freed, then pull out the bones.

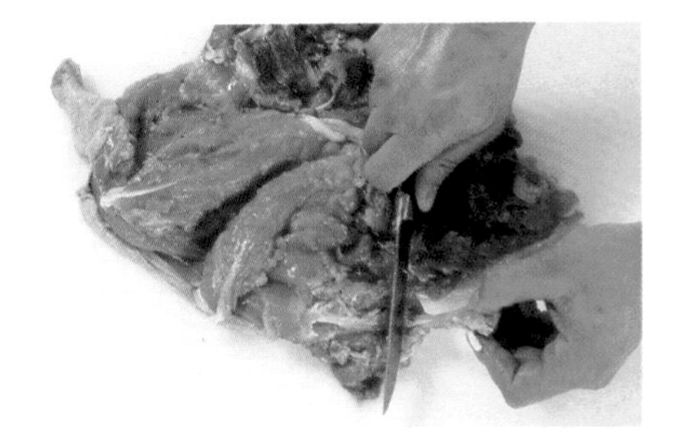

5 Bone the wings in the same way as the legs. The chicken is now ready for stuffing and rolling. Keep the carcass and bones of the bird for making chicken stock.

BONING A QUAIL

For a special occasion, tiny quail can be boned, but left whole. It's then quite simple to fill them with a savoury stuffing and secure with a cocktail stick ready for roasting. Make sure you use a very small knife and be careful not to pierce the skin.

1 With your fingers, carefully loosen the skin at the neck of the quail, and push it back to reveal the wishbone. With a small, sharp knife, cut the flesh from around the wishbone to remove it.

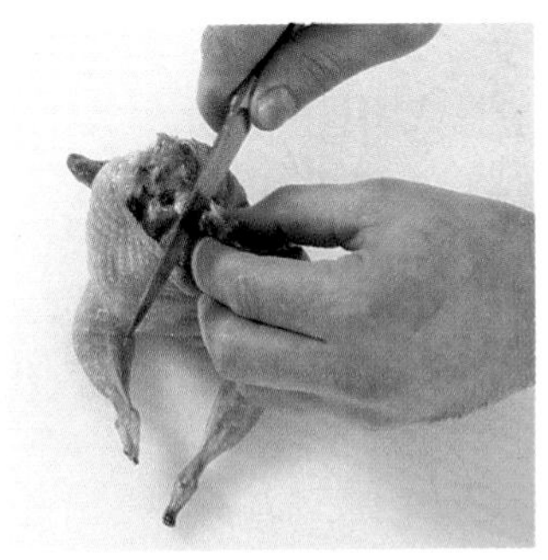

2 Loosen 1 wing by carefully cutting through the tendon at the base. Repeat with the other wing.

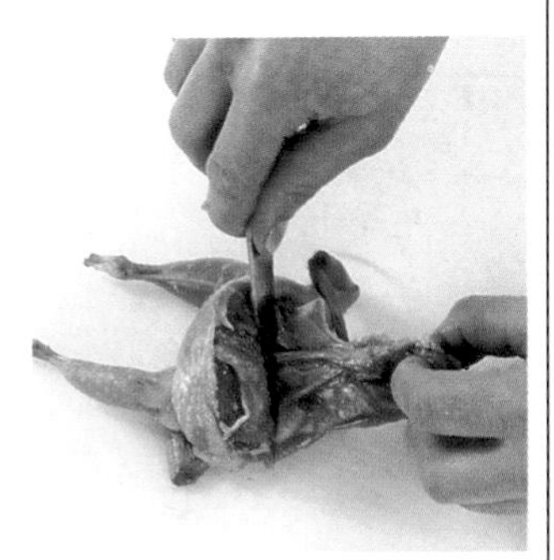

3 Insert the knife between the ribcage and the flesh and, working all around the bird, scrape the flesh from the bones, pushing it back as you go. Remove the ribcage. The bird is now ready to stuff.

SPATCHCOCKING

This method of splitting and flattening a bird makes it quicker to cook and suitable for grilling or cooking over a barbecue. Poussins, chickens, guinea fowl, and game birds can all be spatchcocked.

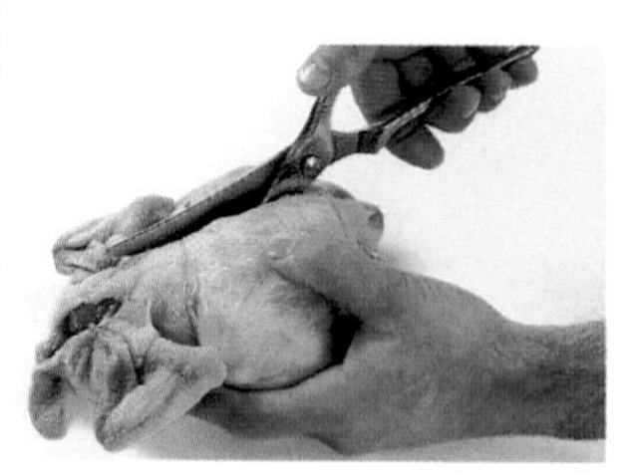

1 With poultry shears or a knife, cut along both sides of the backbone and discard. Cut off the wing tips and the ends of the legs. Remove the wishbone.

2 Turn the bird over. Put your hands on top of the breast and press down firmly with the heels of your hands to break the breastbone and flatten the bird.

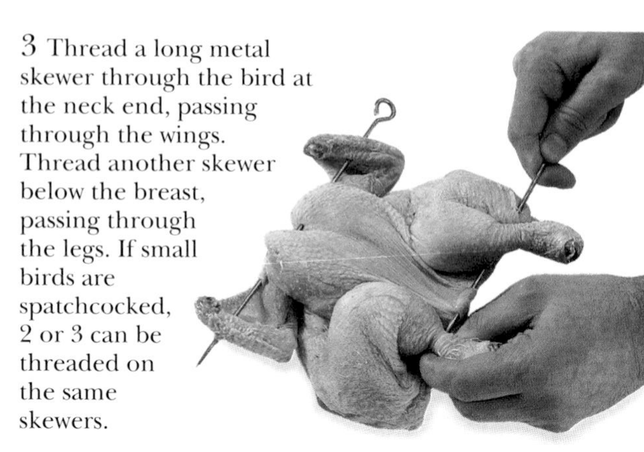

3 Thread a long metal skewer through the bird at the neck end, passing through the wings. Thread another skewer below the breast, passing through the legs. If small birds are spatchcocked, 2 or 3 can be threaded on the same skewers.

PREPARING POULTRY FOR ROASTING

Tying or skewering a bird before roasting holds it together so that it keeps a neat shape during cooking. It will also prevent any stuffing from falling out. Only put stuffing into the neck end of a bird and not into the large body cavity.

Trussing with string

1 Thread a trussing needle with string. Put the bird breast-side up. Push the legs back and down. Insert the needle into a knee joint, through the bird, and then out through the other knee.

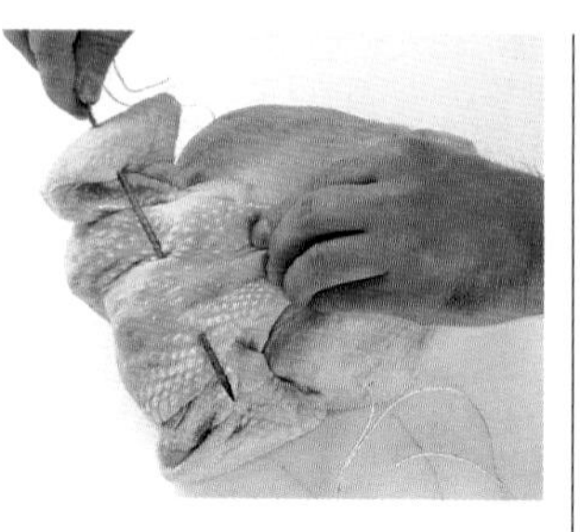

2 Pull the neck skin over the cavity and tuck the wing tips over it. Push the needle through both sections of each wing, through the neck skin, and beneath the backbone.

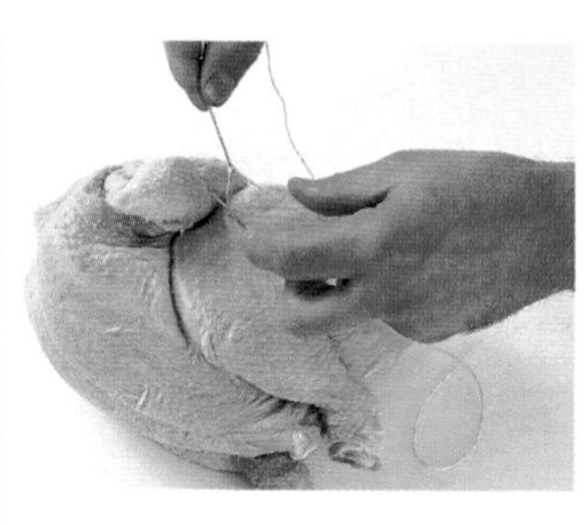

3 With the bird on its side, pull the string tightly, tie the ends together, and trim. Tuck the tail into the cavity and fold the top skin over it.

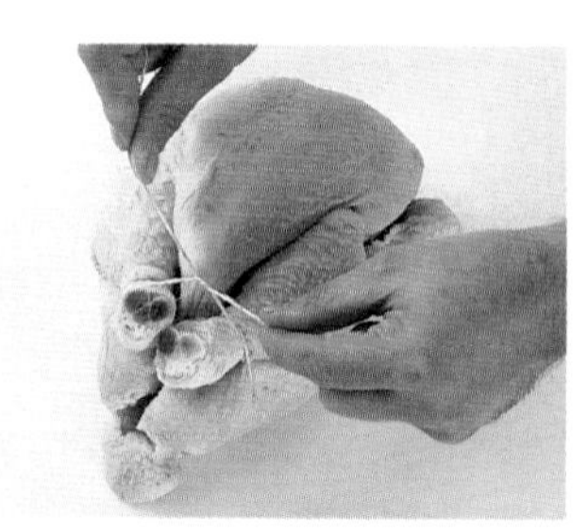

4 Push the needle through the top skin. Loop the string around one of the drumsticks, under the breastbone, and around the other drumstick. Pull the string tight and tie the ends.

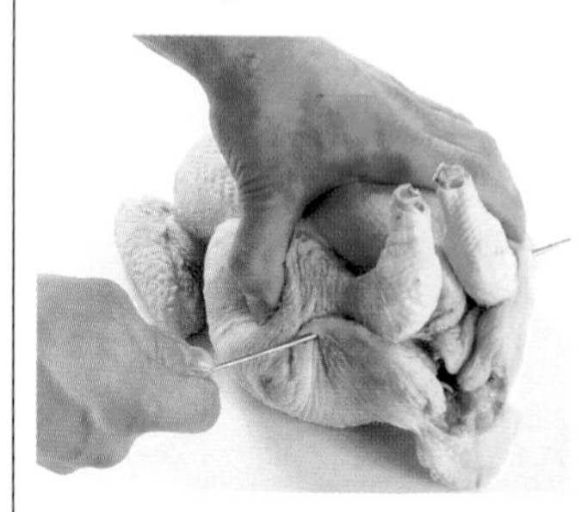

Simple trussing

1 Put the bird breast-side up and push the legs back and down. Hold the legs with one hand, insert a skewer below the knee joint, and push it through the bird.

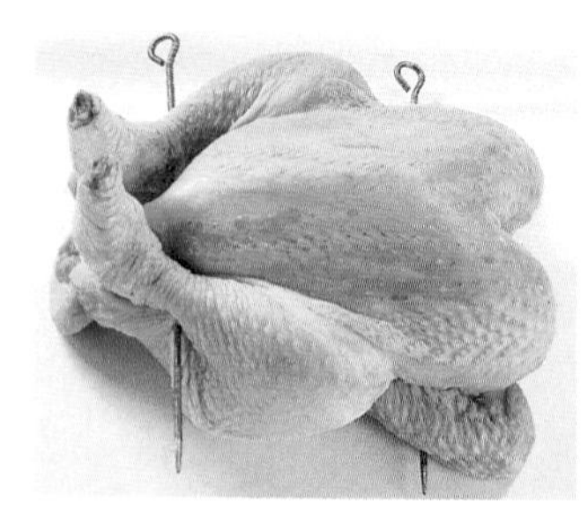

2 Turn the bird over. Pull the neck skin over the cavity and tuck the wing tips over it. Push a skewer through 1 wing, the neck skin, and out through the other wing.

REMOVING THE WISHBONE

A bird is easier to carve if the wishbone is removed before cooking.

With your fingers, loosen the skin from the flesh at the neck end. Fold back the skin to expose the breastbone. Use a small, sharp knife to cut the wishbone free, taking any fat with it.

CARVING DUCKS & GEESE

Once cooked, small ducks need simply to be cut into quarters or even halves for serving. Larger ducks and geese can be carved as for other poultry (below).

1 Remove trussing. Cut through the joints between legs and body to remove the legs. (Cook them further if necessary). Cut the wings in the same way.

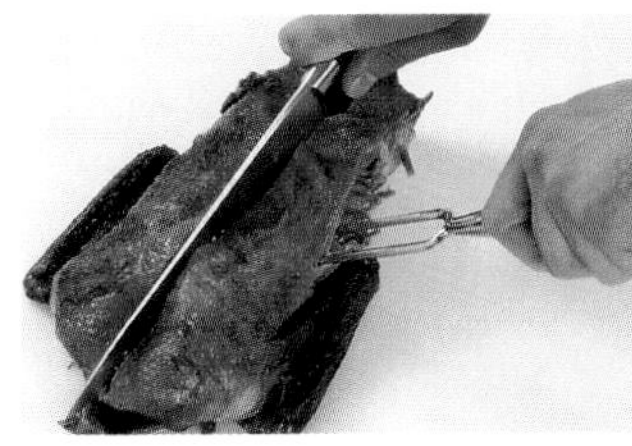

2 Slit the skin along both sides of the breastbone. Slide the knife blade into the cut on one side to free the breast meat in a single piece. Repeat on the other side.

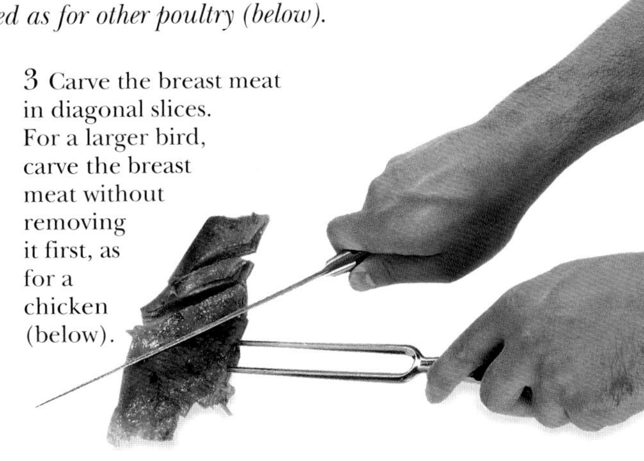

3 Carve the breast meat in diagonal slices. For a larger bird, carve the breast meat without removing it first, as for a chicken (below).

CARVING POULTRY

Leave a bird to rest for about 15 minutes before carving. First remove any trussing string or skewers, then spoon stuffing into a serving dish.

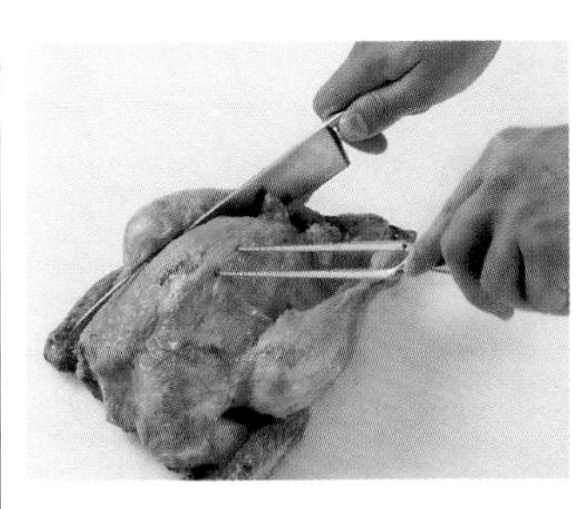

1 Put the bird breast-side up on a carving board (ideally one with a well to catch all the juices). Insert a carving fork into one breast to keep the bird steady, then cut in to the joint between the far leg and body.

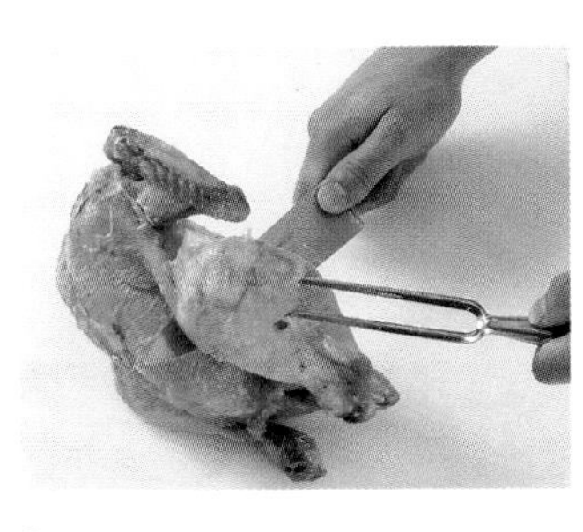

2 Turn the bird on its side and cut away the meat close to the backbone, cutting around the "oyster" meat on the back so that it remains attached to the thigh. Turn the bird over.

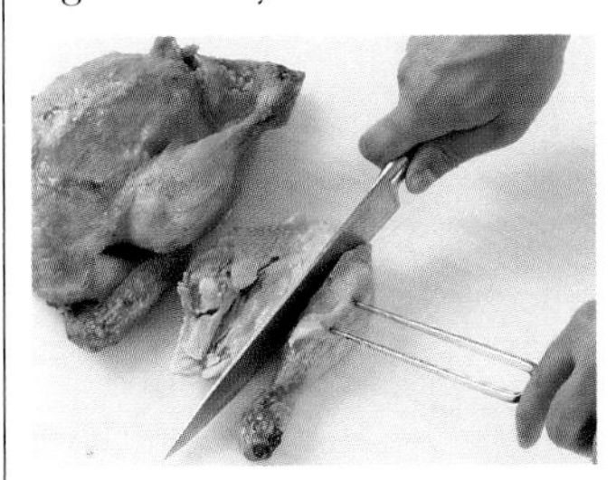

3 Twist the leg outwards to break the joint, then cut it to remove the leg and the thigh. If preferred, divide into thigh and drumstick, cutting through the ball and socket joint. Remove the other leg.

4 Make a horizontal cut into the breast above the wing joint on one side, cutting all the way to the bone. Carve neat slices from the breast, holding the knife blade parallel to the ribcage. Repeat on the other side.

ROASTING TIMES

These times are a guide only; always test a bird to make sure it is thoroughly cooked (page 147).

BIRD	OVEN TEMPERATURE	TIME
Poussin	190°C (375°F, Gas 5)	40–45 minutes total cooking, depending on size
Chicken	190°C (375°F, Gas 5)	20 minutes per 500 g (1 lb) plus 20 minutes
Duck	200°C (400°F, Gas 6)	25 minutes per 500 g (1 lb) for "just cooked"
Goose	180°C (350°F, Gas 4)	20 minutes per 500 g (1 lb) plus 20 minutes
Pheasant	200°C (400°F, Gas 6)	50 minutes total cooking
Turkey		
3.5–4.5 kg (7–9 lb)	190°C (375°F, Gas 5)	2½–3 hours total cooking
5–6 kg (10–12 lb)	190°C (375°F, Gas 5)	3½–4 hours total cooking
6.5–8.5 kg (13–17 lb)	190°C (375°F, Gas 5)	4½–5 hours total cooking

Roasting know-how

To calculate roasting time, weigh the bird after you have added any stuffing. Do not stuff duck or goose.

◆

Cover large birds loosely with foil to prevent the skin from becoming too browned.

◆

Place fatty birds, such as duck and goose, on a rack, to allow the fat to drain away and keep the skin crisp.

SUNDAY ROAST CHICKEN

Amid the many exotic recipes available today, traditional Sunday roast chicken sometimes gets overlooked. However, with its crisp skin, light, juicy stuffing of onion, apple, herbs, and lemon zest, and accompaniment of rich gravy, it is hard to better.

Serves 4

a few parsley and thyme sprigs

1.7–2 kg (3 1/2–4 lb) chicken, with giblets reserved for stock

1/2 lemon, sliced (optional)

1/2 onion, sliced (optional)

60 g (2 oz) butter, softened

APPLE & HERB STUFFING

30 g (1 oz) butter

1 small onion, finely chopped

1 cooking apple, peeled, cored, and grated

60 g (2 oz) fresh white breadcrumbs

1 small egg, beaten

1 tbsp chopped parsley

1 tbsp chopped fresh thyme

grated zest of 1 lemon

salt and black pepper

GRAVY

2 tsp plain flour

300 ml (1/2 pint) chicken giblet stock (page 148)

1 Make the apple and herb stuffing: melt the butter in a saucepan, add the onion, and cook gently for a few minutes until softened. Remove from the heat, leave to cool slightly, then stir in the apple, breadcrumbs, egg, parsley, thyme, lemon zest, and salt and pepper to taste. Leave to cool completely.

2 Put the parsley and thyme sprigs into the cavity of the chicken, add the lemon and onion, if using, and season well with black pepper. Truss the chicken, if preferred (page 150).

3 Spoon the stuffing into the neck end of the chicken, secure the skin flap over the stuffing with a small skewer, and pat into a rounded shape. Put any leftover stuffing into a small ovenproof dish.

4 Weigh the stuffed chicken, then rub the butter over the breast, and season with salt and pepper.

5 Place the chicken, breast-side down, in a roasting tin. Cook in a preheated oven at 190°C (375°F, Gas 5) for 20 minutes per 500 g (1 lb), plus an extra 20 minutes. Turn the chicken over when lightly browned. Continue cooking, basting every 20 minutes. Cook any leftover stuffing with the chicken for the last 40 minutes of cooking time.

6 Test the chicken: insert a skewer into the thigh – the juices will run clear when the chicken is cooked.

7 Transfer to a warmed serving platter, and keep warm while you make the gravy (see box, right).

8 Remove the stuffing from the neck cavity and transfer to a serving dish with any leftover stuffing. Carve the chicken, and serve with the gravy.

Making gravy

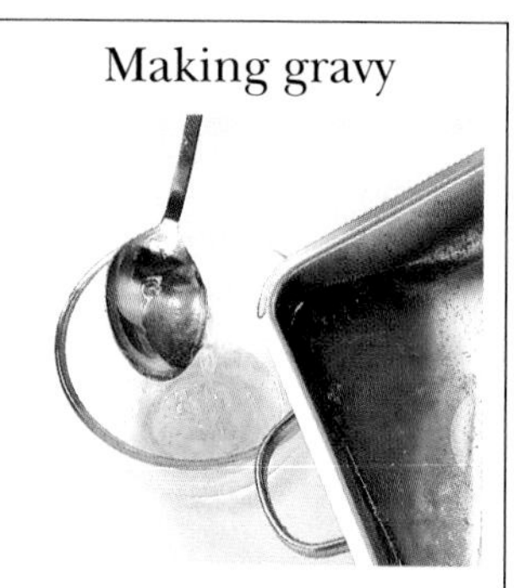

Tilt the roasting tin, and spoon off all but 1 tbsp of the fat that rises to the surface, leaving behind the cooking juices and sediment. Put the roasting tin on top of the stove.

Add the flour, and cook over a medium heat for 1–2 minutes, stirring constantly with a whisk or metal spoon to dissolve any sediment from the bottom of the tin.

Pour in the stock, and bring to a boil, stirring constantly until the gravy thickens. Simmer for 2 minutes, then taste for seasoning. Strain into a warmed gravy boat, and serve at once.

FRENCH ROAST CHICKEN

The flesh of a chicken roasted in the traditional French style remains particularly moist and succulent because of the stock added to the roasting tin. In France, the chicken liver is cooked in a little butter, then sliced and added to the gravy, but this is optional.

 **Serves 4**

- *1 tarragon or rosemary sprig*
- *90 g (3 oz) butter, softened, plus extra for greasing*
- *1.7–2 kg ($3^{1}/_{2}$–4 lb) chicken, with giblets reserved for stock*
- *black pepper*
- *300 ml ($^{1}/_{2}$ pint) chicken giblet stock (page 148)*
- *2 tsp plain flour*
- *4 roast garlic flowers (see box, right) to serve*

1 Put the tarragon sprig and 30 g (1 oz) of the butter into the cavity of the chicken, and season well with black pepper. Truss the chicken, if preferred (page 150). Rub the remaining butter over the breast.

2 Weigh the chicken, then put it, breast-side down, into a small roasting tin. Pour over the stock, and cover with buttered greaseproof paper. Cook in a preheated oven at 190°C (375°F, Gas 5) for 20 minutes per 500 g (1 lb), plus an extra 20 minutes, turning the chicken on to its sides, and finally on to its back, basting occasionally, to brown all over.

3 Test the chicken by inserting a fine skewer into the thickest part of a thigh: the juices will run clear when the chicken is cooked. Transfer to a warmed serving platter, and keep warm. Reserve the cooking juices.

4 Spoon off all but 1 tbsp fat from the tin. Make the gravy (steps 2 and 3, page 152), using the flour and reserved stock.

ITALIAN ROAST CHICKEN

Omit the roast garlic flowers. Put the chicken into a large roasting tin, and add 2 trimmed and sliced fennel bulbs 30 minutes before the end of the cooking time. Remove with a slotted spoon before making the gravy, and keep warm.

Roast garlic flowers

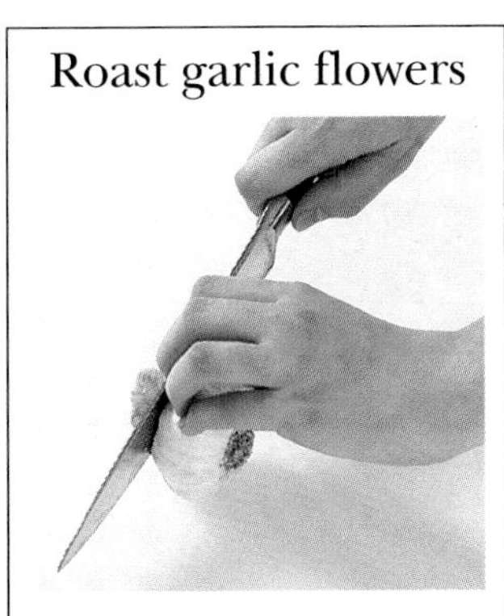

Cut the stalk ends off *4 heads of garlic*, arrange in an oiled baking dish, and drizzle a little olive oil over the tops. Cook in a preheated oven at 190°C (375°F, Gas 5) for 45–60 minutes. To eat, squeeze the soft cloves of garlic from the papery skins.

ROAST CHICKEN WITH ORANGE & PEPPERS

Serves 4

3 oranges

1.5 kg (3 lb) chicken, with giblets removed

a few parsley sprigs

1 head of garlic, separated into cloves

salt and black pepper

1 tsp paprika

pinch of cayenne pepper

15 g (1/2 oz) butter, softened

1 red pepper, cored, seeded, and diced

75 ml (2 1/2 fl oz) brandy

90 ml (3 fl oz) orange juice

chopped fresh basil to garnish

1 Cut 2 of the oranges lengthwise into quarters, leaving them unpeeled. Peel the remaining orange, and separate it into segments.

2 Fill the chicken cavity with the parsley, orange quarters, and half the garlic.

3 Rub the chicken with salt, pepper, paprika, cayenne, and butter. Place the chicken, breast-side down, in a roasting tin. Add the red pepper and the remaining garlic.

4 Roast in a preheated oven at 190°C (375°F, Gas 5) for 20 minutes per 500 g (1 lb), plus an extra 20 minutes, turning the chicken breast-side up halfway through cooking.

5 Heat the brandy in a small saucepan, pour it over the chicken, and light it with a match.

6 When the flames have died down, remove the chicken, red pepper, and garlic from the tin. Carve the chicken, discarding the parsley, orange, and garlic from the cavity. Arrange the sliced chicken, red pepper, and garlic cloves on a warmed serving platter, and keep warm.

7 Spoon off all but 1 tbsp fat from the roasting tin, leaving behind the cooking juices. Add the orange juice and boil until reduced. Add the orange segments and heat through.

8 Spoon the orange segments and sauce over the chicken, sprinkle with the basil, and serve at once.

PROVENÇAL POT ROAST CHICKEN

Serves 4

1 large head of garlic, separated into cloves

1.5–1.7 kg (3–3 1/2 lb) chicken, with giblets removed

salt and cayenne pepper

6 parsley sprigs

1 red pepper, cored, seeded, and diced

1 carrot, diced

350 ml (12 fl oz) chicken stock

250 ml (8 fl oz) red wine vinegar

1 tbsp tomato purée

1/4 tsp herbes de Provence

chopped parsley to garnish

1 Peel half of the garlic cloves. Season the chicken inside and out with salt and cayenne pepper. Put the unpeeled garlic cloves and the parsley sprigs inside the chicken.

2 Place the chicken in a casserole, arrange the red pepper, carrot, and peeled garlic cloves around it, then pour in the stock. Cover and roast in a preheated oven at 190°C (375°F, Gas 5) for 1 1/2 hours.

3 Remove the chicken from the casserole. Pour the pan juices, carrot, red pepper, and garlic into a food processor, and purée until smooth. Return the sauce to the casserole, and if very liquid, boil it until thickened. In another saucepan, boil the vinegar until it is reduced to 3 tbsp.

4 Stir the vinegar, tomato purée, and herbes de Provence into the sauce and taste for seasoning. Return the chicken to the casserole, spoon the sauce over the chicken, and heat through.

5 Garnish with chopped parsley and serve at once.

WINTER POT ROAST CHICKEN

Substitute 2 sliced celery stalks, 1 diced parsnip, and 1/4 tsp celery salt, for the red pepper and herbes de Provence, and proceed as directed.

CHICKEN POT PIE

This recipe makes a great family dish, packed with tender chicken and a variety of colourful vegetables. You can vary the vegetables according to season and availability. The pie will be a great success any time of the year.

Serves 6

1 kg (2 lb) chicken, with giblets removed

1.25 litres (2 pints) chicken stock

1 onion, quartered

1 celery stalk, thickly sliced

2 garlic cloves, crushed

2 small carrots

2 small waxy potatoes

45 g (1 1/2 oz) butter

3 tbsp plain flour, plus extra for dusting

pinch of grated nutmeg

salt and black pepper

125 g (4 oz) frozen peas

1 tbsp chopped parsley

175 g (6 oz) shortcrust pastry

beaten egg yolk for glazing

⋆ 2 litre (3 1/2 pint) pie dish

1 In a large pan, bring the chicken, stock, onion, celery, and garlic to a boil. Simmer for 30 minutes.

2 Add the carrots and potatoes, and simmer for 20 minutes or until all the vegetables are cooked and the chicken is just tender. Leave to cool.

3 Remove the meat from the chicken, and cut it into bite-sized pieces, discarding the skin and bones. Dice the vegetables and set aside.

4 Skim the fat from the stock, then bring 600 ml (1 pint) of the stock to a boil. Melt the butter in a large pan, add the flour, and cook, stirring occasionally, for 1 minute. Stir in the hot stock, whisking until it comes to a boil and thickens. Add the nutmeg, and salt and pepper to taste.

5 Stir the chicken, diced vegetables, peas, and parsley into the sauce, then set aside until cold.

6 On a lightly floured work surface, roll out the pastry, then cut out the lid, and fill, cover, and decorate the pie (see box, right).

7 Bake in a preheated oven at 190°C (375°F, Gas 5) for 30 minutes or until the top is crisp and golden brown. Serve hot.

CHICKEN, LEEK, & MUSHROOM PIE

Omit the celery and carrots. Trim and slice 1 leek, and cook in a little butter for 5 minutes or until soft. Add 60 g (2 oz) sliced mushrooms, and cook for 2 minutes. Remove with a slotted spoon; add to the sauce with the chicken and vegetables.

Filling, covering, and decorating the pie

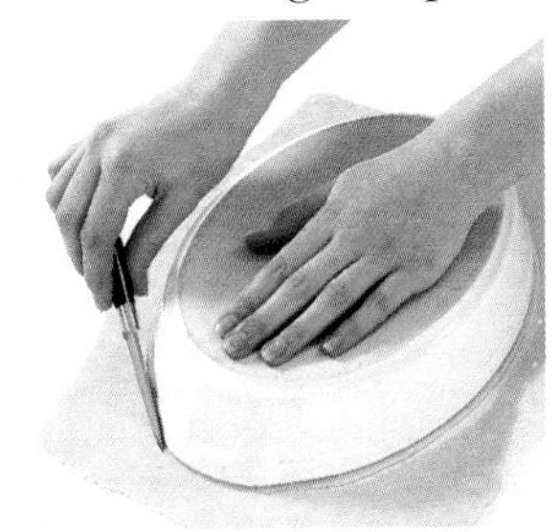

Invert the pie dish on to the pastry, and use a small knife to cut around the edge, keeping the blade close to the dish. Reserve all trimmings. Transfer the filling to the pie dish, and top with the pastry.

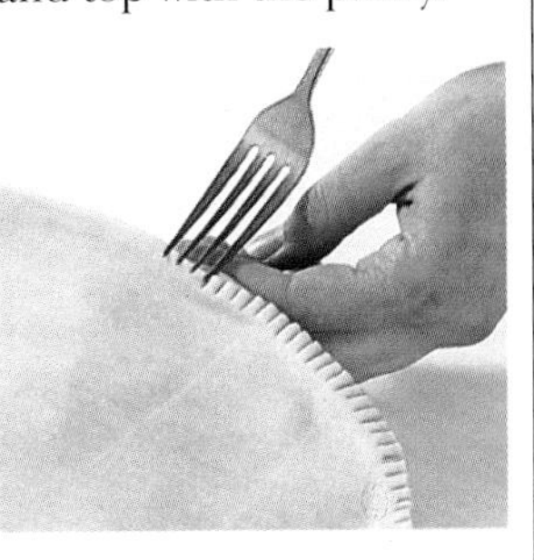

Press the pastry with your fingertips on to the rim of the pie dish. Crimp the edge of the pastry with a fork. Brush the pastry with the beaten egg yolk, making a lattice pattern.

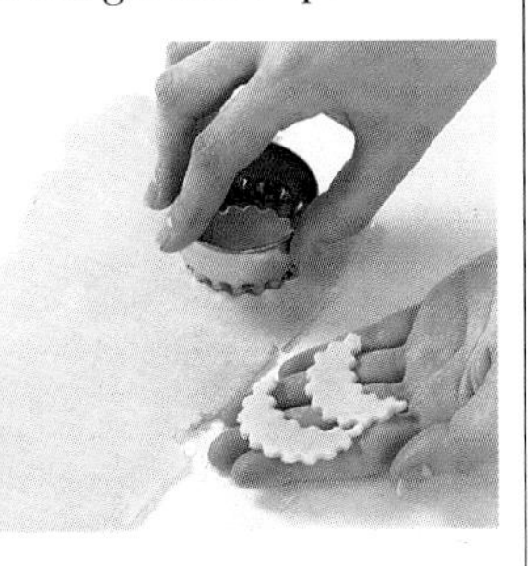

Cut decorative shapes from the reserved pastry trimmings with a pastry cutter. Arrange on top of the pie, and glaze the shapes with the beaten egg yolk.

MOROCCAN POUSSINS

Serves 2

2 x 375 g (12 oz) poussins, spatchcocked (page 150)

MARINADE

3 tbsp olive oil

grated zest of 1/4 lime and juice of 2 limes

1 small onion, finely chopped

5 garlic cloves, crushed

2 tbsp chopped fresh coriander

2 tsp paprika

1 tsp curry powder

1 tsp ground cumin

large pinch of saffron strands

salt and cayenne pepper

1 Make the marinade: in a non-metallic dish, mix the olive oil, lime zest and juice, onion, garlic, coriander, paprika, curry powder, cumin, saffron, and salt and cayenne pepper to taste.

2 Turn the poussins in the marinade, cover, and leave to marinate in the refrigerator, turning the poussins occasionally, for about 3 hours.

3 Place the poussins under a hot grill, 15 cm (6 ins) from the heat, and grill, brushing occasionally with the marinade, for 15–20 minutes on each side. Serve at once.

LEMON POUSSINS WITH MARINATED ARTICHOKE HEARTS

Roasting poussins with lemon, rosemary, and whole cloves of garlic in the cavity makes them fragrant and juicy. The marinated artichokes also give an interesting twist to this classic Italian dish – add some sun-dried tomatoes as well, if you like.

Serves 4

4 x 375 g (12 oz) poussins

salt and black pepper

4 garlic cloves

1 lemon, cut into quarters lengthwise

4 rosemary sprigs

60 g (2 oz) butter, softened

2 x 400 g (13 oz) cans artichoke hearts, drained and halved

175 ml (6 fl oz) dry white wine

fresh rosemary and lemon wedges to garnish

MARINADE

4 tbsp olive oil

2 tbsp lemon juice

3 garlic cloves, crushed

1 tbsp chopped parsley

2 tsp chopped fresh thyme

1 Season the poussins inside and out with salt and pepper, and put a garlic clove, lemon quarter, and rosemary sprig into each one. Truss (page 150). Rub with butter (see box, right).

2 Put the poussins on a rack in a roasting tin. Roast in a preheated oven at 190°C (375°F, Gas 5), basting, for 40–45 minutes until they are golden brown.

3 Meanwhile, combine the marinade ingredients, adding salt and pepper to taste. Turn the artichokes in the marinade and leave to stand for at least 30 minutes.

4 Boil the wine for about 15 minutes until it reduces to 90 ml (3 fl oz). Set aside.

5 Remove the poussins from the tin, and keep warm. Spoon off all but 1 tbsp fat from the tin, leaving the cooking juices.

6 Add the reduced wine to the tin, and mix with the juices. Stir in the artichokes, add 2–3 tbsp marinade, and bring to a boil. Serve the poussins with the artichokes and sauce, garnished with rosemary and lemon wedges.

Rubbing poussins with butter

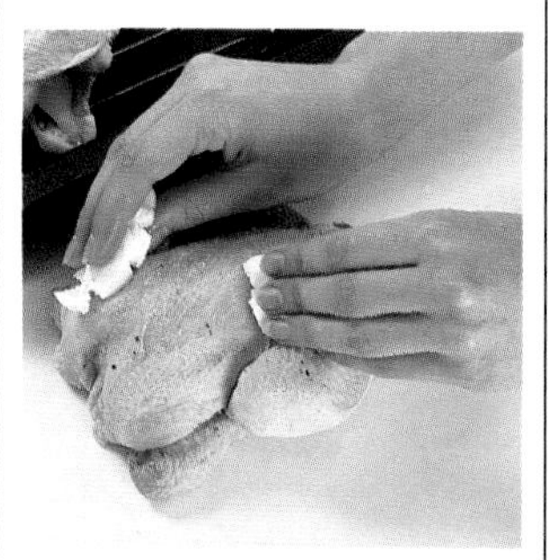

Cut the butter into pieces, and use your fingertips to rub it generously on to the skin of the poussins.

POUSSINS WITH MUSHROOMS

Substitute 375 g (12 oz) halved chestnut mushrooms for the artichoke hearts, and proceed as directed.

POUSSINS WITH ROMESCO SAUCE

Serves 2

2 x 375 g (12 oz) poussins, spatchcocked (page 150)
8 spring onions, trimmed
coriander sprigs to garnish

MARINADE
2 tbsp olive oil
1 tbsp balsamic vinegar
4 garlic cloves, crushed
1/2 tsp ground cinnamon
salt and black pepper

ROMESCO SAUCE
3 tomatoes, peeled (page 39), seeded, and chopped
90 g (3 oz) flaked almonds
1 slice of stale bread, crusts removed, coarsely chopped
2 tbsp olive oil
1 tbsp balsamic vinegar
1 garlic clove
1 small dried red chilli, cored, seeded, and chopped
1 tbsp chopped parsley
1/2 tsp ground cinnamon

1 Make the marinade: combine the oil, vinegar, garlic, cinnamon, and salt and black pepper to taste. Brush over the poussins and spring onions, cover, and leave to marinate in the refrigerator for 1 hour.

2 Place the poussins under a hot grill, 15 cm (6 ins) from the heat, and grill for 15–20 minutes on each side until lightly browned. Grill the spring onions close to the heat for 5–8 minutes on each side until the onions are slightly charred.

3 Meanwhile, make the romesco sauce: purée the tomatoes, almonds, bread, olive oil, balsamic vinegar, garlic, chilli, parsley, and cinnamon in a food processor until smooth. Add salt and pepper to taste.

4 Serve the poussins at once, with the spring onions and the romesco sauce. Garnish each serving with a coriander sprig.

POUSSINS WITH NIÇOISE SAUCE

Make the romesco sauce as directed, but omit the cinnamon and add 2 tbsp ready-made black olive paste (tapenade). *Garnish with black olives before serving.*

ORIENTAL POUSSINS

Serves 4

2 x 625 g (1 1/4 lb) poussins
125 ml (4 fl oz) dark soy sauce
3 tbsp dry sherry
3 tbsp hoisin sauce
3 tbsp sunflower oil
6 garlic cloves, crushed
2 tbsp brown sugar
1 tsp five-spice powder
1 cm (1/2 in) piece of fresh root ginger, peeled and chopped
spring onions to garnish
blanched mangetout and red pepper strips to serve

1 Halve the poussins, and remove the backbones (see box, right).

2 Combine the soy sauce, sherry, hoisin sauce, oil, garlic, sugar, five-spice powder, and ginger. Brush this mixture on both sides of the poussin halves.

3 Put the poussins, skin-side up, into a roasting tin, and roast in a preheated oven at 190°C (375°F, Gas 5), basting occasionally with any remaining soy sauce mixture, for 30 minutes or until cooked through.

4 With a sharp knife, thinly slice just the green tops of the spring onions. Garnish the poussin halves with the spring onion slices, and serve with the mangetout and red pepper strips.

Halving a poussin

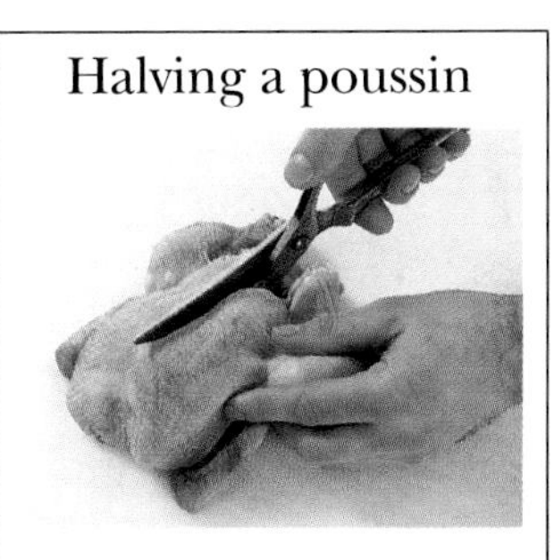

Cut along the middle of the poussin breast with a pair of poultry shears. Take the 2 sides and open out slightly.

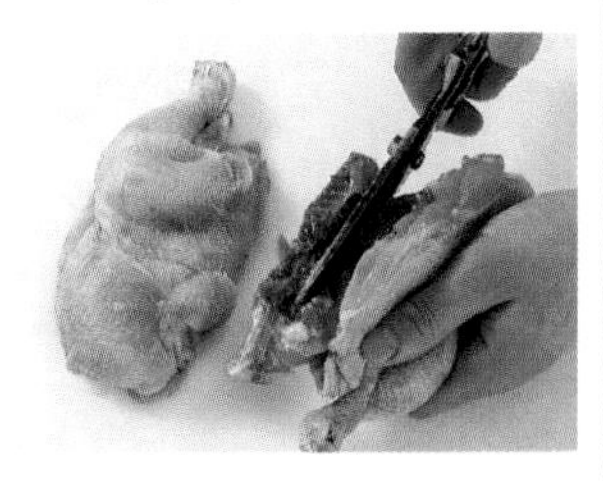

Turn the poussin over and cut in half, along one side of the backbone. Remove and discard the backbone.

FAMILY CHICKEN CASSEROLE

 **Serves 4**

2 tbsp sunflower oil
4 chicken quarters
125 g (4 oz) streaky bacon rashers, cut into strips
250 g (8 oz) carrots, thickly sliced
2 celery stalks, thickly sliced
1 large onion, sliced
30 g (1 oz) plain flour
600 ml (1 pint) chicken stock
1 bay leaf
1 thyme sprig
1 parsley sprig
salt and black pepper
4 potatoes, cut into large chunks
chopped parsley to garnish

1 Heat the oil in a large flameproof casserole. Add the chicken, skin-side down, and cook for 10–12 minutes until browned all over. Lift out and drain on paper towels. Add the bacon, carrots, celery, and onion, and cook over a high heat, stirring, until golden. Lift out with a slotted spoon, and drain on paper towels.

2 Spoon off all but 1 tbsp fat from the casserole. Add the flour, and cook, stirring constantly, for 3–5 minutes until lightly browned. Gradually pour in the chicken stock, stirring until smooth. Add the bay leaf, thyme, parsley, and salt and pepper to taste.

3 Return the chicken, bacon, carrots, celery, and onion to the casserole, add the potatoes, and bring to a boil. Cover and cook in a preheated oven at 160°C (325°F, Gas 3) for 1¼ hours or until the chicken is cooked through. Garnish with chopped parsley.

ITALIAN CHICKEN CASSEROLE

Substitute 250 g (8 oz) sliced courgettes for the carrots, and 1 x 400 g (13 oz) can chopped tomatoes and 1 tbsp tomato purée for the chicken stock. Proceed as directed in the recipe, adding water if the mixture is too thick.

CHICKEN CACCIATORE

Serves 4

1.5 kg (3 lb) chicken, cut into 8 serving pieces (page 148)
salt and black pepper
1 tbsp chopped fresh thyme
plain flour for dusting
3–4 tbsp olive oil
90 g (3 oz) streaky bacon rashers, cut into strips
1 large onion, chopped
1 small green pepper, cored, seeded, and diced
4 garlic cloves, crushed
250 g (8 oz) mushrooms, quartered
125 ml (4 fl oz) red wine
1 x 400 g (13 oz) can chopped tomatoes
75 ml (2½ fl oz) tomato purée
2 tsp chopped fresh sage
4 tbsp chopped parsley
grated zest of 1 lemon
2 tbsp capers
fresh sage to garnish

1 Sprinkle the chicken pieces with salt, pepper, and thyme, then lightly dust them with flour, shaking off any excess.

2 Heat half of the oil in a large frying pan, add the bacon and chicken, and cook for 10–12 minutes until browned all over. Transfer to a casserole.

3 Pour the fat from the frying pan, and wipe clean with a paper towel. Heat the remaining oil, add the onion, green pepper, and half of the garlic, and cook gently, stirring, for 5 minutes until soft but not coloured. Transfer to the casserole with a slotted spoon. Add the mushrooms, and cook for 2 minutes. Add to the casserole.

4 Pour the red wine into the frying pan, and boil for 10 minutes until reduced to about 4 tbsp. Add to the casserole with the tomatoes, tomato purée, and sage. Cover and cook in a preheated oven at 180°C (350°F, Gas 4) for 1 hour or until the chicken is cooked.

5 Combine the remaining garlic with the chopped parsley, lemon zest, and capers. Stir into the casserole, and heat through. Taste for seasoning. Serve at once, garnished with sage.

Cacciatore

Meaning "hunter" in English, cacciatore *is the Italian word used to describe dishes containing mushrooms, tomatoes, herbs, and wine.*

CHICKEN MARENGO

Serves 4

30 g (1 oz) butter
1 tbsp sunflower oil
1.5 kg (3 lb) chicken, cut into 8 serving pieces (page 148)
6 shallots
30 g (1 oz) plain flour
300 ml (1/2 pint) dry white wine
150 ml (1/4 pint) chicken stock
1 x 400 g (13 oz) can chopped tomatoes
250 g (8 oz) button mushrooms
1 tbsp tomato purée
2 garlic cloves, crushed
1 parsley sprig
1 thyme sprig
1 bay leaf
salt and black pepper
250 g (8 oz) cooked peeled prawns
chopped parsley to garnish

1 Melt the butter with the oil in a large flameproof casserole. When the butter is foaming, add the chicken pieces, and cook for 10–12 minutes until browned all over. Lift out and drain.

2 Add the shallots, and cook over a high heat for about 8 minutes until browned all over. Lift out and drain on paper towels.

3 Spoon off all but 1 tbsp of the fat from the casserole. Add the flour, and cook, stirring, for 3–5 minutes until lightly browned. Lower the heat, and blend in the wine and stock, stirring until well combined. Add the tomatoes, mushrooms, tomato purée, garlic, parsley, thyme, bay leaf, and salt and pepper to taste.

4 Return the shallots and chicken to the casserole, and bring to a boil. Cover and cook in a preheated oven at 180°C (350°F, Gas 4) for 1 hour or until the chicken is almost tender. Stir in the prawns, and return to the oven for 10 minutes. Garnish each serving with chopped parsley and serve at once.

Chicken Marengo

This dish takes its name from the battle of Marengo in 1800, when Napoleon defeated the Austrians. The original version, improvised on the battlefield by Napoleon's chef, was made with a chicken, tomatoes, eggs, crayfish, garlic, and a splash of brandy from the General's flask.

COQ AU VIN

Serves 4

30 g (1 oz) butter
1 tbsp sunflower oil
1.5 kg (3 lb) chicken, cut into 8 serving pieces (page 148)
125 g (4 oz) streaky bacon rashers, cut into strips
8 shallots
250 g (8 oz) button mushrooms
30 g (1 oz) plain flour
300 ml (1/2 pint) chicken stock
300 ml (1/2 pint) red wine
1 bay leaf
1 thyme sprig
1 parsley sprig
1 large garlic clove, crushed
salt and black pepper
4 slices of white bread, crusts removed, to serve
2 tbsp chopped parsley to garnish

1 Melt the butter with the oil in a large flameproof casserole. When the butter is foaming, add the chicken pieces, and cook for 10–12 minutes until browned all over. Lift out and drain on paper towels.

2 Spoon off any excess fat, then add the bacon, shallots, and mushrooms, and cook over a high heat, stirring, until golden brown. Lift out with a slotted spoon and drain thoroughly on paper towels.

3 Add the flour, and cook for 3–5 minutes, stirring constantly until lightly browned. Gradually pour in the stock, then the wine, stirring until smooth.

4 Return the chicken, bacon, shallots, and mushrooms to the casserole, and add the bay leaf, thyme, parsley, garlic, and salt and pepper to taste. Bring to a boil, cover, and cook in a preheated oven at 180°C (350°F, Gas 4) for 45–60 minutes until the chicken is cooked through.

5 Towards the end of the cooking time, toast the bread slices. Cut each slice into 4 triangles.

6 Garnish the chicken with the chopped parsley, and serve at once with the toasted bread triangles.

PERFECT AMERICAN FRIED CHICKEN

 **Serves 4**

350 ml (12 fl oz) buttermilk

1.25–1.5 kg (2 1/2– 3 lb) chicken, cut into 8 serving pieces (page 148)

125 g (4 oz) plain flour

1 1/2 tsp salt

1 tsp paprika

1/2 tsp black pepper

1/2 tsp garlic granules

large pinch of grated nutmeg

sunflower oil for deep-frying

4 streaky bacon rashers, rinds removed, to serve

parsley sprigs to garnish

1 Pour the buttermilk into a large non-metallic bowl. Add the chicken, and turn to coat. Cover and chill, turning occasionally, for 2–3 hours.

2 In a large bowl, combine the flour with the salt, paprika, pepper, garlic granules, and nutmeg.

3 Lift the chicken pieces out of the buttermilk and shake off any excess liquid. Coat with the seasoned flour (see box, right).

4 Pour 2 cm (3/4 in) of oil into a deep frying pan, and heat to 180°C (350°F), or until a cube of bread browns in 1 minute.

5 Fry the chicken pieces in the hot oil, in 2–3 batches if necessary, turning them several times so they cook evenly, for 10–15 minutes until golden brown. Drain the chicken on paper towels.

6 Put the bacon under a hot grill, 10 cm (4 ins) from the heat, and cook for 3–4 minutes on each side until crisp. Serve the chicken pieces at once, garnished with the bacon and parsley.

Coating chicken

Dip the chicken pieces, one at a time, into the seasoned flour, turning to coat evenly.

HERB GRILLED CHICKEN

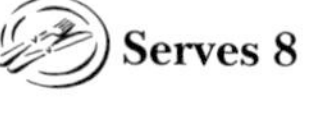 **Serves 8**

8 chicken quarters

HERB BUTTER

90 g (3 oz) butter

3 tbsp chopped parsley

3 tbsp snipped fresh chives

2 garlic cloves, crushed (optional)

salt and black pepper

1 Melt the butter in a small saucepan. Add the parsley, chives, and garlic, if using, and add salt and pepper to taste.

2 Brush the chicken with the herb butter, and put, skin-side down, over a hot barbecue, or skin-side up under a hot grill, 10 cm (4 ins) from the heat. Cook, brushing with the butter, for 10 minutes on each side, until cooked through.

Cook's know-how

To prepare this dish in advance, don't melt the butter, just soften it, and blend with the herbs and garlic. Chill until needed. Melt the butter, and brush over the chicken before cooking.

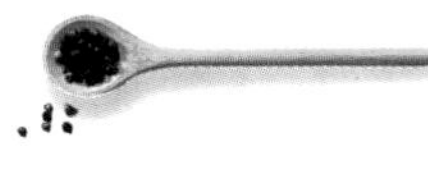

JAMAICAN CHICKEN

Substitute 1/2 tsp crushed tropical peppercorns, 1/2 tsp chopped fresh thyme, and 3 chopped spring onions for the parsley, chives, and garlic. Melt the butter, add the flavourings, and proceed as directed.

ROSY PAPRIKA CHICKEN

Substitute 2 tsp paprika and 2 tsp mustard powder for the parsley, chives, and garlic. Melt the butter, add the flavourings, and proceed as directed.

ASIAN CORIANDER CHICKEN

Substitute 1–2 tbsp chopped fresh coriander, 1–2 cored, seeded, and chopped fresh green chillies, and 1/4 tsp cumin seeds for the parsley and chives.

JERK CHICKEN

Serves 4

1 kg (2 lb) chicken, cut into 4 serving pieces (page 148)

chopped fresh thyme to garnish

grilled pineapple rings to serve

JERK PASTE

3 tbsp lime juice

2 tbsp dark rum

2 tbsp sunflower oil

1 tsp soy sauce

4 spring onions, thinly sliced

1–2 fresh green chillies, cored, seeded, and coarsely chopped

2 garlic cloves, coarsely chopped

2 tbsp ground allspice

1/2 tsp ground cinnamon

pinch of grated nutmeg

2 tsp chopped fresh thyme

salt and black pepper

1 Make the jerk paste: purée the lime juice, rum, oil, soy sauce, spring onions, chillies, garlic, spices, thyme, and salt and pepper in a food processor until smooth.

2 Brush the chicken pieces with the jerk paste (see box, right). Leave to marinate in the refrigerator for 30 minutes.

3 Put the chicken over a hot barbecue, or under a hot grill, 10 cm (4 ins) from the heat. Cook for about 10 minutes on each side until the juices run clear. Serve the chicken at once, garnished with thyme and accompanied by grilled pineapple rings.

Jerk

Jerk is a spicy paste from the West Indies. It is spread over chicken or meat, which is left to marinate, then barbecued or grilled. The rum and lime juice tenderize the meat.

Jerking the chicken

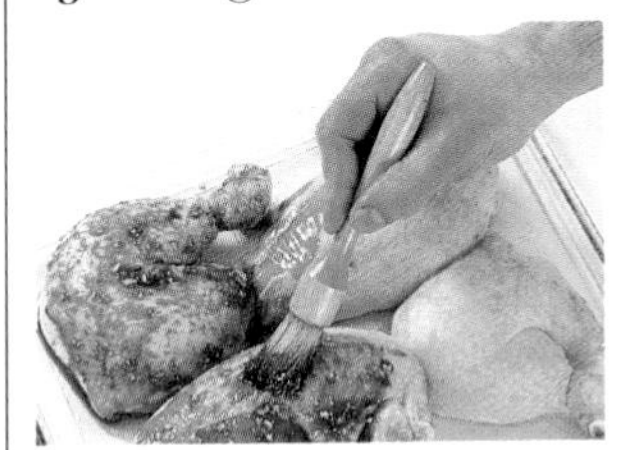

Brush a layer of jerk paste over both sides of each piece of chicken with a pastry brush.

TEX-MEX CHICKEN

Serves 4

4 skinless, boneless chicken breasts

2 avocados

2 tbsp lime juice

1 red onion, finely chopped

MARINADE

4 tbsp olive oil

4 tbsp orange juice

1/2 tsp ground cumin

SALSA

500 g (1 lb) tomatoes, peeled (page 39), seeded, and diced

1 small onion, diced

3 tbsp olive oil

2 tbsp lime juice

3 tbsp chopped fresh coriander

2 garlic cloves, crushed

1 fresh green chilli, cored, seeded, and chopped

salt

1 Make several diagonal slashes in each chicken breast, and put in a shallow dish. Make the marinade: combine the oil, orange juice, and cumin, and pour over the chicken. Cover and leave to marinate in the refrigerator for 30 minutes.

2 Make the salsa: combine the tomatoes, onion, oil, lime juice, coriander, garlic, chilli, and salt to taste. Cover the salsa and chill until ready to serve.

3 Remove the chicken from the marinade, put under a hot grill, 10 cm (4 ins) from the heat, and grill for 6 minutes on each side until golden and cooked through.

4 Meanwhile, halve, stone (page 68), and peel the avocados. Slice lengthwise, and brush with lime juice.

5 Thinly slice the chicken breasts (see box, below). Arrange the avocado and chicken on individual plates, and sprinkle the chopped red onion around the edges. Spoon a little of the salsa into the middle of each serving, and hand the remainder separately. Serve at once.

Slicing the chicken

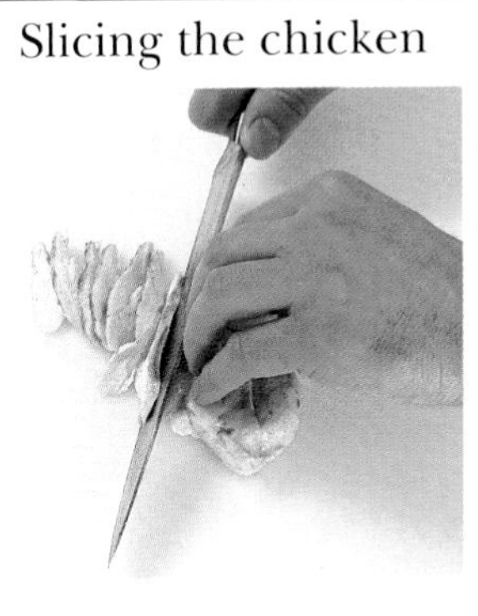

Cut the chicken breasts into 3 mm (1/8 in) slices with a sharp chef's knife, carefully following the diagonal slashes.

FRAGRANT CHICKEN CURRY WITH ALMONDS

The spices in this recipe are among those used in ready-made curry powders, but using your own individual blend of spices gives a truly authentic flavour to a curry. This is a creamy, mild dish – not too hot and spicy.

Serves 4

2 tbsp sunflower oil
4 skinless, boneless chicken breasts
2.5 cm (1 in) piece of cinnamon stick
seeds of 4 cardamom pods, crushed
4 cloves
2 tsp cumin seeds, ground
1 bay leaf
1 large onion, finely chopped
2 garlic cloves, crushed
2.5 cm (1 in) piece of fresh root ginger, peeled and grated
1/4 tsp garam masala
pinch of cayenne pepper
salt and black pepper
150 ml (1/4 pint) single cream
3 tbsp water
150 g (5 oz) plain yogurt
60 g (2 oz) sultanas and 60 g (2 oz) whole almonds, blanched, shredded, and toasted (see box, right), to garnish

1 Heat the oil in a small flameproof casserole. Add the chicken breasts, and cook for 5 minutes on each side until golden. Lift out and drain on paper towels.

2 Add the cinnamon, cardamom seeds, cloves, cumin seeds, and bay leaf to the hot oil, and stir over a high heat for 1 minute.

3 Add the onion, garlic, and ginger, and cook gently, stirring occasionally, for a few minutes until just beginning to soften. Stir in the garam masala and cayenne pepper.

4 Return the chicken to the casserole, and season to taste. Pour in the cream and measured water, and bring to a boil. Cover and simmer very gently for 20 minutes or until the chicken is tender. Remove and discard the cinnamon stick, cloves, and bay leaf.

5 Stir in the yogurt, taste for seasoning, then heat through very gently. Spoon into a serving dish, and sprinkle with the sultanas and toasted shredded almonds. Serve at once.

Cook's know-how

Cardamom comes in 3 forms: as pods, whole seeds, or ground seeds. As the seeds lose their flavour quickly, it is best to buy whole cardamom pods and remove the seeds when you need them. As with the other spices in this recipe, frying cardamom seeds over a high heat releases their full flavour.

Blanching, shredding, and toasting almonds

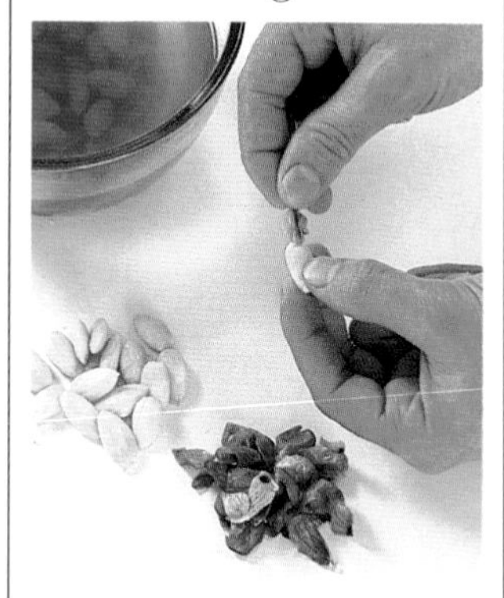

Blanch the almonds and loosen the skins: immerse in a bowl of boiling water. When cool enough to handle, squeeze the almonds between your fingers to slide and pull off the skin.

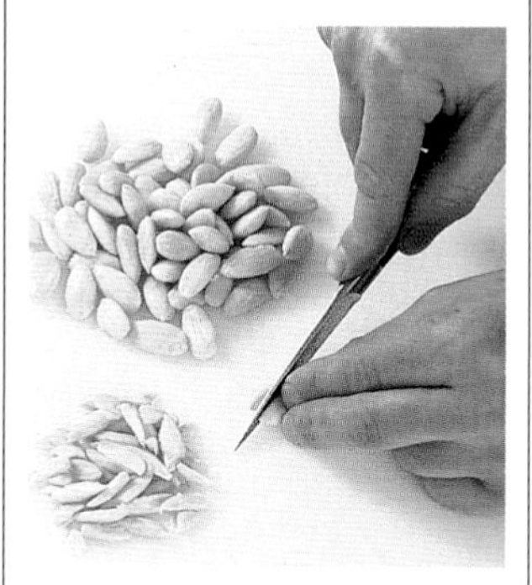

Slice the almonds in half lengthwise. Cut the halves into shreds.

Place the shredded almonds on a baking tray, and toast in a preheated oven at 180°C (350°F, Gas 4), stirring the almonds occasionally to ensure that they colour evenly, for 8–10 minutes until lightly browned.

SAFFRON CHICKEN

 **Serves 6**

6 boneless chicken breasts, with the skin left on

1 tbsp olive oil

200 ml (7 fl oz) crème fraîche

salt and black pepper

chopped parsley to garnish

MARINADE

2 pinches of saffron threads

2.5 cm (1 in) piece of fresh root ginger, peeled and chopped

juice of 1 lemon

1 tsp ground cardamom

1 tsp ground coriander

1 tsp ground cinnamon

1 Make the marinade: put the saffron and the ginger into a mortar and grind with a pestle until smooth. Add the lemon juice, cardamom, coriander, and cinnamon, and mix well.

2 Put the chicken breasts into a shallow non-metallic dish. Pour the marinade over them, and turn to coat evenly. Cover and leave to marinate in the refrigerator for about 20 minutes.

3 Pour the oil into a small roasting tin. Turn the chicken breasts in the oil, and put them, skin-side up, in the roasting tin. Cook in a preheated oven at 190°C (375°F, Gas 5) for 20–25 minutes. Remove from the tin and keep warm.

4 Put the roasting tin on top of the stove, pour in the crème fraîche, and stir to combine with the juices. Add salt and pepper to taste, and heat through.

5 Divide the sauce among 6 warmed plates. Place the chicken breasts on top, sprinkle them lightly with chopped parsley, and serve at once.

TURMERIC CHICKEN

Substitute 1 tsp ground turmeric for the saffron threads. Mix with the ginger, lemon juice, cardamom, coriander, and cinnamon, and proceed as directed.

CHICKEN TIKKA

750 g (1 1/2 lb) skinless, boneless chicken breasts, cut into 2.5 cm (1 in) cubes

cucumber raita (see box, right) to serve

MARINADE

2 tbsp plain yogurt

2 tbsp tomato purée

1 small onion, finely chopped

3 garlic cloves, crushed

1 tbsp tamarind paste

1 tbsp paprika

1 tsp ground ginger

1/2 tsp salt

1/2 tsp ground cumin

large pinch of cayenne pepper

large pinch of grated nutmeg

☆ *4 metal skewers*

1 Make the marinade: in a bowl, combine the yogurt, tomato purée, onion, garlic, tamarind paste, paprika, ginger, salt, cumin, cayenne pepper, and nutmeg.

2 Toss the chicken in the marinade. Cover and marinate in the refrigerator for at least 2 hours.

3 Thread the chicken on to skewers, put under a hot grill, 10 cm (4 ins) from the heat, and cook for 3–5 minutes on each side. Serve at once, with the raita.

Cucumber raita

Cut *half a cucumber* in half lengthwise. Scoop out the seeds, and coarsely grate the cucumber. Put the cucumber in a sieve over a bowl, and leave to drain for 10 minutes. Press the cucumber into the sieve to extract the juices.

Combine the cucumber with *3 thinly sliced spring onions,* reserving some green slices for garnish, *250 g (8 oz) plain yogurt,* and *salt and pepper to taste.* Garnish with the spring onion slices, and serve.

STIR-FRIED CHICKEN WITH VEGETABLES

Serves 4

4 skinless, boneless chicken breasts, cut diagonally into 5 mm (1/4 in) strips

8 spring onions

3 tbsp sunflower oil

250 g (8 oz) carrots, cut into matchstick-thin strips

175 g (6 oz) baby sweetcorn

175 g (6 oz) sugar snap peas

2–3 tbsp lemon juice

2 tbsp clear honey

2.5 cm (1 in) piece of fresh root ginger, peeled and grated

125 g (4 oz) bean sprouts, soaked in cold water for 10 minutes, then drained

DRY MARINADE

1 tsp caster sugar

1/2 tsp ground ginger

1/2 tsp mustard powder

1/4 tsp turmeric

1/4 tsp mild curry powder

salt and black pepper

1 Make the dry marinade: in a large bowl, combine the sugar, ginger, mustard, turmeric, mild curry powder, and salt and pepper to taste. Toss the chicken strips in the dry marinade, cover, and leave to stand for a few minutes.

2 Finely slice the spring onions, reserving the green tops to make spring onion tassels (page 115) to garnish the finished dish.

3 Heat 2 tbsp of the oil in a wok or large frying pan. Add the carrots and baby sweetcorn, and stir-fry over a high heat for 2–3 minutes until they just begin to colour. Lift out with a slotted spoon and drain on paper towels.

4 Add the sugar snap peas and spring onions, and stir-fry over a high heat for 1–2 minutes. Remove with a slotted spoon and drain on paper towels.

5 Heat the remaining oil, add the chicken strips, and stir-fry for 5 minutes or until golden. Add the lemon juice, honey, and ginger, and cook for 3–4 minutes until the chicken is tender.

6 Return all the cooked vegetables to the wok, add the bean sprouts, and stir-fry over a high heat for 1–2 minutes until all the vegetables are heated through. Serve at once, garnished with the spring onion tassels.

THAI CHICKEN WITH WATER CHESTNUTS

Serves 4

375 g (12 oz) skinless, boneless chicken breasts, cut into 2.5 cm (1 in) pieces

3 tbsp sunflower oil

5 garlic cloves, chopped

2.5 cm (1 in) piece of fresh root ginger, peeled and grated

salt and black pepper

1 x 200 g (7 oz) can water chestnuts, drained, rinsed, and sliced

600 ml (1 pint) chicken stock

1 tsp sliced fresh lemon grass

1 small bunch of fresh coriander, coarsely chopped

4 large lettuce leaves, coarsely chopped

1/2 –1 fresh green chilli, cored, seeded, and chopped

1 tsp light soy sauce

1/2 tsp sugar

1/2 tsp fennel seeds

175 g (6 oz) firm tofu, cut into bite-sized pieces

lime wedges, sliced spring onions, and skinned natural peanuts to garnish

1 Put the chicken into a dish, sprinkle with the oil, half of the garlic and ginger, and salt and pepper to taste; leave to stand for 3 minutes.

2 Heat a wok or frying pan, add the chicken mixture and sliced water chestnuts, and stir-fry for 8–10 minutes. Remove the wok from the heat and set aside.

3 Pour half of the stock into a pan, add the lemon grass, bring to a boil, and simmer for 5 minutes.

4 Meanwhile, purée the remaining stock, garlic, and ginger with the coriander, lettuce, chilli, light soy sauce, sugar, and fennel seeds in a food processor until smooth.

5 Add the simmering stock, the puréed coriander mixture, and the tofu pieces to the chicken and water chestnuts in the wok. Stir well, and heat through.

6 Serve at once, garnished with lime wedges, spring onion slices, and peanuts.

SWEET & SOUR CHINESE CHICKEN

Serves 4–6

- *500 g (1 lb) skinless, boneless chicken breasts, cut into 2.5 cm (1 in) pieces*
- *1 x 250 g (8 oz) can pineapple chunks in natural juice, drained and juice reserved*
- *2 tbsp cornflour*
- *3 tbsp sunflower oil*
- *1 green pepper, cored, seeded, and cut into bite-sized pieces*
- *1 red pepper, cored, seeded, and cut into bite-sized pieces*
- *1 celery stalk, thickly sliced*
- *1 onion, cut into bite-sized chunks*
- *4 tbsp tomato ketchup*
- *250 g (8 oz) canned lychees, drained and juice reserved*
- *salt and black pepper*
- *chopped fresh coriander to garnish*

MARINADE

- *2 tbsp dark soy sauce*
- *1 tbsp Chinese rice wine or dry sherry*
- *1 tbsp water*

1 Make the marinade: in a large bowl, combine the soy sauce, rice wine, and measured water.

2 Toss the chicken pieces in the marinade, cover, and leave to marinate in the refrigerator for 30 minutes.

3 Make the reserved pineapple juice up to 250 ml (8 fl oz) with water and blend with the cornflour. Set aside.

4 Heat the oil in a wok or large frying pan, add the chicken, and stir-fry for 8–10 minutes until golden all over. Lift out with a slotted spoon and drain on paper towels.

5 Add the green and red peppers, celery, and onion to the wok, and stir-fry for 5 minutes.

6 Add the cornflour and pineapple juice mixture, ketchup, and reserved lychee juice to the wok, and cook for 3–5 minutes until thickened.

7 Return the chicken to the wok with the lychees and pineapple chunks, and heat through. Add salt and pepper to taste, and serve at once, garnished with chopped fresh coriander.

MUSTARD CHICKEN

Serves 4

- *1 tbsp olive oil*
- *1 garlic clove, crushed*
- *4 skinless, boneless chicken breasts, cut diagonally into 2.5 cm (1 in) strips*
- *250 ml (8 fl oz) single cream*
- *1 tbsp plain flour*
- *1 tbsp coarse-grain mustard*
- *salt and black pepper*
- *flat-leaf parsley sprigs to garnish*

1 Heat the oil in a frying pan, add the garlic, and cook, stirring, for 1–2 minutes. Add the chicken strips, then lower the heat and cook, stirring frequently, for 10 minutes.

2 With a slotted spoon, lift the chicken strips out of the frying pan, and keep them warm.

3 In a small bowl, mix a little of the cream with the flour to make a smooth paste, and set aside.

4 Pour the remaining cream into the pan and stir to mix with the cooking juices. Bring to a boil, stir in the cream and flour mixture, then lower the heat and cook for 2 minutes, stirring constantly until the sauce has thickened. Stir in the mustard and heat through gently, then add salt and pepper to taste.

5 Return the chicken to the pan, coat with the sauce, and reheat gently. Serve at once, garnished with parsley sprigs.

Cook's know-how

Do not let the sauce boil once you have added the mustard or it will taste bitter. Coarse-grain mustard gives an interesting texture to this dish, but if you prefer a smooth sauce, use Dijon mustard.

CHICKEN SATAY

This is a traditional Indonesian speciality that is becoming popular around the world. The rich satay sauce, made from peanuts and coconut, complements the pieces of chicken tenderized by a tangy marinade. Serve as a starter or a buffet party dish.

 **Serves 4**

4 skinless, boneless chicken breasts, cut into 2 cm (3/4 in) pieces

flat-leaf parsley sprigs and coarsely chopped skinned natural peanuts to garnish

MARINADE

90 ml (3 fl oz) dark soy sauce

juice of 1 lemon

3 tbsp sunflower oil

2 tbsp dark brown sugar

3 garlic cloves, crushed

3 spring onions, thinly sliced

** 12 bamboo skewers*

SATAY SAUCE

250 g (8 oz) peanut butter

2 garlic cloves, crushed

175 ml (6 fl oz) water

30 g (1 oz) creamed coconut, coarsely chopped

1 tbsp dark soy sauce

1 tbsp dark brown sugar

1 cm (1/2 in) piece of fresh root ginger, peeled and finely chopped

1 tbsp lemon juice

cayenne pepper

salt and black pepper

1 Make the marinade: in a bowl, combine the soy sauce, lemon juice, oil, sugar, garlic, and spring onions.

2 Toss the chicken with the marinade. Cover and leave to marinate in the refrigerator for 30 minutes.

3 Soak the skewers in warm water for 30 minutes.

4 Make the satay sauce: heat the peanut butter with half of the garlic for 2 minutes. Add the water, creamed coconut, soy sauce, sugar, and ginger, and cook, stirring, for 2 minutes or until the sauce is smooth.

5 Add the lemon juice and remaining garlic, and season to taste with cayenne pepper, salt, and black pepper. Keep warm.

6 Thread the chicken pieces on to the skewers. Place under a hot grill, 10 cm (4 ins) from the heat, and grill for 2–3 minutes on each side until cooked through.

7 Serve the chicken satay at once, garnishing the sauce with parsley sprigs and peanuts.

Cook's know-how

Soaking the bamboo skewers in warm water before threading with the chicken prevents the skewers from burning when under the grill.

CHICKEN KEBABS

Serves 4

4 skinless, boneless chicken breasts, cut into 2.5 cm (1 in) pieces

2 green peppers, cored, seeded, and cut into 2.5 cm (1 in) pieces

500 g (1 lb) cherry tomatoes

375 g (12 oz) button mushrooms

MARINADE

175 ml (6 fl oz) olive oil

125 ml (4 fl oz) light soy sauce

4 tbsp red wine vinegar

1 tsp dried thyme

freshly ground black pepper

** 12 bamboo skewers*

1 Soak the skewers in warm water for 30 minutes.

2 Make the marinade: in a large bowl, combine the oil, soy sauce, wine vinegar, thyme, and pepper to taste. Add the chicken and stir to mix well. Cover and leave to marinate in the refrigerator for at least 10 minutes.

3 Lift the chicken out of the marinade, reserving the marinade. Thread the skewers, alternating green pepper, tomatoes, chicken, and mushrooms.

4 Place the kebabs under a hot grill, 10 cm (4 ins) from the heat, and grill, basting with the marinade, for 3–5 minutes on each side until cooked through.

CHICKEN PINWHEELS

An elegant dinner party dish that's simple and economical to make, yet looks stunning. An accompaniment of fresh tagliatelle goes well with the tomato and herb sauce and makes a light meal that will appeal to everyone.

Serves 4

4 skinless, boneless chicken breasts

melted butter for greasing

basil sprigs to garnish

FILLING

125 g (4 oz) full-fat soft cheese with garlic and herbs

2 tbsp sun-dried tomatoes in oil, drained and chopped

4 tbsp shredded fresh basil

salt and black pepper

TOMATO & HERB SAUCE

1 tbsp olive oil

1 small onion, chopped

1 x 400 g (13 oz) can chopped tomatoes

1 tbsp chopped fresh herbs, such as parsley, chives, and thyme

1 Make the filling: combine the cheese, sun-dried tomatoes, basil, and salt and pepper to taste. Mix well.

2 Put the chicken breasts between sheets of greaseproof paper, and pound with a rolling pin until 5 mm (1/4 in) thick. Spread one-quarter of the filling over each breast, and tightly roll up each one.

3 Brush 4 squares of greaseproof paper with melted butter, and wrap each chicken roll in a square. Wrap each roll in foil, twisting the ends to seal them tightly. Put the rolls into a shallow pan of gently simmering water, cover, and simmer for 15 minutes.

4 Meanwhile, make the tomato and herb sauce: heat the oil in a pan, add the onion, and cook, stirring often, for a few minutes until soft. Stir in the tomatoes with half of their juice, bring to a boil, and simmer for 3 minutes.

5 Purée the tomato mixture in a food processor until smooth. Work the purée through a sieve, stir in the chopped fresh herbs, and add salt and pepper to taste.

6 Unwrap the chicken, and cut into pinwheels (see box, below). Serve with the tomato and herb sauce, and garnish with basil.

Making the pinwheels

Cut each chicken roll on the diagonal into 1 cm (1/2 in) slices, using a sharp knife.

CHICKEN STIR-FRY

Serves 4

3 tbsp sunflower oil

4 spring onions, sliced

2.5 cm (1 in) piece of fresh root ginger, peeled and chopped

3 carrots, thinly sliced

1 red pepper, cored, seeded, and cut into thin strips

1 yellow pepper, cored, seeded, and cut into thin strips

4 tbsp dark soy sauce

2 tbsp dry sherry mixed with 2 tsp cornflour

4 skinless, boneless chicken breasts, cut into 1 cm (1/2 in) strips

125 ml (4 fl oz) water

1 Heat 1 tbsp of the oil in a wok or large frying pan, add the spring onions and ginger, and stir-fry for 1 minute.

2 Heat the remaining oil, add the carrots and peppers, and stir-fry over a high heat for 2–3 minutes. Add the soy sauce, sherry mixture, and chicken strips, and stir-fry for 3–4 minutes.

3 Add the measured water and continue stir-frying for 1–2 minutes until the liquid boils and thickens slightly. Serve at once.

TARRAGON CHICKEN WITH LIME

Serves 4

60 g (2 oz) butter, softened

grated zest of 1 lime and juice of 2 limes

4 skinless, boneless chicken breasts

1 tbsp chopped fresh tarragon

salt and black pepper

1 tbsp water

150 ml (1/4 pint) low-fat crème fraîche

lime segments and fresh tarragon to garnish

1 Put the butter into a bowl, and beat in the lime zest. Prepare the chicken breasts (see box, right).

2 Put the chicken breasts into a roasting tin. Sprinkle with the lime juice, tarragon, and salt and pepper to taste, and bake in a preheated oven at 200°C (400°F, Gas 6) for 20 minutes or until the chicken is cooked through.

3 Transfer the chicken breasts to warmed serving plates and keep warm.

4 Put the tin on top of the stove, add the measured water to the cooking juices, stirring to dissolve the sediment, and bring to a boil, stirring. Cook, stirring, for 1–2 minutes. Stir in the crème fraîche and heat gently until warmed through.

5 Serve the chicken with the sauce, and garnish each serving with the lime segments and fresh tarragon.

Preparing the chicken

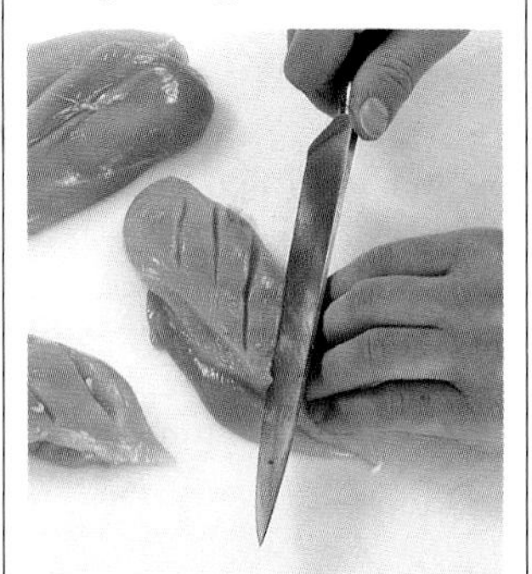

Make 3–4 deep diagonal cuts in each chicken breast with a sharp knife. Spread the top of each breast with one-quarter of the lime butter.

CHEESE & GARLIC STUFFED CHICKEN

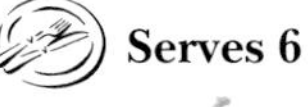

Serves 6

6 boneless chicken breasts, with the skin left on

melted butter for brushing

STUFFING

30 g (1 oz) butter

1 onion, finely chopped

2 large garlic cloves, crushed

250 g (8 oz) full-fat soft cheese

1 tbsp chopped fresh tarragon

1 egg yolk

pinch of grated nutmeg

salt and black pepper

1 Make the stuffing: melt the butter in a small saucepan, add the onion and garlic, and cook gently, stirring occasionally, for a few minutes until soft but not coloured. Turn the onion mixture into a bowl, and leave to cool slightly.

2 Add the soft cheese to the onion mixture with the tarragon, egg yolk, nutmeg, and salt and pepper to taste and mix well.

3 Stuff the chicken breasts (see box, right). Put the chicken breasts into an ovenproof dish, and brush with the melted butter.

4 Bake the chicken in a preheated oven at 190°C (375°F, Gas 5) for 25–30 minutes until the chicken is cooked through. Cut each breast into diagonal slices, remove the cocktail sticks, and serve hot.

Stuffing a chicken breast

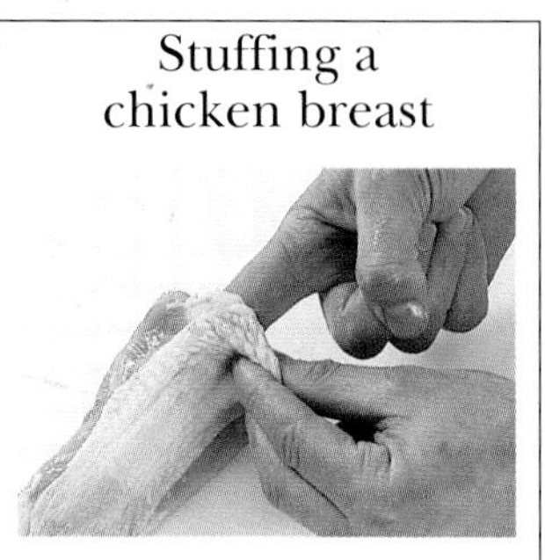

Loosen the skin from one end of the chicken breast. Push a finger between the skin and the flesh, leaving the skin attached at the sides, to form a pouch.

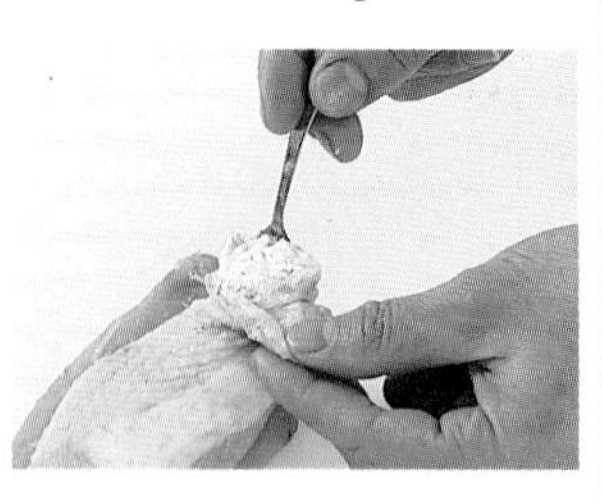

Fill the pouch with the stuffing. Secure the open end of the breast with a wooden cocktail stick.

BACON-WRAPPED CHICKEN BREASTS

Serves 6

6 skinless, boneless chicken breasts
4 tbsp coarse-grain mustard
black pepper
18 streaky bacon rashers, rinds removed
snipped fresh chives to garnish

1 Spread both sides of the chicken breasts with the mustard, and season with black pepper.

2 Take 3 bacon rashers, stretch them with the back of a knife, and arrange them side by side and slightly overlapping. Wrap a chicken breast with the bacon (see box, right). Repeat with the remaining bacon and chicken breasts.

3 Place the chicken breasts in a roasting tin, and bake in a preheated oven at 190°C (375°F, Gas 5) for 25–30 minutes until the bacon is crisp and brown and the chicken cooked through. Serve at once, garnished with snipped chives.

Wrapping a chicken breast in bacon

Place a chicken breast at one end of the bacon rashers, and then wrap the rashers diagonally around the breast.

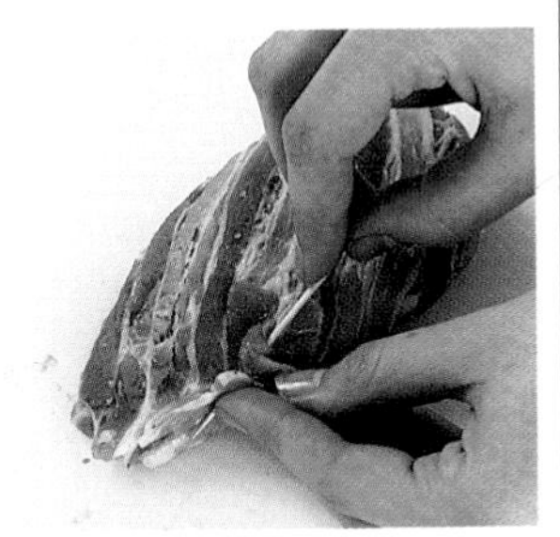

Secure the bacon rashers around the chicken by threading a wooden cocktail stick or small skewer through the loose ends of the rashers.

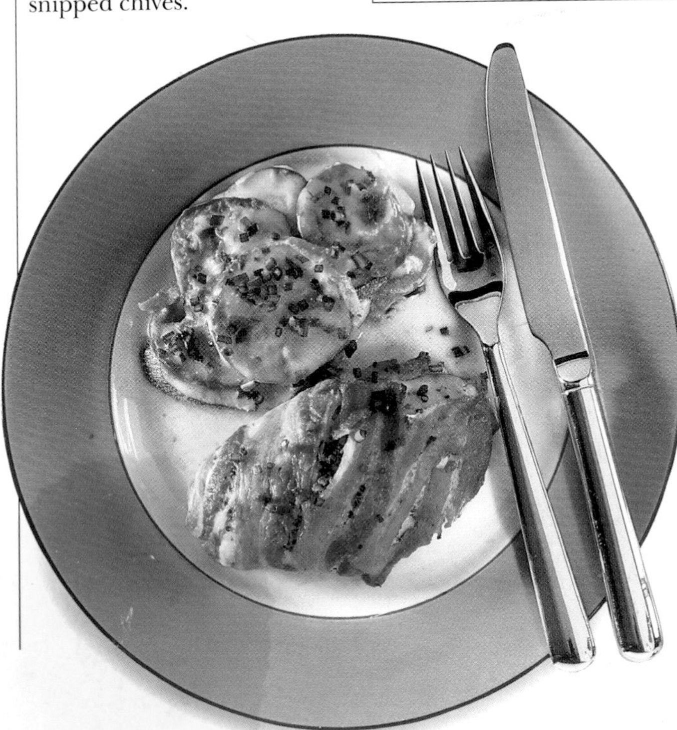

CHICKEN WITH SAGE & ORANGE

Serves 6

6 boneless chicken breasts, with the skin left on
1 tbsp plain flour
orange segments and fresh sage leaves to garnish

MARINADE

300 ml (1/2 pint) orange juice
1 tbsp light soy sauce
2 garlic cloves, crushed
2 tbsp chopped fresh sage
1 cm (1/2 in) piece of fresh root ginger, peeled and finely chopped
salt and black pepper

1 Make the marinade: combine the orange juice, soy sauce, garlic, sage, ginger, and season to taste. Toss the chicken in the marinade, cover, and leave to marinate in the refrigerator for 20–30 minutes.

2 Reserve the marinade, and arrange the chicken breasts, skin-side up, in a large roasting tin.

3 Bake the chicken in a preheated oven at 190°C (375°F, Gas 5) for about 20 minutes. Pour the reserved marinade over the chicken, and return to the oven for 5–10 minutes until the chicken is cooked through.

4 Remove the chicken with a slotted spoon, and arrange on a warmed platter. Cover and keep warm.

5 Pour all but 2 tbsp of the marinade into a jug, and reserve. Add the flour to the marinade remaining in the roasting tin, and mix to a smooth paste.

6 Put the roasting tin on top of the stove, and cook, stirring, for 1 minute. Gradually stir in the reserved marinade. Bring to a boil, simmer for 2 minutes, and taste for seasoning. Strain, pour a little around the chicken breasts, and garnish with the orange segments and fresh sage. Serve the remaining sauce separately.

CHICKEN CORDON BLEU

Serves 4

4 skinless, boneless chicken breasts

4 thin slices of Gruyère cheese

4 thin slices of cooked ham

salt and black pepper

1 egg, beaten

125 g (4 oz) fresh white breadcrumbs

30 g (1 oz) butter

3 tbsp sunflower oil

1 With a sharp knife, cut each chicken breast horizontally, leaving it attached at one side.

2 Open out each chicken breast, place between 2 sheets of greaseproof paper, and pound to a 3 mm (1/8 in) thickness with a rolling pin. Fill and fold the chicken breasts (see box, right).

3 Dip each folded chicken breast into the beaten egg, then dip each breast into the breadcrumbs, making sure each one is evenly coated. Cover and chill for 15 minutes.

4 Melt the butter with the sunflower oil in a large frying pan. When the butter is foaming, add the chicken breasts, and cook for 10 minutes on each side or until the breadcrumb coating is crisp and golden and the chicken is cooked through. Remove the chicken breasts with a slotted spoon and drain thoroughly on paper towels. Cut into 1 cm (1/2 in) slices, and serve at once.

Folding the chicken

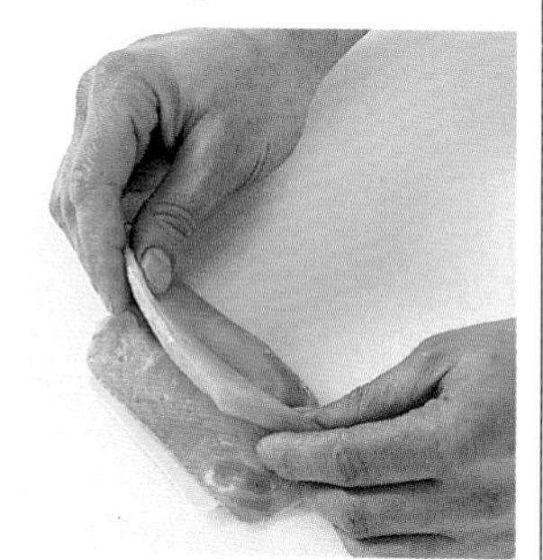

Place 1 slice of cheese and 1 slice of ham on half of each chicken breast, season to taste, and fold the breast to cover the filling. Secure with a wooden cocktail stick.

HERB-MARINATED CHICKEN BREASTS

Serves 4

4 boneless chicken breasts, with the skin left on

30 g (1 oz) plain flour

30 g (1 oz) butter

2 tbsp sunflower oil

150 ml (1/4 pint) chicken stock

1 bunch of watercress, tough stalks removed, to serve

chopped parsley to garnish

MARINADE

2 tbsp olive oil

1 tbsp lemon juice

3 garlic cloves, crushed

3 tbsp chopped parsley

1/2 tsp herbes de Provence

salt and black pepper

1 Make the marinade: combine the oil, lemon juice, garlic, parsley, herbes de Provence, and seasoning to taste. Turn the chicken in the marinade, cover, and leave to marinate in the refrigerator for 30 minutes.

2 Remove the chicken from the marinade, and dry on paper towels. Lightly coat the chicken breasts with the flour, shaking off the excess.

3 Melt the butter with the oil in a large frying pan. When the butter is foaming, add the chicken breasts, skin-side down, and cook for 10 minutes. Turn the chicken, and cook for a further 10 minutes or until golden and cooked through.

4 Using a slotted spoon, remove the chicken breasts and keep warm. Pour off the fat, and discard any dark brown sediment.

5 Pour the chicken stock into the pan, and boil for 8 minutes or until reduced to about 2–3 tbsp.

6 Arrange the chicken breasts on beds of watercress, and then pour over the hot sauce. Serve at once, garnished with chopped parsley.

SPICY CHICKEN BREASTS

Substitute 1/4 tsp crushed chillies for the herbes de Provence in the marinade. Add 1 tsp paprika to the flour for coating, and proceed as directed.

CHICKEN THIGHS WITH CHESTNUT STUFFING

You don't need to roast a whole bird to enjoy the classic combination of chicken with a savoury stuffing. This dish features chicken thighs wrapped around a nutty filling of chestnuts and bacon, and served with cranberry sauce.

Serves 4

8 boneless chicken thighs, with the skin left on
150 ml (1/4 pint) chicken stock
1 tbsp cranberry jelly

STUFFING

15 g (1/2 oz) butter
2 streaky bacon rashers, rinds removed, diced
1 small onion, finely chopped
125 g (4 oz) frozen chestnuts, thawed and finely chopped
30 g (1 oz) fresh brown breadcrumbs
1 tbsp chopped parsley
salt and black pepper
1 egg yolk

1 Make the stuffing: melt the butter in a frying pan, add the bacon and onion, and cook over a medium heat for 3–5 minutes until the bacon is crisp and the onion soft but not coloured.

2 Add the chestnuts, and cook, stirring occasionally, for 5 minutes. Remove from the heat, add the breadcrumbs, parsley, and salt and pepper to taste, then bind with the egg yolk.

3 Place the chicken thighs, skin-side down, on a chopping board, and divide the stuffing among them. Roll up each thigh to enclose the stuffing, and fasten with a wooden cocktail stick or tie with string.

4 Arrange the chicken thighs in a single layer in a roasting tin, and cook in a preheated oven at 190°C (375°F, Gas 5) for 20–25 minutes until the chicken is lightly browned and cooked through.

5 Lift the chicken thighs out of the roasting tin, remove the cocktail sticks or string, and keep warm.

6 Spoon off any excess fat, put the tin on top of the stove, and pour in the stock. Bring to a boil, and boil for 3–5 minutes until syrupy, stirring to dissolve any sediment and cooking juices. Stir in the cranberry jelly, and cook for 1 minute to melt the jelly. Taste for seasoning. Strain the sauce, and serve at once, with the chicken thighs.

CHICKEN THIGHS WITH PINE NUTS

Substitute 100 g (3 1/2 oz) chopped pine nuts for the chestnuts in the stuffing, and proceed as directed.

CHICKEN THIGHS NORMANDE

Serves 4

3 leeks, trimmed and thinly sliced
4 lean back bacon rashers, rinds removed, diced
5 garlic cloves, crushed
350 ml (12 fl oz) strong dry cider
8 chicken thighs, with the bone in and skin left on
1/2 tsp chopped fresh thyme
salt and black pepper
125 ml (4 fl oz) crème fraîche

1 Put the leeks, bacon, and garlic into a roasting tin. Pour in the cider, and put the chicken on top. Sprinkle with the thyme, and season.

2 Bake in a preheated oven at 190°C (375°F, Gas 5) for 20–25 minutes until the chicken is tender and cooked through. Remove the chicken thighs, bacon, and vegetables, and keep warm.

3 Spoon off any excess fat from the roasting tin. Put the tin on top of the stove, and boil the cooking juices until reduced by half. Stir in the crème fraîche, and heat gently. Pour the sauce on to serving plates, arrange the bacon, vegetables, and chicken on top, and serve hot.

MARINATED BARBECUED CHICKEN

Smoke-scented, crisp-skinned, and with juicy tender flesh, marinated chickens and poussins are delicious when cooked over a barbecue. Use chicken portions or spatchcocked whole birds, so that they can be cooked quickly and easily.

ORANGE & BASIL

 **Serves 4**

1.5 kg (3 lb) chicken, cut into 4 (page 148)

MARINADE

75 ml (2 1/2 fl oz) olive oil

75 ml (2 1/2 fl oz) dry white wine

1 orange, sliced

5–8 garlic cloves, crushed

2 tbsp shredded fresh basil

salt and black pepper

PINEAPPLE SALSA

90 g (3 oz) fresh or canned pineapple, diced

1 orange, peeled, segmented, and diced

1/4 red pepper, cored, seeded, and diced

1/4 tsp crushed chillies

1/4 tsp caster sugar

juice of 1/4 lime or lemon

1 Combine the marinade ingredients in a shallow non-metallic dish. Add the chicken, turn to coat, and leave to marinate in the refrigerator for at least 12 hours.

2 Cook the chicken over a barbecue, turning and basting, for 20 minutes or until the juices run clear. Remove the orange slices from the marinade and grill until lightly browned.

3 Mix together the ingredients for the salsa. Serve the chicken hot with the orange slices and the salsa.

FRUITY CORIANDER

Serves 4

2 x 375 g (12 oz) poussins, spatchcocked (page 150)

MARINADE

75 ml (2 1/2 fl oz) olive oil

juice of 1 orange

1 lime and 1 lemon, sliced

2.5 cm (1 in) piece of fresh root ginger, peeled and grated

30 g (1 oz) fresh coriander, chopped

salt and black pepper

NECTARINE SALSA

1 ripe nectarine, peeled and diced

1 cm (1/2 in) piece of fresh root ginger, peeled and grated

1/2 banana, diced

1 spring onion, thinly sliced

1 tsp lime juice

1/4 tsp crushed chillies

1 Combine the marinade ingredients in a non-metallic dish. Add the poussins and marinate for 12 hours.

2 Cook the poussins, turning and basting, for 15 minutes or until the juices run clear. Remove the fruit slices from the marinade and barbecue.

3 Mix together the ingredients for the salsa. Serve the poussins hot with the lime and lemon slices and the salsa.

LEMON & MARJORAM

 **Serves 4**

1.5 kg (3 lb) chicken, spatchcocked (page 150)

MARINADE

75 ml (2 1/2 fl oz) olive oil

juice of 2 lemons

3 garlic cloves, crushed

30 g (1 oz) fresh marjoram, chopped

salt and black pepper

CURRY SAUCE

4 tbsp plain yogurt

1 tbsp mayonnaise

1 tbsp chopped fresh marjaram

1 garlic clove, crushed

1/2 tsp mild curry powder

1/4 tsp lemon juice

1/4 tsp each ground cumin and turmeric

1 Combine the marinade ingredients in a non-metallic dish. Add the chicken, turn to coat, and marinate in the refrigerator for at least 12 hours.

2 Cook the chicken over a barbecue, turning and basting, for 20 minutes or until the juices run clear.

3 Combine the sauce ingredients. Cut up the chicken; serve with the sauce.

Clockwise from top: *Fruity Coriander Poussins, Lemon & Marjoram Chicken, Orange & Basil Chicken.*

Successful marinating

A marinade will give poultry or meat extra flavour before it is cooked over a barbecue. Here are some useful points to remember:

- A marinade is a mixture of liquids and seasonings. There is always an acid such as lemon juice, wine, or vinegar, which makes poultry or meat more tender.
- An oil, such as olive, sesame, or sunflower, keeps the meat or poultry moist and carries the flavours of the seasonings into the food.
- Seasonings usually include salt and pepper, but all kinds of spices and herbs can be used as well. Marinades often include garlic, onions, and celery, which also add flavour.
- Allow enough time for large pieces of poultry or meat to pick up the flavour of the marinade. Smaller pieces will pick up the flavour more quickly.
- Turn the food in the marinade occasionally to ensure an even coating, and baste with the marinade when barbecuing.

LEMON & HERB DRUMSTICKS

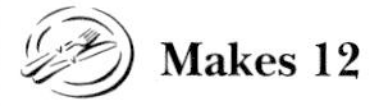 **Makes 12**

12 chicken drumsticks

MARINADE

150 ml (1/4 pint) olive oil

grated zest and juice of 1 lemon

6 large parsley sprigs, chopped

1 onion, thinly sliced

2 large garlic cloves, crushed

salt and black pepper

1 Make the marinade: in a large bowl, combine the olive oil, lemon zest and juice, parsley sprigs, onion, garlic, and salt and pepper to taste.

2 Turn the drumsticks in the marinade. Cover and leave to marinate in the refrigerator for at least 30 minutes.

3 Place the drumsticks under a hot grill, 10 cm (4 ins) from the heat, and grill, turning frequently and basting with the marinade, for 20 minutes until crisp, brown, and cooked through. Serve the drumsticks hot or cold.

Cook's know-how

It is a good idea to wrap the bone ends of the drumsticks in a little foil to make them easier to eat with the fingers, especially if you are serving them hot.

HONEYED DRUMSTICKS

Omit the lemon and parsley marinade. In a large bowl, combine 250 g (8 oz) plain yogurt, 2 tbsp honey, 1 tsp ground coriander, and salt and pepper to taste. Add the drumsticks, turn to coat, and leave to marinate in the refrigerator for 30 minutes. Remove the drumsticks from the marinade, and proceed as directed, brushing frequently with the marinade.

DEVILLED CHICKEN DRUMSTICKS

Makes 12

12 chicken drumsticks

2 tbsp sesame seeds

SPICY COATING

2 tbsp olive oil

2 tbsp white wine vinegar

2 tbsp tomato ketchup

1 tbsp Dijon mustard

1 small onion, quartered

2 tbsp dark muscovado sugar

1 large garlic clove, coarsely crushed

1/4 tsp chilli powder

salt and black pepper

tortilla chips to serve

1 Make the spicy coating: purée the oil, vinegar, ketchup, mustard, onion, sugar, garlic, chilli powder, and salt and pepper to taste in a food processor until fairly smooth.

2 Make 3 deep cuts in each chicken drumstick, arrange in a single layer in a shallow ovenproof dish, and spoon the spicy coating over them. Sprinkle with half of the sesame seeds.

3 Bake in a preheated oven at 190°C (375°F, Gas 5), basting, for 30 minutes until the drumsticks are cooked through. Turn halfway through cooking, and sprinkle with the remaining sesame seeds. Serve hot or cold with tortilla chips.

RED CHILLI ROASTED DRUMSTICKS

Omit the spicy coating. Combine 3 tbsp lemon juice, 4 crushed garlic cloves, 1 1/2 tbsp paprika, 1 tbsp mild chilli powder, 1 tsp ground cumin, and 1/4 tsp oregano. Coat the drumsticks with the mixture, then wrap each one in a streaky bacon rasher. Cover and leave to marinate in the refrigerator for at least 1 hour. Bake in a preheated oven at 190°C (375°F, Gas 5) for 30 minutes or until the drumsticks are cooked through.

CORONATION CHICKEN

Serves 6

- *1 tbsp sunflower oil*
- *125 g (4 oz) spring onions, chopped*
- *4 tsp mild curry paste*
- *150 ml (1/4 pint) red wine*
- *pared zest and juice of 1 lemon*
- *1 tbsp tomato purée*
- *2 tbsp apricot jam*
- *300 ml (1/2 pint) mayonnaise*
- *150 g (5 oz) plain yogurt*
- *salt and pepper*
- *500 g (1 lb) cooked chicken, cut into bite-sized pieces*
- *watercress sprigs to garnish*

1 Heat the oil in a small saucepan, add the spring onions, and cook for about 2 minutes until beginning to soften but not colour. Stir in the curry paste and cook, stirring, for 1 minute.

2 Add the red wine, lemon zest and juice, and tomato purée. Simmer, uncovered, stirring, for 5 minutes or until reduced to 4 tbsp. Strain into a bowl, cover, and leave to cool.

3 Work the apricot jam through the sieve, then stir it into the curry paste and wine mixture. Add the mayonnaise, yogurt, and salt and pepper to taste, stirring well to blend evenly. The mixture should be of a coating consistency and the colour of pale straw.

4 Add the chicken pieces to the mayonnaise mixture, and stir to coat evenly. Garnish with watercress sprigs before serving.

CHICKEN VERONIQUE

Substitute white wine for the red wine. Add 175 g (6 oz) halved, seedless green grapes to the mayonnaise mixture when you add the chicken.

MARINATED CHICKEN WITH PEPPERS

Serves 4–6

- *1.7 kg (3 1/2 lb) chicken, with giblets removed*
- *2 tbsp olive oil*
- *1 large red pepper, cored, seeded, and cut into thin strips*
- *1 large yellow pepper, cored, seeded, and cut into thin strips*
- *125 g (4 oz) pitted black olives*

MARINADE

- *4 tbsp olive oil*
- *2 tbsp clear honey*
- *juice of 1/2 lemon*
- *1 tbsp chopped mixed fresh herbs, such as parsley, thyme, and basil*
- *salt and black pepper*

1 Put the chicken into a roasting tin, rub the breast with oil, and cook in a preheated oven at 190°C (375°F, Gas 5) for 20 minutes per 500 g (1 lb). Spoon off the fat and juices, and then add the peppers. Return to the oven for 20 minutes.

2 Remove the chicken and peppers from the tin, and leave to stand until cool enough to handle.

3 Meanwhile, make the marinade: in a large bowl, combine the olive oil, honey, lemon juice, herbs, and salt and pepper to taste.

4 Strip the chicken flesh from the carcass, and cut it into small bite-sized strips. Toss the strips in the marinade, stirring gently to coat them evenly. Cover the chicken and leave to cool completely.

5 Spoon the chicken on to a serving platter, arrange the peppers and the olives around the edge, and serve at room temperature.

CHICKEN WITH SHALLOTS

Substitute 250 g (8 oz) peeled shallots for the red and yellow peppers, and proceed as directed.

GREEK SPICED CHICKEN

Serves 6

500 g (1 lb) cooked chicken, cut into bite-sized pieces

pitta bread to serve

1 spring onion, cut into strips, to garnish

MARINADE

150 g (5 oz) Greek yogurt

150 ml (1/4 pint) crème fraîche

8 spring onions, thinly sliced

2 tbsp chopped fresh coriander

1 tbsp chopped parsley

1 1/2 tsp ground coriander

1 1/2 tsp ground cumin

salt and black pepper

1 Make the marinade: in a large bowl, combine the yogurt, crème fraîche, spring onions, fresh coriander, parsley, ground coriander, cumin, and salt and pepper to taste.

2 Toss the chicken pieces in the marinade.

3 Sprinkle the pitta bread with a little water and cook under a hot grill for 1 minute on each side. Garnish the chicken with the spring onion strips, and serve with the pitta bread.

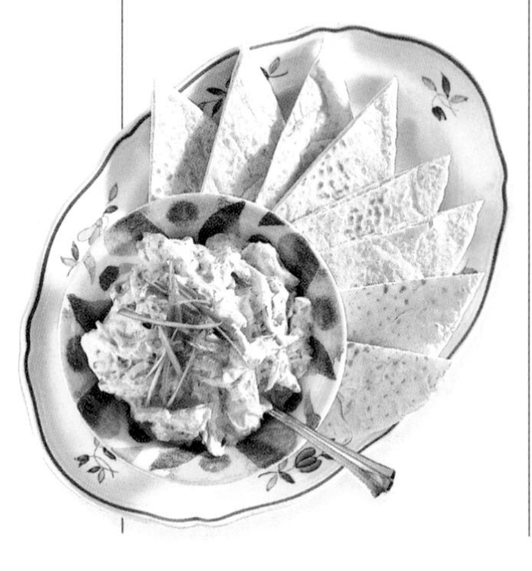

WARM CHICKEN SALAD WITH MANGO & AVOCADO

This unusual salad combines refreshing slices of mango and avocado with spicy chicken breast and a warm, rum-flavoured dressing. The combination of flavours makes a truly tropical dish.

Serves 4

3 skinless, boneless chicken breasts, cut into 2.5 cm (1 in) strips

1 round lettuce, leaves separated

1 bunch of watercress, trimmed

1 avocado, peeled, stoned (page 68), and sliced lengthwise

1 mango, peeled, stoned (page 430), and sliced lengthwise

4 tbsp dark rum

paprika to garnish

MARINADE

2 tbsp olive oil

2 tbsp lemon juice

2 tsp balsamic vinegar

2 garlic cloves, crushed

1 tbsp paprika

1 mild fresh red chilli, cored, seeded, and finely chopped

1/2 tsp ground cumin

salt

1 Make the marinade: combine the oil, lemon juice, vinegar, garlic, paprika, chilli, cumin, and salt to taste. Toss the chicken strips in the marinade, cover, and leave to marinate for a few minutes.

2 Arrange beds of lettuce and watercress on 4 serving plates. Arrange the avocado and mango slices on top.

3 Heat a large frying pan, and add the chicken strips with the marinade. Cook over a high heat, stirring, for 5–6 minutes until golden on all sides and cooked through.

4 Using a slotted spoon, remove the chicken strips from the pan, and arrange on top of the avocado and mango.

5 Return the frying pan to the heat, and pour in the rum. Let it bubble, stirring constantly to dissolve any sediment in the frying pan and incorporate the cooking juices, for about 1 minute. Pour the hot rum mixture over the salads, sprinkle with a little paprika, and serve at once.

Balsamic vinegar

Made in Italy from grape juice aged in wooden casks, balsamic vinegar is a high-quality, expensive vinegar with a smooth, mellow taste. Less expensive, mass-produced versions are available but wine vinegar can be used instead, if you prefer.

BALLOTINE OF CHICKEN

A ballotine is a bird or cut of meat which has been boned, stuffed, and rolled. It is slowly cooked in the oven, allowed to cool, then chilled for several hours or overnight until firm. With its colourful, pistachio-studded filling, it makes an excellent centrepiece for a buffet party, and is easy to slice and serve.

Serves 8–10

2 kg (4 lb) chicken, boned (page 149)
4 thin slices of cooked ham
125 g (4 oz) pistachio nuts, shelled
60 g (2 oz) butter, softened
600 ml (1 pint) chicken stock

STUFFING

500 g (1 lb) belly pork
375 g (12 oz) chicken livers, trimmed
250 g (8 oz) streaky bacon rashers, rinds removed, coarsely chopped
2 shallots, quartered
2 garlic cloves
4 tbsp brandy
2 tsp chopped fresh thyme
1 tsp chopped fresh sage
1/2 tsp ground ginger
1/2 tsp ground cinnamon
salt and black pepper

1 Make the stuffing: chop the pork into 5 mm (1/4 in) pieces, and place in a bowl.

2 Purée the chicken livers, bacon, shallots, garlic, and brandy in a food processor until smooth. Add to the pork in the bowl with the thyme, sage, ginger, and cinnamon, and season generously with salt and pepper. Stir well to combine.

3 Place the boned chicken, skin-side down, between 2 sheets of greaseproof paper and pound to an even thickness with a rolling pin.

4 Remove the greaseproof paper from the chicken, and assemble the ballotine (see box, right). Tie several pieces of string around the chicken to keep it in shape.

5 Spread the softened butter over the chicken skin, and season generously with salt and pepper.

6 Roll the chicken tightly in a piece of muslin and tie the ends. Place the chicken roll on a wire rack in a roasting tin.

7 Bring the stock to a boil, and pour over the chicken in the roasting tin. Cook in a preheated oven at 160°C (325°F, Gas 3), basting occasionally and adding more stock if necessary, for 2 hours or until the juices run clear when the chicken is pierced.

8 Remove the muslin, put the ballotine on to a plate, and leave to cool. Cover and chill overnight. Cut into thin slices to serve.

Assembling the ballotine

Spread half of the stuffing over the chicken, to within 2.5 cm (1 in) of the edges. Arrange the ham slices on top. Scatter the pistachio nuts on top of the ham.

Spoon on and spread the remaining stuffing over the pistachio nuts.

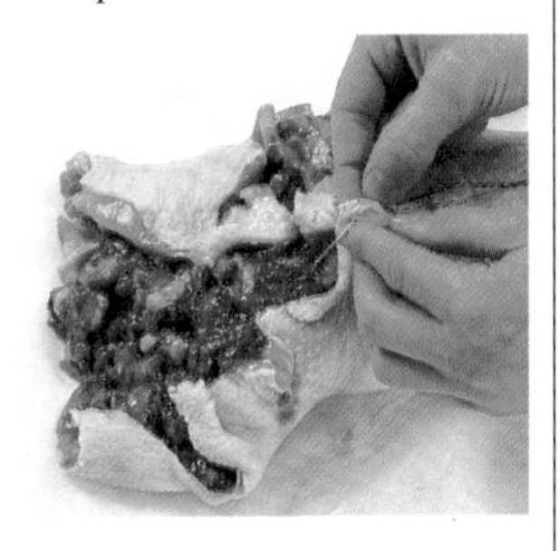

Fold the chicken over the stuffing to form a sausage shape, and sew the edges together with thin string or fasten them with small metal skewers.

Christmas roast turkey

If you've got a large number to cater for at Christmas, be sure to order a fresh turkey well in advance from your butcher; you can collect it on Christmas Eve or store it for up to 3 days in the refrigerator. If you buy a frozen turkey, make sure that it is thoroughly thawed before cooking.

Serves 12

pared zest of 1 lemon
a few parsley stalks
a few thyme sprigs
2 celery stalks, roughly sliced
5 kg (10 lb) oven-ready turkey, with giblets
125 g (4 oz) butter, softened
salt and black pepper
250 g (8 oz) streaky bacon rashers

CHESTNUT STUFFING

30 g (1 oz) butter
1 onion, finely chopped
90 g (3 oz) streaky bacon, finely chopped
375 g (12 oz) frozen chestnuts, thawed, or 175 g (6 oz) dried chestnuts, soaked, finely chopped
175 g (6 oz) pork sausagemeat
3 tbsp chopped parsley
1 tbsp chopped fresh thyme
salt and black pepper
1 small egg, beaten

GRAVY

30 g (1 oz) plain flour
600 ml (1 pint) giblet stock (page 148)
salt and black pepper

TO SERVE

bread sauce
cranberry sauce
bacon rolls
chipolatas

1 Prepare the stuffing: melt the butter in a frying pan, add the onion and bacon, and cook until the onion is soft and both the onion and bacon are golden. Transfer to a large bowl. Add the remaining stuffing ingredients and mix well. Leave to cool completely.

2 Place the lemon zest, parsley stalks, thyme, and celery into the cavity of the turkey. Fill the neck end with stuffing. Put any leftover stuffing into an ovenproof dish and set aside.

3 Shape the stuffed end of the turkey into a neat round and secure the loose skin with fine skewers. Tie the legs with string to give a neat shape.

4 Weigh the turkey and calculate the cooking time, allowing 20 minutes per 500 g (1 lb). Arrange 2 large sheets of foil across a large roasting tin. Place the turkey on top and spread the butter thickly over the bird, concentrating on the breast in particular.

5 Season with a little salt and plenty of pepper, then overlap the bacon rashers across the turkey, again concentrating on the breast.

6 Fold the sheets of foil loosely over the turkey, leaving a large air gap between the turkey and the foil. Cook the turkey in a preheated oven at 220°C (425°F, Gas 7) for 30 minutes.

7 Reduce the oven temperature to 160°C (325°F, Gas 3) and cook for the remaining calculated cooking time.

8 Thirty minutes before the end of the cooking time, fold back the foil, and remove the bacon, to allow the breast to brown. Baste occasionally with cooking juices. Pierce the thickest part of the thigh with a fine skewer: the juices will run clear when the turkey is cooked. Lift on to a warmed serving platter and leave to stand for 30 minutes before carving.

9 Meanwhile, put the reserved stuffing in the oven and cook for 25–30 minutes.

10 Make the gravy: spoon all but 2 tbsp of fat from the roasting tin, leaving behind the cooking juices. Place the roasting tin over a low heat and add the flour. Cook, stirring, for 1 minute. Add the stock and cook, stirring, until thickened. Season to taste.

11 Carve the turkey and serve with the extra stuffing, gravy, bread sauce, cranberry sauce, bacon rolls, and chipolatas.

Bread sauce

Insert *8 whole cloves* into *1 onion.* Put it into a pan with *900 ml ($1\frac{1}{2}$ pints) milk, 1 bay leaf,* and *6 whole black peppercorns.* Bring to a boil, remove from the heat, cover, and leave to infuse for 1 hour. Strain the milk and return to the pan. Gradually add about *175 g (6 oz) fresh white breadcrumbs,* then bring to a boil, stirring. Simmer for 2–3 minutes. Add *salt and black pepper to taste* and stir in *60 g (2 oz) butter.* If liked, stir in *4 tbsp double cream* before serving. Serve hot.

Cranberry sauce

Put *500 g (1 lb) fresh cranberries* into a saucepan with *125 ml (4 fl oz) water.* Bring to a boil and simmer for about 5 minutes, until the cranberries have begun to break down. Stir in *125 g (4 oz) caster sugar* and simmer until the sugar has dissolved. Stir in *2 tbsp port* before serving. Serve hot or cold.

Bacon rolls

With the back of a knife, stretch *6 streaky bacon rashers* until twice their original size. Cut in half and roll up loosely. Thread on to skewers and cook under a hot grill, turning, for 6 minutes or until browned.

Chipolatas

Twist *6 chipolata sausages* in the centre and cut in half, to make 12 small sausages. Cook under a hot grill for 10–15 minutes until cooked through and browned all over.

TURKEY WITH SOURED CREAM & CHIVES

 **Serves 4**

30 g (1 oz) butter

2 tbsp sunflower oil

4 turkey breast fillets, cut diagonally into 1 cm (1/2 in) strips

4 streaky bacon rashers, rinds removed, diced

1 large onion, sliced

250 g (8 oz) button mushrooms, halved

30 g (1 oz) plain flour

150 ml (1/4 pint) turkey or chicken stock

salt and black pepper

150 g (5 oz) soured cream

2 tbsp snipped fresh chives

1 Melt the butter with the oil in a large frying pan. When the butter is foaming, add the turkey strips, and cook over a high heat, stirring, for 8 minutes. Remove the turkey strips from the pan with a slotted spoon and keep warm.

2 Lower the heat and add the bacon, onion, and mushrooms. Cook gently, stirring occasionally, for 3–5 minutes until the onion is soft but not coloured. Add the flour and cook, stirring, for 1 minute.

3 Pour in the stock, and bring to a boil, stirring until thickened. Return the turkey to the pan, and season to taste. Cover and simmer for 5 minutes or until the turkey is tender.

4 Stir the soured cream into the turkey and mushroom mixture, and gently heat the mixture without boiling. Serve at once, sprinkled with the snipped chives.

ROAST TURKEY WITH GARLIC & TARRAGON

Serves 4

1.25 kg (2 1/2 lb) turkey breast joint

1 tsp plain flour

300 ml (1/2 pint) chicken stock

salt and black pepper

watercress sprigs to garnish

MARINADE

3 tbsp sunflower oil

grated zest and juice of 1 lemon

1 small onion, sliced

1 garlic clove, crushed

1 large tarragon sprig

1 large lemon thyme sprig

1 Make the marinade: combine the sunflower oil, lemon zest and juice, onion, garlic, tarragon, and lemon thyme. Spoon the marinade over the turkey, cover, and leave to marinate in the refrigerator, turning occasionally, for 8 hours.

2 Put the turkey into a roasting tin. Strain the marinade, and pour around the turkey. Cover with foil, and cook in a preheated oven at 190°C (375°F, Gas 5) for 20 minutes per 500 g (1 lb). Remove the foil after 20 minutes of cooking to brown the turkey.

3 Test whether the turkey is done by inserting a fine skewer into the thickest part: the juices will run clear when it is cooked. Remove the turkey from the roasting tin, and keep warm while you make the gravy.

4 Put the tin on top of the stove, add the flour to the juices in the tin, and cook, stirring, for 1 minute until lightly browned. Add the stock, and bring to a boil, stirring constantly until lightly thickened. Simmer for 2–3 minutes. Add salt and pepper to taste. Strain into a warmed gravy boat.

5 Garnish the turkey with watercress, and serve the gravy separately.

Cook's know-how

Turkey joints are now available from supermarkets; they are excellent if you like roast turkey but don't want to buy a whole bird. Turkey breast joints usually come with the backbone and wing attached, making a joint which is easy to carve. Turkey breasts which have been boned and rolled are also widely available.

TURKEY & LEMON STIR-FRY

Serves 4

4 turkey breast fillets, cut diagonally into 2.5 cm (1 in) strips

375 g (12 oz) courgettes

1 large green pepper, cored and seeded

1 tbsp olive oil

250 g (8 oz) baby sweetcorn

chopped parsley and lemon twists to garnish

MARINADE

125 ml (4 fl oz) dry white wine

grated zest and juice of 1 large lemon

2 tbsp olive oil

salt and black pepper

1 Make the marinade: combine the wine, lemon zest and juice, oil, and salt and pepper to taste. Toss the turkey strips in the marinade, cover, and leave to marinate in the refrigerator for at least 30 minutes.

2 Slice the courgettes thickly on the diagonal, and cut the green pepper into long thin strips.

3 Heat the oil in a wok, add the courgettes, sweetcorn, and green pepper, and stir-fry over a high heat for 2 minutes. Remove with a slotted spoon, and keep warm.

4 Remove the turkey strips from the marinade, reserving the marinade. Add the turkey to the wok, and stir-fry over a high heat for 5 minutes or until golden.

5 Pour the reserved marinade over the turkey and cook for 3 minutes or until tender. Return the vegetables to the wok, and heat through. Taste for seasoning. Serve at once, garnished with parsley and lemon twists.

Baby sweetcorn

This is corn on the cob, picked when not fully grown. Often used in oriental dishes, it should be cooked only briefly to preserve its sweetness.

TURKEY SCHNITZEL

Serves 4

3 tbsp plain flour

salt and black pepper

1 large egg, beaten

60 g (2 oz) fresh white breadcrumbs

4 x 175 g (6 oz) turkey breast escalopes

2 tbsp sunflower oil

15 g (1/2 oz) butter

lemon slices and chopped parsley to garnish

1 Sprinkle the flour on to a plate, and season generously with salt and pepper. Pour the beaten egg on to another plate, and sprinkle the breadcrumbs on to a third plate.

2 Coat each escalope with the seasoned flour, shaking off any excess. Dip each floured escalope into the beaten egg, then dip into the breadcrumbs.

3 With a sharp knife, score the escalopes in a criss-cross pattern. Cover and chill in the refrigerator for about 30 minutes.

4 Heat the oil with the butter in a large frying pan. When the butter is foaming, add the escalopes, and cook over a high heat until golden on both sides.

5 Lower the heat and cook for 10 minutes or until the escalopes are tender. Test the escalopes by piercing with a fine skewer: the juices should run clear.

6 Lift the escalopes out of the pan, and drain on paper towels. Garnish with lemon slices and chopped parsley, and serve at once.

Cook's know-how

If you can't find turkey breast escalopes, buy breast fillets: put them between 2 sheets of greaseproof paper, and pound with a rolling pin until 5 mm (1/4 in) thick.

TURKEY MOLE

 **Serves 4**

- *2 tbsp sunflower oil*
- *750 g (1½ lb) turkey pieces*
- *300 ml (½ pint) turkey or chicken stock*
- *salt and black pepper*

MOLE SAUCE

- *1 x 400 g (13 oz) can chopped tomatoes*
- *1 small onion, coarsely chopped*
- *90 g (3 oz) blanched almonds*
- *30 g (1 oz) raisins (optional)*
- *20 g (¾ oz) plain chocolate, coarsely chopped*
- *1 garlic clove*
- *1 tbsp sesame seeds*
- *1 tbsp hot chilli powder*
- *1 tsp ground cinnamon*
- *½ tsp ground cloves*
- *½ tsp ground coriander*
- *½ tsp ground cumin*
- *¼ tsp ground aniseed*
- *4 tbsp water*

1 Make the mole sauce: put the tomatoes, onion, almonds, raisins, if using, chocolate, garlic, sesame seeds, chilli powder, cinnamon, cloves, coriander, cumin, aniseed, and the measured water into a food processor and process briefly.

2 Heat the sunflower oil in a large saucepan, add the turkey pieces, and cook over a high heat for about 5 minutes until golden on all sides.

3 Add the mole sauce mixture, and cook, stirring, for 2 minutes. Pour in the stock, and bring to a boil. Cover and simmer very gently for 40 minutes or until the turkey is tender. Add salt and pepper to taste. Serve at once.

Turkey mole

Pronounced "molay", this is an ancient Mexican dish. The hot spicy sauce, often served with turkey, is given depth of flavour by a little plain chocolate, which often features in Mexican dishes. For an authentic touch, serve with tortillas, red kidney beans, avocado, and red onion rings.

TURKEY CASSEROLE WITH PEPPERS & CIDER

Serves 4

- *30 g (1 oz) butter*
- *1 tbsp sunflower oil*
- *750 g (1½ lb) turkey pieces*
- *1 onion, sliced*
- *1 garlic clove, crushed*
- *1 red pepper, cored, seeded, and thinly sliced*
- *1 yellow pepper, cored, seeded, and thinly sliced*
- *300 ml (½ pint) dry cider*
- *salt and black pepper*
- *chopped parsley to garnish*

1 Melt the butter with the oil in a flameproof casserole. When the butter is foaming, add the turkey pieces, and cook over a high heat for 5 minutes or until golden on all sides. Lift out with a slotted spoon, and drain on paper towels.

2 Lower the heat, add the onion, garlic, and red and yellow pepper slices to the casserole, and cook for 5 minutes or until the vegetables are just beginning to soften.

3 Return the turkey to the casserole, pour in the cider, and bring to a boil. Add salt and pepper to taste, cover, and cook in a preheated oven at 160°C (325°F, Gas 3) for 1 hour or until the turkey is tender.

4 Using a slotted spoon, transfer the turkey and vegetables to a warmed platter. Put the casserole on top of the stove and boil, stirring, until the cooking juices are thickened. Taste for seasoning.

5 Spoon the sauce over the turkey and vegetables, garnish with chopped parsley, and serve at once.

TURKEY & APPLE CASSEROLE

Substitute 2 cored, halved, and sliced dessert apples for the red and yellow peppers, and add to the casserole 20 minutes before the end of cooking time.

STIR-FRIED TURKEY MEATBALLS

Serves 4

3 tsp sunflower oil
1 onion, thinly sliced
1 green pepper, cored, seeded, and cut into bite-sized pieces
1 courgette, sliced
4–6 mushrooms, thinly sliced
125 g (4 oz) bean sprouts

MEATBALLS

375 g (12 oz) minced turkey
45 g (1 1/2 oz) parsley stuffing mix
1 onion, finely chopped
4 garlic cloves, crushed
3 tbsp soy sauce
1 cm (1/2 in) piece of fresh root ginger, peeled and chopped
salt and black pepper

1 Make the meatballs: in a bowl, combine the turkey, stuffing mix, onion, garlic, 1 tbsp of the soy sauce, the ginger, and salt and pepper to taste. Shape into meatballs (see box, right).

2 Heat 1 tsp of the oil in a wok, add the onion, green pepper, and courgette, and stir-fry for 2–3 minutes. Remove with a slotted spoon, and keep warm.

3 Heat another 1 tsp of the oil, add the mushrooms, and stir-fry for 2–3 minutes. Remove with a slotted spoon, and keep warm.

4 Heat the remaining oil in the wok, add the turkey meatballs, and cook gently, turning, for 6–7 minutes until cooked through. Return the vegetables to the wok, add the bean sprouts, sprinkle with the remaining soy sauce, and cook for 1 minute to heat through. Serve at once.

Shaping meatballs

Break off pieces of the turkey mixture and, with dampened hands to prevent the mixture sticking, roll into 5 cm (2 in) meatballs.

TURKEY BURGERS HOLSTEIN

Serves 4

60 g (2 oz) butter
1 small onion, very finely chopped
500 g (1 lb) minced turkey
90 g (3 oz) sliced cooked ham, finely chopped
1 tbsp chopped parsley
salt and black pepper
2 tbsp sunflower oil
4 eggs to serve

1 Melt half of the butter in a small saucepan, add the onion, and cook gently, stirring occasionally, for 3–5 minutes until soft but not coloured. Leave to cool.

2 Put the onion into a large bowl, add the turkey, ham, parsley, and salt and pepper to taste, and mix thoroughly. Shape into 4 burgers. Cover and chill for 30 minutes.

3 Melt the remaining butter with the oil in a frying pan. When the butter is foaming, add the burgers, and cook over a high heat for 2–3 minutes on each side until golden.

4 Lower the heat, and cook, turning once, for about 10 minutes until the burgers are cooked through.

5 Lift the burgers out of the frying pan with a slotted spoon and drain on paper towels.

6 Break the eggs into the frying pan, and fry over a medium heat until the whites are firm and the yolks are still soft. Divide the turkey burgers among serving plates, top each burger with an egg, and serve at once.

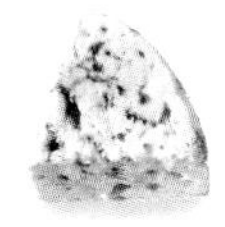

BLUE CHEESE TURKEY BURGERS

Omit the eggs. Make the burgers as directed. Crumble 125 g (4 oz) blue cheese, such as Roquefort, Stilton, or Danish Blue, and arrange on top of the burgers 5 minutes before the end of the cooking time.

TURKEY WITH CHEESE & PINEAPPLE

Serves 6

60 g (2 oz) butter

1 onion, sliced

60 g (2 oz) plain flour

450 ml (3/4 pint) turkey or chicken stock

1 x 250 g (8 oz) can pineapple pieces in natural juice, drained and juice reserved

250 g (8 oz) mature Cheddar cheese, grated

salt and black pepper

500 g (1 lb) cooked turkey, cut into bite-sized pieces

3 tbsp fresh brown breadcrumbs

chopped parsley to garnish

1 Melt the butter in a saucepan, add the onion, and cook gently, stirring occasionally, for 3–5 minutes until soft but not coloured. Add the flour, and cook, stirring, for 1 minute.

2 Gradually blend in the stock and the pineapple juice, and bring to a boil, stirring until thickened.

3 Add the pineapple pieces, reserving 6 for garnish. Stir in three-quarters of the cheese, and salt and pepper to taste.

4 Divide the turkey pieces among 6 individual gratin dishes, or put into 1 large ovenproof dish. Pour the sauce over the turkey, and sprinkle with the remaining cheese and then the breadcrumbs.

5 Bake in a preheated oven at 200°C (400°F, Gas 6) for 15–20 minutes until the turkey has heated through and the topping is golden. Garnish with chopped parsley and the reserved pineapple pieces, and serve at once.

TURKEY SALAD WITH MANGO & GRAPES

 **Serves 4**

1.25 kg (2 1/2 lb) turkey breast joint

1 onion, quartered

1 carrot, sliced

a few parsley sprigs

pared zest of 1 lemon

6 black peppercorns

1 bay leaf

200 ml (7 fl oz) lemon mayonnaise

1 bunch of watercress, tough stalks removed

1 ripe mango, peeled, stoned, and cut into cubes (page 430)

125 g (4 oz) seedless green grapes

90 g (3 oz) walnut pieces

1 Put the turkey joint into a large saucepan, and cover with cold water. Add the onion, carrot, parsley, lemon zest, peppercorns, and bay leaf, and bring to a boil. Cover and simmer very gently for 1 hour or until the turkey is tender. Remove from the heat, and leave the turkey to cool completely in the poaching liquid.

2 Lift the turkey out of the poaching liquid, and remove the flesh from the carcass. Discard the skin and bones, then cut the meat into bite-sized pieces.

3 Put the turkey pieces into a large bowl, and add the lemon mayonnaise. Stir well to coat the turkey pieces thoroughly and evenly.

4 Arrange the watercress on individual serving plates, and pile the turkey mixture on top. Arrange the mango cubes and grapes around the edge, sprinkle with the walnut pieces, and serve at room temperature.

Cook's know-how

Cooling the turkey in the poaching liquid helps to keep the flesh moist. Reserve the poaching liquid, and use it as stock for soups and sauces.

WALDORF TURKEY SALAD

Substitute 2 cored and cubed red dessert apples, and 2 sliced celery stalks for the mango and grapes, and then add to the turkey and lemon mayonnaise mixture. Proceed as directed in the recipe.

CHRISTMAS ROAST GOOSE

Goose is the traditional Christmas bird in Britain and northern Europe, and is a favourite festive choice. It is simple to cook and tastes delicious with a fruit stuffing and spicy accompaniments. Try it for an extra special Christmas lunch or dinner.

Serves 8

5–6 kg (10–12 lb) goose, with giblets reserved for stock

1 onion, quartered

1 cooking apple, quartered

a few sage sprigs

salt and black pepper

30 g (1 oz) plain flour

450 ml (3/4 pint) goose giblet stock (page 148)

150 ml (1/4 pint) dry white wine

spiced stuffed apples (see box, right) to serve

watercress sprigs to garnish

PORK & APPLE STUFFING

300 g (10 oz) pork sausagemeat

60 g (2 oz) fresh breadcrumbs

2 tsp dried sage

30 g (1 oz) butter

1 onion, finely chopped

1 large cooking apple, peeled, cored, and finely chopped

1 Make the pork and apple stuffing: in a bowl, combine the sausagemeat, breadcrumbs, and sage.

2 Melt the butter in a pan, add the onion, and cook gently, stirring occasionally, for 3–5 minutes until soft but not coloured.

3 Add the cooking apple, and cook for 5 minutes. Stir the onion and apple into the sausagemeat mixture, add salt and pepper to taste, and leave to cool.

4 Remove any fat from the cavity of the goose. Put the onion and apple quarters into the cavity together with the sage. Spoon the stuffing into the neck end of the goose, pat it into a rounded shape, and secure the skin flap with a small skewer. Weigh the goose.

5 Prick the skin of the goose all over with a fork, and rub with salt and pepper. Place the goose, breast-side down, on a wire rack in a large roasting tin, and cook in a preheated oven at 220°C (425°F, Gas 7) for 30 minutes.

6 Turn the goose breast-side up, and cook for 20 minutes. Reduce the oven temperature to 180°C (350°F, Gas 4) and cook for 20 minutes per 500 g (1 lb).

7 Test the goose by inserting a fine skewer into the thickest part of a thigh: the juices should run clear when the meat is thoroughly cooked.

8 Lift the goose on to a warmed serving platter, and then leave to stand, covered with foil, for about 20 minutes.

9 Make the gravy while the goose is standing: pour off all but 2 tbsp of the fat from the roasting tin. Put the tin on top of the stove, add the flour, and cook, stirring, for 1 minute. Add the stock and wine, and bring to a boil, stirring constantly. Simmer for 2–3 minutes, then taste for seasoning. Strain into a warmed gravy boat.

10 To serve, arrange the spiced stuffed apples around the goose, and garnish with watercress. Hand the gravy separately.

Cook's know-how

Goose is even richer and fattier than duck. Putting it on a wire rack set in a roasting tin ensures it does not sit in the fat during cooking and so gives a good, crisp skin.

Spiced stuffed apples

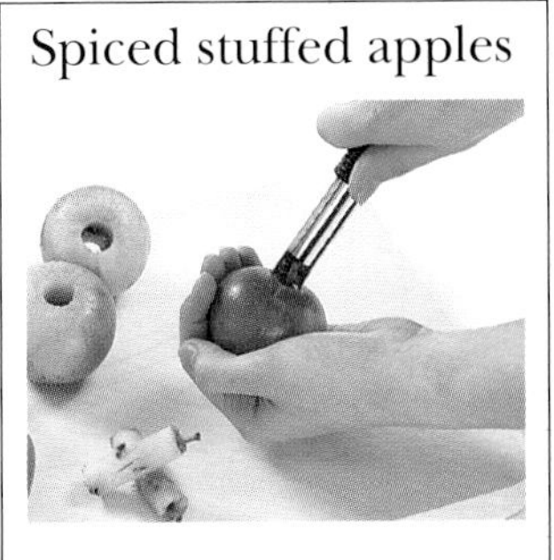

Core *8 dessert apples,* keeping them whole. Combine *2 tbsp Calvados, 1 tsp ground cinnamon, 1/2 tsp ground allspice, and 8 finely chopped ready-to-eat prunes* in a small bowl for the stuffing.

Place the apples in a buttered ovenproof dish, and spoon a little of the stuffing into the centres. Melt *60 g (2 oz) butter,* pour over the apples, and cover with foil. Bake in a preheated oven at 180°C (350°F, Gas 4) for 1 hour or until tender.

PEKING DUCK

This traditional Chinese dish is great fun to eat and ideal for serving at an informal dinner party. Let everyone help themselves to some crispy-skinned duck, spring onions, cucumber, and hoisin sauce, so they can assemble their own pancakes.

 **Serves 6**

2.5 kg (5 lb) duck, with giblets removed

3 tbsp dry sherry

3 tbsp clear honey

3 tbsp soy sauce

CHINESE PANCAKES

275 g (9 oz) plain flour

200 ml (7 fl oz) boiling water

2 tbsp sesame oil

TO SERVE

6 spring onions, cut into matchstick-thin strips

1/2 cucumber, peeled and cut into matchstick-thin strips

90 ml (3 fl oz) hoisin sauce, sprinkled with sesame seeds

6 spring onion tassels (page 115) to garnish

1 Remove any fat from the cavity of the duck. Put into a bowl; pour boiling water over the duck. Dry inside and out. Brush with the sherry, tie, and hang (see box, right).

2 Mix together the honey and soy sauce, and brush over the duck. Leave to hang for a further 4 hours or until the skin is dry again.

3 Put the duck, breast-side down, on a wire rack in a roasting tin, and cook in a preheated oven at 200°C (400°F, Gas 6) for 25 minutes or until browned. Turn over and cook for 1–1 1/4 hours until tender.

4 Meanwhile, make the pancake dough: sift the flour into a large bowl, add the boiling water, and mix to form a soft dough. Knead until smooth. Cover and leave to stand for about 30 minutes.

5 Knead the dough for 5 minutes. Shape into a roll about 2.5 cm (1 in) in diameter. Cut into 18 pieces, then roll into balls. Shape and cook the pancakes (see box, far right).

6 Leave the duck to stand for about 15 minutes. Meanwhile, arrange the pancakes on a plate in a steamer, cover, and steam for 10 minutes. Cut the duck into small pieces. Serve with the pancakes, spring onions, cucumber, and hoisin sauce, and garnish with onion tassels.

Hanging the duck

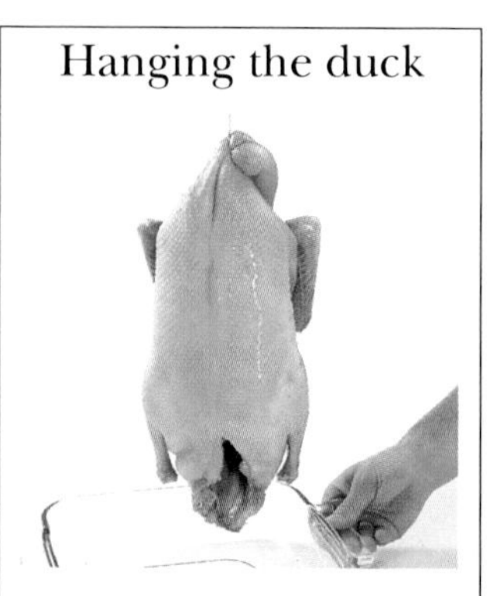

Tie a long piece of string around the skin at the neck opening. Hang the duck in a cool, draughty place for 4 hours, until the skin is dry.

Shaping and cooking Chinese pancakes

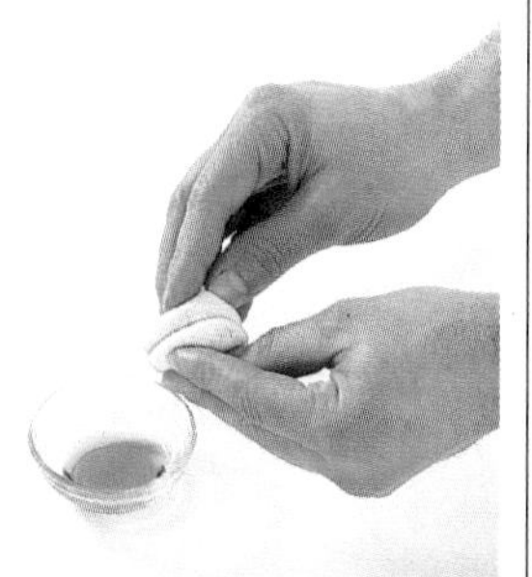

Pour the sesame oil into a bowl. Take 2 balls of dough, dip half of 1 ball into the oil, then press the oiled half on to the second ball.

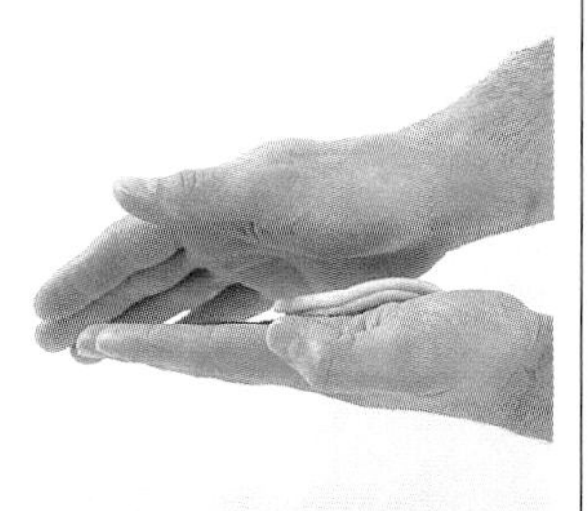

Flatten the dough balls with the palms of your hands and roll out to a pancake about 15 cm (6 ins) in diameter. Heat a frying pan. Put the double pancake into the pan and cook for 1 minute. Flip over and cook the other side for 1 minute.

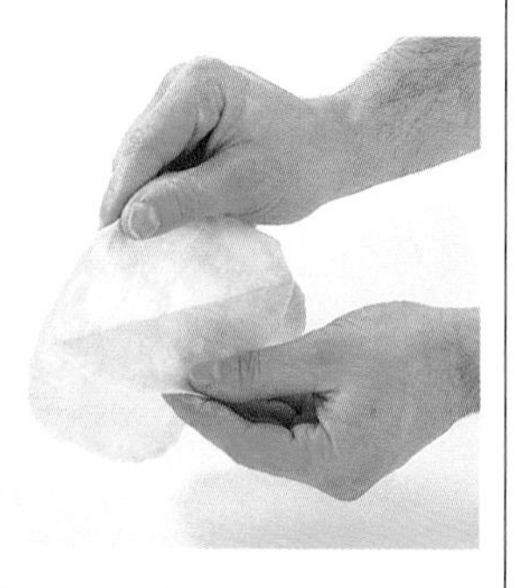

Remove from the pan, and peel the 2 pancakes apart. Repeat with the remaining dough, to make 18 pancakes in all. Cover the pancakes with a damp tea towel to stop them drying out.

ROAST DUCK WITH CRANBERRIES

Many people like the flesh of roast duck breast a little pink. However, the legs need to be well cooked, otherwise they may be tough. To accommodate the difference, serve the breast meat first, and return the duck to the oven for 15 minutes to finish cooking the legs.

Serves 4

2.5 kg (5 lb) duck, with giblets reserved for stock
cranberry sauce to serve (page 178)
watercress sprigs to garnish
CRANBERRY STUFFING
30 g (1 oz) butter
1 small onion, finely chopped
175 g (6 oz) fresh brown breadcrumbs
125 g (4 oz) cranberries
1 tbsp chopped parsley
1/4 tsp ground mixed spice
salt and black pepper
1 egg, beaten
GRAVY
1 tsp plain flour
300 ml (1/2 pint) duck giblet stock (page 148)

1 Make the cranberry stuffing: melt the butter in a pan, add the onion, and cook gently for 3–5 minutes until softened.

2 Stir in the breadcrumbs, cranberries, parsley, mixed spice, and salt and pepper to taste. Bind with the egg, and leave to cool.

3 Remove any fat from the cavity of the duck. Spoon the stuffing into the neck end of the duck, secure the skin flap over the stuffing with a small skewer, and pat into a rounded shape. Put any leftover stuffing into an ovenproof dish and set aside.

4 Prick the skin of the duck all over with a fork, and rub salt and pepper into the skin. Place the duck, breast-side down, on a wire rack in a deep roasting tin, and cook in a preheated oven at 200°C (400°F, Gas 6) for 25 minutes or until golden brown.

5 Pour off some of the fat from the tin to reduce spitting. Turn the duck breast-side up, and cook for 20 minutes or until brown.

6 Reduce the oven temperature to 180°C (350°F, Gas 4), and cook the duck, without basting, for 1–1 1/4 hours. Cook any leftover stuffing with the duck for the last 40 minutes.

7 Test the duck by inserting a fine skewer into the thickest part of a thigh: the juices will run clear when it is cooked. Keep warm, uncovered, while you make the gravy.

8 Pour off all but 1 tbsp of the fat from the roasting tin. Set the tin on top of the stove, add the flour, and cook, stirring constantly, for 2 minutes. Pour in the stock, and bring to a boil, stirring until lightly thickened. Taste for seasoning, and strain into a warmed gravy boat.

9 Put the stuffing into a serving dish, carve the duck (page 151), and garnish with watercress. Serve with the gravy and cranberry sauce.

SAUCES FOR DUCK

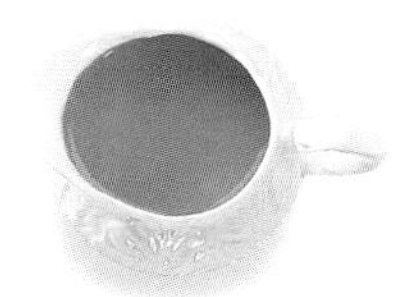

ORANGE SAUCE

Put *2 finely chopped shallots, 300 ml (1/2 pint) chicken stock,* and the *juice of 2 oranges* into a pan, and bring to a boil. Simmer until reduced by half. Add *salt and pepper to taste.* Push through a sieve, add the *pared zest of 1 large orange, cut into fine strips,* and reheat gently. Serve hot.

HONEY SAUCE

Cook *2 finely chopped shallots* in *30 g (1 oz) butter* until soft. Add *1 tbsp plain flour,* and cook, stirring, for 1 minute. Blend in *300 ml (1/2 pint) chicken stock* and *75 ml (2 1/2 fl oz) dry white wine.* Boil, stirring, until thick. Add *3 tbsp clear honey, 1 tbsp white wine vinegar,* and *salt and pepper to taste,* and cook for 1 minute. Push through a sieve, and add *3 tbsp finely chopped parsley.* Serve hot.

BLACKCURRANT SAUCE

Put *250 g (8 oz) blackcurrants* and *300 ml (1/2 pint) water* into a saucepan, and bring slowly to a boil. Simmer for 10 minutes until tender. Add *250 g (8 oz) caster sugar* and *1 tbsp port,* and cook gently until the sugar has dissolved. Serve hot or cold.

DUCK BREASTS WITH RASPBERRY SAUCE

Serves 4

4 x 250–300 g (8–10 oz) duck breasts, with the skin left on

salt and black pepper

RASPBERRY SAUCE

150 ml (¼ pint) port

75 ml (2½ fl oz) water

45 g (1½ oz) caster sugar

250 g (8 oz) raspberries

1 tsp cornflour

juice of 2 oranges

salt and black pepper

1 Make the raspberry sauce: pour the port, measured water, and sugar into a small saucepan, and bring to a boil, stirring until the sugar has dissolved. Add the raspberries, and bring back to a boil. Cover and simmer very gently for 5 minutes.

2 With a wooden spoon, push the raspberry mixture through a nylon sieve to extract the seeds. Return the raspberry purée to the saucepan, and bring back to a boil.

3 Mix the cornflour with the orange juice. Add a little of the raspberry purée to the cornflour mixture, and blend together. Return to the saucepan, and bring back to a boil, stirring constantly until thickened. Add salt and pepper to taste and set aside.

4 Score each duck breast (see box, below right), and rub with a little salt and pepper.

5 Place the duck breasts under a hot grill, 10 cm (4 ins) from the heat, and cook for 8 minutes on each side or until the skin is crisp and the duck is tender but still slightly pink inside.

6 Slice the duck breasts, skin-side up, and arrange in a fan shape on warmed serving plates. Spoon a little raspberry sauce around each of the servings, and hand the remainder separately.

DUCK BREASTS WITH RED WINE SAUCE

 **Serves 4**

4 x 250–300 g (8–10 oz) duck breasts, with the skin left on

125 ml (4 fl oz) beef stock

125 ml (4 fl oz) red wine

1 tsp tomato purée

1 tsp lemon juice

15 g (½ oz) butter

salt and black pepper

1 tbsp chopped fresh rosemary to garnish

MARINADE

5 garlic cloves, sliced

2 tbsp balsamic vinegar

1 tbsp chopped fresh rosemary

1 Make the marinade: in a bowl, combine the garlic, vinegar, and rosemary. Score the duck breasts, and spread with the marinade (see box, below). Chill for 30 minutes.

2 Put the duck breasts, skin-side down, with the marinade, in a frying pan and cook for 5–7 minutes. Turn, and cook for a further 5 minutes. Remove from the pan, and keep warm.

3 Spoon any excess fat from the frying pan. Add the stock and wine and bring to a boil. Cook over a high heat until reduced to a dark glaze, then add the tomato purée and lemon juice.

4 Remove from heat, and whisk in the butter, letting it thicken the sauce as it melts. Taste for seasoning.

5 Slice the duck breasts, and arrange on warmed serving plates. Spoon the sauce around the duck, sprinkle with chopped rosemary, and serve at once.

Scoring and marinating the duck breasts

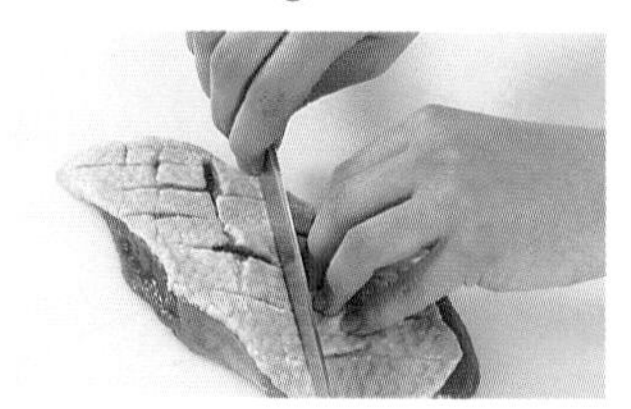

Score the skin of each duck breast with criss-cross lines. Season both sides with salt and pepper.

Put the duck breasts in a shallow dish, skin-side down, and spoon the marinade over the top.

HOT & SPICY STIR-FRIED DUCK

Serves 4

4 x 250–300 g (8–10 oz) skinless duck breasts, cut diagonally into 1 cm (1/2 in) strips

2 tbsp sunflower oil

8 spring onions, cut into 2.5 cm (1 in) lengths

125 g (4 oz) carrots, cut into matchstick-thin strips

250 g (8 oz) mangetout

1 x 200 g (7 oz) can water chestnuts, drained, rinsed, and sliced

MARINADE

2 tsp dark soy sauce

2 tsp red wine vinegar

2.5 cm (1 in) piece of fresh root ginger, peeled and grated

2 fresh red chillies, cored, seeded, and coarsely chopped

grated zest and juice of 1 orange

1 tsp sesame oil

1 tsp cornflour

1 tsp caster sugar

salt and black pepper

1 Make the marinade: in a large bowl, combine the soy sauce, vinegar, ginger, chillies, orange zest and juice, sesame oil, cornflour, sugar, and salt and pepper to taste.

2 Toss the duck strips in the marinade, cover, and leave to stand for 10 minutes.

3 Lift the duck strips out of the marinade, reserve the marinade, and drain the duck on paper towels.

4 Heat the oil in a wok or large frying pan, add the duck, and stir-fry over a high heat for 5 minutes or until browned all over. Add the spring onions and carrots, and stir-fry for 2–3 minutes. Add the mangetout, and stir-fry for 1 minute.

5 Pour the marinade into the wok, and stir-fry for a further 2 minutes or until the duck is just tender. Stir in the water chestnuts, heat through, and season to taste.

ORIENTAL DUCK WITH GINGER

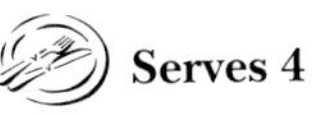

Serves 4

4 x 250–300 g (8–10 oz) skinless duck breasts

1 tbsp sunflower oil

8 baby sweetcorn

bean sprouts and 1 tbsp toasted sesame seeds to garnish

MARINADE

200 ml (7 fl oz) orange juice

3 tbsp dark soy sauce

1 tbsp sesame oil

1 tbsp Chinese rice wine or dry sherry

1 tbsp clear honey

3.5 cm (1 1/2 in) fresh root ginger, peeled and chopped

1 garlic clove, crushed

1 tsp ground ginger

salt and black pepper

1 Make the marinade: in a large bowl, combine the orange juice, soy sauce, sesame oil, rice wine, honey, fresh root ginger, garlic, ground ginger, and salt and pepper to taste.

2 With a sharp knife, make several diagonal slashes in each duck breast. Pour the marinade over the duck breasts, turn, then cover, and marinate in the refrigerator for 30 minutes.

3 Lift the duck breasts out of the marinade, reserving the marinade. Heat the oil in a large frying pan, add the duck breasts, and cook over a high heat, turning frequently, for 10–12 minutes until tender. Add the marinade and simmer for 2–3 minutes until slightly reduced.

4 Meanwhile, blanch the baby sweetcorn in boiling salted water for 1 minute. Drain, then make lengthwise cuts in each one, leaving them attached at the stem.

5 To serve, slice each duck breast, and arrange on 4 individual serving plates. Spoon the hot sauce over the duck, add the sweetcorn tassels, then garnish with bean sprouts and the toasted sesame seeds.

ORIENTAL DUCK WITH PLUMS

Substitute 250 g (8 oz) finely sliced dark red plums for the baby sweetcorn and bean sprouts. Add to the wok with the marinade. Simmer for 3–4 minutes, and serve as above.

GUINEA FOWL MADEIRA

Serves 6

2 tbsp sunflower oil
2 x 1.25 kg (2½ lb) guinea fowl, cut into serving pieces (page 148)
4 shallots, halved
1 tbsp plain flour
600 ml (1 pint) chicken stock
150 ml (¼ pint) dry white wine
4 tbsp Madeira
salt and black pepper
375 g (12 oz) seedless green grapes
150 ml (¼ pint) double cream
chopped parsley to garnish

1 Heat the oil in a flameproof casserole, and cook the guinea fowl pieces in batches for a few minutes until browned all over. Lift out and drain.

2 Lower the heat, add the shallots, and cook, stirring, for 5 minutes or until softened. Lift out and drain.

3 Add the flour, and cook, stirring, for 1 minute. Pour in the stock, and bring to a boil, stirring. Add the wine, Madeira, and season to taste. Add the guinea fowl and shallots, and bring to a boil. Cook in a preheated oven at 160°C (325°F, Gas 3) for about 1 hour until tender.

4 Add the grapes and cook for 15 minutes. Add the cream, and heat gently. Garnish with parsley.

MUSHROOM-STUFFED QUAIL

Whole quail make a very impressive dinner party dish. They can be quite fiddly to eat, so boning and stuffing them makes it much easier for your guests. Ask your butcher if he can bone the birds for you, but if not, it's quite simple to do at home.

Serves 6

12 quail, boned (page 149)
30 g (1 oz) butter, plus extra for greasing
1 tbsp lime marmalade

MUSHROOM STUFFING
60 g (2 oz) butter
3 shallots, finely chopped
375 g (12 oz) button mushrooms, coarsely chopped
60 g (2 oz) fresh white breadcrumbs
salt and black pepper
1 egg, beaten

LIME SAUCE
150 ml (¼ pint) chicken stock
juice of 1 lime
200 ml (7 fl oz) crème fraîche
4 tbsp chopped parsley

1 Make the mushroom stuffing: melt the butter in a saucepan, add the shallots, and cook gently, stirring occasionally, for 3–5 minutes until soft but not coloured.

2 Add the mushrooms and cook for 2 minutes, then remove from the heat. Stir in the breadcrumbs, salt and pepper to taste, and the egg, then leave to cool. Stuff the quail (see box, right).

3 Put the quail into a buttered roasting tin. Melt the butter gently in a saucepan, add the lime marmalade, and heat gently, stirring, until combined. Brush over the quail, and cook in a preheated oven at 200°C (400°F, Gas 6) for 15–20 minutes until golden brown and tender. Remove from the tin and keep warm.

4 Make the lime sauce: put the roasting tin on top of the stove. Add the stock, and bring to a boil, then stir for 5 minutes or until reduced a little.

5 Stir in the lime juice and crème fraîche, and heat gently, stirring constantly, until the sauce has a smooth, creamy consistency.

6 Add half of the parsley and salt and pepper to taste. Serve the quail with the lime sauce, and garnish with the remaining parsley.

Stuffing the quail

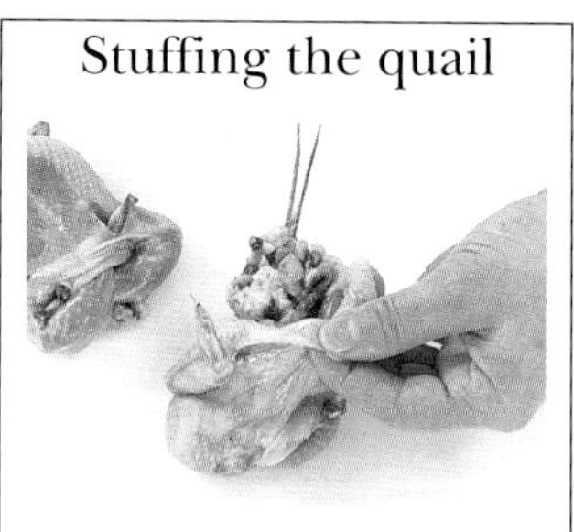

Spoon some of the stuffing into the cavity of each quail; secure the skin with a wooden cocktail stick.

STUFFED PHEASANT BREASTS

Substitute 6 pheasant breasts with skin for the quail, put the stuffing beneath the skin, and proceed as directed, cooking for 35 minutes.

TRADITIONAL ROAST PHEASANT

Pheasants are often sold in a brace – a cock and a hen. Make sure you get young pheasants for this recipe; old ones are not suitable for roasting and can be very tough unless slowly cooked in a casserole.

Serves 4

- *2 oven-ready pheasants, with giblets reserved for stock*
- *90 g (3 oz) butter, softened*
- *salt and black pepper*
- *4 streaky bacon rashers*
- *1 tsp plain flour*
- *300 ml (1/2 pint) pheasant giblet stock (page 148)*
- *1 tsp redcurrant jelly*
- *watercress sprigs to garnish*

TO SERVE

- *fried breadcrumbs (far right)*
- *game chips (far right)*
- *bread sauce (page 178)*

1 Prepare the oven-ready pheasants for roasting (see box, right).

2 Put the pheasants into a roasting tin, and cook in a preheated oven at 200°C (400°F, Gas 6), basting once, for 1 hour or until tender.

3 Test the pheasants by inserting a fine skewer in the thickest part of a thigh: the juices should run clear when they are cooked.

4 Lift the pheasants on to a warmed serving platter, cover with foil, and keep warm. Pour off all but 1 tbsp of the fat from the roasting tin, reserving any juices. Put the tin on top of the stove, add the flour, and cook, stirring, for 1 minute.

5 Add the stock and redcurrant jelly, and bring to a boil, stirring until lightly thickened. Simmer for 2–3 minutes, then taste for seasoning. Strain into a warmed gravy boat.

6 To serve, garnish the pheasants with the watercress sprigs, and serve with fried breadcrumbs, game chips, bread sauce, and the gravy.

Preparing pheasants for roasting

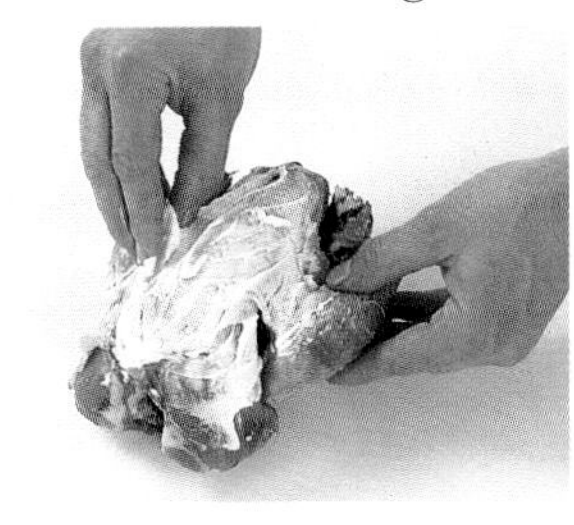

Rub the pheasants all over with the softened butter, and season with salt and black pepper.

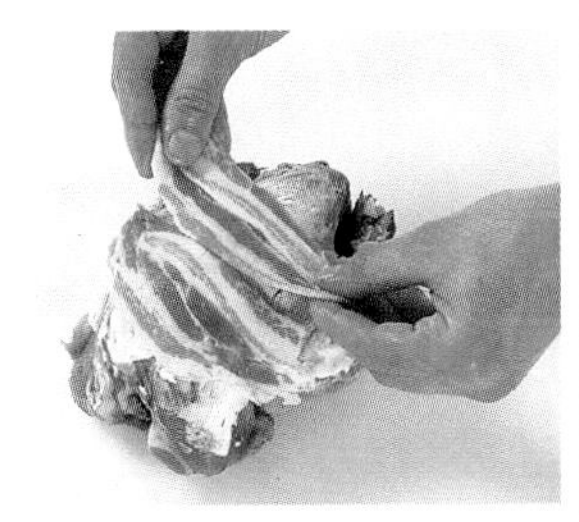

Lay the bacon rashers crosswise over the breast of each pheasant.

EXTRAS FOR GAME

These traditional accompaniments can be served with roast pheasant and many other game dishes, including grouse and partridge.

FRIED BREADCRUMBS

Melt *30 g (1 oz) butter* with *1 tbsp sunflower oil.* When the butter is foaming, add *90 g (3 oz) fresh white breadcrumbs* and cook, stirring, for 3–5 minutes until golden.

GAME CHIPS

Using a mandoline or the finest blade on a food processor, slice *500 g (1 lb) old potatoes* finely, then dry them. Heat some *sunflower oil* in a deep-fat fryer, add the potato slices, and deep-fry for 3 minutes or until crisp and golden. Drain, then sprinkle with *salt.*

FORCEMEAT BALLS

Combine *125 g (4 oz) fresh white breadcrumbs, 60 g (2 oz) grated cold butter, 1 beaten egg, 2 tbsp chopped parsley, grated zest of 1 lemon,* and *salt and pepper to taste.* Stir to mix, then roll into 12 small balls. *Melt 30 g (1 oz) butter* with *1 tbsp olive oil* in a frying pan. When the butter is foaming, add the forcemeat balls, and cook for 5 minutes or until golden all over. Drain thoroughly.

PHEASANT STEW

Serves 6–8

- *2 tbsp sunflower oil*
- *2 pheasants, cut into serving pieces (page 148)*
- *375 g (12 oz) shallots, chopped*
- *125 g (4 oz) piece of smoked streaky bacon, cut into strips*
- *3 garlic cloves, crushed*
- *1 tbsp plain flour*
- *600 ml (1 pint) game stock (page 148)*
- *300 ml (1/2 pint) red wine*
- *1 head of celery, separated into stalks, sliced*
- *250 g (8 oz) button mushrooms*
- *1 tbsp tomato purée*
- *salt and black pepper*
- *chopped parsley to garnish*

1 Heat the oil in a large flameproof casserole. Add the pheasant pieces and cook over a high heat until browned. Lift out and drain.

2 Add the shallots and bacon and cook for 5 minutes. Add the garlic and flour and cook, stirring, for 1 minute. Add the stock and wine and bring to a boil. Add the celery, mushrooms, tomato purée, and season. Simmer for 5 minutes.

3 Add the pheasant, bring back to a boil, cover, and cook in a preheated oven at 160°C (325°F, Gas 3) for 2 hours. Garnish with parsley.

NORMANDY PHEASANT

Apples and cream are traditional ingredients in the cuisine of Normandy. Here, apples and a rich sauce perfectly complement the pheasant, which is cooked slowly and gently in wine and stock to keep it moist and tender.

Serves 6–8

- *30 g (1 oz) butter*
- *1 tbsp sunflower oil*
- *2 pheasants, cut into serving pieces (page 148)*
- *2 cooking apples, quartered, cored, and sliced*
- *4 celery stalks, sliced*
- *1 onion, sliced*
- *1 tbsp plain flour*
- *300 ml (1/2 pint) chicken or game stock (page 148)*
- *150 ml (1/4 pint) dry white wine*
- *salt and black pepper*
- *150 ml (1/4 pint) double cream*
- *apple rings to serve (see box, right)*
- *chopped parsley to garnish*

1 Melt the butter with the oil in a flameproof casserole. When the butter is foaming, add the pheasant pieces and cook for about 5 minutes until browned. Lift out and drain.

2 Lower the heat, add the apples, celery, and onion, and cook for 5–6 minutes until soft.

3 Add the flour and cook, stirring, for 1 minute. Pour in the stock and wine, add salt and pepper to taste, and bring to a boil, stirring until lightly thickened.

4 Return the pheasant to the casserole and spoon the sauce over the top. Bring back to a boil, cover with greaseproof paper and the casserole lid, and cook in a preheated oven at 180°C (350°F, Gas 4) for 1–1 1/2 hours until tender. Remove the pheasant from the casserole with a slotted spoon and keep warm.

5 Strain the sauce into a saucepan. Whisk in the cream, taste for seasoning, then reheat gently. Arrange the pheasant on serving plates with the apple rings. Spoon the sauce over the pheasant and serve at once, garnished with parsley.

Apple rings

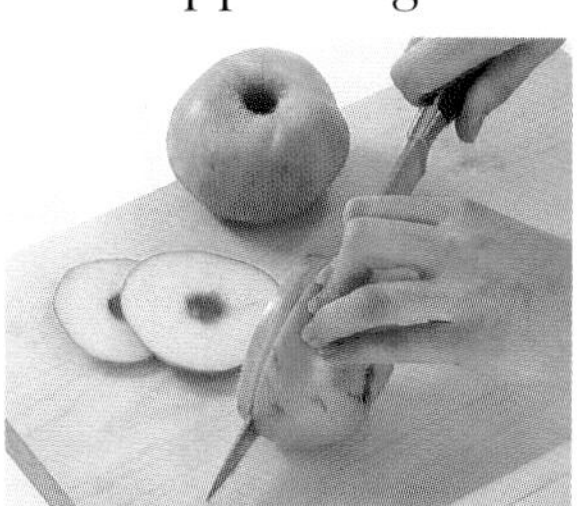

Core *2 cooking apples,* leaving them whole, and slice crosswise into 5 mm (1/4 in) rings.

Melt *30 g (1 oz) butter* in a frying pan, add the apple rings, and sprinkle with *a little caster sugar.* Cook over a high heat, turning once, for 3 minutes or until the sugar has caramelized and the apples are golden brown. Lift out and keep warm.

PIGEON PIE WITH FENNEL & CARROTS

Serves 6

2 tbsp sunflower oil
4 pigeons, breasts removed and cut into strips, and carcasses used for stock
2 large carrots, sliced
1 fennel bulb, sliced
1 large onion, chopped
2 tsp plain flour
300 ml (1/2 pint) game stock (page 148)
150 ml (1/4 pint) red wine
1 tbsp redcurrant jelly
salt and black pepper
plain flour for dusting
250 g (8 oz) ready-made puff pastry
beaten egg for glazing
chopped parsley to garnish
⋆ 2 litre (3 1/2 pint) pie dish

1 Heat the oil in a large flameproof casserole. Add the pigeon in batches and cook over a high heat until browned all over. Lift out and drain on paper towels.

2 Lower the heat, add the carrots, fennel, and onion, and cook, stirring occasionally, for 5 minutes or until softened. Add the flour and cook, stirring, for about 1 minute.

3 Gradually pour in the stock and bring to a boil, stirring all the time until lightly thickened. Add the pigeon, wine, redcurrant jelly, and salt and pepper to taste. Cover tightly and simmer very gently for 1 hour. Leave to cool.

4 Lightly flour a work surface. Roll out the puff pastry until 2.5 cm (1 in) larger than the pie dish. Invert the pie dish on to the dough and cut around the edge. Cut a long strip of pastry from the trimmings and press on to the rim of the pie dish. Reserve the remaining trimmings. Spoon in the pigeon and vegetable mixture. Brush the pastry strip with water, top with the pastry lid, and crimp the edge with a fork.

5 Make a hole in the top of the pie to let the steam escape. Roll out the reserved pastry and cut decorative shapes with a pastry cutter. Brush the bottoms of the shapes with beaten egg, and arrange on the pie. Glaze the top with beaten egg.

6 Bake the pie in a preheated oven at 200°C (400°F, Gas 6) for 25–30 minutes until the pastry is well risen and golden. Garnish with parsley.

CASSEROLE OF HARE

Serves 6

1 hare, cut into serving pieces
30 g (1 oz) butter
2 tbsp olive oil
125 g (4 oz) piece of streaky bacon, cut into strips
16 small shallots
250 g (8 oz) chestnut mushrooms, halved
30 g (1 oz) plain flour
900 ml (1 1/2 pints) game stock (page 148)
2 large thyme sprigs
2 large parsley sprigs
salt and black pepper
forcemeat balls (page 191)
fresh thyme to garnish

MARINADE
300 ml (1/2 pint) ruby port
4 tbsp olive oil
1 large onion, sliced
2 bay leaves

1 Make the marinade: in a large bowl, combine the port, oil, onion, and bay leaves. Add the hare pieces, turn in the marinade, cover, and leave to marinate in the refrigerator for 8 hours.

2 Remove the hare from the marinade, reserving the marinade. Melt the butter with the oil in a large flameproof casserole. When the butter is foaming, add the hare pieces and cook over a high heat until browned all over. Lift out and drain on paper towels.

3 Lower the heat, add the bacon and shallots, and cook for 5 minutes or until lightly browned. Add the mushrooms and cook for 2–3 minutes. Remove and drain on paper towels. Add the flour and cook, stirring, for 1 minute. Gradually add the stock and bring to a boil, stirring until thickened.

4 Return the hare, bacon, shallots, and mushrooms to the casserole with the strained marinade. Add the thyme, parsley, and salt and pepper to taste, and bring to a boil. Cover and cook in a preheated oven at 160°C (325°F, Gas 3) for 2 hours.

5 Taste for seasoning. Place the forcemeat balls on top, garnish with fresh thyme, and serve at once.

RABBIT WITH MUSTARD & MARJORAM

Serves 4

4 tbsp Dijon mustard
1 tsp chopped fresh marjoram
1 rabbit, cut into serving pieces
30 g (1 oz) butter
2 tbsp olive oil
1 large onion, chopped
2 garlic cloves, crushed
90 g (3 oz) piece of smoked streaky bacon, cut into pieces
1 tsp plain flour
450 ml (3/4 pint) chicken stock
salt and black pepper
150 ml (1/4 pint) single cream
2 tbsp chopped parsley to garnish

1 Mix the mustard and marjoram and spread over the rabbit pieces. Place in a shallow dish, cover, and leave to marinate in the refrigerator for 8 hours.

2 Melt the butter with the oil in a large flameproof casserole. When the butter is foaming, add the rabbit pieces and cook for about 5 minutes until browned all over. Lift out and drain on paper towels.

3 Add the onion, garlic, and bacon to the casserole and cook for 3–5 minutes until the onion is soft and the bacon golden. Add the flour and cook, stirring, for 1 minute. Gradually blend in the stock and bring to a boil, stirring until thickened.

4 Return the rabbit to the casserole, add salt and pepper to taste, and bring back to a boil. Cover and cook in a preheated oven at 160°C (325°F, Gas 3) for 1 1/2 hours or until the rabbit is tender.

5 Transfer the rabbit to a warmed platter and keep warm. Boil the sauce for 2 minutes or until reduced to a coating consistency. Stir in the cream. Taste for seasoning, reheat gently, and spoon the sauce over the rabbit. Serve at once, garnished with parsley.

BRAISED RABBIT WITH MUSHROOMS & CIDER

Serves 4

30 g (1 oz) butter
1 tbsp sunflower oil
1 rabbit, cut into serving pieces
8 small shallots
375 g (12 oz) mushrooms, quartered
300 ml (1/2 pint) dry cider
a few parsley sprigs
3–4 tarragon sprigs
salt and black pepper
300 ml (1/2 pint) single cream
2 tbsp chopped parsley to garnish

1 Melt the butter with the oil in a flameproof casserole. When the butter is foaming, add the rabbit pieces and cook for about 5 minutes until browned all over. Lift out the rabbit with a slotted spoon and drain on paper towels.

2 Add the shallots to the casserole and cook over a high heat, stirring, for about 3 minutes until golden. Add the mushrooms, and cook, stirring occasionally, for 3–4 minutes until softened.

3 Return the rabbit joints to the casserole, add the cider, parsley sprigs, tarragon, and salt and pepper to taste, and bring to a boil. Cover and cook in a preheated oven at 160°C (325°F, Gas 3) for 1 1/2 hours or until the rabbit is tender.

4 Transfer the rabbit to a warmed platter and keep warm. Remove and discard the parsley and tarragon. Bring the sauce in the casserole to a boil, then boil until slightly reduced. Stir in the cream. Taste for seasoning and reheat gently.

5 Pour the sauce over the rabbit, and serve at once, garnished with parsley.

BRAISED RABBIT WITH PRUNES

Substitute 125 g (4 oz) ready-to-eat prunes for the mushrooms. Add to the casserole 30 minutes before the end of cooking time.

POT ROAST VENISON

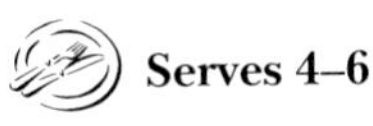 **Serves 4–6**

1.25–1.5 kg ($2^1/_2$–3 lb) shoulder of venison, rolled and tied
30 g (1 oz) butter
2 tbsp sunflower oil
1 large onion, chopped
2 large carrots, sliced
2 celery stalks, sliced
300 ml ($^1/_2$ pint) beef stock
salt and black pepper
1 tbsp redcurrant jelly

MARINADE

300 ml ($^1/_2$ pint) red wine
2 tbsp olive oil
pared zest of 1 orange
pared zest of 1 lemon
2 tsp crushed juniper berries
6 black peppercorns
1 garlic clove, crushed
1 large thyme sprig
1 large parsley sprig

1 Make the marinade: in a large bowl, combine the wine, oil, orange and lemon zests, juniper berries, black peppercorns, garlic, thyme, and parsley. Turn the venison in the marinade, cover, and leave to marinate in the refrigerator, turning occasionally, for 2–3 days.

2 Lift the venison out of the marinade, straining and reserving the marinade, and pat dry. Melt the butter with the oil in a large flameproof casserole. When the butter is foaming, add the venison and cook over a high heat for 5 minutes or until well browned all over. Remove the venison from the casserole.

3 Lower the heat and add the onion, carrots, and celery to the casserole. Cover and cook very gently for 10 minutes. Place the venison on top of the vegetables, add the stock, the strained marinade, and salt and pepper to taste, and bring to a boil. Cover with a layer of greaseproof paper and the casserole lid and cook in a preheated oven at 160°C (325°F, Gas 3) for $2^1/_2$–3 hours until tender.

4 Lift out the venison and keep warm. Strain the liquid in the casserole, spoon off the fat, then return to the casserole. Add the redcurrant jelly, and boil for a few minutes until syrupy. Slice the venison, and arrange on a warmed platter. Pour over the sauce, and serve at once.

HEARTY VENISON CASSEROLE

Serves 4

1 kg (2 lb) stewing venison, cut into 2.5 cm (1 in) cubes
2 tbsp olive oil
6 celery stalks, thickly sliced on the diagonal
150 g (5 oz) chestnut mushrooms, quartered
30 g (1 oz) plain flour
salt and black pepper
125 g (4 oz) small carrots
chopped parsley to garnish

MARINADE

450 ml ($^3/_4$ pint) red wine
3 tbsp sunflower oil
1 onion, sliced
1 tsp ground allspice
a few parsley sprigs
1 bay leaf

1 Make the marinade: in a large bowl, combine the red wine, oil, onion, allspice, parsley sprigs, and bay leaf. Toss the venison cubes in the marinade to coat them thoroughly, cover, and leave to marinate in the refrigerator, turning occasionally, for 2 days.

2 Lift the venison and onion out of the marinade and pat dry. Strain and reserve the marinade.

3 Heat the oil in a large flameproof casserole, add the venison and onion, and cook for 3–5 minutes until well browned. Lift out and drain on paper towels.

4 Lower the heat, add the celery and mushrooms, and cook for 2–3 minutes until softened. Remove with a slotted spoon. Add the flour and cook, stirring, for 1 minute. Gradually blend in the marinade and bring to a boil, stirring until thickened.

5 Return the venison, onion, celery, and mushrooms to the casserole, and season to taste. Bring to a boil, cover, and cook in a preheated oven at 160°C (325°F, Gas 3) for $1^1/_2$ hours.

6 Add the carrots, and return to the oven for 30 minutes or until the venison is tender. Serve at once, garnished with parsley.

TRADITIONAL GAME PIE

This raised game pie follows a classic recipe which takes about 6 hours to make, over 3 days, but it's well worth the effort. Boned mixed game meats – usually pheasant, hare, and venison – are available in the best supermarkets. There is chicken in the pie too, which goes very well with game, but you could use turkey.

Serves 18

2 kg (4 lb) chicken, boned and skinned (page 149)

1 kg (2 lb) boneless mixed game meats, cut into 1 cm (½ in) pieces

375 g (12 oz) belly pork, coarsely chopped

500 g (1 lb) piece of streaky bacon, cut into small pieces

butter for greasing

hot-water crust pastry (see box, right)

about 2 tsp salt

black pepper

1 egg, beaten

450 ml (¾ pint) jellied stock (page 148)

MARINADE

150 ml (¼ pint) port

1 small onion, finely chopped

3 garlic cloves, crushed

leaves of 4 thyme sprigs, chopped

1 tsp grated nutmeg

⋆ *29 cm (11½ in) springform or loose-bottomed cake tin*

1 Make the marinade: in a bowl, combine the port, onion, garlic, thyme, and grated nutmeg.

2 Cut the chicken breast into long strips, about 1 cm (½ in) wide, and set aside. Cut the rest of the chicken into 1 cm (½ in) chunks. Add the chunks to the marinade with the game meats, belly pork, and bacon. Cover and leave to marinate in the refrigerator for 8 hours.

3 Lightly butter the tin. Take two-thirds of the hot-water crust pastry, pat it out over the bottom of the tin, and push it up the side, until it stands 1 cm (½ in) above the rim.

4 Season the meat mixture with plenty of salt and pepper and spoon half into the pastry shell. Smooth the surface evenly.

5 Arrange the reserved chicken breast strips on top of the meat, radiating from the middle. Season with salt and pepper.

6 Top with the remaining meat mixture. Brush the top edge of the pastry with beaten egg. Roll out the remaining pastry, and cover the pie, reserving the trimmings. Pinch around the edge to seal, then crimp.

7 Decorate the pie with the pastry trimmings, attaching them with beaten egg. Make 3 steam holes in the pastry lid, and glaze the pie with beaten egg.

8 Bake in a preheated oven at 220°C (425°F, Gas 7) for 1 hour. If the pastry browns too quickly, cover with foil. Reduce the heat to 160°C (325°F, Gas 3) and cook for 2–2¼ hours.

9 Test the pie by piercing the centre with a skewer: the juices will run clear and the meat will feel tender when it is done. Leave the pie to cool in the tin for 8 hours.

10 Put the jellied stock into a saucepan and heat until melted. Using a funnel, slowly pour the stock through the steam holes in the pie. Cover and chill for 6 hours or until the stock has set. Unmould the pie and cut into wedges to serve.

Making the pastry

Sift *750 g (1½ lb) plain flour* and *1 tsp salt* into a large bowl. Put *400 ml (14 fl oz) water* and *300 g (10 oz) white vegetable fat* into a saucepan and heat until the water is boiling and the fat has melted.

Pour on to the flour and mix quickly with a wooden spoon until the mixture holds together.

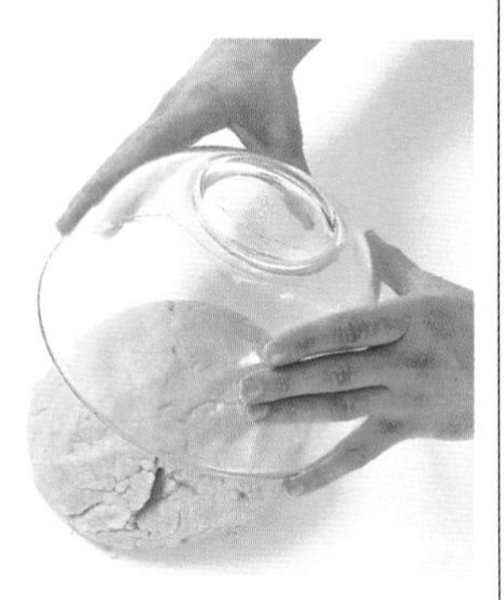

Turn the dough on to a floured surface, invert the bowl over the top to keep the dough moist, and leave to cool until lukewarm.

MEAT DISHES

UNDER 30 MINUTES

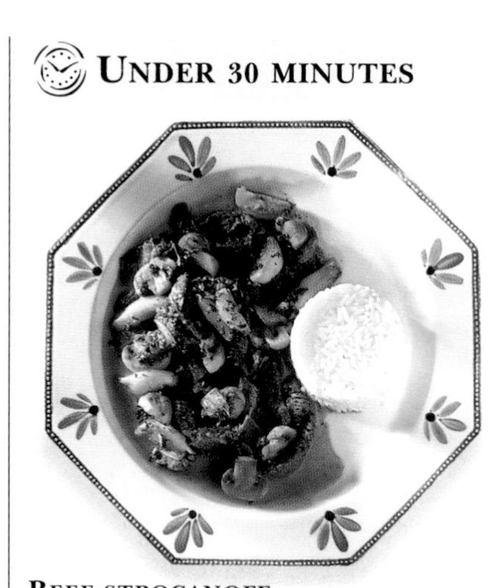

BEEF STROGANOFF

Classic Russian dish: strips of rump steak cooked with shallots and button mushrooms, and mixed with soured cream.

SERVES 4 493 calories per serving
Takes 20 minutes **PAGE 223**

LAMB CHOPS WITH MINTED HOLLANDAISE SAUCE

Grilled chops served with hollandaise sauce, flavoured with lemon juice and fresh mint.

SERVES 4 611 calories per serving
Takes 20 minutes **PAGE 252**

STEAK DIANE

Flambéed rump steaks served with a light sauce combining onion, beef stock, lemon juice, Worcestershire sauce, and parsley.

SERVES 4 373 calories per serving
Takes 25 minutes **PAGE 222**

STEAKS WITH SMOKED OYSTER RELISH

Steaks rubbed with garlic, and sprinkled with smoked oyster relish flavoured with parsley.

SERVES 4 278 calories per serving
Takes 15–20 minutes **PAGE 221**

HERBED BUTTERFLY CHOPS

Lamb chops brushed with olive oil, sprinkled with pepper, and flavoured with rosemary, mint, and thyme sprigs, then grilled.

SERVES 4 320 calories per serving
Takes 15 minutes **PAGE 252**

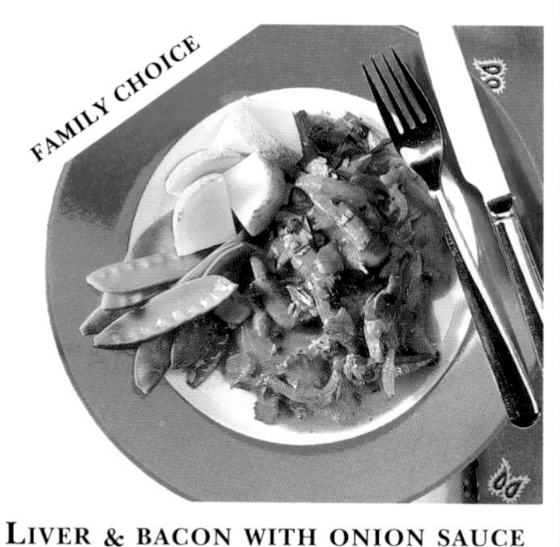

LIVER & BACON WITH ONION SAUCE

Strips of liver cooked with onion and bacon. Simmered with beef stock, tomato ketchup, tarragon, and Worcestershire sauce.

SERVES 4 441 calories per serving
Takes 15 minutes **PAGE 243**

TOURNEDOS ROQUEFORT

Crunchy and nutritious: grilled tournedos steaks topped with a mixture of melted Roquefort cheese, butter, and chopped walnuts.

SERVES 4 430 calories per serving
Takes 20 minutes **PAGE 222**

PEPPER STEAKS

Piquant and creamy: fillet steak encrusted with black peppercorns. Served in a pool of cream and brandy sauce.

SERVES 4 489 calories per serving
Takes 25 minutes **PAGE 220**

CALF'S LIVER WITH SAGE

Slices of calf's liver, coated with seasoned flour, and cooked quickly. Served with pan juices flavoured with sage and lemon juice.

SERVES 4 364 calories per serving
Takes 10 minutes **PAGE 244**

UNDER 30 MINUTES

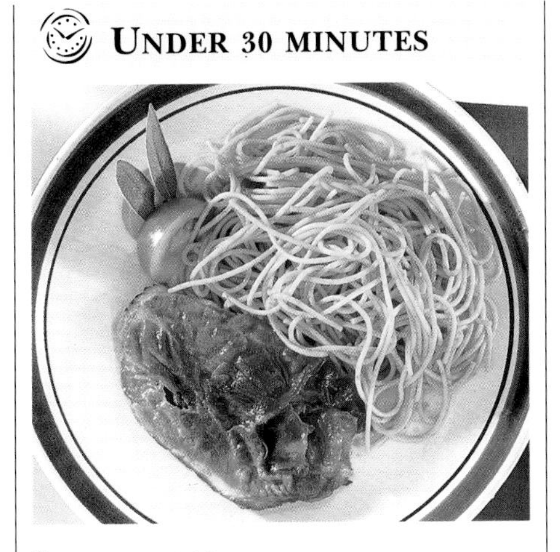

SALTIMBOCCA

Veal escalopes topped with sage leaves and Parma ham, and cooked with garlic. Served with a wine and cream sauce.

SERVES 4 342 calories per serving

Takes 25 minutes **PAGE 241**

BEEF TACOS

Minced beef and tomatoes richly seasoned with garlic, chilli, and coriander. Served in taco shells with lettuce and soured cream.

SERVES 4 407 calories per serving

Takes 25 minutes **PAGE 237**

CHATEAUBRIAND WITH BEARNAISE SAUCE

Grilled steak basted with butter, served with a béarnaise sauce flavoured with tarragon.

SERVES 2 761 calories per serving

Takes 25 minutes **PAGE 220**

30–60 MINUTES

VEAL MARSALA

Veal escalopes lightly coated in seasoned flour and cooked until golden. Served in a Marsala sauce, and garnished with parsley.

SERVES 4 239 calories per serving

Takes 30 minutes **PAGE 242**

CORNED BEEF HASH

Quick and nourishing: chunks of corned beef cooked with onion, pieces of potato, and stock, and grilled until crispy and brown.

SERVES 2–3 887–591 calories per serving

Takes 30 minutes **PAGE 232**

BEEF & BEAN BURRITOS

Popular and piquant: strips of rump steak cooked with garlic, chilli, tomatoes, and pinto beans. Wrapped in tortillas.

SERVES 4 471 calories per serving

Takes 35 minutes **PAGE 223**

GRILLED PORK CHOPS WITH MANGO SAUCE

Sweet and tender: chops served with a sauce combining fresh mango and mango chutney.

SERVES 4 347 calories per serving

Takes 35 minutes **PAGE 262**

PORK CHOPS WITH ORANGES

Fresh and tangy: pork chops spread with wholegrain mustard, topped with orange slices and sugar, and baked.

SERVES 6 361 calories per serving

Takes 55 minutes **PAGE 263**

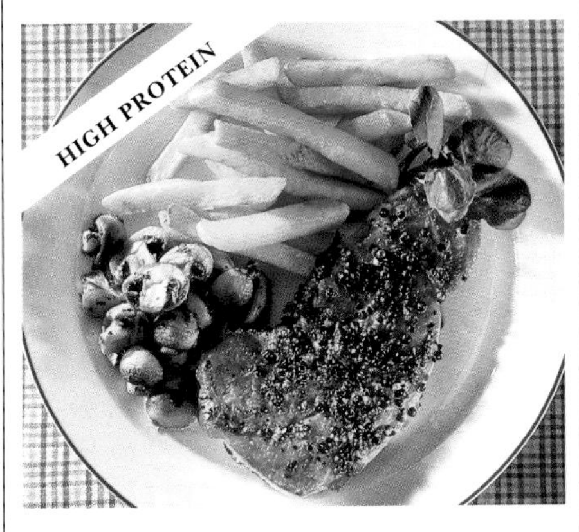

PORK STEAKS WITH MIXED PEPPERCORNS

Lean pork steaks encrusted with mixed peppercorns, served with a sauce of white wine, beef stock, and double cream.

SERVES 4 567 calories per serving

Takes 30 minutes, plus standing **PAGE 264**

30–60 MINUTES

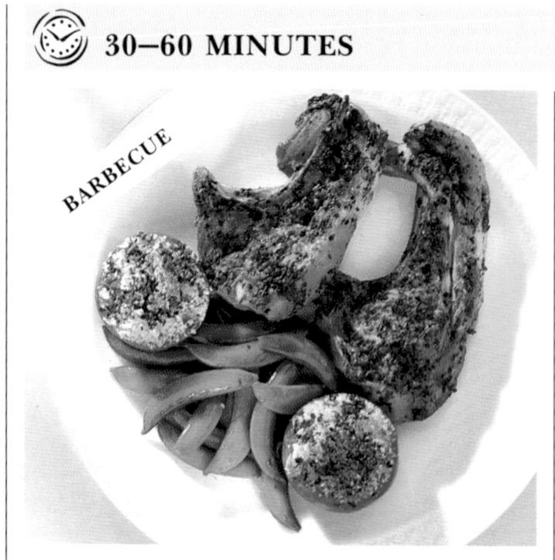

LAMB WITH MINT GLAZE

Best end lamb chops glazed with white wine, vinegar, mint sprigs, honey, and Dijon mustard, then barbecued or grilled.

SERVES 4 304 calories per serving

Takes 15 minutes, plus marinating **PAGE 251**

MADEIRA PORK WITH PAPRIKA

Rich and creamy: pork fillet simmered with Madeira, stock, onion, mushrooms, red pepper, and paprika, then mixed with cream.

SERVES 4 560 calories per serving

Takes 50 minutes **PAGE 261**

VEAL CHOPS WITH MUSHROOMS & CREAM

Veal chops cooked with mushrooms, cream, shallots, garlic, wine, and tarragon.

SERVES 4 604 calories per serving

Takes 30 minutes, plus soaking **PAGE 240**

MEATBALLS IN CIDER

Balls of minced beef and pork in a sauce of cider and tomato purée, with onion, garlic, celery, red pepper, and mushrooms.

SERVES 4 416 calories per serving

Takes 40 minutes **PAGE 233**

KIDNEYS TURBIGO

Lamb's kidneys cooked with chipolata sausages, then simmered with stock, sherry, onions, mushrooms, and bay leaf.

SERVES 4 455 calories per serving

Takes 50 minutes **PAGE 258**

VEAL SCHNITZELS

A classic Viennese dish: veal escalopes coated in beaten egg and fresh white breadcrumbs, chilled, then cooked until light golden brown. Traditionally served with piquant anchovy fillets, chopped capers, lemon wedges, and a few parsley sprigs.

SERVES 4 373 calories per serving

Takes 20 minutes, plus chilling **PAGE 241**

Over 60 minutes

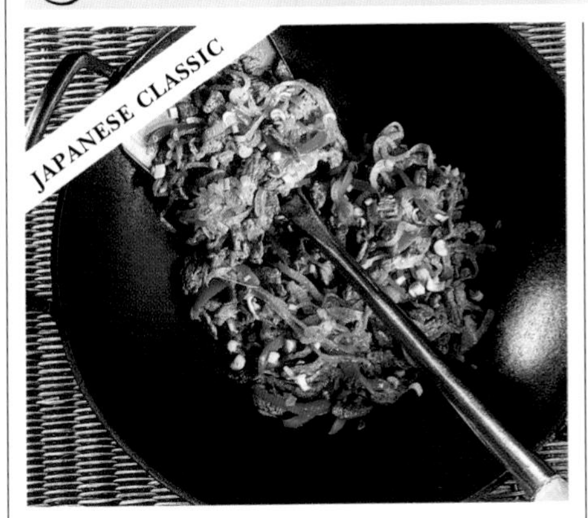

Teriyaki beef

Strips of tender rump steak marinated in soy sauce, Japanese rice wine, and sugar. Stir-fried with onion and red pepper.

SERVES 4 329 calories per serving

Takes 15 minutes, plus marinating **PAGE 226**

Lamb noisettes with orange & honey

Noisettes marinated in honey, orange, olive oil, garlic, and herbs, and grilled. Served with a sauce made from the marinade.

SERVES 4 457 calories per serving

Takes 20 minutes, plus marinating **PAGE 253**

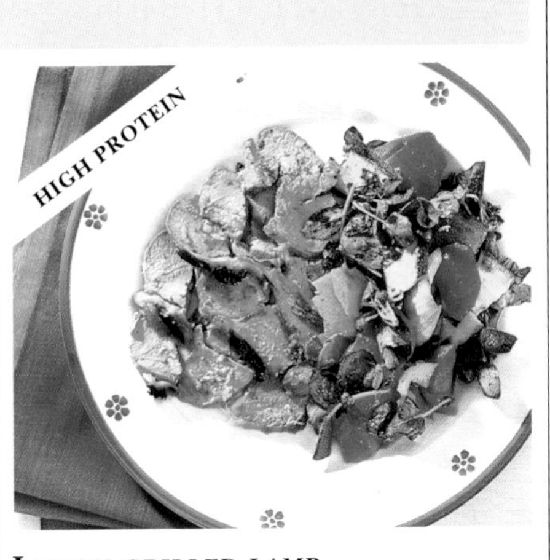

Lemon grilled lamb

Butterflied leg of lamb marinated in a tangy mixture of lemon juice, honey, garlic, and mustard, and grilled.

SERVES 6–8 425–318 calories per serving

Takes 45 minutes, plus marinating **PAGE 247**

Bacon-wrapped pork in vermouth sauce

Pork fillets wrapped in bacon and served with a vermouth and mushroom sauce.

SERVES 6 547 calories per serving

Takes 1¼ hours **PAGE 261**

Fajitas

Chuck steak marinated in orange and lime juices, tequila, garlic, coriander, and chilli, and grilled. Served with relish and tortillas.

SERVES 4 543 calories per serving

Takes 40 minutes, plus marinating **PAGE 226**

Meat loaf

Minced beef mixed with tomatoes, stuffing, onion, carrot, parsley, and garlic, wrapped in bacon and baked.

SERVES 4–6 717–478 calories per serving

Takes 1½ hours **PAGE 236**

Pork with chilli & coconut

Strips of pork in a dry marinade of ginger, chilli, and curry powder. Cooked with coconut, spring onions, and red pepper.

SERVES 4 498 calories per serving

Takes 40 minutes, plus marinating **PAGE 262**

Creamed sweetbreads

Calf's sweetbreads simmered with onion, parsley, and bay leaf. Served with a lemon-flavoured sauce.

SERVES 4 345 calories per serving

Takes 40 minutes, plus soaking **PAGE 244**

Spinach-stuffed pork chops

Loin chops stuffed with spinach, bacon, Parmesan cheese, and herbs, cooked in wine, and topped with Gruyère cheese.

SERVES 4 737 calories per serving

Takes 1¼ hours **PAGE 263**

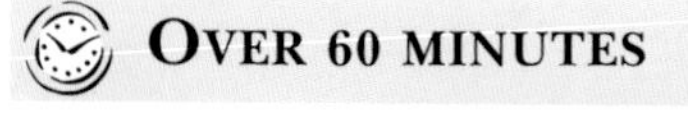

OVER 60 MINUTES

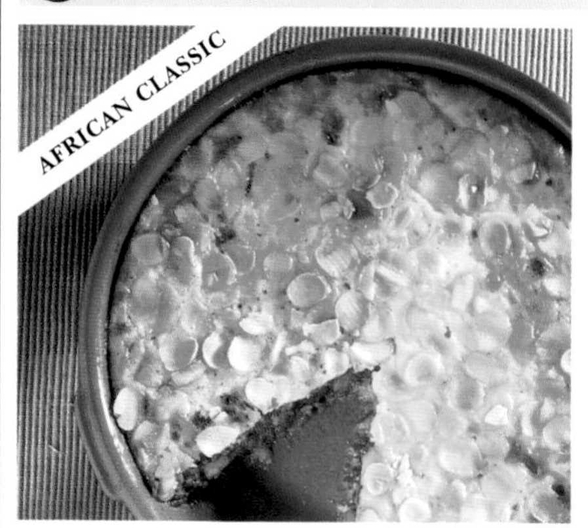

BOBOTIE

Minced beef baked with garlic, apricots, almonds, chutney, lemon, and milk-soaked bread. Topped with eggs and almonds.

SERVES 6–8 656–492 calories per serving
Takes 1 hour 5 minutes **PAGE 237**

DANISH MEATBALLS

Minced pork seasoned with onion, thyme, and paprika and shaped into ovals. Cooked in a tomato sauce, and topped with Greek yogurt.

SERVES 4 586 calories per serving
Takes 1½ hours **PAGE 266**

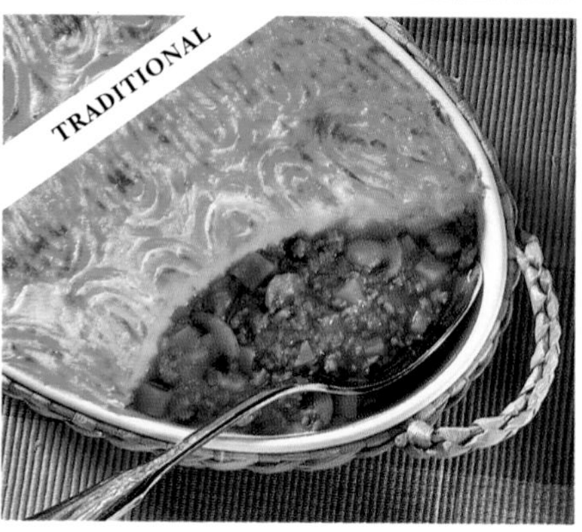

SHEPHERD'S PIE

Minced lamb baked with mushrooms, carrot, onion, garlic, stock, and mushroom ketchup. Topped with mashed potato.

SERVES 4 574 calories per serving
Takes 1½ hours **PAGE 257**

SPICED LAMB WITH COCONUT

Cubes of lamb, dry marinated in ginger and spices, are cooked with tomato, lime, mango chutney, and coconut, then mixed with yogurt.

SERVES 4–6 745–496 calories per serving
Takes 1¼ hours **PAGE 256**

PASTICCIO

Minced pork simmered with red wine, tomatoes, garlic, herbs, and cinnamon. Baked with macaroni and cheese custard.

SERVES 4–6 1019–679 calories per serving
Takes 1¼ hours **PAGE 266**

BEEF WITH ROAST VEGETABLE SALAD

Roast beef served with a salad of roasted aubergine, courgettes, fennel, and peppers.

SERVES 4–6 522–348 calories per serving
Takes 1¾ hours, plus cooling **PAGE 218**

MERGUEZ WITH POTATOES & PEPPERS

Bite-sized pieces of spicy merguez sausage in a casserole with potatoes, red and green peppers, and garlic.

SERVES 4 381 calories per serving
Takes 1¼ hours, plus cooling **PAGE 258**

MARINATED LOIN OF PORK WITH PINEAPPLE

Pork marinated in pineapple juice, maple syrup, soy sauce, and herbs, then roasted.

SERVES 6–8 426–320 calories per serving
Takes 2½ hours, plus marinating **PAGE 260**

BEEF FLORENTINE

Layer of minced beef, tomato, and garlic, topped with spinach and three types of cheese. Covered with filo pastry.

SERVES 8 576 calories per serving
Takes 1½ hours **PAGE 233**

OVER 60 MINUTES

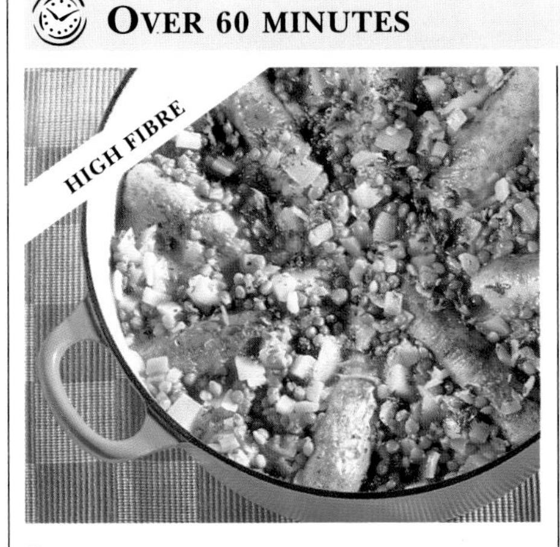

SAUSAGE & LENTIL CASSEROLE

Herby pork sausages baked with lentils, stock, and vegetables. Flavoured with bay leaves, parsley, and sage.

SERVES 4 783 calories per serving

Takes 1$\frac{3}{4}$ hours **PAGE 270**

RACK OF LAMB WITH A WALNUT & HERB CRUST

Rack of lamb coated with a walnut and parsley crust, and roasted.

SERVES 6 626–417 calories per serving

Takes 1$\frac{3}{4}$ hours, plus chilling **PAGE 251**

BLANQUETTE OF LAMB

Chunks of lamb simmered with onion, carrot, bay leaves, lemon juice, and mushrooms. Served with a cream and egg sauce.

SERVES 4–6 658–439 calories per serving

Takes 2 hours **PAGE 255**

MOUSSAKA

Minced lamb flavoured with garlic, onion, passata, and red wine, layered with aubergines, and topped with cheese sauce.

SERVES 6–8 653–490 calories per serving

Takes 1$\frac{3}{4}$ hours, plus standing **PAGE 257**

TOAD IN THE HOLE WITH ONION SAUCE

Pork sausagemeat combined with leek, sage, and parsley, and baked in a batter.

SERVES 4 802 calories per serving

Takes 45 minutes, plus standing **PAGE 270**

COTTAGE PIES WITH CHEESY POTATO TOPPING

Minced beef cooked with vegetables and stock. Topped with mashed potato and cheese.

SERVES 4 850 calories per serving

Takes 1$\frac{1}{2}$ hours **PAGE 236**

LEMON ROAST VEAL WITH SPINACH STUFFING

Veal marinated in lemon and thyme, with a stuffing of spinach, shallot, and bacon.

SERVES 4–6 666–444 calories per serving

Takes 1$\frac{3}{4}$ hours, plus marinating **PAGE 239**

ROAST LEG OF LAMB WITH RED WINE GRAVY

Lamb flavoured with herbs, roasted and served with red wine gravy and mint sauce.

SERVES 4–6 517–344 calories per serving

Takes 2 hours **PAGE 245**

LAMB TAGINE

Cubes of lamb cooked with apricots, fennel, green peppers, and stock. Flavoured with saffron, ginger, and orange.

SERVES 6–8 550–412 calories per serving

Takes 1$\frac{3}{4}$ hours **PAGE 256**

OVER 60 MINUTES

CHILLI CON CARNE

Tex-Mex speciality: cubes of chuck steak cooked with red kidney beans, chilli, onion, garlic, stock, tomato purée, and red pepper.

SERVES 4 543 calories per serving

Takes 3¼ hours, plus soaking **PAGE 231**

SPINACH-STUFFED LAMB

Succulent and nutritious: boned leg of lamb stuffed with spinach and garlic, and roasted with wine and anchovies.

SERVES 6–8 459–344 calories per serving

Takes 2½ hours, plus cooling **PAGE 246**

SHOULDER OF LAMB WITH GARLIC & HERBS

Lamb flavoured with garlic, rosemary, mint, and thyme. Served with haricot beans.

SERVES 6 464 calories per serving

Takes 1¾ hours **PAGE 250**

FARMER'S BACON BAKE

Joint of bacon simmered with vegetables, parsley, and peppercorns, cut into pieces, and baked with a cheese sauce.

SERVES 4 765 calories per serving

Takes 2¼ hours **PAGE 268**

AFELIA

Cubes of pork marinated in red wine, coriander seeds, and cinnamon, cooked with wine, and sprinkled with cumin seeds.

SERVES 4 582 calories per serving

Takes 2 hours, plus marinating **PAGE 265**

WINTER BEEF CASSEROLE

Cubes of chuck steak and strips of bacon cooked with stock, celery, and carrots, and flavoured with wine and passata.

SERVES 4–6 680–454 calories per serving

Takes 2¾ hours **PAGE 227**

SWEET & SOUR CHINESE SPARE RIBS

Spare ribs baked until tender, and coated in a sauce combining ginger, garlic, soy and hoisin sauces, tomato purée, and sherry.

SERVES 4 491 calories per serving

Takes 2 hours **PAGE 264**

CURRIED LAMB WITH ALMONDS

Rich and creamy: chunks of lamb marinated in yogurt and garam masala, and cooked with ginger, garlic, almonds, and spices.

SERVES 6–8 855–642 calories per serving

Takes 2½ hours, plus marinating **PAGE 254**

BEEF OLIVES WITH VEGETABLE JULIENNE

Slices of topside wrapped around stir-fried vegetables, and cooked with beef stock.

SERVES 4 386 calories per serving

Takes 2¼ hours **PAGE 231**

Over 60 minutes

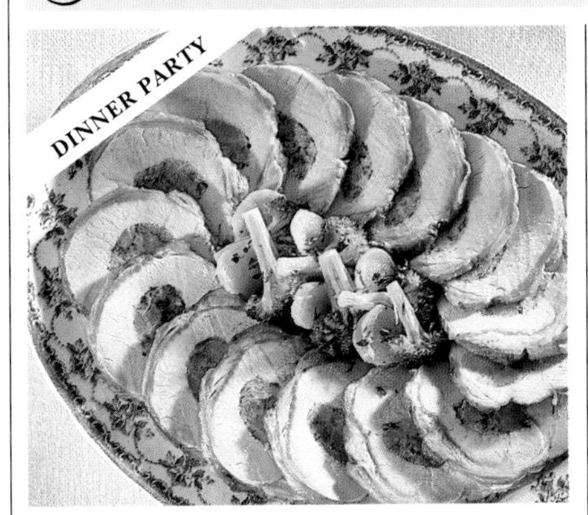

Boned loin of pork with apricot stuffing

Pork filled with an apricot and herb stuffing, then rolled and roasted.

SERVES 6–8 571–428 calories per serving

Takes 2 1/4 hours, plus cooling **PAGE 259**

Latimer beef with horseradish

Chuck steak cooked with stock, shallots, curry powder, sugar, ginger, and horseradish cream, and garnished with parsley.

SERVES 4–6 448–298 calories per serving

Takes 3 hours **PAGE 229**

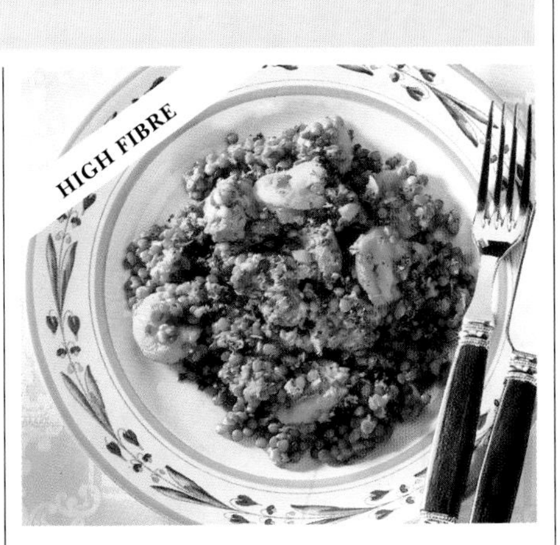

Aromatic lamb with lentils

Chunks of lamb marinated in orange juice, garlic, ginger, and coriander. Cooked with apricots, stock, onion, and lentils.

SERVES 6–8 633–475 calories per serving

Takes 2 1/2 hours, plus marinating **PAGE 255**

Salt beef with mustard sauce

Boned salt beef cooked with carrots, celery, potatoes, turnips, and leeks. Served with a mustard sauce flavoured with wine vinegar.

SERVES 4–6 863–575 calories per serving

Takes 2 1/4 hours, plus soaking **PAGE 217**

Hungarian goulash

Cubes of chuck steak cooked with stock, onion, tomatoes, red pepper, potatoes, paprika, and soured cream.

SERVES 4–6 711–474 calories per serving

Takes 2 1/2 hours **PAGE 228**

Chianti beef casserole

Cubes of chuck steak marinated in Chianti, garlic, and thyme, and cooked with sun-dried tomatoes, artichoke hearts, and olives.

SERVES 4–6 815–543 calories per serving

Takes 2 1/2 hours, plus marinating **PAGE 229**

Thai red beef curry

Cubes of chuck steak cooked with cardamom, cinnamon, bay leaves, cloves, ginger, garlic, paprika, tomatoes, yogurt, and red pepper.

SERVES 4–6 490–327 calories per serving

Takes 2 1/2 hours **PAGE 230**

Beef Wellington

Roasted fillet of beef coated with mushrooms, onion, and liver pâté, and encased in puff pastry. Served with a mushroom gravy.

SERVES 8 580 calories per serving

Takes 2 1/4 hours, plus cooling **PAGE 219**

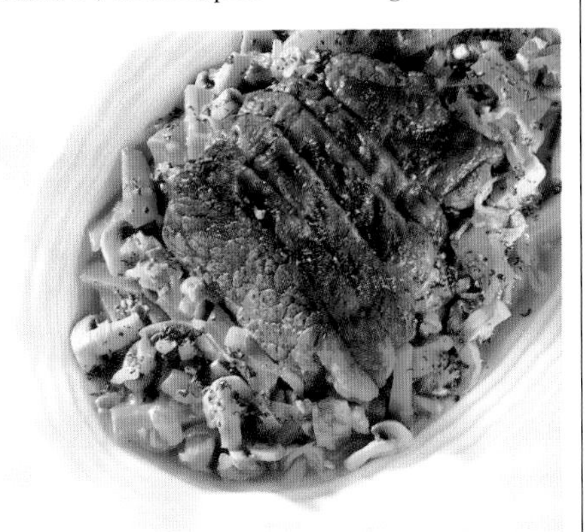

French-style braised beef

Beef marinated in wine, vinegar, garlic, orange, and herbs, and cooked with bacon, carrots, mushrooms, tomatoes, and olives.

SERVES 4–6 604–402 calories per serving

Takes 2 1/2 hours, plus marinating **PAGE 217**

OVER 60 MINUTES

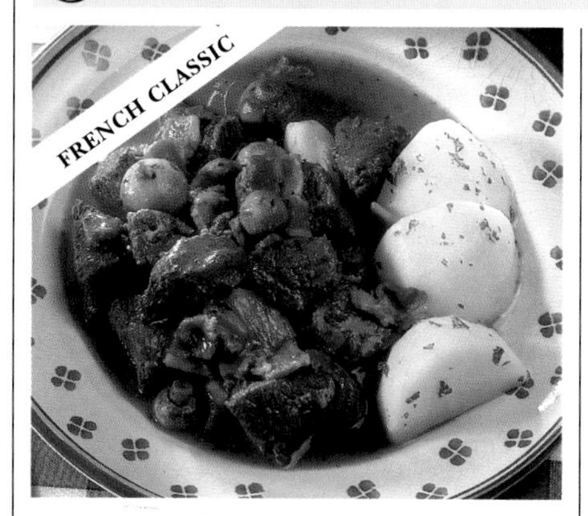

BOEUF BOURGUIGNON

Rich casserole: cubes of chuck steak cooked with shallots, bacon, red Burgundy, beef stock, mushrooms, and herbs.

SERVES 4–6 735–490 calories per serving
Takes 2 3/4 hours **PAGE 227**

OSSO BUCO

Slices of veal shin cooked with onion, tomato, carrots, celery, garlic, white wine, and stock. Sprinkled with gremolata.

SERVES 6 354 calories per serving
Takes 2 3/4 hours **PAGE 242**

COUNTRY BEEF CASSEROLE

Chunky and nourishing: cubes of chuck steak cooked in a casserole with stock and vegetables. Served with herb dumplings.

SERVES 6–8 540–405 calories per serving
Takes 3 hours **PAGE 230**

VEAL STEW WITH OLIVES & PEPPERS

Cubes of veal cooked in a casserole of peppers, wine, tomatoes, and olives, and flavoured with garlic and rosemary.

SERVES 6–8 473–355 calories per serving
Takes 2 hours **PAGE 243**

SHOULDER OF LAMB WITH LEMON & OLIVE STUFFING

Lamb rolled with an olive, lemon, and herb stuffing, and roasted in wine and stock.

SERVES 6–8 460–345 calories per serving
Takes 2 3/4 hours **PAGE 247**

ENGLISH ROAST BEEF

Traditional succulent family roast: rolled beef sirloin basted and cooked until deliciously tender. Served with a variety of vegetables, traditional Yorkshire puddings, a rich red wine gravy, and creamy horseradish sauce.

SERVES 8 394 calories per serving
Takes 3 1/4 hours **PAGE 215**

OVER 60 MINUTES

ROAST LEG OF PORK

Tender and nourishing: pork roasted with carrot and onion until crackling is crisp. Served with gravy and apple sauce.

SERVES 6 338 calories per serving

Takes 2¼ hours **PAGE 260**

IRISH STEW

Traditional Irish family meal: lamb chops cooked in layers of potato and onion, and flavoured with bay leaf, thyme, and parsley.

SERVES 4 539 calories per serving

Takes 3¼ hours **PAGE 254**

WILTSHIRE PORK CASSEROLE

Shoulder of pork cut into cubes, cooked in a casserole with stock, white wine vinegar, honey, soy sauce, mushrooms, and prunes.

SERVES 6–8 536–402 calories per serving

Takes 3¼ hours **PAGE 265**

LANCASHIRE HOT POT

Lamb chops and kidneys cooked with potatoes, carrots, and onions, and flavoured with thyme, parsley, and bay leaf.

SERVES 4 689 calories per serving

Takes 3 hours **PAGE 253**

TEXAS BARBECUE BEEF BRISKET

Spicy and rich: beef baked in a marinade of barbecue sauce, pale ale, lemon juice, onions, garlic, and Worcestershire sauce.

SERVES 6 693 calories per serving

Takes 3½ hours, plus marinating **PAGE 216**

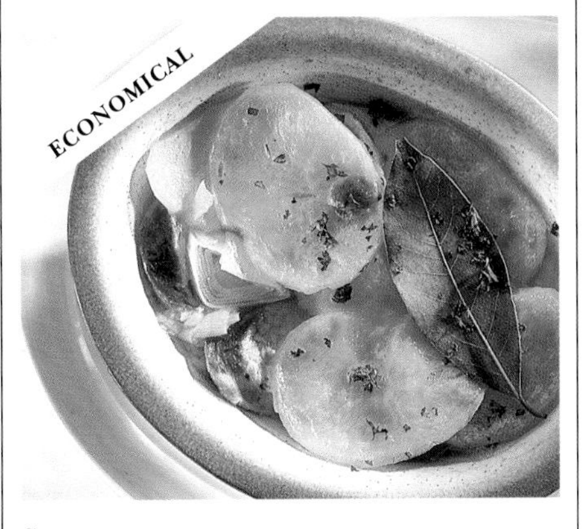

SAUSAGE BAKE

Slices of pork sausage with layers of vegetables, lentils, and potatoes, cooked in a casserole with stock, bay leaves, and cloves.

SERVES 6 712 calories per serving

Takes 3¼ hours **PAGE 269**

TRADITIONAL STEAK & KIDNEY PIE

Rich and satisfying: cubes of beef and kidney cooked with stock, Worcestershire sauce, and mushrooms. Topped with shortcrust pastry.

SERVES 4–6 865–577 calories per serving

Takes 3¼ hours, plus cooling **PAGE 232**

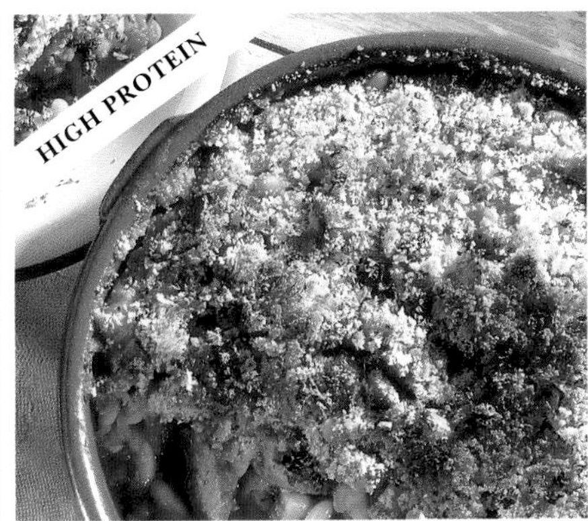

SAUSAGE CASSOULET

Garlic sausage, pork sausages, and bacon baked with beans, tomatoes, wine, onion, and herbs. Topped with breadcrumbs.

SERVES 8 619 calories per serving

Takes 3 hours, plus soaking **PAGE 269**

TRINIDAD PEPPERPOT BEEF

Boneless beef simmered with stock, vinegar, Worcestershire sauce, chillies, sugar, parsley, peppercorns, cinnamon, and thyme.

SERVES 4–6 697–465 calories per serving

Takes 3¾ hours **PAGE 218**

OVER 60 MINUTES

BEEF POT ROAST WITH WINTER VEGETABLES

Topside of beef in a casserole with onions, swede, celery, carrot, wine, and herbs.

SERVES 6 360 calories per serving

Takes 3 1/2 hours **PAGE 216**

GREEK ROAST LAMB

Traditional Greek dish: leg of lamb richly flavoured with garlic, rosemary, and lemon juice, and cooked until tender.

SERVES 6 328 calories per serving

Takes 4 1/4 hours **PAGE 246**

OXTAIL STEW

Tender thick stew: slices of oxtail simmered slowly with beef stock, onions, tomato purée, celery, and herbs.

SERVES 4 505 calories per serving

Takes 4 1/2 hours **PAGE 238**

CARBONNADE OF BEEF

Cubes of chuck steak cooked with onion, garlic, fresh herbs, brown ale, and stock, and topped with mustard croûtes.

SERVES 4–6 698–465 calories per serving

Takes 3 1/2 hours **PAGE 228**

INDIAN SPICED LAMB

Lamb coated in a mixture of spices, honey, yogurt, and saffron, roasted, and garnished with cashew nuts and chopped coriander.

SERVES 4–6 569–379 calories per serving

Takes 4 1/4 hours, plus marinating **PAGE 250**

BOSTON BAKED BEANS

Haricot beans, bacon, and onions cooked with muscovado sugar, tomato purée, treacle, golden syrup, and mustard powder.

SERVES 4 650 calories per serving

Takes 5 3/4 hours, plus soaking **PAGE 268**

VEAL WITH TUNA MAYONNAISE

Veal flavoured with garlic and rosemary, and roasted in white wine. Served cold with a tuna mayonnaise.

SERVES 6–8 848–636 calories per serving

Takes 3 1/2 hours, plus cooling **PAGE 240**

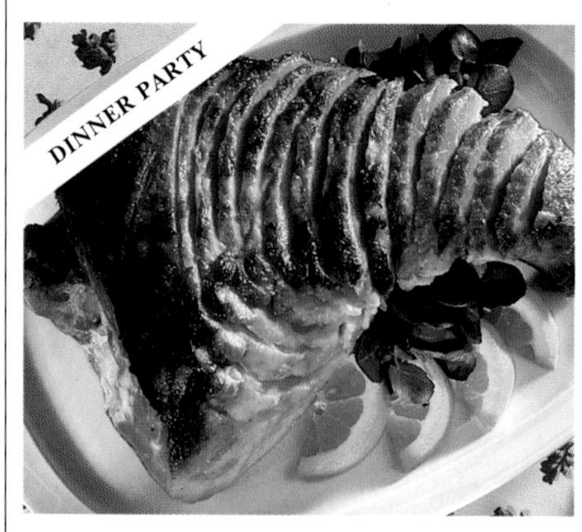

MUSTARD GLAZED HAM

Smoked gammon cooked with cider, glazed with sugar and mustard, roasted, and served with a lemon mustard sauce.

SERVES 16–20 477–382 calories per serving

Takes 4 hours, plus soaking **PAGE 267**

PRESSED TONGUE

Salted ox tongue simmered with bay leaf and onion, then covered with gelatine, pressed, and chilled until set.

SERVES 10 392 calories per serving

Takes 4 1/4 hours, plus chilling **PAGE 238**

MEAT KNOW-HOW

FOR CENTURIES, MEAT HAS BEEN the protein food around which the majority of meals have been planned. And even though more and more people are changing their diets, to include more pasta, rice, and pulses, meat is nevertheless enjoyed by most families several times a week, and it still forms the traditional centrepiece for many celebration meals. Make sure the cooking method suits the cut of meat you are preparing. Lean meats are best cooked quickly, while tougher cuts of meat are made more tender with long, slow cooking.

BUYING & STORING

If possible, buy your meat from a butcher because he's most likely to have just the cut you want (or will be prepared to cut it for you), and he will also advise you how to cook it. Wherever you shop, choose meat that looks fresh and moist (not wet), with a good colour and no greyish tinge. If possible, smell the meat: it should smell fresh. Check that pieces are neatly trimmed, without excess fat and splinters of bone. Appetites vary, but as a general guide, allow 125–200 g (4–7 oz) of lean boneless meat per person, and about 250 g (8 oz) each if the meat has a reasonable amount of bone.

Store meat, both raw and cooked, in the refrigerator. Mince and offal are more perishable than other kinds of meat, so cook them within 1–2 days of purchase. Chops, steaks, and joints can be kept for 2–4 days: remove the wrapping and replace with a loose covering. Eat cooked meat within 2–3 days.

PREPARING MEAT FOR COOKING

Trim off excess fat before cooking. If grilling or frying steaks, chops, or bacon rashers, slash or snip the fat at intervals to prevent the meat from curling up during cooking. If necessary, trim away sinew and tough connective tissue.

Lean joints which are to be roasted usually require barding. This means protecting them with a thin layer of fat such as bacon or pork fat, tied in place with string. Alternatively, lean joints can be larded with fat: use a long larding needle to insert strips of fat evenly through the meat.

MICROWAVING

Because microwave cooking is so fast, meat does not have time to brown and become crisp. This can be overcome by using a special browning dish which sears meat in the way a frying pan does.

The microwave oven is very useful for defrosting frozen meat. This must be done evenly at the manufacturer's recommended setting to prevent some parts of the meat beginning to cook before others are totally defrosted. All wrapping should be removed from the meat before defrosting to ensure that the meat does not start cooking.

FREEZING

Meat to be frozen must be very fresh. Wrap it tightly and thoroughly so that all the air is excluded. Pad any sharp bones so that they don't pierce the wrapping. If packing chops, cutlets, steaks, or hamburgers, separate them with freezerproof cling film or freezer wrap. The larger the piece of meat the longer it will keep. Mince and sausages can be stored in a freezer for 3 months; offal, chops, and cutlets for 4 months; joints and steaks for 6 months. Thaw frozen meat, in its wrapping and on a plate to catch any juices, in the refrigerator.

MEAT STOCK

Ask your butcher to saw 2 kg (4 lb) bones into 6 cm (2½ in) pieces. Beef and veal bones are best.

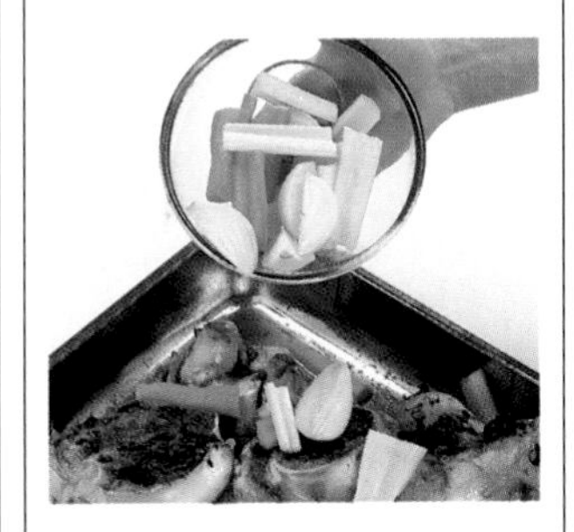

1 Roast the bones in a preheated oven at 230°C (450°F, Gas 8) for about 30 minutes. Add *2–3 roughly chopped onions, carrots, and celery stalks.* Roast for 30 minutes.

2 Transfer the browned bones and vegetables to a large stockpot. Add *4 litres (7 pints) water, a bouquet garni made of 1–2 bay leaves, a few parsley stalks, and 1–2 sprigs of thyme,* and *a few black peppercorns.*

3 Bring to a boil, skim off scum, then simmer for 4–6 hours. Using a ladle, strain through a sieve. Skim off fat, or let cool and lift off solidified fat.

BASIC COOKING TECHNIQUES

Tougher pieces of meat should be cooked slowly by stewing or braising. More tender pieces can be cooked quickly by frying or grilling. Beef and lamb when roasted, grilled, or fried can be served pink in the middle, but pork should be thoroughly cooked.

Stewing
Cut the meat into even cubes. Put into a casserole with any vegetables and liquid to cover. Bring to a boil, cover, and simmer on top of the stove or in the oven.

Alternatively, to seal in juices, heat some oil in the casserole and brown the cubes. Brown the vegetables, add liquid and flavourings, bring to a boil, cover, and simmer as above.

Braising
1 Brown the meat in the casserole, to add flavour and to seal in the cooking juices. Remove the meat from the casserole.

2 Add chopped vegetables and cook until beginning to brown. Return the meat and add liquid and flavourings. Bring to a boil, cover, and cook gently, according to the recipe.

Frying and sautéing
1 Dry the meat with paper towels (if too moist it will not brown quickly and evenly). Heat oil or a mixture of oil and butter in a heavy frying pan until it is very hot and add the meat, taking care not to crowd the pan.

2 Cook until well browned on both sides. Reduce the heat and continue until the meat is cooked to your taste. When turning meat, use tongs rather than a fork as a fork pierces the meat and allows the juices to run out.

Roasting
1 Take the joint from the refrigerator and allow it to come to room temperature.

2 Preheat the oven. Rub the meat with fat or oil and seasonings, or make incisions all over and insert herbs or slivers of garlic. Insert a meat thermometer, if using.

3 Put the joint and any vegetables in a roasting tin. Roast in the preheated oven, basting with the juices, until cooked to your taste (page 214). If not using a meat thermometer, test whether the meat is cooked by inserting a skewer into the centre. If the juices that run out are bloody, the meat is rare; if pink, medium; if clear, well-done.

4 Transfer the joint to a carving board and leave to rest for 10–15 minutes while making gravy. Carve the joint (page 213) and serve.

Grilling and barbecuing
1 Preheat the grill to hot, or light the barbecue (it will take 20–30 minutes to reach cooking temperature unless it is a gas barbecue which will heat up immediately).

2 Arrange the meat on the grill rack and put under the hot grill, or arrange on the grid over the charcoal fire. Brush with oil or melted butter and cook the meat until it is browned all over.

3 For sausage, or thicker pieces of meat that needs to be thoroughly cooked, reduce the heat or move the meat further away from the heat, and complete cooking.

Stir-frying
1 Cut the meat into uniform pieces for even cooking. Heat a wok or heavy frying pan, then add a little oil.

2 When the oil is hot, start adding the meat, a little at a time – adding too much at once will lower the temperature of the oil. Using a slotted spoon or a spatula, stir and toss the meat constantly until it is evenly browned.

3 If some pieces of meat are cooked before others, they can be pushed up the side of the wok or to the side of the pan where they will keep warm but not overcook.

BONING & BUTTERFLYING A LEG OF LAMB

A boned leg of lamb is much easier to carve than meat still on the bone. Tunnel boning leaves a pocket that can be filled with a savoury stuffing. If the leg is cut open to lie flat, this is known as butterflying.

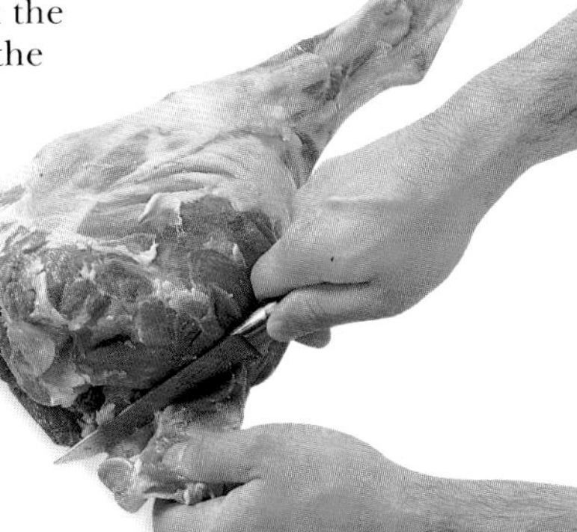

1 To tunnel bone, trim the skin and most or all of the fat from the lamb. Cut around the pelvic bone, at the wide end of the leg, to separate it from the meat. Sever the tendons that connect it to the leg bone. Remove the pelvic bone.

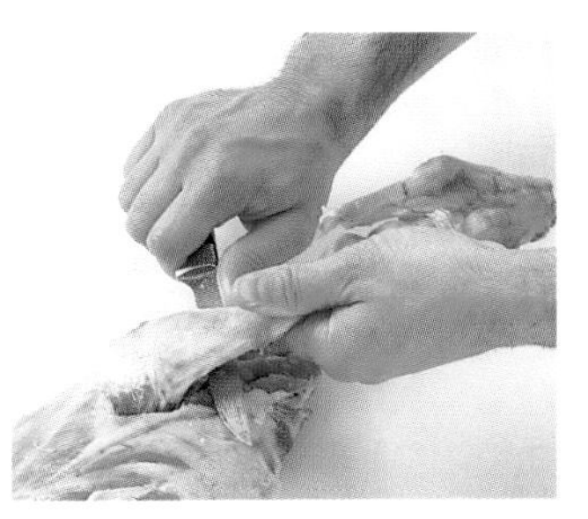

2 At the narrow end of the leg, cut around the shank bone and then scrape the meat away from the whole length of the bone using short strokes.

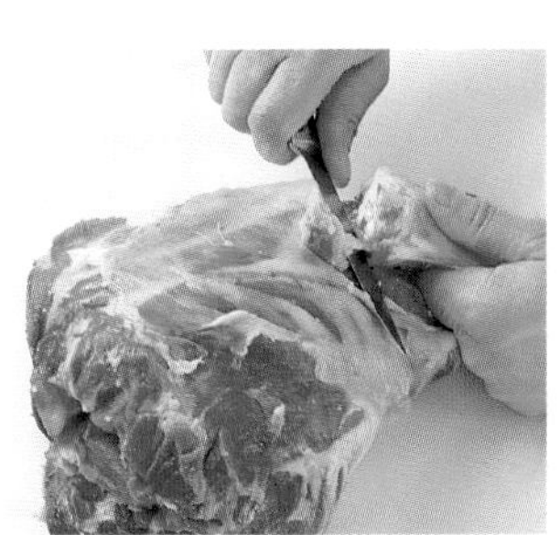

3 Cut away the meat to expose the joint that joins the shank bone to the leg bone. Sever the tendons and then remove the shank bone.

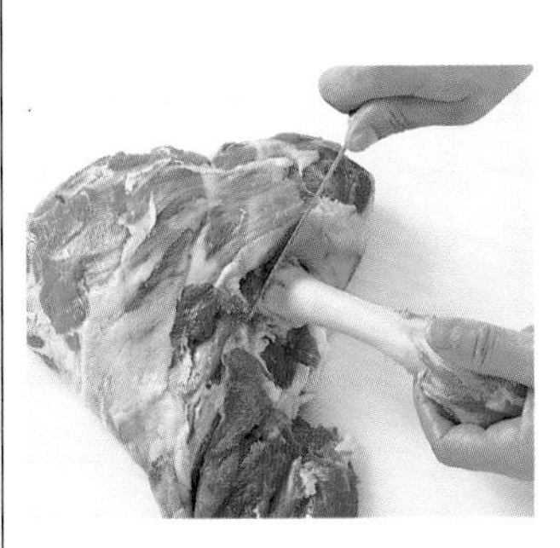

4 Cut around each end of the leg bone. Ease the leg bone out, cutting and scraping away the meat as you twist and pull it out. Trim off the tendons.

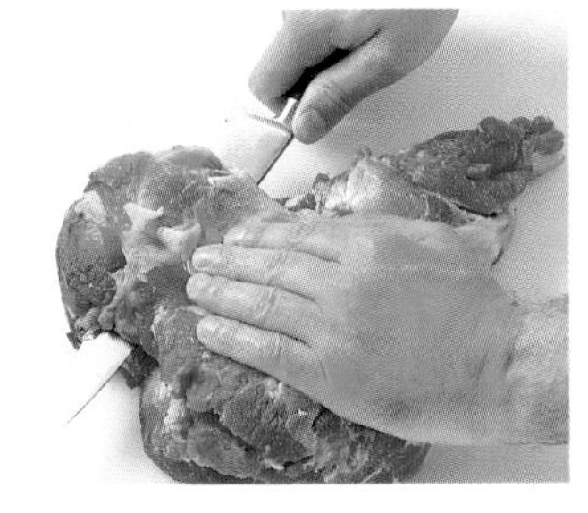

5 If you want to butterfly the boned leg, carefully insert a large chef's knife into the cavity left by the leg bone and cut to one side to slit open the meat.

6 Open out the boned leg into a "butterfly" shape. Cut through any thick portions of meat so that the whole leg can be opened out flat and is roughly even in thickness. Trim off excess fat and any remaining tendons.

BONING A SHOULDER OF LAMB

A special boning knife, with a narrow, pointed blade, is useful for preparing shoulders of lamb, pork, and veal. If you don't have one, a small, sharp chef's knife can be used instead.

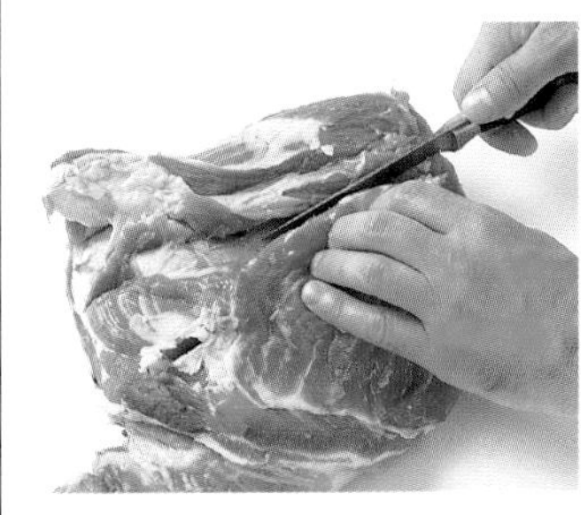

1 Remove the skin and fat. Set the shoulder meat-side up. Cut through the meat to the blade bone, and then cut away the meat on either side, keeping the knife as close to the bone as possible, until the bone is revealed.

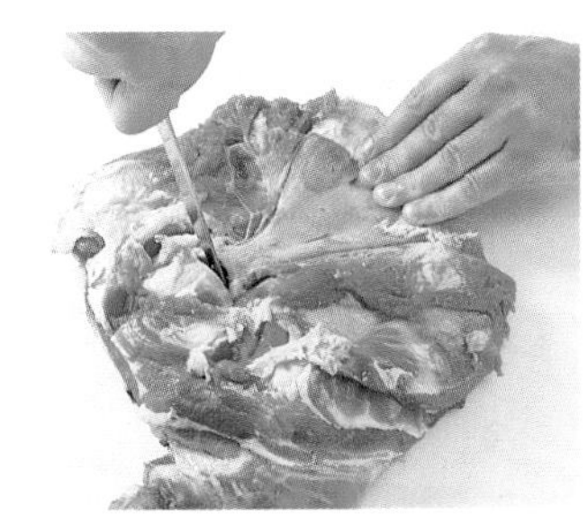

2 Cut through the ball and socket joint between the blade bone and the central shoulder bone, to separate the 2 bones.

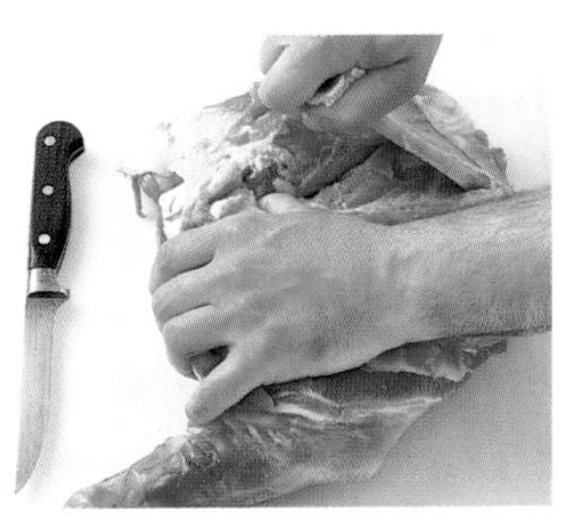

3 Cut beneath the ball and socket joint to free the end. Hold it firmly in one hand and pull the blade bone away from the meat.

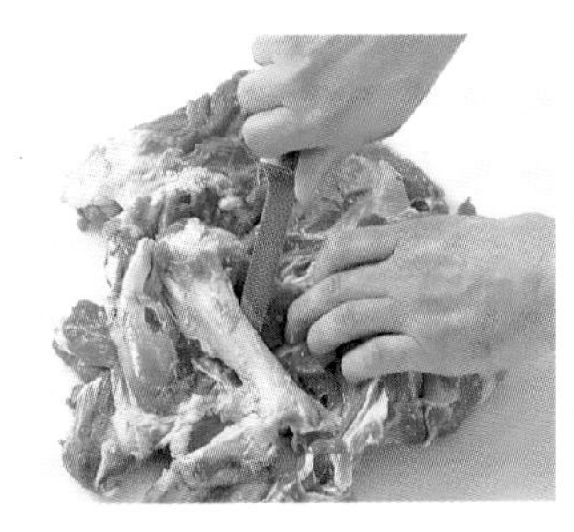

4 Cut around the central shoulder bone, severing the tendons, and cutting and scraping away the meat. Pull out the bone. If necessary, enlarge the pocket left by the bone so that it will accommodate a stuffing.

PREPARING A BEST END OF NECK OR RACK OF LAMB

Best end of neck, or rack of lamb, is a tender joint for roasting or grilling. A single rack, which is one side of the upper ribcage, comprises 6–9 cutlets and serves 2–3 people. Two racks can be used to make impressive joints such as a guard of honour or crown roast.

Rack of lamb

1 Set the rack on a board and cut away the cartilage at one end. Pull off the skin. Score the fat and meat 5 cm (2 ins) from the ends of the rib bones.

2 Turn the rack over and set it at the edge of the chopping board, so the ends of the rib bones are suspended. Score the meat along the rack, about 5 cm (2 ins) from the ends of the rib bones, cutting through to the bones.

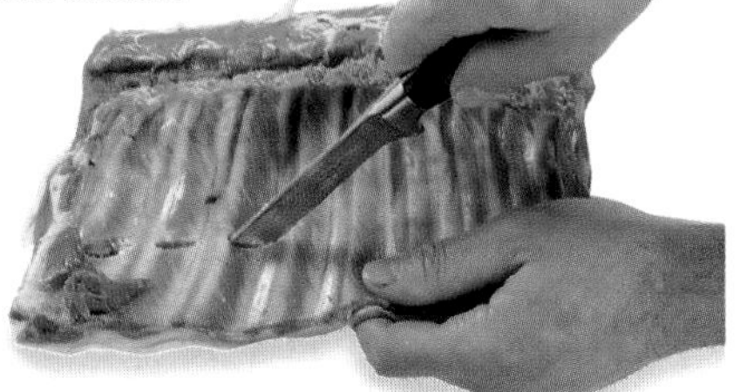

3 Cut out the meat from between the bones, cutting from the crosswise cuts to the ends. Turn the rack over and scrape the ends of the bones clean.

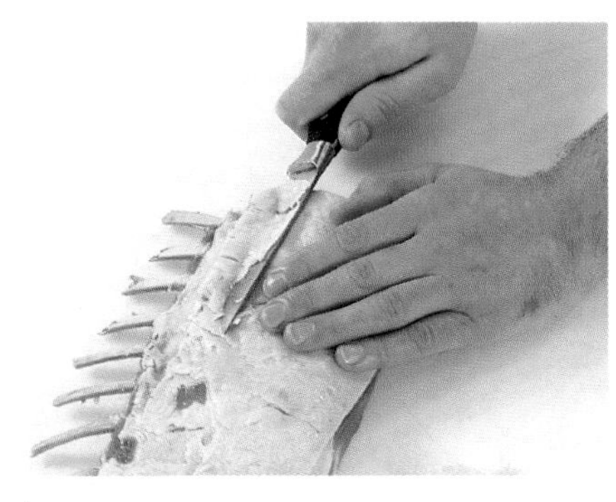

4 Trim away most of the fat from the meat. Repeat the preparation process with the second rack, if using.

Guard of honour

Hold 1 rack in each hand, fat-side outwards, and push them together, interlocking the rib bones. Cook as directed, covering the rib bones with foil, if desired, to prevent them from charring during cooking.

CROWN ROAST

Two racks of lamb are tied together in the shape of a crown.

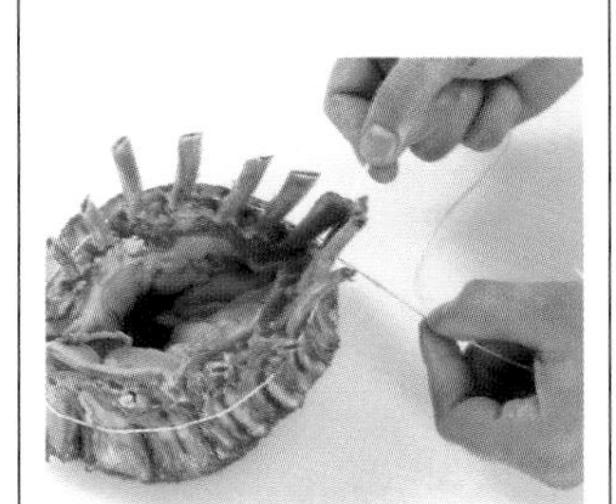

1 Prepare 2 racks as above. Slit the membrane between the rib bones at the meaty end so that the racks can be bent.

2 Stand the racks, meat-side innermost, on a work surface and curve to form a crown shape. Bend the bones so that the crown will stand upright.

3 Tie string around the middle of the 2 racks, to hold them in place.

4 Fill the centre of the roast with a stuffing, or add a filling just before serving. Carve the roast by cutting down between the rib bones.

STUFFING, ROLLING, & TYING A JOINT

Joints that have been boned and opened out can be rolled around a savoury stuffing, which gives both moisture and flavour to the meat during cooking.

1 Open out the meat and spread with an even layer of stuffing, leaving a small margin around the edge of the meat.

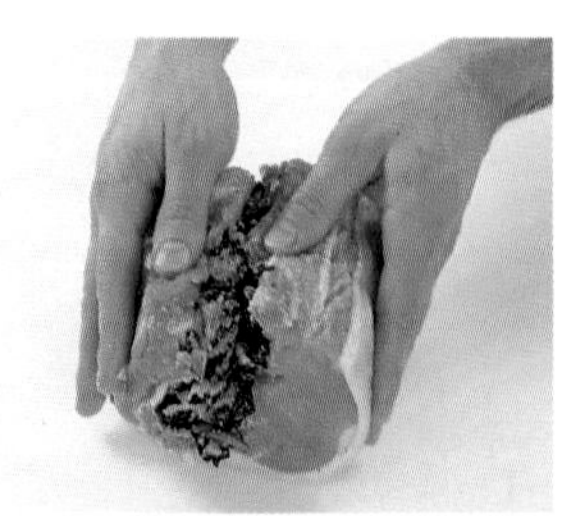

2 Roll up or fold the joint around the stuffing, to make a compact bolster shape. Turn it so that the join is underneath.

3 Tie string around the meat at regular intervals, to hold it in shape during cooking. Remove the string before carving.

CARVING A JOINT

Once a joint of meat has finished cooking, transfer it to a carving board and let it "rest" in a warm place for 10–15 minutes. During this time, the temperature of the joint will even out, and the flesh will reabsorb most of the juices. To carve, use a 2-pronged carving fork and a long carving knife.

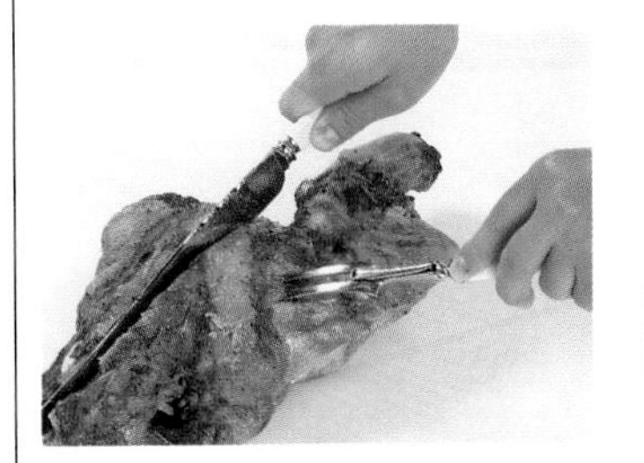

Shoulder of lamb

1 Insert the fork into the shank end. Cut a narrow, wedge-shaped piece from the centre, in the meatiest part between the angle formed by the blade bone and the shoulder bone.

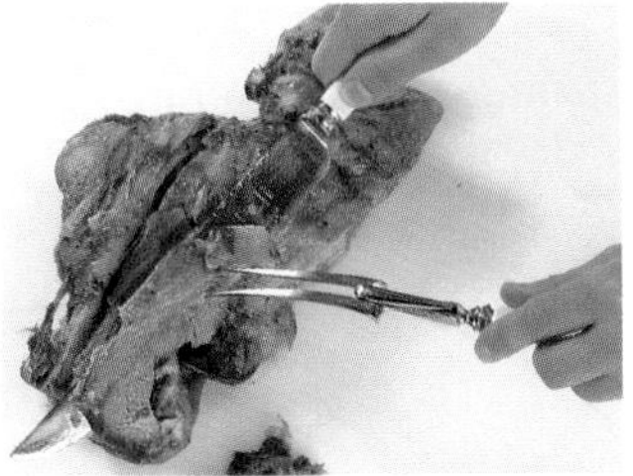

2 Carve neat slices from either side of this wedge-shaped cut until the blade and central shoulder bones are reached. Turn the shoulder over and cut horizontal slices lengthwise.

Rib of beef

1 Set the roast upright on a carving board, insert the carving fork into the meaty side, to steady the joint, and cut close to the large rib bones at the base of the meat, to remove them.

2 With the meat on its side, hold the knife at a slight angle and carve the meat into slices, 2 cm (3/4 in) thick.

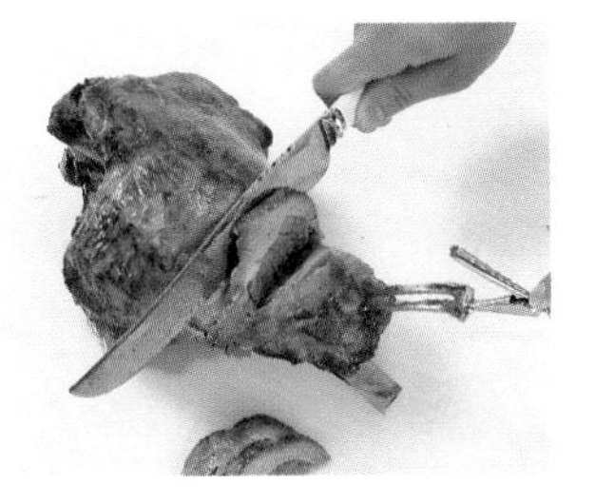

Leg of lamb

1 Set the joint with the meaty side upwards, and insert the carving fork firmly into the knuckle end. Cut a narrow, wedge-shaped piece from the centre of the meaty portion, cutting all the way to the bone.

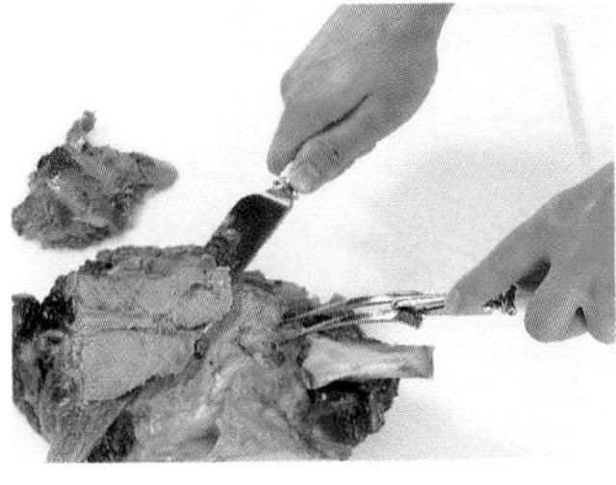

2 Carve neat slices from either side of this wedge-shaped cut, gradually changing the angle of the knife to make the slices larger. Turn the leg over. Trim off the fat, then carve off horizontal slices.

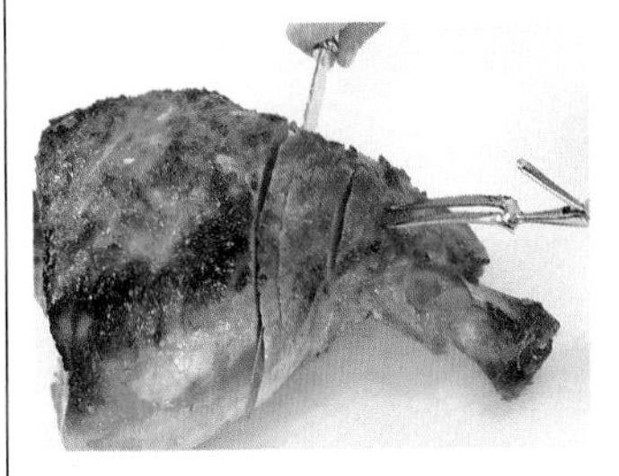

Whole ham

1 Cut a few horizontal slices from one side of the ham, to make a flat surface. Turn the ham over on to this surface. Insert the carving fork in the shank end. Make 3 or 4 cuts through to the bone at the shank end.

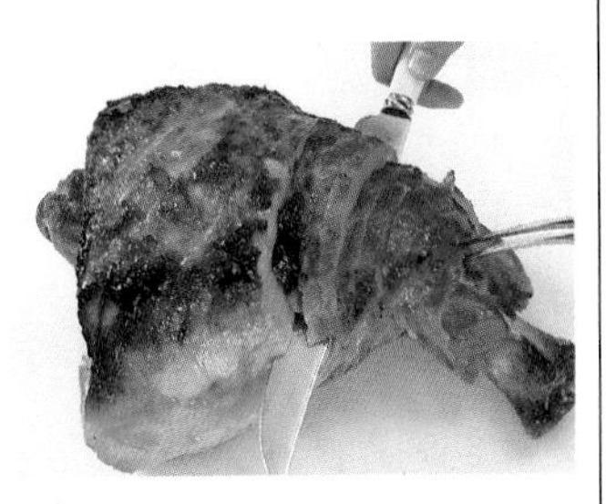

2 Insert the knife into the last cut and slide it along the bone, to detach the slices. Make a few more cuts in the ham and continue to remove the slices in the same way. Turn over and carve off horizontal slices.

MAKING GRAVY

A delicious gravy can be made from a good stock and the richly flavoured sediments and juices left after roasting meat. Add a little gravy browning to improve the colour of the gravy.

1 Pour all but *1 tbsp fat* from the roasting tin, leaving the juices. Set the tin on top of the stove and heat until sizzling. Stir in *1 tbsp plain flour*.

2 Whisk or stir briskly to mix the flour with the juices, and scrape the bottom and sides of the tin to dissolve any sediment. Keep stirring to form a well browned paste.

3 Gradually add *1 litre (1 3/4 pints) stock or other liquid*, whisking constantly to combine with the flour paste. Whisk until smooth. Simmer, stirring frequently, until the gravy reaches the desired consistency. Season to taste, strain into a warmed gravy boat, and serve.

ROASTING MEATS

As all ovens are different, these times are intended as a general guide and may vary according to the thickness of the meat. When calculating oven times, allow an extra 500 g (1 lb) on the weight of your joint.

MEAT		OVEN TEMPERATURE	TIME	INTERNAL TEMPERATURE
Beef	Rare	180°C (350°F, Gas 4)	15 mins per 500 g (1 lb)	60°C (140°F)
	Medium	180°C (350°F, Gas 4)	20 mins per 500 g (1 lb)	70°C (160°F)
	Well-done	180°C (350°F, Gas 4)	25 mins per 500 g (1 lb)	75°C (170°F)
Veal	Well-done	180°C (350°F, Gas 4)	25 mins per 500 g (1 lb)	75°C (170°F)
Lamb	Medium	180°C (350°F, Gas 4)	20 mins per 500 g (1 lb)	75°C (170°F)
	Well-done	180°C (350°F, Gas 4)	25 mins per 500 g (1 lb)	80°C (175°F)
Pork	Well-done	180°C (350°F, Gas 4)	30 mins per 500 g (1 lb)	90°C (190°F)

USING A MEAT THERMOMETER

The most accurate way to test if a large piece of meat is cooked is to use a meat thermometer, which registers the internal temperature of the joint. Before cooking, insert the spike of the thermometer into the middle or thickest part of the joint. Make sure that the thermometer does not touch a bone as bones become hotter than meat and will therefore give a false reading. Start checking the temperature reading towards the end of the suggested cooking time. A joint will continue to cook by retained heat for 5–10 minutes after it is removed from the oven, so take it out as soon as the thermometer reaches the desired temperature.

PREPARING OFFAL

Sweetbreads are glands from the throat and heart of calves or lambs. They have a delicate flavour and a rich, creamy texture. Lamb, beef, and veal kidneys are sometimes sold surrounded by a layer of hard, white fat – this is suet which can be grated and used in the same way as shredded suet.

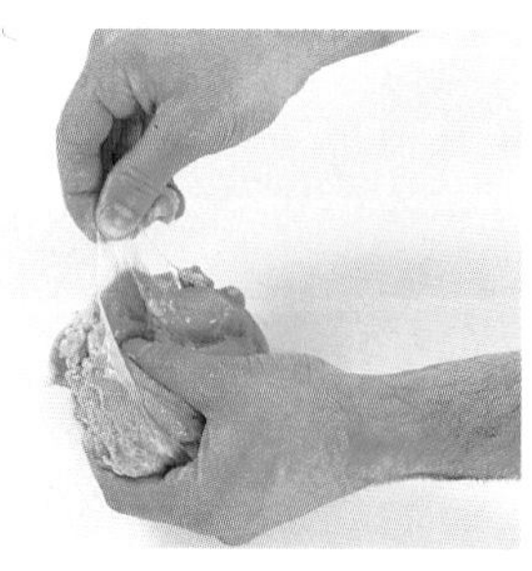

Sweetbreads

1 Soak the sweetbreads in cold water with 1 tbsp lemon juice for 2–3 hours to clean them. Drain, and rinse well. Cut away any discoloured parts. Use your fingers to carefully peel off the thin membrane surrounding the sweetbreads.

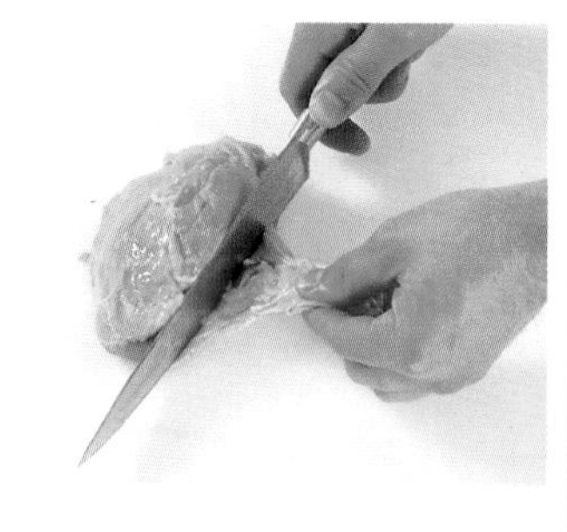

2 Cut away the ducts and any fat and discard. Don't remove too much or the sweetbreads will break up. Put into a saucepan of cold water and bring to a boil. Blanch calf's sweetbreads for 5 minutes, lamb's sweetbreads for 3 minutes.

Lamb's kidneys

1 If the kidneys are surrounded by suet, pull it away. Separate the kidneys (if using beef or veal). Carefully cut through the fine membrane around each kidney and use your fingers to peel it off (cut the ducts from beef or veal kidneys).

2 Set each kidney round-side up and slice lengthwise in half (or leave attached at the base, according to recipe directions). With a sharp pair of scissors, snip out the small fatty, white core and the tubes.

ENGLISH ROAST BEEF

 **Serves 8**

3.25 kg (6½ lb) rolled beef sirloin

60 g (2 oz) butter, melted

2 tbsp plain flour

salt and black pepper

1 onion, quartered

horseradish sauce and Yorkshire puddings to serve (see boxes, below and right)

GRAVY

150 ml (¼ pint) red wine

150 ml (¼ pint) beef stock

1 Insert a meat thermometer, if using, into the middle of the meat. Put the beef into a roasting tin and brush with the butter. Sprinkle with the flour and season. Add the onion and roast with the beef in a preheated oven at 200°C (400°F, Gas 6) for 20 minutes. Make the Yorkshire pudding batter and set aside.

2 Baste the beef with the juices from the tin and lower the oven temperature to 180°C (350°F, Gas 4).

3 Roast, basting frequently, for a further 1½ hours for rare beef, 1¾ hours for medium, and 2 hours for well-done, or until the meat thermometer registers 60°C (140°F), 70°C (160°F), or 75°C (170°F).

4 Transfer the beef to a carving board, cover with foil, and leave to stand in a warm place. Increase the oven temperature and bake the Yorkshire puddings.

5 Meanwhile, make the gravy: spoon the excess fat from the roasting tin. Put the tin on top of the stove, add the wine and stock, and bring to a boil, stirring constantly to dissolve the cooking juices. Simmer for 5 minutes or until the gravy has a syrupy consistency.

6 Season to taste and strain into a gravy boat. Transfer the beef to a platter, and serve with the gravy, horseradish sauce, and Yorkshire puddings.

Horseradish sauce

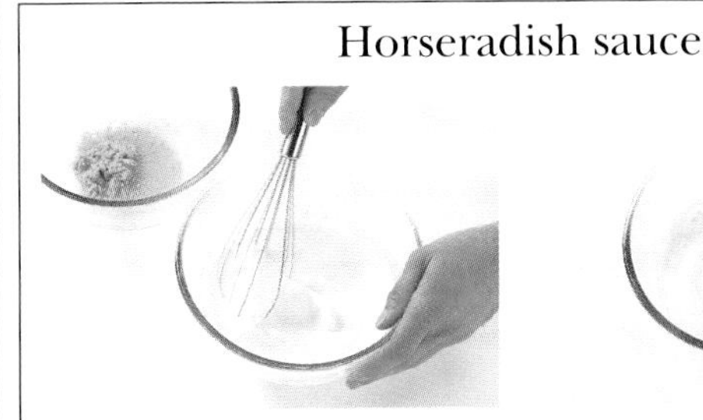

Mix *2–3 tbsp grated fresh horseradish* with *1 tbsp white wine vinegar* in a bowl. In another bowl, whisk *150 ml (¼ pint) whipping cream* until thick.

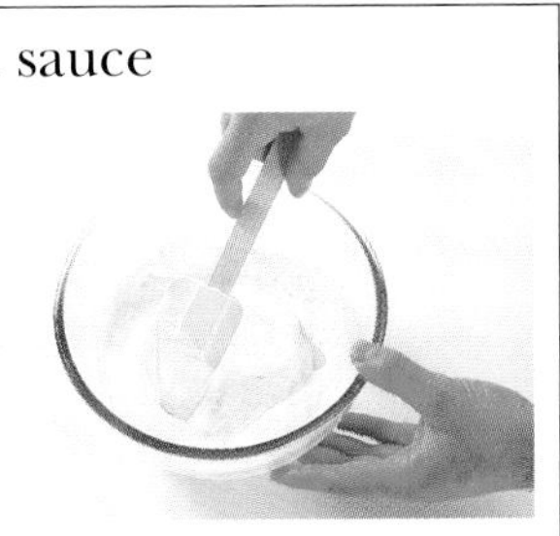

Fold the cream into the horseradish mixture, and add *salt, black pepper,* and *caster sugar to taste.* Cover and leave to chill until ready to serve.

Yorkshire puddings

Sift *125 g (4 oz) plain flour* and *a pinch of salt* into a bowl. Make a well in the middle and add *2 beaten eggs* and *a little milk.*

Whisk the milk and egg, then whisk in *125 ml (4 fl oz) milk,* drawing in the flour to make a smooth batter. Stir in another *125ml (4 fl oz) milk.* Cover and stand for at least 30 minutes.

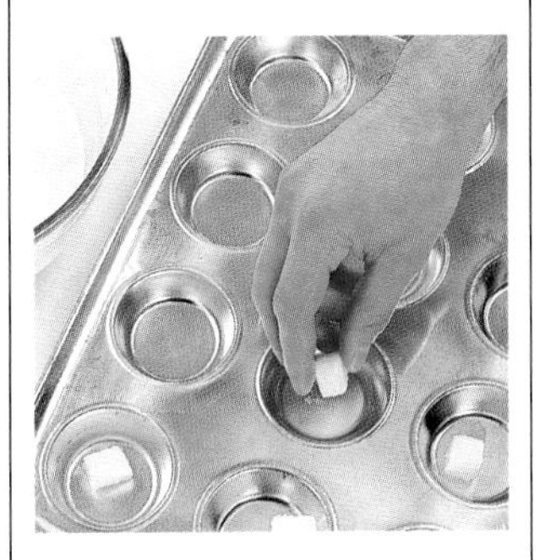

Put *some white vegetable fat* into each cup of a 12-hole bun tin and heat in a preheated oven at 220°C (425°F, Gas 7) until very hot. Remove the tin from the oven. Whisk the batter and pour into the cups in the tin. Bake the Yorkshire puddings in the oven for 15 minutes or until well risen, golden, and crisp. Serve immediately.

BEEF POT ROAST WITH WINTER VEGETABLES

 **Serves 6**

2 tbsp sunflower oil
1.15 kg (2 1/2 lb) beef topside or silverside
4 onions, quartered
1 large swede, cut into thick chunks
2 celery stalks, thickly sliced
2 large carrots, thickly sliced
150 ml (1/4 pint) dry white wine
150 ml (1/4 pint) hot water
a few parsley sprigs
2 fresh thyme sprigs
1 bay leaf
salt and black pepper
chopped parsley to garnish

1 Heat the sunflower oil in a large flameproof casserole. Add the beef and cook, turning, for about 10 minutes until browned all over.

2 Lift the beef out of the casserole and put in the onions, swede, celery, and carrots. Stir well to coat the vegetables in the oil, then cook, stirring occasionally, for about 5 minutes.

3 Insert a meat thermometer, if using, into the middle of the beef. Push the vegetables to the side of the casserole, and place the meat in the middle, arranging the vegetables around it.

4 Add the wine, measured water, parsley, thyme, bay leaf, and salt and pepper to taste. Bring to a boil, then cover tightly, and cook in a preheated oven at 150°C (300°F, Gas 2) for 2 1/2–3 hours until the meat is tender. The meat thermometer should register well-done: 75°C (170°F).

5 Transfer the meat and vegetables to a warmed platter, cover, and keep warm.

6 Spoon the fat from the surface of the cooking liquid, then boil over a high heat until the liquid is reduced by half. Taste for seasoning, and strain into a warmed gravy boat. Carve the meat into thin slices, garnish with parsley, and serve with the gravy.

TEXAS BARBECUE BEEF BRISKET

Serves 6

1.15–1.5 kg (2 1/2–3 lb) beef brisket
2 tbsp sunflower oil
cayenne pepper

MARINADE

750 ml (1 1/4 pints) spicy barbecue sauce
250 ml (8 fl oz) pale ale or lager
juice of 1 lemon
2 tbsp Worcestershire sauce
3 onions, chopped
5 garlic cloves, crushed
3 tbsp brown sugar
2 tsp ground cumin
1/2 tsp ground ginger

1 Make the marinade: in a large bowl, combine the barbecue sauce, pale ale, lemon juice, Worcestershire sauce, onions, garlic, brown sugar, cumin, and ginger. Turn the brisket in the marinade, cover loosely, and leave to marinate in the refrigerator, turning occasionally, for 1–2 days.

2 Remove the beef from the marinade, reserving the marinade, and pat dry with paper towels.

3 Heat the vegetable oil in a flameproof casserole, add the brisket, and brown.

4 Insert a meat thermometer, if using, into the middle of the brisket. Pour over the marinade, cover, and cook in a preheated oven at 160°C (325°F, Gas 3) for 2 1/2–3 hours until tender, adding a little water if the sauce becomes too thick. The meat thermometer should register well-done: 75°C (170°F).

5 Remove the casserole from the oven and leave to stand for 15–20 minutes. Remove the meat and slice. Season the sauce with cayenne pepper to taste, then heat through. Arrange the meat on a serving platter, and pour over the sauce.

Cook's know-how

This dish can be cooked a day ahead. As it cools, the fat will rise to the surface and solidify, so it can then be lifted off, producing a less fatty dish.

French-style Braised Beef

Serves 4–6

1 kg (2 lb) piece of chuck steak
2 tbsp olive oil
125 g (4 oz) piece of lean bacon, cut into strips
1 onion, sliced
250 g (8 oz) carrots, thickly sliced
250 g (8 oz) mushrooms, quartered
500 g (1 lb) tomatoes, peeled (page 39), seeded, and chopped
125 g (4 oz) pitted black olives
600 ml (1 pint) beef stock
salt and black pepper
chopped parsley to garnish

MARINADE

500 ml (16 fl oz) red wine
3 tbsp red wine vinegar
2 large garlic cloves
1 strip of orange zest
2 bay leaves
1 thyme sprig
1 parsley sprig

1 Make the marinade: combine the wine, vinegar, garlic, orange zest, and herbs. Add the beef, cover, and leave to marinate in the refrigerator overnight.

2 Remove the beef from the marinade and pat dry with paper towels. Strain the marinade and reserve. Heat the oil in a large flameproof casserole, add the beef and bacon, and brown all over. Lift out and drain on paper towels.

3 Add the onion, carrots, and mushrooms and cook, stirring, for 5 minutes or until lightly browned.

4 Add the beef, bacon, tomatoes, olives, and reserved marinade. Insert a meat thermometer, if using, into the middle of the beef. Pour in sufficient stock to cover the meat and season.

5 Bring to a boil, cover tightly, and cook in a preheated oven at 180°C (350°F, Gas 4) for 1½–2 hours or until the meat is very tender.

6 Slice the meat and arrange on a warmed platter with the vegetables. Skim the sauce and pour over the meat. Garnish with parsley before serving.

Salt Beef with Mustard Sauce

Serves 6–8

1 kg (2 lb) boned and rolled salt beef
500 g (1 lb) baby carrots
8 potatoes, halved
8 celery stalks, cut into chunks
250 g (8 oz) turnips, cut into chunks
chopped parsley to garnish

MUSTARD SAUCE

30 g (1 oz) butter
30 g (1 oz) plain flour
150 ml (¼ pint) milk
4 tsp white wine vinegar
2 tsp mustard powder
2 tsp caster sugar
salt and black pepper

1 Put the salt beef into a large bowl. Cover with cold water and leave to soak overnight to remove any excess salt.

2 Rinse the beef under cold running water, place in a large saucepan, and cover with cold water. Cover the pan with its lid, bring to a boil, and simmer very gently, topping up the water in the pan when necessary, for about 1 hour.

3 Add the carrots, potatoes, celery, and turnips and cook for 40 minutes or until the beef and vegetables are tender.

4 Transfer the meat to a warmed platter. Lift out the vegetables with a slotted spoon, reserving the liquid, and arrange around the meat. Cover and keep warm.

5 Make the sauce: melt the butter in a saucepan, add the flour, and cook, stirring, for 1 minute. Remove from the heat and gradually blend in the milk and 150 ml (¼ pint) of the cooking liquid from the beef. Bring to a boil, stirring constantly, until the sauce thickens. Simmer for 2 minutes.

6 In a jug, combine the vinegar, mustard powder, and sugar, and stir into the sauce. Cook for 1 minute, then add salt and pepper to taste. (Be careful not to add too much salt because the liquid from the beef is salty.)

7 Slice the beef and arrange on warmed serving plates with the vegetables. Pour the mustard sauce over the beef, and sprinkle with parsley.

TRINIDAD PEPPERPOT BEEF

Serves 4–6

1 kg (2 lb) boneless beef, such as brisket, trimmed
2–3 litres (3 1/2–5 pints) beef stock
2 large onions, coarsely chopped
2–4 fresh red chillies, cored, seeded, and chopped
2 tbsp chopped parsley
4 tbsp vinegar, plus extra if necessary
2 tbsp dark brown sugar
1 tbsp Worcestershire sauce
1 tbsp tropical peppercorns, coarsely crushed, plus extra if necessary
1 tsp ground cinnamon
1 tsp dried thyme
large pinch of ground allspice
salt

1 Put the beef into a large pan, add enough stock to cover, and bring to a boil, skimming off any scum that rises to the surface. Lower the heat, cover, and simmer for 1 1/2 hours or until the meat feels just tender when pierced with a skewer.

2 Add the onions, chillies, and half of the parsley, then add the vinegar, sugar, Worcestershire sauce, peppercorns, cinnamon, thyme, allspice, and salt to taste. Cover and simmer for 2 hours or until the beef is very tender.

3 Transfer the beef to a carving board, cover, and keep warm.

4 Skim any fat from the cooking liquid, and boil for about 10 minutes until reduced to 300 ml (1/2 pint). Season, adding more vinegar and peppercorns if needed. Slice the beef thickly, discarding the fat. Pour the sauce over the beef, and sprinkle with the parsley.

Tropical peppercorns

Also known as mixed peppercorns, tropical peppercorns are a mixture of black, white, green, and pink peppercorns.

BEEF WITH ROAST VEGETABLE SALAD

Serves 4–6

1 kg (2 lb) beef fillet cut from the centre, trimmed
2 tbsp black olive paste
1 tbsp black peppercorns, coarsely crushed
2 tbsp olive oil
chopped parsley to garnish

ROAST VEGETABLE SALAD

1–2 tbsp olive oil
1 aubergine, cut into 5 mm (1/4 in) slices
3 courgettes, cut into 5 mm (1/4 in) slices
1 fennel bulb, cut lengthwise into 5 mm (1/4 in) pieces
1 red pepper, cored, seeded, and cut into 5 mm (1/4 in) strips
1 yellow pepper, cored, seeded, and cut into 5 mm (1/4 in) strips
salt and black pepper
2 tsp balsamic vinegar

1 Tie the beef to retain its shape, if necessary. Spread the black olive paste all over the beef, then press on the peppercorns.

2 Pour the oil into a roasting tin and heat in a preheated oven at 230°C (450°F, Gas 8).

3 Insert a meat thermometer, if using, into the middle of the beef, put the joint into the hot oil, and roast for 20 minutes.

4 Lower the heat to 220°C (425°F, Gas 7) and roast for a further 15 minutes for rare beef, 20 minutes for medium, or 25 minutes for well-done, or until the meat thermometer registers 60°C (140°F), 70°C (160°F), or 75°C (170°F). Leave to cool.

5 Make the roast vegetable salad: put the olive oil into a large bowl. Add the aubergine, courgettes, fennel, and red and yellow peppers, and toss in the oil.

6 Turn the vegetables into the roasting tin and add salt and pepper to taste. Cook in the oven at 200°C (400°F, Gas 6), turning the vegetables once, for 30 minutes or until tender. Leave to cool, then toss with the balsamic vinegar.

7 When the beef is cold, slice very thinly and serve with the roast vegetable salad. Garnish with parsley.

BEEF WELLINGTON

Inside a puff pastry case is a succulent piece of prime beef and a rich stuffing of liver pâté and mushrooms. The pastry locks in all the juices and ensures none of the wonderful flavours are lost. Serve with a mushroom and red wine gravy.

Serves 8

1.5 kg (3 lb) beef fillet, trimmed and tied

salt and black pepper

2 tbsp sunflower oil

45 g (1 1/2 oz) butter

1 small onion, finely chopped

250 g (8 oz) flat mushrooms, finely chopped

175 g (6 oz) smooth liver pâté

400 g (13 oz) ready-made puff pastry

1 egg, beaten

thin mushroom gravy to serve (page 239)

1 Season the beef with black pepper. Heat the oil in a large frying pan, add the beef, and cook over a high heat until browned all over.

2 Put the beef fillet in a roasting tin and cook in a preheated oven at 220°C (425°F, Gas 7) for 25 minutes for rare beef, 30 minutes for medium, or 40 minutes for well-done. Leave to cool completely.

3 Meanwhile, melt the butter in the frying pan, add the onion and mushrooms, and cook, stirring, for 3 minutes or until softened. Increase the heat to high, and cook until the excess moisture has evaporated. Turn into a bowl and leave to cool completely.

4 Add the liver pâté to the mushroom and onion mixture and stir well to combine. Add salt and pepper to taste.

5 Wrap the beef in the pastry (see box, right).

6 Bake at 220°C (425°F, Gas 7) for 45 minutes or until the pastry is crisp and golden. Cover with foil after 30 minutes to prevent the pastry becoming too brown. Leave to stand for about 10 minutes, then slice and serve with the gravy.

INDIVIDUAL BEEF WELLINGTONS

Cut the raw beef into 8 slices. Brown the slices in a frying pan, then wrap each one in pastry with a little of the pâté mixture. Bake for 25–30 minutes.

Wrapping the beef in pastry

Roll out 300 g (10 oz) of the pastry to a 30 x 40 cm (12 x 16 in) rectangle. Spread half of the pâté mixture down the middle, leaving a 10 cm (4 in) border on each side.

Remove the string from the beef and place on the pâté mixture. Cover with remaining pâté mixture.

Brush the pastry border with beaten egg. Fold the short sides of the pastry over the beef.

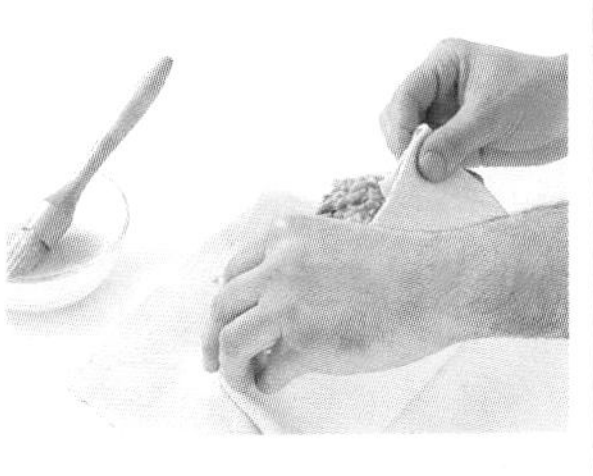

Fold over the long ends and turn the parcel over. Brush with beaten egg. Roll out the remaining pastry, and cut into strips, 5 mm (1/4 in) wide. Arrange in a lattice pattern on top of the pastry, then glaze the strips with beaten egg.

PEPPER STEAKS

Serves 4

4 x 150–175 g (5–6 oz) fillet steaks, about 2.5 cm (1 in) thick, trimmed

salt and black pepper

2 tbsp black peppercorns

30 g (1 oz) butter

1 tbsp sunflower oil

2 tbsp brandy

150 ml (1/4 pint) double cream

chopped parsley to garnish

1 Season the steaks on both sides with salt. Crush the peppercorns and spread them on a plate. Coat the steaks with the peppercorns (see box, right).

2 Melt the butter with the oil in a frying pan. When the butter is foaming, add the steaks and cook over a high heat for 2 minutes on each side.

3 Lower the heat and continue cooking until the steaks are to your liking: rare steaks need 1–2 minutes on each side, medium steaks 3 minutes on each side, and well-done steaks 4–5 minutes on each side. Lift out of the pan and keep warm.

4 Pour the brandy into the frying pan, remove from the heat, and set the brandy alight. When the flames have died down, stir in the cream, and add salt and pepper to taste. Gently reheat the sauce, pour it over the steaks, and garnish with parsley. Serve at once.

Coating steaks

Press each steak firmly on to the peppercorns, until both sides are well coated.

Cook's know-how

It is easiest to crush peppercorns using a pestle and mortar. Alternatively, put the peppercorns on a board and crush them with a rolling pin.

CHATEAUBRIAND WITH BEARNAISE SAUCE

Serves 2

400 g (13 oz) Chateaubriand steak

30 g (1 oz) butter, melted

black pepper

béarnaise sauce (see box, right)

1 Cut the steak crosswise in half. Brush one side of each half with melted butter and season with pepper.

2 Put the steaks, buttered-side up, under a hot grill, 7 cm (3 ins) from the heat, and cook for 2 minutes or until browned. Turn the steaks over, brush with melted butter, and season with pepper. Grill for about 2 minutes until browned.

3 Lower the heat and cook, turning once and brushing with the butter, for 4–5 minutes. Cover and leave to stand for 5 minutes. Slice the steaks, and serve with the béarnaise sauce.

Chateaubriand

A thick piece of fillet steak from the centre of the tenderloin, ideal for serving 2 people.

Béarnaise sauce

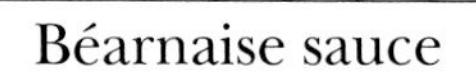

Put *4 tbsp tarragon vinegar, 1 finely chopped shallot,* and *1 tbsp chopped tarragon* into a pan and boil for a few minutes until reduced by one-third. Leave to cool.

Pour *2 egg yolks* into a bowl over a saucepan of simmering water, add the vinegar mixture, and whisk over a gentle heat until thick and fluffy.

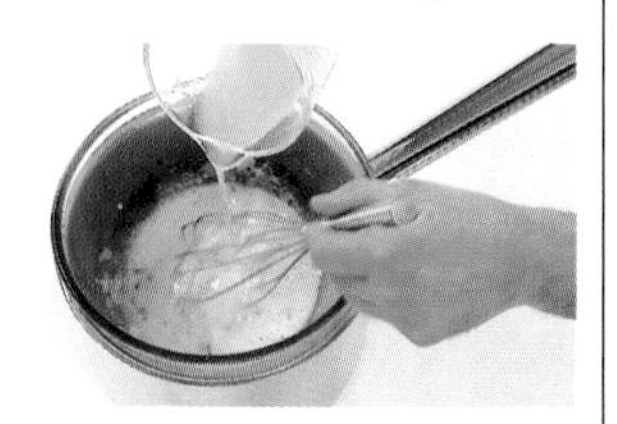

Melt *90 g (3 oz) butter* and gradually add to the sauce, whisking constantly until thick. Add *salt and white pepper to taste.*

STEAKS WITH SMOKED OYSTER RELISH

 **Serves 4**

4 x 175 g (6 oz) rump steaks

salt and black pepper

2 garlic cloves, crushed

1 tbsp olive oil

smoked oyster relish (see box, below) and lemon wedges to serve

1 Season the steaks with salt and pepper, rub with the garlic, and brush with the oil.

2 Heat a frying pan over a high heat, add the steaks, and cook for 3–4 minutes on each side for rare steaks, 4–5 minutes for medium steaks, or 7–8 minutes for well-done steaks. Transfer the steaks to warmed serving plates.

3 Generously spoon the smoked oyster relish over the steaks, and serve at once, accompanied by lemon wedges.

CARPETBAG STEAKS

Melt 15 g (1/2 oz) butter and cook 2 chopped shallots until softened. Remove from the heat and add 6 chopped fresh oysters, 125 g (4 oz) fresh breadcrumbs, 1 tbsp chopped parsley, and salt and pepper. Cut a pocket in each steak and fill with the stuffing. Cook as directed.

Smoked oyster relish

Drain *1 x 100 g (3 1/2 oz) can smoked oysters.* Finely chop *1 small onion* and *1 handful of parsley sprigs.*

Chop the drained smoked oysters with a large, sharp chef's knife.

Put the oysters, onion, and parsley into a small bowl and mix well. Chill until needed.

SAVOURY BUTTERS

These simple butters are ideal for livening up plain grilled meats such as steaks, chops, and noisettes.

CORIANDER BUTTER

Soften *125 g (4 oz) butter* and blend in *2 tbsp chopped fresh coriander, 1 tbsp lemon juice, 1 tsp ground coriander,* and *salt and black pepper to taste.* Chill. Garnish with *a coriander sprig* and *a sprinkling of ground coriander.*

ANCHOVY BUTTER

Soften *125 g (4 oz) butter* and blend in *2 tbsp finely chopped anchovies, 1 tbsp lemon juice, 1 tsp ground coriander,* and *black pepper to taste.* Chill. Garnish with *anchovy fillets.*

PARSLEY BUTTER

Soften *125 g (4 oz) butter* and blend in *2 tbsp chopped parsley, 1 tbsp lemon juice,* and *salt and black pepper to taste.* Chill. Garnish with *a lemon twist* and *a parsley sprig.*

MUSTARD BUTTER

Soften *125 g (4 oz) butter* and blend in *2 tbsp Dijon mustard, 2 tbsp chopped fresh tarragon,* and *salt and black pepper to taste.* Chill. Garnish with *a tarragon sprig.*

STEAK DIANE

Serves 4

4 x 150–175 g (5–6 oz) rump steaks, trimmed
30 g (1 oz) butter
2 tbsp sunflower oil
1 small onion, finely chopped
300 ml (1/2 pint) beef stock
2 tbsp Worcestershire sauce
1 tbsp lemon juice
1 tbsp chopped parsley
salt and black pepper
3 tbsp brandy

1 Place the steaks between 2 sheets of greaseproof paper and pound with a rolling pin until 5 mm (1/4 in) thick.

2 Melt the butter with the sunflower oil in a large frying pan. When the butter is foaming, add the pounded steaks and cook over a high heat for about 3 minutes on each side until browned. Lift the steaks out of the frying pan and cover with foil to keep warm.

3 Add the onion and cook gently, stirring, for a few minutes until softened. Stir in the stock, Worcestershire sauce, lemon juice, parsley, and salt and pepper to taste, and cook for 2 minutes.

4 Return the steaks to the pan and remove from the heat. Flambé the steaks (see box, below). Let the flames die down and serve.

Flambéing steaks

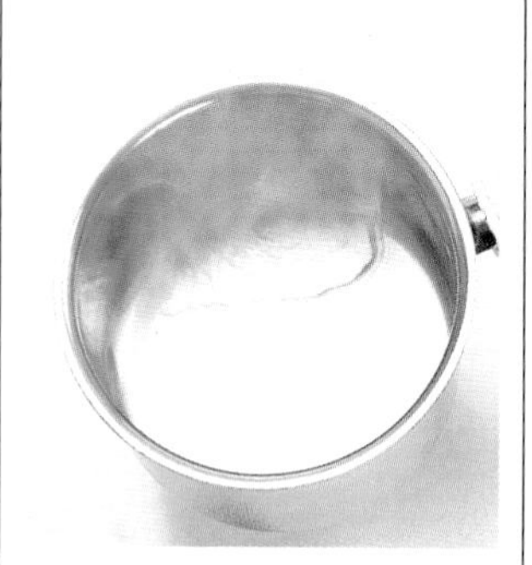

Warm the brandy gently in a small saucepan. Light it with a taper and pour over the steaks.

TOURNEDOS ROQUEFORT

Serves 4

125 g (4 oz) Roquefort cheese, crumbled
60 g (2 oz) walnut pieces, roughly chopped
30 g (1 oz) butter, softened
salt and black pepper
4 x 125 g (4 oz) tournedos steaks, 2.5 cm (1 in) thick
chopped parsley to garnish

1 In a small bowl, combine the Roquefort, walnuts, butter, and pepper to taste.

2 Season the tournedos steaks on both sides with salt and pepper, and place them under a hot grill, 7–10 cm (3–4 ins) from the heat. Grill for 3–4 minutes on each side for rare steaks, 4–5 minutes for medium steaks, or 7–8 minutes for well-done steaks.

3 Two minutes before the steaks are ready, sprinkle with the Roquefort mixture, and return to the hot grill until the cheese has melted. Serve hot, garnished with chopped parsley.

TOURNEDOS WITH MUSHROOMS

Substitute a mushroom topping for the cheese and walnut topping. Coarsely chop 1 garlic clove, 1 shallot, and 60 g (2 oz) streaky bacon, put into a food processor, and process to a paste. Transfer to a frying pan and cook for 3 minutes or until browned. Process 250 g (8 oz) chestnut mushrooms in a food processor until finely chopped. Add to the mixture in the frying pan and cook for 15 minutes. Stir in 2 tbsp chopped parsley, 1 tsp grated lemon zest, and salt and pepper to taste. Arrange the mushroom mixture on top of the steaks just before serving.

BEEF & BEAN BURRITOS

Serves 4

- *375 g (12 oz) rump steak, trimmed and cut into thin strips*
- *salt and black pepper*
- *2 tbsp olive oil*
- *1 garlic clove, crushed*
- *1/2–1 fresh red chilli, cored, seeded, and chopped*
- *1/2 tsp cumin seeds*
- *1 x 400 g (13 oz) can tomatoes, drained, juice reserved*
- *1 x 400 g (13 oz) can pinto or black beans, drained*
- *8 flour tortillas*
- *4 tbsp soured cream or crème fraîche*
- *chopped fresh coriander to garnish*

1 Season the steak strips with salt and pepper. Heat the olive oil in a large frying pan, add the steak, crushed garlic, chopped chilli, and cumin seeds, and cook, stirring, for 5 minutes or until lightly browned.

2 Add the tomatoes to the pan and cook for about 3 minutes. Pour in the reserved tomato juice and boil for 8–10 minutes until the liquid is reduced.

3 Add the beans and cook until heated through. Taste for seasoning, cover, and keep warm.

4 Warm the tortillas (page 226).

5 Divide the steak and tomato mixture among the tortillas and roll them up. Serve topped with soured cream and garnished with coriander.

Burritos

These take their name from the Spanish word, burro, *meaning donkey – like a donkey, a burrito is heavily laden. Flour tortillas are the usual, traditional choice for burritos, but if you cannot find them, pita bread can be used instead.*

PORK & BEAN BURRITOS

Substitute 375 g (12 oz) pork fillet for the rump steak, and proceed as directed.

BEEF STROGANOFF

Serves 4

- *30 g (1 oz) butter*
- *1 tbsp sunflower oil*
- *750 g (1 1/2 lb) rump steak, trimmed and cut into strips (see box, right)*
- *8 shallots, quartered*
- *300 g (10 oz) button mushrooms, halved*
- *salt and black pepper*
- *300 ml (1/2 pint) soured cream*
- *chopped parsley to garnish*

1 Melt the butter with the oil in a large frying pan. When the butter is foaming, add the steak strips, in batches if necessary, and cook over a high heat for 5 minutes or until browned all over. Remove from the pan with a slotted spoon.

2 Add the shallots and mushrooms and cook for about 5 minutes until soft and browned.

3 Return the steak strips to the pan, and add salt and pepper to taste. Stir in the soured cream and heat gently. Garnish with parsley, and serve at once.

Cutting the beef

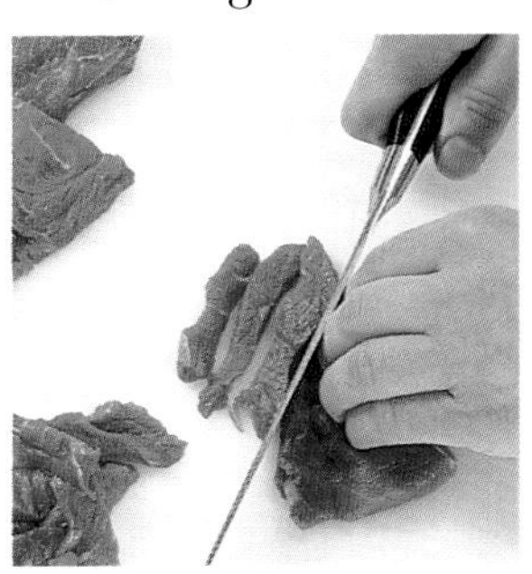

Slice the beef into thin strips, 5 mm (1/4 in) wide and 5 cm (2 ins) long, using a sharp chef's knife.

Beef Stroganoff

This classic Russian dish has been known in western Europe since the 18th century. It takes its name from the Stroganoffs, a family of wealthy merchants from Novgorod. A family member had a French cook and it is thought that he gave his employer's name to the dish.

Mexican steak platter

A traditional Mexican meal usually includes a number of separate dishes to be eaten together, with the classic accompaniments of refried beans and guacamole. Prepare this selection of dishes for a special family meal or, if you prefer, try just one or two of them – each dish tastes just as good on its own.

Steaks with roasted pepper sauce

Serves 4

4 x 175 g (6 oz) rump steaks

MARINADE

4 tbsp sunflower oil

1/4 tsp ground allspice

1/4 tsp black pepper

2 tbsp lime juice

ROASTED PEPPER SAUCE

1 tbsp sunflower oil

1/2 onion, thinly sliced

1 garlic clove, crushed

1 green and 1 red pepper, roasted, peeled (page 354), and cut into strips

90 ml (3 fl oz) crème fraîche

1/4 tsp dried mixed herbs

salt and black pepper

chopped parsley to garnish

1 Make the marinade: heat the oil in a small saucepan and add the allspice and pepper. Remove from the heat and leave to cool, then add the lime juice. Put the rump steaks into a shallow non-metallic dish and brush with the marinade. Cover and chill, turning occasionally, for 8 hours.

2 Make the roasted pepper sauce: heat the oil in a frying pan, add the onion, and cook gently, stirring, for 5 minutes or until golden.

3 Add the garlic and pepper strips and cook for 2 minutes. Stir in the crème fraîche and herbs and season with salt. Simmer for 3–5 minutes until the sauce is reduced and just coats the vegetables. Set aside.

4 Remove the steaks from the marinade, drain, but do not dry completely. Season with salt and pepper to taste. Heat another frying pan, add the steaks, and cook for 3–6 minutes on each side. Top the steaks with the roasted pepper sauce and sprinkle with chopped parsley.

Enchiladas

Serves 4

4 tbsp sunflower oil

4 flour tortillas

60 g (2 oz) queso fresco or feta cheese, crumbled

1 onion, finely chopped

chopped parsley to garnish

MEXICAN TOMATO SAUCE

750 g (1 1/2 lb) ripe tomatoes, peeled (page 39), cored, and chopped

1 fresh green chilli, cored, seeded, and chopped

1/2 small onion, chopped

1 garlic clove, chopped

1 tbsp sunflower oil

salt

1 Make the Mexican tomato sauce: put the tomatoes, chilli, onion, and garlic into a food processor. Process briefly until combined but still retaining a little texture. Heat the oil in a frying pan and add the tomato mixture. Cook, stirring, for 5 minutes or until the sauce thickens. Season with salt and keep warm.

2 Put the oil in another frying pan and heat over a medium-high heat. Add the tortillas, one at a time, and fry for about 3 seconds on each side until golden. Drain on paper towels.

3 Fill each tortilla with a little tomato sauce, roll up, and arrange on a serving plate. Top with the remaining tomato sauce, and sprinkle with the cheese, chopped onion, and parsley.

Guacamole

Put the flesh of *1 large ripe avocado* into a bowl and roughly mash with a fork. Add *1/2 finely chopped onion, 1 tbsp chopped fresh coriander* and *the juice of 1 lime* and mix well. Chill for no more than 30 minutes before serving.

Mexican rice

Serves 4

1 tbsp sunflower oil

1 onion, finely chopped

200 g (7 oz) long grain rice

1 garlic clove, crushed

1 x 200 g (7 oz) can chopped tomatoes

375 ml (13 fl oz) hot chicken stock

salt and black pepper

125 g (4 oz) frozen peas, thawed and drained

30 g (1 oz) fresh coriander, chopped

1 Heat the oil in a large saucepan, add the onion and rice, and cook for 8–10 minutes, until lightly browned. Add the garlic and cook for 2 minutes.

2 Add the tomatoes and stock and season with salt and pepper. Bring to a boil, cover tightly, and simmer over a very gentle heat for 15 minutes.

3 Remove from the heat and leave to stand, still covered, for 10 minutes until all the liquid has been absorbed.

4 Stir in the peas, and sprinkle with the coriander.

Refried beans

Heat *1–2 tbsp sunflower oil* in a frying pan. Add *1/2 finely chopped onion,* and cook for 8 minutes, until lightly browned. Add *1 crushed garlic clove,* and cook for 2 minutes. Drain *1 x 400 g (13 oz) can red kidney beans,* and add to the pan. Cook over a gentle heat until warmed through, mashing the beans with a potato masher or fork and adding *1–2 tbsp water* if necessary, to prevent sticking.

Clockwise from top: *Refried Beans, Enchiladas, Steaks with Roasted Pepper Sauce, Guacamole, Mexican Rice.*

TERIYAKI BEEF

Serves 4

500 g (1 lb) rump steak, trimmed and cut into thin strips

2 tbsp sunflower oil

1 large onion, thinly sliced

1 red pepper, cored, seeded, and cut into strips

2 spring onions, sliced, to garnish

MARINADE

125 ml (4 fl oz) dark soy sauce

90 ml (3 fl oz) Japanese rice wine or dry sherry

2 tbsp caster sugar

1 Make the marinade: in a bowl, combine the soy sauce, rice wine, and sugar. Toss the steak strips in the marinade, cover, and leave in the refrigerator overnight.

2 Remove the steak strips from the marinade, reserving the marinade. Heat 1 tbsp of the oil in a wok, add the onion and red pepper, and stir-fry for about 2 minutes. Remove from the wok with a slotted spoon and set aside. Heat the remaining oil, and stir-fry the steak strips for 5 minutes or until just cooked through.

3 Return the onion and red pepper to the wok with the marinade and cook for 2 minutes or until heated through. Garnish with the spring onions before serving.

FAJITAS

This Mexican speciality features slices of steak marinated in spices, and laced with tequila. Serve with tortillas, avocado, soured cream, and pico de gallo *relish.*

Serves 4

500 g (1 lb) piece of chuck steak

8 flour tortillas

chopped coriander to garnish

1 avocado, stoned, peeled (page 336), and diced

soured cream

MARINADE

juices of 1 orange and 1 lime

2 tbsp tequila or brandy

3 garlic cloves, crushed

2 tbsp chopped fresh coriander

1 tbsp chilli powder

1 tbsp paprika

1 tsp cumin

salt and black pepper

PICO DE GALLO RELISH

6 tomatoes, peeled (page 39), seeded, and diced

10 radishes, coarsely chopped

5 spring onions, thinly sliced

1–2 green chillies, cored, seeded, and chopped

4 tbsp chopped fresh coriander

juice of 1/2 lime

1 Make the marinade: in a large bowl, combine the orange and lime juices, tequila, garlic, coriander, chilli powder, paprika, cumin, and salt and pepper to taste. Turn the steak in the marinade, cover, and leave to marinate in the refrigerator overnight.

2 Make the pico de gallo relish: in a bowl, combine the tomatoes, radishes, spring onions, chillies, coriander, lime juice, and salt to taste. Cover and chill until ready to serve.

3 Remove the steak from the marinade and pat dry. Put the steak under a hot grill, 7–10 cm (3–4 ins) from the heat, and grill for 3 minutes on each side for rare steak, 4 minutes for medium steak, or 5–6 minutes for well-done steak. Cover with foil and leave to stand for 5 minutes.

4 Meanwhile, warm the tortillas (see box, right).

5 Slice the steak, arrange on serving plates, and sprinkle with coriander. Serve with the tortillas, pico de gallo relish, diced avocado, and soured cream.

Warming tortillas

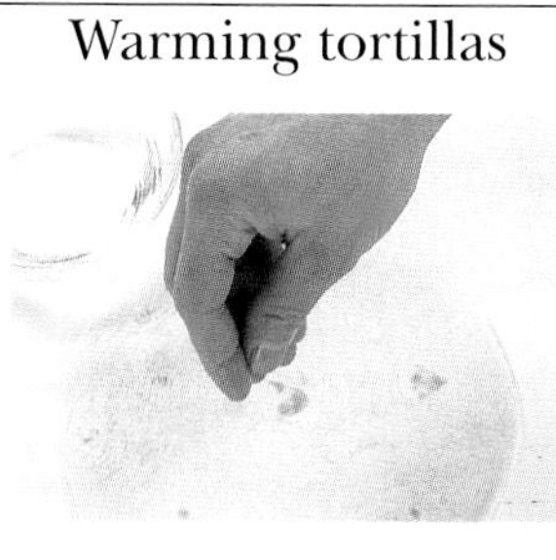

Sprinkle each tortilla with a little water, and stack the tortillas in a pile.

Wrap the tortillas in foil and warm in a preheated oven at 140°C (275°F, Gas 1) for 10 minutes.

WINTER BEEF CASSEROLE

Serves 4–6

- *2 tbsp sunflower oil*
- *1 kg (2 lb) chuck steak, trimmed and cut into 2.5 cm (1 in) cubes*
- *3 streaky bacon rashers, rinds removed, cut into strips*
- *1 large onion, chopped*
- *45 g (1½ oz) plain flour*
- *500 g (1 lb) passata*
- *450 ml (¾ pint) beef stock*
- *150 ml (¼ pint) red wine*
- *6 celery stalks, sliced*
- *250 g (8 oz) carrots, cut into thin strips*
- *1 garlic clove, crushed*
- *1 tsp chopped fresh marjoram*
- *salt and black pepper*
- *chopped parsley to garnish*

1 Heat the oil in a large flameproof casserole, add the beef and bacon, and cook over a moderate to high heat for 2–3 minutes until browned all over. Using a slotted spoon, lift out and drain on paper towels.

2 Add the onion and cook, stirring occasionally, for a few minutes until soft but not coloured.

3 Add the flour and cook, stirring, for 1 minute. Add the passata, stock, and red wine and bring to a boil, stirring until smooth and thickened. Return the meat to the casserole, add the celery, carrots, garlic, marjoram, and salt and pepper to taste, and bring back to a boil.

4 Cover and cook in a preheated oven at 160°C (325°F, Gas 3) for 2 hours or until the beef is tender. Taste for seasoning and garnish with chopped parsley before serving.

Passata

This is made from puréed, sieved tomatoes and makes an ideal base for all kinds of casseroles, sauces, and soups. It is available from most supermarkets and Italian delicatessens.

BOEUF BOURGUIGNON

Serves 4–6

- *2 tbsp sunflower oil*
- *1 kg (2 lb) chuck steak, trimmed and cut into 5 cm (2 in) cubes*
- *250 g (8 oz) thickly sliced smoked bacon, rinds removed, cut into strips*
- *12 shallots*
- *30 g (1 oz) plain flour*
- *300 ml (½ pint) red Burgundy*
- *150 ml (¼ pint) beef stock*
- *a few parsley sprigs*
- *1 thyme sprig*
- *1 bay leaf*
- *1 garlic clove, crushed*
- *salt and black pepper*
- *250 g (8 oz) button mushrooms*

1 Heat the oil in a large flameproof casserole, add the beef in batches, and cook over a high heat until browned all over. Remove with a slotted spoon and drain on paper towels.

2 Add the bacon and shallots and cook gently, stirring occasionally, for 3 minutes or until the bacon is crisp and the shallots are softened. Lift out and drain on paper towels.

3 Add the flour and cook, stirring, for 1 minute. Gradually blend in the wine and stock and bring to a boil, stirring until thickened.

4 Return the beef and bacon to the casserole, and add the parsley, thyme, bay leaf, garlic, and salt and pepper to taste. Cover and cook in a preheated oven at 160°C (325°F, Gas 3) for 1½ hours.

5 Return the shallots to the casserole, add the mushrooms, and cook for 1 hour or until the beef is very tender.

6 Remove the parsley and thyme sprigs and the bay leaf and discard. Taste the sauce for seasoning before serving.

Boeuf Bourguignon

Bourguignon describes dishes which come from the Burgundy region of central France, an area renowned for its fine red wines.

CARBONNADE OF BEEF

Serves 4–6

2 tbsp sunflower oil

1 kg (2 lb) chuck steak, trimmed and cut into 5 cm (2 in) cubes

2 large onions, sliced

1 garlic clove, crushed

2 tsp light muscovado sugar

1 tbsp plain flour

450 ml (3/4 pint) brown ale

150 ml (1/4 pint) beef stock

1 tbsp red wine vinegar

a few parsley sprigs

1 thyme sprig

1 bay leaf

salt and black pepper

thyme sprigs to garnish

MUSTARD CROUTES

1/2 baguette, cut into 1.25 cm (1/2 in) slices

Dijon mustard for spreading

1 Heat the oil in a large flameproof casserole, add the beef in batches, and cook over a high heat for a few minutes until browned. Lift out with a slotted spoon. Lower the heat and add the onions, garlic, and sugar. Cook, stirring, for 4 minutes or until browned.

2 Add the flour and cook, stirring, for 1 minute. Add the brown ale and stock, and bring to a boil, stirring until thickened.

3 Return the meat to the casserole, and add the red wine vinegar, parsley sprigs, thyme sprig, bay leaf, and salt and pepper to taste. Bring back to a boil, cover, and cook in a preheated oven at 150°C (300°F, Gas 2) for 2 1/2 hours or until the meat is really tender. Remove the herbs and discard. Taste for seasoning.

4 Increase the oven temperature to 190°C (375°F, Gas 5). Make the croûtes (see box, below).

5 Return the casserole to the oven, uncovered, for 10 minutes or until the croûtes are just crisp. Garnish with thyme sprigs before serving.

Making croûtes

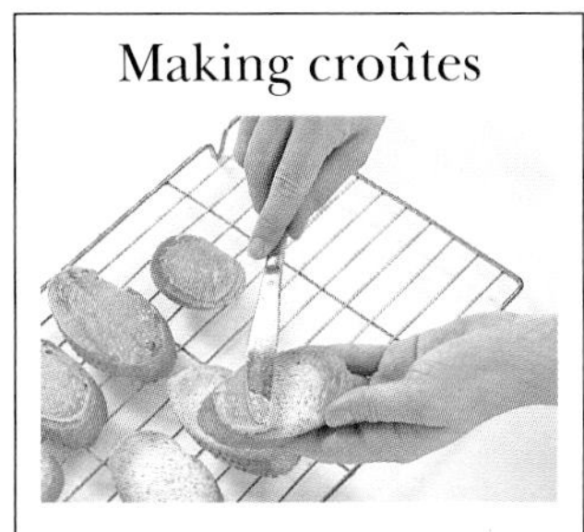

Toast the slices of baguette on both sides and spread one side with mustard. Put the croûtes, mustard-side up, on top of the casserole and baste with the sauce.

HUNGARIAN GOULASH

Serves 4–6

2 tbsp sunflower oil

1 kg (2 lb) chuck steak, trimmed and cut into 5 cm (2 in) cubes

2 large onions, sliced

1 garlic clove, crushed

1 tbsp plain flour

1 tbsp paprika

600 ml (1 pint) beef stock

1 x 400 g (13 oz) can tomatoes

2 tbsp tomato purée

salt and black pepper

2 large red peppers, cored, seeded, and cut into 2.5 cm (1 in) pieces

4 potatoes, peeled and quartered

150 ml (1/4 pint) soured cream

paprika to garnish

1 Heat the sunflower oil in a large flameproof casserole, add the beef in batches, and cook over a high heat until browned.

2 Lift out the beef with a slotted spoon. Lower the heat slightly, add the onions and garlic, and cook gently, stirring occasionally, for a few minutes until soft but not coloured.

3 Add the flour and paprika and cook, stirring, for 1 minute. Pour in the stock and bring to a boil, stirring until thickened.

4 Return the meat to the casserole and add the tomatoes, tomato purée, and salt and pepper to taste. Bring back to a boil, cover, and cook in a preheated oven at 160°C (325°F, Gas 3) for 1 hour.

5 Add the red peppers and potatoes and return the casserole to the oven for 1 hour or until the potatoes and meat are tender.

6 Taste for seasoning, and stir in the soured cream. Sprinkle with a little paprika before serving.

CHIANTI BEEF CASSEROLE

Serves 4–6

1 kg (2 lb) chuck steak, trimmed and cut into 5 cm (2 in) cubes
3 tbsp olive oil
30 g (1 oz) plain flour
300 ml (1/2 pint) beef stock
60 g (2 oz) sun-dried tomatoes, roughly chopped
1 x 400 g (13 oz) can artichoke hearts, drained and halved
1 x 185 g (6 1/2 oz) can pitted black olives, drained
thyme sprigs to garnish

MARINADE

75 cl bottle of Chianti
3 tbsp olive oil
2 tbsp tomato purée
1 large onion, chopped
2 garlic cloves, crushed
a few thyme sprigs
salt and black pepper

1 Make the marinade: in a large bowl, combine the Chianti, oil, tomato purée, onion, garlic, thyme, and salt and pepper to taste. Toss the beef in the marinade, cover, and leave to marinate in the refrigerator overnight.

2 Remove the beef from the marinade, reserving the marinade. Heat the oil in a large flameproof casserole, add the beef in batches, and cook over a high heat until browned. Remove the beef.

3 Add the flour and cook, stirring, for 1 minute. Pour in the marinade and stock and bring to a boil, stirring until thickened. Return the beef to the casserole and add the sun-dried tomatoes. Bring back to a boil, cover, and cook in a preheated oven at 160°C (325°F, Gas 3) for 2 hours.

4 Add the artichokes and olives and return to the oven for 15 minutes. Taste for seasoning and garnish with thyme before serving.

Chianti

This is a fruity Italian red wine, well known for the raffia-covered bottles in which it is often sold.

LATIMER BEEF WITH HORSERADISH

Serves 4–6

2 tbsp sunflower oil
1 kg (2 lb) chuck steak, trimmed and cut into strips
12 shallots or button onions
30 g (1 oz) plain flour
2 tsp mild curry powder
2 tsp light muscovado sugar
1 tsp ground ginger
600 ml (1 pint) beef stock
2 tbsp Worcestershire sauce
salt and black pepper
3 tbsp chopped parsley
2 tbsp horseradish cream
extra chopped parsley to garnish

1 Heat the sunflower oil in a large flameproof casserole, and cook the beef strips over a high heat until browned all over. Lift out with a slotted spoon and drain on paper towels.

2 Lower the heat, add the shallots, and cook gently, stirring occasionally, for a few minutes until softened. Lift out with a slotted spoon and drain on paper towels.

3 Add the flour, curry powder, sugar, and ginger to the casserole and cook, stirring, for 1 minute. Pour in the stock and bring to a boil, stirring until smooth and thickened. Add the Worcestershire sauce, and salt and pepper to taste, and return to a boil.

4 Return the beef and shallots to the casserole and stir in the parsley. Bring back to a boil, cover, and cook in a preheated oven at 160°C (325°F, Gas 3) for 2–2 1/2 hours until the meat is tender.

5 To serve, stir in the horseradish cream, taste for seasoning, and garnish with parsley.

Cook's know-how

Horseradish cream is a simple blend of grated horseradish, cream, vinegar, and seasoning. It is widely available in jars at large supermarkets and delicatessens.

THAI RED BEEF CURRY

Serves 4–6

3 tbsp sunflower oil

1 kg (2 lb) chuck steak, trimmed and cut into 2.5 cm (1 in) cubes

8 cardamom pods, split

2.5 cm (1 in) piece of cinnamon stick

2 bay leaves

6 cloves

8 black peppercorns

1 large onion, chopped

5 cm (2 in) piece of fresh root ginger, peeled and grated

4 garlic cloves, crushed

4 tsp paprika

2 tsp cumin seeds, coarsely ground

1 tsp coriander seeds, coarsely ground

1 tsp salt

1/2 tsp cayenne pepper

600 ml (1 pint) water

90 g (3 oz) plain yogurt

1 x 400 g (13 oz) can chopped tomatoes

1 large red pepper, cored, seeded, and cut into chunks

1 Heat the oil in a large flameproof casserole, add the beef in batches, and cook over a high heat until browned all over. Lift out with a slotted spoon and drain on paper towels.

2 Add the cardamom pods, cinnamon stick, bay leaves, cloves, and peppercorns, and cook over a high heat, stirring, for 1 minute. Remove from the pan and tie in a muslin bag.

3 Add the onion to the pan and cook over a high heat, stirring, for about 3 minutes until beginning to brown. Add the ginger, garlic, paprika, cumin and coriander seeds, salt, cayenne pepper, and 4 tbsp of the water. Cook, stirring, for about 1 minute.

4 Return the beef and spices to the casserole, then gradually add the yogurt, stirring. Stir in the remaining water. Add the tomatoes and red pepper, and bring to a boil. Cover and cook in a preheated oven at 160°C (325°F, Gas 3) for 2 hours or until tender. Remove the bag of spices before serving.

Cook's know-how

Many curries benefit from being made a day in advance and left overnight. This brings out their flavours and allows them to permeate the meat. Ensure the dish is well heated before serving.

COUNTRY BEEF CASSEROLE

Serves 6–8

3 tbsp sunflower oil

1 kg (2 lb) chuck steak, trimmed and cut into 5 cm (2 in) cubes

500 g (1 lb) carrots, thickly sliced

250 g (8 oz) turnips, cut into large chunks

250 g (8 oz) parsnips, thickly sliced

2 onions, sliced

1 large leek, sliced

1 tbsp plain flour

600 ml (1 pint) beef stock

1 x 400 g (13 oz) can chopped tomatoes

2 tbsp chopped fresh herbs, such as parsley and thyme

1 large bay leaf

salt and black pepper

herb dumplings (see box, right)

1 Heat the oil in a large flameproof casserole, add the beef in batches, and cook over a high heat until browned. Lift out the beef with a slotted spoon.

2 Add the carrots, turnips, parsnips, onions, and leek, and cook over a high heat, stirring occasionally, for 5 minutes or until the vegetables are softened.

3 Add the flour and cook, stirring, for 1 minute. Add the stock, tomatoes, half of the herbs, and salt and pepper to taste, and bring to a boil. Return the meat to the casserole and bring to a boil. Cover and cook in a preheated oven at 160°C (325°F, Gas 3) for 2 hours.

4 Place the dumplings on the meat. Increase the oven temperature to 190°C (375°F, Gas 5) and cook for 20–25 minutes until the dumplings are firm. Sprinkle with the remaining herbs before serving.

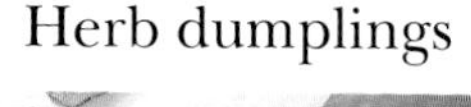

Herb dumplings

Sift *125 g (4 oz) self-raising flour* into a bowl, and add *60 g (2 oz) shredded vegetable suet, 1 tbsp chopped fresh thyme or parsley,* and *salt and pepper.* Add *4–5 tbsp water* to make a soft dough. Shape into 12–16 balls with your hands.

CHILLI CON CARNE

Serves 4

- *250 g (8 oz) dried red kidney beans*
- *2 tbsp sunflower oil*
- *750 g (1½ lb) chuck steak, trimmed and cut into 3.5 cm (1½ in) cubes*
- *2 onions, chopped*
- *2 fresh red chillies, cored, seeded, and finely chopped*
- *1 garlic clove, crushed*
- *1 tbsp plain flour*
- *900 ml (1½ pints) beef stock*
- *2 tbsp tomato purée*
- *1 square of plain chocolate, grated*
- *salt and black pepper*
- *1 large red pepper, cored, seeded, and cut into chunks*
- *chopped coriander to garnish*

1 Put the red kidney beans into a large bowl, cover generously with cold water, and leave to soak overnight.

2 Drain the beans, rinse under cold running water, and drain again. Put the beans into a large saucepan. Cover with cold water, bring to a boil, and boil rapidly for 10 minutes. Lower the heat and simmer, partially covered, for 50 minutes or until the beans are just tender. Drain.

3 Heat the oil in a large flameproof casserole. Add the beef and cook in batches over a high heat for 5–7 minutes until browned. Lift out with a slotted spoon.

4 Lower the heat, add the onions, chillies, and garlic, and cook, stirring occasionally, for a few minutes until softened.

5 Add the flour and cook, stirring, for 1 minute. Add the stock, tomato purée, chocolate, and salt and pepper to taste. Return the beef to the casserole, add the beans, and bring to a boil. Cover and cook in a preheated oven at 150°C (300°F, Gas 2) for 1½ hours.

6 Add the red pepper and cook for 30 minutes. Taste for seasoning, and garnish with coriander.

QUICK CHILLI CON CARNE

Substitute 1 x 400 g (13 oz) can red kidney beans for the dried beans, and minced beef for the chuck steak. Simmer gently on top of the stove for 45 minutes.

BEEF OLIVES WITH VEGETABLE JULIENNE

Serves 4

- *8 thin slices of beef topside, total weight about 750 g (1½ lb)*
- *2 tbsp sunflower oil*
- *375 g (12 oz) piece of celeriac, peeled and cut into matchstick-thin strips*
- *250 g (8 oz) carrots, cut into matchstick-thin strips*
- *2 small leeks, cut into matchstick-thin strips*
- *salt and black pepper*
- *30 g (1 oz) plain flour*
- *1 onion, sliced*
- *1 garlic clove, sliced*
- *450 ml (¾ pint) beef stock*

1 Put each slice of topside between 2 sheets of greaseproof paper and pound to a 3 mm (⅛ in) thickness with a rolling pin.

2 Heat 1 tbsp of the oil in a large frying pan, add the celeriac, carrots, and leeks, and stir-fry over a high heat for 1 minute. Add salt and pepper to taste, then lift out and drain. Leave to cool.

3 Divide the vegetables among the beef slices. Roll up and secure with wooden cocktail sticks.

4 Lightly coat the beef olives in half of the flour, shaking off any excess. Heat the remaining oil in a flameproof casserole, add the beef olives, and cook over a high heat for 5–7 minutes until browned. Lift out with a slotted spoon.

5 Add the onion and garlic and cook gently until softened. Add the remaining flour and cook, stirring, for 1 minute. Gradually blend in the stock, add salt and pepper to taste, and bring to a boil, stirring until thick.

6 Return the beef olives to the casserole, bring back to a boil, cover, and cook in a preheated oven at 180°C (350°F, Gas 4) for 1½ hours. Lift out the beef olives and remove the cocktail sticks. Slice and arrange on serving plates. Work the sauce through a sieve, and serve with the beef olives.

Beef olives

This refers to any dish of beef slices wrapped around a savoury stuffing.

CORNED BEEF HASH

 **Serves 2–3**

60 g (2 oz) butter

1 large onion, chopped

750 g (1½ lb) potatoes, cut into small chunks

300 ml (½ pint) beef stock

salt and black pepper

1 x 325 g (11 oz) can corned beef, cut into chunks

chopped parsley to garnish

1 Melt the butter in a large frying pan, add the onion, and cook gently, stirring occasionally, for a few minutes until softened.

2 Add the potatoes and stir to coat in the butter. Pour in the stock, and add salt and pepper to taste. Simmer for 10–15 minutes until the potatoes are tender and the stock absorbed.

3 Gently stir in the corned beef and heat to warm through. Put the pan under a hot grill, 7 cm (3 ins) from the heat, to brown the top. Garnish with chopped parsley before serving.

Cook's know-how

Corned beef hash can be made ahead and then re-fried to warm through. You can add other vegetables, or a splash of Worcestershire sauce or Tabasco sauce, or top each portion with a fried egg, if you like.

TRADITIONAL STEAK & KIDNEY PIE

This pie is a family favourite, with its tender steak and kidney filling and shortcrust pastry topping. For convenience, the meat can be cooked a day in advance, then all you have to do on the day of serving is make the pastry and pop the pie in the oven.

Serves 4–6

2 tbsp sunflower oil

1 large onion, chopped

750 g (1½ lb) beef skirt, cut into 2.5 cm (1 in) cubes

250 g (8 oz) beef kidney, trimmed (page 214), and cut into 2.5 cm (1 in) cubes

30 g (1 oz) plain flour

300 ml (½ pint) beef stock

½ tsp Worcestershire sauce

salt and black pepper

250 g (8 oz) button mushrooms

beaten egg for glazing

SHORTCRUST PASTRY

250 g (8 oz) plain flour

125 g (4 oz) butter

about 3 tbsp cold water

1 Heat the oil in a large saucepan, add the onion, and cook, stirring from time to time, for a few minutes until soft but not coloured.

2 Add the beef and kidney and cook until browned. Add the flour and cook, stirring, for 1 minute. Add the stock, Worcestershire sauce, and salt and pepper to taste, and bring to a boil, stirring. Partially cover, and simmer gently for 1½ hours.

3 Add the mushrooms and cook for 30 minutes or until the meat is tender. Taste for seasoning, then leave to cool completely.

4 Make the pastry: sift the flour into a bowl. Add the butter and rub in lightly with your fingertips until the mixture looks like fine breadcrumbs. Add the water and mix with a flat-bladed knife until the dough comes together to form a ball.

5 Roll out the pastry on a floured work surface until 2.5 cm (1 in) larger than the pie dish. Invert the dish over the pastry and cut around the dish. Brush the rim of the dish with water and press on a strip of pastry cut from the trimmings.

6 Put a pie funnel into the middle of the dish, then spoon in the meat mixture.

7 Lightly brush the pastry strip with water and top with the pastry lid. Seal the edges and crimp with a fork. Make a hole in the pastry lid above the pie funnel to let the steam escape, and decorate with pastry trimmings, attaching them with beaten egg.

8 Brush the pastry all over with beaten egg, and bake in a preheated oven at 200°C (400°F, Gas 6) for 25–30 minutes until the pastry is crisp and golden. Serve at once.

STEAK & KIDNEY PUDDING

Mix 300 g (10 oz) self-raising flour, 150 g (5 oz) shredded suet, salt and pepper, and 200 ml (7 fl oz) water. Use ¾ pastry to line a 1.7 litre (3 pint) basin. Add the uncooked filling, top with pastry, and steam for 5 hours.

BEEF FLORENTINE

Ready-made filo pastry provides a quick and easy way to cover a pie, and it gives a lovely crisp, golden topping. In this dish it is cooked with a delicious combination of minced beef in tomato sauce, and fresh spinach mixed with three types of cheese.

 **Serves 8**

11 sheets of filo pastry
60 g (2 oz) butter, melted

BEEF LAYER

30 g (1 oz) butter
1 kg (2 lb) lean minced beef
1 tbsp plain flour
1 x 400 g (13 oz) can chopped tomatoes
2 tbsp tomato purée
2 garlic cloves, crushed
1 tsp caster sugar
salt and black pepper

SPINACH & CHEESE LAYER

625 g (1¼ lb) spinach, tough stalks removed, roughly chopped
90 g (3 oz) mature Cheddar cheese, grated
90 g (3 oz) Gruyère or Emmental cheese, grated
125 g (4 oz) full-fat soft cheese
2 eggs, lightly beaten

1 Prepare the beef layer: melt the butter in a large saucepan, add the minced beef, and cook, stirring, for 10–15 minutes or until the meat is browned all over.

2 Add the flour and cook, stirring, for 1 minute. Add the tomatoes, tomato purée, garlic, sugar, and salt and pepper to taste, and bring to a boil. Cover and simmer, stirring occasionally, for 35 minutes. Taste for seasoning.

3 Meanwhile, prepare the spinach and cheese layer: wash the spinach and put it into a large saucepan with only the water that clings to the leaves. Cook over a gentle heat until the spinach has just wilted. Drain thoroughly, squeezing to remove excess water. Mix the spinach with the Cheddar, Gruyère, soft cheese, eggs, and salt and pepper to taste.

4 Spoon the beef mixture into a shallow ovenproof dish, then spoon the spinach mixture over the top.

5 Prepare the filo topping (see box, right).

6 Bake in a preheated oven at 200°C (400°F, Gas 6) for 20–25 minutes until the filo pastry is crisp and golden. Serve at once.

Preparing the filo topping

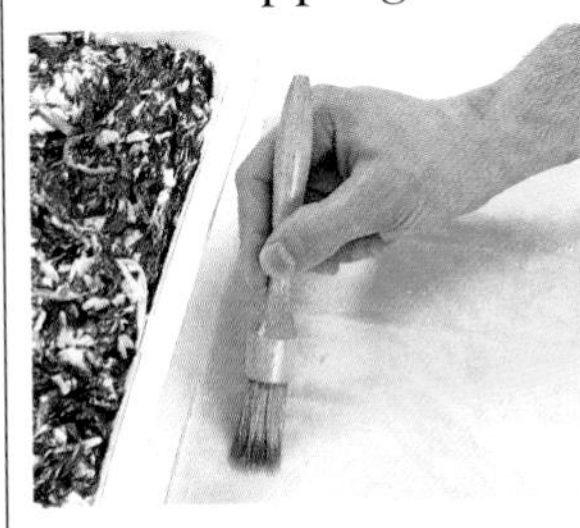

Brush 3 of the filo pastry sheets with a little of the melted butter and layer them on top of the spinach mixture, trimming to fit the dish if necessary.

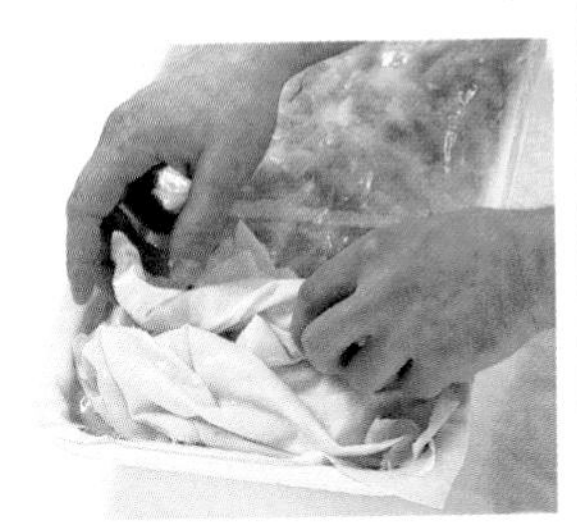

Arrange the remaining 8 filo pastry sheets over the dish, lightly brushing with a little butter and scrunching each one up, in order to completely cover the lower layer of filo pastry.

MEATBALLS IN CIDER

Serves 4

250 g (8 oz) minced beef
125 g (4 oz) minced pork
salt and black pepper
plain flour for dusting
2 tbsp sunflower oil
2 large onions, sliced
1 garlic clove, crushed
300 ml (½ pint) dry cider
3 tbsp tomato purée
4 celery stalks, thickly sliced
1 large red pepper, cored, seeded, and cut into strips
125 g (4 oz) mushrooms, sliced
2 tsp caster sugar

1 Mix together the beef and pork, and add salt and pepper to taste. On a floured work surface, shape into 16 even-sized balls.

2 Heat the oil in a flameproof casserole, add the meatballs, and cook over a high heat until browned. Remove and drain on paper towels. Lower the heat, add the onions and garlic, and cook gently, stirring occasionally, for a few minutes until softened.

3 Return the meatballs to the casserole, add the cider, tomato purée, celery, red pepper, mushrooms, sugar, and salt and pepper to taste, and bring to a boil. Cover and simmer for 20 minutes or until the meatballs are cooked through. Serve at once.

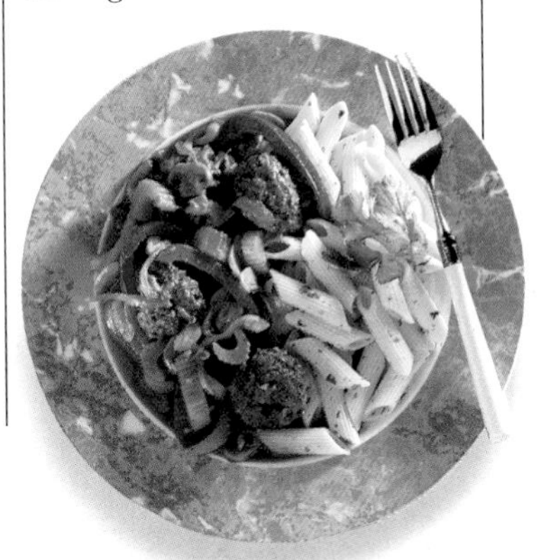

Hamburgers

Hamburgers, especially home-made ones, are hard to resist, but there's no need to stick to the basic minced beef on a burger bun every time. All kinds of meat can be used, and by adding different flavourings, serving burgers on a variety of breads and rolls, and topping them with tasty sauces, the possibilities are limitless.

Roquefort beef burgers

Serves 4

500 g (1 lb) lean minced beef

5 shallots, finely chopped

salt and black pepper

125 g (6 oz) Roquefort or other blue cheese, cut into slices

ciabatta and green salad to serve

1 Put the minced beef and shallots into a bowl, season, and mix well.

2 Divide the mixture into 8 balls, then flatten each ball to form a thin patty. Place a slice of cheese on top of half of the patties, then top with the remaining patties. Press the edges together to enclose the filling.

3 Cook the burgers over a medium heat for 3–4 minutes on each side until the burgers are brown and feel firm when pressed.

4 Serve the burgers on toasted sliced ciabatta, accompanied by a tossed green salad.

Provençal pork burgers

Serves 4

500 g (1 lb) minced pork

juice of 1/2 lemon

2–3 tbsp olive oil

1/4 tsp herbes de Provence

1/2 onion, finely chopped

90 g (3 oz) garlic and herb cream cheese

1/2 tsp each fennel seeds and dried oregano

salt and black pepper

baguette, sliced tomatoes, and pitted black olives to serve

1 Put the minced pork into a bowl with the lemon juice, oil, herbes de Provence, onion, cream cheese, fennel seeds, oregano, and salt and pepper to taste, and mix well. Divide the mixture into 4 balls and flatten to form patties.

2 Cook the burgers over a medium heat for 3–4 minutes on each side until browned and firm when pressed. Serve between slices of baguette with tomatoes and olives.

Turkish lamb burgers

Serves 4

500 g (1 lb) minced lamb

4 garlic cloves, crushed

60 g (2 oz) fresh breadcrumbs

1 tbsp each chopped fresh coriander and plain yogurt

1 tsp each ground cumin, paprika, curry powder, and tomato purée

1/4 tsp each ground cinnamon, turmeric, and salt

pita bread, plain yogurt, mint, and cucumber slices to serve

1 Put the minced lamb into a bowl with the remaining ingredients and mix well. Shape into 4 patties.

2 Put under a hot grill, 10 cm (4 ins) from the heat, and cook for 3–4 minutes on each side until browned and firm. Serve in pita bread with yogurt, mint, and cucumber slices.

Clockwise from top: *Turkish Lamb Burgers, Roquefort Beef Burgers, Provençal Pork Burgers.*

Toppings for hamburgers

Aubergine & fennel

Slice *1/2 aubergine* and *1 fennel bulb* and brush with *olive oil.* Cook under a hot grill, 10 cm (4 ins) from the heat, for 3–5 minutes on each side until lightly browned and tender. Cut into strips and put into a bowl. Mix together *2 tbsp olive oil, the juice of 1/2 lemon, 1/4 tsp herbes de Provence* and *salt and pepper to taste.* Pour over the aubergine and fennel strips and stir to coat. Serve hot or cold.

Chilli aioli

In a small bowl, combine *2 egg yolks , 1 tbsp lemon juice, 1 tsp Dijon mustard,* and *salt and pepper to taste,* and whisk until thick. Gradually add *250 ml (8 fl oz) olive oil,* whisking constantly until the mixture is very thick. Stir in *1 crushed garlic clove, 1/2 tsp chilli powder,* and *1/4 tsp ground cumin.* Taste for seasoning. Cover and leave to chill in the refrigerator until ready to serve.

Barbecue sauce

Heat *1 tbsp sunflower oil* in a saucepan and cook *1 finely chopped onion* and *1 crushed garlic clove* until soft but not coloured. Add *1 x 400 g (13 oz) can chopped tomatoes, 2 tbsp water, 2 tbsp lemon juice, 1 tbsp brown sugar, 1 tbsp Worcestershire sauce, 2 tsp Dijon mustard, 1/2 tsp paprika, 1/2 tsp chilli powder,* and *salt and pepper to taste.* Bring to a boil, and simmer for 20 minutes. Serve warm.

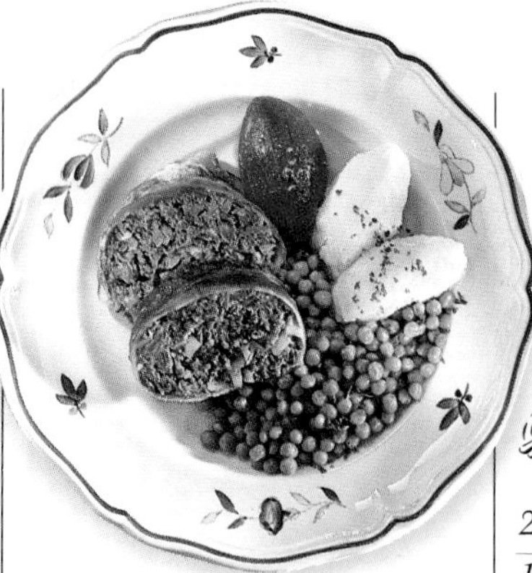

MEAT LOAF

Serves 4–6

750 g (1½ lb) minced beef
1 x 400 g (13 oz) can chopped tomatoes
90 g (3 oz) herby stuffing mix
1 onion, chopped
1 carrot, coarsely shredded
3 garlic cloves, crushed
2 tbsp chopped parsley
1 egg, beaten
1 tbsp Worcestershire sauce
salt and black pepper
4–5 streaky bacon rashers, rinds removed
★ 1 kg (2 lb) loaf tin

1 Combine the minced beef, tomatoes, stuffing mix, onion, carrot, garlic, parsley, beaten egg, Worcestershire sauce, and salt and pepper to taste.

2 Arrange bacon rashers crosswise in the loaf tin, letting them hang over the sides. Put the beef mixture into the tin and fold over the bacon. Turn the loaf out into a roasting tin and bake in a preheated oven at 190°C (375°F, Gas 5), basting once or twice, for 1 hour.

3 Increase the heat to 230°C (450°F, Gas 8) and bake for 15 minutes or until the meat loaf is firm. Spoon off any fat, slice the meat loaf, and serve hot.

COTTAGE PIES WITH CHEESY POTATO TOPPING

A savoury mixture of minced beef and vegetables lies beneath a lightly browned topping of cheesy mashed potato. Cook it in 4 small dishes if you have them, then everyone can have an individual pie.

Serves 4

2 tbsp sunflower oil
1 large onion, finely chopped
1 celery stalk, finely chopped
1 large carrot, finely chopped
750 g (1½ lb) minced beef
2 tsp plain flour
300 ml (½ pint) beef stock
1 tbsp tomato purée
2 tbsp Worcestershire sauce
salt and black pepper

TOPPING

750 g (1½ lb) potatoes, cut into chunks
30 g (1 oz) butter
2–3 tbsp hot milk
125 g (4 oz) mature Cheddar cheese, grated

1 Heat the oil in a large saucepan, add the onion, celery, and carrot, and cook for 3 minutes. Add the minced beef, and cook for 5 minutes or until browned.

2 Add the flour and cook, stirring, for 1 minute. Add the stock, tomato purée, Worcestershire sauce, and salt and pepper to taste, and bring to a boil. Cover and simmer, stirring occasionally, for 45 minutes.

3 Meanwhile, prepare the potato topping: cook the potatoes in boiling salted water for 20 minutes or until tender. Drain. Add the butter and milk to the potatoes, and mash until soft. Add salt and pepper to taste, and stir in the cheese.

4 Spoon the minced beef mixture into 4 individual ovenproof dishes, or 1 large dish, and cover with the mashed potato mixture (see box, right). Cook the pies in a preheated oven at 200°C (400°F, Gas 6) for 20–25 minutes until the potato topping is golden brown and the meat mixture is bubbling. Serve hot.

Covering the pies

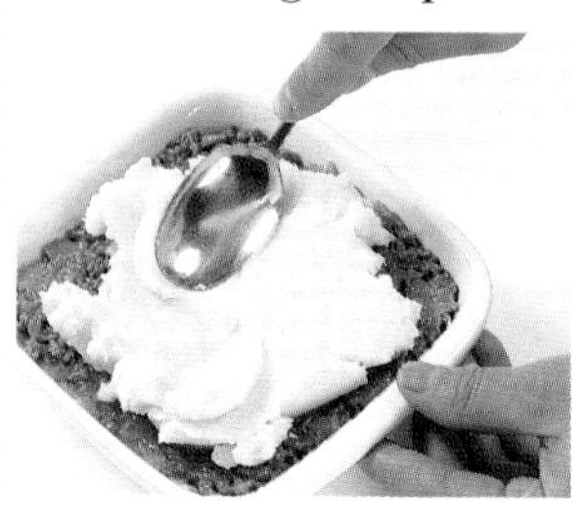

Spoon the mashed potato on to the beef mixture, and spread over the top to cover completely.

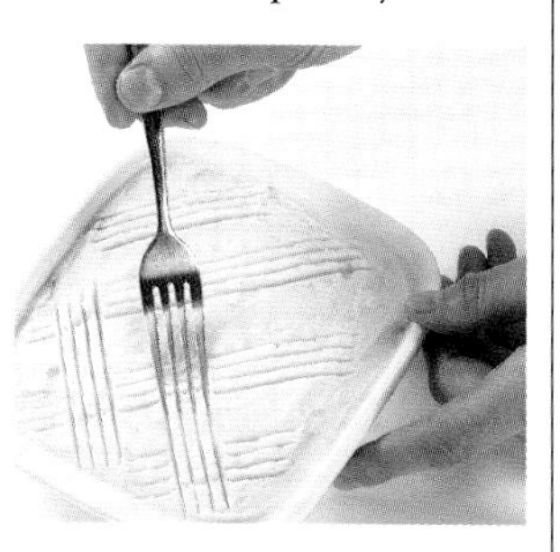

Score the surface of the mashed potato, using a fork, to make a decorative topping.

BOBOTIE

Serves 6–8

1 slice of white bread, crusts removed
300 ml (1/2 pint) milk
30 g (1 oz) butter
1 large onion, chopped
2 garlic cloves, crushed
1 kg (2 lb) minced beef
1 tbsp medium-hot curry powder
90 g (3 oz) ready-to-eat dried apricots, coarsely chopped
90 g (3 oz) blanched almonds, coarsely chopped
2 tbsp fruit chutney
1 tbsp lemon juice
salt and black pepper
2 eggs
30 g (1 oz) flaked almonds

1 Put the bread into a shallow dish. Sprinkle over 2 tbsp of the milk and leave to soak for 5 minutes.

2 Meanwhile, melt the butter in a large frying pan, add the onion and garlic, and cook gently, stirring occasionally, for a few minutes until soft.

3 Increase the heat, add the minced beef, and cook, stirring, for 5 minutes or until browned. Spoon any excess fat from the pan.

4 Add the curry powder and cook, stirring, for 2 minutes. Add the chopped apricots and almonds, the chutney, lemon juice, and salt and pepper to taste.

5 Mash the bread with the milk in the dish, then stir into the minced beef mixture. Turn into an ovenproof dish and bake in a preheated oven at 180°C (350°F, Gas 4) for 35 minutes.

6 Break the eggs into a bowl, and whisk in the remaining milk, and salt and pepper to taste. Pour over the minced beef mixture, sprinkle with the almonds, and bake for 25–30 minutes until the topping is set.

BEEF TACOS

Serves 4

1 tbsp sunflower oil
375 g (12 oz) minced beef
1 onion, chopped
3 garlic cloves, crushed
1 tsp mild chilli powder
1 tsp paprika
1/2 tsp ground cumin
3 ripe tomatoes, peeled (page 39), seeded, and diced
salt and black pepper
1 fresh green chilli, cored, seeded, and thinly sliced
2 tbsp chopped fresh coriander
8 taco shells
8 lettuce leaves, finely shredded
4 tbsp soured cream
chopped coriander to garnish

1 Heat the oil in a large frying pan, add the minced beef, onion, and garlic, and cook, stirring, for 5 minutes or until the beef is browned and the onion and garlic are softened.

2 Add the chilli powder, paprika, and cumin, and cook, stirring, for 2 minutes. Stir in the tomatoes, cover, and cook over a medium heat for 5 minutes. Add salt and pepper to taste, remove from the heat, and stir in the chilli and coriander.

3 Place the taco shells on a baking tray, and heat in a preheated oven at 180°C (350°F, Gas 4) for 2–3 minutes or according to packet instructions.

4 Fill the taco shells (see box, below), and serve at once.

Filling taco shells

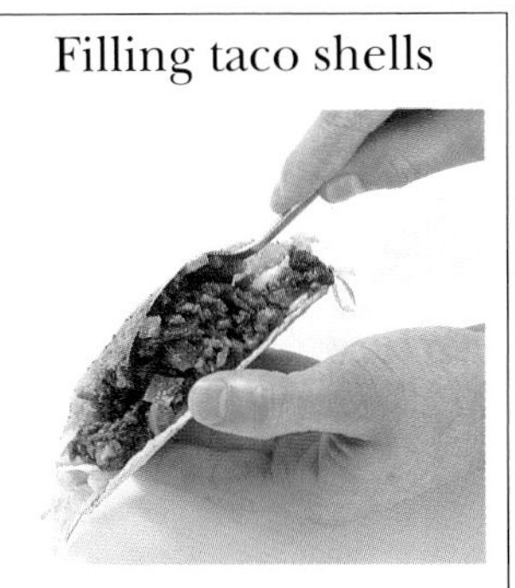

Holding each shell in one hand, put a layer of shredded lettuce into the bottom. Add a generous spoonful of the meat mixture and top with soured cream and a sprinkling of chopped coriander.

Pressed tongue

Serves 10

2–2.5 kg (4–5 lb) salted ox tongue, trimmed
1 onion, quartered
1 bay leaf
1 tbsp gelatine
3 tbsp cold water
⭑ 15 cm (6 in) round cake tin

1 Put the ox tongue, onion, and bay leaf into a large saucepan, cover with cold water, and bring to a boil. Simmer very gently for 3–4 hours until tender. Test the water after 2 hours; if it is very salty, replace it with fresh water.

2 Lift the tongue out of the saucepan, reserving the cooking liquid, and leave to cool slightly. Remove and discard the skin, then cut the tongue in half lengthwise.

3 Sprinkle the gelatine over the measured water in a small bowl. Leave to stand for 3 minutes or until the gelatine is spongy. Put the bowl into a saucepan of gently simmering water and leave for 3 minutes or until the gelatine has dissolved.

4 Add 150 ml (¼ pint) of the cooking liquid to the gelatine and mix well.

5 Arrange one half of the tongue, cut-side down, in the cake tin, and put in the other half, cut-side up. Cover with the gelatine mixture (see box, below). Cover with a small plate and weigh down with weights or heavy cans. Chill in the refrigerator overnight.

6 Dip the base of the cake tin into a bowl of hot water, just long enough to melt the jelly slightly and free it from the edges of the tin. Serve the tongue very thinly sliced.

Covering with gelatine

Pour the gelatine mixture over the tongue, until well covered.

Oxtail stew

Serves 4

1 tbsp sunflower oil
1.25 kg (2½ lb) oxtail, cut into 5 cm (2 in) slices and trimmed
30 g (1 oz) plain flour
900 ml (1½ pints) beef stock
2 large onions, sliced
1 tbsp tomato purée
1 tbsp chopped parsley
1 tbsp chopped fresh thyme
1 bay leaf
salt and black pepper
8 celery stalks, thickly sliced
chopped parsley to garnish

1 Heat the oil in a large flameproof casserole, add the oxtail, and cook over a high heat for 10 minutes or until browned all over. Remove the oxtail and drain on paper towels.

2 Add the flour and cook, stirring occasionally, for about 1 minute. Blend in the beef stock and bring to a boil, stirring until the sauce has thickened.

3 Return the oxtail to the casserole, add the onions, tomato purée, parsley, thyme, bay leaf, and salt and pepper to taste, and bring to a boil. Cover and simmer gently for 2 hours.

4 Add the celery and cook for a further 1½–2 hours until the meat can be easily removed from the bones. Skim any fat from the top of the casserole, then taste for seasoning. Sprinkle with parsley before serving.

Cook's know-how

Oxtail stew needs long, slow cooking to develop its rich brown gravy and to make the meat so soft that it falls off the bone. If possible, make the stew the day before serving; the excess fat can then be easily lifted from the surface of the cooled stew. If you make the stew with lots of sauce, this can be used, thinned down and with added vegetables, for a tasty soup.

LEMON ROAST VEAL WITH SPINACH STUFFING

Veal can be quite dry, because it is so lean. Marinating the joint for 2 days before roasting makes it more succulent.

Serves 4–6

1.25 kg (2½ lb) boned veal roasting joint, such as loin
150 ml (¼ pint) dry white wine
150 ml (¼ pint) chicken stock

MARINADE

3 tbsp olive oil
grated zest and juice of 1 lemon
4 thyme sprigs
black pepper

STUFFING

30 g (1 oz) butter
1 shallot, finely chopped
2 streaky bacon rashers, rinds removed, finely chopped
175 g (6 oz) spinach leaves, coarsely shredded
grated zest of 1 lemon
60 g (2 oz) fresh brown breadcrumbs
salt and black pepper
1 small egg, lightly beaten

1 Combine the marinade ingredients. Turn the veal in the marinade, cover, and leave to marinate in the refrigerator for 2 days.

2 Make the stuffing: melt the butter, add the shallot and bacon, and cook for 5 minutes or until the shallot is softened. Stir in the spinach and cook for 1 minute. Remove from the heat, and add the lemon zest, breadcrumbs, and salt and pepper to taste. Mix well, then bind with the egg. Leave to cool completely.

3 Remove the veal from the marinade, reserving the marinade. Spread the stuffing over the veal and roll up (see box, right).

4 Weigh the veal, insert a meat thermometer, if using, into the middle of the meat, and place in a roasting tin. Pour the marinade around the meat. Roast in a preheated oven at 180°C (350°F, Gas 4) for 25 minutes per 500 g (1 lb), until the juices run clear or until the thermometer registers 75°C (170°F). Transfer to a platter, cover loosely with foil, and leave to stand in a warm place for 10 minutes.

5 Meanwhile, spoon the fat from the tin, and remove the thyme sprigs. Put the tin on top of the stove, add the wine and stock, and bring to a boil, stirring to dissolve the sediment from the bottom of the tin. Boil for 5 minutes or until thickened and reduced by about half.

6 Taste the gravy for seasoning, and pour into a warmed gravy boat. Carve the veal, and serve at once.

Rolling up the veal

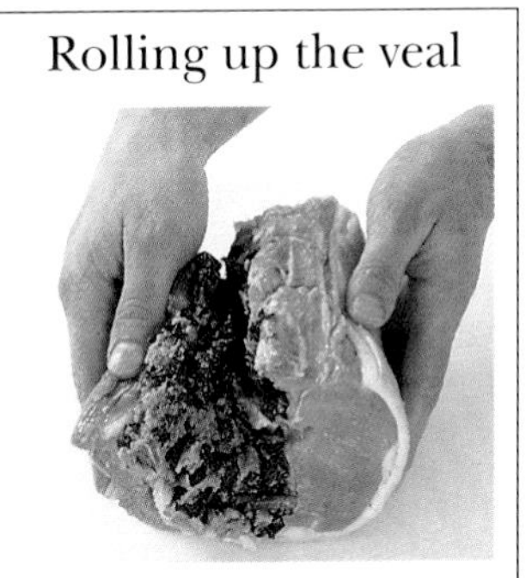

Bring the 2 sides of the veal together, enclosing the stuffing completely. Tie fine string around the veal to secure.

GRAVIES FOR MEAT

MUSHROOM GRAVY

Melt *30 g (1 oz) butter* in a saucepan. Add *1 finely chopped shallot* and cook for 2 minutes until softened. Add *250 g (8 oz) sliced mushrooms* and cook gently for 5 minutes. Pour in *300 ml (½ pint) beef stock*, and simmer for about 5 minutes. Add *1 tbsp chopped parsley*, *1 tsp chopped fresh thyme*, and *salt and pepper to taste.*

ONION GRAVY

Heat *1 tbsp sunflower oil* and *30 g (1 oz) butter* in a saucepan. Add *1 sliced onion* and cook for 5–7 minutes until golden. Add *1 tbsp plain flour* and cook, stirring, for 1 minute. Add *300 ml (½ pint) chicken stock.* Simmer for about 5 minutes. Add *salt and pepper to taste.*

RED WINE GRAVY

Melt *30 g (1 oz) butter* in a saucepan. Add *1 sliced small onion* and cook for 5 minutes or until beginning to brown. Add *1 tbsp plain flour* and cook, stirring, for 1 minute. Add *100 ml (3½ fl oz) red wine* and *300 ml (½ pint) beef stock.* Simmer for about 5 minutes. Pour in any juices from the meat, and add *salt and pepper to taste.*

VEAL WITH TUNA MAYONNAISE

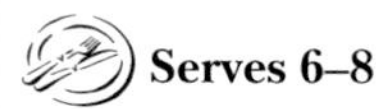 **Serves 6–8**

1.5 kg (3 lb) veal roasting joint
2 large rosemary sprigs
2 garlic cloves, cut into slivers
salt and black pepper
250 ml (8 fl oz) dry white wine

TUNA MAYONNAISE

1 x 200 g (7 oz) can tuna in oil, drained
2 tbsp lemon juice
1 garlic clove, coarsely chopped
2 tbsp capers
1 tsp chopped fresh thyme
dash of Tabasco sauce
125 ml (4 fl oz) olive oil
250 ml (8 fl oz) mayonnaise
1 tbsp mustard seeds

TO GARNISH

black olives
1 red pepper, cored, seeded, and cut into strips
fresh basil

1 Make incisions in the veal and push 1 or 2 rosemary leaves and a sliver of garlic into each incision. Season, and rub with any remaining rosemary and garlic.

2 Place the veal in a large roasting tin and pour the wine around it. Cover with foil and roast in a preheated oven at 160°C (325°F, Gas 3) for 2–2½ hours or until the veal is tender.

3 Remove the veal from the oven, and leave to cool completely in the cooking liquid. Remove any fat that solidifies on the surface. Slice the veal thinly and arrange the slices on a serving platter.

4 Make the tuna mayonnaise: purée the tuna, reserving a little for the garnish, with the lemon juice, garlic, capers, thyme, and Tabasco sauce in a food processor until smooth. Gradually blend in the oil, then add the mayonnaise, mustard seeds, and salt and pepper to taste.

5 Pour the tuna mayonnaise over the veal, and garnish with the reserved tuna, the black olives, red pepper, and basil. Serve at room temperature.

VEAL CHOPS WITH MUSHROOMS & CREAM

Serves 4

15 g (½ oz) dried porcini mushrooms
2 tbsp plain flour
salt and black pepper
4 x 250 g (8 oz) veal loin chops
45 g (1½ oz) butter
8 shallots, chopped
3 garlic cloves, crushed
250 g (8 oz) button mushrooms, thinly sliced
250 ml (8 fl oz) dry white wine
300 ml (½ pint) single cream
1 tbsp chopped fresh tarragon
pinch of grated nutmeg
chopped fresh tarragon to garnish

1 Put the dried mushrooms into a bowl, cover with warm water, and soak for 30 minutes or until soft.

2 Sprinkle the flour on to a plate, and season with salt and pepper. Lightly coat the chops with the flour.

3 Melt half of the butter in a frying pan, add the veal chops, and cook for about 4 minutes on each side.

4 Remove the chops and keep warm. Melt the remaining butter in the pan, add the shallots and garlic, and cook gently, stirring occasionally, for a few minutes until softened.

5 Drain the dried mushrooms, reserving the soaking liquid. Rinse under cold running water, and drain on paper towels. Add the dried and button mushrooms to the pan and cook for 3 minutes or until tender. Remove the shallots and mushrooms from the pan and keep warm.

6 Pour in the wine and boil until reduced to about 3 tbsp. Add the mushroom liquid and boil until reduced to about 125 ml (4 fl oz).

7 Stir in the cream and heat gently. Add the tarragon, nutmeg, and salt and pepper to taste. Return the chops, shallots, and mushrooms to the pan and heat through gently. Transfer to serving plates, sprinkle with chopped tarragon, and serve at once.

VEAL SCHNITZELS

Serves 4

4 x 60–90 g (2–3 oz) veal escalopes
salt and black pepper
1 egg, beaten
125 g (4 oz) fresh white breadcrumbs
60 g (2 oz) butter
1 tbsp sunflower oil

TO SERVE

8 anchovy fillets, drained and halved lengthwise
2 tbsp coarsely chopped capers
lemon wedges
parsley

1 Put each veal escalope between 2 sheets of greaseproof paper and pound to a 3 mm (1/8 in) thickness with a rolling pin. Season with salt and pepper.

2 Pour the egg on to a plate, and sprinkle the breadcrumbs on to another plate. Dip each escalope into the beaten egg, then into the breadcrumbs, to coat evenly. Cover and chill.

3 Melt the butter with the oil in a large frying pan. When the butter is foaming, add 2 of the escalopes and cook for 2 minutes on each side until golden. Drain on paper towels and keep warm while cooking the remaining 2 escalopes.

4 Serve the escalopes with anchovy fillets, capers, lemon wedges, and parsley.

Veal schnitzels

Known in German as Wiener schnitzel, *this is the name given to a veal escalope cooked the Viennese way. Traditionally served garnished with anchovies and capers, Wiener schnitzel is known as* Holsteiner schnitzel *when topped with a fried egg.*

SALTIMBOCCA

Serves 4

4 x 60–90 g (2–3 oz) veal escalopes
8–12 fresh sage leaves
4 thin slices of Parma ham
2 tbsp plain flour
salt and black pepper
30 g (1 oz) butter
1 garlic clove, crushed
125 ml (4 fl oz) dry white wine
4 tbsp double cream

1 Put each veal escalope between 2 sheets of greaseproof paper and pound to a 3 mm (1/8 in) thickness with a rolling pin.

2 Lay 2 or 3 sage leaves on each escalope, and press a slice of Parma ham firmly on top. Sprinkle the flour on to a plate and season with salt and pepper. Lightly coat both sides of the escalopes with the flour, shaking off any excess.

3 Melt half of the butter in a large frying pan. When the butter is foaming, add the escalopes, and cook in batches, sprinkling them with the garlic as they cook, and adding more butter when needed, for 2 minutes on each side. Lift out and keep warm.

4 Pour the white wine into the pan and boil for a few minutes until it is reduced to about 2 tbsp. Stir in the cream and heat gently, then taste for seasoning. Pour the sauce over the escalopes on warmed plates, and serve at once.

Saltimbocca

Translated literally, saltimbocca *means "jump in the mouth", presumably because this classic Italian dish is so delicious that it almost leaps into one's mouth. If veal is not available, saltimbocca can also be made with either pork, turkey, or chicken escalopes.*

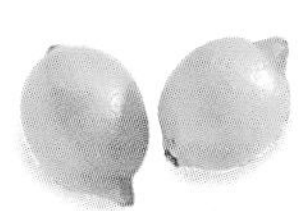

VEAL WITH LEMON & BASIL

Omit the sage leaves and Parma ham. Coat the veal with seasoned flour and cook as directed. While still in the pan, sprinkle over the juice of 1 lemon, 2 tbsp shredded fresh basil, and season to taste.

VEAL MARSALA

Serves 4

4 x 60–90 g (2–3 oz) veal escalopes
1 tbsp plain flour
salt and black pepper
45 g (1 1/2 oz) butter
1 large onion, finely chopped
125 ml (4 fl oz) Marsala
125 ml (4 fl oz) veal or chicken stock
chopped parsley to garnish

1 Put each veal escalope between 2 sheets of greaseproof paper and pound to a 3 mm (1/8 in) thickness with a rolling pin.

2 Season the flour with salt and pepper and use to lightly coat the escalopes.

3 Melt 30 g (1 oz) of the butter in a frying pan, and cook the escalopes, in batches if necessary, for 2 minutes on each side or until golden. Remove from the pan and keep warm.

4 Melt the remaining butter, add the onion, and cook gently for about 5 minutes until soft and lightly browned. Pour in the Marsala and boil, stirring, until reduced to 2 tbsp. Add the stock and boil until reduced to 90 ml (3 fl oz).

5 Return the escalopes to the pan, spoon over the sauce, and warm the escalopes through. Sprinkle with chopped parsley.

OSSO BUCO

The name of this Italian classic, originally from Milan, means "bone with a hole" as it is made from thick slices of veal shin that have the central bone containing marrow left in. For authenticity, serve with gremolata *and a creamy risotto Milanese (page 322).*

Serves 6

30 g (1 oz) plain flour
salt and black pepper
6 slices of veal shin with bones, 3.5–5 cm (1 1/2–2 ins) thick
30 g (1 oz) butter
2 tbsp olive oil
2 onions, finely chopped
175 g (6 oz) carrots, finely chopped
2 celery stalks, finely chopped
2 garlic cloves, crushed
300 ml (1/2 pint) dry white wine
300 ml (1/2 pint) veal or chicken stock
1 x 400 g (13 oz) can chopped tomatoes
2 tsp chopped fresh oregano
1 bay leaf
gremolata (see box, right) to serve

1 Put the flour into a large plastic bag and season with salt and pepper. Put the veal into the bag and shake until all the meat is evenly coated with flour.

2 Melt the butter with the oil in a large flameproof casserole. When the butter is foaming, add the veal slices and cook in batches, for 10 minutes or until golden all over. Lift out and drain on paper towels. Lower the heat, add the onions, carrots, celery, and garlic, and cook for 5 minutes.

3 Pour in the wine and boil until reduced by half. Add the stock, tomatoes, oregano, and bay leaf, and bring to a boil. Return the veal to the casserole, bring back to a boil, cover, and cook in a preheated oven at 160°C (325°F, Gas 3) for 1 1/2–2 hours until very tender.

4 If the sauce in the casserole is too liquid, lift out the veal slices, keep warm, and boil the sauce until reduced to a thick consistency. Taste for seasoning. Sprinkle the gremolata over the veal just before serving.

Gremolata

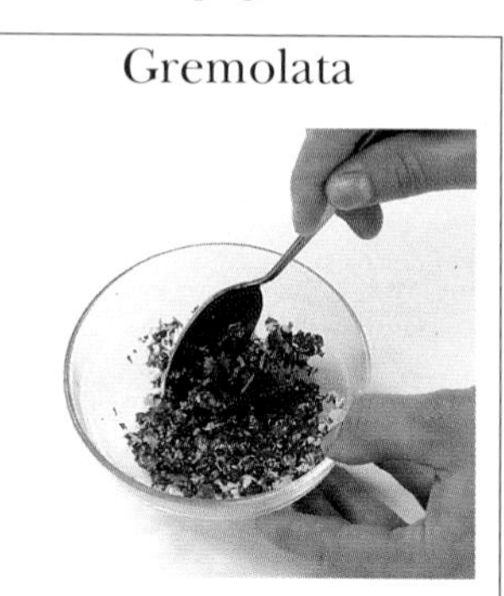

Put *2 tbsp chopped parsley*, the *grated zest of 1 lemon*, and *1 finely chopped garlic clove* into a small bowl and stir to mix thoroughly. Chill until needed.

Cook's know-how

Make sure the slices of veal you buy have the bone in, as the marrow is the most important part of this traditional Italian dish. Scoop it out of the bone and eat it with the meat.

VEAL STEW WITH OLIVES & PEPPERS

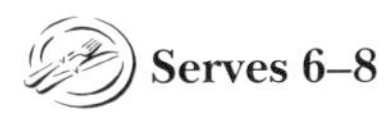

Serves 6–8

2 tbsp plain flour

salt and black pepper

1.5 kg (3 lb) stewing veal, cut into 3.5 cm (1½ in) cubes

2–3 tbsp olive oil

2 garlic cloves, crushed

1 red, 1 green, and 1 yellow pepper, cored, seeded, and cut into strips

250 ml (8 fl oz) dry white wine

500 g (1 lb) tomatoes, peeled (page 39), seeded, and chopped

4 tbsp tomato purée

4 rosemary sprigs, chopped

250 g (8 oz) pitted black olives

1 tbsp chopped fresh rosemary to garnish

1 tbsp chopped parsley to garnish

1 Put the flour into a plastic bag and season with salt and pepper. Toss the veal in the seasoned flour to coat lightly.

2 Heat the oil in a large flameproof casserole, add the veal, sprinkle with half of the garlic, and cook for 5–7 minutes until browned all over. Lift out the veal and set aside.

3 Add the peppers and cook, stirring, for 3 minutes, until almost soft. Remove from the casserole and set aside.

4 Return the veal to the casserole, and add the wine, tomatoes, tomato purée, remaining garlic, and rosemary. Cover and simmer for 1 hour.

5 Return the peppers to the casserole and cook for a further 30 minutes or until the meat is very tender.

6 Stir the olives into the casserole and heat through. Serve hot, lightly sprinkled with rosemary and parsley.

LIVER & BACON WITH ONION SAUCE

Serves 4

2 tbsp sunflower oil

1 large onion, thinly sliced

125 g (4 oz) streaky bacon rashers, rinds removed, cut into strips

500 g (1 lb) calf's liver, trimmed and cut into 1 cm (½ in) strips

2 tbsp plain flour

600 ml (1 pint) beef stock

3 tbsp tomato ketchup

dash of Worcestershire sauce

salt and black pepper

chopped fresh tarragon to garnish

1 Heat the oil in a large frying pan, add the onion and bacon, and cook gently, stirring occasionally, for a few minutes until the onion is soft and the bacon crisp. Add the liver and cook, stirring, for 2 minutes. Remove with a slotted spoon and keep warm.

2 Add the flour to the pan and cook, stirring, for 1 minute. Pour in the stock and bring to a boil, stirring until thickened.

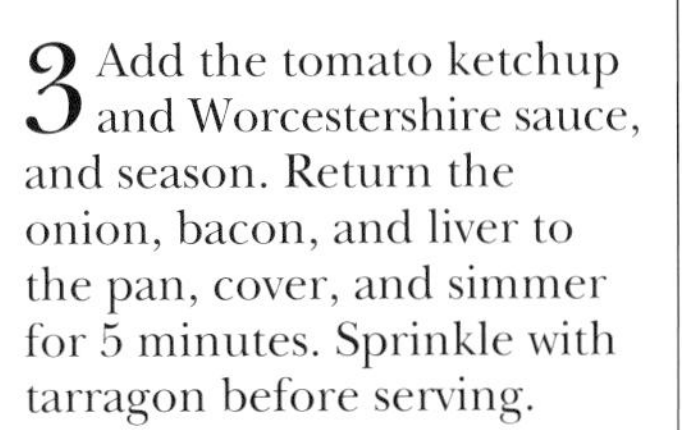

3 Add the tomato ketchup and Worcestershire sauce, and season. Return the onion, bacon, and liver to the pan, cover, and simmer for 5 minutes. Sprinkle with tarragon before serving.

Cook's know-how

Lamb's liver can also be used in this recipe. Pig's liver is a less expensive alternative to calf's or lamb's liver but it has a stronger flavour. To reduce its pronounced taste, soak it in milk for about 30 minutes.

LIVER STROGANOFF

Use 150 ml (¼ pint) chicken stock instead of the beef stock and omit the ketchup and Worcestershire sauce. Stir in 150 ml (¼ pint) soured cream.

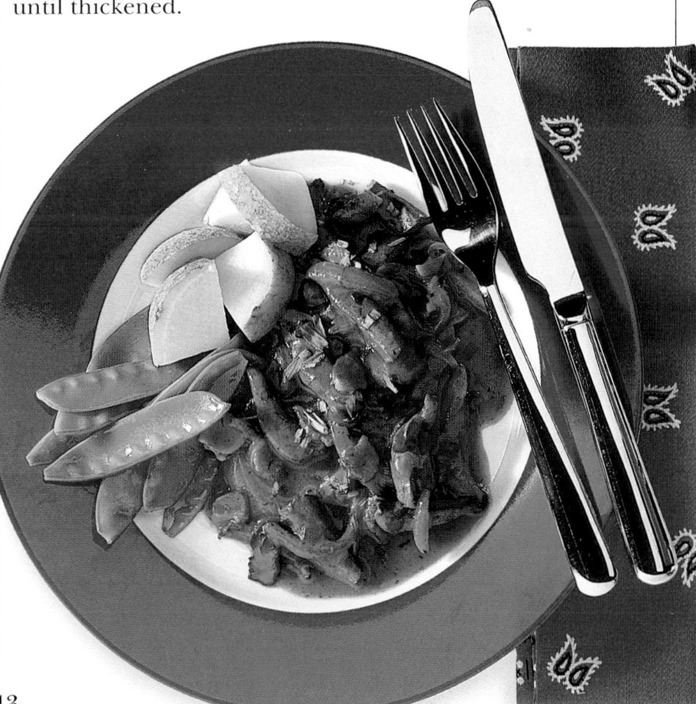

CALF'S LIVER WITH SAGE

Serves 4

2 tbsp plain flour

salt and black pepper

500 g (1 lb) calf's liver

60 g (2 oz) butter

1 tbsp sunflower oil

juice of 1 lemon

3 tbsp chopped fresh sage

sage leaves and lemon slices to garnish

1 Sprinkle the flour on to a large plate and season with salt and pepper. Use to coat both sides of the liver, shaking off any excess.

2 Melt half of the butter with the oil in a large frying pan. When the butter is foaming, add half of the liver and cook over a high heat for 2–3 minutes on each side until browned all over. Lift out with a slotted spoon and keep warm. Repeat with the remaining liver.

3 Melt the remaining butter in the pan, and add the lemon juice and sage, stirring to dissolve any sediment from the bottom of the pan. Pour the pan juices over the liver, garnish with sage leaves and lemon slices, and serve at once.

Cook's know-how

Overcooking liver will toughen it, so make sure that the butter and oil are really hot, then the liver will cook quickly.

CALF'S LIVER WITH APPLE

Halve and slice 1 dessert apple and add to the pan with the lemon juice and sage. Cook, stirring, for 3 minutes, and serve with the liver.

CREAMED SWEETBREADS

Serves 4

500 g (1 lb) calf's sweetbreads

2 tbsp lemon juice

1 small onion, chopped

a few parsley sprigs

1 bay leaf

salt and black pepper

45 g (1½ oz) butter

45 g (1½ oz) plain flour

300 ml (½ pint) milk

chopped parsley to garnish

1 Put the sweetbreads into a bowl, cover with cold water, add 1 tbsp of the lemon juice, and leave to soak for 2–3 hours.

2 Drain, rinse, and trim the sweetbreads (page 214).

3 Put the sweetbreads into a large saucepan with the onion, parsley, bay leaf, and salt and pepper to taste. Cover with cold water and bring slowly to a boil. Simmer gently for 15 minutes or until just tender, skimming off any scum as it rises to the surface.

4 Drain the sweetbreads, reserving 300 ml (½ pint) of the cooking liquid. Rinse again, and shape (see box, right).

5 Melt the butter in a saucepan, add the flour, and cook, stirring, for 1 minute. Remove the pan from the heat, and gradually blend in the milk and reserved cooking liquid. Bring to a boil, stirring constantly, and boil for 2–3 minutes until the mixture thickens. Add the remaining lemon juice and salt and pepper to taste.

6 Unwrap the sweetbreads and slice into thin rounds. Add to the sauce, and simmer gently for about 5 minutes to warm through. Transfer to warmed plates and garnish with chopped parsley before serving.

Shaping sweetbreads

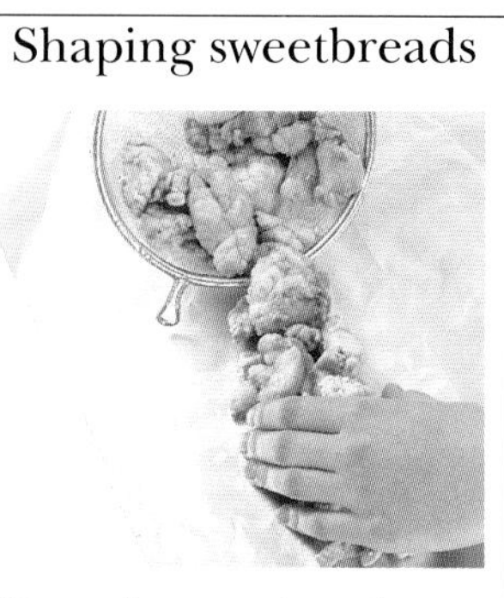

Place the sweetbreads on a large piece of foil, and roll it up very tightly, twisting the ends to make a sausage shape. Chill for 2 hours or until firm.

ROAST LEG OF LAMB WITH RED WINE GRAVY

Roast leg of lamb, a traditional British dish, is served here with a rich gravy that incorporates all the flavoursome juices from the meat as well as a dash of red wine. A bowl of freshly made mint sauce completes the scene for a perfect Sunday lunch.

Serves 4–6

2 kg (4 lb) leg of lamb
salt and black pepper
1 tbsp chopped fresh rosemary
1 tbsp chopped fresh thyme
1 tbsp plain flour
300 ml (1/2 pint) lamb stock
90 ml (3 fl oz) red wine
rosemary and thyme to garnish
mint sauce (see far right) to serve

1 Trim the skin and excess fat from the lamb. Score the fat (see box, right).

2 Insert a meat thermometer, if using, into the middle of the meat. Put the lamb, fat-side up, on a rack in a roasting tin, and sprinkle with pepper and the herbs. Roast in a preheated oven at 200°C (400°F, Gas 6) for 20 minutes.

3 Lower the oven temperature to 180°C (350°F, Gas 4) and cook for 20 minutes per 500 g (1 lb) for well-done meat, or until the meat thermometer registers 80°C (175°F), and the fat is crisp and golden.

4 Remove the lamb, cover loosely with foil, and leave to stand for 10 minutes.

5 Meanwhile, make the gravy: spoon all but 1 tbsp fat from the tin. Put the roasting tin on top of the stove, add the flour, and cook, stirring, for 1 minute. Pour in the stock or water and wine, and bring to a boil, stirring to dissolve any sediment from the bottom and sides of the tin. Simmer for about 3 minutes, add salt and pepper to taste, and strain.

6 Transfer the leg of lamb to a warmed serving platter, and garnish with rosemary and thyme sprigs. Hand the red wine gravy and mint sauce separately.

Scoring the fat

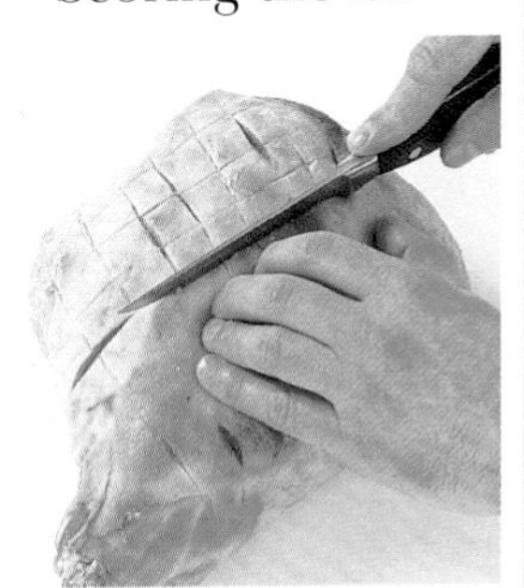

Score the fat in a criss-cross pattern using a small, sharp knife, making sure that only the fat is cut, and that the meat underneath remains completely untouched.

SAUCES FOR LAMB

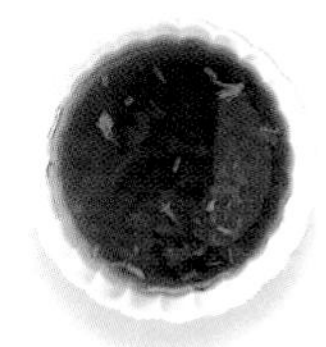

MINT SAUCE

In a small bowl, combine *3 tbsp chopped fresh mint* and *1–2 tsp caster sugar.* Pour over *2 tbsp boiling water,* and stir until the sugar has completely dissolved. Add *2 tbsp wine vinegar* and leave to cool before serving.

CUMBERLAND SAUCE

Put *2 tbsp redcurrant jelly* into a small saucepan and heat gently until melted. Add *300 ml (1/2 pint) red wine* and the *grated zest of 1 orange.* Bring to simmering point, and simmer, whisking constantly, for 5 minutes. Add *the juices of 1 orange and 1/2 lemon* and simmer for a further 5 minutes. Strain, then add *salt and pepper to taste.* Serve hot.

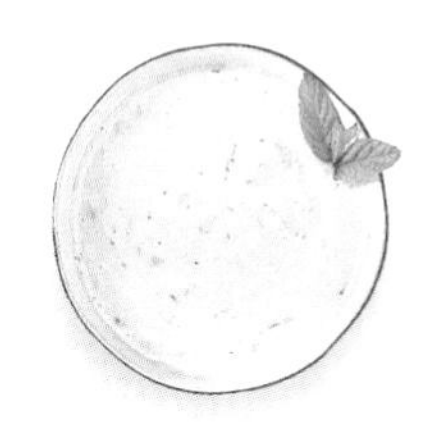

YOGURT & LIME SAUCE

Put *150 g (5 oz) Greek yogurt,* the *grated zest and juice of 1 lime, 1 crushed garlic clove, 1 tbsp chopped fresh mint,* and *salt and pepper to taste* into a small bowl. Mix well to combine. Cover and chill until required.

GREEK ROAST LAMB

Serves 6

2 kg (4 lb) leg of lamb

4 garlic cloves, cut into slivers

2 large rosemary sprigs, chopped

juice of 1/2 lemon

salt and black pepper

chopped fresh rosemary to garnish

1 With a sharp chef's knife, carefully make small incisions in the lamb and insert a sliver of garlic into each incision.

2 Put the lamb into a casserole with the rosemary sprigs, sprinkle with the lemon juice, and add salt and pepper to taste.

3 Roast in a preheated oven at 220°C (425°F, Gas 7) for 30 minutes or until the lamb is browned. Lower the oven temperature to 140°C (275°F, Gas 1), cover, and cook for a further 3 1/2 hours or until the lamb is very tender. Leave to stand for 10 minutes.

4 Remove the lamb from the casserole, and spoon off any fat from the cooking juices. Taste for seasoning, and strain into a gravy boat. Carve the lamb, garnish with rosemary, and serve at once.

SPINACH-STUFFED LAMB

The lamb in this recipe is distinctively flavoured with spinach, wine, and anchovies. Stuffed mushrooms are a perfect accompaniment.

Serves 6–8

2 kg (4 lb) leg of lamb, boned but left whole (page 211)

150 ml (1/4 pint) dry white wine

4 anchovy fillets, chopped

150 ml (1/4 pint) lamb stock or water

salt and black pepper

stuffed mushrooms (page 349)

SPINACH STUFFING

30 g (1 oz) butter

3–4 garlic cloves, crushed

250 g (8 oz) spinach leaves, coarsely shredded

60 g (2 oz) fresh brown breadcrumbs

1 egg, beaten

1 Make the stuffing: melt butter in a saucepan. Add the garlic and cook, stirring, for 2–3 minutes until softened. Stir in the spinach, add salt and pepper to taste, and cook for 1 minute. Add the breadcrumbs and leave to cool. Bind with the egg.

2 Stuff the lamb (see box, right). Secure with fine skewers or thin string.

3 Put the lamb on a rack in a roasting tin and roast in a preheated oven at 200°C (400°F, Gas 6) for 15 minutes. Turn, insert a meat thermometer, if using, and cook for 15 minutes.

4 Drain the fat from the tin. Add the wine and anchovies. Cover the lamb loosely with foil, lower the oven temperature to 180°C (350°F, Gas 4), and cook for 1 1/2 hours or until the juices run slightly pink. The meat thermometer should register 75–80°C (170–175°F).

5 Remove the lamb, cover loosely with foil, and leave to stand for 10 minutes.

6 Pour the cooking liquid into a measuring jug and make up to 300 ml (1/2 pint) with the stock or water.

7 Return the cooking liquid to the tin. Bring to a boil, stirring to dissolve the sediment. Season, and strain into a warmed gravy boat. Serve the lamb with the stuffed mushrooms, and hand the gravy separately.

Stuffing the lamb

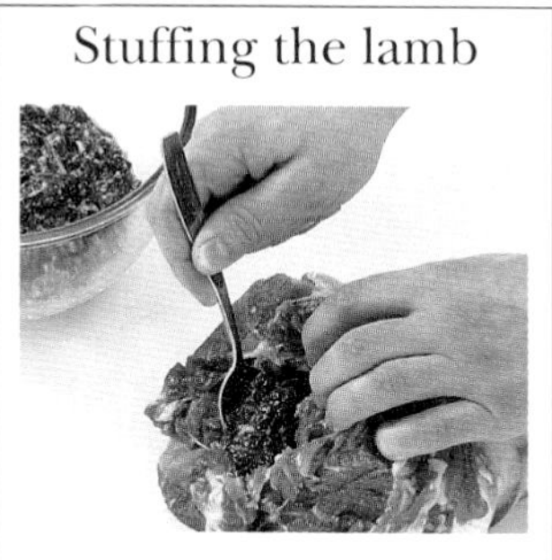

Season the cavity of the lamb with salt and pepper, then spoon in the spinach stuffing, packing it in tightly.

SHOULDER OF LAMB WITH LEMON & OLIVE STUFFING

The flavours of lemon zest, black olives, and fresh herbs combine together to make a glorious stuffing, which is especially good with succulent lamb. Boning the lamb before cooking makes it easier to carve into neat slices.

Serves 6–8

2 kg (4 lb) shoulder of lamb, boned

2 garlic cloves, cut into slivers

150 ml (1/4 pint) dry white wine

150 ml (1/4 pint) lamb stock or water

LEMON & OLIVE STUFFING

1 tbsp olive oil

1 shallot, finely chopped

125 g (4 oz) fresh breadcrumbs

30 g (1 oz) pitted black olives, roughly chopped

grated zest of 1 lemon

1 tbsp chopped fresh thyme

1 tbsp chopped fresh rosemary

1 small egg, beaten

salt and black pepper

1 Make the stuffing: heat the olive oil in a small pan, add the shallot, and cook for about 5 minutes. Remove from the heat and add the breadcrumbs, olives, lemon zest, herbs, egg, and salt and pepper to taste. Leave to cool.

2 Stuff and roll the lamb (see box, right). Weigh the lamb.

3 Put the lamb into a roasting tin and insert a meat thermometer, if using, into the middle of the meat. Pour over the wine and stock and cook in a preheated oven at 200°C (400°F, Gas 6) for 20–25 minutes. Lower the temperature to 180°C (350°F, Gas 4) and cook for 20 minutes per 500 g (1 lb) or until the juices run clear. The meat thermometer should register 75–80°C (170–175°F).

4 Remove the lamb, cover loosely with foil, and leave to stand for 10 minutes.

5 Make the gravy: spoon any fat from the cooking juices. Put the tin on top of the stove. Bring to a boil, and boil for 5 minutes, stirring to dissolve any sediment from the bottom of the tin. Taste for seasoning, strain, and serve with the lamb.

Stuffing and rolling the lamb

Make incisions in the meat side of the lamb using a small knife, and push a sliver of garlic into each incision. Season the lamb with salt and pepper.

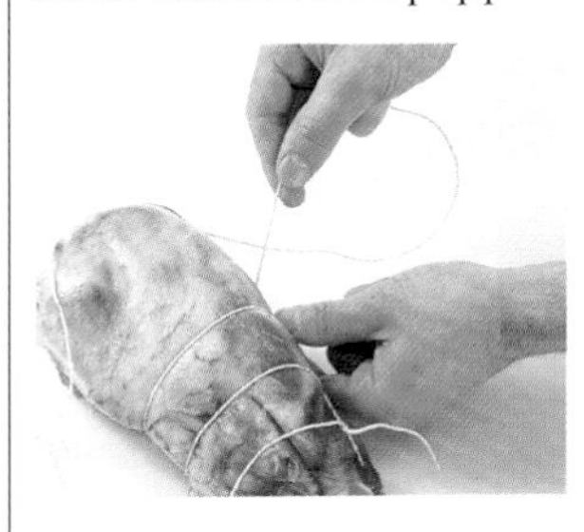

Spread the lemon and olive stuffing over the lamb. Roll up the lamb, and secure with string.

LEMON GRILLED LAMB

Serves 6–8

2–2.5 kg (4–5 lb) leg of lamb, butterflied (page 211)

MARINADE

juice of 3 lemons

4 tbsp clear honey

3 large garlic cloves, quartered

1 tbsp mustard powder

1 tbsp coarse-grain mustard

1 Make the marinade: in a non-metallic dish, mix together the lemon juice, honey, garlic, and mustards. Turn the lamb in the marinade, cover loosely, and leave to marinate in the refrigerator, turning the lamb occasionally, for 1–2 days.

2 Remove the lamb from the marinade. Strain and reserve the marinade. Cook the lamb under a hot grill, 15 cm (6 ins) from the heat, basting from time to time with the marinade, for 20–25 minutes on each side.

3 Test the lamb: insert a skewer into the thickest part – the juices will run clear when it is cooked.

4 Leave the lamb to stand, covered loosely with foil, in a warm place for 5–10 minutes. Spoon the fat from the grill pan, strain the juices into a gravy boat, and serve with the lamb.

KEBABS

Cooking food over a barbecue is a sociable, enjoyable way to cook, but if you're tired of the usual barbecue fare, here's a selection of kebabs to choose from, with mouth-watering marinades or flavoured butter to enhance each one. There's bound to be a kebab to suit everyone's taste.

BEEF & ONION

Serves 4

500 g (1 lb) rump steak, cut into chunks

2 onions, cut into chunks

salt and black pepper

fresh tarragon to garnish

MARINADE

125 ml (4 fl oz) olive oil

90 ml (3 fl oz) port

6–8 shallots, finely chopped

2 tbsp Dijon mustard

1 tbsp chopped fresh tarragon

1 Combine the marinade ingredients, add the beef, and stir well. Cover and chill for at least 2 hours.

2 Thread the beef and onions on to skewers. Season and cook for 2–3 minutes on each side for rare beef, 3–4 for medium, and 4–5 for well-done.

CURRIED LAMB

Serves 4

500 g (1 lb) lamb neck fillet, trimmed and cut into chunks

lime wedges to serve

MARINADE

3 tbsp plain yogurt

juice of 1/2 lime

4 garlic cloves, crushed

3 tbsp chopped fresh coriander

1 tbsp chopped fresh mint

1 tsp each curry powder and cumin

pinch each of salt and cayenne pepper

1 Combine the marinade ingredients in a large bowl. Add the lamb and stir. Cover and chill for at least 2 hours.

2 Thread the lamb on to skewers, then cook for 4 minutes on each side for medium lamb, or 5 minutes for well-done lamb. Serve with lime wedges.

ORIENTAL PORK

Serves 4

500 g (1 lb) pork fillet, cut into chunks

1 red pepper, cored, seeded, and cut into chunks

1 green pepper, cored, seeded, and cut into chunks

1 onion, cut into chunks

1/4 fresh pineapple, peeled and cut into chunks

MARINADE

90 ml (3 fl oz) sunflower oil

90 ml (3 fl oz) soy sauce

juice of 1 lime

3 garlic cloves, crushed

3 tbsp sugar

1/4 tsp ground ginger

1/4 tsp fennel seeds

1 Combine the marinade ingredients in a bowl. Add the pork, peppers, onion, and pineapple, and stir well. Cover and chill for at least 2 hours.

2 Thread the meat on to skewers, alternating with the peppers, onions, and pineapple. Baste the kebabs with any remaining marinade. Cook for 4–5 minutes on each side, basting occasionally, until the pork is cooked through.

LIVER & SAUSAGE

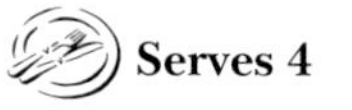

Serves 4

8 streaky bacon rashers, cut into 3.5 cm (1 1/2 in) pieces

125 g (4 oz) chicken livers, trimmed and cut into bite-sized pieces

2 Toulouse sausages or other coarse-cut sausages, cut into bite-sized pieces

salt and black pepper

chopped parsley to garnish

lemon wedges to serve

MUSTARD BUTTER

45 g (1 1/2 oz) butter

2 garlic cloves, crushed

1 tbsp chopped fresh rosemary

1 tbsp wholegrain mustard

1 Wrap the bacon pieces around the chicken livers and thread on to skewers, alternating with the sausages. Soften the butter slightly, then mix in the garlic, rosemary, and mustard.

2 Spread half of the butter over the kebabs. Cook for 4–5 minutes on each side, until cooked through. Season, garnish, and serve with the remaining butter and the lemon wedges.

Clockwise from top: *Curried Lamb Kebabs, Oriental Pork Kebabs, Beef & Onion Kebabs, Mustard Butter, Liver & Sausage Kebabs.*

Successful barbecues

It's not very difficult to get successful results when cooking over charcoal. Just remember a few simple points.

- It is usually best to marinate meat to be cooked over a barbecue. The basis of a marinade should be an oil, to keep the food moist; an acid such as lemon or lime juice, which tenderizes the meat; and herbs, spices, or other seasonings to add flavour. Baste with the marinade while the meat is cooking, if stated in the recipe.
- Start to cook when the coals have stopped glowing, which takes about 30 minutes.
- Some metal skewers have wooden handles, but if not, handle with care as they become very hot. Soak bamboo skewers in water for 30 minutes before use so that they don't burn.

SHOULDER OF LAMB WITH GARLIC & HERBS

Serves 6

2 kg (4 lb) shoulder of lamb, trimmed of excess fat

creamed haricot beans (page 347) to serve

HERB BUTTER

90 g (3 oz) butter, softened

2 garlic cloves, crushed

1 tbsp chopped fresh thyme

1 tbsp chopped fresh rosemary

1 tbsp chopped fresh mint

2 tbsp chopped parsley

salt and black pepper

GRAVY

1 tbsp plain flour

150 ml (1/4 pint) red wine

150 ml (1/4 pint) lamb stock or water

1 Make the herb butter: mix the butter, garlic, thyme, rosemary, mint, parsley, and salt and pepper to taste.

2 Using a knife, slash the lamb at regular intervals and push a little of the herb butter into each cut. Rub any remaining butter over the lamb. Weigh the lamb.

3 Put the lamb on a rack in a roasting tin and insert a meat thermometer, if using, into the middle of the meat. Cook in a preheated oven at 200°C (400°F, Gas 6) for 30 minutes.

4 Lower the temperature to 180°C (350°F, Gas 4) and cook for 20 minutes per 500 g (1 lb). The thermometer should register 75–80°C (170–175°F).

5 Remove the lamb. Cover loosely with foil and leave to stand for 10 minutes.

6 Make the gravy: drain all but 1 tbsp of the fat from the tin. Set the tin on top of the stove, add the flour, and cook, stirring, for 1 minute. Pour in the wine and stock, bring to a boil, and simmer for 2–3 minutes. Taste for seasoning, and strain into a warmed gravy boat. Serve with the lamb and creamed haricot beans.

INDIAN SPICED LAMB

Serves 4–6

1.5 kg (3 lb) shoulder or leg of lamb

1/2 tsp lemon juice

salt and black pepper

cashew nuts and chopped coriander to garnish

SPICED YOGURT MARINADE

8 garlic cloves, coarsely chopped

7 cm (3 in) piece of fresh root ginger, chopped

2 tbsp clear honey

1 tbsp lemon juice

seeds of 5 cardamom pods

1 tsp cumin seeds

1 tsp turmeric

1 tsp cayenne pepper

1 tsp salt

1/2 tsp ground cinnamon

1/4 tsp ground cloves

150 g (5 oz) Greek yogurt

large pinch of saffron threads, crumbled

1 Make the spiced yogurt marinade: purée the garlic, ginger, honey, lemon juice, cardamom and cumin seeds, turmeric, cayenne, salt, cinnamon, cloves, yogurt, and saffron in a food processor until smooth.

2 Spread the mixture over the lamb (see box, right).

3 Cover the lamb and leave to marinate in the refrigerator for 2 hours.

4 Put the lamb on a rack in a roasting tin and cook in a preheated oven at 160°C (325°F, Gas 3) for 3 1/2 hours or until the meat is tender.

5 Remove the lamb and keep warm. Spoon the fat from the tin. Set the tin on top of the stove and add the lemon juice. Boil until thickened, and season with salt and pepper to taste.

6 Cut the lamb from the bone, then cut the meat into chunks. Mix with the sauce, and serve at once, garnished with cashew nuts and chopped coriander.

Coating the lamb

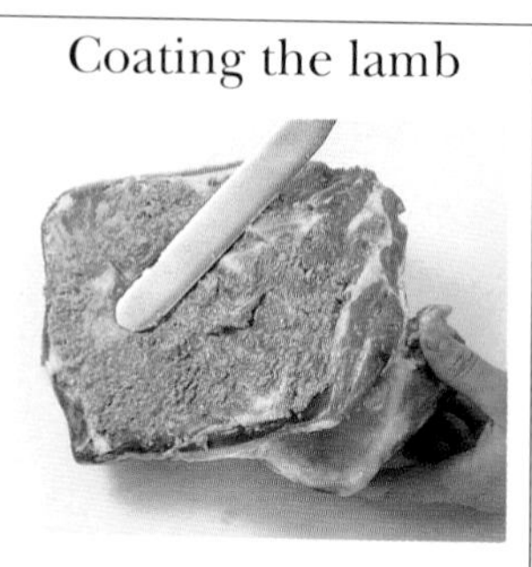

Make incisions in the lamb and, using a spatula, spread the spiced yogurt marinade over the lamb to cover it completely.

Rack of Lamb with a Walnut & Herb Crust

Also called best end of neck, a rack of lamb comprises 8 chops. The walnut and herb crust and light wine and grape sauce make this cut of lamb the perfect main course.

Serves 4–6

2 prepared racks of lamb (page 212)

1 egg, beaten

WALNUT & HERB CRUST

30 g (1 oz) fresh wholemeal breadcrumbs

30 g (1 oz) parsley, chopped

2 tbsp coarsely chopped walnut pieces

2 large garlic cloves, crushed

finely grated zest of 1 lemon

1 tbsp walnut oil

salt and black pepper

WINE & GRAPE SAUCE

150 ml (1/4 pint) dry white wine

150 ml (1/4 pint) lamb stock or water

125 g (4 oz) seedless green grapes, halved

1 Brush the outsides of the racks of lamb with some of the beaten egg.

2 Prepare the walnut and herb crust: combine the breadcrumbs, parsley, walnuts, garlic, lemon zest, oil, and salt and pepper to taste, and bind with the remaining beaten egg. Chill for 30 minutes.

3 Coat the lamb with the walnut and parsley crust (see box, right). Weigh each rack and put them crust-side up into a roasting tin. Cook in a preheated oven at 200°C (400°F, Gas 6) for 20 minutes per 500 g (1 lb) plus 20 minutes for medium meat, or plus 30 minutes for well-done.

4 Remove the lamb, cover loosely with foil, and leave to stand in a warm place for 10 minutes.

5 Meanwhile, make the sauce: spoon all but 1 tbsp of the fat from the roasting tin. Set the tin on top of the stove, pour in the wine, and bring to a boil, stirring to dissolve any sediment from the bottom of the tin.

6 Add the stock and boil, stirring occasionally, for 2–3 minutes. Taste the sauce for seasoning, strain into a warmed sauce boat, and stir in the grapes. Serve with the lamb.

Crown Roast with Red Wine

Shape 2 prepared racks of lamb into a crown roast (page 212). Weigh, then place in a roasting tin with 2 tbsp oil, and cook as for rack of lamb. Make the gravy from the juices and 1 tbsp fat in the roasting tin, stirring in 1 tbsp plain flour, and adding 300 ml (1/2 pint) lamb stock or water and 90 ml (3 fl oz) red wine. To serve, put a bunch of watercress inside the crown.

Coating the lamb

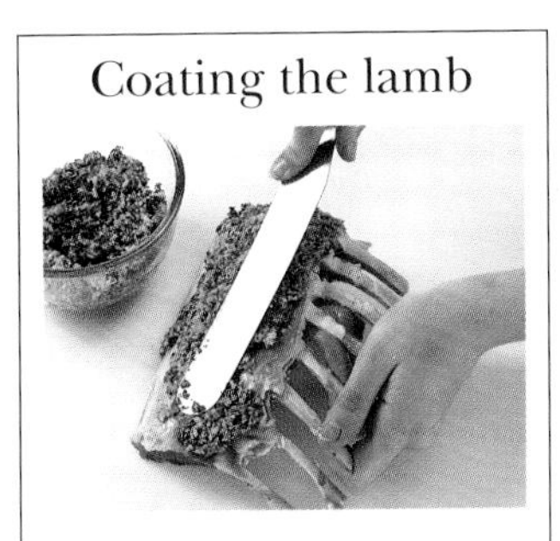

Press half of the walnut and herb crust mixture on to the skin side of each rack of lamb, using a palette knife.

Lamb with Mint Glaze

Serves 4

8 best end lamb chops, trimmed

MINT GLAZE

3 tbsp dry white wine

1 tbsp white wine vinegar

4 mint sprigs, leaves stripped and chopped

1 tbsp clear honey

1 tsp Dijon mustard

salt and black pepper

1 Make the mint glaze: combine the wine, vinegar, mint, honey, mustard, and salt and pepper to taste. Brush the glaze over the chops, and leave to marinate for about 30 minutes.

2 Place the chops over a barbecue or under a hot grill, 7 cm (3 ins) from the heat, and cook, brushing often with the glaze, for 4–6 minutes on each side, until done to your liking.

Lamb with Orange Glaze

Omit the mint glaze. Combine 3 tbsp orange juice with 1 tbsp each white wine vinegar, orange marmalade, and chopped fresh thyme, 1 tsp Dijon mustard, and salt and pepper to taste. Glaze the chops with the mixture.

HERBED BUTTERFLY CHOPS

Serves 4

4 butterfly lamb chops
1 tbsp olive oil
black pepper
4 rosemary sprigs
4 mint sprigs
4 thyme sprigs

1 Place the lamb chops on a grill rack. Brush each chop with half of the oil, and sprinkle with black pepper. Arrange 1 rosemary sprig, 1 mint sprig, and 1 thyme sprig on each chop.

2 Place the chops under a hot grill, 10 cm (4 ins) from the heat, and cook for 4–6 minutes. Remove from the heat, lift off the herbs, and turn the chops over. Brush the chops with the remaining oil, replace the herbs, and grill for 4–6 minutes until done to your liking. Serve at once.

Butterfly chops

These are double-sided chops, cut from a saddle of lamb, or double loin. They are also known as Barnsley chops.

LAMB CHOPS WITH MINTED HOLLANDAISE SAUCE

Instead of the traditional mint sauce, lamb chops are served here with a creamy hollandaise sauce flavoured with fresh mint. The sauce is not difficult to make, as long as it is cooked over a gentle heat.

Serves 4

4 chump lamb chops
a little olive oil
salt and black pepper
minted hollandaise sauce to serve (see box, below)

1 Brush the chops on both sides with a little oil, and season with black pepper.

2 Put the chops under a hot grill, 10 cm (4 ins) from the heat, and cook for 3–4 minutes on each side for medium-rare chops, slightly longer for well-done.

3 Arrange the lamb chops on warmed serving plates and serve at once with the warm minted hollandaise sauce.

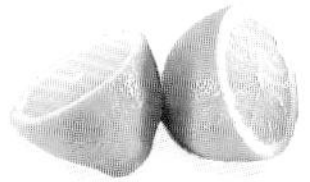

LAMB CHOPS WITH LEMON & THYME HOLLANDAISE

Make the sauce as directed, substituting 1 tsp grated lemon zest and 1 tbsp chopped fresh thyme for the chopped mint. Serve with the lamb chops.

Minted hollandaise sauce

Whisk together *2 tsp lemon juice, 2 tsp white wine vinegar,* and *3 egg yolks at room temperature.* Put over a saucepan of simmering water and whisk until thick.

Melt *125 g (4 oz) unsalted butter,* and add, a little at a time, to the egg-yolk mixture, whisking constantly until the sauce thickens.

Stir in *2 tbsp chopped fresh mint* and season with *salt and pepper to taste.* Transfer to a sauce boat and serve at once.

LANCASHIRE HOT POT

 **Serves 4**

2 tbsp sunflower oil

1 kg (2 lb) middle neck lamb chops, trimmed

3 lamb's kidneys, trimmed (page 214) and halved

1 kg (2 lb) potatoes, cut into 5 mm (1/4 in) slices

500 g (1 lb) carrots, sliced

2 large onions, chopped

1 tsp caster sugar

salt and black pepper

1 bay leaf

1 rosemary sprig

a few parsley sprigs

600–750 ml (1–1 1/4 pints) lamb stock or water

chopped parsley to garnish

1 Heat the oil in a flameproof casserole, add the lamb in batches, and brown over a medium heat for 5 minutes. Remove and set aside. Add the kidneys and cook for 3–5 minutes. Remove and set aside.

2 Add the potatoes, carrots, and onions, and cook for 5 minutes. Remove from the casserole.

3 Make layers of lamb chops, kidneys, and vegetables in the casserole, adding sugar, and salt and pepper to taste, and putting the herbs in the middle. Top with a neat layer of potatoes. Pour in enough stock to come up to the potato layer. Cover tightly and cook in a preheated oven at 160°C (325°F, Gas 3) for 2 hours or until the meat and vegetables are tender.

4 Remove the casserole lid, increase the oven temperature to 220°C (425°F, Gas 7), and cook for 20–30 minutes to brown the potato topping. Sprinkle with parsley before serving.

COUNTRY HOT POT

Omit the kidneys, and substitute 250 g (8 oz) swede for half of the carrots. Layer the meat and vegetables, and add 60 g (2 oz) pearl barley. Proceed as directed.

LAMB NOISETTES WITH ORANGE & HONEY

 **Serves 4**

8 lamb noisettes

2 lamb's kidneys, trimmed (page 214) and quartered (optional)

chopped fresh thyme and rosemary to garnish

MARINADE

grated zest and juice of 1 orange

4 tbsp clear honey

3 tbsp olive oil

2 garlic cloves, crushed

1 tbsp chopped fresh thyme

1 tbsp chopped fresh rosemary

salt and black pepper

1 Make the marinade: in a shallow, non-metallic dish, combine the orange zest and juice, honey, oil, garlic, thyme, rosemary, and salt and pepper to taste. Add the lamb noisettes to the marinade, turn them, then cover, and leave to marinate in the refrigerator overnight.

2 Lift the lamb noisettes out of the marinade, reserving the marinade. Place a piece of kidney, if using, in the middle of each lamb noisette.

3 Put under a hot grill, 10 cm (4 ins) from the heat, and cook for 7 minutes on each side until the lamb is tender.

4 Meanwhile, strain the marinade into a small saucepan, bring to a boil, and simmer for a few minutes until it reaches a syrupy consistency. Taste for seasoning, spoon over the lamb noisettes, and garnish with thyme and rosemary.

Lamb noisettes

These are taken from the loin. The eye of meat is cut away, then rolled, tied, and cut into thick slices. It is an expensive cut but gives neat portions of tender, lean meat.

IRISH STEW

Serves 4

- *1 kg (2 lb) old potatoes, cut into 5 mm (1/4 in) slices*
- *2 large onions, sliced*
- *1 kg (2 lb) middle neck lamb chops, trimmed*
- *a few parsley stalks*
- *1 thyme sprig*
- *1 bay leaf*
- *salt and black pepper*
- *300–500 ml (10–16 fl oz) water*
- *chopped parsley to garnish*

1 Put half of the potatoes into a flameproof casserole, cover with half of the onions, then add the chops, parsley, thyme, bay leaf, and salt and pepper to taste. Add the remaining onions, then the remaining potatoes, seasoning each layer with salt and pepper.

2 Pour in enough water to half-fill the casserole, and then bring to a boil. Cover tightly and cook in a preheated oven at 160°C (325°F, Gas 3) for 2–2 1/2 hours until the lamb and potatoes are just tender.

3 Remove the lid, increase the oven temperature to 220°C (425°F, Gas 7), and cook for 20–30 minutes to brown the topping. Sprinkle with parsley before serving.

CURRIED LAMB WITH ALMONDS

In this rich and aromatic lamb dish, the lamb is marinated in creamy yogurt and spicy garam masala, flavoured with ground almonds, and garnished with mint and paprika. For an authentic accompaniment, serve with spiced red lentils.

Serves 6–8

- *125 g (4 oz) plain yogurt*
- *1 tsp garam masala*
- *1.5 kg (3 lb) lamb neck fillet, trimmed and cut into chunks*
- *90 ml (3 fl oz) sunflower oil*
- *4 onions, sliced*
- *5 cm (2 in) piece of fresh root ginger, peeled and chopped*
- *4–5 garlic cloves, crushed*
- *1/2 tsp caster sugar*
- *salt and black pepper*
- *300 ml (1/2 pint) lamb stock or water*
- *4 tbsp ground almonds*
- *4 bay leaves*
- *1 cardamom pod, crushed*
- *250 ml (8 fl oz) double cream*
- *juice of 1/4 lemon*
- *1/2 tsp ground coriander*
- *1/4 tsp ground cinnamon*
- *1/4 tsp cayenne pepper*
- *chopped fresh mint and paprika to garnish*

1 In a large bowl, combine the yogurt and garam masala. Add the meat, and turn to coat in the yogurt. Cover and leave to marinate in the refrigerator for 3–4 hours.

2 Heat the oil in a large flameproof casserole, add the onions, ginger, garlic, sugar, and 1/2 tsp salt, and cook very gently, stirring occasionally, for about 10 minutes until the onions are soft and golden brown.

3 Add the stock, almonds, bay leaves, and cardamom and bring to a boil, stirring constantly.

4 Remove the meat from the marinade. Add to the casserole and stir to coat evenly with the sauce. Cover and cook in a preheated oven at 160°C (325°F, Gas 3) for 2 hours or until the meat is tender.

5 Lift the meat out of the casserole and keep warm. Skim any fat from the juices in the casserole. If the cooking juices are too liquid, boil until reduced to a thick consistency. Stir in the cream, lemon juice, coriander, cinnamon, cayenne pepper, and salt and pepper to taste, and heat through.

6 Return the meat to the casserole and heat through. Garnish with mint and paprika before serving.

Garam masala

Garam masala is an Indian blend of spices usually sold ready mixed. The spices vary according to individual brands, but usually include cumin, coriander, cardamom, cinnamon, cloves, mace, bay leaves, and pepper.

BLANQUETTE OF LAMB

Serves 4–6

1 kg (2 lb) boneless shoulder of lamb, trimmed and cut into chunks
1.25 litres (2 pints) water
8 button onions
2 large carrots, thickly sliced
2 bay leaves
juice of 1/2 lemon
salt and black pepper
250 g (8 oz) button mushrooms
45 g (1 1/2 oz) butter
45 g (1 1/2 oz) plain flour
150 ml (1/4 pint) single cream
1 egg yolk
chopped parsley to garnish

1 Put the chunks of lamb into a large saucepan, cover with cold water, and bring to a boil. Strain, and rinse the meat thoroughly to remove the scum.

2 Return the meat to the saucepan and pour in the measured water. Add the button onions, carrots, bay leaves, lemon juice, and salt and pepper to taste. Bring to a boil, cover, and simmer gently for 1 hour.

3 Add the mushrooms and simmer for 30 minutes. Lift out the lamb and vegetables, reserving the liquid, and keep warm.

4 Melt the butter in a small pan. Add the flour and cook, stirring occasionally, for 1 minute. Gradually blend in the reserved cooking liquid, stirring constantly. Bring to a boil, stirring, then simmer until the sauce thickens.

5 In a bowl, whisk together the cream and egg yolk. Blend in 2 tbsp of the hot sauce. Take the saucepan off the heat, stir the cream mixture into the sauce, then reheat very gently. Taste for seasoning. Pour the sauce over the lamb and garnish with parsley before serving.

LAMB & TOMATO CASSEROLE

Substitute 1 x 400 g (13 oz) can chopped tomatoes and 300 ml (1/2 pint) dry white wine for the water. Cook the lamb as directed, but do not make the white sauce.

AROMATIC LAMB WITH LENTILS

Serves 6–8

1.5 kg (3 lb) lamb neck fillet, trimmed and cut into chunks
2 tbsp olive oil
2 onions, chopped
125 g (4 oz) brown lentils, rinsed
175 g (6 oz) ready-to-eat dried apricots
salt and black pepper
600 ml (1 pint) lamb or chicken stock

MARINADE

175 ml (6 fl oz) orange juice
2 tbsp olive oil
3 garlic cloves, crushed
1 tsp ground ginger
1 tsp ground coriander
1/2 tsp ground cinnamon

1 Make the marinade: in a large bowl, combine the orange juice, olive oil, garlic, ginger, coriander, and cinnamon.

2 Turn the chunks of lamb in the marinade, cover loosely, and then leave to marinate in the refrigerator overnight.

3 Remove the lamb from the marinade, reserving the marinade. Heat the olive oil in a large flameproof casserole, add the lamb in batches, and cook over a high heat for 5 minutes or until browned all over. Lift out the lamb chunks with a slotted spoon.

4 Lower the heat slightly, add the onions, and cook gently, stirring occasionally, for a few minutes until just soft but not coloured. Lift out of the casserole.

5 Make layers of lamb, onions, lentils, and apricots in the casserole, seasoning each layer with salt and pepper to taste. Pour in the stock and reserved marinade and bring to a boil. Cover and cook in a preheated oven at 160°C (325°F, Gas 3) for 2 hours or until the meat is tender. Taste for seasoning before serving.

LAMB TAGINE

Serves 6–8

1/4 tsp saffron threads
150 ml (1/4 pint) hot water
3 tbsp olive oil
1.5 kg (3 lb) boneless shoulder of lamb, trimmed and cut into 2.5 cm (1 in) cubes
1 fennel bulb, trimmed and sliced crosswise
2 green peppers, cored, seeded, and cut into strips
1 large onion, sliced
30 g (1 oz) plain flour
1/2 tsp ground ginger
450 ml (3/4 pint) lamb stock or water
grated zest and juice of 1 orange
125 g (4 oz) ready-to-eat dried apricots
salt and black pepper
mint sprigs to garnish

1 Prepare the saffron (see box, right). Heat the oil in a flameproof casserole, add the lamb in batches, and cook over a high heat for 5 minutes or until browned. Lift out and drain on paper towels.

2 Lower the heat, add the fennel, peppers, and onion, and cook gently, stirring, for 5 minutes.

3 Add the flour and ground ginger to the vegetables and cook, stirring occasionally, for about 1 minute. Add the saffron liquid to the casserole, return the cubes of lamb, then add the stock, orange zest, and salt and black pepper to taste. Bring to a boil, cover, and cook in a preheated oven at 160°C (325°F, Gas 3) for 1 hour.

4 Add the orange juice and apricots and cook for about 30 minutes until the lamb is very tender. Taste for seasoning and garnish with mint sprigs before serving.

Preparing saffron

Put the saffron threads into a small bowl, add the measured hot water, and soak for 10 minutes.

SPICED LAMB WITH COCONUT

Serves 4–6

1 kg (2 lb) lamb neck fillet, trimmed and cut into 2.5 cm (1 in) cubes
30 g (1 oz) butter
1 tbsp sunflower oil
1 large Spanish onion, sliced
2 large garlic cloves, crushed
1 tbsp plain flour
1 x 400 g (13 oz) can chopped tomatoes
150 ml (1/4 pint) lamb stock or water
grated zest and juice of 1 lime
2 tbsp mango chutney
60 g (2 oz) creamed coconut, chopped
250 g (8 oz) Greek yogurt
coriander sprigs to garnish

DRY MARINADE

2.5 cm (1 in) piece of fresh root ginger, peeled and grated
1 tbsp ground cumin
1 tbsp ground coriander
1 tbsp mild curry powder
1 tsp turmeric
salt and black pepper

1 Make the dry marinade: combine the ginger, cumin, coriander, curry powder, turmeric, and salt and pepper to taste.

2 Toss the lamb in the marinade, cover, and leave to marinate in the refrigerator overnight.

3 Melt the butter with the oil in a large flameproof casserole. When the butter is foaming, add the lamb in batches, and cook over a high heat for about 5 minutes until browned all over.

4 Lift out with a slotted spoon and set aside. Lower the heat, add the onion and garlic, and cook gently, stirring occasionally, for a few minutes until soft but not coloured.

5 Add the flour and cook, stirring, for 1 minute. Add the tomatoes, stock, lime zest and juice, chutney, and salt and pepper to taste. Bring to a boil, stirring.

6 Return the lamb to the casserole, add the coconut, and bring back to a boil. Cover and cook in a preheated oven at 160°C (325°F, Gas 3) for 1 hour or until the lamb is tender.

7 Stir in the yogurt and taste for seasoning. Garnish with coriander sprigs before serving.

SHEPHERD'S PIE

 **Serves 4**

750 g (1½ lb) minced lamb
125 g (4 oz) mushrooms, sliced
2 carrots, diced
1 large onion, chopped
1 garlic clove, crushed
30 g (1 oz) plain flour
300 ml (½ pint) lamb stock or water
1 tbsp mushroom ketchup
salt and black pepper
750 g (1½ lb) potatoes
about 4 tbsp hot milk
30 g (1 oz) butter

1 Put the minced lamb into a large frying pan and heat gently until the fat runs. Increase the heat and cook, turning and mashing the meat, until it browns. Using a slotted spoon, lift the lamb out of the pan and spoon off the excess fat.

2 Add the mushrooms, carrots, onion, and garlic to the pan, and cook gently, stirring occasionally, for a few minutes until just beginning to soften.

3 Return the lamb to the frying pan. Add the flour and cook, stirring, for about 1 minute.

4 Add the stock, mushroom ketchup, and salt and pepper to taste, and bring to a boil. Cover and simmer very gently for 30 minutes.

5 Meanwhile, cook the potatoes in boiling salted water for 15–20 minutes until tender. Drain. Add the milk and butter to the potatoes and mash until soft, adding salt and pepper to taste.

6 Taste the lamb mixture for seasoning. Turn into an ovenproof dish, then spread the potato on top. With a fork, score the potato in a decorative pattern. Cook in a preheated oven at 200°C (400°F, Gas 6) for about 20 minutes until the potato topping is golden and the meat mixture bubbling.

MONDAY LAMB PIE

Substitute 750 g (1½ lb) cooked, leftover lamb, finely chopped, for the minced lamb. Cook the mushrooms, carrots, onions, and garlic as directed, and add the cooked lamb after 15 minutes. Proceed as directed.

MOUSSAKA

 **Serves 6–8**

2 large aubergines, sliced
750 g (1½ lb) minced lamb
3 onions, chopped
3 garlic cloves, crushed
45 g (1½ oz) plain flour
500 ml (16 fl oz) passata
150 ml (¼ pint) red wine
2 tbsp tomato purée
2 tsp dried oregano
olive oil for brushing
salt and black pepper
chopped parsley to garnish

CHEESE SAUCE

45 g (1½ oz) butter
45 g (1½ oz) plain flour
450 ml (¾ pint) milk
125 g (4 oz) Gruyère cheese, grated
1½ tsp Dijon mustard
pinch of grated nutmeg
1 large egg, beaten

1 Put the aubergine slices into a colander, sprinkle generously with salt, and leave to stand for 30 minutes.

2 Put the minced lamb into a frying pan and heat gently until the fat runs. Increase the heat and cook, stirring, until browned. Spoon off the excess fat.

3 Add the onions and garlic and cook until softened. Add the flour and cook, stirring, for 1 minute. Add the passata, wine, tomato purée, oregano, and salt and pepper to taste, and bring to a boil. Cover and simmer for 20 minutes.

4 Rinse the aubergine slices and pat dry. Place on a grill rack and brush with oil. Cook under a hot grill, 10 cm (4 ins) from the heat, for 5–6 minutes until golden on both sides.

5 Make the cheese sauce: melt the butter in a pan, add the flour, and cook, stirring, for 1 minute. Remove from the heat and gradually blend in the milk. Bring to a boil, stirring constantly until thick. Simmer for 2–3 minutes. Add the cheese, mustard, nutmeg, and salt and pepper to taste. Leave to cool slightly, then stir in the egg.

6 Spoon half of the meat mixture into a shallow ovenproof dish and top with half of the aubergine slices. Repeat with the remaining meat and aubergines, then pour over the cheese sauce. Cook in a preheated oven at 180°C (350°F, Gas 4) for 45 minutes or until golden.

KIDNEYS TURBIGO

Serves 4

6 lamb's kidneys
60 g (2 oz) butter
250 g (8 oz) chipolata sausages
12 button onions, peeled, with roots left intact
250 g (8 oz) button mushrooms
1 tbsp plain flour
300 ml (1/2 pint) lamb stock or water
1 tbsp medium sherry
2 tsp tomato purée
1 bay leaf
salt and black pepper
2 tbsp chopped parsley to garnish
croûtes (page 31) to serve

1 Prepare the kidneys (page 214).

2 Melt the butter in a large frying pan, add the kidneys, and cook, stirring, over a high heat for about 3 minutes until browned. Lift out and drain on paper towels. Add the sausages and cook for 3 minutes or until browned. Lift out and drain on paper towels.

3 Add the onions and mushrooms to the pan and cook for 3–5 minutes until browned.

4 Add the flour and cook, stirring, for 1 minute. Add the stock, sherry, and tomato purée, and bring to a boil, stirring constantly. Add the bay leaf, and salt and pepper to taste.

5 Slice the sausages thickly and return to the pan with the kidneys. Cover and simmer gently for 20–25 minutes until tender.

6 Spoon the kidney mixture on to a warmed platter, garnish with the chopped parsley, and serve with croûtes.

Kidneys Turbigo

This classic French dish is named after the town of Turbigo in Lombardy, the site of two French victories over the Austrians in the 19th century.

MERGUEZ WITH POTATOES & PEPPERS

Serves 4

3 large potatoes, unpeeled
salt and black pepper
1 red pepper
1 green pepper
250 g (8 oz) merguez, cut into bite-sized pieces
3 garlic cloves, crushed
1/2 tsp ground cumin
1–2 tbsp olive oil, more if needed
chopped fresh coriander to garnish

1 Put the potatoes into a large saucepan of boiling salted water and cook for 10 minutes. Drain the potatoes and leave to cool.

2 Put the peppers under a hot grill, 10 cm (4 ins) from the heat, and grill, turning as needed, for 10–12 minutes until charred and blistered. Put the peppers into a plastic bag, seal, and leave to cool.

3 Peel the peppers, rinse under running water, and pat dry. Core and seed the peppers and slice the flesh lengthwise into strips.

4 Cut the potatoes into wedges and put into a casserole with the peppers and merguez. Stir in the garlic, cumin, salt and pepper to taste, and the oil. Cook in a preheated oven at 190°C (375°F, Gas 5), turning occasionally, for 45 minutes or until the potatoes are tender and the sausages cooked through, adding a little more oil if the potatoes look dry.

5 Remove the casserole from the oven, and spoon off any excess fat. Garnish with coriander before serving.

FRANKFURTERS WITH POTATOES & PEPPERS

Substitute 250 g (8 oz) frankfurters, cut into bite-sized pieces, for the merguez, and proceed as directed.

BONED LOIN OF PORK WITH APRICOT STUFFING

Succulent boned loin of pork, with an apricot stuffing flavoured with lemon juice and lemon thyme, is served here with a white wine gravy. The crackling is cooked separately, in the top half of the oven, to ensure that it is deliciously crisp.

 **Serves 6–8**

1.5 kg (3 lb) boned loin of pork

sunflower oil for brushing

APRICOT STUFFING

30 g (1 oz) butter

1 small onion, finely chopped

90 g (3 oz) fresh brown breadcrumbs

90 g (3 oz) ready-to-eat dried apricots, coarsely chopped

1 tbsp chopped parsley

1 tbsp lemon juice

2 tsp chopped fresh lemon thyme

1 egg, beaten

salt and black pepper

GRAVY

1 tbsp plain flour

150 ml (1/4 pint) chicken stock

150 ml (1/4 pint) dry white wine

1 Make the apricot stuffing: melt the butter in a small saucepan, add the onion, and cook gently, stirring occasionally, for a few minutes until just soft but not coloured.

2 Remove the pan from the heat and stir in the breadcrumbs, apricots, parsley, lemon juice, lemon thyme, egg, and salt and black pepper to taste. Leave to cool completely.

3 With the point of a small knife, score the pork skin in long strokes, about 1 cm (1/2 in) apart. Cut the skin off the meat, brush with a little oil, and sprinkle generously with salt and pepper. Place the skin on a rack in a small roasting tin.

4 Stuff and roll the pork (see box, right). Weigh the stuffed pork.

5 Place the pork skin in the top of a preheated oven at 180°C (350°F, Gas 4). Put the pork into another roasting tin. Brush with oil and season generously. Insert a meat thermometer, if using, into the middle of the loin, and cook the pork in the oven for about 2 hours or until the thermometer registers 90°C (190°F).

6 Transfer the pork to a carving board, cover loosely with foil, and leave to stand for 10 minutes. If the crackling is not really crisp, increase the oven temperature to 200°C (400°F, Gas 6) and let it continue to cook while making the gravy.

7 Put the roasting tin on top of the stove and spoon off all but 1 tbsp of the fat. Add the flour, and cook, stirring to dissolve any sediment from the bottom of the tin, for 1 minute. Pour in the stock and wine, and bring to a boil, stirring constantly. Simmer for 3 minutes. Season to taste and strain into a gravy boat. Serve with the pork.

Stuffing and rolling a loin of pork

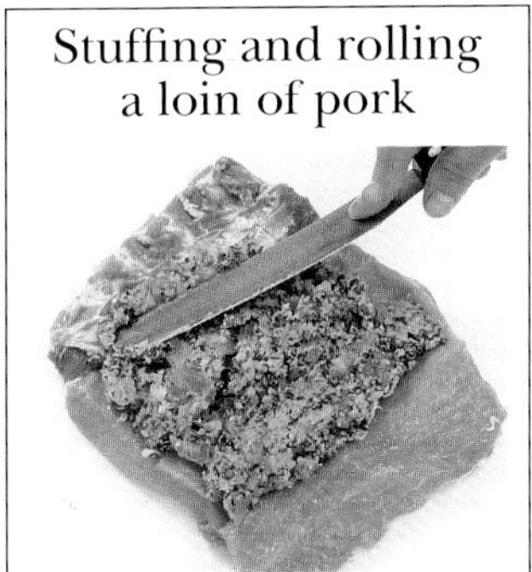

Open out the loin of pork and spread the stuffing over the meat.

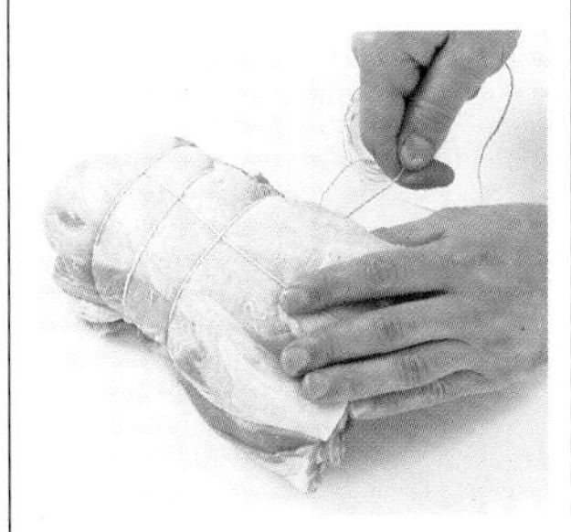

Roll the pork around the stuffing and tie at intervals with fine string.

SAUCES FOR PORK

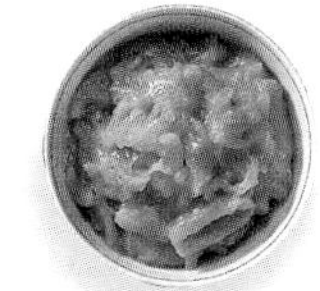

APRICOT SAUCE

Melt *30 g (1 oz) butter*, and cook *1 thinly sliced small onion* until soft. Add *125 g (4 oz) halved ready-to-eat dried apricots, 150 ml (1/4 pint) chicken stock, 150 ml (1/4 pint) dry white wine, 1/4 tsp ground cinnamon*, and *salt and black pepper to taste*. Simmer for about 20 minutes.

APPLE SAUCE

Peel, core, and slice *500 g (1 lb) cooking apples* and put into a saucepan with the *grated zest of 1 lemon*, and *2–3 tbsp water*. Cover tightly and cook gently for about 10 minutes until soft. Stir in *30 g (1 oz) caster sugar*. Beat the sauce until smooth, or push through a nylon sieve. Stir in *15 g (1/2 oz) butter*.

SWEET & SOUR SAUCE

Finely slice *1 onion, 1 leek, and 2 celery stalks*. Cut *2 carrots* into matchstick-thin strips. Heat *2 tbsp oil* in a pan and cook the vegetables for 3 minutes or until softened. Blend *2 tbsp tomato ketchup, 1 tbsp soy sauce, 1 tbsp white wine vinegar, 4 tsp cornflour, and 2 tsp caster sugar*, then blend in *300 ml (1/2 pint) water*. Add this mixture to the pan and bring to a boil, stirring until thickened.

MARINATED LOIN OF PORK WITH PINEAPPLE

Serves 6–8

1.5 kg (3 lb) boned loin of pork, skin removed

grilled pineapple rings to serve

MARINADE

250 ml (8 fl oz) pineapple juice

2 tbsp maple syrup

2 tbsp soy sauce

2 garlic cloves, crushed

2 tbsp chopped fresh thyme

1 tsp ground coriander

1 Make the marinade: in a large non-metallic bowl, combine the pineapple juice, maple syrup, soy sauce, garlic, thyme, and coriander. Add the pork, cover, and leave to marinate in the refrigerator, turning occasionally, for 8 hours.

2 Remove the pork from the marinade, reserving the marinade. Put the pork flat, fat-side up, in a small roasting tin. Insert a meat thermometer, if using, into the middle of the pork. Cover loosely with foil and cook in a preheated oven at 220°C (425°F, Gas 7) for 1 hour.

3 Remove the foil and pour the marinade over the pork. Return to the oven and cook for 20–30 minutes or until the marinade has darkened and the meat juices run clear when tested with a fine skewer. The meat thermometer should register 90°C (190°F).

4 Transfer the pork to a carving board, cover loosely with foil, and leave to stand for 10 minutes. Strain the marinade and remove the fat (see box, below). Gently heat the marinade to warm through. Serve the pork with the marinade and grilled pineapple rings.

Removing the fat

Skim the layer of fat from the surface of the marinade, using a spoon.

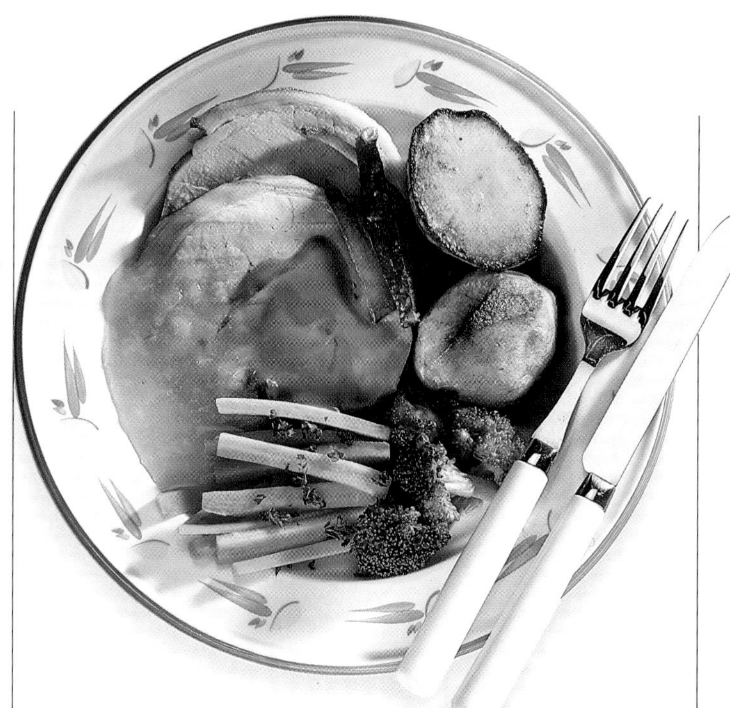

ROAST LEG OF PORK

Serves 6

2 kg (4 lb) leg of pork

sunflower oil for brushing

salt and black pepper

1 carrot, thickly sliced

1 onion, thickly sliced

1 tbsp plain flour

300 ml (1/2 pint) chicken stock

apple sauce to serve (page 259)

1 With the point of a small knife, score the pork skin in long strokes, about 1 cm (1/2 in) apart. Cut the skin off the meat, brush with a little oil, and sprinkle generously with salt and black pepper. Place on a rack in a small roasting tin.

2 Place the pork skin in the top of a preheated oven at 180°C (350°F, Gas 4).

3 Put the pork into another roasting tin, and arrange the carrot and onion around it. Brush the meat with a little oil and season well. Insert a meat thermometer, if using, into the middle of the pork and cook in the oven for 2 1/2 hours or until the thermometer registers 90°C (190°F).

4 Transfer the pork to a carving board, cover loosely with foil, and leave to stand for 10 minutes. If the crackling is not really crisp, increase the oven temperature to 200°C (400°F, Gas 6) and let it continue to cook while making the gravy.

5 Put the roasting tin on top of the stove. Remove and discard the carrot and onion and spoon off all but 1 tbsp of the fat from the tin.

6 Add the flour and cook, stirring to dissolve any sediment from the bottom of the tin, for 1 minute. Pour in the stock and bring to a boil. Simmer for 3 minutes, then season, and strain into a gravy boat. Serve the pork with the gravy and apple sauce.

Cook's know-how

The high oven temperature needed for crisp crackling can make meat tough and dry. Removing the skin and cooking it separately, above the pork, avoids this problem.

MADEIRA PORK WITH PAPRIKA

Serves 4

- *30 g (1 oz) butter*
- *2 tbsp sunflower oil*
- *750 g (1 1/2 lb) pork fillet, trimmed and cut diagonally into 1 cm (1/2 in) slices*
- *1 onion, chopped*
- *1 large red pepper, cored, seeded, and cut into strips*
- *1 tbsp paprika*
- *1 tbsp plain flour*
- *300 ml (1/2 pint) chicken stock*
- *75 ml (2 1/2 fl oz) Madeira*
- *175 g (6 oz) button mushrooms*
- *1 tsp tomato purée*
- *150 ml (1/4 pint) single cream*
- *salt and black pepper*

1 Melt the butter with the oil in a large frying pan. When the butter is foaming, add the pork fillet slices, in batches if necessary, and cook over a high heat for about 3 minutes until just beginning to brown. Lift out with a slotted spoon and drain on paper towels.

2 Add the onion and red pepper and cook, stirring, for 2 minutes. Add the paprika and flour, and cook, stirring, for 1 minute. Remove the pan from the heat and blend in the stock. Return to the heat and add the Madeira, mushrooms, and tomato purée. Simmer for 2–3 minutes.

3 Return the pork to the pan and season to taste. Cover and simmer very gently for 20 minutes or until the pork is tender and cooked through.

4 Stir the cream into the pork mixture, taste for seasoning, and heat through gently. Serve hot.

Cook's know-how

Madeira is a fortified wine from the Portuguese island of the same name. Ruby port can be used as a substitute if preferred.

BACON-WRAPPED PORK IN VERMOUTH SAUCE

Serves 6

- *2 pork fillets, about 375 g (12 oz) each, trimmed*
- *2 tbsp Dijon mustard*
- *salt and black pepper*
- *375 g (12 oz) streaky bacon rashers, rinds removed*

VERMOUTH SAUCE

- *30 g (1 oz) butter*
- *1 tbsp olive oil*
- *1 shallot, finely chopped*
- *1 tbsp plain flour*
- *200 ml (7 fl oz) chicken stock*
- *90 ml (3 fl oz) dry vermouth*
- *125 g (4 oz) button or chestnut mushrooms, sliced*

1 Spread the pork fillets with the mustard and season with salt and pepper. Stretch the bacon rashers with the back of a knife and wrap around the fillets (see box, right).

2 Place the fillets in a roasting tin and cook in a preheated oven at 220°C (425°F, Gas 7), turning the fillets halfway through cooking, for 30–35 minutes until the juices from the pork run clear and the bacon is crisp and golden.

3 Meanwhile, make the sauce: melt the butter with the oil in a small pan. When the butter is foaming, add the shallot, and cook gently until softened.

4 Add the flour and cook, stirring, for 1 minute. Gradually blend in the stock and vermouth. Bring to a boil, add the mushrooms, and simmer for 15 minutes.

5 Transfer the pork to a warmed platter. Spoon off the fat from the roasting tin and strain the juices into the sauce. Heat through and taste for seasoning. Serve with the pork.

Wrapping pork fillets

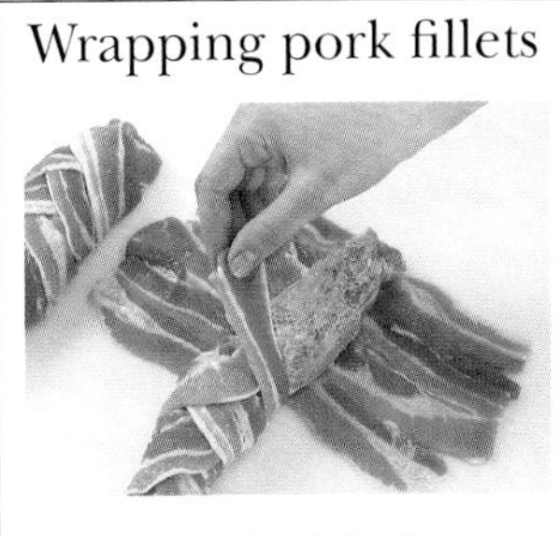

Overlap half of the bacon rashers on a work surface. Lay 1 pork fillet across the bacon and plait the rashers around the meat. Secure with a fine skewer. Repeat with the second pork fillet.

PORK WITH CHILLI & COCONUT

Serves 4

750 g ($1^1/_2$ lb) pork fillet, trimmed and cut into 5 mm ($^1/_4$ in) strips

2 tbsp sunflower oil

8 spring onions, cut into 2.5 cm (1 in) pieces

1 large red pepper, cored, seeded, and cut into thin strips

1 x 400 g (13 oz) can chopped tomatoes

60 g (2 oz) creamed coconut, coarsely chopped

4 tbsp water

2 tbsp chopped fresh coriander

1 tbsp lemon juice

salt and black pepper

coriander sprigs to garnish

DRY MARINADE

2.5 cm (1 in) piece of fresh root ginger, peeled and grated

2 fresh red chillies, cored, seeded, and finely chopped

1 garlic clove, crushed

1 tbsp mild curry powder

$^1/_4$ tsp ground turmeric

$^1/_4$ tsp garam masala

1 Make the dry marinade: in a bowl, combine the ginger, chillies, garlic, curry powder, turmeric, garam masala, and salt and pepper to taste. Turn the pork in the marinade, cover, and leave to marinate in the refrigerator for 2 hours.

2 Heat a wok or large frying pan, add the oil, and heat until hot. Add the strips of pork in batches, and stir-fry over a high heat for 5 minutes or until browned all over.

3 Add the spring onions and stir-fry for 1 minute. Add the red pepper and stir-fry for 1 minute, then add the tomatoes, coconut, and measured water. Bring to a boil, cover, and simmer very gently for 15 minutes or until the pork is tender.

4 Add the chopped coriander, lemon juice, and salt and pepper to taste. Garnish with coriander sprigs before serving.

GRILLED PORK CHOPS WITH MANGO SAUCE

Serves 4

4 pork loin chops, on the bone

sunflower oil for brushing

salt and black pepper

1 ripe mango

flat-leaf parsley to garnish

MANGO SAUCE

1 ripe mango

150 ml ($^1/_4$ pint) chicken stock

1 tbsp mango chutney

1 Prepare the pork chops (see box, right). Brush the chops on each side with oil and sprinkle with black pepper. Put under a hot grill, 10 cm (4 ins) from the heat, and grill for 8–10 minutes on each side until cooked through.

2 Meanwhile, make the mango sauce: peel, stone, and cube the mango (page 430). Purée in a food processor until smooth. Put into a small saucepan with the stock, mango chutney, and salt and pepper to taste. Bring to a boil and simmer for about 3 minutes until heated through. Taste for seasoning.

Preparing a pork chop

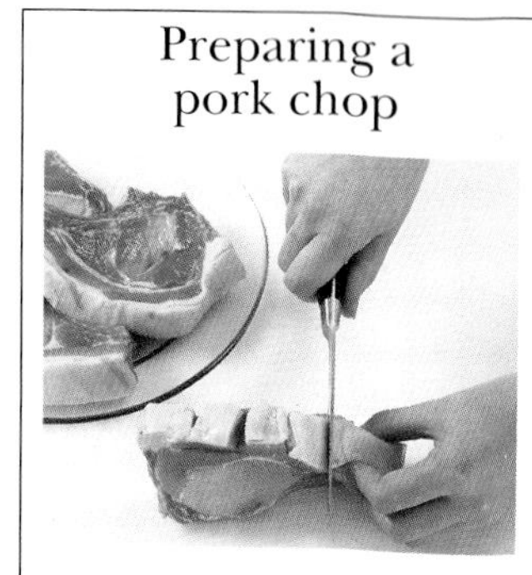

Cut the fat along the outside of the chop at regular intervals. This will prevent it curling up when under the grill.

3 Peel the remaining mango and cut it into 2 pieces lengthwise, slightly off-centre to miss the stone. Cut the flesh from around the stone. Slice the flesh into thin strips.

4 Arrange the mango strips on the chops, garnish with the flat-leaf parsley, and serve with the mango sauce.

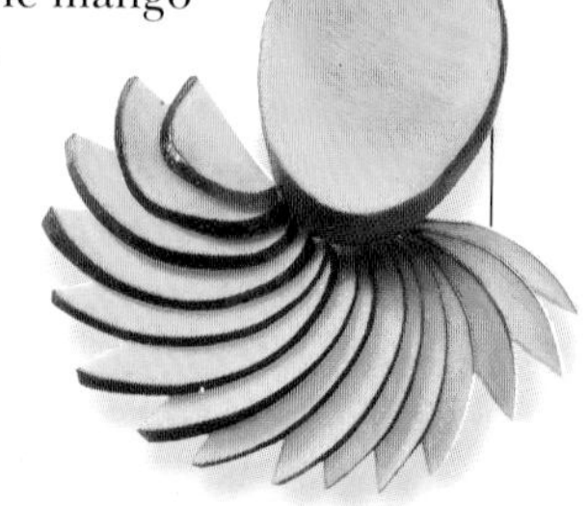

SPINACH-STUFFED PORK CHOPS

Tender pork loin chops, with a stuffing of finely chopped spinach, Parmesan cheese, cream, bacon, and herbs, are cooked in dry white wine and topped with melted Gruyère cheese. A hearty main course for a cold winter's day.

Serves 4

4 pork loin chops, on the bone

350 ml (12 fl oz) dry white wine

175 g (6 oz) Gruyère cheese, thinly sliced

salt and black pepper

SPINACH STUFFING

500 g (1 lb) spinach

60 g (2 oz) herby stuffing mix

60 g (2 oz) streaky bacon rashers, rinds removed, finely chopped

60 g (2 oz) Parmesan cheese, freshly grated

1 egg, beaten

2 garlic cloves, crushed

2 tbsp double cream

1 tbsp chopped parsley

2 tsp chopped fresh rosemary

1 Make the stuffing: wash and trim the spinach, put it into a pan with only the water that clings to the leaves, and cook gently until it has just wilted.

2 Drain the spinach, reserving the cooking liquid, then chop finely. In a bowl, mix the spinach with the cooking liquid, stuffing mix, bacon, Parmesan cheese, egg, garlic, cream, parsley, and rosemary. Add a little of the wine, if needed, to make the stuffing moist.

3 Cut and stuff the chops (see box, right). Put into an ovenproof dish just large enough to hold the chops, and pour in the wine. Cover and cook in a preheated oven at 160°C (325°F, Gas 3) for 50 minutes or until the pork is cooked through.

4 Remove the dish from the oven and increase the oven temperature to 220°C (425°F, Gas 7).

5 If the sauce is too liquid, pour it into a small pan and boil it until it has thickened and reduced to a sauce-like consistency.

6 Put the cheese slices on top of the chops, pour the sauce around them, and return to the oven. Cook for 10–15 minutes until the cheese has melted. Serve hot.

Cutting and stuffing the pork chops

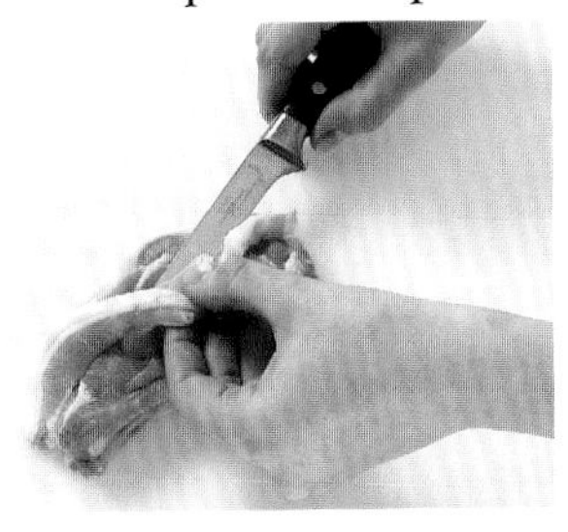

Cut into each chop horizontally with a sharp knife, cutting through to the bone to make a pocket. Sprinkle each chop inside and out with salt and pepper.

Spoon the spinach stuffing into the pockets in the chops. If there is any extra stuffing, put it into a small dish and cook it in the oven at the same time as the chops.

PORK CHOPS WITH ORANGES

Serves 6

6 boneless pork loin chops

3 tbsp wholegrain mustard

125 g (4 oz) demerara sugar

3 small oranges

90 ml (3 fl oz) orange juice

salt and black pepper

1 Spread both sides of each pork chop with the mustard, and sprinkle one side with half of the demerara sugar. Arrange the chops, sugared-side down, in a single layer in a shallow ovenproof dish.

2 With a sharp knife, carefully peel the oranges, removing all the pith. Cut the oranges into thin slices.

3 Cover the chops with the orange slices. Pour the orange juice over the top, add salt and pepper to taste, and sprinkle with the remaining sugar.

4 Cook, uncovered, in a preheated oven at 200°C (400°F, Gas 6) for about 35 minutes, basting the chops occasionally, until cooked through.

Pork steaks with mixed peppercorns

Serves 4

4 lean boneless pork steaks
salt
3–4 tbsp mixed peppercorns
30 g (1 oz) butter
350 ml (12 fl oz) dry white wine
350 ml (12 fl oz) beef stock
175 ml (6 fl oz) double cream

1 Season the steaks on each side with salt. Coarsely crush the peppercorns and spread them on a plate. Press the steaks on to the peppercorns to encrust the surface of the meat, then turn them over and repeat on the other side. Cover and set aside for 30 minutes.

2 Melt the butter in a large frying pan, add the steaks, and cook for 5–7 minutes on each side until the meat is just cooked through but still juicy. Lift the steaks out of the pan, and keep warm.

3 Pour the wine into the pan and boil until it has reduced by half, stirring to mix in the peppercorns and the sediment from the bottom of the pan.

4 Pour in the stock and cook for 5 minutes. Strain the sauce to remove the peppercorns, then return to the pan and boil for 3 minutes or until the sauce is reduced but not too thick.

5 Add the cream and cook, stirring, over a high heat until the sauce is reduced and thickened. Return the pork steaks to the pan, heat through, and serve at once.

Crispy pork steaks with apple

Dip the pork steaks into beaten egg and then into breadcrumbs. Proceed as directed. Meanwhile, peel, core, and slice 2 dessert apples. Wipe the pan and add 15 g (1/2 oz) butter. Add the apple slices, and cook until golden. Serve with the chops.

Sweet & sour Chinese spare ribs

Serves 4

1.25 kg (2 1/2 lb) pork spare ribs
salt and black pepper
spring onion tassels to garnish

SWEET & SOUR SAUCE

2.5 cm (1 in) piece of fresh root ginger, peeled and grated
2 garlic cloves, crushed
2 tbsp soy sauce
2 tbsp dry sherry
2 tbsp hoisin sauce
2 tbsp tomato purée
1 tbsp sesame oil
1 tbsp caster sugar

1 Arrange the ribs in 1 layer in a roasting tin, season, and cook in a preheated oven at 140°C (275°F, Gas 1) for 1 1/2 hours.

2 Make the sauce: combine the ginger, garlic, soy sauce, sherry, hoisin sauce, tomato purée, sesame oil, and caster sugar.

3 Spoon the sauce over the ribs, turning them to coat. Increase the oven temperature to 180°C (350°F, Gas 4), and cook for 25–30 minutes. Garnish with spring onion tassels before serving.

Cook's know-how

Sweet and sour spare ribs are excellent for a barbecue. Cook them in the oven and coat with the sweet and sour sauce, then cook over hot charcoal for 15 minutes on each side.

Spicy spare ribs

Mix together the ginger, garlic, soy sauce, dry sherry, and sesame oil as directed. Add 1 tbsp brown sugar, 1/2 tsp grated nutmeg, 1/4 tsp ground cloves, and 1/4 tsp ground cinnamon. Cook the spare ribs as directed.

Afelia

Serves 4

750 g (1½ lb) boneless spare rib pork chops, cut into 3.5 cm (1½ in) cubes
90 ml (3 fl oz) olive oil
1 large onion, chopped
3 garlic cloves, crushed
250 ml (8 fl oz) beef stock
250 ml (8 fl oz) red wine
½ tsp cumin seeds

MARINADE
250 ml (8 fl oz) red wine
2 tbsp crushed coriander seeds
½ tsp ground cinnamon
salt and black pepper

1 Make the marinade: in a large bowl, combine the red wine, coriander seeds, cinnamon, and salt and pepper to taste. Toss the pork in the marinade, cover, and leave to marinate in the refrigerator overnight.

2 Remove the pork from the marinade, reserving the marinade. Pat dry with paper towels.

3 Heat the oil in a large frying pan, add the onion and garlic, and cook gently, stirring occasionally, for a few minutes until soft but not coloured.

4 Add the pork and cook over a medium to high heat for 5 minutes or until golden brown all over. Discard any excess fat. Pour in the reserved marinade, the stock, and wine, and bring to a boil. Simmer for 1 hour or until the meat is tender.

5 Remove the meat with a slotted spoon and transfer to a shallow ovenproof dish into which it just fits in 1 layer. Skim any fat from the sauce, then strain to remove the coriander seeds. Pour the sauce over the meat, sprinkle with cumin seeds and salt, and cook in a preheated oven at 200°C (400°F, Gas 6) for 40 minutes or until the top is crisp and browned.

Cook's know-how

This stew, in which the pork is marinated then cooked in red wine, is a speciality of Cyprus. Crushed coriander seeds are the classic seasoning, and, in this recipe, the cumin seeds add extra interest. Afelia can be marinated and cooked ahead of time, frozen, then thawed and reheated for 40 minutes when required.

Wiltshire pork casserole

Serves 6–8

2 tbsp sunflower oil
1.5 kg (3 lb) shoulder of pork, trimmed and cut into 3.5 cm (1½ in) cubes
60 g (2 oz) plain flour
450 ml (¾ pint) chicken stock
4 tbsp white wine vinegar
3 tbsp clear honey
2 tbsp soy sauce
250 g (8 oz) large mushrooms, quartered
250 g (8 oz) ready-to-eat stoned prunes
salt and black pepper
chopped parsley to garnish

1 Heat the oil in a large flameproof casserole. Add the pork in batches and cook over a medium to high heat for 5 minutes or until golden brown all over.

2 Return all of the meat to the casserole, sprinkle in the flour, and cook, stirring, for 1 minute.

3 Stir in the chicken stock, white wine vinegar, honey, soy sauce, and salt and pepper to taste, and bring to a boil. Cover and cook in a preheated oven at 160°C (325°F, Gas 3) for 2 hours.

4 Stir the mushrooms and prunes into the casserole and cook for 1 hour or until the pork is tender. Taste for seasoning and garnish with parsley before serving.

Boston pork & bean casserole

Add 2 tbsp tomato purée with the stock and substitute 1 x 400 g (13 oz) can haricot beans for the mushrooms and prunes. Proceed as directed.

DANISH MEATBALLS

 **Serves 4**

500 g (1 lb) minced pork
1 small onion, very finely chopped
30 g (1 oz) plain flour, plus extra for coating
1 tsp chopped fresh thyme
1/4 tsp paprika
salt and black pepper
1 egg, beaten
a little milk
30 g (1 oz) butter
1 tbsp sunflower oil
Greek yogurt to serve
chopped fresh thyme to garnish

TOMATO SAUCE
30 g (1 oz) butter
30 g (1 oz) plain flour
450 ml (3/4 pint) chicken stock
1 x 400 g (13 oz) can chopped tomatoes
1 tbsp tomato purée
1 garlic clove, crushed
1 bay leaf

1 Mix the pork and onion in a large bowl, then stir in the flour, thyme, paprika, and salt and pepper to taste. Bind with the egg, adding enough milk to give a soft but not sticky texture.

2 Using 2 dessertspoons, shape the mixture into 20 ovals. Roll lightly in flour, and chill in the refrigerator.

3 Make the tomato sauce: melt the butter in a pan, add the flour, and cook, stirring, for 1 minute. Blend in the stock, then add the tomatoes, tomato purée, garlic, bay leaf, and salt and pepper to taste. Bring to a boil, stirring until thickened. Cover and simmer for 20–25 minutes.

4 Work the sauce through a nylon sieve, then taste for seasoning. Set aside.

5 Melt the butter with the oil in a flameproof casserole. Cook the meatballs in batches, for 5 minutes or until browned all over. Lift out the meatballs and drain on paper towels.

6 Pour the fat out of the casserole. Return the meatballs, add the sauce, and bring to a boil. Cover and cook in a preheated oven at 180°C (350°F, Gas 4) for 30 minutes. Spoon over a little yogurt and garnish with thyme before serving.

PASTICCIO

Serves 4

1 tbsp sunflower oil
500 g (1 lb) minced pork or beef
2 onions, chopped
3–5 garlic cloves, crushed
1 x 400 g (13 oz) can chopped tomatoes
150 g (5 oz) tomato purée
90 ml (3 fl oz) red wine
2 bay leaves
1 tsp sugar
1/2 tsp chopped fresh oregano
1/2 tsp ground cinnamon
250 g (8 oz) elbow macaroni
salt and black pepper

CHEESE CUSTARD
20 g (3/4 oz) butter
20 g (3/4 oz) plain flour
300 ml (1/2 pint) milk
250 g (8 oz) mature Cheddar cheese, grated
2 eggs, lightly beaten
large pinch of grated nutmeg

1 Heat the sunflower oil in a large frying pan, add the meat, onions, and garlic, and cook over a medium heat for 5 minutes or until lightly browned.

2 Add the tomatoes, tomato purée, and wine. Bring to a boil and simmer for 15 minutes.

3 Add the bay leaves, sugar, oregano, cinnamon, and salt and pepper to taste. Simmer gently for 10 minutes or until the sauce is thickened.

4 Meanwhile, cook the macaroni in boiling salted water for 8–10 minutes until just tender. Drain and set aside.

5 Spoon half of the meat mixture into an ovenproof dish and add half of the macaroni. Cover with the remaining meat mixture, then top with the remaining macaroni. Bake in a preheated oven at 180°C (350°F, Gas 4) for 20 minutes.

6 Make the cheese custard: melt the butter in a saucepan, add the flour, and cook, stirring, for 1 minute. Remove from the heat and gradually blend in the milk. Bring to a boil, stirring constantly, until the mixture thickens. Simmer for 2–3 minutes. Remove from the heat and stir in the cheese, eggs, nutmeg, and salt and pepper to taste.

7 Remove the dish from the oven, pour over the cheese custard, and bake for a further 20 minutes or until the custard is golden.

MUSTARD-GLAZED HAM

Gammon tastes best when it is cooked on the bone, especially if it is home-baked and coated with a tangy glaze as in this recipe. Here, gammon slowly steam-roasts in its own juices, spiked with cider. Watercress and orange slices are the perfect finishing touch. Once gammon is cooked it is commonly known as ham.

Serves 16–20

4–5 kg (8–10 lb) smoked gammon

400 ml (14 fl oz) cider or apple juice

3 tbsp English mustard

90 g (3 oz) demerara sugar

LEMON MUSTARD SAUCE

4 tbsp olive oil

juice of 1 lemon

1 tbsp caster sugar

2 tsp coarse-grain mustard

salt and black pepper

150 ml (1/4 pint) crème fraîche

1 Put the gammon into a large container, cover with cold water, and leave to soak for at least 12 hours.

2 Drain and rinse the gammon. Arrange 2 pieces of foil, long enough to cover the gammon, across a large roasting tin.

3 Pour the cider into the foil. Stand a wire rack on the foil and stand the gammon on the rack. Insert a meat thermometer, if using, into the thickest part of the meat.

4 Wrap the foil loosely over the gammon, leaving plenty of space for air to circulate. Place the gammon just below the centre of a preheated oven and cook at 160°C (325°F, Gas 3) for 20 minutes per 500 g (1 lb). The meat thermometer should register 75°C (170°F). Remove the gammon from the oven and leave to cool for a few minutes.

5 Increase the oven temperature to 230°C (450°F, Gas 8). Transfer the gammon to a board, drain the cooking juices from the foil, and discard. Glaze the gammon with the mustard and sugar (see box, right).

6 Return the gammon to the rack in the roasting tin. Cover any lean parts of the gammon with foil, return to the oven, and cook, turning the roasting tin if necessary, for 15–20 minutes until the glaze is golden brown all over.

7 Meanwhile, make the lemon mustard sauce: put the olive oil, lemon juice, caster sugar, mustard, and salt and pepper to taste into a screw-top jar and shake vigorously to mix the ingredients together.

8 Put the crème fraîche into a bowl and stir in the lemon and mustard mixture. Taste for seasoning and leave to chill in the refrigerator until needed.

9 Carve the ham into slices and serve either warm or cold, with the lemon mustard sauce.

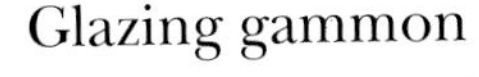

Glazing gammon

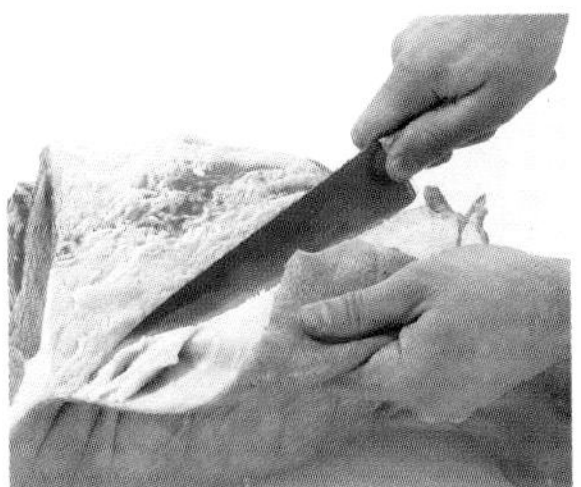

Cut away the skin with a sharp knife, leaving behind a thin layer of fat. Discard the skin.

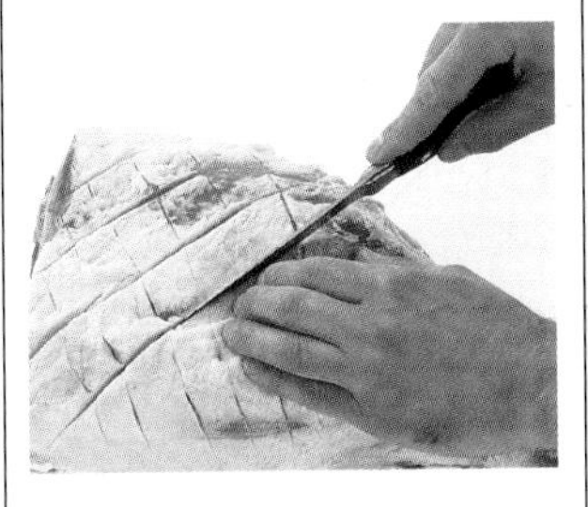

Score the fat all over in a diamond pattern, so that the glaze penetrates the fat.

Spread a generous layer of mustard over the fat, using a palette knife or your hands.

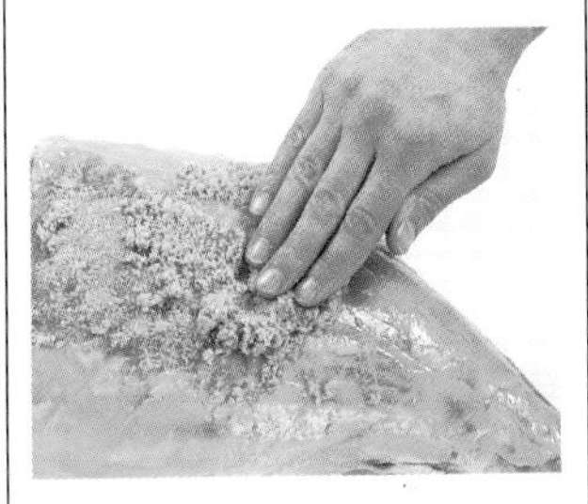

Press the demerara sugar on to the layer of mustard, making sure it is evenly coated all over.

BOSTON BAKED BEANS

 **Serves 4**

375 g (12 oz) dried haricot beans
60 g (2 oz) dark muscovado sugar
2 tbsp tomato purée
2 tsp black treacle
2 tsp golden syrup
2 tsp mustard powder
2 tsp salt
black pepper
250 g (8 oz) piece of streaky bacon, cut into 2.5 cm (1 in) cubes
3 onions, quartered
600 ml (1 pint) water

1 Put the haricot beans into a large bowl, cover with plenty of cold water, and leave to soak overnight.

2 Drain the beans, and rinse under cold running water. Put the beans into a saucepan, cover with cold water, and bring to a boil. Boil rapidly for 10 minutes, then partially cover the pan and simmer for 30 minutes. Drain and set aside.

3 Put the sugar, tomato purée, black treacle, golden syrup, mustard, salt, and pepper to taste into a large flameproof casserole and heat gently, stirring constantly.

4 Add the bacon and onions to the casserole with the drained beans and measured water. Bring to a boil, cover tightly, and cook in a preheated oven at 140°C (275°F, Gas 1), stirring occasionally, for 4½–5 hours. Taste for seasoning before serving.

Boston baked beans

This classic American dish needs long slow cooking to let the flavours mingle and mellow. It dates back to the early days of the Puritan settlers in New England. As no cooking was allowed on the Sabbath, the dish was cooked on Saturday and then served for Saturday dinner, Sunday breakfast, and Sunday lunch.

FARMER'S BACON BAKE

Serves 4

750 g (1½ lb) bacon joint
a few parsley stalks
6 black peppercorns
1 bay leaf
4 potatoes, cut into large chunks
4 carrots, thickly sliced
4 celery stalks, thickly sliced
chopped parsley to garnish

CHEESE SAUCE

45 g (1½ oz) butter
45 g (1½ oz) plain flour
200 ml (7 fl oz) milk
90 g (3 oz) mature Cheddar cheese, grated
salt and black pepper

1 Put the bacon joint into a large pan, cover with cold water, and bring to a boil. Drain, rinse, and cover with fresh cold water. Add the parsley stalks, peppercorns, and bay leaf, and bring to a boil. Cover and simmer very gently for 45 minutes.

2 Add the potatoes, carrots, and celery and bring back to a boil. Cover and simmer very gently for 20 minutes or until the meat and vegetables are tender. Drain, reserving the cooking liquid, and allow the bacon to cool slightly.

3 Remove all of the rind and fat from the bacon, cut the meat into bite-sized pieces, and arrange in a shallow ovenproof dish with the vegetables. Keep warm.

4 Make the cheese sauce: melt the butter in a saucepan, add the flour, and cook, stirring, for 1 minute. Remove from the heat and gradually blend in the milk and 250 ml (8 fl oz) of the reserved cooking liquid. Bring to a boil, stirring constantly until the mixture thickens. Simmer for 2–3 minutes. Add three-quarters of the cheese, and salt and pepper to taste.

5 Pour the sauce over the meat and vegetables and sprinkle with the remaining cheese. Bake in a preheated oven at 180°C (350°F, Gas 4) for 30 minutes or until the cheese topping is bubbling. Garnish with chopped parsley before serving.

SAUSAGE CASSOULET

Cassoulet is a hearty dish from Languedoc in the south west of France. This is a simple and satisfying version. The types of meat used in more traditional recipes may include duck, goose, or lamb.

Serves 8

- *375 g (12 oz) dried haricot beans*
- *2 tbsp olive oil*
- *500 g (1 lb) coarse pork sausages*
- *250 g (8 oz) piece of smoked bacon, cut into strips*
- *2 large onions, sliced*
- *250 g (8 oz) piece of garlic sausage, cut into 2.5 cm (1 in) chunks*
- *2 x 400 g (13 oz) cans chopped tomatoes*
- *300 ml (1/2 pint) chicken stock*
- *150 ml (1/4 pint) dry white wine*
- *2 tbsp tomato purée*
- *2 garlic cloves, crushed*
- *3 thyme sprigs*
- *a few parsley stalks*
- *salt and black pepper*
- *125–175 g (4–6 oz) fresh white breadcrumbs*
- *chopped parsley to garnish*

1 Put the haricot beans into a large bowl, cover with plenty of cold water, and leave to soak overnight.

2 Drain the beans, and rinse under cold running water. Put the beans into a saucepan, cover with fresh cold water, and bring to a boil. Boil rapidly for 10 minutes, then simmer for 30 minutes or until just tender. Drain.

3 Heat the olive oil in a large flameproof casserole, add the sausages and bacon, and cook for 5 minutes or until browned all over. Lift out and drain on paper towels. Thickly slice the sausages.

4 Pour off all but 1 tbsp of the fat from the casserole. Add the onions and cook gently, stirring occasionally, for a few minutes until soft but not coloured.

5 Return the bacon and sausages to the casserole, add the beans, the garlic sausage, tomatoes, stock, wine, tomato purée, garlic, thyme, parsley stalks, and salt and pepper to taste and bring back to a boil.

Adding the topping to the cassoulet

Remove the cassoulet from the oven and sprinkle with a thick, even layer of breadcrumbs.

6 Cover and cook in a preheated oven at 160°C (325°F, Gas 3) for 1 hour. Add the breadcrumb topping (see box, above). Return the casserole to the oven and cook, uncovered, for 30 minutes or until the topping is golden brown. Taste for seasoning. Garnish with chopped parsley before serving.

SAUSAGE BAKE

Serves 6

- *1 tbsp sunflower oil*
- *1 kg (2 lb) coarse-cut pork sausages*
- *500 g (1 lb) leeks, thickly sliced*
- *750 g (1 1/2 lb) potatoes, cut into 5 mm (1/4 in) slices*
- *90 g (3 oz) red lentils*
- *salt and black pepper*
- *2 bay leaves*
- *2 cloves*
- *1 garlic clove, crushed*
- *900 ml (1 1/2 pints) chicken stock*
- *chopped parsley to garnish*

1 Heat the oil in a large flameproof casserole and brown the sausages. Lift out, then cut into thick slices.

2 Layer the leeks, potatoes, sausages, and lentils in the casserole, adding seasoning to taste, and placing the bay leaves, cloves, and garlic among the layers. Top with a layer of potatoes.

3 Pour in the stock and bring to a boil. Cover tightly and cook in a preheated oven at 160°C (325°F, Gas 3), checking the liquid level occasionally, for 2 1/2 hours.

4 Remove the lid, increase the oven temperature to 200°C (400°F, Gas 6) and cook for 20–25 minutes until the potato is browned. Garnish with parsley.

TOAD IN THE HOLE WITH ONION SAUCE

Serves 4

400 g (13 oz) pork sausagemeat
1 leek, finely chopped
2 tbsp chopped fresh sage
1 tbsp chopped parsley
3 tbsp sunflower oil
3 onions, chopped
2 tbsp plain flour
300 ml (1/2 pint) milk
250 ml (8 fl oz) chicken stock
chopped parsley to garnish

BATTER

125 g (4 oz) self-raising flour
3 eggs, beaten
300 ml (1/2 pint) milk
1 tbsp chopped parsley
pinch of grated nutmeg
salt and black pepper

1 Make the batter: sift the flour into a bowl. Make a well in the middle and add the eggs and a little milk. Blend to a smooth paste, then gradually whisk in the remaining milk until the batter has the pouring consistency of cream.

2 Add the chopped parsley, nutmeg, and salt and pepper to taste. Cover and leave to stand for 30 minutes.

3 Meanwhile, combine the sausagemeat, leek, sage, parsley, and salt and pepper to taste. Shape the mixture into 12 balls and set aside.

4 Heat the oil in a saucepan, add the onions, and cook for a few minutes until soft but not coloured. Transfer one-third of the onions to 4 small ovenproof dishes or 1 large dish. Set aside the remainder.

5 Add the sausage balls to the dishes and bake in a preheated oven at 220°C (425°F, Gas 7) for about 10 minutes until brown.

6 Add the batter mixture, and return at once to the oven. Bake for 20–25 minutes until the batter is well risen and golden.

7 Meanwhile, add the plain flour to the onions in the pan and cook, stirring, for 1 minute. Remove from the heat and gradually blend in the milk and stock. Bring to a boil, stirring constantly, and simmer for 2–3 minutes until the mixture thickens. Serve the toad in the hole sprinkled with parsley, with the sauce handed separately.

SAUSAGE & LENTIL CASSEROLE

Serves 4

300 g (10 oz) brown lentils
2 bay leaves
2 tbsp sunflower oil
2 large onions, chopped
1 large potato, chopped
1 celery stalk, diced
1 carrot, diced
2 tomatoes, peeled (page 39), seeded, and diced
2 tbsp plain flour
250 ml (8 fl oz) chicken or vegetable stock
2–3 tbsp chopped parsley
1 tbsp chopped fresh sage
salt and black pepper
375 g (12 oz) herby pork sausages
chopped parsley to garnish

1 Put the lentils and bay leaves into a saucepan, cover with cold water, and bring to a boil. Cover and simmer for 30 minutes or until the lentils are just tender. Drain, and set aside.

2 Heat the oil in a large saucepan, add the onions, and cook gently, stirring occasionally, for a few minutes until softened.

3 Add the potato, celery, carrot, and tomatoes, and cook for 10 minutes or until the onions are browned and the other vegetables are softened. Using a slotted spoon, lift out the vegetables and set aside.

4 Add the flour to the pan and cook, stirring, for 1 minute. Remove the pan from the heat and gradually blend in the stock. Bring to a boil, stirring constantly, and simmer for 2–3 minutes until the sauce thickens.

5 Add the lentils to the sauce with the vegetables, parsley, sage, and salt and pepper to taste. Mix well and turn into a large ovenproof casserole.

6 Arrange the sausages on top and cook in a preheated oven at 190°C (375°F, Gas 5) for about 30 minutes until the sausages are browned all over and cooked through. Garnish with chopped parsley before serving.

7

VEGETARIAN DISHES

UNDER 30 MINUTES

HALLOUMI & VEGETABLE KEBABS

Cubes of halloumi cheese, cherry tomatoes, baguette slices, and red pepper threaded on to skewers, then briefly marinated, and grilled.

SERVES 4 722 calories per serving

Takes 25 minutes PAGE 293

RED BEAN & TOMATO CURRY

Rich and spicy: red kidney beans cooked with tomatoes, garlic, chilli, ginger, curry powder, turmeric, coriander, and cayenne.

SERVES 4 218 calories per serving

Takes 20 minutes PAGE 292

VEGETABLE STIR-FRY WITH TOFU

Tofu marinated in soy sauce and sherry, stir-fried with carrots, ginger, mushrooms, bean sprouts, chicory, and spring onions.

SERVES 4 335 calories per serving

Takes 15 minutes, plus marinating PAGE 294

30–60 MINUTES

COUSCOUS WITH ROASTED PEPPERS

Tasty and simple to make: couscous with chick peas, courgettes, carrots, and spices. Topped with peppers and almonds.

SERVES 4 418 calories per serving

Takes 45 minutes PAGE 287

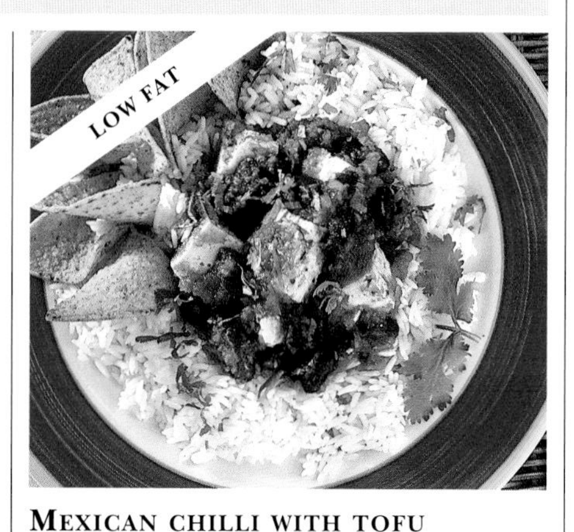

MEXICAN CHILLI WITH TOFU

Bite-sized pieces of tofu cooked with red kidney beans and tomato sauce seasoned with garlic, chilli, paprika, cumin, and oregano.

SERVES 4–6 386–257 calories per serving

Takes 35 minutes PAGE 294

FELAFEL WITH SESAME YOGURT SAUCE

Blended chick peas, spring onions, herbs, and spices, shaped into patties, and cooked until golden. Served with sesame yogurt sauce.

SERVES 4–6 489–326 calories per serving

Takes 20 minutes, plus standing PAGE 293

CARROT ROULADE

Fresh and creamy: carrot mixed with garlic, red pepper, tomatoes, and eggs, baked, then rolled around a cheese and cucumber filling.

SERVES 4 725 calories per serving

Takes 30 minutes, plus chilling PAGE 297

SPINACH & RICOTTA PARCELS

Light and crispy: spinach combined with ricotta cheese, onion, and nutmeg, and baked in cases of filo pastry until golden.

MAKES 4 307 calories per serving

Takes 40 minutes PAGE 289

VEGETARIAN BURGERS

Soya beans combined with tomato juice, soya mince, sesame seeds, and herbs. Shaped into burgers, and served with lettuce dressing.

SERVES 6 380 calories per serving

Takes 30 minutes, plus chilling PAGE 295

30–60 MINUTES

MIXED BEAN BAKE

Aduki and butter beans simmered with mushrooms, tomatoes, and parsley. Topped with leeks and a cheese sauce.

SERVES 4 564 calories per serving

Takes 60 minutes **PAGE 279**

SPINACH ROULADE

Combined spinach, butter, and eggs, briefly baked, sprinkled with Parmesan, and rolled with a crème fraîche and mushroom filling.

SERVES 6–8 250–187 calories per serving

Takes 30 minutes, plus chilling **PAGE 297**

ITALIAN STUFFED COURGETTES

Baked courgettes with a delicious tomato and basil stuffing. Topped with capers and Fontina cheese.

SERVES 4 437 calories per serving

Takes 50 minutes **PAGE 284**

RED LENTIL & COCONUT CURRY

Lentils cooked with coconut and seasoned with ginger, chilli, garlic, and turmeric. Topped with mustard-seed butter.

SERVES 4–6 722–481 calories per serving

Takes 40 minutes **PAGE 292**

VEGETABLE BAKE NIÇOISE

Rich and aromatic: black olives, courgettes, tomatoes, red onion, and garlic, sprinkled with capers, herbes de Provence, and pepper, and baked. Garnished with shredded fresh basil. It is delicious served hot or cold with croûtons or toasted baguette.

SERVES 4 237 calories per serving

Takes 60 minutes **PAGE 278**

OVER 60 MINUTES

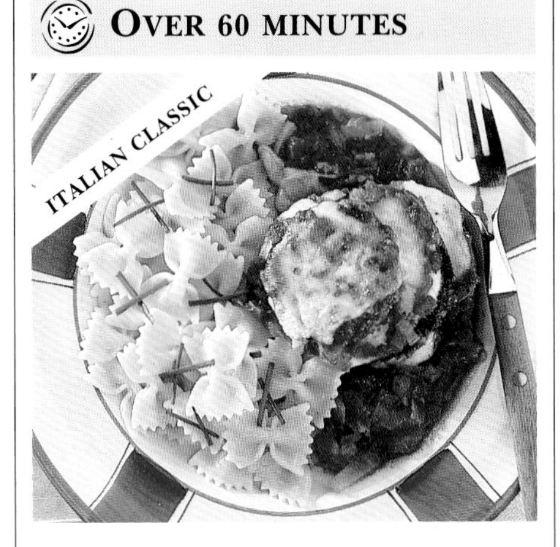

AUBERGINE PARMIGIANA

Rich and tangy: aubergine slices layered with garlic- and basil-flavoured tomato sauce, and mozzarella and Parmesan cheeses.

SERVES 4–6 774–516 calories per serving

Takes 1 1/4 hours, plus standing **PAGE 282**

POLENTA WITH GRILLED VEGETABLES

Barbecued strips of polenta served with marinated and barbecued courgettes, fennel, tomatoes, and red onion.

SERVES 4–6 479–319 calories per serving

Takes 45 minutes, plus marinating **PAGE 286**

GLAMORGAN SAUSAGES

Caerphilly and goat's cheeses combined with breadcrumbs, leek, walnuts, sage, lemon zest, mustard, and eggs, and fried until crisp.

SERVES 4 526 calories per serving

Takes 35 minutes, plus chilling **PAGE 295**

OVER 60 MINUTES

MUSHROOM GOUGERE

Savoury choux pastry with a filling of mixed mushrooms, flavoured with tarragon, and baked until golden brown.

SERVES 4 558 calories per serving

Takes 1 1/2 hours, plus chilling **PAGE 288**

SPINACH GNOCCHI WITH TOMATO SAUCE

Dumplings of spinach, ricotta and Parmesan cheeses, and eggs, served with tomato sauce.

SERVES 4 738 calories per serving

Takes 1 1/4 hours, plus chilling **PAGE 286**

COUNTRY VEGETABLE PIES

Carrots and parsnips baked with onion, garlic, and parsley sauce. Topped with mashed potato for a nourishing meal.

SERVES 4 642 calories per serving

Takes 1 1/4 hours **PAGE 279**

VEGETABLE & BARLEY CASSEROLE

Pearl barley, shallots, carrots, parsnips, courgettes, mangetout, and cauliflower, cooked with stock. Topped with dumplings.

SERVES 4 509 calories per serving

Takes 1 1/4 hours **PAGE 287**

POTATO, CELERIAC, & PARMESAN GRATIN

Potatoes and celeriac baked with cream and ricotta cheese, breadcrumbs and Parmesan.

SERVES 4 676 calories per serving

Takes 1 3/4 hours **PAGE 282**

CHESTNUT LOAF

Chestnuts baked with potatoes and celery, flavoured with garlic, parsley, soy sauce, and tomato purée. Served with spicy tomato salsa.

SERVES 6 226 calories per serving

Takes 1 1/4 hours **PAGE 296**

TOMATO & OLIVE FLAN

Poppyseed pastry base baked with a topping of onions, tomatoes, tomato purée, basil, garlic, vignotte cheese, and black olives.

SERVES 6 502 calories per serving

Takes 60 minutes, plus chilling **PAGE 288**

STUFFED RED PEPPERS

Baked peppers with a nourishing stuffing of button mushrooms, onion, rice, red lentils, stock, pine nuts, and parsley.

SERVES 4 622 calories per serving

Takes 1 1/2 hours **PAGE 283**

CHEESE-TOPPED BAKED AUBERGINES

Aubergines spiked with garlic slivers dipped in herbs and olive oil. Topped with Gorgonzola and Cheddar cheeses.

SERVES 4 447 calories per serving

Takes 1 1/4 hours **PAGE 283**

OVER 60 MINUTES

MUSHROOM LASAGNE

Lasagne layered with mushroom and tomato sauce, spinach balls, béchamel sauce, and grated Cheddar cheese, then baked.

SERVES 6 684 calories per serving
Takes 1 1/4 hours **PAGE 285**

DAIRY-FREE LASAGNE

Tomato sauce layered with lasagne, lightly browned aubergine slices, and spinach, topped with courgettes, and baked.

SERVES 4–6 364–243 calories per serving
Takes 60 minutes, plus standing **PAGE 285**

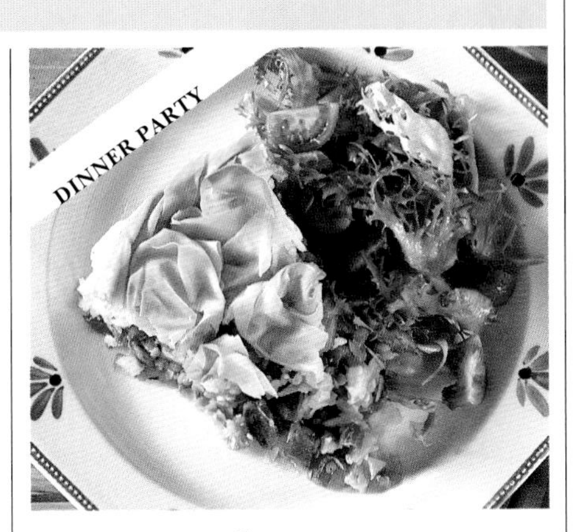

AUBERGINE & CAERPHILLY FILO PIE

Diced aubergine, onions, Caerphilly cheese, lentils, red peppers, spices, and oregano, combined and baked in filo pastry.

SERVES 6 569 calories per serving
Takes 1 1/4 hours, plus standing **PAGE 289**

CHRISTMAS NUT LOAF

Brown rice blended with ceps, mushrooms, carrots, parsley, and rosemary, and baked in a loaf tin with walnuts, Brazil nuts, pine nuts, and Cheddar cheese. Garnished with rosemary sprigs, served in slices, and accompanied by cranberry sauce.

SERVES 6–8 600–450 calories per serving
Takes 2 1/2 hours, plus soaking **PAGE 296**

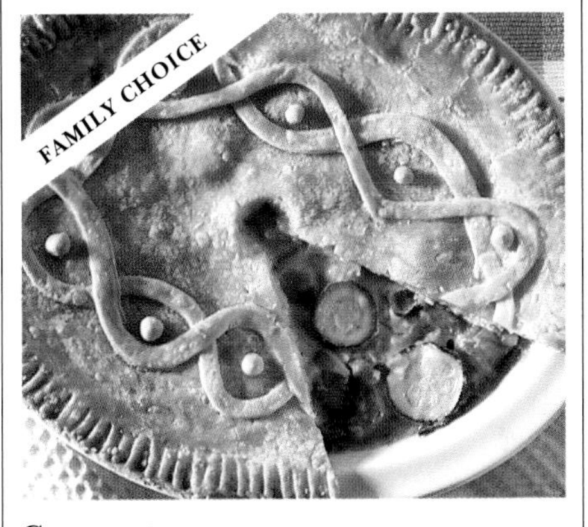

CHEESE & VEGETABLE PIE

A variety of vegetables mixed with parsley and marjoram, in a Cheddar cheese and mustard sauce. Topped with cheese pastry.

SERVES 4–6 610–406 calories per serving
Takes 1 1/2 hours, plus chilling **PAGE 278**

WINTER VEGETABLE TERRINE

Three colourful layers of puréed carrot, celeriac, and broccoli, baked and served in slices.

SERVES 4–6 142–95 calories per serving
Takes 1 3/4 hours, plus chilling **PAGE 298**

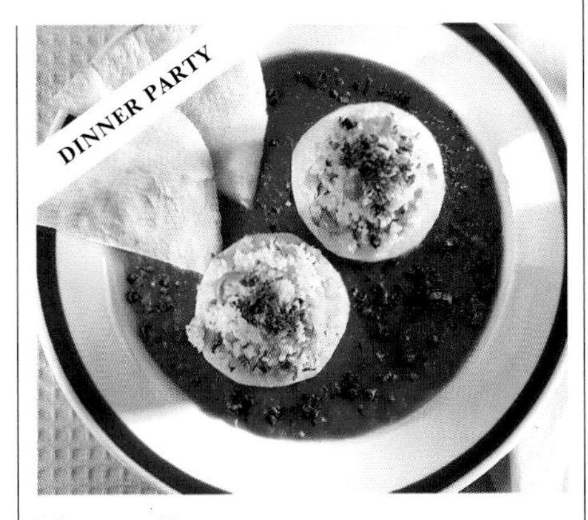

MIDDLE-EASTERN STUFFED MARROW

Marrow slices filled with a mixture of steamed couscous, mushrooms, lemon, spring onions, yogurt, mint, and olives, then baked.

SERVES 4 247 calories per serving
Takes 1 1/4 hours **PAGE 284**

CREAM CHEESE TERRINE

Aubergine and red and yellow peppers layered with a cream cheese mixture, wrapped in spinach leaves, and baked.

SERVES 8 194 calories per serving
Takes 2 1/4 hours, plus chilling **PAGE 298**

VEGETARIAN KNOW-HOW

THERE ARE THREE BASIC types of vegetarian diet. A vegan diet is the strictest – vegans do not eat any meat, fish, eggs, or dairy products. A vegetarian diet excludes meat, poultry, and fish and may or may not include eggs and dairy products. A demi-vegetarian diet can include fish and poultry. With such a great variety of foods from which to choose, vegetarian diets, based largely on complex carbohydrates, pulses, vegetables, fruits, nuts, and seeds, can be quite imaginative and nutritious.

MAINTAINING A BALANCED DIET

Fish, meat, poultry, dairy products, and eggs are complete protein foods, which means that they contain almost all the essential dietary amino acids that the body needs. Many vegetarians replace fish, meat, and poultry with eggs, cheese, and other dairy products, but this is not the ideal solution as dairy foods are high in saturated fats and calories. Instead, complete protein can be obtained by combining two or more vegetable protein sources, or adding non-animal complete protein foods to the diet, such as tofu, TVP (textured vegetable protein) and quorn, a mild-flavoured vegetarian food made from a mushroom.

Pulses, grains, nuts, and seeds, although rich in protein, are deficient in one or more of the essential amino acids, but by combining vegetable protein sources, the protein becomes complete. Examples of complete vegetarian protein combinations drawn from cuisines around the world are beans and rice, hummus and pita bread, or a mixed nut, lentil, and vegetable salad.

Another dietary interaction that vegetarians should be aware of is that between iron and vitamin C. The form of iron found in meat is easily absorbed by the body, but the iron in vegetables, nuts, grains, pulses, and eggs needs a helping hand, and this is provided by vitamin C. Be sure to include a green vegetable, tomatoes, or citrus fruit when serving these foods.

ALTERNATIVE PROTEIN FOODS

Tofu and TVP are complete protein foods that are low in fat, calories, and cholesterol, and so make a healthy basis for a great variety of dishes.

Tofu
Made from processed, pressed soya beans, tofu has no taste of its own, unless it is the smoked variety, but it quickly takes on the flavours of marinades and sauces. It contains no fat. Silken tofu has a soft, creamy texture: use it in sauces, dips, and puddings. Firm tofu can be stir-fried, grilled, or casseroled. Before use, drain and pat dry with paper towels.

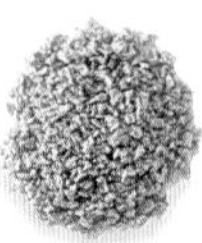

TVP
Textured vegetable protein, or TVP, is made from soya flour and is virtually fat free. It is available as chunks or as mince and has a rather chewy texture, like meat. It is often used in commercial vegetarian products such as sausages. It keeps well, so keep a pack in the store-cupboard and use it in home-made burgers or cook it in a stew or casserole.

A gelatine substitute

Gelatine is a natural protein found in the bones, skin, and connective tissues of animals. Commercial powdered gelatine is derived from pig skin, and is thus unacceptable in a vegetarian diet. The most common substitute is agar agar, a tasteless dried seaweed sold in stick or powder form. Before use, stir the agar agar into boiling water and simmer for 5 minutes, to dissolve. It has stronger setting properties than gelatine, so less needs to be used.

VEGETABLE STOCK

Add any vegetable trimmings you have (celery tops or tomato skins, for example), or vary the ingredients to emphasize the flavour of the dish in which you want to use the stock.

1 Coarsely chop *2 onions, 2–3 carrots, 3 celery stalks,* and *1 leek.* Put into a large saucepan or stockpot and add *1 large bouquet garni.* Add *1 crushed garlic clove* too, if wished.

2 Add *1.25 litres (2 pints) water* and bring to the boil. Skim off any scum that rises to the surface. Lower the heat and simmer for 30 minutes.

3 Strain the stock through a sieve. If not using immediately, leave to cool, cover, and store in the refrigerator for up to 5 days or in the freezer for up to 1 month.

COOKING PULSES

Pulses are the dried, edible seeds of the legume family – beans, peas, and lentils. Stored in a cool, dark place, they will keep for up to 6 months. Many types are now available in cans, and need no soaking or cooking, but if you want to prepare your own, it's quite simple.

1 Put the pulses into a large bowl and cover with plenty of cold water. Leave to soak for the required time (see below). Drain and rinse under cold running water.

2 Put into a saucepan and add cold water to cover – about twice their volume. Bring to a boil. Lower the heat, cover, and simmer until tender (see below).

Warning

If cooking pulses such as red kidney beans, soya beans, or black-eyed beans, it is vital to boil them rapidly for 10 minutes first, to destroy toxins. Drain, add fresh water, and return to a boil. If in doubt, treat all pulses (except split peas and lentils) in this way.

Pulses know-how

Pulses can be left to soak for 8 hours, but if you prefer, you can speed up the process by boiling them for 3 minutes, then leaving them to soak, covered, for 1–2 hours before cooking as usual.

◆

Add salt towards the end of cooking time; if it is added at the beginning, it will toughen the skins of the pulses.

◆

Pulses double in size and weight when cooked, so if a recipe calls for 250 g (8 oz) cooked pulses, you will need 125 g (4 oz) before cooking.

SOAKING & COOKING TIMES OF PULSES

Cooking times depend on the age of the pulse: the older pulses are the longer they will take to cook. The cooking times given below are therefore only a guide.

PULSE	SOAKING	COOKING
Aduki beans	8–12 hours	30–45 minutes
Black-eyed beans	8–12 hours	1 hour
Butter beans	8–12 hours	1 hour
Cannellini beans	8–12 hours	1¼ hours
Chick peas	8–12 hours	1½–2 hours
Flageolet beans	8–12 hours	1 hour
Haricot beans	8–12 hours	1–1½ hours
Red lentils	not required	20–30 minutes
Green lentils	not required	30–45 minutes
Mung beans	8–12 hours	45 minutes
Red kidney beans	8–12 hours	1¼–1½ hours
Soya beans	8–12 hours	1½ hours

GRAINS

Whole grains are first-class sources of carbohydrate, fibre, vitamins, and minerals.

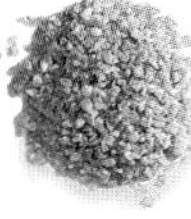

Bulgur wheat Also known as burghul wheat. Made from steamed, dried, and crushed wheat kernels, it cooks very quickly. It can also be soaked and used in salads.

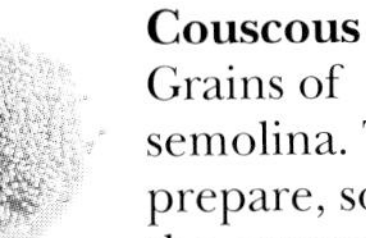

Couscous Grains of semolina. To prepare, soak the couscous first to allow the grains to swell and soften. For extra flavour, steam the couscous over vegetables in a colander set over a large pot.

Polenta Made from ground maize or corn, and also known as cornmeal. Cook in simmering water, stirring constantly until the water is absorbed. Cook, stirring, for 10–20 minutes until thick. Serve warm, or leave to cool, then grill.

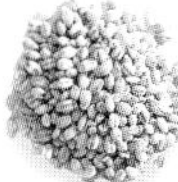

Pearl barley Has a nutty flavour and chewy texture. Add to vegetable soups and stews to thicken them.

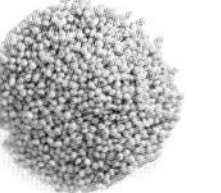

Millet Available as flakes or grains, millet can be cooked with water, stock, or milk. Add a small handful to soups to thicken them.

Oats Available in various sizes and textures. Oatflakes are used in porridge and muesli; fine oatmeal can be used to make biscuits or to thicken soups.

VEGETABLE BAKE NIÇOISE

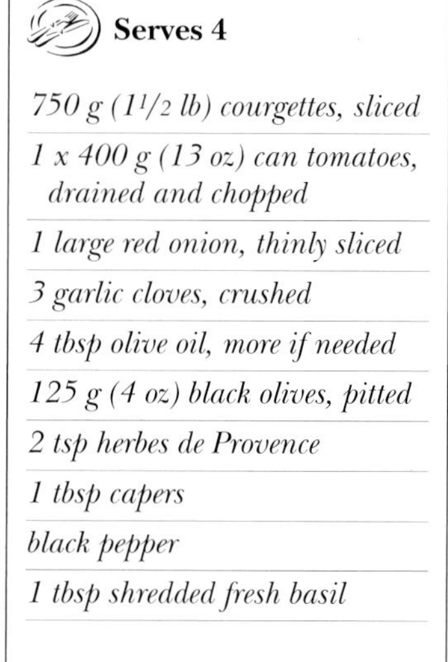

Serves 4

750 g (1½ lb) courgettes, sliced
1 x 400 g (13 oz) can tomatoes, drained and chopped
1 large red onion, thinly sliced
3 garlic cloves, crushed
4 tbsp olive oil, more if needed
125 g (4 oz) black olives, pitted
2 tsp herbes de Provence
1 tbsp capers
black pepper
1 tbsp shredded fresh basil

1 In an ovenproof dish, toss the courgettes, tomatoes, onion, and garlic, and drizzle the oil over the top.

2 Arrange the black olives on top of the vegetables, then sprinkle with the herbes de Provence, capers, and black pepper to taste.

3 Bake in a preheated oven at 190°C (375°F, Gas 5) for 45 minutes or until the courgettes and onion are tender, checking occasionally to see if the surface is getting too dry. If it is, drizzle a little more olive oil over the vegetables.

4 Sprinkle the dish with the shredded fresh basil. Serve hot or cold.

CHEESE & VEGETABLE PIE

Serves 4–6

30 g (1 oz) butter
1 onion, chopped
2 carrots, sliced
500 g (1 lb) courgettes, sliced
2 large tomatoes, peeled (page 39), seeded, and chopped
125 g (4 oz) mushrooms, sliced
2 tbsp chopped parsley
1 tsp chopped fresh marjoram
salt and black pepper

CHEESE SAUCE

30 g (1 oz) butter
30 g (1 oz) plain flour
300 ml (½ pint) milk
60 g (2 oz) mature Cheddar cheese, grated
1 tsp English mustard
pinch of cayenne pepper

CHEESE PASTRY

125 g (4 oz) plain flour
60 g (2 oz) butter
60 g (2 oz) mature Cheddar cheese, grated
1 small egg, beaten

1 Make the cheese pastry: sift the flour into a bowl. Add the butter and rub in lightly until the mixture resembles fine breadcrumbs. Stir in the cheese, then bind to a soft but not sticky dough with 1 tbsp of the beaten egg and 1 tbsp cold water. Chill for 30 minutes.

2 Melt the butter in a large pan, add the onion, and cook gently for 3–5 minutes until softened. Add the carrots and cook for about 5 minutes.

3 Add the courgettes, tomatoes, mushrooms, parsley, marjoram, and salt and pepper to taste, and cook over a gentle heat, stirring occasionally, for 10–15 minutes until just softened. Set aside.

4 Make the cheese sauce: melt the butter in a saucepan, add the flour, and cook, stirring, for 1 minute. Remove from the heat and gradually blend in the milk.

5 Bring to a boil, stirring until the mixture thickens. Simmer for 2–3 minutes, then stir in the cheese, mustard, cayenne, and salt and pepper to taste. Stir the vegetables into the sauce, remove from the heat, and leave to cool.

6 Roll out the pastry on a floured work surface. Invert a pie dish on to the pastry and cut around the edge. Reserve the trimmings.

7 Transfer the vegetable and sauce mixture to the pie dish and top with the pastry. Crimp the edges with a fork and make a hole in the top of the pastry to allow steam to escape.

8 Decorate the pie with the pastry trimmings, attaching them with beaten egg. Brush the pastry all over with the remaining beaten egg. Bake in a preheated oven at 200°C (400°F, Gas 6) for 30 minutes or until the pastry is crisp and golden.

COUNTRY VEGETABLE PIES

Serves 4

8 carrots, diced
8 parsnips, diced
300 ml (1/2 pint) vegetable stock
2 tbsp olive oil
1 onion, chopped
1 head of garlic, separated into cloves and peeled
750 g (1 1/2 lb) potatoes, diced
salt and black pepper
45 g (1 1/2 oz) butter
4 tbsp hot milk
paprika to garnish (optional)

PARSLEY SAUCE

45 g (1 1/2 oz) butter
45 g (1 1/2 oz) plain flour
150 ml (1/4 pint) milk
4 tbsp chopped parsley

1 Blanch the carrots and parsnips in the stock for 1 minute. Drain, reserving the stock. Put the oil into an ovenproof dish, add the vegetables, and half of the garlic. Bake in a preheated oven at 200°C (400°F, Gas 6) for about 30 minutes.

2 Meanwhile, cook the potatoes and the remaining garlic in boiling salted water for 15–20 minutes until tender. Drain. Add 30 g (1 oz) of the butter and the milk. Mash, adding salt and pepper to taste.

3 Remove the vegetables with a slotted spoon and divide among 4 individual ovenproof dishes. Add salt and pepper to taste.

4 Make the parsley sauce: melt the butter in a small pan, add the flour, and cook, stirring, for 1 minute. Remove from the heat and blend in the milk and reserved stock. Bring to a boil, stirring, until thick. Simmer for 2–3 minutes, then stir in the parsley and salt and pepper to taste.

5 Pour the sauce over the vegetables. Top with the mashed potato, dot with the remaining butter, and bake for 20 minutes. Serve at once, sprinkled with paprika, if you prefer.

MIXED BEAN BAKE

Serves 4

2 tbsp olive oil
3 large leeks, trimmed and sliced
1 garlic clove, crushed
250 g (8 oz) mushrooms, sliced
1 x 400 g (13 oz) can aduki beans, drained
1 x 400 g (13 oz) can butter beans, drained
1 x 400 g (13 oz) can chopped tomatoes
3 tbsp tomato purée
4 tbsp chopped parsley
salt and black pepper

CHEESE SAUCE

30 g (1 oz) butter
30 g (1 oz) plain flour
300 ml (1/2 pint) milk
1 egg, beaten
125 g (4 oz) Cheddar cheese, grated

1 Heat the olive oil in a large saucepan. Add the leeks and cook gently, stirring, for a few minutes until softened but not coloured. Lift out with a slotted spoon and set aside.

2 Add the garlic and mushrooms and cook, stirring occasionally, for 5 minutes. Add the aduki and butter beans, tomatoes, tomato purée, 3 tbsp of the parsley, and salt and pepper to taste. Bring to a boil. Cover and simmer very gently for about 20 minutes.

3 Meanwhile, make the cheese sauce: melt the butter in a small saucepan, add the flour, and cook, stirring, for 1 minute. Remove the pan from the heat and gradually blend in the milk. Bring to a boil, stirring constantly until the mixture thickens. Simmer for 2–3 minutes, then leave to cool slightly. Stir in the egg and cheese and add salt and pepper to taste.

4 Transfer the bean mixture to an ovenproof dish and arrange the leek slices on top. Pour the cheese sauce over the leeks, and bake in a preheated oven at 190°C (375°F, Gas 5) for 30 minutes or until the topping is golden. Garnish with the remaining parsley, and serve at once.

Vegetable casseroles

Fresh vegetables make delicious, satisfying casseroles whatever the season, and particularly when the herbs, spices, and flavourings are carefully chosen to bring out the best in the vegetables. For even more variety, add some simple toppings or a puff pastry lid to any of these casseroles to create a whole new dish.

Baby vegetable medley

Serves 4

90 g (3 oz) butter
3 fresh sage leaves, chopped
3 thyme sprigs, chopped
leaves from 1 small sprig of rosemary
salt and black pepper
125 g (4 oz) small new potatoes
8 baby carrots, scrubbed and trimmed
4 baby cauliflowers, broken into florets
8 pickling onions, peeled
2 garlic cloves, crushed
150 ml (1/4 pint) dry white wine
125 g (4 oz) French beans
125 g (4 oz) cherry tomatoes
60 g (2 oz) canned butter beans
2 tbsp balsamic vinegar
2 tbsp coarse-grain mustard
fresh rosemary to garnish

1 Melt the butter in a flameproof casserole with the herbs and salt and pepper. Add the potatoes, carrots, cauliflowers, onions, and garlic, and cook, stirring, for 3 minutes.

2 Add the white wine, bring to a boil, cover, and simmer for 10 minutes.

3 Add the remaining vegetables, cover and simmer for 3–4 minutes. Stir in the vinegar. Increase the heat and cook, stirring, for 1 minute until the sauce has reduced and thickened. Stir in the mustard, and garnish with rosemary.

Baby vegetable gratin

Transfer the vegetables to an ovenproof dish. Sprinkle the vegetables with *90 g (3 oz) grated smoked Cheddar cheese* and *60 g (2 oz) fresh breadcrumbs.* Cook under a hot grill until golden.

Mushroom Stroganoff

Serves 4

20 g (3/4 oz) dried mushrooms
150 ml (1/4 pint) boiling water
60 g (2 oz) butter
1 onion, chopped
1 garlic clove, crushed
salt and black pepper
200 g (7 oz) mixed mushrooms
1 red pepper, cored, seeded, and sliced
1/2 tsp paprika
150 g (5 oz) canned artichoke hearts
300 ml (1/2 pint) vegetable stock
2 tbsp red wine
1 tbsp tomato purée
150 ml (1/4 pint) single cream

1 Soak the dried mushrooms in the boiling water for 20 minutes. Line a sieve with paper towels and drain the mushrooms, reserving the water.

2 Melt half of the butter in a large flameproof casserole, add the onion and garlic, and cook, stirring occasionally, for 3–5 minutes until softened. Season well to taste.

3 Add the remaining butter, all of the mushrooms, and the red pepper. Cook, stirring, for 5 minutes. Add the paprika, artichokes, stock, red wine, reserved mushroom water, tomato purée, and cream and bring to a boil. Simmer gently for 10–15 minutes. Taste for seasoning. Serve hot.

Mushroom vol-au-vent

When cooking the mushrooms, increase the heat to reduce and thicken the sauce. Warm through a *ready-made large vol-au-vent shell.* Fill the shell with the Mushroom Stroganoff and serve.

Pumpkin casserole

Serves 4

2 tbsp olive oil
15 g (1/2 oz) butter
1 onion, cut into 8 segments
salt and black pepper
1 turnip, diced
1 potato, diced
500 g (1 lb) pumpkin, peeled and cut into 2.5 cm (1 in) cubes
1 parsnip, cut into 2.5 cm (1 in) cubes
1 tsp medium curry powder or paste
375 ml (13 fl oz) vegetable stock
90 ml (3 fl oz) soured cream or crème fraîche
chopped fresh coriander to garnish

1 Heat the olive oil and butter in a flameproof casserole. Add the onion and cook gently for 3–5 minutes or until softened. Season well.

2 Add the vegetables, curry powder, and stock, and bring to a boil. Cover and simmer, stirring, for 20 minutes.

3 Remove the vegetables with a slotted spoon and transfer to a warmed serving dish. Bring the sauce to a boil and stir in the cream. Cook gently, stirring, until thickened. Spoon the sauce over the vegetables, garnish with coriander, and serve hot.

Clockwise from top: *Baby Vegetable Medley, Mushroom Stroganoff, Pumpkin Casserole.*

Hearty pumpkin pie

Put the vegetables and sauce into a pie dish. Mix *250 g (8 oz) self-raising flour, 150 g (5 oz) shredded vegetable suet, 2 tbsp chopped parsley* and *water* to bind. Bake at 190°C (375°F, Gas 5) for 15 minutes.

POTATO, CELERIAC, & PARMESAN GRATIN

Serves 4

60 g (2 oz) butter, plus extra for greasing
1 onion, sliced
2 garlic cloves, crushed
1 kg (2 lb) potatoes, thinly sliced
375 g (12 oz) celeriac, peeled and thinly sliced
300 ml (1/2 pint) single cream
150 ml (1/4 pint) milk
250 g (8 oz) ricotta cheese
1 tsp chopped fresh rosemary
1/2 tsp paprika
salt and black pepper
2 tbsp fresh breadcrumbs
3 tbsp grated Parmesan cheese, plus extra for serving
rosemary sprigs to garnish

1 Melt the butter in a frying pan, add the onion and garlic, and cook gently, stirring occasionally, for 3–5 minutes until softened but not coloured. Lightly butter a large gratin dish.

2 Arrange the potatoes, celeriac, and the onion mixture in layers in the prepared gratin dish, finishing with a neat layer of potatoes.

3 In a large bowl, combine the cream, milk, ricotta cheese, rosemary, paprika, and salt and pepper to taste. Beat well together, and pour over the vegetables.

4 In a small bowl, combine the breadcrumbs and grated Parmesan cheese, and then sprinkle evenly over the potatoes.

5 Bake in a preheated oven at 180°C (350°F, Gas 4) for 1 1/2 hours or until the potatoes and celeriac are tender and the top is a golden brown colour.

6 Serve the gratin hot, sprinkled with grated Parmesan cheese and garnished with a few rosemary sprigs.

AUBERGINE PARMIGIANA

Serves 4–6

1.5 kg (3 lb) aubergines
salt and black pepper
2 eggs, lightly beaten
60 g (2 oz) plain flour
2–3 tbsp olive oil
2 onions, chopped
3 x 400 g (13 oz) cans chopped tomatoes, drained
1 x 140 g (4 3/4 oz) can tomato purée
2 garlic cloves, crushed
2 tbsp chopped fresh basil
1/4 tsp caster sugar
300–375 g (10–12 oz) mozzarella cheese, sliced
125 g (4 oz) Parmesan cheese, grated

1 Cut the aubergines into 1 cm (1/2 in) slices. Place in a colander, sprinkle with salt, and leave to stand for 30 minutes. Rinse the slices and pat dry with paper towels.

2 Dip the aubergines into the beaten eggs, then into the flour, shaking off any excess.

3 Heat 1 tbsp of the oil in a large frying pan, add the aubergine slices in batches, and cook for 3–4 minutes on each side until golden, adding more oil between batches if necessary. Lift out with a slotted spoon and drain on paper towels.

4 Heat 1 tbsp oil in a saucepan, add the onions, and cook gently until soft. Stir in the tomatoes, tomato purée, garlic, and basil. Bring to a boil, then simmer for 10–15 minutes until thickened. Add sugar and salt and pepper to taste.

5 Spoon some of the tomato mixture into a shallow ovenproof dish and cover with a layer of aubergine slices, then a layer each of mozzarella and Parmesan. Continue layering, finishing with tomato mixture, mozzarella, and Parmesan.

6 Bake in a preheated oven at 190°C (375°F, Gas 5) for 15–20 minutes until the cheese is lightly browned.

STUFFED RED PEPPERS

 **Serves 4**

8 small red peppers
4 tbsp water

STUFFING

4 tbsp olive oil
1 large onion, finely chopped
1 garlic clove, crushed
175 g (6 oz) button mushrooms, chopped
250 g (8 oz) long grain rice
90 g (3 oz) red lentils
450 ml (¾ pint) vegetable stock
salt and black pepper
60 g (2 oz) pine nuts, toasted
4 tbsp chopped parsley
fresh coriander to garnish

1 Slice off the tops from the peppers and reserve. Cut out and discard the cores, seeds, and white ribs, and set the peppers aside.

2 Make the stuffing: heat the oil in a pan. Add the onion and garlic and cook gently, stirring occasionally, for 3–5 minutes until soft but not coloured. Add the button mushrooms and cook for 10 minutes.

3 Add the rice and lentils and stir to coat in the oil. Pour in the stock, season to taste, and bring to a boil. Cover and simmer very gently for 15–20 minutes until the rice is tender and the liquid has been absorbed. Stir in the pine nuts and parsley, then taste for seasoning.

4 Divide the stuffing among the peppers and replace the tops.

5 Stand the peppers upright in an ovenproof casserole that just contains them. Pour the measured water into the casserole, cover, and bake in a preheated oven at 180°C (350°F, Gas 4) for about 40 minutes until the peppers are tender. Serve at once, garnished with coriander.

Cook's know-how

If the peppers will not stand upright, slice a little off the bases before stuffing them, to give a more even surface.

CHEESE-TOPPED BAKED AUBERGINES

Serves 4

5 tbsp chopped fresh basil
2 tbsp chopped parsley
2 tbsp olive oil
1 tsp salt
4 medium aubergines
6 garlic cloves, cut into thin slivers
175 g (6 oz) Gorgonzola or Danish blue cheese, crumbled
175 g (6 oz) Cheddar or mozzarella cheese, grated

1 In a small bowl, combine 4 tbsp of the basil, the parsley, olive oil, and salt.

2 Prepare the aubergines (see box, right). Put the aubergines into an ovenproof dish and bake in a preheated oven at 180°C (350°F, Gas 4) for 40–50 minutes until they are very tender and soft to the touch.

3 Remove the aubergines from the oven, sprinkle with the Gorgonzola and Cheddar cheeses, and bake for 5 minutes or until the cheese is melted. Serve at once, sprinkled with the remaining basil.

Preparing the aubergines

Cut diagonal slits one-third of the way into 1 aubergine. Repeat.

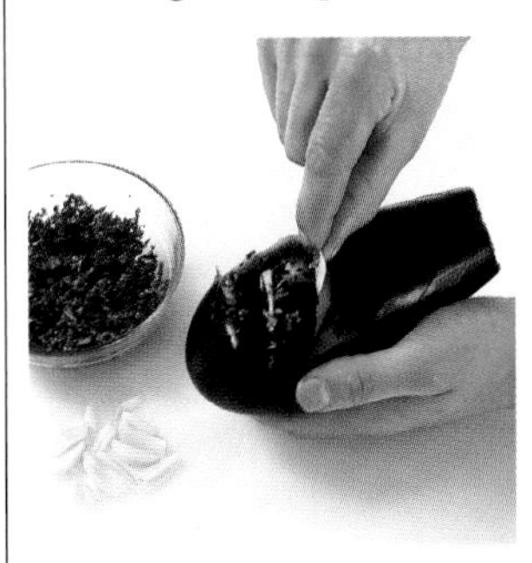

Stuff the garlic slivers and chopped herb mixture into each slit.

ITALIAN STUFFED COURGETTES

Serves 4

4 large courgettes

30 g (1 oz) butter

2 tbsp olive oil, plus extra for greasing

1 small onion, finely chopped

4 ripe tomatoes, peeled (page 39), seeded, and chopped

4 tbsp chopped fresh basil

salt and black pepper

2 tbsp capers, drained and coarsely chopped

250 g (8 oz) Fontina cheese, grated

1 Cut the courgettes in half lengthwise. Scoop out the flesh and chop finely.

2 Melt the butter with 1 tbsp of the olive oil in a saucepan.

3 When the butter is foaming, add the onion and cook gently, stirring occasionally, for 3–5 minutes until softened but not coloured. Add the courgette flesh, tomatoes, basil, and salt and pepper to taste, and cook, stirring, for 5 minutes.

4 Brush the insides of the courgette shells with the remaining oil and arrange in a lightly oiled shallow ovenproof dish. Bake the shells in a preheated oven at 180°C (350°F, Gas 4) for 5–10 minutes.

5 Divide half of the tomato mixture among the courgette shells. Cover with the chopped capers and a thin layer of cheese. Spoon over the remaining tomato mixture and top with the remaining cheese. Return to the oven and bake for 10–15 minutes until the cheese topping is bubbling.

Fontina

This Italian cheese is made in the region of Val d'Aosta. It is pale yellow, with a scattering of small holes, a dark brown rind, and a sweet, nutty flavour. It is most frequently used in an Italian dish similar to a fondue, but as it melts so well, it can be used in many other cooked dishes. Parmesan cheese may be used as a substitute.

MIDDLE-EASTERN STUFFED MARROW

Serves 4

250 g (8 oz) couscous

150 ml (1/4 pint) hot vegetable stock

1 kg (2 lb) marrow

salt and black pepper

butter for greasing

1 tbsp olive oil

1 shallot, finely chopped

125 g (4 oz) button mushrooms, sliced

grated zest and juice of 1/2 lemon

2 spring onions, finely chopped

4 tbsp Greek yogurt

1 tbsp chopped fresh mint

12 pitted green olives, chopped

chopped parsley to garnish

tomato sauce (page 286) to serve

1 Put the couscous into a bowl and add the stock. Leave to stand for about 10 minutes. Put into a sieve over a pan of boiling water, cover, and steam for 10 minutes.

2 Prepare the marrow (see box, right). Blanch in boiling salted water for 2 minutes. Arrange the marrow slices in a lightly buttered ovenproof dish.

3 Heat the oil in a saucepan, add the shallot, and cook gently for a few minutes until softened. Add the mushrooms, lemon zest and juice, and salt and pepper to taste, and cook for 8 minutes or until tender.

4 Strain the mushroom mixture and stir into the couscous. Add the spring onions, yogurt, mint, olives, and salt and pepper to taste.

5 Spoon the couscous mixture into the marrow slices. Cover loosely with foil and bake in a preheated oven at 190°C (375°F, Gas 5) for 20–25 minutes. Serve at once, with the tomato sauce, and garnished with parsley.

Preparing the marrow

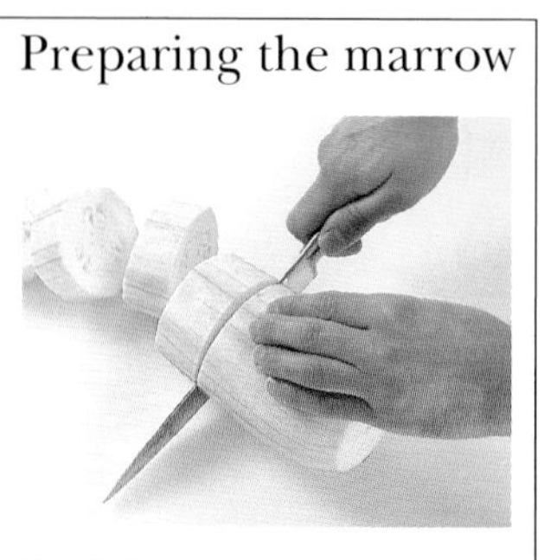

Peel the marrow, cut it into 5 cm (2 in) slices, and scoop out and discard the seeds from the middle.

MUSHROOM LASAGNE

Serves 6

- *2 tbsp olive oil*
- *1 large onion, chopped*
- *500 g (1 lb) mushrooms, sliced*
- *2 large garlic cloves, crushed*
- *30 g (1 oz) plain flour*
- *2 x 400 g (13 oz) cans chopped tomatoes*
- *1 tbsp chopped fresh basil*
- *1 tsp caster sugar*
- *salt and black pepper*
- *500 g (1 lb) frozen whole leaf spinach, thawed and drained*
- *300 g (10 oz) mature Cheddar cheese, grated*
- *150 g (5 oz) pre-cooked lasagne*

WHITE SAUCE

- *90 g (3 oz) butter*
- *90 g (3 oz) plain flour*
- *900 ml (1½ pints) milk*
- *1 tsp Dijon mustard*

1 Heat the oil in a large saucepan, add the onion, and cook gently for 3–5 minutes until softened. Add the mushrooms and garlic and cook for 5 minutes. Add the flour and cook, stirring, for 1 minute.

2 Add the tomatoes, basil, sugar, and salt and pepper to taste. Cover and simmer for 20 minutes.

3 Make the white sauce: melt the butter in a saucepan, add the flour, and cook, stirring, for 1 minute. Remove from the heat and gradually blend in the milk. Bring to a boil, stirring, until thickened. Simmer for 2–3 minutes. Add the mustard and season. Set aside.

4 Season the spinach with salt and pepper. Taking 1 teaspoonful at a time, shape it loosely into 24 balls.

5 Spoon one-third of the mushroom mixture into a large ovenproof dish, and place 8 of the spinach balls on top. Cover with one-third of the sauce and one-third of the cheese. Arrange half of the lasagne on top. Repeat the layers, finishing with the cheese.

6 Bake in a preheated oven at 190°C (375°F, Gas 5) for 35 minutes or until the pasta is tender.

DAIRY-FREE LASAGNE

Serves 4–6

- *1 aubergine, cut into 5 mm (¼ in) slices*
- *salt and black pepper*
- *3 tbsp olive oil*
- *2 courgettes, sliced*
- *250 g (8 oz) frozen chopped spinach, thawed and drained*
- *2 onions, chopped*
- *1 red pepper, cored, seeded, and diced*
- *2 garlic cloves, crushed*
- *2 x 400 g (13 oz) cans chopped tomatoes*
- *1 x 140 g (4¾ oz) can tomato purée*
- *¼ tsp caster sugar*
- *3 tbsp chopped fresh basil*
- *150 g (5 oz) pre-cooked lasagne*

1 Place the aubergine slices in a colander, sprinkle generously with salt, and leave to stand for about 30 minutes.

2 Heat 1 tbsp of the oil in a large frying pan, add the courgettes, and cook for 3 minutes. Turn into a bowl, and add salt to taste. Season the spinach with salt and pepper and set aside.

3 Rinse the aubergine and pat dry with paper towels. Heat the remaining oil in the frying pan, and cook the aubergines for 3–5 minutes on each side until golden. Remove and set aside.

4 Add the onions, red pepper, and garlic to the pan, and cook gently, stirring, for 3–5 minutes until softened. Add the tomatoes, tomato purée, and sugar and bring to a boil. Simmer for 10 minutes until thickened, stir in the basil, and season with salt and pepper.

5 Spoon one-third of the tomato sauce into a large ovenproof dish and cover with one-third of the lasagne. Add the aubergine, then half of the remaining tomato sauce. Add half of the remaining lasagne, then the spinach. Add the remaining lasagne and tomato sauce, and finish with an overlapping layer of courgettes.

6 Bake in a preheated oven at 190°C (375°F, Gas 5) for 35 minutes or until tender and golden.

SPINACH GNOCCHI WITH TOMATO SAUCE

Serves 4

1 kg (2 lb) spinach
375 g (12 oz) ricotta cheese
3 eggs
4 tbsp grated Parmesan cheese
pinch of grated nutmeg
salt and black pepper
60–75 g (2–2½ oz) plain flour

TOMATO SAUCE

30 g (1 oz) butter
1 small onion, chopped
1 small carrot, chopped
30 g (1 oz) plain flour
1 x 400 g (13 oz) can chopped tomatoes
300 ml (½ pint) vegetable stock
1 bay leaf
1 tsp caster sugar

TO SERVE

125 g (4 oz) butter
grated Parmesan cheese and Parmesan shavings

1 Wash the spinach and put into a saucepan with only the water remaining on the leaves. Cook over a gentle heat until just wilted. Drain the spinach throughly, squeezing to remove any excess water.

2 Put the spinach, ricotta, eggs, Parmesan, nutmeg, and salt and pepper to taste into a food processor and purée until smooth. Turn into a bowl. Gradually add flour until the mixture just holds its shape.

3 Using 2 dessertspoons, form the mixture into 20 oval shapes. Cover and chill in the refrigerator for 1 hour.

4 Make the tomato sauce: melt the butter in a pan, add the onion and carrot, and cook for 10 minutes or until softened. Add the flour and cook, stirring, for 1 minute. Add the tomatoes, stock, bay leaf, sugar, and salt and pepper to taste, and bring to a boil. Cover and simmer for 30 minutes. Purée in a food processor until smooth. Keep warm.

5 Cook the gnocchi in batches in boiling salted water for 5 minutes or until they float to the surface. Lift out and keep warm.

6 Melt the butter and pour over the gnocchi. Serve with the tomato sauce, grated Parmesan, and Parmesan shavings.

POLENTA WITH GRILLED VEGETABLES

Serves 4–6

175 g (6 oz) polenta
150 ml (¼ pint) cold water
600 ml (1 pint) boiling salted water
30 g (1 oz) butter
2 courgettes, halved and thickly sliced lengthwise
1 fennel bulb, trimmed and quartered lengthwise
2 tomatoes, cored and sliced
1 red onion, thickly sliced
melted butter for brushing

MARINADE

4 tbsp olive oil
2 tbsp red wine vinegar
3 garlic cloves, chopped
2–3 tbsp chopped parsley
salt and black pepper

1 Put the polenta into a saucepan, cover with the measured cold water, and leave to stand for 5 minutes.

2 Add the boiling salted water to the pan, return to a boil, and simmer for 10–15 minutes, stirring, until smooth and thickened.

3 Sprinkle a baking tray with water. Stir the butter into the polenta, then spread the mixture over the baking tray in a 1 cm (½ in) layer. Leave to cool.

4 Make the marinade: combine the oil, vinegar, garlic, parsley, and salt and pepper to taste. Add the courgettes, fennel, tomatoes, and onion. Cover and leave to marinate in the refrigerator for 30 minutes.

5 Lift the vegetables out of the marinade and cook over a hot barbecue for 2–3 minutes on each side. Cut the polenta into strips and cook over a hot barbecue, brushing with melted butter, for 1–2 minutes on each side until golden. Serve hot.

Cook's know-how

Outside the barbecue season, cook the polenta and vegetables under a hot grill, 10 cm (4 ins) from the heat.

COUSCOUS WITH ROASTED PEPPERS

Serves 4

1 large red pepper
1 large yellow pepper
175 g (6 oz) couscous
600 ml (1 pint) hot vegetable stock
2 tbsp olive oil
60 g (2 oz) blanched almonds
2 courgettes, sliced
1 large red onion, chopped
1 large carrot, thinly sliced
1–2 garlic cloves, crushed
1 x 400 g (13 oz) can chick peas, drained
1/2 tsp ground cumin
1/2 tsp curry powder
1/4–1/2 tsp crushed chillies
salt and black pepper
chopped coriander to garnish

1 Cook the peppers under a hot grill, 10 cm (4 ins) from the heat, for 10 minutes or until charred. Seal in a plastic bag and leave to cool.

2 Put the couscous into a bowl and add the stock. Cover and leave to stand for 10 minutes or until absorbed.

3 Meanwhile, heat the oil in a large frying pan, add the almonds, and cook gently, stirring, for 3 minutes or until lightly browned.

4 Lift out with a slotted spoon and drain on paper towels. Add the courgettes, onion, carrot, and garlic to the pan, and cook, stirring, for 5 minutes.

5 Stir in the chick peas, cumin, curry powder, and crushed chillies, and cook, stirring occasionally, for a further 5 minutes. Stir in the couscous, and cook for 3–4 minutes until heated through. Season to taste.

6 Peel, core, and seed the peppers and cut into thin strips.

7 Divide the couscous among warmed serving plates and arrange the pepper strips on top. Serve at once, sprinkled with the almonds and chopped coriander.

VEGETABLE & BARLEY CASSEROLE

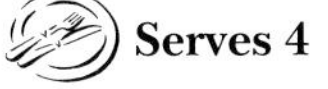 **Serves 4**

60 g (2 oz) butter
125 g (4 oz) shallots or small onions, halved
1.25 litres (2 pints) vegetable stock
250 g (8 oz) baby carrots
250 g (8 oz) baby parsnips
60 g (2 oz) pearl barley
1 bay leaf
2 courgettes, sliced
1 small cauliflower, separated into florets
125 g (4 oz) mangetout
1 tbsp chopped fresh mixed herbs

DUMPLINGS

125 g (4 oz) self-raising flour
60 g (2 oz) shredded vegetable suet
1 tbsp chopped fresh mixed herbs
salt and black pepper

1 Make the dumplings: sift the flour into a bowl, and add the suet, herbs, and salt and pepper to taste. Add enough water to make a soft but not sticky dough. Shape into 16 balls. Cover and set aside.

2 Melt the butter in a large flameproof casserole. When the butter is foaming, add the shallots and cook gently, stirring occasionally, for 3–5 minutes until soft but not coloured.

3 Add the stock, carrots, parsnips, pearl barley, and bay leaf, and bring to a boil. Cover and bake in a preheated oven at 190°C (375°F, Gas 5) for about 30 minutes.

4 Remove the casserole from the oven, and stir in the courgettes, cauliflower, mangetout, herbs, and salt and pepper to taste.

5 Arrange the dumplings on top of the casserole, cover, and return to the oven for 20 minutes or until the dumplings are cooked. Remove and discard the bay leaf and serve at once.

TOMATO & OLIVE FLAN

 Serves 6

3 tbsp olive oil

2 large onions, coarsely chopped

3 garlic cloves, crushed

1 x 400 g (13 oz) can chopped tomatoes

1 x 140 g (4 3/4 oz) can tomato purée

2 tsp chopped fresh basil

1 tsp caster sugar

125 g (4 oz) vignotte or mozzarella cheese, grated

90 g (3 oz) pitted black olives

shredded fresh basil to garnish

POPPYSEED BASE

250 g (8 oz) plain flour

125 g (4 oz) butter

90 g (3 oz) poppyseeds

1 tbsp light muscovado sugar

salt and black pepper

about 4 tbsp cold water

1 Make the poppyseed base: work the flour, butter, poppyseeds, sugar, and salt and pepper to taste in a food processor until the mixture resembles fine breadcrumbs. Add the measured water and work until the mixture forms a ball. Knead lightly. Shape the base (see box, right).

2 Heat the oil in a pan, add the onions and garlic, and cook gently for 3–5 minutes until soft. Add the tomatoes, tomato purée, basil, and sugar. Season to taste and bring to a boil. Boil for 5–7 minutes until thick. Leave to cool slightly.

3 Bake the flan base in a preheated oven at 220°C (425°F, Gas 7) for 15 minutes. Spread the tomato mixture over the base, sprinkle with the cheese and olives, and bake for 15–20 minutes. Serve hot or cold, sprinkled with basil.

Shaping the flan base

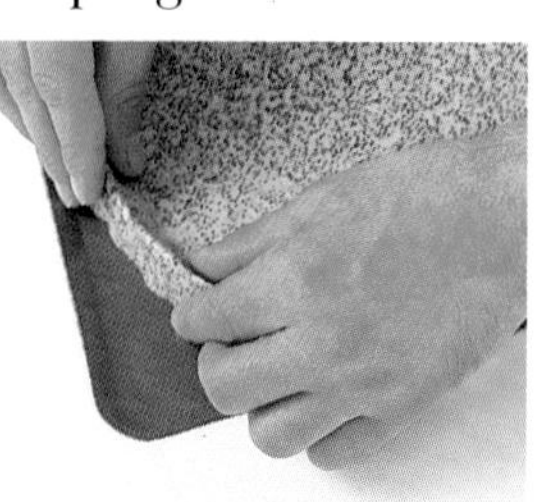

Roll out the pastry into a 30 cm (12 in) round on a baking tray, then pinch the edge to form a small rim. Prick the pastry base all over with a fork. Chill for 30 minutes.

MUSHROOM GOUGERE

 Serves 4

60 g (2 oz) butter

375 g (12 oz) mixed mushrooms, such as oyster, shiitake, and button, sliced

60 g (2 oz) plain flour

450 ml (3/4 pint) milk

1 tsp chopped fresh tarragon

tarragon leaves to garnish

CHOUX PASTRY

125 g (4 oz) plain flour

salt and black pepper

300 ml (1/2 pint) water

60 g (2 oz) butter, plus extra for greasing

4 eggs, beaten

1 Make the choux pastry: sift the flour with a pinch of salt. Put the measured water and butter into a saucepan and bring to a boil.

2 Remove from the heat and add the flour. Beat well until the mixture is smooth and glossy and leaves the side of the pan clean. Leave to cool slightly.

3 Beat the eggs into the flour mixture until smooth and glossy. Make the gougère (see box, right). Cover and chill while preparing the filling.

4 Melt the butter in a large saucepan, add the mushrooms, and cook gently for 3–4 minutes. Lift out with a slotted spoon and set aside. Add the flour and cook, stirring, for 1 minute. Remove from the heat and gradually blend in the milk. Bring to a boil, stirring until the mixture thickens. Simmer for 2–3 minutes.

5 Return the mushrooms to the pan, add the tarragon, and season. Pour into the middle of the choux ring and bake in a preheated oven at 220°C (425°F, Gas 7) for 35–40 minutes until well risen and golden. Garnish with tarragon, and serve hot.

Making the gougère

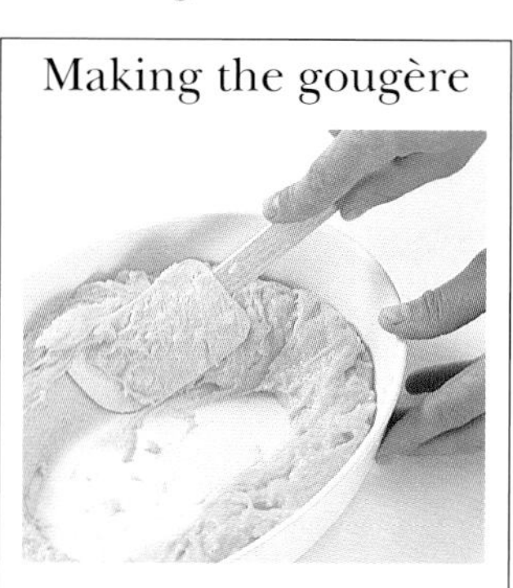

Butter a large shallow ovenproof dish, and lightly press the choux pastry around the edge.

SPINACH & RICOTTA PARCELS

Serves 4

4 sheets of filo pastry
60 g (2 oz) melted butter, plus extra for greasing

FILLING

30 g (1 oz) butter
1 small onion, finely chopped
300 g (10 oz) spinach, shredded
125 g (4 oz) ricotta cheese
pinch of grated nutmeg
salt and black pepper
tomato sauce (page 286) to serve

1 Make the filling: melt the butter in a saucepan, add the onion, and cook gently for 3–5 minutes until softened.

2 Add the spinach to the onion and cook for 1–2 minutes. Leave to cool. Add the ricotta cheese, nutmeg, and salt and pepper to taste, and mix well. Divide into 8 portions.

3 Lightly butter a baking tray. Cut each sheet of filo pastry lengthwise into 2 long strips. Brush 1 strip with melted butter, covering the remaining strips with a damp tea towel. Fill and fold the parcels (see box, right).

4 Bake in a preheated oven at 200°C (400°F, Gas 6) for 20 minutes or until the pastry is crisp and golden. Serve with the tomato sauce.

Filling and folding the parcels

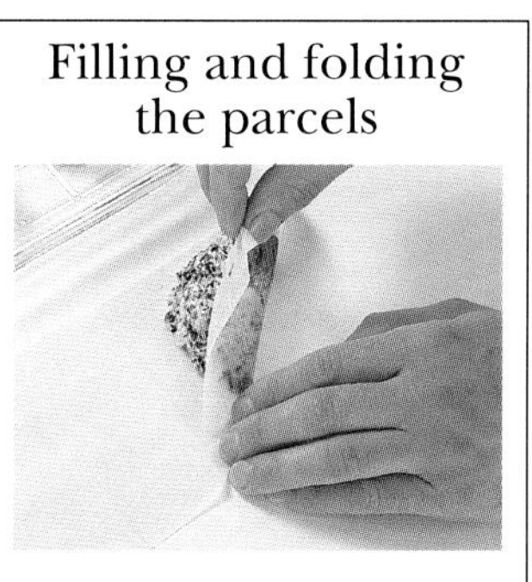

Spoon 1 portion of filling on to a corner of the filo strip. Fold over opposite corner to form a triangle.

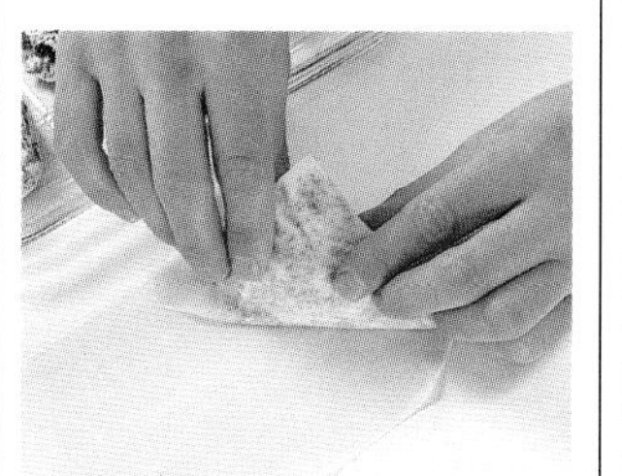

Fold the filled triangle until you reach the end of the strip. Brush with melted butter and put on to the baking tray. Butter, fill, and fold the remaining filo strips.

AUBERGINE & CAERPHILLY FILO PIE

Serves 6

2 aubergines, cut into 1 cm (1/2 in) dice
salt and black pepper
2 tbsp olive oil
2 large onions, chopped
2 tsp ground cumin
2 tsp ground coriander
2 tsp mild curry paste
2 red peppers, cored, seeded, and diced
175 g (6 oz) red lentils
250 g (8 oz) Caerphilly cheese, diced
4 tbsp chopped fresh oregano
1 x 300 g (10 oz) packet filo pastry
60 g (2 oz) melted butter
** 26 cm (10 1/2 in) springform cake tin*

1 Put the aubergines into a colander, sprinkle generously with salt, and leave to stand for 30 minutes.

2 Heat the oil in a large pan. Cook the onions for 3–5 minutes. Add the cumin, coriander, and curry paste, and cook for 2 minutes.

3 Drain the aubergines and pat dry with paper towels. Add to the onion mixture with the red peppers and cook for 10–15 minutes until soft. Add salt and pepper to taste and leave to cool.

4 Meanwhile, put the lentils into a pan, cover with water, and bring to a boil. Simmer for 15 minutes or until just soft. Drain and cool.

5 Stir the lentils, Caerphilly cheese, and oregano into the aubergine mixture. Taste for seasoning.

6 Using two-thirds of the filo pastry, line the bottom and side of the cake tin, brushing each sheet with butter, and letting the sheets overhang the rim of the tin. Spoon in the aubergine mixture and fold the filo sheets over the top. Brush the remaining filo with butter, crumple up, and arrange on top of the pie.

7 Bake in a preheated oven at 190°C (375°F, Gas 5) for 40 minutes or until the pastry is golden. Serve hot.

Vegetarian curries

The cuisine of India, with its use of aromatic spices to enhance the flavour of vegetables and pulses, is one in which vegetarians can find a whole range of dishes to whet their appetites. The tradition of eating a selection of small dishes, accompanied by rice and breads, makes for well-balanced, nutritious meals.

Mixed vegetable curry

Serves 4

2 tbsp sunflower oil
2 tsp ground coriander
1/4–1/2 tsp chilli powder
1/4 tsp turmeric
2.5 cm (1 in) piece of fresh root ginger, peeled and grated
1 large onion, chopped
2 garlic cloves , crushed
1 small cauliflower, cut into florets
2 potatoes, cut into chunks
2 large carrots, sliced
45 g (1 1/2 oz) creamed coconut, grated
150 ml (1/4 pint) boiling water
1 green pepper, cored, seeded, and cut into chunks
1 fresh green chilli, cored, seeded, and finely chopped
1 x 400 g (13 oz) can chopped tomatoes
salt and black pepper
juice of 1/2 lemon
fresh coriander leaves to garnish

1 Heat the oil in a large saucepan, add the coriander, chilli powder, and turmeric, and cook, stirring constantly, for 1 minute. Add the ginger, onion, and garlic, and cook, stirring, for 3–5 minutes until the onion is softened but not coloured.

2 Add the cauliflower, potatoes, and carrots to the pan, and stir well to coat in the spices. Cook, stirring occasionally, for 5 minutes.

3 Put the creamed coconut into a jug, add the boiling water, and stir until dissolved. Add the green pepper, chilli, tomatoes, and coconut milk to the pan, with salt and pepper to taste. Stir well.

4 Bring to a boil. Cover and simmer gently for 25–30 minutes until the vegetables are just tender. Stir in the lemon juice. Serve at once, garnished with coriander leaves.

Sag aloo

Serves 4

500 g (1 lb) new potatoes
salt
500 g (1 lb) frozen spinach, thawed
250 ml (8 fl oz) water
30 g (1 oz) butter
1 onion, chopped
3 garlic cloves, chopped
2.5 cm (1 in) piece of fresh root ginger, peeled and grated
1 small fresh green chilli, cored, seeded, and finely chopped
1 tsp ground coriander
1/2 tsp ground cumin
1/2 tsp turmeric
1/2 tsp garam masala
2 tbsp lime or lemon juice
2–3 tbsp chopped fresh coriander leaves

1 Cook the potatoes in a saucepan of boiling salted water for 10 minutes. Drain and leave to cool. Cut into bite-sized pieces and set aside.

2 In a food processor or blender, purée the spinach with the measured water. Set aside.

3 Melt the butter in a large, heavy frying pan. When the butter is foaming, add the onion, garlic, ginger, and chilli and cook for about 5 minutes until soft.

4 Add 1 tsp salt, the ground coriander and cumin, turmeric, and garam masala. Cook, stirring, for 1 minute. Add the potatoes and turn to coat in the spices. Cover and cook over a gentle heat for 15 minutes or until the potatoes are tender.

5 Remove the lid and add the spinach purée. Increase the heat and cook for about 10 minutes until the spinach thickens into a sauce-like consistency. Stir in the lime juice and coriander leaves, and serve at once.

Dhal

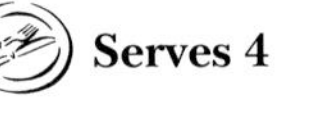

Serves 4

4 tbsp olive oil
2 onions, thinly sliced
1 large garlic clove, crushed
2 tsp cumin seeds
2 tsp hot Madras curry powder
2 tsp ground coriander
1 cinnamon stick
8 cloves
250 g (8 oz) red lentils
900 ml (1 1/2 pints) vegetable stock
2 bay leaves
salt and black pepper

1 Heat the oil in a saucepan, add the onions, garlic, and cumin, and cook for 3–5 minutes until the onions are soft. Add the curry powder and coriander, increase the heat, and cook, stirring, until the onions begin to brown.

2 Add the cinnamon, cloves, and lentils. Cook, stirring, for 1 minute. Add the stock and bring to a boil.

3 Add the bay leaves and salt and pepper to taste, cover, and simmer, stirring occasionally, for about 1 hour until the lentils are tender and the liquid has reduced. Remove the cinnamon stick. Serve at once.

Clockwise from top: *Mixed Vegetable Curry, Dhal, Sag Aloo.*

Curry accompaniments

Serve some of these side dishes for an authentic Indian meal:

- tomato and coriander relish
- plain yogurt and cucumber
- grated carrot salad
- mango chutney
- poppadoms
- basmati rice
- naan bread

RED LENTIL & COCONUT CURRY

Serves 4–6

300 g (10 oz) red lentils
900 ml (1½ pints) water
2.5 cm (1 in) piece of fresh root ginger, peeled and chopped
1½ fresh green chillies, cored, seeded, and finely chopped
4 garlic cloves
90 g (3 oz) creamed coconut, grated
1/2 tsp turmeric
1/2 tsp ground ginger
1 tbsp lemon juice
salt
30 g (1 oz) butter
4 tsp black mustard seeds

1 Put the lentils into a pan and add the water. Bring to a boil and simmer for 20 minutes or until tender.

2 Using a pestle and mortar, crush the fresh root ginger, two-thirds of the chillies, and 2 of the garlic cloves until smooth. Add to the lentils.

3 Add the creamed coconut, turmeric, ground ginger, lemon juice, and salt to taste. Cook gently, stirring, until the coconut dissolves, then increase the heat and cook for 5 minutes or until any excess liquid has evaporated. Taste for seasoning.

4 Crush the remaining garlic and set aside. Melt the butter in a frying pan and add the mustard seeds. As soon as they begin to pop, remove the frying pan from the heat and stir in the crushed garlic and the remaining chopped chilli.

5 Transfer the lentil mixture to a warmed serving dish, top with the garlic, chilli, and mustard seed butter. Serve at once.

RED BEAN & TOMATO CURRY

Serves 4

2 tbsp sunflower oil
1 large onion, sliced
5 garlic cloves, crushed
1–2 fresh green chillies, cored, seeded, and sliced
2.5 cm (1 in) piece of fresh root ginger, peeled and chopped
1 tsp curry powder
1 tsp turmeric
1/2 tsp ground coriander
pinch of cayenne pepper
salt
1 x 400 g (13 oz) can chopped tomatoes
600 g (20 oz) canned red kidney beans, drained
1 tbsp lemon juice
fresh coriander leaves to garnish

1 Heat the sunflower oil in a large frying pan, add the onion, garlic, chillies, and ginger, and cook, stirring occasionally, for a few minutes until all the aromas are released, and the onion is softened but not coloured.

2 Add the curry powder, turmeric, ground coriander, cayenne pepper, and salt to taste, and cook, stirring, for 2 minutes.

3 Add the tomatoes with most of their juice and cook for about 3 minutes. Add the beans and cook for a further 5 minutes or until the beans are warmed through and the sauce is thickened. Add the lemon juice and serve hot, garnished with coriander.

CHICK PEA, RED BEAN, & TOMATO CURRY

Substitute 400 g (13 oz) chick peas for 400 g (13 oz) red kidney beans and proceed as directed in the recipe.

FELAFEL WITH SESAME YOGURT SAUCE

Serves 4–6

1 x 400 g (13 oz) can chick peas, drained

6 spring onions, finely chopped

30 g (1 oz) fresh white breadcrumbs

1 egg, lightly beaten

grated zest and juice of 1/2 lemon

1 garlic clove, crushed

2 tbsp chopped fresh coriander

2 tbsp chopped parsley

1 tbsp tahini paste

1 tsp ground coriander

1 tsp ground cumin

1/2 tsp ground cinnamon

pinch of cayenne pepper

salt and black pepper

sunflower oil for deep-frying

warmed mini pita bread to serve

chopped fresh coriander to garnish

SESAME YOGURT SAUCE

4 tbsp plain yogurt

2 tbsp olive oil

1 tbsp lemon juice

1 tbsp tahini paste

1 In a food processor, purée the chick peas, onions, breadcrumbs, egg, lemon zest and juice, garlic, coriander, parsley, tahini, ground coriander, cumin, cinnamon, cayenne pepper, and salt and pepper to taste until smooth.

2 Turn into a bowl, cover, and leave to stand for at least 30 minutes.

3 Meanwhile, make the sesame yogurt sauce: in a bowl, combine the yogurt, oil, lemon juice, tahini, and salt and pepper to taste. Cover and set aside.

4 With dampened hands, shape the felafel mixture into balls about the size of a walnut, then flatten them into patties.

5 In a deep-fat fryer, heat the oil to 190°C (375°F). Lower the felafel into the fryer in batches and cook for 2–3 minutes until golden. Lift out and drain on paper towels. Serve warm, with pita bread and sesame yogurt sauce, garnished with chopped coriander.

Tahini

This is a paste made from ground sesame seeds which has a rich smoky aroma and flavour. It is available in jars in most supermarkets and Middle-Eastern delicatessens.

HALLOUMI & VEGETABLE KEBABS

Serves 4

1 small baguette

250 g (8 oz) halloumi cheese

1 small red pepper, cored and seeded

150 ml (1/4 pint) olive oil, plus extra for greasing

16 large cherry tomatoes

grated zest and juice of 1 lemon

1 garlic clove, crushed

2 tbsp chopped fresh basil

1 tbsp snipped fresh chives

salt and black pepper

⭑ 8 metal skewers

1 Cut the bread into 8 thick slices and cut each slice in half. Cut the halloumi into 16 cubes and cut the red pepper into 8 pieces.

2 Oil the skewers and thread alternately with the tomatoes, bread, cheese, and pepper. Place in a shallow flameproof dish.

3 Mix the oil, lemon zest and juice, garlic, herbs, and salt and pepper to taste. Drizzle over the kebabs. Leave to stand for 10 minutes.

4 Cook the kebabs over a hot barbecue or under a hot grill, 10 cm (4 ins) from the heat, and cook, turning once and basting with the marinade, for 3–4 minutes until the cheese is lightly browned.

Cook's know-how

Halloumi is a semi-hard Greek cheese which is usually made from ewe's milk. It has a chewy texture and needs to be eaten while still hot or it becomes slightly rubbery.

TOFU & VEGETABLE KEBABS

Substitute smoked tofu for the halloumi cheese, and 8 whole button mushrooms for the red pepper, and proceed as directed.

VEGETABLE STIR-FRY WITH TOFU

Serves 4

- *250 g (8 oz) firm tofu, cut into bite-sized pieces*
- *2 tbsp sesame oil*
- *1 tbsp sunflower oil*
- *1 head of chicory, halved lengthwise*
- *4 carrots, thinly sliced diagonally*
- *5 cm (2 in) piece of fresh root ginger, peeled and finely chopped*
- *250 g (8 oz) shiitake mushrooms, sliced*
- *8 spring onions, sliced into 2.5 cm (1 in) pieces*
- *250 g (8 oz) bean sprouts*
- *3 tbsp toasted sesame seeds*

MARINADE

- *3 tbsp soy sauce*
- *3 tbsp dry sherry*
- *1 garlic clove, crushed*
- *salt and black pepper*

1 Make the marinade: in a bowl, combine the soy sauce, sherry, garlic, and salt and pepper to taste. Turn the tofu in the marinade, cover, and leave to marinate at room temperature for at least 15 minutes.

2 Drain the tofu, reserving the marinade. Heat the sesame and sunflower oils in a wok or large frying pan, add the tofu, and carefully stir-fry over a high heat for 2–3 minutes, being careful not to break up the tofu. Remove from the wok with a slotted spoon and drain on paper towels.

3 Separate the chicory halves into leaves. Add the carrots and ginger to the wok and stir-fry for about 2 minutes. Add the mushrooms and spring onions and stir-fry for a further 2 minutes, then add the bean sprouts and chicory leaves and stir-fry for 1 minute.

4 Return the tofu to the wok, pour the reserved marinade over the top, and boil quickly until almost all of the marinade has evaporated and the tofu has warmed through. Generously sprinkle with the toasted sesame seeds, taste for seasoning, and serve at once.

MEXICAN CHILLI WITH TOFU

Serves 4–6

- *3 onions, chopped*
- *3 garlic cloves*
- *1 fresh green chilli, cored, seeded, and chopped*
- *2 tsp paprika*
- *2 tsp mild chilli powder*
- *1 tsp ground cumin*
- *1/2 tsp dried oregano*
- *4 tbsp sunflower oil*
- *1 x 400 g (13 oz) can chopped tomatoes, drained and juice reserved*
- *500 ml (16 fl oz) hot vegetable stock*
- *625 g (1 1/4 lb) firm tofu, cut into bite-sized pieces*
- *1 x 400 g (13 oz) can red kidney beans, drained*
- *salt and black pepper*
- *chopped fresh coriander to garnish*

1 Put the onions, garlic, green chilli, spices, and oregano into a food processor and work until smooth.

2 Heat the oil in a large frying pan. Add the onion mixture and cook until fragrant.

3 Add half of the tomatoes to the pan and cook until reduced and thickened. Add the remaining tomatoes, allowing them to reduce and thicken. Pour in the stock and cook for 5–10 minutes until the mixture thickens.

4 Add the tofu, kidney beans, and the reserved tomato juice, and cook, spooning the sauce over the tofu pieces, for 5–8 minutes until heated through. Do not stir the tofu as it may break up. Season, and serve hot, sprinkled with coriander.

Cook's know-how

Reducing a sauce involves cooking it over a high heat to allow the moisture to evaporate and the flavours to become concentrated.

VEGETARIAN BURGERS

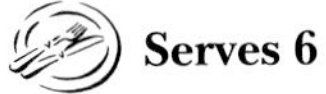 **Serves 6**

1 x 400 g (13 oz) can soya beans, drained

125 ml (4 fl oz) tomato juice or water

90 g (3 oz) flavoured soya mince

1 onion, chopped

30 g (1 oz) fresh white breadcrumbs

1 egg

2 tbsp lightly crushed sesame seeds

1 tbsp chopped parsley

1 vegetable stock cube, crumbled

1/2 tsp dried oregano

salt and black pepper

45 g (1 1/2 oz) plain flour

4 tbsp olive oil

LETTUCE DRESSING

4 tbsp mayonnaise

2 tbsp Dijon mustard

dash of lemon juice

1/2 small iceberg lettuce, finely shredded

1/4 onion, thinly sliced

1 Purée the soya beans in a food processor. Put into a bowl, add the tomato juice, soya mince, onion, breadcrumbs, egg, sesame seeds, parsley, stock cube, oregano, and salt and pepper to taste. Chill for 30 minutes.

2 Shape the mixture into 6 burgers. Sprinkle the flour on to a plate. Dip each burger into the flour, coating both sides.

3 Heat the oil in a frying pan, add the burgers, and cook for 1–2 minutes on each side until browned.

4 Arrange the burgers on a baking tray and cook in a preheated oven at 180°C (350°F, Gas 4) for about 20 minutes until cooked through.

5 Make the lettuce dressing: combine the mayonnaise, mustard, and lemon juice. Stir in the lettuce and onion. Serve the burgers at once, with the dresssing.

SPICY RED BEAN BURGERS

Substitute 1 x 400 g (13 oz) can red kidney beans for the soya beans. Proceed as directed, adding 1 tbsp chopped parsley, 1 tsp paprika, 1 tsp mild chilli powder, and 1/2 tsp ground cumin.

GLAMORGAN SAUSAGES

 **Serves 4**

150 g (5 oz) fresh white breadcrumbs

125 g (4 oz) Caerphilly or Cheddar cheese, grated

1 small leek, finely chopped

30 g (1 oz) walnuts, finely ground

2 tbsp chopped fresh sage

1 tsp grated lemon zest

1 tsp mustard powder

60 g (2 oz) Welsh goat's cheese, coarsely chopped

2 eggs

1 tbsp milk

salt and black pepper

45 g (1 1/2 oz) plain flour

2 tbsp sunflower oil

shredded fresh sage to garnish

1 In a bowl, combine the breadcrumbs, cheese, leek, walnuts, sage, lemon zest, and mustard powder. Gradually blend the goat's cheese into the mixture.

2 Separate 1 egg, reserving the white and adding the yolk to the remaining egg. Beat the egg and yolk into the cheese mixture with the milk. Season to taste.

3 Divide the mixture into 8 pieces and roll into sausages about 7 cm (3 ins) long. Cover and chill for about 1 hour to allow the flavours to develop.

4 Sprinkle the flour on to a plate. Brush the sausages with the reserved egg white, then dip into the flour until lightly coated all over. Shake off any excess flour.

5 Heat the oil in a frying pan, add the sausages, and cook over a medium heat, turning occasionally, for 8–10 minutes until golden. Drain on paper towels, and serve at once, garnished with sage.

GOAT'S CHEESE NUGGETS

Cut the goat's cheese into 16 cubes. Combine the breadcrumbs with the other ingredients as above. Mould the mixture around the goat's cheese cubes, forming small balls. Chill, and proceed as directed.

CHESTNUT LOAF

Serves 6

- *250 g (8 oz) frozen chestnuts, thawed*
- *1 tbsp olive oil, plus extra for greasing*
- *1 onion, coarsely chopped*
- *2 celery stalks, chopped*
- *2 garlic cloves, crushed*
- *250 g (8 oz) potatoes, boiled and mashed*
- *125 g (4 oz) fresh wholemeal breadcrumbs*
- *1 egg, beaten*
- *2 tbsp chopped parsley*
- *1 tbsp soy sauce*
- *1 tbsp tomato purée*
- *salt and black pepper*
- *red pepper strips and watercress sprigs to garnish*
- *spicy tomato salsa (see box, right) to serve*
- ⋆ *1 kg (2 lb) loaf tin*

1 Coarsely chop half of the chestnuts, and finely chop the remainder.

2 Heat the oil in a pan, add the onion, celery, and garlic, and cook, stirring, for 3–5 minutes until soft.

3 Remove from the heat. Stir in all of the chestnuts, potatoes, breadcrumbs, egg, parsley, soy sauce, and tomato purée. Season to taste.

4 Lightly grease the loaf tin, spoon in the mixture, and level the top. Cover with foil and cook in a preheated oven at 180°C (350°F, Gas 4) for 1 hour or until firm.

5 Turn out, cut into slices, and garnish. Serve hot or cold, with the salsa.

Spicy tomato salsa

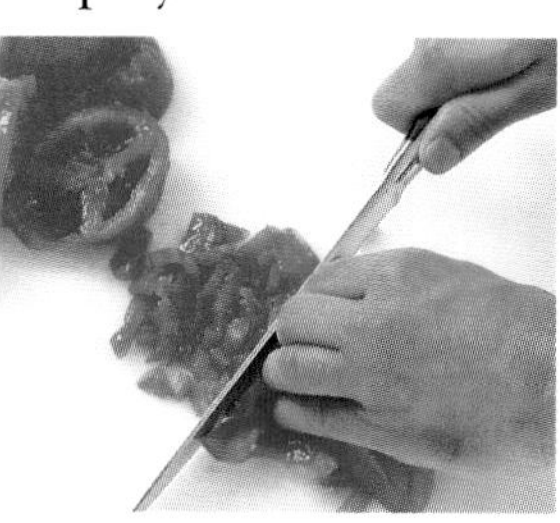

Peel (page 39) and seed *8 large tomatoes*. Dice and put into a bowl.

Stir in *2 chopped spring onions, 1 chopped fresh green chilli, zest and juice of 2 limes, 3 tbsp chopped fresh coriander, 1 tsp caster sugar,* and *salt and pepper*. Chill.

CHRISTMAS NUT LOAF

Serves 6–8

- *75 g (2½ oz) brown rice*
- *salt and black pepper*
- *15 g (½ oz) dried ceps*
- *30 g (1 oz) butter*
- *2 carrots, grated*
- *1 small onion, finely chopped*
- *1 garlic clove, crushed*
- *250 g (8 oz) button mushrooms, chopped*
- *2 tbsp chopped parsley*
- *1 tbsp chopped fresh rosemary*
- *125 g (4 oz) walnuts, toasted and chopped*
- *125 g (4 oz) Brazil nuts, toasted and chopped*
- *60 g (2 oz) pine nuts, toasted*
- *175 g (6 oz) Cheddar cheese, grated*
- *1 egg, beaten*
- *sunflower oil for greasing*
- *rosemary sprigs to garnish*
- *cranberry sauce (page 178) to serve*
- ⋆ *1 kg (2 lb) loaf tin*

1 Cook the rice in boiling salted water for 30–35 minutes until tender. Drain.

2 Cover the ceps with boiling water, and leave to soak for 30 minutes.

3 Drain the ceps, rinse under cold water, and pat dry. Chop finely.

4 Melt the butter in a frying pan, add the carrots, onion, and garlic, and cook gently, stirring occasionally, for 5 minutes. Stir in the mushrooms, rice, ceps, parsley, and rosemary, and cook until softened.

5 Purée the mixture in a food processor. Stir in the walnuts, Brazil nuts, pine nuts, cheese, egg, and salt and pepper to taste.

6 Lightly grease the loaf tin, spoon in the mixture, and level the top. Cover with foil and bake in a preheated oven at 190°C (375°F, Gas 5) for 1½ hours or until firm. Turn out, cut into slices, and garnish. Serve hot, with cranberry sauce.

Ceps

Known as porcini *in Italian, ceps are small, well-flavoured mushrooms, often sold dried.*

Spinach roulade

Serves 6–8

560 g (1 lb 2 oz) spinach

30 g (1 oz) butter, plus extra for greasing

4 eggs, separated

pinch of grated nutmeg

1 tbsp finely grated Parmesan cheese

FILLING

15 g (1/2 oz) butter

250 g (8 oz) button mushrooms, sliced

juice of 1/2 lemon

salt and black pepper

200 ml (7 fl oz) crème fraîche

2 tbsp chopped parsley

* *33 x 23 cm (13 x 9 in) Swiss roll tin*

1 Make the filling: melt the butter in a pan, add the mushrooms, lemon juice, and salt and pepper to taste, and cook for 3 minutes until just softened. Leave to cool.

2 Wash the spinach and put into a saucepan with only the water remaining on the leaves. Cook over a gentle heat for 1–2 minutes until the spinach has just wilted. Drain well, squeezing to remove excess water.

3 Butter the tin and line with baking parchment. Butter the parchment.

4 Coarsely chop the spinach, turn into a large bowl, and beat in the butter, egg yolks, nutmeg, and salt and pepper to taste. In another bowl, whisk the egg whites until firm but not dry, then fold gently into the spinach mixture.

5 Pour the spinach mixture into the Swiss roll tin and bake in a preheated oven at 220°C (425°F, Gas 7) for 10–12 minutes until firm.

6 Sprinkle the Parmesan cheese on to a sheet of baking parchment. Turn the roulade out on to the cheese, leave to cool for 5–10 minutes, then peel off the lining paper. Trim.

7 Drain the mushrooms, reserving some of the cooking liquid. Put them into a bowl, add the crème fraîche, parsley, and season to taste. Add a little of the reserved liquid if too thick. Spread the filling over the roulade, leaving a 2.5 cm (1 in) border. Roll up from the long side. Cover and chill for 30 minutes. Cut into slices to serve.

Carrot roulade

Serves 4

125 g (4 oz) butter, plus extra for greasing

1 large garlic clove, crushed

1/2 red pepper, cored, seeded, and finely chopped

1 x 200 g (7 oz) can tomatoes

750 g (1 1/2 lb) carrots, grated

6 eggs, separated

FILLING

1 cucumber, diced

salt and black pepper

125 g (4 oz) goat's cheese

125 g (4 oz) full-fat soft cheese

3 spring onions, thinly sliced

1 large garlic clove, crushed

2–3 tbsp finely chopped parsley

1/4 tsp dried thyme

Greek yogurt if needed

* *33 x 23 cm (13 x 9 in) Swiss roll tin*

1 Put the cucumber into a colander, sprinkle with salt, and leave to stand for 20 minutes.

2 Butter the tin and line with baking parchment. Butter the parchment.

3 Melt the butter, add half of the garlic, the red pepper, and tomatoes, and cook gently for 5 minutes.

4 Add the carrots and cook gently for 2 minutes or until soft. Turn the carrot mixture into a large bowl and beat in the egg yolks, and salt and pepper to taste. In another bowl, whisk the egg whites until firm but not dry, then fold into the carrot mixture.

5 Pour the carrot mixture into the Swiss roll tin and bake in a preheated oven at 200°C (400°F, Gas 6) for 10 minutes or until golden. Cover and leave to cool.

6 Make the filling: rinse the cucumber and pat dry with paper towels. Turn into a bowl and combine with the goat's cheese, soft cheese, spring onions, the garlic, parsley, thyme, and black pepper to taste. If the mixture is very thick, stir in 1–2 tbsp Greek yogurt.

7 Turn the roulade out on to a sheet of baking parchment and peel off the lining paper. Trim the edges. Spread the filling over the roulade, leaving a 2.5 cm (1 in) border on each side. Roll up the roulade from the long side, using the paper for support. Cover and chill for 30 minutes. Cut into slices to serve.

CREAM CHEESE TERRINE

Serves 8

12–16 large spinach leaves

salt and black pepper

1 aubergine, sliced lengthwise

1 tbsp olive oil, plus extra for greasing

2 large red peppers, cored, seeded, and halved

1 large yellow pepper, cored, seeded, and halved

500 g (1 lb) low-fat soft cheese

2 eggs, lightly beaten

4 tbsp single cream

30 g (1 oz) Parmesan cheese, grated

2 tbsp ready-made pesto

** 1 kg (2 lb) loaf tin or terrine*

1 Blanch the spinach in boiling salted water for 30 seconds. Drain, rinse in cold water, and pat dry. Line the loaf tin (see box, right).

2 Brush the aubergine with the oil, and cook under a hot grill for 6–8 minutes on each side. Roast and peel the peppers (page 354). Cut the pepper halves into strips.

3 Combine the soft cheese, eggs, cream, grated Parmesan, pesto, and salt and pepper to taste.

Lining the loaf tin

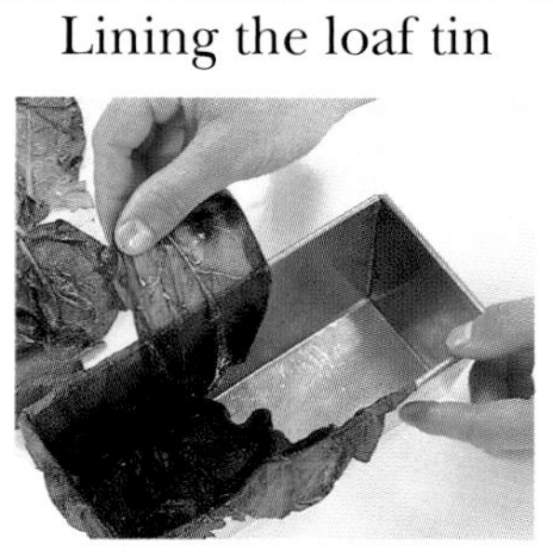

Oil the loaf tin and line with the spinach leaves, letting 5 cm (2 ins) overhang the sides.

4 Cover the bottom of the tin with some of the cheese mixture. Layer half of the red pepper, half of the aubergine, the yellow pepper, then the remaining aubergine and red pepper, spreading cheese mixture between each layer. Finish with the remaining cheese. Fold over the spinach leaves.

5 Oil a piece of foil and tightly cover the tin. Put the tin into a roasting tin and pour in boiling water to come halfway up the side. Cook in a preheated oven at 180°C (350°F, Gas 4) for 1½ hours or until firm. Remove from the water and leave to cool, then chill thoroughly. Slice and serve.

WINTER VEGETABLE TERRINE

Serves 4–6

375 g (12 oz) carrots, coarsely chopped

2.5 cm (1 in) piece of fresh root ginger, peeled and chopped

salt and black pepper

375 g (12 oz) celeriac, peeled and coarsely chopped

375 g (12 oz) broccoli

sunflower oil for greasing

3 eggs

** 1 kg (2 lb) loaf tin or terrine*

1 Cook the carrots and fresh root ginger in boiling salted water for 10–15 minutes until just tender. Cook the celeriac in boiling salted water for 8–10 minutes until tender.

2 Cut the stalks off the broccoli and cook them in boiling salted water for 8–10 minutes until almost tender, then add the broccoli florets and cook for 1 minute longer.

3 Drain all of the vegetables separately and rinse in cold running water. Lightly oil the loaf tin and line the bottom with greaseproof paper.

4 Purée the broccoli, 1 of the eggs, and salt and pepper to taste in a food processor until smooth. Turn the mixture into the loaf tin and level the surface with a palette knife.

5 Purée the celeriac, 1 of the eggs, and salt and pepper to taste in the food processor until smooth. Spread over the broccoli mixture and level the surface.

6 Purée the carrots, ginger, the remaining egg, and salt and pepper to taste in the food processor until smooth. Spread over the celeriac layer and level the surface.

7 Oil a piece of foil and tightly cover the tin. Put the tin into a roasting tin and pour in boiling water to come halfway up the side of the tin. Cook in a preheated oven at 180°C (350°F, Gas 4) for 1 hour or until firm.

8 Remove from the water, and leave to cool in the loaf tin. Chill thoroughly in the refrigerator. Turn out the terrine, and cut into slices to serve.

8

PASTA & RICE

UNDER 30 MINUTES

PENNE WITH SPINACH & STILTON

Pasta quills with mushrooms, cream, and garlic, mixed with spinach, Stilton cheese, and lemon juice.

SERVES 4 976 calories per serving
Takes 15 minutes **PAGE 309**

PASTA ALLA MARINARA

Pasta bows combined with squid, scallops, prawns, button mushrooms, white wine, onion, and parsley. Enriched with cream.

SERVES 4 797 calories per serving
Takes 15 minutes **PAGE 307**

SPAGHETTI ALLA CARBONARA

Crisp-cooked strips of bacon mixed with garlic, eggs, and Parmesan cheese, then tossed with spaghetti and single cream.

SERVES 4 906 calories per serving
Takes 20 minutes **PAGE 312**

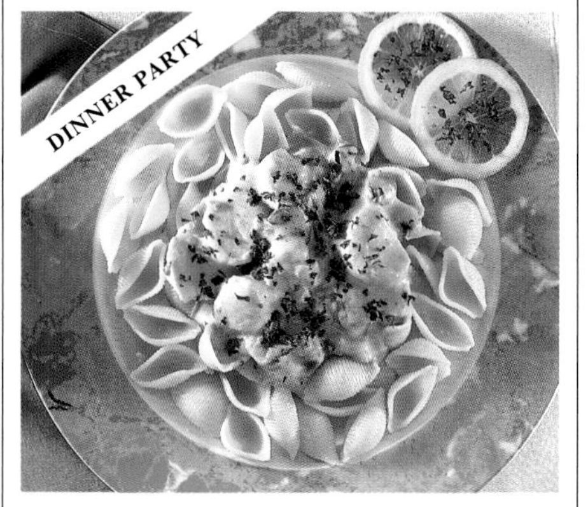

PASTA SHELLS WITH SCALLOPS

Scallops simmered with lemon juice, onion, peppercorns, and bay leaf. Served with a creamy mushroom sauce and pasta shells.

SERVES 4 753 calories per serving
Takes 25 minutes **PAGE 308**

TAGLIATELLE WITH VEGETABLE RIBBONS

Courgette and carrot ribbons cooked with tagliatelle. Mixed with coriander sauce.

SERVES 4 878 calories per serving
Takes 25 minutes **PAGE 309**

EGG-FRIED RICE

Delicious and simple: long grain rice boiled then stir-fried with bacon, peas, eggs, and bean sprouts. Sprinkled with spring onions.

SERVES 4 441 calories per serving
Takes 25 minutes **PAGE 326**

PENNE WITH ASPARAGUS

Bite-sized pieces of asparagus and pasta quills in a light, aromatic mixture of olive oil, garlic, basil, and goat's cheese.

SERVES 4 693 calories per serving
Takes 20 minutes **PAGE 310**

TORTELLINI WITH PEAS & BACON

Rich and creamy: petits pois and diced bacon combined with double cream, salt, black pepper, and a pinch of grated nutmeg. This delicious sauce is tossed with tortellini, and servings are sprinkled generously with grated Parmesan cheese.

SERVES 4 965 calories per serving
Takes 25 minutes **PAGE 311**

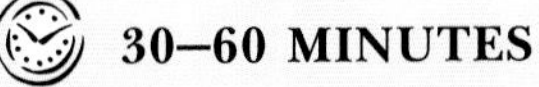

30–60 MINUTES

STIR-FRIED CHINESE NOODLES

Egg noodles stir-fried with mangetout, bean sprouts, shiitake mushrooms, garlic, and ginger, served sprinkled with spring onions.

SERVES 4 476 calories per serving

Takes 20 minutes, plus soaking **PAGE 311**

CARIBBEAN RICE & PEAS

Traditional West Indian dish: rice cooked with kidney beans, stock, spring onions, bacon, garlic, tomatoes, herbs, and spices.

SERVES 4 435 calories per serving

Takes 35 minutes **PAGE 319**

RISI E BISI

Risotto rice cooked with peas, stock, and Parma ham. Flavoured with garlic, onion, Parmesan cheese, and parsley.

SERVES 4–6 585–390 calories per serving

Takes 40 minutes **PAGE 320**

SUMMER RISOTTO AL VERDE

Risotto rice cooked with stock and garlic, mixed with cream, blue cheese, pesto, and pine nuts. Served sprinkled with basil.

SERVES 4 734 calories per serving

Takes 35 minutes **PAGE 323**

KEDGEREE

Anglo-Indian breakfast dish: long grain rice baked with smoked haddock, hard-boiled eggs, cream, and lemon juice. Mixed with parsley.

SERVES 4 470 calories per serving

Takes 45 minutes **PAGE 323**

TAGLIATELLE WITH PRAWNS

Ribbon pasta served with a sauce of button mushrooms, tomatoes, prawns, and crème fraîche, garnished with parsley.

SERVES 4 734 calories per serving

Takes 35 minutes **PAGE 308**

SAVOURY RICE

Long grain rice simmered with tomatoes, stock, sweetcorn, onion, carrot, and peas, and flavoured with garlic.

SERVES 4 356 calories per serving

Takes 30 minutes **PAGE 319**

PASTA SPIRALS WITH MEATBALLS

Meatballs of minced veal, Parmesan cheese, breadcrumbs, and parsley in a tomato and basil sauce. Served with pasta spirals.

SERVES 4–6 1022–681 calories per serving

Takes 35 minutes **PAGE 313**

PERSIAN PILAF

Rice cooked with cumin and cardamom seeds, cinnamon, cloves, and bay leaves. Combined with pistachio nuts and raisins.

SERVES 4 426 calories per serving

Takes 40 minutes **PAGE 321**

30–60 MINUTES

SPAGHETTI ALLE VONGOLE

Fresh clams cooked in tomatoes and wine, and seasoned with onion, garlic, chilli powder, and parsley. Served with spaghetti.

SERVES 4 626 calories per serving
Takes 40 minutes **PAGE 307**

WILD RICE BAKE

Basmati and wild rice baked with broccoli, garlic, onions, soured cream, mozzarella and Parmesan cheeses, and rosemary.

SERVES 4 669 calories per serving
Takes 60 minutes **PAGE 320**

FETTUCCINE PRIMAVERA

Asparagus, broccoli, courgette, pepper, garlic, tomatoes, petits pois, and cream mixed with fettuccine. Served with basil and Parmesan.

SERVES 4 831 calories per serving
Takes 35 minutes **PAGE 312**

RISOTTO MILANESE

Rice cooked with stock and onion, flavoured with saffron, and mixed with Parmesan cheese. Served with Parmesan shavings.

SERVES 4 604 calories per serving
Takes 45 minutes **PAGE 322**

PORTUGUESE RICE WITH TUNA

Nourishing meal: brown rice simmered with stock, bacon, and onion. Combined with fresh tuna, pimientos, and olives.

SERVES 4 603 calories per serving
Takes 45 minutes **PAGE 321**

TUNA & FENNEL PASTA BAKE

Fresh and aromatic: fennel and onion baked with white sauce, pasta shells, tuna, eggs, and Cheddar cheese.

SERVES 4 768 calories per serving
Takes 45 minutes **PAGE 316**

SPAGHETTI ALL' AMATRICIANA

Diced bacon cooked with tomatoes, garlic, red and green peppers, fresh chilli, and herbs, then tossed with spaghetti.

SERVES 4 646 calories per serving
Takes 40 minutes **PAGE 310**

CHICKEN LIVER RISOTTO

Wild and risotto rice cooked with stock and bacon. Combined with chicken livers, mushrooms, and sun-dried tomatoes.

SERVES 4 619 calories per serving
Takes 40 minutes **PAGE 322**

VEGETABLES NAPOLETANA

Broccoli, shiitake mushrooms, red pepper, courgettes, and mustard-flavoured white sauce baked with pasta twists.

SERVES 4 713 calories per serving
Takes 55 minutes **PAGE 316**

OVER 60 MINUTES

THREE-CHEESE MACARONI

Macaroni baked with a sauce flavoured with Fontina, mozzarella, and Parmesan cheeses, and topped with breadcrumbs.

SERVES 4–6 1272–848 calories per serving

Takes 1 hour 5 minutes **PAGE 317**

CLASSIC LASAGNE

Pasta layered with minced beef, simmered with stock, tomatoes, celery, white sauce, and Cheddar and Parmesan cheeses.

SERVES 6 854 calories per serving

Takes $1^1/_2$ hours, plus simmering **PAGE 318**

CANNELLONI WITH RICOTTA & SPINACH

Cannelloni tubes filled with spinach and ricotta cheese, and topped with tomato sauce.

SERVES 4–6 694–462 calories per serving

Takes 40 minutes, plus simmering **PAGE 318**

FISHERMAN'S LASAGNE

Pasta layered with haddock, prawns, courgettes, and parsley sauce. Sprinkled with Cheddar and Parmesan cheeses.

SERVES 6 636 calories per serving

Takes $1^1/_4$ hours **PAGE 317**

SPAGHETTI BOLOGNESE

Traditional Italian dish: spaghetti served with a sauce of minced beef simmered with celery, garlic, tomato, and redcurrant jelly.

SERVES 4 904 calories per serving

Takes 15 minutes, plus simmering **PAGE 313**

PAELLA

Chicken and rice are cooked in the oven with bacon, stock, tomatoes, onion, peppers, peas, and saffron. Mussels and prawns are stirred in and cooked gently on top of the stove, then the dish is served garnished with jumbo prawns, lemon wedges, olives, and parsley.

SERVES 6 718 calories per serving

Takes $1^1/_4$ hours **PAGE 326**

PASTA & RICE KNOW-HOW

BOTH PASTA AND RICE are natural convenience foods. They're endlessly versatile, and are easily combined with almost any ingredient imaginable to make starters, soups, main dishes, side dishes, salads, snacks, and even desserts.

Pasta and rice are very quick to cook and don't need any elaborate preparation. They are healthy too, providing essential nutrients, fibre, and, most important of all, carbohydrate for energy. And, as long you don't overdo the rich ingredients such as butter, cream, and cheese, pasta and rice dishes can be very low in fat and calories.

BUYING & STORING

Pasta is now available both fresh and dried, in a variety of shapes. Commercial dried pasta is made from durum wheat semolina mixed with water. Egg is sometimes added to dried pasta, and the fresh pasta available in supermarkets is normally enriched with eggs. Fresh pasta is convenient because it cooks quickly, but its texture and absorbency are not necessarily as good as some dried pasta. A good Italian brand of dried pasta, made from 100% durum wheat semolina (*semola di grano duro*), is often of superior quality.

Dried pasta, in a tightly closed packet, will keep almost indefinitely in the store cupboard (up to 2 years); fresh pasta must be refrigerated and can only be kept for 2–3 days (check the use-by date).

Rice is another good store cupboard stand-by. As long as it is stored in an airtight container in a dry, dark place, it will keep indefinitely. But make sure that the container is tightly closed to prevent moisture or insects getting in. Store any left-over cooked pasta in a tightly closed container in the refrigerator and use it within 2 days. Rice should be eaten on the day it is cooked as it is susceptible to food poisoning bacteria.

MICROWAVING

There is no advantage to cooking pasta in a microwave oven as it takes just as long as cooking in a pan of boiling water. Many pasta sauces, however, are quickly prepared in the microwave, and dishes containing layered or filled pasta can also be cooked in the microwave. Another use for the microwave is reheating cooked pasta; be careful not to overcook it. The microwave is ideal for cooking rice, whether it is steamed or turned into a pilaf or risotto. The liquid does not have to be brought to a boil before the rice is added. Also, a risotto can be left unattended in the microwave and will turn out as tender and creamy as one made by the classic method.

FREEZING

Fresh pasta can be frozen for up to 3 months and then cooked from frozen. Layered or filled pasta dishes such as cannelloni, lasagne, and macaroni cheese freeze very well and can also be stored for up to 3 months. Put them in foil or other freezer-proof containers that can go straight from the freezer into the oven.

There is no advantage to freezing cooked rice as it takes a long time to thaw – longer than it would take to cook a fresh batch.

It's not advisable to freeze pasta and rice in soups and other dishes that contain a lot of liquid because the pasta and rice become mushy when thawed. Instead, add when reheating the soup or casserole.

ORIENTAL NOODLES

Oriental noodles are made from wheat, potato, or rice flour, and from soya or mung bean starch. The most popular types are available in supermarkets and delicatessens; fresh varieties can be found in Chinese or Japanese shops.

Egg noodles The most common of Oriental noodles. Made from wheat flour and egg and used in dishes such as chow mein. They are sold in flat sheets, which separate when cooked.

Cellophane noodles Sometimes referred to as transparent noodles or bean thread noodles. They are made from ground mung bean flour.

Rice noodles Long, thin, white strands, also called rice vermicelli. They are sold dried or fresh in bundles, and will cook very quickly if soaked in water first.

Rice sticks Made from ground rice and water. Similar to rice noodles but sold dried, as broad ribbons. They need to be soaked before cooking.

Noodles know-how

Allow 90–125 g (3–4 oz) or one flat sheet of noodles per person.

◆

Store dried noodles in the same way as pasta.

◆

Fresh noodles will keep for 3 days in the refrigerator.

PASTA SHAPES

Of the many pasta shapes available there are some which are traditionally served with certain sauces – spaghetti with bolognese sauce, for example. But you can mix and match as you wish.

Long, thin varieties Capelli d'angelo or angel hair, vermicelli, spaghettini, spaghetti, and bucatini are best served with a thin oily sauce that clings without making the strands stick together.

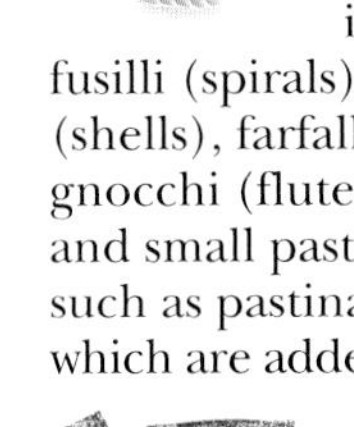

Other shapes These include fusilli (spirals), conchiglie (shells), farfalle (bows), gnocchi (fluted shells), and small pasta shapes such as pastina and orzo, which are added to soups.

Long flat ribbons Pastas such as linguine, fettuccine, and tagliatelle are usually served with a creamy sauce such as *alfredo*.

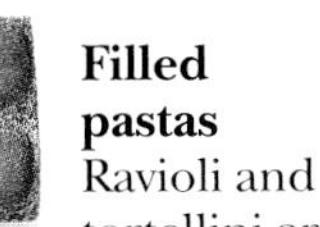

Filled pastas Ravioli and tortellini are stuffed with ground meats or mixtures such as spinach and ricotta, and served with a simple sauce.

Tubular pasta Macaroni, penne (quills), and rigatoni are best with rich sauces that will coat them all over.

Sheet pasta Flat sheets of lasagne are layered with sauce and baked. They can be rolled to make cannelloni for filling.

PRE-COOKED LASAGNE

Sheets of dried lasagne, known as pre-cooked lasagne, are a great boon to the cook because they can be taken straight from the packet and layered with the other ingredients. However, this lasagne needs to absorb liquid during cooking, so if you are using pre-cooked lasagne in a recipe that calls for fresh pasta or for ordinary dried lasagne, increase the quantity of sauce and make it thinner. Or briefly soak the pre-cooked lasagne in a bowl of hot water to soften it before layering in the baking dish.

Coloured & flavoured pasta

Not only does pasta come in a vast range of shapes, you can also choose from a variety of colours and flavours. Green is the most common colour, and is derived from spinach. Other colours include red, made with tomato purée, pink, dyed with beetroot, yellow, dyed with saffron, and even black pasta, made from squid ink. These colourings affect the taste very little. Flavoured pasta usually has ingredients such as herbs, garlic, or black pepper added to the dough. Serve with a complementary sauce.

COOKING PASTA

There is one golden rule when cooking pasta: use plenty of salted water – at least 2 litres (3 1/2 pints) water and 2 tsp salt for every 250 g (8 oz) of pasta.

1 Bring the salted water to a boil. Add the pasta and stir to separate. If cooking spaghetti, let the ends soften before stirring. Return the water to a boil as quickly as possible. Reduce the heat so that the water is bubbling briskly and cook, uncovered.

2 Immediately remove the pan from the heat and drain in a large colander, shaking the colander to drain the pasta thoroughly.

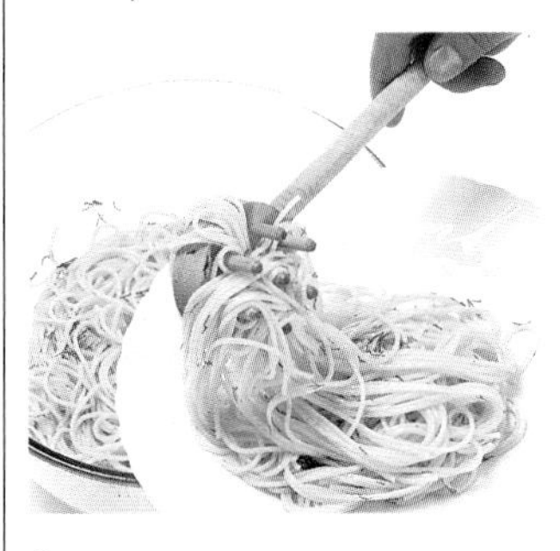

3 Return the pasta to the pan or transfer to a warmed bowl. Toss with olive oil or butter, add plenty of ground black pepper and chopped fresh herbs, if preferred, and serve immediately.

Pasta know-how

To test pasta, lift out a piece and bite it – it should be tender but still a little firm. The Italians call this al dente, literally "to the tooth".

◆

If you are going to use the pasta in a baked dish such as lasagne, undercook it slightly. This stops it from becoming overcooked as it cooks in its own heat.

COOKING TIMES & QUANTITIES

These times can only be a guide because they depend on the freshness of fresh pasta and the age of dried pasta, as well as shape and thickness. Start timing as soon as the water returns to a boil, and for fresh pasta, start testing three-quarters of the way through the suggested cooking time. If using dried pasta, start testing as soon as the minimum time given on the packet is reached. Fresh, store-bought pasta takes 2–4 minutes, 7–10 minutes if filled. Most dried pastas cook in 8–12 minutes (less for fine pasta such as capelli d'angelo and vermicelli).

In Italy, pasta is usually eaten as a first course. Use 500 g (1 lb) fresh or dried pasta (uncooked weight) to serve 6 people as a first course and 4 people as a main dish. If the dish has a rich sauce or filling it will stretch even farther. As an accompaniment to another dish, this amount would serve 6–8 people.

COOKING WITH RICE

The length of the rice grain determines the cooking method and its use. Short grain rice is almost round in shape. It is very starchy and best cooked by absorption, so after cooking it remains moist and sticky. Use short grain rice for puddings, risottos, moulded rice dishes, stir-fried rice, and croquettes. The grains of long grain rice are separate, dry, and fluffy after cooking. Use it in pilafs, for rice salads, or other savoury dishes.

White rice has been milled to remove the husk, bran, and germ, whereas for brown rice only the tough outer husk has been removed, leaving the nutritious bran layer which gives it its distinctive colour and nutty flavour.

COOKING RICE BY ABSORPTION

Cook the rice very gently in simmering salted water. Use 2 parts water to 1 part rice.

1 Bring the salted water to a boil and add the rice. Return to a boil and stir once. Cover, reduce the heat, and cook gently until the water is absorbed.

2 Remove the pan from the heat and leave to stand, covered, for at least 5 minutes. Fluff it up with chopsticks or a fork just before serving.

BOILING RICE

Long grain rice should be rinsed well before and after boiling, to remove starch that would cause stickiness.

1 Put the rice into a large bowl of cold water. Swirl it around with your fingertips until the water becomes milky. Drain and repeat until the water runs clear. Drain again. Bring a large pan of salted water to a boil and add the rice.

2 Bring the water back to a boil. Reduce the heat so that the water is simmering quite vigorously. Cook until the rice is just tender. Drain well and rinse with boiling water to remove any excess starch.

COOKING RISOTTO RICE

An authentic risotto requires constant attention as the liquid (usually stock) must be stirred into the rice very gradually. The stock must be hot, so bring it to a boil and keep it at a gentle simmer.

1 Heat butter or oil in a large saucepan and soften the onion, garlic, or other flavourings as specified in the recipe.

2 Add the rice and stir to coat the grains with the oil (this will keep them separate during cooking). Cook, stirring, for 1–2 minutes or until the rice grains look translucent.

3 Add a ladleful, about 150 ml (1/4 pint), of the stock. Cook until absorbed. Add another ladleful and cook until absorbed.

4 Continue adding stock, stirring, for 25–30 minutes. When the rice is tender but still firm to the bite, you have added enough stock.

RICE VARIETIES

There are many varieties of rice, each with a distinct flavour and aroma. Here are the most common.

Long grain Mild in flavour. The most widely used type of white rice. Cook for 12–15 minutes.

Easy-cook Processed so the grains separate after cooking. Cook for 10–12 minutes.

Basmati Available both brown and white. Used in Indian dishes. Cook for 10–15 minutes.

Risotto A short grain Italian variety, also called arborio rice. Cook for 20–25 minutes.

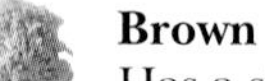

Brown Has a slightly chewy texture with a mild nutty flavour. Cook for 30–35 minutes.

Wild Not a true rice, but an aquatic grass from the USA. Cook for 35–40 minutes.

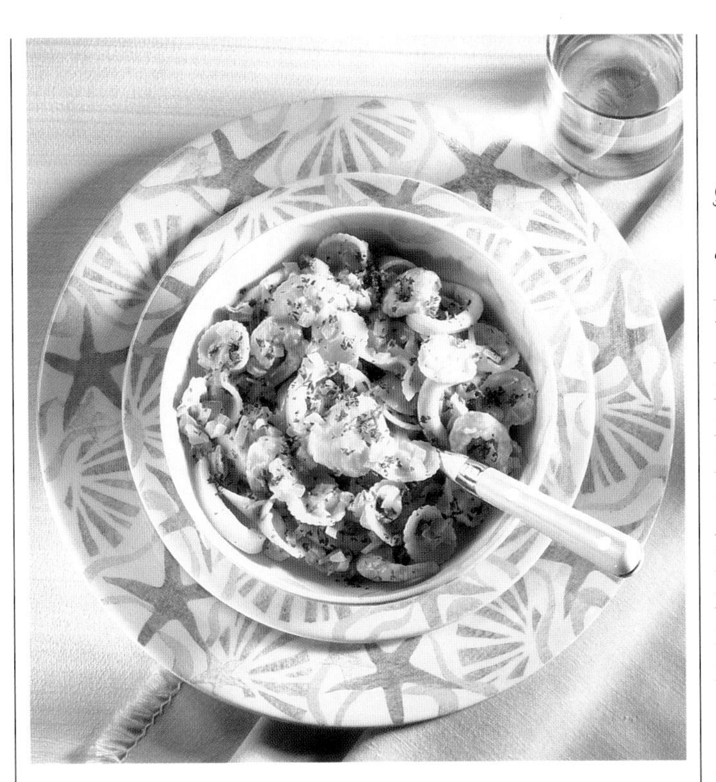

PASTA ALLA MARINARA

Serves 4

- *500 g (1 lb) pasta bows*
- *salt and black pepper*
- *2 tbsp olive oil*
- *1 large onion, finely chopped*
- *1 large garlic clove, crushed*
- *125 ml (4 fl oz) dry white wine*
- *125 g (4 oz) squid, cut into strips or rings*
- *60 g (2 oz) button mushrooms, sliced*
- *125 g (4 oz) scallops, halved*
- *125 g (4 oz) cooked peeled prawns*
- *150 ml (1/4 pint) double cream*
- *4 tbsp chopped parsley*

1 Cook the pasta bows in a large saucepan of boiling salted water for 8–10 minutes until just tender.

2 Meanwhile, heat the oil in a large pan, add the onion and garlic, and cook gently, stirring occasionally, for 3–5 minutes until softened but not coloured.

3 Pour in the white wine and boil to reduce the liquid in the saucepan to about 2 tbsp, stirring constantly. Add the squid and cook for 1 minute, then add the mushrooms and scallops, and cook, stirring, for a further 2 minutes. Add the prawns, double cream, and half of the parsley, and heat through.

4 Drain the pasta bows thoroughly, and add to the seafood mixture, stirring well to combine. Season with salt and black pepper to taste, and serve at once, garnished with the remaining chopped parsley.

Cook's know-how

If you prefer, replace the squid, scallops, and prawns with 375 g (12 oz) mixed seafood, packets of which are available in supermarkets. The mixture contains ready-prepared squid, prawns, and mussels.

SPAGHETTI ALLE VONGOLE

Serves 4

- *about 32 fresh clams in their shells, cleaned (page 106)*
- *2 tbsp olive oil, plus extra for tossing*
- *1 onion, chopped*
- *1 garlic clove, crushed*
- *1/4 tsp chilli powder*
- *1 x 400 g (13 oz) can chopped tomatoes*
- *4 tbsp dry white wine*
- *salt and black pepper*
- *500 g (1 lb) spaghetti*
- *2 tbsp chopped parsley*

1 Holding each clam in a tea towel, insert a thin knife blade between the shells and twist the knife to open the shells. Reserve 4 clams for garnish. Remove the remaining clams from their shells, cut them into bite-sized pieces, and set aside with any juices.

2 Heat the olive oil in a large pan, add the onion and garlic, and cook gently, stirring occasionally, for 3–5 minutes until softened but not coloured. Add the chilli powder and cook gently, stirring, for 1 minute.

3 Add the tomatoes, wine, and salt and pepper to taste, and bring to a boil. Simmer, uncovered, for 15 minutes or until the mixture has thickened.

4 Meanwhile, cook the spaghetti in a large saucepan of boiling salted water for 8–10 minutes until just tender. Drain, then toss the spaghetti in a little olive oil to prevent sticking. Transfer to warmed serving plates.

5 Add the parsley, and the clams and their juices to the tomato mixture, and cook for 2 minutes. Do not cook any longer or the clams will toughen.

6 Taste for seasoning, then spoon the sauce over the spaghetti. Serve at once, garnished with the reserved clams in their shells.

Cook's know-how

Live clams should have tightly closed shells. Discard any that do not close when tapped.

TAGLIATELLE WITH PRAWNS

Serves 4

2 tbsp olive oil

1 large onion, chopped

1 garlic clove, crushed

375 g (12 oz) button mushrooms, halved

500 g (1 lb) tomatoes, peeled (page 39), seeded, and chopped

salt and black pepper

500 g (1 lb) tagliatelle

375 g (12 oz) cooked peeled prawns

125 ml (4 fl oz) crème fraîche

4 tbsp chopped parsley to garnish

1 Heat the oil in a large pan, add the onion and garlic, and cook gently, stirring, for 3–5 minutes until softened but not coloured. Add the mushrooms and cook over a high heat, stirring, for about 5 minutes.

2 Add the tomatoes, season to taste, and simmer gently, uncovered, for about 20 minutes or until the mixture has thickened.

3 Meanwhile, cook the tagliatelle in a large saucepan of boiling salted water for 8–10 minutes until just tender.

4 Add the prawns and crème fraîche to the tomato mixture and cook gently for about 2 minutes until the prawns are heated through. Season to taste.

5 Drain the tagliatelle thoroughly and transfer to warmed serving plates. Arrange the prawn mixture on top, and serve at once, garnished with parsley.

PASTA WITH SMOKED SALMON

Substitute 125 g (4 oz) smoked salmon for 125 g (4 oz) of the prawns. Proceed as directed, adding the smoked salmon just before serving.

PASTA SHELLS WITH SCALLOPS

Serves 4

8 large scallops, each cut into 3 slices

75 ml ($2^{1}/_{2}$ fl oz) water

juice of 1 lemon

1 slice of onion

6 black peppercorns

1 small bay leaf

500 g (1 lb) pasta shells

15 g ($^{1}/_{2}$ oz) butter

chopped parsley and lemon slices to garnish

SAUCE

45 g ($1^{1}/_{2}$ oz) butter

125 g (4 oz) button mushrooms, sliced

30 g (1 oz) plain flour

250 ml (8 fl oz) single cream

1 tbsp tomato purée

salt and black pepper

1 Put the scallops into a pan with the water, half of the lemon juice, the onion, peppercorns, and bay leaf, and bring to a boil.

2 Cover and simmer until the scallops are opaque. Remove the scallops, strain the liquid, and reserve.

3 Make the sauce: melt the butter in a saucepan, add the mushrooms, and cook gently, stirring occasionally, for 2 minutes. Add the flour and cook, stirring, for 1 minute. Remove from the heat and blend in the strained poaching liquid. Cook, stirring, for 1 minute until thickened.

4 Add the cream and tomato purée and bring to a boil, stirring constantly until the mixture thickens. Simmer for 2 minutes, then add salt and pepper to taste.

5 Cook the pasta shells in a large saucepan of boiling salted water for 8–10 minutes or until tender.

6 Drain the pasta shells, then toss with the butter and the remaining lemon juice. Add the scallops to the sauce, and heat through. Transfer to serving plates.

7 Spoon the sauce over the pasta shells, and serve at once, garnished with the parsley and lemon slices.

TAGLIATELLE WITH VEGETABLE RIBBONS

Serves 4

500 g (1 lb) courgettes
250 g (8 oz) carrots
500 g (1 lb) tagliatelle

CORIANDER SAUCE
60 g (2 oz) fresh coriander leaves
125 ml (4 fl oz) olive oil
2 tbsp pine nuts
2 garlic cloves
salt and black pepper
60 g (2 oz) Parmesan or pecorino cheese, grated

1 Make the coriander sauce: put the coriander, olive oil, pine nuts, garlic, and salt and pepper to taste into a food processor and work until smooth. Fold in the grated cheese.

2 Cut the courgettes and carrots into wide ribbons (page 335).

3 Cook the tagliatelle in a large saucepan of boiling salted water for 8 minutes.

4 Add the courgettes and carrots to the pan of tagliatelle and cook for 1–2 minutes until the pasta and vegetables are just tender.

5 Drain the tagliatelle and vegetables thoroughly and return to the saucepan. Add the coriander sauce and toss over a high heat to warm through fully. Taste for seasoning, and serve at once.

Cook's know-how

The coriander sauce can be made in advance and kept in an airtight container in the refrigerator for up to 2 weeks.

PENNE WITH SPINACH & STILTON

Serves 4

500 g (1 lb) penne
salt and black pepper
45 g (1½ oz) butter
2 large garlic cloves, crushed
250 g (8 oz) chestnut mushrooms, sliced
300 ml (½ pint) double cream
1 egg, lightly beaten
90 g (3 oz) spinach, coarsely shredded
90 g (3 oz) blue Stilton cheese, crumbled
juice of ½ lemon
pinch of grated nutmeg

1 Cook the pasta quills in boiling salted water for 8–10 minutes until just tender.

2 Meanwhile, melt the butter in a large pan, add the garlic, and cook, stirring, for 1 minute. Add the mushrooms and cook, stirring occasionally, for 2 minutes. Stir in the cream and boil for 2–3 minutes until the mixture reaches a coating consistency.

3 Drain the pasta quills, add to the mushroom and cream mixture with the egg, stirring well, and heat through. Add the spinach, Stilton cheese, lemon juice, nutmeg, and pepper to taste, and stir well to coat the pasta. Serve at once.

Cook's know-how

For best results use young spinach leaves. No extra salt is needed in the sauce as Stilton is a salty cheese.

PENNE WITH BROCCOLI & STILTON

Substitute 125 g (4 oz) small broccoli florets for the spinach. Cook in boiling salted water for 5 minutes or until just tender. Add to the pasta with the cheese, lemon juice, nutmeg, and pepper, omitting the egg. Stir well, and serve at once.

PENNE WITH ASPARAGUS

Serves 4

125 g (4 oz) goat's cheese, cut into small pieces
3 tbsp olive oil
3 garlic cloves, crushed
3 tbsp shredded fresh basil
500 g (1 lb) penne or spaghetti
salt and black pepper
500 g (1 lb) asparagus

1 In a small bowl, combine the goat's cheese, olive oil, garlic, and shredded fresh basil. Set aside.

2 Cook the pasta in a large saucepan of boiling salted water for 8–10 minutes until just tender.

3 Meanwhile, trim the woody ends from the asparagus. Cut the asparagus into bite-sized pieces and cook in boiling salted water for about 3 minutes until just tender.

4 Drain the pasta thoroughly, add the goat's cheese mixture, and toss together. Drain the asparagus and add to the pasta mixture. Toss lightly together, add salt and black pepper to taste, and serve at once.

SPAGHETTI ALL' AMATRICIANA

A speciality of Amatrice, near Rome, this tomato-based sauce is spiced with chillies and garlic, and richly flavoured with diced bacon and roast peppers.

Serves 4

1 red pepper
1 green pepper
4 tbsp olive oil
5 unsmoked bacon rashers, rinds removed, diced
1/2–1 fresh green chilli, cored, seeded, and thinly sliced
5 garlic cloves, crushed
2 ripe tomatoes, peeled (page 39), seeded, and diced
2 tbsp chopped parsley
1/2 tsp dried oregano
salt and black pepper
500 g (1 lb) spaghetti
grated Parmesan cheese to serve

1 Remove and discard the cores and seeds from the peppers and cut each pepper in half. Roast and peel the peppers (page 354). Cut the flesh into thin strips.

2 Heat the oil in a frying pan, add the bacon and cook over a high heat for 5 minutes or until crisp. Add the red and green peppers and the chilli, and cook for 2 minutes. Stir in the garlic and cook for about 1 minute.

3 Add the tomatoes and parsley and cook for 3 minutes or until thickened. Remove the frying pan from the heat and add the oregano and salt and pepper to taste.

4 Cook the spaghetti in a large saucepan of boiling salted water for 8–10 minutes until just tender.

5 Drain the spaghetti thoroughly. Add the sauce and toss with the spaghetti. Generously sprinkle with grated Parmesan cheese, and serve at once.

SPAGHETTI ALL' ARRABIATA

Melt 30 g (1 oz) butter with 2 tbsp oil in a frying pan, add 3 crushed garlic cloves and 1/2–1 tsp crushed chillies, and cook gently. Drain and stir in 1 x 400 g (13 oz) can chopped tomatoes, and bring slowly to a boil. Simmer until reduced and thickened. Add 1/4 tsp dried oregano and season. Toss with the spaghetti, and serve at once.

Spaghetti all' amatriciana

This recipe originates in the Abruzzo region of Italy. This is where peperoncino *or green chillies are grown and widely used to flavour pasta sauces.*

STIR-FRIED CHINESE NOODLES

Serves 4

5 dried shiitake mushrooms
250 ml (8 fl oz) hot vegetable stock
375 g (12 oz) Chinese egg noodles
salt
about 2 tsp soy sauce
1 tbsp sunflower oil
250 g (8 oz) mangetout
3 garlic cloves, crushed
5 mm (1/4 in) piece of fresh root ginger, peeled and chopped
1/4 tsp sugar (optional)
125 g (4 oz) bean sprouts
about 1/2 tsp crushed chillies

TO SERVE
3 spring onions, sliced
2 tsp sesame oil
1 tbsp chopped fresh coriander

1 Put the mushrooms into a bowl, cover with the hot vegetable stock, and leave to soak for about 30 minutes.

2 Drain the mushrooms, reserving the liquid.

3 Pour the soaking liquid through a sieve lined with a paper towel to remove any grit, and reserve the liquid. Squeeze the shiitake mushrooms dry, then cut into thin strips.

4 Cook the noodles in a large saucepan of boiling salted water for 3 minutes or according to packet instructions. Drain the noodles, toss with soy sauce to taste, and set aside.

5 Heat the sunflower oil in a wok or large frying pan, add the mushrooms, mangetout, garlic, and ginger, and stir-fry for 2 minutes. Add the sugar, if using, bean sprouts, crushed chillies to taste, and 3 tbsp of the reserved mushroom soaking liquid, and stir-fry for 2 minutes.

6 Add the egg noodles and stir-fry for 2 minutes or until heated through. Serve at once, sprinkled with the spring onions, sesame oil, and coriander.

TORTELLINI WITH PEAS & BACON

Serves 4

500 g (1 lb) tortellini
salt and black pepper
1 tbsp sunflower oil
250 g (8 oz) bacon rashers, rinds removed, diced
175 g (6 oz) frozen petits pois
300 ml (1/2 pint) double cream
pinch of grated nutmeg
grated Parmesan cheese to serve

1 Cook the tortellini in boiling salted water for about 10–12 minutes, or according to packet instructions, until tender.

2 Meanwhile, heat the oil in a frying pan, add the bacon, and cook over a high heat, stirring, for 3 minutes or until crisp.

3 Cook the petits pois in boiling salted water for about 2 minutes until just tender. Drain.

4 Drain the tortellini thoroughly and return to the saucepan. Add the bacon, petits pois, cream, nutmeg, and salt and pepper to taste, and heat gently for 1–2 minutes to warm through. Serve at once, sprinkled with the grated Parmesan cheese.

Tortellini

These are small, circular pieces of pasta enclosing a stuffing such as spinach and ricotta, or ground meats. In Bologna, Northern Italy, their place of origin, tortellini are traditionally served in a broth or with a cream sauce.

Fettuccine Primavera

Serves 4

125 g (4 oz) asparagus, trimmed and cut into bite-sized pieces

125 g (4 oz) broccoli florets

1 courgette, sliced

salt and black pepper

3 tbsp olive oil

1/2 red and 1/2 yellow pepper, cored, seeded, and diced

3 garlic cloves, crushed

1 x 200 g (7 oz) can plum tomatoes, drained and juice reserved, diced

90 g (3 oz) frozen petits pois, thawed

125 ml (4 fl oz) double cream

500 g (1 lb) fettuccine

4 tbsp chopped fresh basil

90 g (3 oz) Parmesan cheese, grated, to serve

1 Cook the asparagus, broccoli, and courgette in boiling salted water for 3 minutes or until just tender. Drain, rinse, and set aside.

2 Heat the oil in a frying pan, add the peppers and garlic, and cook, stirring, for 4 minutes or until the peppers are softened.

3 Add the tomatoes, 3 tbsp of their juice, and the petits pois, and cook for 5 minutes or until the liquid in the pan is reduced by half.

4 Add the asparagus, broccoli, and courgette, stir in the cream, and boil for 1–2 minutes to reduce the liquid and concentrate the flavour. Add salt and pepper to taste.

5 Cook the fettuccine in a large saucepan of boiling salted water for 8–10 minutes until just tender.

6 Drain the fettuccine thoroughly and toss with the vegetables and sauce. Stir in the basil and serve at once, sprinkled with Parmesan cheese.

Fettuccine

The Roman equivalent of tagliatelle, these egg noodles are cut into flat, narrow strips, about 1 cm (3/8 in) wide.

Spaghetti alla Carbonara

Serves 4

500 g (1 lb) spaghetti

salt and black pepper

175 g (6 oz) streaky bacon rashers, rinds removed, cut into strips

1 garlic clove, crushed

4 eggs

125 g (4 oz) Parmesan cheese, grated

150 ml (1/4 pint) single cream

chopped parsley to garnish

1 Cook the spaghetti in a large saucepan of boiling salted water for 8–10 minutes until just tender.

2 Meanwhile, put the bacon into a frying pan and heat gently for 7 minutes until the fat begins to run, then increase the heat. Add the garlic and cook quickly for 2–3 minutes until the bacon is crisp.

3 Break the eggs into a bowl. Add the bacon and garlic mixture, using a slotted spoon. Add the Parmesan cheese, season generously with salt and pepper, and whisk until well blended.

4 Drain and return the spaghetti to the hot pan. Stir in the bacon and egg mixture and cook gently until the egg just begins to set. Stir in the cream and heat gently. Serve at once, garnished with parsley.

Cook's know-how

It's best to buy a whole piece of Parmesan cheese and grate the quantity you need for a given dish. Ready-grated Parmesan in packets is less economical and lacks the flavour of freshly grated Parmesan.

Spaghetti Alfredo

Heat 150 ml (1/4 pint) double cream with 30 g (1 oz) butter until the mixture has thickened. Set aside. Cook the pasta, drain, then add to the cream mixture. Add 90 ml (3 fl oz) more cream, 90 g (3 oz) Parmesan cheese, a pinch of grated nutmeg, and season to taste. Heat gently until thickened, and serve.

SPAGHETTI BOLOGNESE

Serves 4

3 tbsp olive oil
500 g (1 lb) minced beef
1 large onion, finely chopped
2 celery stalks, sliced
1 tbsp plain flour
2 garlic cloves, crushed
90 g (3 oz) tomato purée
150 ml (1/4 pint) beef stock
150 ml (1/4 pint) red wine
1 x 400 g (13 oz) can chopped tomatoes
1 tbsp redcurrant jelly
salt and black pepper
500 g (1 lb) spaghetti
grated Parmesan cheese to serve

1 Heat 2 tbsp of the oil in a saucepan. Add the minced beef, onion, and celery, and cook, stirring, for 5 minutes or until the beef is browned. Add the flour, garlic, and tomato purée, and cook, stirring, for about 1 minute.

2 Pour in the stock and wine. Add the tomatoes, redcurrant jelly, and salt and pepper to taste, and bring to a boil. Cook, stirring, until the mixture has thickened.

3 Lower the heat, partially cover the pan, and simmer very gently, stirring occasionally, for about 1 hour.

4 Meanwhile, cook the spaghetti in boiling salted water for 8–10 minutes until just tender. Drain thoroughly.

5 Return the spaghetti to the saucepan, add the remaining oil, and toss gently to coat.

6 Divide the spaghetti among warmed serving plates and ladle some of the sauce on top of each serving. Sprinkle with a little Parmesan cheese and hand the remainder separately.

PASTA SPIRALS WITH MEATBALLS

Serves 4

2 tbsp olive oil
500 g (1 lb) pasta spirals
shredded basil to garnish

TOMATO BASIL SAUCE
1 tbsp olive oil
1 small onion, chopped
1 x 400 g (13 oz) can chopped tomatoes, drained and juice reserved
1 tbsp chopped fresh basil
salt and black pepper

MEATBALLS
500 g (1 lb) minced veal
150 g (5 oz) fresh white breadcrumbs
150 g (5 oz) Parmesan cheese, grated
1 large egg, beaten
4 tbsp chopped parsley
90 ml (3 fl oz) water

1 Make the tomato basil sauce: heat the oil in a saucepan, add the onion, and cook gently, stirring occasionally, for 3–5 minutes until soft but not coloured. Stir in the tomatoes with half of their juice, bring to a boil, and simmer for 3 minutes. Stir in the basil and season to taste. Set aside.

2 Make the meatballs: in a large bowl, combine the minced veal, breadcrumbs, Parmesan cheese, egg, parsley, and salt and pepper to taste. Gradually add the measured water, mixing it in well. With dampened hands, shape the veal mixture into balls about the size of large walnuts.

3 Heat the oil in a large non-stick frying pan, add the meatballs, and cook for 10–15 minutes until browned and cooked through. Lift out with a slotted spoon and drain on paper towels. Add to the tomato basil sauce and heat gently for about 5 minutes.

4 Meanwhile, cook the pasta spirals in a large saucepan of boiling salted water for 8–10 minutes until just tender. Drain the pasta spirals thoroughly, top with the meatballs and sauce, and serve, garnished with shredded basil.

Ravioli

Ravioli is one of the easiest home-made pastas to prepare; roll out the dough, then fill with a savoury stuffing. It is so delicious that it needs only a simple accompaniment of melted butter and freshly grated Parmesan cheese.

Basic pasta dough

Serves 3

300 g (10 oz) semolina flour or strong plain white flour
3 eggs
1 tsp salt
1 tbsp olive oil

1 Sift the flour into a mound on a work surface. Make a well in the middle of the flour and add the eggs, salt, and oil. Using your fingertips, gradually draw the flour into the egg mixture until a sticky ball of dough is formed.

2 Knead the dough on a floured work surface for 10 minutes or until the pasta dough is smooth and no longer sticks to the work surface.

3 Shape the dough into a ball, put into an oiled plastic bag, and leave to rest at room temperature for about 30 minutes.

4 On a lightly floured work surface, roll out the dough very thinly into a 37 cm (15 in) square. Leave the pasta uncovered for about 20 minutes to dry out slightly. Cut the pasta in half, fill and cook the ravioli (see box, right).

Crab & prawn

90 g (3 oz) cooked white crabmeat, flaked
90 g (3 oz) cooked peeled prawns, chopped
60 g (2 oz) cream cheese
1 spring onion, very finely chopped
salt and black pepper
coriander sauce (page 309) to serve
Parmesan shavings and coriander sprigs to garnish

1 Combine the crabmeat and prawns with the cream cheese, spring onion, and salt and pepper.

2 Fill and cook the ravioli (see box, right). Toss in coriander sauce and serve at once, garnished with Parmesan shavings and coriander sprigs.

Veal & prosciutto

15 g (1/2 oz) butter
90 g (3 oz) cooked veal or beef, minced
75 g (2 1/2 oz) prosciutto, finely chopped
1 tbsp fresh white breadcrumbs
1 tbsp chopped parsley
2 tsp each water and tomato purée
salt and black pepper
1 egg
tomato basil sauce (page 313) to serve
basil sprigs to garnish

1 Melt the butter in a saucepan. Add the veal and fry for 5 minutes. Stir in the remaining ingredients.

2 Fill and cook the ravioli (see box, below). Toss in the tomato basil sauce, and serve at once, garnished with basil sprigs.

Cheese & spinach

125 g (4 oz) ricotta cheese
60 g (2 oz) Parmesan cheese, grated
1 egg, beaten
pinch of grated nutmeg
250 g (8 oz) frozen chopped spinach, thawed and squeezed dry
salt and black pepper
30 g (1 oz) butter to serve

1 Beat together the ricotta, half of the Parmesan, the egg, nutmeg, spinach, and salt and pepper to taste.

2 Fill and cook the ravioli (see box, below). Serve with butter, the remaining Parmesan, and black pepper.

Clockwise from top: *Cheese & Spinach Ravioli, Veal & Prosciutto Ravioli, Crab & Prawn Ravioli.*

Filling and cooking the ravioli

1 Place 18 spoonfuls of filling at regular intervals on to one half of the pasta. Lightly brush the pasta between the filling with water.

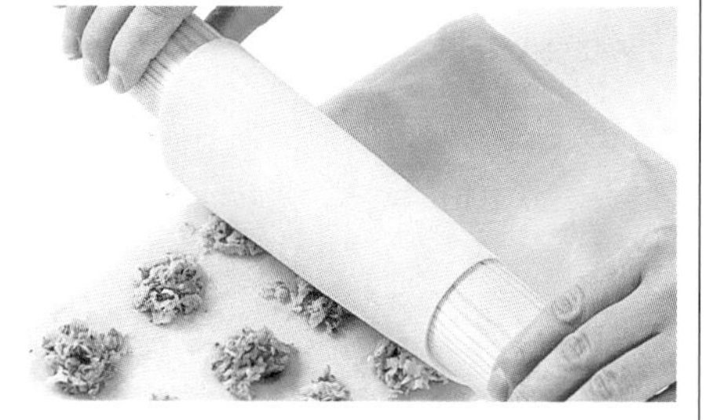

2 Roll the remaining pasta around a rolling pin and unroll over the bottom sheet. Use your hand to press the pasta together between the filling.

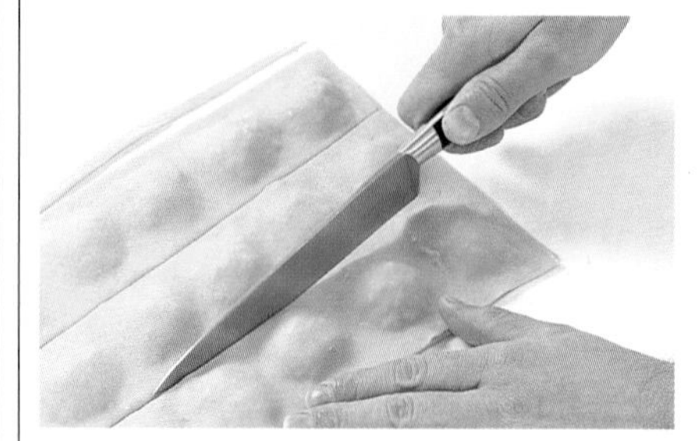

3 With a sharp knife, pastry wheel, or pastry cutter, cut into round or square ravioli. Leave to stand, turning once, for about 30 minutes until dried out.

4 Add a little oil to a large saucepan of boiling salted water, add the ravioli, and cook for 4–5 minutes until just tender. Serve immediately.

TUNA & FENNEL PASTA BAKE

 **Serves 4**

- *250 g (8 oz) pasta shells or spirals*
- *salt and black pepper*
- *1 tbsp sunflower oil*
- *1 fennel bulb, trimmed and finely sliced*
- *1 onion, finely sliced*
- *60 g (2 oz) butter*
- *60 g (2 oz) plain flour*
- *600 ml (1 pint) milk*
- *1 x 200 g (7 oz) can tuna in brine, drained and flaked*
- *3 hard-boiled eggs, coarsely chopped*
- *125 g (4 oz) mature Cheddar cheese, grated*
- *2 tbsp chopped parsley to garnish*

1 Cook the pasta shells in boiling salted water for 8–10 minutes until just tender. Drain thoroughly and set aside.

2 Heat the sunflower oil in a large frying pan, add the fennel and onion, and cook for 3–5 minutes until softened but not coloured. Set aside.

3 Melt the butter in a large saucepan, add the flour, and cook, stirring, for 1 minute. Remove from the heat and gradually blend in the milk. Bring to a boil, stirring constantly until the mixture thickens. Simmer for 2–3 minutes.

4 Stir in the pasta shells, the fennel and onion mixture, tuna, eggs, and Cheddar cheese. Add salt and pepper to taste, then turn the mixture into a shallow ovenproof dish.

5 Bake in a preheated oven at 200°C (400°F, Gas 6) for about 30 minutes or until heated through and golden brown on top. Serve at once, lightly sprinkled with chopped parsley.

TUNA & SWEETCORN PASTA BAKE

Substitute 1 x 200 g (7 oz) can sweetcorn and 90 g (3 oz) frozen peas, thawed, for the fennel bulb, and proceed as directed.

VEGETABLES NAPOLETANA

Serves 4

- *250 g (8 oz) pasta twists*
- *salt and black pepper*
- *250 g (8 oz) broccoli*
- *15 g (1/2 oz) butter*
- *1 tbsp olive oil*
- *1 large onion, chopped*
- *2 large garlic cloves, crushed*
- *150 g (5 oz) shiitake mushrooms, coarsely chopped*
- *1 red pepper, cored, seeded, and sliced*
- *250 g (8 oz) courgettes, sliced*
- *75 g (3 oz) mature Cheddar cheese, grated*

SAUCE

- *60 g (2 oz) butter*
- *60 g (2 oz) plain flour*
- *600 ml (1 pint) milk*
- *1 tsp Dijon mustard*
- *pinch of grated nutmeg*

1 Cook the pasta twists in boiling salted water for 8–10 minutes until just tender. Drain thoroughly.

2 Cut the stalks off the broccoli and cook them in boiling salted water for 3 minutes, then add the florets, and cook for 2 minutes longer. Drain and rinse in cold water.

3 Melt the butter with the oil in a large frying pan, add the onion and garlic, and cook gently for 3–5 minutes until softened.

4 Add the mushrooms, red pepper, and courgette slices, and cook, stirring occasionally, for 3 minutes. Remove from the heat and stir in the broccoli.

5 Make the sauce: melt the butter in a large saucepan, add the flour and cook, stirring, for 1 minute. Remove from the heat and gradually blend in the milk. Bring to a boil, stirring constantly until thickened. Simmer for 2–3 minutes. Add the mustard, nutmeg, and salt and pepper to taste.

6 Remove the sauce from the heat, add the vegetables and pasta, and stir well to coat.

7 Divide the mixture among 4 individual gratin dishes, sprinkle with the Cheddar cheese, and bake in a preheated oven at 200°C (400°F, Gas 6) for 20–25 minutes until golden. Serve at once.

FISHERMAN'S LASAGNE

Serves 6

625 g (1 1/4 lb) haddock fillet
1 slice of onion
1 bay leaf
4 black peppercorns
300 ml (1/2 pint) dry white wine
250 g (8 oz) cooked peeled prawns
30 g (1 oz) butter
500 g (1 lb) courgettes, thickly sliced
1 garlic clove, crushed
175 g (6 oz) pre-cooked lasagne
60 g (2 oz) Cheddar cheese, grated
2 tbsp grated Parmesan cheese

SAUCE

90 g (3 oz) butter
90 g (3 oz) plain flour
300 ml (1/2 pint) single cream
3 tbsp chopped parsley
1 tbsp chopped fresh dill
salt and black pepper

1 Put the haddock into a large pan with the onion, bay leaf, peppercorns, and wine. Add enough water to cover, bring to a boil, and simmer for 5 minutes or until the fish is just cooked. Lift out, remove the skin and bones, and flake the flesh. Mix with the prawns.

2 Strain the liquid and make up to 900 ml (1 1/2 pints) with water. Set aside.

3 Melt the butter in a saucepan, add the courgettes and garlic, and cook for 3 minutes until beginning to soften.

4 Make the sauce: melt the butter in a saucepan, add the flour, and cook, stirring, for 1 minute. Remove the pan from the heat, and gradually blend in the reserved cooking liquid. Bring to a boil, stirring until thickened. Simmer for 2–3 minutes. Stir in the cream, parsley, dill, and salt and pepper to taste.

5 Spoon one-third of the haddock and prawn mixture into a shallow ovenproof dish, top with one-third of the courgettes, and pour over one-third of the sauce. Arrange half of the lasagne in a single layer. Repeat the layers, finishing with the sauce.

6 Sprinkle with the Cheddar and Parmesan cheeses and bake in a preheated oven at 200°C (400°F, Gas 6) for about 40 minutes until golden.

THREE-CHEESE MACARONI

Serves 4

250 g (8 oz) short-cut macaroni
salt and black pepper
90 g (3 oz) butter, plus extra for greasing
45 g (1 1/2 oz) plain flour
1 bay leaf
900 ml (1 1/2 pints) milk
375 g (12 oz) Fontina cheese, grated
175 g (6 oz) mozzarella cheese, chopped
125 g (4 oz) Parmesan cheese, grated
large pinch of grated nutmeg
60 g (2 oz) fresh white breadcrumbs

1 Cook the macaroni in boiling salted water for 8–10 minutes until just tender. Drain and set aside.

2 Melt the butter in a large saucepan. Add the flour and bay leaf, and cook, stirring, for 1 minute. Remove the pan from the heat and gradually blend in the milk. Bring to a boil, stirring constantly until the mixture thickens. Simmer for 2–3 minutes.

3 Remove and discard the bay leaf, then stir in the Fontina and mozzarella cheeses, 90 g (3 oz) of the Parmesan cheese, and the cooked macaroni. Add the nutmeg and salt and pepper to taste.

4 Lightly butter a large shallow ovenproof dish and spoon in the macaroni mixture. Sprinkle with the breadcrumbs and the remaining Parmesan cheese and bake in a preheated oven at 180°C (350°F, Gas 4) for about 40 minutes until golden and bubbling.

CHEESE & LEEK MACARONI

Omit the mozzarella cheese. Melt 30 g (1 oz) butter in a saucepan, add 2–3 trimmed and finely sliced leeks, and cook gently for 3–5 minutes until softened. Add to the sauce with the Fontina and Parmesan cheeses and macaroni, and proceed as directed.

CANNELLONI WITH RICOTTA & SPINACH

Serves 4–6

butter for greasing
18 pre-cooked cannelloni
30 g (1 oz) Parmesan cheese, grated

TOMATO SAUCE

1 tbsp olive oil
2 celery stalks, chopped
1 small onion, chopped
1 carrot, chopped
1 garlic clove, crushed
300 ml (1/2 pint) chicken or vegetable stock
2 x 400 g (13 oz) cans chopped tomatoes
2 tbsp tomato purée
salt and black pepper
60 g (2 oz) sun-dried tomatoes in oil, drained and chopped

FILLING

2 tbsp olive oil
1 small onion, chopped
1 garlic clove, crushed
500 g (1 lb) spinach, chopped
500 g (1 lb) ricotta cheese
pinch of grated nutmeg

1 Make the tomato sauce: heat the oil in a saucepan, add the celery, onion, carrot, and garlic, and cook gently for 3–5 minutes until softened. Stir in the stock, tomatoes, tomato purée, and salt and pepper to taste, and bring to a boil. Cover and simmer, stirring occasionally, for 30 minutes.

2 Meanwhile, make the filling: heat the oil in a large pan, add the onion and garlic, and cook for 3–5 minutes until softened. Add the spinach and cook over a high heat for 1–2 minutes. Leave to cool slightly, then add the ricotta, nutmeg, and salt and pepper to taste.

3 Purée the tomato sauce in a food processor, then stir in the sun-dried tomatoes.

4 Grease an ovenproof dish. Spoon the spinach filling into the cannelloni. Arrange in the dish, spoon over the sauce, sprinkle with Parmesan, and bake in a preheated oven at 200°C (400°F, Gas 6) for 30 minutes.

CLASSIC LASAGNE

Serves 6

125 g (4 oz) mature Cheddar cheese, grated
30 g (1 oz) Parmesan cheese, grated
175 g (6 oz) pre-cooked lasagne
chopped parsley to garnish

MEAT SAUCE

2 tbsp olive oil
1 kg (2 lb) minced beef
45 g (11/2 oz) plain flour
300 ml (1/2 pint) beef stock
1 x 400 g (13 oz) can chopped tomatoes
6 celery stalks, sliced
2 onions, chopped
2 large garlic cloves, crushed
4 tbsp tomato purée
1 tsp sugar
salt and black pepper

WHITE SAUCE

60 g (2 oz) butter
45 g (11/2 oz) flour
600 ml (1 pint) milk
1 tsp Dijon mustard
pinch of grated nutmeg

1 Make the meat sauce: heat the oil, add the beef, and cook, stirring, until browned. Add the flour and cook, stirring, for 1 minute.

2 Add the stock, tomatoes, celery, onions, garlic, tomato purée, sugar, and salt and pepper to taste, and bring to a boil. Cover and simmer for 1 hour.

3 Meanwhile, make the white sauce: melt the butter in a saucepan, add the flour and cook, stirring, for 1 minute. Remove from the heat and gradually blend in the milk. Bring to a boil, stirring constantly until the mixture thickens. Simmer for 2–3 minutes. Stir in the mustard, nutmeg, and salt and pepper to taste.

4 Spoon one-third of the meat sauce into a large shallow ovenproof dish, cover with one-third of the white sauce, and one-third of the Cheddar and Parmesan cheeses. Arrange half of the lasagne in a single layer. Repeat the layers, finishing with the Cheddar and Parmesan cheeses.

5 Bake in a preheated oven at 190°C (375°F, Gas 5) for 45–60 minutes until the pasta is tender and the topping is a golden brown colour. Serve at once, garnished with parsley.

CARIBBEAN RICE & PEAS

Serves 4

2 tbsp olive oil

8 spring onions, sliced

3 smoked bacon rashers, rinds removed, diced

2 garlic cloves, crushed

250 g (8 oz) long grain rice

1 x 200 g (7 oz) can tomatoes

3 tbsp chopped parsley

2 bay leaves

1 small green chilli, cored, seeded, and thinly sliced

1/2 tsp turmeric

1/2 tsp cumin seeds

1/2 tsp dried thyme

1 x 400 g (13 oz) can red kidney beans or black-eyed beans, drained

375 ml (13 fl oz) chicken stock

1 lime, cut into wedges, to serve

1 Heat the oil in a pan, add the spring onions and bacon, and cook for about 5 minutes or until the bacon is crisp. Add the garlic and cook for 2 minutes.

2 Add the rice and stir to coat the grains in the oil. Add the tomatoes with their juice, 2 tbsp of the parsley, the bay leaves, chilli, turmeric, cumin, and thyme, and cook for 2 minutes.

3 Add the beans and stock and bring to a boil. Cover and cook over a low heat for 15 minutes until the rice is tender and the liquid has been absorbed.

4 Sprinkle with remaining parsley, and serve at once, with lime wedges.

Rice and peas

Variations of this dish, both simple and elaborate, are found all over the West Indies. In the Caribbean, the word peas means beans, and small round beans, known as pigeon peas, are traditionally used for this dish. Red kidney beans make a particularly colourful, and very good substitute.

SAVOURY RICE

Serves 4

2 tbsp olive oil

1 onion, chopped

1 carrot, diced

200 g (7 oz) long grain rice

250 g (8 oz) tomatoes, peeled (page 39), seeded, and diced

500 ml (16 fl oz) hot chicken or vegetable stock

150 g (5 oz) sweetcorn kernels

90 g (3 oz) frozen peas

2 tbsp tomato purée

salt and black pepper

1 garlic clove, crushed

chopped parsley to garnish

1 Heat the oil in a frying pan, add the onion and carrot, and cook gently, stirring, for 3–5 minutes until the onion is softened but not coloured.

2 Add the rice, and stir to coat the grains in the oil. Add the tomatoes and stock.

3 Add the sweetcorn, peas, and tomato purée, and bring to a boil. Simmer, stirring occasionally, for 12–15 minutes or until the rice is tender and the liquid has been absorbed.

4 Add salt and pepper to taste, and stir in the garlic. Serve at once, garnished with parsley.

Cook's know-how

Savoury rice is a delicious accompaniment to simple grilled or roasted foods. Spoon any extra into a hot home-made chicken or vegetable soup. Add a little chopped fresh coriander, onion, or crushed chillies for extra flavour. Use the same day.

RISI E BISI

 **Serves 4–6**

60 g (2 oz) butter

1 onion, finely chopped

60 g (2 oz) Parma ham, diced, or 90 g (3 oz) unsmoked lean bacon rashers, rinds removed, diced

2 garlic cloves, crushed

300 g (10 oz) risotto rice

300 g (10 oz) frozen peas, thawed

salt and black pepper

1 litre (1 3/4 pints) hot chicken or vegetable stock

60 g (2 oz) Parmesan cheese, grated, and 2 tbsp chopped parsley to garnish

1 Melt the butter in a large pan. When it is foaming, add the onion, Parma ham, and garlic, and cook gently, stirring occasionally, for 3–5 minutes until the onion is soft but not coloured.

2 Add the rice and stir to coat in the butter. Add the peas and seasoning.

3 Pour in half of the stock and cook, stirring constantly, over a low heat until it is absorbed. Add a little more stock and cook, stirring constantly until it has been absorbed.

4 Continue adding the stock in this way until the rice is just tender and the mixture is thick and creamy. It should take about 25 minutes.

5 Serve hot, sprinkled with chopped parsley and Parmesan cheese.

Risi e bisi

This is a classic Venetian dish meaning rice and peas. In the days when Venice was a republic, it was traditionally served at a dinner held by the doge, the city's chief magistrate, on 25 April in honour of St Mark, the patron saint of Venice.

WILD RICE BAKE

Serves 4

375 g (12 oz) mixed basmati and wild rice

salt and black pepper

250–375 g (8–12 oz) broccoli

15 g (1/2 oz) butter

2 onions, chopped

3 garlic cloves, crushed

125 ml (4 fl oz) soured cream or crème fraîche

125 g (4 oz) mozzarella cheese, grated

60 g (2 oz) Parmesan cheese, grated

1 tbsp chopped fresh rosemary

1 Cook the rice in boiling salted water for about 35 minutes, or according to packet instructions. Drain thoroughly and rinse with cold water. Drain again.

2 Meanwhile, cut the stalks off the broccoli and cook them in boiling salted water for 8–10 minutes until almost tender, then add the florets, and cook for 2 minutes longer. Drain and rinse in cold water. Drain again and set aside.

3 Melt the butter in a frying pan, add the onions, and cook gently, stirring occasionally, for 3–5 minutes until softened. Add the garlic, and cook, stirring occasionally, for 3–5 minutes until the onion is lightly browned.

4 Coarsely chop the broccoli, then stir into the rice with the onion and garlic mixture, soured cream, three-quarters of the mozzarella and Parmesan cheeses, the rosemary, and salt and pepper to taste.

5 Turn the mixture into an ovenproof dish and sprinkle with the remaining mozzarella and Parmesan cheeses. Bake in a preheated oven at 180°C (350°F, Gas 4) for about 20 minutes until heated through and the cheese is melted. Serve at once.

PERSIAN PILAF

Serves 4

1 small cinnamon stick

2 tsp cumin seeds

6 black peppercorns

seeds of 4 cardamom pods, crushed

3 cloves

2 tbsp sunflower oil

1 small onion, chopped

1 tsp turmeric

250 g (8 oz) long grain rice

1.25 litres (2 pints) hot chicken stock

2 bay leaves, torn into pieces

salt and black pepper

60 g (2 oz) shelled pistachio nuts, coarsely chopped

30 g (1 oz) raisins

fresh coriander to garnish

1 Heat a heavy pan and add the cinnamon stick, cumin seeds, peppercorns, cardamom seeds, and cloves.

2 Dry-fry the spices over a medium heat for 2–3 minutes until they begin to release their distinctive flavours and aromas.

3 Add the oil to the pan and, when it is hot, add the onion and turmeric. Cook gently, stirring occasionally, for about 10 minutes until the onion is softened.

4 Add the rice and stir to coat the grains in the oil. Slowly pour in the hot stock, add the bay leaves, and salt and pepper to taste, and bring to a boil. Lower the heat, cover, and cook very gently for about 10 minutes without lifting the lid.

5 Remove the saucepan from the heat and leave to stand, still covered, for about 5 minutes.

6 Add the pistachio nuts and raisins to the pilaf, and fork them in gently to fluff up the rice. Garnish with fresh coriander, and serve at once.

PORTUGUESE RICE WITH TUNA

Serves 4

3 streaky bacon rashers, rinds removed, cut into strips

3 tbsp olive oil

1 small onion, thinly sliced

250 g (8 oz) long grain brown rice

600 ml (1 pint) hot chicken stock

salt and black pepper

375 g (12 oz) fresh tuna, cut into chunks

1 x 400 g (13 oz) can pimientos, drained and cut into strips

16 black olives

dill sprigs and lemon slices to garnish

1 Put the bacon into a large, heavy saucepan and heat until it begins to sizzle. Add the olive oil and onion, and cook gently, stirring occasionally, for 3–5 minutes until soft but not coloured. Add the rice and stir to coat the grains in the oil.

2 Pour the hot stock into the pan, add salt and pepper to taste, and bring to a boil. Cover and simmer for 25–30 minutes.

3 Add the tuna, pimientos, and olives, and cook for 5 minutes or until all the liquid has been absorbed and the rice and tuna are tender. Season, garnish with dill sprigs and lemon slices, and serve at once.

PORTUGUESE RICE WITH CANNED TUNA

Substitute 2 x 200 g (7 oz) cans tuna in brine for the fresh tuna. Flake the tuna roughly, and proceed as directed.

CHICKEN LIVER RISOTTO

 **Serves 4**

75 g (2 1/2 oz) butter
1 tbsp sunflower oil
125 g (4 oz) smoked bacon rashers, rinds removed, diced
1 onion, chopped
1 garlic clove, crushed
175 g (6 oz) risotto rice
60 g (2 oz) wild rice
600 ml (1 pint) hot chicken stock
250 g (8 oz) chicken livers, sliced
125 g (4 oz) wild mushrooms, for example, oyster mushrooms or ceps, sliced
60 g (2 oz) sun-dried tomatoes in oil, drained and chopped
salt and black pepper
30 g (1 oz) Parmesan cheese, grated
1 tbsp chopped fresh rosemary

1 Melt 60 g (2 oz) of the butter with the oil in a large frying pan. When the butter is foaming, add the bacon, onion, and garlic, and cook gently, stirring occasionally, for 3–5 minutes until the onion is soft but not coloured.

2 Add the risotto rice and wild rice, stirring to coat the grains in the oil, then pour in the hot chicken stock. Cover and simmer for 25 minutes.

3 Meanwhile, melt the remaining butter in a saucepan. Add the chicken livers, and cook, stirring, for 2–3 minutes until a rich brown colour. Add the mushrooms, and cook, stirring occasionally, for 5–7 minutes.

4 Stir the chicken liver mixture into the rice. Add the sun-dried tomatoes and salt and pepper to taste. Cook for 5 minutes or until all the liquid has been absorbed. Serve hot, garnished with Parmesan and rosemary.

Cook's know-how

Wild mushrooms add a special touch to this risotto. Chanterelles, ceps, morels, or oyster mushrooms would all be equally suitable.

RISOTTO MILANESE

Serves 4

90 g (3 oz) butter
1 onion, chopped
375 g (12 oz) risotto rice
1.25 litres (2 pints) hot chicken stock
a few pinches of saffron strands
salt and black pepper
60 g (2 oz) Parmesan cheese, grated
Parmesan shavings to serve

1 Melt 30 g (1 oz) of the butter in a large saucepan, add the chopped onion, and cook gently, stirring occasionally, for 3–5 minutes until softened but not coloured.

2 Add the rice, stirring to coat the grains in the butter, and cook for 1 minute. Add a ladleful of hot chicken stock to the pan, and cook gently, stirring constantly, until all the stock has been absorbed.

3 Add the saffron and salt and pepper to taste. Continue to add the stock, a ladleful at a time, stirring constantly, until the risotto is thick and creamy and the rice tender. This will take 20–25 minutes.

4 Stir in the remaining butter and the Parmesan cheese, and season to taste. Top with Parmesan shavings, and serve at once.

Cook's know-how

Risotto milanese *is the traditional accompaniment to* Osso buco *(page 242), but also complements many other meat and poultry dishes. In the past, it was always cooked with beef bone marrow. Many Italians now top the finished risotto with a few spoonfuls of the juices from a veal roast to give it a more traditional and authentic flavour.*

KEDGEREE

Serves 4

175 g (6 oz) long grain rice
1/4 tsp turmeric
375 g (12 oz) smoked haddock fillet
2 hard-boiled eggs
60 g (2 oz) butter, plus extra for greasing
juice of 1/2 lemon
150 ml (1/4 pint) single cream
salt
cayenne pepper
2 tbsp finely chopped parsley

1 Simmer the rice and turmeric, covered, in boiling salted water for 12–15 minutes until tender. Rinse with boiling water, drain, and keep warm.

2 Meanwhile, put the haddock, skin-side down, in a frying pan, cover with cold water, and poach for 8–10 minutes.

3 Cut 1 egg lengthwise into quarters and reserve for garnish. Coarsely chop the second egg.

4 Drain the haddock, remove the skin and bones, then flake the fish. Put into a large bowl, add the rice, chopped egg, butter, lemon juice, and cream, and season with salt and cayenne pepper. Stir gently to mix.

5 Butter an ovenproof dish, add the kedgeree, and bake in a preheated oven at 180°C (350°F, Gas 4), stirring occasionally, for 10–15 minutes.

6 To serve, stir in the parsley and garnish with the reserved egg quarters.

Cook's know-how

Some smoked haddock is dyed bright yellow, so look out for smoked haddock that is pale in colour or is labelled "un-dyed" if you particularly want to avoid artificial colourings.

SUMMER RISOTTO AL VERDE

Serves 4

15 g (1/2 oz) butter
3 garlic cloves, crushed
250 g (8 oz) risotto rice
1 litre (1 3/4 pints) hot vegetable stock
175 ml (6 fl oz) single cream
90 g (3 oz) blue cheese, crumbled
4 tbsp ready-made pesto
90 g (3 oz) Parmesan cheese, grated
4 tbsp pine nuts, lightly toasted
4 tbsp shredded fresh basil

1 Melt the butter in a large saucepan. When it is foaming, add the garlic and cook gently for 1 minute.

2 Add the risotto rice, stirring to coat the grains in the butter, and cook for 2 minutes. Add a ladleful of the hot vegetable stock, and cook gently, stirring constantly, until the stock has been absorbed. Continue to add the stock, a ladleful at a time, and cook for 20–25 minutes or until the rice is just tender.

3 Add the cream, and cook gently, stirring, until it has been absorbed. Stir in the blue cheese, then the pesto, Parmesan, and pine nuts. Garnish with shredded fresh basil, and serve.

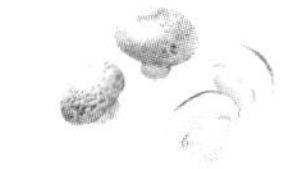

CHICKEN & MUSHROOM RISOTTO

Substitute chicken stock for the vegetable stock and omit the blue cheese and pesto. Add 250 g (8 oz) cooked diced chicken and 125 g (4 oz) sliced mushrooms to the saucepan with the garlic, and proceed as directed.

ASPARAGUS RISOTTO

Omit the blue cheese and pesto. Add 1 finely chopped onion to the pan with the garlic and cook for 3–5 minutes until soft. Add 375 g (12 oz) trimmed and chopped asparagus, and proceed as directed.

Nasi goreng

The name of this Indonesian recipe simply means fried rice. Prepared with a variety of ingredients, it is one of the best known Indonesian dishes, and one of the easiest to make. Traditional garnishes such as crushed peanuts and omelette strips give contrasting flavours and textures to the finished dish.

Chicken nasi goreng

Serves 6

- *375 g (12 oz) long grain rice*
- *90 ml (3 fl oz) olive oil*
- *6 streaky bacon rashers, chopped*
- *2 large onions, chopped*
- *3 garlic cloves, crushed*
- *1/4 tsp chilli powder*
- *2 tsp mild curry powder*
- *2 cooked chicken breasts, skinned and cubed*
- *90 ml (3 fl oz) soy sauce*
- *salt and pepper*
- *6 spring onions, chopped*
- *60 g (2 oz) cooked peeled prawns*
- *60 g (2 oz) almonds, halved, and toasted (page 162)*
- *coriander sprigs to garnish*
- *prawn crackers to serve*

1 Cook the rice in boiling salted water for 12–15 minutes until tender. Drain, rinse with boiling water, drain again, and set aside.

2 Heat 1 tbsp of the oil in a large frying pan or wok, add the bacon, and cook for 3–5 minutes until browned. Add the remaining oil, the onions, and garlic, and cook over a gentle heat for 3–5 minutes until the onions are soft but not coloured.

3 Add the chilli and curry powders and cook, stirring, for 1 minute or until fragrant. Add the chicken and cook for 5–6 minutes until just beginning to brown.

4 Add the soy sauce and half of the rice and stir well. Add the remaining rice and salt and pepper to taste. Cook over a gentle heat, stirring, for 7–8 minutes until the rice is heated through.

5 Stir in the spring onions, prawns, and almonds, and heat through. Garnish with coriander sprigs and serve with prawn crackers.

Vegetarian nasi goreng

Serves 6

- *375 g (12 oz) long grain rice*
- *salt*
- *2 tbsp tamarind paste*
- *2 tbsp vegetable oil*
- *8 shallots, chopped*
- *3 garlic cloves, crushed*
- *1 cm (1/2 in) piece of fresh root ginger, grated*
- *2 tsp curry powder*
- *1/4 tsp each crushed chillies and turmeric*
- *1/2 small cabbage, thinly sliced*
- *2 medium tomatoes, peeled (page 39), seeded, and diced*
- *3 tbsp soy sauce*
- *1 tbsp dark muscovado sugar*

TO GARNISH

- *3 tomatoes, coarsely chopped*
- *1/2 red pepper, cored, seeded, and diced*
- *1/2 cucumber, diced*
- *1 celery stalk, diced*
- *omelette strips (see right)*

1 Cook the rice in boiling salted water for 12–15 minutes until tender. Drain, rinse, and drain again. Stir in the tamarind paste and set aside.

2 Heat 1 tbsp of the oil in a large frying pan or wok, add the shallots, and cook for 3–5 minutes until softened. Add the garlic, ginger, curry powder, crushed chillies, and turmeric, and cook gently, stirring, for 1 minute.

3 Add the cabbage and cook for 3–5 minutes. Add the tomatoes and cook for 2–3 minutes. Remove from pan.

4 Heat the remaining oil in the pan, add the rice, and cook gently until lightly browned. Return the vegetables to the pan. Add the soy sauce and sugar and heat gently to warm through.

5 Serve hot, garnished with tomatoes, red pepper, cucumber, celery, and omelette strips.

Quick nasi goreng

Serves 6

- *375 g (12 oz) long grain rice*
- *2 tbsp vegetable oil*
- *1 onion, chopped*
- *1/2 tsp paprika*
- *1 tsp ground ginger*
- *125 g (4 oz) button mushrooms, sliced*
- *60 g (2 oz) bean sprouts*
- *1 tsp soy sauce*
- *125 g (4 oz) cooked peeled prawns*
- *2 spring onions, finely sliced*
- *chopped coriander to garnish*

1 Cook the rice in boiling salted water, for 12–15 minutes until tender. Drain, rinse with boiling water, drain again, and set aside.

2 Heat 1 tbsp of the oil in a frying pan or wok, add the onion, and cook for 3–5 minutes until soft. Add the paprika and ginger, and cook over a low heat for 1 minute. Add the mushrooms and bean sprouts and cook for 2–3 minutes until softened. Remove from the pan.

3 Heat the remaining oil in the pan, add the rice, and cook over a gentle heat, stirring, for 7–8 minutes to warm through. Stir in the soy sauce. Return the vegetables to the pan and add the prawns and onions. Garnish and serve.

Omelette garnish

Whisk *2 eggs* with plenty of *salt and pepper*. Melt *30 g (1 oz) butter* in an omelette pan or small frying pan. Add the eggs to the pan and cook until set. Leave to cool. Roll up the omelette and slice across into fine strips.

Clockwise from top: *Vegetarian Nasi Goreng, Prawn Crackers, Quick Nasi Goreng, Chicken Nasi Goreng.*

Egg-Fried Rice

 **Serves 4**

250 g (8 oz) long grain rice
salt and black pepper
3 tbsp sunflower oil
60 g (2 oz) bacon rashers, rinds removed, diced
125 g (4 oz) frozen peas, thawed
2 eggs, beaten
125 g (4 oz) bean sprouts
6 spring onions, sliced

1 Cook the rice in boiling salted water for 12–15 minutes until tender. Drain.

2 Heat the oil in a wok or large frying pan, add the bacon, and cook over a high heat, stirring, for 2 minutes. Add the rice and peas and cook, stirring, for 5 minutes.

3 Add the eggs and bean sprouts, and stir-fry for 2 minutes until the eggs have just set. Taste for seasoning, sprinkle with the sliced spring onions, and serve at once.

Special Egg-Fried Rice

Add 125 g (4 oz) cooked peeled prawns when you add the rice and peas, and cook as directed. Sprinkle with 60 g (2 oz) toasted cashew nuts just before serving.

Paella

Serves 6

3 tbsp olive oil
6 chicken thighs
250 g (8 oz) smoked bacon, rind removed, cut into strips
1 large onion, chopped
1 litre (1 3/4 pints) chicken stock
250 g (8 oz) tomatoes, peeled (page 39), seeded, and chopped
2 garlic cloves, crushed
a few pinches of saffron threads, soaked in a little hot water
500 g (1 lb) long grain rice
1 red and 1 green pepper, cored, seeded, and sliced
125 g (4 oz) frozen peas, thawed
salt and black pepper
500 g (1 lb) mussels, cleaned (page 106)
125 g (4 oz) cooked peeled prawns

TO GARNISH
9 pitted black olives
6 large cooked prawns
lemon wedges
2 tbsp chopped parsley

1 Heat the oil in a paella pan or a large flameproof casserole. Add the chicken and cook over a medium heat for about 10 minutes until browned all over. Add the bacon and onion and cook for 5 minutes.

2 Stir in the stock, tomatoes, garlic, and the saffron with its soaking liquid, and bring to a boil. Add the rice, red and green peppers, peas, and salt and pepper to taste. Cover and bake in a preheated oven at 180°C (350°F, Gas 4) for 35–40 minutes until the rice is nearly tender and the stock has been absorbed.

3 Meanwhile, put the mussels into a large saucepan with about 1 cm (1/2 in) boiling water. Cover tightly, and cook, shaking the pan occasionally, for 5 minutes or until the shells open. Drain the mussels, and throw away any which have not opened: do not try to force them open.

4 Stir the mussels and peeled prawns into the chicken and rice mixture, then cook gently on top of the stove for 5 minutes. Taste for seasoning. Arrange the olives, large prawns, and lemon wedges on top, and sprinkle with parsley.

Paella

*A traditional Spanish rice dish, paella is originally from Valencia. The basic ingredients are shellfish, chicken, peas, and saffron, which gives the rice its characteristic yellow colour. Variations may include spicy sausage (*chorizo*), red and green peppers, or other types of poultry. It is best cooked in a traditional large, shallow two-handled paella pan.*

9

VEGETABLES & SALADS

UNDER 30 MINUTES

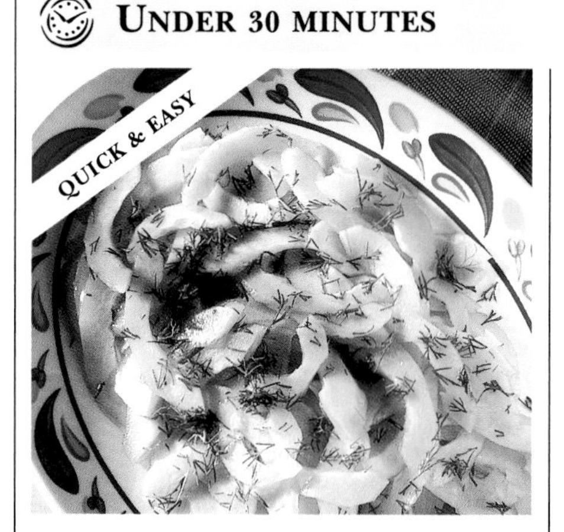

CUCUMBER & DILL SALAD

Light and summery: thin cucumber slices in a vinaigrette dressing of white wine vinegar and sunflower oil, sprinkled with dill.

SERVES 4–6 75–50 calories per serving

Takes 10 minutes **PAGE 359**

SPRING GREENS WITH GARLIC

Light and nutritious: spring greens cut into thin strips, then blanched and stir-fried with olive oil and garlic.

SERVES 4 154 calories per serving

Takes 15 minutes **PAGE 345**

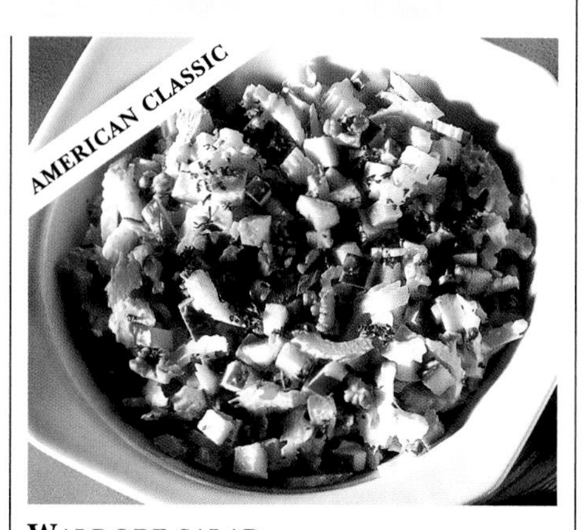

WALDORF SALAD

Fruity salad: celery and apple flavoured with lemon and coated with mayonnaise. Mixed with pieces of walnut.

SERVES 4 469 calories per serving

Takes 15 minutes, plus chilling **PAGE 356**

GREEK SALAD

Tomato wedges with cucumber, green pepper, feta cheese, and olives. Flavoured with olive oil, lemon, and oregano.

SERVES 4–6 503–335 calories per serving

Takes 10 minutes **PAGE 359**

MIXED VEGETABLE STIR-FRY

Sliced courgette stir-fried with yellow pepper and a variety of mushrooms. Flavoured with lemon juice, and sprinkled with almonds.

SERVES 4 155 calories per serving

Takes 10 minutes **PAGE 350**

FRENCH CELERIAC SALAD

Matchstick-thin strips of celeriac tossed with yogurt and mayonnaise dressing flavoured with capers and mustard.

SERVES 4–6 100–66 calories per serving

Takes 15 minutes **PAGE 357**

MIXED LEAF SALAD

Crisp lettuce, lamb's lettuce, watercress, and rocket leaves tossed with vinaigrette dressing, and sprinkled with herbs.

SERVES 4–6 117–78 calories per serving

Takes 10 minutes **PAGE 355**

RED SALAD BOWL

Bite-sized pieces of radicchio and oak leaf and lollo rosso lettuces mixed with onion, grapes, and balsamic vinegar dressing.

SERVES 4–6 387–258 calories per serving

Takes 15 minutes **PAGE 355**

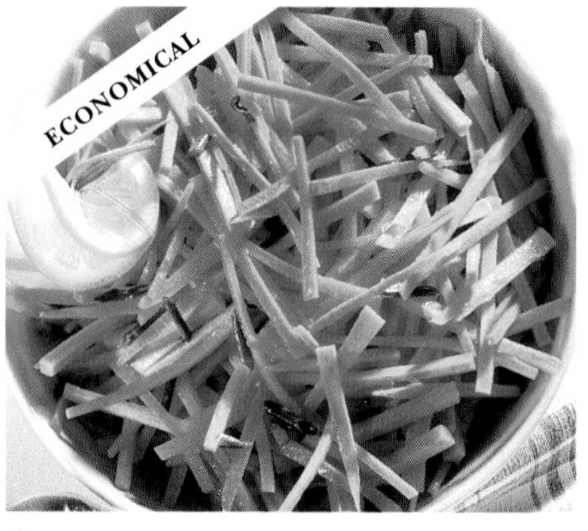

CARROT JULIENNE SALAD

Matchstick-thin strips of carrot briefly cooked, then coated in a dressing of olive oil, white wine vinegar, garlic, and parsley.

SERVES 4–6 79–53 calories per serving

Takes 20 minutes **PAGE 357**

UNDER 30 MINUTES

CABBAGE & MIXED PEPPER STIR-FRY

Crunchy and nourishing: shredded white cabbage stir-fried with onion, celery, red and yellow peppers, and mushrooms.

SERVES 6–8 128–96 calories per serving

Takes 15 minutes **PAGE 345**

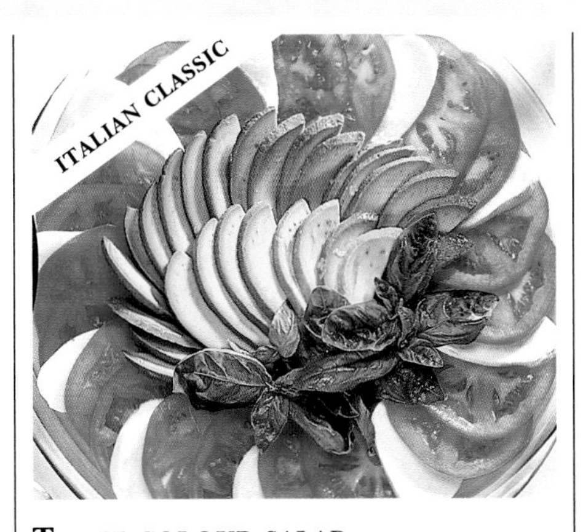

THREE-COLOUR SALAD

Thinly sliced beefsteak tomatoes arranged with slices of mozzarella cheese and avocado, and drizzled with olive oil.

SERVES 4 509 calories per serving

Takes 20 minutes **PAGE 358**

OKRA WITH CHILLI

Hot and spicy: okra, onion, garlic, and fresh red chilli, stir-fried until just tender but still slightly crisp.

SERVES 4 152 calories per serving

Takes 15 minutes **PAGE 350**

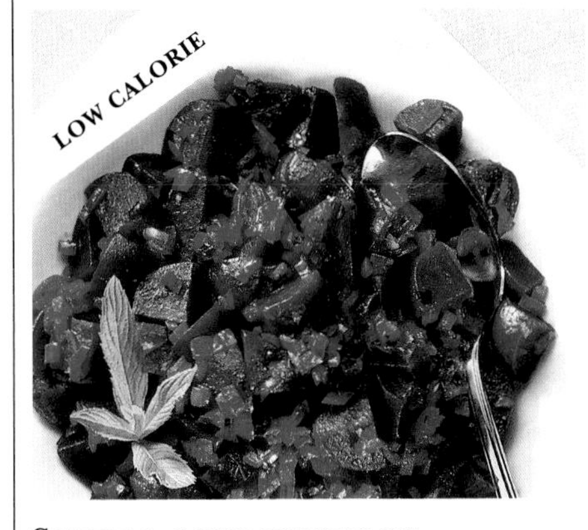

SWEET & SOUR BEETROOT

Juicy and well-flavoured: diced beetroot cooked with onions, garlic, lemon juice, and mint. Served warm or cold.

SERVES 4 242 calories per serving

Takes 20 minutes **PAGE 344**

CHIPS

Popular accompaniment or snack: potatoes, cut into sticks, then deep fried until crispy and brown.

SERVES 4 422 calories per serving

Takes 20 minutes, plus soaking **PAGE 340**

CRUNCHY SALAD

Iceberg lettuce, bean sprouts, spring onions, and green pepper tossed with ginger dressing, and sprinkled with sesame seeds.

SERVES 6 141 calories per serving

Takes 10 minutes, plus soaking **PAGE 355**

CREAMED SPINACH

Creamy and nutritious: lightly cooked spinach mixed with crème fraîche, Parmesan cheese, chives, and nutmeg, then grilled.

SERVES 4 250 calories per serving

Takes 20 minutes **PAGE 344**

SPROUTS WITH MUSTARD SEEDS

Tender and tangy: Brussels sprouts simmered, then tossed with mustard-seed butter, and flavoured with lemon juice.

SERVES 4 188 calories per serving

Takes 15 minutes **PAGE 345**

CAESAR SALAD

Pieces of cos lettuce tossed with olive oil, lemon juice, and hard-boiled egg quarters. Mixed with croûtons and Parmesan cheese.

SERVES 4 421 calories per serving

Takes 20 minutes **PAGE 356**

UNDER 30 MINUTES

AVOCADO SALAD

Fresh and tangy: avocado with orange, pine nuts, and mixed salad leaves, tossed with orange and walnut oil dressing.

SERVES 6 240 calories per serving

Takes 20 minutes **PAGE 358**

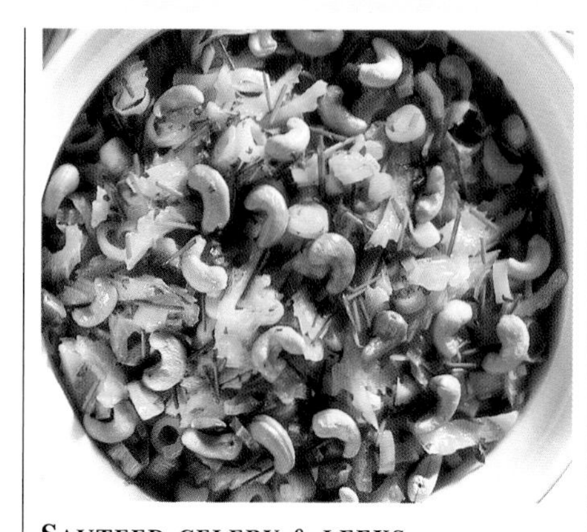

SAUTEED CELERY & LEEKS

Fresh and summery: sliced young leeks cooked with sliced celery, mixed with chives, and garnished with cashew nuts.

SERVES 6 235 calories per serving

Takes 20 minutes **PAGE 348**

SUMMER PEAS & BEANS

Shelled peas cooked with French beans, then combined with cooked young broad beans, butter, and mint.

SERVES 6 107 calories per serving

Takes 20 minutes **PAGE 347**

SALADE NIÇOISE

Lettuce, French beans, and cucumber topped with tomatoes, eggs, tuna, anchovies, olives, and a garlic and mustard dressing.

SERVES 4 530 calories per serving

Takes 25 minutes **PAGE 360**

GLAZED CARROTS & TURNIPS

Strips of carrot and whole baby turnips glazed with chicken stock, butter, and sugar. Flavoured with fresh mint and parsley.

SERVES 4 115 calories per serving

Takes 20 minutes **PAGE 344**

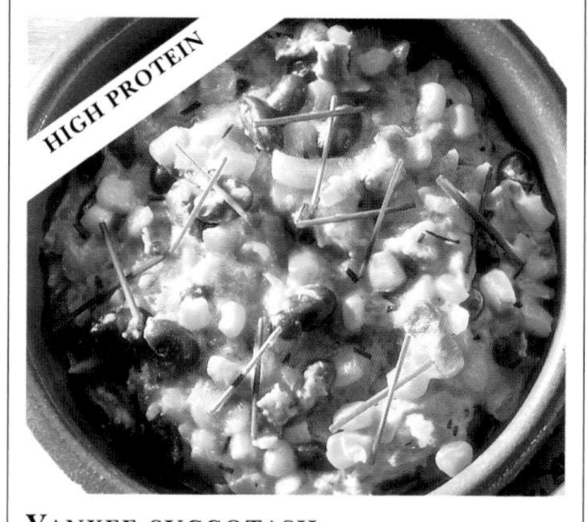

YANKEE SUCCOTASH

Hearty and wholesome: sweetcorn kernels simmered with cream, borlotti beans, bacon, and onion. Flavoured with chives.

SERVES 4 736 calories per serving

Takes 25 minutes **PAGE 348**

SPINACH & BACON SALAD

Pieces of spinach and crispy bacon lightly tossed with vinaigrette or blue cheese dressing, and topped with croûtons.

SERVES 6 436 calories per serving

Takes 25 minutes **PAGE 355**

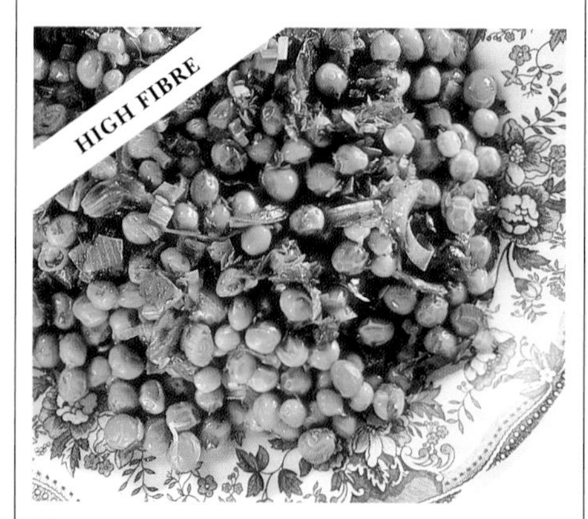

FRENCH-STYLE PEAS

Light and summery: sweetened shelled peas simmered with shredded lettuce, chopped spring onions, butter, and parsley.

SERVES 4 237 calories per serving

Takes 25 minutes **PAGE 347**

STUFFED MUSHROOMS

Tasty and healthy: mushrooms stuffed with chopped mushroom stalks, carrots, courgettes, and parsley, then baked.

SERVES 6 91 calories per serving

Takes 25 minutes **PAGE 349**

30–60 MINUTES

WATERCRESS & ROAST VEGETABLE SALAD

Courgette slices tossed with roasted peppers, watercress, and vinaigrette dressing.

SERVES 4–6 310–207 calories per serving

Takes 20 minutes, plus cooling **PAGE 354**

SAVOURY PUMPKIN

Chunks of pumpkin sprinkled with a mixture of oil, balsamic vinegar, garlic, thyme, and paprika. Baked until tender.

SERVES 4 140 calories per serving

Takes 30 minutes **PAGE 350**

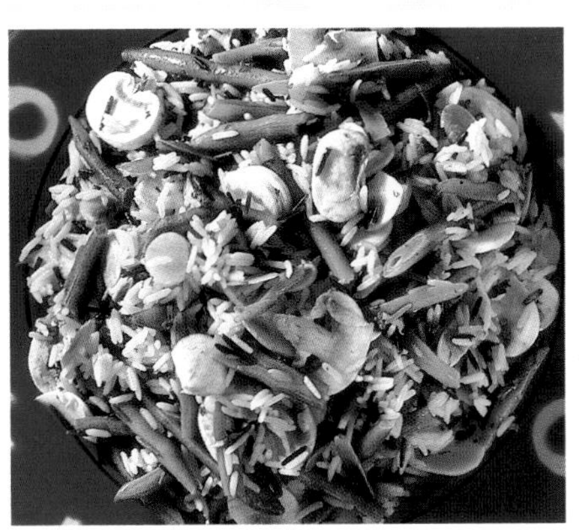

WILD RICE SALAD

Wild and long grain rice in a dressing of oils, vinegar, and mustard. Mixed with French beans, mushrooms, parsley, and walnuts.

SERVES 4–6 554–369 calories per serving

Takes 30 minutes **PAGE 361**

TOMATOES WITH CORIANDER

Cherry tomatoes baked until lightly browned and tender. Dotted with butter combined with coriander, garlic, and lemon juice.

SERVES 4 106 calories per serving

Takes 35 minutes **PAGE 350**

GINGER PARSNIPS

Matchstick-thin strips of parsnip lightly cooked with ginger, covered with crème fraîche, then baked until tender.

SERVES 6 332 calories per serving

Takes 30 minutes **PAGE 344**

TOMATO & COURGETTE BAKE

Light and delicious: layers of sliced courgette and tomato baked in a white sauce flavoured with nutmeg.

SERVES 4–6 238–159 calories per serving

Takes 40 minutes **PAGE 351**

SPICED YAMS

Chunky and spicy: cubed yams cooked with tomatoes, garlic, cumin, and cinnamon. Spiked with chilli powder and paprika.

SERVES 4 381 calories per serving

Takes 30 minutes **PAGE 343**

ASPARAGUS WITH PARMESAN

Asparagus marinated in olive oil, wine, vinegar, and garlic. Rolled in Parmesan cheese, and baked with marinade.

SERVES 4 215 calories per serving

Takes 35 minutes, plus marinating **PAGE 349**

PASTA SALAD WITH PEPPERS

Cooked pasta bows combined with diced red and green peppers and spring onions. Coated in mayonnaise.

SERVES 4–6 556–370 calories per serving

Takes 20 minutes, plus chilling **PAGE 362**

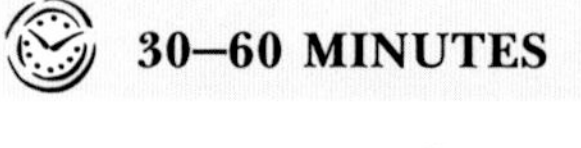

30–60 MINUTES

SWEET & SOUR RED CABBAGE

Shredded red cabbage cooked with bacon, apple, sugar, red wine, vinegar, sultanas, caraway seeds, cinnamon, and nutmeg.

SERVES 4–6 450–300 calories per serving

Takes 55 minutes **PAGE 346**

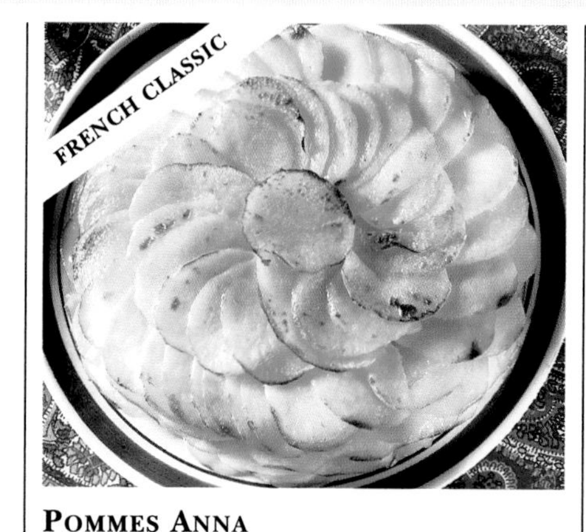

POMMES ANNA

Thinly sliced potatoes, layered in a frying pan, dotted with butter, and seasoned with salt and pepper, then cooked until tender.

SERVES 4 307 calories per serving

Takes 55 minutes **PAGE 341**

COUSCOUS SALAD

Couscous cooked with sultanas and ginger. Mixed with chilli oil, raspberry vinegar, tomatoes, onion, spring onions, and mint.

SERVES 4–6 420–280 calories per serving

Takes 20 minutes, plus cooling **PAGE 361**

GARLIC CREAMED POTATOES

Hearty and satisfying: boiled potato, mashed, then mixed with roasted garlic, warm milk, and butter. Sprinkled with chives.

SERVES 4 282 calories per serving

Takes 45 minutes **PAGE 341**

CAULIFLOWER & BROCCOLI LAYERS

Florets of cauliflower and broccoli layered in rings, and moulded in a basin. Topped with almonds and breadcrumbs.

SERVES 4–6 341–227 calories per serving

Takes 35 minutes **PAGE 346**

RICE SALAD

Long grain rice in a dressing flavoured with mustard and garlic. Mixed with peas, red pepper, sweetcorn, and coriander.

SERVES 4–6 517–345 calories per serving

Takes 25 minutes, plus cooling **PAGE 361**

ITALIAN FENNEL

Quartered fennel bulbs lightly cooked until tender, topped with mozzarella cheese, and baked until golden.

SERVES 6–8 145–108 calories per serving

Takes 30 minutes **PAGE 349**

GLAZED SHALLOTS

Whole shallots simmered in water, butter, caster sugar, and thyme until glazed and golden brown.

SERVES 4 225 calories per serving

Takes 30 minutes **PAGE 348**

TABBOULEH

Fresh and herby: bulgur wheat mixed with vinaigrette dressing, lemon juice, tomatoes, spring onions, parsley, and mint.

SERVES 4 276 calories per serving

Takes 10 minutes, plus standing **PAGE 361**

OVER 60 MINUTES

TOMATO & BASIL SALAD

Assortment of tomatoes and chunks of yellow pepper dressed in oil and balsamic vinegar. Sprinkled with basil.

SERVES 4–6 146–97 calories per serving

Takes 10 minutes, plus standing **PAGE 359**

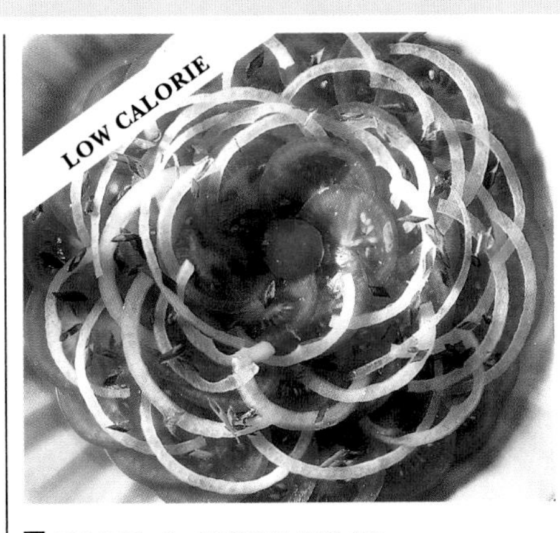

TOMATO & ONION SALAD

Thinly sliced tomatoes and mild onion dressed in olive oil, red wine vinegar, and caster sugar. Sprinkled with snipped chives.

SERVES 6 166 calories per serving

Takes 15 minutes, plus chilling **PAGE 359**

AUBERGINE WITH FRESH PESTO

Mediterranean flavours: slices of aubergine grilled until lightly browned, cooled, then spread with pesto, and sprinkled with basil.

SERVES 4 499 calories per serving

Takes 20 minutes, plus standing **PAGE 354**

POTATO, APPLE, & CELERY SALAD

Hearty salad: pieces of boiled potato tossed with vinaigrette dressing, mixed with apple, celery, onion, and mayonnaise.

SERVES 6 332 calories per serving

Takes 30 minutes, plus chilling **PAGE 357**

THREE-BEAN SALAD

French beans, chick peas, and red kidney beans combined with olives in a Greek yogurt dressing, flavoured with vinegar and mustard.

SERVES 4 315 calories per serving

Takes 15 minutes, plus standing **PAGE 360**

COLESLAW

Shredded white cabbage tossed with onion, celery, carrot, sultanas, vinaigrette dressing, mustard, and mayonnaise.

SERVES 8 245 calories per serving

Takes 15 minutes, plus chilling **PAGE 356**

PASTA & MACKEREL SALAD

Pasta shells tossed with courgettes, French beans, orange segments, mackerel, walnuts, and a dressing of oils and orange juice.

SERVES 4–6 965–643 calories per serving

Takes 30 minutes, plus chilling **PAGE 362**

FRENCH POTATO SALAD

Tender new potatoes and onion coated in vinaigrette dressing, then mixed with chives and mayonnaise.

SERVES 4–6 714–476 calories per serving

Takes 30 minutes, plus chilling **PAGE 358**

MUSHROOM & YOGURT SALAD

Mushrooms cooked with coriander, then dressed in yogurt flavoured with mustard and garlic. Chilled, and mixed with celery.

SERVES 6 102 calories per serving

Takes 15 minutes, plus chilling **PAGE 358**

OVER 60 MINUTES

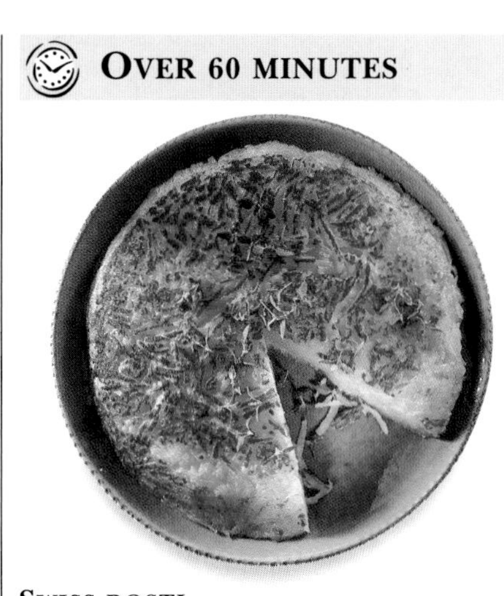

SWISS ROSTI

Grated potatoes seasoned with pepper, and shaped into a cake. Lightly cooked in butter until golden.

SERVES 8 230 calories per serving

Takes 45 minutes, plus chilling **PAGE 339**

POTATOES LYONNAISE

Mouthwateringly delicious: thickly sliced potatoes layered with onion. Baked until the potatoes are tender.

SERVES 4 369 calories per serving

Takes 1 3/4 hours **PAGE 340**

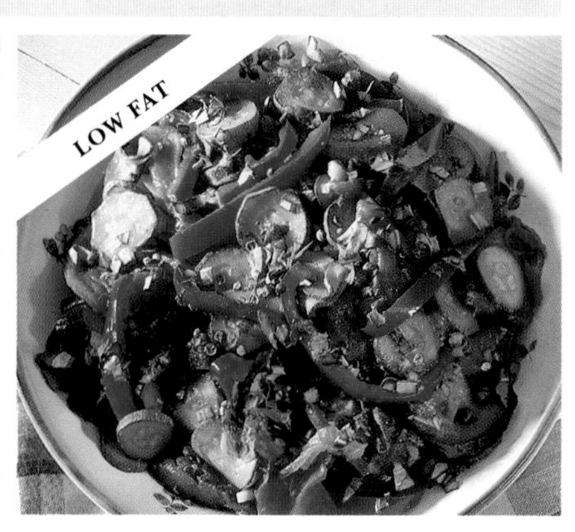

RATATOUILLE

Slices of aubergine, courgette, and red pepper cooked with tomatoes. Flavoured with onion, garlic, and basil.

SERVES 4–6 236–157 calories per serving

Takes 1 1/2 hours, plus standing **PAGE 351**

ROAST POTATOES

Classic accompaniment to roast meat or poultry: briefly simmered pieces of potato roasted in a little fat until crisp and golden.

SERVES 4 288 calories per serving

Takes 1 1/4 hours **PAGE 340**

SWEET POTATOES WITH GINGER BUTTER

Baked sweet potatoes, flavoured with soy sauce, and served with ginger and garlic butter. Sprinkled with sesame seeds.

SERVES 4 381 calories per serving

Takes 1 hour 5 minutes **PAGE 343**

SPINACH & CHEESE BAKED POTATOES

Hearty and healthy: baked potatoes scooped out and mixed with spinach, onion, and ricotta cheese. Flavoured with nutmeg.

SERVES 4 291 calories per serving

Takes 1 3/4 hours **PAGE 342**

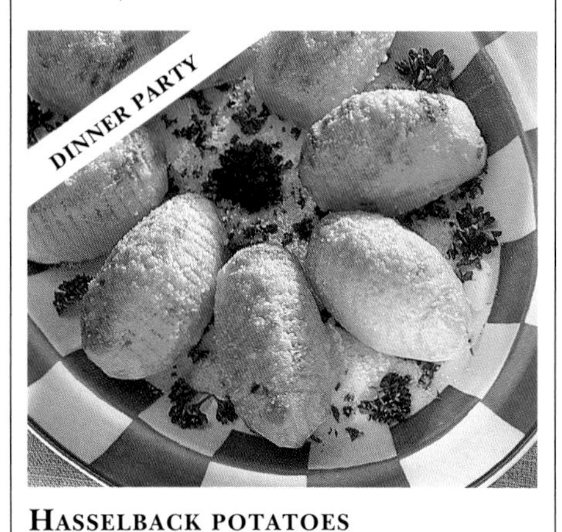

HASSELBACK POTATOES

Simple to make: whole potatoes sliced almost through at intervals. Brushed with butter, sprinkled with Parmesan, and baked.

SERVES 4–6 366–244 calories per serving

Takes 1 hour 5 minutes **PAGE 342**

CREAMED HARICOT BEANS

Hearty dish: haricot beans simmered with carrot, onion, parsley, thyme, and bay leaf. Thickened with puréed beans.

SERVES 6 167 calories per serving

Takes 1 1/2 hours, plus soaking **PAGE 347**

GRATIN DAUPHINOIS

Rich and creamy: thinly sliced potato layered with cream, garlic, and grated Gruyère cheese, then baked until golden.

SERVES 6 372 calories per serving

Takes 1 3/4 hours **PAGE 339**

VEGETABLES & SALADS KNOW-HOW

THE SELECTION OF VEGETABLES available from the greengrocer and supermarket seems to increase all the time. With every shopping trip there are new varieties of potatoes and tomatoes, pumpkins and other squashes, a wide variety of baby vegetables, and peppers of all colours. The choice is no longer limited by the season: vegetables once available only in spring and summer are now imported from sunnier climes during the winter. This wonderful bounty helps the cook to be innovative, trying new combinations and creating nutritious, appetizing dishes. Salad has never been more exciting – exotic salad greens such as rocket, radicchio, and frisée are just a few of the leafy ingredients widely available to brighten up the salad bowl.

BUYING AND STORING

When choosing vegetables, look for the freshest available. Their colour should be bright and their texture firm and crisp. Any vegetables that are bruised or show signs of age – those that are discoloured, shrivelled, or flabby – are past their best. In general, small, young vegetables are more tender and have a better flavour than large, older ones, although very small baby vegetables can sometimes be quite tasteless.

Many vegetables, including onions, potatoes, garlic, swede, and pumpkin, can be stored in a cool, dark, well-ventilated place. More perishable vegetables, such as peas, sweetcorn, celery, lettuces, spinach, and ripe tomatoes, should be chilled. Keep them in the special salad drawer in the refrigerator, unwrapping them or piercing their bags to prevent moisture build-up. Rinse any leafy green vegetables, lettuces, or herbs, wrap in paper towels, and store in a plastic bag.

CUTTING VEGETABLES

Keep pieces to a unifom size and shape to ensure they cook evenly.

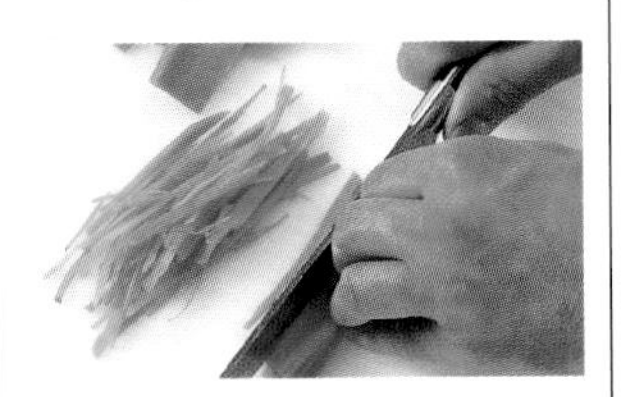

Julienne
Cut into 5 mm (1/4 in) slices. Stack the slices then cut into sticks, 5 mm (1/4 in) thick.

Dice
Cut into 1 cm (1/2 in) strips, then cut across the strips to form neat dice.

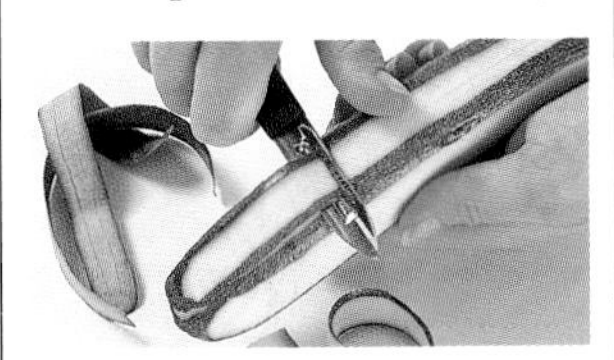

Ribbons
Using a vegetable peeler, carefully shave off thin, wide ribbons.

NUTRITION

A healthy, well-balanced diet should include plenty of vegetables, because they supply essential vitamins, minerals, fibre, and vegetable protein. Despite their reputation, starchy vegetables such as potatoes are not fattening in themselves – calories are increased by the oil they are fried in or the butter that is added to them. To get the maximum benefit from the vegetables you eat:

- choose the freshest produce
- keep all vegetables in a cool, dark place and use as quickly as possible
- rinse thoroughly but don't soak before cooking, particularly if peeled
- prepare as close to cooking time as possible
- never add bicarbonate of soda to the cooking water as this destroys vitamin C.

MICROWAVING

The microwave oven is ideal for cooking vegetables: very little water is used so they retain their nutrients as well as their colours and flavours. Cut vegetables into uniform pieces, or pierce skins of those that are left whole. Arrange them so that the tender parts are in the centre of the dish, to prevent overcooking. Add salt when serving. Keep the dish tightly covered during cooking, and turn or stir once or twice if necessary.

FREEZING

Most vegetables freeze very well, whether plain, in a sauce, or in a prepared dish. Potatoes, however, do not freeze successfully. Vegetables that are to be frozen plain should first be blanched in boiling water, then cooled quickly in iced water before freezing; this will set the colour and prevent vitamin loss. Vegetables can be kept in the freezer for at least 6 months, and can be cooked directly from frozen.

PREPARING VEGETABLES

Learning the correct way to prepare vegetables will save you time and effort in the kitchen. For most tasks, a chopping board and a sharp chef's knife, small knife, or a vegetable peeler are all you'll need. Here's how the professionals deal with more unusual vegetables.

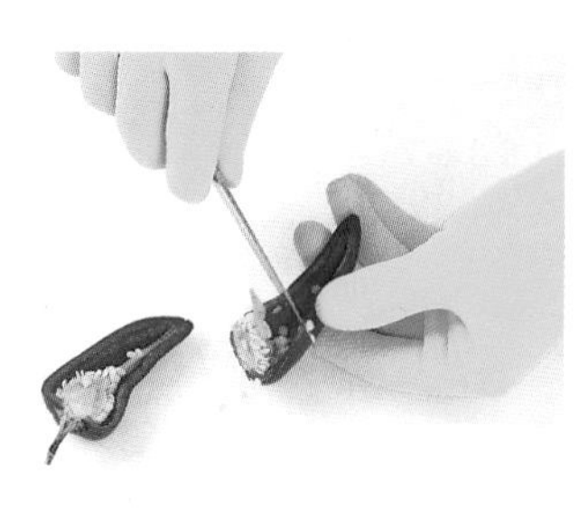

Fresh chilli
1 Cut the chilli in half lengthwise. Remove the stalk and core and scrape out the fleshy white ribs and seeds.

2 Set the chilli cut-side up and cut into thin strips. Hold the strips together and cut across to make dice.

Pepper
1 Cut around the stalk and the core. Twist and pull them out in one piece.

2 Cut the pepper in half. Scrape out the fleshy white ribs and the seeds.

Fresh root ginger
1 With a small knife, peel off the skin. Slice the ginger across the fibrous grain.

2 Set the flat of a knife on top and crush the slices. Chop the crushed slices.

Aubergine
Cut the aubergine as specified in the recipe. Put the pieces on to a plate or into a colander, sprinkle with salt (on all cut sides if possible), and leave for about 30 minutes. Rinse and dry with paper towels. This process, known as salting, removes any bitter juices from the aubergine.

Asparagus
Cut off any woody ends from the asparagus to make the spears uniform in length. Using a vegetable peeler, and working down towards the end of the spear, shave off the tough layer of skin in thin strips.

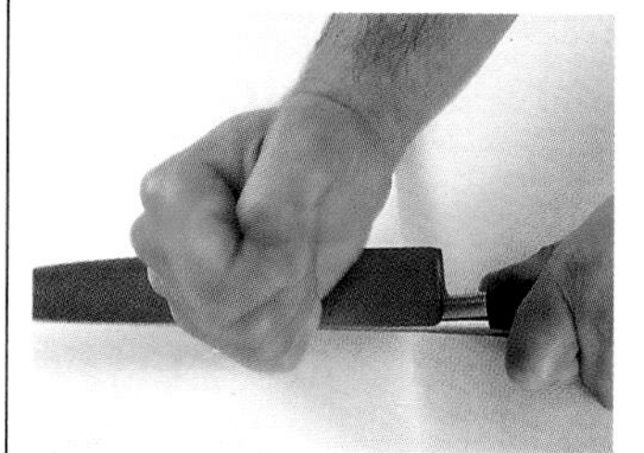

Garlic
1 Set the flat side of a knife on top of the clove and crush it lightly. Peel off the skin.

2 With a sharp chef's knife, chop the crushed garlic clove finely.

Avocado
Cut the avocado in half lengthwise and twist the 2 halves to separate them. Embed the blade of a chef's knife into the stone and pull it out. If the avocado is to be mashed, the flesh can simply be scooped out with a teaspoon. To serve in slices, lightly score the skin into 2 or 3 strips. Peel off the strips of skin and slice.

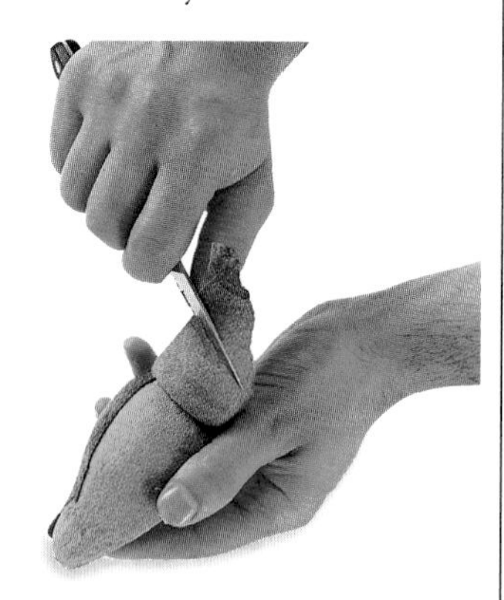

Preparing vegetables know-how

The juices produced by fresh chillies can burn the skin, so it's best to wear rubber gloves when cutting them and to avoid any contact with the eyes.

◆

Large courgettes, which may be bitter, can be salted in the same way as aubergines.

◆

The more finely you chop garlic, the stronger the flavour.

◆

Avocados discolour quickly, so brush cut surfaces with lemon juice, and use as soon as possible.

COOKING VEGETABLES

Choose the right cooking method to bring out the best in vegetables and create an exciting accompaniment to a main dish. If cooking a variety of vegetables at the same time, remember that some take longer to cook than others, so you may have to add them in stages.

Baking
Potatoes, sweet potatoes, aubergines, and pumpkin are all delicious baked. Prick the skins of whole vegetables or, if cut, moisten cut surfaces with oil or butter. Push a skewer through the centres of large vegetables to conduct heat and speed up cooking time.

Grilling
Many types of quick-cooking vegetables can be grilled under a conventional grill or over a barbecue. Halve the vegetables or cut into thick slices. Brush with oil and grill, turning at least once, until tender. For extra flavour, marinate vegetables first (page 352).

Braising
Carrots, celery, and other root vegetables are ideal for braising. Put the vegetables into a heavy pan or casserole, add a small amount of water or stock, and bring to a boil. Cover tightly and cook over a gentle heat until just tender.

Sautéing
Vegetables can be sautéed in oil or a mixture of oil and butter. Butter alone burns if it becomes too hot. Cook the vegetables over a high heat, stirring and turning, until they start to brown. Reduce the heat and cook, stirring occasionally, until tender.

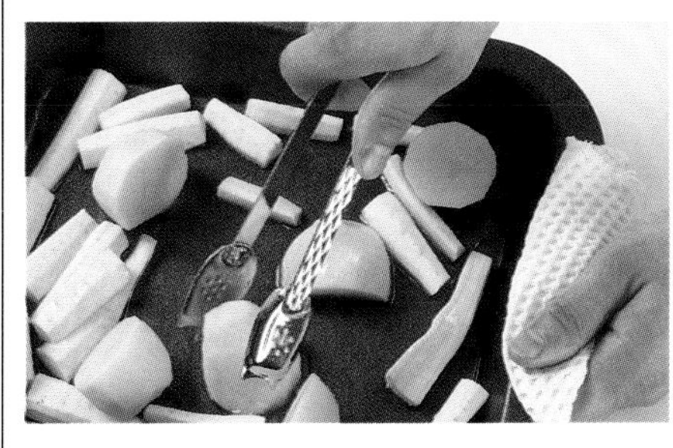

Roasting
Put olive oil or duck fat into a roasting tin and put in a preheated oven until hot. Cut any root vegetables into large chunks and parboil them. Add to the roasting tin, turning to coat with the fat. Roast, at 180°C (350°F, Gas 4), turning occasionally, until well browned.

Boiling
Green vegetables should be dropped into a pan of boiling salted water; root vegetables should be put in a pan of cold water and brought to a boil. Cover and simmer until just tender, then drain. To stop further cooking and set the colour, rinse in cold water.

Deep-frying
Apart from root vegetables, most vegetables need a protective coating such as batter before being deep-fried. Heat the oil in a deep-fat fryer to the required temperature. Add the vegetables in batches and fry until golden, bringing the oil to the required temperature between each batch.

Stir-frying
Cut the vegetables into small, even-sized pieces. Heat a little oil in a wok. When it is hot, add the vegetables, starting with those that need the longest cooking time. Keep the heat high, and toss and stir the vegetables for just a few minutes until they are tender but still crisp.

Steaming
This method is ideal for delicate vegetables such as cauliflower, broccoli, or asparagus. Bring water to a boil in a steamer. Put the vegetables in a single layer on the rack, cover, and steam until just tender. If you don't have a steamer, use a large saucepan with a steamer basket, or a wok and a bamboo steamer.

VEGETABLE GARNISHES

Vegetables cut into attractive shapes or decoratively assembled can add a distinctive finishing touch to dishes, and will make a meal more special.

Carrot flowers
With a channelling or canelle knife, cut lengthwise grooves at regular intervals all around the carrot, then slice thinly. Cucumber can also be prepared in this way.

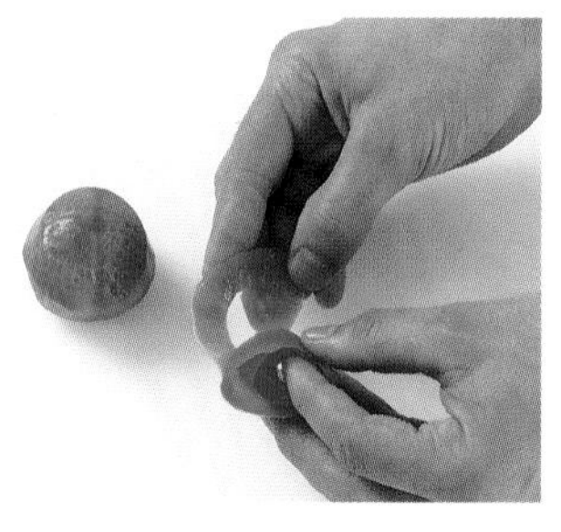

Tomato roses
Peel a length of skin from a tomato. Hold the flat end of the strip and wind the rest of the strip around into a loose spiral, turning as you wind. Tuck in the other end of the strip.

French bean bundles
1 Gather together small bundles of cooked French beans and cut the beans to the same length, about 7 cm (3 ins).

2 With a vegetable peeler, shave a thin strip of skin from a courgette. Cut the strip into very fine "strings". Tie each French bean bundle around the middle with a courgette "string".

SALAD DRESSINGS

All of the following dressings can be made by hand, with a balloon whisk, but if you prefer, a screw-topped jar is a handy alternative for mixing a vinaigrette, while a food processor or blender can produce mayonnaise or blue cheese dressing in a matter of seconds.

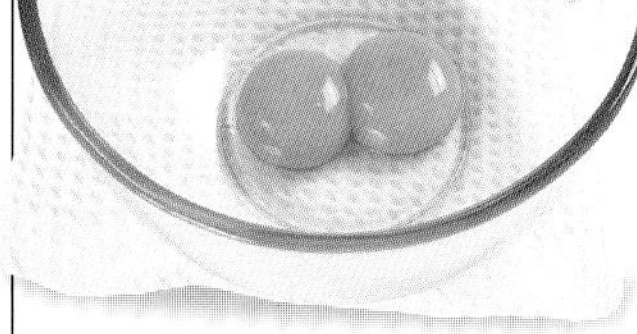

Mayonnaise
1 Put a bowl on a tea towel to steady it. Add *2 egg yolks, 1 tsp Dijon mustard,* and *salt and pepper to taste* and beat together with a balloon whisk until the egg yolks have thickened slightly.

2 Whisk in *150 ml (1/4 pint) olive or sunflower oil,* just a drop at a time at first, whisking until the mixture is thick. Stir in *2 tsp white wine vinegar* and serve at once, or chill. Makes 200 ml (7 fl oz).

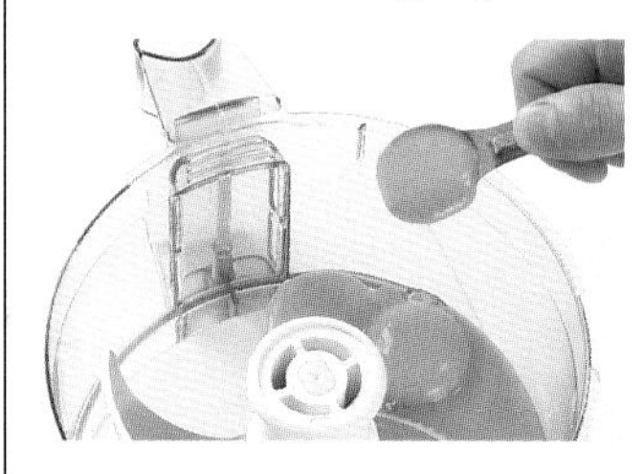

Food processor mayonnaise
1 Put *2 egg yolks, 1 tsp Dijon mustard,* and *salt and pepper to taste* in the bowl of a food processor or blender. Process briefly to combine.

2 With the blades turning, gradually add *150 ml (1/4 pint) olive or sunflower oil,* pouring it through the funnel in a slow, continuous stream.

Vinaigrette dressing
Put *6 tbsp olive oil, 2 tbsp white wine vinegar, 1 tbsp lemon juice, 1 tbsp Dijon mustard, 1/4 tsp caster sugar,* and *salt and pepper* into a screw-topped jar. Shake until combined. Makes 150 ml (1/4 pint).

Blue cheese dressing
Put *150 ml (1/4 pint) each of mayonnaise and soured cream, 90 g (3 oz) crumbled blue cheese, 1 tsp white wine vinegar, 1 crushed garlic clove,* and *black pepper to taste* into a bowl and whisk until smooth.

Salad dressings know-how

If mayonnaise curdles, add 1 tbsp hot water and beat well, or start again with fresh egg yolks and oil and slowly add the curdled mixture once the eggs and oil thicken.

◆

Ensure the eggs for mayonnaise are at room temperature.

◆

Keep mayonnaise, covered, in the refrigerator for up to 3 days. Bring to room temperature, stir, and serve.

◆

Keep vinaigrette dressings at room temperature for up to 1 week. Whisk before serving.

GRATIN DAUPHINOIS

Serves 6

butter for greasing

150 ml (1/4 pint) single cream

150 ml (1/4 pint) double cream

1 large garlic clove, crushed

1 kg (2 lb) old potatoes

salt and black pepper

125 g (4 oz) Gruyère cheese, grated

1 Lightly butter a shallow gratin dish. Put the single and double creams into a bowl, add the garlic, and stir to mix.

2 Thinly slice the potatoes, preferably with the slicing disc of a food processor.

3 Prepare the gratin dauphinois (see box, right).

4 Bake in a preheated oven at 160°C (325°F, Gas 3) for 1 1/2 hours or until the potatoes are tender and the topping is golden brown. Serve at once.

Preparing the gratin dauphinois

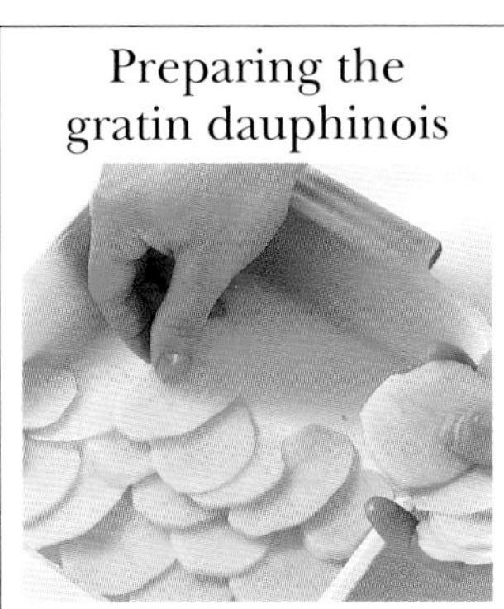

Arrange a layer of potatoes in the bottom of the gratin dish and add salt and pepper to taste.

Pour a little of the cream mixture over the potatoes, then sprinkle with cheese. Continue layering the potatoes, cream, and cheese, adding salt and pepper, and finishing with a layer of cheese.

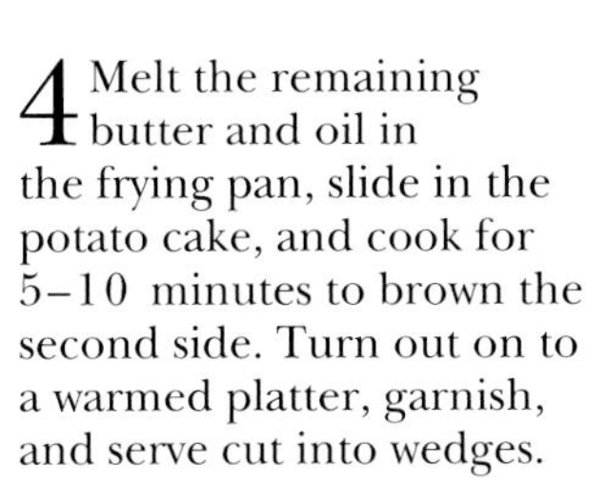

SWISS ROSTI

Serves 8

1.5 kg (3 lb) large baking potatoes, scrubbed

black pepper

60 g (2 oz) butter

2 tbsp sunflower oil

fresh thyme to garnish

1 Cook the potatoes in boiling salted water for about 10 minutes until just tender. Drain the potatoes thoroughly, leave to cool, then peel. Cover and chill for about 4 hours.

2 Coarsely grate the potatoes into a large bowl, add pepper to taste, and stir carefully to mix.

3 Melt 30 g (1 oz) of the butter with 1 tbsp of the oil in a frying pan, add the grated potato, and flatten into a cake with a fish slice. Cook over a low heat for about 15 minutes until the base is crisp and golden brown. Turn on to a large buttered plate.

4 Melt the remaining butter and oil in the frying pan, slide in the potato cake, and cook for 5–10 minutes to brown the second side. Turn out on to a warmed platter, garnish, and serve cut into wedges.

CELERIAC ROSTI

Substitute 750 g (1 1/2 lb) celeriac for half of the potato. Toss in lemon juice to prevent discoloration, then proceed as directed.

ONION ROSTI

Heat 1 tbsp sunflower oil in a frying pan, add 1 large chopped onion, and cook for 3–5 minutes until softened but not coloured. Fork the onion into 2 1/2 lb grated potato, add the pepper, and proceed as directed.

POTATOES LYONNAISE

 **Serves 4**

90 g (3 oz) butter, plus extra for greasing

1 large onion, sliced

1 kg (2 lb) old potatoes, thickly sliced

salt and black pepper

chopped parsley to garnish

1 Lightly butter a gratin dish. Melt the butter in a frying pan, add the onion, and cook gently, stirring occasionally, for 3–5 minutes until the onions are softened but not coloured.

2 Layer the potatoes and onion in the gratin dish, seasoning each layer with salt and pepper, and finishing with a neat layer of potatoes.

3 Pour any butter left in the frying pan over the potatoes. Bake in a preheated oven at 190°C (375°F, Gas 5) for 1–1½ hours until the potatoes are tender. Garnish with parsley, and serve hot.

CHIPPED POTATOES

Serves 4

750 g (1½ lb) old potatoes

sunflower oil for deep-frying

salt

** deep-fat fryer*

1 Cut the potatoes into 5 x 1 cm (2 x ½ in) sticks, put into a bowl of cold water, and leave to soak for 5–10 minutes.

2 Heat the oil in a deep-fat fryer to 160°C (325°F). Dry the chips thoroughly, then lower them into the deep-fat fryer, in batches if necessary, and deep-fry for 5–6 minutes until soft.

3 Lift the basket out of the fryer. Increase the temperature of the oil to 190°C (375°F). Carefully return the basket of chips to the fryer and deep-fry for 3–4 minutes until crisp and brown. Lift out the basket and drain the chips on paper towels. Sprinkle with salt, and serve hot.

Cook's know-how

Good chips should be crisp and golden on the outside and soft and tender in the middle. The secret is to cook the potatoes first in medium-hot oil until tender, then lift them out, increase the temperature of the oil, and cook the chips quickly to brown and crisp the outsides. Drain on paper towels.

FRENCH FRIES

Cut the potatoes into 5 cm x 5 mm (2 x ¼ in) sticks and leave to soak as directed. Heat the oil as directed and deep-fry the sticks for 4–5 minutes. Lift out of the fryer, increase the heat as directed, return and deep-fry the sticks for 1–2 minutes. Sprinkle with salt, and serve at once.

ROAST POTATOES

Serves 4

1 kg (2 lb) old potatoes, cut into even-sized pieces

3 tbsp duck or goose fat, dripping, or sunflower oil

salt

1 Put the potatoes into a large saucepan, cover with cold water, and bring to a boil. Simmer for 1 minute, then drain.

2 Return the potatoes to the saucepan and shake over a gentle heat to roughen the surfaces and dry the potatoes thoroughly.

3 Put the fat into a roasting tin, heat until very hot, then add the potatoes, turning to coat them in the fat. Roast the potatoes in a preheated oven at 220°C (425°F, Gas 7), turning and basting occasionally, for 45–60 minutes until tender, crisp, and golden. Sprinkle with salt, and serve at once.

Cook's know-how

Roughening the surfaces of the potatoes before roasting gives them a particularly crisp texture. If you prefer, you can also score the surfaces with a fork.

POMMES ANNA

 **Serves 4**

750 g (1½ lb) old potatoes

90 g (3 oz) butter, plus extra for greasing

salt and black pepper

1 Slice the potatoes very thinly, preferably with the slicing disc of a food processor.

2 Generously butter the bottom and side of an ovenproof frying pan. Layer the potatoes in the frying pan, seasoning each layer with salt and pepper to taste, and dotting with the butter.

3 Cover the pan tightly with buttered foil and the lid, and cook over a medium heat for about 15 minutes or until the base of the potato cake is light golden brown.

4 Transfer the pan to a preheated oven and cook at 190°C (375°F, Gas 5) for 30 minutes or until the potato cake is tender.

5 Invert a warmed serving platter over the frying pan, and turn out the potato cake so that the crisp layer is on the top. Serve at once, cut into wedges.

Cook's know-how

Arrange the potatoes in the frying pan as soon as they have been sliced; if you put them into water the starch contained in them will be washed away and they won't hold together.

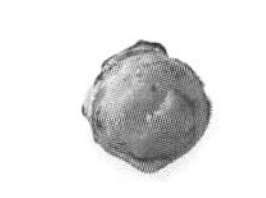

INDIVIDUAL POMMES ANNA

Layer the sliced potatoes in well-buttered individual patty tins. Cook the potatoes in the top half of a preheated oven at 220°C (425°F, Gas 7) for 30–35 minutes.

GARLIC CREAMED POTATOES

 **Serves 4**

750 g (1½ lb) old potatoes, cut into large chunks

salt and black pepper

4 garlic cloves

about 150 ml (¼ pint) milk

60 g (2 oz) butter

2 tbsp snipped fresh chives

1 Cook the potatoes in boiling salted water for 20–30 minutes until tender. Drain thoroughly.

2 Meanwhile, roast the garlic cloves in a preheated oven at 180°C, (350°F, Gas 4) for 10 minutes until softened. Remove the skins.

3 Return the potatoes to the saucepan and toss over a gentle heat for a few seconds to dry thoroughly, shaking the saucepan so that the potatoes do not burn.

4 Mash the potatoes or work through a sieve, then push them to one side of the pan.

5 Pour the milk into the saucepan and heat until almost boiling. Beat the milk into the potatoes with the garlic, butter, and salt and pepper to taste. Sprinkle with chives, and serve hot.

HERB & CHEESE CREAMED POTATOES

Omit the garlic, and add 2 tbsp chopped parsley and 60 g (2 oz) finely grated Cheddar cheese when you beat in the milk, then proceed as directed.

CREAMED POTATOES WITH SWEDE

Omit the garlic and fresh chives. Substitute 250 g (8 oz) swede, cut into small chunks, for 250 g (8 oz) of the potatoes and proceed as directed, adding a pinch of grated nutmeg just before serving.

HASSELBACK POTATOES

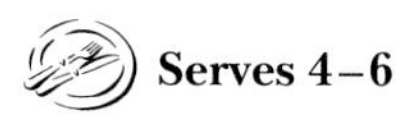 **Serves 4–6**

1 kg (2 lb) old potatoes

60 g (2 oz) butter, melted, plus extra for greasing

salt and black pepper

4 tbsp grated Parmesan cheese

parsley to garnish

1 Slice the potatoes (see box, right).

2 Put the potatoes into a buttered roasting tin and brush with the melted butter, separating the slices slightly so a little of the butter goes between them. Season with salt and pepper.

3 Bake in a preheated oven at 220°C (425°F, Gas 7) for 45 minutes. Sprinkle the potatoes with 3 tbsp of the Parmesan cheese and return to the oven until tender.

4 Transfer to a serving platter, and sprinkle with the remaining Parmesan. Garnish, and serve at once.

Slicing the potatoes

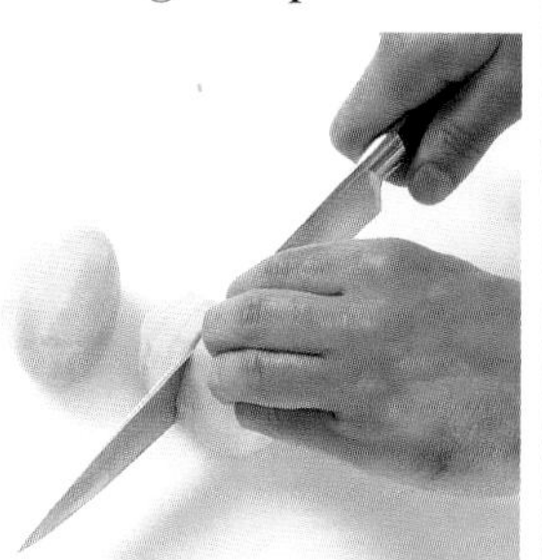

Cut a thin slice off one side of each potato, if necessary, to steady it. Slice each potato, three-quarters of the way through, at 5 mm (1/4 in) intervals.

Cook's know-how

To make it easier to slice the potatoes, push a skewer lengthwise through the lower part of each potato, and slice as far down as the skewer. Remove the skewer before cooking.

SPINACH & CHEESE BAKED POTATOES

Serves 4

4 baking potatoes, scrubbed

250 g (8 oz) spinach

1 tbsp olive oil

1 small onion, finely chopped

125 g (4 oz) ricotta cheese

pinch of grated nutmeg

salt and black pepper

1 Prick the potatoes all over with a fork. Bake in a preheated oven at 220°C (425°F, Gas 7) for 1–1 1/4 hours until tender.

2 Meanwhile, wash the spinach and put it into a saucepan with only the water remaining on the leaves. Cook over a gentle heat for 1–2 minutes until the spinach has just wilted. Drain thoroughly, squeezing to remove excess water. Chop the spinach finely.

3 Heat the olive oil in a small saucepan, add the onion, and cook gently, stirring occasionally, for 3–5 minutes until softened but not coloured.

4 Cut the potatoes in half lengthwise, scoop out the flesh and turn it into a bowl. Add the spinach, onion, any oil left in the pan, the ricotta cheese, nutmeg, and salt and pepper to taste, and mix thoroughly. Fill the potato skins with the mixture, return to the oven, and cook for 20 minutes or until piping hot. Serve at once.

SPRING ONION & HUMMUS BAKED POTATOES

Bake the potatoes, cut in half lengthwise, and scoop out the flesh as directed. Mix with 4 finely chopped spring onions, 150 g (5 oz) hummus, and salt and pepper to taste. Fill the potato skins and proceed as directed in the recipe.

SWEET POTATOES WITH GINGER BUTTER

Serves 4

4 sweet potatoes, scrubbed

125 g (4 oz) sesame seeds

soy sauce to taste

GINGER BUTTER

45 g (1½ oz) butter, softened

1 garlic clove, crushed

1 cm (½ in) piece of fresh root ginger, peeled and chopped

1 Lightly prick the skins of the sweet potatoes with a fork. Bake in a preheated oven at 180°C (350°F, Gas 4) for 1 hour or until tender.

2 Meanwhile, make the ginger butter: put the butter into a small bowl and blend in the garlic and chopped ginger.

3 Put the sesame seeds into a frying pan and toss over a low heat for 2–3 minutes until golden brown. Remove from the frying pan. Lightly crush about half of the sesame seeds to release more of their fragrance. Set aside.

4 Cut the sweet potatoes into wedges and arrange on a serving plate with the ginger butter. Sprinkle with soy sauce and sesame seeds, and serve at once.

Sweet potatoes

Sweet potatoes feature a great deal in North American cooking and are often served roasted as accompaniments to barbecued meats and chicken. The most popular varieties are a pale-skinned sweet potato with pale yellow flesh and a dark-skinned variety with orange, yellow, or white flesh. They have a deliciously sweet, chestnut flavour, and honey and sweet spices are often added to accentuate this.

SPICED YAMS

Serves 4

45 g (1½ oz) butter

2 garlic cloves, crushed

2 yams, total weight about 1 kg (2 lb), trimmed but unpeeled, cubed

½ tsp mild chilli powder

¼ tsp paprika

¼ tsp ground cumin

¼ tsp ground cinnamon

1 x 200 (7 oz) can tomatoes, juice reserved, diced

salt

plain yogurt and chopped parsley to garnish

1 Melt the butter in a large pan. When it is foaming, add the garlic, and cook gently, stirring occasionally, for 1–2 minutes until soft but not coloured.

2 Add the yams to the pan and toss over a medium to high heat for 1–2 minutes.

3 Stir in the chilli powder, paprika, cumin, and cinnamon, then add the tomatoes, and cook the mixture over a medium heat for 1–2 minutes.

4 Add the juice from the tomatoes and salt to taste. Cover and simmer, gently turning the yams from time to time with a palette knife, for 15–20 minutes until the yams are tender. Do not stir or they will break up. Serve at once, garnished with yogurt and parsley.

CREAMED SPINACH

 **Serves 4**

750 g (1½ lb) frozen leaf spinach, thawed and drained
45 g (1½ oz) butter
125 ml (4 fl oz) crème fraîche or double cream
1–2 tbsp grated Parmesan cheese
1 tsp snipped fresh chives
large pinch of grated nutmeg
salt and black pepper

1 Coarsely chop the spinach leaves and set aside.

2 Melt the butter in a saucepan, add the spinach, and stir until it has absorbed the butter.

3 Add half of the crème fraîche or double cream, the Parmesan cheese, chives, nutmeg. Season with salt and pepper to taste, and heat through.

4 Transfer to a shallow flameproof dish, pour the remaining crème fraîche or double cream over the spinach mixture, and put under a hot grill for 4–5 minutes until lightly browned. Taste for seasoning, and serve hot.

SWEET & SOUR BEETROOT

Serves 4

3 tbsp olive oil
2 onions, chopped
2 garlic cloves, crushed
4 cooked beetroot, diced
30 g (1 oz) caster sugar
juice of 1 lemon
2 tsp chopped fresh mint
salt and black pepper
fresh mint to garnish

1 Heat the olive oil in a large saucepan, add the onions and garlic, and cook gently, stirring occasionally, for 3–5 minutes until the onions are softened but not coloured.

2 Stir in the beetroot, sugar, half of the lemon juice, the mint, and salt and pepper to taste, and cook gently, stirring, for 10 minutes. Taste for seasoning, adding more lemon juice if needed.

3 Serve warm or cold, garnished with fresh mint.

GINGER PARSNIPS

Serves 6

1 kg (2 lb) parsnips, cut into matchstick-thin strips
salt and black pepper
60 g (2 oz) butter
2.5 cm (1 in) piece of fresh root ginger, peeled and finely chopped
300 ml (½ pint) crème fraîche

1 Blanch the parsnips in a large saucepan of boiling salted water for 2 minutes. Drain the parsnips.

2 Melt the butter in the saucepan. Add the ginger and cook gently, stirring, for 2–3 minutes. Add the parsnips, tossing to coat in the butter. Add salt and pepper to taste, then turn the mixture into a large, shallow ovenproof dish.

3 Pour the crème fraîche over the parsnip mixture and bake in a preheated oven at 190°C (375°F, Gas 5) for 10–15 minutes until tender. Serve at once.

GLAZED CARROTS & TURNIPS

Serves 4

375 g (12 oz) carrots, cut into 5 cm (2 in) strips
375 g (12 oz) baby turnips
300 ml (½ pint) chicken stock
30 g (1 oz) butter
1 tsp caster sugar
salt and black pepper
1 tbsp mixed chopped fresh mint and parsley

1 Put the vegetables into a pan with the stock, butter, sugar, and salt and pepper to taste, and bring to a boil. Cover and cook for about 10 minutes until the vegetables are almost tender.

2 Remove the lid and boil rapidly until the liquid in the pan has evaporated and formed a glaze on the vegetables. Stir in the herbs, and serve at once.

CABBAGE & MIXED PEPPER STIR-FRY

Serves 6–8

- *2–3 tbsp olive oil*
- *1 large onion, finely sliced*
- *6 celery stalks, sliced diagonally*
- *1 small white cabbage, finely shredded*
- *2 red peppers, cored, seeded, and cut into thin strips*
- *1 yellow pepper, cored, seeded, and cut into thin strips*
- *175 g (6 oz) mushrooms, quartered*
- *salt and black pepper*

1 Heat 1 tbsp of the olive oil in a wok or large frying pan, add the sliced onion, and stir-fry over a high heat for about 2 minutes until beginning to brown.

2 Add the sliced celery and stir-fry for about 1 minute, then lower the heat and stir-fry for 2 minutes.

3 Add a further 1 tbsp of olive oil to the wok, add the cabbage, and stir-fry for 2 minutes.

4 Add the peppers and mushrooms, with the remaining oil, if needed, and stir-fry for 3 minutes. Add salt and pepper to taste, and serve at once.

Cook's know-how

This is a good vegetable dish to serve when entertaining. Prepare and stir-fry the vegetables up to the end of step 2. The final cooking can be done in minutes, just before serving.

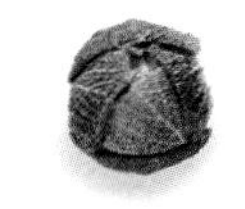

SAVOY CABBAGE STIR-FRY

Heat 1 tbsp sunflower oil in a wok and stir-fry 1 finely sliced large onion, and 2 crushed garlic cloves for 2 minutes. Add a further 1 tbsp sunflower oil, then 1 shredded small Savoy cabbage, and stir-fry for 2 minutes. Sprinkle with 2 tbsp soy sauce and 1 tsp sesame oil.

SPRING GREENS WITH GARLIC

Serves 4

- *1 kg (2 lb) spring greens, tough stalks removed*
- *salt*
- *2 tbsp olive oil*
- *3 garlic cloves, coarsely chopped*

1 Roll up the spring greens, a few at a time, and cut across into thin strips. Blanch in boiling salted water for 2 minutes.

2 Drain and rinse in iced water to cool. Drain thoroughly, squeezing to remove excess water.

3 Heat the olive oil in a large saucepan, add the garlic, and cook gently for 1 minute or until lightly browned. Add the spring greens, toss to coat thoroughly in the garlic and oil, and cook for 2–3 minutes until the spring greens are heated through.

4 Season with salt to taste. Serve hot or cold.

SPROUTS WITH MUSTARD SEEDS

Serves 4

- *1 kg (2 lb) Brussels sprouts*
- *salt and black pepper*
- *45 g (1½ oz) butter*
- *2 tsp mustard seeds*
- *1 tbsp lemon juice*

1 Cut a cross in the base of each sprout, and simmer the sprouts in boiling salted water for 5–10 minutes until just tender. Drain.

2 Melt the butter in a large saucepan, add the mustard seeds, cover, and cook over a low heat for 1–2 minutes until the mustard seeds have stopped popping and the butter is lightly browned. Do not let the butter burn.

3 Add the sprouts to the pan, tossing to heat them through and coat them in the mustard-seed butter. Add the lemon juice, and salt and black pepper to taste, and serve at once.

CAULIFLOWER & BROCCOLI LAYERS

Serves 4–6

500 g (1 lb) broccoli florets

500 g (1 lb) cauliflower florets

salt and black pepper

60 g (2 oz) butter, plus extra for greasing

60 g (2 oz) flaked almonds

4 tbsp fresh white breadcrumbs

1 garlic clove, crushed

⋆ *1 litre (1¾ pint) pudding basin*

1 Cook the broccoli and cauliflower in boiling salted water for 10 minutes or until just tender. Drain.

2 Butter the basin and layer the cauliflower and broccoli (see box, right).

3 Cover the basin with a small plate and press down lightly to mould the vegetables. Leave in a warm place for 5 minutes.

4 Melt the remaining butter in a frying pan. Add the almonds, breadcrumbs, and garlic, and cook, stirring, for 3–5 minutes until golden. Add salt and pepper to taste.

Layering the vegetables

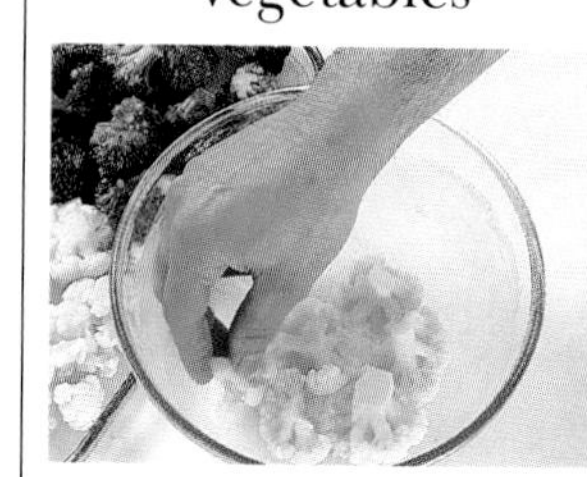

Arrange a layer of cauliflower florets, stalk-sides up, in the bottom of the pudding basin.

Place a ring of outward-facing broccoli florets, then of cauliflower florets on top. Continue layering alternately. Tightly pack the middle of the mould with the remaining florets.

5 Invert the pudding basin on to a warmed platter. Spoon the almond mixture over the top and serve.

SWEET & SOUR RED CABBAGE

Serves 4–6

1 tbsp sunflower oil

4 streaky bacon rashers, rinds removed, diced

125 g (4 oz) light soft brown sugar

2 onions, chopped

1 red cabbage, weighing about 1 kg (2 lb), shredded

1 tart apple, cored and diced

250 ml (8 fl oz) red wine

4 tbsp red wine vinegar

60 g (2 oz) sultanas

2 tsp caraway seeds

¼ tsp ground cinnamon

pinch of grated nutmeg

salt and black pepper

1 Heat the sunflower oil in a large saucepan, add the diced bacon, and cook for about 5 minutes until crisp and browned.

2 Stir in 90 g (3 oz) of the sugar and cook gently, stirring constantly, for 1–2 minutes, taking care that it does not burn.

3 Add the onions, cabbage, and apple, and cook, stirring occasionally, for about 5 minutes.

4 Pour in the wine and half of the vinegar, then add the sultanas, caraway seeds, cinnamon, nutmeg, and salt and pepper to taste. Cover and cook over a low heat for 30 minutes or until the cabbage is tender but still firm. If there is too much liquid, uncover, and boil rapidly until the liquid evaporates completely.

5 Stir in the remaining sugar and vinegar, heat through, and serve.

RED CABBAGE WITH CHESTNUTS

Omit the sultanas. Add 125 g (4 oz) coarsely chopped chestnuts with the chopped onions, shredded cabbage, and diced apple, and proceed as directed in the recipe.

Creamed Haricot Beans

Serves 6

- *250 g (8 oz) dried haricot beans*
- *30 g (1 oz) butter*
- *1 small carrot, finely chopped*
- *1 small onion, finely chopped*
- *a few parsley stalks*
- *1 fresh thyme sprig*
- *1 bay leaf*
- *salt and black pepper*
- *2 tbsp chopped parsley*

1 Put the beans into a large bowl, cover with cold water, then leave to soak for at least 8 hours.

2 Drain the beans. Rinse under cold water and drain again. Put the beans into a saucepan and cover with cold water. Bring to a boil and boil rapidly for 10 minutes. Drain.

3 Melt the butter in a heavy saucepan, add the carrot and onion, and cook, stirring, for 3–4 minutes until beginning to soften.

4 Add the beans, parsley, thyme, and bay leaf, and pour in enough cold water to just cover the beans. Bring to a boil, cover, and simmer gently for 1 hour or until the beans are soft but not breaking up.

5 Strain the bean mixture, reserving the cooking liquid. Purée one-third of the mixture in a food processor.

6 Stir the purée back into the bean mixture, adding a little of the reserved cooking liquid to make a sauce-like consistency. Add salt and pepper to taste. Reheat gently, sprinkle with chopped parsley, and serve at once.

French-Style Peas

Serves 4

- *1 small round lettuce, shredded*
- *6 spring onions, chopped*
- *60 g (2 oz) butter*
- *1 tbsp chopped parsley*
- *1 tsp caster sugar*
- *500 g (1 lb) shelled peas*
- *4 tbsp water*
- *salt and black pepper*

1 Line the bottom of a saucepan with the lettuce. Add the spring onions, butter, parsley, and sugar, and top with the peas. Add the measured water and salt and pepper to taste.

2 Simmer gently for 15–20 minutes until the liquid has evaporated and the peas are tender. Taste for seasoning and serve at once.

Summer Peas & Beans

Serves 6

- *250 g (8 oz) shelled young broad beans*
- *salt and black pepper*
- *250 g (8 oz) shelled peas*
- *250 g (8 oz) French beans, halved*
- *30 g (1 oz) butter*
- *2 tbsp chopped fresh mint*
- *fresh mint to garnish*

1 Cook the broad beans in a saucepan of boiling salted water for 10–15 minutes until just tender. Cook the peas and French beans in a second pan of boiling salted water for 5–10 minutes until tender.

2 Drain all the vegetables, and return to one pan. Add the butter and mint and stir until the butter melts. Taste for seasoning, garnish with fresh mint, and serve hot.

GLAZED SHALLOTS

Serves 4

750 g (1½ lb) shallots
90 g (3 oz) butter
1 tbsp caster sugar
1 tbsp chopped fresh thyme
salt and black pepper
chopped parsley to garnish

1 Place the shallots in a single layer in a large frying pan and cover with cold water.

2 Add the butter, sugar, thyme, and salt and pepper to taste, cover, and bring to a boil. Remove the lid, and simmer gently, shaking the pan vigorously at intervals to prevent the shallots from sticking and burning, for 10–15 minutes until the liquid has almost evaporated and the shallots are golden brown.

3 Garnish the shallots with parsley, and serve hot.

SAUTEED CELERY & LEEKS

Serves 6

30 g (1 oz) butter
2 tbsp olive oil
500 g (1 lb) young leeks, trimmed and thinly sliced
12 celery stalks, thinly sliced diagonally
salt and black pepper
2 tbsp snipped fresh chives
125 g (4 oz) salted cashew nuts to garnish

1 Melt the butter with the olive oil in a wok or large frying pan.

2 When the butter is foaming, add the leeks, and cook over a high heat, stirring occasionally, for 7–10 minutes.

3 Add the celery, and cook for 3–5 minutes. Add salt and pepper to taste, then stir in the snipped fresh chives.

4 Garnish with the salted cashew nuts, and serve at once.

YANKEE SUCCOTASH

Serves 4

2 tbsp sunflower oil
1 large onion, chopped
8 thick streaky bacon rashers, rinds removed, diced
500 g (1 lb) sweetcorn kernels
250 ml (8 fl oz) single cream
1 x 400 g (13 oz) can beans, such as borlotti or broad beans, drained
salt
Tabasco sauce
3–4 tbsp snipped fresh chives
fresh chives to garnish

1 Heat the sunflower oil in a large frying pan, add the onion and bacon, and cook gently, stirring occasionally, for 7 minutes or until lightly browned.

2 Stir in the sweetcorn and cream and simmer for 2 minutes. Purée 3–4 tbsp of the sweetcorn mixture in a food processor until quite smooth, then stir back into the frying pan.

3 Add the beans and return to a boil. Simmer, stirring occasionally, for 5–10 minutes until the mixture is thickened.

4 Add salt and Tabasco sauce to taste, and stir in the snipped chives. Serve at once, garnished with chives.

Succotash

This is a native American dish. Any type of bean may be used in succotash and both dried and canned are suitable for this recipe. Sometimes, for a summer succotash, large chunks of courgette are simmered with the sweetcorn. It is a highly nutritious dish – the combination of sweetcorn and beans alone provides as much protein as a thick steak.

STUFFED MUSHROOMS

Serves 6

250 g (8 oz) mushrooms
60 g (2 oz) butter
125 g (4 oz) carrots, diced
125 g (4 oz) courgettes, diced
1 tbsp chopped parsley
salt and pepper

1 Remove the stalks from the mushrooms and chop the stalks finely.

2 Melt the butter in a frying pan. When it is foaming, add the mushroom stalks, carrots, and courgettes, and cook, stirring, for 1 minute. Add the parsley and salt and pepper to taste.

3 Put the mushroom cups in a single layer in a shallow ovenproof dish. Fill with the vegetable mixture.

4 Cook in a preheated oven at 180°C (350°F, Gas 4) for 15 minutes. Serve at once.

GARLIC-STUFFED MUSHROOMS

Substitute 60 g (2 oz) fresh white breadcrumbs and 4 crushed garlic cloves for the carrots and courgettes.

ITALIAN FENNEL

Serves 6–8

4 fennel bulbs, trimmed and quartered lengthwise
salt and black pepper
butter for greasing
250 g (8 oz) mozzarella cheese, grated
chopped parsley to garnish

1 Cook the fennel in boiling salted water for 3–5 minutes until just tender. Drain thoroughly.

2 Butter a shallow ovenproof dish. Add the fennel and salt and pepper to taste. Arrange the mozzarella cheese on top.

3 Bake in a preheated oven at 200°C (400°F, Gas 6) for 15–20 minutes until the cheese topping is golden and bubbling.

4 Sprinkle with chopped parsley, and serve hot.

ASPARAGUS WITH PARMESAN

Serves 4

625 g ($1\frac{1}{4}$ lb) asparagus
90 g (3 oz) Parmesan cheese, grated
lemon wedges and flat-leaf parsley sprigs to garnish

MARINADE

2 tbsp olive oil
1 tbsp dry white wine
1 tsp red or white wine vinegar
3 garlic cloves, crushed
$\frac{1}{4}$ tsp herbes de Provence
salt and black pepper

1 Trim the woody ends from the asparagus.

2 Make the marinade: combine the oil, wine, wine vinegar, garlic, herbes de Provence, and salt and pepper to taste. Toss the asparagus in the marinade, cover, and leave to marinate for 15 minutes.

3 Sprinkle the Parmesan on to a plate. Roll the asparagus in the Parmesan, then arrange in a single layer in a large ovenproof dish.

4 Pour any remaining marinade over the asparagus, and bake in a preheated oven at 200°C (400°F, Gas 6) for 15–20 minutes until lightly browned and sizzling hot. Garnish with the lemon wedges and parsley sprigs, and serve at once.

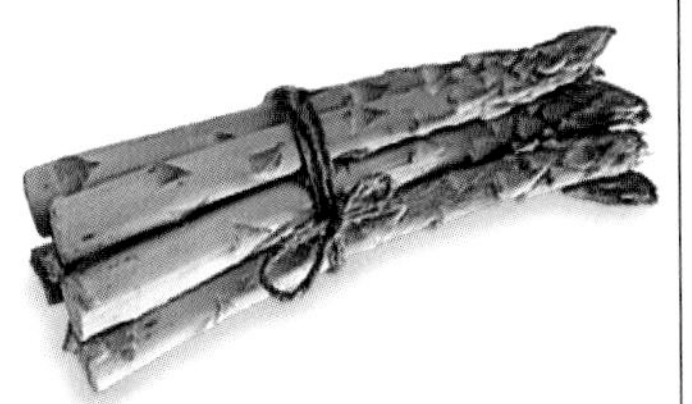

TOMATOES WITH CORIANDER

Serves 4

500 g (1 lb) cherry tomatoes
fresh coriander to garnish

CORIANDER BUTTER

45 g (1 1/2 oz) butter, softened
2 tbsp chopped fresh coriander
1 garlic clove, crushed
1/2 tsp lemon juice
salt

1 Arrange the cherry tomatoes in a single layer in an ovenproof dish. Cook in a preheated oven at 230°C (450°F, Gas 8) for 25–30 minutes until the tomatoes are lightly browned and tender but still retain their shape.

2 Meanwhile, make the coriander butter: put the butter into a small bowl and beat in the chopped fresh coriander, garlic, lemon juice, and salt to taste.

3 Garnish the tomatoes, and serve hot, dotted with coriander butter.

SAVOURY PUMPKIN

Serves 4

1 kg (2 lb) piece of pumpkin
2–3 tbsp olive oil
1 tsp balsamic or red wine vinegar
3 garlic cloves, crushed
1/2 tsp chopped fresh thyme
1/2 tsp paprika
salt and black pepper
fresh thyme to garnish

1 Cut the flesh of the pumpkin into large chunks and arrange on a baking tray.

2 Combine the olive oil, vinegar, garlic, thyme, paprika, and salt and pepper to taste, and pour over the pumpkin.

3 Bake in a preheated oven at 190°C (375°F, Gas 5) for 15–20 minutes until the pumpkin is just tender and lightly browned on top. Garnish with thyme, and serve at once. If preferred, leave to cool and serve with a vinaigrette dressing (page 338).

OKRA WITH CHILLI

Serves 4

3 tbsp sunflower oil
1 small onion, sliced
1 garlic clove, crushed
500 g (1 lb) okra, trimmed
1 large fresh red chilli, cored, seeded, and diced
salt and black pepper

1 Heat the oil in a wok or large frying pan, add the onion, and stir-fry over a high heat for 3 minutes or until golden. Add the garlic and stir-fry for 1 minute.

2 Add the okra and chilli and stir-fry over a high heat for 5–10 minutes until the okra is tender, but still retains some crispness. Add salt and pepper to taste. Serve at once.

Cook's know-how

Because of its shape, okra is sometimes known as ladies' fingers. Trim the ends carefully so that the sticky juices and seeds are not exposed and released.

MIXED VEGETABLE STIR-FRY

Serves 4

1 tbsp olive oil
250 g (8 oz) courgettes, sliced diagonally
1 yellow pepper, cored, seeded, and thinly sliced
250 g (8 oz) mixed mushrooms, sliced
salt and black pepper
1 tbsp lemon juice
60 g (2 oz) flaked almonds, toasted

1 Heat the olive oil in a wok or large frying pan, add the courgettes, and stir-fry for 3–4 minutes until the courgettes are just beginning to colour.

2 Add the yellow pepper and mushrooms and stir-fry for 2 minutes. Add salt and pepper to taste, stir in the lemon juice, and leave the mixture to bubble for about 1 minute. Sprinkle with the toasted flaked almonds, and serve at once.

TOMATO & COURGETTE BAKE

Serves 4–6

2 courgettes, sliced
salt and black pepper
3 large tomatoes, sliced
snipped fresh chives to garnish

WHITE SAUCE

30 g (1 oz) butter
30 g (1 oz) plain flour
300 ml (1/2 pint) milk
pinch of grated nutmeg

1 Arrange half of the courgette slices in the bottom of a shallow ovenproof dish. Season with a little salt and pepper.

2 Arrange half of the tomato slices in a layer on top of the courgettes. Season to taste.

3 Layer the remaining courgette and tomato slices in the dish, adding salt and pepper to taste.

4 Make the white sauce: melt the butter in a small saucepan. Add the flour, and cook, stirring, for 1 minute. Remove from the heat and gradually blend in the milk. Bring to a boil, stirring, until the mixture thickens. Simmer for 2–3 minutes. Add the nutmeg, and salt and pepper to taste.

5 Pour the white sauce over the vegetables. Cook in a preheated oven at 190°C (375°F, Gas 5) for 15–20 minutes until the vegetables are just cooked. Sprinkle with snipped chives, and serve at once.

TOMATO & LEEK BAKE

Substitute 2 sliced leeks for the courgettes. Stir-fry in 1 tbsp olive oil for 2–3 minutes, then layer with the tomatoes. Make the white sauce, substituting 1 tbsp Dijon mustard for the nutmeg, and proceed as directed.

RATATOUILLE

Serves 4–6

1 large aubergine
salt and black pepper
4 tbsp olive oil
1 large onion, sliced
1 large garlic clove, crushed
4 courgettes, sliced
6 tomatoes, peeled (page 39), quartered, and seeded
1 large red pepper, cored, seeded, and sliced
1/4 tsp caster sugar
1/4 tsp crushed coriander seeds (optional)
1 tbsp chopped fresh basil

1 Cut the aubergine into 1 cm (1/2 in) slices. Place in a colander, sprinkle generously with salt, and leave to stand for about 30 minutes. Rinse the aubergine slices and pat dry with paper towels.

2 Heat the olive oil in a large frying pan, add the onion and garlic, and cook gently, stirring occasionally, for 3–5 minutes until softened.

3 Add the aubergine slices, cover, and simmer gently for 20 minutes.

4 Add the courgettes, tomatoes, red pepper, sugar, and salt and pepper to taste, and cook gently, covered, for 45–60 minutes until the vegetables are soft but still retain their shape. Do not stir vigorously or you may break them up.

5 Ten minutes before the end of cooking time, add the coriander seeds, if using, and taste for seasoning. Serve hot or cold, sprinkled with the chopped fresh basil.

Cook's know-how

A classic from the south of France, ratatouille may be served by itself as a starter or as an accompaniment to cold or grilled meats; it goes particularly well with lamb. It tastes just as good warm or cold.

CHARGRILLED VEGETABLE PLATTER

Vegetables are delicious chargrilled – their flesh is tender and smoky in flavour. Serve them hot as a side dish with roast meat, poultry, or grilled fish, or cold as an unusual salad with picnics and barbecues. Experiment with different vegetables, oils, and marinades to suit your taste.

 **Serves 4**

4 baby aubergines
salt and black pepper
4 baby courgettes
2 red peppers, cored and seeded
500 g (1 lb) asparagus
4 large mushrooms
175 g (6 oz) pattypan squash
175 g (6 oz) baby sweetcorn
olive oil for brushing
⋆ *8–10 wooden cocktail sticks*

1 Prepare the vegetables. Trim the aubergines, cut in half lengthwise, and score a criss-cross pattern on the cut surfaces. Sprinkle the cut surfaces with salt and set aside for 30 minutes.

2 Meanwhile, cut the courgettes in half lengthwise. Cut the red peppers in half lengthwise and cut out the fleshy ribs. Trim the woody ends from the asparagus and cut all the spears to an even length.

3 Gently wipe the mushrooms with damp paper towels and remove the stalks. Trim the squash if necessary.

4 Rinse the aubergines under cold running water, and pat dry with paper towels.

5 Place the asparagus spears side by side in groups of 3 or 4 (depending on thickness). Gently push a cocktail stick through the asparagus, about 1 cm (1/2 in) from the tips, until they are all skewered. Insert a second cocktail stick at the bases of the spears. Repeat for the remaining groups of asparagus spears.

6 Brush all of the vegetables generously with olive oil and season with salt and pepper to taste.

7 Cook over a hot barbecue or under a hot grill a batch at a time, turning occasionally, for 15–20 minutes until the outer skins are charred. Keep each batch warm while you cook the remaining vegetables.

VEGETABLE MARINADES

For extra flavour, soak the vegetables in a marinade for 1 hour before cooking.

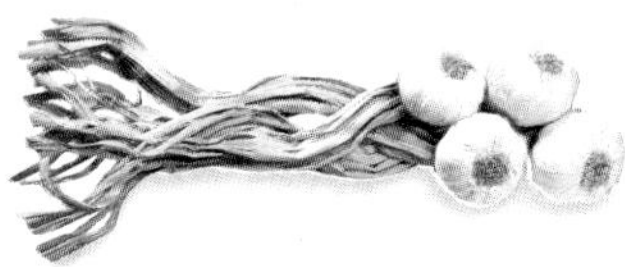

HERB & GARLIC

Put *250 ml (8 fl oz) olive oil, 2 finely chopped garlic cloves, 1 tbsp chopped fresh rosemary, oregano, or thyme,* and *salt and pepper to taste* into a bowl and whisk to mix thoroughly.

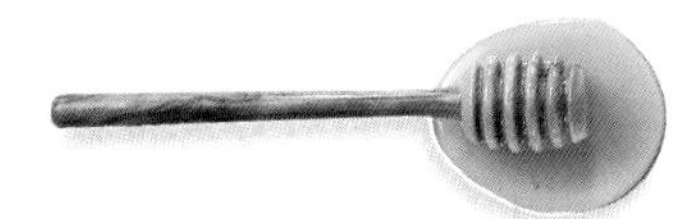

HONEY & MUSTARD

Put *250 ml (8 fl oz) sunflower oil, 2 tbsp soy sauce, 1 tbsp clear honey, 2 tsp Dijon mustard,* and *salt and pepper to taste* into a small bowl and whisk to mix.

FLAVOURED OILS

Flavoured oils are easy to make and add an individual touch. One of these flavoured oils can be used to baste the vegetables during chargrilling instead of the olive oil in the recipe above.

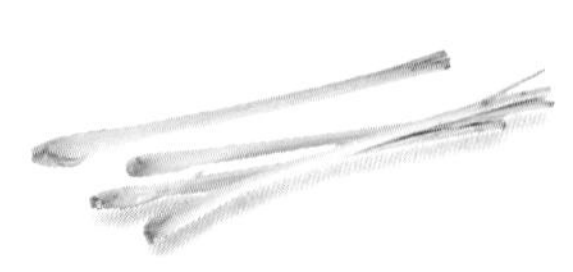

THAI PERFUMED OIL

Lightly bruise *2–3 sprigs coriander* and *3 x 5 cm (2 in) pieces fresh lemon grass.* Put the coriander, lemon grass, and *2 dried chillies* into a clean jar or bottle. Pour in *500 ml (16 fl oz) rapeseed oil or corn oil* and seal the bottle. Leave in a cool, dark place for 2 weeks, remove the coriander and lemon grass, and use to baste as directed.

PAPRIKA OIL

Spoon *2 tbsp paprika* into a clean jar or bottle. Pour in *500 ml (16 fl oz) extra-virgin olive oil* and seal the bottle. Leave in a cool, dark place, shaking the bottle from time to time, for 1 week. Line a funnel with a double layer of muslin and then strain the oil into another bottle. Use the oil to baste as directed.

MIXED HERB OIL

Lightly bruise *1 rosemary sprig* and *1 thyme sprig.* Peel and finely slice *1 pickling onion.* Put the herbs, onion, *1 bay leaf,* and *6 black peppercorns* into a clean jar or bottle. Pour in *500 ml (16 fl oz) extra-virgin olive oil* and seal the bottle. Leave in a cool, dark place for about 2 weeks. Use to baste as directed.

WATERCRESS & ROAST VEGETABLE SALAD

Serves 4–6

2 courgettes, sliced lengthwise
1 tbsp olive oil
2 red peppers
2 yellow peppers
150 g (5 oz) watercress
vinaigrette dressing (page 338)

1 Brush the courgette slices on both sides with the olive oil, and cook under a hot grill, 10 cm (4 ins) from the heat, for 1–2 minutes on each side until golden. Leave to cool.

2 Core, seed, and halve the peppers. Roast and peel the peppers (see box, right). Cut the flesh into chunks. Cut the courgette slices crosswise.

3 Put the watercress into a large serving bowl. Add the peppers and courgettes and mix together. Pour over the vinaigrette dressing and toss to coat. Serve at once.

Roasting and peeling peppers

Cook the pepper halves under a hot grill, 10 cm (4 ins) from the heat, until the skin is black and blistered. Put into a plastic bag, seal, and leave to cool.

Peel away the skin, using a small knife.

AUBERGINE WITH FRESH PESTO

Serves 4

1 large aubergine
salt
75 ml (2 1/2 fl oz) olive oil, plus extra for greasing
2–3 tsp balsamic or wine vinegar
fresh pesto (see box, below)
shredded fresh basil to garnish

1 Cut the aubergine crosswise into thin slices. Put the slices into a colander, sprinkle generously with salt, and leave to stand for about 30 minutes. Rinse and pat dry with paper towels.

2 Lightly grease a baking tray with a little olive oil, and arrange the aubergine slices in a single layer. Brush with one-quarter of the oil, place under a hot grill, 7 cm (3 ins) from the heat, and grill for 5 minutes or until lightly browned. Turn, brush with one-third of the remaining oil, and grill for a further 5 minutes.

3 Sprinkle the remaining oil and the vinegar over the aubergine slices. Leave to cool. Spread pesto over one side of each slice, garnish with fresh basil, and serve at room temperature.

Fresh pesto

Purée *60 g (2 oz) grated Parmesan cheese, 1 garlic clove, 60 g (2 oz) pine nuts, 60 g (2 oz) fresh basil leaves,* and *salt and pepper to taste* in a food processor until almost smooth.

Add *4 tbsp olive oil* gradually, with the blades turning, scraping the side of the bowl occasionally with a rubber spatula to ensure that all of the mixture is incorporated.

MIXED LEAF SALAD

Serves 4–6

1 crisp lettuce, such as iceberg

1 bunch of watercress, tough stalks removed

60 g (2 oz) lamb's lettuce

60 g (2 oz) rocket

about 4 tbsp vinaigrette dressing (page 338)

1 tbsp snipped fresh chives to garnish

1 Tear the lettuce leaves into bite-sized pieces. Put the lettuce into a large salad bowl. Add the watercress, lamb's lettuce, and rocket and mix together.

2 Pour the dressing over the salad and toss gently. Sprinkle with the chives, and serve at once.

Cook's know-how

The important thing to remember about making a mixed leaf salad is not to drown the leaves in the vinaigrette dressing; there should be just enough to cling to the leaves. Adding the dressing just before serving ensures they retain crispness.

RED SALAD BOWL

Serves 4–6

1 small head of radicchio

1 small oak leaf lettuce

1 small lollo rosso lettuce

1 small red onion, thinly sliced

125 g (4 oz) seedless red grapes

DRESSING

150 ml (1/4 pint) olive oil

3 tbsp balsamic vinegar

1 garlic clove, crushed (optional)

1/2 tsp caster sugar

salt and black pepper

1 Tear the radicchio leaves and the oak leaf and lollo rosso lettuce leaves into bite-sized pieces. Put them into a large salad bowl and mix together, then add the onion and grapes.

2 Make the dressing: combine the oil, vinegar, garlic, if using, sugar, and salt and pepper to taste.

3 Pour just enough dressing over the salad to cling to the leaves, toss gently, and serve at once.

CRUNCHY SALAD

Serves 6

175 g (6 oz) bean sprouts

1 iceberg lettuce

6 spring onions, thinly sliced diagonally

1 green pepper, cored, seeded, and thinly sliced

2 tbsp toasted sesame seeds

DRESSING

3 tbsp sunflower oil

1 tbsp white wine vinegar

1 tsp sesame oil

1 garlic clove, crushed

1 cm (1/2 in) piece of fresh root ginger, peeled and grated

1/2 tsp caster sugar

salt and black pepper

1 Soak the bean sprouts in cold water for 10 minutes. Drain. Tear the lettuce leaves into bite-sized pieces. Put the lettuce, bean sprouts, spring onions, and pepper into a salad bowl and mix together.

2 Make the dressing: combine the sunflower oil, vinegar, sesame oil, garlic, ginger, sugar, and salt and pepper to taste.

3 Toss the salad with the dressing, sprinkle with the sesame seeds, and serve.

SPINACH & BACON SALAD

Serves 6

500 g (1 lb) spinach

3 large slices of thick-cut white bread, crusts removed

4 tbsp sunflower oil

1 garlic clove, crushed

12 streaky bacon rashers, rinds removed, cut into strips

4–5 tbsp vinaigrette or blue cheese dressing (page 338)

salt and black pepper

1 Tear the spinach leaves into large pieces and put them into a salad bowl.

2 Make the croûtons: cut the bread into small cubes. Heat the sunflower oil in a frying pan, add the garlic, and cook for 1 minute. Add the bread cubes and cook, stirring, for 1–2 minutes until golden and crisp. Lift out the croûtons and drain on paper towels.

3 Add the bacon to the pan and fry for 5 minutes or until crisp. Lift out and drain on paper towels.

4 Sprinkle the bacon over the spinach leaves. Spoon the dressing over the salad, add salt and pepper to taste, and toss gently. Scatter the croûtons over the salad, and serve at once.

WALDORF SALAD

 **Serves 4**

500 g (1 lb) crisp red-skinned apples, cored and diced
juice of 1/2 lemon
4 celery stalks, thickly sliced
150 ml (1/4 pint) mayonnaise (page 338)
salt and black pepper
90 g (3 oz) walnut pieces, coarsely chopped
chopped parsley to garnish

1 Put the diced apples into a bowl, pour the lemon juice over the top, and stir to coat thoroughly to prevent discoloration. Transfer to a salad bowl and add the celery.

2 Spoon the mayonnaise over the salad, add salt and pepper to taste, and toss gently to mix. Cover and chill until required. Stir in the walnut pieces and garnish with chopped parsley just before serving.

Waldorf salad

This classic salad recipe was created at the turn of the 20th century by Oscar, the maître d'hôtel at the Waldorf-Astoria Hotel in New York.

COLESLAW

Serves 8

1 white cabbage, weighing about 750 g (1 1/2 lb)
150 ml (1/4 pint) vinaigrette dressing (page 338)
1 small onion, finely chopped
1 tsp Dijon mustard
salt and black pepper
3 celery stalks, thinly sliced
2 carrots, grated
60 g (2 oz) sultanas
75–90 ml (2 1/2–3 fl oz) mayonnaise (page 338)

1 Cut the cabbage into quarters lengthwise and cut out the core. Shred the cabbage finely, using either a sharp knife or the slicing blade of a food processor.

2 Put the cabbage into a large bowl, add the vinaigrette dressing, onion, Dijon mustard, and salt and black pepper to taste, and toss to mix thoroughly. Cover the bowl tightly, and leave to chill for about 8 hours.

3 Add the celery, carrots, and sultanas, and toss to mix thoroughly. Stir in the mayonnaise. Cover and leave to chill for 1 hour. Taste the coleslaw for seasoning, and serve.

CAESAR SALAD

Serves 4

1 cos lettuce
4 tbsp olive oil
2 tbsp lemon juice
salt and black pepper
2 hard-boiled eggs
30 g (1 oz) Parmesan cheese, coarsely grated

CROUTONS

3 large slices of thick-cut white bread, crusts removed
4 tbsp olive oil
1 garlic clove, crushed

1 Make the croûtons: cut the bread into small cubes. Heat the olive oil in a frying pan, add the garlic, and cook for 1 minute. Add the bread cubes and cook, stirring, for 1–2 minutes until crisp. Lift out and drain on paper towels.

2 Tear the lettuce leaves into bite-sized pieces and put them into a salad bowl. Add the oil, lemon juice, and seasoning to taste, and toss to coat.

3 Cut the hard-boiled eggs into quarters, and add to the salad. Add the croûtons and Parmesan cheese and toss gently. Serve at once.

Caesar salad

This recipe, said to have been created by restaurateur Caesar Cardini in Tijuana, Mexico in the 1920s, has deservedly become a classic. Only crisp salad leaves, preferably cos lettuce leaves, should be used. Some versions replace the hard-boiled eggs with soft-boiled ones, while others break a raw egg into the salad and toss it in with the dressing.

CAESAR SALAD WITH ANCHOVIES

Coarsely chop 6 anchovy fillets and add to the salad with the hard-boiled eggs. Proceed as directed in the recipe.

POTATO, APPLE, & CELERY SALAD

Serves 6

750 g (1½ lb) new potatoes, scrubbed

salt and black pepper

75 ml (2½ fl oz) vinaigrette dressing (page 338)

6 celery stalks, sliced

1 small red onion, very finely sliced

2 red-skinned apples, such as Red Delicious or Spartan, cored and diced

125 ml (4 fl oz) mayonnaise (page 338)

2 tbsp snipped fresh chives to garnish

1 Put the potatoes into a large saucepan of boiling salted water and simmer gently for 10–15 minutes until just tender. Drain, leave to cool, then cut the potatoes in half.

2 Put the potatoes into a large salad bowl, add the vinaigrette dressing, and toss gently while the potatoes are still warm.

3 Add the celery, onion, and apples to the potatoes. Mix together gently so that all the ingredients are thoroughly coated with the dressing, then add salt and pepper to taste. Cover and chill for at least 1 hour.

4 Gently stir in the mayonnaise, taste for seasoning, then sprinkle with the chives, and serve at once.

POTATO & TOMATO SALAD

Substitute 250 g (8 oz) peeled and chopped tomatoes for the apples and proceed as directed.

FRENCH CELERIAC SALAD

 **Serves 4–6**

500 g (1 lb) celeriac

juice of 1 lemon

1 tsp sliced gherkins and 2 tbsp chopped parsley to garnish

DRESSING

150 ml (¼ pint) plain yogurt

2 tbsp mayonnaise (page 338)

1 tsp finely chopped capers

½ tsp Dijon mustard

salt and black pepper

1 Peel the celeriac, cut into matchstick-thin strips, and place in a bowl of cold water. Add the lemon juice and toss to prevent discoloration.

2 Make the dressing: combine the yogurt, mayonnaise, capers, Dijon mustard, and salt and pepper to taste.

3 Drain the celeriac and transfer to a salad bowl. Pour over the dressing and toss gently to mix. Garnish with the gherkins and chopped parsley, and serve at once.

CARROT JULIENNE SALAD

 **Serves 4–6**

5 carrots

salt and black pepper

DRESSING

1 tbsp olive oil

1 tsp white wine vinegar

1 garlic clove, crushed

1 tsp chopped parsley

lemon twists and snipped fresh chives to garnish

1 Cut the carrots into matchstick-thin strips. Simmer in a saucepan of boiling salted water until just tender. Drain.

2 Make the dressing: combine the oil, white wine vinegar, garlic, parsley, and salt and pepper to taste.

3 Put the carrots into a salad bowl, pour over the dressing, and toss to coat evenly. Leave to cool. Garnish with lemon twists and chives, and serve.

FRENCH POTATO SALAD

 **Serves 4–6**

1 kg (2 lb) new potatoes, scrubbed
salt and black pepper
1 small mild onion, very finely chopped
4 tbsp vinaigrette dressing (page 338)
250 ml (8 fl oz) mayonnaise (page 338)
2 tbsp snipped fresh chives
fresh chives to garnish

1 Put the potatoes into a large saucepan of boiling salted water and simmer for 10–15 minutes until tender. Drain the potatoes thoroughly. Cut them into even-sized pieces.

2 Put the potatoes into a large salad bowl and add the chopped onion.

3 While the potatoes are still quite warm, spoon the vinaigrette dressing over them and then toss to mix thoroughly.

4 Add the mayonnaise and the chives, and mix together gently. Add salt and pepper to taste, cover, and chill for about 30 minutes. Garnish with chives, and serve at once.

MUSHROOM & YOGURT SALAD

 **Serves 6**

3 tbsp sunflower oil
1/2 tsp ground coriander
750 g (1 1/2 lb) button mushrooms
salt and black pepper
4 celery stalks, thinly sliced
shredded fresh basil to garnish

DRESSING

150 ml (1/4 pint) plain yogurt
1 tbsp lemon juice
1 tbsp white wine vinegar
1 tsp Dijon mustard
1 garlic clove, crushed

1 Heat the oil in a frying pan, add the coriander, and cook gently, stirring, for 1 minute. Add the mushrooms, and salt and pepper to taste, and cook over a high heat, stirring, for 5 minutes. Lift out with a slotted spoon, and leave to cool.

2 Make the dressing: combine the yogurt, lemon juice, vinegar, Dijon mustard, garlic, and salt and pepper to taste. Pour the dressing over the mushrooms, and toss to mix. Cover and leave to chill for 8 hours. Stir in the celery, garnish with basil, and serve.

AVOCADO SALAD

 **Serves 6**

60 g (2 oz) pine nuts
250 g (8 oz) mixed salad leaves
2 oranges
2 avocados

DRESSING

finely grated zest of 1 orange
3 tbsp orange juice
1 tbsp walnut oil
1–2 tsp caster sugar
salt and pepper

1 Spread the pine nuts on a baking tray, and cook under a grill for 2 minutes.

2 Put the salad leaves into a large salad bowl. Peel the oranges, removing the rind and pith, and separate into segments (page 430).

3 Halve, stone, and peel the avocados (page 336). Slice lengthwise and mix with the orange segments and pine nuts.

4 Make the dressing: combine the ingredients and pour over the salad. Toss gently and serve.

THREE-COLOUR SALAD

Serves 4

4 beefsteak or slicing tomatoes
salt and black pepper
250 g (8 oz) mozzarella cheese
2 avocados
2 tbsp lemon juice
3–4 tbsp olive oil
basil sprigs to garnish

1 Slice the tomatoes thinly, put into a bowl, and sprinkle with salt and pepper. Cut the mozzarella into thin slices.

2 Cut the avocados in half lengthwise. Twist to loosen the halves and pull them apart. Remove the stones (page 336), score and peel off the skin, then cut the halves in half again.

3 Cut the avocado quarters into slices lengthwise, then sprinkle with lemon juice to prevent discoloration.

4 Arrange the tomato, mozzarella, and avocado slices on a serving platter. Drizzle with the olive oil, garnish with basil sprigs, and serve at once.

CUCUMBER & DILL SALAD

Serves 4–6

1 cucumber, peeled and cut in half lengthwise

1 tbsp chopped fresh dill

DRESSING

2 tbsp hot water

2 tbsp white wine vinegar

1 tbsp sunflower oil

2 tbsp caster sugar

salt and black pepper

1 Scoop out the cucumber seeds. Cut the flesh into thin slices, and arrange in a serving dish.

2 Make the dressing: combine the measured water, vinegar, oil, sugar, and salt and pepper to taste.

3 Pour the dressing over the cucumber, sprinkle with dill, and serve at once.

Cook's know-how

This Danish-style salad makes a particularly good accompaniment to cold fish.

GREEK SALAD

Serves 4–6

4 beefsteak or slicing tomatoes

1 cucumber, sliced

250 g (8 oz) feta cheese, diced

24 pitted black olives

125 ml (4 fl oz) olive oil

4 tbsp lemon juice

salt and black pepper

2 tbsp chopped fresh oregano

1 Cut the tomatoes in half lengthwise, cut out the core, and cut each half into 4 wedges.

2 Put the tomatoes into a large salad bowl, and add the cucumber, feta cheese, and olives.

3 Spoon over the olive oil, lemon juice, and add salt and black pepper to taste (do not use too much salt as feta is a salty cheese), then toss gently to mix.

4 Sprinkle the salad with the oregano, and serve at once.

TOMATO & ONION SALAD

Serves 6

1 mild onion, cut in half lengthwise and thinly sliced

750 g (1½ lb) ripe firm tomatoes, peeled (page 39) and thinly sliced

1 tbsp snipped fresh chives

DRESSING

90 ml (3 fl oz) olive oil

2 tbsp red wine vinegar

¼ tsp caster sugar

salt and black pepper

1 Separate the onion slices into half-rings. Overlap the tomato slices in circles of diminishing size in a large shallow dish. Arrange the onions on top.

2 Make the dressing: combine the olive oil, red wine vinegar, caster sugar, and add salt and pepper to taste.

3 Spoon the dressing over the tomatoes and onions, cover, and leave to chill for about 2 hours. Sprinkle with the snipped chives, and serve at once.

TOMATO & BASIL SALAD

Serves 4–6

2 beefsteak or slicing tomatoes

4 ripe salad tomatoes

125 g (4 oz) cherry tomatoes

1 yellow pepper, cored, seeded, and cut into chunks

2 tbsp shredded fresh basil

DRESSING

3 tbsp olive oil

2 tsp balsamic vinegar

¼ tsp caster sugar

salt and black pepper

1 Make the dressing: combine the olive oil, vinegar, sugar, and salt and pepper to taste.

2 Cut the tomatoes in half lengthwise, cut out the core, and cut each half into 4 wedges. Thickly slice the salad tomatoes. Halve the cherry tomatoes.

3 Put all the tomatoes and the yellow pepper into a salad bowl, and sprinkle with the dressing. Cover and leave to stand for 1 hour to let the flavours mingle. Sprinkle with the basil just before serving.

SALADE NIÇOISE

 **Serves 4**

250 g (8 oz) French beans, cut in half crosswise

salt and black pepper

2 hard-boiled eggs

1 cos lettuce

1/2 cucumber, sliced

4 tomatoes, peeled (page 39) and quartered

1 x 200 g (7 oz) can tuna, drained

1/2 mild onion, very thinly sliced

1 x 50 g (1 3/4 oz) can anchovy fillets, drained

12 pitted black olives

chopped parsley to garnish

DRESSING

150 ml (1/4 pint) olive oil

3 tbsp white wine vinegar

1 garlic clove, crushed

1/2 tsp Dijon mustard

1 Cook the French beans in boiling salted water for 4–5 minutes until just tender. Drain, rinse in cold water, and drain again.

2 Peel the shells from the eggs, and cut the eggs into wedges lengthwise.

3 Make the dressing: combine the oil, vinegar, garlic, mustard, and salt and pepper to taste.

4 Tear the lettuce leaves into pieces and place on a large serving plate. Arrange the cucumber and beans on top of the lettuce.

5 Arrange the tomatoes and eggs on the serving plate. Coarsely flake the tuna with a fork and place in the middle. Arrange the onion, anchovy fillets, and olives over the tuna. Pour over the dressing, garnish with parsley, and serve at once.

Salade niçoise

A great favourite from Nice in the south of France, there are many variations of this recipe, and much debate about which particular ingredients are needed for an authentic Salade niçoise. *New potatoes are included in some versions.*

THREE-BEAN SALAD

 **Serves 4**

250 g (8 oz) French beans, cut in half crosswise

salt and black pepper

1 x 400 g (13 oz) can chick peas, drained and rinsed

1 x 400 g (13 oz) can red kidney beans, drained and rinsed

10 pitted black olives, halved

chopped parsley to garnish

DRESSING

4 tbsp Greek yogurt

3 tbsp olive oil

3 tbsp red wine vinegar

2 tsp Dijon mustard

1/4 tsp caster sugar

1 Cook the French beans in boiling salted water for 4–5 minutes until just tender. Drain, rinse in cold water, and drain again.

2 Make the dressing: combine the Greek yogurt, oil, red wine vinegar, mustard, caster sugar, and salt and pepper to taste.

3 Put the chick peas, red kidney beans, and French beans into a large bowl. Pour the dressing over the beans and stir gently to mix. Cover and leave to stand for 1 hour. Add the olives, sprinkle with chopped parsley, and serve at once.

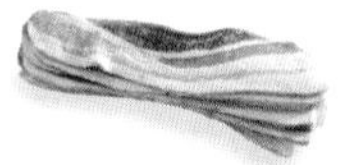

THREE-BEAN SALAD WITH BACON

Substitute 250 g (8 oz) broad beans for the chick peas, and omit the olives. Cut 60 g (2 oz) streaky bacon rashers into strips, and dry-fry until crisp and golden. Sprinkle over the salad just before serving.

TABBOULEH

 **Serves 4**

175 g (6 oz) bulgur wheat

4–5 tbsp vinaigrette dressing (page 338)

juice of 1 lemon

3 tomatoes, peeled (page 39), seeded, and diced

4 spring onions, chopped

3 tbsp chopped parsley

3 tbsp chopped fresh mint

salt and black pepper

parsley sprigs to garnish

1 Put the bulgur wheat into a large bowl, cover with cold water, and leave to stand for 30 minutes.

2 Drain the bulgur wheat, pressing out as much of the liquid as possible. Transfer to a salad bowl, and mix in the vinaigrette dressing, lemon juice, tomatoes, spring onions, parsley, mint, and salt and pepper to taste. Garnish with parsley, and serve at once.

Bulgur wheat

Bulgur wheat is also known as burghul and is available from a variety of good supermarkets and health food stores.

COUSCOUS SALAD

Serves 4–6

1/2 tsp crushed chillies

90 ml (3 fl oz) olive oil

250 g (8 oz) couscous

500 ml (16 fl oz) boiling water

3–4 tbsp sultanas

5 cm (2 in) piece of fresh root ginger, peeled and chopped

pinch of salt

3–4 tbsp raspberry vinegar

5 ripe tomatoes, peeled (page 39), seeded, and diced

1 onion, chopped

3 spring onions, thinly sliced

2 tbsp chopped fresh mint

mint sprigs to garnish

1 Combine the chillies and olive oil, and set aside.

2 Put the couscous into a large saucepan. Stir in the measured water, sultanas, ginger, and salt to taste, and cook over a medium-high heat for 5–10 minutes. Remove from heat, cover, and leave to cool.

3 Stir in the chilli oil, vinegar, tomatoes, onion, spring onions, and mint. Garnish with mint sprigs, and serve at once.

WILD [illegible] SALA[illegible]

Serves 4-

250 g (8 oz) mi[illegible] and wild rice

salt and black [illegible]

175 g (6 oz) [illegible] in half cros[illegible]

2 tbsp chopp[illegible]

60 g (2 oz) button mushroo[illegible], thinly sliced

60 g (2 oz) walnut pieces

DRESSING

4 tbsp sunflower oil

2 tbsp walnut oil

2 tbsp white wine vinegar

1 tsp Dijon mustard

1 Cook the rice in boiling salted water for about 20 minutes, or according to packet instructions, until just tender. Drain, rinse in boiling water, and drain again. Transfer to a bowl.

2 Meanwhile, cook the beans in boiling salted water for 4–5 minutes until just tender. Drain, rinse in cold water, and drain again.

3 Make the dressing: combine the oils, vinegar, mustard, and salt and pepper to taste. Pour over the rice while still warm, stir, and leave to cool.

4 Add the beans, parsley, mushrooms, and walnuts to the rice. Stir well, and serve at once.

diced

2 tbsp chopped fresh coriander

DRESSING

90 ml (3 fl oz) olive oil

3 tbsp white wine vinegar

1 tsp Dijon mustard

1 garlic clove, crushed

1 Cook the rice in boiling salted water for 12–15 minutes until just tender. Drain, rinse in boiling water, and drain again. Transfer to a salad bowl.

2 Make the dressing: combine the olive oil, wine vinegar, mustard, garlic, and salt and pepper to taste. Pour over the rice while still warm, stir gently, and leave to cool.

3 Add the peas, sweetcorn, red pepper, and coriander to the rice, and stir gently to combine. Serve at once.

PASTA & MACKEREL SALAD

 **Serves 4–6**

500 g (1 lb) pasta shells

salt and black pepper

2 courgettes, sliced

125 g (4 oz) French beans, cut in half crosswise

2 oranges

375 g (12 oz) peppered smoked mackerel fillets

30 g (1 oz) walnut pieces

DRESSING

juice of 1 orange

2 tbsp sunflower oil

1 tbsp walnut oil

2 tbsp chopped parsley

1 Cook the pasta shells in a large saucepan of boiling salted water for 8–10 minutes until just tender. Drain, rinse in cold water, and drain again.

2 Meanwhile, cook the courgettes and French beans in another pan of boiling salted water for 4–5 minutes until tender. Drain, rinse in cold water, and drain again.

3 Peel and segment the oranges (page 430) and set aside. Remove the skin and any bones from the mackerel, then flake the flesh into large pieces.

4 Make the dressing: combine the orange juice, sunflower and walnut oils, parsley, and salt and pepper to taste.

5 Put the pasta, courgettes, French beans, orange segments, flaked mackerel, and walnut pieces into a large salad bowl. Add the dressing and toss gently so that the fish does not break up. Leave to chill in the refrigerator for at least 30 minutes before serving.

Cook's know-how

Smoked mackerel is a rich, oily fish that goes well with citrus fruits such as oranges. If you prefer, replace the mackerel with smoked trout, which has a milder flavour.

PASTA SALAD WITH PEPPERS

 **Serves 4–6**

500 g (1 lb) pasta bows

salt and black pepper

1 red pepper, cored, seeded, and diced

1 green pepper, cored, seeded, and diced

3 spring onions, sliced diagonally

4 tbsp mayonnaise (page 338)

spring onion tops, sliced, to garnish

1 Cook the pasta bows in a large saucepan of boiling salted water for 8–10 minutes until just tender.

2 Drain, rinse under cold running water, and drain again. Leave to cool.

3 Put the pasta into a salad bowl, add the peppers and spring onions, and season. Add the mayonnaise, then stir well to coat all of the ingredients evenly. Chill for 30 minutes. Garnish with the spring onion tops, and serve.

PASTA SALAD WITH MANGETOUT & SESAME SEEDS

Substitute 125 g (4 oz) blanched mangetout for the red and green peppers. Omit the mayonnaise. Mix together 2 tbsp white wine vinegar, 3 tsp sunflower oil, 1 tsp sesame oil, and salt and pepper to taste, and pour over the salad. Substitute 2 tbsp toasted sesame seeds for the spring onion tops, and serve at once.

Cook's know-how

If you are concerned about the raw eggs used in the mayonnaise, substitute the yolks from 3 hard-boiled eggs, and combine with 150 ml (1/4 pint) soured cream and 1 tbsp Dijon mustard.

10

YEAST COOKERY

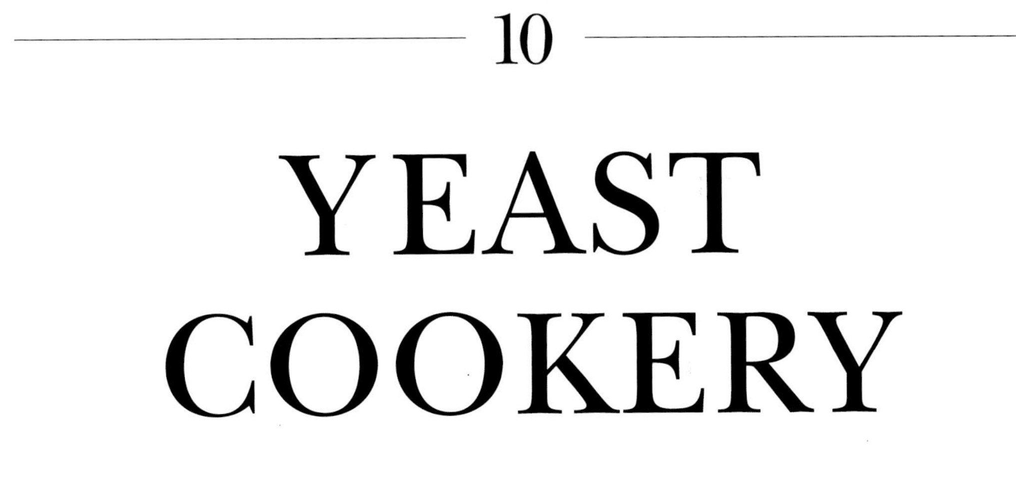

OVER 60 MINUTES

FOCACCIA

Italian classic: flat pizza-like bread flavoured with olive oil and fresh rosemary. Sprinkled with coarse sea salt.

MAKES 1 LOAF 2989 calories per loaf

Takes 35 minutes, plus rising **PAGE 375**

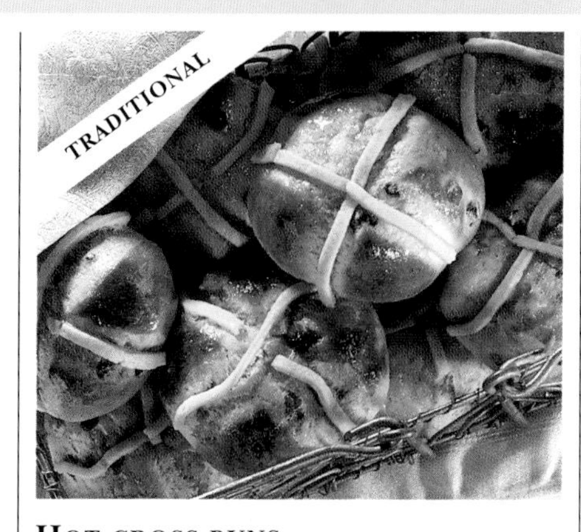

HOT CROSS BUNS

Slightly sweet spiced buns studded with currants and mixed peel, decorated with pastry crosses, and baked until golden.

MAKES 12 279 calories each

Takes 35 minutes, plus rising **PAGE 386**

DINNER ROLLS

A simple dough shaped into rolls and baked until golden. Served warm or cool and spread with butter.

MAKES 18 95 calories each

Takes 40 minutes, plus rising **PAGE 371**

BRIOCHES

Classic and rich: an egg- and butter-enriched dough baked until dark golden brown in characteristic fluted moulds.

MAKES 12 149 calories each

Takes 35 minutes, plus rising **PAGE 380**

WHOLEMEAL CROWN LOAF

Hearty and flavourful: a close-textured loaf made from wholemeal flour, shaped into a crown, and baked until golden.

MAKES 1 LOAF – 2975 calories per loaf

Takes 50 minutes, plus rising **PAGE 372**

CINNAMON ROLLS

Breakfast treat: a plain dough enriched with egg, kneaded with cinnamon and raisins, rolled into spirals, baked, and glazed.

MAKES 16 450 calories each

Takes 60 minutes, plus rising **PAGE 386**

BATH BUNS

Sweetened rich dough with sultanas and mixed peel. Shaped into buns, topped with crushed sugar, and baked until golden.

MAKES 18 196 calories each

Takes 40 minutes, plus rising **PAGE 385**

MILK ROLLS

Attractive rolls in a variety of shapes: knots, twists, and rosettes. Decorated with poppyseeds and sesame seeds, and baked until golden.

MAKES 18 188 calories each

Takes 50 minutes, plus rising **PAGE 371**

CROISSANTS

Classic French breakfast roll: made rich and flaky with butter. Shaped into crescents, glazed, and baked until golden.

MAKES 12 352 calories each

Takes 55 minutes, plus chilling **PAGE 379**

OVER 60 MINUTES

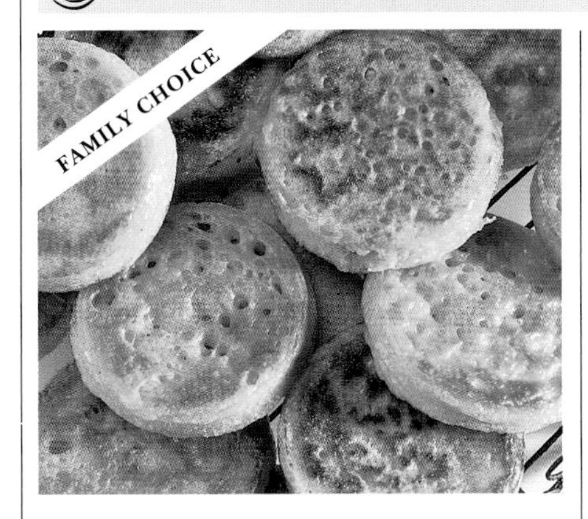

CRUMPETS

Golden and fresh from the griddle: a simple batter cooked until light and tender. Served warm spread with butter.

MAKES 20 73 calories each

Takes 50 minutes, plus rising **PAGE 384**

FLAT DEVON BAPS

Soft-crusted rolls made slightly sweet with the addition of honey. Dusted with flour and baked until golden.

MAKES 16 135 calories each

Takes 45 minutes, plus rising **PAGE 370**

CHEESE & HERB BREAD

Hearty and flavourful: Cheddar and Parmesan cheeses, chopped parsley, and mustard flavour this crisp-crusted bread.

MAKES 1 LOAF 2707 calories per loaf

Takes 55 minutes, plus rising **PAGE 374**

CALZONE

A delicious and aromatic mixture of Mediterranean ingredients wrapped in pizza dough and baked until golden.

MAKES 4 637 calories each

Takes 35 minutes, plus rising **PAGE 378**

SPICY DEEP-PAN PIZZA

Thick, crisp-crusted pizza covered with tomatoes, pepperoni sausage, mozzarella, and Parmesan cheeses. Spiked with green chillies.

MAKES 1 LARGE PIZZA 3596 calories

Takes 35 minutes, plus rising **PAGE 378**

JAM DOUGHNUTS

Old-fashioned favourite: doughnuts filled with raspberry jam, deep-fried, and sprinkled with cinnamon and sugar.

MAKES 16 269 calories each

Takes 40 minutes, plus rising **PAGE 381**

WALNUT BREAD

Hearty and rustic: a coarse-textured loaf studded with chopped walnuts and parsley. Slashed in a criss-cross pattern, dusted with flour, then baked until golden brown. This bread is the classic accompaniment to a traditional ploughman's lunch.

MAKES 2 LOAVES 1657 calories per loaf

Takes 55 minutes, plus rising **PAGE 373**

FARMHOUSE LOAF

TRADITIONAL

Simple to make: white flour loaf dusted with flour and baked until well risen and golden. It has a large and tender crumb.

MAKES 1 LOAF 2790 per loaf

Takes 50 minutes, plus rising **PAGE 370**

OVER 60 MINUTES

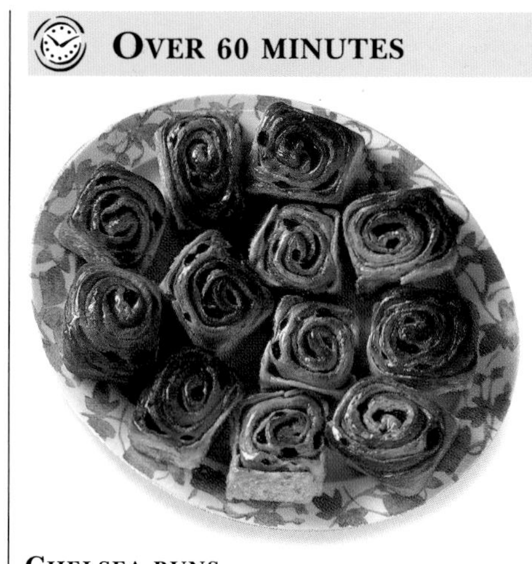

CHELSEA BUNS

A plain dough rolled with a filling of sultanas, currants, orange zest, and mixed spices. Sliced, baked, and glazed with honey.

MAKES 12 298 calories each

Takes 60 minutes, plus rising **PAGE 385**

CHALLAH

Tender and golden: an egg-enriched dough, shaped into a plait, and baked until golden. Excellent toasted or used to make French toast.

MAKES 2 PLAITS 1144 calories per loaf

Takes 60 minutes, plus rising **PAGE 380**

OLIVE & SUN-DRIED TOMATO BREAD

The flavours of Provence: pungent olives and sun-dried tomatoes are kneaded into a dough darkened with buckwheat flour.

MAKES 2 LOAVES 1139 calories per loaf

Takes 60 minutes, plus rising **PAGE 374**

POTATO BREAD

Old-fashioned favourite: mashed potato and butter enrich this simple bread. Makes 2 hearty, coarse-textured loaves.

MAKES 2 LOAVES 1002 calories per loaf

Takes 60 minutes, plus rising **PAGE 373**

SOURDOUGH RYE BREAD

Sourdough starter gives a slightly tangy flavour to this hearty loaf. Studded with caraway seeds.

MAKES 2 LOAVES 3329 calories per loaf

Takes 1 hour 5 minutes, plus rising **PAGE 375**

LARDY CAKE

Traditional English cake made tender and crisp with lard and studded with mixed fruit. Baked until dark golden brown.

MAKES 2 LOAVES 4093 calories per loaf

Takes 1 hour 5 minutes, plus rising **PAGE 381**

WHOLEMEAL ENGLISH MUFFINS

Savoury quick bread: wholemeal flour is used to make these muffins. Cooked on a hot griddle. Served spread with butter and jam.

MAKES 12 158 calories each

Takes 60 minutes, plus rising **PAGE 384**

MULTI-GRAIN LOAF

A nutritious, coarse-textured wholemeal and white flour loaf studded with a combination of wheat flakes, linseed and sunflower seeds. The loaves are lightly brushed with milk, generously sprinkled with wheat flakes, and baked until golden brown.

MAKES 2 LOAVES 1495 calories per loaf

Takes 60 minutes, plus rising **PAGE 372**

YEAST COOKERY KNOW-HOW

THE PLEASURE of baking bread is legendary. From making and kneading the dough to slicing a freshly baked loaf, the experience is a thoroughly satisfying one that cooks the world over have shared for centuries. Indeed, yeast cookery is perhaps the most popular of all kitchen crafts.

From this rich history comes a wide variety of recipes, both sweet and savoury, some of which are easily made while others are more time-consuming to prepare. Crumpets and hot cross buns, Danish pastries and croissants, wholemeal bread and crispy, thin-crusted pizzas are all equally delicious.

Yeast know-how

Yeast is a living organism, activated by warmth and moisture. It converts natural sugars to gases and alcohol, causing dough to rise. Fast-action dried yeast (also known as easy-blend) is used throughout this chapter. If you prefer, an equal quantity of ordinary dried yeast may be substituted, or fresh yeast may be used (see box, below).

FREEZING

Bread tends to dry out if stored in the refrigerator, so if you aren't going to use it quickly it should be frozen. Pack it in moisture-proof wrapping and seal well. Ordinary loaves can be frozen for up to 4 months; if enriched with milk or fruit, storage time is 3 months. Thaw the bread, still wrapped, at room temperature.

Successful home baking

The quantity of liquid given in a recipe can only be a guide because the absorbency of flour can vary. The quantity of liquid flour can absorb depends on temperature and humidity, and how much hard wheat the flour contains (proportions vary from one brand to another). Add a small amount of liquid at first, then gradually add more if needed.

◆

Dough can be kneaded in a food processor or an electric mixer fitted with a dough hook, as well as by hand.

◆

Dough rises quickest in a warm environment. The process slows as the temperature drops.

◆

To test if the dough has risen sufficiently, push in a finger; when withdrawn, an indentation should remain in the dough.

YEAST COOKERY INGREDIENTS

There is a large range of flours to choose from, each one with its own unique texture and flavour. The different types of yeast, on the other hand, vary simply in their method of preparation.

Flour
The best flours to use for yeast doughs are those labelled "strong". These are milled from hard wheat with a high gluten content that produces a good open-textured bread. Ordinary plain flour, which contains a higher proportion of soft wheat, can be used for yeast doughs, but the result will be a much more close-textured and crumbly loaf.

The flour most commonly used for bread-making is white wheat flour. Other wheat flours include wholemeal flour, also called whole wheat, which is milled from the entire wheat kernel, including the bran and germ; brown flour, which contains more of the bran and wheat germ than white flour; and granary flour, which is brown flour with malted wheat flakes added.

Many other grains, such as barley, buckwheat, maize (polenta), millet, oats, and rye may be milled and used to make bread. Soya beans are also ground into a flour-like powder. Many of these grains are low in gluten, so they are normally combined with stronger flours that have a much higher gluten content.

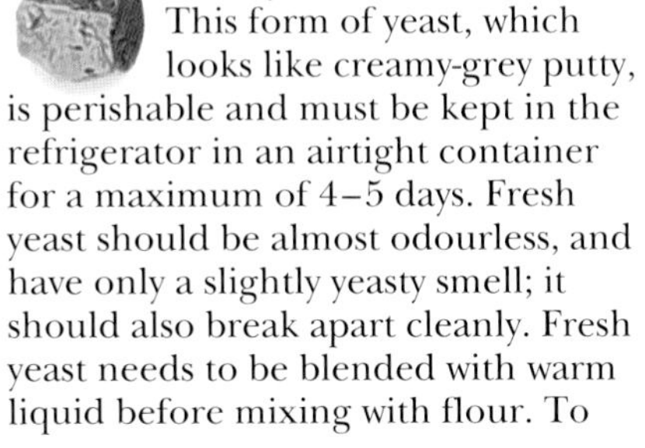

Fresh yeast
This form of yeast, which looks like creamy-grey putty, is perishable and must be kept in the refrigerator in an airtight container for a maximum of 4–5 days. Fresh yeast should be almost odourless, and have only a slightly yeasty smell; it should also break apart cleanly. Fresh yeast needs to be blended with warm liquid before mixing with flour. To substitute fresh yeast for fast-action or for ordinary dried yeast, use double the weight, for example, 15 g (1/2 oz) fresh yeast for 7 g (1/4 oz) dried.

Dried yeast
If stored in a cool place, dried yeast will keep up to 6 months. Fast-action dried yeast (also known as easy-blend) is added directly to flour with other dry ingredients. Ordinary dried yeast, however, needs to be blended with warm liquid and a little sugar before mixing with flour. After about 5 minutes, the yeast should dissolve and the mixture should be foamy. If this is not the result, discard the yeast and start again.

Tepid water (40–43°C/105–110°F) should be used to blend and dissolve fresh and ordinary dried yeast.

MAKING A YEAST DOUGH

Making bread is not difficult, nor does it take up a lot of time – the most lengthy parts of the procedure, the rising and baking, are done by the bread itself.

1 Sift the flour into a large mixing bowl with the yeast and any other dry ingredients. Make a well in the middle and then gradually add the liquid ingredients.

2 Using your fingers, mix the liquid ingredients together, and then gradually incorporate the flour. Mix thoroughly until a soft but not sticky dough is formed.

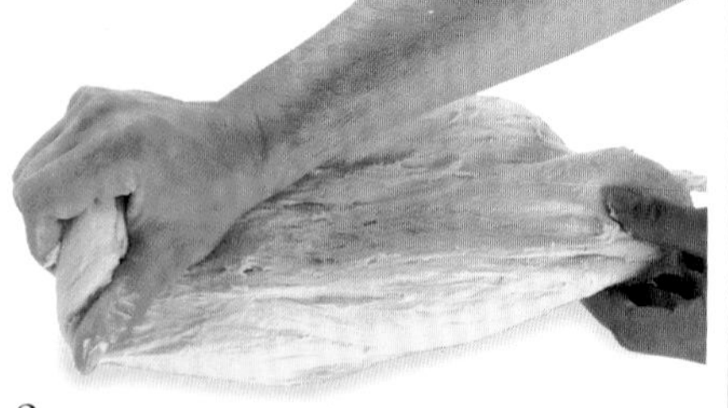

3 Turn the dough on to a floured work surface and knead: fold it over towards you, then push it down and away with the heel of your hand. Turn the dough, fold it, and push it away again. Continue kneading for 5–10 minutes until the dough is elastic and smooth. Doughs made with strong wheat flour take longer to knead than those made with soft wheat flour.

4 Shape the dough into a ball. Put the dough into an oiled bowl and turn to coat. Cover with oiled cling film or a damp tea towel and leave in a warm, draught-free place such as an airing cupboard to rise.

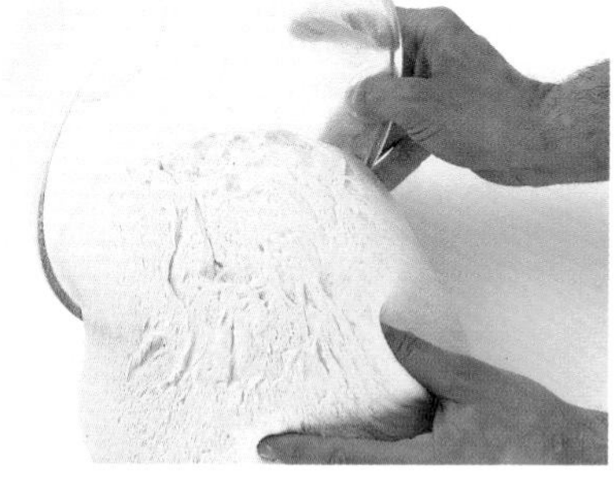

5 When the dough has doubled in size, turn it on to a lightly floured work surface and knock out the air by punching the dough gently. Knead the dough vigorously for 2–3 minutes until smooth and elastic.

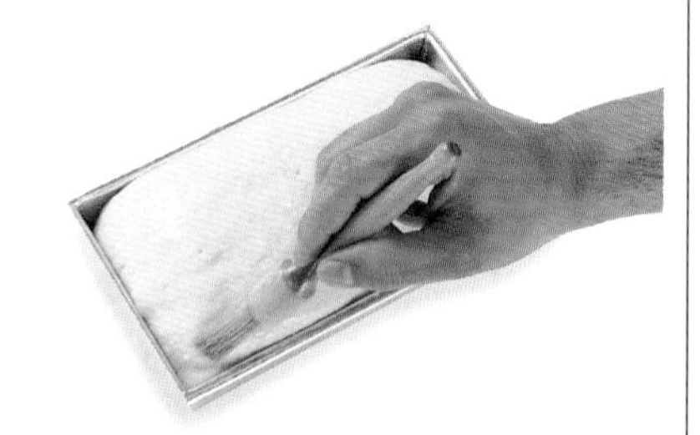

6 Shape the dough as directed. Cover loosely with cling film or a dry tea towel and leave in a warm, draught-free place to rise until doubled in size again. Bake according to recipe.

SHAPING LOAVES

Because of the elastic quality of dough, it can very easily be formed into a variety of different shapes. Here are some of the more traditional shapes.

Cottage loaf
Cut off one-third of the dough. Roll each piece into a ball and put the small ball on top of the large ball. Push a forefinger through the middle to the base.

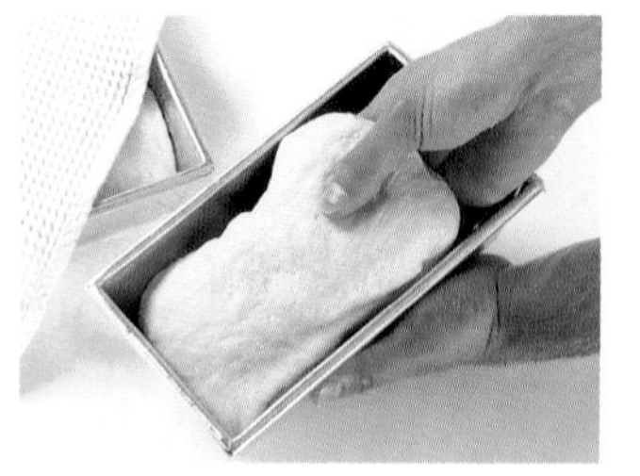

Tin loaf
Shape the dough into a cylinder a little longer than the tin and tuck the ends under to just fit into the tin. Place the dough in the tin, with the joins underneath.

Round loaf
Roll the dough into a ball, then fold the sides of the ball to the middle, to make a tight, round ball. Turn the ball over and put on a baking tray.

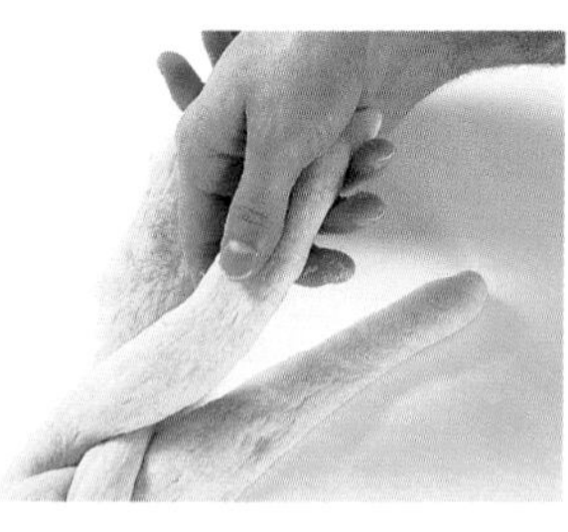

Plaited loaf
Divide and roll the dough into 3 strands. Place side by side and pinch together at one end. Plait the strands, pinching them together at the other end to secure.

GLAZES & TOPPINGS

Breads and rolls can be glazed before or after baking to add flavour and, depending on the glaze, to make the crust soft, or shiny and crisp. Apply the glaze thinly, using a pastry brush. Here are a few suggestions for different glazes:

- water (before baking) for a crisp crust
- milk or cream (before baking) for a soft crust
- egg or egg yolk beaten with a pinch of salt (before baking) for a shiny, crisp crust
- butter (after baking) for a shiny crust
- sugar and water (after baking) for a shiny crust.

Toppings such as wheat or barley flakes, herbs, sunflower or sesame seeds, poppyseeds, grated cheese, chopped nuts, and coarse sea salt can be sprinkled over glazed breads and rolls before baking. Sweetened breads are often sprinkled with sugar or a spice and sugar mixture after cooking.

TESTING LOAVES

At the end of cooking, bread should be well risen, firm, and golden brown. To test if it is thoroughly cooked, tip out of the tin or lift off the baking tray and tap the base. The bread should have a hollow, drum-like sound. If it doesn't sound hollow, return it to the oven for a further 5 minutes, then remove it and test again.

MAKING BUTTER SHAPES

Attractive butter shapes are perfect served with home-baked breads and rolls. They can be prepared in advance, tray frozen, then packed in freezer bags, and thawed when needed. If you like, flavour them with herbs, garlic, or mustard for savoury breads, and spices, honey, or sugar for sweet breads.

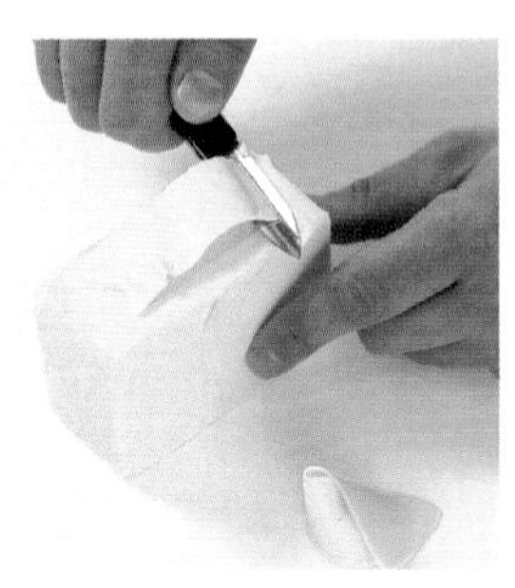

Rose

1 Chill a block of butter in the refrigerator until quite firm. Using a vegetable peeler, shave a strip of butter from the block. Curl the strip, overlapping the ends, to form a cone. Stand the cone on the wide base on a work surface.

2 Using the vegetable peeler, shave off another strip of butter and wrap it about two-thirds of the way around the cone. Carefully press the strip on to the cone at the base, to secure it. Gently shape the butter strip so that it curves outwards at the top.

3 Continue cutting strips from the butter block and wrapping them around the cone as before, overlapping each layer and pinching and curling the edges to imitate rose petals. The finished rose can be kept chilled in the refrigerator or frozen until required.

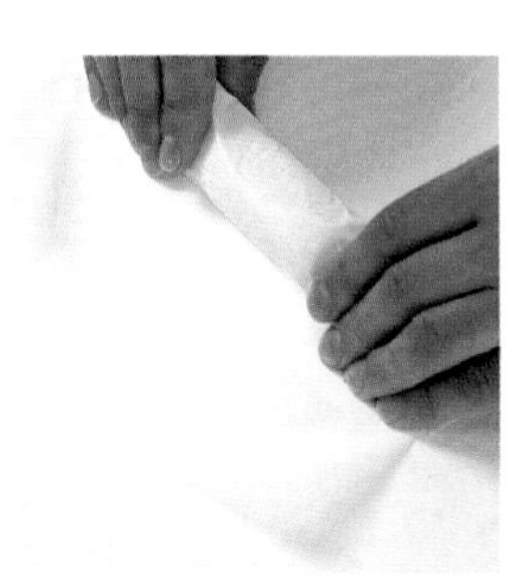

Discs

1 Use butter at room temperature. Beat it with a wooden spoon until it is soft, then beat in any flavourings. Put on to a sheet of greaseproof paper and roll it in the paper until it forms a neat sausage shape.

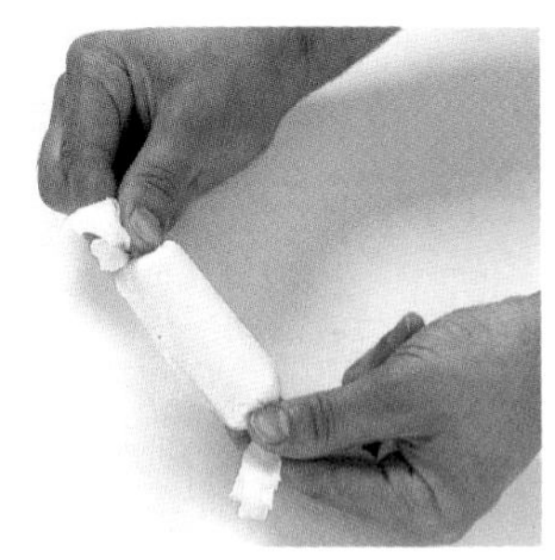

2 Wrap the butter tightly in the greaseproof paper and twist the ends to secure. Chill in the refrigerator until firm. Unwrap and slice the butter crosswise into thin discs. Use immediately, leave to chill, or freeze until required.

Curls

Chill a block of butter. Warm a butter curler in hot water, then dry it. Pull the curler lengthwise along the surface of the block, to shave off curls. Use immediately, or keep the curls in iced water in the refrigerator until required.

FARMHOUSE LOAF

Makes 1 large loaf

750 g (1½ lb) strong white flour, plus extra for dusting

30 g (1 oz) butter or margarine

2 tsp salt

1 x 7 g (¼ oz) sachet fast-action dried yeast

about 450 ml (¾ pint) tepid water

sunflower oil for greasing

☆ 1 kg (2 lb) loaf tin

1 Put the flour into a bowl, rub in the butter with the fingertips until the mixture resembles breadcrumbs, then stir in the salt and yeast. Make a well in the middle and pour in the water. Using a wooden spoon, mix to a soft but not sticky dough.

2 Lightly oil a large bowl. Knead the dough until smooth and elastic. Shape into a round and place in the bowl. Cover with oiled cling film and leave in a warm place to rise for 1–1½ hours until the dough has doubled in size.

3 Turn out the dough on to a lightly floured work surface and knock back with your fists. Knead vigorously for 2–3 minutes until the dough is smooth and elastic.

4 Lightly oil the loaf tin. Shape the dough to fit the tin, tucking the ends underneath to give a smooth top, and place in the tin. Cover loosely with oiled cling film and leave in a warm place to rise for about 30 minutes until the dough reaches the top of the tin.

5 Lightly dust the top of the loaf with flour and bake in a preheated oven at 230°C (450°F, Gas 8) for 30–35 minutes until well risen and golden. Turn the loaf out of the tin and tap the base to see if it is cooked: it should sound hollow. Leave the loaf to cool on a wire rack.

FLAT DEVON BAPS

Makes 16

500 g (1 lb) strong white flour, plus extra for dusting

45 g (1½ oz) butter

1 tsp salt

1 tsp fast-action dried yeast

about 150 ml (¼ pint) tepid water

about 150 ml (¼ pint) tepid milk

1 tsp clear honey

sunflower oil for greasing

1 Put the flour into a large bowl. Add the butter and rub in with the fingertips until the mixture resembles fine breadcrumbs. Stir in the salt and yeast. Make a well in the middle and pour in the water, milk, and honey. Using a wooden spoon, mix to a soft but not sticky dough.

2 Lightly oil a large bowl. Knead the dough until smooth and elastic. Shape into a round and place in the bowl. Cover with oiled cling film and leave in a warm place to rise for 1–1½ hours until the dough has doubled in size.

3 Turn out the dough on to a lightly floured work surface and knock back with your fists. Knead for 2–3 minutes until the dough is smooth and elastic.

4 Lightly oil 2 baking trays. Divide the dough into 16 even-sized pieces. Knead and roll into rounds and place well apart on the baking trays. With the heel of your hand, flatten each round so that it measures 7 cm (3 ins) across.

5 Cover loosely with oiled cling film and leave in a warm place to rise for about 30 minutes until the dough has doubled in size.

6 Lightly dust the baps with flour and bake in a preheated oven at 200°C (400°F, Gas 6) for 15–20 minutes until well risen and golden. Tap the bases to see if they are cooked: they should sound hollow. Leave the baps to cool on a wire rack.

Milk rolls

Makes 18

750 g (1½ lb) strong white flour, plus extra for dusting

60 g (2 oz) butter or white vegetable fat

2 tsp salt

1 x 7 g (¼ oz) sachet fast-action dried yeast

about 450 ml (¾ pint) tepid milk

sunflower oil for greasing

1 egg, beaten

poppyseeds and sesame seeds for sprinkling

1 Put the flour into a large bowl, rub in the butter, then stir in the salt and yeast. Make a well in the middle and pour in the milk. Using a wooden spoon, mix to a soft but not sticky dough.

2 Lightly oil a large bowl. Knead the dough until smooth and elastic. Shape into a round and place in the bowl. Cover with oiled cling film and leave in a warm place for 1–1½ hours until doubled in size.

3 Turn out the dough on to a lightly floured work surface and knock back with your fists. Knead for 2–3 minutes until the dough is smooth and elastic.

4 Divide the dough into 18 even-sized pieces and shape into balls, folding the sides to the middles to form tight round balls, or shape as required (see box, right).

5 Lightly oil 2 or 3 baking trays. Arrange the rolls on the baking trays, leaving enough room between them for the dough to expand, cover loosely with oiled cling film, and leave in a warm place to rise for 15–20 minutes until the dough has doubled in size.

6 Brush the rolls with the beaten egg to glaze and sprinkle with poppyseeds and sesame seeds. Bake in a preheated oven at 230°C (450°F, Gas 8) for about 15 minutes until well risen and golden. Tap the bases to see if the rolls are cooked: they should sound hollow. Leave to cool on a wire rack.

Shaping milk rolls

Form each piece of dough into a long rope and tie into a single knot.

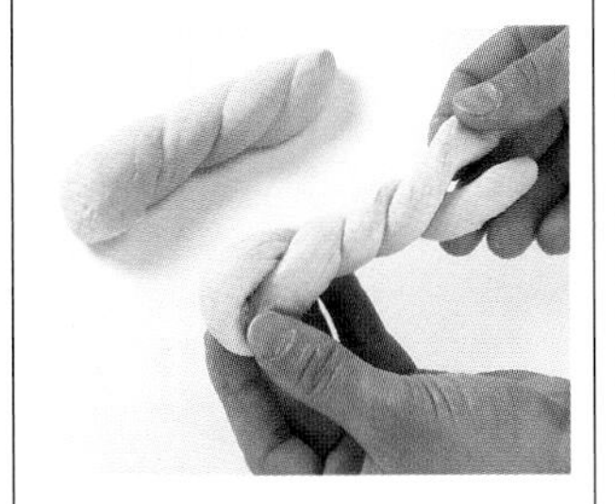

Roll each piece of dough into a thin strand. Fold in half and twist together, sealing the ends well to form a twist.

Shape each piece of dough into a ball or an oval. Snip tops with scissors.

Dinner rolls

Makes 18

500 g (1 lb) strong white flour

1 tsp salt

1 tsp fast-action dried yeast

about 350 ml (12 fl oz) tepid water

sunflower oil for greasing

1 Put the flour into a large bowl, then stir in the salt and yeast. Make a well in the middle and pour in the water. Work to a soft but not sticky dough.

2 Lightly oil a large bowl. Knead the dough until smooth and elastic. Shape into a round and place in the bowl. Cover with oiled cling film and leave in a warm place to rise for 1–1½ hours until doubled in size.

3 Lightly oil 2 or 3 baking trays. Divide the dough into 18 even-sized pieces. Shape into balls, folding the sides to the middles to form round balls. Arrange on the trays, leaving room for the dough to expand, cover loosely with oiled cling film, and leave in a warm place to rise for 20 minutes or until doubled in size.

4 Bake the rolls in a preheated oven at 190°C (375°F, Gas 5) for 20 minutes or until golden. Tap the bases to see if they are cooked: they should sound hollow. Leave to cool.

WHOLEMEAL CROWN LOAF

Makes 1 large loaf

750 g (1½ lb) strong wholemeal flour, plus extra for dusting
30 g (1 oz) butter or margarine
1 tbsp caster sugar
2 tsp salt
1 x 7 g (¼ oz) sachet fast-action dried yeast
about 450 ml (¾ pint) tepid water
sunflower oil for greasing
milk for glazing
cracked wheat for sprinkling
☆ 20 cm (8 in) round cake tin

1 Put the flour into a large bowl. Rub in the butter with the fingertips, then stir in the sugar, salt, and yeast, and mix thoroughly. Make a well in the middle of the ingredients and pour in the water. Using a wooden spoon, mix to a soft but not sticky dough.

2 Lightly oil a large bowl. Knead the dough until smooth and elastic and shape into a round. Place the dough in the bowl, cover with oiled cling film, and leave in a warm place to rise for 1–1½ hours until the dough has doubled in size.

3 Turn out the dough on to a lightly floured work surface and knock back with your fists. Knead for 2–3 minutes until smooth.

4 Oil the cake tin. Shape the loaf (see box, below). Cover loosely with oiled cling film and leave in a warm place to rise for 1–1½ hours until doubled in size.

5 Brush the loaf with milk to glaze and sprinkle with cracked wheat. Bake in a preheated oven at 230°C (450°F, Gas 8) for 20–25 minutes until well risen. Tap the base to see if the loaf is cooked: it should sound hollow. Leave to cool on a wire rack.

Shaping a crown loaf

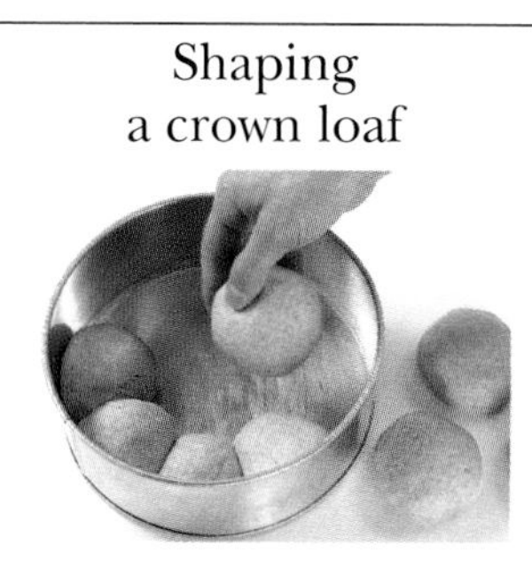

Divide the dough into 8 even-sized pieces, shape into rounds, and place in the cake tin to form a crown. The rounds will rise to fill the tin.

MULTI-GRAIN LOAF

Makes 2 small loaves

150 g (5 oz) wheat flakes
45 g (1½ oz) linseed
300 ml (½ pint) boiling water
500 g (1 lb) strong white flour, plus extra for dusting
125 g (4 oz) strong wholemeal flour
60 g (2 oz) sunflower seeds
20 g (¾ oz) salt
1 x 7 g (¼ oz) sachet fast-action dried yeast
about 350 ml (12 fl oz) tepid water
sunflower oil for greasing
milk for glazing
wheat flakes to decorate
☆ 2 x 500 g (1 lb) loaf tins

1 Put the wheat flakes and linseed into a large bowl, pour the boiling water over, and stir. Cover and set aside for 30 minutes or until the water has been absorbed.

2 Stir the flours, sunflower seeds, salt, and yeast into the wheat-flake mixture. Make a well in the middle of the ingredients and pour in the tepid water. Using a wooden spoon, mix to a soft but not sticky dough.

3 Lightly oil a large bowl. Knead the dough until smooth and elastic. Shape into a round and place in the bowl. Cover with oiled cling film and leave in a warm place for 1–1½ hours until doubled in size.

4 Turn out the dough on to a floured work surface and knock back with your fists. Knead for 2–3 minutes until smooth and elastic once again.

5 Oil the tins. Divide the dough in half, and shape into oblongs, tucking the ends underneath to give smooth tops. Place in the tins. Alternatively, shape into 2 rounds and place on oiled baking trays. Cover loosely with oiled cling film and leave in a warm place to rise for 20–30 minutes.

6 Brush the loaves with milk to glaze and sprinkle with wheat flakes. Bake in a preheated oven at 230°C (450°F, Gas 8) for 10 minutes; reduce the oven temperature to 200°C (400°F, Gas 6), and bake for 20–25 minutes. Tap the bases to see if the loaves are cooked: they should sound hollow. Leave to cool.

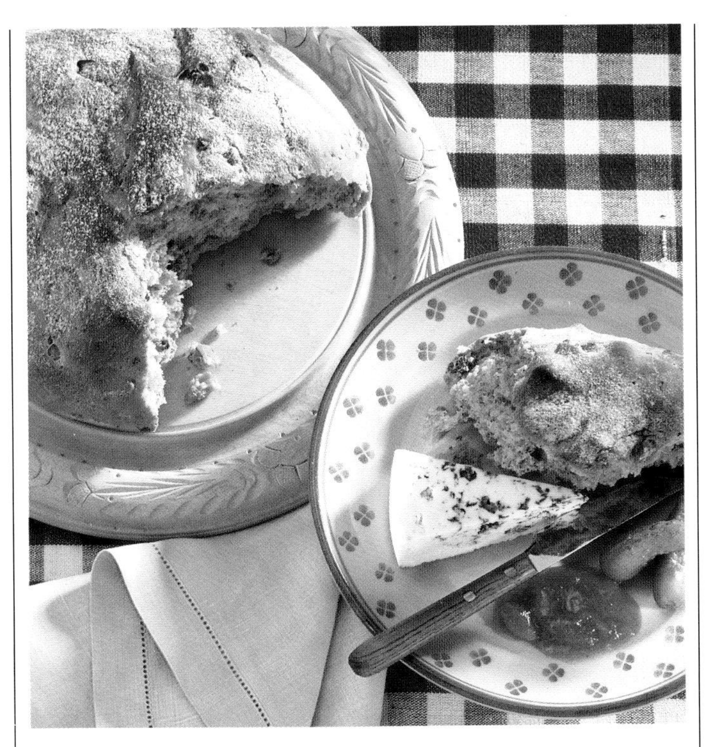

WALNUT BREAD

Makes 2 small loaves

- *650 g (1 lb 5 oz) strong white flour, plus extra for dusting*
- *2 tsp salt*
- *30 g (1 oz) butter or margarine*
- *125 g (4 oz) walnut pieces, coarsely chopped*
- *2 tbsp chopped parsley*
- *1 x 7 g (1/4 oz) sachet fast-action dried yeast*
- *about 400 ml (14 fl oz) tepid water*
- *sunflower oil for greasing*

1 Put the flour and salt into a large bowl. Rub in the butter, then stir in the walnuts, parsley, and yeast. Make a well in the middle of the ingredients. Pour in the tepid water, and mix to a soft but not sticky dough.

2 Lightly oil a large bowl. Knead the dough until smooth and elastic, then shape into a round. Place the dough in the bowl, cover loosely with oiled cling film, and leave in a warm place to rise for 1–1 1/2 hours until doubled in size.

3 Lightly oil 2 baking trays. Knock back the dough with your fists, then knead for 2–3 minutes until smooth and elastic.

4 Divide the dough in half, shape each half into a round, and then place on a baking tray.

5 Cover the rounds loosely with oiled cling film, and leave in a warm place to rise for 20–30 minutes.

6 Dust each loaf with flour, slash the tops in a criss-cross pattern, and bake in a preheated oven at 220°C (425°F, Gas 7) for about 10 minutes; reduce the oven temperature to 190°C (375°F, Gas 5), and bake for 20 minutes or until the bread is well risen and golden brown.

7 Tap the bases to see if the loaves are cooked: they should sound hollow. Leave to cool on a wire rack.

POTATO BREAD

Makes 2 small loaves

- *500 g (1 lb) strong white flour, plus extra for dusting*
- *1 tsp salt*
- *15 g (1/2 oz) butter*
- *1 tsp fast-action dried yeast*
- *250 g (8 oz) cold mashed potato*
- *about 250 ml (8 fl oz) tepid water*
- *sunflower oil for greasing*
- ⋆ *2 x 500 g (1 lb) loaf tins*

1 Put the flour and salt into a large bowl, rub in the butter, then stir in the yeast. Add the potato, rubbing it loosely into the flour.

2 Make a well in the middle of the ingredients and pour in the tepid water. Using a wooden spoon, mix to form a soft dough.

3 Lightly oil a large bowl. Knead the dough until smooth and elastic, then shape into a round. Place in the bowl, cover with oiled cling film, and leave in a warm place to rise for 1 hour or until doubled in size.

4 Turn out the dough on to a lightly floured work surface and knock back with your fists. Knead until smooth and elastic.

5 Lightly oil the loaf tins. Divide the dough into 2, and shape to fit the tins, tucking the ends underneath. Place in the tins. Cover loosely with oiled cling film and leave in a warm place to rise for 30 minutes or until the dough reaches the tops of the tins.

6 Bake in a preheated oven at 230°C (450°F, Gas 8) for 10 minutes; reduce the oven temperature to 200°C (400°F, Gas 6), and bake for 20–25 minutes until well risen and golden. Tap the bases of the loaves to see if they are cooked: they should sound hollow. Leave to cool on a wire rack.

Cook's know-how

This recipe is ideal for using up leftover mashed potato. If you use freshly cooked and mashed potatoes, make sure that they are completely cold before use.

CHEESE & HERB BREAD

Makes 1 medium loaf

- *500 g (1 lb) strong white flour, plus extra for dusting*
- *90 g (3 oz) mature Cheddar cheese, grated*
- *30 g (1 oz) Parmesan cheese, grated*
- *2 tsp mustard powder*
- *2 tbsp chopped parsley*
- *1½ tsp salt*
- *1 x 7 g (¼ oz) sachet fast-action dried yeast*
- *about 350 ml (12 fl oz) tepid milk*
- *sunflower oil for greasing*
- *beaten egg for glazing*
- *2 tbsp grated Cheddar cheese for sprinkling*

1 Put the flour into a large bowl and stir in the cheeses, mustard powder, parsley, salt, and yeast, mixing thoroughly. Make a well in the middle and pour in the tepid milk. Mix to a soft but not sticky dough.

2 Lightly oil a large bowl. Knead the dough until smooth and elastic, then shape into a round.

3 Place the dough in the bowl, cover with oiled cling film, and leave in a warm place to rise for 1–1½ hours until doubled in size.

4 Turn out the dough on to a floured surface and knock back with your fists. Knead for 2–3 minutes until smooth and elastic.

5 Lightly flour a baking tray. Shape the dough into a 15 cm (6 in) round and place on the baking tray. Cover loosely with oiled cling film and leave in a warm place to rise for 20–30 minutes.

6 Brush with the egg to glaze, cut a shallow cross in the top, and sprinkle with the grated Cheddar cheese. Bake in a preheated oven at 230°C (450°F, Gas 8) for 10 minutes; reduce the oven temperature to 200°C (400°F, Gas 6), and bake for 20 minutes or until well risen.

7 Cover with foil halfway through baking if the bread is browning too much. Leave to cool on a wire rack.

OLIVE & SUN-DRIED TOMATO BREAD

Makes 2 small loaves

- *400 g (13 oz) strong white flour*
- *60 g (2 oz) buckwheat flour*
- *1 tsp salt*
- *1 x 7 g (¼ oz) sachet fast-action dried yeast*
- *black pepper*
- *about 300 ml (½ pint) tepid water*
- *1 tbsp olive oil, plus extra for greasing*
- *125 g (4 oz) pitted black olives, coarsely chopped*
- *125 g (4 oz) sun-dried tomatoes in oil, drained and chopped*
- *1 tbsp chopped parsley*
- *1 tbsp chopped fresh basil*
- *1 tbsp coarse sea salt*

1 Put the flours into a large bowl. Stir in the salt and yeast and season with black pepper. Make a well in the middle. Pour in the water and oil and mix to a soft but not sticky dough.

2 Lightly oil a large bowl. Knead until smooth and elastic, then shape into a round. Place the dough in the bowl, cover with oiled cling film, and leave in a warm place to rise for 1–1½ hours until doubled in size.

3 Lightly oil a baking tray. Knock back the dough, then knead for 2–3 minutes. Divide the dough into 2 pieces. Roll out each piece to a 23 x 25 cm (9 x 10 in) rectangle. Spread one of the rectangles with the olives and the other with the sun-dried tomatoes, parsley, and basil.

4 Roll up each rectangle of dough from 1 long end and place, seam-side down, on the tray. Make 4–5 diagonal slashes on the top of each loaf, cover loosely with oiled cling film, and leave in a warm place to rise for 20–30 minutes.

5 Brush the top of each loaf with water and lightly sprinkle with sea salt. Bake in a preheated oven at 230°C (450°F, Gas 8) for 15 minutes; reduce the oven temperature to 190°C (375°F, Gas 5), and bake for a further 15 minutes or until well risen and golden.

6 Tap the bases to see if the loaves are cooked: they should sound hollow. Leave to cool on a wire rack.

SOURDOUGH RYE BREAD

A satisfying and tasty country bread from Eastern Europe, this rye bread is not difficult to make but, because the starter has to be left to ferment for a couple of days, it does require a little forward planning.

Makes 2 large loaves

1.5 kg (3 lb) strong white flour, plus extra for sprinkling
1 x 7 g (1/4 oz) sachet fast-action dried yeast
250 ml (8 fl oz) tepid water
3 tbsp caraway seeds (optional)
1 tbsp salt
sunflower oil for greasing
polenta for sprinkling

SOURDOUGH STARTER
250 g (8 oz) strong white flour
1 tsp fast-action dried yeast
250 ml (8 fl oz) tepid water

SPONGE
200 g (7 oz) rye flour
250 ml (8 fl oz) tepid water

1 Make the sourdough starter: put the flour into a large bowl and stir in the yeast. Make a well in the middle, pour in the tepid water, and mix together.

2 Cover tightly and leave at room temperature for 2 days. Alternatively, leave the starter in the refrigerator for up to 1 week.

3 Make the sponge: put the rye flour into a large bowl, add the sourdough starter and the water, and stir to mix. Cover tightly and leave at room temperature for 8 hours or chill in the refrigerator for up to 2 days.

4 Put the flour into a bowl, add the sponge mixture, yeast, measured water, caraway seeds, if using, and salt, and mix to a soft and slightly sticky dough.

5 Turn the dough into a large ungreased bowl, sprinkle the top with flour, cover loosely with oiled cling film, and leave in a warm place to rise for about 2 hours until doubled in size.

6 Lightly sprinkle 2 baking trays with polenta. Turn out the dough on to a lightly floured work surface and knock back with your fists. Knead for 3–4 minutes until smooth and elastic. Halve the dough and form each half into a round. Score the tops with a sharp knife.

7 Place on the baking trays, cover loosely with oiled cling film, and leave in a warm place for 45 minutes or until doubled in size.

8 Place the loaves in a preheated oven at 220°C (425°F, Gas 7). Fill a roasting tin with boiling water and place at the bottom of the oven. Bake the loaves for about 35 minutes until they are lightly browned. Tap the bases to see if the loaves are cooked: they should sound hollow. Leave to cool on wire racks.

FOCACCIA

Makes 1 large loaf

750 g (1 1/2 lb) strong white flour, plus extra for dusting
1 x 7 g (1/4 oz) sachet fast-action dried yeast
3–4 tbsp chopped fresh rosemary
3 tbsp olive oil, plus extra for greasing
250 ml (8 fl oz) tepid water
2 tsp coarse sea salt

1 Put the flour into a bowl, and add the yeast and rosemary. Make a well in the middle, add the oil and the water, and work to a soft but not sticky dough. Lightly oil a large bowl. Knead the dough until smooth and elastic, then shape into a round.

2 Place the dough in the bowl, cover loosely with oiled cling film, and leave in a warm place to rise for about 1 hour until the dough has doubled in size.

3 Turn out the dough on to a lightly floured work surface and knock back with your fists. Knead for 2–3 minutes until smooth. Roll out the dough to form a round 5 cm (2 ins) thick. Cover loosely with oiled cling film and leave in a warm place to rise for 1 hour or until doubled in size.

4 Brush with olive oil and sprinkle with sea salt. Bake in a preheated oven at 190°C (375°F, Gas 5) for 20 minutes or until golden.

THIN-CRUST PIZZAS

Tomatoes, cheese, herbs, and olive oil are just a few characteristic pizza toppings, but there are endless combinations. Pizza bases can be bought ready-made, but if you follow the steps illustrated below it is easy to make them at home.

TUNA & CAPER

 **Makes 1 large pizza**

- *90 ml (3 fl oz) passata*
- *1 pizza base (see box, below)*
- *1 x 200 g (7 oz) can tuna in brine, drained*
- *2 tbsp capers*
- *125 g (4 oz) mozzarella cheese, chopped*
- *1 tsp dried oregano*
- *2 tbsp olive oil*

Spread the passata over the pizza base. Top with the remaining ingredients.

NAPOLETANA

Makes 1 large pizza

- *90 ml (3 fl oz) passata*
- *1 pizza base (see box, below)*
- *1 x 60 g (2 oz) can anchovy fillets, drained*
- *125 g (4 oz) mozzarella cheese, chopped*
- *2 tbsp olive oil*

Spread passata over the pizza base. Halve the anchovies and arrange on top with the remaining ingredients.

FOUR SEASONS

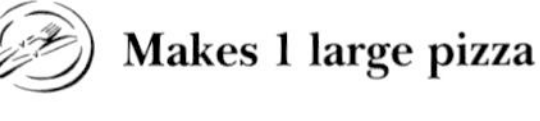 **Makes 1 large pizza**

- *90 ml (3 fl oz) passata*
- *1 pizza base (see box, below)*
- *salt and black pepper*
- *60 g (2 oz) salami*
- *1/2 tsp dried oregano*
- *45 g (1 1/2 oz) mushrooms, sliced*
- *30 g (1 oz) mozzarella cheese, chopped*
- *30 g (1 oz) anchovy fillets, drained*
- *12 pitted black olives*
- *1/2 red and 1/2 green pepper, thinly sliced*
- *1 tbsp shredded fresh basil*
- *2 tbsp olive oil*

1 Spread the passata over the pizza base and season with salt and pepper to taste.

2 Arrange the salami and oregano on 1 quarter, the sliced mushrooms and mozzarella on a second quarter, the anchovies and black olives on a third, and the red and green peppers and basil on the final quarter. Lightly sprinkle with olive oil.

MINI PIZZAS

 **Makes 12**

- *90 ml (3 fl oz) passata*
- *1 quantity pizza dough (see box, below), shaped into 12 x 7 cm (3 in) rounds*
- *salt and black pepper*
- *2 tbsp olive oil*

SUN-DRIED TOMATO TOPPING

- *8 sun-dried tomatoes, diced*
- *15 g (1/2 oz) pitted black olives, diced*
- *2 garlic cloves, chopped*
- *1 tbsp shredded fresh basil*
- *45 g (1 1/2 oz) goat's cheese, diced*

PARMA HAM TOPPING

- *15 g (1/2 oz) Parma ham, diced*
- *90 g (3 oz) artichoke hearts in oil, drained and quartered*
- *60 g (2 oz) Parmesan cheese, grated*

Spread passata over the rounds and season. Top half with the sun-dried tomatoes, olives, garlic, basil, and goat's cheese, and half with the Parma ham, artichokes, and cheese. Sprinkle with oil.

Clockwise from top: *Napoletana Pizza, Mini Pizzas, Tuna & Caper Pizza, Four Seasons Pizza*

Making the thin-crust pizza base

1 Sift *250 g (8 oz) strong white flour* on to a work surface and add *1/2 tsp fast-action dried yeast* and *1/2 tsp salt.* Make a well in the middle and add about *175 ml (6 fl oz) tepid water* and *1 tbsp olive oil.* Draw in the flour with your fingertips or a pastry scraper and work to form a smooth dough.

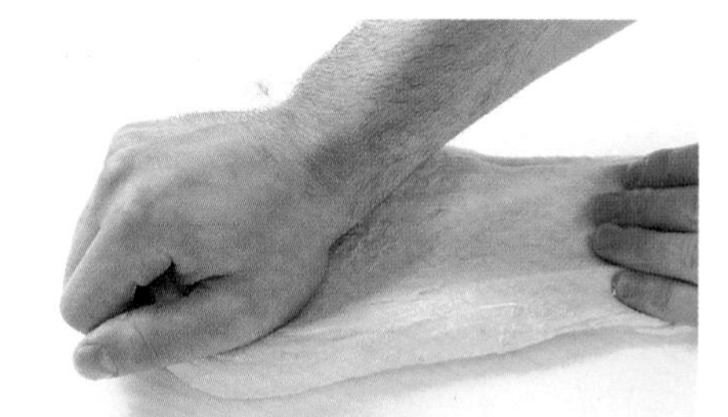

2 Lightly oil a large bowl. Knead the dough for 10 minutes until smooth. Shape into a round and put in the bowl. Cover loosely with oiled cling film and leave in a warm place to rise for 1 hour or until doubled in size. Turn out of the bowl and knead for 2–3 minutes until smooth.

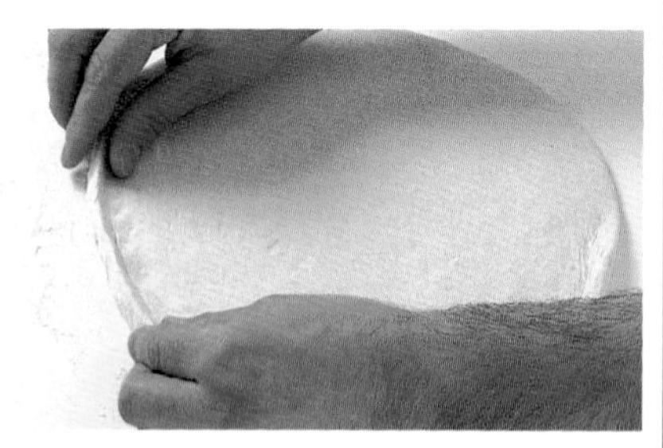

3 Roll and stretch the dough until it forms a round 1 cm (1/2 in) thick and 35 cm (14 ins) in diameter. Press around the edge to form a rim. Put on a baking tray, add topping, and bake in a preheated oven at 220°C (425°F, Gas 7) for 20–30 minutes. Bake mini pizzas for 12–15 minutes.

CALZONE

Makes 4

125 g (4 oz) ricotta cheese
8 oz (250 g) tomatoes, peeled (page 39), seeded, and chopped
60 g (2 oz) mozzarella cheese, chopped
2 garlic cloves, chopped
30 g (1 oz) pitted black olives, chopped
60 g (2 oz) mushrooms, sliced
1 green pepper, cored, seeded, and sliced
1/2 tsp dried oregano
salt and black pepper
beaten egg for glazing

DOUGH

1 x 7 g (1/4 oz) sachet fast-action dried yeast
1/2 tsp caster sugar
500 g (1 lb) strong white flour
1/2 tsp salt
2 tbsp olive oil, plus extra for greasing
about 275 ml (9 fl oz) tepid water

1 Mix the dough ingredients to a soft but not sticky dough. Lightly oil a large bowl. Knead the dough for 5–10 minutes until smooth.

2 Shape into a round and place in the bowl. Cover with oiled cling film and leave in a warm place to rise until doubled in size.

3 Knock back the dough on a floured work surface, and shape into four 20 cm (8 in) rounds. Combine the ricotta, tomatoes, mozzarella, garlic, olives, mushrooms, green pepper, and oregano, and season. Fill the calzone (see box, below).

4 Put on an oiled baking tray and bake in a preheated oven at 240°C (475°F, Gas 9) for 15 minutes.

Filling the calzone

Put one-quarter of the ricotta mixture on to half of each dough round.

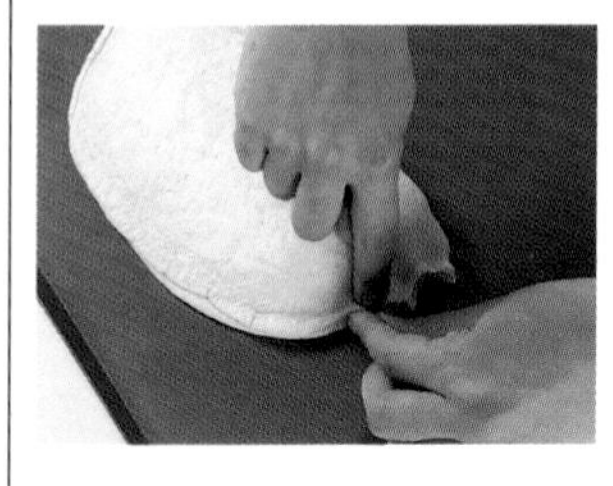

Brush the edge of the dough with beaten egg and fold over to enclose the filling. Seal the edges and brush the top with egg.

SPICY DEEP-PAN PIZZA

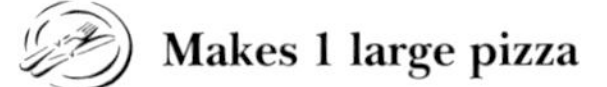

Makes 1 large pizza

125 g (4 oz) tomato purée
1 x 400 g (13 oz) can chopped tomatoes, drained
60 g (2 oz) pepperoni sausage, sliced
300 g (10 oz) mozzarella cheese, grated
60 g (2 oz) Parmesan cheese, grated
2 tbsp sliced pickled green chillies

DOUGH

1 x 7 g (1/4 oz) sachet fast-action dried yeast
1/2 tsp caster sugar
500 g (1 lb) strong white flour
1/2 tsp salt
2 tbsp olive oil, plus extra for greasing
about 150 ml (1/4 pint) tepid water
⋆ *deep dish 35 cm (14 in) round pizza pan*

1 Make the dough: mix the yeast, sugar, flour, and salt in a bowl. Add the oil and water and mix to a soft dough. Knead for 5–10 minutes until smooth and elastic.

2 Put into an oiled bowl, turn to coat with the oil, cover with oiled cling film and leave in a warm place to rise for 1 hour or until doubled in size.

3 Lightly oil the pizza pan. Knock back the dough on a floured work surface, roll out, and shape into a 35 cm (14 in) round. Put into the pan and shape the edge to form a rim.

4 Spread the tomato pureé over the base. Top with the tomatoes and pepperoni. Sprinkle over the mozzarella, Parmesan, and green chillies.

5 Bake in a preheated oven at 240°C (475°F, Gas 9) for 10–15 minutes until the crust is golden and the cheese topping melted. Serve hot.

Pickled green chillies

Jalapeño *are a variety of chilli often sold pickled in fruit vinegars and a variety of herbs and spices.*

CROISSANTS

Croissant is the French word for crescent, the traditional shape for this classic breakfast roll. Quite delicious on their own, croissants are also good served warm with butter and jam, or marmalade. They can also have savoury fillings, such as ham and cheese.

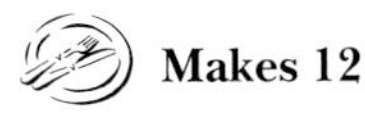

Makes 12

500 g (1 lb) strong white flour

1/2 tsp salt

300 g (10 oz) butter, at room temperature

1 tsp fast-action dried yeast

30 g (1 oz) caster sugar

about 150 ml (1/4 pint) tepid milk

about 150 ml (1/4 pint) tepid water

sunflower oil for greasing

beaten egg for glazing

1 Put the flour and salt into a large bowl, add 60 g (2 oz) of the butter, and rub in with your fingertips until the mixture resembles fine breadcrumbs. Stir in the yeast and sugar.

2 Make a well in the middle of the dry ingredients and add the milk and water all at once. Mix together with a wooden spoon until smooth. Cover the bowl with oiled cling film and chill the dough for 2 hours.

3 Meanwhile, on a sheet of baking parchment, spread out the remaining butter into a 12 x 20 cm (5 x 8 in) rectangle. Cover with another sheet of baking parchment and leave to chill.

4 Roll out the dough on to a floured work surface into an 18 x 35 cm (7 x 14 in) rectangle, and place the chilled butter on top so that it covers the top two-thirds of the rectangle.

5 Fold the bottom third of the dough over the middle third, and fold the top third, with the butter, over the top to form a neat parcel. Seal the edges with the edge of your hand. Wrap and chill for 30 minutes.

6 Roll out the dough parcel into an 18 x 35 cm (7 x 14 in) rectangle, fold into 3 as before, and seal the edges of the parcels.

7 Wrap and chill for a few hours until firm enough to roll and shape.

8 Shape the croissants (see box, right). Place on 2 baking trays and leave for about 30 minutes until almost doubled in size.

9 Lightly brush the croissants with the beaten egg and bake in a preheated oven at 220°C (425°F, Gas 7) for 12–15 minutes until crisp and golden brown. Leave to cool slightly before serving.

CHOCOLATE CROISSANTS

Make the dough as directed. Before rolling the triangles into sausage shapes, sprinkle them with 90 g (3 oz) plain chocolate chips. Roll the triangles, and proceed as directed.

Shaping the croissants

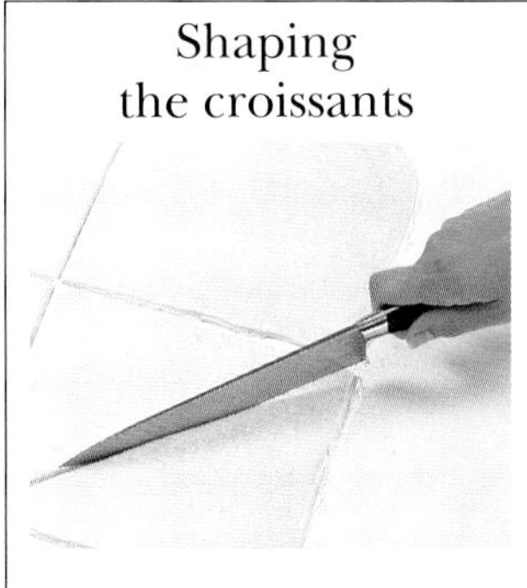

Roll out the dough into a 35 x 53 cm (14 x 21 in) rectangle, and cut into 12 triangles.

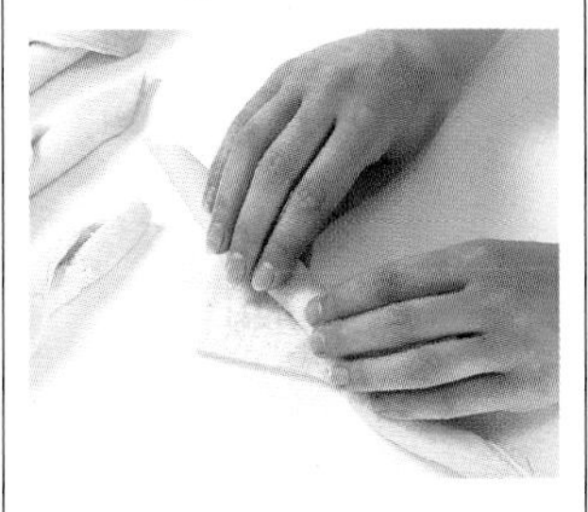

Roll each triangle into a sausage shape, starting from the long side and ending with the point of the triangle.

Bend the ends of each croissant to give the traditional shape.

CHALLAH

Makes 2 small loaves

500 g (1 lb) strong white flour, plus extra for dusting
1 tbsp caster sugar
2 tsp salt
1 x 7 g (1/4 oz) sachet fast-action dried yeast
about 250 ml (8 fl oz) tepid water
2 eggs, beaten
2 tbsp sunflower oil, plus extra for greasing
beaten egg for glazing
poppyseeds for sprinkling

1 Put the flour, sugar, and salt into a bowl. Stir in the yeast. Make a well in the middle. Combine the water, eggs, and oil, and pour into the well. Mix to a soft but not sticky dough.

2 Lightly oil a large bowl. Knead the dough until firm and elastic. Shape into a round and place in the bowl. Cover with oiled cling film and leave in a warm place to rise for 1–1 1/2 hours until doubled in size.

3 Turn out the dough on to a lightly floured work surface and knock back with your fists. Knead for 2–3 minutes until smooth and elastic. Divide the dough into 2 pieces.

4 Lightly oil a baking tray. Divide each piece of dough into 3 even-sized strands, and shape into a plait (page 368). Place on the baking tray, cover loosely with oiled cling film, and leave in a warm place to rise for 30 minutes or until doubled in size.

5 Brush the loaves with the beaten egg and sprinkle generously with poppyseeds. Bake in a preheated oven at 230°C (450°F, Gas 8) for 10 minutes; reduce the oven temperature to 200°C (400°F, Gas 6), and bake for 20 minutes or until the loaves are well risen and a rich brown colour. Tap the bases to see if the loaves are cooked: they should sound hollow. Leave to cool on a wire rack.

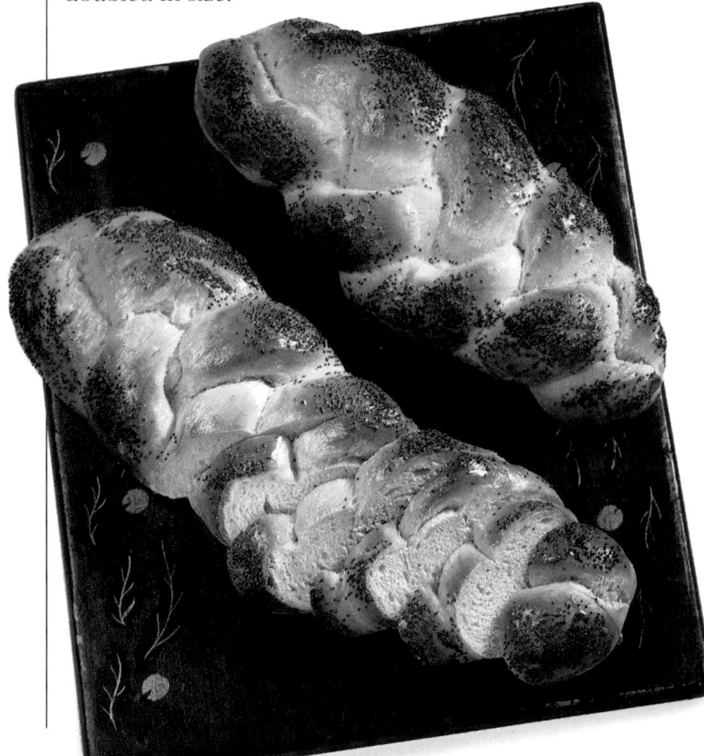

BRIOCHES

Makes 12

275 g (9 oz) strong white flour, plus extra for dusting
30 g (1 oz) caster sugar
60 g (2 oz) butter
1 x 7 g (1/4 oz) sachet fast-action dried yeast
2 eggs, beaten
about 3 tbsp tepid milk
sunflower oil for greasing
beaten egg for glazing
⋆ 12 individual brioche moulds

1 Sift the flour and sugar into a large bowl. Rub in the butter until the mixture resembles fine breadcrumbs, then stir in the yeast. Make a well in the middle and pour in the eggs and milk. Mix to a soft but not sticky dough.

2 Lightly oil a large bowl. Knead the dough until smooth and elastic. Shape into a round and place in the bowl. Cover with oiled cling film and leave in a warm place to rise for 1–1 1/2 hours until the dough has doubled in size.

3 Turn out the dough on to a lightly floured work surface and knock back with your fists. Knead the dough for 2–3 minutes until smooth.

4 Lightly oil the brioche moulds. Shape the brioches (see box, below).

5 Cover loosely with oiled cling film and leave in a warm place for 20 minutes or until doubled in size.

6 Brush the brioches with a little beaten egg and bake in a preheated oven at 200°C (400°F, Gas 6) for 10–12 minutes until well risen and golden brown. Tap the bases to see if the brioches are cooked through: they should sound hollow. Leave to cool on a wire rack.

Shaping brioches

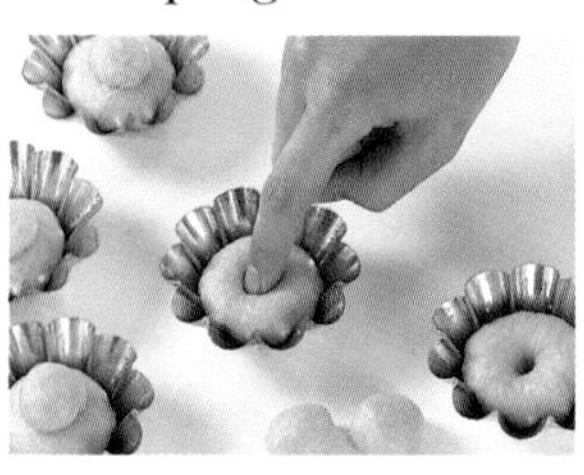

Divide the dough into 12 pieces, cutting one-quarter from each. Shape each piece into a ball. Place the large balls in the moulds, and press a hole in the middle of each. Place the small balls over the holes and press down to seal.

JAM DOUGHNUTS

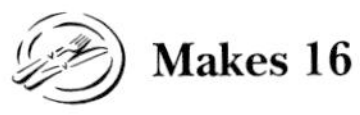 **Makes 16**

500 g (1 lb) plain white flour, plus extra for dusting

30 g (1 oz) butter or margarine

90 g (3 oz) caster sugar

1 x 7 g (1/4 oz) sachet fast-action dried yeast

2 eggs, beaten

about 90 ml (3 fl oz) tepid milk

about 90 ml (3 fl oz) tepid water

sunflower oil for greasing and deep-frying

150 g (5 oz) raspberry jam

125 g (4 oz) caster sugar

2 tsp ground cinnamon

1 Put the flour into a large bowl and rub in the butter with the fingertips until the mixture resembles fine breadcrumbs. Stir in the sugar and yeast. Make a well in the middle of the dry ingredients, pour in the eggs, milk, and water, and mix to a smooth dough.

2 Lightly oil a large bowl. Knead the dough until smooth and elastic. Shape into a round and place in the bowl. Cover with oiled cling film and leave in a warm place to rise for 1–1 1/2 hours until doubled in size.

3 Turn out the dough on to a lightly floured work surface, and knock back with your fists. Knead for 2–3 minutes until smooth.

4 Divide the dough into 16 pieces. Shape each one into a ball, then flatten slightly. Fill the doughnuts (see box, below). Place the doughnuts on oiled baking trays, cover with oiled cling film, and leave in a warm place to rise for 30 minutes.

5 Heat the oil in a deep-fat fryer to 160°C (325°F), and cook the doughnuts in batches for 5 minutes until golden. Drain on paper towels. Combine the sugar and cinnamon and coat the doughnuts. Serve at once.

Filling the doughnuts

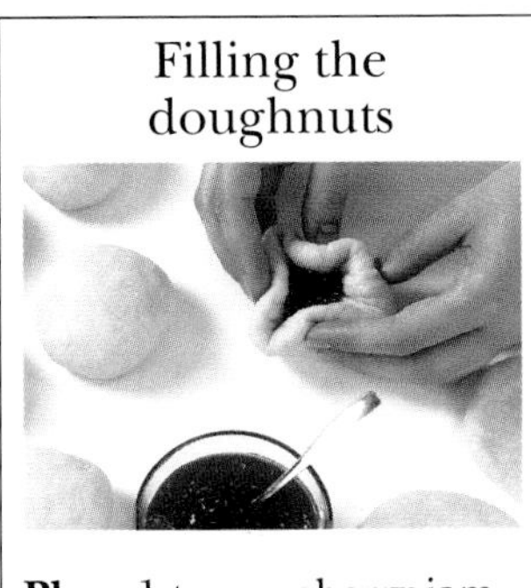

Place 1 tsp raspberry jam in the middle of each doughnut. Gather the edges over the jam and pinch firmly to seal.

LARDY CAKE

Makes 1 large loaf

500 g (1 lb) strong white flour, plus extra for dusting

1 tsp salt

30 g (1 oz) caster sugar

1 x 7 g (1/4 oz) sachet fast-action dried yeast

15 g (1/2 oz) white vegetable fat

about 300 ml (1/2 pint) tepid water

sunflower oil for greasing

FILLING

90 g (3 oz) lard or white vegetable fat

60 g (2 oz) butter, plus extra for greasing

90 g (3 oz) currants

90 g (3 oz) sultanas

60 g (2 oz) chopped mixed candied peel

90 g (3 oz) light muscovado sugar

GLAZE

1 tbsp caster sugar

1 tbsp boiling water

⋆ 23 x 30 cm (9 x 12 in) roasting tin

1 Mix the flour, salt, sugar, and yeast in a bowl. Rub in the fat. Make a well in the middle and pour in the water. Mix to a soft dough.

2 Knead until smooth and elastic, place in an oiled bowl, and cover with oiled cling film. Leave to rise.

3 Turn out the dough on to a lightly floured work surface and roll out to a rectangle about 5 mm (1/4 in) thick. Dot with one-third each of the vegetable fat and butter. Sprinkle over one-third each of the dried fruit, mixed peel, and sugar.

4 Fold into three, folding the bottom third up and the top third down on top of it. Seal the edges to trap the air, then give the dough a quarter turn. Repeat the rolling and folding twice more, with the remaining fat, fruit, peel, and sugar.

5 Lightly butter the roasting tin. Roll out the dough to fit the tin, and lift it into the tin. Cover with oiled cling film and leave to rise in a warm place for about 30 minutes until doubled in size.

6 Score the top of the dough in a criss-cross pattern, and bake in a preheated oven at 200°C (400°F, Gas 6) for about 30 minutes until well risen and golden brown.

7 Leave to cool in the roasting tin for about 10 minutes. Meanwhile, make the glaze: dissolve the caster sugar in the measured water. Brush the glaze on top of the warm cake and leave to cool.

DANISH PASTRIES

These tender and flaky pastries are quick and easy to make and are particularly good for breakfast. Vary the fillings, bake them ahead, and freeze. Warm the pastries, loosely covered with foil, in a low oven, and serve for a special breakfast or brunch.

Makes 16

500 g (1 lb) strong white flour, plus extra for dusting

1/2 tsp salt

375 g (12 oz) butter, plus extra for greasing

1 x 7 g (1/4 oz) sachet fast-action dried yeast

60 g (2 oz) caster sugar

150 ml (1/4 pint) tepid milk

2 eggs, beaten

beaten egg to glaze

FILLING & TOPPING

250 g (8 oz) white almond paste

4 apricot halves, canned or fresh

about 2 tsp water

125 g (4 oz) icing sugar

60 g (2 oz) flaked almonds

60 g (2 oz) glacé cherries

1 Put the flour and salt into a bowl and rub in 60 g (2 oz) of the butter. Stir in the yeast and sugar. Make a well in the middle, add the tepid milk and eggs, and mix to a soft dough.

2 Turn out the dough on to a floured surface and knead for 10 minutes or until smooth. Shape into a round and place in an oiled bowl. Cover with oiled cling film and leave in a warm place to rise for 1 hour or until doubled in size.

3 Turn out the dough on to a lightly floured work surface and knead for 2–3 minutes until smooth. Roll out into a 20 x 35 cm (8 x 14 in) rectangle. Dot the top two-thirds of the dough with half of the remaining butter. Fold the bottom third up and the top third down to form a parcel. Seal the edges, then give the dough a quarter turn so the folded side is to the left.

4 Roll out the dough into a 20 x 35 cm (8 x 14 in) rectangle as before. Dot with the remaining butter, fold, and chill for 15 minutes. Roll, fold, and chill twice more.

5 Divide the dough into 4 pieces. Shape and fill the pastries (see box, below). Arrange on buttered baking trays and leave to rise in a warm place for 20 minutes. Brush with beaten egg and bake in a preheated oven at 220°C (425°F, Gas 7) for 15 minutes or until golden brown. Transfer to a wire rack.

6 Mix the water and icing sugar and spoon a little over each pastry while still warm. Decorate kites with flaked almonds and pinwheels with glacé cherries. Leave to cool.

Clockwise from top: *Pinwheels, Kites, Crescents, Envelopes.*

Shaping Danish pastries

Crescents

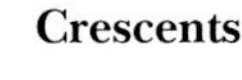

1 Roll out the dough into a 23 cm (9 in) round. Cut into quarters. Place a small roll of almond paste at the wide end of each piece.

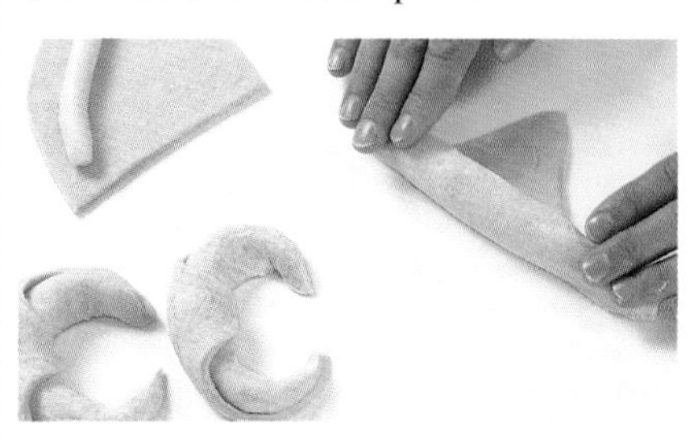

2 Starting from the wide end, roll up each dough quarter loosely around the almond paste, then curve the ends to form a crescent.

Kites

1 Roll out the dough into a 20 cm (8 in) square. Cut into 4 squares. Make cuts around 2 corners of each square, 1 cm (1/2 in) in from the edge.

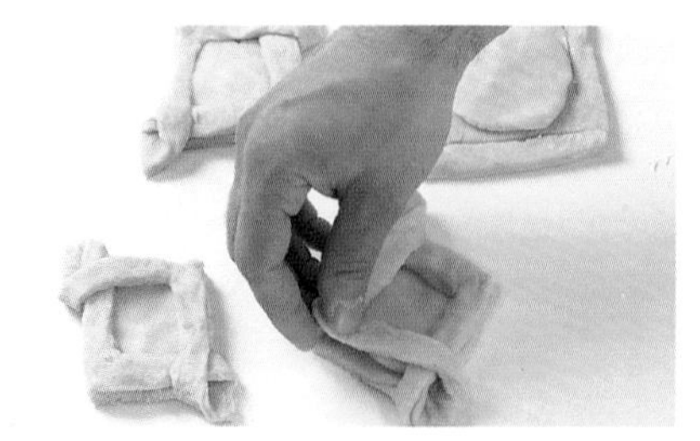

2 Place a round of almond paste in the middle of each square. Lift each cut corner and cross it over the almond paste to the opposite corner.

Pinwheels & Envelopes

1 Roll out dough and cut into 4 squares as for kites. Put almond paste in middle of each. Cut from the corners almost to the middle. Fold in alternate points.

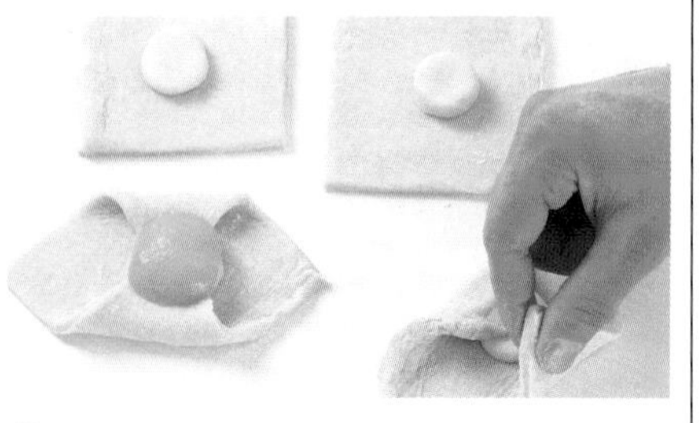

2 Roll out the dough, cut into 4, and fill as for pinwheels. Fold 2 opposite corners into the middle. Top with an apricot half, cut-side down.

WHOLEMEAL ENGLISH MUFFINS

Makes about 12

500 g (1 lb) strong wholemeal flour, plus extra for dusting

1 tsp caster sugar

1 tsp salt

1 tsp fast-action dried yeast

about 250 ml (8 fl oz) tepid milk

about 125 ml (4 fl oz) tepid water

sunflower oil for greasing

⋆ 7 cm (3 in) pastry cutter

1 Put the flour and sugar into a large bowl and stir in the salt and yeast. Make a well in the middle, pour in the milk and water all at once, and mix to a soft but not sticky dough.

2 Knead until smooth and elastic, then shape into a round. Oil a large bowl. Place the dough in the bowl, cover with oiled cling film, and leave in a warm place to rise for 45–60 minutes until doubled in size.

3 Knock back the dough, then turn out on to a lightly floured work surface and knead for 2–3 minutes until smooth and elastic.

4 Roll out the dough to a 1 cm (1/2 in) thickness and, using the cutter, cut into 12 rounds, re-rolling and kneading the dough as necessary.

5 Lightly dust 2 baking trays with flour, arrange the rounds on the trays, and cover loosely with oiled cling film. Leave in a warm place to rise for 30 minutes or until doubled in size.

6 Lightly oil a griddle or frying pan, and cook the muffins over a medium heat, 3 or 4 at a time, for about 7 minutes on each side until golden and cooked through. Do not allow the griddle to get too hot or the outside of the muffins will burn before the inside is cooked.

CRUMPETS

Makes 20

375 g (12 oz) strong white flour

1/2 tsp caster sugar

1/2 tsp salt

1 tsp fast-action dried yeast

about 300 ml (1/2 pint) tepid water

about 250 ml (8 fl oz) tepid milk

sunflower oil for greasing

⋆ 4 crumpet rings or 4 x 7 cm (3 in) pastry cutters

1 Put the flour and caster sugar into a large bowl and stir in the salt and yeast. Make a well in the middle, pour in the water and milk, and beat to form a smooth, thick batter.

2 Cover and leave in a warm place to rise for 1 hour or until the surface is bubbling.

3 Beat the batter mixture for 2 minutes, then pour into a jug.

4 Lightly oil the crumpet rings or pastry cutters and oil a griddle or frying pan. Place the rings or cutters on the griddle and then leave for 1–2 minutes to heat through.

5 Pour 2 cm (3/4 in) of batter into each ring and cook for 5–7 minutes until the surface is dry and full of holes, and the crumpets are shrinking away from the sides of the rings.

6 Lift off the rings, turn the crumpets over, and cook for 1 minute until pale golden. Transfer the crumpets to a wire rack and leave to cool.

7 Repeat with the remaining batter, lightly greasing the griddle and rings between each batch. Serve warm.

Cook's know-how

Any leftover crumpets can be successfully frozen, but make sure they are fully cooled first. They can be toasted straight from the freezer.

CHELSEA BUNS

Makes 12

500 g (1 lb) strong white flour
1 tsp salt
60 g (2 oz) butter
1 x 7 g (1/4 oz) sachet fast-action dried yeast
30 g (1 oz) caster sugar
about 200 ml (7 fl oz) tepid milk
1 large egg, beaten
sunflower oil for greasing
4 tbsp clear honey

FILLING

60 g (2 oz) butter
30 g (1 oz) light muscovado sugar
60 g (2 oz) sultanas
60 g (2 oz) currants
grated zest of 1 orange
1 tsp ground mixed spice

1 Put the flour into a large bowl and stir in the salt. Rub in the butter and yeast. Stir in the sugar. Make a well in the middle, pour in the milk and egg, and mix to a soft dough.

2 Oil a large bowl. Knead the dough until smooth and elastic, then shape into a round and place in the bowl. Cover with oiled cling film and leave in a warm place to rise for 1–1 1/2 hours until doubled in size.

3 Make the filling: cream the butter with the muscovado sugar. In another bowl, combine the sultanas, currants, orange zest, and mixed spice.

4 Lightly oil an 18 x 28 cm (7 x 11 in) roasting tin. Turn out the dough on to a lightly floured work surface, and knock back with your fists. Knead for 2–3 minutes until smooth.

5 Roll out into a 30 cm (12 in) square and dot with the butter mixture. Fold in half and roll out into a 30 cm (12 in) square. Sprinkle with the fruit mixture, then roll up.

6 Cut the roll into 12 pieces and arrange cut-side up in the roasting tin. Cover with oiled cling film. Leave in a warm place to rise for 30 minutes or until the pieces are touching.

7 Bake in a preheated oven at 220°C (425°F, Gas 7) for 20–25 minutes until well risen, covering the buns loosely with foil after about 15 minutes to prevent them from browning too much. Transfer to a wire rack.

8 Warm the honey in a small pan and brush over the buns to glaze. Pull the buns apart, and serve warm.

BATH BUNS

Makes 18

500 g (1 lb) strong white flour
60 g (2 oz) caster sugar
1 tsp salt
1 x 7 g (1/4 oz) sachet fast-action dried yeast
about 150 ml (1/4 pint) tepid milk
60 g (2 oz) butter, melted and cooled slightly
1 egg and 2 egg yolks, beaten
150 g (5 oz) sultanas
90 g (3 oz) chopped mixed peel
sunflower oil for greasing

TOPPING

1 egg, beaten
30 g (1 oz) nibbed sugar or coarsely crushed sugar cubes

1 Put the flour and sugar into a large bowl and stir in the salt and yeast. Make a well in the middle and add the milk, butter, egg and egg yolks, sultanas, and mixed peel. Mix to a soft dough.

2 Knead the dough until smooth and elastic. Shape into a round and place in an oiled bowl.

3 Cover with oiled cling film and leave in a warm place to rise for 1–1 1/2 hours until the dough has doubled in size.

4 Turn out the dough on to a lightly floured work surface and knock back with your fists. Knead the dough for 2–3 minutes until smooth and elastic.

5 Lightly oil 2 or 3 baking trays. Divide the dough into 18 pieces, shape into rolls, and place on the baking trays. Cover loosely with oiled cling film and leave in a warm place to rise for about 30 minutes until doubled in size.

6 Brush the tops of the buns with the beaten egg and sprinkle with the sugar. Bake in a preheated oven at 190°C (375°F, Gas 5) for 15 minutes or until well risen and golden brown.

7 Tap the bases of the buns to see if they are cooked through: they should sound hollow. Leave to cool on a wire rack.

CINNAMON ROLLS

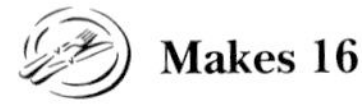 **Makes 16**

1 kg (2 lb) plain flour
425 g (14 oz) caster sugar
1 x 7 g (1/4 oz) sachet fast-action dried yeast
1 tsp salt
about 350 ml (12 fl oz) tepid milk
2 eggs, lightly beaten
30 g (1 oz) butter, melted
250 g (8 oz) raisins
3 tbsp ground cinnamon
sunflower oil for greasing
milk for glazing

GLAZE
200 g (7 oz) icing sugar
4 tbsp water
1 tsp vanilla essence

1 Sift the flour and 375 g (12 oz) of the sugar into a bowl and stir in the yeast and salt. Make a well in the middle, pour in the milk, eggs, and butter, and stir to make a sticky dough.

2 Knead the dough until smooth and elastic. Knead in the raisins and 1 tbsp of the cinnamon.

3 Divide the dough into 16 even-sized pieces. Shape each piece into a 20–25 cm (8–10 in) strand, then flatten.

4 Combine the remaining sugar and cinnamon, sprinkle the mixture over the strips of dough, then roll up tightly into spirals.

5 Lightly oil 2 baking trays. Arrange the rolls on the trays, cover loosely with oiled cling film, and leave in a warm place to rise for about 1 hour until doubled in size.

6 Brush the rolls with milk to glaze, then bake them in a preheated oven at 190°C (375°F, Gas 5) for 30–40 minutes until lightly browned. Transfer the rolls to a wire rack.

7 Meanwhile, make the glaze: in a small bowl, combine the icing sugar, measured water, and vanilla essence. As soon as the cinnamon rolls come out of the oven, brush them with the glaze. Serve the rolls warm or cold.

HOT CROSS BUNS

Makes 12

500 g (1 lb) strong white flour
60 g (2 oz) caster sugar
1 x 7 g (1/4 oz) sachet fast-action dried yeast
1 tsp salt
1 tsp ground mixed spice
1 tsp ground cinnamon
1/2 tsp grated nutmeg
60 g (2 oz) butter, melted and cooled slightly
about 150 ml (1/4 pint) tepid milk
about 75 ml (2 1/2 fl oz) tepid water
1 egg, beaten
90 g (3 oz) currants
60 g (2 oz) chopped mixed peel
sunflower oil for greasing
60 g (2 oz) shortcrust pastry

GLAZE
2 tbsp caster sugar
2 tbsp water

1 Sift the flour into a large bowl, and stir in the sugar, yeast, salt, mixed spice, cinnamon, and nutmeg. Make a well in the middle, and pour in the butter, milk, water, egg, currants, and mixed peel. Mix to a soft dough.

2 Knead the dough on a floured work surface until smooth and elastic, then shape into a round.

3 Put into an oiled bowl, cover with oiled cling film, and leave in a warm place to rise for 1–1 1/2 hours until doubled in size.

4 Knock back the dough with your fists, then turn out on to a lightly floured work surface and knead for 2–3 minutes until smooth and elastic. Divide the dough into 12 pieces and shape into round rolls.

5 Roll out the shortcrust pastry to 5 mm (1/4 in) thickness, cut it into 24 narrow strips, and press 2 strips in the form of a cross on the top of each bun. Secure with a little water.

6 Lightly oil 2 baking trays, arrange the buns on the trays, and cover with oiled cling film. Leave in a warm place to rise for 30 minutes or until doubled in size.

7 Bake the buns in a preheated oven at 220°C (425°F, Gas 7) for 15 minutes or until well risen and browned. Transfer to a wire rack.

8 Meanwhile, make the glaze: put the sugar and water into a pan and heat gently, stirring, until the sugar has dissolved. As soon as the buns come out of the oven, brush them with the glaze. Serve warm or cold.

11

PIES, TARTS, & HOT DESSERTS

UNDER 30 MINUTES

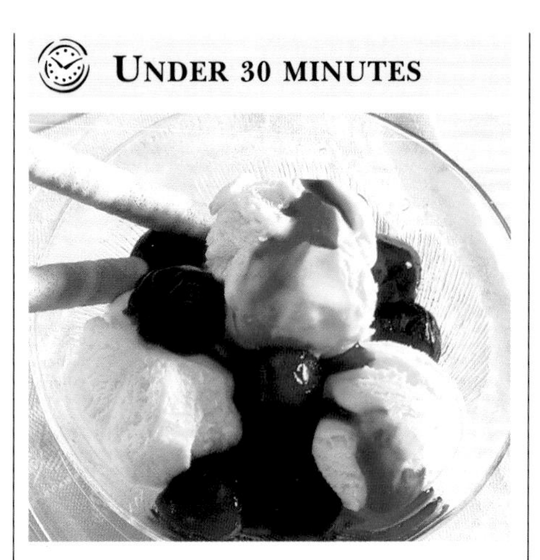

FLAMBEED CHERRIES JUBILEE

Morello cherries simmered in sugar and flavoured with almond essence, then flambéed in brandy. Served with ice cream.

SERVES 4 162 calories per serving

Takes 20 minutes **PAGE 399**

WARM JAMAICAN BANANAS

Banana halves coated in a rich caramel and cinnamon sauce, and flambéed in rum. Served with vanilla ice cream.

SERVES 4 269 calories per serving

Takes 15 minutes **PAGE 398**

FRUIT FRITTERS

Bite-sized pieces of apple and banana coated in batter, and deep-fried until golden. Sprinkled with sugar and cinnamon.

SERVES 4 541 calories per serving

Takes 25 minutes **PAGE 399**

30–60 MINUTES

FRENCH APRICOT PANCAKES

Small golden pancakes, baked, then folded over a filling of apricot jam, and sprinkled with caster sugar.

SERVES 4 378 calories per serving

Takes 35 minutes **PAGE 400**

BAKED APPLES

Cooking apples filled with sugar and butter, then baked until soft and served hot with their juices spooned over.

SERVES 6 235 calories per serving

Takes 55 minutes **PAGE 397**

CREPES SUZETTE

Delicious crêpes coated with a sweet orange sauce. Flambéed in brandy and orange liqueur and served hot.

SERVES 4 604 calories per serving

Takes 55 minutes **PAGE 400**

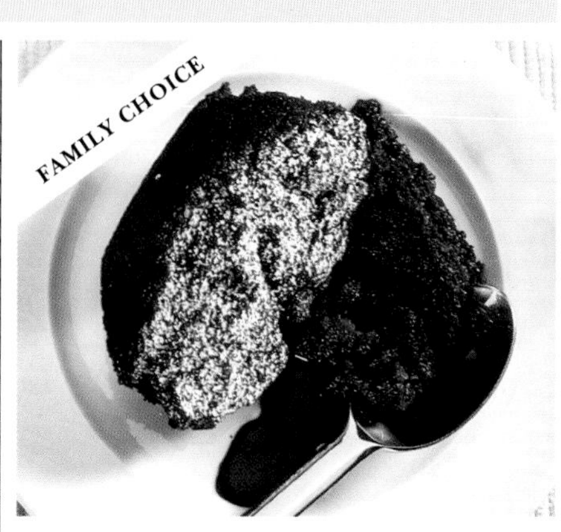

SAUCY CHOCOLATE PUDDING

Irresistible light chocolate sponge flavoured with cocoa and vanilla essence, and baked in a chocolate sauce.

SERVES 4 361 calories per serving

Takes 45 minutes **PAGE 404**

APPLE BROWN BETTY

Layers of spiced apple slices and buttered breadcrumbs sprinkled with caster sugar, then baked until golden brown.

SERVES 4–6 426–284 calories per serving

Takes 55 minutes **PAGE 397**

PLUM CRUMBLE

Sweet and crunchy: juicy plums sprinkled with sugar and cinnamon, and baked beneath a golden brown topping.

SERVES 6 436 calories per serving

Takes 50 minutes **PAGE 398**

OVER 60 MINUTES

MAGIC LEMON PUDDING
Fresh and tangy: a light lemony mixture separates during cooking into a sponge on top and a delicious lemon sauce underneath.
SERVES 4 295 calories per serving
Takes 1 hour 5 minutes **PAGE 401**

APPLE BREAD PUDDING
Slices of buttered bread covered with an apple and apricot jam mixture, and topped with a layer of bread triangles.
SERVES 4–6 642–428 calories per serving
Takes 1 hour 5 minutes **PAGE 396**

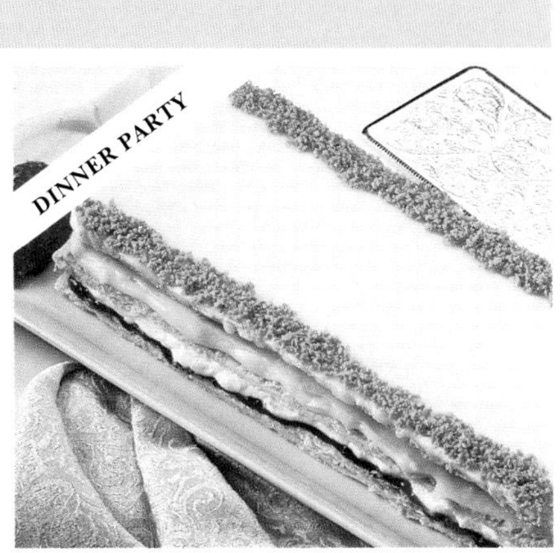

MILLE-FEUILLE
Melt-in-the-mouth puff pastry layered with whipped cream, jam, and crème pâtissière, and topped with glacé icing.
SERVES 6 486 calories per serving
Takes 45 minutes, plus chilling **PAGE 486**

KEY LIME PIE
Creamy, lime-flavoured filling is baked in a pastry shell, then covered with whipped cream and decorated with lime slices.
SERVES 8 489 calories per serving
Takes 60 minutes, plus chilling **PAGE 418**

PINEAPPLE UPSIDE-DOWN PUDDING
Pineapple rings and chopped apricots beneath a light and springy sponge topping, turned out and served "upside-down".
SERVES 4–6 749–499 calories per serving
Takes 1 hour 5 minutes **PAGE 401**

EVE'S PUDDING
Warming and filling: sweetened sliced cooking apples, and lemon zest and juice, are topped with a golden sponge.
SERVES 6 414 calories per serving
Takes 1 hour 5 minutes **PAGE 396**

BANOFFI PIE
Rich and creamy: crushed biscuit base with a caramel filling, topped with banana slices, whipped cream, and grated chocolate.
SERVES 6 1210–901 calories per serving
Takes 20 minutes, plus chilling **PAGE 418**

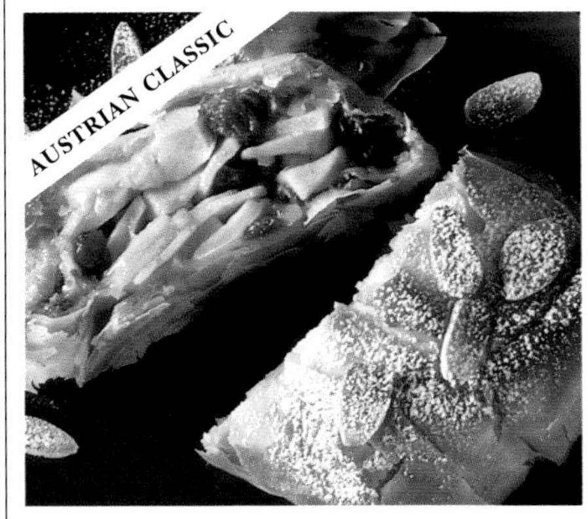

APPLE STRUDEL
Sheets of filo pastry enclosing apples, lemon zest and juice, sugar, spices, and sultanas, and sprinkled with almonds.
SERVES 8 278 calories per serving
Takes $1^1/_4$ hours **PAGE 411**

FRUITY CREAM PIE
Muesli pastry shell filled with layers of creamy custard and fresh fruit, and covered with whipped cream.
SERVES 6–8 787–590 calories per serving
Takes 60 minutes, plus chilling **PAGE 419**

OVER 60 MINUTES

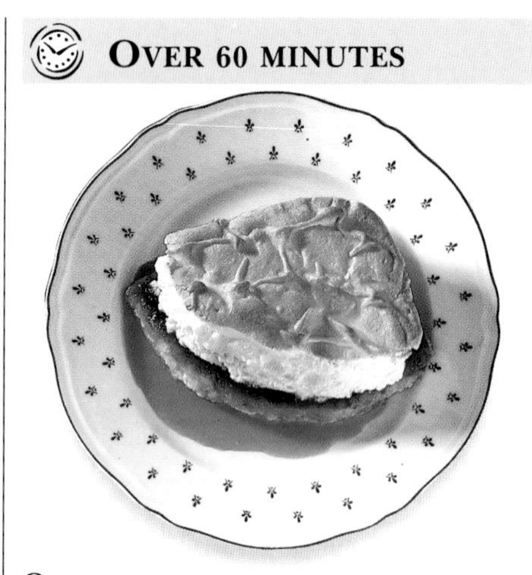

QUEEN OF PUDDINGS

Old-fashioned favourite: smooth set creamy custard is flavoured with orange zest, spread with melted jam, and topped with meringue.

SERVES 6 386 calories per serving

Takes 60 minutes, plus standing **PAGE 405**

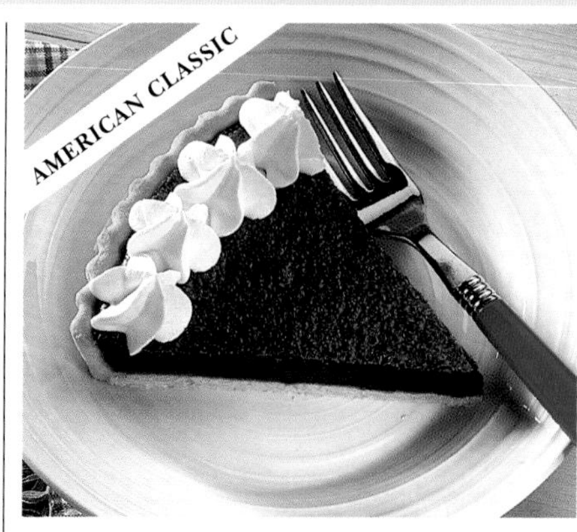

MISSISSIPPI MUD PIE

Popular American dessert: pastry shell with a sweetened chocolate and coffee filling, decorated with whipped cream.

SERVES 8–10 692–553 calories per serving

Takes 1 1/4 hours, plus chilling **PAGE 419**

TREACLE TART

Rich and sweet: pastry shell filled with golden syrup, breadcrumbs, and lemon zest and juice. Served warm.

SERVES 8 386 calories per serving

Takes 60 minutes, plus chilling **PAGE 414**

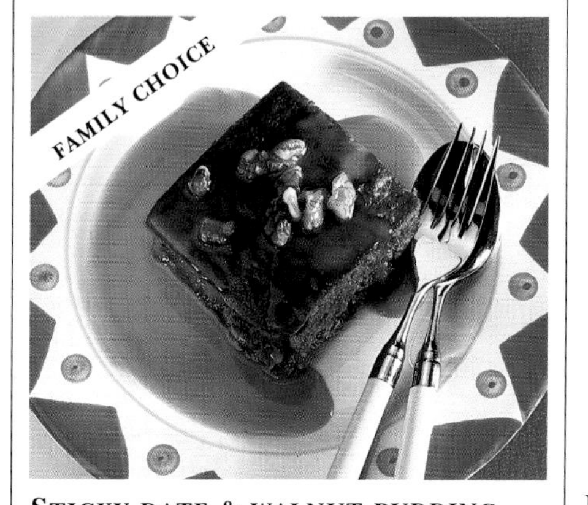

STICKY DATE & WALNUT PUDDING

Rich pudding flavoured with coffee essence, dates, and walnuts, and served with a deliciously sticky toffee sauce.

SERVES 8 690 calories per serving

Takes 1 hour 5 minutes **PAGE 404**

HOT CHOCOLATE SOUFFLES

Light and airy: individual soufflés made from dark chocolate, baked until well risen and fluffy, then dusted with icing sugar.

SERVES 4 494 calories per serving

Takes 1 1/4 hours **PAGE 405**

BAKLAVA

Traditional Greek pastry: layers of buttered filo pastry and walnuts soaked in honey and lemon juice, and cut into squares.

MAKES 20 SQUARES 249 calories per serving

Takes 60 minutes, plus cooling **PAGE 422**

BAKED APPLE DUMPLINGS

Cooking apples filled with sugar and cinnamon, enclosed in decorative pastry case, and baked until golden.

SERVES 4 781 calories per serving

Takes 60 minutes, plus chilling **PAGE 409**

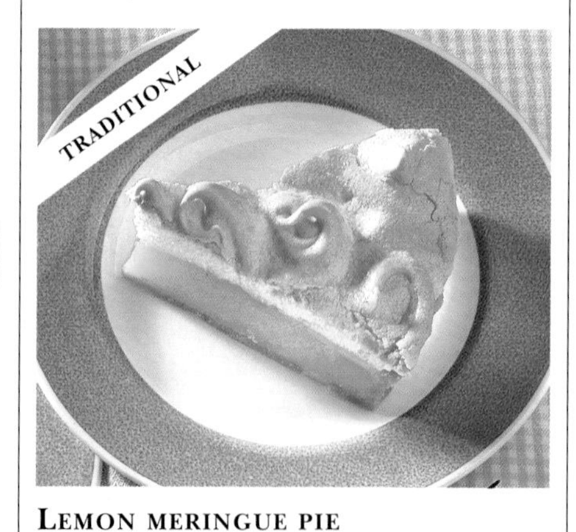

LEMON MERINGUE PIE

Deliciously sweet: golden brown pastry with tangy lemon filling, topped with light and fluffy meringue.

SERVES 8–10 537–430 calories per serving

Takes 1 1/4 hours, plus chilling **PAGE 417**

DOUBLE CRUST APPLE PIE

Family favourite: light and golden puff pastry encases tender apple slices in this traditional apple pie.

SERVES 6 432 calories per serving

Takes 60 minutes, plus cooling **PAGE 410**

OVER 60 MINUTES

BAKEWELL TART

Traditional sweet dessert: pastry shell spread with jam, topped with an almond-flavoured sponge and a pastry lattice.

SERVES 6 560 calories per serving

Takes 1 1/4 hours, plus chilling **PAGE 415**

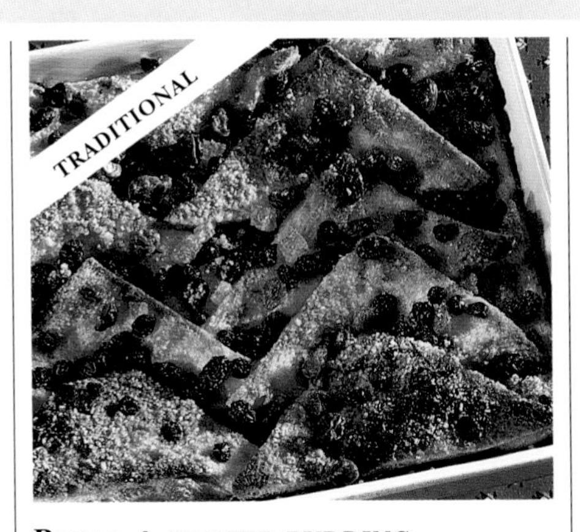

BREAD & BUTTER PUDDING

Slices of white bread thickly spread with butter, layered with dried fruit, lemon zest, and sugar, and baked in a custard.

SERVES 6 516 calories per serving

Takes 60 minutes, plus standing **PAGE 406**

STRAWBERRY & RHUBARB PIE

Sweet strawberries and rhubarb are lightly spiced, and baked in a pastry shell with a lattice topping.

SERVES 6–8 371–278 calories per serving

Takes 1 1/4 hours, plus chilling **PAGE 409**

FRENCH APRICOT & ALMOND TART

French classic: apricots in lemon juice, on a bed of crème pâtissière in a pastry shell. Glazed with brandy and flaked almonds.

SERVES 10 398 calories per serving

Takes 45 minutes, plus chilling **PAGE 416**

TARTE AU CITRON

Light and tangy: pastry shell with a cream and lemon filling, baked until set, and lightly dusted with icing sugar.

SERVES 10–12 572–476 calories per serving

Takes 1 1/4 hours, plus chilling **PAGE 417**

RICE PUDDING

Rich and creamy: pudding rice, milk, caster sugar, and lemon zest mixed together, then sprinkled with freshly grated nutmeg and dotted with small knobs of butter. Baked slowly in the oven until the top turns golden brown.

SERVES 4 210 calories per serving

Takes 2 3/4 hours, plus standing **PAGE 406**

OVER 60 MINUTES

PECAN PIE

Deliciously rich: pecan pie is an American classic originating from the Southern States of America. The buttery rich pecan kernels are toasted, then mixed with a lightly spiced syrup, and flavoured with brandy and vanilla essence.

SERVES 6–8 611–458 calories per serving
Takes 1¼ hours, plus chilling

PAGE 415

FRENCH APPLE TART

Apple chunks, jam, sugar, and lemon zest, puréed, and spooned into a pastry shell, and topped with apple slices and jam glaze.

SERVES 8–10 593–474 calories per serving
Takes 2 hours, plus chilling

PAGE 414

SYRUP PUDDING

Wonderfully sweet and sticky: a simple, traditional steamed pudding, deliciously sweetened with golden syrup.

SERVES 4–6 619–413 calories per serving
Takes 3¼ hours

PAGE 408

TARTE TATIN

Rich and fruity: crisp pastry baked over caramel and apple slices, then turned out with the glazed apples on top.

SERVES 6 511 calories per serving
Takes 60 minutes, plus chilling

PAGE 411

MINCEMEAT & ALMOND TART

A pastry shell filled with mincemeat and topped with a light, creamy almond mixture, then baked until golden.

SERVES 8–10 856–685 calories per serving
Takes 60 minutes, plus chilling

PAGE 408

STEAMED JAM PUDDING

Traditional pudding: a temptingly light sponge mixture is steamed over rich plum jam. A firm family favourite.

SERVES 4–6 573–382 calories per serving
Takes 1¾ hours

PAGE 407

CHRISTMAS PUDDING

Rich, dark and fruity traditional Christmas pudding: dried fruits are combined with nuts, and lemon zest and juice. Grated carrots ensure that the pudding stays deliciously moist. Once steamed, the pudding is liberally laced with rum.

SERVES 8–10 522–418 calories per serving
Takes 6¼ hours, plus storing

PAGE 407

PIES, TARTS, & HOT DESSERTS KNOW-HOW

PUDDINGS MAY NO longer be a feature of every family meal, but few people can say that they don't enjoy something sweet from time to time, especially to round off a special meal. From warming steamed puddings, to golden pastries filled with fresh fruit, there's a mouth-watering dessert for every season and occasion. Since a pie or tart made at home tastes so much better than a commercially made version, it's worth learning the art of pastry making – you'll find it surprisingly simple once you understand the basic principles.

TYPES OF PASTRY

All pastries are based on a mixture of flour, fat, and a liquid to bind them. Plain flour is usually used, although wholemeal or a mixture of the two gives a "nuttier" pastry. The liquid used for binding may be water, milk, or egg; the fat may be butter, margarine, lard, white vegetable fat, or a combination.

Shortcrust pastry
A blend of 2 parts flour, 1 part fat, and usually water, shortcrust pastry (page 394) is used for sweet and savoury pies and tarts.

Pâte sucrée
Bound with egg yolks, pâte sucrée (page 394) is richer than shortcrust pastry and is used for sweet tarts and tartlets. The classic method for mixing the dough is on a flat marble work surface.

Puff pastry
A light, flaky pastry made by rolling and folding the dough, each time making more layers of dough and butter. Ready-made fresh or frozen pastry is very convenient, but is usually not made with butter. Puff pastry is often used as a top crust for sweet and savoury pies, to wrap beef Wellington, and to make mille-feuille.

Flaky pastry
This is a short-cut version of puff pastry. The rolling and folding is repeated only a few times. It is used for pies and tarts.

Rough puff pastry
Like puff and flaky pastry, this is rolled and folded, but all the butter is added at once, in large cubes (page 394). Rough puff pastry can be used as flaky pastry and for dishes normally made with puff pastry.

Filo & strudel pastry
These are similar types of pastry made from a pliable dough that is stretched and rolled until extremely thin. It is then rolled around a filling or layered with melted butter. Filo and strudel pastries are difficult to make at home, but ready-made varieties are available fresh and frozen. Common uses include strudel and baklava.

MICROWAVING

The microwave can be a helpful tool when preparing pies, tarts, and hot desserts. When it comes to baking pastry-based pies and tarts, however, there really is no substitute for the conventional oven.

The microwave is perfect for cooking fruit fillings for pies and tarts. The fruit remains plump and colourful. It can also be used to melt or soften butter and to heat liquids in which fruit is left to soak. Under careful watch, the microwave can be used to melt chocolate and make caramel.

FREEZING

Most puddings freeze well, particularly baked sponge and steamed suet puddings (before or after cooking), bread and butter pudding (before cooking), crumbles (before or after cooking), and pancakes.

Custard-based and milk puddings are not as successful because they tend to separate. Raw pastry can be frozen for up to 3 months and baked pastries will keep for up to 6 months. Pastries baked before freezing will not be as crisp as those frozen unbaked. Thaw in wrappings at room temperature.

MAKING A PASTRY SHELL

Careful handling of pastry should ensure it doesn't shrink or distort when baking.

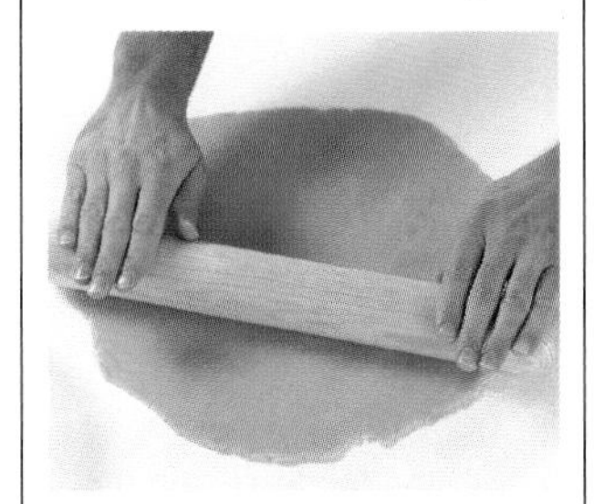

1 Put the pastry on a floured work surface and flour the rolling pin. Roll out from the middle outwards, giving the pastry a quarter turn occasionally.

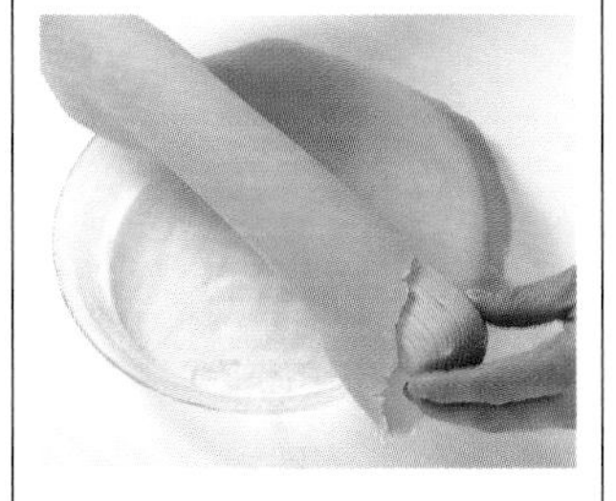

2 If lining a pie dish, roll the pastry to a round 5 cm (2 ins) larger than the top of the dish. Roll it loosely around the rolling pin, and unroll over the dish. A pastry lid should also be 5 cm (2 ins) larger.

3 Gently ease the pastry into the pie dish, pressing it firmly but neatly into the bottom edge of the dish, being very careful not to overstretch the pastry. Carefully trim the excess pastry with a table knife.

ROUGH PUFF PASTRY

Ideal for both sweet and savoury pies. These quantities make sufficient pastry for a 25 cm (10 in) double-crust pie.

1 Sift *250 g (8 oz) plain flour* into a bowl. Add *90 g (3 oz) each of cubed butter and white vegetable fat,* and then stir to coat in flour. Add *150 ml (1/4 pint) cold water* and *a squeeze of lemon juice,* and with a table knife bind to a fairly stiff, lumpy dough.

2 Roll the dough into a rectangle 3 times as long as it is wide. Fold the bottom third up and the top third down. Press the edges with the side of your hand, to seal. Wrap the dough and chill in the refrigerator for 15 minutes.

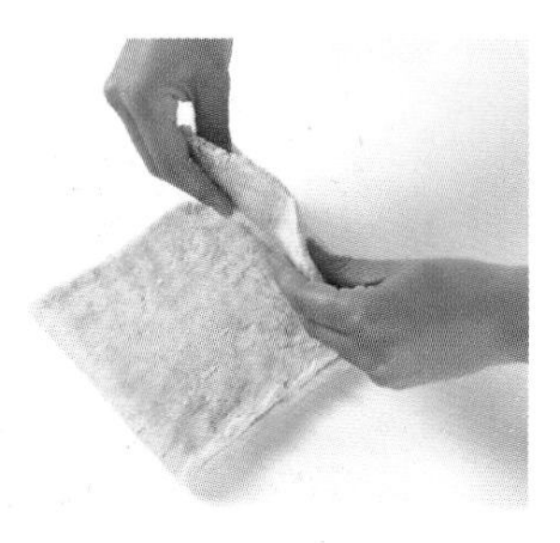

3 With the unfolded edges at top and bottom, roll the dough into a rectangle and fold as before. Turn the dough and repeat rolling, folding, and turning, twice more. Wrap the dough and chill in the refrigerator for 30 minutes.

PATE SUCREE

Traditionally made on a marble surface. These quantities make sufficient pastry to line a 25 cm (10 in) flan dish, tin, or pie dish.

1 Sift *200 g (7 oz) plain flour* and *a pinch of salt, if preferred,* on to a work surface. Make a well in the middle and add *90 g (3 oz) softened butter, 60 g (2 oz) caster sugar,* and *3 egg yolks.* With your fingertips, mix the butter, sugar, and egg yolks until well blended.

2 Using your fingertips, gradually work the sifted flour into the butter mixture until the mixture resembles coarse crumbs; if the butter mixture seems too sticky, work in a little more flour.

3 With your fingers or a pastry scraper, gather the dough into a ball then knead until it is smooth and pliable. Shape the kneaded dough into a ball again, wrap, and chill in the refrigerator for 30 minutes or until just firm.

SHORTCRUST PASTRY

This basic recipe may be flavoured or sweetened as preferred. For best results, the fat should be well chilled. Handle the dough as little as possible, or the pastry will become tough. These quantities make sufficient pastry to line a 23–25 cm (9–10 in) flan dish, flan tin, or pie dish.

1 Sift *175 g (6 oz) plain flour* and *a pinch of salt, if preferred,* into a bowl. Cut *90 g (3 oz) chilled butter, margarine, or other fat* into small pieces and add to the bowl. Stir to coat in the flour.

2 Using your fingertips, quickly and lightly rub the fat into the flour, lifting the mixture to incorporate air, until the mixture resembles fine breadcrumbs. Sprinkle *about 2 tbsp cold water* over the mixture. Stir gently with a table knife to mix. If the mixture seems too dry, add a little more liquid.

3 Gather the mixture together and knead very briefly until smooth. If the dough feels at all sticky, add a little more flour. Shape into a ball, wrap, and chill for 30 minutes.

BAKING BLIND

A pastry shell may be partly baked before adding a filling, to help it stay crisp, or it may be fully baked if the filling itself does not need to be cooked. The shell is filled with baking beans to weigh down the pastry.

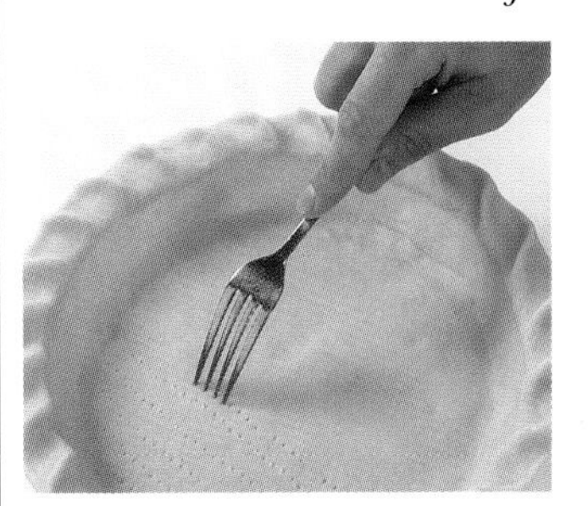

1 Prick the pastry shell all over with a fork. Press a piece of foil or greaseproof paper into the pastry shell, smoothing it over the bottom and up the side of the shell.

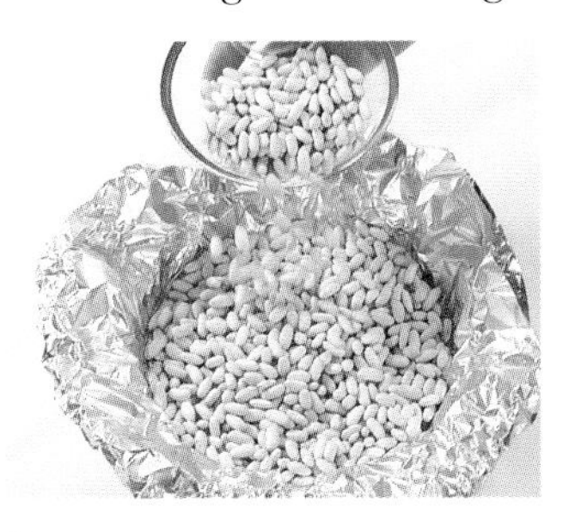

2 Fill the shell with ceramic baking beans, dried pulses, or uncooked rice, and bake in a preheated oven at 200°C (400°F, Gas 6) for 10–15 minutes or until browning at the edges.

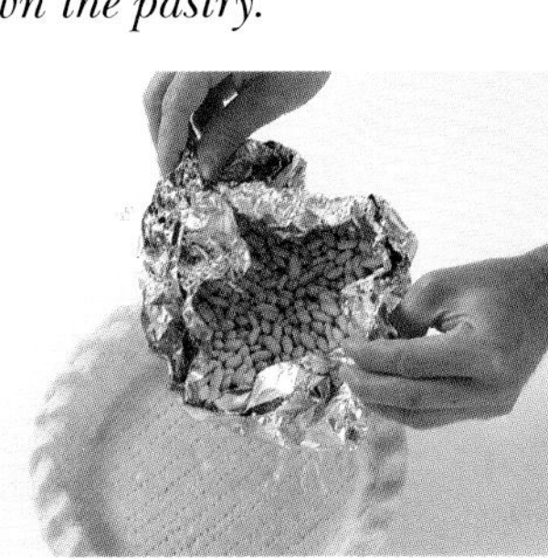

3 Remove the beans and foil and bake for 5 minutes for a part-baked shell, or 15 minutes for a fully baked shell. If the pastry rises during baking, gently press it down with your hand.

STEAMED PUDDINGS

Light sponges and rich suet mixtures can both be gently cooked by steaming. Be sure to make the seal tight so that steam can't get in. It's important to keep the water in the saucepan topped up, so boil some water ready to add to the pan when needed.

1 Turn the mixture into a greased, heatproof basin. Take a piece of buttered greaseproof paper, lay a piece of foil on top, and make a pleat across the middle, to allow for expansion.

2 Lay the paper and foil over the top of the basin. Secure by tying string under the rim of the basin. Form a handle with another piece of string. Trim away excess paper and foil.

3 Lower the basin into a saucepan containing enough simmering water to come halfway up the side of the basin. Cover tightly and steam for the required time. Make sure that the water stays at simmering point and top up with more boiling water when necessary.

DECORATIVE EDGES

Many decorative finishes can be given to the edge of a pastry lid. The simplest is to press all around the edge at regular intervals with the floured prongs of a fork. Alternatively, crimp the pastry with your fingers: place the thumb and forefinger of one hand just inside the edge of the pastry. With the forefinger of your other hand, push outwards, and pinch the pastry between finger and thumb to make a rounded "V" shape. Repeat this action all around the pastry lid.

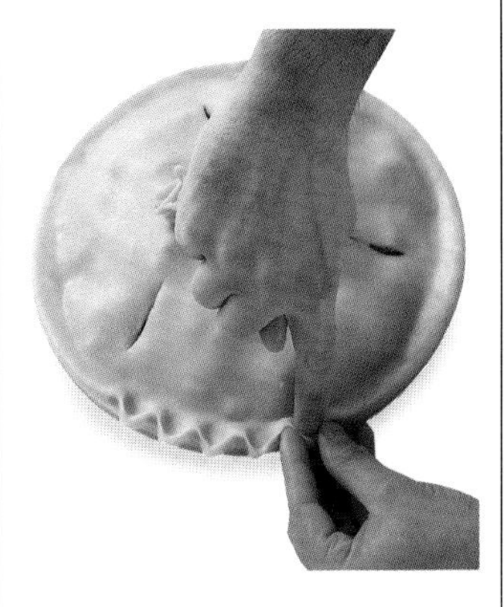

Decorating pies & tarts

A pastry lid can be given an attractive sheen by being brushed with a glaze before baking. A beaten egg or an egg yolk lightly mixed with 1 tsp water will give a golden finish. Milk or cream will give a shine. Brush with water, then sprinkle with sugar for a crisp, sweet glaze.

◆

Keep pastry trimmings to make small decorative shapes. Cut them freehand or use pastry cutters. They can be fixed to the edge of a pastry shell or arranged on a lid. If the pastry has a glaze, use it to attach the shapes, or brush them with a little water.

APPLE BREAD PUDDING

Serves 4–6

1 kg (2 lb) cooking apples, peeled, cored, and sliced

125 g (4 oz) caster sugar

3 tbsp water

2 tbsp apricot jam

125 g (4 oz) butter, softened, plus extra for greasing

12 medium slices of bread, crusts removed

** 15 cm (6 in) square cake tin*

1 Put the apples into a large saucepan with the sugar and measured water. Cook gently until soft, then beat well with a wooden spoon until smooth. Add the apricot jam, and heat gently to melt the jam, stirring occasionally to combine with the apples.

2 Spread the butter on one side of each slice of bread. Lightly butter the cake tin and assemble the pudding (see box, right).

3 Bake in a preheated oven at 200°C (400°F, Gas 6) for about 40 minutes until crisp and golden. Serve hot.

Assembling the pudding

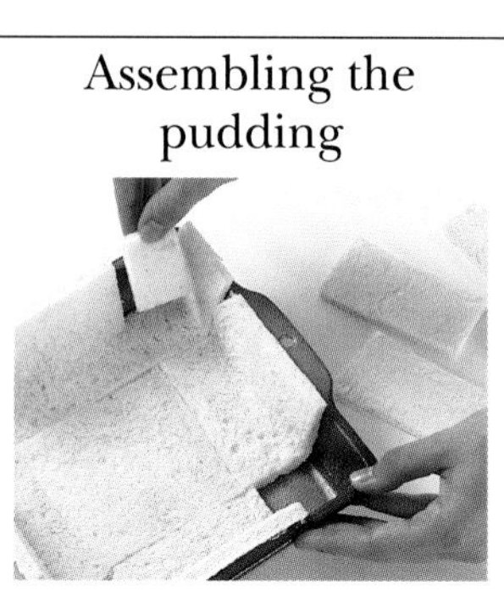

Use 8 of the bread slices to line the tin, cutting them into strips or squares as necessary, and placing them buttered-side down. Spoon in the apple mixture.

Cut the remaining slices into quarters diagonally. Arrange the quarters on top of the apple mixture, buttered-side up.

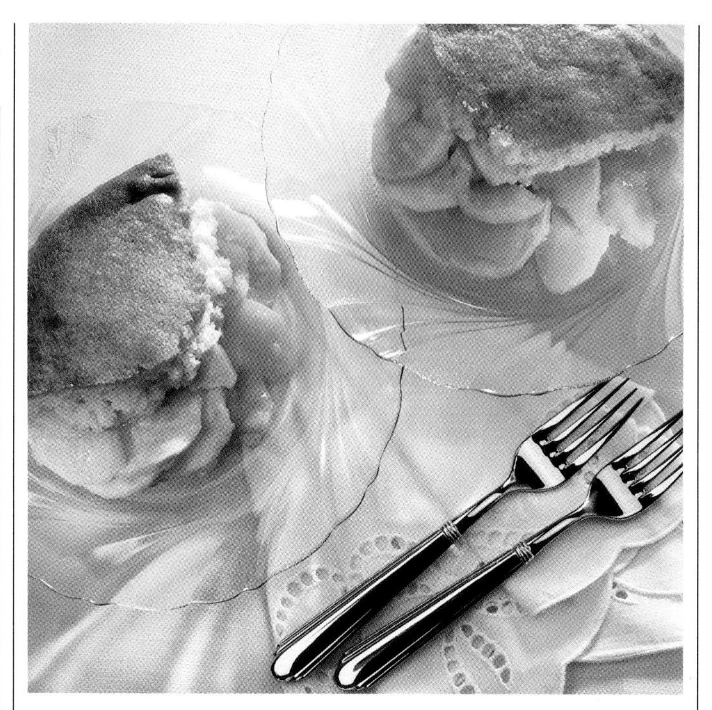

EVE'S PUDDING

Serves 6

butter for greasing

500 g (1 lb) cooking apples, peeled, cored, and sliced

90 g (3 oz) demerara sugar

grated zest and juice of 1 lemon

SPONGE TOPPING

125 g (4 oz) soft margarine

125 g (4 oz) caster sugar

2 eggs, beaten

125 g (4 oz) self-raising flour

1 tsp baking powder

** 1.25 litre (2 pint) ovenproof dish*

1 Lightly butter the ovenproof dish and arrange the apples in the bottom. Sprinkle over the demerara sugar and the lemon zest and juice.

2 Make the sponge topping: put the margarine, caster sugar, eggs, flour, and baking powder into a large bowl, and beat until smooth and thoroughly blended. Spoon the mixture on top of the apple slices, and level the surface.

3 Bake in a preheated oven at 180°C (350°F, Gas 4) for about 45 minutes until the sponge topping is well risen, golden, and springy to the touch. Serve hot.

SPICED EVE'S PUDDING

Add 1 tsp ground cinnamon to the sponge topping, and 60g (2 oz) raisins, 1 tsp ground cinnamon, and 1 tsp ground mixed spice to the apple mixture. Proceed as directed.

Cook's know-how

Double the sponge ingredients and use half to make a sponge cake, or add some dried fruit and make buns to bake at the same time as the Eve's Pudding. There will be enough cake mixture to make 2 x 18 cm (7 in) sponges or about 18 fruit buns.

Apple brown Betty

Easy to prepare from ingredients often to hand, this pudding is deliciously satisfying, and can be made with fruits other than apples if you prefer. Serve it with vanilla ice cream, frozen vanilla yogurt, or whipped cream.

Serves 4–6

30–45 g (1–1½ oz) butter

175 g (6 oz) fresh breadcrumbs

1 kg (2 lb) cooking apples, peeled, cored, and thinly sliced

125 g (4 oz) caster sugar, plus extra for sprinkling

1 tbsp lemon juice

1–2 tsp ground cinnamon

pinch of grated nutmeg

⋆ deep 1.5–2 litre (2½–3½ pint) ovenproof dish

1 Melt the butter in a frying pan. Add the breadcrumbs and stir over a medium heat for 5 minutes or until the crumbs are crisp and golden. Remove from the heat.

2 Toss the apples with the caster sugar, lemon juice, ground cinnamon, and nutmeg.

3 Press one-quarter of the crisp breadcrumbs over the bottom of the dish. Cover with half of the apple mixture and sprinkle with a further one-quarter of the breadcrumbs.

4 Arrange the remaining apple mixture on top of the breadcrumbs, spoon over any juices, and cover with the remaining breadcrumbs. Sprinkle the top of the pudding lightly with caster sugar.

5 Cover the dish with foil. Bake in a preheated oven at 200°C (400°F, Gas 6) for about 20 minutes.

6 Remove the foil and continue baking for a further 20 minutes or until the apples are tender and the top is golden brown. Serve warm.

Apple & cranberry brown Betty

Add 175 g (6 oz) fresh or thawed frozen cranberries to the apple mixture. Add a little more sugar if necessary.

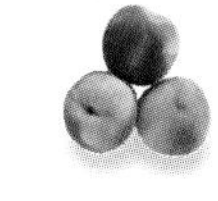

Peach Melba brown Betty

Substitute 3 peeled and sliced peaches, and 250 g (8 oz) raspberries for the apples. Omit the lemon juice, cinnamon, nutmeg, and salt.

Cook's know-how

White or brown bread can be used for the breadcrumbs. Wholemeal gives a nutty flavour and granary gives an interesting texture. For best results, the bread should be 2 days old.

Baked apples

Serves 6

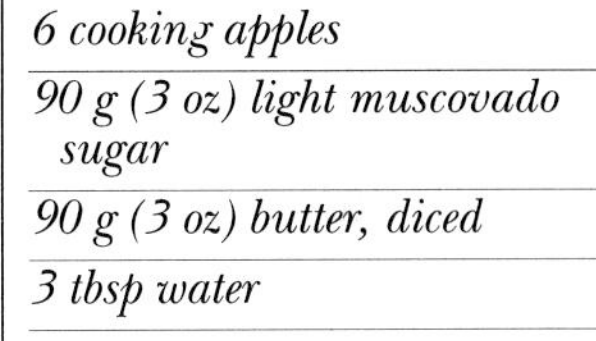

6 cooking apples

90 g (3 oz) light muscovado sugar

90 g (3 oz) butter, diced

3 tbsp water

1 Wipe the apples, and remove the cores using an apple corer. Make a shallow cut through the skin around the middle of each apple.

2 Put the apples into an ovenproof dish and fill the centres with the sugar and butter. Pour the water around the apples.

3 Bake in a preheated oven at 190°C (375°F, Gas 5) for 40–45 minutes until the apples are soft. Serve hot, spooning all the juices from the dish over the apples.

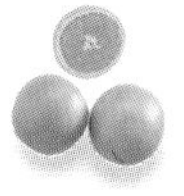

Citrus baked apples

Add the grated zest of 1 orange or 1 lemon to the muscovado sugar, and proceed as directed.

Baked apples with mincemeat

Use 125 g (4 oz) mincemeat instead of the sugar and butter, and proceed as directed.

WARM JAMAICAN BANANAS

Serves 4

30–45 g (1–1½ oz) unsalted butter

2–3 tbsp dark muscovado sugar

½ tsp ground cinnamon

4 firm but ripe bananas, cut in half lengthwise

60 ml (2 fl oz) dark rum

vanilla ice cream to serve

1 Put the butter and sugar into a large heavy frying pan, and heat gently until the butter has melted and sugar dissolved. Stir to blend together, then cook gently, stirring, for about 5 minutes.

2 Stir the cinnamon into the caramel mixture, then add the banana halves. Cook for 3 minutes on each side until warmed through.

3 Gently warm the rum in a saucepan, remove from the heat, and set alight. Pour the flaming rum over the banana halves.

4 When the flames have died down, transfer the bananas and hot sauce to serving plates. Serve at once, with scoops of vanilla ice cream.

Cook's know-how

Great care must be taken when flambéing food with alcohol. Never pour the alcohol directly from the bottle into a hot pan as it may ignite and flames can quickly lick back up the bottle to your hand. Use only a small amount of alcohol, and warm it very gently, removing it from the heat before setting it alight. Don't lean over the pan, and keep young children and pets well away from the stove. Flames can leap extremely high, so don't attempt to do any flambéing if you have a low extractor hood or cupboards over the top of the stove.

PLUM CRUMBLE

Serves 6

1 kg (2 lb) plums, halved and stoned

60 g (2 oz) light muscovado sugar

1 tsp ground cinnamon

CRUMBLE TOPPING

250 g (8 oz) plain wholemeal flour

1 tsp baking powder

90 g (3 oz) butter

150 g (5 oz) light muscovado sugar

1 Put the plums into a shallow ovenproof dish and sprinkle with the sugar and cinnamon.

2 Make the topping: put the flour and baking powder into a bowl, and rub in the butter with the fingertips until the mixture resembles fine breadcrumbs. Stir in the sugar.

3 Sprinkle the topping evenly over the plums, without pressing it down, and bake in a preheated oven at 180°C (350°F, Gas 4) for 30–40 minutes until golden. Serve hot.

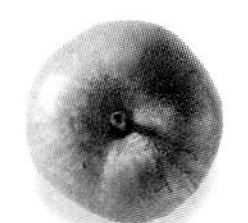

CRUNCHY APPLE CRUMBLE

Substitute 1 kg (2 lb) peeled, cored, and sliced cooking apples for the plums. Put into a saucepan with the sugar and cinnamon and 2 tbsp water. Cook gently until soft. Substitute porridge oats or muesli for half of the flour in the crumble topping, and proceed as directed in the recipe.

RHUBARB & GINGER CRUMBLE

Substitute 1 kg (2 lb) rhubarb, cut into 2.5 cm (1 in) pieces, for the plums. Put into a saucepan with the sugar, 2 tbsp water, and 1 tsp ground ginger instead of the cinnamon, and cook gently until soft. Spoon into the dish, and proceed as directed in the recipe.

FLAMBEED CHERRIES JUBILEE

 **Serves 4**

1 x 425 g (14 oz) jar Morello cherries in syrup

2–3 tbsp caster sugar

few drops of almond essence

75 ml (2½ fl oz) brandy

vanilla ice cream to serve

1 Drain the cherries, reserving 125 ml (4 fl oz) of the syrup. Put the cherries into a saucepan with the syrup and sugar. Heat gently, stirring, until the sugar dissolves, then bring to a boil. Simmer for about 5 minutes until the liquid has thickened and reduced by about half. Stir in the almond essence.

2 Pour half of the brandy over the cherries. Pour the remainder of the brandy into a small saucepan and warm gently. Remove from the heat, and set the brandy alight. Pour the flaming brandy over the cherries.

3 When the flames have died down, spoon the hot cherries and syrup over servings of vanilla ice cream, and serve at once.

FRESH CHERRIES JUBILEE

Replace the Morello cherries with 500 g (1 lb) fresh cherries. Pit the cherries and poach them in 250 ml (8 fl oz) red wine and 100 g (3½ oz) caster sugar until tender. Substitute the poaching liquid for the syrup, and proceed as directed.

Cherries

These are classified as sweet or sour. Morello cherries, which are used to make jam or syrup, are a sour variety. If you use fresh cherries, make sure you choose sweet dark ones.

FRUIT FRITTERS

Serves 4

2 apples, peeled and cored

3 bananas

juice of ½ lemon

sunflower oil for deep-frying

60 g (2 oz) caster sugar

1 tsp ground cinnamon

BATTER

125 g (4 oz) plain flour

1 tbsp icing sugar

1 egg, separated

150 ml (¼ pint) mixed milk and water

1 Cut the apples and bananas into bite-sized pieces. Toss the pieces in the lemon juice to prevent discoloration.

2 Make the batter: sift the flour and icing sugar into a bowl, and make a well in the middle. Add the egg yolk and a little of the milk mixture and whisk together. Whisk in half of the remaining milk mixture, drawing in the flour to form a smooth batter. Add the remaining milk mixture.

3 Whisk the egg white until stiff but not dry. Fold into the batter.

4 Heat the oil in a deep-fat fryer to 190°C (375°F). Pat the fruit dry. Dip each piece of fruit into the batter, lower into the hot oil, and cook in batches for 3–4 minutes until golden and crisp. Drain on paper towels and keep warm while cooking the remainder.

5 Combine the caster sugar and cinnamon, sprinkle generously over the fritters, and serve at once.

Cook's know-how

For a light, crisp batter, the egg white should be whisked and folded in just before you are ready to cook the fritters – don't leave the batter to stand or it will lose its airy texture.

FRENCH APRICOT PANCAKES

Serves 4

60 g (2 oz) butter, softened, plus extra for greasing
60 g (2 oz) caster sugar
2 eggs, beaten
60 g (2 oz) self-raising flour
300 ml (1/2 pint) milk
apricot jam and caster sugar to serve
⋆ *8-hole bun tin with 7 cm (3 in) cups*

1 Combine the butter and sugar in a bowl and cream together until soft. Beat in the eggs, a little at a time, then fold in the flour.

2 In a small saucepan, heat the milk to just below boiling point. Stir into the creamed mixture.

3 Lightly butter the bun tin cups, and divide the batter equally among them. Bake in a preheated oven at 190°C (375°F, Gas 5) for about 20 minutes until the pancakes are well risen and golden brown.

4 Slide the pancakes out of the cups, and serve with apricot jam and caster sugar. To eat, place a little jam in the middle of each pancake, fold in half, and sprinkle with caster sugar.

CREPES SUZETTE

Serves 4

juice of 2 oranges
125 g (4 oz) unsalted butter
60 g (2 oz) caster sugar
1 tbsp orange liqueur
3 tbsp brandy

CREPES
125 g (4 oz) plain flour
pinch of salt
1 egg
1 tbsp oil, plus extra for frying
300 ml (1/2 pint) milk
⋆ *18 cm (7 in) frying pan*

1 Make the crêpes: sift the flour and salt into a bowl. Make a well in the middle. Mix together the egg, oil, and milk, and pour into well. Gradually beat in the flour, to make a fairly thin batter.

2 Heat a little oil in the frying pan, then wipe away the excess oil. Add about 2 tbsp batter to the pan, tilting it to coat the frying pan evenly. Cook for about 1 minute, then turn over, and cook the other side for about 1 minute. Turn out on to a warmed plate.

3 Repeat to make 7 more crêpes. Stack the crêpes with greaseproof paper between each one to prevent them sticking together.

4 Make the orange sauce and add and fold the crêpes (see box, below). Heat to warm through.

5 Gently warm the liqueur and brandy in a pan. Remove from heat, set alight, and pour over the crêpes. When the flames have died down, transfer to hot serving dishes, and serve at once.

Making the sauce and adding and folding the crêpes

Put the orange juice, butter, and sugar into a large frying pan, and simmer for 5 minutes.

Place 1 crêpe in the pan, coat with sauce, fold in half, then in half again. Move to one side of pan.

Add another crêpe. Coat with the sauce, and fold as before. Repeat with the remaining crêpes.

MAGIC LEMON PUDDING

Serves 4

60 g (2 oz) butter, softened, plus extra for greasing

grated zest and juice of 1 large lemon

90 g (3 oz) caster sugar

2 eggs, separated

30 g (1 oz) plain flour

175 ml (6 fl oz) milk

lemon twists to decorate

⭑ 600 ml (1 pint) shallow ovenproof dish

1 Put the butter, lemon zest, and sugar into a bowl and beat together until pale and fluffy.

2 Add the egg yolks, flour, and lemon juice, and stir to combine. Gradually stir in the milk.

3 Whisk the egg whites until stiff but not dry. Gradually fold into the lemon mixture.

4 Lightly butter the ovenproof dish. Pour the lemon mixture into the dish, and put the dish into a roasting tin. Add enough hot water to the roasting tin to come almost to the rim of the dish. Bake in a preheated oven at 160°C (325°F, Gas 3) for 40 minutes or until the sponge is springy to the touch. Serve at once, decorated with lemon twists.

Cook's know-how

This "magic" pudding separates during cooking to form a sponge topping with a tangy lemon sauce beneath.

PINEAPPLE UPSIDE-DOWN PUDDING

Serves 4–6

60 g (2 oz) butter, softened, plus extra for greasing

60 g (2 oz) light muscovado sugar

1 x 225 g ($7^{1/2}$ oz) can pineapple rings in natural juice, drained, and juice reserved

4 ready-to-eat dried apricots, coarsely chopped

SPONGE

125 g (4 oz) butter, softened

125 g (4 oz) caster sugar

2 eggs, beaten

175 g (6 oz) self-raising flour

1 tsp baking powder

⭑ 18 cm (7 in) round cake tin

1 Lightly butter the tin and line the bottom with baking parchment. Cream together the butter and sugar and spread evenly over the baking parchment.

2 Arrange the pineapple rings on top of the butter and sugar mixture, and sprinkle the chopped dried apricots between the pineapple rings.

3 Make the sponge: put the butter, caster sugar, eggs, flour, and baking powder into a bowl with 2 tbsp of the reserved pineapple juice. Beat for 2 minutes or until smooth and well blended. Spoon the mixture on top of the pineapple rings and level the surface.

4 Bake in a preheated oven at 180°C (350°F, Gas 4) for about 45 minutes until the sponge is well risen and springy to the touch. Invert the sponge on to a warmed serving plate, and serve at once.

APRICOT UPSIDE-DOWN PUDDING

Substitute 1 x 400 g (13 oz) can apricot halves for the pineapple and 2 tbsp chopped stem ginger for the dried apricots, and proceed as directed.

Chocolate fondue

We're all familiar with savoury fondues, but why not try a sweet one to round off a meal? Sweet fondues are becoming so popular that you can now buy small fondue pots specially designed for the purpose. Choose a good selection of accompaniments and let everyone gather round to dip them into the luscious warm chocolate sauce.

Serves 6

1 x 250 g (8 oz) packet ready-made croissant dough

beaten egg for glazing

60 g (2 oz) desiccated coconut

60 g (2 oz) strawberries

60 g (2 oz) cape gooseberries (physalis)

1 star fruit

1 fresh fig

125 g (4 oz) cherries

60 g (2 oz) blackberries

squares of cake, such as Iced Lime Traybake (page 472, icing omitted)

CHOCOLATE SAUCE

200 g (7 oz) plain chocolate, chopped

125 ml (4 fl oz) water

30 g (1 oz) caster sugar

grated zest of 2 oranges (optional)

1 Cut each triangle of croissant dough into 3 smaller triangles. Roll up into 18 mini croissant shapes and glaze with beaten egg. Bake in a preheated oven at 190°C (375°F, Gas 5) for 10–15 minutes until golden. Set aside.

2 Spread the coconut on a baking tray and toast in the oven, turning once, for a few minutes until golden.

3 Rinse and dry the fruit. Halve any large strawberries. Peel back the papery covering from the gooseberries to reveal the fruit. Cut the star fruit into slices crosswise. Cut the fig into 8 segments.

4 Arrange the croissants and squares of cake on serving plates and set aside. Arrange the strawberries, gooseberries, star fruit, fig, cherries, and blackberries on another serving plate and set aside. Put the toasted coconut into a small bowl and set aside.

5 Make the sauce: put the chocolate into a heatproof bowl and put over a saucepan of hot water, making sure the bowl does not touch the water. Heat gently until the chocolate has melted. Remove from the heat, keeping the bowl over the water.

6 In another saucepan, combine the measured water and sugar and bring to a boil. Simmer for 5 minutes. Slowly stir the sugar syrup into the chocolate and whisk until smooth. Stir in the orange zest, if using.

7 Transfer the chocolate sauce to a fondue pot and place over a low flame to keep warm. Serve with the fruit, mini croissants, and cake for dipping, and with the toasted coconut for sprinkling.

Fondue sauces

White chocolate sauce

Roughly chop *175 g (6 oz) good quality white chocolate* and put the pieces into a heatproof bowl. Put the bowl over a saucepan of hot water, making sure the bowl does not touch the water, and heat gently until melted. Put *150 ml (1/4 pint) double cream* into a saucepan and bring almost to boiling point. Slowly pour the hot cream into the melted chocolate, stirring well. Transfer to a fondue pot or warmed serving bowl, and serve at once.

Black cherry sauce

Purée *1 x 400 g (13 oz) can pitted black cherries, including the juice.* Make the white chocolate sauce as above. After adding the double cream, stir in the puréed cherries. Heat gently to warm. Transfer the sauce to a fondue pot or warmed serving bowl, and serve at once.

Chocolate fudge sauce

Roughly chop *1* x *125 g (4 oz) bar caramel and fudge chocolate* and *90 g (3 oz) plain chocolate.* Put into a small saucepan with *125 g (4 oz) butter* and *60 g (2 oz) golden syrup* and cook over a very low heat, stirring the mixture once or twice, for 10–12 minutes. Whisk together until smooth. Whisk in *4 tbsp double cream.* Transfer to a fondue pot or warmed serving bowl, and serve at once.

Extra fondue accompaniments

A fondue can be served with a whole range of accompaniments other than those listed in the recipe above. Here are some suggestions.

- Sliced peaches and nectarines, which go particularly well with White Chocolate Sauce.
- Pieces of pineapple: either a fresh pineapple, peeled, sliced, and cut into wedges, or canned pineapple in natural juice – spears are an ideal shape for dipping.
- Chunks of nougat, fudge, or Turkish delight.
- Mini profiteroles; make the pastry (page 484), and shape into small rounds before baking.
- Seedless grapes.
- Finger-shaped cakes or biscuits, such as shortcake, sponge fingers, or Viennese fingers.
- Kiwi fruit, peeled and cut into segments lengthwise.
- Apple and pear slices, which go well with Chocolate Fudge Sauce.

SAUCY CHOCOLATE PUDDING

 **Serves 4**

60 g (2 oz) caster sugar
60 g (2 oz) fine semolina
30 g (1 oz) cocoa powder
1 tsp baking powder
30 g (1 oz) butter, melted, plus extra for greasing
2 eggs, beaten
2–3 drops of vanilla essence
icing sugar for dusting

SAUCE
90 g (3 oz) light muscovado sugar
2 tbsp cocoa powder
300 ml (1/2 pint) hot water
⋆ 1 litre (1 3/4 pint) ovenproof dish

1 Mix together the sugar and semolina in a large bowl. Sift the cocoa powder and baking powder into the bowl, and mix thoroughly.

2 In a separate bowl, whisk together the melted butter, eggs, and vanilla essence with an electric whisk. Add this mixture to the dry ingredients and stir with a wooden spoon until well blended.

3 Lightly butter the ovenproof dish. Pour the mixture into the dish.

4 Make the sauce: mix together the muscovado sugar and cocoa powder, and gradually stir in the measured hot water. Pour the liquid over the pudding.

5 Bake the pudding in a preheated oven at 180°C (350°F, Gas 4) for 30 minutes or until the liquid has sunk to the bottom and the sponge is well risen and springy to the touch. Sprinkle with icing sugar, and serve at once.

NUTTY CHOCOLATE PUDDING

Add 60 g (2 oz) chopped pecan nuts or walnuts to the dry ingredients, and proceed as directed.

STICKY DATE & WALNUT PUDDING

Serves 8

90 g (3 oz) butter, softened, plus extra for greasing
150 g (5 oz) light muscovado sugar
2 eggs, beaten
1 tbsp coffee essence
175 g (6 oz) self-raising flour
1 tsp baking powder
175 g (6 oz) stoned dates, roughly chopped
90 g (3 oz) walnuts, roughly chopped
175 ml (6 fl oz) hot water

TOFFEE SAUCE
125 g (4 oz) butter
175 g (6 oz) light muscovado sugar
6 tbsp double cream
60 g (2 oz) walnuts, roughly chopped
⋆ deep 18 cm (7 in) square cake tin

1 Butter the cake tin and line the bottom with baking parchment.

2 Put the butter, sugar, eggs, coffee essence, flour, and baking powder into a large bowl. Beat well until smooth and thoroughly blended.

3 Stir in the dates and walnuts, and then the measured hot water. Pour the mixture into the tin.

4 Bake in a preheated oven at 180°C (350°F, Gas 4) for 45–50 minutes until the pudding is well risen, browned on top, and springy to the touch.

5 About 10 minutes before the pudding is ready, make the toffee sauce: put the butter and sugar into a small saucepan, and heat gently, stirring, until the butter has melted and the sugar dissolved. Stir in the cream and walnuts and heat gently to warm through.

6 Cut the pudding into 8 even-sized squares, and transfer to serving plates. Spoon over the toffee sauce, and serve at once.

Cook's know-how

Serve the toffee sauce with other hot or cold desserts, such as steamed puddings or ice cream.

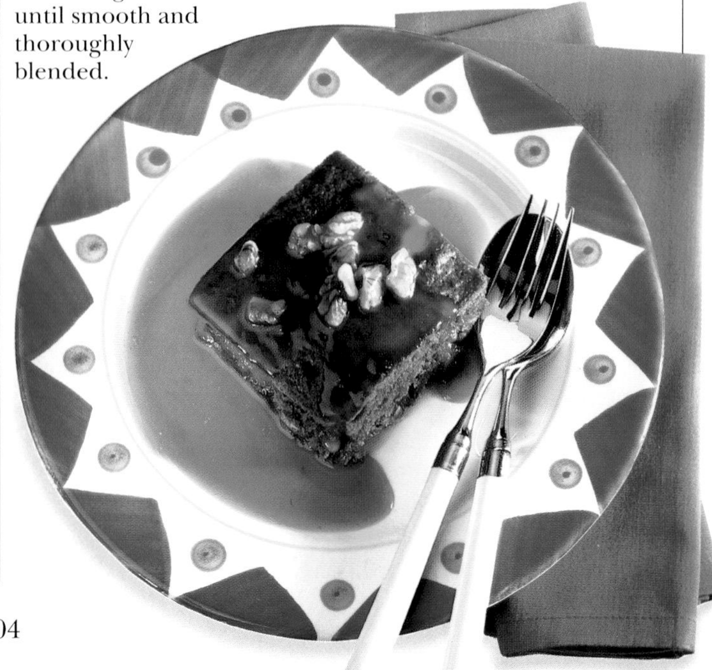

QUEEN OF PUDDINGS

Serves 6

4 egg yolks
600 ml (1 pint) milk
30 g (1 oz) butter, plus extra for greasing
60 g (2 oz) caster sugar
grated zest of 1 orange
90 g (3 oz) fresh white breadcrumbs
3 tbsp strawberry or raspberry jam

MERINGUE TOPPING

4 egg whites
175 g (6 oz) caster sugar
⭑ 1.25 litre (2 pint) shallow ovenproof dish

1 In a large bowl, lightly beat the egg yolks. Set aside. Heat the milk in a small saucepan until bubbles appear around the edge. Add the butter, sugar, and orange zest, and heat gently until the butter has melted and the sugar dissolved.

2 Lightly butter the ovenproof dish and set aside. Gradually add the hot milk mixture to the egg yolks, whisking all the time.

3 Stir in the breadcrumbs, then pour into the ovenproof dish. Leave to stand for 15 minutes.

4 Bake the pudding in a preheated oven at 180°C (350°F, Gas 4) for about 30 minutes until just set. Remove from the oven and set aside.

5 Warm the jam in a small saucepan until melted. Spread the warmed jam evenly over the surface of the pudding.

6 Make the meringue topping: whisk the egg whites until stiff but not dry. With an electric mixer, whisk in the caster sugar, 1 tsp at a time, keeping the mixer at full speed.

7 Spoon the meringue on top of the pudding, spreading it to the edge and pulling it up to form peaks.

8 Return the pudding to the oven and bake for a further 10–15 minutes until the top of the meringue is crisp and golden brown. Serve at once.

HOT CHOCOLATE SOUFFLES

Serves 4

125 g (4 oz) plain chocolate
2 tbsp water
300 ml ($^{1}/_{2}$ pint) milk
45 g ($1^{1}/_{2}$ oz) butter, plus extra for greasing
45 g ($1^{1}/_{2}$ oz) plain flour
2–3 drops of vanilla essence
60 g (2 oz) caster sugar
4 egg yolks
5 egg whites
sifted icing sugar for dusting
⭑ 4 x 300 ml ($^{1}/_{2}$ pint) soufflé dishes

1 Break the chocolate into pieces, and put into a small saucepan with the meaured water and a few tablespoons of the milk. Heat gently, stirring, until the chocolate has melted. Add the remaining milk, stirring to blend.

2 Melt the butter in a pan, add the flour, and cook, stirring, for 1 minute. Remove from the heat, and gradually add the chocolate and milk mixture. Bring to a boil, stirring, until the sauce has thickened. Stir in the vanilla essence and caster sugar, and leave to cool.

3 Beat the egg yolks into the cooled chocolate mixture. Lightly butter the individual soufflé dishes and set aside.

4 Whisk the egg whites until stiff but not dry. Stir 1 large spoonful of the chocolate egg whites into the chocolate mixture, then carefully fold in the remainder. Divide the mixture between the 4 soufflé dishes.

5 Place on a hot baking tray and bake in a preheated oven at 190°C (375°F, Gas 5) for 40–45 minutes until the soufflés are well risen and firm. Dust with sifted icing sugar. Serve the soufflés at once.

Cook's know-how

If you prefer, you can make 1 large soufflé instead of individual soufflés. Simply use 1 x 1.25 litre (2 pint) soufflé dish and bake for 45–50 minutes. You may need to tie a collar of greaseproof paper around the outside of the dish (page 429), to support the soufflé as it rises.

BREAD & BUTTER PUDDING

 **Serves 6**

12 thin slices of white bread, crusts removed

about 125 g (4 oz) butter, softened, plus extra for greasing

175 g (6 oz) mixed dried fruit

grated zest of 2 lemons

125 g (4 oz) demerara sugar

600 ml (1 pint) milk

2 eggs

⭑ 1.7 litre (3 pint) ovenproof dish

1 Spread one side of each slice of bread with a thick layer of butter. Cut each slice of bread in half diagonally. Lightly butter the ovenproof dish and arrange 12 of the triangles, buttered-side down, in the bottom of the dish.

2 Sprinkle over half of the dried fruit, lemon zest, and sugar. Top with the remaining bread, buttered-side up. Sprinkle over the remaining dried fruit, lemon zest, and sugar.

3 Beat together the milk and eggs, and strain over the bread. Leave for 1 hour so that the bread can absorb some of the liquid.

4 Bake in a preheated oven at 180°C (350°F, Gas 4) for about 40 minutes until the bread slices on the top of the pudding are a golden brown colour and crisp, and the custard mixture has set completely. Serve at once.

BREAD & BUTTER PUDDING WITH MARMALADE

Spread 6 of the slices of bread with thick-cut marmalade after spreading them with the butter. Halve the slices, and arrange the triangles, buttered-side down, in the dish. Sprinkle with the dried fruit, lemon zest, and sugar, then arrange the remaining triangles, marmalade-side up, on top. Proceed as directed.

BREAD & BUTTER PUDDING WITH APRICOTS

Add 60 g (2 oz) roughly chopped ready-to-eat dried apricots to the dried fruit, and proceed as directed.

RICE PUDDING

 **Serves 4**

15 g (1/2 oz) butter, plus extra for greasing

60 g (2 oz) pudding rice

600 ml (1 pint) milk

30 g (1 oz) caster sugar

1 strip of lemon zest

1/4 tsp grated nutmeg

⭑ 900 ml (1 1/2 pint) ovenproof dish

1 Lightly grease the ovenproof dish with butter. Rinse the rice under cold running water and drain well.

2 Put the rice into the ovenproof dish and stir in the milk. Leave for about 30 minutes to allow the rice to soften.

3 Add the caster sugar and lemon zest to the rice mixture, and stir to mix. Sprinkle the surface of the milk with freshly grated nutmeg and dot with small knobs of butter.

4 Bake in a preheated oven at 150°C (300°F, Gas 2) for 2–2 1/2 hours until the skin of the pudding is brown. Serve at once.

Cook's know-how

Pudding rice has short, rounded grains which absorb a great deal of liquid and give a rich, creamy consistency. For the creamiest pudding, use full-fat milk.

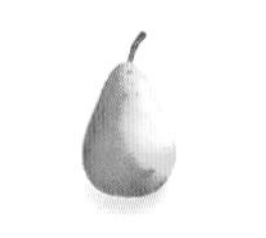

CHILLED RICE WITH PEARS

Leave the rice pudding to cool. Remove and discard the skin. Chill the pudding in the refrigerator and serve with poached fresh pears or canned pear halves.

CHRISTMAS PUDDING

A steamed pudding, with its dried fruit, spices, and rum, is the traditional way to end a family Christmas meal. This is a rich, dark, heavily fruited version, delicious served with brandy butter.

Serves 8–10

- *90 g (3 oz) self-raising flour*
- *125 g (4 oz) shredded vegetable suet*
- *30 g (1 oz) almonds, blanched and shredded*
- *125 g (4 oz) carrot, grated*
- *250 g (8 oz) raisins*
- *125 g (4 oz) currants*
- *125 g (4 oz) sultanas*
- *125 g (4 oz) fresh white breadcrumbs*
- *1/4 tsp grated nutmeg*
- *60 g (2 oz) mixed candied peel, chopped*
- *90 g (3 oz) light muscovado sugar*
- *grated zest and juice of 1 lemon*
- *2 eggs, beaten*
- *butter for greasing*
- *75 ml (2 1/2 fl oz) dark rum*
- *brandy butter to serve*
- ** 1.25 litre (2 pint) pudding basin*

1 In a large bowl, combine the flour, suet, almonds, carrot, raisins, currants, sultanas, breadcrumbs, nutmeg, candied peel, sugar, and lemon zest. Add the lemon juice and eggs, and stir until well combined.

2 Lightly butter the pudding basin. Spoon in the pudding mixture and level the surface.

3 Cover with buttered greaseproof paper, then foil, both pleated in the middle. Secure the paper and foil in place by tying string under the rim of the basin (page 395).

4 Put the basin into a steamer or saucepan of simmering water, making sure the water comes halfway up the side of the basin. Cover and steam, topping up with boiling water as necessary, for about 6 hours.

5 Remove the basin from the steamer or pan and leave to cool. Remove the paper and foil covering. Make a few holes in the pudding with a fine skewer, and pour in the rum.

6 Cover the pudding with fresh greaseproof paper and foil. Store in a cool place for up to 3 months.

7 To reheat for serving, steam the pudding for 2–3 hours. Serve at once, with brandy butter.

Cook's know-how

Make your own brandy butter by creaming together 250 g (8 oz) each of unsalted butter and caster sugar or icing sugar, and 90 ml (3 fl oz) brandy. The brandy butter can be frozen for up to 3 months.

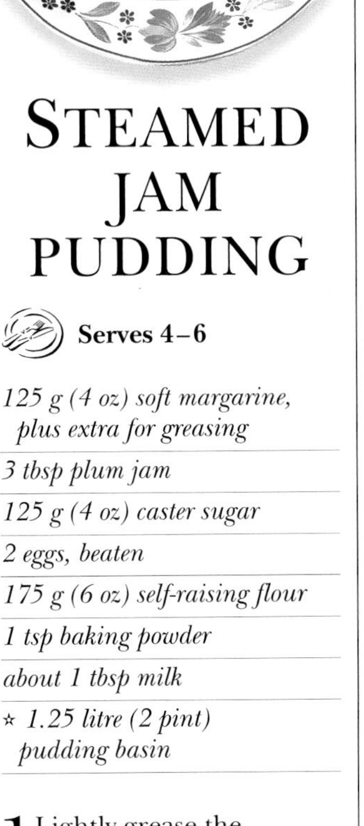

STEAMED JAM PUDDING

Serves 4–6

- *125 g (4 oz) soft margarine, plus extra for greasing*
- *3 tbsp plum jam*
- *125 g (4 oz) caster sugar*
- *2 eggs, beaten*
- *175 g (6 oz) self-raising flour*
- *1 tsp baking powder*
- *about 1 tbsp milk*
- ** 1.25 litre (2 pint) pudding basin*

1 Lightly grease the pudding basin with margarine, and spoon the jam into the bottom.

2 Put the margarine, sugar, eggs, flour, and baking powder into a large bowl, and beat until smooth and thoroughly blended. Add enough milk to give a dropping consistency.

3 Spoon the mixture into the pudding basin, and smooth the surface. Cover with greased greaseproof paper and foil, both pleated in the middle. Secure with string (page 395).

4 Put the basin into a steamer or saucepan of simmering water, making sure the water comes halfway up the side of the basin. Cover and steam, topping up with boiling water as needed, for about 1 1/2 hours. Turn the pudding out on to a warmed plate, and serve hot.

SYRUP PUDDING

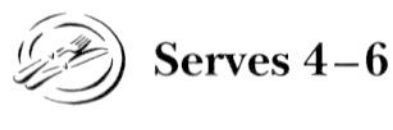 **Serves 4–6**

butter for greasing

90 ml (3 fl oz) golden syrup

125 g (4 oz) self-raising flour

125 g (4 oz) shredded vegetable suet

125 g (4 oz) fresh white breadcrumbs

60 g (2 oz) caster sugar

about 125 ml (4 fl oz) milk

⋆ *900 ml (1½ pint) pudding basin*

1 Lightly butter the basin and spoon the golden syrup into the bottom.

2 Put the flour, suet, breadcrumbs, and sugar into a bowl and stir to combine. Stir in enough milk to give a dropping consistency. Spoon into the basin on top of the syrup.

3 Cover the basin with buttered baking parchment and foil, both pleated in the middle. Secure by tying string under the rim of the basin (page 395).

4 Put the basin into a steamer or saucepan of simmering water, making sure the water comes halfway up the side of the basin if using a saucepan. Cover and steam, topping up with boiling water as necessary, for about 3 hours. Turn out the pudding, and serve.

MINCEMEAT & ALMOND TART

This is a rich and spicy dessert, ideal for Christmas and during the cold winter months. If you prefer, you can use a little less mincemeat and add some stewed apple, which gives a lighter, fruitier flavour.

Serves 8–10

175 g (6 oz) butter, softened

175 g (6 oz) caster sugar

4 eggs

175 g (6 oz) ground almonds

1 tsp almond essence

about 8 tbsp good-quality mincemeat

PASTRY

250 g (8 oz) plain flour

125 g (4 oz) chilled butter, cut into cubes

60 g (2 oz) caster sugar

1 egg, beaten

TOPPING

175 g (6 oz) icing sugar, sifted

juice of ½ lemon

1–2 tbsp water

60 g (2 oz) flaked almonds

⋆ *deep 28 cm (11 in) loose-bottomed fluted flan tin*

1 Make the pastry: put the flour into a large bowl. Add the butter and rub in with the fingertips until the mixture resembles fine breadcrumbs. Stir in the sugar, then mix in the egg to bind to a soft pliable dough. Wrap the dough in cling film and chill for about 30 minutes.

2 Roll out the dough on a lightly floured work surface and use to line the tin. Prick the bottom with a fork. Cover and chill while preparing the filling.

3 Put the butter and sugar into a large bowl and cream together until pale and fluffy. Add the eggs one at a time, beating well after each addition, then mix in the ground almonds and almond essence.

4 Spread the mincemeat evenly over the bottom of the pastry shell. Pour the almond mixture over the mincemeat.

5 Bake in a preheated oven at 190°C (375°F, Gas 5) for about 40 minutes until the filling is golden and firm to the touch. Cover loosely with foil if it is browning too much.

6 Meanwhile, make the topping: stir together the icing sugar, lemon juice, and enough water to make a thin glacé icing. Spread evenly over the tart, then sprinkle with the almonds.

7 Return to the oven and bake for about 5 minutes until the icing is shiny and the almonds lightly coloured. Serve warm.

STRAWBERRY & RHUBARB PIE

Serves 6–8

150 g (5 oz) caster sugar, plus extra for sprinkling

45 g (1 1/2 oz) cornflour

750 g (1 1/2 lb) rhubarb, cut into 1 cm (1/2 in) slices

2 cinnamon sticks, halved

375 g (12 oz) strawberries, hulled and halved

SHORTCRUST PASTRY

175 g (6 oz) plain flour

90 g (3 oz) chilled butter, cut into cubes

about 2 tbsp cold water

** 23 cm (9 in) flan dish*

1 Make the pastry: put the flour into a large bowl, add the butter, and rub in with the fingertips until the mixture resembles fine breadcrumbs. Add enough water to bind to a soft, but not sticky dough. Wrap the pastry in cling film and leave to chill in the refrigerator for about 30 minutes.

2 Meanwhile, combine the sugar with the cornflour and toss with the rhubarb, cinnamon, and strawberries. Leave to macerate for 15–20 minutes.

3 On a lightly floured work surface, divide the dough in half and roll out one half into a round to line the bottom and side of the flan dish.

4 Put the macerated fruit into the pastry shell, removing the cinnamon.

5 Roll out the second half of pastry to the same size as the first round. Cut a 1 cm (1/2 in) strip from around the edge of the pastry.

6 Cut the remaining pastry into 1 cm (1/2 in) strips and arrange in a lattice on top of the pie. Brush the ends with water and attach the long strip around the rim of the pie. Sprinkle with 1–2 tbsp sugar.

7 Bake in a preheated oven at 220°C (425°F, Gas 7) for 10 minutes; reduce the oven temperature to 180°C (350°F, Gas 4), and bake for a further 30–40 minutes until the fruit is just cooked, and the pastry golden.

8 Remove from the oven and leave to cool. Serve warm or cold.

BAKED APPLE DUMPLINGS

Serves 4

4 cooking apples, peeled and cored

60 g (2 oz) demerara sugar

1/2 tsp ground cinnamon

milk for glazing

SHORTCRUST PASTRY

375 g (12 oz) plain flour

90 g (3 oz) chilled butter, cut into cubes, plus extra for greasing

90 g (3 oz) chilled white vegetable fat, cut into cubes

3–4 tbsp cold water

1 Make the pastry: put the flour into a large bowl. Add the butter and white vegetable fat, and rub in with the fingertips until the mixture resembles fine breadcrumbs. Mix in enough water to make a soft, pliable dough. Wrap the dough in cling film and chill for about 30 minutes.

2 Divide the dough into 4 pieces. Roll out each piece on a lightly floured work surface and cut into an 18 cm (7 in) round. Reserve the trimmings. Put an apple in the centre of each round and make 4 dumplings (see box, right).

Making the apple dumplings

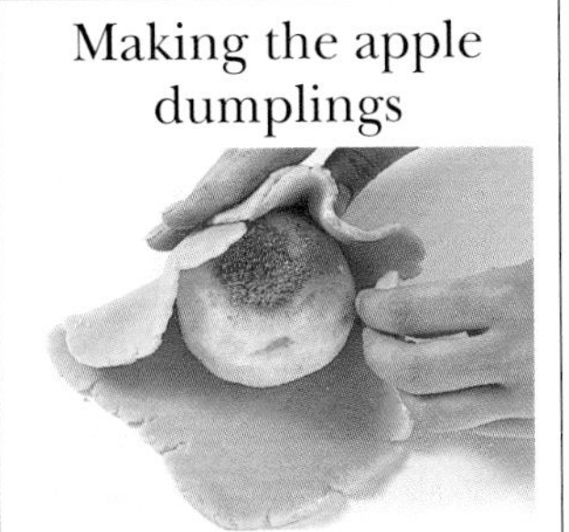

Fill the apples with the demerara sugar and cinnamon. Draw up a pastry round to enclose each apple, sealing the joins with a little water. Place, with the joins underneath, on a lightly buttered baking tray.

3 Cut leaf shapes from the pastry trimmings, and use to decorate the tops of the dumplings, attaching them with a little water. Make a hole in the top of each dumpling, and lightly brush all over with milk.

4 Bake in a preheated oven at 200°C (400°F, Gas 6) for 35–40 minutes until the pastry is golden and the apples tender. Serve hot.

DOUBLE CRUST APPLE PIE

For a successful double crust pie, the pastry shell should be properly cooked. Putting the pie dish on a baking tray ensures the heat is transferred to the base.

Serves 6

500 g (1 lb) cooking apples, preferably Bramley apples, peeled, cored, and sliced

250 g (8 oz) Cox's apples, peeled, cored, and sliced

about 30 g (1 oz) caster sugar, plus extra for sprinkling

2 tbsp water

rough puff pastry (page 394)

milk for glazing

★ *24 cm (9 1/2 in) pie dish*

1 Put the apples into a large pan and add the sugar and water. Cover and cook gently, stirring, for about 10 minutes until the apples are soft and fluffy. Taste for sweetness and add more sugar if necessary. Turn into a bowl and leave to cool.

2 Divide the pastry into 2 portions, 1 portion slightly larger than the other. Roll out the larger portion on a lightly floured work surface and use to line the pie dish.

3 Spoon the apple filling on to the pastry shell, spreading it almost to the edge and then doming it in the middle.

4 Roll out the remaining pastry. Brush the edge of the pastry shell with a little water, then lay the pastry lid over the apple filling. Trim the edge, then crimp to seal. Make a small hole in the pastry lid to allow the steam to escape.

5 Use the pastry trimmings to make leaves to decorate the pie, attaching them with milk. Brush the pastry lid with milk and sprinkle with sugar.

6 Put a baking tray in the oven and preheat the oven to 220°C (425°F, Gas 7). Put the pie dish on the hot baking tray (this helps ensure a crisp pastry base) and bake for 25–30 minutes until the pastry is golden.

DUTCH APPLE PIE

When cooking the apples, substitute light muscovado sugar for the caster sugar, and add 90 g (3 oz) raisins, 1/2 tsp ground cinnamon, 1/4 tsp ground cloves, and 1/4 tsp grated nutmeg to the apple filling. Proceed as directed in the recipe.

CITRUS APPLE PIE

When cooking the apples, add the grated zest and juice of 1 large lemon, and 3 tbsp fine-cut orange marmalade to the apples.

SAUCES FOR PUDDINGS

SWEET WHITE SAUCE

Blend *1 tbsp cornflour* with *1 tbsp caster sugar,* and a little milk taken from *300 ml (1/2 pint).* Bring the remaining milk to a boil and stir into the cornflour mixture. Return to the saucepan and heat gently, stirring, until thickened. If preferred, add flavourings such as *grated orange zest, brandy, rum,* or *vanilla essence* to the sauce. Serve warm.

POURING CUSTARD

Blend together *3 eggs, 30 g (1 oz) caster sugar,* and *1 tsp cornflour.* Heat *600 ml (1 pint) milk* to just below boiling and stir into the egg mixture. Return to the pan and heat gently, stirring, until thickened. Strain into a cold bowl to prevent further cooking, and serve warm or cold.

SABAYON SAUCE

Put *4 egg yolks, 60 g (2 oz) caster sugar,* and *150 ml (1/4 pint) dry white wine* into a bowl over a saucepan of gently simmering water. Whisk for 5–8 minutes or until the mixture is frothy and thick. Remove from the heat and whisk in the *grated zest of 1 orange.* Serve at once or, to serve cool, continue whisking the mixture until cool.

TARTE TATIN

Serves 6

90 g (3 oz) butter
90 g (3 oz) demerara sugar
1 kg (2 lb) Cox's apples or similar firm dessert apples
grated zest and juice of 1 lemon

PASTRY
175 g (6 oz) plain flour
125 g (4 oz) chilled butter, cut into cubes
30 g (1 oz) icing sugar
1 egg yolk
about 1 tbsp cold water
☆ shallow 23 cm (9 in) round cake tin

1 Make the pastry: put the flour into a large bowl and add the butter. Rub in until the mixture resembles fine breadcrumbs. Stir in the icing sugar, then mix in the egg yolk and enough water to make a soft but not sticky dough. Wrap and chill for 30 minutes.

2 Put the butter and sugar into a pan and heat very gently until the sugar dissolves. Increase the heat and cook gently for 4–5 minutes until the mixture turns dark golden brown and is thick, but pourable. Pour evenly over the bottom of the tin.

3 Peel, core, and slice the apples. Toss them with the lemon zest and juice. Arrange in the cake tin (see box, below).

4 Roll out the pastry on a lightly floured work surface into a round slightly larger than the tin. Lay the pastry over the apples, tucking the excess down the side of the tin.

5 Bake in a preheated oven at 200°C (400°F, Gas 6) for 25–30 minutes until the pastry is crisp and golden. Invert a serving plate on top of the tin, turn the tin and plate over, and lift the tin to reveal the caramelized apples. Serve warm or cold.

Arranging the apples in the cake tin

Arrange a single layer of the best apple slices in a circular pattern on top of the caramel mixture. Cover evenly with the remaining apple slices.

APPLE STRUDEL

Serves 8

four 25 x 45 cm (10 x 18 in) sheets of filo pastry
60 g (2 oz) butter, melted
30 g (1 oz) fresh white breadcrumbs
15 g (1/2 oz) flaked almonds
icing sugar for dusting

FILLING
750 g (1 1/2 lb) cooking apples, peeled, cored, and sliced
grated zest and juice of 1 lemon
3 tbsp light muscovado sugar
1/2 tsp ground mixed spice
1/2 tsp ground cinnamon
125 g (4 oz) sultanas
60 g (2 oz) blanched almonds, roughly chopped

1 Make the filling: mix together the apples, lemon zest and juice, sugar, mixed spice, cinnamon, sultanas, and almonds.

2 Lightly brush 1 sheet of filo pastry with melted butter. Cover with the remaining sheets, brushing each with butter. Add the filling and finish the strudel (see box, right).

3 Brush the strudel with melted butter and sprinkle with the almonds. Bake in a preheated oven at 190°C (375°F, Gas 5) for 40–45 minutes until the pastry is crisp and golden. Dust with icing sugar. Serve warm or cold.

Finishing the strudel

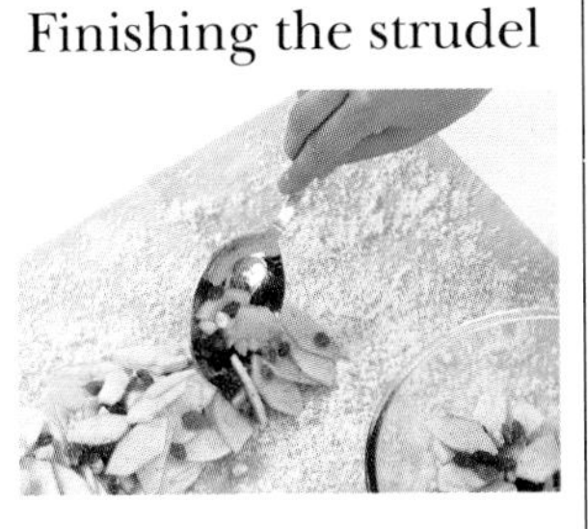

Sprinkle the breadcrumbs over the pastry. Spoon the apple mixture along the middle of the pastry.

Fold the pastry to enclose the filling, turn over on to a baking tray, and bend into a horseshoe shape.

Fruit puddings

Make the most of the fruits of all seasons with these delicious recipes. Just add an unusual topping, and any fruit can be turned into a pudding no-one can resist. Here are 3 recipes, with a couple of extra toppings so you can ring the changes. If you're feeling really self-indulgent, serve them with custard, cream, or ice cream.

Nutty peach streusel

Serves 4

6 ripe peaches
1/2 tsp ground ginger
1/2 tsp ground cinnamon
60 g (2 oz) caster sugar
4 tbsp water

STREUSEL TOPPING

60 g (2 oz) plain flour
60 g (2 oz) caster sugar
60 g (2 oz) butter, diced
125 g (4 oz) skinned hazelnuts, chopped

1 Score the bottoms of the peaches and immerse them in boiling water for a few seconds. Peel off the skins, remove the stones, and cut into quarters.

2 Put the peaches into a saucepan with the ginger, cinnamon, sugar, and water. Bring to a boil and simmer for 10 minutes. Remove from the heat.

3 Make the streusel: put the flour and sugar into a bowl and stir together. Add the butter and rub in with the fingertips. Stir in the hazelnuts.

4 Transfer the peaches to a shallow ovenproof dish and spoon over the topping: it should be no more than 1 cm (1/2 in) deep. Bake in a preheated oven at 200°C (400°F, Gas 6) for 20 minutes. Serve hot.

Nutty shortcake

Cream *90 g (3 oz) butter* and *75 g (2 1/2 oz) caster sugar* until very light and fluffy. Sift *90 g (3 oz) self-raising flour* and *45 g (1 1/2 oz) cornflour* and add to the mixture with *30 g (1 oz) chopped walnuts.* Mix to form a stiff dough. Knead the dough lightly for 3 minutes. Cut out rounds and arrange on top of the fruit. Bake in a preheated oven at 190°C (375°F, Gas 5) for 45 minutes.

Winter fruit with dumplings

Serves 4–6

250 g (8 oz) caster sugar
200 ml (7 fl oz) water
125 g (4 oz) ready-to-eat dried apricots
125 g (4 oz) raisins
125 g (4 oz) dried apple rings
125 g (4 oz) ready-to-eat prunes
1 orange, segmented
2 tbsp whisky

DUMPLINGS

60 g (2 oz) fresh white breadcrumbs
175 g (6 oz) self-raising flour
125 g (4 oz) shredded vegetable suet
pinch of salt
about 150 ml (1/4 pint) water
pared orange zest to decorate

1 Put the sugar and water into a large saucepan and bring to a boil. Add the apricots, raisins, apple rings, prunes, orange, and whisky. Cover and simmer for 10 minutes. Leave to stand for about 2 hours.

2 Make the dumplings: combine the breadcrumbs, flour, suet, and salt in a bowl. Add enough water to bind to a smooth dough. Knead briefly. Shape into 2.5 cm (1 in) dumplings.

3 Transfer the fruit to an ovenproof dish, arrange the dumplings on top, and bake in a preheated oven at 200°C (400°F, Gas 6) for 20 minutes. Serve hot.

Cinnamon croutons

Melt *125 g (4 oz) butter* in a frying pan over a gentle heat. Add *1 tsp ground cinnamon* and triangles of crustless white bread, and fry for 1–2 minutes on each side until lightly golden. Arrange on top of the fruit before serving.

Blackberry & apple cobbler

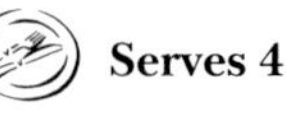

Serves 4

2 Bramley apples
500 g (1 lb) blackberries
60 g (2 oz) caster sugar
grated zest and juice of 1 lemon

TOPPING

250 g (8 oz) self-raising flour
60 g (2 oz) butter
90 g (3 oz) caster sugar
90 ml (3 fl oz) milk, plus extra for glazing
⋆ star-shaped and crescent-shaped pastry cutters

1 Peel the apples and cut into large slices, about 1 cm (1/2 in) thick. Use the star-shaped cutter to cut shapes out of the apple slices.

2 Put the star-shaped pieces of apple as well as the offcuts into a pan with the blackberries, sugar, and lemon zest and juice. Cover and simmer gently for 10–15 minutes until the apple pieces are tender but not broken up.

3 Meanwhile, make the topping: put the flour into a bowl, add the butter, and rub in with the fingertips until the mixture resembles fine breadcrumbs. Stir in the sugar, add the milk, and mix to form a soft dough.

4 Roll out on a lightly floured surface until 1 cm (1/2 in) thick. Cut into shapes with the crescent pastry cutter.

5 Transfer the fruit to an ovenproof dish, arranging the star-shaped pieces of apple on the top. Arrange the pastry crescents on top of the fruit and brush with milk to glaze.

6 Bake in a preheated oven at 220°C (425°F, Gas 7) for 15–20 minutes until golden. Serve hot.

Clockwise from top: *Winter Fruit with Dumplings, Nutty Peach Streusel, Blackberry & Apple Cobbler.*

TREACLE TART

 **Serves 8**

375 g (12 oz) golden syrup

about 200 g (7 oz) fresh white or brown breadcrumbs

grated zest and juice of 1 large lemon

PASTRY

175 g (6 oz) plain flour

90 g (3 oz) chilled butter, cut into cubes

about 2 tbsp cold water

** 25 cm (10 in) loose-bottomed fluted flan tin*

1 Make the pastry: put the flour into a large bowl, add the butter, and rub in with the fingertips until the mixture resembles fine breadcrumbs. Mix in enough water to make a soft pliable dough.

2 Wrap the dough in cling film and leave to chill in the refrigerator for about 30 minutes.

3 Roll out the dough on a lightly floured surface and use to line the flan tin.

4 Gently heat the golden syrup in a saucepan until melted, and stir in the breadcrumbs and lemon zest and juice. Pour into the pastry shell.

5 Bake in a preheated oven at 200°C (400°F, Gas 6) for 10 minutes; reduce the oven temperature to 180°C (350°F, Gas 4), and bake for a further 30 minutes or until the pastry is golden and the filling firm.

6 Leave to cool in the tin for a few minutes. Serve warm, cut into slices.

Cook's know-how

An easy way to measure the golden syrup in this recipe is to put the saucepan on the scales, set the scales at zero, then measure the syrup directly into the saucepan.

FRENCH APPLE TART

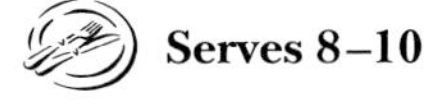 **Serves 8–10**

90 g (3 oz) butter

1.5 kg (3 lb) cooking apples, cored and cut into chunks

3 tbsp water

6 tbsp apricot jam

125 g (4 oz) caster sugar

grated zest of 1 large lemon

APPLE TOPPING & GLAZE

375 g (12 oz) dessert apples, peeled, cored, and sliced

juice of 1 lemon

1 tbsp caster sugar

6 tbsp apricot jam

PASTRY

250 g (8 oz) plain flour

125 g (4 oz) chilled butter, cubed

125 g (4 oz) caster sugar

4 egg yolks

** 28 cm (11 in) loose-bottomed fluted flan tin*

** baking beans*

1 Make the pastry: put the flour into a large bowl. Add the butter and rub in until the mixture resembles fine breadcrumbs. Stir in the sugar, then mix in the egg yolks and a little cold water, if necessary, to make a soft dough. Wrap in cling film and chill for 30 minutes.

2 Melt the butter in a large saucepan, and add the cooking apples and water. Cover and cook very gently for 20–25 minutes until the apples are soft.

3 Rub the apples through a nylon sieve into a clean pan. Add the jam, sugar, and lemon zest. Cook over a high heat for 15–20 minutes, stirring constantly, until all the liquid has evaporated and the apple purée is thick. Leave to cool.

4 Roll out the pastry on a lightly floured work surface and use to line the flan tin. Bake blind (page 395) in a preheated oven at 190°C (375°F, Gas 5) for 10–15 minutes. Remove the beans and foil and bake for 5 minutes. Leave to cool.

5 Spoon the apple purée into the shell. Arrange the apple slices on top, brush with lemon juice, and sprinkle with caster sugar. Return to the oven and bake for 30–35 minutes until the apples are tender and their edges lightly browned.

6 Heat the jam, work through a sieve, then brush over the apples. Serve.

BAKEWELL TART

Serves 6

125 g (4 oz) butter
125 g (4 oz) caster sugar
1 egg, lightly beaten
125 g (4 oz) ground rice
1/2 tsp almond essence
2 tbsp raspberry jam
icing sugar for sprinkling

PASTRY

175 g (6 oz) plain flour
45 g (1 1/2 oz) chilled butter, cut into cubes
45 g (1 1/2 oz) chilled white vegetable fat, cut into cubes
about 2 tbsp cold water
milk for glazing
☆ 19 cm (7 1/2 in) loose-bottomed fluted flan tin

1 Make the pastry: put the flour into a large bowl. Add the butter and white vegetable fat and rub in until the mixture resembles fine breadcrumbs. Mix in enough water to make a soft pliable dough. Wrap in cling film and chill for 30 minutes.

2 Roll out the pastry on a lightly floured work surface and use to line the flan tin. Reserve trimmings.

3 Melt the butter in a saucepan, stir in the caster sugar, and cook for about 1 minute. Remove from the heat, leave to cool a little, then gradually stir in the egg, ground rice, and almond essence.

4 Spread the jam over the bottom of the pastry shell, and pour the almond mixture on top.

5 Roll out the reserved pastry trimmings, and cut into thin strips, long enough to fit across the tart. Arrange the strips on top of the almond filling to form a lattice, attaching them to the edge of the pastry shell with a little milk.

6 Bake in a preheated oven at 200°C (400°F, Gas 6) for 45–50 minutes until the filling is well risen and golden and springs back when lightly presssed with a finger. If the pastry is browning too much, cover the tart loosely with foil.

7 Remove the tart from the oven. Sprinkle with icing sugar and serve the tart warm or cold.

PECAN PIE

Serves 6–8

150 g (5 oz) pecan halves
30 g (1 oz) unsalted butter
60 g (2 oz) light muscovado sugar
30 g (1 oz) caster sugar
125 ml (4 fl oz) golden syrup
3 tbsp brandy
1 tsp vanilla essence
2 tbsp single cream
1/4 tsp ground cinnamon
pinch of grated nutmeg
1 large egg, lightly beaten
2 egg yolks

PASTRY

175 g (6 oz) plain flour
90 g (3 oz) chilled butter, cubed
about 2 tbsp cold water
1 egg white, lightly beaten
☆ 23 cm (9 in) loose-bottomed fluted flan tin
☆ baking beans

1 Make the pastry: put the flour into a bowl, add the butter, and rub in with the fingertips until the mixture resembles fine breadcrumbs. Add enough water to make a soft dough. Leave to chill for about 30 minutes.

2 Roll out the pastry on a lightly floured work surface and line the flan tin. Bake blind (page 395) in a preheated oven at 180°C (350°F, Gas 4) for 10 minutes.

3 Remove the beans and foil, lightly brush the pastry shell with egg white, and return to the oven for 1–2 minutes.

4 Meanwhile, toast the pecans in a preheated oven at 180°C (350°F, Gas 4), turning occasionally, for 10–15 minutes. Reserve a few pecan halves and coarsely chop the remainder.

5 Put the butter into a heavy saucepan and cook over a gentle heat until it turns golden brown. Add the sugars and golden syrup, and heat gently until the sugars dissolve. Add the brandy, bring to a boil, and cook for 5 minutes.

6 Remove from the heat and stir in the vanilla essence, cream, cinnamon, and nutmeg.

7 Whisk together the egg and egg yolks. Whisk a little hot syrup into the eggs. Add half of the syrup, little by little, then add the remainder. Leave to cool.

8 Arrange the chopped pecans and pecan halves in the pastry shell. Pour the syrup and egg mixture over them. Bake in a preheated oven at 180°C (350°F, Gas 4) for about 40 minutes until golden brown and set. Leave to cool before serving.

FRENCH APRICOT & ALMOND TART

So often the star of French pâtisserie, this golden fruit tart is not too difficult to make at home. Fresh apricots really make it special, but if they are not available, canned apricots can be used instead.

Serves 10

1 kg (2 lb) fresh apricots, halved and stoned

juice of 1 lemon

125 ml (4 fl oz) water

75 g (2½ oz) caster sugar

crème pâtissière (see box, right)

1 tsp arrowroot

1 tbsp brandy

30 g (1 oz) flaked almonds, toasted

PASTRY

250 g (8 oz) plain flour

125 g (4 oz) chilled butter, cubed

60 g (2 oz) caster sugar

1 egg, beaten

* *28 cm (11 in) loose-bottomed fluted flan tin*
* *baking beans*

1 Sift the flour into a large bowl. Add the butter and rub in until the mixture resembles fine breadcrumbs.

2 Stir in the sugar, then mix in the egg to make a soft pliable dough. Wrap in cling film and chill for 30 minutes.

3 Roll out the pastry on a lightly floured work surface and use to line the flan tin. Bake blind (page 395) in a preheated oven at 200°C (400°F, Gas 6) for 10 minutes until the pastry shell is beginning to brown at the edge. Remove the beans and foil and bake for 5–10 minutes. Leave to cool.

4 Put the apricots, cut-side down, in a shallow pan with the lemon juice, water, and sugar. Cover tightly and bring to a boil. Lower the heat and simmer gently for 3 minutes or until just soft.

5 Remove the apricots with a slotted spoon, reserving the juices. Drain on paper towels, and leave to cool.

6 Remove the pastry shell from the flan tin and put on a serving plate. Spread the crème pâtissière over the pastry shell, and smooth the surface.

7 Arrange the apricots, cut-side down, on the crème pâtissière. Combine the arrowroot and brandy in a small bowl and stir in the reserved apricot juices.

8 Return the mixture to the pan and bring to a boil, stirring until thick. Add the toasted flaked almonds.

9 Spoon the glaze over the apricots, making sure they are evenly coated. (Add a little water to the glaze if it is too thick.) Leave to stand until the glaze has cooled and set. Serve the tart cold.

Crème pâtissière

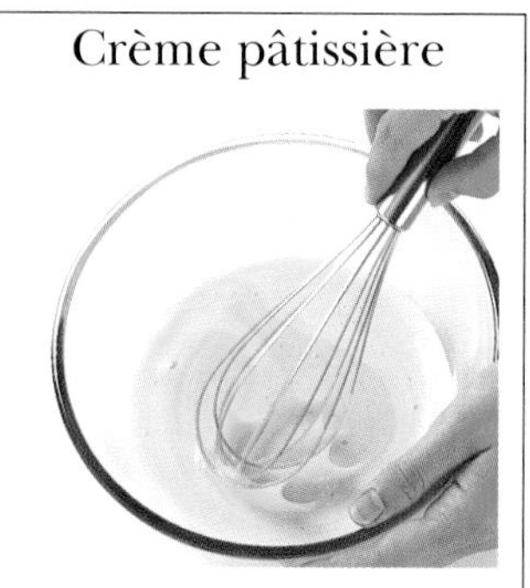

Put *3 eggs, 90 g (3 oz) vanilla sugar,* and *60 g (2 oz) plain flour* into a large bowl, add a little milk taken from *400 ml (14 fl oz)*, and mix until smooth. Pour the remaining milk into a heavy saucepan and bring almost to a boil. Pour on to the egg mixture, whisking well.

Rinse out the saucepan, return the egg mixture to the pan, and cook over a gentle heat, stirring, for 15–20 minutes until thickened.

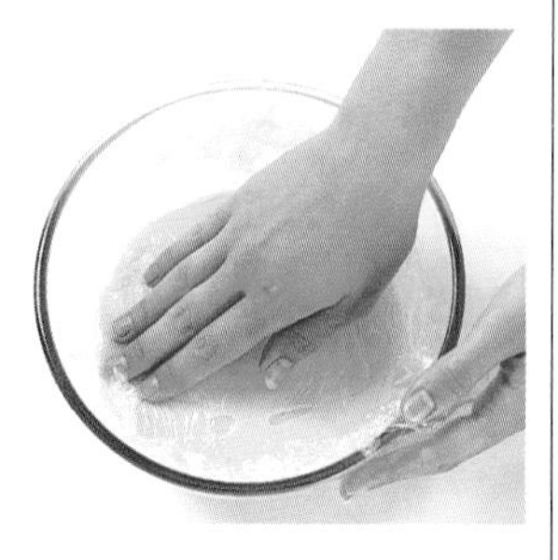

Pour into a bowl and cover with cling film, gently pressing it over the surface of the custard to prevent a skin from forming. Leave to cool.

LEMON MERINGUE PIE

Serves 8–10

grated zest and juice of 4 large lemons
90 g (3 oz) cornflour
600 ml (1 pint) water
4 egg yolks
175 g (6 oz) caster sugar

MERINGUE
5 egg whites
250 g (8 oz) caster sugar

PASTRY
250 g (8 oz) plain flour
30 g (1 oz) icing sugar
125 g (4 oz) chilled butter, cut into cubes
1 egg yolk
2 tbsp cold water
⋆ 25 cm (10 in) loose-bottomed fluted flan tin
⋆ baking beans

1 Make the pastry: sift the flour and icing sugar into a large bowl. Add the butter and rub in with the fingertips until the mixture resembles fine breadcrumbs.

2 Mix in the egg yolk and enough cold water to make a soft pliable dough. Wrap the dough in cling film and chill in the refrigerator for about 30 minutes.

3 Roll out the dough on a lightly floured surface and use to line the flan tin. Bake blind (page 395) in a preheated oven at 200°C (400°F, Gas 6) for 10 minutes.

4 Remove the baking beans and foil and bake the pastry shell for 5 minutes or until the base has dried out. Remove from the oven and reduce the temperature to 150°C (300°F, Gas 2).

5 Mix the lemon zest and juice with the cornflour. Bring the water to a boil, then stir into the lemon mixture. Return to the pan and bring back to a boil, stirring, until the mixture thickens. Remove from heat.

6 Leave to cool slightly, then stir in the egg yolks and sugar. Return to a low heat and cook, stirring, until just simmering. Pour into the pastry shell.

7 Whisk the egg whites until stiff but not dry. Whisk in the sugar 1 tsp at a time. Pile on top of the filling and spread over evenly. Bake for 45 minutes or until crisp and brown. Serve warm or cold.

TARTE AU CITRON

Serves 10–12

9 eggs
300 ml (1/2 pint) double cream
grated zest and juice of 5 large lemons
375 g (12 oz) caster sugar
icing sugar for dusting
lemon twists to decorate

PASTRY
250 g (8 oz) plain flour
125 g (4 oz) chilled butter, cut into cubes
60 g (2 oz) caster sugar
1 egg
⋆ 28 cm (11 in) loose-bottomed fluted flan tin
⋆ baking beans

1 Make the pastry: put the flour into a large bowl. Add the butter and rub in with the fingertips until the mixture resembles fine breadcrumbs.

2 Stir in the caster sugar, then bind together with the egg to make a soft pliable dough. Wrap in cling film and chill for 30 minutes.

3 Roll out the dough on a lightly floured work surface and use to line the flan tin. Bake blind (page 395) in a preheated oven at 200°C (400°F, Gas 6) for 10 minutes.

4 Remove the baking beans and foil and bake the pastry shell for 5 minutes or until the base has dried out. Remove from the oven and reduce the oven temperature to 180°C (350°F, Gas 4).

5 Beat the eggs in a bowl and add the cream, lemon zest and juice, and caster sugar. Stir until smooth, and pour into the pastry shell.

6 Bake for 35–40 minutes until the lemon filling has set. Cover the tart loosely with foil if the pastry begins to brown too much.

7 Leave the tart to cool a little, then dust with icing sugar. Decorate with lemon twists, and serve warm or at room temperature.

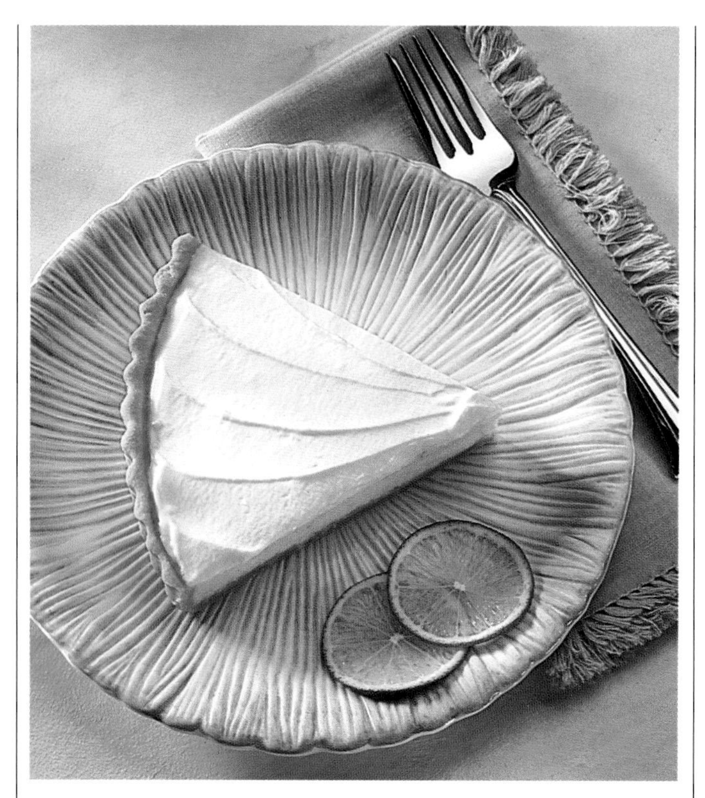

KEY LIME PIE

Serves 8

4 egg yolks
1 x 400 g (13 oz) can sweetened condensed milk
grated zest and juice of 1 lime
250 ml (8 fl oz) whipping or double cream, chilled
2 tbsp caster sugar
lime slices to decorate

PASTRY

175 g (6 oz) plain flour
90 g (3 oz) chilled butter, cut into cubes
2 tbsp cold water
⋆ 23 cm (9 in) loose-bottomed fluted flan tin
⋆ baking beans

1 Make the pastry: put the flour into a large bowl, add the butter, and rub in until the mixture resembles fine breadcrumbs. Add enough cold water to make a soft pliable dough.

2 Wrap the dough and chill for 30 minutes.

3 Roll out the dough on a lightly floured surface and use to line the flan tin.

4 Bake the pastry shell blind (page 395) in a preheated oven at 200°C (400°F, Gas 6) for about 10 minutes. Remove the baking beans and foil and return the shell to the oven for 5 minutes. Cool slightly.

5 Mix together the egg yolks, condensed milk, and lime zest. Slowly stir in the lime juice. Pour the filling into the shell and bake for 15–20 minutes until the filling has set and the pastry edge is a golden brown colour.

6 Leave to cool, then chill in the refrigerator for at least 1 hour.

7 Whip the cream until it forms soft peaks, and fold in the sugar. Spread decoratively over the pie. Serve chilled, decorated with lime slices.

BANOFFI PIE

Serves 6

175 g (6 oz) butter
175 g (6 oz) caster sugar
1 x 400 g (13 oz) can sweetened condensed milk
2 bananas, sliced
300 ml (1/2 pint) double cream, lightly whipped
30 g (1 oz) plain chocolate, grated, to decorate

BISCUIT SHELL

125 g (4 oz) butter
275 g (9 oz) ginger biscuits, crushed
⋆ 23 cm (9 in) loose-bottomed fluted flan tin

1 Make the biscuit shell (see box, right).

2 Combine the butter and sugar in a non-stick pan. Heat, stirring occasionally, until the butter has melted and the sugar has dissolved.

3 Add the condensed milk and heat gently, stirring, until the mixture reaches simmering point. Simmer, stirring occasionally, for about 5 minutes.

4 Pour the mixture into the biscuit shell and leave to cool. Chill until the caramel filling is set.

5 Arrange the banana slices evenly over the caramel filling. Top with the whipped cream, and decorate with the grated chocolate. Serve chilled.

Making the biscuit shell

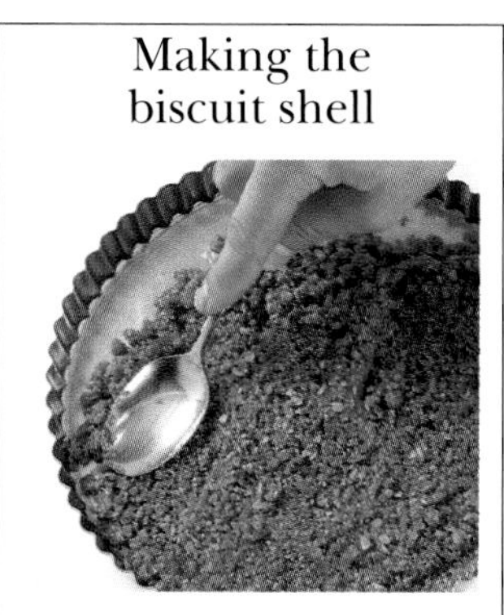

Melt the butter in a saucepan, add the crushed biscuits, and stir well to combine. Press on to the bottom and side of the flan tin. Chill until set.

MISSISSIPPI MUD PIE

Serves 8–10

200 g (7 oz) plain chocolate
125 g (4 oz) butter
1 tbsp coffee essence
3 eggs
150 ml (1/4 pint) single cream
175 g (6 oz) dark muscovado sugar
150 ml (1/4 pint) whipping cream to decorate

PASTRY

250 g (8 oz) plain flour
125 g (4 oz) chilled butter, cut into cubes
about 2–3 tbsp cold water
⋆ 25 cm (10 in) loose-bottomed fluted flan tin
⋆ baking beans

1 Make the pastry: put the flour into a large bowl. Add the butter and rub in until the mixture resembles fine breadcrumbs. Add enough cold water to make a soft pliable dough.

2 Wrap the dough and chill for 30 minutes.

3 Roll out the dough on a lightly floured surface and use to line the flan tin.

4 Bake the pastry shell blind (page 395) in a preheated oven at 200°C (400°F, Gas 6) for about 10 minutes until the pastry edge begins to brown.

5 Remove the baking beans and foil and bake for a further 5 minutes or until the base has dried out. Remove the pastry shell from the oven, and reduce the oven temperature to 190°C (375°F, Gas 5).

6 Break the chocolate into pieces, and place in a heavy pan with the butter and coffee essence. Heat gently, stirring occasionally, until the chocolate and butter have melted. Remove from the heat. Leave the mixture to cool slightly.

7 Beat the eggs, then add to the saucepan with the cream and sugar. Stir thoroughly to mix.

8 Pour the filling into the pastry shell. Bake for 30–35 minutes until the filling has set. Leave to cool.

9 Pipe whipped cream rosettes around the edge of the pie before serving.

FRUITY CREAM PIE

Serves 6–8

200 g (7 oz) sugar
3 tbsp cornflour
1 tbsp plain flour
pinch of salt
2 egg yolks, lightly beaten
175 ml (6 fl oz) milk
175 ml (6 fl oz) double cream
1 tsp vanilla essence
1 ripe banana, sliced
5 strawberries, sliced
1 ripe nectarine, sliced
60 g (2 oz) blackberries
60 g (2 oz) raspberries
250 ml (8 fl oz) whipping or double cream, chilled
2 tbsp caster sugar

PASTRY

175 g (6 oz) plain flour
90 g (3 oz) chilled butter, cubed
3 tbsp muesli
about 2–3 tbsp cold water
⋆ 23 cm (9 in) loose-bottomed fluted flan tin
⋆ baking beans

1 Make the pastry: put the flour into a bowl, add the butter, and rub in with the fingertips until it resembles fine breadcrumbs. Mix in the muesli. Add enough cold water to make a soft pliable dough. Chill for 30 minutes.

2 Roll out the pastry on a lightly floured work surface and use to line the tin (patch it with your fingers if the dough breaks).

3 Bake blind (page 395) in a preheated oven at 200°C (400°F, Gas 6) for about 10 minutes. Remove the beans and foil and bake for a further 10–15 minutes.

4 Combine the sugar, cornflour, flour, and salt. Mix together the egg yolks, milk, and cream, and whisk into the cornflour mixture.

5 Cook over a medium heat, stirring constantly, until the mixture boils and thickens. If the egg begins to curdle or stick, lower the heat. Remove from the heat, stir in the vanilla essence, and leave to cool.

6 Spread half of the custard over the pastry shell and arrange the fruit on top, reserving some berries for decoration. Spread with the remaining custard. Chill until serving time.

7 Before serving, whip the cream until it forms stiff peaks. Fold in the sugar, spread over the pie, and decorate with reserved fruit.

FRUIT TARTLETS

A mouth-watering combination of crisp golden pastry, creamy filling, and refreshing fruits always makes a special treat, whether served as a dessert or as part of a teatime spread. For convenience, use the same pastry and filling, but vary the toppings for a stunning display.

FRESH FRUIT TARTLETS

 **Makes 16**

250 g (8 oz) low-fat soft cheese
2 tsp lemon juice
2 tbsp sugar
2 kiwi fruit, sliced
60 g (2 oz) seedless green grapes, halved
1 piece of stem ginger in syrup, chopped
2 ripe pears, cored, quartered, and sliced
apricot jam or ginger marmalade for glazing

PASTRY

250 g (8 oz) plain flour
125 g (4 oz) chilled butter, cut into cubes
2 tbsp caster sugar
3–4 tbsp cold water
☆ 7 cm (3 in) pastry cutter
☆ 16 x 6 cm (2 1/2 in) round tartlet tins

1 Make the pastry: put the flour into a bowl, add the butter, and rub in with the fingertips until the mixture resembles fine breadcrumbs. Stir in the sugar, then add enough cold water to bind to a soft pliable dough. Wrap and chill for at least 30 minutes.

2 On a lightly floured work surface, roll out the pastry thinly. Using the pastry cutter, cut out 16 rounds.

3 Gently press the rounds into the tartlet tins. Prick all over with a fork and bake in a preheated oven at 190°C (375°F, Gas 5) for 12–15 minutes until golden. Leave in the tins for 10 minutes then remove and transfer to a wire rack. Leave to cool completely.

4 Beat together the soft cheese, lemon juice, and sugar. Divide half between 8 of the shells. Arrange kiwi slices and grapes on top and set aside. Add the ginger to the remaining cheese mixture and divide between the remaining shells. Top with pears.

5 Melt the jam or marmalade in a saucepan. Sieve and brush over the fruits. Serve immediately.

FRUIT PUFFS

Makes 8

500 g (1 lb) ready-made puff pastry
beaten egg
60 g (2 oz) strawberries, halved
60 g (2 oz) blueberries
150 ml (1/4 pint) double cream
1 tbsp caster sugar
1 ripe nectarine, sliced
icing sugar for dusting

1 Roll out the pastry until 5 mm (1/4 in) thick. Cut into strips 7 cm (3 in) wide, then cut the strips diagonally into 8 diamond shapes.

2 With a sharp knife, score each pastry diamond 1 cm (1/2 in) from the edge, taking care not to cut all the way through. Place on a dampened baking tray and glaze with beaten egg.

3 Bake in a preheated oven at 230°C (450°F, Gas 8) for 10–15 minutes until golden. Transfer to a wire rack. Remove the pastry centres, reserving them for lids if desired. Leave to cool.

4 Divide half of the strawberries and blueberries among the pastry shells. Whip the cream and sugar and divide among the shells. Top with nectarine slices, and the remaining strawberries and blueberries. Dust the pastry lids with icing sugar, replace, and serve at once.

TROPICAL TARTLETS

 **Makes 10**

3 tbsp desiccated coconut
crème pâtissière (page 416)
1 x 200 g (7 oz) can mandarin oranges in natural juice, drained
1 x 200 g (7 oz) can pineapple slices in natural juice, drained and cut into pieces

ALMOND PASTRY

60 g (2 oz) ground almonds
125 g (4 oz) plain flour
2 tbsp caster sugar
90 g (3 oz) chilled butter, cut into cubes
3 tbsp cold water
☆ 10 x 7 cm (3 in) round tartlet tins or boat-shaped tins (barquette moulds)

1 Make the pastry: combine the ground almonds, flour, and sugar in a bowl. Add the butter and rub in with the fingertips until the mixture resembles fine breadcrumbs. Add enough cold water to make a soft pliable dough. Wrap and chill for 1 hour.

2 Put the pastry on a floured work surface and flatten slightly. Place a large sheet of baking parchment on top and roll out the pastry, beneath the parchment, until 3 mm (1/8 in) thick.

3 Line the tartlet tins with pastry and chill for 2 hours. Prick the pastry all over and bake in a preheated oven at 190°C (375°F, Gas 5) for 10 minutes.

4 Leave the shells to cool in the tins for 10 minutes. Remove and transfer to a wire rack. Leave to cool.

5 Toast the coconut under a hot grill until golden. Spoon a little crème pâtissière into each shell. Top with the mandarin oranges and pineapple, sprinkle with the toasted coconut, and serve at once.

Tartlet toppings

Many other combinations of fruit work equally well.

- Cranberry purée and apple slices.
- Segments of orange and grapefruit.
- Raspberries and blackberries.
- Halved and stoned plums.
- Sliced star fruit.

Clockwise from top: *Tropical Tartlets, Fresh Fruit Tartlets, Fruit Puffs.*

MILLE-FEUILLE

Serves 6

250 g (8 oz) puff pastry, thawed if frozen

3 tbsp raspberry jam

150 ml (1/4 pint) double cream, whipped

CREME PATISSIERE

2 eggs, beaten

60 g (2 oz) vanilla sugar

sugar

30 g (1 oz) plain flour

300 ml (1/2 pint) milk

ICING

125 g (4 oz) icing sugar

about 1 tbsp water

1 Make the crème pâtissière (page 416). Set aside.

2 Roll out the pastry on a floured work surface to make a thin, 28 x 33 cm (11 x 13 in) rectangle. Lay it over a dampened baking tray.

3 Prick the pastry with a fork. Bake in a preheated oven at 220°C (425°F, Gas 7) for 10–15 minutes until the pastry is crisp and a deep brown colour.

4 Remove from the oven and leave to cool. Reduce the oven temperature to 180°C (350°F, Gas 4).

5 Trim the edges of the pastry to a rectangle, then cut into 3 equal rectangles, 10 cm (4 ins) wide. Crush the pastry trimmings and set aside.

6 Mix the icing sugar and enough water to make a smooth glacé icing. Spread over 1 of the rectangles, and place on a baking tray.

7 Bake for 2 minutes or until the icing has just set and has a slight sheen. Leave to cool.

8 Place a second pastry rectangle on a serving plate. Spread evenly with the jam and then the whipped cream. Set the third rectangle on top and cover with the crème pâtissière.

9 Top with the iced pastry rectangle. Decorate the long edges of the rectangle with thin rows of crushed pastry trimmings.

10 Chill the mille-feuille in the refrigerator until ready to serve.

Cook's know-how

It doesn't matter if the edges of the pastry are uneven because they will be trimmed after cooking. To cut the mille-feuille, use a serrated knife, holding it almost vertically, and cut with a sawing action. If you prefer, cut the mille-feuille before cooking to provide individual servings.

BAKLAVA

Makes 20 squares

250 g (8 oz) walnut pieces, finely chopped

60 g (2 oz) light muscovado sugar

1 tsp ground cinnamon

175 g (6 oz) butter, melted, plus extra for greasing

24 sheets of filo pastry, weighing about 500 g (1 lb)

90 ml (3 fl oz) clear honey

2 tbsp lemon juice

** shallow 18 x 23 cm (7 x 9 in) rectangular cake tin*

1 Mix together the walnuts, sugar, and cinnamon.

2 Lightly butter the cake tin and lay 1 sheet of filo pastry in the bottom of the tin, allowing the pastry to come up the sides. (If necessary, cut the sheets in half to fit in the tin.) Brush the pastry with a little melted butter.

3 Repeat with 5 more filo sheets, layering and brushing each one with the butter. Sprinkle with one-third of the nut mixture.

4 Repeat this process twice, using 6 more sheets of filo pastry each time, brushing each sheet with butter and sprinkling the nut mixture over each sixth sheet. Finish with 6 buttered sheets of filo pastry, and lightly brush the top with melted butter.

5 Trim the edges of the filo, then, using a sharp knife, cut about halfway through the pastry layers to make 20 squares.

6 Bake in a preheated oven at 220°C (425°F, Gas 7) for 15 minutes, then reduce the oven temperature to 180°C (350°F, Gas 4) and bake for 10–15 minutes until the pastry is crisp and golden brown. Remove the baklava from the oven.

7 Heat the honey and lemon juice in a heavy saucepan until the honey has melted. Spoon over the hot baklava. Leave to cool in the tin for 1–2 hours. Cut into the marked squares, and serve the baklava at room temperature.

12

CHILLED DESSERTS

UNDER 30 MINUTES

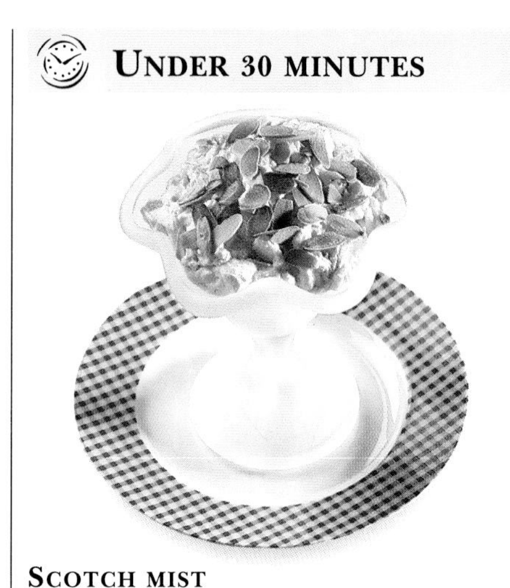

SCOTCH MIST

Rich double cream whipped with whisky and crushed meringues, chilled, and sprinkled with toasted flaked almonds.

SERVES 6 446 calories per serving

Takes 10 minutes, plus chilling **PAGE 436**

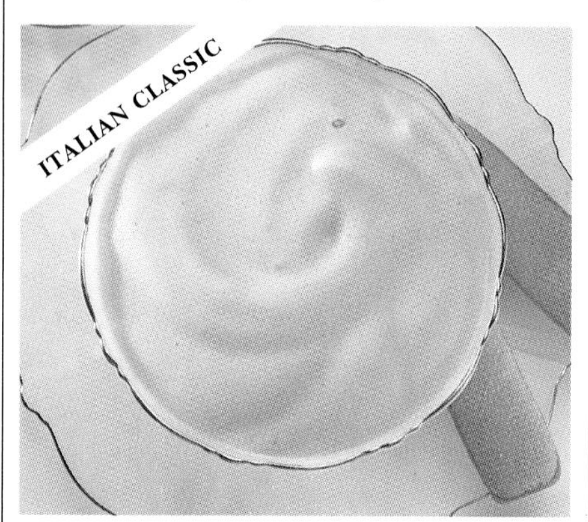

ZABAGLIONE

Light dessert: egg yolks, sugar, and Marsala whisked until creamy, and served with boudoir biscuits.

SERVES 6 114 calories per serving

Takes 20 minutes **PAGE 447**

PEACH MELBA

Deliciously ripe peaches and raspberries, topped with a large scoop of vanilla ice cream and a sweet raspberry sauce.

SERVES 4 273 calories per serving

Takes 15 minutes **PAGE 454**

30–60 MINUTES

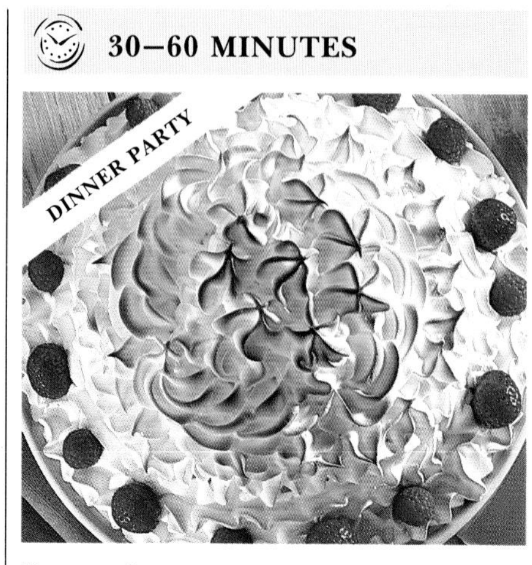

BAKED ALASKA

Stunning dessert: sponge case filled with layers of raspberries and strawberries, topped with ice cream and meringue, and browned.

SERVES 8 256 calories per serving

Takes 30 minutes **PAGE 455**

GOOSEBERRY FOOL

Fresh gooseberries are lightly cooked with fragrant elderflowers until soft, mixed with whipped cream, and decorated with lime zest.

SERVES 6 396 calories per serving

Takes 30 minutes, plus chilling **PAGE 433**

LEMON SYLLABUB

Lemon zest and juice, whipped double cream, sweet white wine, and whisked egg whites, folded together, and topped with lemon zest.

SERVES 4 470 calories per serving

Takes 20 minutes, plus standing **PAGE 435**

OVER 60 MINUTES

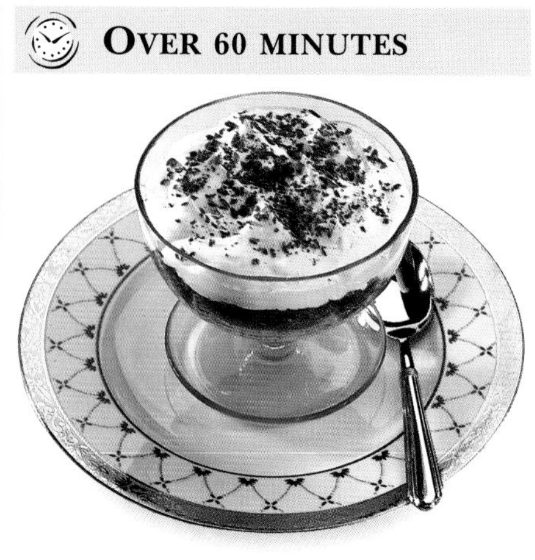

HELEN'S PUDDING

Easy and delicious: chocolate and coffee flavoured breadcrumbs are layered with whipped cream, and sprinkled with chocolate.

SERVES 6 510 calories per serving

Takes 15 minutes, plus chilling **PAGE 448**

FRESH FRUIT SALAD

Light and refreshing: a variety of fruit including pink grapefruit, oranges, green grapes, pears, and bananas coated in syrup.

SERVES 6 173 calories per serving

Takes 25 minutes, plus chilling **PAGE 432**

POTS AU CHOCOLAT

Rich and smooth: chocolate, coffee, butter, egg yolks, and vanilla essence mixed with egg whites and decorated with whipped cream.

SERVES 6 324 calories per serving

Takes 15 minutes, plus chilling **PAGE 446**

OVER 60 MINUTES

FROZEN LEMON FLUMMERY

Whipped double cream, lemon zest and juice, caster sugar, and milk, frozen, and decorated with strips of lemon zest.

SERVES 4 391 calories per serving

Takes 20 minutes, plus freezing **PAGE 456**

CHOCOLATE & BRANDY MOUSSE

Smooth and delicious: an egg and whipped cream mousse flavoured with chocolate and brandy. Topped with cream and chocolate.

SERVES 6 585 calories per serving

Takes 45 minutes, plus chilling **PAGE 449**

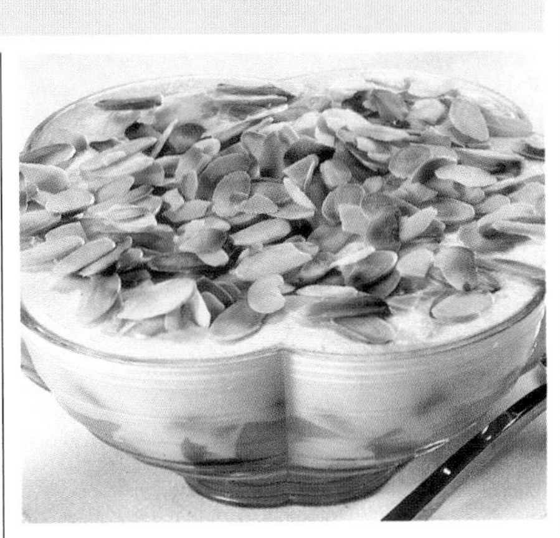

OLD ENGLISH TRIFLE

Family favourite: sponges layered with white peaches, crisp biscuits, custard, and whipped cream. Decorated with toasted almonds.

SERVES 6–8 534–401 calories per serving

Takes 35 minutes, plus chilling **PAGE 432**

SUMMER PUDDING

Ripe and juicy strawberries, redcurrants, blackcurrants, cherries, and raspberries wrapped in juice-soaked bread.

SERVES 6 240 calories per serving

Takes 35 minutes, plus chilling **PAGE 433**

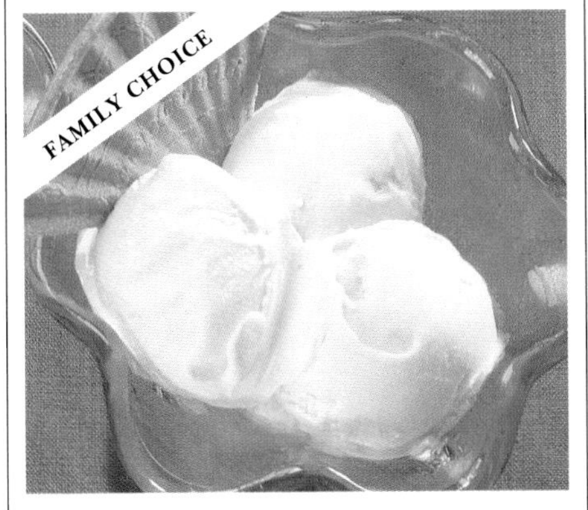

QUICK VANILLA ICE CREAM

Plain and simple: fresh eggs and double cream flavoured with vanilla sugar, whisked until light and creamy, and frozen.

SERVES 4–6 799–533 calories per serving

Takes 20 minutes, plus freezing **PAGE 451**

CHOCOLATE CHIP CHEESECAKE

Rich and delicious: a crunchy muesli base is topped with a creamy mixture enriched with both melted chocolate and chocolate chips.

SERVES 8 628 calories per serving

Takes 50 minutes, plus chilling

The cheesecake is decorated with piped rosettes of whipped cream and chocolate caraque for a luscious finish.

PAGE 446

OVER 60 MINUTES

PAVLOVA WITH PINEAPPLE & GINGER

Crisp meringue case filled with whipped double cream and ginger, and topped with pineapple rings and strips of ginger.

SERVES 6–8 504–378 calories per serving

Takes 2 1/2 hours, plus cooling **PAGE 436**

TIRAMISU

Traditional Italian dessert: a sponge base layered with creamy mascarpone cheese flavoured with brandy, chocolate, and coffee.

SERVES 12 556 calories per serving

Takes 45 minutes, plus chilling **PAGE 449**

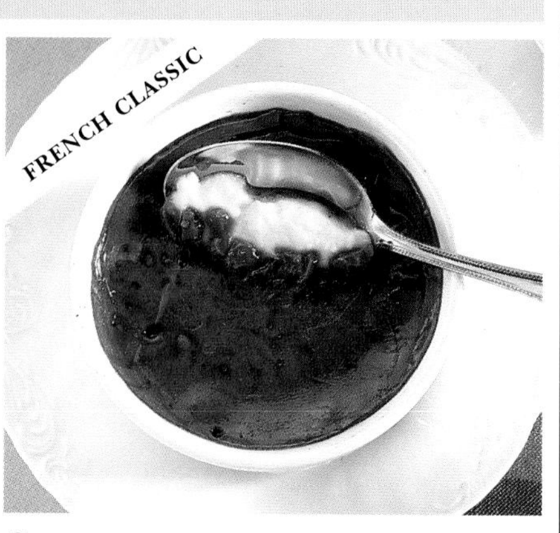

CREME BRULEE

Simple and delicious: egg and cream custard baked until tender, finished with crisp, caramelized sugar on top.

SERVES 6 302 calories per serving

Takes 45 minutes, plus chilling **PAGE 450**

MANGO & LIME MOUSSE

Light and refreshing: mangoes and tangy lime zest and juice mixed with whipped cream. Decorated with lime slices and cream.

SERVES 6 354 calories per serving

Takes 40 minutes, plus chilling **PAGE 434**

CHOCOLATE ROULADE

Rich and creamy: a chocolate-flavoured sponge with a deliciously rich cream and chocolate filling.

SERVES 6 677 calories per serving

Takes 60 minutes, plus cooling **PAGE 447**

ICED CHRISTMAS PUDDING

Easy and delicious: dried fruit, apricots, cherries, and brandy combined with custard and whipped cream, and frozen.

SERVES 8 437 calories per serving

Takes 20 minutes, plus freezing **PAGE 455**

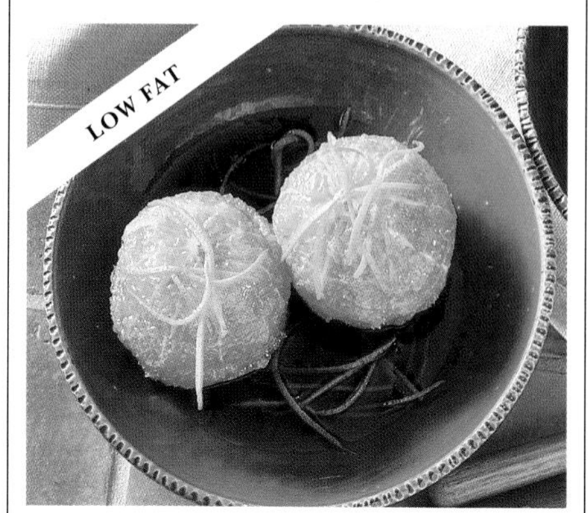

CARAMELIZED ORANGES

Quick and easy: oranges caramelized and served in their own juices, and decorated with strips of orange zest.

SERVES 4 388 calories per serving

Takes 30 minutes, plus chilling **PAGE 434**

CHILLED LEMON SOUFFLE

Light and fluffy: refreshing, smooth dessert with a citrus tang, decorated with whipped cream and toasted almonds.

SERVES 4 883 calories per serving

Takes 40 minutes, plus chilling **PAGE 435**

FLOATING ISLANDS

Fluffy oval-shaped meringues are served floating on a smooth and creamy vanilla custard. Decorated with almonds.

SERVES 4 412 calories per serving

Takes 40 minutes, plus cooling **PAGE 441**

OVER 60 MINUTES

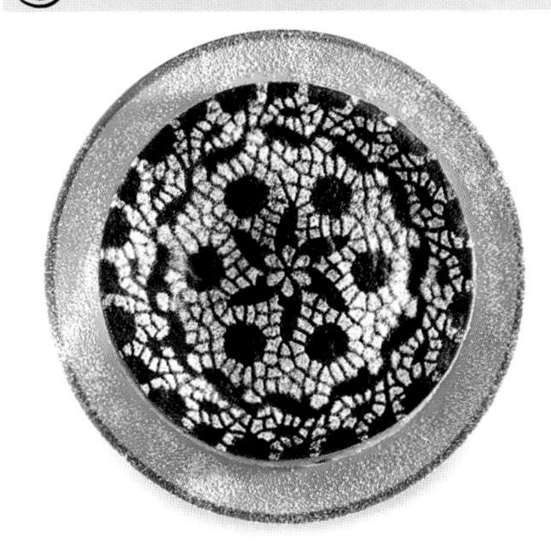

AUSTRIAN CHEESECAKE

Smooth and creamy: curd cheese, butter, egg, almonds, and semolina folded with sultanas and lightened with egg whites.

SERVES 8 331 calories per serving

Takes 50 minutes, plus cooling **PAGE 443**

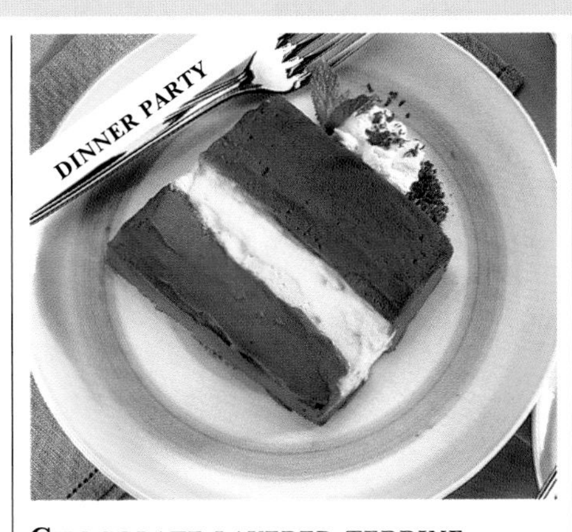

CHOCOLATE LAYERED TERRINE

Two chocolate and brandy mousse-like layers sandwiched with white chocolate. Decorated with whipped cream and chocolate shavings.

SERVES 8–10 641–513 calories per serving

Takes 45 minutes, plus chilling **PAGE 448**

TROPICAL FRUIT CHEESECAKE

Crunchy coconut biscuit base topped with a creamy mango mixture, and decorated with tropical fruits.

SERVES 10 396 calories per serving

Takes 1 1/4 hours **PAGE 443**

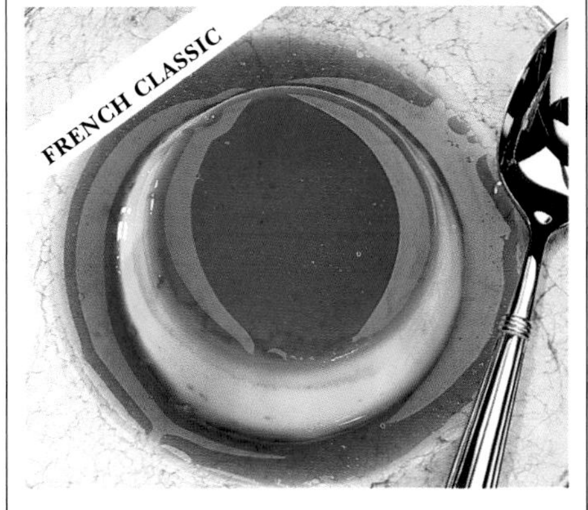

CREME CARAMEL

Easy and delicious: velvety vanilla-flavoured custard coated with a tempting golden brown caramel sauce.

SERVES 6 255 calories per serving

Takes 60 minutes, plus chilling **PAGE 450**

CHERRY CHEESECAKE

Black cherries flavoured with Kirsch top a slightly sweet and creamy cheese filling with a crisp biscuit base.

SERVES 8 530 calories per serving

Takes 60 minutes, plus chilling **PAGE 441**

RICH VANILLA ICE CREAM

Creamy and irresistible: rich egg custard mixed with double cream, flavoured with vanilla essence, churned, and then frozen.

SERVES 4–6 577–385 calories per serving

Takes 30 minutes, plus freezing

A delicious and versatile recipe every cook should know. Colourful strawberry fans highlight each serving.

PAGE 454

OVER 60 MINUTES

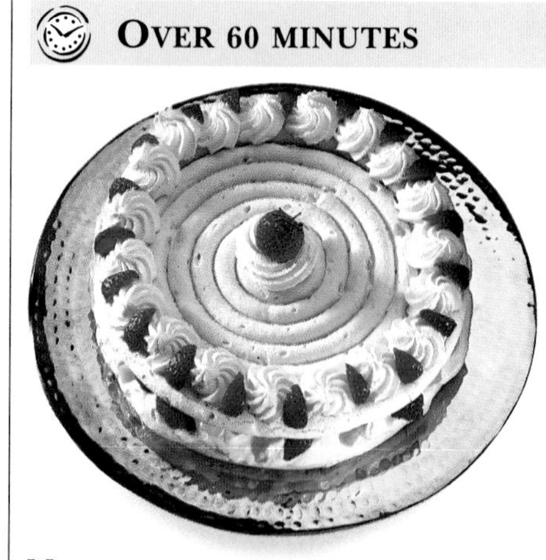

MANGO & PASSION FRUIT MERINGUE

Two light and crunchy meringue rounds are sandwiched together with cream, mango slices, strawberries, and passion fruit.

SERVES 6 503 calories per serving

Takes 1 1/2 hours, plus cooling PAGE 437

CASSATA

Layers of ice cream, rum-soaked fruit, and sorbet are frozen to make this traditional Italian dessert.

SERVES 8 364 calories per serving

Takes 30 minutes, plus freezing PAGE 456

MARBLED RASPBERRY CHEESECAKE

Crunchy base of walnuts and oats is topped with a creamy raspberry and cheese filling. Decorated with whipped cream.

SERVES 10 439 calories per serving

Takes 45 minutes, plus chilling PAGE 442

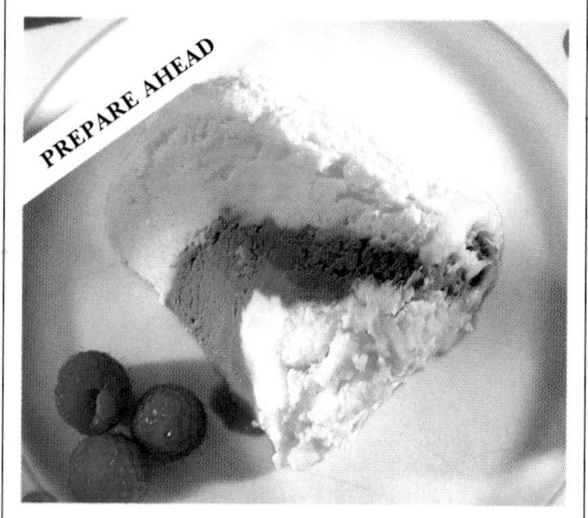

CHOCOLATE & MERINGUE BOMBE

Delicious layers of vanilla and chocolate ice cream with a surprise centre of whipped cream and meringue.

SERVES 8 413 calories per serving

Takes 45 minutes, plus freezing PAGE 451

HAZELNUT MERINGUE GATEAU

Toasted hazelnuts add a rich flavour to meringue rounds, which are sandwiched with cream and served with raspberry sauce.

SERVES 8 429 calories per serving

Takes 1 1/4 hours PAGE 440

STRAWBERRY MERINGUE ROULADE

A light meringue layer scattered with flaked almonds, spread with whipped double cream and strawberries, and rolled into a roulade. Chilled, then lightly dusted with icing sugar before serving. A perfect and attractive end to a special dinner.

SERVES 8 349 calories per serving

Takes 55 minutes, plus chilling PAGE 437

CHILLED DESSERTS KNOW-HOW

CHILLED DESSERTS ARE ideal for family suppers as well as special entertaining because they can be made well in advance. Fruit salads and fools, trifles, creamy mousses, light chilled soufflés, meringue baskets, and gateaux, luxurious cheesecakes, layered terrines, ice creams, and sorbets – all can be kept in the refrigerator or freezer, to be served when you're ready.

FREEZING

Many completed desserts, as well as ingredients and accompaniments for desserts, can be stored in the freezer. Freeze chocolate, caramel, or fruit sauces, then thaw at room temperature, or reheat from frozen if serving warm. Tray freeze piped rosettes of cream, pack in a freezer bag, and use frozen – they will thaw in minutes. Freeze citrus zest, then thaw, unwrapped, at room temperature. Chocolate decorations should be packed in rigid containers and used frozen. Tray freeze baked meringue shells, gateau layers, and cheesecake. Unwrap and thaw in the refrigerator. Crème caramel should be frozen uncooked in the mould and baked from frozen, allowing extra time.

Warning

Some of the chilled desserts in this book, such as mousses and soufflés, contain uncooked eggs. Because of the risk of salmonella poisoning from raw eggs, the Department of Health recommend that in order to be completely safe no one should eat raw eggs.

WHISKING EGG WHITES

Ensure all your equipment is clean, dry, and grease-free, and that the egg whites are at room temperature. Use a balloon whisk, and a glass, stainless steel, or copper bowl, or an electric mixer with a balloon beater.

Whisk the whites slowly until they look foamy, then increase the whisking speed, incorporating as much air as possible. Stop whisking when the whites are just smooth and will stand in stiff peaks. Use immediately.

DISSOLVING GELATINE

Gelatine is a flavourless setting agent used in many chilled desserts, including mousses and fruit jellies. It is most commonly available in a powdered form, which is usually sold in sachets. However, if you prefer to use leaf gelatine, follow the packet instructions, because sheets of gelatine vary in size.

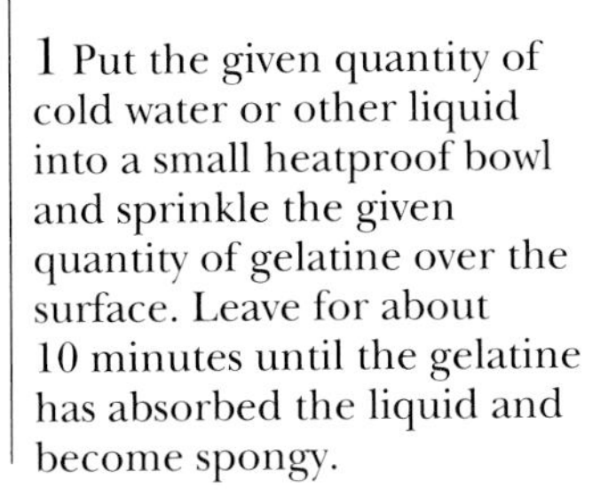

1 Put the given quantity of cold water or other liquid into a small heatproof bowl and sprinkle the given quantity of gelatine over the surface. Leave for about 10 minutes until the gelatine has absorbed the liquid and become spongy.

2 Put the bowl of gelatine into a pan of hot water and heat until the gelatine has dissolved and is clear. Use a metal spoon to check that there are no granules left. Use the gelatine at the same temperature as the mixture it is setting.

PREPARING A SOUFFLE DISH

To give a chilled soufflé the appearance of its baked counterpart, it is set in a dish with a raised collar.

Cut a piece of foil or greaseproof paper 5 cm (2 ins) longer than the circumference of the dish and wide enough to stand 5 cm (2 ins) above it when folded. Fold in half. Wrap around the dish and secure with tape or string. Remove before serving.

FOLDING EGG WHITES

Folding combines light and heavy mixtures. Work quickly and gently, to keep in as much air as possible.

Mix a spoonful of the whites into the heavy mixture to lighten it. Using a rubber spatula or metal spoon, fold in the remaining whites using a "figure of eight" motion, cutting straight through the mixture, then turning it over until well blended.

PREPARING CITRUS FRUITS

When taking the zest from citrus fruits, first scrub the fruit with hot soapy water, rinse well, and dry. This will remove any wax coating on the skin.

Grating
Hold the grater on a plate. Rub the fruit over the medium grid of the grater, removing the zest and leaving behind the bitter white pith. Use a pastry brush to remove all the zest from the grater.

Paring
Use a vegetable peeler or small knife to pare strips of zest, trying not to take any of the white pith with the zest. Cut the pieces of zest lengthwise into very fine strips or "julienne".

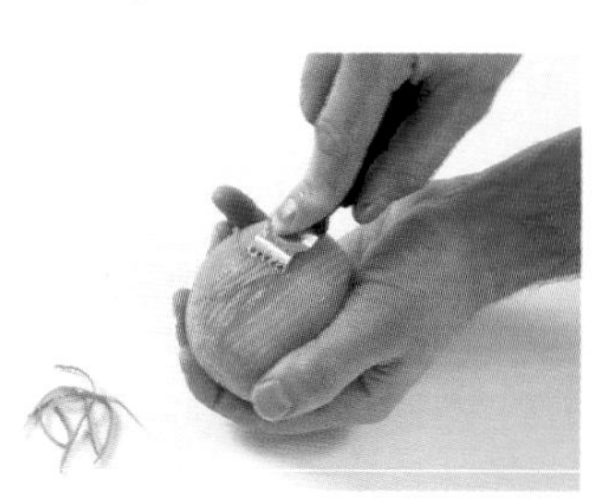

Zesting
For speedy removal of zest, a special tool known as a "zester" is used.

Peeling
Use a small sharp knife. Cut a slice across the top and the base, cutting through to the flesh. Hold the fruit upright on a chopping board and cut away the peel from top to bottom, following the curve of the fruit and cutting away the white pith as well.

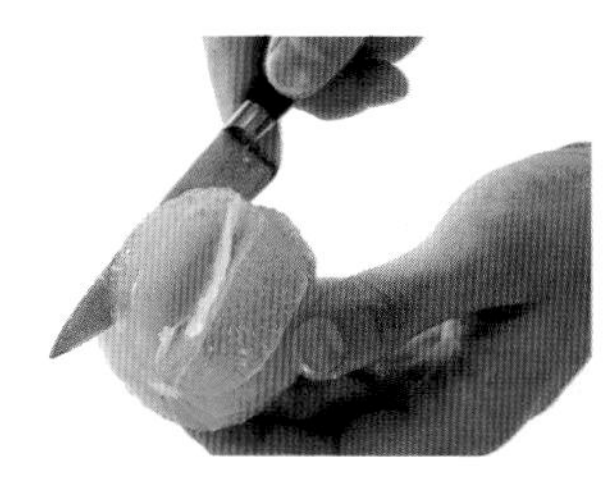

Segmenting
Hold the peeled fruit over a bowl to catch the juice. With a sharp knife, cut down one side of a segment, cutting it from the membrane. Cut away from the membrane on the other side, and remove the segment. Continue all around the fruit.

Citrus tips

To get the maximum juice from citrus fruits, first roll the fruit gently on a work surface, pressing lightly. Or heat in the microwave, on HIGH (100% power) for 30 seconds, just until the fruit feels warm.

◆

If a recipe includes grated citrus zest, add it immediately after grating, preferably to any sugar in the recipe. Then the zest won't discolour or dry out, and all the flavoursome oils from the zest will be absorbed by the sugar.

PREPARING A PINEAPPLE

When peeling pineapple, cut away the skin in strips, taking out all the "eyes". If there are any left after peeling, cut them out with the tip of a knife.

Wedges or cubes
1 Cut off the green crown, then cut a slice from the base. Hold the pineapple upright on a chopping board and slice away strips of the skin.

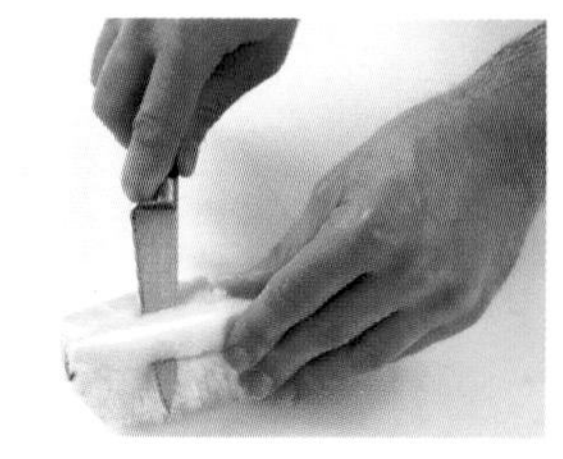

2 To remove the core, cut the pineapple into quarters lengthwise. Cut the central core from each quarter. Cut the quarters into wedges or cubes as required.

Rings
Do not cut the pineapple lengthwise, but cut crosswise into 1 cm (1/2 in) slices. Stamp out the central core from each slice using a biscuit or pastry cutter.

PREPARING MANGOES

Mangoes have a large, flat central stone and the flesh clings to it tightly. There are 2 methods of preparation, depending on how the flesh is to be used.

Slicing
For flesh to be sliced or puréed, cut the flesh from each side of the stone with a sharp knife. Cut the flesh from the edges of the stone, then peel and slice or purée.

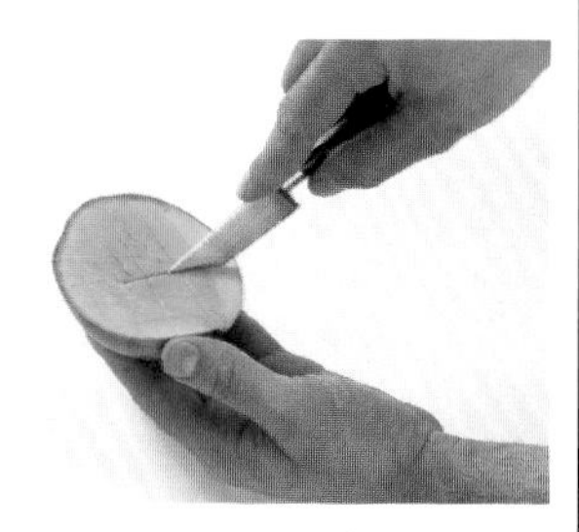

Dicing
1 Cut the unpeeled fruit away from each side of the stone. With a sharp knife, score the flesh in a criss-cross pattern, cutting through as far as the skin.

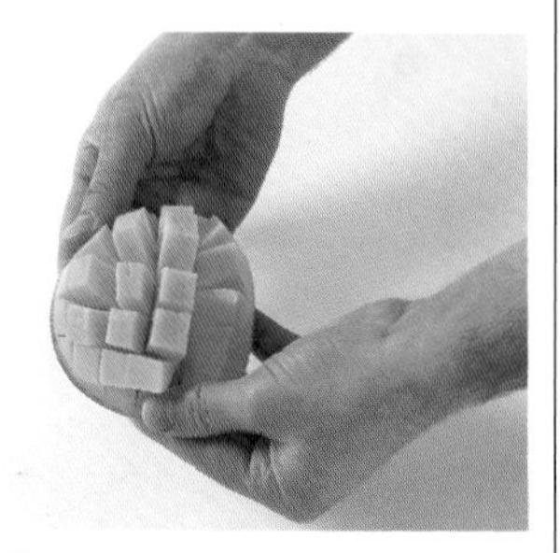

2 Press the middle of the skin to open out the cubes of flesh, then cut them away from the skin with a sharp knife.

DECORATING WITH CHOCOLATE

Chocolate decorations can transform a dessert, and you don't have to reserve them for desserts made only from chocolate; fruit fools and mousses can also benefit from a contrasting finishing touch.

Grating chocolate
Use chilled chocolate and hold it firmly in a piece of greaseproof paper. Hold the grater on a sheet of greaseproof paper and rub chocolate over the large grid of the grater.

Chocolate curls
With the chocolate at room temperature, use a vegetable peeler to shave off long curls on to a sheet of greaseproof paper. Use the paper to tip the curls on to the dessert.

Chocolate caraque
1 Spread a smooth, thin layer of melted chocolate about 1.5 mm (1/16 in) thick, on to a cool work surface (preferably marble), and leave to cool until nearly set.

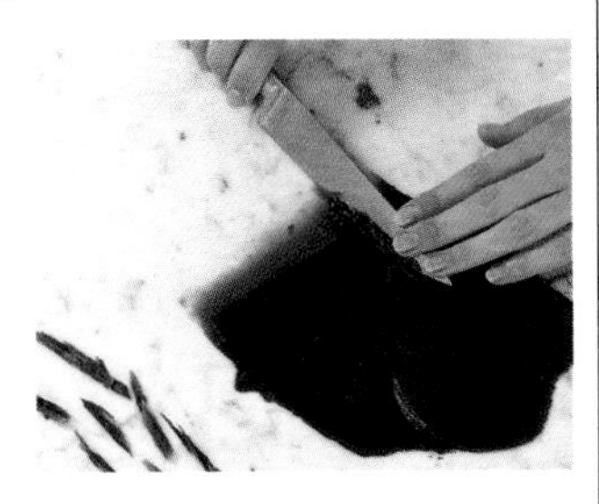

2 Using a long, sharp knife held at an angle, push across the chocolate with a slight sawing action, to shave it into "caraque" curls. Use a cocktail stick to pick up the caraque.

MELTING CHOCOLATE

A gentle touch is needed when melting chocolate, especially white chocolate. Don't allow it to overheat or come into contact with any steam as it may scorch or harden.

Chop the chocolate and put into a heatproof bowl over a pan of hot, not boiling, water. The bowl should not be touching the water. Heat gently, without stirring, until the chocolate becomes soft, then stir until very smooth and creamy. Remove from the heat, but leave over the water to keep the chocolate soft.

DECORATING WITH CREAM

Piping whipped cream adds a professional touch to desserts and cakes, and with a little practice and some confidence it's not so difficult to do. A star-shaped nozzle is the most useful.

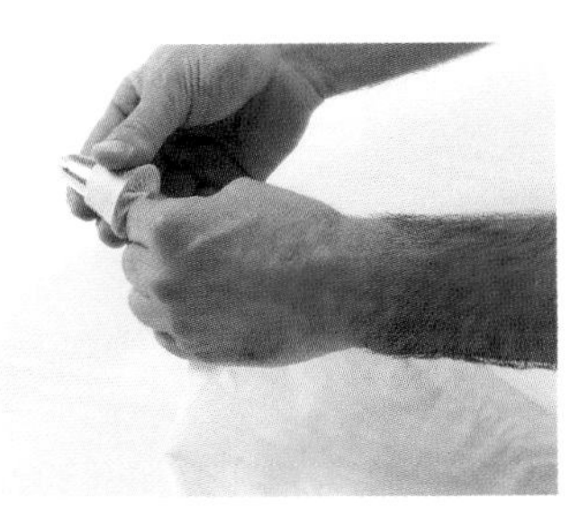

1 Drop the nozzle into the piping bag, then tuck the lower half of the piping bag into the nozzle, to prevent the cream from leaking out when filling the bag.

2 Hold the bag in one hand, and fold the top of the bag over your hand. Spoon in the cream.

3 When the bag is full, twist the top until there is no air left. Pipe the cream as desired, gently squeezing the twisted end to force out the cream in a steady stream.

Rosette
Hold the bag upright, just above the surface of the cake. Squeeze, moving the bag in a small circle. Stop squeezing before you lift the nozzle away.

Swirl
Hold the bag upright, just above the surface of the cake. Squeeze the bag and pipe the cream in a steady stream, guiding the nozzle in an "S" shape.

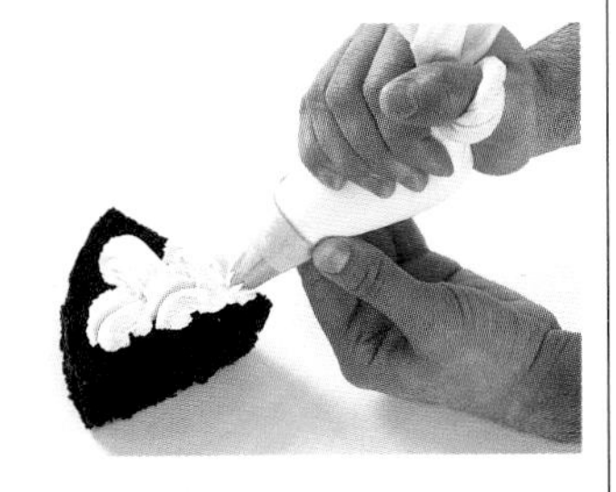

Rope
Hold the bag at a 45° angle. Pipe a short length of cream to 1 side. Pipe another length of cream to the opposite side, overlapping the first one.

OLD ENGLISH TRIFLE

 **Serves 6–8**

- *1 x 400 g (13 oz) can white peach halves*
- *6 trifle sponges*
- *4 tbsp blackcurrant jam*
- *60 g (2 oz) ratafia biscuits*
- *75 ml (2½ fl oz) sherry*
- *3 egg yolks*
- *30 g (1 oz) caster sugar*
- *1 tsp cornflour*
- *300 ml (½ pint) milk*
- *300 ml (½ pint) double cream*
- *30 g (1 oz) flaked almonds, toasted, to decorate*

1 Drain the peaches and reserve the juice. Slice and set aside.

2 Cut the trifle sponges in half horizontally and sandwich the halves together with the blackcurrant jam.

3 Use the trifle sponges to line the bottom of a glass serving bowl, and arrange the peaches and ratafia biscuits on top. Drizzle over the sherry and reserved peach juice, and leave to soak while you make the custard.

4 In a bowl, mix together the egg yolks, sugar, and cornflour. Warm the milk in a heavy saucepan, then pour it into the egg yolk mixture, stirring constantly. Return the mixture to the pan and cook over a low heat, stirring constantly, until the custard thickens. Leave the custard to cool slightly.

5 Pour the custard over the sponges, peaches, and biscuits in the glass bowl. Cover the surface of the custard with a layer of cling film, to prevent a skin from forming, and chill until set.

6 Whip the cream until thick and spread over the custard. Scatter the almonds over the top to decorate. Serve chilled.

APRICOT & GINGER TRIFLE

Substitute 1 x 400 g (13 oz) can apricot halves for the peaches. Sandwich the sponges with apricot jam and sprinkle with 1 piece of stem ginger in syrup, chopped, instead of the almonds.

FRESH FRUIT SALAD

 **Serves 6**

- *60 g (2 oz) caster sugar*
- *90 ml (3 fl oz) water*
- *zest of ½ lemon*
- *2 pink grapefruit*
- *2 oranges*
- *250 g (8 oz) seedless green grapes, halved*
- *2 ripe pears, peeled, cored, and sliced*
- *2 bananas, sliced*

1 Put the sugar and water into a saucepan and heat gently until the sugar has dissolved. Add the lemon zest and bring the syrup to a boil. Boil for 1 minute, then strain into a serving bowl. Leave to cool.

2 Using a sharp serrated knife, cut the peel and pith from each grapefruit and orange. Remove the segments by cutting between each membrane. Add the segments to the bowl.

3 Add the grapes, pears, and bananas to the serving bowl and gently mix to coat all of the fruit in the sugar syrup.

4 Cover and chill the fruit salad for up to 1 hour before serving.

FRESH BERRY SALAD

Halve 750 g (1½ lb) strawberries, then mix them with 250 g (8 oz) raspberries and 250 g (8 oz) blueberries. Sift 3 tbsp icing sugar over the fruit, and pour the juice of 2 oranges on top. Stir gently, cover, and chill for 1 hour.

Cook's know-how

In order to prevent the pears and bananas from discolouring when sliced and exposed to the air, toss the pieces in lemon juice.

Summer pudding

This classic summer-time treat is as easy to make as it is delicious to eat, and not at all high in calories. Reserve half of the cooking juices and pour them over any pale patches of bread after turning out the pudding, for a perfect, evenly coloured result.

Serves 6

8 slices of stale medium-sliced white bread, crusts removed

875 g (1 3/4 lb) mixed summer fruits such as strawberries, redcurrants, blackcurrants, cherries, and raspberries

150 g (5 oz) caster sugar

75 ml (2 1/2 fl oz) water

2 tbsp framboise or crème de cassis liqueur

crème fraîche or Greek yogurt to serve

⋆ 1.25 litre (2 pint) pudding basin

1 Line the pudding basin with the slices of stale white bread (see box, right).

2 Hull and halve the strawberries if very large, strip the redcurrants and blackcurrants from their stalks, and pit the cherries.

3 Place the redcurrants, blackcurrants, and cherries in a saucepan with the sugar and measured water. Heat gently until the juices begin to run. Stir until the sugar has dissolved, and cook until all of the fruit is just tender.

4 Remove from the heat and add the strawberries, raspberries, and liqueur.

5 Spoon the fruit and half of the juice into the bread-lined basin, reserving remaining juice. Cover the top of the fruit with the 2 reserved slices of bread.

6 Stand the bowl in a shallow dish to catch any juices that may overflow, then put a saucer on top of the bread lid. Place a kitchen weight (a can of food will do) on top of the saucer. Leave to chill for 8 hours.

7 Remove the weight and saucer and invert the pudding on to a serving plate. Spoon the reserved juices over the top, paying particular attention to any pale areas, and serve with either crème fraîche or Greek yogurt.

Lining the pudding basin

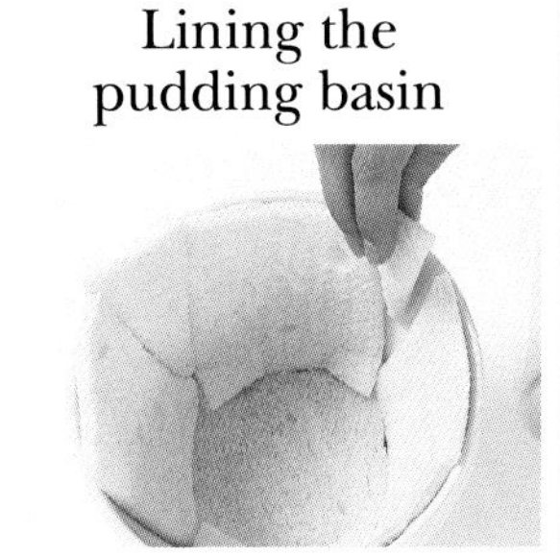

Reserve 2 slices of bread for the top of the pudding, and use the remainder to line the basin, making sure that the bread fits snugly together, leaving no gaps.

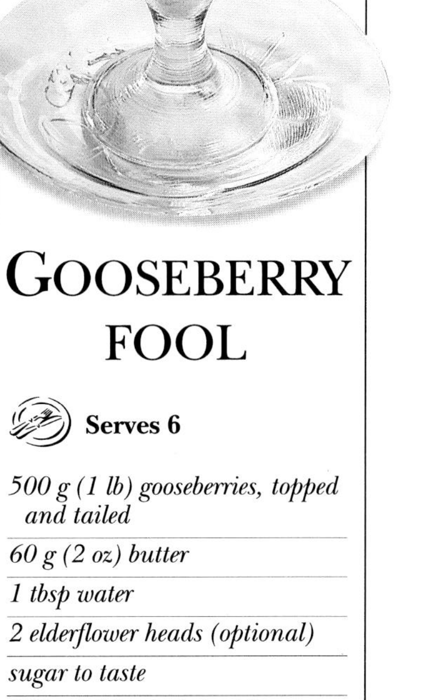

Gooseberry fool

Serves 6

500 g (1 lb) gooseberries, topped and tailed

60 g (2 oz) butter

1 tbsp water

2 elderflower heads (optional)

sugar to taste

300 ml (1/2 pint) double cream, whipped until thick

strips of blanched lime zest to decorate

1 Put the gooseberries into a pan with the butter, water, and elderflowers, if using. Cover and cook gently for 5–10 minutes until the gooseberries are soft.

2 Beat with a wooden spoon until smooth, and add sugar to taste. Leave to cool.

3 Fold mixture into cream. Turn into serving glasses and chill for 30 minutes. Decorate with lime zest.

Rhubarb & orange fool

Substitute 500 g (1 lb) chopped rhubarb for the gooseberries. Omit the elderflower heads. Cook until soft with the grated zest and juice of 1 large orange. Sweeten, and proceed as directed.

CARAMELIZED ORANGES

Serves 4

250 g (8 oz) granulated sugar
150 ml (1/4 pint) cold water
150 ml (1/4 pint) tepid water
3 tbsp orange liqueur
8 thin-skinned oranges

1 Put the sugar and measured cold water into a heavy pan and heat gently until the sugar dissolves.

2 When all the sugar has dissolved, bring to a boil and boil steadily until a rich brown colour. (If the caramel is too light in colour it will be very sweet, but be careful not to let it burn.)

3 Protect your hand by covering it with a cloth, and remove the pan from the heat. Pour the measured tepid water into the caramel.

4 Return the pan to the heat and stir to melt the caramel. Pour the caramel into a heatproof serving dish. Leave to cool for 30 minutes. Stir in the orange liqueur.

5 Pare the zest from 1 of the oranges, using a vegetable peeler. Cut the zest into very thin strips (page 430). Cook for 1 minute in boiling water, drain, rinse thoroughly under cold running water, and set aside.

6 Using a sharp knife, remove the peel and pith from each orange, catching any juice to add to the caramel in the dish. Cut each orange into slices crosswise, then reassemble the oranges, holding the slices together with cocktail sticks.

7 Place the oranges in the dish of caramel and spoon the caramel over them. Scatter the strips of orange zest over the top. Chill for about 30 minutes. Remove the cocktail sticks before transferring the oranges to individual bowls to serve.

MANGO & LIME MOUSSE

Serves 6

2 large ripe mangoes
grated zest and juice of 2 limes
2 tbsp powdered gelatine
3 eggs, plus 1 egg yolk
45 g (1 1/2 oz) caster sugar
150 ml (1/4 pint) double cream, whipped until thick

DECORATION

150 ml (1/4 pint) double cream, whipped until thick
1 lime, thinly sliced

1 Slice the mango flesh away from the stones (page 430). Peel the flesh, then purée in a blender or food processor. Add the lime zest to the purée.

2 Put the lime juice into a small bowl, sprinkle the gelatine over the top, and leave for 10 minutes until it becomes spongy. Stand the bowl in a pan of hot water and heat until the gelatine has dissolved.

3 Combine the eggs, egg yolk, and sugar in a large bowl and whisk vigorously for about 10 minutes until the mixture is pale and very thick. Gradually add the mango purée, whisking between each addition to keep the mixture thick.

4 Fold the whipped cream into the mango mixture. Add the dissolved gelatine in a steady stream, stirring gently to mix. Pour the mixture into a glass serving bowl and chill until set.

5 To decorate, pipe rosettes of whipped cream (page 431) on top of the mousse. Cut the lime slices in half, place 2 slices between each rosette of cream, and serve chilled.

LEMON SYLLABUB

Serves 4

150 ml (1/4 pint) dessert wine or sweet white wine

2 large lemons

90 g (3 oz) caster sugar

300 ml (1/2 pint) double cream

2 egg whites

1 Put the wine into a bowl with the grated zest and juice of 1 of the lemons, and the sugar. Stir to mix, then leave to stand for about 15 minutes, stirring occasionally, until the sugar has dissolved.

2 Meanwhile, pare the zest from the remaining lemon in long thin strips. Blanch the strips in a small saucepan of boiling water for 1 minute. Drain, rinse under cold running water, pat dry, and set aside.

3 In a medium bowl, whip the cream until it just holds its shape. Add the wine mixture very slowly, whisking well between each addition to ensure that the mixture remains thick.

4 In a separate bowl, whisk the egg whites until stiff but not dry. Carefully fold into the cream and wine mixture. Spoon into 4 tall syllabub glasses. Decorate the top of each syllabub with a strip of lemon zest, and serve at once.

Cook's know-how

For a less rich lemon syllabub, use half whipped double cream and half Greek yogurt. Serve with shortbread biscuits, if preferred.

CHILLED LEMON SOUFFLE

Serves 4

3 tbsp cold water

2 tbsp powdered gelatine

3 eggs, size 2, separated

250 g (8 oz) caster sugar

grated zest and juice of 3 lemons

300 ml (1/2 pint) double cream, whipped until thick

DECORATION

30 g (1 oz) nibbed almonds, lightly toasted

150 ml (1/4 pint) double cream, whipped until stiff

⋆ *1 litre (1 3/4 pint) soufflé dish*

1 Prepare the soufflé dish: tie a band of double thickness greaseproof paper or foil around the outside so that it stands about 5 cm (2 ins) above the top of the dish (page 429).

2 Put the water into a small bowl and sprinkle the gelatine over the top. Leave for about 10 minutes until it becomes spongy. Stand in a pan of hot water and heat until dissolved.

3 Put the egg yolks and sugar into a heatproof bowl and put over a pan of gently simmering water. Do not let the bottom of the bowl touch the water. Using an electric hand-held mixer, whisk together. Add the lemon zest and juice and whisk at full speed until the mixture is pale and thick.

4 Fold the whipped double cream into the lemon mixture, then fold in the dissolved gelatine.

5 In a separate large bowl, whisk the egg whites until stiff but not dry. Fold into the lemon mixture, and carefully pour into the prepared soufflé dish. Level the surface, then chill for about 4 hours until set.

6 Carefully remove the paper collar. Decorate the outside edge of the soufflé with the lightly toasted almonds and sprinkle some in the middle. Pipe the cream (page 431) around the edge of the soufflé, and serve chilled.

SCOTCH MIST

Serves 6

450 ml (3/4 pint) double cream

4 tbsp whisky

90 g (3 oz) meringues, coarsely crushed

30 g (1 oz) flaked almonds, toasted

1 Whip the cream with the whisky until it just holds its shape. Fold in the crushed meringues.

2 Spoon the mixture into 6 glass serving bowls, cover, and chill for about 20 minutes or until firm.

3 Scatter the toasted flaked almonds over the desserts just before serving.

ETON MESS

Substitute 4 tbsp brandy for the whisky, and add 500 g (1 lb) chopped strawberries to the cream mixture. Decorate with strawberry halves and mint leaves instead of the almonds.

PAVLOVA WITH PINEAPPLE & GINGER

A light, delicate, and crisp meringue serves as the base for this delicious dessert. The meringue is crisp and golden on the outside, but soft and chewy beneath. A pineapple and ginger topping provides the ideal complement.

Serves 6–8

4 egg whites

250 g (8 oz) caster sugar

1 1/2 tsp cornflour

1 1/2 tsp white wine vinegar

TOPPING

375 ml (13 fl oz) double cream

60 g (2 oz) stem ginger in syrup, cut into matchstick-thin strips

1 x 400 g (13 oz) can pineapple rings, drained

1 Preheat the oven to 160°C (325°F, Gas 3). Mark a 23 cm (9 in) circle on a sheet of non-stick baking parchment, turn the paper over, and line a baking tray.

2 Whisk the egg whites until stiff, then add the sugar, 1 tsp at a time, whisking the mixture constantly.

3 Blend the cornflour and vinegar and whisk into the egg white mixture.

4 Spread the mixture inside the circle on the baking parchment, building up the side so that it is higher than the middle. Place in the oven, then immediately reduce the heat to 150°C (300°F, Gas 2).

5 Bake the meringue for 1 hour or until firm to the touch. Turn off the oven and leave the meringue inside for another hour.

6 Peel the lining paper from the meringue, and transfer the meringue to a serving plate. Leave to cool.

7 Before serving, whip the double cream until stiff, and stir in half of the stem ginger strips. Spoon the mixture into the middle of the meringue. Top with the pineapple rings and the remaining stem ginger strips.

Cook's know-how

Keep the oven door closed when you leave the meringue to dry out. If you have a fan-assisted oven, however, the door should be slightly ajar. The meringue base can be made a day in advance and kept in an airtight container in a cool place until needed. Add the cream and fruit topping just before serving.

MANGO & PASSION FRUIT MERINGUE

Serves 6

4 egg whites

250 g (8 oz) caster sugar

FILLING

1 ripe mango

1 passion fruit

300 ml (1/2 pint) whipping cream, whipped until thick

125 g (4 oz) strawberries, sliced

DECORATION

150 ml (1/4 pint) double cream, whipped until stiff

a few strawberries

1 Mark 2 x 20 cm (8 in) circles on 2 sheets of non-stick baking parchment, turn the paper over, and use to line 2 baking trays.

2 Whisk the egg whites with a hand-held electric mixer until stiff but not dry. Add the sugar, 1 tsp at a time, and continue to whisk until all the sugar has been incorporated and the mixture is stiff and glossy.

3 Pipe the meringue, in concentric circles, inside the marked circles on the paper-lined baking trays.

4 Bake the meringue rounds in a preheated oven at 140°C (275°F, Gas 1) for 1–1 1/4 hours until crisp and dry. Leave to cool, then carefully peel off the paper.

5 Dice the mango very fine (page 430). Halve the passion fruit and scoop out the pulp.

6 Spread the whipped cream over 1 of the meringue rounds. Arrange the mango, passion fruit pulp, and strawberries on top, and cover with the remaining meringue round.

7 Decorate with piped rosettes of cream (page 431), strawberry slices, and a whole strawberry.

PEACH MERINGUE

Substitute 2 peeled and sliced peaches for the mango, and 125 g (4 oz) raspberries for the strawberries. Proceed as directed in the recipe, decorating the top of the peach meringue with a few whole raspberries.

STRAWBERRY MERINGUE ROULADE

Serves 8

sunflower oil for greasing

4 egg whites

250 g (8 oz) caster sugar

45 g (1 1/2 oz) flaked almonds

icing sugar for dusting

FILLING

300 ml (1/2 pint) double cream, whipped until thick

250 g (8 oz) strawberries, quartered

☆ 23 x 33 cm (9 x 13 in) Swiss roll tin

1 Lightly oil the Swiss roll tin and line with a sheet of baking parchment.

2 Whisk the egg whites until stiff but not dry. Add the sugar, 1 tsp at a time, and continue to whisk, until all the sugar has been incorporated and the mixture is stiff and glossy.

3 Spoon the meringue into the lined tin and tilt to level the surface. Sprinkle over the flaked almonds.

4 Bake near the top of a preheated oven at 220°C (425°F, Gas 7) for about 8 minutes until the top is golden brown.

5 Reduce the oven temperature to 160°C (325°F, Gas 3), and continue baking for 10 minutes or until the meringue is firm to the touch.

6 Remove the meringue from the oven and turn out on to a sheet of baking parchment. Peel the lining paper from the base and leave the meringue to cool for 10 minutes.

7 Spread the whipped cream evenly over the meringue, and scatter the strawberries over the cream.

8 Roll up the meringue from a long end, using the lining paper to help lift it. Wrap the roulade in baking parchment and leave to chill in the refrigerator for about 30 minutes. Lightly dust with sifted icing sugar before serving.

MERINGUES

Meringues are very quick and easy to prepare, and as they can be made weeks in advance and kept in the freezer, they're ideal for impromptu entertaining and special occasions of all kinds. Contrast their crisp, light texture with fillings and toppings of cream, chocolate, and fruit.

BASIC MERINGUE

4 egg whites
250 g (8 oz) caster sugar

1 Whisk the egg whites with an electric mixer until firm. Add the caster sugar, 1 tsp at a lime, and whisk until the mixture is stiff and shiny.

2 Pipe the meringue as preferred and bake as directed.

BERRY BASKETS

Makes 8

1 quantity basic meringue (above)
250 ml (8 fl oz) double cream
selection of berries and mint sprigs to decorate
raspberry or peach sauce (page 440) to serve

1 Pipe 8 meringue baskets (see box, below). Bake in a preheated oven at 120°C (250°F, Gas 1/2) for 1–1 1/2 hours until firm. Leave to cool.

2 Whip the cream until it forms stiff peaks. Fill the baskets with the cream and top with berries and mint sprigs. Serve with raspberry sauce.

COFFEE & ALMOND ROUNDS

Makes 6

1 quantity basic meringue (left)
125 g (4 oz) slivered almonds
icing sugar for dusting
COFFEE CHANTILLY CREAM
2 tbsp instant coffee granules
1 tbsp hot milk
250 ml (8 fl oz) double cream
2–3 tbsp caster sugar

1 Pipe 18 meringue rounds (see box, below). Sprinkle the almonds over the rounds. Bake in a preheated oven at 120°C (250°F, Gas 1/2) for 1–1 1/2 hours until firm. Leave to cool.

2 Make the coffee Chantilly cream: dissolve the coffee in the milk and cool. Put the cream into a chilled bowl and whip until it forms soft peaks. Add the coffee mixture and sugar to the cream and whip until stiff peaks form.

3 Sandwich together the meringue rounds, 3 at a time, with the coffee Chantilly cream. Dust with a little icing sugar before serving.

CHOCOLATE ROSETTES

Makes 12

1 quantity basic meringue (left)
125 g (4 oz) plain chocolate, chopped
CHOCOLATE GANACHE
125 g (4 oz) plain chocolate, chopped
125 ml (4 fl oz) double cream

1 Pipe 24 rosettes (see box, below). Bake in a preheated oven at 120°C (250°F, Gas 1/2) for 1–1 1/2 hours until firm. Leave to cool. Put the chocolate into a heatproof bowl over a pan of hot water and heat until melted. Drizzle over the meringues and leave to set.

2 Make the ganache: put the chocolate into a bowl. Put the cream into a pan and bring just to a boil. Pour over the chocolate and stir until the chocolate has melted.

3 Whisk for about 5 minutes until the mixture is fluffy and cooled. Sandwich the meringues together with the chocolate ganache.

Clockwise from top: *Berry Baskets, Coffee & Almond Rounds, Chocolate Rosettes.*

Piping meringue shapes

Baskets

Mark 8 x 10 cm (4 in) circles on non-stick baking parchment; turn over. Put the meringue into a piping bag fitted with a medium star nozzle, and pipe inside the circles, building up the sides to form baskets.

Rounds

Mark 18 x 7 cm (3 in) circles on non-stick baking parchment; turn over. Put the meringue into a piping bag fitted with a medium plain nozzle. Pipe the meringue inside the circles, in concentric rings.

Rosettes

Put the meringue into a piping bag fitted with a medium star nozzle. Pipe the meringue on to non-stick baking parchment to form 24 even-sized rosettes, about 5 cm (2 ins) in diameter at the base.

SAUCES FOR DESSERTS

HOT CHOCOLATE SAUCE

Heat *175 g (6 oz) plain chocolate, broken into pieces, 2 tsp instant coffee granules, 125 ml (4 fl oz) hot water* and *90 g (3 oz) caster sugar* in a pan until the chocolate has melted. Serve hot.

CHOCOLATE MARSHMALLOW SAUCE

Heat *60 g (2 oz) chopped plain chocolate, 100 g (3 1/2 oz) marshmallows, 75 ml (2 1/2 fl oz) double cream,* and *75 ml (2 1/2 fl oz) honey* in a pan until the chocolate and marshmallows have melted. Serve hot.

BUTTERSCOTCH SAUCE

Heat *60 g (2 oz) butter, 150 g (5 oz) light muscovado sugar,* and *150 g (5 oz) golden syrup* in a pan until melted. Remove from the heat and add *150 ml (1/4 pint) double cream* and *a few drops of vanilla essence,* stirring until smooth. Serve hot.

PEACH SAUCE

Put *400 g (13 oz) canned peaches and their juice* into a food processor or blender with *1/4 tsp almond essence.* Work to a smooth purée. Serve chilled.

HAZELNUT MERINGUE GATEAU

Crisp meringues made with toasted hazelnuts are sandwiched with a whipped cream filling. The attractive decoration is easy to create: piped rosettes of cream are topped with hazelnuts and raspberries, and the gateau is accompanied by a raspberry sauce.

Serves 8

125 g (4 oz) shelled hazelnuts
4 egg whites
275 g (9 oz) caster sugar
1/2 tsp white wine vinegar
300 ml (1/2 pint) whipping cream, whipped until thick
icing sugar for dusting

RASPBERRY SAUCE

250 g (8 oz) raspberries
about 4 tbsp icing sugar, sifted

1 Mark 2 x 20 cm (8 in) circles on 2 sheets of non-stick baking parchment. Turn the paper over and use to line 2 baking trays.

2 Spread the hazelnuts on another baking tray and toast in a preheated oven at 190°C (375°F, Gas 5) for about 10 minutes. Continue to heat the oven.

3 Tip the hazelnuts on to a clean tea towel and rub together inside the towel to remove the skins. Reserve 8 whole nuts for decoration and grind the remaining nuts in a food processor.

4 Whisk the egg whites until stiff but not dry (if using an electric mixer turn it to high speed). Add the caster sugar, 1 tsp at a time, and continue to whisk, still at high speed, until all of the caster sugar has been incorporated and the mixture is stiff and glossy.

5 Whisk in the white wine vinegar, then fold in the ground hazelnuts.

6 Divide the hazelnut meringue mixture equally between the baking trays, spreading it out evenly within the marked circles.

7 Bake in the oven for about 30 minutes until the top of each meringue round is crisp and a pale beige colour. The insides of the meringues should still be soft like marshmallow.

8 Lift the meringue rounds off the baking trays and peel the lining paper from the bases. Leave to cool on a wire rack.

9 Make the raspberry sauce: reserve 8 whole raspberries for decoration, and put the remainder of the raspberries into a food processor. Blend until smooth, then push through a nylon sieve to remove the pips. Gradually whisk in icing sugar to taste.

10 Use two-thirds of the whipped cream to sandwich the meringue rounds together. Dust the top with sifted icing sugar and decorate with piped rosettes (page 431) of the remaining whipped cream. Top the rosettes with the reserved whole hazelnuts and raspberries. Serve with the raspberry sauce.

Cook's know-how

This kind of raspberry sauce is known as raspberry coulis. It makes a colourful accompaniment to many chilled and frozen desserts.

FLOATING ISLANDS

Serves 4

butter for greasing

3 eggs, separated

30 g (1 oz) vanilla sugar (page 450)

1 tsp cornflour

600 ml (1 pint) milk

175 g (6 oz) caster sugar

30 g (1 oz) flaked almonds, toasted

1 Butter 4 individual serving dishes. Line a baking tray with a sheet of baking parchment.

2 In a large bowl, mix together the egg yolks, vanilla sugar, and cornflour. In a heavy saucepan, bring the milk to a boil. Add the boiling milk to the egg-yolk mixture, stirring constantly, then pour the mixture back into the pan.

3 Return to the heat and cook gently, stirring constantly, until the froth disappears and the custard is thickened. Pour the custard into the buttered dishes, and leave to cool.

4 Whisk the egg whites until stiff but not dry. Add the caster sugar, 1 tsp at a time, and continue to whisk until all the sugar has been incorporated and the mixture is stiff and glossy.

5 Shape the meringue (see box, below).

6 Cook in a preheated oven at 160°C (325°F, Gas 3) for 20 minutes until the meringues are set and no longer sticky. Leave to cool, then arrange on top of the dishes of custard. Sprinkle with almonds before serving.

Shaping the meringue

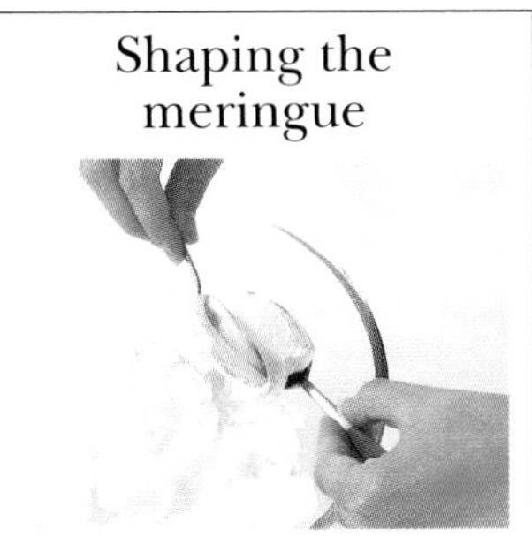

Shape the meringue into 8 ovals, using 2 tablespoons, and place the ovals on the baking tray lined with baking parchment.

CHERRY CHEESECAKE

Serves 8

375 g (12 oz) full-fat soft cheese

125 g (4 oz) caster sugar

2 eggs, beaten

a few drops of vanilla essence

1 tbsp lemon juice

BISCUIT SHELL

175 g (6 oz) digestive biscuits, crushed

90 g (3 oz) butter, melted

2 tbsp demerara sugar

TOPPING

1 tsp arrowroot

1 x 400 g (13 oz) can pitted black cherries

a few drops of kirsch

⋆ 23 cm (9 in) springform cake tin

1 Make the biscuit shell: mix together the crushed biscuits, melted butter, and sugar, and press evenly over the bottom and up the side of the cake tin.

2 Put the soft cheese into a bowl and beat until smooth. Add the caster sugar and beat until well blended. Add the eggs, vanilla essence, and lemon juice. Mix until smooth and creamy.

3 Pour the filling into the biscuit shell. Bake in a preheated oven at 180°C (350°F, Gas 4) for 25–30 minutes until just set. Leave to cool completely, then transfer to the refrigerator and leave to chill.

4 Make the topping: dissolve the arrowroot in a little of the cherry juice. Put the cherries and their juice into a small pan and add the arrowroot mixture with the kirsch. Bring to a boil, stirring, until thick. Leave to cool completely.

5 Spoon the cherries on top of the cheese filling. Chill. Use a knife to loosen the side of the cheesecake from the tin, then remove the cheesecake. Serve chilled.

Cook's know-how

Cheesecakes freeze well, but should always be frozen without the topping. Thaw in the refrigerator, then decorate. Fruit toppings may be prepared at the same time and frozen separately. Thaw and add to the cheesecake just before serving.

MARBLED RASPBERRY CHEESECAKE

The crunchy base of this cheesecake, made with crushed oat biscuits and walnuts, provides a delicious contrast to the creamy filling, marbled with streaks of fresh raspberry purée. It's a delicate cheesecake, so for best results be sure to chill it well before slicing and serving.

Serves 10

3 tbsp cold water
2 tbsp powdered gelatine
500 g (1 lb) raspberries
4 tbsp framboise liqueur
250 g (8 oz) full-fat soft cheese, at room temperature
150 ml (1/4 pint) soured cream
2 eggs, separated
125 g (4 oz) caster sugar

BISCUIT BASE

125 g (4 oz) sweet oat biscuits, coarsely crushed
60 g (2 oz) butter, melted
30 g (1 oz) demerara sugar
45 g (1 1/2 oz) walnuts, chopped

DECORATION

150 ml (1/4 pint) whipping cream, whipped until stiff
a few raspberries
mint sprigs
⋆ *23 cm (9 in) loose-bottomed or springform cake tin*

1 Make the biscuit base: mix together the biscuits, butter, demerara sugar, and walnuts and press evenly over the bottom of the tin.

2 Put the measured water into a heatproof bowl, sprinkle the gelatine over the top, and leave for about 10 minutes until spongy.

3 Meanwhile, purée the raspberries in a food processor, then push them through a nylon sieve to remove the pips. Stir in the framboise liqueur. Set aside.

4 Put the soft cheese into a large bowl, and beat until soft and smooth. Add the soured cream and egg yolks, and beat until well blended.

5 Stand the bowl of gelatine in a saucepan of hot water and heat gently until it dissolves. Stir into the cheese mixture.

6 Make the filling (see box, right).

7 Use a knife to loosen the side of the cheesecake from the tin, then remove the cheesecake. Slide on to a serving plate. Pipe whipped cream (page 431) around the edge and decorate with raspberries and mint sprigs.

Cook's know-how

To achieve an attractive marbled effect, fold in the raspberry purée lightly but thoroughly, so that it forms thin streaks. If there are large areas of raspberry purée, they will not set with the rest of the mixture.

Making the filling

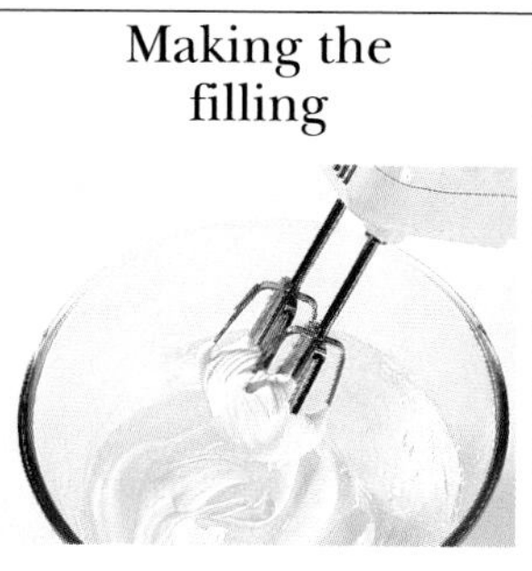

Whisk the egg whites until stiff but not dry. Add the caster sugar, 1 tsp at a time, and whisk until all the sugar is incorporated and the meringue mixture is stiff and glossy.

Turn the cheese mixture into the meringue and fold together, blending well. Leave the mixture to thicken slightly.

Fold in the raspberry purée, swirling it in just enough to give an attractive marbled effect.

Pour the mixture carefully on to the biscuit base and chill until set.

AUSTRIAN CHEESECAKE

Serves 8

- *90 g (3 oz) butter, at room temperature, plus extra for greasing*
- *150 g (5 oz) caster sugar*
- *300 g (10 oz) curd cheese*
- *2 eggs, separated*
- *60 g (2 oz) ground almonds*
- *2 tbsp semolina*
- *grated zest and juice of 1 large lemon*
- *60 g (2 oz) sultanas*
- *icing sugar for dusting*
- ⋆ *20 cm (8 in) loose-bottomed or springform cake tin*

1 Lightly butter the tin and line the bottom with a round of baking parchment.

2 Beat the butter with the sugar and curd cheese until light and creamy. Beat in the egg yolks, then stir in the almonds, semolina, and lemon zest and juice. Leave the mixture to stand for 10 minutes, then fold in the sultanas.

3 In a separate bowl, whisk the egg whites until stiff but not dry. Carefully fold into the cheese mixture.

4 Turn into the prepared tin and level the surface. Bake in a preheated oven at 190°C (375°F, Gas 5) for 30–35 minutes until browned and firm to the touch. Turn off the oven and leave the cheesecake inside to cool for about 1 hour. Chill before serving.

5 Use a knife to loosen the side of the cheesecake from the tin, then remove the cheesecake. Slide on to a serving plate, and dust with sifted icing sugar (see below).

Cook's know-how

For a decorative pattern on top of the cheesecake, place a doily on top, dust with icing sugar, then carefully lift off the doily.

TROPICAL FRUIT CHEESECAKE

Serves 10

- *2 ripe mangoes*
- *150 ml (1/4 pint) mango and apple fruit juice*
- *2 tbsp powdered gelatine*
- *250 g (8 oz) full-fat soft cheese, at room temperature*
- *125 g (4 oz) caster sugar*
- *2 eggs, separated*
- *150 ml (1/4 pint) whipping cream, whipped until thick*

BISCUIT BASE

- *125 g (4 oz) coconut biscuits, crushed*
- *60 g (2 oz) butter, melted*
- *30 g (1 oz) demerara sugar*

DECORATION

- *2 kiwi fruit, peeled and sliced*
- *1 x 250 g (8 oz) can pineapple pieces in natural juice, drained*
- ⋆ *23 cm (9 in) loose-bottomed or springform cake tin*

1 Make the biscuit base: mix together the biscuits, melted butter, and sugar, and press evenly over the bottom of the tin.

2 Slice the mango flesh away from the stones (page 430). Peel, then purée in a food processor.

3 Pour the fruit juice into a heatproof bowl, and sprinkle the gelatine over the top. Leave for about 10 minutes until it becomes spongy. Stand the bowl in a small pan of hot water, and heat gently until the gelatine has dissolved.

4 In a large bowl, beat the soft cheese until smooth and creamy. Beat in half of the caster sugar, the egg yolks, and the mango purée. Gradually beat in the gelatine mixture.

5 In a separate bowl, whisk the egg whites until stiff but not dry. Whisk in the remaining sugar, 1 tsp at a time, and continue to whisk at high speed until the sugar is incorporated and the mixture is stiff and glossy.

6 Fold the whipped cream into the cheese and mango mixture, then fold in the egg whites. Pour on to the biscuit base and chill until set.

7 Use a knife to loosen the side of the cheesecake, then remove from the tin. Slide on to a serving plate. Decorate the top with slices of kiwi fruit and pieces of pineapple before serving.

Fruit jellies

Jellies are not just for children's birthday parties. Made from fresh fruits and fruit juices, they make a wonderfully light dessert worthy of any sophisticated dinner party. What's more, they can be prepared the day before and simply turned out, decorated, and served without too much last-minute fuss.

Layered fruit terrine

Serves 4–6

2 oranges
175 g (6 oz) raspberries
175 g (6 oz) strawberries
175 g (6 oz) seedless green grapes
150 ml (¼ pint) cold water
2 tbsp powdered gelatine
90 g (3 oz) granulated sugar
500 ml (16 fl oz) dry white wine
juice of ½ lemon
⋆ 1.25 litre (2 pint) terrine or loaf tin

1 Peel the oranges and cut out the segments (page 430). Pick over the raspberries. Hull the strawberries and cut in half if large. Reserve a few for decoration. Halve the grapes.

2 Put 4 tbsp of the measured water into a small heatproof bowl and sprinkle the gelatine over the top. Leave for 10 minutes or until spongy. Put the bowl into a pan of hot water and heat gently until the gelatine dissolves.

3 Put the remaining water into a large saucepan, add the sugar, and heat, stirring occasionally, until dissolved. Bring to a boil and simmer the syrup for 5 minutes.

4 While the gelatine is still warm, pour it into the sugar syrup and stir well. Add the wine and lemon juice and stir well to mix.

5 Pour a little of the mixture into the terrine to make a 1 cm (½ in) layer. Chill for about 30 minutes until the jelly is set.

6 Arrange the fruit in layers on top of the jelly. Pour the remaining wine mixture into the terrine, a ladleful at a time, gently shaking the terrine to remove any air bubbles. Chill for about 6 hours until set. Turn out the jelly, slice, then decorate with the reserved strawberries. Serve chilled.

Starburst jellies

Serves 6

100 ml (3½ fl oz) cold water
2 tbsp powdered gelatine
1 x 400 g (13 oz) can peach halves in syrup
6 passion fruit
6 slices of star fruit
1 pink grapefruit, peeled and segmented
125 ml (4 fl oz) whipping cream
30 g (1 oz) icing sugar
passion fruit to decorate
⋆ 6 x 250 ml (8 fl oz) jelly moulds

1 Put the water into a heatproof bowl and sprinkle the gelatine over the top. Leave for 10 minutes or until spongy. Put the bowl into a pan of hot water and heat gently until dissolved.

2 Purée the peaches and their syrup in a food processor or blender. Remove the pulp from the passion fruit, add to the purée, and process briefly to combine. Push through a nylon sieve. Stir in the gelatine.

3 Dip the star fruit slices into the peach mixture and place 1 in each mould. Arrange the grapefruit around the star fruit. Divide the peach mixture among the moulds. Chill for 1–2 hours until set.

4 Whip the cream until stiff. Sift the icing sugar and fold into the cream. Turn out the jellies, pipe with whipped cream, and decorate with passion fruit.

Elderflower & grape jellies

Serves 4–6

200 ml (7 fl oz) cold water
3 tbsp powdered gelatine
750 ml (1¼ pints) rosé wine
30 g (1 oz) caster sugar
juice of ½ lemon
4 tbsp elderflower cordial
150 g (5 oz) seedless red grapes, halved
lemon twists and mint sprigs to decorate
⋆ 4 wine glasses

1 Put the water into a heatproof bowl and sprinkle the gelatine over the top. Leave for 10 minutes or until spongy. Put the bowl into a pan of hot water and heat gently until dissolved.

2 Put half of the wine and the sugar into a saucepan. Heat gently until the sugar dissolves. Bring to a boil and simmer for 5 minutes. Add the lemon juice, elderflower cordial, and the remaining wine. Stir in the gelatine.

3 Arrange the grape halves in the glasses. Pour a little of the jelly mixture into each glass. Chill for 10 minutes. Pour the remaining mixture into the glasses. Chill for 1–2 hours until set. Decorate with lemon twists and mint sprigs before serving.

Clockwise from top: *Starburst Jellies, Elderflower & Grape Jellies, Layered Fruit Terrine.*

Successful fruit jellies

Almost all fruits make successful jellies, with the exception of pineapples and kiwi fruit, which contain an enzyme that prevents gelatine setting.

- Wash and dry all fruit, or the jelly may go cloudy or not set.
- To turn out, pull the edge of the jelly away from the mould. Dip the mould in hot water for 2–3 seconds, then turn out on to a wet plate (this allows repositioning).

POTS AU CHOCOLAT

Serves 6

175 g (6 oz) plain chocolate, broken into pieces

3 tbsp strong black coffee

15 g (1/2 oz) butter

a few drops of vanilla essence

3 eggs, separated

150 ml (1/4 pint) double cream, whipped until stiff, to decorate

1 Put the chocolate pieces into a saucepan with the strong black coffee. Heat gently, stirring, until the chocolate melts.

2 Leave the chocolate mixture to cool slightly, then add the butter, vanilla essence, and egg yolks and stir until well blended.

3 Whisk the egg whites until stiff but not dry. Fold gently but thoroughly into the chocolate mixture.

4 Pour the mixture into 6 small custard pots, ramekins, or other serving dishes, and leave to chill for about 8 hours.

5 Decorate each pot of chocolate with a piped rosette of whipped cream (page 431) before serving.

CHOCOLATE CHIP CHEESECAKE

This delicious dessert, with its crunchy muesli base and rich chocolate filling, is ideal for parties. It can be prepared up to a month in advance and frozen in freezer foil. Thaw, wrapped, in the refrigerator for 8 hours, then decorate.

Serves 8

125 g (4 oz) plain chocolate, broken into pieces

3 tbsp cold water

2 tbsp powdered gelatine

250 g (8 oz) full-fat soft cheese

2 eggs, separated

60 g (2 oz) caster sugar

150 ml (1/4 pint) soured cream

30 g (1 oz) plain chocolate chips, coarsely chopped

BASE

125 g (4 oz) muesli

90 g (3 oz) butter, melted

30 g (1 oz) demerara sugar

DECORATION

300 ml (1/2 pint) whipping cream, whipped until stiff

chocolate curls or caraque (page 431)

⭑ 20 cm (8 in) loose-bottomed or springform cake tin

1 Make the base: mix together the muesli, melted butter, and sugar, and press evenly over the bottom of the tin. Chill.

2 Meanwhile: put the chocolate into a small heatproof bowl over a pan of hot water. Heat gently to melt the chocolate, stirring occasionally. Leave to cool.

3 Put the measured water into a heatproof bowl and sprinkle the gelatine over the top. Leave for 10 minutes until spongy. Stand the bowl in a pan of hot water and heat gently until the gelatine has dissolved.

4 Beat the cheese until smooth. Add the egg yolks and sugar and beat until blended. Stir in the soured cream, melted chocolate, chocolate chips, and gelatine. Mix well.

5 In a separate bowl, whisk the egg whites until stiff but not dry. Fold carefully into the chocolate mixture. Pour on to the muesli base and chill until set.

6 Use a knife to loosen the side of the cheesecake from the tin, then remove the cheesecake. Slide on to a serving plate. Pipe rosettes of whipped cream (page 431) on top and decorate with chocolate curls or caraque.

Cook's know-how

Chocolate chips are convenient, but if you don't have any to hand, chop squares taken from a chocolate bar.

CHOCOLATE ROULADE

This impressive dessert is made from a baked chocolate soufflé rolled around a cream and chocolate filling. It is important to cut the roulade cleanly, so use a long serrated knife and dip it in hot water before cutting each slice.

Serves 6

sunflower oil for greasing

175 g (6 oz) plain chocolate, broken into pieces

6 eggs, size 2, separated

175 g (6 oz) caster sugar

icing sugar for dusting

FILLING

90 g (3 oz) plain chocolate, broken into pieces

300 ml (1/2 pint) double cream, whipped until thick

⋆ *23 x 33 cm (9 x 13 in) Swiss roll tin*

1 Lightly grease the tin with sunflower oil and line with baking parchment.

2 Put the chocolate into a small heatproof bowl over a pan of hot water and heat gently, stirring occasionally, to melt the chocolate. Leave to cool.

3 Combine the egg yolks and sugar in a large bowl and whisk together until light and creamy. Add the cooled chocolate and stir to blend evenly.

4 In a separate bowl, whisk the egg whites until stiff but not dry. Carefully fold into the chocolate mixture.

5 Turn the chocolate mixture into the tin, tilting it so that the mixture spreads evenly into the corners. Bake in a preheated oven at 180°C (350°F, Gas 4) for 20 minutes or until firm to the touch.

6 Remove from the oven. Place a clean, dry tea towel on top of the cake and on top of this lay another tea towel that has been soaked in cold water and well wrung out. Leave in a cool place for 8 hours.

7 Make the filling: put the chocolate into a heatproof bowl over a pan of hot water and heat gently, stirring occasionally, to melt the chocolate. Cool.

8 Remove the tea towels from the sponge, and turn it out on to a piece of baking parchment that has been liberally sprinkled with sifted icing sugar. Peel the lining paper from the cake.

9 Spread the melted chocolate over the cake, then spread the whipped cream evenly on top.

10 Roll up the cake from a long edge, using the sugared paper to help lift the cake and roll it forward.

11 Dust the roulade with more sifted icing sugar before serving.

ZABAGLIONE

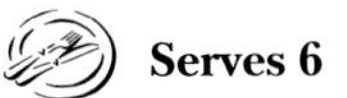

Serves 6

4 egg yolks

75 g (2 1/2 oz) caster sugar

125 ml (4 fl oz) Marsala

boudoir biscuits (Italian sponge fingers) to serve

1 Put the egg yolks and sugar into a heatproof bowl. Whisk together until light and foamy, then add the Marsala. Whisk to blend.

2 Put the bowl over a pan of simmering water, making sure it does not touch the water. Heat gently, whisking the mixture until it becomes thick and creamy and stands in soft peaks.

3 Remove from the heat and whisk until cool. Pour into 6 glass dishes and serve with boudoir biscuits.

Zabaglione

This Italian dessert may also be served warm. As soon as the mixture has thickened, remove from the heat and pour into serving dishes.

HELEN'S PUDDING

Serves 6

125 g (4 oz) fresh brown breadcrumbs
90 g (3 oz) demerara sugar
75 g (2 1/2 oz) drinking chocolate powder
2 tbsp instant coffee granules
300 ml (1/2 pint) double cream
150 ml (1/4 pint) single cream
60 g (2 oz) plain chocolate, grated

1 In a bowl, mix together the breadcrumbs, sugar, drinking chocolate, and coffee granules. In another bowl, whip together the double and single creams until they form soft peaks.

2 Spoon half of the cream into 6 glass serving dishes. Cover with the breadcrumb mixture and then with the remaining cream. Chill for at least 6 hours or 8 hours for best results.

3 Sprinkle generously with the grated chocolate just before serving.

Cook's know-how

For best results, make sure the chocolate is well chilled before you grate it. Use the large grid on the grater.

CHOCOLATE LAYERED TERRINE

This rich and creamy dessert is ideal for a dinner party or special family treat. A layer of white chocolate and double cream is sandwiched between layers of plain chocolate and double cream flavoured with brandy.

Serves 8–10

PLAIN CHOCOLATE LAYERS
250 g (8 oz) plain chocolate
2 tbsp brandy
2 eggs
375 ml (13 fl oz) double cream
WHITE CHOCOLATE LAYER
90 g (3 oz) white chocolate
1 egg
150 ml (1/4 pint) double cream
DECORATION
150 ml (1/4 pint) double cream, whipped, grated chocolate, and mint sprigs to decorate
☆ 1 kg (2 lb) loaf tin

1 Make the plain chocolate layers: break the plain chocolate into pieces and place in a heatproof bowl with the brandy over a pan of hot water. Heat gently to melt, then leave to cool.

2 Line the loaf tin with cling film. Set aside.

3 Put the eggs into a heatproof bowl over a pan of hot water. Whisk until the eggs are thick and mousse-like, and leave a trail when the whisk is lifted. Remove from the heat and whisk until the bowl is completely cold.

4 Whip the cream until it just holds its shape. Fold the whisked eggs into the cooled chocolate mixture, then fold in the cream.

5 Pour half of the plain chocolate mixture into the prepared tin, then place in the freezer for about 15 minutes until firm. Reserve the remaining plain chocolate mixture.

6 Meanwhile, make the white chocolate mixture in the same way as the plain chocolate mixture.

7 Pour the white chocolate mixture on top of the firm layer in the tin, and freeze for 15 minutes.

8 Spoon the reserved plain chocolate mixture on top of the white chocolate layer and freeze for about 30 minutes until it is firm enough to slice.

9 Invert the tin on to a serving plate, and remove the cling film. Decorate the terrine with piped rosettes of whipped cream (page 431), grated chocolate, and mint sprigs. Slice thinly to serve.

Cook's know-how

Keep this terrine well chilled for easy slicing and serving. Substitute Greek yogurt for one-third of the double cream to give a less rich flavour, if preferred.

CHOCOLATE & BRANDY MOUSSE

Serves 6

250 g (8 oz) plain chocolate, broken into pieces

3 tbsp brandy

3 tbsp cold water

2 tsp powdered gelatine

4 eggs, plus 2 egg yolks

90 g (3 oz) caster sugar

150 ml (1/4 pint) whipping cream, whipped until thick

DECORATION

150 ml (1/4 pint) double cream, whipped until stiff

chocolate curls or caraque (page 431) to decorate

1 Put the chocolate into a heatproof bowl with the brandy over a pan of hot water. Heat gently until melted. Leave to cool.

2 Put the cold water into a heatproof bowl and sprinkle the gelatine over the top. Leave for about 10 minutes until spongy. Stand the bowl in a pan of hot water and heat gently until dissolved.

3 Combine the eggs, egg yolks, and sugar in a large heatproof bowl, and put over a saucepan of simmering water. Whisk with a hand-held electric mixer until the egg mixture is very thick and mousse-like. Whisk in the dissolved gelatine.

4 Fold the whipped cream into the cooled chocolate, then fold into the egg mixture. Carefully pour into a glass serving bowl, cover, and leave in the refrigerator until set.

5 Decorate with piped rosettes of cream and chocolate curls or caraque (page 431). Serve the mousse chilled.

Cook's know-how

Make sure you use good quality chocolate. For the best flavour, look for the brand with the highest percentage of cocoa solids.

TIRAMISU

Serves 12

1 1/2 tsp instant coffee granules

175 ml (6 fl oz) boiling water

150 ml (1/4 pint) brandy

3 eggs

125 g (4 oz) caster sugar

425 g (14 oz) mascarpone cheese

450 ml (3/4 pint) double cream

150 g (5 oz) plain chocolate chips

1 packet trifle sponges

60 g (2 oz) white chocolate, grated, to decorate

1 Dissolve the coffee in the measured boiling water and mix with the brandy.

2 Combine the eggs and caster sugar in a large bowl and whisk together until thick and light. The mixture should be thick enough to leave a trail on the surface.

3 Put the mascarpone cheese into a large bowl. Stir in a little of the egg mixture. Fold in the remaining egg mixture. Fold in the double cream.

4 Chop the chocolate chips in a food processor until they form a powder with some larger pieces of chocolate for texture.

5 Cut the trifle sponges horizontally in half. Layer the tiramisu (see box, below).

6 Decorate with the remaining plain chocolate and the white chocolate. Cover and chill for 4 hours.

Layering the tiramisu

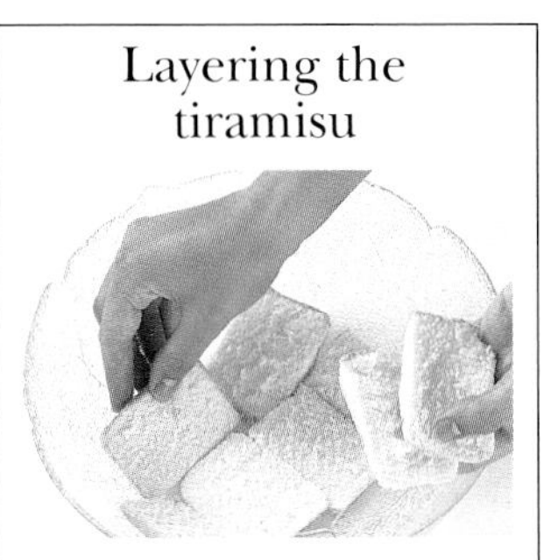

Line the bottom of a large glass serving bowl with half of the sponge pieces. Drizzle half of the coffee and brandy mixture over the sponges.

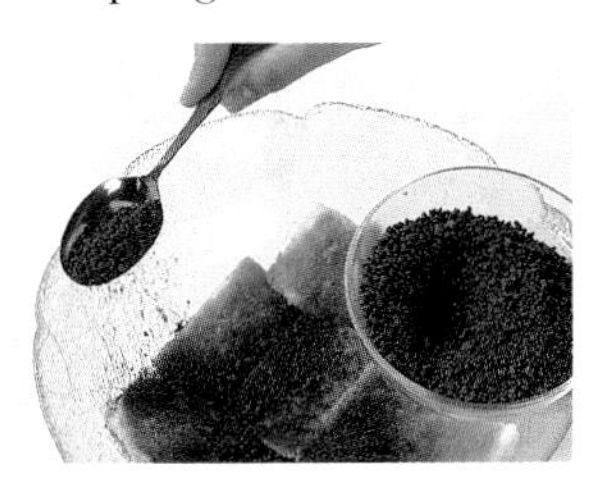

Scatter over one-third of the chocolate, then spoon half of the mascarpone mixture on top. Level the surface. Repeat the layers.

CREME CARAMEL

 **Serves 6**

175 g (6 oz) granulated sugar

150 ml (1/4 pint) water

4 eggs

30 g (1 oz) vanilla sugar (see Cook's know-how, right)

600 ml (1 pint) milk

☆ *6 small ramekins*

1 Combine the sugar and water in a saucepan and heat gently until all the sugar has dissolved. Bring to a boil, and cook without stirring, until golden. Pour into the ramekins.

2 Whisk the eggs and vanilla sugar in a bowl. Heat the milk until just warm, then pour into the egg mixture, stirring well. Strain into the ramekins.

3 Put the ramekins in a roasting tin and add enough hot water to come halfway up the sides of the ramekins. Bake in a preheated oven at 160°C (325°F, Gas 3) for about 40 minutes until just set and firm to the touch but not solid. Cool, then chill for about 8 hours.

4 Turn out on to individual plates to serve.

Cook's know-how

To make your own vanilla sugar, store a vanilla pod in a jar of sugar, and the sugar will absorb the vanilla flavour. You can then use the sugar when making custards and sauces.

CREME BRULEE

Serves 6

butter for greasing

4 egg yolks

30 g (1 oz) vanilla sugar (see Cook's know-how, left)

600 ml (1 pint) single cream

60 g (2 oz) demerara sugar

☆ *6 small ramekins or shallow 900 ml (1 1/2 pint) ovenproof dish*

1 Lightly butter the individual ramekins or ovenproof dish.

2 In a large bowl, beat the egg yolks with the vanilla sugar. Heat the cream to just below boiling point, then pour into the egg-yolk mixture, stirring well.

3 Pour the custard into the ramekins or the large ovenproof dish. Set in a roasting tin and add enough hot water to come halfway up the sides of the ramekins or dish.

4 Bake in a preheated oven at 160°C (325°F, Gas 3) for about 25 minutes for the individual ramekins or about 45 minutes for the large ovenproof dish, until just set and firm to the touch. Leave to cool.

5 Sprinkle the demerara sugar evenly over the top of the set custard. Place under a very hot grill until the sugar melts and caramelizes to a rich golden brown colour.

6 Chill for no more than 2 hours before serving.

Cook's know-how

The caramel topping should be hard and crisp; don't chill crème brûlée for too long, or the caramel will begin to soften. To reach the rich and creamy custard beneath, crack the hard caramel with the edge of a spoon.

QUICK VANILLA ICE CREAM

Serves 4–6

6 eggs, separated

175 g (6 oz) vanilla sugar (see Cook's know-how, page 450)

450 ml (3/4 pint) double cream, whipped until thick

1 Whisk the egg whites (at high speed if using an electric mixer) until stiff but not dry. Add the vanilla sugar, 1 tsp at a time, and continue whisking until the sugar has been incorporated and the egg-white mixture is very stiff and glossy.

2 Put the egg yolks into a separate bowl and whisk at high speed with an electric mixer until the mixture is blended thoroughly.

3 Gently fold the whipped cream and egg yolks into the egg-white mixture. Turn into a large shallow freezerproof container, cover, and leave the mixture to freeze for 8 hours.

4 Transfer the ice cream to the refrigerator for about 10 minutes before serving so that it softens slightly.

COFFEE BRANDY ICE CREAM

Substitute caster sugar for the vanilla sugar, and add 3 tbsp each coffee essence and brandy when folding the mixtures.

LEMON ICE CREAM

Substitute caster sugar for the vanilla sugar, and add the grated zest and juice of 3 large lemons when folding.

STRAWBERRY ICE CREAM

Substitute caster sugar for the vanilla sugar. Purée 375 g (12 oz) strawberries and add when folding the mixtures.

CHOCOLATE & MERINGUE BOMBE

Serves 8

600 ml (1 pint) vanilla ice cream

600 ml (1 pint) chocolate ice cream

150 ml (1/4 pint) whipping cream

1 tbsp brandy

125 g (4 oz) meringues, coarsely crushed

⋆ *1.5 litre (2 1/2 pint) bombe mould or pudding basin*

1 Chill the bombe mould in the freezer. Fill the mould with the vanilla and chocolate ice creams (see box, right).

2 Whip the cream with the brandy until it just holds its shape. Gently fold in the crushed meringues. Spoon the meringue mixture into the bombe mould. Cover and freeze for 8 hours.

3 Dip the mould into cold water and invert the chocolate and meringue bombe on to a large serving plate. Slice and serve.

Filling the mould

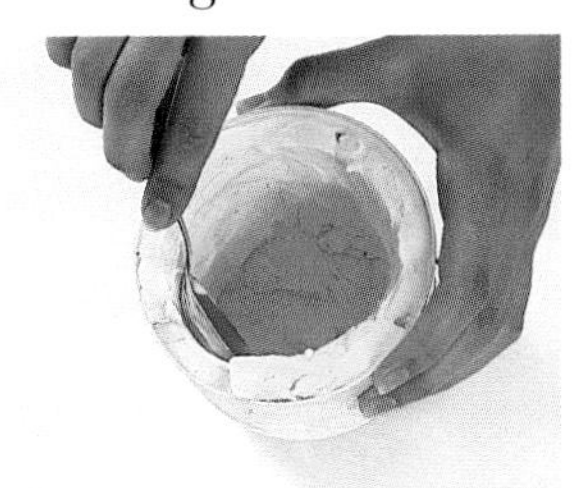

Allow the vanilla ice cream to soften at room temperature for about 20 minutes. Spread it over the base and up the side of the mould. Chill in the freezer until solid.

Soften the chocolate ice cream, then spread it evenly over the vanilla ice cream to make a hollow inner layer. Return to the freezer until solid.

Sorbets

Light and refreshing, sorbets are the perfect ending to a rich meal. Flavoured with fresh fruits and made from a basic mixture of sugar, water, and egg white, they're also low in fat. Decorate each sorbet with its key ingredient or with an ingredient complementary in flavour.

Lime

Serves 6–8

250 g (8 oz) granulated sugar
600 ml (1 pint) water
grated zest and juice of 6 limes
2 egg whites
strips of lime zest to decorate

1 Put the sugar and measured water into a saucepan and heat gently until the sugar dissolves. Bring to a boil and boil for 2 minutes. Remove from the heat, add the lime zest, and leave to cool completely. Stir in the lime juice.

2 Strain the lime syrup into a shallow freezerproof container and freeze for about 2 hours until just mushy. Turn the mixture into a bowl and whisk gently to break down any large crystals.

3 Whisk the egg whites until stiff but not dry, then fold into the lime mixture. Return to the freezer and freeze until firm. Transfer the sorbet to the refrigerator to soften for about 30 minutes. Decorate before serving.

Apricot

Serves 6–8

90 g (3 oz) granulated sugar
300 ml (1/2 pint) water
juice of 1 lemon
750 g (1 1/2 lb) apricots, halved and stoned
2 egg whites

1 Put the sugar, measured water, and lemon juice into a saucepan and heat gently until the sugar has dissolved. Bring to a boil, add the apricots, and simmer for 15 minutes or until very tender. Leave to cool.

2 Peel and slice a few apricots for decoration. Press the remainder through a nylon sieve. Pour with the syrup into a freezerproof container, then follow steps 2 and 3 of Lime Sorbet (above). Decorate before serving.

Pear & Ginger

Serves 6–8

90 g (3 oz) granulated sugar
300 ml (1/2 pint) water
1 tbsp lemon juice
750 g (1 1/2 lb) pears, peeled and cored
1 piece of stem ginger in syrup, finely chopped
2 egg whites
strips of stem ginger to decorate

1 Put the sugar, measured water, and lemon juice into a saucepan and heat gently until the sugar dissolves. Bring to a boil, add the pears, and poach gently, basting with the sugar syrup from time to time, for 20–25 minutes until the pears are tender. Cool, then purée in a food processor.

2 Add the chopped stem ginger to the pear purée. Pour the pear mixture into a freezerproof container, then follow steps 2 and 3 of Lime Sorbet (left). Decorate before serving.

Raspberry

Serves 6–8

500 g (1 lb) raspberries
175 g (6 oz) granulated sugar
600 ml (1 pint) water
juice of 1 orange
3 egg whites
raspberries and mint sprigs to decorate

1 Purée the raspberries in a food processor, then push through a nylon sieve to remove the pips. Put the sugar and measured water into a saucepan and heat gently until the sugar dissolves. Bring to a boil, then boil for 5 minutes.

2 Pour into a bowl and cool. Stir in raspberry purée and orange juice. Pour into a freezerproof container, then follow steps 2 and 3 of Lime Sorbet (left). Decorate before serving.

Granitas

Granitas are similar to sorbets but even easier to make: they're simply flavoured ice crystals.

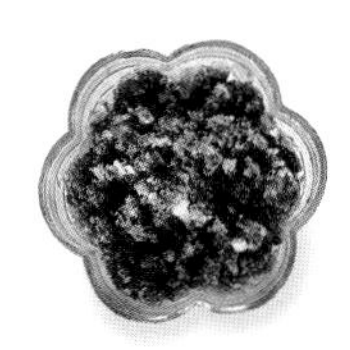

Coffee

Put *60 g (2 oz) caster sugar* and *4 tbsp instant coffee granules* into a pan with *750 ml (1 1/4 pints) water* and bring to a boil. Simmer for about 5 minutes. Leave to cool, then pour into a freezerproof container. Freeze, stirring occasionally, for 5 hours.

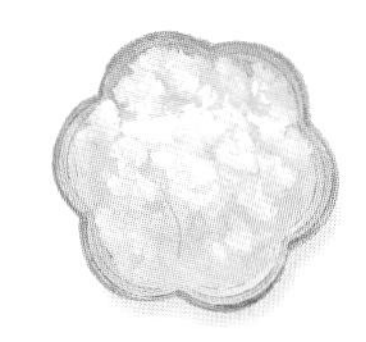

Lemon

Put *200 g (7 oz) caster sugar* into a saucepan, add *500 ml (16 fl oz) water*, and bring to a boil. Simmer for 5 minutes. Leave to cool. Add *2 tsp grated lemon zest* and the *juice of 4 lemons* to the sugar syrup. Pour into a freezerproof container and freeze, stirring occasionally, for 5 hours.

Watermelon

Remove and discard the rind and seeds from *1 kg (2 lb) watermelon.* Purée the flesh in a food processor. Pour into a freezerproof container and mix in *30 g (1 oz) icing sugar* and *1 1/2 tsp lemon juice.* Freeze, stirring occasionally, for 5 hours.

Clockwise from top: *Apricot, Pear & Ginger, Lime, and Raspberry Sorbets.*

PEACH MELBA

 **Serves 4**

4 ripe peaches, peeled, stoned, and sliced
8 scoops of vanilla ice cream
mint sprigs to decorate
MELBA SAUCE
375 g (12 oz) raspberries
about 4 tbsp icing sugar

1 Make the Melba sauce (see box, below).

2 Arrange the peach slices in 4 glass serving dishes. Top with 2 scoops of ice cream each and some sauce. Decorate with the remaining raspberries and mint sprigs.

Making Melba sauce

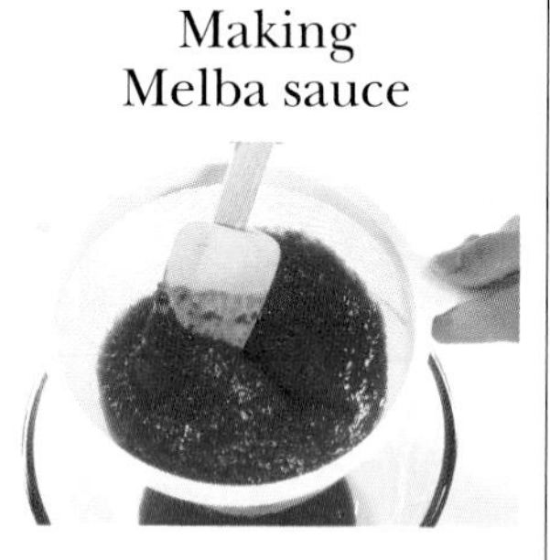

Purée 250 g (8 oz) of the raspberries. Push through a nylon sieve to remove the pips.

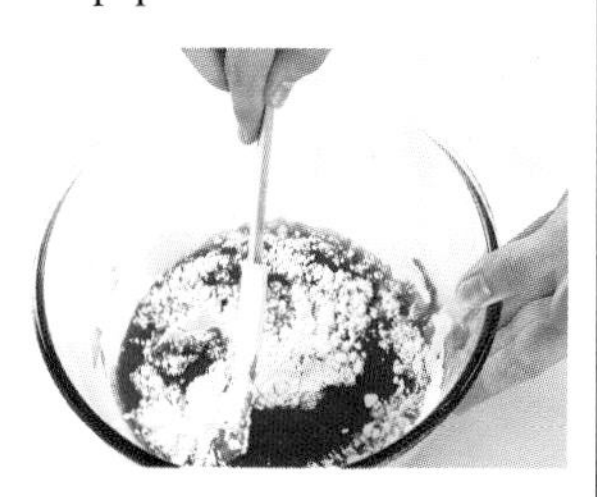

Sift the icing sugar over the purée and stir in.

RICH VANILLA ICE CREAM

Home-made ice cream tastes much better than any commercially made ice cream, and, despite its reputation, it is not at all difficult to make. It will keep for up to 1 month in the freezer.

Serves 4–6

4 egg yolks
125 g (4 oz) caster sugar
300 ml (1/2 pint) milk
300 ml (1/2 pint) double cream
1 1/2 tsp vanilla essence
strawberry fans to decorate

1 Put the egg yolks and sugar into a bowl and whisk until light in colour.

2 Heat the milk in a heavy pan to just below boiling point. Add a little of the hot milk to the egg-yolk mixture and stir to blend, then pour in the remaining milk.

3 Pour back into the pan and heat gently, stirring, until the froth disappears and the mixture coats the back of a spoon. Do not boil.

4 Leave the custard to cool, then stir in the cream and vanilla essence.

5 Pour into a container and freeze for 3 hours. Tip into a bowl and mash to break down the ice crystals. Return to container. Freeze for 2 hours. Mash and freeze for another 2 hours. Remove from the freezer 30 minutes before serving, and decorate.

CHOCOLATE ICE CREAM

Heat the milk with 125 g (4 oz) pieces of plain chocolate. Allow the chocolate to melt, then proceed as directed.

COCONUT ICE CREAM

Heat the milk with 175 g (6 oz) grated creamed coconut. Allow the coconut to melt, then proceed as directed.

CHOCOLATE CHIP ICE CREAM

Heat the milk with 125 g (4 oz) chopped white chocolate. Allow the chocolate to melt, then proceed as directed. Stir 60 g (2 oz) plain chocolate chips into the custard with the cream.

BANANA & HONEY ICE CREAM

Mash 500 g (1 lb) bananas with 3 tbsp lemon juice and 2 tbsp honey. Add to the custard with the double cream, then proceed as directed.

BAKED ALASKA

Serves 8

1 x 20 cm (8 in) sponge flan case

250 g (8 oz) raspberries, sliced strawberries, or other summer fruits

450 ml (3/4 pint) vanilla ice cream

2 egg whites

125 g (4 oz) caster sugar

whole berries to decorate

1 Put the sponge flan case into a shallow ovenproof serving dish. Arrange the fruits in the case.

2 Put the ice cream on top of the fruits and put in the freezer to keep the ice cream frozen while making the meringue.

3 Whisk the egg whites (an electric mixer can be used) until stiff but not dry.

4 Add the caster sugar, 1 tsp at a time, and continue to whisk until the sugar has been incorporated and the meringue mixture is stiff and glossy.

5 Pipe or spoon the meringue over the ice cream, covering it completely.

6 Bake immediately in a preheated oven at 230°C (450°F, Gas 8) for 3–4 minutes until the meringue is tinged with brown. Serve at once, decorated with raspberries and strawberries.

Cook's know-how

A block of ice cream is best for this recipe. Don't use soft-scoop ice cream. Make sure the ice cream is completely covered by the egg white, which stops the ice cream melting.

ICED CHRISTMAS PUDDING

Serves 8

175 g (6 oz) mixed dried fruit

60 g (2 oz) ready-to-eat dried apricots, chopped

60 g (2 oz) glacé cherries, halved

3 tbsp brandy

3 eggs

125 g (4 oz) caster sugar

450 ml (3/4 pint) milk

450 ml (3/4 pint) double cream

150 ml (1/4 pint) single cream

⋆ *1.75 litre (3 pint) pudding basin*

1 Combine the dried fruit, apricots, glacé cherries, and brandy. Cover and leave to soak for 8 hours.

2 In a large bowl, whisk together the eggs and sugar. Heat the milk in a heavy saucepan to just below boiling point. Pour into the egg mixture, stirring.

3 Pour back into the pan. Cook gently, stirring with a wooden spoon, until the froth disappears and the mixture thickens. Do not boil. Remove from the heat and leave to cool.

4 Whip 300 ml (1/2 pint) double cream and the single cream together until they are just beginning to hold their shape. Fold into the custard with the fruit and brandy mixture.

5 Turn into a shallow freezerproof container and freeze for 2 hours or until beginning to set but still slightly soft.

6 Remove the pudding from the freezer and mix well to distribute the fruit evenly. Spoon into the pudding basin, cover, and return to the freezer. Freeze for 3 hours or until firm.

7 Remove from the freezer about 20 minutes before serving to soften. Turn out on to a serving plate, and spoon the remaining cream, lightly whipped, on top. Slice and serve at once.

CASSATA

 **Serves 8**

30 g (1 oz) candied angelica, rinsed, dried, and chopped

30 g (1 oz) glacé cherries, rinsed, dried, and chopped

30 g (1 oz) chopped mixed candied peel

2 tbsp dark rum

600 ml (1 pint) raspberry sorbet

150 ml (1/4 pint) double cream, whipped until thick

600 ml (1 pint) vanilla ice cream

⭑ *900 ml (1 1/2 pint) terrine*

1 Chill the terrine. Put the angelica, glacé cherries, and candied peel in a bowl.

2 Add the rum and stir well, then leave to soak while preparing the ice cream layers.

3 Allow the sorbet to soften, then spread it evenly over the bottom of the chilled terrine. Chill in the freezer until solid.

4 Fold the fruit and rum mixture into the whipped cream. Spoon into the terrine and level the surface. Return to the freezer until firm.

5 Allow the vanilla ice cream to soften, then spread it evenly over the fruit layer. Cover and leave to freeze for 8 hours.

6 To turn out, dip the terrine into warm water and invert the cassata on to a large serving plate. Slice, and serve at once.

FROZEN LEMON FLUMMERY

 **Serves 4**

150 ml (1/4 pint) double cream

grated zest and juice of 1 large lemon

175 g (6 oz) caster sugar

300 ml (1/2 pint) milk

pared zest of 1 lemon, cut into strips, to decorate

1 Whip the cream until it forms soft peaks. Add the lemon zest and juice, caster sugar, and milk, and mix until evenly blended.

2 Pour into a shallow freezerproof container, cover, and freeze for at least 6 hours until firm.

3 Cut the mixture into chunks, then transfer to a food processor and work until smooth and creamy. Pour into 4 individual freezerproof dishes and freeze for about 8 hours.

4 Blanch the strips of lemon zest in boiling water for 1 minute. Drain, rinse, and pat dry.

5 Decorate the flummery with the strips of lemon zest and serve.

FROZEN ORANGE FLUMMERY

Substitute the grated zest and juice of 1 orange for the lemon, reduce the caster sugar to 125 g (4 oz), and proceed as directed. Decorate with blanched strips of orange zest.

13

CAKES & TEABREADS

30–60 MINUTES

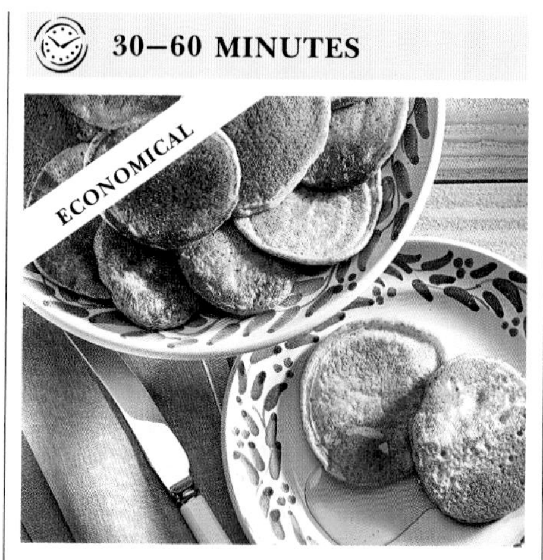

WHOLEMEAL DROP SCONES

Family favourite: a simple batter made with wholemeal flour for nutty flavour. Dropped on to a hot griddle and served with syrup.

MAKES 20 55 calories each

Takes 30 minutes **PAGE 481**

BRANDY SNAPS

A delicate batter flavoured with ground ginger and lemon juice, baked until golden, and rolled before crisp.

MAKES 15 107 calories each

Takes 40 minutes, plus cooling **PAGE 483**

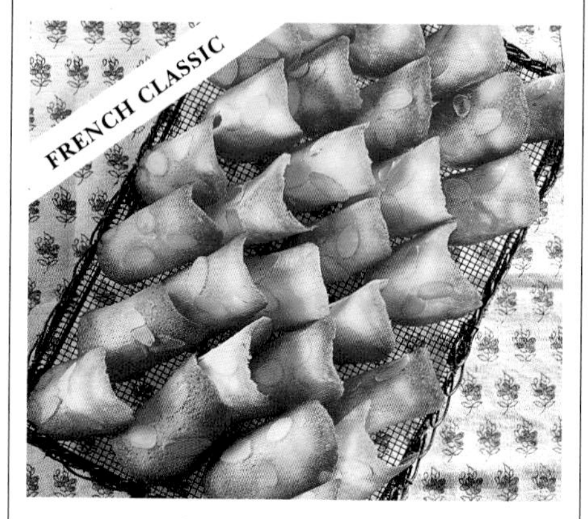

ALMOND TUILES

Crisp and delicate: a sweet, almond-flavoured batter baked until golden brown, then shaped into curves before crisp.

MAKES 30 45 calories each

Takes 30 minutes, plus cooling **PAGE 482**

OVER 60 MINUTES

VICTORIA SANDWICH CAKE

Two light and golden layers of sponge sandwiched with jam, and sprinkled generously with caster sugar.

SERVES 6–8 515–386 calories per serving

Takes 35 minutes, plus cooling **PAGE 472**

CORNBREAD

An American favourite: a simple, slightly sweet batter made from polenta. Baked until golden and served warm.

MAKES 9 SQUARES 230 calories each

Takes 40 minutes, plus cooling **PAGE 478**

DEVON SCONES

An English teatime favourite: a simple dough makes featherweight scones. Serve spread with butter and jam.

MAKES 12 133 calories each

Takes 30 minutes, plus cooling **PAGE 480**

FORK BISCUITS

Plain and simple: a butter-enriched dough, imprinted with a fork pattern and baked until crisp and golden.

MAKES 32 104 calories each

Takes 30 minutes, plus cooling **PAGE 483**

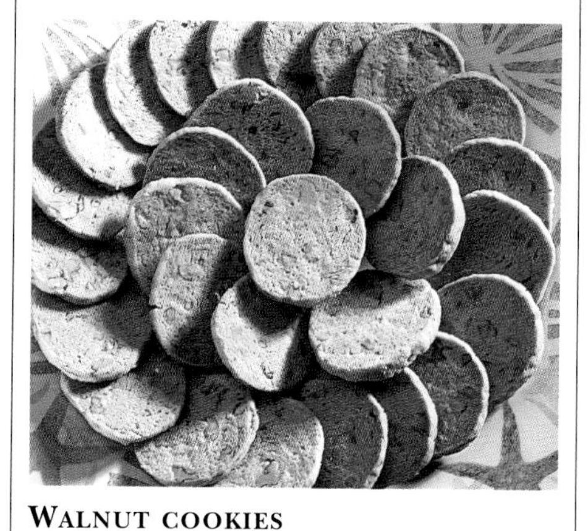

WALNUT COOKIES

Crisp and sweet: a walnut-studded dough, shaped into a roll, cut into thin slices, and baked until golden. Very easy to make.

MAKES 50 59 calories each

Takes 35 minutes, plus chilling **PAGE 486**

MINCEMEAT BUNS

Rich and fruity: a miniature and quick version of mince pies. Baked in individual cake cases.

MAKES 32 137 calories each

Takes 40 minutes, plus cooling **PAGE 474**

OVER 60 MINUTES

SWISS ROLL

An old favourite: a light golden sponge spread generously with a layer of raspberry jam, rolled up, and decorated with sugar.

SERVES 6–8 260–195 calories per serving

Takes 45 minutes, plus cooling **PAGE 469**

VIENNESE FINGERS

Pretty and delicious: a rich butter dough piped into fingers, baked until golden brown, and each end dipped in chocolate.

MAKES 12 215 calories each

Takes 30 minutes, plus cooling **PAGE 482**

PINWHEEL BISCUITS

Attractive and easy: vanilla and coffee doughs rolled together, cut into thin slices, and baked.

MAKES 18 98 calories each

Takes 45 minutes, plus chilling **PAGE 486**

COCONUT MACAROONS

Almonds and coconut flavour these macaroons. Crisp and golden on the outside and deliciously tender on the inside.

MAKES 26 116 calories each

Takes 40 minutes, plus cooling **PAGE 482**

POTATO FARLS

An old-fashioned treat: a biscuit dough made with mashed potatoes and baked until crisp. Simple and delicious.

MAKES 12 113 calories each

Takes 40 minutes, plus cooling **PAGE 481**

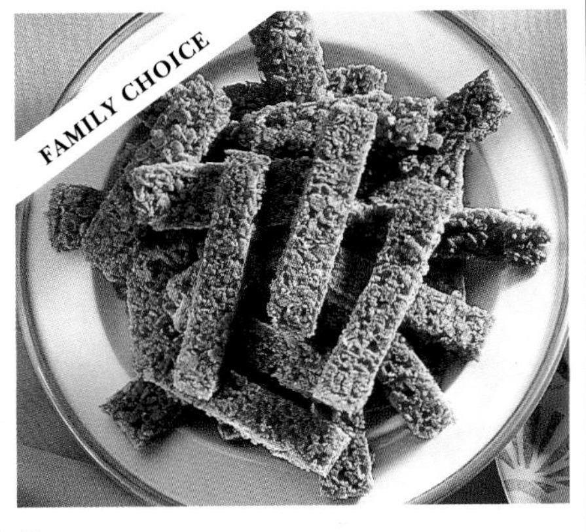

FLAPJACKS

Rich, chewy, and very easy to make: an oat-studded batter is spread into a roasting tin, baked, and cut into fingers.

MAKES 24 102 calories each

Takes 45 minutes, plus cooling **PAGE 486**

GINGER SNAPS

Crisp and spicy: ginger and cinnamon spice a dough enriched with butter and baked until dark golden brown.

MAKES 15 81 calories each

Takes 30 minutes, plus cooling **PAGE 483**

SUMMER STRAWBERRY SPONGE

Two layers of golden sponge filled with freshly whipped cream, sweet and juicy strawberries, and tropical passion fruit.

SERVES 8 260 calories per serving

Takes 60 minutes, plus cooling **PAGE 469**

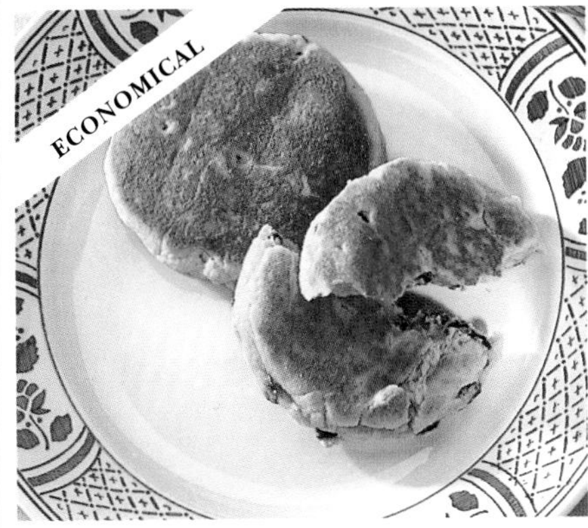

WELSH CAKES

Old-fashioned griddle cakes studded with currants and flavoured with mixed spice. Served hot from the pan or left to cool slightly.

MAKES 12 204 calories each

Takes 30 minutes, plus cooling **PAGE 480**

Over 60 minutes

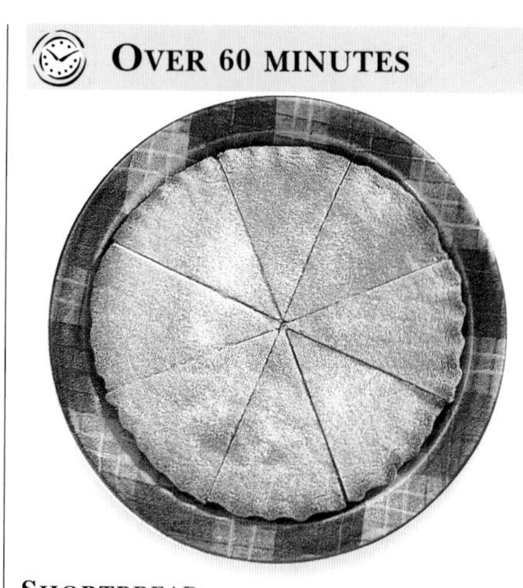

Shortbread

Highland classic: a dough made rich with butter, baked until golden, and sprinkled with sugar.

MAKES 8 WEDGES 233 calories each

Takes 55 minutes, plus cooling **PAGE 478**

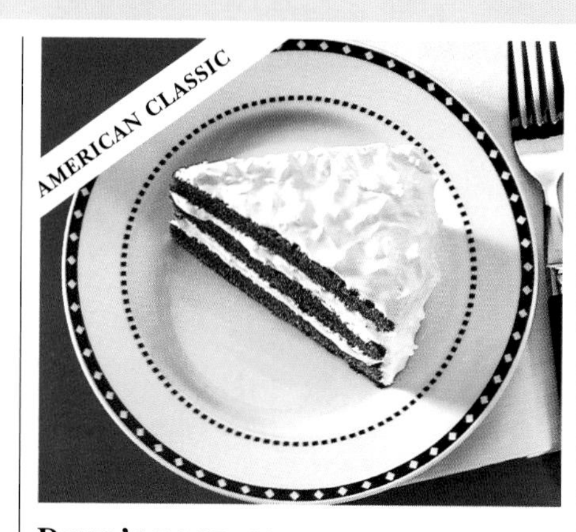

Devil's food cake

Layers of moist, rich chocolate sponge spread with a sweet, white American icing. Perfect for family gatherings.

SERVES 8–10 769–615 calories per serving

Takes 60 minutes, plus cooling **PAGE 466**

Carrot cake

American favourite: moist cake with chopped walnuts, mashed banana, and grated carrot. Cream cheese icing is spread on top.

SERVES 8–10 515–412 calories per serving

Takes 1¼ hours, plus cooling **PAGE 465**

Marbled coffee ring cake

Two batters, one coffeee flavoured and one plain, swirled together, baked, and topped with coffee icing and white chocolate.

SERVES 8–10 707–565 calories per serving

Takes 1¼ hours **PAGE 467**

Irish soda bread

A traditional bread made light and tasty with buttermilk. Scored and baked until golden brown.

MAKES 1 LOAF 1816 calories per loaf

Takes 45 minutes, plus cooling **PAGE 481**

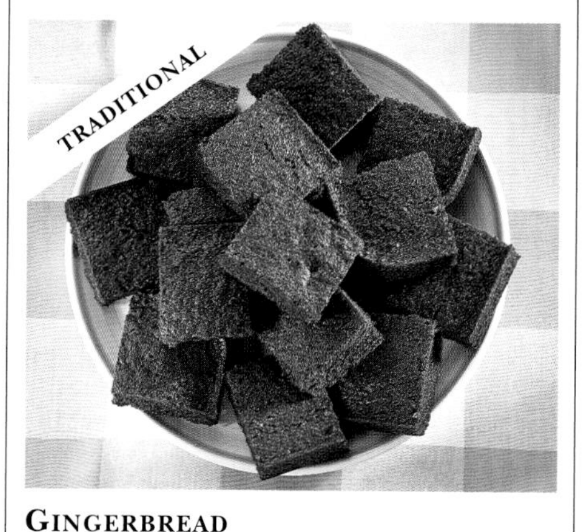

Gingerbread

Moist and tasty: a batter made dark and delicious with treacle and spices. Best when baked ahead.

MAKES 15 SQUARES 349 calories each

Takes 1¼ hours, plus cooling **PAGE 478**

Iced lime traybake

Light and delicious: a lime-flavoured cake batter baked in a rectangular tin, topped with tangy lime icing, and cut into squares.

MAKES 9 SQUARES 453 calories each

Takes 50 minutes, plus cooling **PAGE 472**

Chocolate & orange mousse cake

Two layers of delicate chocolate sponge filled with chocolate and orange flavoured mousse.

SERVES 8–10 626–500 calories per serving

Takes 1¼ hours, plus chilling **PAGE 468**

White chocolate gateau

Rich and attractive: delicious whipped cream hides a cocoa-flavoured sponge. Perfect for special occasions.

SERVES 8–10 684–547 calories per serving

Takes 1¼ hours, plus cooling **PAGE 467**

OVER 60 MINUTES

FRUITED BANANA LOAF

A hearty loaf made from a spiced fruit batter. Perfect use for ripe bananas. Serve sliced and spread with butter.

SERVES 8-10 501–401 calories per serving

Takes 1 1/2 hours, plus cooling **PAGE 475**

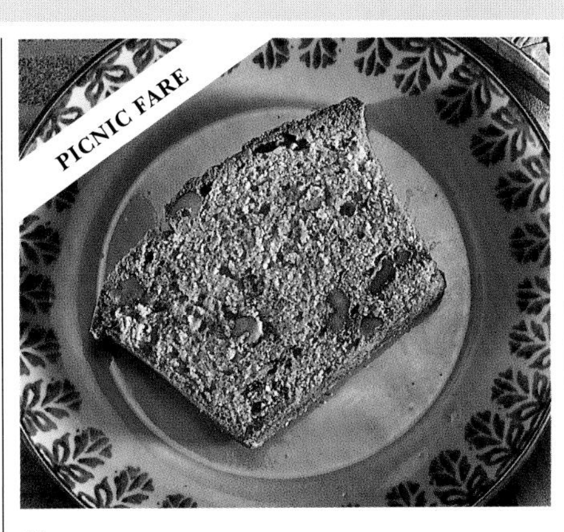

COURGETTE LOAF

American favourite: courgettes baked until sweet and tender in a deliciously spiced and walnut-studded batter.

SERVES 8–10 496–397 calories per serving

Takes 1 1/2 hours, plus cooling **PAGE 465**

DATE & WALNUT LOAF

Sweet dates and crunchy walnuts are baked in a lightly sweetened batter. Delicious sliced and spread with butter.

SERVES 8 404 calories per serving

Takes 1 3/4 hours, plus cooling **PAGE 479**

CHOCOLATE & VANILLA BATTENBURG

Classic cake made from chocolate and vanilla batters wrapped with almond paste.

SERVES 8 425 calories per serving

Takes 60 minutes, plus cooling **PAGE 473**

BARA BRITH

A deliciously tender loaf studded with tea-soaked dried fruit. Serve sliced and spread with butter.

SERVES 8 385 calories per serving

Takes 2 hours, plus soaking **PAGE 479**

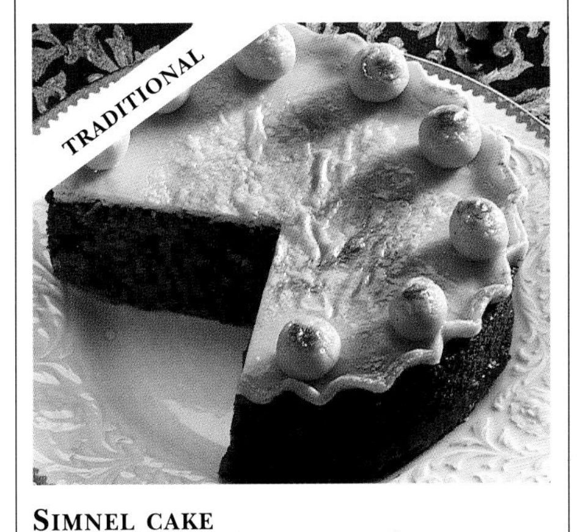

SIMNEL CAKE

Moist and tender fruit cake, brushed with apricot jam, topped with almond paste, and decorated with balls of almond paste.

SERVES 8–10 742–593 calories per serving

Takes 2 3/4 hours, plus cooling **PAGE 474**

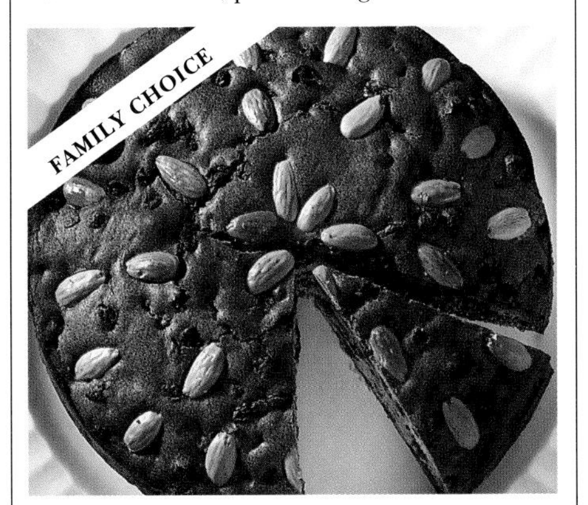

DUNDEE CAKE

Rich and fruity: sultanas, currants, raisins, cherries, and lemon, baked in a batter until golden, and decorated with almonds.

SERVES 8–10 576–461 calories per serving

Takes 1 3/4 hours, plus cooling **PAGE 475**

HEAVENLY CHOCOLATE CAKE

A rich chocolate and almond sponge cut in half, filled and covered with fudge icing, and decorated with white chocolate curls.

SERVES 6 820 calories per serving

Takes 1 1/2 hours, plus cooling **PAGE 466**

FRUIT CAKE

Classic: raisins, sultanas, glacé cherries, spices, and brandy flavour this moist cake. Best when baked ahead.

SERVES 8–10 712–570 calories per serving

Takes 2–2 1/4 hours, plus cooling **PAGE 473**

CAKES & TEABREADS KNOW-HOW

CAKE-MAKING is often seen as the test of a cook's skills, but there are lots of cakes and teabreads, as well as scones, biscuits, cookies, and American-style muffins that are really quite simple to make and just as delicious as more elaborate creations. If you are a beginner, just remember to follow recipes carefully, and make sure your weighing and measuring is accurate. Use the right equipment and tins, and take the time to prepare cakes properly, and you'll achieve perfect results every time. You'll find that once you've gained confidence, you'll be able to experiment with more difficult recipes.

STORING

Most cakes are best eaten freshly made, particularly sponge cakes made without fat, but if you do want to keep a cake, be sure to store it in an airtight container. Put the cake on the upturned lid of the cake tin, then put the tin over the top. This makes it easy to remove the cake from the tin. Fruit cakes and cakes made by the melting method, such as gingerbread, will improve with keeping if kept in an airtight tin. Wrap fruit cake in greaseproof paper and then overwrap in foil. Don't put foil directly in contact with a fruit cake as the acid in the fruit may react with the foil. Any cake that has a filling or icing of whipped cream, butter-icing, or soft-cheese should be kept in the refrigerator. Scones, American-style muffins, and most teabreads are best eaten freshly made.

Most biscuits can be stored in an airtight tin for a few days; if they soften, crisp them up in a warm oven. Allow cakes and biscuits to cool completely on a wire rack before putting them into a tin. Do not store cakes and biscuits together as the moisture from the cake will soften the biscuits.

MICROWAVING

Microwave-baked cakes and biscuits can be disappointingly pale in colour and gluey in texture. In baking, the microwave oven comes into its own when used as an accessory to the conventional oven.

- Break chocolate into small pieces, put into a bowl, and cook on LOW for 3–5 minutes until melted and shiny.
- Melt crystallized honey or syrup on HIGH for 1–2 minutes.
- Soften hardened, set sugar by cooking on HIGH for 30–40 seconds.
- Place hazelnuts on paper towels and cook on HIGH for 30 seconds; remove skins, and cook until golden.

FREEZING

This is a good way of keeping cakes fresh if they are not eaten immediately. Cakes, teabreads, biscuits, American-style muffins, and scones freeze well. Wrap cakes and teabreads in foil or freezer wrap. If a cake has been iced or decorated, tray freeze, then place in a rigid container or freezer bag. Fruit cakes can be stored for up to 12 months; un-iced cakes for 4–6 months; iced cakes for 2–3 months. Unwrap decorated cakes before thawing, but leave other cakes in their wrapping. Interleave biscuits with foil or freezer wrap. Biscuits, muffins, and scones can be stored for 6 months. Thaw at room temperature; scones can be successfully reheated or toasted from frozen.

BAKING INGREDIENTS

In baking it is important to use ingredients as they are specified. Choose the best quality available.

Butter and other fats
In simple cakes, biscuits, and teabreads, where flavour is important, always use butter. In other cakes, margarine is acceptable. Soft margarine should be used in all-in-one mixtures as it is made up of 80% fat and blends easily. Low-fat spreads are not suitable for baking because of their high water content, so check before you buy. If oil is called for, use a mild one such as sunflower oil.

Flour
Both plain and self-raising flours are used in baking. Self-raising flour includes a raising agent, so if you want to substitute plain flour, add 2 tsp baking powder to each 250 g (8 oz) flour.

Raising agents
Baking powder and bicarbonate of soda are used in cakes, teabreads, and biscuits. When using baking powder, or self-raising flour, bake the mixture within 1 hour, while the chemicals are still active.

Sugar
For most mixtures, it is essential to use a sugar that dissolves easily, such as caster sugar or muscovado. Granulated sugar can be used in rubbed-in mixtures. Coarse demerara sugar can be used in melted mixtures and is ideal for sprinkling on the top of cakes.

Eggs
Eggs at room temperature are more easily aerated than cold eggs taken from the refrigerator. Cold eggs can also cause some cake mixtures to curdle.

BAKING BISCUITS

When arranging biscuits on prepared baking trays, leave enough space between them to allow for spreading, if necessary. As biscuits cook quickly, they can easily be baked in batches if you don't have enough baking trays.

At the end of the baking time, many biscuits will still feel a little soft in the middle: they will continue to bake on the tray after being removed from the oven. If the recipe directs, leave them to firm up for 1–2 minutes before transferring to a wire rack. Avoid letting biscuits cool completely on the tray or they may stick.

ALL-IN-ONE CAKES

Be sure to use a soft margarine for this quick, simple technique.

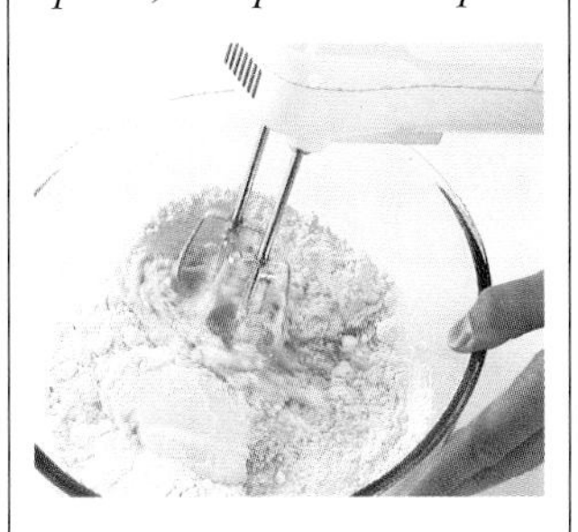

Put all the ingredients into a large bowl and beat together with a hand-held electric mixer until combined. You can also do this in a food processor or by hand.

WHISKED CAKES

This method is used for light, fatless sponges. Use a hand-held or table-top electric mixer. If using a hand-held mixer, set it at high speed.

1 Whisk the eggs, or egg yolks, with the sugar until the mixture is light, pale, and thick enough to leave a trail on the surface. This will take about 5 minutes.

2 Gently fold in the flour and any other ingredients. If the eggs have been separated, the whisked egg whites should be folded into the mixture last of all.

CREAMED CAKES

Creaming is used for both cakes and biscuits. Use a wooden spoon, rubber spatula, or electric whisk, and soften the butter or margarine first.

1 Cream the fat and sugar together until the mixture is pale in colour and fluffy in texture, scraping the side of the bowl with a wooden spoon to incorporate all of the mixture.

2 Lightly beat the eggs. Gradually add the eggs to the creamed mixture, beating well between each addition. If the mixture curdles, which will result in a dense-textured cake, beat in a spoonful of the flour.

3 Sift over the flour and any other dry ingredients. Using a wooden spoon, gently fold the 2 mixtures together until well combined. Any liquid ingredients should also be added at this stage.

PREPARING CAKE TINS

Lightly greasing the tin ensures a cake will turn out easily. Some recipes also call for the tin to be floured or lined with greaseproof paper or baking parchment.

Greasing and flouring
Use melted or softened butter or margarine, or oil, according to the recipe. Brush over the bottom and side of the tin using a pastry brush or paper towels. Add a spoonful of flour and tilt the tin to coat it with a thin layer. Tip out any excess flour.

Lining
1 Set the cake tin on a sheet of greaseproof paper or parchment and mark around the base with a pencil or the tip of a knife.

2 Cut out the shape, cutting just inside the line, and press smoothly over the bottom of the tin. Lightly grease if directed in recipe.

BAKING, TESTING, & COOLING CAKES

Before baking cakes, teabreads, and biscuits, be sure to preheat the oven to the correct temperature. If you need to, adjust the position of the shelves before you turn on the oven.

1 As soon as the mixture is prepared, turn it into the tin and level the surface. Tap the tin on the work surface to break any large air bubbles. Transfer immediately to the oven.

2 When cooked, a cake will shrink slightly from the side of the tin. To test, lightly press the middle with a fingertip; the cake should spring back. Rich cakes should feel firm to the touch.

Testing dense cakes
For fruit cakes and fruited teabreads, insert a metal skewer or wooden cocktail stick into the middle: it should come out clean, without any crumbs sticking to it.

3 Set the tin on a wire rack and leave to cool for about 10 minutes. Run a knife around the side of the cake to free it from the tin.

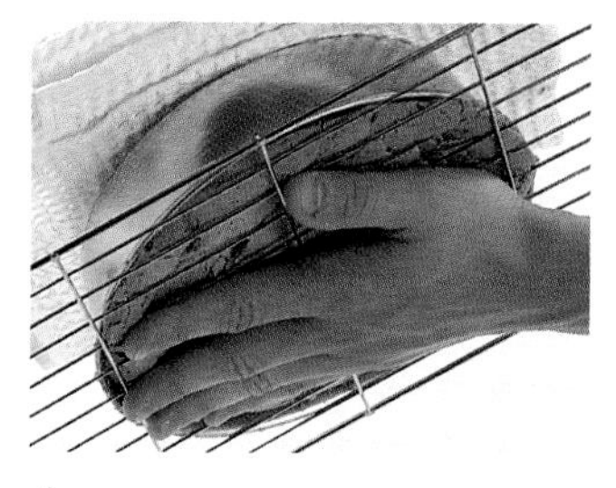

4 Hold a wire rack over the top of the tin, then invert the rack and tin so that the cake falls on to the rack. Carefully lift the tin away from the cake.

5 Peel off the lining paper. With a light-textured cake, turn it over again so the base is on the rack; this will prevent the rack marking the top.

Baking know-how

To check the dimensions of a cake tin, measure inside the top rim. To work out the depth, measure from the bottom to the top rim on the inside of the tin. To check the capacity of a tin, measure how much water is needed to fill it to the brim.

◆

Bake for the minimum time given in the recipe before opening the oven door. If the door is opened too soon it may cause some cakes to deflate.

◆

If a cake looks as though it is browning too quickly, cover the top loosely with foil.

◆

If baking several cake layers, stagger them on the oven shelves so one is not directly beneath another.

◆

When measuring ingredients with a spoon, don't hold the spoon directly over the bowl or you may accidentally add too much.

CUTTING A CAKE

A cake can be cut into layers and sandwiched with cream or another filling. Use a long serrated knife.

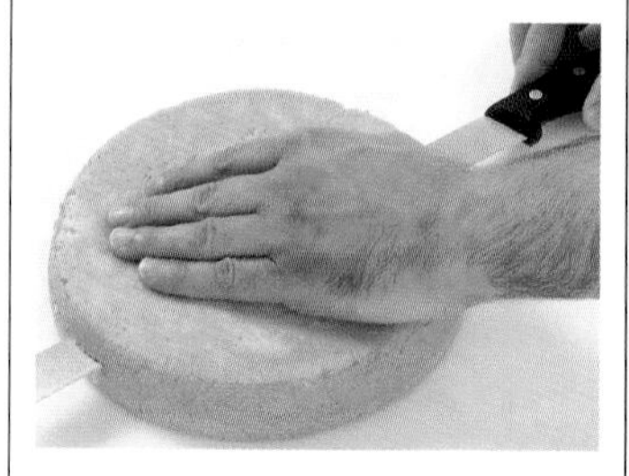

Steady the cake by holding the top with one hand. Cut the cake horizontally, using a gentle sawing action.

FILLING & ICING CAKES

There are many simple ways to fill or decorate cakes. Whipped cream, jam, or chocolate spread make quick and easy fillings. Butter-icing can be made in a variety of flavours, to complement the flavour of the cake.

Chocolate butter-icing
In a bowl, soften *150 g (5 oz) butter*, then add *30 g (1 oz) cocoa powder* and *250 g (8 oz) sifted icing sugar*, and beat together until smooth. Add *a little milk* if necessary to give a spreading consistency. For a citrus icing, omit the cocoa powder and add *finely grated orange or lemon zest.*

Spreading icing
Only ice a cake when it has cooled completely. Use a large palette knife and spread the icing with long, smooth strokes over the top and side of the cake. Dip the palette knife in warm water if the icing sticks to it.

Courgette loaf

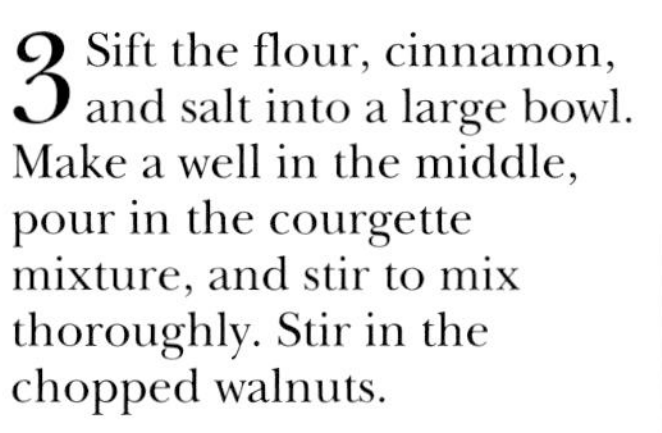

Serves 8–10

- *250 g (8 oz) courgettes*
- *2 eggs*
- *125 ml (4 fl oz) sunflower oil, plus extra for greasing*
- *250 g (8 oz) caster sugar*
- *1/4 tsp vanilla essence*
- *375 g (12 oz) self-raising flour*
- *1 tsp ground cinnamon*
- *1/2 tsp salt*
- *60 g (2 oz) walnut pieces, coarsely chopped*
- *☆ 1 kg (2 lb) loaf tin*

1 Coarsely grate the courgettes, put them into a sieve, and leave for about 30 minutes to drain.

2 Beat the eggs until light and foamy. Add the sunflower oil, sugar, vanilla essence, and courgettes and mix lightly until combined.

3 Sift the flour, cinnamon, and salt into a large bowl. Make a well in the middle, pour in the courgette mixture, and stir to mix thoroughly. Stir in the chopped walnuts.

4 Pour the mixture into the greased loaf tin and bake in a preheated oven at 180°C (350°F, Gas 4) for about 50 minutes until firm. Turn out and cool.

Cook's know-how

For best results, the courgettes should be thoroughly drained. Press into the sieve with your hand or the back of a spoon to extract the excess juices.

Carrot cake

Serves 8–10

- *150 ml (1/4 pint) sunflower oil, plus extra for greasing*
- *250 g (8 oz) wholemeal self-raising flour*
- *2 tsp baking powder*
- *150 g (5 oz) light muscovado sugar*
- *60 g (2 oz) walnuts, coarsely chopped*
- *125 g (4 oz) carrots, grated*
- *2 ripe bananas, mashed*
- *2 eggs*
- *1 tbsp milk*

TOPPING

- *250 g (8 oz) low-fat soft cheese, at room temperature*
- *2 tsp clear honey*
- *1 tsp lemon juice*
- *chopped walnuts to decorate*
- *☆ 18 cm (7 in) square cake tin*

1 Lightly grease the tin and line the bottom with baking parchment.

2 Combine all the cake ingredients in a large bowl. Mix well until thoroughly blended. Turn into the prepared cake tin and level the surface.

3 Bake in a preheated oven at 180°C (350°F, Gas 4) for about 50 minutes until the cake is well risen, firm to the touch, and beginning to shrink away from the sides of the tin.

4 Leave the cake to cool in the tin for a few minutes. Turn out on to a wire rack, peel off the lining paper, and leave to cool completely.

5 Make the topping: mix together the cheese, honey, and lemon juice. Spread on top of the cake and sprinkle the walnuts over the top. Store the cake in the refrigerator until ready to serve.

Cook's know-how

Spices enhance the flavour of all kinds of vegetable cakes; ground mace, cinnamon, coriander, and cloves, and freshly grated nutmeg are particularly complementary. Add 1 tsp ground cinnamon to this cake, if preferred.

HEAVENLY CHOCOLATE CAKE

Serves 6

- *125 g (4 oz) butter, plus extra for greasing*
- *200 g (7 oz) plain chocolate, broken into pieces*
- *2 tbsp water*
- *3 eggs, separated*
- *125 g (4 oz) caster sugar*
- *90 g (3 oz) self-raising flour*
- *60 g (2 oz) ground almonds*

FUDGE ICING

- *60 g (2 oz) butter*
- *30 g (1 oz) cocoa powder*
- *3 tbsp milk*
- *250 g (8 oz) icing sugar, sifted*
- *white chocolate curls (page 431) to decorate*
- *⋆ deep 20 cm (8 in) cake tin*

1 Lightly butter the tin and line the bottom.

2 Put the chocolate into a heatproof bowl with the butter and water. Put the bowl over a pan of hot water and heat gently, stirring, until the mixture has melted. Leave to cool.

3 Combine the egg yolks and caster sugar in a large bowl and whisk together with an electric whisk until fluffy and very light in colour. Stir in the cooled chocolate mixture. Carefully fold in the flour and ground almonds.

4 In a separate bowl, whisk the egg whites until stiff but not dry. Fold into the sponge mixture, gently but thoroughly. Pour the mixture into the prepared tin. Bake in a preheated oven at 180°C (350°F, Gas 4) for 50 minutes or until well risen and firm to the touch.

5 Leave the cake to cool in the tin for a few minutes, turn out on to a wire rack, and peel off the lining paper. Cool completely.

6 Make the fudge icing: melt the butter in a pan, add the cocoa powder, and cook, stirring, for 1 minute. Stir in the milk and icing sugar. Beat well until smooth. Leave to cool until thickened.

7 Split the cake in half horizontally and sandwich the layers together with half of the fudge icing. With a palette knife, spread the remaining icing over the top and side of the cake. Decorate with white chocolate curls.

DEVIL'S FOOD CAKE

Serves 8–10

- *175 g (6 oz) soft margarine, plus extra for greasing*
- *90 g (3 oz) plain chocolate, broken into pieces*
- *175 ml (6 fl oz) hot water*
- *300 g (10 oz) light muscovado sugar*
- *3 eggs, beaten*
- *300 g (10 oz) plain flour*
- *1 1/2 tsp bicarbonate of soda*
- *1 1/2 tsp baking powder*
- *1 tsp vanilla essence*
- *150 ml (1/4 pint) soured cream*

AMERICAN FROSTING

- *400 g (13 oz) caster sugar*
- *2 egg whites*
- *4 tbsp hot water*
- *pinch of cream of tartar*
- *⋆ 3 x 20 cm (8 in) sandwich cake tins*

1 Grease the tins and line the bottoms with baking parchment.

2 Put the chocolate into a pan with the water. Heat gently, stirring, until the chocolate melts. Cool.

3 Combine the margarine and sugar in a bowl and beat until light and fluffy. Gradually add the eggs, beating well.

4 Stir in the melted chocolate. Sift together the flour, bicarbonate of soda, and baking powder. Fold into the chocolate mixture until evenly blended, then fold in the vanilla essence and soured cream.

5 Divide the mixture evenly among the prepared tins. Bake in a preheated oven at 190°C (375°F, Gas 5) for about 25 minutes until well risen, springy to the touch, and just shrinking away from the sides of the tins.

6 Turn out the cakes on to a wire rack, peel off the lining paper, and leave to cool.

7 Make the American frosting: combine all the ingredients in a heatproof bowl. Set the bowl over a pan of hot water and whisk with an electric mixer for about 12 minutes until the mixture is white, thick, and stands in peaks.

8 Use half of the American frosting to sandwich the 3 layers together, then spread the remainder over the top and side of the cake, swirling it decoratively and pulling it into peaks with a small palette knife.

MARBLED COFFEE RING CAKE

Serves 8–10

250 g (8 oz) soft margarine, plus extra for greasing

250 g (8 oz) caster sugar

4 eggs

250 g (8 oz) self-raising flour

2 tsp baking powder

2 tsp instant coffee granules

1 tbsp hot water

30 g (1 oz) white chocolate

ICING

60 g (2 oz) butter, softened

3 tbsp milk

2 tbsp instant coffee granules

250 g (8 oz) icing sugar, sifted

⋆ *1.75 litre (2¾ pint) ring mould*

1 Lightly grease the ring mould with margarine.

2 Combine the margarine, sugar, eggs, flour, and baking powder in a large bowl. Beat until smooth.

3 Put half of the mixture into another bowl. Dissolve the instant coffee granules in the measured hot water and stir into one half of the cake mixture.

4 Drop tablespoonfuls of the plain mixture into the ring mould, then tablespoonfuls of the coffee mixture on top of the plain mixture. Marble by swirling together with a skewer.

5 Bake in a preheated oven at 180°C (350°F, Gas 4) for 40 minutes or until well risen and firm to the touch. Leave to cool for a few minutes, then turn out on to a wire rack set over a tray, and cool completely.

6 Make the icing: combine the butter, milk, and coffee in a pan and heat, stirring, until smooth. Remove from the heat and beat in the icing sugar until smooth and glossy.

7 Leave to cool, then pour over the cake, spreading it over the sides to cover completely. Leave to set.

8 Melt the white chocolate in a heatproof bowl over a pan of hot water. Leave to cool slightly, then spoon into a plastic bag. Snip off a corner of the bag and drizzle the chocolate over the cake. Leave to set.

WHITE CHOCOLATE GATEAU

Serves 8–10

90 g (3 oz) butter, melted and cooled slightly, plus extra for greasing

6 eggs, size 2

175 g (6 oz) caster sugar

125 g (4 oz) self-raising flour

30 g (1 oz) cocoa powder

2 tbsp cornflour

FILLING AND TOPPING

300 ml (½ pint) double cream, whipped until thick

white chocolate curls (optional) (page 431)

⋆ *deep 23 cm (9 in) round cake tin*

1 Lightly butter the cake tin and line the bottom of the tin with a sheet of baking parchment.

2 Put the eggs and sugar into a large bowl and whisk together with an electric mixer at high speed until the mixture is pale and thick enough to leave a trail on itself when the whisk is lifted out.

3 Sift together the flour, cocoa powder, and cornflour, and fold half into the egg mixture. Pour half of the cooled butter around the edge of the mixture and fold in gently.

4 Repeat with the remaining flour mixture and butter, folding gently.

5 Turn the mixture into the prepared cake tin and tilt the tin to level the surface. Bake in a preheated oven at 180°C (350°F, Gas 4) for 35–40 minutes until the sponge is well risen and firm to the touch. Turn out on to a wire rack, peel off the lining paper, and cool.

6 Cut the cake in half horizontally and sandwich the layers together with half of the whipped cream. Cover the cake with a thin layer of cream, then pipe the remainder around the top and bottom edges.

7 Press the chocolate curls over the top and side of the cake, if preferred.

CHOCOLATE & ORANGE MOUSSE CAKE

This cake is made of chocolate sponge layers sandwiched together with a deliciously fluffy chocolate and orange mousse. When making the mousse, don't overwhisk the egg whites; when they just flop over at the tip they are ready to fold into the chocolate mixture.

Serves 8–10

butter for greasing
4 eggs
125 g (4 oz) caster sugar
90 g (3 oz) self-raising flour
30 g (1 oz) cocoa powder

MOUSSE

175 g (6 oz) plain chocolate, broken into pieces
grated zest and juice of 1 orange
1 tsp powdered gelatine
2 eggs, separated
300 ml (1/2 pint) double cream, whipped until thick

DECORATION

300 ml (1/2 pint) double cream, whipped until thick
strips of orange zest, blanched
⋆ deep 23 cm (9 in) springform cake tin

1 Lightly butter the tin and line the bottom with baking parchment. Make the sponge (see box, right).

2 Bake the sponge in a preheated oven at 180°C (350°F, Gas 4) for 40–45 minutes until the sponge is well risen and beginning to shrink away from the side of the tin. Turn out on to a wire rack, peel off the lining paper, and leave to cool.

3 Cut the cake in half horizontally. Put one half back into the clean tin.

4 Make the mousse: put the chocolate into a heatproof bowl set over a pan of hot water. Heat gently, stirring occasionally, until the chocolate has melted. Leave to cool slightly.

5 Strain the orange juice into a small heatproof bowl and sprinkle over the gelatine. Leave for 3 minutes or until spongy, then stand the bowl in a saucepan of gently simmering water for 3 minutes or until the gelatine has dissolved.

6 Stir the egg yolks and orange zest into the cooled chocolate. Slowly stir in the dissolved gelatine, then fold in the whipped cream. In a separate bowl, whisk the egg whites until stiff but not dry, then gently fold into the chocolate mixture until well blended.

7 Pour the mousse on top of the cake layer in the tin. Put the remaining cake layer on top. Cover and chill in the refrigerator until the mousse filling is set.

8 Remove the side of the tin and slide the cake on to a serving plate. Decorate with cream and orange zest.

Making the sponge

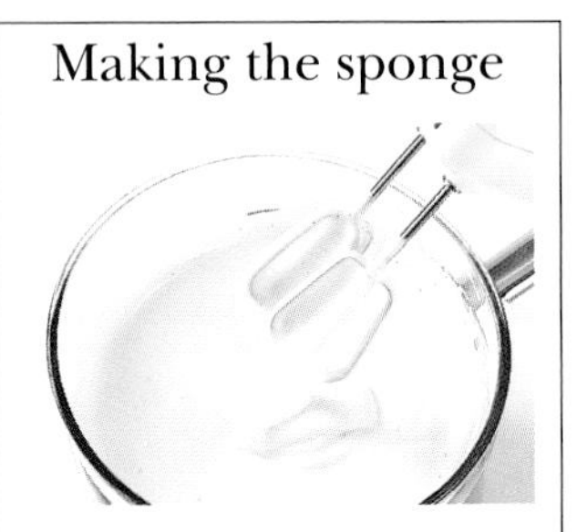

Combine the eggs and sugar in a large bowl and whisk with an electric mixer at high speed until the mixture is pale and thick enough to leave a trail on itself when the whisk is lifted out.

Sift the flour and cocoa powder over the surface.

Fold in the flour and cocoa until blended.

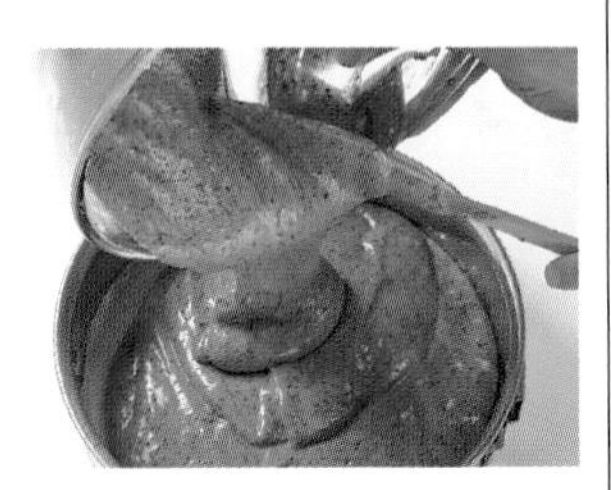

Turn the mixture into the prepared tin and tilt to level the surface.

SUMMER STRAWBERRY SPONGE

Serves 8

butter for greasing

3 eggs

90 g (3 oz) caster sugar

90 g (3 oz) self-raising flour

FILLING AND TOPPING

300 ml (1/2 pint) whipping cream, whipped until thick

125 g (4 oz) strawberries, sliced

1 passion fruit, halved

strawberries, halved, to decorate

⋆ 2 x 18 cm (7 in) sandwich cake tins

1 Lightly butter the cake tins, line the bottoms with baking parchment, then butter the parchment.

2 Put the eggs and sugar into a large bowl. Whisk with an electric mixer at high speed until the mixture is pale and thick enough to leave a trail when the whisk is lifted out.

3 Sift in half of the flour and fold in gently. Repeat with the remaining flour.

4 Divide the mixture between the tins. Tilt to spread the mixture evenly.

5 Bake in a preheated oven at 190°C (375°F, Gas 5) for 20–25 minutes until well risen, golden, and beginning to shrink away from the sides of the tins. Turn out on to a wire rack, peel off the lining paper, and leave to cool.

6 Spread half of the whipped cream over 1 of the sponges. Top with the sliced strawberries and passion fruit pulp. Put the other sponge on top and press down gently.

7 Spread the remaining cream on top of the cake, smoothing it neatly with a palette knife. Decorate with strawberry halves.

Cook's know-how

Sponges made without fat do not keep well, so be sure to eat the cake on the day of baking.

SWISS ROLL

Serves 6–8

butter for greasing

4 eggs, size 2

125 g (4 oz) caster sugar, plus extra for sprinkling

125 g (4 oz) self-raising flour

icing sugar for sprinkling

FILLING

about 4 tbsp raspberry jam

⋆ 23 x 33 cm (9 x 13 in) Swiss roll tin

1 Lightly butter the Swiss roll tin, line with baking parchment, then lightly butter the parchment.

2 Put the eggs and sugar into a large bowl. Whisk together with an electric mixer at high speed until the mixture is pale and thick enough to leave a trail when the whisk is lifted out.

3 Sift the flour into the egg mixture and fold in gently but thoroughly. Turn the mixture into the prepared tin and tilt to spread the mixture evenly, particularly into the corners.

4 Bake in a preheated oven at 220°C (425°F, Gas 7) for about 10 minutes until the sponge is golden and beginning to shrink away from the sides of the tin.

5 Invert the sponge on to a large piece of baking parchment which has been liberally sprinkled with caster sugar. Peel off the lining paper and trim the edges of the sponge with a sharp knife.

6 Roll up the sponge and the baking parchment together. Leave to stand for 2–3 minutes.

7 Unroll the sponge, and remove the baking parchment. Spread the sponge with warmed jam and roll up again. Wrap tightly in baking parchment and leave to cool. Unwrap, dust with icing sugar, and serve in slices.

Cook's know-how

Don't spread the cake mixture in the tin with a palette knife as this will knock the air out of the mixture.

American muffins

Not to be confused with their British counterparts, American muffins are small, moist cakes made with self-raising flour and flavoured with endless combinations of ingredients. Here are 3 of the tastiest, together with some complementary butters for spreading while the muffins are still warm.

Cranberry & pecan

Makes 12

1 egg, lightly beaten
60 g (2 oz) butter, melted, plus extra for greasing
250 ml (8 fl oz) orange juice
375 g (12 oz) self-raising flour, sifted
175 g (6 oz) caster sugar
3 tbsp porridge oats
pinch of salt
200 g (7 oz) pecan halves, coarsely chopped
125 g (4 oz) cranberries
** 12-hole muffin tin*

1 Mix together the egg, butter, and orange juice. Combine the flour, sugar, porridge oats, and salt and stir into the orange juice mixture with the pecans and cranberries. Make sure the ingredients are well combined and that the mixture has a thick consistency.

2 Butter each cup of the muffin tin, then spoon in the muffin mixture, filling the cups almost to the tops.

3 Bake in a preheated oven at 200°C (400°F, Gas 6) for 10 minutes; reduce the oven temperature to 180°C (350°F, Gas 4), and bake for about 15 minutes until the muffins are golden and firm. Serve warm.

Apricot & bran flake

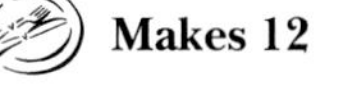

Makes 12

90 g (3 oz) ready-to-eat dried apricots, diced
1 egg, lightly beaten
30 g (1 oz) butter, melted, plus extra for greasing
2 tbsp clear honey
125 ml (4 fl oz) milk
1 tsp vanilla essence
125 g (4 oz) plain yogurt
200 g (7 oz) self-raising flour, sifted
175 g (6 oz) caster sugar
125 g (4 oz) sultana bran cereal
pinch of salt
** 12-hole muffin tin*

1 Mix the apricots with the egg, butter, honey, milk, vanilla essence, and yogurt. Combine the flour, sugar, sultana bran, and salt, add to the milk mixture, and stir until well combined.

2 Butter each cup of the muffin tin, then spoon in the muffin mixture, filling the cups almost to the tops.

3 Bake in a preheated oven at 200°C (400°F, Gas 6) for 10 minutes; reduce the oven temperature to 180°C (350°F, Gas 4), and bake for 15 minutes or until golden and firm. Serve warm.

Double-chocolate

Makes 12

2 eggs, lightly beaten
125 g (4 oz) plain yogurt
125 ml (4 fl oz) strong brewed coffee
125 ml (4 fl oz) milk
250 g (8 oz) self-raising flour, sifted
250 g (8 oz) caster sugar
75 g (2½ oz) cocoa powder
pinch of salt
100 g (3½ oz) plain chocolate chips
melted butter for greasing
** 12-hole muffin tin*

1 Combine the eggs, yogurt, coffee, and milk in a large bowl.

2 Sift together the flour, sugar, cocoa powder, and salt, and stir into the milk mixture. Mix well. Stir in the chocolate chips.

3 Butter each cup of the muffin tin, then spoon in the muffin mixture, filling the cups almost to the tops.

4 Bake the muffins in a preheated oven at 200°C (400°F, Gas 6) for about 10 minutes; reduce the oven temperature to 180°C (350°F, Gas 4), and continue to bake for about 15 minutes until the muffins are golden and firm. Serve warm.

Clockwise from top: *Apricot & Bran Flake Muffins, Double-chocolate Muffins, Double-chocolate Muffin served with Honey & Spice Butter, Apricot & Bran Flake Muffin served with Chocolate & Nut Butter, Cranberry & Pecan Muffins.*

Butters for muffins

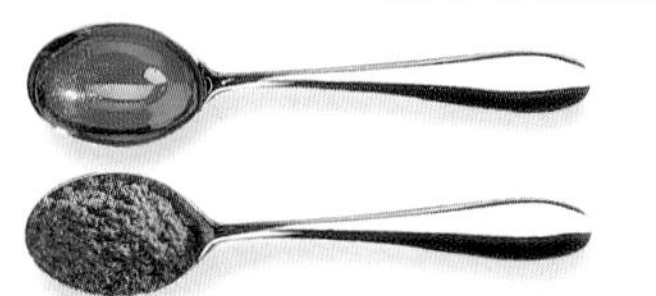

Honey & spice

Put *125 g (4 oz) butter* into a bowl and beat with a wooden spoon until softened. Add *2 tbsp clear honey, ½ tsp ground cinnamon,* and *¼ tsp grated nutmeg.* Stir until well combined. Roll the butter in cling film to make a log shape, and chill until firm. Remove the cling film and cut into slices.

Chocolate & nut

Combine *20 g (¾ oz) chopped plain chocolate, 1 tsp caster sugar,* and *1 tbsp brandy,* and heat over a pan of simmering water until melted. Cool. Soften *125 g (4 oz) butter,* and stir in the chocolate mixture and *30 g (1 oz) ground hazelnuts.* Shape into a block and wrap in cling film. Chill and slice.

VICTORIA SANDWICH CAKE

Serves 6–8

- *175 g (6 oz) soft margarine, plus extra for greasing*
- *175 g (6 oz) caster sugar*
- *3 eggs*
- *175 g (6 oz) self-raising flour*
- *1 1/2 tsp baking powder*

FILLING

- *4 tbsp raspberry or strawberry jam*
- *caster sugar for sprinkling*
- ☆ *2 x 18 cm (7 in) sandwich tins*

1 Lightly grease the tins and line the bottoms with baking parchment.

2 Combine all the cake ingredients in a large bowl. Beat well for about 2 minutes until smooth.

3 Divide the mixture between the prepared tins and level the surfaces. Bake in a preheated oven at 180°C (350°F, Gas 4) for about 25 minutes until the cakes are well risen, golden, and springy to the touch.

4 Turn out on to a wire rack, peel off the lining paper, and leave to cool.

5 Sandwich the 2 cakes together with jam and sprinkle the top of the cake with caster sugar.

CHOCOLATE SANDWICH CAKE

Mix 2 tbsp cocoa powder with 3 tbsp boiling water and leave to cool. Add to the cake ingredients before beating. Sandwich together and cover with chocolate butter icing (page 464). Decorate the top of the cake with chocolate curls (page 431).

LEMON SANDWICH CAKE

Add the grated zest of 1 lemon to the cake ingredients before beating. Sandwich the cakes together with lemon curd and 150 ml (1/4 pint) whipping cream, whipped until thick.

ICED LIME TRAYBAKE

Makes 9 squares

- *175 g (6 oz) soft margarine, plus extra for greasing*
- *175 g (6 oz) caster sugar*
- *250 g (8 oz) self-raising flour*
- *1 1/2 tsp baking powder*
- *3 eggs*
- *3 tbsp milk*
- *grated zest of 2 limes*

ICING

- *250 g (8 oz) icing sugar*
- *juice of 2 limes*
- ☆ *23 x 30 cm (9 x 12 in) cake tin*

1 Lightly grease the tin and line the bottom with baking parchment.

2 Combine all the cake ingredients in a large bowl and beat well for about 2 minutes until smooth and thoroughly blended.

3 Turn into the prepared tin and level the surface. Bake in a preheated oven at 180°C (350°F, Gas 4) for 35–40 minutes until the cake is well risen, springy to the touch, and beginning to shrink away from the sides of the cake tin.

4 Leave to cool slightly in the tin, then turn out on to a wire rack, peel off the lining paper, and cool.

5 Make the icing: sift the icing sugar into a bowl. Mix in enough of the lime juice to give a runny consistency. Pour over the cooled cake, spreading carefully with a palette knife, and leave to set. When cold, cut into squares and serve.

CHOCOLATE & MINT TRAYBAKE

Mix 4 tbsp cocoa powder with 4 tbsp hot water and leave to cool. Add to the basic cake ingredients with 4 tbsp chopped fresh mint. For the icing, break 250 g (8 oz) plain chocolate into pieces and put into a heatproof bowl with 90 g (3 oz) margarine and 4 tbsp hot water. Put the bowl over a saucepan of hot water and heat gently until the chocolate has melted. Beat together until smooth and shiny, then spread over the top of the cooled cake.

Chocolate & Vanilla Battenburg Cake

Serves 8

125 g (4 oz) soft margarine, plus extra for greasing
125 g (4 oz) caster sugar
2 eggs, size 2
60 g (2 oz) ground rice
125 g (4 oz) self-raising flour
½ tsp baking powder
a few drops of vanilla essence
1½ tsp cocoa powder
3 tbsp apricot jam
250 g (8 oz) almond paste
⭑ shallow 18 cm (7 in) square cake tin

1 Lightly grease the cake tin with margarine and line the bottom with greaseproof paper.

2 Combine the margarine, sugar, eggs, ground rice, flour, baking powder, and vanilla essence in a large bowl. Beat well for 2 minutes or until the mixture is smooth and evenly combined.

3 Spoon half of the mixture into one half of the prepared tin. Dissolve the cocoa in a little hot water to make a thick paste and add to the remaining cake mixture in the bowl. Mix well, then spoon into the remaining half of the tin.

4 Bake the mixture in a preheated oven at 160°C (325°F, Gas 3) for 35 minutes or until the cake is well risen and springy to the touch. Turn out on to a wire rack, peel off the lining paper, and leave to cool.

5 Trim the edges of the cake. Cut it into 4 equal strips down the length of the 2 colours.

6 Warm the apricot jam in a small saucepan. Stack the cake strips, alternating the colours to give a chequerboard effect and sticking them together with the apricot jam.

7 Roll out the almond paste into an oblong that is the same length as the cake and wide enough to wrap around it. Put the cake on top, then brush with jam. Wrap the paste around the cake (see box, below).

8 Score the top with a criss-cross pattern and crimp the edges with your fingers to decorate.

Wrapping the cake

Wrap the almond paste around the cake, pressing it on gently and making the join in 1 corner. Turn to hide the join.

Fruit Cake

Serves 8–10

250 g (8 oz) soft margarine, plus extra for greasing
250 g (8 oz) light muscovado sugar
4 eggs
250 g (8 oz) self-raising flour
250 g (8 oz) raisins
250 g (8 oz) sultanas
125 g (4 oz) glacé cherries, halved and rinsed
½ tsp ground mixed spice
1 tbsp brandy
⭑ deep 20 cm (8 in) round cake tin

1 Lightly grease the tin and line the bottom with greaseproof paper.

2 Combine all the ingredients in a large bowl and mix well until combined. Turn the mixture into the prepared cake tin and level the surface.

3 Bake in a preheated oven at 140°C (275°F, Gas 1) for 2–2¼ hours. Cover the top of the cake with greaseproof paper after about 1 hour to prevent the top becoming too brown.

4 When cooked, the cake should be firm to the touch and a fine skewer inserted in the middle of the cake should come out clean. Leave the cake to cool in the tin before turning out. Store in an airtight container.

MINCEMEAT BUNS

Makes 32

375 g (12 oz) mincemeat
250 g (8 oz) currants
2 eggs
150 g (5 oz) caster sugar
150 g (5 oz) soft margarine
250 g (8 oz) self-raising flour
⋆ 32 paper cake cases

1 Combine all the ingredients in a large bowl and beat well for about 2 minutes.

2 Divide the cake mixture evenly among the paper cases, putting them into bun tins if preferred.

3 Bake in a preheated oven at 160°C (325°F, Gas 3) for 25–30 minutes until golden and springy to the touch. Transfer the cases to a wire rack and leave to cool.

Cook's know-how

Mincemeat is traditionally made with beef suet. If you want a vegetarian version, use vegetable suet. Home-made mincemeat is best, but you can improve on commercial ones by adding a variety of different ingredients, such as chopped nuts, angelica, glacé cherries, or dried apricots, peaches, or pears.

SIMNEL CAKE

This is now a traditional Easter cake, but originally it was given by girls to their mothers on Mothering Sunday. The almond paste balls represent the 11 disciples of Christ, excluding Judas Iscariot.

Serves 8–10

175 g (6 oz) soft margarine, plus extra for greasing
175 g (6 oz) light muscovado sugar
3 eggs
175 g (6 oz) self-raising flour
175 g (6 oz) sultanas
90 g (3 oz) currants
90 g (3 oz) glacé cherries, quartered, rinsed, and dried
30 g (1 oz) candied peel, roughly chopped
grated zest of 1 large lemon
1 tsp ground mixed spice

FILLING AND DECORATION

500 g (1 lb) almond paste
2 tbsp apricot jam
1 egg white
⋆ deep 18 cm (7 in) round loose-bottomed cake tin

1 Roll out one-third of the almond paste. Using the base of the cake tin as a guide, cut out an 18 cm (7 in) round.

2 Grease the cake tin and line the bottom and side with greaseproof paper.

3 Combine all the cake ingredients in a bowl. Beat well until thoroughly blended. Spoon half of the cake mixture into the prepared tin and smooth the surface. Top with the round of almond paste.

4 Spoon the remaining cake mixture on top and level the surface.

5 Bake in a preheated oven at 150°C (300°F, Gas 2) for 2¼ hours or until golden brown and firm to the touch.

6 Cover the top of the cake with greaseproof paper if it is browning too quickly. Leave to cool for 10 minutes, then remove from the tin, and leave to cool completely.

7 Warm the jam and use to brush the top of the cake.

8 To decorate the cake, roll out half of the remaining almond paste and use the tin to cut out an 18 cm (7 in) round. Put on top of the jam and crimp the edges. Roll the remaining almond paste into 11 even-sized balls. Place around the edge of the cake, using the egg white to attach them.

9 Brush the tops of the balls and the almond paste with egg white. Place under a hot grill for 1–2 minutes, until the balls are golden.

DUNDEE CAKE

Serves 8–10

150 g (5 oz) butter, at room temperature, plus extra for greasing
150 g (5 oz) light muscovado sugar
3 eggs
250 g (8 oz) plain flour
1 tsp baking powder
175 g (6 oz) sultanas
90 g (3 oz) currants
90 g (3 oz) raisins
60 g (2 oz) glacé cherries, quartered, rinsed, and dried
60 g (2 oz) chopped mixed candied peel
2 tbsp ground almonds
grated zest of 1 large lemon
60 g (2 oz) whole almonds, blanched and halved, to decorate
⋆ deep 20 cm (8 in) round loose-bottomed cake tin

1 Lightly butter the cake tin and line the bottom with greaseproof paper.

2 Combine the butter, sugar, eggs, flour, and baking powder in a bowl and beat for 2 minutes or until well blended. Stir in the fruit, mixed peel, ground almonds, and lemon zest.

3 Spoon the mixture into the prepared tin. Level the surface and arrange the halved almonds neatly in concentric circles on top.

4 Bake in a preheated oven at 160°C (325°F, Gas 3) for 1½ hours or until well risen, golden, and firm to the touch. A fine skewer inserted into the middle of the cake should come out clean. Cover the cake with greaseproof paper halfway through baking if it is browning too quickly.

5 Leave the cake to cool in the tin for a few minutes, then turn out on to a wire rack and leave to cool completely. Store the cake in an airtight container for about 1 week before eating.

FRUITED BANANA LOAF

Serves 8–10

125 g (4 oz) margarine, plus extra for greasing
250 g (8 oz) self-raising flour
175 g (6 oz) caster sugar
125 g (4 oz) sultanas
60 g (2 oz) walnuts, roughly chopped
125 g (4 oz) glacé cherries, quartered, rinsed, and dried
2 eggs, size 2, beaten
500 g (1 lb) bananas, weight with peel, peeled and mashed
⋆ 1 kg (2 lb) loaf tin

1 Grease the loaf tin and line the bottom with greaseproof paper.

2 Put the flour into a bowl, add the margarine, and rub in with the fingertips until the mixture resembles fine breadcrumbs. Add the caster sugar, sultanas, chopped walnuts, and glacé cherries, and mix well.

3 Add the eggs and mashed bananas and beat the mixture until well blended. Spoon into the prepared tin.

4 Bake in a preheated oven at 160°C (325°F, Gas 3) for about 1¼ hours until well risen and firm to the touch. A fine skewer inserted into the middle of the loaf should come out clean.

5 Leave the loaf to cool slightly in the tin, then turn out on to a wire rack, and peel off the lining paper. Leave the loaf to cool completely before slicing and serving.

Cook's know-how

If you like, you can add some grated lemon zest or 1 tsp ground mixed spice to the mixture, for extra flavouring.

Christmas cakes

One of the focal points of Christmas is a specially decorated cake. As rich fruit cake is usually eaten over a period of days, the decoration should be as attractive and long-lasting as possible. Here are 3 different presentation ideas, each of which is easy to adapt according to available ingredients and personal taste.

Rich fruit cake

Makes 1 x 23 cm (9 in) cake

- *425 g (14 oz) currants*
- *250 g (8 oz) sultanas*
- *250 g (8 oz) raisins*
- *300 g (10 oz) glacé cherries, quartered, rinsed, and dried*
- *75 g (2 1/2 oz) mixed candied peel, roughly chopped*
- *4 tbsp brandy, plus extra for soaking*
- *300 g (10 oz) plain flour*
- *1 tsp ground mixed spice*
- *1/2 tsp grated nutmeg*
- *300 g (10 oz) soft margarine, plus extra for greasing*
- *300 g (10 oz) dark muscovado sugar*
- *5 eggs*
- *60 g (2 oz) whole unblanched almonds, roughly chopped*
- *1 tbsp black treacle*
- *grated zest of 1 large lemon*
- *grated zest of 1 large orange*
- *⋆ deep 23 cm (9 in) round or 20 cm (8 in) square cake tin*

1 Combine the fruit and candied peel in a large bowl. Add the brandy and stir to mix well. Cover and leave to macerate overnight.

2 Put the remaining ingredients into a large bowl and beat well with an electric mixer until thoroughly blended. Stir in the macerated fruits and any liquid.

3 Grease the cake tin with margarine, line the bottom and side with a double layer of greaseproof paper, and grease the paper. Spoon the mixture into the prepared tin. Level the surface and cover the top of the cake with greaseproof paper.

4 Bake in a preheated oven at 140°C (275°F, Gas 1) for 4 3/4–5 hours until firm to the touch and a skewer inserted into the middle of the cake comes out clean. Leave the cake to cool in the tin.

5 When the cake has cooled, pierce it in several places with a fine skewer and pour over a little brandy. Remove the cake from the tin, but leave the lining paper on. Wrap the cake in more greaseproof paper, then overwrap with foil. Store the cake in a cool place for up to 3 months, to mature, unwrapping and spooning over more brandy (1–2 tbsp) occasionally.

6 Decorate the cake with glacé fruit, almond paste, or ready-to-use icing (see box, right). Tie a ribbon around the cake, if wished.

Making holly leaves and berries

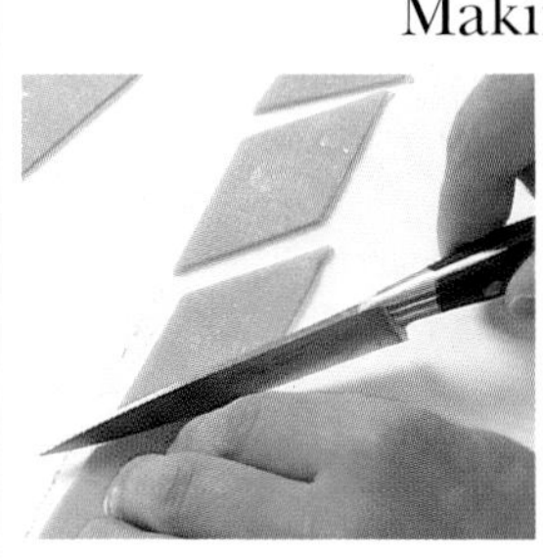

1 On a work surface lightly dusted with icing sugar, thinly roll out the green icing. Cut the icing into diamond shapes with a small, sharp knife.

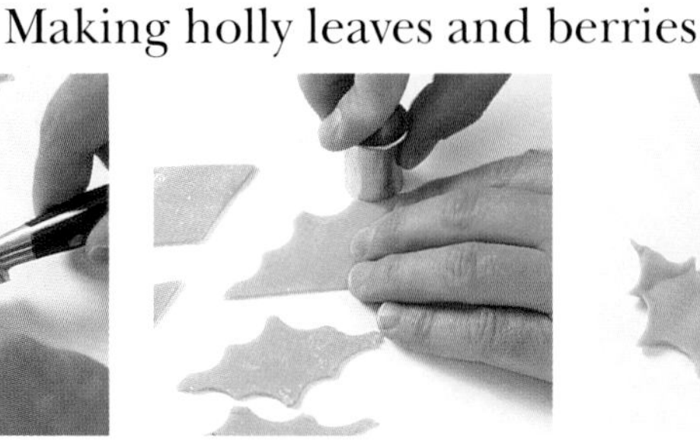

2 With a small pastry cutter or the tip of a small, sharp knife, cut a series of curves out of the edges of the diamond-shaped icing to form holly leaves.

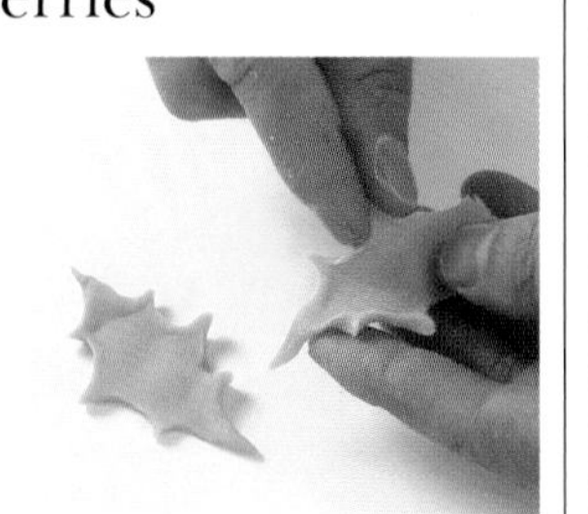

3 Mould the holly leaves to form pointed tips. Roll the red icing into small balls to represent holly berries. Brush with water and attach to cake.

Cake decorations

Christmas cakes can be decorated with a variety of ingredients, many of which are available ready-prepared. These are a few of my favourites.

Glace fruit cake

Put *90 g (3 oz) apricot jam* into a small saucepan and stir over a low heat until melted. Brush the melted jam over the fruit cake with a pastry brush. Decorate the top of the cake with *glacé fruit* and *nuts*, and glaze the topping with more apricot jam.

Festive dragee cake

Brush the cake with *3 tbsp melted apricot jam*. Roll out *750 g (1 1/2 lb) almond paste* and use to cover the cake. Leave to dry for 1 week. Decorate with *gold and silver dragées*.

Holly berry cake

Brush the cake with *3 tbsp melted apricot jam*. Roll out *750 g (1 1/2 lb) almond paste* to cover the cake. Leave for 1 week to dry. Roll out *500 g (1 lb) icing*. Brush the almond paste with *a little sherry*, then lift the icing on to the cake. Smooth and trim. Use green and red food colourings to colour the trimmings. Make holly leaves and berries (see box, left).

Clockwise from top: *Glacé Fruit Cake, Holly Berry Cake, Festive Dragée Cake.*

CORNBREAD

Makes 9 squares

sunflower oil for greasing
175 g (6 oz) polenta or fine yellow cornmeal
125 g (4 oz) plain flour
2–3 tbsp brown sugar
2 tsp baking powder
1 tsp salt
300 ml (1/2 pint) tepid milk
2 eggs, lightly beaten
60 g (2 oz) butter, melted and cooled slightly
⋆ 18 cm (7 in) square cake tin

1 Lightly oil the cake tin. Put the polenta, flour, sugar, baking powder, and salt into a large bowl and make a well in the middle. Pour in the milk, eggs, and butter, and beat the ingredients to form a batter.

2 Pour the mixture into the cake tin and bake in a preheated oven at 200°C (400°F, Gas 6) for 25–30 minutes until golden. Leave the cornbread to cool, then cut into squares.

CHILLI & CHEESE CORNBREAD

For a savoury variation to serve with Chilli con Carne, add 250 g (8 oz) grated Cheddar cheese and 1 cored, seeded, and finely chopped fresh green chilli to the cornbread mixture, and proceed as directed.

SHORTBREAD

Makes 8 wedges

125 g (4 oz) plain flour
60 g (2 oz) ground rice
125 g (4 oz) butter, plus extra for greasing
60 g (2 oz) caster sugar, plus extra for sprinkling

1 Mix the flour with the ground rice in a bowl. Add the butter and rub in with the fingertips. Stir in the sugar. Knead the mixture lightly until it forms a smooth dough.

2 Lightly butter a baking tray. Roll out the dough on a lightly floured work surface into an 18 cm (7 in) round. Lift on to the baking tray. Crimp the edges to decorate, prick all over with a fork, and mark into 8 wedges with a sharp knife. Chill until firm.

3 Bake in a preheated oven at 160°C (325°F, Gas 3) for 35 minutes or until a pale golden brown colour. Mark the wedges again and lightly sprinkle the shortbread with sugar.

4 Allow the shortbread to cool on the baking tray for 5 minutes, then lift off carefully with a palette knife and transfer to a wire rack. Leave to cool completely. Cut the shortbread into wedges to serve.

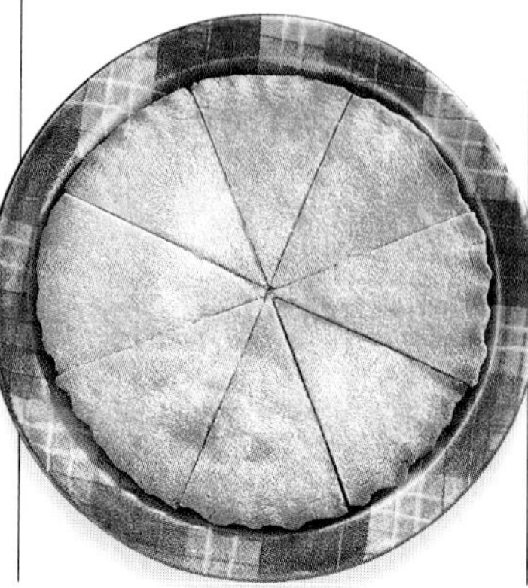

GINGERBREAD

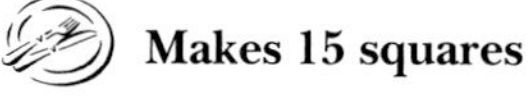

Makes 15 squares

250 g (8 oz) margarine or butter, plus extra for greasing
250 g (8 oz) dark muscovado sugar
250 g (8 oz) black treacle
375 g (12 oz) plain flour
5 tsp ground ginger
2 tsp ground cinnamon
2 eggs, beaten
3 pieces of stem ginger in syrup, drained and roughly chopped
300 ml (1/2 pint) milk
2 tsp bicarbonate of soda
⋆ 23 x 30 cm (9 x 12 in) cake tin

1 Lightly grease the tin and line the bottom with greaseproof paper.

2 Combine the margarine, sugar, and treacle in a pan, stirring, and heat until smooth. Cool slightly.

3 Sift the flour and ground spices into the mixture. Stir well, then beat in the eggs and stem ginger.

4 Warm the milk in a small heavy saucepan, and add the bicarbonate of soda. Pour into the gingerbread mixture and stir gently until thoroughly blended.

5 Pour the mixture into the prepared tin. Bake in a preheated oven at 160°C (325°F, Gas 3) for about 1 hour until well risen and springy to the touch.

6 Leave to cool in the tin for a few minutes, then turn out on to a wire rack, and peel off the lining paper. Leave to cool completely. Cut into even-sized squares to serve.

Cook's know-how

Gingerbread improves with keeping and is best made 2–3 days before eating. Store in an airtight container to keep the gingerbread moist until serving.

BARA BRITH

Serves 8

375 g (12 oz) mixed dried fruit
250 g (8 oz) light muscovado sugar
300 ml (1/2 pint) strong hot tea, strained
butter for greasing
300 g (10 oz) self-raising flour
1 egg, beaten
⋆ *1 kg (2 lb) loaf tin*

1 Combine the dried fruit, sugar, and hot tea in a large bowl. Stir the mixture, then cover and leave to steep for at least 8 hours.

2 Lightly butter the loaf tin and line the bottom with greaseproof paper. Stir the flour and egg into the dried fruit and tea mixture, mixing thoroughly. Turn the mixture into the loaf tin and level the surface.

3 Bake in a preheated oven at 150°C (300°F, Gas 2) for 1 1/2–1 3/4 hours until well risen and firm to the touch. A fine skewer inserted into the middle should come out clean.

4 Leave to cool in the tin for about 10 minutes, then turn out on to a wire rack, and peel off the lining paper. Leave to cool completely. Serve sliced and buttered, if wished.

Cook's know-how

Mixed dried fruit is steeped in strong tea so that it is well plumped by the time the bara brith is mixed.

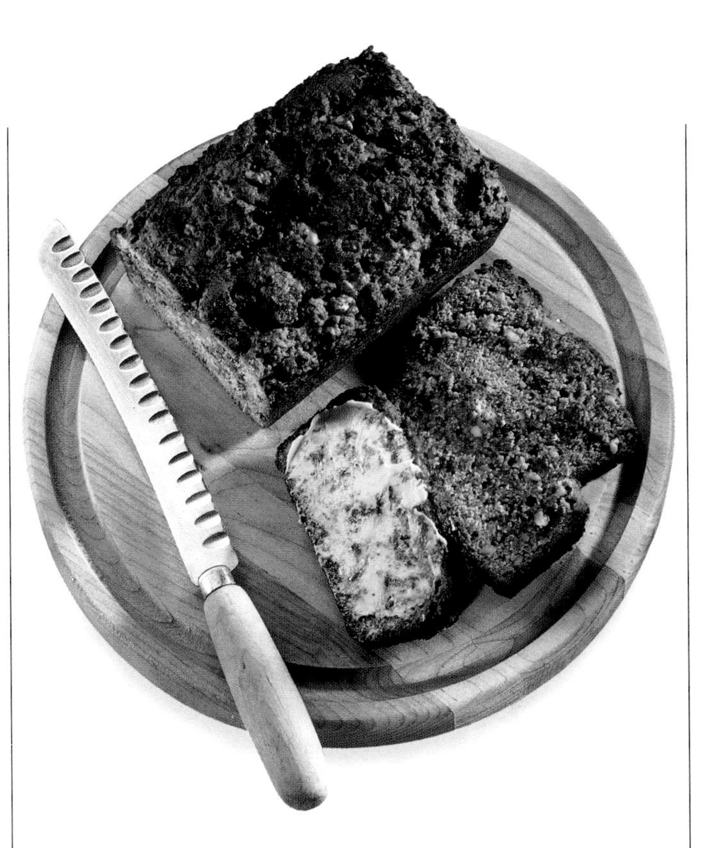

DATE & WALNUT LOAF

Serves 8

90 g (3 oz) soft margarine, plus extra for greasing
250 g (8 oz) dates, stoned and roughly chopped
150 ml (1/4 pint) boiling water
90 g (3 oz) caster sugar
1 egg
250 g (8 oz) self-raising flour
1 tsp baking powder
90 g (3 oz) walnuts, roughly chopped
⋆ *1 kg (2 lb) loaf tin*

1 Lightly grease the loaf tin with margarine and line with greaseproof paper.

2 Put the dates into a bowl, pour over the measured boiling water, and leave for about 15 minutes.

3 Combine the margarine, sugar, egg, flour, and baking powder in a large bowl and beat until well blended. Add the walnuts and dates, plus the soaking liquid, and stir to mix.

4 Spoon into the prepared loaf tin and bake in a preheated oven at 180°C (350°F, Gas 4) for 1 1/4–1 1/2 hours until well risen and firm to the touch. A fine skewer inserted into the middle of the loaf should come out clean.

5 Leave to cool in the loaf tin for a few minutes, then turn out on to a wire rack, and peel off the lining paper. Leave to cool completely. Serve sliced and buttered, if wished.

CHERRY & BANANA LOAF

Omit the dates and walnuts, and add 125 g (4 oz) quartered glacé cherries, and 2 mashed large ripe bananas. Proceed as directed in the recipe.

WELSH CAKES

Makes 12

250 g (8 oz) self-raising flour
1 tsp baking powder
125 g (4 oz) butter
90 g (3 oz) caster sugar
90 g (3 oz) currants
1/2 tsp ground mixed spice
1 egg, beaten
about 2 tbsp milk
sunflower oil for greasing
** 7 cm (3 in) pastry cutter*

1 Sift the flour and baking powder into a large bowl. Add the butter and rub in with the fingertips until the mixture resembles fine breadcrumbs.

2 Add the sugar, currants, and mixed spice, and stir to mix. Add the egg and enough milk to form a soft but not sticky dough.

3 On a lightly floured work surface, roll out the dough to a thickness of 5 mm (1/4 in). Cut into rounds with pastry cutter.

4 Heat a griddle or a heavy frying pan and grease with a little oil. Cook the Welsh cakes on the hot griddle or pan over a low heat for about 3 minutes on each side until cooked through and golden brown.

5 Leave to cool on a wire rack. Serve on the day of making, if possible.

Cook's know-how

If preferred, serve the Welsh cakes hot, lightly sprinkled with sugar, straight from the griddle or frying pan.

DEVON SCONES

Makes 12

60 g (2 oz) butter, plus extra for greasing
250 g (8 oz) self-raising flour
2 tsp baking powder
30 g (1 oz) caster sugar
1 egg
about 150 ml (1/4 pint) milk, plus extra for glazing
butter and jam to serve
** 5 cm (2 in) pastry cutter*

1 Lightly butter a large baking tray.

2 Sift the flour and baking powder into a bowl. Rub in the butter with the fingertips until the mixture resembles fine breadcrumbs. Stir in the sugar.

3 Break the egg into a measuring jug and make up to 150 ml (1/4 pint) with milk. Beat lightly to mix. Add to the bowl and mix to a soft dough.

4 Lightly knead the dough until smooth. Roll out until 1 cm (1/2 in) thick, cut into rounds with the pastry cutter, and put on the baking tray. Brush with milk.

5 Bake in a preheated oven at 220°C (425°F, Gas 7) for about 10 minutes until risen and golden. Cool on a wire rack. Serve on the day of making, if possible, with butter and jam.

CHEESE SCONES

Omit the sugar, and add 125 g (4 oz) grated mature Cheddar cheese and 1/2 tsp mustard powder to the dry ingredients before mixing in the egg and milk. Roll out the dough into a 15 cm (6 in) round and cut it into wedges. Brush with milk and sprinkle with finely grated cheese. Bake as directed.

Wholemeal Drop Scones

Makes 20

- *175 g (6 oz) wholemeal self-raising flour*
- *1 tsp baking powder*
- *45 g ($1^1/_2$ oz) caster sugar*
- *1 egg, size 1*
- *200 ml (7 fl oz) milk*
- *sunflower oil for greasing*
- *golden syrup or butter and jam to serve*

1 Combine the flour, baking powder, and sugar in a bowl, and stir to mix. Make a well in the middle and add the egg and half of the milk. Beat well to make a smooth, thick batter.

2 Add enough milk to give the batter the consistency of thick cream.

3 Heat a griddle or heavy frying pan and grease with oil. Drop spoonfuls of batter on to the hot griddle or pan, spacing them well apart. When bubbles rise to the surface, turn the scones over and cook until golden.

4 As each batch is cooked, wrap the scones in a clean tea towel to keep them soft. Serve warm, with syrup or butter and jam.

Plain Drop Scones

Substitute plain self-raising flour for the wholemeal self-raising flour, use a little less milk, and proceed as directed.

Cook's know-how

Drop scones are also known as Scotch pancakes. They freeze well if you have any left over. Interleave with freezer wrap or greaseproof paper and freeze for up to 6 months.

Irish Soda Bread

Makes 1 loaf

- *500 g (1 lb) plain white flour, plus extra for dusting*
- *1 tsp bicarbonate of soda*
- *1 tsp salt*
- *300 ml ($^1/_2$ pint) buttermilk, or half milk and half plain yogurt*
- *90 ml (3 fl oz) tepid water*
- *sunflower oil for greasing*

1 Sift the flour, bicarbonate of soda, and salt into a large bowl. Pour in the buttermilk, or milk and yogurt, and the measured water. Mix with a wooden spoon or your hands to form a very soft dough.

2 Lightly oil a baking tray. Turn out the dough on to a lightly floured work surface and shape into a round measuring 18 cm (7 ins) in diameter.

3 Place the loaf on the prepared baking tray and cut a deep cross in the top.

4 Bake in a preheated oven at 200°C (400°F, Gas 6) for 30 minutes. Turn the bread over and bake for a further 10 minutes or until the loaf sounds hollow when tapped on the base. Leave to cool on a wire rack. Serve on the day of making.

Potato Farls

Makes 12

- *175 g (6 oz) plain flour*
- *1 tbsp baking powder*
- *60 g (2 oz) butter, plus extra for greasing*
- *45 g ($1^1/_2$ oz) caster sugar*
- *125 g (4 oz) freshly boiled and mashed potato*
- *3 tbsp milk*

1 Sift the flour and baking powder into a bowl. Rub in the butter until the mixture resembles fine breadcrumbs. Stir in the sugar and mashed potato. Add enough milk to bind to a soft but not sticky dough.

2 Turn out the dough on to a floured surface and knead lightly until blended. Roll out until 1 cm ($^1/_2$ in) thick and cut into rectangles.

3 Place the rectangles on a buttered baking tray and bake in a preheated oven at 220°C (425°F, Gas 7) for 12–15 minutes until risen and golden. Leave to cool on a wire rack. Serve on the day of making.

Farls

Traditionally, farls are triangular in shape. Instead of rectangles as here, cut 12 triangles from the dough.

ALMOND TUILES

 **Makes 30**

- *2 egg whites*
- *125 g (4 oz) caster sugar*
- *60 g (2 oz) plain flour*
- *1/2 tsp vanilla essence*
- *60 g (2 oz) butter, melted and cooled*
- *30 g (1 oz) flaked almonds*

1 Line a baking tray with baking parchment. Put the egg whites into a bowl and beat in the sugar until frothy. Stir in the flour and vanilla essence, then add the melted butter.

2 Put 6 teaspoonfuls of the mixture on to the baking tray, spacing them well apart to allow for spreading. Flatten each with a fork.

3 Sprinkle with the almonds. Bake in a preheated oven at 180°C (350°F, Gas 4) for about 6 minutes until golden brown around the edges but still pale in the middle.

4 Allow the biscuits to cool on the baking tray for a few seconds, then lift off with a fish slice and gently lay them over a greased rolling pin to give the traditional curved shape.

5 Allow the biscuits to set, then lift off on to a wire rack and leave to cool.

6 Cook and shape the remaining mixture in batches, cooking 1 batch while another is setting on the rolling pin.

Tuiles

These biscuits take their name from the French word "tuile" meaning roof tile, which they resemble in shape.

VIENNESE FINGERS

 **Makes 12**

- *175 g (6 oz) butter, plus extra for greasing*
- *60 g (2 oz) caster sugar*
- *175 g (6 oz) self-raising flour*
- *a few drops of vanilla essence*
- *90 g (3 oz) plain chocolate, broken into pieces*

1 Lightly butter 2 baking trays. Combine the butter and sugar in a bowl and cream together until pale and fluffy. Stir in the flour and vanilla essence and beat until well combined.

2 Spoon the mixture into a piping bag with a medium star nozzle. Pipe into 7 cm (3 in) lengths on the baking trays. Bake in a preheated oven at 160°C (325°F, Gas 3) for about 20 minutes until golden. Cool on a wire rack.

3 Put the chocolate into a heatproof bowl. Set the bowl over a pan of hot water and heat gently until the chocolate has melted. Dip both ends of each biscuit into the chocolate. Leave to set on the wire rack.

COCONUT MACAROONS

Makes 26

- *3 egg whites*
- *175 g (6 oz) icing sugar*
- *175 g (6 oz) ground almonds*
- *a few drops of almond essence*
- *175 g (6 oz) desiccated coconut*
- *about 13 whole almonds, blanched and halved*

1 Line 2 baking trays with baking parchment.

2 Whisk the egg whites thoroughly until stiff but not dry. Sift in the icing sugar and fold it in gently. Fold in the ground almonds, almond essence, and desiccated coconut.

3 Put teaspoonfuls of the coconut mixture on to the baking trays. Top each with an almond half.

4 Bake in a preheated oven at 150°C (300°F, Gas 2) for about 25 minutes until golden brown and crisp on the outside and soft in the middle.

5 Leave the macaroons to cool on a wire rack. Best served on the day of making.

BRANDY SNAPS

Makes 15

90 g (3 oz) butter
90 g (3 oz) demerara sugar
90 g (3 oz) golden syrup
90 g (3 oz) plain flour
3/4 tsp ground ginger
3/4 tsp lemon juice

1 Line a baking tray with baking parchment.

2 Combine the butter, sugar, and syrup in a saucepan and heat gently until the ingredients have melted and dissolved. Cool slightly, then sift in the flour and ginger. Add the lemon juice and stir to mix well.

3 Place 3–4 teaspoonfuls of the mixture on to the baking tray, leaving plenty of room for the biscuits to spread out.

4 Bake in a preheated oven at 160°C (325°F, Gas 3) for about 8 minute until the mixture spreads out to form large, thin, dark golden rounds. While the biscuits are baking, oil the handles of 4 wooden spoons.

5 Remove the biscuits from the oven and leave for 1–2 minutes to firm slightly. Shape the brandy snaps (see box, below).

6 Continue baking, shaping, and cooling the remaining mixture in batches until all is used.

Shaping the brandy snaps

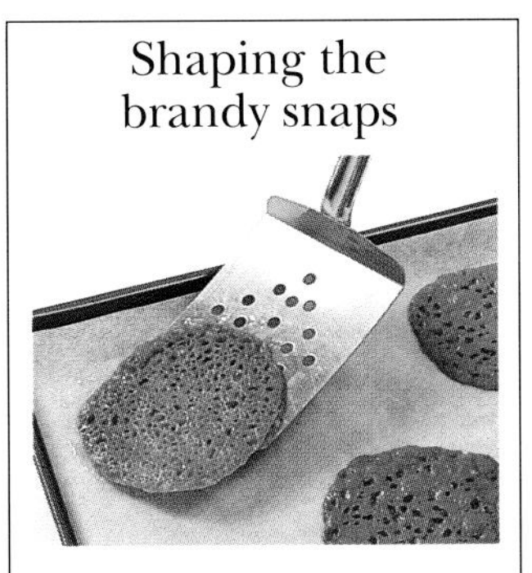

Lift 1 biscuit from the paper using a fish slice or palette knife, turn the biscuit over so that the rough side is on the outside, and wrap around an oiled wooden spoon handle. Repeat with the remaining biscuits. Transfer to a wire rack and cool until firm. Slip from the spoon handles.

GINGER SNAPS

Makes 15

60 g (2 oz) butter, plus extra for greasing
90 g (3 oz) golden syrup
125 g (4 oz) self-raising flour
2 tsp ground ginger
1 tsp ground cinnamon
1/2 tsp bicarbonate of soda
1 tbsp caster sugar

1 Lightly grease 2 baking trays with butter.

2 Combine the butter and golden syrup in a small saucepan and heat gently until melted. Leave the mixture to cool slightly.

3 Sift the flour, spices, and bicarbonate of soda into a bowl, and stir in the sugar. Add the cooled syrup mixture, and stir to mix to a soft but not sticky dough.

4 Roll the dough into balls about the size of walnuts and place well apart on the baking trays. Flatten the dough balls slightly with the heel of your hand.

5 Bake in a preheated oven at 190°C (375°F, Gas 5) for about 15 minutes. Leave the biscuits to cool on the baking trays for a few minutes, then transfer them to a wire rack and leave to cool completely.

FORK BISCUITS

Makes 32

250 g (8 oz) butter, at room temperature, plus extra for greasing
125 g (4 oz) caster sugar
300 g (10 oz) self-raising flour

1 Lightly grease 2 baking trays with butter.

2 Put the butter into a large bowl and beat with a wooden spoon to soften it. Gradually beat in the caster sugar, then stir in the flour. Use your hands to gather the mixture together into a soft but not sticky dough.

3 Roll the dough into balls about the size of walnuts and place well apart on the baking trays. Dip a fork into cold water and press on top of each ball to flatten it and imprint the fork pattern.

4 Bake in batches in a preheated oven at 180°C (350°F, Gas 4) for 15–20 minutes until the biscuits are a very pale golden colour. Transfer the biscuits from the baking tray to a wire rack and leave to cool completely.

CHOUX PASTRIES

Quite unlike any other pastry, choux is a thick paste that can be piped into any shape you like. Once baked, the light-as-air pastry can be served with sweet or savoury fillings. Try ever-popular éclairs, classic profiteroles filled with ice cream, or innovative pastry hearts sandwiched with cream and tropical fruits.

COFFEE ECLAIRS

 **Makes 8**

butter for greasing
1 quantity choux pastry (see box, below)
1 egg, beaten
300 ml (1/2 pint) whipping cream
ground cinnamon for sprinkling

COFFEE ICING
1 tsp instant coffee granules
15 g (1/2 oz) butter
2 tbsp water
90 g (3 oz) icing sugar

1 Lightly butter a baking tray and sprinkle with water. Spoon the choux pastry into a piping bag fitted with a 1 cm (1/2 in) plain nozzle. Pipe the pastry into 7 cm (3 in) lengths, leaving enough space between them to spread. Brush with the beaten egg.

2 Bake in a preheated oven at 220°C (425°F, Gas 7) for 10 minutes; reduce the oven temperature to 190°C (375°F, Gas 5), and bake for a further 20 minutes until golden brown. Split in half and leave to cool on a wire rack.

3 Whip the cream until stiff. Pipe into the bottom halves of the éclairs and sprinkle the cream with cinnamon.

4 Make the icing: put the coffee, butter, and measured water into a heatproof bowl over a pan of simmering water. Heat gently until the butter melts. Remove from the heat and beat in the icing sugar. Dip the top half of each eclair into the warm icing, then place on top of the cream. Leave the icing to cool before serving.

PROFITEROLES

 **Makes 12**

butter for greasing
1 quantity choux pastry (see box, below)
1 egg, beaten
vanilla ice cream and chocolate sauce (page 440) to serve

1 Lightly butter a baking tray and sprinkle with water. Place 12 tablespoonfuls of choux pastry on to the tray and brush with the beaten egg.

2 Bake in a preheated oven at 220°C (425°F, Gas 7) for 10 minutes; reduce the oven temperature to 190°C (375°F, Gas 5), and bake for 20 minutes until golden brown. Split in half and leave to cool on a wire rack.

3 Fill the profiteroles with ice cream and serve with chocolate sauce.

CHOUX HEARTS

 **Makes 4**

butter for greasing
1 quantity choux pastry (see box, below)
1 egg, beaten
300 ml (1/2 pint) whipping cream
exotic fruits to serve
icing sugar for dusting

1 Lightly butter a baking tray and sprinkle with water. Spoon the choux pastry into a piping bag fitted with a 1 cm (1/2 in) plain nozzle. Pipe 4 heart shapes, about 7 cm (3 ins) across. Brush with the beaten egg.

2 Bake in a preheated oven at 220°C (425°F, Gas 7) for 10 minutes; reduce the oven temperature to 190°C (375°F, Gas 5), and bake for a further 20 minutes until golden brown.

3 Cut in half horizontally and leave to cool on a wire rack. Whip the cream until stiff. Pipe the cream on to the bottom halves of the hearts and top with exotic fruits. Dust the top halves of the hearts with icing sugar and replace on the bottom halves.

Clockwise from top: *Coffee Eclairs, Choux Hearts, Profiteroles.*

Basic choux pastry

1 Put *60 g (2 oz) butter, cut into cubes,* into a heavy saucepan with *150 ml (1/4 pint) water* and heat until the butter melts. Bring to a boil.

2 Remove from the heat and add *75 g (2 1/2 oz) sifted plain flour* and *a pinch of salt, if preferred.* Stir vigorously until the mixture forms a soft ball.

3 Leave to cool slightly, then gradually add *2 lightly beaten eggs,* beating well between each addition, to form a smooth, shiny paste.

FLAPJACKS

 **Makes 24**

125 g (4 oz) butter, plus extra for greasing

90 g (3 oz) golden syrup

90 g (3 oz) light muscovado sugar

250 g (8 oz) rolled oats

⋆ roasting tin or shallow cake tin, about 20 x 30 cm (8 x 12 ins)

1 Lightly butter the roasting tin or cake tin.

2 Combine the butter, syrup, and sugar in a saucepan and heat gently until the ingredients have melted and dissolved. Stir in the oats and mix well.

3 Spoon into the prepared tin and smooth the surface with a palette knife. Bake in a preheated oven at 180°C (350°F, Gas 4) for about 30 minutes.

4 Leave to cool in the tin for about 5 minutes, then mark into 24 fingers. Leave to cool completely, then cut and remove from the tin.

WALNUT COOKIES

Makes 50

250 g (8 oz) plain flour

1 tsp baking powder

125 g (4 oz) butter, plus extra for greasing

175 g (6 oz) caster sugar

60 g (2 oz) walnuts, finely chopped

1 egg, beaten

1 tsp vanilla essence

1 Sift the flour and baking powder into a bowl. Rub in the butter with the fingertips until the mixture resembles breadcrumbs. Mix in the sugar and walnuts. Add the beaten egg and vanilla essence, and stir to form a smooth dough.

2 Shape the dough into a long cylinder about 5 cm (2 ins) in diameter. Wrap in foil, roll to give smooth sides, and chill for about 8 hours.

3 Lightly butter several baking trays. Cut the cylinder into thin slices and place the biscuits on the baking trays. Bake in a preheated oven at 190°C (375°F, Gas 5) for 10–12 minutes until golden.

PINWHEEL BISCUITS

Makes 18

VANILLA DOUGH

60 g (2 oz) butter, at room temperature

30 g (1 oz) caster sugar

90 g (3 oz) plain flour

a few drops of vanilla essence

about 1 tbsp water

COFFEE DOUGH

60 g (2 oz) butter, at room temperature

30 g (1 oz) caster sugar

90 g (3 oz) plain flour

1 tbsp coffee essence

milk for brushing

1 Combine the ingredients for the vanilla dough in a bowl and mix well, adding just enough water to bind. Knead lightly, then wrap and chill for at least 2 hours until very firm.

2 Mix the ingredients for the coffee dough, using the coffee essence to bind. Wrap and chill for at least 2 hours until very firm.

3 On a lightly floured work surface, roll out each dough to a rectangle about 18 x 25 cm (7 x 10 ins).

4 Brush the coffee dough with a little milk, then place the vanilla dough on top. Roll up together like a Swiss roll, starting at a narrow end.

5 Wrap the roll tightly in foil and leave to chill in the refrigerator for about 30 minutes or until firm.

6 Lightly grease 1–2 baking trays. Cut the dough roll into about 18 thin slices and place them well apart on the baking trays.

7 Bake in a preheated oven at 180°C (350°F, Gas 4) for about 20 minutes until the vanilla dough is a very pale golden colour.

8 Leave the biscuits to cool on the baking trays for a few minutes, then lift off on to a wire rack and leave to cool completely.

Cook's know-how

If the doughs become too soft and difficult to roll out, put each piece of dough between sheets of greaseproof paper before rolling.

USEFUL INFORMATION

On the following pages you'll find practical information on Herbs, Spices, Microwaving, and Freezing, and advice on Healthy Eating. All of this will help you get more from the recipes in this book – and from all of your cooking.

HERBS

WITH THEIR WONDERFUL flavours, scents, and colours, herbs can transform even the simplest dish into something very special, accenting and enhancing other ingredients. Most savoury dishes benefit from the inclusion of one or more herbs to add flavour during cooking, or as a garnish to be sprinkled over the top of a dish just before serving. Sweet dishes, too, can be perfumed with herbs such as mint and lemon balm, and decorated with delicate herb flowers such as borage. Herbs are also used to make drinks known as infusions or tisanes, to be served hot or cold.

PRESERVING HERBS

You can preserve your own herbs by drying or freezing them. The best herbs for drying are bay, lovage, marjoram, oregano, mint, rosemary, spearmint, and thyme. When drying herbs, spread the sprigs out on trays or racks, cover with muslin, and leave in a warm, airy place for about 24 hours. Alternatively, tie the stalks in bunches and hang them upside down in a warm, airy place. When dry, remove the leaves or sprigs from the stalks, crumble them if they are large, pack into small jars, and seal tightly. The seeds of coriander, dill, and fennel are ideal for drying. If you have herbs with seedheads that are ripe (the seeds will have started to change from green to brown), pack the seedheads loosely in a paper bag. Leave to dry for 10–14 days, then shake out the seeds, and pack into small jars.

Herbs such as basil, chervil, dill, fennel, parsley, sorrel, and tarragon can be frozen successfully. Pack leaves or small sprigs in small plastic bags, or mix chopped herbs with water and freeze in ice-cube trays. Freezing is generally considered to be a better method of preserving than drying as a fresher flavour is retained.

PREPARING HERBS

Rinse and dry the herbs, then remove the leaves or sprigs from the stalks.

Chopping
Gather the leaves together on a chopping board. Chop the leaves with a sharp knife, rocking it back and forth, chopping as finely as necessary.

Snipping
A pair of scissors is best for snipping chives. Hold the stalks in one hand and snip into short lengths, either into a bowl or directly into the dish you are flavouring.

GROWING YOUR OWN HERBS

The range of fresh herbs available in shops and supermarkets is extensive, but there are still some, such as the more unusual varieties of mint, that are more difficult to find. Also, buying fresh herbs is much more expensive than using those you grow yourself, particularly if you use large amounts.

The cultivation of herbs, indoors or out, is simple and satisfying. You can start from seed or from a small plant; the latter is the quicker and easier method. Herbs can be grown outdoors in the garden, in pots on a paved terrace or patio, in a rock garden, in a hanging basket, or simply in a window box. Inside the house, herbs will grow satisfactorily in a box or in pots on a window sill.

Most herbs need as much sunshine as possible during the growing season, so they should be grown in a sunny spot that offers protection from cold winds. The only other requirement, for your own convenience, is to site them as near to the kitchen as possible.

STORING & USING FRESH HERBS

Buy or gather fresh herbs only when they are needed. If you have to store them for a day or so, keep them in a cool place or in the refrigerator. If they have stalks, stand them in a jug of water, just as you would cut flowers. Herb leaves can be spread on damp paper towels, rolled up, and put into a plastic bag.

Most herbs, should be chopped before being added to a dish, and this is usually best at the last possible moment. The volatile oils in herbs are released by heat or oxidation, so unless fresh herbs are used as soon as they are prepared, they will quickly lose their flavours, and colours.

Bay leaves are among the few herbs that are best used whole. They should always be added at the start of cooking, and removed just before serving. Whole sprigs are also used if flavour is needed in a dish but not colour – the herbs should be lifted out before serving. For easy removal, tie with string or wrap in muslin.

HERB MIXTURES

There are certain combinations of herbs that are often used in dishes. The most common herb mixture is a bouquet garni (see box, right). *Herbes de Provence,* an aromatic mixture of sage, basil, savory, thyme, rosemary, and marjoram, is another popular combination, good in stews, but should be used sparingly. *Fines herbes* combines equal quantities of tarragon, chervil, parsley, and chives, and is good with omelettes, fish and poultry.

These mixtures can be made with fresh or dried herbs. Tie fresh herbs together with string or wrap dried herbs in a muslin bag. Remember to remove the bundle or bag of herbs before serving.

MAKING A BOUQUET GARNI

A bouquet garni may vary, but always includes parsley stalks, thyme, and a bay leaf. Remove before serving.

1 With a length of string, tie together *2–3 sprigs of thyme, 5–6 parsley stalks, and 1 bay leaf.*

2 Add to the saucepan or casserole – tie it to the handle for easy removal. Remove before serving.

STORING & USING DRIED HERBS

Whether they are shop-bought or prepared at home, dried herbs must be stored correctly or they will quickly lose their flavour. Dark glass jars or earthenware pots with airtight lids are excellent for storage; if you use clear glass jars keep them in a dark cupboard or drawer because light causes dried herbs to deteriorate. Make sure they are in a cool, dry place, away from kitchen heat and steam.

Dried herbs will not keep forever, even if they are stored correctly. Home-dried herbs should stay flavourful for 1 year, but shop-bought ones will last only 6 months. It is best to buy dried herbs in small quantities from shops that have a rapid turnover.

Dried herbs can be substituted for fresh ones in most recipes. Dried herbs are more pungent than fresh, so a smaller quantity is required. Use 1/2 teaspoon finely powdered dried herb or 1 teaspoon crumbled dried herb to 1 tablespoon chopped fresh herb.

HERBS & THEIR USES

These are some of the most commonly used herbs, their flavours, and the foods or dishes they complement best.

HERB	FLAVOUR	USE WITH
Basil	*sweet, spicy, aromatic*	beef, lamb, pork, and veal; white fish; salad greens; tomatoes; eggs; pasta sauces
Bay	*aromatic, pungent*	soups and stocks; casseroles; sauces
Chervil	*delicate, fresh*	chicken; omelettes; delicate sauces
Chives	*delicate, oniony*	fish; egg dishes; salads; garnish for creamy soups
Coriander	*aromatic, spicy*	curries; salsa; stir-fries; salads; yogurt; guacamole
Dill	*tangy, pungent*	salmon and herrings; veal; carrots, cucumber, and potatoes; eggs and cheese
Fennel	*anise-like*	pork; seafood; eggs
Lemon balm	*fragrant, lemon-like*	salads; eggs; soups; garnish for desserts
Lemon grass	*delicate, fresh, lemon-like*	Oriental curries and soups, particularly Thai
Marjoram	*sweet, aromatic*	lamb, pork, and veal; chicken; tomatoes; Italian dishes; eggs and cheese; pasta dishes
Mint	*strong, sweet, cooling*	cucumber, new potatoes, and peas; melon; garnish for many savoury and sweet dishes
Oregano	*sweet, aromatic*	as for marjoram
Parsley	*fresh, slightly spicy*	eggs; fish; almost every savoury dish
Rosemary	*pungent, oily*	lamb and pork; chicken; breads; potatoes
Sage	*aromatic, slightly bitter*	pork and veal; duck, goose, and turkey; beans; eggs and cheese; risotto
Tarragon	*piquant, anise-like*	chicken; fish; eggs; béarnaise sauce

SPICES

THE USE OF SPICES in cooking has a very long history – they were often used to mask the taste of less than perfect food or to liven up bland-tasting food. At one time, spices were so precious and expensive that even in the wealthiest of households they would be locked away in special spice boxes or cupboards. Today, most spices are no longer a luxury seasoning, and modern cooks use them to enhance flavours rather than to disguise them, as well as to provide vibrant colours and enticing aromas.

BUYING & STORING

Spices don't deteriorate as quickly as herbs, particularly if they are whole (which is why it's a good idea to buy them whole and grind them as you need them). When buying spices – whole or ground – sniff them if you can: the more pungent they smell, the fresher they are. Store spices in tightly sealed containers in a cool, dark, dry place. Whole spices can be kept for at least 1 year, often longer, and ground spices will keep for about 6 months.

COOKING WITH SPICES

Because spices need time to release their aromas and flavours, they are usually added near the start of cooking.

If the cooking process is prolonged, spices that are whole, cracked, or bruised are normally used rather than ground spices, which could become bitter. Large spices, such as cinnamon sticks and cloves, are best removed before serving.

In Oriental cooking, whole spices are toasted in a heavy frying pan until they smell aromatic, then ground. Toasting or warming in this way brings out the flavour of most spices, particularly if they are to be used in a dish that is cooked for only a short time. When toasting whole spices, cook them over a low heat because they scorch easily. Use oil to prevent ground spices from scorching.

TYPES OF SPICES

Spicy food does not simply mean a fiery flavour – spices lend all kinds of qualities to dishes.

Hot spices
These spices stimulate the palate and sharpen the appetite as well as encouraging the body to produce perspiration – an excellent means of cooling down in a hot climate.

The best known of the hot spices include ground and crushed chillies, chilli powder (which is usually a blend of chillies and other spices), cayenne (ground from red chilli peppers) which is very strong and so should be used sparingly, and paprika (made from sweet peppers and very mild). Be careful to avoid contact with your eyes when using these spices because they can sting.

Peppercorns are a hot spice with a more aromatic flavour. Black, white, green, and pink varieties are available. If sold together, they are known as tropical or mixed peppercorns.

Fragrant spices
Spices such as allspice, cardamom, cloves, cinnamon, coriander, mace, juniper, and nutmeg add a pungent, sweet note to all kinds of dishes, both sweet and savoury. Most can be used whole or ground, and they are usually added at the beginning of cooking so that their flavour and perfume can permeate and enhance the dish.

Colouring spices
A dish can be coloured as well as flavoured by a spice. Saffron is the most expensive spice in the world, but only a pinch is needed to give a dish such as paella a vibrant yellow colour. Turmeric is often used as an alternative and gives a rich yellow hue to many Indian dishes. The dark red colour of goulash and chorizo sausages comes from paprika.

PREPARING SPICES

The way in which spices are prepared depends on the recipe in which they are used and the depth of flavour required.

Whole spices
Whole spices and herbs that are to be removed before serving are best tied in a piece of muslin, which allows them to be lifted out of the dish all at once.

Toasting spices
Heat a heavy frying pan until hot. Add the spices and cook over a low heat for 1–2 minutes, stirring occasionally, until the aromas are released. The spices can then be ground.

Grinding spices
Put the whole spices into a mortar and use a pestle to crush them to the required consistency. Electric spice grinders are also available.

SPICES & THEIR USES

Here are some of the most commonly used spices, their flavours, the forms in which they are sold, and the foods or dishes they complement best.

SPICE	FLAVOUR	FORM	USE WITH
Allspice	*sweet, like a mixture of cloves and cinnamon*	whole berries or ground	meat stews, particularly lamb; spiced vinegar; poached fruits; cakes, breads, and pies
Caraway	*aromatic, strong*	whole seeds	meat stews; sausages; cabbage and sauerkraut; breads; cheese
Cardamom	*pungent*	pods that contain whole seeds or ground	curries; pickled herrings; punches; pastries and cakes; fruit dishes
Cayenne	*spicy, very hot*	ground	Indian, Mexican, and Cajun dishes; eggs
Chilli powder	*spicy, hot*	ground	Indian and Mexican dishes; eggs and cheese; soups and stews
Cinnamon	*sweet, aromatic*	sticks or ground	Middle-Eastern dishes; curries; fruit desserts; cakes and breads; milk and rice puddings
Cloves	*sweet, strong*	whole or ground	ham and pork; sweet potatoes; pumpkin; spiced cakes; apples and other fruits
Coriander	*fragrant, lemony*	whole berries or ground	Indian dishes; meat; chicken; pickled fish; mushrooms; breads, cakes, and pastries; custards
Cumin	*pungent, slightly bitter*	whole seeds or ground	Indian and Mexican dishes; pork; chicken; cheese; soups
Curry powder	*mild to hot*	ground mixture of turmeric, fenugreek, coriander, cumin, cardamom, chilli	poultry; fish; eggs; vegetables; sauces for meat
Garam masala	*aromatic*	ground mixture of spices such as cumin, coriander, cardamom, cinnamon, pepper, cloves, mace	Indian dishes
Ginger	*pungent, spicy*	fresh root or ground	Oriental and Indian dishes; chicken; vegetables, particularly pumpkin and carrots; fruit such as melon and rhubarb; cakes and biscuits
Juniper	*pungent*	berries	pork and pork sausage; pâtés and terrines; game, particularly venison; cabbage; stuffings
Mace	*sweet, fragrant*	whole blades or ground	as for nutmeg
Mixed spice	*sweet, aromatic*	ground mixture of cinnamon, allspice, cloves, nutmeg, ginger	Middle-Eastern dishes; cakes, puddings, and biscuits
Mustard	*pungent, hot*	whole seeds or ground	pork and beef; chicken; rabbit; vegetables; pickles and relishes; sauces and dressings
Nutmeg	*sweet, fragrant*	whole or ground	meat sauces; tomatoes, spinach, and potatoes; cakes and biscuits; milk puddings and custards; mulled wine
Paprika	*pungent, mild or hot*	ground	meat stews; eggs and cream cheese
Pepper	*pungent, mild or hot*	berries (peppercorns) or ground	almost every savoury dish and a few sweet ones, such as strawberries

MICROWAVING

THE MICROWAVE OVEN has revolutionized cooking for many people. Those whose busy lifestyles don't allow time to devote to conventional cooking find it a boon. Vegetables and fish are quickly cooked to perfection, retaining vitamins, colour, and texture. Stews and casseroles made with good cuts of meat are tender and succulent, and stocks and steamed puddings can be made in a fraction of the time taken by the conventional method. For most cooks, however, the microwave is one tool among many, used to speed preparation, but not used to cook a dish from start to finish.

HOW A MICROWAVE OVEN WORKS

Cooking in a microwave oven is very different from cooking in a conventional oven, so an understanding of the basic principles is essential in order to achieve the best results. A microwave oven contains a device known as a magnetron. This converts electricity into microwaves, which pass through materials such as china, glass, and plastic and are absorbed by the moisture molecules in food. The microwaves penetrate food up to a depth of about 5 cm (2 ins), where they cause the molecules to vibrate so quickly that they create heat. The heat created spreads to the rest of the food and cooks, but does not brown it.

Most microwave ovens contain a turntable which rotates the food and exposes it evenly to the microwaves. Stirring foods also ensures even cooking. As microwaves continue to produce heat when the power has been turned off, standing times are often given with recipes, to allow the food to finish cooking.

The microwave oven is ideal for cooking fish, vegetables, and other foods that are normally cooked using moisture methods such as steaming or poaching. Combination ovens also use conventional energy, similar to a grill, which browns and crisps food.

Microwaving safety

A microwave oven is quite safe if used properly. The door of every oven has a special seal to ensure the waves do not escape. The oven will only work if the door is closed; if the door is accidentally opened during cooking, the power cuts off automatically. Always have the oven checked for leakage if it has been dropped or damaged.

◆

A microwave can be positioned wherever convenient, but make sure that any vents, which allow steam to escape, are not obstructed.

◆

Never switch on the microwave when it is empty; with nothing to absorb them, the waves will simply bounce back and damage the magnetron.

◆

Do not put metal into a microwave – it reflects the waves and causes "arcing", producing sparks which can damage the magnetron.

MICROWAVING EQUIPMENT

Special equipment is not essential for cooking in a microwave oven; many containers and implements used for conventional cooking are suitable.

Round or oval dishes are the most efficient for even heat distribution, particularly large containers with straight sides which allow the heat to spread in an even layer. Rectangular and square dishes are the least successful in a microwave because the corners cook faster than the middles.

Although metal should not be put in a microwave, small amounts of foil may be used, dull-side out, for shielding areas of food, but make sure its surface is smooth and keep it well away from the oven walls.

Paper towels are useful for soaking up moisture and covering foods, but make sure it is not recycled paper which can contain impurities such as tiny fragments of metal. If cooking in a dish that does not have a lid, cover it with special microwave cling film, or put the food directly into a roasting bag, fastened with a plastic tie.

Ovenproof glass and ceramic dishes are excellent, as are plastics specially made for the microwave. Plastic containers not specifically made for the microwave may soften and distort. Foods containing a high percentage of fat or sugar will get very hot and are not suitable for cooking in thin plastic containers. Wicker, wooden, or paper containers can be used for very short cooking times, such as for warming bread rolls, etc.

One special piece of equipment is a browning dish, which is usually made from a ceramic material that gets very hot when preheated and browns any food in contact with it.

Microwaving know-how

Remove eggs from their shells before cooking, otherwise they will explode.

◆

Use large containers for liquids, and keep stirring to avoid a build up of hot spots which can cause the liquid to boil over.

◆

Foods with a skin or membrane, such as sausages or egg yolks, must be pierced before cooking.

◆

Don't use empty yogurt pots for heating foods – they will melt and collapse.

ARRANGING FOODS

The shape and texture of food determines how it is best cooked in a microwave oven. Remember that microwaves penetrate food from the outside towards the middle, so arrange foods properly to ensure even cooking.

Uneven shapes
Arrange unevenly shaped foods, such as broccoli, in a circle with the densest parts facing outwards. Chicken drumsticks should be arranged with the bones pointing towards the middle of the dish.

Delicate areas
The heads and tails of fish will cook too quickly and must be shielded with small pieces of smooth foil. Protruding bones on chops and chicken pieces should also be covered with smooth strips of foil.

Even shapes
Foods of the same size and shape, or small individual dishes, should be arranged in a circle, with plenty of space between them, to enable the microwaves to reach the food from all sides.

COVERING & WRAPPING

Covering food with cling film prevents it drying out during cooking and traps steam which helps to heat the food. A loose covering of greaseproof paper or paper towels prevents spattering.

1 Stretch microwave cling film over the dish, then either pierce several times or peel back a small corner to allow some of the steam to escape.

2 After cooking, carefully remove the cling film from the edge of the dish furthest away from you first, as the rush of steam is very hot and can scald.

POWER LEVELS

Most recipes are designed for 600–700 watt output ovens; smaller ovens may have an output of 400–600 watts. Cooking times are longer the lower the output, so some recipes may need to be adapted. Descriptions of the power levels of microwave ovens vary, but in general you can follow this guide:

HIGH = 100% full power

MEDIUM = 50–60% of full power

DEFROST = 30–40% of full power

LOW = 10–20% of full power

THAWING & COOKING

A microwave oven can thaw frozen foods in a fraction of the time it normally takes. Thawing must be done slowly and gently – always use the defrost setting, so that the outside does not begin to cook before the inside is thawed. Break up and stir the food as it thaws. Bread, pastry, and cakes are best thawed on paper towels that absorb moisture. Meat and poultry must be completely thawed before cooking to ensure they are at the same temperature all the way through. Cook food as soon as possible once thawed.

Quick cooking know-how

Soften a wedge of Brie on LOW or DEFROST for 20–30 seconds. A whole Camembert will take longer. Allow to stand for several minutes before serving.

◆

Use the microwave to gently warm bread and rolls; 4 rolls will take approximately 20–30 seconds on HIGH.

◆

Soften cold butter for 20–30 seconds on MEDIUM.

◆

Soften hard ice-cream for 30–60 seconds on MEDIUM and leave to stand for 1 minute.

◆

To soften crystallized honey, remove the lid from the jar and microwave on HIGH for 30 seconds.

◆

To toast nuts, heat on HIGH for 2–4 minutes, stirring occasionally.

◆

Melt chocolate on HIGH for 2 minutes, stirring halfway.

FREEZING

HOME FREEZERS offer one of the most natural and economical methods of food preservation and storage, and when used in conjunction with a microwave oven, they are invaluable in a busy household. Fresh foods need no longer be bought every day – you can buy most of the food you need for a week, or even a month, in just one shopping trip and freeze it until needed. Follow the correct procedures and the food will lose none of the flavour, texture, and quality it had on the day you bought it.

FREEZING FOOD

Freezing halts the growth of bacteria, but only temporarily. It does not kill bacteria, so remember that when food thaws it will be in the same condition as it was before freezing, and the food must then be treated in the same way as any fresh produce. A temperature of -18°C (0°F) is essential. A freezer thermometer will reassure you that your freezer is at the correct temperature. The freezer compartment of a refrigerator rarely reaches this temperature so food can be stored there only for a few days. Turn the temperature to its coldest setting to speed the process several hours before freezing food. Quick freezing ensures that only small, round ice crystals form. In food frozen slowly, the ice crystals are larger and jagged; they puncture the cell walls causing the loss of moisture, texture, and flavour.

SPECIAL EQUIPMENT

Use rigid polythene containers with lids, foil containers with lids, or freezer bags. Special freezer-quality cling film or freezer wrap is convenient for interleaving and wrapping foods. Freezer tape should be used for sealing packages as ordinary sticky tape peels off. Colour-coded sticky labels are useful for indicating different types of food — it can be very difficult to identify unmarked packages once frozen.

Freezing know-how

Try to keep your freezer 75–100% full – this will keep the temperature down and make the freezer more economical to run. Bread is always a good space-filler.

◆

Mark each item with details of the contents, weight or number of servings, and the date of freezing.

◆

Do not allow frozen foods to partially thaw when shopping. Immediately wrap them in newspaper or invest in an insulated bag.

POWER CUTS

An unexpected power failure that causes the contents of your freezer to thaw can cause hundreds of pounds worth of damage.

If you have advance warning, fill any spaces in the freezer with towels, newspapers, or plastic boxes three-quarters filled with cold water. Switch on to "fast freeze". During the power cut, keep the door closed. Turn on to "fast freeze" as soon as power is restored. Food in a chest freezer will be safe for about 48 hours, and in an upright freezer for about 36 hours.

If you have no warning of a power failure, food, except for ice-cream, in a chest freezer will be safe for 30–35 hours, and in an upright freezer for about 30 hours.

PREPARING FOOD

Food should be packed in airtight, moisture-proof materials to avoid "freezer burn" – dry grey patches that form on the surface.

Tray freezing
Arrange items in a single layer, without touching, on a tray and freeze. Once frozen, transfer to a rigid container or freezer bag. Items can then be used "free-flow".

Interleaving
Place a sheet of freezer wrap or greaseproof paper between foods such as steaks and chops before wrapping. This makes them easier to separate before thawing.

Liquids
Pour liquid into a rigid polythene container, leaving roughly 1 cm (1/2 in) headroom per 600 ml (1 pint) liquid, to allow for expansion.

FOODS FOR FREEZING

The size, content, and texture of food largely determine how well it freezes, but you'll find that most foods can be frozen with great success as long as you follow the correct procedures.

Fruits and vegetables
Raw fruits tend to suffer a slight loss of quality when frozen and will always be softer once thawed. Soft fruits are best tray frozen. Treat pineapple and rhubarb in the same way. Freeze apples and pears in syrup, apple juice, or water, and add lemon juice to prevent discolouring. Strawberries become soft when thawed so are best frozen as a purée.

Vegetables such as green beans, peas, carrots, Brussels sprouts, sweetcorn, and mangetout should be blanched first. Most vegetables freeze well in cooked dishes such as soups or casseroles. However, potatoes don't freeze particularly well; if uncooked they will discolour, if part of a prepared dish, they will become floury.

Meat and poultry
Smaller pieces of meat give the best results. Poultry and larger pieces of meat are best bought ready-frozen. Interleave individual items, then bag.

Fish and shellfish
Fish must be as fresh as possible when frozen. Whole fish should be scaled, gutted, rinsed, and dried, then wrapped in freezer wrap or foil. Interleave fillets or steaks before wrapping. Crabs, lobsters, and prawns are best bought ready-frozen.

Pasta and rice
Fresh pasta, both filled and unfilled, freezes well. Pasta in sauces tends to turn soft when thawed. Rice dishes can be frozen but there is no advantage in freezing plain cooked rice.

Dairy products
The higher the fat content the better the product will freeze. Creams with over 40% fat freeze very well. Cheeses can be frozen but they are best used in cooking; full-fat hard cheeses and grated cheeses are most successful. Lightly whisk uncooked eggs, then add 1/2 tsp salt or sugar per 6 eggs or yolks to prevent thickening. Hard-boiled eggs become rubbery but dishes such as quiches freeze well.

Breads, pastries, and cakes
Wrap bread in airtight polythene or foil. Thaw at room temperature. Sliced bread can be toasted when still frozen. Both cooked and uncooked pastry freezes well. Cakes can be frozen in individual portions, but for best results freeze before filling or icing.

RECOMMENDED STORAGE TIMES

Some frozen foods are harmed if stored too long. Follow these guidelines to avoid loss of quality.

FOOD	STORAGE TIME
Bread	6 months
Butter	3 months
Cakes and pastries	3 months
Cheese	
Hard cheeses	6 months
Soft cheeses	6 weeks
Fish	
White fish	3 months
Oily fish and shellfish	2 months
Fruit and vegetables	12 months
Meat	
Beef	8 months
Lamb, veal, pork	6 months
Bacon, sausages	1 month
Milk, cream, and yogurt	1 month
Poultry	8 months
Soups and sauces	3 months

THAWING & REHEATING

For some foods, thawing before cooking is totally unnecessary. Vegetables and pasta can be added directly to boiling water. Put frozen sauces and soups into a saucepan and heat very gently until thawed. Thin pieces of meat, bacon, and chipolata sausages can be cooked straight from frozen, although thicker pieces of meat should be thawed first to ensure that they reach the right internal temperature. A meat thermometer can be used to check this at the end of cooking. If in doubt, simply thaw food before cooking.

It is vital that all poultry is thoroughly thawed before cooking. Thaw poultry and all other foods in the refrigerator: bacteria will soon begin to multiply if thawed at room temperature.

To thaw, remove food from wrappings and put on a lipped plate or in a bowl, in order to prevent any juices from spilling. Cover loosely and then put in the refrigerator.

Frozen food must be cooked immediately after thawing, to kill any bacteria. Use a food thermometer to check the temperature in the centre of the food. Never refreeze foods that have already been thawed.

HEALTHY EATING

UNDER THE BANNER OF PROGRESS the food we eat has changed radically in the last few decades. Large amounts of money are being spent spreading the word that we can improve our general health and longevity if we improve our diets. Sorting through all of the research and nutritional trends can be quite difficult, but most experts agree on the basics behind a healthy diet: reduce the amount of fats in your diet; increase the complex carbohydrates by eating more wholegrain cereals, rice, pasta, and bread; and eat a wide variety of fruits and vegetables every day.

BALANCING YOUR DIET

A healthy, balanced diet need not mean excluding any particular foods, as long as they are eaten in the correct proportions.

Foods belong to different groups, depending on their properties and the nutrients they contain. A healthy diet includes a variety of foods, some from each group.

The food pyramid is a very easy way to remember how to plan your diet. It shows the different food groups and the proportion of our diet they should make up.

Fats, oils, sugars

Dairy products, meat, fish, poultry, pulses, nuts

Fruits & vegetables

Potatoes, pasta, bread, cereals, rice

ARTIFICIAL ADDITIVES

Colourings, flavourings, and preservatives have had a very bad press in recent years and many new products now claim to be completely free of them. It is important to be aware what this claim really means. Many foods still contain flavourings and colourings which, although natural (for example, beetroot is used to give a pink colour) are still added ingredients. Nature-identical flavours and colours are artificially created but with the same chemical make-up as the natural product. Read labels carefully before buying processed foods.

Preservatives are necessary to maintain the shelf-life of food. Antioxidants retard rancidity in fats and oils, and nitrites and nitrates in cured meats such as bacon help to prevent food poisoning. Because they are potentially harmful, avoid eating too much of any single additive or preservative by eating a wide variety of foods.

If you buy foods free from preservatives, you must remember that they will not keep for as long as other foods and therefore must be eaten or cooked as soon as possible after purchase.

For foods that are as natural as possible, however, choose organic ones. Organic grains, fruits, and vegetables are grown without the use of chemical fertilizers or pesticides. Organic meats come from animals that have received no growth promoters or hormones.

HEALTHY COOKING TECHNIQUES

Changing the way we prepare food is one of the simplest ways to a healthier diet. Use one of the following cooking methods next time you prepare a meal.

Steaming
An ideal way to cook most vegetables. Arrange them in a single layer in a metal or bamboo steamer and put over a saucepan or wok of boiling water. Vegetables that are boiled lose many of their nutrients in the cooking water, whereas steaming ensures their goodness is retained.

Grilling and barbecuing
Cooking under a hot grill or over hot charcoal is a good way to cook poultry, fish, tender cuts of meat, and even many vegetables. Some foods benefit from being lightly brushed with oil to prevent them drying out, but meats that already contain fat, such as bacon, need no added fat. As the food cooks, the fat melts and drips away.

Stir-frying
Meat, poultry, fish, and vegetables can all be stir-fried. The food is cooked quickly, only small amounts of fat are needed, and the fat is usually a light one, such as sunflower oil. Use a well-seasoned wok or frying pan, or a non-stick one that requires even less oil.

Microwaving
Because microwave ovens often speed up the cooking process (pages 492–493), fewer essential nutrients are lost. Vegetables need only have a small amount of water in the cooking dish, and therefore many types of food can be successfully cooked with no added fat.

WEIGHT CONTROL

It is generally known that a healthy diet which results in a steady weight loss is much better than a very low-calorie diet which may promote a faster, but not always permanent weight loss.

To maintain the correct weight for your height and build you need to balance calorie intake with calorie output. If you take in more calories than you need to produce energy, then that energy will be stored as fat. If you want to lose weight you have to take in less calories than you need, so that your body burns off some of the energy stored as fat. Very low-calorie diets can therefore be dangerous because they don't contain enough calories to produce the energy needed for basic body functions. You will feel ill, tired, and lacking in energy.

Reduce the total intake of fats and sugars, and replace some of the calories with complex carbohydrates, fruits, and vegetables. Together with an increase in the amount of exercise you do, this should not only make you feel healthier, but should also result in a steady weight loss.

CUTTING DOWN ON FAT

Advice on reducing the amount of fat in your diet can be quite confusing, and simply cutting down on all fats is not the answer. Generally, fats should make up 30–35% of your total calorie intake, but bear in mind that there are different types of fat.

Saturated fat is usually of animal origin. Avoid saturated fat if you want to reduce the risk of heart disease: it blocks the arteries and also increases the level of cholesterol in the blood.

Unsaturated fats may be either polyunsaturated, such as sunflower oil, or mono-unsaturated, such as olive oil. These fats, in small amounts, are actually beneficial to the health as they may help to prevent cholesterol building up in the arteries, thereby lowering the risk of heart disease.

It is important to be aware that when an unsaturated oil is treated or hydrogenated, it becomes a saturated fat. Read labels.

Quick ways to a healthier diet

Replace creams with yogurt – low-fat yogurts are the best, but even Greek yogurt, which has a thick, creamy texture, contains much less fat than double cream. Fromage frais is available in a low-fat form and is a good replacement for cream in cooked dishes.

◆

Eat less red meat.

◆

Increase the carbohydrates in your meals and reduce the proteins.

◆

Add salt or sugar sparingly to foods and avoid processed foods which often contain large quantities of salt and sugar.

◆

Eat fresh or frozen vegetables rather than canned. Vegetables lose nutrients from the moment they're picked, so frozen ones are often better than fresh.

◆

Buy wholemeal bread and flour, and brown rice.

◆

Reduce the fat content of your meals wherever possible: remove any skin and fat from poultry and meat before cooking; skim any fat from the surface of casseroles, soups, or gravies; drain foods on paper towels before serving.

◆

Leave the nutritious skin on vegetables such as potatoes and carrots: simply scrub them before cooking.

◆

Instead of frying food, steam, grill or stir-fry.

CALORIE COUNTS

The following calorific values are per 100 g (3½ oz) of each item.

Cereals	
Bread, white	235
Bread, wholemeal	215
Brown rice, boiled	141
Cornflakes	360
Muesli	363
Spaghetti, boiled	104
Dairy products	
Butter	737
Cheddar cheese	412
Cottage cheese, plain	98
Double cream	449
Eggs, whole	147
Full-fat soft cheese	313
Margarine	739
Plain yogurt, low-fat	56
Single cream	198
Skimmed milk	33
Whole milk	66
Fish	
Cod, grilled	95
Mackerel, grilled	239
Tuna, canned in brine	99
Tuna, canned in oil	189
Fruits	
Apple, raw	47
Avocado, flesh only	190
Banana, flesh only	95
Kiwi fruit, flesh only	49
Orange, flesh only	37
Pear, raw	40
Pineapple, raw	41
Strawberries, raw	27
Meats	
Back bacon, grilled lean and fat	405
Chicken, roast meat only	148
Frozen beefburger, fried	264
Ham, cooked	120
Lamb chop, grilled lean only	222
Mince, cooked	229
Pork chop, grilled lean only	226
Pork sausage, grilled	318
Rump steak, grilled lean and fat	218
Vegetables	
Broccoli, boiled	24
Carrots, boiled	24
Courgettes, boiled	19
Frozen peas, boiled	69
Home-made chips, deep-fried	183
Potato, boiled	72
Sweetcorn kernels, canned	122
Tomatoes, canned	16

COOK'S NOTES

ALL THE RECIPES IN THIS BOOK have been carefully tested to ensure they produce successful results. It is important, however, to bear a few essential points in mind when shopping for and preparing any of the ingredients.

- Be sure to follow either all metric or all imperial measurements in a recipe. They are not interchangeable, so don't combine the two.
- The tablespoons used throughout the book are 15 ml, the teaspoons are 5 ml. They are always level measurements.
- All eggs are size 3 unless otherwise stated. Fruits and vegetables are medium-sized unless otherwise specified in a recipe.
- If you want to replace fresh herbs with dried in any of the recipes, use 1 teaspoon dried herbs for 1 tablespoon fresh.
- When a dish is cooked in the oven, always use the middle shelf unless otherwise stated.
- Because ingredients can vary, calorie counts are approximate only.
- Any serving suggestions given with the recipes are not included in the calorie counts.

MEASUREMENTS

METRIC	IMPERIAL
5 mm	1/4 in
1 cm	1/2 in
2.5 cm	1 in
5 cm	2 ins
7 cm	3 ins
10 cm	4 ins
12 cm	5 ins
15 cm	6 ins
18 cm	7 ins
20 cm	8 ins
23 cm	9 ins
25 cm	10 ins
28 cm	11 ins
30 cm	12 ins

VOLUME

METRIC	IMPERIAL
125 ml	4 fl oz
150 ml	1/4 pint
175 ml	6 fl oz
250 ml	8 fl oz
300 ml	1/2 pint
350 ml	12 fl oz
400 ml	14 fl oz
450 ml	3/4 pint
500 ml	16 fl oz
550 ml	18 fl oz
600 ml	1 pint
750 ml	1 1/4 pints
900 ml	1 1/2 pints
1 litre	1 3/4 pints

WEIGHT

METRIC	IMPERIAL
15 g	1/2 oz
30 g	1 oz
60 g	2 oz
90 g	3 oz
125 g	4 oz
175 g	6 oz
250 g	8 oz
300 g	10 oz
375 g	12 oz
400 g	13 oz
425 g	14 oz
500 g	1 lb
750 g	1 1/2 lb
1 kg	2 lb

OVEN TEMPERATURES

CELSIUS	FAHRENHEIT	GAS	DESCRIPTION
110°C	225°F	1/4	Cool
120°C	250°F	1/2	Cool
140°C	275°F	1	Very slow
150°C	300°F	2	Very slow
160°C	325°F	3	Slow
180°C	350°F	4	Moderate
190°C	375°F	5	Moderate
200°C	400°F	6	Moderately hot
220°C	425°F	7	Hot
230°C	450°F	8	Hot
240°C	475°F	9	Very hot

INDEX

Page numbers in *italic* type refer to illustrations.

A

B

◆ D ◆

◆ E ◆

◆ F ◆

G

• H •

• I •

• J •

• L •

N

O

P

Q

R

• S •

◆ T ◆

U

V

W

Y

Z

Acknowledgments

◆

Food preparation
Eric Treuille
Annie Nichols
Cara Hobday
Sandra Baddeley
Elaine Ngan

◆

Assisted by
Maddalena Bastianelli
Sarah Lowman

◆

Photographers' assistants
Nick Allen
Sid Sideris

◆

Additional recipes/Contributors
Marlena Spieler
Sue Ashworth
Louise Pickford
Cara Hobday
Norma MacMillan
Anne Gains

◆

Nutritional Consultant
Anne Sheasby

◆

Index
Madeline Weston

◆

Typesetting
Axis Design (DTP)

◆

Production Consultant
Lorraine Baird